The Princeton Handbook of Poetic Terms

PRINCETON
REFERENCE

The Princeton Handbook of Poetic Terms

Third Edition

EDITED BY
Roland Greene and
Stephen Cushman

PRINCETON UNIVERSITY PRESS

PRINCETON AND OXFORD

Library of Congress Cataloging-in-Publication Data

Names: Greene, Roland, 1957– editor. | Cushman, Stephen, 1956– editor.
Title: The Princeton handbook of poetic terms / edited by Roland Greene,
    Stephen Cushman.
Description: Third edition. | Princeton, New Jersey : Princeton University
    Press, 2016. | Includes bibliographical references and index.
Identifiers: LCCN 2015044023| ISBN 9780691171999 (hardback)
    | ISBN 9780691170435 (paperback)
Subjects: LCSH: Poetry—Dictionaries. | Poetics—Dictionaries. | Poetry—History
    and criticism. | BISAC: LITERARY CRITICISM / Poetry. | LITERARY
    CRITICISM / Reference. | POETRY / General.
Classification: LCC PN1021 .N39 2016 | DDC 808.1/03—dc23
    LC record available at http://lccn.loc.gov/2015044023

British Library Cataloging-in-Publication Data is available

This book has been composed in Adobe Garamond Pro

Printed on acid-free paper. ∞

Printed in the United States of America

10 9 8 7 6 5 4 3 2 1

Contents

Preface

How does one begin to study poetry? This volume, derived from the fourth edition of the *Princeton Encyclopedia of Poetry and Poetics*, provides a rich store of technical and conceptual information, and invites its readers to commence their study with fundamental ideas, facts, and practices. Poetics, the discipline out of which this book comes, is concerned with the nature of poetry across times and cultures. Those of us who are committed to the discipline often find ourselves trying to balance the kind of technical, highly particular materials collected here with larger questions that open outward from them: What is the character of the poetic? How does poetic description change the world it represents? Who speaks in a poem, and who listens? While these are broad, durable questions, our consideration of them is indivisible from our knowledge of rhythm and meter, rhyme and its shadings, line and stanza, scheme and trope, or a fixed form and its history. To make that knowledge attainable, this *Handbook* gathers authoritative accounts of basic, essential terms.

The entries selected for this volume are chosen for their value in a classroom, a reading community, or a personal experience of poetry. For some readers, the *Handbook* will be a threshold across which they will move in search of greater knowledge. The *Princeton Encyclopedia* includes not only the entries collected here but many more that complement them and lend them context; moreover, the bibliographies for every item in the *Handbook* and the *Encyclopedia* make a virtually boundless resource for further exploration.

The present volume maintains several conventions of the *Princeton Encyclopedia*. Translations are generally given within parentheses, without quotation marks if no other words appear in the parenthetical matter, but set off within quotation marks when some qualification is needed, as in the form of many etymologies: for example, arsis and thesis (Gr., "raising and lowering"). Translated titles of works generally appear in the most comprehensive articles; entries of smaller scope often give original titles without translation, although some contributors have translated titles where doing so clarifies the argument. (We tolerate inconsistency that reflects to some degree the field at hand: thus some entries, such as "eclogue" or "ode," rarely translate titles because many readers of those genres are familiar with the original languages; others, such as "love poetry," give only translated titles.) Translated titles of books are italicized when the title refers to a published English translation: for example, Joachim du Bellay's *Les Antiquités de Rome* (*Ruins of Rome*). For poems, translated titles are given with quotation marks when the translation has been published under that title, but without quotation marks when the translated title is ad hoc.

This convention sometimes entails reproducing a nonliteral rendering that appears in a published translation, such as Francisco de Quevedo's *Canta sola a Lisi* as *Poems to Lisi*. We believe that the value of indicating an extant translation outweighs the occasional infelicity. At the same time, it is likely we have overlooked some published translations, and many new ones will appear over the life of this book.

Dates of the lives and works of poets and critics often appear in the most comprehensive entries on a given topic (e.g., "lyric"), showing up less often as topics become narrower ("alba," "envoi"). Dates of works in the age of print refer to publication unless otherwise indicated.

Articles contain two types of cross-references: those that appear within the body of an entry (indicated with asterisks or in parentheses with small capitals), and those that follow an entry, just before the bibliographies. The former are often topics that extend the fabric of the definition at hand; the latter often indicate adjacent topics of broader interest. Of course, both kinds of cross-reference hold out the danger of infinite connection: nearly every entry could be linked to many others, and the countless usages of terms such as *line*, *metaphor*, and *poetics* cannot all be linked to the entries concerned with those terms. Accordingly we have tried to apply cross-references judiciously, indicating where further reading in a related entry really complements the argument at hand.

The bibliographies are intended not only as lists of works cited in the entries but as guides to relevant scholarship of the distant and recent past. The bibliographies have been lightly standardized, but some entries—say, those that narrate the development of a field—gain from citing works of scholarship in their original iterations (John Crowe Ransom's essay "Criticism, Inc." in its first appearance in the *Virginia Quarterly Review* of 1937) or in their original languages, while many others choose to cite later editions or translations into English as a convenience for the reader.

At a time in which poetry is thriving as an art, and poetics is gaining fresh disciplinary force, the study of poetry at the secondary and college level depends on maintaining a living connection to these scenes of renewal. With hundreds of contributors active in the field (including many poets) and access to advanced thinking, this *Handbook* is that connection.

Acknowledgments

We gratefully acknowledge the following authors, publishers, and agents for granting us permission to use brief selections from the copyrighted material listed below. Great care has been taken to trace all the owners of copyrighted material used in this book. Any inadvertent omissions pointed out to us will be gladly acknowledged in future printings.

Faber and Faber Ltd. for two lines of "The Hollow Men" by T. S. Eliot from *Collected Poems 1909–1962* by T. S. Eliot, copyright © 1974 by Faber and Faber, Ltd. Reprinted by permission of Faber and Faber, Ltd.

Harvard University Press for five lines of "Artifice of Absorption" from *A Poetics* by Charles Bernstein, Cambridge, Mass.: Harvard University Press, copyright © 1992 by Charles Bernstein, and four lines of *The Kalevala: Or, Poems of the Kalevala District*, compiled by Elias Lönnrot, translated by Francis Peabody Magoun, Jr., Cambridge, Mass.: Harvard University Press, copyright © 1963 by the President and Fellows of Harvard College. Both reprinted by permission of the publisher.

Houghton Mifflin Harcourt Publishing Company for excerpts from "The Hollow Men" from *Collected Poems 1909–1962* by T. S. Eliot, copyright © 1936 by Harcourt, Inc. and renewed by T. S. Eliot. Reprinted by permission of Houghton Mifflin Harcourt Publishing Company. All rights reserved.

New Directions Publishing Corporation for five lines of "The Five Day Rain" by Denise Levertov, from *Collected Earlier Poems 1940–1960*, copyright © 1960 by Denise Levertov, and four lines of "Poems" by Dylan Thomas, from *Collected Poems*, copyright © 1952 by Dylan Thomas. Both reprinted by permission of New Directions Publishing Corp.

Society of Biblical Literature for six lines of "Kirta," from *Ugaritic Narrative Poetry*, edited by Simon B. Parker, copyright © 1997. Reprinted by permission of the Society of Biblical Literature.

University of Virginia Press for four lines of "A Warm Day in Winter" by Paul Laurence Dunbar from *The Collected Poetry of Paul Laurence Dunbar*, edited by Joanne M. Braxton, copyright © 1993 Rector and Visitors of the University of Virginia. Reprinted by permission of the University of Virginia Press.

Wesleyan University Press for eight lines of "Spring Images" by James Wright from *Collected Poems*, copyright © 1971 by James Wright. Reprinted by permission of Wesleyan University Press.

Alphabetical List of Entries

accent
accentual-syllabic verse
accentual verse
air
alba
alexandrine
alliteration
ambiguity
anacoluthon
anacreontic
anadiplosis
analogy. *See* METAPHOR;
    SIMILE; SYMBOL
anapest
anaphora
antistrophe
antithesis
antonomasia
aporia
apostrophe
assonance
asyndeton
audience. *See* PERFORMANCE
ballad
ballad meter, hymn meter
beat
Biblical poetry. *See* HYMN;
    PSALM
blank verse
blason
blues
broken rhyme
burlesque. *See* PARODY
caesura
canon
carpe diem
catachresis
catalexis
catalog
chain rhyme
chiasmus
Christabel meter
closure
colon
complaint
composition. *See* POET;
    VERSIFICATION
composition by field
conceit
concrete poetry

confessional poetry
consonance
convention
couplet
cross rhyme
dactyl
decasyllable
decorum
deixis
demotion
devotional poetry
dialogue
diction
dimeter
dozens
dramatic monologue. *See*
    MONOLOGUE
dramatic poetry
dream vision
eclogue
ekphrasis
elegiac distich
elegiac stanza
elegy
elision
ellipsis
encomium
English prosody
enjambment
envoi
epic
epigram
epitaph
epithalamium
epithet
epode
euphony
eye rhyme
fabliau
foot (modern)
form
fourteener
free verse
genre
georgic
haiku, western
hemistich
hendecasyllable
hendiadys
heptameter

heroic couplet
heroic verse
hexameter
hiatus
homoeoteleuton
hymn
hyperbaton
hyperbole
hypotaxis and parataxis
iambic
idyll
image
imagery
indeterminacy
In Memoriam stanza
internal rhyme
invective
irony
isocolon and parison
kenning
lament
leonine rhyme, verse
letter, verse. *See* VERSE EPISTLE
limerick
line
litotes
love poetry
lyric
lyric sequence
madrigal
masculine and feminine
metaphor
meter
metonymy
mimesis
mock epic, mock heroic
monologue
narrative poetry
narrator. *See* PERSONA; VOICE
near rhyme
nonsense verse
octave
octosyllable
ode
onomatopoeia
ottava rima
palinode
panegyric
paradox
paralipsis

Bibliographical Abbreviations

Abrams   M. H. Abrams, *The Mirror and the Lamp: Romantic Theory and the Critical Tradition*, 1953
AION-SL   *Annali dell'Istituto Universitario Orientale di Napoli: sezione filologico-letteraria*
AJP   *American Journal of Philology*
AJS   *American Journal of Semiotics*
AL   *American Literature*
Allen   W. S. Allen, *Accent and Rhythm*, 1973
Analecta hymnica   *Analecta hymnica medii aevi*, ed. G. M. Dreves, C. Blume, and H. M. Bannister, 55 v., 1886–1922
Attridge, Poetic Rhythm   D. Attridge, *Poetic Rhythm: An Introduction*, 1995
Attridge, Rhythms   D. Attridge, *The Rhythms of English Poetry*, 1982
Auerbach   E. Auerbach, *Mimesis: The Representation of Reality in Western Literature*, trans. W. R. Trask, 1953

Beare   W. Beare, *Latin Verse and European Song*, 1957
Bec   P. Bec, *La Lyrique Française au moyen âge (XIIe–XIIIe siècles): Contribution à une typologie des genres poétiques médiévaux*, 2 v., 1977–78
Benjamin   W. Benjamin, "The Work of Art in the Age of Mechanical Reproduction," *Illuminations*, trans. H. Zohn, 1968
BGDSL (H)   *Beiträge zur Geschichte de deutschen Sprache und Literatur (Halle)*
BGDSL (T)   *Beiträge zur Geschichte de deutschen Sprache und Literatur (Tübingen)*
BHS   *Bulletin of Hispanic Studies*
BJA   *British Journal of Aesthetics*
Bowra   C. M. Bowra, *Greek Lyric Poetry from Alcman to Simonides*, 2d ed., 1961
Bridges   R. Bridges, *Milton's Prosody*, rev. ed., 1921
Brogan   T.V.F. Brogan, *English Versification, 1570–1980: A Reference Guide with a Global Appendix*, 1981
Brooks   C. Brooks, *The Well Wrought Urn*, 1947
Brooks and Warren   C. Brooks and R. P. Warren, *Understanding Poetry*, 3d ed., 1960

Carper and Attridge   T. Carper and D. Attridge, *Meter and Meaning: An Introduction to Rhythm*, 2003
CBEL   *Cambridge Bibliography of English Literature*, ed. F. W. Bateson, 4 v., 1940; v. 5, *Supplement*, ed. G. Watson, 1957

CBFL   *A Critical Bibliography of French Literature*, gen. ed. D. C. Cabeen and R. A. Brooks, 6 v., 1947–1994
CE   *College English*
Chambers   F. M. Chambers, *An Introduction to Old Provençal Versification*, 1985
Chatman   S. Chatman, *A Theory of Meter*, 1965
CHCL   *Cambridge History of Classical Literature*, v. 1, *Greek Literature*, ed. P. E. Easterling and B.M.W. Knox, 1985; v. 2, *Latin Literature*, ed. E. J. Kenney and W. V. Clausen, 1982
CHEL   *Cambridge History of English Literature*, ed. A. W. Ward and A. R. Waller, 14 v., 1907–16
CHLC   *Cambridge History of Literary Criticism*, 9 v., 1989–2005
Chomsky and Halle   N. Chomsky and M. Halle, *The Sound Pattern of English*, 1968
CJ   *Classical Journal*
CL   *Comparative Literature*
CML   *Classical and Modern Literature*
Corbett   E.P.J. Corbett, *Classical Rhetoric for the Modern Student*, 3d ed., 1990
CP   *Classical Philology*
CQ   *Classical Quarterly*
Crane   *Critics and Criticism, Ancient and Modern*, ed. R. S. Crane, 1952
CritI   *Critical Inquiry*
Crusius   F. Crusius, *Römische Metrik: ein Einführung*, 8th ed., rev. H. Rubenbauer, 1967
Culler   J. Culler, *Structuralist Poetics: Structuralism, Linguistics, and the Study of Literature*, 1975
Cureton   R. D. Cureton, *Rhythmic Phrasing in English Verse*, 1992
Curtius   E. Curtius, *European Literature and the Latin Middle Ages*, trans. W. R. Trask, 1953
CW   *Classical World*

DAI   *Dissertation Abstracts International*
Dale   A. M. Dale, *The Lyric Meters of Greek Drama*, 2d ed., 1968
DDJ   *Deutsches Dante-Jahrbuch*
de Man   P. de Man, *Blindness and Insight: Essays in the Rhetoric of Contemporary Criticism*, 2d ed., 1983
Derrida   J. Derrida, *Of Grammatology*, trans. G. C. Spivak, 2d ed., 1998
DHI   *Dictionary of the History of Ideas*, ed. P. P. Weiner, 6 v., 1968–74
Dronke   P. Dronke, *Medieval Latin and the Rise of European Love Lyric*, 2d ed., 2 v., 1968

Duffell   M. J. Duffell, *A New History of English Metre*, 2008

E&S   *Essays and Studies of the English Association*
ELH   *ELH* (formerly *English Literary History*)
Eliot, Essays   T. S. Eliot, *Selected Essays*, rev. ed., 1950
Elwert   W. T. Elwert, *Französische Metrik*, 4th ed., 1978
Elwert, Italienische   W. T. Elwert, *Italienische Metrik*, 2d ed., 1984
Empson   W. Empson, *Seven Types of Ambiguity*, 3d ed., 1953
ENLL   *English Language and Linguistics*

Fabb et al.   N. Fabb, D. Atridge, A. Durant, and C. MacCabe, *The Linguistics of Writing*, 1987
Faral   E. Faral, *Les arts poétique du XIIe et du XIIIe siècles*, 1924
Finch and Varnes   *An Exaltation of Forms: Contemporary Poets Celebrate the Diversity of Their Art*, ed. A. Finch and K. Varnes, 2002
Fish   S. Fish, *Is There a Text in This Class? The Authority of Interpretive Communities*, 1980
Fisher   *The Medieval Literature of Western Europe: A Review of Research, Mainly 1930–1960*, ed. J. H. Fisher, 1965
FMLS   *Forum for Modern Language Studies*
Fontanier   P. Fontanier, *Les figures du discours*, 1977
Fowler   A. Fowler, *Kinds of Literature: An Introduction to the Theory of Genres and Modes*, 1982
Frye   N. Frye, *Anatomy of Criticism: Four Essays*, 1957
FS   *French Studies*

Gasparov   M. L. Gasparov, *Sovremennyj russkij stix: Metrika i ritmika*, 1974
Gasparov, History   M. L. Gasparov, *A History of European Versification*, trans. G. S. Smith and M. Tarlinskaja, 1996
GRLMA   *Grundriss der romanischen Literaturen des Mittelalters*, ed. H. R. Jauss and E. Köhler, 11 v., 1968–
Group μ   Group μ (J. Dubois, F. Edeline, J.-M. Klinkenberg, P. Minguet, F. Pire, H. Trinon), *A General Rhetoric*, trans. P. B. Burrell and E. M. Slotkin, 1981

Halporn et al.   J. W. Halporn, M. Ostwald, and T. G. Rosenmeyer, *The Meters of Greek and Latin Poetry*, 2d ed., 1980
Hardie   W. R. Hardie, *Res Metrica*, 1920
HJAS   *Harvard Journal of Asiatic Studies*
Hollander   J. Hollander, *Vision and Resonance: Two Senses of Poetic Form*, 2d ed., 1985

Hollier   *A New History of French Literature*, ed. D. Hollier, 1989
HQ   *Hopkins Quarterly*
HR   *Hispanic Review*
HudR   *Hudson Review*

ICPhS   *International Congress of Phonetic Sciences* (journal)
IJCT   *International Journal of Classical Tradition*

JAAC   *Journal of Aesthetics and Art Criticism*
JAC   *JAC: A Journal of Rhetoric, Culture, and Politics*
JAF   *Journal of American Folklore*
Jakobson   R. Jakobson, *Selected Writings*, 8 v., 1962–88
Jakobson and Halle   R. Jakobson and M. Halle, *Fundamentals of Language*, 1956
JAOS   *Journal of American Oriental Society*
Jarman and Hughes   *A Guide to Welsh Literature*, ed. A.O.H. Jarman and G. R. Hughes, 2 v., 1976–79
Jeanroy   A. Jeanroy, *La Poésie lyrique des Troubadours*, 2 v., 1934
Jeanroy, Origines   A. Jeanroy, *Les origines de la poésie lyrique en France au moyen âge*, 4th ed., 1965
JEGP   *Journal of English and Germanic Philology*
JFLS   *Journal of French Language Studies*
JHS   *Journal of Hellenic Studies*
JL   *Journal of Linguistics*
Jour. P. Society   *Journal of Polynesian Society*
JPhon   *Journal of Phonetics*

Kastner   L. E. Kastner, *A History of French Versification*, 1903
Keil   *Grammatici Latini*, ed. H. Keil, 7 v., 1855–80; v. 8, *Anecdota helvitica: Supplementum*, ed. H. Hagen, 1870
Koster   W.J.W. Koster, *Traité de métrique greque suivi d'un précis de métrique latine*, 5th ed., 1966
KSMB   *Keats-Shelley Journal*
KR   *Kenyon Review*

L&S   *Language and Speech*
Lang   *Language*
Lang&S   *Language and Style*
Lanham   R. A. Lanham, *A Handlist of Rhetorical Terms*, 2d ed., 1991
Lausberg   H. Lausberg, *Handbook of Literary Rhetoric: A Foundation for Literary Study*, trans. M. T. Bliss, A. Jansen, and D. E. Orton, 1998
Le Gentil   P. Le Gentil, *La Poésie lyrique espagnole et portugaise à la fin du moyen âge*, 2 v., 1949–53
Lewis   C. S. Lewis, *The Allegory of Love*, 1936
LingI   *Linguistic Inquiry*

Lord   A. B. Lord, *The Singer of Tales*, 2d ed., 2000
Lote   G. Lote, *Histoire du vers française*, 9 v., 1940

M&H   *Medievalia et Humanistica: Studies in Medieval and Renaissance Culture*
Maas   P. Maas, *Greek Metre*, trans. H. Lloyd-Jones, 3d ed., 1962
Manitius   M. Manitius, *Geschichte der lateinischen Literatur des Mittelalters*, 3 v., 1905–36
Mazaleyrat   J. Mazaleyrat, *Éléments de métrique française*, 3d ed., 1981
Meyer   W. Meyer, *Gesammelte Abhandlungen zur mittelateinischen Rhythmik*, 3 v., 1905–36
MGG   *Die Musik in Geschichte und Gegenwart: Allegemeine Enzyklopaedia der Musik*, ed. F. Blume, 16 v., 1949–79
MGH   *Monumenta germaniae historica*
MHRA   Modern Humanities Research Association
Michaelides   S. Michaelides, *The Music of Ancient Greece: An Encyclopaedia*, 1978
MidwestQ   *Midwest Quarterly*
Migne, PG   *Patrologiae cursus completus, series graeca*, ed. J. P. Migne, 161 v., 1857–66
Migne, PL   *Patrologiae cursus completus, series latina*, ed. J. P. Migne, 221 v., 1844–64
Miner et al.   E. Miner, H. Odagiri, and R. E. Morrell, *The Princeton Companion to Classical Japanese Literature*, 1986
MLN   *Modern Language Notes*
MLQ   *Modern Language Quarterly*
MLQ (London)   *Modern Language Quarterly (London)*
MLR   *Modern Language Review*
Morier   H. Morier, *Dictionnaire de poétique et de rhétorique*, 5th ed., rev. and exp., 1998
Morris-Jones   J. Morris-Jones, *Cerdd Dafod*, 1925, rpt. with index, 1980
MP   *Modern Philology*
Murphy   J. J. Murphy, *Rhetoric in the Middle Ages: A History of Rhetorical Theory from St. Augustine to the Renaissance*, 1974

N&Q   *Notes & Queries*
Navarro   T. Navarro, *Métrica española: Reseña histórica y descriptiva*, 6th ed., 1983
NER/BLQ   *New England Review / Bread Loaf Quarterly*
New CBEL   *New Cambridge Bibliography of English Literature*, ed. G. Watson and I. R. Willison, 5 v., 1969–77
New Grove   *New Grove Dictionary of Music and Musicians*, ed. S. Sadie, 20 v., 1980
Nienhauser et al.   W. H. Nienhauser, Jr., C. Hartman, Y. W. Ma, and S. H. West, *The Indiana Companion to Traditional Chinese Literature*, 1986
NLH   *New Literary History*

NM   *Neuphilologische Mitteilungen (Bulletin of the Modern Language Society)*
Norberg   D. Norberg, *Introduction a l'étude de la versification latine médiévale*, 1958
Norden   E. Norden, *Die antike Kunstprosa*, 9th ed., 2 v., 1983

OED   *Oxford English Dictionary*
OL   *Orbis Litterarum: International Review of Literary Studies*
Olson   C. Olson, "Projective Verse," *Collected Prose*, ed. D. Allen and B. Friedlander, 1997
Omond   T. S. Omond, *English Metrists*, 1921

P&R   *Philosophy and Rhetoric*
Parry   M. Parry, *The Making of Homeric Verse*, ed. A. Parry, 1971
Parry, History   T. Parry, *A History of Welsh Literature*, trans. H. I. Bell, 1955
Patterson   W. F. Patterson, *Three Centuries of French Poetic Theory: A Critical History of the Chief Arts of Poetry in France (1328–1630)*, 2 v., 1935
Pauly-Wissowa   *Paulys Realencyclopädie der classischen Alterumswissenschaft*, ed. A. Pauly, G. Wissowa, W. Kroll, and K. Mittelhaus, 24 v. (A–Q), 10 v. (R–Z, Series 2), and 15 v. (Supplements), 1894–1978
PBA   *Proceedings of the British Academy*
Pearsall   D. Pearsall, *Old English and Middle English Poetry*, 1977
PMLA   *Publications of the Modern Language Association of America*
PoT   *Poetics Today*
PQ   *Philological Quarterly*
PsychologR   *Psychological Review*
Puttenham   G. Puttenham, *The Arte of English Poesie*, ed. F. Whigham and W. A. Rebhorn, 2007

QJS   *Quarterly Journal of Speech*

Raby, Christian   F.J.E. Raby, *A History of Christian-Latin Poetry from the Beginnings to the Close of the Middle Ages*, 2d ed., 1953
Raby, Secular   F.J.E. Raby, *A History of Secular Latin Poetry in the Middle Ages*, 2d ed., 2 v., 1957
Ransom   *Selected Essays of John Crowe Ransom*, ed. T. D. Young and J. Hindle, 1984
Reallexikon I   *Reallexikon der deutschen Literaturgeschichte*, 1st ed., ed. P. Merker and W. Stammler, 4 v., 1925–31
Reallexikon II   *Reallexikon der deutschen Literaturgeschichte*, 2d ed., ed. W. Kohlschmidt and W. Mohr (v. 1–3), K. Kanzog and A. Masser (v. 4), 1958–84

Reallexikon III   *Reallexikon der deutschen Literatur-wissenschaft*, 3d ed, ed. H. Fricke, K. Frubmüller, J.-D. Müller, and K. Weimar, 3 v., 1997–2003

REL   *Review of English Literature*

RES   *Review of English Studies*

Richards   I. A. Richards, *Principles of Literary Criticism*, 1925

RLC   *Revue de littérature compareé*

RPh   *Romance Philology*

RQ   *Renaissance Quarterly*

RR   *Romanic Review*

SAC   *Studies in the Age of Chaucer*

Saintsbury, Prose   G. Saintsbury, *A History of English Prose Rhythm*, 1912

Saintsbury, Prosody   G. Saintsbury, *A History of English Prosody, from the Twelfth Century to the Present Day*, 2d ed., 3 v., 1961

Saisselin   R. G. Saisselin, *The Rule of Reason and the Ruses of the Heart: A Philosophical Dictionary of Classical French Criticism, Critics, and Aesthetic Issues*, 1970

Sayce   O. Sayce, *The Medieval German Lyric, 1150–1300: The Development of Its Themes and Forms in Their European Context*, 1982

Scherr   B. P. Scherr, *Russian Poetry: Meter, Rhythm, and Rhyme*, 1986

Schipper   J. M. Schipper, *Englische Metrik*, 3 v., 1881–88

Schipper, History   J. M. Schipper, *A History of English Versification*, 1910

Schmid and Stählin   W. Schmid and O. Stählin, *Geschichte der griechischen Literatur*, 7 v., 1920–48

Scott   C. Scott, *French Verse-Art: A Study*, 1980

Sebeok   *Style in Language*, ed. T. Sebeok, 1960

SEL   *Studies in English Literature 1500–1900*

ShQ   *Shakespeare Quarterly*

Sievers   E. Sievers, *Altergermanische Metrik*, 1893

SIR   *Studies in Romanticism*

Smith   *Elizabethan Critical Essays*, ed. G. G. Smith, 2 v., 1904

Snell   B. Snell, *Griechesche Metrik*, 4th ed., 1982

SP   *Studies in Philology*

Spongano   R. Spongano, *Nozioni ed esempi di metric italiana*, 2d ed., 1974

SR   *Sewanee Review*

Stephens   *The Oxford Companion to the Literature of Wales*, ed. M. Stephens, 1986

TAPA   *Transactions of the American Philological Association*

Tarlinskaja   M. Tarlinskaja, *English Verse: Theory and History*, 1976

Terras   *Handbook of Russian Literature*, ed. V. Terras, 1985

Thieme   H. P. Thieme, *Essai sur l'histoire du vers française*, 1916

Thompson   J. Thompson, *The Founding of English Metre*, 2d ed., 1989

Trypanis   C. A. Trypanis, *Greek Poetry from Homer to Seferis*, 1981

TPS   *Transactions of the Philological Society*

TSL   *Tennessee Studies in Literature*

TSLL   *Texas Studies in Literature and Language*

Vickers   B. Vickers, *Classical Rhetoric in English Poetry*, 2d ed., 1989

Vickers, Defence   B. Vickers, *In Defence of Rhetoric*, 1988

VP   *Victorian Poetry*

VQR   *Virginia Quarterly Review*

Weinberg   B. Weinberg, *A History of Literary Criticism in the Italian Renaissance*, 2 v., 1961

Wellek   R. Wellek, *A History of Modern Criticism, 1750–1950*, 8 v., 1955–92

Wellek and Warren   R. Wellek and A. Warren, *Theory of Literature*, 3d ed., 1956

Welsh   A. Welsh, *Roots of Lyric*, 1978

West   M. L. West, *Greek Metre*, 1982

WHB   *Wiener Humanistische Blätter*

Wilamowitz   U. von Wilamowitz-Moellendorf, *Griechesche Verkunst*, 1921

Wilkins   E. H. Wilkins, *A History of Italian Literature*, rev. T. G. Bergin, 1974

Williams and Ford   J.E.C. Williams and P. K. Ford, *The Irish Literary Tradition*, 1992

Wimsatt   *Versification: Major Language Types*, ed. W. K. Wimsatt, 1972

Wimsatt and Beardsley   W. K. Wimsatt and M. C. Beardsley, "The Concept of Meter: An Exercise in Abstraction," *PMLA* 74 (1959); rpt. in *Hateful Contraries*, W. K. Wimsatt, 1965

Wimsatt and Brooks   W. K. Wimsatt and C. Brooks, *Literary Criticism: A Short History*, 1957

YFS   *Yale French Studies*

YLS   *Yearbook of Langland Studies*

ZCP   *Zeitschrift für celtische Philologie*

ZDA   *Zeitschrift für deutsches Altertum*

ZFSL   *Zeitschrift für französische Sprache und Literatur*

ZRP   *Zeitschrift für Romanische Philologie*

ZVS   *Zeitschrift für Vergleichende Sprachforschung*

General Abbreviations

The abbreviations below are used throughout the volume to conserve space. General abbreviations may also show plural forms, e.g., "cs." for "centuries."

Af. African
Af. Am. African American
Am. American
anthol. anthology
Ar. Arabic
Assoc. Association

b. born
bibl. bibliography
Brit. British

c./cs. century
ca. *circa*, about
cf. *confer*, compare
ch. chapter
cl. classical
contemp. contemporary
crit. criticism

d. died
devel./devels. development
dict. dictionary
diss. dissertation

ed./eds. edition, editor, edited by
e.g. *exempla gratia*, for example
Eng. English
esp. especially
et al. *et alii*, and others
Eur. European

ff. following
fl. *floruit*, flourished
Fr. French

Ger. German
Gr. Greek

Heb. Hebrew
hist./hists. history

IE Indo-Euopean
i.e. *id est*, that is
incl. including
intro./intros. introduction
Ir. Irish
It. Italian

jour./jours. journal

lang./langs. language
Lat. Latin
ling. linguistics, linguistic
lit./lits. literature
lit. crit. literary criticism
lit. hist. literary history

ME Middle English
med. medieval
MHG Middle High German
mod. modern
ms./mss. manuscript

NT New Testament

OE Old English
OF Old French
OHG Old High German
ON Old Norse
OT Old Testament

p./pp. page
pl. plural
Port. Portuguese
postmod. postmodern
premod. premodern
pseud. pseudonym
pub. published

r. reigned
Ren. Renaissance
rev. revised
Rev. Review
rhet./rhets. rhetoric
rpt. reprinted
Rus. Russian

sing. singular
Sp. Spanish
supp. supplement(ed)

temp. temporary
trad./trads. tradition
trans. translation, translated

v. volume(s)

Contributors

This list includes all contributors credited in this volume, including some whose articles from the previous edition have been updated by the editors or other contributors. Those with names preceded by a dagger (†) are deceased.

†Percy G. Adams, English, University of Tennessee

Cécile Alduy, French, Stanford University

Roger M. A. Allen, Arabic Languages and Literatures (emeritus), University of Pennsylvania

Robert Alter, Hebrew and Comparative Literature, University of California, Berkeley

Hélio J. S. Alves, Portuguese and Comparative Literature, University of Évora

†John Arthos, English, University of Michigan

Derek Attridge, English and Related Literature, University of York

Timothy Bahti, German and Comparative Literature (emeritus), University of Michigan

†Ernst H. Behler, Germanics and Comparative Literature, University of Washington

Sandra L. Bermann, Comparative Literature, Princeton University

Eleanor Berry, independent scholar

Stanley S. Bill, Slavic Languages and Literatures, Northwestern University

Frederick L. Blumberg, English, University of Hong Kong

Gordon Braden, English (emeritus), University of Virginia

Jacqueline Vaught Brogan, English, University of Notre Dame

†T.V.F. Brogan, independent scholar

†Huntington Brown, English, University of Minnesota

Sidney Burris, English, University of Arkansas

John Burt, English, Brandeis University

Stephen Burt, English, Harvard University

Thomas Cable, English (emeritus), University of Texas

Kolter M. Campbell, Slavic Languages and Literatures, Northwestern University

David Caplan, English, Ohio Wesleyan University

Thomas Carper, English (emeritus), University of Southern Maine

Max Cavitch, English, University of Pennsylvania

Mary Ann Caws, Comparative Literature, English, and French, Graduate Center, City University of New York

Seeta Chaganti, English, University of California, Davis

Jennifer Chang, English, George Washington University

A. Thomas Cole, Classics (emeritus), Yale University

Claire Colebrook, English, Pennsylvania State University

James M. Cocola, English, Worcester Polytechnic Institute

Ann Baynes Coiro, English, Rutgers University

†Gregory G. Colomb, English, University of Virginia

J. E. Congleton, Humanities and Sciences (emeritus), University of Findlay

Eleanor Cook, English (emerita), University of Toronto

G. Burns Cooper, English, University of Alaska, Fairbanks

Ian D. Copestake, British Culture, University of Bamberg

Holly Crocker, English Language and Literature, University of South Carolina

Jennifer Croft, Comparative Literary Studies, Northwestern University

Stephen Cushman, English, University of Virginia

Andrew M. Devine, Classics, Stanford University

Joanne Diaz, English, Illinois Wesleyan University

Jeffrey Dolven, English, Princeton University

Daniel G. Donoghue, English, Harvard University

†Edward Doughtie, English (emeritus), Rice University

Johanna Drucker, Information Studies, University of California, Los Angeles

Heather Dubrow, English, Fordham University

Martin J. Duffell, Modern Languages, Queen Mary, University of London

Dianne Dugaw, English, University of Oregon

Rachel Blau DuPlessis, English, Temple University

†Gerald F. Else, Classical Studies, University of Michigan

†Alfred Garvin Engstrom, French, University of North Carolina, Chapel Hill

David Evans, Modern Languages, University of St. Andrews

†Robert O. Evans, English and Comparative Literature (emeritus), University of New Mexico

Harris Feinsod, English, Northwestern University

Frances Ferguson, English, University of Chicago

Margaret W. Ferguson, English, University of California, Davis

Jordan Finkin, Klau Library, Hebrew Union College

†Stephen F. Fogle, English, Adelphi Suffolk College

Stephen Foley, English and Comparative Literature, Brown University

Elizabeth Fowler, English, University of Virginia

Lisa Freinkel, Comparative Literature, University of Oregon

Amanda L. French, Center for History and New Media, George Mason University

Nila Friedberg, Russian, Portland State University

Norman Friedman, English (emeritus), Queens College, City University of New York

Paul H. Fry, English, Yale University

Marisa Galvez, French, Stanford University

Mary Malcolm Gaylord, Romance Languages and Literatures, Harvard University

Natalie Gerber, English, State University of New York, Fredonia

†Robert J. Getty, Classics, University of North Carolina

Brian Glavey, English Language and Literature, University of South Carolina

Kevis Goodman, English, University of California, Berkeley

Stathis Gourgouris, Classics, Columbia University

Kenneth J. E. Graham, English Language and Literature, University of Waterloo

Roland Greene, Comparative Literature and English, Stanford University

Edward L. Greenstein, Bible, Bar-Ilan University

Tobias B. Gregory, English, Catholic University of America

Kathryn Gutzwiller, Classics, University of Cincinnati

Stephen Halliwell, Greek and Classics, University of St. Andrews

†James W. Halporn, Classical Studies, Indiana University

†Albert W. Halsall, French, Carleton University

†O. B. Hardison, English, Georgetown University

William Harmon, English and Comparative Literature (emeritus), University of North Carolina, Chapel Hill

Robert L. Harrison, independent scholar

Henry Hart, English, College of William and Mary

Charles O. Hartman, English, Connecticut College

Daniel Hoffman, English (emeritus), University of Pennsylvania

†Urban T. Holmes, Romance Languages, University of North Carolina, Chapel Hill

†Roger A. Hornsby, Classics, University of Iowa

Walter Hunter, English, Clemson University

Linda Hutcheon, English and Comparative Literature (emerita), University of Toronto

Oren Izenberg, English, University of California, Irvine

Virginia Jackson, English, University of California, Irvine

Alessandro Michelangelo Jaker, Alaska Native Language Center, University of Alaska, Fairbanks

Christopher Johnson, Comparative Literature, Harvard University

Jeffrey Johnson, English Language and Literature, Daito Bunka University

Eileen Tess Johnston, English, United States Naval Academy

William R. Jones, English and Philosophy, Murray State University

Elise Bickford Jorgens, English (emerita), College of Charleston

Julie Kane, English, Northwestern State University of Louisiana

Ruth Kaplan, English, Quinnipiac University

Clare R. Kinney, English, University of Virginia

Christopher Kleinhenz, French and Italian (emeritus), University of Wisconsin–Madison

Peter Kline, English, James Madison University

David Kovacs, Classics, University of Virginia

Theresa Krier, English, Macalester College

Christoph Küper, English Linguistics, University of Vechta

Keith D. Leonard, Literature, American University

Jennifer Lewin, Writing, Sewanee School of Letters

Franklin D. Lewis, Persian Language and Literature, University of Chicago

Joel Lidov, Classics, Graduate Center, City University of New York

Eva Lilja, Comparative Literature, University of Gothenburg

John Lindow, Scandinavian, University of California, Berkeley

Lawrence Lipking, English (emeritus), Northwestern University

Lawrence Manley, English, Yale University

Jenny C. Mann, English, Cornell University

David Marno, English, University of California, Berkeley

Meredith Martin, English, Princeton University

†Wallace Martin, English, University of Toledo

Krystyna Mazur, American Studies, University of Warsaw

Russ McDonald, English and Comparative Literature, Goldsmiths, University of London

Kevin McFadden, Virginia Foundation for the Humanities

Jerome McGann, English, University of Virginia

Talya Meyers, English, Stanford University

W. J. T. Mitchell, English and Art History, University of Chicago

Steven Monte, English, College of Staten Island, City University of New York

Colin H. Moore, Comparative Literature, Stanford University

J. K. Newman, Classics (emeritus), University of Illinois

B. Ashton Nichols, English, Dickinson College

†Michael Patrick O'Connor, Semitics, Catholic University of America

†Richard H. Osberg, English, Santa Clara University

Stephen Owen, Comparative Literature, Harvard University

†Douglass S. Parker, Classics, University of Texas, Austin

Walter Ward Parks, independent scholar

Mark Payne, Classics, University of Chicago

†Erskine A. Peters, English, University of Notre Dame

Guillaume Peureux, French, University of California, Davis

William Bowman Piper, English (emeritus), Rice University

Noam Pines, Comparative Literature, University at Buffalo, The State University of New York

†Alex Preminger, independent scholar

William H. Race, Classics, University of North Carolina, Chapel Hill

Virginia Ramos, Comparative Literature, Stanford University

Brian M. Reed, English, University of Washington

Elizabeth Renker, English, Ohio State University

Eric J. Rettberg, English, Georgia Institute of Technology

Eliza Richards, English and Comparative Literature, University of North Carolina, Chapel Hill

Hallie Smith Richmond, English, University of Virginia

Phillip Rollinson, English Language and Literature (emeritus), University of South Carolina

Susan Rosenbaum, English, University of Georgia

Patricia A. Rosenmeyer, Classics, University of Wisconsin–Madison

David J. Rothman, Creative Writing, Western State Colorado University

Joshua Scodel, English and Comparative Literature, University of Chicago

Clive Scott, European Literature (emeritus), University of East Anglia

Robert B. Shaw, English, Mount Holyoke College

†Isidore Silver, Humanities, Washington University in Saint Louis

Barbara Herrnstein Smith, Comparative and English Literature (emerita), Duke University and Brown University

G. Gabrielle Starr, English, New York University

Timothy Steele, English, California State University, Los Angeles

†Martin Steinmann, English, University of Illinois, Chicago

Laurence D. Stephens, Classics, University of North Carolina, Chapel Hill

Robert S. Stilling, English, Florida State University

†Roy Arthur Swanson, Comparative Literature, University of Wisconsin–Milwaukee

Jeffrey S. Sychterz, English, Fayetteville State University

Bronwen Tate, Comparative Literature, Stanford University

Herbert F. Tucker, English, University of Virginia

John Van Sickle, Classics, Brooklyn College, City University of New York

Daniel Veraldi, independent scholar

Amanda Walling, English, University of Hartford

James Perrin Warren, English, Washington and Lee University

William Waters, Modern Languages and Comparative Literature, Boston University

Amanda Watson, Research and Instruction Librarian, Connecticut College

Jessica Weare, Microsoft

Madeline Weinstein, English, Harvard University

†Edward R. Weismiller, English (emeritus), George Washington University

Andrew Welsh, English (emeritus), Rutgers University

James I. Wimsatt, English (emeritus), University of Texas, Austin

Rosemary (Gates) Winslow, English, Catholic University of America

Susan J. Wolfson, English, Princeton University

Dafydd Wood, English and Comparative Literature, McNeese State University

Malcolm Woodland, English, University of Toronto

W. B. Worthen, Theatre, Barnard College

George T. Wright, English (emeritus), University of Minnesota

†Lawrence J. Zillman, English, University of Washington

The Princeton Handbook of Poetic Terms

A

ACCENT. In Eng., accent is the auditory prominence perceived in one syllable as compared with others in its vicinity. Accent and stress are often treated as synonymous, though some literary scholars and linguists distinguish the two terms according to a variety of criteria. Disagreements persist about the source and acoustical nature of syllabic prominence—loudness, volume, pitch, duration, or some combination of factors—but they are arguably of peripheral relevance to the understanding of accent within Eng. poetics.

The phenomena of accent vary among langs. and the poetics associated with them. The Eng. lexical contrast between *convict* as noun and as verb has no parallel in Fr. (Sp. resembles Eng. in this regard, while Finnish resembles Fr.) For Fr. speakers, stress contours are perceived on the level of the phrase or clause, and learning Eng. entails acquiring the ability to hear contrastive accent in words, just as a Japanese speaker learning Eng. must acquire the distinction between the liquids *l* and *r*. A consequence is that, while Fr. *meters count only syllables, Eng. meters conventionally also govern the number and distribution of accents.

In Eng. speech, accent operates in various ways on scales from the word (*convict*) through the sentence. As the units grow larger, accent becomes increasingly available to choice and conscious use for rhetorical emphasis. One step beyond the accents recorded in dicts. is the difference between "Spanish teacher" as a compound (a person who teaches Sp.) and as a phrase (a teacher from Spain). Eng. phonology enjoins stronger accent on "Spanish" in the compound and "teacher" in the phrase.

These lexical accents and differences in accent between compounds and phrases are "hardwired" into the Eng. lang. Beyond those, speakers exercise more deliberate choice when they employ contrasting accent to create rhetorical or logical emphases that are intimately entwined with semantic context. In the opposition Chicago White Sox vs. Chicago Cubs, it is the variable rather than the fixed element that receives the accent. Consequently, the question "Are you a fan of the Chicago *Cubs*?" accords with what we know about the world of baseball, while "Are you a fan of the *Chicago* Cubs?"

implies a Cubs team from some other city. This kind of contrastive stress, so dynamic in Eng. speech, also plays a variety of important roles in the poetic manipulation of lang., perhaps esp. in how written poetry contrives to convey the rhetorical and intonational contours of speech. When a line break, for instance, encourages the reader to place an accent on some word where it would not normally be expected, the emphasis may suggest an unanticipated logical contrast. This foregrounding of accent may have rhetorical implications: "The art of losing isn't hard to master; / so many things seem filled with the intent / to *be* lost that their loss is no disaster" (emphasis inferred; Elizabeth Bishop, "One Art"); "The sound of horns and motors, which shall bring / Sweeney to Mrs. Porter [not Actaeon to Diana] in the spring" (T. S. Eliot, *The Waste Land*).

Within the specific realm of traditional Eng. metrical verse, words are treated as bearing an accent if they are short polysyllables (whose stress can be looked up in a dict.) or monosyllables that belong to an open class (noun, verb, adjective, adverb, interjection). Other syllables tend to be unstressed. Yet several factors can alter this perception. One is the kind of rhetorical force created by contrastive stress, esp. in the volatile case of pronouns. Another, more pervasive influence arises from the complex interaction between the abstract, narrowly constrained pattern of meter and the concrete, highly contingent *rhythm of the spoken words. This fundamental distinction—meter and rhythm are related similarly to "the human face" and "a human's face"—crucially conditions how we perceive accent; it accounts for some difficulties that an unpracticed reader of metrical verse, though a native of Eng. speech, may have in locating the accents in a line.

Some of the confusion surrounding the term may be reduced if we recognize that *accent* names phenomena on two different levels of abstraction, the acoustical and the metrical. There is an analogy with phonemes. Speakers of Eng. unconsciously insert a puff of air after the *p* in *pan*, but not in *span*. The difference can be detected by using acoustic instruments or by holding a palm in front of the mouth, yet is not detected by speakers in the absence of exceptional

1

attention. The *p* in both cases represents the same phoneme, the same distinctive feature in the Eng. phonetic system—a system that does not merely divide the continuous acoustic stream of speech but abstracts from it a small set of three or four dozen discrete items. Similarly, various acoustical phenomena (pitch, loudness, etc.) give rise to an indefinitely large number of degrees and perhaps even kinds of accent; yet within a metrical context, the accustomed reader—analogous to a native speaker—reduces this continuum to an abstraction of (usually) two opposed values, stressed vs. unstressed. (The analogy fails to capture how the reader is simultaneously aware of a continuum of stress weights in the speech rhythm and a binary feature in the metrical pattern, both embodied in a single set of words.)

Differences of accent between compounds and phrases, or introduced for the sake of rhetorical contrast, which operate prominently within the larger manifold of rhythm, make no difference on the level of meter. "Spanish teacher" in either sense would be scanned as two *trochees, and the stronger stress on one word or the other has no specifically metrical effect. The four degrees of stress adopted by Chatman and others from Trager and Smith, while useful in the phonological analysis of Eng. and in the poetic understanding of rhythm, are unnecessary in the specifically metrical treatment of accent. The "four levels" represent an intermediate abstraction, as does the more traditional compromise of secondary stress or the hovering accent of Brooks and Warren. "Trager and Smith . . . demonstrated that stress and pitch are much more complex and variable phenomena than could be accounted for by the binary unstress-stress relation of traditional prosody" (Bradford 1994)—but this important truth should not mislead us into trying to weld speech rhythm and metrical pattern into an unwieldy whole, rather than hearing their interplay.

Readers are sensitive to a far wider range of rhythmic phenomena in poetry than those that are encoded within a metrical system. The nuanced stress patterns of speech, though they are foregrounded in nonmetrical or *free verse, do not disappear from the reader's awareness in metrical verse with its two-valued feature of accent. Rather, the give and take between the claims of meter and rhythm become a major source of auditory richness. Syllables may be heard as stressed either because of their prominence in speech or because of their position within the metrical line.

Any of the kinds of speech accent—lexical, phrasal, rhetorical—may coincide with a stressed position within the metrical line (as in the even-numbered positions within an *iambic *pentameter); or the speech and metrical accents may be momentarily out of phase. Within the accentual-syllabic system of Eng. metrics, these possibilities give rise to a repertoire of more or less common or striking variations. When speech accents occur in metrically unstressed positions, they give rise to metrical substitutions of one foot for another, such as the trochee or the *spondee for the iamb:

/ x   /   /
Singest of summer in full-throated ease

When metrical accents occur where no speech accent is available to embody them, the syllable receives "promoted" stress. The conjunction in the middle of W. B. Yeats's line, "We loved each other and were ignorant," which might pass unstressed in speech, exhibits this kind of promoted accent. It may render the verse line different from and semantically richer than its speech equivalent. The metrical expectation of accent in this position in the line is presumably the initial cause of the promotion; whether the rhetorical point—that love and ignorance are not at odds as one might think, but inextricable—is an effect or another kind of cause would be difficult to decide.

The phonological and metrical understandings of accent can sometimes even be directly at odds. In a compound word like *townsman*, the second syllable is not unstressed (its vowel is not reduced to schwa). Phonologically, then, the syllable sequence "townsman of" presents three descending levels of stress. In A. E. Housman's line, however, "Townsman of a stiller town," the reader hears "of" with an accent created or promoted by the underlying metrical pattern of iambic *tetrameter; and in comparison, the syllable "-man" is heard as unstressed. The case is complicated by the copresence of other details: because the line is headless, e.g., we know not to scan the initial compound word as a spondee only once we get the following syllables ("a still-"); the unambiguous accent on the last of those syllables (confirmed by the final alternation, "-er town") anchors the whole iambic matrix and retrospectively clarifies the metrical role of "Townsman of." Complications of this kind are typical in the interaction between metrical pattern and speech rhythms and constitute a primary reason for apparent ambiguities of accent in lines of Eng. verse.

See DEMOTION.

■ G. L. Trager and H. L. Smith Jr., *An Outline of English Structure* (1951); W. K. Wimsatt and M. C. Beardsley, "The Concept of Meter: An Exercise in Abstraction," *PMLA* 74 (1959); Brooks and Warren; Chatman, ch. 3, 4, appendix; N. Chomsky and M. Halle, *The Sound Pattern of English* (1968); M. Halle and S. J. Keyser, *English Stress* (1971); R. Vanderslice and P. Ladefoged, "Binary Suprasegmental Features and Transformational Word-Accentuation Rules," *Lang* 48 (1972); P. Kiparsky, "Stress, Syntax, and Meter," *Lang* 51 (1975); M. Liberman and A. S. Prince, "On Stress and Linguistic Rhythm," *LingI* 8 (1977); E. O. Selkirk, *Phonology and Syntax* (1984); B. Hayes, "The Prosodic Hierarchy in Meter," *Phonetics and Phonology*, ed. P. Kiparsky and G. Youmans (1989); R. Bradford, *Roman Jakobson* (1994).

C. O. HARTMAN

ACCENTUAL-SYLLABIC VERSE.

In Eng. poetry that is not written in *free verse, the most common and traditional metrical system is called "accentual-syllabic" because it combines a count of syllables per line with rules for the number and position of *accents in the line.

Metrical systems in different langs. measure lines by various linguistic elements and combinations of elements. Some systems are based on counting a single kind of element (syllables in Fr., monosyllabic words in Chinese). Others—such as the Lat. quantitative meters and the accentual-syllabic system used in mod. Eng., mod. Gr., Ger., and many other langs.—coordinate two different measures, such as syllables and their length or syllables and their stress. Cl. theorists provided a method of analyzing these meters by dividing them into feet, small units defined by various permutations of the two kinds of elements. Thus, the iamb orders a slack syllable and a stressed one (in Eng.) or a short syllable and a long one (in Lat.), while the *trochee reverses the iamb's order and the *anapest extends the iamb by doubling the initial weak syllable position.

Two-element *meters tend to maintain the stability of the lines' measure without as much rigidity in adherence to the meter's defining rules as single-element meters require. Consequently, much of the richness of variation in a two-element meter such as the accentual-syllabic can be captured at least crudely by analysis of substituted feet, metrical inversions, promoted stresses, and similar concepts that build on the notion of the *foot. This variety can be sketched or roughly diagrammed by *scansion of the lines.

Particular meters in such a two-element system are conventionally named by combining an adjectival form of the name of the base foot (iambic, dactylic, trochaic, etc.) with a noun made of a Lat. number word plus "-meter": trimeter, tetrameter, pentameter, hexameter, and so on.

See DEMOTION, PROSODY.

C. O. HARTMAN

ACCENTUAL VERSE.

Verse organized by count of stresses, not by count of syllables. Many prosodists of the 18th, 19th, and early 20th cs. looked upon most med. verse, a large amount of Ren. verse, and all popular verse down to the present as loose, rough, or irregular in number of syllables and in placement of stresses; from this assumption (not demonstration), they concluded that regulated count of stresses was the only criterion of the *meter. Schipper, e.g., effectually views most ME and mod. Eng. four-stress verse as descended from OE alliterative verse. But in this, he misconceived the nature of OE prosody. Other prosodists, too, have lumped together verse of very different rhythmic textures drawn from widely different social registers and textual contexts, treating all of them under the general rubric of accentual verse. This generalization masks differences that should probably be characterized in metrical (and not merely more broadly rhythmic) terms. Ideally, we would isolate the similarities among species of accentual verse and then identify either features or gradations in strictness of form that differentiate them. No clear theoretical foundation has been established to accomplish this.

Several varieties of accentual verse have been proposed in the Western langs.: (1) folk verse as opposed to art verse, i.e., the large class of popular (e.g., greeting card) verse, nursery rhymes, college cheers and chants, slogans, logos, and jingles—both Malof and Attridge rightly insist on the centrality of the four-stress line here; (2) *ballad and *hymn meter, specifically the meter of the Eng. and Scottish popular ballads and of the metrical psalters in the Sternhold-Hopkins line; (3) popular *song—an extremely large class; (4) literary imitations of genuine ballad meter such as the *Christabel meter; (5) genuine oral poetry, which indeed seems to show a fixed number of stresses per line but, in fact, is constructed by lexico-metrical formulaic phrases; (6) simple doggerel, i.e., lines that hardly scan at all except for stress count, whether because of authorial ineptitude, scribal misprision, textual corruption, or reader misperception—there are many scraps of late med. verse that *seem* to be so; (7) literary verse (often stichic) that is less regular than accentual-syllabic principles would demand but clearly not entirely free, e.g., the four-stress lines that Helen Gardner has pointed out in T. S. Eliot's *Four Quartets*; (8) Ger. *knittelvers*, both in a freer, late med. variety subsequently revived for literary and dramatic purposes by J. W. Goethe and Bertholt Brecht, and in a stricter, 16th-c. variety (*Hans-Sachs verse*) in octosyllabic couplets; and (9) Rus. *dol'nik* verse, a 20th-c. meter popularized by Alexander Blok, mainly in three-stress lines (interestingly, this form devolved from literary verse, not folk verse as in Eng. and Ger.). In all the preceding, there has been an assumption that accentual verse is isoaccentual; if one defines it more broadly (organized only on stresses but not always the same number per line), one would then admit Ger. *freie Rhythmen* and *freie Verse* and possibly Fr. 19th-c. *vers libéré*. But these verge on *free verse.

When Robert Bridges, the Eng. poet and prosodist, studied accentual verse at the turn of the 20th c., he believed he discovered a paradox in claims that accentual verse works by counting the natural stresses in the line. For example, despite S. T. Coleridge's claims that "Christabel" is in a "new" *meter* and that every line in it will be found to have exactly four stresses, the poem actually contains a number of problematic lines, like "How drowsily it crew," which cannot by any reasonable standard carry four natural accents. Of this line Bridges remarks: "In stress-verse this line can have only two accents . . . but judging from other lines in the poem, it was almost certainly meant to have three, and if so, the second of these is a conventional accent; it does not occur in the speech but in the metre, and has to be imagined because the metre suggests or requires it; and it is plain that *if the stress is to be the rule of the metre, the metre cannot be called on to provide the stress*" (italics added). For Bridges, the definition of true "accentual verse" is that it operates on only two principles: "*the stress governs the rhythm*" and "*the stresses must all be true speech-stresses*" (Bridges set these sentences in all capitals). This two-part

definition, he asserts, strictly distinguishes accentual verse from *accentual-syllabic verse, in which it is the function of the meter to establish and preserve in the mind's ear a paradigm, an abstract pattern, such that, if the line itself does not supply the requisite number of accents, the pattern shall supply them mentally. But Bridges's view is complicated by the dominance of accentual-syllabism in so much mod. Eng. verse that poets and readers may hear promoted stresses even in a mostly accentual context. In many poems by Elizabeth Bishop, such as "The Fish" (three-stress), e.g., the near regularity of accent counts encourages us to fill out some shorter lines with stresses that, while strong relative to surrounding syllables, would not be heard in the speech rhythm of the line; analyzing the verse as either strictly accentual or as consistently but roughly accentual-syllabic requires acknowledging exceptions, but calling the result "free verse" ignores important gestures toward regularity.

In Eng. as in other Teutonic langs., accentual verse has some claim to being fundamental; it is "the simplest, oldest, and most natural poetic measure in English" (Gioia). It lies near the root of poetry, as it were, and near the point where poetry and music diverge (and reconverge in song). It comes closer than accentual-syllabic meters to manifesting the *beat that defines the term *meter* in the musical sense of that word. Perhaps partly for this reason, versions of accentual verse (measuring lines in four, three, or even two stresses) have been popular alongside mod. free verse, sometimes only notionally distinct from it.

See ALLITERATION, BALLAD METER, VERSIFICATION.

■ Schipper; Bridges, "Appendix on Accentual Verse"; G. Saintsbury, *History of English Prosody* (1906–10); W. Kayser, *Kleine deutsche Versschule* (1946); H. Gardner, *The Art of T. S. Eliot* (1949); J. Bailey, "The Stress-Meter of Goethe's *Der Erlkönig,*" *Lang&S* 2 (1969); J. Malof, *A Manual of English Meters* (1970), chs. 3–4; M. G. Tarlinskaja, "Meter and Rhythm of Pre-Chaucerian Rhymed Verse," *Linguistics* 121 (1974) and *English Verse: Theory and History* (1976); Scott; Brogan, 319–37; Attridge; Scherr; D. Gioia, "Accentual Verse," http://www.danagioia.net/essays/eaccentual.htm.

T.V.F. BROGAN; C. O. HARTMAN

AIR. (1) Described as a "musico-poetic miniature" by Fischlin, *air* (ayre, Fr. *air de cour*) most aptly refers to a style of song that flourished in courtly social circles in England and France in the 16th and 17th cs. Airs are typically solo songs (though sometimes printed in such a way that they can be accompanied by additional singers), accompanied by a lute or other plucked instrument and featuring a refined and intimate style appropriate to the courts in which they were sung. A hallmark of the genre is clear presentation of the text, sometimes with illustrative musical devices highlighting specific words. Many airs take their lyrics from the noted poets of the day; many are Petrarchan, and most are love songs; many are strophic (see STROPHE); and they range in quality from exquisite gems to cliché-ridden rhymes. These stylistic features distinguish the air from other types of song that coexisted with it (e.g., Eng. *ballad, Eng. or It. *madrigal) or that evolved into more dramatic or elaborate vocal compositions (Ger. *lied*, It. *aria*). (2) By extension, *air* frequently designates a melody or tune, apart from any harmony or accompaniment, and thus a musical composition, usually brief, in which the melody is dominant. In the same courtly circles, an air was sometimes an instrumental dance tune with a prominent melody. (3) *Air* has also come to be associated with the texts or lyrics, especially of the Eng. variety, which themselves have been the subject of stylistic and historical investigation in the 20th and 21st cs. (4) In the writings of some of the late 16th- and 17th-c. Eng. musical theorists such as Thomas Morley and Charles Butler, *air* denotes the mode or key of a piece.

See SONG.

■ T. Morley, *A Plaine and Easie Introduction to Practicall Musicke* (1597); C. Butler, *Principles of Musick* (1636); P. Warlock, *The English Ayre* (1926); *Roger North on Music*, ed. J. Wilson (1959); U. Olshausen, *Das lautenbegleitete Sololied in England um 1600* (1963); *Lyrics from English Airs, 1596–1622*, ed. E. Doughtie (1970); I. Spink, *English Song* (1974); N. Fortune and D. Greer, "Air," *New Grove*; E. Jorgens, *The Well-Tun'd Word* (1982); L. Schleiner, *The Living Lyre in English Verse* (1984); E. Doughtie, *English Renaissance Song* (1986); W. Maynard, *Elizabethan Lyric Poetry and Its Music* (1986); L. Auld, "Text as Pretext: French Court Airs," *Literature and the Other Arts*, ed. D. L. Rubin (1993); D. Fischlin, *In Small Proportions* (1998).

E. B. JORGENS

ALBA (Occitan, Sp., "dawn"; OF *aube, aubade*; Galician-Port. *alva*; Ger. *Tagelied*). A dawn song about adulterous love, expressing one or both lovers' regret over the coming of dawn after a night of love. A third voice, a watchman, may announce the coming of dawn and the need for the lovers to separate. An Occitan *alba* may contain a dialogue (or serial monologues) between lover and beloved or a lover and the watchman or a combination of monologue with a brief narrative intro. The voices may fear the jealous husband (*gilos*) and the lovers' secret being discovered. In its staging of a secret, consummated love under the threat of the coming of dawn, the alba, unlike the *canso*, imagines a love of mutual but nonetheless illicit attraction. The alba has no fixed metrical form, but in Occitan each stanza usually ends with a *refrain that contains the word *alba*. The earliest examples date from the end of the 12th c. By the turn of the 13th c., the alba belongs to the technical vocabulary of troubadours and later appears in the grammatical manual *Doctrina de compondre dictats* (late 13th c.).

Various theories of origins remain hypothetical. The earliest attributed alba, Giraut de Bornelh's "Reis glorios, verais lums e clartatz," bears a melodic resemblance to the Lat. hymn to the Virgin, "Ave maris stella" (ca. 9th c.) and the 11th-c. Occitan *versus* "O Maria, Deu maire"; this song as well as an earlier bilingual Lat.-Occitan alba ("Alba de Fleury-sur-Loire") attests to the likely dialogue between the secular alba and the long trad. of Lat. religious dawn hymns such as those by Prudentius (ca. 348–405) and Ambrose (4th c.) that figure dawn as announcing the light of salvation. In Mozarabic *zéjels* and *kharjas*, songs about the parting of lovers incorporating the word *alba* suggest a relation with an independent Romance trad. that exerted an influence on the Occitan alba. Likewise, the courtly Occitan alba perhaps developed in conjunction with a popular pan-Romance lyric trad. that includes OF *chanson de femme* and the Galician-Port. *cantigas d'amigo*, as well as similar Catalan, Sp., and It. compositions. This trad. consists of dialogue or women's songs about separation, the arrival of dawn signaled by light and bird's song, and the risk of being seen; the adulterous situation of the husband or presence of a watchman seems to have been a significant devel. of the genre (Jeanroy). The watchman plays an important role as mediator between the two symbolic worlds of night (illicit love in an enclosed space) and day (courtly society, *lauzengiers* or evil gossips or enemies of love; Saville). Eng. examples can be found in Chaucer (*Troilus and Criseyde*, 3.1415–1533, 1695–1712 and "Reeve's Tale" 4236–47), Shakespeare (*Romeo and Juliet* 3.5.1–64), John Donne ("The Sun Rising," "The Good Morrow"), and Robert Browning ("Parting at Morning"). In the 20th c., the genre was attempted by Ezra Pound ("Alba"), W. H. Auden ("Aubade"), Philip Larkin ("Aubade"), and Robert Creeley ("Alba").

■ **Anthologies**: *Eos: An Enquiry into the Theme of Lovers' Meetings and Partings at Dawn in Poetry*, ed. A.T. Hatto (1965); *Et ades sera l'alba. Angoisse de l'aube: Recueil des chansons d'aube des troubadours*, ed. G. Gouiran (2005).

■ **Criticism and History**: Jeanroy; R. E. Kaske, "An Aube in the *Reeve's Tale*," *ELH* 26 (1959), and "The Aube in Chaucer's *Troilus*," *Troilus and Criseyde and the Minor Poems, Chaucer Criticism 2*, ed. R. J. Schoeck and J. Taylor (1961); J. Saville, *The Medieval Erotic Alba* (1972); D. Rieger, *GRLMA* 2.1B (1979); E. W. Poe, "The Three Modalities of the Old Provençal Dawn Song," *RPh* 37 (1984), and "New Light on the *Alba*: A Genre Redefined," *Viator* 15 (1984); H. U. Seeber, "Intimität und Gesellschaft. Zur Renaissance der Aubade in der englischen Lyrik des 20. Jahrhunderts," *Gattungsprobleme in der anglo-amerikanischen Literatur*, ed. R. Borgmeir (1986); T. F. Cornejo, *La canción de alba en la lírica románica medieval* (1999); F. Bauer, "L'aube et la nuit," *Revue des langues romanes* 110 (2006); C. Chaguinian, "L'alba dans le système des genres troubadouresques: Réflexions sur le rapport des troubadours à la production non troubadouresque," *Cahiers de Civilisation Médiévale* 50 (2007).

M. GALVEZ

ALEXANDRINE. The grand line of Fr. poetry since the 16th c., the alexandrine is made of 12 countable vowels (or 13 vowels in a feminine verse line: see MASCULINE AND FEMININE) and divided in two *hemistichs (6-6), as in the following lines from Sonnet 31 of *Les Regrets* (1558) by Joachim du Bellay:

Heureux qui, comme Ulysse, + a fait un beau voyage
    1   2   3   4   5 6   7 8 9 10 11 12 (13)
(Happy the man who, like Ulysses, completed a great voyage)

Ou comme cestuy-là + qui conquit la toison
  1   2   3 4 5 6   7   8   9 10 11 12
(Or like he who won the Golden Fleece)

Although its name comes from the *Roman d'Alexandre* (The Romance of Alexander, 1170), the alexandrine had been used previously in the *Pèlerinage de Charlemagne* (The Pilgrimage of Charlemagne, 1150). Hypotheses about its origins are numerous (from the most credible to the least, as follows: imitation of Lat. verse; length matched to the number of syllables that can be read in one breath; combination of two six-syllable lines). As the longest Fr. cl. verse line, it was at first seen as resembling discourse in prose; du Bellay, for instance, wrote the *Regrets* in alexandrines because his book was meant to express an intimate and informal type of inspiration. Considered to be less noble than the more common ten-syllable line, the alexandrine was associated primarily with popular poetry. In 1572, Pierre de Ronsard wrote in the preface to the *Franciade*, "It would have been much easier to write my book in alexandrines, since this is the longest verse line, were it not for the scruple that they sound too much like prose." Nevertheless, between the 16th and 17th cs., the alexandrine became not only the most widely used verse line in Fr. poetry but the preferred form of elevated and even "noble" genres such as *epic and tragedy. Thus, a name that referred to the med. heroic poem was elevated to the status of national symbol and eventually came to typify Fr. poetry overall (Halévy). In reality, Ronsard's reluctance to espouse the alexandrine bears witness to its success after 1555, when it began to displace the ten-syllable line as the new *vers héroïque*. This agreement on what had become the most common verse line in Fr. poetry of the Ren. illustrates the dedication of poets in their efforts to forge a national lang.

Since the exact number of syllables that speakers of Fr. can routinely identify with certainty in a given verse line is limited to eight or fewer, the alexandrine is heard not as a whole but as two hexasyllabic units. But the cl. 6-6 alexandrine is just one of the possible 12-syllable meters in Fr., along with 8-4, 4-4-4, 3-5-4, 5-7, and 7-5, all of which appeared during the second half of the 19th c. Strictly speaking, the designation "alexandrine" should be reserved for 6-6 lines and not all dodecasyllabic lines.

Given its status as the favorite Fr. meter, the alexandrine has always been criticized. Poets and theorists of the 18th c. (e.g., François Neuf-Château, Toussaint Rémond de Saint-Mard, Jean-François Marmontel, Louis-Sébastien Mercier, André Chénier, Jean-Antoine Roucher) judged its structure to be too rigid, an obstacle to the expression of poets' voices and passions. Traditional theatrical declamation of the line, which was based on a rising tone for the first six syllables and a falling tone for the final six, was felt to be monotonous and little conducive to rhythm (Lote 1940). Later, Hugo heroically claimed he had "disloqué ce grand niais d'alexandrin" (dislocated the alexandrine, that great simpleton [*Les Contemplations*, 1856]). Though in his poetry Hugo never changed the alexandrine's fundamental 6-6 structure, even as he straddled line-limits (through *rejets* and *enjambments*), he launched a radical change that some romantics demanded. Subsequent generations from Charles Baudelaire to Arthur Rimbaud, including such figures as Paul Verlaine and Théodore de Banville but excluding Gérard de Nerval and Théophile Gautier, investigated ways to renew the "grand vers" by inventing new scansions that first could accommodate the 6-6 structure ("mesures d'accompagnement"; Cornulier 1995): alternative scansions appeared, such as the 8-4 as in "Comme César pour un sourire, Ô Cléopâtre" (Like Caesar for a smile, O Cleopatra; Verlaine, "Lettre," *Fêtes galantes*, 1869); the 4-8 as in "Entendez-vous? C'est la marmite qu'accompagne / L'horloge du tic-tac allègre de son pouls" (Do you hear? It is the pot / That accompanies the blithe pulse of the clock; Verlaine, "L'Auberge," *Jadis et naguère*, 1881); the 4-4-4 as in "Mais de ceci, pour mon malheur, ne sachant rien" (But knowing nothing about this, unfortunately; Charles-Marie Leconte de Lisle, "Le corbeau," *Poèmes barbares*, 1862); and the rare 3-5-4 as in "Ô malheur ! je me sens frémir, la vieille terre . . ." (Oh misfortune! I tremble, the old earth . . .; "Qu'est-ce pour nous, mon coeur . . ." Rimbaud, *Derniers vers*, 1872). Then, increasingly bold in their line construction, poets weakened the usual syntactic pause of the *caesura by placing in the sixth position words that could not receive vocal emphasis, such as the proclitic article *un*: "Chacun plantant, comme *un* outil, son bec impur" (Each [bird] planting his unclean beak as if it were a tool; "Un voyage à Cythère," Baudelaire, *Les Fleurs du mal*, 1857).

Experiments with the alexandrine (but also with the decasyllable) led to the emergence of *vers libre* (free verse) at the turn of the 20th c. But in spite of free verse's liberties, poets have maintained a system of echoes and resemblances with the alexandrine, which remains the most prominent poetic line in Fr.

See SYLLABIC VERSE.

■ G. Lote, *L'Alexandrin d'après la phonétique expérimentale* (1919); J. Roubaud, *La Vieillesse d'Alexandre* (1978); B. de Cornulier, *Théorie du vers* (1982); S. P. Verluyten, "Analyse de l'alexandrin: Mètre ou rythme?" in *Le Souci des apparences*, ed. M. Dominicy (1989); H. Morier, "L'Alexandrin classique était bel et bien un tétramètre," in *Langue, littérature du XVIIᵉ et du XVIIIᵉ siècle* (1990); G. Lote, *Histoire du vers français* (VIII) (1994 [1953]); B. de Cornulier, *Art poëtique* (1995); J.-M. Gouvard, *Critique du vers* (2000); O. Halévy, "La vie d'une forme: l'alexandrin renaissant (1452–1573)," *L'Information littéraire* (2004); J. Gros de Gasquet, *En disant l'alexandrin renaissant* (2006); G. Peureux, *La Fabrique du vers* (2009).

G. PEUREUX

ALLITERATION. The repetition of the *sound of an initial consonant or consonant cluster in stressed syllables close enough to each other for the ear to be affected. The term is sometimes also used for the repetition of an initial consonant in unstressed syllables, as in E. A. Poe's "lost Lenore," where the weak second *l* affects the ear less than the long *o* followed by *r*, but this less direct patterning is arguably not of the same class as stress-enhanced alliteration. From cl. times up to the 20th c., *alliteration* as a figure in rhet. means the repetition of the initial *letter* of words. Alliteration formerly included the echo of initial vowels, even of initial letters in weak syllables—a fact that explains Charles Churchill's 18th-c. attack on those who unsuccessfully "pray'd / For apt alliteration's Artful aid." In mod. scholarship, *vowel alliteration* usually refers only to the older Germanic langs. It must constantly be borne in mind that, since alliteration is a device of the *sound* stratum of poetry, the vagaries of spelling systems must be discounted: it is sounds, not letters, that count, as in Emily Dickinson's "The cricket sang / And set the sun" ("The Cricket Sang") or John Dryden's "Thy force, infus'd, the fainting Tyrians prop'd, / And haughty Pharoah found his fortune stop'd" (*Absalom and Achitophel*, 842–43), where the *f* phone begins six stressed syllables, one in a medial syllable, one spelled *Ph*.

In the alliterative meters of the older Germanic langs., including *Beowulf* (see ENGLISH PROSODY, Old English), alliteration binds the two *hemistichs, as in "Oft Scyld Scefing sceathena threatum." The alliteration is usually on initial consonants or on certain consonant clusters, but any vowel may alliterate with any other. In Old Saxon, a weakening of phonological stress apparently caused alliterating syllables to be reinforced by a higher proportion of identical vowels, whether the syllable began with the vowel or with a consonant (Suzuki). In poetry after ME, alliteration is neither linear nor structural; in fact, it is often carried through several lines. Today, then, alliteration is one of the four most significant devices of phonic echo in poetry (see ASSONANCE, CONSONANCE, RHYME).

One must remember that unintentional alliteration will occur less often than unintentional assonance, since in IE langs. consonants outnumber vowels. Certain consonant clusters (e.g., *st* and *sp*) alliterate only with themselves in the older Germanic langs. A. E. Housman, aware of this trad., lets his poet in "The Grecian Galley" alliterate seven *st* clusters in three lines.

Almost every major poetry in the world except Hebrew, Persian, and Arabic seems to have made considerable use of alliteration, which has been more popular and persistent than rhyme. Although there is disagreement about the nature or importance of stress in Gr. and Lat. poetry, it is certain that cl. poets understood the uses of alliteration. Aeschylus echoed initials to emphasize key words and phrases, to point up a pun, to aid *onomatopoeia, or simply to please the ear (Stanford). Lucretius reveled in phonic echoes, incl. alliteration, while Virgil, a quieter poet, wrote many lines like these two, heavy with assonance, in which eight important syllables also bear initial *k* or *l*: "cuncta mihi Alpheum linquens locusque Molorchi / cursibus et crudo decernet Graecia caestu."

More than most others, the Romance langs. have neglected alliteration in favor of assonance, the reason perhaps being that It., Sp., and Port. poetry have traditionally preferred short lines with vowel (often followed by consonant) echoes in the final two syllables. Even though it is said that Fr. poetry by the 17th c. considered alliteration "mauvaise" (Thieme), the Fr. cl. *alexandrine did make some use of it, as in Nicolas Boileau's "Des traits d'esprit semés de temps en temps pétillent." But most Fr. poets from Victor Hugo to Saint-John Perse have found other devices more appealing to the ear.

Even the Asian tonal langs. have been as fond of alliteration as of other phonic echoes. Chinese, a monosyllabic lang. with short-line poems based on parallel structure and patterning of rising vs. falling tones, insists on rhyme and plays much with repeated vowels and consonants, as with *ch* in the opening lines of "Fu on Climbing a Tower" by Wang Can (ca. 200 CE; Frankel). Also tonal, but polysyllabic, Japanese poetry has from ancient times employed much alliteration (Brower).

All the Celtic langs., but esp. Ir. and Welsh, have been renowned for their elaborate schemes of phonic ornamentation. Early Welsh and Ir. "cadenced" verse was seldom rhymed but used much alliteration for linking words and lines. By the 6th c., this verse gave way to "rhyming" verse in which each line has stressed word pairs that alliterate or assonate, all to go with the "generic rhyming" that links lines of a stanza. By the 14th c., Welsh bards had evolved the elaborately decorated *cynghanedd* based on exact rhymes in couplets and complex echoes of vowels and consonants, incl. alliteration (Dunn).

Of the poetry in Germanic langs., mod. Ger. has employed alliteration consistently, while Eng. has liked it perhaps even more. J. W. Goethe used alliteration much as Shakespeare did, in conjunction with other phonic devices and normally with restraint. He might, however, open a lyric (e.g., "Hochzeitlied") with heavy alliteration or help elevate Faust's most important speech to Mephistopheles with "Dann will ich gern zu Grunde gehn!" Heinrich Heine preferred rhymed short-line verse and needed alliteration less, but he often tended to heavy ornament (e.g., "Ein Wintermarchen"). Gottfried Benn and R. M. Rilke were perhaps more sound-conscious than most other 20th-c. Ger. poets; and while they too preferred assonance, Benn could write dozens of lines like this one in "Untergrundbahn": "Druch all den Frühling kommt die fremde Frau," a line no more ornate than some by Rilke.

Although alliteration was disparaged by Chaucer's Parson, a southern man, as "rum, ram, ruf," Eng. poets continued to use it widely after the 14th-c. revival of alliterative verse in England and Scotland. The later usage shows no knowledge of the precise rules of meter that have been discovered for alliterative verse of the 14th and early 15th cs. (see ENGLISH PROSODY, Middle English). Edmund Spenser makes use of it in the *Shepheardes Calender*; and in *The Faerie Queene*, the first 36 lines have seven instances of triple alliteration—by some standards very heavy. In *A Midsummer Night's Dream* (5.1.147–48), Shakespeare makes fun of alliteration, but he employs it heavily in the early long poems (e.g., *Lucrece*)—less so in the lyrics, sonnets, and plays—though alliteration is often conspicuous in the plays. John Milton, who loved the sound of words even before his blindness, preferred assonance, but he also liked alliteration, e.g., in "L'Allegro" ("And to the stack, or the barn door, / Stoutly struts his Dames before") and in *Paradise Lost* ("Moping melancholy, / And moonstruck madness" [2.424–25]). Eng. poets from 1660 to 1780 worked hard with phonic echoes in order to vary not only their couplets but their *blank verse and octosyllables. Dryden, Alexander Pope, John Gay, and James Thomson used alliteration best to tie adjectives to nouns, to balance nouns or verbs or adjectives, to stress the *caesura and end rhyme, to join sound to sense, and to decorate their lines. After 1780, poets used alliteration less; still, almost every poet from William Blake to G. M. Hopkins to Housman used it well, sometimes excessively, as with this typical burst in Robert Browning's "The Bishop Orders His Tomb": "And stretch my feet forth straight as stone can point." Alfred, Lord Tennyson is reported to have said, "When I spout my lines first, they come out so alliteratively that I have sometimes no end of trouble to get rid of the alliteration."

In the 20th c., Robert Frost, Ezra Pound, and W. C. Williams are relatively unornamental, though Frost could sometimes alliterate heavily—"Nature's first green is gold, / Her hardest hue to hold" ("Nothing Gold Can Stay"). Others—Wallace Stevens, T. S. Eliot, W. B. Yeats—are less sparing with alliteration, as Eliot is in the Sweeney poems and "The Love Song of J. Alfred Prufrock," though sometimes they indulge sudden excesses, as with Stevens's "Winding across wide waters." But there is a larger group of more recent poets who, learning from Hopkins and Thomas Hardy, have depended very much on phonic echoes, esp. in unrhymed verse. Among these are Wilfred Owen and Dylan Thomas in Britain and Robinson Jeffers, Marianne Moore, Hart Crane, Theodore Roethke, Robert Lowell, Richard Wilbur, and Mary Oliver in the U.S. Crane, typical of this group, echoes not only initial consonants but important vowels in almost every line—"Sun-silt rippled them / Asunder" ("Repose of Rivers") and "Rail-squatters ranged in nomad raillery" (*The Bridge*). Oliver, whose poems show an awareness of rhetorical figures and prosodical turns, alliterates *s* four times and *f* twice in two lines: "It is the light at the center

of every cell. / It is what sent the snake coiling and flowing forward" ("The Black Snake").

All these literary patterns depend for their effectiveness on the salience of alliteration in everyday speech. In the Germanic langs. esp., alliterative formulas have been in common use historically, incl. alliterating names for siblings, e.g., *Heorogar, Hrothgar,* and *Halga* (Minkova). It appears that nonliterary usage both preceded the literary forms and survived them after fashions in verse changed. Recent research using the databases of corpus ling. has revealed the pervasiveness of alliterative formulas in early ME, influenced partly by the alliterative collocations of western Scandinavia (Markus). ME prose with an affinity to the registers of spoken lang. suggests that these collocations were a part of common speech, as they continue to be in present-day Eng.—e.g., *fit as a fiddle, ship-shape, tit for tat, topsy turvy, down in the dumps, worse for wear,* and so on.

■ H. Tennyson, *Alfred, Lord Tennyson: A Memoir By His Son* (1897); R. E. Deutsch, *The Patterns of Sound in Lucretius* (1939); W. B. Stanford, *Aeschylus in His Style* (1942); N. I. Hérescu, *La poésie latine* (1960); L. P. Wilkinson, *Golden Latin Artistry* (1963); W. B. Stanford, *The Sound of Greek* (1967); J. D. Allen, *Quantitative Studies in Prosody* (1968); Wimsatt, esp. essays by Frankel, Brower, Lehmann, and Dunn; P. G. Adams, *Graces of Harmony: Alliteration, Assonance, and Consonance in Eighteenth-Century British Poetry* (1977); J.T.S. Wheelock, "Alliterative Functions in the *Divina Comedia,*" *Lingua e Stile* 13 (1978); Brogan, esp. items C111–C170, L65, L406 (Jakobson), L150, L474, L564, L686, and pp. 479–585; D. Minkova, *Alliteration and Sound Change in Early English* (2003); S. Suzuki, *The Metre of Old Saxon Poetry* (2004); M. Markus, "*Bed & Board*: The Role of Alliteration in Twin Formulas of Middle English Prose," *Folia Linguistica Historica* 26 (2005).

P. G. ADAMS; T. CABLE

AMBIGUITY (Lat. *ambiguitas,* from *ambigere,* "to dispute about," literally "to wander"). In lit. crit., *ambiguity* is primarily defined as the simultaneous availability of more than one meaning or interpretation. It has been variously identified as a property of verbal structure (lexical, semantic, and syntactic), of literary forms and genres themselves, and of readerly practices. Aristotle regarded ambiguity as a type of fallacious argument that he called *sophistic syllogism*, an argument that defends something false in order to confuse an adversary. For Aristotle, there were only two types of arguments: true and untrue. An ambiguous argument was an argument that appeared to be true and untrue at the same time and was, thus, logically untrue. Aristotle's principle of noncontradiction is at the root of scientific and logical thought. But in a literary context, Virgil's suggestive use of the noun *ambages* in *Aeneid* 6.99 to denote the ambiguous prophecy of the Cumaean Sibyl was noticed by Dante, Boccaccio, Chaucer, and others, who introduce the Lat. term directly into their vernaculars to suggest perniciously doubled meanings ("with double words slye, / Swiche as men clepen a worde with two visages," *Troilus and Criseyde* 5.898–99). By the 16th c., *ambiguity* is established in Eng. (and its counterparts in the other vernaculars) to refer to multiple meanings that may be dangerous, productive, or aporetic (see APORIA), in keeping with the Ren. rupturing of monologic paradigms. For instance, the Rus. theorist Mikhail Bakhtin in the first half of the 20th c. identifies in the works of François Rabelais a socially and historically conditioned use of ambiguity involving multiple meanings in not only words but discourses of all kinds; and in the second half of the century, a train of critics from Leo Spitzer to Claudio Guillén argue that literary works embody contrasting perspectives, the basis of *genres such as the Cervantine novel and the picaresque. The fact that many mod. critics develop theories of ambiguity with reference to Ren. works implies that the concept has a special purchase in the period.

In Anglo-Am. New Criticism, the broad use of the term *ambiguity* as making available more than one meaning or interpretation became common practice with William Empson's *Seven Types of Ambiguity* (1930), where he defines the term as "any verbal nuance, however slight, which gives room to alternative reactions to the same piece of language." Empson drew attention to ambiguity as constitutive of the lang. of poetry and valued it positively as a source of richness rather than imprecision. Empson offers a taxonomy of ambiguity: *metaphor is the first type of ambiguity; followed by ambiguity as two or more meanings that become another meaning; two concepts inextricably connected via context; two meanings that combine to illuminate the author's state of mind; two opposite meanings that illuminate a division within the

author; the lack of apparent meaning and the need for the reader's creation of meaning; and, finally, ambiguity as the act of writing, a channel halfway between the text and the writer.

In the 1960s, literary theorists such as Genette, Barthes, and Wheelwright proposed ambiguity as an intrinsic capacity of poetic lang. Genette theorizes the notion of a nonempty "gap" as the essence of poetry, while Wheelwright and Barthes observe not only the capacity to hold more than one meaning or interpretation but the open state of oscillation between them, which is variously called *plurisignation* (Wheelwright) or *infinite plurality* (Barthes).

In contrast to Barthes's description of an open work that lacks or deliberately eschews centers of orientation, Rimmon considers an ambiguous work to possess marked centers that polarize data and create mutually exclusive systems of meaning. Rimmon distinguishes ambiguity from double meaning, multiple meaning, plurisignation, or infinite plurality, which she refers to as types of *conjunctive ambiguity*. For Rimmon, however, ambiguity is disjunctive, that which both "calls for choice and makes it impossible." According to her, the essential difference between the multiplicity of subjective interpretations given to a work of fiction and ambiguity proper is that, while the subjectivity of reading is conditioned mainly by the psyche of the reader, ambiguity is "a fact in the text— a double system of mutually exclusive clues." While Rimmon emphasizes the function of the reader by offering ambiguity as a plurality of readings from which we are to determine our own, at the same time she sees such a subjectivity as invited by the text itself and considers each meaning clearly based in a function of the text and context. Rimmon considers Empson's approach too broad, as he analyzes ambiguity by the conjunction or synthesis or fusion or multiplication of meaning, but she ultimately sides with him in locating ambiguity in the verbal structure itself.

For the poststructuralist Kristeva, "communication and that which breaks communication apart" are located not only in the verbal structure but, following Jacques Lacan, in the unconscious. For Kristeva, ambiguity "provides the creative and innovative impulse of modern poetic structure" and is closely related to *significance* or "the eruption of the semiotic within the symbolic." The ambiguity that characterizes modernism is the unleashing of the semiotic, i.e., the preverbal impulses and bodily drives discharged into signification. Other critics such as Trujillo move even further away from the verbal structure, considering ambiguity not as inherent in lang. but as a performative mechanism used at will by the writing subject.

With its cl. origins and early mod. provenance, ambiguity differs from concepts such as polysemy or *indeterminacy. Unlike indeterminacy, it refers not to the instability of meaning itself but to the existence of multiple meanings at the same time. And unlike polysemy, it emphasizes not discrete meanings but their simultaneity, thus placing signification in a state of oscillation between meanings but also interpretations, where context and subjectivity play a main role. Ambiguity is an openness to the potentiality of a multiplicity of interpretations, not because all are equally important or relevant at the same time and for the same reader but because they all exist equally within the field and will emerge eventually as actualized—as De Beauvoir puts it, "reinvested with [a particular] human signification."

■ M. Black, "Vagueness: An Exercise in Logical Analysis," *Philosophy of Science* 4 (1937); I. M. Copilowish, "Borderline Cases: Vagueness and Ambiguity," and C. G. Hempel, "Vagueness and Logic," *Philosophy of Science* 6 (1939); W. B. Stanford, *Ambiguity in Greek Literature* (1939); S. de Beauvoir, *The Ethics of Ambiguity*, trans. B. Frechtman (1948); G. W. Cunningham, "On the Meaningfulness of Vague Language," *Philosophy Review* 58 (1949); M. C. Beardsley, *Thinking Straight* (1954); S. Dawson, "Infinite Types of Ambiguity," *BJA* 5 (1965); P. Wheelwright, "On the Semantics of Poetry," *Essays on the Language of Literature*, ed. S. Chatman and S. R. Levin (1967); R. Barthes, *S/Z*, trans. R. Miller (1970); C. Guillén, *Literature as System* (1971); R. Trujillo, *Elementos de semántica lingüística* (1976); R. Barthes, "From Work to Text," *Image, Music, Text*, trans. S. Heath (1977); S. Rimmon, *The Concept of Ambiguity* (1977); G. Pérez Firmat, "Genre as Text," *Comparative Literature Studies* 17 (1980); J. Kristeva, *Desire in Language*, trans. T. Gora et al. (1980); M. M. Bakhtin, *The Dialogic Imagination*, ed. M. Holquist, trans. C. Emerson and M. Holquist (1981); J. Derrida, *Dissemination*, trans. B. Johnson (1981); M. Perloff, *The Poetics of Indeterminacy* (1981); G. Genette, *Figures of Literary Discourse*, trans. A. Sheridan (1982); D. Wallace, "Chaucer's Ambages," *American Notes and Queries* 23 (1984); J. Ferrater Mora,

Diccionario de la Filosofía (1988); U. Eco, *The Open Work*, trans. A. Cancogni (1989).

V. RAMOS

ANACOLUTHON (Gr., "wanting sequence"). A term of grammar designating a change of construction in the middle of a sentence that leaves its beginning uncompleted. In rhet., however, *anacoluthon* has been treated as a figure, a natural and often effective mode of expression in spoken discourse. Hervey cites Matt. 7:9, which runs, in the Authorized Version, "Or what man is there of you, whom if his son ask bread, will he give him a stone?" Shakespeare sometimes shows depth of feeling in his characters by this means, as at *Henry V* 4.3.34–36, where the king says: "Rather proclaim it, Westmoreland, through my host, / That he which hath no stomach to this fight, / Let him depart." Lausberg finds the commonest form of anacoluthon to be the so-called absolute nominative (as in the Shakespeare above).

Related to anacoluthon is the absence of the second of a pair of correlative expressions, which is known as *particula pendens* when it has to do with correlative particles (e.g., "either . . . or," "both . . . and"), otherwise by the related term *anapodoton* (Gr., "wanting the apodosis," i.e., the main clause in a conditional sentence). Ernesti cites the authority of a Scholiast on Thucydides 3.3; the passage goes, "If the attempt succeeds," the understood but unexpressed apodosis being, "it will be well"; so also Lausberg. Anapodoton includes a subset called *anantapodoton*, in which even the subordinate clause is incomplete.

Group μ classifies anacoluthon among "metataxes" that act on the form of sentences by focusing on syntax. Like syllepsis, which includes "any rhetorical omission relating to the rules of agreement between morphemes and syntagms, whether it is agreement of gender, number, person, or tense," anacoluthon produces through bifurcation a break in sentence structure. Mod. poetry's frequent suppression of punctuation removed anacoluthon from the list of taboo figures drawn up by prescriptive rhetoricians. The deletion of punctuation produces rhetorical effects by combining in a single utterance large numbers of agrammatical or potentially incoherent units of discourse. Much poetry after about 1950 draws on anacoluthon for diverse effects, incl. the late poetry of Paul Celan reflecting on human suffering (e.g., *Fadensonnen* [*Threadsuns*], 1968); John Ashbery's plain-lang. meditations on being and becoming; and the verbal artist Kenneth Goldsmith's transcriptive work (e.g., *Fidget*, 2000).

■ C. T. Ernesti, *Lexicon technologiae graecorum rhetoricae* (1795); H. Bahrs, *Die Anacoluthe bei Shakespeare* (1893); G. W. Hervey, *Christian Rhetoric* (1873); Group μ; L. Edelman, *Transmemberment of Song* (1987); N. E. Enkvist, "A Note on the Definition and Description of True Anacolutha," *On Language: Rhetorica, Phonologica, Syntactica*, ed. C. Duncan-Rose, C. Vennemann, T. Vennemann (1988); E. Bloch, "Spoken and Written Syntax: Anacoluthon," *Literary Essays*, trans. A. Joron et al. (1998); Lausberg; Morier.

H. BROWN; A.W. HALSALL

ANACREONTIC. The term *anacreontic* denotes both a *meter and a literary mode. The anacreontic meter (anaclasts: ∪ ∪ – ∪ – ∪ – – or hemiambs: x – ∪ – ∪ – x) is named after the ancient Gr. poet Anacreon of Teos (6th c. BCE), who used it frequently in his verses. The meter was not originally associated with a particular mood: thus, Aeschylus used anacreontics in an emotional graveside speech (*Choephoroi* 327–30), while Euripides included them in his satyr play *Cyclops* (495–500). But by 250 BCE, Anacreon was best known for his sympotic verses, and the meter accordingly was associated with youthful hedonism and a *carpe diem* theme. At about this time, anonymous poets started to write in imitation of Anacreon; these *Anacreontea* were later preserved in one 10th-c. ms. The collection consists of 60 short poems in anacreontic meter on topics of love, wine, and song, composed over a span of 600 years, from the Hellenistic well into the Byzantine era. Lat. poets also experimented with anacreontic meter on different themes (e.g., Hadrian, Boethius); Christian bishops even wrote anacreontic religious *hymns (e.g., Gregory of Nazianzus, Synesius of Cyrene). But it was the Gr. imitative *Anacreontea* that most strongly influenced early mod. and later Eur. poets.

In 1554, Henricus Stephanus (Henri Estienne), convinced that the recently rediscovered collection was genuinely archaic, published the *Anacreontea* to great public acclaim. In Paris, Pierre de Ronsard enthused about the recovery of "du vieil Anacréon perdu / La douce lyre Teienne." In Italy, Torquato Tasso was an early admirer, as were the Eng. poets Robert Herrick and Abraham Cowley. For the next three centuries, the *Anacreontea* were read as archaic artifacts, inspiring trans. and imitators across Europe. J. W. Goethe wrote an elegiac "Anakreons Grab," while Lord Byron teased the Ir. poet Thomas Moore for his devotion to the anacreontic mode. Eur. poets reveal a remarkable consistency in tone and theme, inspired by what Voltaire approvingly called "ces riens naïfs et pleins de grace." By the mid-19th c., however, mod. philology had condemned the *Anacreontea* as products of the postclassical age and removed them from the canon of great lit. With this reclassification came a rejection of their poetic quality: the Ger. philologist Ulrich von Wilamowitz-Moellendorff found them tasteless compared to the "pure Hellenic wine" of the archaic period. Only in the late 20th c. was the collection recognized by scholars as a worthy mode of poetry in its own right.

■ H. Zeman, *Die deutsche Anakreontische Dichtung* (1972); M. Baumann, *Die Anakreonteen in englischen Übersetzungen* (1974); G. Braden, *The Classics and English Renaissance Poetry* (1978); M. Brioso-Sánchez, *Anacreónticas* (1981); J. Labarbe, "Un curieux phénomène littéraire, l'anacréontisme," *Bulletin de la Classe des Lettres de l'Académie Royale de Belgique* 68 (1982); M. L. West, *Carmina Anacreontea* (1984) and "The *Anacreontea*," *Sympotica*, ed. O. Murray (1990); P. A. Rosenmeyer, *The Poetics of Imitation* (1992) and "Greek Lyric Poetry in the French Renaissance," *The Classical Heritage in France*, ed. G. Sandy (2002); F. Budelmann, "Anacreon and the Anacreontea," *Cambridge Companion to Greek Lyric*, ed. F. Budelmann (2009).

P. A. ROSENMEYER

ANADIPLOSIS, also *epanadiplosis* (Gr., "doubled back"). In cl. rhet., a figure of word *repetition that links two phrases, clauses, lines, or stanzas by repeating the word at the end of the first one at the beginning of the second: "The crime was common, common be the pain" (Alexander Pope, "Eloisa to Abelard"); "More safe I Sing with mortal voice, unchang'd / To hoarse or mute, though fall'n on evil dayes, / On evil dayes though fall'n, and evil tongues" (John Milton, *Paradise Lost* 7.24–26). Sometimes more than one word repeats: "When I give I give myself" (Walt Whitman, "Song of Myself"). As such, *anadiplosis* is the mechanism of concatenation and is the usual vehicle for the rhetorical strategy of climax. It can also be used to link speeches in drama, the second character picking up the train of thought of the first from his or her last word:

Othello: What dost thou think?
Iago: Think, my lord?
Othello: Think, my lord? By heaven he
echoes me. (3.3.104–07)

Among the Ren. sonneteers, the use of ana-diplosis both within the sonnet and to link sonnets together was common practice—visible in Petrarch, Torquato Tasso, Pierre de Ronsard, Joachim du Bellay, Philip Sidney, Samuel Daniel, and many others—Shakespeare showing rather less interest in such effects than most. But Shakespeare's sonnet 129 has "On purpose laid to make the taker mad. / Mad in pursuit and in possession so" (8–9). Anadiplosis fixed at the level of the line and adapted into prosody as a figure of rhyme was practiced by the *rhétoriqueurs*, who called it *rime annexée* and *rime fratrisée*.

See CHAIN RHYME.

■ Patterson; M. Joseph, *Shakespeare's Use of the Arts of Language* (1947); A. Quinn, *Figures of Speech* (1982); Vickers; Corbett.

T.V.F. BROGAN

ANALOGY. *See* METAPHOR; SIMILE; SYMBOL.

ANAPEST, anapaest (Gr.; of uncertain meaning, perhaps "beaten back," i.e., a reversed *dactyl). In the quantitative meters of cl. poetry, a metrical foot of two short syllables followed by one long (◡ ◡ −, e.g., *děĭtās*), or, in verse-systems based on accent, two unstressed syllables followed by one stressed (x x /, e.g., *interrupt*). In Gr., the anapest usually appears as a dipody or metron with the form ◡ ◡ − ◡ ◡ −. The metron shows total equivalence of single longs and double shorts, unique in Gr.; consequently, in the dimeter (the commonest form), there is usually diaeresis between metra. Anapests were used first as a warlike marching rhythm, then later in Gr. drama as a song meter, both purely, as in the choruses of tragedy and comedy, commonly anapestic *tetrameter catalectic, and in combination with other meters. Runs of anapests are often closed with a catalectic *dimeter or paroemiac. With the Romans, the single foot replaced the metron as the unit of measure. Plautus made wide use of anapests, esp. in four-foot units (anapestic quaternarii), and acatalectic and catalectic eight-foot units (anapestic septenarii and octonarii). Seneca, however, uses anapests in the Gr. manner (i.e., in metra, not feet) in his tragedies, as anapaestic dimeters, a form used later by Boethius and Prudentius.

In the accentual prosodies of the Ren. and after, the anapest was used in Eng. mainly for popular verse until the beginning of the 18th c.; serious anapestic poems were later written by William Cowper, Walter Scott, Lord Byron, Robert Browning ("How They Brought the Good News"), William Morris, and esp. A. C. Swinburne, who used it in lines of every possible length ("Dolores"). Contemp. poets like Annie Finch have revived interest in anapests and other triple meters as alternatives to canonical iambic meters; they have also challenged common conceptions of anapests as limited to humorous verse (e.g., the *limerick); to depicting mimetic action (typically, hurried motion), e.g., "The Assyrian came down like a wolf on the fold" (Byron, "The Destruction of Sennacherib"); or to conveying excitement, or less frequently, mourning (Matthew Arnold's "Rugby Chapel"). Nonetheless, pure anapests remain comparatively rare in Eng. and can be difficult to distinguish in running series both from other triple meters such as dactylic and amphibrachic or from some loose duple meters with extensive trisyllabic substitutions, although prosodists have proposed promising solutions to some of these descriptive problems.

■ A. Raabe, *De metrorum anapaesticorum apud poetas Graecos usu* (1912); J. W. White, *The Verse of Greek Comedy* (1912); Hardie, ch. 4; Wilamowitz, pt. 2, ch. 11; Koster, ch. 7; Crusius; C. Questa, *Introduzione alle metrica de Plauto* (1967); Dale, ch. 4; D. Korzeniewski, *Griechische Metrik* (1968); D. Hascall, "Triple Meter in English," *Poetics* 12 (1974); Halporn et al.; Snell, 30 ff.; West, passim; J. G. Fitch, *Seneca's Anapaests* (1987); K. Hanson, "English Iambic-Anapestic Meter," "Resolution in Modern Meters" (diss., Stanford University, 1991); A. Finch, "Metrical Diversity," *Meter in English*, ed. D. Baker (1996); T. Steele, *All The Fun's In How You Say a Thing* (1999); C. Hartman, "Anapestics," Finch and Varnes; N. Fabb and M. Halle, *The Meter of a Poem* (2008).

D. S. PARKER; J. W. HALPORN;
T.V.F. BROGAN; N. GERBER

ANAPHORA (Gr., "a carrying up or back"). *Anaphora* (or *epanaphora*) is the *repetition of the same word or words at the beginning of successive phrases, clauses, sentences, or lines. *Epistrophe* (also *epiphora* or *antistrophe*) reverses the figure, repeating words at the ends of poetic units; anaphora and epistrophe combine in *symploce*. In *epanalepsis*, the same word is repeated at the beginning *and* end of phrases, clauses, or lines. Duplicating the end of one clause or line at the beginning of the next is *anadiplosis*. (In ling., *anaphora* refers to a grammatical system of reference; in musicology, *anaphora* can be used to discuss the rhetorical and poetic effects described above but also names a part of the Christian liturgical service, or music composed to accompany those rites.)

Because it consists of simple repetition, anaphora is a versatile, translatable, and ubiquitous poetic tool: present in the *Epic of Gilgamesh* and the fragments of Sappho; noted by cl. rhetoricians such as Demetrius, Alexander, and Longinus; dominating sections of the Bible and Philip Sidney's *Astrophil and Stella*; and figuring prominently in the work of 20th-c. poets such as H.D., André Breton, Attila Jósef, Allen Ginsberg, and T. S. Eliot, whose "The Love Song of J. Alfred Prufrock" contains anaphora, epistrophe, symploce, and a loose form of epanalepsis.

Anaphora can serve as the main structuring element of *free verse, as in the poetry of Walt Whitman, but it also fits into closed forms (for anaphora in *sonnets, see E. B. Browning's "The Ways of Love" and Bartholomew Griffin's "Most true that I must fair Fidessa love," the latter demonstrating perfect symploce). However, anaphora neither results from nor signifies any poetic stricture; free verse featuring anaphora is still free verse. Anaphora spans generic boundaries as well as formal ones, as it is often used in political and religious rhet. to build cohesion or emphasis (see M. L. King Jr.'s "I have a dream" speech or Winston Churchill's "We shall fight on the beaches"). The natural sound of anaphora—which could plausibly occur spontaneously and unremarkably in speech—may account for its flexibility.

The seemingly straightforward repetitions of anaphora and its related figures can produce contradictory and complicated poetic effects: the devices can both accentuate and undercut a point, can produce both momentum and stasis. W. H. Auden's use of anaphora goes beyond simple adductive emphasis to unpack the contradictory connotations of a repeated word ("Law Like Love") or track a shifting political ideology ("Spain"). In such nuanced uses of anaphora, repetition compels continual reassessment of the repeated terms.

Whereas some poetic devices (meter, slant rhyme) may become apparent only on close or repeated readings, anaphora thrusts itself into the reader's attention: each line begins with an unmistakable reminder of the unfolding pattern. Thus, anaphora highlights poetic lines as discrete units while simultaneously binding those lines together.

Perhaps because of its ubiquity, natural sound, or ostensible simplicity, the definitive critical hist. of anaphora remains to be written; the device is often noted rather than examined.

See HYPOTAXIS AND PARATAXIS.

■ M. Joseph, *Shakespeare's Use of the Arts of Language* (1947); Vickers, *Defence*; D.A.H. Elworthy, "A Theory of Anaphoric Information," *Linguistics and Philosophy* 18 (1995).

J. WEARE

ANTISTROPHE (Gr., "counterturning"). (1) In cl. prosody, the second part of the regular *ode in Gr. choral dance and poetry. The antistrophe follows the first part, the *strophe, and is followed by the third and concluding section, the *epode. The antistrophe corresponds to the strophe exactly in meter, while the epode does not, giving a double-triple *aab* structure that is replicated in several other major verse forms. (2) In cl. rhet., the repetition of words in reversed order, e.g., "the master of the servant and the servant of the master" (cf. CHIASMUS). *Antistrophe* is also occasionally used as a term for repetition of a word at the end of successive phrases or clauses, but the preferable term is *epistrophe*.

R. A. HORNSBY; T.V.F. BROGAN

ANTITHESIS, *antitheton* (Gr., "opposition"; Lat. *contentio*). The juxtaposition of contraries: the contrast of ideas, sharpened or pointed up by the use of words of opposite or conspicuously different meaning in contiguous or parallel phrases or clauses. Antithesis is a form of expression recommended as satisfying by Aristotle "because contraries are easily understood and even more so when placed side by side, and also because antithesis resembles a syllogism, for it is by putting opposing conclusions side by side that you refute one of them" (*Rhetoric* 3.9.8). The anonymous *Rhetorica ad Alexandrum* (3rd c. BCE, ch. 26) observes that antithesis may oppose words or ideas or both, and later authorities likewise stress the clarity and force that an antithesis may impart to an idea (e.g., *Rhetorica ad Herennium* [86–82 BCE], 4.15.21; Johannes Susenbrotus, *Epitome troporum ac schematum et Grammaticorum* and *Rhetorme arte rhetorica*

[1541], under *contentio*). Antithesis is one of the two or three fundamental strategies of biblical *parallelism first defined by Bishop Robert Lowth (1753) and is fairly frequent in OE poetry. In both these trads., as in nearly all others, antithesis achieves heightened effect when confined to the two halves of a *hemistichic line or two lines of a couplet, securing thereby the reinforcement of meter. Antithesis was cultivated by the cl. poets, and while these poets sometimes contrive a strict balance of form (the figure of *parison* [see ISOCOLON] in cl. rhet.) or a complex opposition of idea, e.g., "He aims to fetch not smoke from a flash, but light from smoke" (Horace, *Ars poetica* 142–43), this kind of ingenuity is even more characteristic of the Eng. and Fr. poets of the 17th and 18th cs., e.g., "I would and would not, I am on fire yet dare not" (Pierre Corneille, *Cinna* [1643] 1.2.122). A. Albalat once declared antithesis to be "the generating principle of half of French literature, from Montaigne to Hugo" (192–93); certainly, it is the predominant figure in the romantic poetry of Victor Hugo.

In Eng. poetry, William Shakespeare uses antithesis 209 times in the *Sonnets*, i.e., about once per sonnet, both of content and of form (syntax); he also experiments with double antithesis regularly (e.g., 27.12) and at least once with triple (11.5). He particularly exploits antithesis in series, to develop the (Petrarchan) contrariety of emotional conflict (94, 119, 129, 150): love–hate, truth–falsity, beauty–ugliness, fertility–sterility. But it is the *heroic couplet, which emerged in the course of the 17th c. to become the preferred meter of the Restoration and 18th-c. poets, that offered nearly the ideal medium for that balanced, concise, antithetical expression, serious and witty alike, which is the major characteristic of neoclassical style. In John Dryden and Alexander Pope, antithesis becomes an inestimable device for the display of satirical wit: "Thus wicked but in will, of means bereft, / He left not faction, but of that was left" (Dryden, *Absalom and Achitophel* 567–68); "It is the slaver kills, and not the bite" (Pope, "Epistle to Dr. Arbuthnot" 1.106); "Be not the first by whom the new are tried, / Nor yet the last to lay the old aside" (*Essay on Criticism* 2.335–36). In contemp. writing, antithesis continues to be used to achieve effects, as, e.g., in T. S. Eliot: "We are the hollow men / We are the stuffed men" ("The Hollow Men").

The antitheses quoted above are among the many forms of expression that exhibit two or more figures of speech as these were defined in cl. rhet. and may be labeled with one term or another according to the particular feature to be distinguished. Thus, the second line of the quotation from Dryden exhibits *chiasmus, epanalepsis, and isocolon. If the contrastive members of the antithesis are set in adjoining clauses that are not parallel but rather contrastive syntactically, the figure is termed *syncrisis*. Antithesis combined with chiasmus may be seen in the old definition of the scholar: "one who knows something about everything and everything about something." More recently, Group μ describes antithesis as a metalogism of addition, which asserts both "X" and "X is not non-X." Quinn puts this similarly: "rather than saying something and then repeating it in other words, you both deny its contrary and assert it," so that "you have said the thing in two different ways." Antithesis thus offers "the advantage of giving a sense of completeness with only two items."

See EPIGRAM, OXYMORON.

■ A. Albalat, *La Formation du style par l'assimilation des auteurs* (1921); M. Joseph, *Shakespeare's Use of the Arts of Language* (1947); P. Beyer, "Antithese," *Reallexikon II*; A. Kibédi-Varga, *Les Constantes du poème* (1963); G. K. Spring, "An Analysis of Antithesis as a Basis of Epic Rhetorical Patterns," *DAI* 26 (1966): 6030; M. Kallich, "Balance and Antithesis in Pope's *Essay on Criticism*," *TSL* 12 (1967); C. Perelman and L. Olbrechts-Tyteca, *The New Rhetoric*, trans. J. Wilkinson and P. Weaver (1969); Lausberg; Sr. M. M. Holloway, "Hopkins' Theory of 'Antithetical Parallelism,'" *HQ* 1 (1974); M. Isnard, "Antithese et oxymoron chez Wordsworth," *Rhétorique et communication* (1979); R. F. Gleckner, "Antithetical Structure in Blake's *Poetical Sketches*," *SIR* 20 (1981); Group μ, 141–42; A. Quinn, *Figures of Speech* (1982); Corbett, 429–30.

T.V.F. BROGAN; A. W. HALSALL

ANTONOMASIA (Gr., "naming instead"). A figure in which an epithet or appellative or descriptive phrase is substituted for a proper name (e.g., "The Bard" for Shakespeare; "It was visitors' day at the vinegar works / In Tenderloin Town" [W. H. Auden, *For the Time Being*]) or, conversely, in which a proper name is substituted for an individual, a class, or type ("the English Diana" for Queen Elizabeth; "Some mute, inglorious Milton here may rest" [Thomas Gray, "Elegy Written in a Country Churchyard"]). Similar to the first form above is *periphrasis. Group μ (101–3), however, identifies the two types, respectively, as "particularizing" and "generalizing" varieties of *synecdoche.

Quintilian (*Institutio oratoria* 8.6.29) holds that antonomasia, which is very common in poetry but less so in oratory, may be accomplished in two ways—by substitution of epithets for names (such as "Pelides" [i.e., son of Peleus] for Achilles) and by substitution of the most striking characteristic of an individual for his or her name ("Divum pater atque hominum rex" [Father of gods and king of men; Virgil, *Aeneid* 1.65]). To these he adds a third type, wherein acts may indicate the individual; this, however, may be a spurious emendation. He too points to the relation of antonomasia to synecdoche. George Puttenham (*The Arte of English Poesie*, 1589) distinguishes between epitheton ("fierce Achilles," "wise Nestor"), where name and epithet both appear, and antonomasia, use of one for the other.

■ Group μ; Morier; Lausberg; S. Leroy, "Quels fonctionnements discursifs pour l'antonomase du nom propre?" *Cahiers de praxematique* 35 (2000), and *De l'identification à la catégorisation* (2004).

R. O. EVANS; T.V.F. BROGAN

APORIA. A logical impasse in which meaning oscillates between two contradictory imperatives. First described in Gr. philosophy as a seemingly insoluble logical conundrum—aporia translates as "without a passage"—it is an important concept in poststructuralist theory, as a term for interpretive undecidability. In deconstructive criticism, an aporia is the site at which a text undermines its own philosophical structure by revealing the rhetorical nature of that structure (de Man). Consider Derrida's deconstruction of the paradox of structure and event in structuralist theories of lang. According to structuralist ling., the structure of a lang. (*langue*) is a product of past speech acts (*parole*), yet every speech act is itself made possible by prior structures (Saussure). Thus, Derrida argues, any account of linguistic origins must oscillate between these two perspectives on lang., each of which shows the error of the other. Instead of discovering a foundational linguistic structure, one finds an irresolvable aporia between structure and event (*Positions*). Because literary texts foreground their own rhetoricity,

deconstructive theory often identifies lit. as an exemplary location for identifying and examining such philosophical paradoxes.

In cl. rhet., aporia is a figure of speech that professes doubt or deliberation. Aporia allows a speaker to hesitate on both sides of a question, as when Hamlet asks, "to be or not to be?" The figure, thus, signifies indecision—Plato describes the experience of an aporia as paralysis or numbness (*Meno*)—although in rhetorical practice this uncertainty is often feigned. The philosophical and rhetorical senses of aporia suggest how the term can refer to both a philosophical paradox and to the state of being perplexed by such a paradox.

■ F. Saussure, *Cours de linguistique générale*, ed. C. Bally and A. Sechehaye, 3d ed. (1931); P. de Man, *Allegories of Reading* (1979); J. Derrida, *Positions* (1981); J. Culler, *On Deconstruction* (1982); J. Derrida, "*Ousia and Grammē*: Note on a Note from *Being and Time*" and "Signature Event Context," *Margins of Philosophy*, trans. A. Bass (1986); J. Derrida, *Aporias*, trans. T. Dutoit (1993).

J. C. MANN

APOSTROPHE (Gr. "turning away"). Poetic address, esp. to unhearing entities, whether these be abstractions, inanimate objects, animals, infants, or absent or dead people. Examples include Petrarch's "Occhi miei lassi, mentre ch'io vi giro . . ." (*Canzoniere* 14); Shakespeare's "thou age unbred" (sonnet 104); Alphonse de Lamartine's "O lac! rochers muets! grottes! Forêt obscure!" ("Le Lac"); William Blake's "Little lamb, who made thee?" ("The Lamb"); or William Wordsworth's "Milton! Thou shouldst be living at this hour" ("London, 1802"). Some poetry critics have treated the term *apostrophe* as interchangeable with the term *address*, so including poetic speech not only to unhearing entities but to the listening beloved, friend, or patron or to contemp. or later readers. The narrower term is more useful, but, as with all varieties of poetic address, it is best to think in terms of prototypes rather than of sharp-edged categories. The term *apostrophe* originates in cl. oratory. An orator was felt to be addressing his audience at all times, such that there is no rhetorical term for address to the audience; *apostrophe* meant instead "turning aside" from the principal audience to address briefly someone or something else (Quintilian, *Institutio oratoria* 4.1.63–70). (The rhetorical trad. does not distinguish between hearing and unhearing addressees; that distinction emerges only in recent poetry crit.) Such side addresses in oratory were said to convey pathos (as in the cry of *Julius Caesar*'s Mark Antony, "O judgment! thou art fled to brutish beasts"), as poetic apostrophe often does too (John Donne's "Full nakedness! All joys are due to thee," *Elegy* 19). Overlap with the figure of exclamation or ecphonesis is frequent. Dupriez suggests that apostrophe "is rhetorical when one of its elements is unexpected" and characterizes the pretense of address to the unhearing as one form this unexpectedness may take.

In mod. poetry crit., Culler's seminal essay "Apostrophe" highlighted the potential embarrassment in apostrophe's excess of pretense or pathos, seeing in this figure of speech the wager that one can pull off this extravagant verbal gesture and so be proven as the poet one claims to be. To cry "O" to something insentient is self-consciously to stage a drama of the self calling. Culler can thus identify apostrophic invocation as a trope of poetic vocation, the self's performance of itself. Positing, moreover, an opposition between narrative temporality and lyric timelessness, he styles *lyric in general as "the triumph of the apostrophic" because poetic hailing seeks to become an event itself rather than to narrate events.

Numerous critics have responded to Culler. Several have built on the suggestion (also found in de Man's essays) that apostrophe is closely linked to *prosopopoeia, making the inanimate speak; others introduce historical considerations, such as different eras' practices of public utterance or familiarity with rhetorical models. It is also important to recognize differences among apostrophes. For the pathos of address to the unhearing may be of a different kind, not embarrassing but moving, when the unhearing addressee is (as in Elizabeth Bishop's "Insomnia" or "One Art") a forsaking lover who will, to the poet's grief, never read her poem, or (as in Catullus's elegy for his brother, poem 101) not a great figure in hist. but the poet's own loved dead.

See MONOLOGUE.

■ P. de Man, "Autobiography as De-Facement," *The Rhetoric of Romanticism* (1984) and "Lyrical Voice in Contemporary Theory: Riffaterre and Jauss," *Lyric Poetry: Beyond New Criticism*, ed. C. Hošek and P. Parker (1985); B. Johnson, "Apostrophe, Animation, and Abortion," *A World of Difference* (1987); J. Hollander, "Poetic Imperatives," *Melodious Guile: Fictive Pattern in Poetic Language* (1988); B. Dupriez, *A Dictionary of Literary Devices*, trans. A. W. Halsall (1991); J. D. Kneale, "Romantic Aversions: Apostrophe Reconsidered," *ELH* 58 (1991); J. Culler, "Apostrophe," *The Pursuit of Signs*, rev. ed. (2002); Lausberg; W. Waters, *Poetry's Touch: On Lyric Address* (2003); H. Dubrow, *The Challenges of Orpheus* (2008).

W. WATERS

ASSONANCE (Lat. *assonare*, "to sound to" or "to respond to"; Ir. *amus*). The repetition of a vowel or diphthong in nonrhyming stressed syllables near enough to each other for the echo to be discernible. Examples in Eng. would be *back-cast*, *rose-float*, and *feat-seek*, or the echoes of diphthongs such as *fine-bride* and *proud-cowl*. In some verse forms of Celtic prosody, the patterning of assonance is strictly governed by elaborate rules; in other prosodies, it may be an occasional ornament (see, e.g., Gluck or Mariaselvam on assonance in Heb. verse). Between these two extremes fall cases in which assonance substitutes for strict rhyme in a form requiring the latter, as in the case of a poet who ends an Eng. or Shakespearean *sonnet with a *couplet pairing end words that assonate. In a trad. stemming from OF and Old Sp., and until the 20th c. with its more varied versification, assonance served the same function as rhyme, i.e., formalized closures to lines in the poems of most Romance langs. The OF *Chanson de Roland* (early 12th c.) attempts in each *laisse* to have not only the same vowel in the final stressed syllable of each line but the same vowel in the following weak syllable, if there is one. A similar system prevailed in Sp. and Port., as can be seen not only in the great epic *Os Lusíadas* (*The Lusiads*, 1572) by Luís de Camões but also in his lyrics, sonnets, and pastorals. Waley has argued that, because most Chinese syllables end in a vowel or nasal sound, "rhyme" in Chinese poetry is actually assonance, but Liu differentiates assonance from Chinese rhyming compounds, which do require identical final consonants, if there are any. Distinctions between assonance and rhyme are complicated because, as a full taxonomy of rhyme suggests (see RHYME), assonance, like *alliteration and *consonance, falls into the category of sound pairings to which many would assign the larger heading *rhyme*; that *vowel rhyme* or *vocalic rhyme* often appears as a synonym for *assonance* suggests that the latter is a subset of rhyme. But the hist. of the word *assonance* in Eng. suggests that it has served some as the more comprehensive term.

According to the *OED*, the word *assonance* first appeared in Eng. in 1727 and meant "resemblance or correspondence of sound between two words or syllables." This definition, which does not limit *assonance* to "the recurrence of syllable-forming vowels" (Gasparov's formulation; see definition 2 in the *OED*), would make assonance the basis not only of all rhyme but of all *prosody.

Along with the complex end echoes in OF, Old Sp., and Port., Romance poets have employed much internal assonance, partly perhaps because their langs., like Lat., are so rich in vowels. Almost any Lat. or Gr. poet can be shown to have loved vowel play (Wilkinson, Stanford). John Dryden quotes this line from the *Aeneid* to demonstrate Virgil's "musical ear"—"Quo fata trahunt retrahuntque, sequamur"—which stresses *a* four times against a background of three unstressed *u* sounds. In mod. times, internal assonance is as marked an acoustic device of the *alexandrine as of later Fr. poetry, as in *Phèdre*, which has a number of lines with assonance of three syllables, this one (1.3.9) with four—"Tout m'afflige et me nuit et conspire a me nuire." Paul Verlaine with his belief in "musique avant toute chose" is often credited with inspiring poets of his day to employ sonorous sounds; assonance was most important in his own versification.

Far less a subject of traditional interest than alliteration but more noticed than consonance, assonance has often been thought a lesser substitute for rhyme. It is true that the Germanic langs. had an early hist. of alliterative poetries—e.g., *Beowulf*—and continue to employ alliteration, often heavily. True, too, the Celtic langs., notably Welsh, developed schemes of sound correspondence, esp. *cynghanedd*, that have complex alliterative patterns. But it is equally true that in nearly all langs., incl. Ir. and Welsh, poets have continually employed assonance internally if not as a substitute for end rhyme. The term *assonance* was borrowed by Eng. from Sp. and Fr. to describe the various vocalic substitutes for rhyme in the Romance poetries. But end assonance is only a small part of the total phenomenon called *assonance*.

Since vowels and diphthongs change their pronunciation, sometimes radically, over time and from region to region, while consonants change relatively little, a reader needs to know how the vowels were pronounced by the poet being read. Mod. readers can still hear the alliterations of Germanic poetries, e.g., but they may no longer hear what were originally instances of assonance. In Eng., because the "great vowel shift" was largely completed by Shakespeare's time, the verse of Chaucer and other ME poets sounds different from that of later times. Furthermore, a number of vowels continued to change pronunciation after Shakespeare's day; by the 18th c., Eng. poets were still naturally rhyming *Devil-civil*, *stem-stream*, *pull-dull-fool*, *feast-rest*, *tea-obey*, and *join-fine* (Hanson).

Ger. poets seem to have found assonance even more appealing than alliteration, from Clemens Brentano, who has whole poems with a polysyllabic assonance in nearly every line, to J. W. Goethe, Heinrich Heine, and mod. poets. Goethe, in his lyrics and plays, has more assonance than other phonic echoes, as in Faust's contract with Mephistopheles, which in its last three lines has a six-syllable assonance of *aI* as well as other echoes: "Dann bist du *deines* Dienstes fr*ei*, / Die Ühr mag stehn, der Z*eiger* fallen, / Es s*ei* die Z*eit* fur mich vorb*ei*!" And R. M. Rilke, one of the most sonorous of poets, opens "Wendung" with "L*a*nge err*a*ng ers im *A*nschauen."

Rus. poets, too, have employed assonance consistently, esp. Fyodor Tiutchev, Boris Pasternak, Alexander Blok, and Valery Bryusov, the latter two frequently substituting it for end rhyme (Plank, Donchin, Ginzburg).

Finally, the notion that assonance is no longer used for end rhyme must be dispelled. Blok replaced rhyme with assonance in whole series of poems, as did Rilke; Verlaine used assonance instead of rhyme perhaps half the time, and poets such as Dylan Thomas in Britain and Randall Jarrell and Hart Crane in the U.S. have often made such a substitution. It should also be pointed out that poets other than Sp. and It. have dabbled with polysyllabic assonance, the echoes coming only in the weak final syllables. But in Eng. such echoes are rare, difficult, and relatively ineffective. In fact, just as computers would be of little help in finding assonance, any reader should hesitate before including obviously weak syllables in a study of vowel repetitions.

■ *A Hundred and Seventy Chinese Poems,* trans. A. Waley (1919); R. E. Deutsch, *The Pattern of Sound in Lucretius* (1939); W. B. Stanford, *Aeschylus in His Style* (1942); G. Donchin, *The Influence of French Symbolism on Russian Poetry* (1958); N. I. Hérescu, *La poésie latine* (1960); W. Kayser, *Geschichte des deutschen Verses* (1960); P. Delbouille, *Poésie et sonorités*, 2 v. (1961, 1984);

J.J.Y. Liu, *The Art of Chinese Poetry* (1962); W. B. Stanford, *The Sound of Greek* (1967); D. L. Plank, *Pasternak's Lyric* (1966); L. P. Wilkinson, *Golden Latin Artistry* (1963); J. Gluck, "Assonance in Ancient Hebrew Poetry," *De Fructu oris sui*, ed. I. H. Eybers et al. (1971); Wimsatt; P. G. Adams, *Graces of Harmony: Alliteration, Assonance, and Consonance in Eighteenth-Century Britsh Poetry* (1977); R. P. Newton, *Vowel Undersong* (1981); Brogan, esp. items C129–30, C150, C152–53, K2, K116, L233, L322, L406, L518; A. Mariaselvam, *The Song of Songs and Ancient Tamil Love Poems* (1988); Gasparov; K. Hanson, "Vowel Variation in English Rhyme," *Studies in the History of the English Language*, ed. D. Minkova and R. Stockwell (2002); E. Ginzburg, "The Structural Role of Assonance in Poetic Form," *Poetics, Self, Place,* ed. C. O'Neil, N. Boudreau, and S. Krive (2007).

P. G. ADAMS; S. CUSHMAN

ASYNDETON (Gr., "unconnected"). The omission of conjunctions between phrases or clauses; the opposite of *polysyndeton, which is the addition of conjunctions. Omission of conjunctions between words is technically brachylogia—fundamental to all forms of series and *catalogs—but many writers now use asyndeton as the cover term for all types of conjunction deletion. And it is itself, in turn, one species of all the figures of *ellipsis. Asyndeton is used both in rhet. and lit. for the purpose of speed, breathlessness, headlong momentum, and emotional force. Quintilian calls asyndeton *dissolutio* and the Ger. equivalent is *Worthäufung,* "word-piling." Heinrich Lausberg divides forms of asyndeton by two principles of division: according to parts of speech (nominal and verbal asyndeton) and according to length of elements (asyndeton between single words, phrases, and clauses). Also, both Malcolm Hebron and Lausberg organize asyndeton (a.) according to relations of the parts: a. *additivum* (accumulated in list), a. *summativum* (collective sense of list summarized either at beginning or end), a. *disiunctivum* (elements are contradictory or paradoxical), a. *adversativum* (elements are logically antithetical), a. *causale* (reasons following a proposition), a. *explicativum* (elements clarify a preceding proposition), a. *conclusivum* (a series of premises expressed by asyndeton and followed by the logical conclusion). These classifications are neither canonical nor comprehensive. Homer uses it, as does Virgil (e.g., *Aeneid* 4.594), but the classic examples are Aristotle's "I have done; you have heard me. The facts are before you; I ask for your judgment" (*Rhetoric*) and Caesar's *veni, vidi, vici.* Horace and Statius are fond of the device, and their example was followed by many med. Lat. poets. Med. Ger. poets (e.g., Walther von der Vogelweide, Wolfram von Eschenbach) also made much use of asyndeton, but the figure was esp. favored by baroque poets in Germany (Andreas Gryphius), Spain, and France. In the Latinist John Milton one can find numerous examples as well: "Thrones, Dominations, Princedoms, Vertues, Powers" (*Paradise Lost* 5.601); "The first sort by their own suggestion fell, / Self-tempted, self-depraved; man falls, deceived / By the other first: man therefore shall find grace, / The other none" (3.129–32). In Eng., asyndeton has occurred particularly in mod. poetry—in the work of the imagists, e.g., with their cult of brevity—and in W. H. Auden (e.g., "In Memory of W. B. Yeats"), with his fondness for the pithy and loaded phrase.

■ H. Pliester, *Die Worthäufung im Barock* (1930); Curtius, 285; Group μ; A. Quinn, *Figures of Speech* (1982); E. Blettner, "The Role of Asyndeton in Aristotle's Rhetoric," *P&R* 16 (1983); J. P. Houston, *Shakespearean Sentences* (1988); Corbett; W. G. Müller, "Emotional Asyndeton in the Literature of Feeling," *Anglistentag* (1992); Lausberg; M. Hebron, "Seven Types of Asyndeton in *Paradise Lost*," *English* 52 (2003).

A. PREMINGER; T.V.F. BROGAN; A. W. HALSALL; D. VERALDI

AUDIENCE. *See* PERFORMANCE.

B

BALLAD

I. Regional and Linguistic Variation
II. Oral and Written Ballads
III. Scholarship and Influence in Literary
   History

In scholarly discourse since the 18th c., across the disciplines of lang. and lit., musicology, and folklore, a ballad is a narrative song set to a rounded—i.e., stanzaic—tune or a literary poem modeled on such songs. This stanzaic structure distinguishes the ballad from the sung traditional *epic (a longer narrative set to a chant-like, nonstanzaic tune). Ballads present a series of actions involving protagonists and are thus distinguished from *lyric and other nonnarrative songs or verse. Typically, ballads focus on a single episode where the plot involves a small cast of characters and is directed toward a catastrophe. In all Eur. langs. since the Middle Ages, popular narrative song and oral poetry have displayed recognizable links and parallels across regions. Moreover, many of the lang. trads. possess cognate forms of particular ballads. With origins in popular idioms, the ballad form represents a collective cultural sensibility, and anonymous popular ballads persist to the present day as folk songs found in diverse variants.

In common parlance, the term *ballad* has been variously employed from the 16th-c. beginnings of its usage in Eng., when the word appeared in connection with danced songs, and considerable ambiguity can still cloud the term. In the 17th and 18th cs., a ballad meant any popular song, and Samuel Johnson's *Dictionary* (1755) applies the term vaguely to any "trifling verse." In the context of jazz or popular music today, the term designates any song in a slow tempo with a sentimental text.

Ballads exist in both polite and popular culture as oral-performance works as well as literary ones, across a range of social registers. Literary ballads are items of individually authored verse that imitate the structure and style of popular ballads. The latter are typically created, performed, learned, and disseminated as songs. These anonymous ballads are best understood as a species of oral poetry that has for centuries intersected with, influenced, and been influenced by writing, while still maintaining widespread oral circulation in the traditional channels documented by folklorists. The interaction of oral forms with written culture has been pervasive, despite scholarly theories that defined the two expressive realms as entirely in contradistinction to each other. The ballad has commanded literary and scholarly interest across Europe and its colonies, especially beginning in the 18th c. when the form drew attention first as a mode for satire and later as part of a fascination with subaltern expression and sensibility during romanticism. In Eng., the ballad took on renewed importance in 20th-c. modernist poetry and the poetics of New Criticism.

I. Regional and Linguistic Variation. Ballads are found throughout Europe and in Africa, the Americas, and Australia. Analogous popular narrative songs are found as well in Asia and Oceania. Despite nearly global pervasiveness, regional ballad forms and trads. show as many differences as commonalities. Even among Eur. trads., metrical distinctions are obvious. For example, Eng. and other northern Eur. ballads are stanzaic and set to strophic tunes, the words rendered in *accentual-syllabic verse as quatrains of alternating tetrameter and trimeter lines or, less commonly, as four tetrameter lines (if in *accentual verse, as alternating four- and three-stress lines or as four-stress lines, respectively). Many southern and eastern Eur. ballads are, by contrast, stichic with varying verse structures. Sp. ballads, termed *romances*, are for the most part conceived of as octosyllabic with assonant rhyme in the even-numbered lines. However, to underscore their presumed devel. from the earlier epic, these are sometimes typographically rendered in 12 to 16 syllables in *hemistichs linked by rhyme or assonance, as are ballads of Portugal, France, Catalonia, and northern Italy. An octosyllabic line is considered typical of Bulgarian and much Ger. balladry. Romanian ballads, normally in trochaic trimeter or tetrameter, have considerable variation in length as do the Rus. ballads, termed *bylina*.

In all trads., the shaping function of the music is crucial to understanding the rhythmic textual patterns. Seeming prosodic irregularities seen in print almost inevitably disappear in oral performance. Indeed, ballad prosody should be understood as a recognizable yet elastic mode governed by the predilections for shaping songs within the collective song-making trad. of a region. Scholars of ballad style typically study the structures, formulas, and conventional patterns of regional and lang. forms as distinct entities, e.g., Eng. and Scottish ballads, Sp. *romances*, and Rus. *bylina*.

II. Oral and Written Ballads. Popular ballads in Eur. trads. fall into two categories determined by origins, hist., and narrative techniques: (1) the older "traditional" or cl. ballad, usually on a tragic theme, that represents a med. oral poetry reflective of a premod. world; (2) the journalistic or broadside ballad developed with the advent of popular, commercial printing in urban centers in the late 16th c., often chronicling a newsworthy event such as a sensational crime, natural disaster, military conflict, or love scandal. All Eur. lang. groups with print markets display this division between older, oral ballads and more journalistic ballads shaped by writing and print. However, individual ballads of both types have circulated orally as anonymous songs among singers, and many continue to be learned, sung, and reshaped over time through processes of oral trad. While both types of narratives conform to the ballad genre and relate similar kinds of events, each displays distinct stylistic conventions.

A. *Oral-Ballad Traditions and Style.* The older "traditional" or cl. ballads from premod. oral trads. have generated greater literary appreciation and imitation than the later broadside ballads, on the one hand because of their mysterious and almost indefinable artistry and on the other because of their med. archaism. These songs concentrate on two or three characters and develop dramatically and economically through dialogue and action. The plot usually begins in medias res with little attention to settings or circumstantial detail. Cl. ballads present stark and formulaic characters, actions, objects, and scenes. Events are shown with brevity, and *dialogue prevails as protagonists speak to each other, usually without ascription. Individual ballads unfold as a series of gapped paratactic images that Hodgart has likened to the cinematic technique of montage, whereby the narrative develops almost as a series of tableaux. Gummere described this plotting of the

traditional ballad style as an abrupt "leaping and lingering" from scene to scene, and Vargyas as a poetry of conventionalized gestures.

In the cl. ballads, repetitive verbal patterns and tight, balancing scenes create a tone of striking objectivity. Repetition and formulaic expression, both marks of oral artistry, are key to traditional ballad style. Commonplace descriptors serve as formulas for what characterization occurs and for construction of the narrative. In Eng. ballads, protagonists typically mount "milk-white steeds" and write "braid letters signed with their hands"; maidens are "taken by their lily-white hands"; characters enter a scene asking "what news, what news"; and so on. Redundancy shapes individual ballads and marks as well the shared nature of the patterned idiom from song to song across a lang. trad. Incremental repetition is a common strategy in ballad narrative technique, whereby a song unfolds in sequences of repeating lines or stanzas that, with each occurrence, introduce a change of word or phrase that furthers the plot. Thus, "Lord Randall," known across various Eur. langs., unfolds as a question-and-answer dialogue between a mother and son in which details added to each stanza disclose the dying son's report of being poisoned by his lover. The repetition and formulaic structure of the disclosure create the understatement, dramatic irony, and suspense characteristic of oral style.

In all lang. trads., the oral origin and style of cl. ballads is thought to predate the writing-based mode of the broadside ballad, though few individual examples of the oral style are reported before the late 16th and 17th cs. Cl. ballads represent a late-med. world and sensibility. They place their characters in a rural world of feudal objects and settings, med. social roles and practices, and premod. beliefs and mores (castles, knights and ladies, hawks and hounds, herbal potions, supernatural visitants, etc.). Thus, in a typical variant, the eponymous protagonist of the Scottish ballad "Tam Lin" escapes thralldom to the underworld by shape-shifting in the arms of his beloved, who embraces him through a magical rescue as he transforms from one archaic state of being to another: "an esk and adder," "a lion bold," "a burning gleed," and finally, "a naked knight." This counterspell frees him from fairy captivity.

The study of such ballads as representative of oral poetry and of a retrospectively imagined med. past began in the 18th c. with commentary by scholars such as Thomas Percy (1729–1811), the Eng. ed. of *Reliques of Ancient English Poetry* (1765), and the Ger. writer and philosopher J. G. Herder (1744–1803), both influential in Eur. romanticism. For them, ballads posed a collective mythopoetic inheritance for forging a prized national unity. By the 19th c., scholars of the "traditional" ballad—typified by collectors such as the Scottish Walter Scott (1771–1832) and William Motherwell (1795–1835) or the Danish Svend Grundtvig (1824–83)—garnered versions found in mss. and oral variants that they considered purer and more "ancient" for being free from print and commercial associations. The defining collection and cataloging of some 300 narrative songs of this type in Eng. by the Am. medievalist F. J. Child (1825–96) codified the anglophone trad. of these narratives to the extent that scholars refer to them as "Child ballads."

B. Broadside-Ballad Traditions and Style. Originating with print production for a popular readership, the broadside or journalistic ballad is a song reproduced on a single sheet of paper (a broadside) and sold on urban streets, in bookshops, and at such gathering places as docks and fairs. From the late 16th c., such marketing of ballads remained a fixture of popular culture in Europe and its colonies for several hundred years. Typically, a woodcut print included the text of one or more ballads, several images and decorative borders, and sometimes the title of a recommended tune. Musical notation almost never appeared. By the 18th c., broadside-ballad presses operated in provincial centers in Europe and its colonies. Frequent literary attacks on the vulgarity of the form and the large numbers of ballad prints from the 16th through the 19th cs. that remain in archives to this day attest to the popularity of broadside ballads.

As a product of urban journalism, the narrative style of the broadside ballad discloses a contrasting worldview to that of the orally based cl. ballad. The broadside ballad narrates in a straightforwardly linear and expository manner, with little repetition, and offers a journalistic rendering of each story with specifically named and particularized places, people, and events. A realistic and moralizing narrative voice portrays a world of more mod. institutions and commerce. As an example, the paratextual heading of the London broad-side ballad of "The Children in the Wood" (1595) gives details of place and persons as well as the causal outlines of its moralizing plot: "The Norfolk Gentleman, his Will and Testament, and howe he committed the keeping of his children to his own brother whoe delte most wickedly with them, and how god plagued him for it." Not uncommonly, broadside ballads relate first-person stories, identifying precise urban locations, detailed actions, and historical identities. In *The Beggar's Daughter of Bednall Green*, from another Eng. print, the "blind beggar" narrator sings at his daughter's wedding and at the end reveals his true identity as the heir of the rebel earl of Leicester: "And here, noble lordes, is ended the songe / Of one, that once to your owne ranke did belong." These characteristics contrast to the impersonal, third-person narration of orally rooted traditional ballads. Across Eur. and Eur.-colonized regions, song makers and publishers rendered ballad accounts of historical events. Ballads in Eng. from North America exemplify the journalistic specificities of the style: "The Constitution and the Guerrière," an account of an 1812 U.S. sea victory over an Eng. frigate; "Lost Jimmie Whalen," the lamenting story of the death of a 19th-c. lumberman; and murder ballads such as "Charles Guiteau," which tells of the assassination of President James Garfield in 1881, and "Poor Omie," which recounts the 1808 drowning of a North Carolina girl by her former lover.

Many ballads originating in broadsides continued to circulate in oral trads. Typically recomposed through the strategies of repetition and gapped narrative characteristic of oral recall and preservation, some ballads that originated as printed compositions have continued to be passed on for generations—as is the case with the Am. ballads mentioned. Shortened in the process, such orally reformed ballads focus on the central, most patterned, and most emotionally charged points of the story, taking on characteristics of performative orality (repetition, parallel structure, and formulaic expression) not found in the initial broadside version. Conversely, some ballads of the older oral type—"Barbara Allen" and "Lord Beichan" are examples from the Eng. trad.—were sold in printed broadside versions and were refashioned with more details and plot linearity in keeping with the journalistic mode.

Scholars of the printed street ballad amassed collections of ballad broadsides (single-sheet prints) produced by printers from the 16th c. on, a preservation effort that takes on renewed life today with collections made available online. In the 19th c., antiquarian enthusiasm for both traditional and broadside ballads spurred collections of orally disseminated folk songs from live singers, an effort that peaked in the mid-20th c. and amassed an enormous body of ballads and other songs from Europe and Eur.-influenced cultures.

Significant devels. in ballad style have emerged as a result of regional adaptations. Scholars identify in the U.S. the "blues ballad," a narrative song type influenced by Af. Am. oral performance and composition style. With a focus on murder, death, and tragedy typical of all ballads, the blues ballad renders historical events from a contemp. view as did the printed broadside ballads (see BLUES). However, characteristics of the blues ballad also include the call-and-response techniques of Af. Am. arts, a predilection for antiheroes and -heroines, a prominent influence of orality in the ballad's creation and dissemination, and a voice more poetic and celebratory than reportorial. In contrast to the linear, broadside style, such ballads as "John Henry," "Casey Jones," "The Titanic," "Frankie and Albert" ("Frankie and Johnny"), and "Stagolee" tell their stories with an oblique, gapped, and sometimes radial rendering of the narrative and an improvisatory style characterized by repetition, parallelism, and a stock of commonplace images ("rubber-tire hearses," guns that are "38s" and "44s," girls "dressed in blue" followed by those "dressed in red"). Ballads in this mode typically celebrate their transgressing protagonists, who emerge from a world of crime. The narrative song trads. brought with the Sp. conquest display a similar devel. in the Americas, with narrative *corridos* emerging, like the blues ballads, from oral trads., even as journalistic *corridos* in reportorial style were sold on broadsides. In Mexico and the southwestern U.S., *corridos* from the 20th and early 21st cs. often feature antihero *bandidos* and stories of narcotics trafficking.

In Germany from the 17th to the 20th c., sellers of the broadside ballad—termed *Bänkelsang* or *Moritat*—used elaborate pictorial representations of the typically sensational and sentimental narratives. Conventionally, the *Bänkelsanger* sang from a platform and displayed scenes from the story on a large poster as passersby purchased the song sheets. Nineteenth-c. authors adapted the form to literary ballads and satire, especially after 1848. In the 20th c., such ballads featured in Ger. cabaret culture; the best-known adaptation is Bertolt Brecht and Kurt Weill's "Die Moritat von Mackie Messer" from *Driegroschenoper* (1928), a reworking of the Eng. *Beggar's Opera* (1728) by John Gay.

III. Scholarship and Influence in Literary History. Early 20th-c. scholarship divided between theories of the origin of popular ballads in individual or in communal creation, eventually reaching consensus that a particular ballad originates with an individual song maker; subsequently, continuing performance across communities recreates the ballad in numerous variants. Scholars applied this model of dynamic creation and re-creation in their study of individual traditional artistry in both the making and the performance of ballads (Porter and Gower). Theoretical concern about the reliability of ethnographic records has spurred attention to documenting occasions, modes, and contexts for song performance; the social function and reception of songs; and the interpretive framings of oral hist. (Ives 1978). Studies of contexts reveal in ballads an index for diachronic analysis of sociopolitical hist. and paradigms of gender, class, socioeconomics, power dynamics, etc. (Dugaw 1989, Symonds). Individual ballads afford sites for synchronically examining particular historical moments and events (Ives 1997, C. Brown, Long-Wilgus). The broadside ballad has received renewed scholarly attention both with analytic studies of prints from different eras and regions (Würzbach, Cheesman) and with the availability of online databases (English Broadside Ballad Archive, Roud). Analyses of textual form attend to the aesthetic effects of ballads and to their formulaic and performative mechanisms as examples of oral artistry (McCarthy, Andersen, Renwick).

The importance of the ballad to Eng.-lang. lit. hist. has received renewed investigation with regard to the 18th-c. literary interest in and emulation of the form and its engendering of a new ethnographic sensibility that gave rise to ethnopoetics and verse-making beyond the traditional borders of belles lettres (Groom, Newman). Scholars have examined the ballad in connection with the art of particular writers such as John Gay and John Clare (Dugaw 2001, Deacon) as well as the tenets of literary movements such as romanticism (McLane), and in examinations of the historiographical significance of individual ballad scholars (M. E. Brown).

Ballads of every type have influenced lit. in all the lang. trads. E.g., literary poets of early mod. Sp. such as Félix Lope de Vega and Sor Juana Inés de la Cruz wrote *romances* modeled on popular narratives in earlier *cancionero* collections. The prevalence of poets who wrote ballad-inflected poems in Eng. mirrors the importance of the form in lits. elsewhere. Political satire of the late 17th and early 18th cs. enlisted the ballad form in miscellanies such as *The Covent Garden Drollery* and *Poems on Affairs of State*. Gay's *Beggar's Opera* introduced ballad opera as a burlesque in which pointed songs set to popular ballad tunes forwarded the mood and action of spoken drama. The decades-long popularity of this and imitative ballad operas reflected and enhanced interest in ballads. Such antiquarian collections as Percy's *Reliques of Ancient English Poetry* influenced lit. at all levels, shaping the poetics of Eng. and continental romanticism. Wordsworth ("Lucy Gray," "Seven Sisters") and S. T. Coleridge (*The Rime of the Ancient Mariner*, "The Three Graves") wrote verse imitative of ballads. The Preface to the 2d ed. of the *Lyrical Ballads* (1800) articulates a theoretical justification for echoing plebeian forms in order to make poetic expression "real lang." without the obfuscations of literary artifice. Ballad-like poems modeled on both oral-traditional and broadside ballads in Britain are among the works of Gay ("Sweet William's Farewell"), Thomas Tickell ("Lucy and Colin"), Robert Burns ("The Five Carlins," "Kellyburn Braes"), William Blake ("Mary," "Long John Brown and Little Mary Bell"), John Keats ("La Belle Dame sans Merci"), Christina Rossetti ("Maude Clare," "Lord Thomas and Fair Margaret"), A. C. Swinburne ("The Bloody Son," "May Janet"), Thomas Hardy ("The Second Night," "No Bell-Ringing"), Oscar Wilde ("The Ballad of Reading Gaol"), and others.

The interplay, through collection and study, between the street, workplace, or fireside realm of ballads and that of belles lettres is evident in British trads. and throughout Europe. Literary writers—John Clare, e.g., himself a fiddler—participated as well in collecting ballads. In Scotland, 18th-c. ballad collecting by Allan Ramsay and Burns was followed in the 19th c. by James Hogg, in addition to Scott and Motherwell. Ger. poetry through the 19th c. was shaped by Achim von Arnim and Clemens Brentano's *Des Knaben Wunderhorn* (1805–8), a collection prompted by Herder's philosophic championing of popular song.

In the 20th c., the ballad continued as a literary model. In Ireland, modernist writers such as James Joyce, J. M. Synge, and W. B. Yeats identified their work with an Ir. cultural sensibility both ancient and contemp. Yeats collaborated on song and tale collections in Ir. and Eng. with Lady Augusta Gregory and others and also penned ballad-influenced works ("Down by the Salley Gardens," "Moll Magee"). In the U.S., Cleanth Brooks and R. P. Warren formulated a modernist poetics of New Criticism that identified the ballad as a model for an aesthetics of accessibility and collective *voice, echoed in the work of Elizabeth Bishop and others. For Af. Am. modernism and subsequent movements, the blues ballad supplied a model for such poets as Langston Hughes ("Sylvester's Dying Bed," "Ballad of the Landlord") and Gwendolyn Brooks ("of De Witt Williams on his way to Lincoln Cemetery," "The Ballad of Late Annie"). To the present, literary writers from numerous national and ethnic trads. collect and engage ballads in a continuing testimony to the mutually influencing dynamic between literary artistry and the oral and collective realm of popular trads.

■ **Descriptive Catalogs and Research Aids**: G. M. Laws, *American Balladry from British Broadsides* (1957), and *Native American Balladry* (1964); T. P. Coffin, *The British Traditional Ballad in North America*, 2d ed. (1977); B. R. Jonsson et al., *The Types of the Scandinavian Medieval Ballad* (1978); D. Catalán et al., *Catálogo general del romancero*, 3 v. (1984); E. Richmond, *Ballad Scholarship* (1989); L. Syndergaard, *English Translations of the Scandinavian Medieval Ballads* (1995).

■ **Historical Contexts**: A. Paredes, *"With His Pistol in His Hand"* (1958); D. Dugaw, *Warrior Women and Popular Balladry* (1989); M. Herrera-Sobek, *The Mexican Corrido* (1990)—feminist crit.; N. Würzbach, *The Rise of the English Street Ballad 1550–1650*, trans. G. Walls (1990); E. Ives, *The Bonny Earl of Murray* (1997); D. Symonds, *Weep Not for Me* (1997)—ballads in early mod. Scotland; J. McDowell, *Poetry and Violence* (2000)—Mexico's Costa Chica; C. Brown, *Stagolee Shot Billy* (2003); E. Long-Wilgus, *Naomi Wise* (2003).

■ **History of Scholarship**: D. K. Wilgus, *Anglo-American Folksong Scholarship since 1898* (1959); *The Anglo-American Ballad*, ed. D. Dugaw (1995); N. Groom, *The Making of Percy's "Reliques"* (1999); M. E. Brown, *William Motherwell's Cultural Politics* (2001); *Singing*

the Nations: Herder's Legacy, ed. D. Bula and S. Rieuwerts (2008).
■ **Literary Contexts**: M. R. Katz, *The Literary Ballad in Early 19th-Century Russian Literature* (1976); D. Dugaw, *"Deep Play"—John Gay and the Invention of Modernity* (2001); G. Deacon, *John Clare and the Folk Tradition* (2004); S. Newman, *Ballad Collection, Lyric, and the Canon* (2007); M. McLane, *Balladeering, Minstrelsy, and the Making of British Romantic Poetry* (2008).
■ **Origins and Style**: F. B. Gummere, *The Popular Ballad* (1907); H. Rollins, "Black-Letter Broadside Ballad," *PMLA* 35 (1919); W. Entwistle, *European Ballad* (1939); G. Gerould, *The Ballad of Tradition* (1939); M.J.C. Hodgart, *The Ballads* (1962); D. Foster, *The Early Spanish Ballad* (1971); E. Ives, *Joe Scott* (1978); O. Holzapfel, *Det balladeske: fortællemåden i den ældre episke folkevise* (1980); C. later, *Stories on a String: The Brazilian Literatura de Cordel* (1982); F. Andersen, *Commonplace and Creativity* (1985); D. K. Wilgus and E. Long, "The Blues Ballad and the Genesis of Style," *Narrative Folksong*, ed. C. Edwards and K. Manley (1985); W. McCarthy, *The Ballad Matrix* (1990); C. Harvey, *Contemporary Irish Traditional Narrative* (1992); T. Cheesman, *The Shocking Ballad Picture Show* (1994); J. Porter and H. Gower, *Jeannie Robertson* (1995); R. deV. Renwick, *Recentering Anglo/American Folksong* (2001); D. Atkinson, *The English Traditional Ballad* (2002); V. Gammon, *Desire, Drink and Death in English Folk and Vernacular Song* (2008).
■ **Ballad and Tune Collections**: S. Grundtvig et al., *Danmarks gamle folkeviser*, 12 v. (1853–76); F. J. Child, *The English and Scottish Popular Ballads*, 10 v. (1882–98); G. Doncieux and J. Tiersot, *Le Romancéro populaire de la France* (1904); R. Menéndez Pidal, *Poesía popular y poesía tradicional* (1922); *Deutsche Volkslieder mit ihren Melodien: Balladen*, ed. J. Meier et al., 8 v. (1935–88); *Traditional Tunes of the Child Ballads*, ed. B. Bronson, 4 v. (1959–72); E. Janda and F. Nützhold, *Die Moritat vom Bänkelsang oder Lied von der Strasse* (1959); H. Fromm, ed., *Deutsche Balladen*, 4th ed. (1965); C. Simpson, *The British Broadside Ballad and Its Music* (1966); L. Vargyas, *Hungarian Ballads and the European Ballad Tradition*, trans. I. Gombos, 2 v., (1983); J. Jiménez, *Cancionero completo* (2002); *Ballads on Affairs of State*, ed. A. McShane (2009)—17th-c. England.
■ **Web Sites**: English Broadside Ballad Archive, University of California, Santa Barbara: http://emc.english.ucsb.edu/ballad_project/index.asp; Roud Folk Song Index: http://library.efdss.org/cgi-bin/home.cgi; Roud Broadside Index: http://library.efdss.org/cgi-bin/textpage.cgi?file-aboutRoudbroadside&access=off.

D. DUGAW

BALLAD METER, HYMN METER. In Eng. poetry, *ballad meter*—or, as it is sometimes termed, *ballad stanza*—refers to the meter of the traditional ballad, a popular narrative song form since the late Middle Ages, and the written literary adaptation of this oral form. Ambiguities abound with regard to the application of the term, which gained importance in literary parlance only with the 18th-c. rise of interest in plebeian poetic forms. Commonly, ballad meter designates quatrains that alternate iambic tetrameter with iambic trimeter and rhyme at the second and fourth lines. For reasons discussed below, the form corresponds to "hymn meter" or "common meter," whose quatrains, however, can rhyme *abab*, as in the well-known instance of Isaac Watts's setting of Psalm 90: "O God, our help in ages past, / Our hope for years to come, / Our shelter from the stormy blast, / And our eternal home." The use of this iambic tetrameter-trimeter form in the two familiar arenas of popular secular ballads and widely sung hymnody is significant, as this structure and its effects over time draw from and represent collectively widespread and recognizable sung utterance. Moreover, in practice, the distinction between the two, ballad meter and hymn meter, is not made consistently, so that a poem in quatrains with either rhyme scheme, whose iambic lines alternate four stresses and three stresses, may be identified as a ballad. Nor is the requirement of the iambic stress pattern rigidly or universally followed in the application of the term. Thus, literary poets may title a work a "ballad" that varies from the quatrain form, the meter, or other aspects of the usual definition. Oscar Wilde's "Ballad of Reading Gaol," e.g., alternates between unrhymed tetrameters and rhymed trimeters but features stanzas of six rather than four lines.

Collective ongoing oral practice, for hundreds of years, constructs a context for understanding the vitality of the ballad meter form, from its origins in sung verse from popular trads. to the uses both hymnodists and literary poets made of it. Both the meter and the quatrain organization derive from the association of the verse with conventional melodic structures and rhythms: Eng. tunes typically follow patterns of four musical phrases. The popular and orally circulating ballads of the anglophone trad.—e.g., such ballads as are found in F. J. Child's *English and Scottish Popular Ballads*—customarily, though not inevitably, follow the accentual 4-3-4-3 pattern of ballad meter, but the words hew less rigorously to metrical form than do the ballads of consciously literary poets such as William Wordsworth, who adhere to metric strategies of poetic formulation. The shaping function of the music allows for greater flexibility in the verbal patterns of orally circulating folk ballads; sung performance inevitably enlivens and smoothes seeming prosodic irregularities in a text.

The origin, devel., and exact nature of ballad meter have prompted considerable scholarly discussion. One point of dispute concerns whether ballad meter is *accentual verse, i.e., isochronous and counting only stresses, or *accentual-syllabic, regulating syllable count and not timed. The irregularities of the anonymous popular sung ballads and the importance of *caesura and dipodism in their isochronic lines have suggested to metrists the application of the concept of accentual meter used for OE verse to ballad meter. However, ballads do not show evidence of such consciously wrought complexities of OE prosody as formulaic hemistichs, structural alliteration, and clear stichic structure. Nineteenth-c. metrists considered ballad meter to be derived from the med. Lat. *septenarius*, a line of seven stresses and 14 syllables, and proposed that such long couplets, often with internal rhyme, were formulated into quatrains, perhaps because of exigencies of space on a given codex page. However, no plausible or demonstrable link between Church Lat. hymn verse and the oral vernacular ballads has been found. In the Ren., rhyming iambic heptameter couplets—*fourteeners—function with a syntactic and conceptual coherence that corresponds to the quatrain stanzas of alternating tetrameters and trimeters of ballad meter. The more regular meters and not infrequent heptameter form found in early broadside ballads suggest a link to this fashion for heptameter couplets; however, no direct lineage between the 16th-c. literary mode and the popular verse quatrains of ballad meter is discernible, and the term *ballad meter* appears only in the romantic period, long after

the literary vogue of fourteeners had passed. Rather, the ballad and ballad meter's influencing presence assist the occasional use of iambic-heptameter couplets in mod. poetry in connection with topics from the popular realm, as, e.g., in E. L. Thayer's "Casey at the Bat," whose composed heptameter couplets can be "heard" in recitation as ballad meter.

Another set of pertinent analytic terms attests to the significance of orality and singing traditions with regard to the develop. and study of ballad meter. With the 16th-c. emergence of Eng. Protestantism, such writers of *hymns in the vernacular as Thomas Sternhold and John Hopkins brought Martin Luther's Ger. practice into their hymnody and also made use of the conventional ballad meter and sometimes the actual tunes of Eng. popular ballads for settings of psalm and hymn texts. The widespread collective singing of religious song, thus, formed another context in which the metric predilections of ballad meter influenced the writing of poetry in such authors shaped by hymnody as George Herbert and Emily Dickinson. To this day, metrical designations remain a common feature in the indexes of Protestant hymnals with the following categories typically given (numbers denote the stresses per line): long meter (or measure; abbreviated LM): 4-4-4-4; common meter (or measure; CM): 4-3-4-3; short meter (SM): 3-3-4-3; and rarely, half meter (HM): 3-3-3-3. The most common pattern is CM, which conforms metrically to iambic ballad meter and reflects the overlap of the two collective trads. of popular sacred and secular song.

See METER, PSALM.

■ F. B. Gummere, *Old English Ballads* (1894); J. W. Hendren, *A Study of Ballad Rhythm* (1936); E. Routley, *The Music of Christian Hymnody* (1957); Saintsbury, *Prosody*; G. W. Boswell, "Reciprocal Controls Exerted by Ballad Texts and Tunes," *JAF* 80 (1967) and "Stanza Form and Music-Imposed Scansion," *Southern Folklore Quarterly* 31 (1967); B. H. Bronson, *The Ballad as Song* (1969); Brogan; J. Hollander, *Rhyme's Reason* (1981); R. Leaver, *"Goostly psalms and spirituall songes"* (1991)—Eng. and Dutch psalms, 16th c.; Attridge, *Poetic Rhythm*; *Meter in English*, ed. D. Baker (1996); J. R. Watson, *The English Hymn* (1997); T. Steele, *All the Fun's in How You Say a Thing* (1999); Carper and Attridge; L. Turco, *The Book of Forms*, 3d ed. (2000).

D. DUGAW

BEAT. The recurring pulse in a regular *rhythm. Derived from the motion of the conductor's hand or baton indicating the rhythmic pulse in music, in the analysis of verse it refers to the salient elements of a poetic *meter as experienced by the reader or listener. It is generally agreed that spoken lang. is normally too varied to allow for the emergence of beats (but see Couper-Kuhlen for a different view); metered verse, however, arranges words and sentences in controlled ways that produce a regular movement characterized by the alternation of stronger and weaker beats (or "offbeats"). When beats and offbeats are organized into the patterns enshrined in verse trad., the rhythm created is particularly strong; and once sequences of beats are perceived, the expectation is that they will continue. *Free verse and, more rarely, prose can fall into a sequence of alternating beats and offbeats, but without creating metrical patterns. The equivalent term for the beat in cl. prosody is ictus.

Analysis of poetry in terms of beats and offbeats—"beat prosody"—emphasizes the relation of verse to music, without attempting to apply musical notation to the rhythms of lang. Both regular verse and cl. Western music are regarded as building on simple, familiar rhythmic forms, the most ubiquitous of which is the four-beat unit (which is produced by doubling a beat, then doubling it again). In the Eng. trad., the four-beat rhythm is the staple of popular verse and song, children's rhymes, advertising jingles, and *hymns. It is also common in art verse, where, in its most straightforward realization, it becomes *iambic or *trochaic tetrameter. Most commonly, it is found in larger units also created by doubling: four-beat *couplets or, more usually, four groups of four beats. In dipodic verse, beats alternate between stronger and weaker (an alternation that arises from the hierarchic nature of all regular rhythm).

Once a four-beat rhythm is established, the mind can perceive a beat in certain limited positions even when there is no syllable to manifest it; thus, the common *ballad meter omits the last beat of the second and fourth groups. This perceived but not actual beat is termed an "implied beat," a "virtual beat," or an "empty beat." Most line lengths in the Eng. verse trad. are based on the four-beat group or its variants, the two-beat group or the group of three beats plus an implied beat. A significant exception is the five-beat line, which does not fit easily into the four-beat rhythm, a fact that explains many of its special characteristics: it is rare in popular verse and song, it is often unrhymed, and it almost always takes the form of a strict accentual-syllabic or syllable-stress meter, the *iambic pentameter. It is thus clearly distinct from the trad. of song and closer to the rhythms of the spoken lang. (Some prosodists have argued that five-beat lines have a sixth implied beat, but this is not generally accepted.)

The strong pulse of the four-beat rhythm makes it possible to vary the number of offbeats that occur between the beats. Eng. accentual or stress verse has the greatest freedom in this respect, allowing one or two offbeats and, less frequently, three or none at all. Accentual-syllabic verse, by contrast, controls the number of syllables in the line, and hence the character of the offbeats: before or after a double offbeat, there will usually be a missing offbeat, and vice versa. Offbeats at the beginning and end of the line are less strictly controlled; four-beat verse may begin consistently with a beat or with an offbeat, or it may vary between these, as in these lines from John Milton's "L'Allegro" (where *b* indicates the syllables that take a beat):

And young and old come forth to play
   b   b   b   b

On a sunshine holiday,
b b   b b

Till the livelong daylight fail,
b   b   b   b

Then to the spicy nut-brown ale.
b   b b   b

Verse in a triple or ternary rhythm (almost always in four-beat groups) has more double offbeats than single, but it can begin and end with two, one, or no offbeats. When a duple or binary meter begins regularly with an offbeat, it may be labeled "iambic"; when it begins regularly with a beat and ends with an offbeat, it may be labeled "trochaic." When it begins and ends with a beat, it may be termed both "catalectic trochaic" (see CATALEXIS) and "acephalous" or "headless iambic"; more simply, it is four-beat verse without initial or final offbeats.

Beats are realized by the most prominent rhythmic feature of the lang.—in Eng., by stress. However, not every stressed syllable is perceived as a beat and not every unstressed syllable as an offbeat. Under certain conditions, such as its occurrence between two stresses carrying beats, a stressed syllable can be felt as the rhythmic equivalent of an offbeat. Conversely, an unstressed syllable can, under certain conditions, such as its occurrence between two unstressed syllables functioning as offbeats, be experienced as rhythmically doing duty for a beat. These processes, *demotion and promotion, are common in Eng. verse and derive from similar rhythmic processes in spoken Eng. They enable the poet to vary the speed and weight of the verse, the former producing a slower rhythm (since the demoted stress is still given emphasis) and the latter a quicker rhythm (since the promoted nonstress is still uttered lightly).

*Scansion of accentual-syllabic verse in terms of beats and offbeats differs from scansion in terms of cl. feet in that it does not assume the verse line to be divided into units determined by the meter. This difference is particularly evident in their accounts of the patterns / / x x and x x / /, which are frequent in Eng. iambic verse. In foot prosody, the former involves the substitution of a trochaic foot for an iambic foot ($|x/|/x|x/|x/|$), and the latter the substitution of a *pyrrhic and a *spondee for two iambs ($|x/|xx|//|x/|$). In beat prosody, by contrast, the two successive stressed syllables are understood as two beats, and the two unstressed syllables as realizing a double offbeat. By showing the position of the beats, and the composition of the offbeats in the intervals between beats and at the beginning and end of the line, beat scansion indicates the rhythm as perceived by the reader or listener—who may have no training in cl. prosody.

■ W. B. Ker, *Form and Style in Poetry* (1928); G. R. Stewart, *The Technique of English Verse* (1930); J. Malof, "The Native Rhythm of English Meters," *TSLL* 5 (1964); R. Burling, *Man's Many Voices* (1970); G. D. Allen, "The Location of Rhythmic Stress Beats in English," *L&S* 15 (1972); G. Knowles, "The Rhythm of English Syllables," *Lingua* 34 (1974); Attridge, *Rhythms*; E. Couper-Kuhlen, *English Speech Rhythm* (1993); Attridge, *Poetic Rhythm*; Brendan O'Donnell, *The Passion of Meter* (1995)—Wordsworth's use of rhythm; Carper and Attridge; John Creaser, " 'Service Is Perfect Freedom': Paradox and Prosodic Style in *Paradise Lost*," *RES* 58 (2007).

D. ATTRIDGE

BIBLICAL POETRY. *See* HYMN; PSALM.

BLANK VERSE

I. Italian
II. English
III. Spanish and Portuguese
IV. German
V. Scandinavian
VI. Slavic

I. Italian. *Blank verse* is a term for unrhymed lines of poetry, always in lines of a length considered appropriate to serious topics and often in the most elevated, canonical meter in a given national *prosody. The phenomenon first appeared in It. poetry of the 13th c. with "Il Mare Amoroso" (The Sea of Love), an anonymous poem composed of 334 unrhymed *endecasillabo* verses. In the Ren., this form was transplanted to England as the unrhymed decasyllable or iambic *pentameter. Though these lines are thought to have derived metrically from the cl. iambic *trimeter, they were designed to produce, in the vernaculars, equivalents in tone and weight of the cl. "heroic" line, the *hexameter. The unrhymed endecasillabo, while popular and important for certain writers (e.g., Ugo Foscolo, Giacomo Leopardi, and many 20th-c. poets), did not become a major meter in It. as the unrhymed iambic pentameter did in Eng. Fr. poet-critics noted the work of the It. poets and made experiments of their own, but these never took hold in a lang. where word *accent was weak; hence, Fr. poetry never developed a significant blank-verse trad. The Iberian, Ger., Scandinavian, and Slavic trads. are discussed below.

Luigi Alamanni's *Rime toscane* (1532) and other famous It. works in *versi sciolti* (i.e., *versi sciolti da rima*, verse freed from rhyme), such as Giangiorgio Trissino's tragedy *Sophonisba* (1524) and *epic *L'Italia liberata dai Goti* (1547), were important models for other national poetries such as the Eng.; the first poet to write blank verse in Eng., Henry Howard, the Earl of Surrey (1517–47), surely knew of Alamanni, as well as Niccolò Liburnio's 1534 trans. of Virgil or the 1539 trans. by the de' Medici circle.

II. English. Blank verse in England was invented by the Earl of Surrey, who sometime between 1539 and 1546 translated two books of the *Aeneid* (2 and 4) into this "straunge meter." It remains to be shown precisely how the rhythms in Surrey's lines derived from the It. endecasillabo. Rather than the 11 syllables of his It. model, Surrey's lines have 10, in an alternating (*iambic) rhythm, and his more easily identifiable precursors are Eng. writers of rhymed decasyllabic verse such as Thomas Wyatt and (more remotely) Chaucer. Gavin Douglas's Scottish trans. of Virgil's epic (written ca. 1513, pub. 1553), from which Surrey took 40% of his diction, is in rhymed *heroic couplets. Like other pre-Shakespearean blank verse, Surrey's is relatively stiff in rhythm, impeded by end-stops. Dignified in style, it exhibits an extensive network of sound patterning, perhaps to offset absent *rhyme.

As blank verse developed in Eng., generic considerations became important. In Eng., *blank* as used of verse suggests a mere absence of rhyme, not that liberation from a restrictive requirement implied in the It. term. Nevertheless, Eng. defenders of blank verse repeatedly asserted that rhyme acts on poets as a "constraint to express many things otherwise, and for the most part worse than else they would have exprest them" (John Milton). That rhyme has its virtues and beauties needs no argument here. Rhyme does, however, tend to delimit—even to define—metrical structures; it has its clearest effect when the syllables it connects occur at the ends also of syntactic structures, so that *meter and syntax reinforce one another. One associates rhyme with symmetries and closures. Omission of rhyme, by contrast, encourages the use of syntactic structures greater and more various than could be contained strictly within the line and so makes possible an amplitude of discourse, a natural-seeming multiformity, not easily available to rhymed verse. In light of these characteristics, Eng. writers found blank verse a fitting vehicle for long works (for its lack of imposed repetition), drama (for its natural word order), and epic (for its inversion, suspension, and related stylistic devices).

Though blank verse appeared in Eng. first in (trans.) epic, attempts at Eng. *heroic verse after Surrey use, as Hardison remarks, "almost every form *but* blank verse." The form achieved its first great flowering in drama. After Surrey, the dramatic and nondramatic varieties have significantly different hists., suggesting that they differ in nature more than critics once thought. In nondramatic verse, the influence of Petrarchism, manifested in the vogue for the *sonnet sequence, ensured that rhyme held sway in Eng. nondramatic verse up to

Milton. The heavy editorial regularization by the editor of *Tottel's Miscellany* (1557) set the trend up to Philip Sidney, who showed that metrical correctness and natural expressiveness were not mutually exclusive (see Thompson), a demonstration extended even further by John Donne—but again, in rhyme.

The first Eng. dramatic blank verse, Thomas Norton's in the first three acts of *Gorboduc* (1561), is smooth but more heavily end-stopped than Surrey's, giving the impression of contrivance, of a diction shaped—and often padded out—to fit the meter. Thomas Sackville's verse in the last two acts of the play is more alive. But the artificial regularity of Norton's verse came to characterize Eng. *dramatic poetry until Christopher Marlowe came fully into his powers. Marlowe showed what rhetorical and tonal effects blank verse was capable of; his early play *Dido* echoes lines from Surrey's *Aeneid*, and Shakespeare's early works show what he learned from Marlowe.

A. *Shakespeare.* Shakespeare's blank verse, the major verse form of his plays throughout his career, is marked by several features, some of them shared with or derived from earlier Eng. poets (e.g. John Lydgate, Sidney, and Marlowe) but developed with unprecedented coherence. (1) Blank verse is always mixed with other metrical modes (e.g., rhymed verse, songs) and (except for *Richard II* and *King John*) with prose; two plays offer more rhymed verse than blank (*Love's Labour's Lost* and *A Midsummer Night's Dream*), and seven plays (two hists. and five middle-period comedies) are largely or predominantly written in prose. Shifts within a scene from one mode to another are often subtle, gradual, and hard to hear; different metrical registers for different social classes, however, can be heard, and identify sets of characters—as in *MND*. (2) Resourceful use of common Elizabethan conventions of metrical patterning and esp. of metrical variation gives many individual lines great flexibility, variety, melody, and speechlike force. (3) Frequent use of lines deviant in length or pattern (short, long, headless, broken-backed, and epic-caesural) extends the potentialities of expressive variation beyond what was commonly available to Ren. writers of stanzaic verse. (4) Shrewdly deployed syllabic ambiguity, esp. by devices of compression (see ELISION), makes many lines seem packed. (5) Lines become increasingly enjambed: sentences run from midline to midline, and even a speech or a scene may end in midline (see ENJAMBMENT). Conversely, metrically regular lines may comprise several short phrases or sentences and may be shared by characters (*split lines). In the theater, consistently enjambed blank verse, unlike Marlowe's end-stopped "mighty" line, sounds more like speech but also tests the audience's awareness of the meter. Esp. in Shakespeare's later plays, the audience, like the characters it is scrutinizing, follows an uncertain path between comprehension and bafflement. Besides carrying the characters' emotional utterances and conveying (with appropriate intensity) their complex states of mind, Shakespeare's blank verse may figure, through its rich dialectic of pattern and departure-from-pattern, a continuing tension between authority and event, model and story, the measured structures of cosmic order and the wayward motions of erratic individual characters.

B. After Shakespeare, and esp. after Donne's (rhymed) *Satyres*, the dramatic blank-verse line grew looser in form. Feminine endings (see MASCULINE AND FEMININE), infrequent in all early blank verse, became common; in John Fletcher, they often carry verbal stress. Later, true feminine endings become common even in nondramatic rhymed verse. Milton uses feminine endings in *Paradise Lost* and *Paradise Regained* only with great restraint. They occur rather seldom in the early books of *Paradise Lost*, but much more frequently after Eve and Adam's fall and are thereby appropriate to the speech of fallen mortals.

In dramatic blank verse, extrametrical syllables begin to appear within the line—first, nearly always following a strong stress and at the end of a phrase or clause at the *caesura; later, elsewhere within the line. In some late Jacobean and Caroline dramas (e.g., those of John Webster) the line has become so flexible that at times the five points of stress seem to become phrase centers, each capable of carrying with it unstressed syllables required by the sense rather than by the metrical count of syllables. But such "Websterian" lines were to call down the wrath of later critics; and the closing of the theaters in 1642 saw the end of a brilliant—if almost too daring—period of experimentation with the structure of the dramatic blank-verse line. When verse drama was written again, after the Restoration and under the impetus of the newly popular Fr. model, the line was once

again a strict pentameter but now, and for the next century, rhymed. In any event, after the closing of the theaters, blank verse was never to be of major importance in the drama again. The attempt to renew verse drama (incl. blank verse) in the 20th c. never won either popular or critical acclaim.

C. Milton. Milton returned blank verse to its earliest use as a vehicle of epic and to strict, though complex, metrical order; his influence was so powerful that the form bore his impress up to the 20th c. He did, of course, write blank-verse drama—*Comus* (*A Mask*) and *Samson Agonistes*, the first much influenced by Shakespeare. In both, blank verse, though it is unquestionably the central form, is intermingled with other forms—lyric in *Comus*, choric in *Samson Agonistes*—to such effect that we think of both works as being in mixed meters. In *Samson Agonistes*, Milton is trying to produce the effect of Gr. tragedy (though with a biblical subject); but the blank verse is similar enough to Milton's nondramatic blank verse that discussion of the two may be merged.

Milton was profoundly familiar with the *Aeneid* in Lat., perhaps in It. trans., and in some Eng. versions; he was equally familiar with It. epic and romance. As a theorist of form, he wanted to make blank verse in Eng. the instrument that the humanist poets had been attempting to forge since Trissino. For his subject in *Paradise Lost*, he needed a dense, packed line, as various as possible in movement within the limits set by broadly understood but absolute metricality; at the same time, he needed a syntax complex and elaborate enough to overflow line form, to subordinate it to larger forms of thought, appropriately varied in the scope of their articulation—"the sense variously drawn out from one verse into another." The idea was not new, yet no one had managed enjambment in Eng. as skillfully as Milton learned to manage it. Before him—except in Shakespeare's later plays—the congruence of syntax with line form had been too nearly predictable.

Even more than Shakespeare's, Milton's blank-verse line differs from his rhymed pentameter in management of rhythm and through constant variation of the placement of pause within the line. In the course of enjambing lines, Milton writes long periodic sentences, making liberal use of inversion, parenthesis, and other delaying and complicating devices. At times, he uses Italianate stress sequences that disturb the double rhythm and in some instances all but break the meter. Also important, given his refusal of rhyme, is a more extensive (if irregular) deployment of the varied resources of sound patterning. Numerous forms of *internal rhyme occur, as well as final *assonance and half rhyme; and whole passages are woven together by patterns of *alliteration, assonance, and half rhyme.

D. After Milton. Milton's influence on subsequent nondramatic blank verse in Eng. was, as Havens showed, enormous. Yet, all blank verse after Milton became essentially a romantic form—no longer epic and (the dramatic *monologue excepted) no longer dramatic, but the vehicle of rumination and recollection. The line of descent leads through William Wordsworth ("Michael"; *The Prelude*; *The Excursion*) to Alfred, Lord Tennyson ("Ulysses"; "Tithonus"; *Idylls of the King*) and Robert Browning (*The Ring and the Book*). By the mid-18th c., the forces of metrical regularity had begun to weaken; for the first time, extra syllables that cannot be removed by elision begin to appear in the nondramatic line, producing triple rhythm. The Eng. pentameter, both dramatic and nondramatic, between 1540 and 1780 all but disallowed triple rhythms; strict count of syllables was deemed central to line structure. Real, irreducible triple rhythms before 1780 were associated with music; they occur fairly commonly in song lyrics and *ballads but not in *accentual-syllabic verse. After 1780, however, triple rhythms gradually invade poems in double rhythm, in part because the romantics were devoted to the work of their 16th- and 17th-c. predecessors and often used the diction of Edmund Spenser, Shakespeare, and Milton, though without entirely understanding earlier metrical conventions. There was also a revival of interest in the ballads, which varied the basic double rhythms with irreducible triple rhythms, a practice soon evident in William Blake's *Songs* and even occasionally in Wordsworth. As the 19th c. wore on, rhythmic handling might be restrained (Tennyson) or flamboyant (Browning), but the prevailing stylistic tendency was toward effects of speech (a devel. forecast by S. T. Coleridge's term *conversation poem*).

In the early 20th c., such speech qualities were exploited by E. A. Robinson and esp. Robert Frost in his *North of Boston* (1914). The rise of experimental modernism severely challenged the form; T. S. Eliot deprecated

"the inevitable iambic pentameter." Although with scant critical attention and with diminished prestige, much blank verse continued to be written. The impressive works of the post–World War II generation (e.g., Howard Nemerov, Richard Wilbur, Anthony Hecht, James Merrill) followed in the wake of earlier achievements such as W. B. Yeats's "The Second Coming" and Wallace Stevens's "Sunday Morning." In the later 20th c., some poets, evidently with an eye to *free verse, wrote looser versions of the line with added syllables and with stresses erratically clumped or spaced, so that the standard meter seems a distant paradigm rather than an active presence. More traditionally inclined poets—first the Stanford formalists and later the New Formalists—practiced a stricter adherence to the meter. In the 21st c., blank verse continues in wide use among poets attracted to its generic versatility and its expressive pliancy and power.

III. Spanish and Portuguese. In his foundational *Gramática de la lengua castellana* (Grammar of the Castilian Language, 1492), Antonio de Nebrija deplores the use of rhyme for three reasons: the lack of freedom to express the feelings of the poet, the wearisome similarity of sound, and the way the sound distracts from understanding the sense. But the rise of blank verse occurs after Juan Boscán (ca. 1490–1542) wrote a preface to his poems (1543) where he waxed ironic about the readers who felt "nostalgic for the multitude of rhymes" current in traditional courtly poetry. His generation opened the way toward a new Iberian idiom, based on a kind of studied spontaneity, in which rhyme became secondary or nonexistent. Lyric Port. and Sp. rhymed hendecasyllabic poems by Francisco Sá de Miranda (1481–1558) suggest a rhythmical flexibility like that of prose. Boscán himself wrote *Leandro*, a narrative poem of over 2,700 unrhymed lines, and his friend Garcilaso de la Vega (1503–36) composed an epistle in the form. In spite of detractors such as Fernando de Herrera ("Notes on the Poetry of Garcilaso," 1580), blank verse appeared in important *lyric, narrative, and dramatic poetry of the later 16th c. António Ferreira (1528–69) composed the supreme masterwork of 16th-c. Iberian tragedy, *Castro* (first written ca. 1554, pub. 1587, definitive ed. 1598), mostly in blank verse, and expressed elsewhere the same reluctance about rhyme as Nebrija. The first epic poem finished in Port., *Segundo Cerco de Diu*

(Second Siege of Diu, ms. ca. 1568, pub. 1574) by Jerónimo Corte-Real (d. 1588), is entirely in unrhymed verse. The Spaniard Francisco de Aldana (1537–75) wrote the mythological *Fábula de Faetonte* and three long epistles in blank *hendecasyllables (pub. 1589–91). There were influential blank verse Sp. trans. of Homer's *Odyssey* in 1550, Virgil's *Aeneid* in 1555, Ovid's *Metamorphoses* in 1580, and of a mod. poem like Corte-Real's in 1597. Corte-Real himself published two other epics mostly in blank verse that received considerable renown, *Victoria de Lepanto* in Sp. (1578) and *Sepúlveda* in Port. (1594), with intertextual links back to Boscán's *Leandro* and not without influence in authors as canonical as Miguel de Cervantes and Milton. In the 17th c., perhaps the only remarkable poem in blank verse was Félix Lope de Vega's *El arte nuevo de hacer comedias* (*New Art of Writing Comedies*, 1609), and this only for its value as theory of drama (though ironically 17th-c. Sp. drama rejected blank verse). But unrhymed hendecasyllabic verse returned to full effect in some of the best lit. of the 18th c., such as the Brazilian nativist epic *O Uraguai* by Basílio da Gama, the *mock-heroic masterpiece *O Hissope* (The Aspergill) by Antonio Dinis da Cruz e Silva, Leandro Fernández de Moratín's great and moving *Elegía a las Musas* (Elegy to the Muses), and the truculent defense of poetry *Carta a Brito* (Epistle to Brito) by Filinto Elísio. Blank verse was also chosen for the first great work of Port. romanticism, Almeida Garrett's *Camões* (1825), as well as for mod. long poems by major Iberian figures of the time such as Eugénio de Castro (*Constança*, 1900), Teixeira de Pascoaes (*Regresso ao Paraíso*, 1912) and Miguel de Unamuno (*El Cristo de Velásquez*, 1920).

IV. German. The earliest attempt at writing iambic pentameter blank verse in Ger. dates to the beginning of the 17th c., when Johannes Rhenanus wrote a version of Thomas Tomkis's university comedy *Lingua*. In 1682, Rhenanus was followed by E. G. von Berge with a trans. of Milton's *Paradise Lost*. While these attempts were of no further consequence, interest in blank verse was rekindled around the middle of the 18th c., when various writers, incl. J. E. Schlegel and his brother J. H. Schlegel, pub. trans. of Eng. blank-verse lit. (e.g., James Thomson's *Seasons* and some of his tragedies, William Congreve's *The Mourning Bride*) or wrote their own dramas (J. W. von Brawe, *Brutus*; C. F. Weisse, *Atreus und Thyest*;

F. G. Klopstock, *Salomo*). G. A. Bürger applied blank verse to the epic genre in his trans. of passages from Homer's *Iliad*, as did C. M. Wieland in his *Erzählungen* (Tales). The first Ger. blank-verse drama to be performed was Wieland's *Lady Johanna Gray*, staged in Switzerland in 1758. As a translator of Shakespeare's dramatic works into prose, Wieland chose *MND* for a blank-verse trans. (1762). However, it was not until G. E. Lessing's *Nathan der Weise* (1779) that blank verse replaced the *alexandrine as the dominant meter in Ger. cl. and postclassical drama. This change was promoted by K. P. Moritz's handbook on prosody, *Versuch einer deutschen Prosodie* (1786), which J. W. Goethe consulted in rewriting earlier prose versions of his *Iphigenie auf Tauris* (1787) and *Torquato Tasso* (1790). Likewise, Friedrich Schiller rewrote *Don Karlos* (1787) and the second and third parts of his *Wallenstein* trilogy, *Die Piccolomini* and *Wallensteins Tod* (the first part, *Wallensteins Lager*, being in free *knittelvers*). Between 1800 and 1804, Schiller wrote *Maria Stuart*, *Die Jungfrau von Orleans*, *Die Braut von Messina*, and *Wilhelm Tell*, all (apart from the choruses in *Die Braut von Messina*) in blank verse.

A. W. Schlegel's trans. of Shakespeare's plays (14 plays between 1797 and 1810) helped further establish blank verse as the standard meter of Ger. verse drama. His work was later complemented by Ludwig Tieck, his daughter Dorothea Tieck, and Wolf Graf Baudissin, who even took the liberty of translating Molière's alexandrines into blank verse (1865) because he argued that it had the same dominant position in Ger. drama as the alexandrine had in Fr. Thus, most major and minor dramatists of the 19th c. used blank verse exclusively (as is the case with Heinrich von Kleist, although there are some prose passages in *Das Käthchen von Heilbronn*), extensively (as did Franz Grillparzer, C. D. Grabbe, and C. F. Hebbel), or at least occasionally (Karl Immermann, Karl Gutzkow, and Paul Heyse).

While the earliest attempts at blank verse in Ger. clearly reflected the Eng. models on which they were based (e.g., by the avoidance of feminine endings like Thomson or by construing long periodic sentences over many verse lines like Milton), Lessing, Goethe, and Schiller developed their own metrical styles. Lessing almost disregarded the verse line as a metrical unit by using strong enjambments, by frequently splitting the line into short phrases, often uttered by different speakers, and by splitting lines between speakers 70% of the time (see SPLIT LINES). Thus, Lessing made his verse sound "natural" in the sense of sounding like speech or prose. Goethe went to the other extreme and made his blank verse clearly distinct from speech or prose. His lines are mostly end-stopped, and a change of speakers coincides generally (more than 90%) with the end of a line, at a dramatic climax even in the form of *stichomythia. His syntax is complex but well built, rhythmically balanced, and, stylistic devices such as *sententia* or *genitivus explicativus*, at times highly artificial. Schiller's style lies somewhere between Lessing and Goethe, although he moved toward Goethe in his later plays. However, Goethe's verse always has a smooth, lyrical "ring," whereas Schiller adapts his verse to the dramatic function by, e.g., making Mortimer (*Maria Stuart*, 3.6) utter wildly unmetrical lines in order to convey to the listener or reader that he is out of his mind.

Ger. blank-verse dramas like those of Shakespeare often contain lines that are shorter or longer than the standard ten syllables. Kleist, esp. in his comedies, was less strict than Goethe, but both occasionally loaded an ultrashort or an extra-long line with extra meaning. Insertions of a different meter in Goethe's *Iphigenie* or in Schiller's *Braut von Messina* always have a dramatic function.

Even in late 19th- and 20th-c. drama, blank verse was not entirely abandoned (Ernst von Wildenbruch, Gerhart Hauptmann, Hugo von Hofmannsthal, J. R. Becher, and Walter Hasenclever). After 1945, blank verse experienced a kind of renaissance in the works of some East Ger. dramatists (Heiner Müller, Hartmut Lange, Erwin Strittmatter, and Peter Hacks), who introduced more metrical complexity in their verse dramas by frequently—and even verse-internally—placing trochaic words in weak-strong sequences as in Eng. blank verse.

In Ger. poetry, iambic pentameter verse occurred mostly in its rhymed version. However, after Schiller's early specimen *Das verschleierte Bild zu Sais* (1795), early mod. poets like C. F. Meyer, Stefan George, von Hofmannsthal, and R. M. Rilke (in two of his *Duineser Elegien*) used blank verse for some of their best poetry. Despite the predilection among contemp. poets for free verse, blank verse can still be found, be it in the form of entire poems in blank verse (by Arnfrid Astel and Thomas Rosenlöcher in *Jahrbuch der Lyrik 2001*) or intermingled with

shorter lines (Günter Grass) or "hidden" in scattered passages (sometimes incongruent with the printed lines) of free-verse poems (Volker Braun, Norbert Hummelt).

Blank verse in Ger. has at times been criticized as being rhythmically monotonous. Compared to Eng., Ger. blank verse is more "regular" because Ger. lexical words tend to have an unstressed syllable that naturally falls on a weak position, while the lexically stressed syllable falls just as naturally on the strong position (ictus). However, this view overlooks the rhythmic potential of blank verse in the hands of a poet with a fine ear (such as Goethe or Lessing) and ignores the subtleties of meaning created by an interplay between meter and rhythm.

V. Scandinavian. In Scandinavia, blank verse was introduced as an effect of romanticism at the end of the 18th c. It soon replaced the alexandrine in the narrative, philosophical, and dramatic genres. Originally, the Eng. and Ger. varieties were adopted, and trans. of Shakespeare's plays enhanced the reputation of the new meter. The assimilation of blank verse in Scandinavia can be attributed to two factors: the lack of end rhyme in blank verse suited the Scandinavian langs., with their scarcity of rhyme words; and the habit of realizing just four out of five prominence positions brought blank verse close to the med. four-beat line. As it grew in use, the Scandinavian variant of blank verse became distinguished by its alternation between lines of 10 and 11 syllables.

In Denmark, Johannes Ewald initially attempted blank verse in 1768. His music drama *Balders Død* (1773) introduced hendecasyllabic blank verse in Denmark, probably of It. extraction. A. G. Oehlenschläger's first play in blank verse was the comedy *Aladdin* (1805). He used the decasyllable with masculine endings, following the Eng. and the Ger. styles.

The earliest instances of Norwegian blank verse are some farces by Henrik Wergeland, whose versification was probably inspired by Shakespeare. Blank verse in the style of the Danish forerunners dominated Norwegian drama from the middle of the 19th c. Henrik Ibsen tested blank verse in his first play *Catilina* (1850), and Bjønstjerne Bjørnson composed excellent blank verse in his saga dramas *Halte-Hulda* (1858) and *Kong Sverre* (1861).

In Sweden, blank verse was introduced with J. H. Kellgren's narrative fragment *Sigvarth och Hilma* (1788), which was inspired by Ewald's works. The poet F. M. Franzén, influenced by Shakespeare, elaborated blank verse in the 1790s. Since then, blank verse has been a popular Swedish measure in the narrative and philosophical genres, with contributions by poets such as E. J. Stagnelius, Birger Sjöberg, and Gunnar Ekelöf. Most of the space opera *Aniara* (1956) by Harry Martinson is written in blank verse. The versification of Göran Palm's *Sverige—en vintersaga* (1984–2005) is a mod. blank verse that comes close to the rhythm of spoken lang.

VI. Slavic. Rus. blank verse emerged in 18th-c. imitations of antiquity, e.g., Vasily Trediakovsky's syllabic blank-verse version of François Fénelon's *Aventures de Télémaque* (1699) and A. D. Kantemir's renderings of Horace. In the 19th c., under the influence of Vasily Zhukovsky's trans. (1817–21) of Schiller's *Die Jungfrau von Orleans* and Alexander Pushkin's *Boris Godunov* (1825), iambic pentameter blank verse became widely associated with drama. Simultaneously, Rus. blank verse appeared in folk stylizations, e.g., Pushkin's "Tale of the Fisherman and the Fish" (1833) and "Songs of the Western Slavs" (1835), inspired by the Serbo-Croatian epic decasyllable, and Mikhail Lermontov's "Song of the Merchant Kalashnikov" (1837), as well as in lyric monologues such as Pushkin's "Again I visited" (1835), where it acquired a semantic aura later echoed by such 20th-c. poets as Alexander Blok, Vladislav Khodasevich, and Joseph Brodsky.

In Poland, dactylic-hexameter blank verse was employed by Ren. poets writing in Lat. Hendecasyllabic blank verse in Polish-lang. poetry had It. roots; Jan Kochanowski used it in his tragedy *The Dismissal of Greek Envoys* (1578). Polish trans. from antiquity and from Eng., Ger., and It. featured blank verse; however, rhymed verse was the standard for Polish drama. Blank verse plays include Jozef Korzeniowski's *The Monk* (1830) and *Gypsies* (1857), J. C. Słowacki's *Lilla Weneda* (1840, partially rhymed), and Cyprian Norwid's 1880 comedy *Pure Love at a Seaside Spa*.

■ **English:** S. Johnson, *Rambler*, nos. 86–96 (1751); Schipper; J. A. Symonds, *Blank Verse* (1895); J. B. Mayor, *Chapters on English Metre*, 2d ed. (1901); E. Gosse, "Blank Verse," *Encyclopedia Britannica*, 11th ed. (1910–11); Bridges; R. D. Havens, *The Influence of Milton on English Poetry* (1922); A. Oras, *Blank Verse and Chronology in Milton* (1966); R. Beum, "So

Much Gravity and Ease," *Language and Style in Milton*, ed. R. D. Emma and J. T. Shawcross (1967); R. Fowler, "Three Blank Verse Textures," *The Languages of Literature* (1971); E. R. Weismiller, "Blank Verse," "Versification," and J. T. Shawcross, "Controversy over Blank Verse," *A Milton Encyclopedia*, ed. W. B. Hunter Jr., 8 v. (1978–80); Brogan, 356 ff.; H. Suhamy, *Le Vers de Shakespeare* (1984); M. Tarlinskaja, *Shakespeare's Verse* (1987); G. T. Wright, *Shakespeare's Metrical Art* (1988); J. Thompson, *The Founding of English Metre*, 2d ed. (1989); O. B. Hardison Jr., *Prosody and Purpose in the English Renaissance* (1989); A. Hecht, "Blank Verse," Finch and Varnes; R. B. Shaw, *Blank Verse* (2007).

■ **Spanish and Portuguese:** I. Navarrete, *Orphans of Petrarch* (1994); *Historia y Crítica de la Literatura Española*, ed. F. Rico, 7 v. (1991–95); *Juán Boscán, Obra Completa*, ed. C. Clavería (1999); *António Ferreira, Poemas Lusitanos*, ed. T. F. Earle (2000); *Fernando de Herrera, Anotaciones a la poesía de Garcilaso*, ed. I. Pepe and J. M. Reyes (2001); H.J.S. Alves, "Milton after Corte-Real," *MP* 106 (2009).

■ **German:** J. G. Herder, *Ueber die neuere deutsche Literatur. Fragmente,* 2d ed. (1768); F. Zarncke, *Über den fünffüssigen Jambus mit besonderer Rücksicht auf seine Behandlung durch Lessing, Schiller und Goethe* (1865); A. Sauer, *Ueber den fünffüssigen Iambus vor Lessing's "Nathan"* (1878); E. Zitelmann, *Der Rhythmus des fünffüßigen Jambus* (1907); W. Rube, *Der fünffüssige Jambus bei Hebbel* (1910); L. Hettich, *Der fünffüssige Jambus in den Dramen Goethes* (1913); R. Haller, "Studie über den deutschen Blankvers," *Deutsche Vierteljahrsschrift für Literaturwissenschaft und Geistesgeschichte* 31 (1957); R. Bräuer, *Tonbewegung und Erscheinungsformen des sprachlichen Rhythmus* (1964); L. Schädle, *Der frühe deutsche Blankvers unter besonderer Berücksichtigung seiner Verwendung durch Chr. M. Wieland* (1972); B. Bjorklund, *A Study in Comparative Prosody* (1978); D. Chisholm, "Prosodische Aspekte des Blankversdramas," *Literaturwissenschaft und empirische Methoden*, ed. H. Kreuzer and R. Viehoff (1981); C. Küper, *Sprache und Metrum* (1988), and "Blankvers," *Reallexikon III*, v. 1 (1997).

■ **Scandinavian:** O. Sylwan, *Den svenska versen från 1600-talets början*, v. 1–3 (1925–34); O. Sylwan, *Svensk verskonst. Från Wivallius till Karlfeldt* (1934); H. Lie, *Norsk verslære* (1967); J. Fafner, *Dansk vershistorie*, v. 1–3 (1994–2000); E. Lilja, *Svensk metrik* (2006).

■ **Slavic**: K. Estreicher, *Bibliografia Polska*, v. 1 (1870); R. Jakobson, "Slavic Epic Verse," v. 4 (1966); M. Gasparov, *Ocherk istori russkogo stikha* (1984); Terras; M. Wachtel, *Development of Russian Verse* (1999); L. Pszolowska, "Dve literatury i dve modeli stikha," *Slavianskii stikh*, ed. M. Gasparov et al. (2001); S. Zurawski, "Wiersz biały," *Literatura polska. Encyklopedia PWN* (2007).

E. R. WEISMILLER (IT.); T.V.F. BROGAN, R. B. SHAW, E. R. WEISMILLER, G. T. WRIGHT (ENG.); H.J.S. ALVES (SP. AND PORT.); C. KÜPER (GER.); E. LILJA (SCAND.); N. FRIEDBERG (SLAVIC)

BLASON. A descriptive poem in praise or blame of a single object (Thomas Sébillet, *L'art poétique*, 1548). It gained popularity in mid-16th-c. France after Clément Marot's "Blason du beau tétin" (1536) gave rise to the vogue of the *blason anatomique*. However, the term is first used in the late 15th c. with the loose definition of *propos* ("speech") or even "dialogue" in works such as Guillaume Alexis's *Blason des Faulces Amours* (1486) or Guillaume Coquillart's *Blason des armes et des dames* (1484).

The blason received its stricter early mod. definition after Marot's poem, written while in exile in Ferrara and probably influenced by Olimpo da Sassoferrato's love poetry. In response to the poetic competition launched by Marot, dozens of poems celebrating some part of the female body were composed in France and collected in an illustrated anthol., first pub. as a short annex to Leon Battista Alberti's *Hecatomphilia* (1536, 1537, 1539), then as an independent volume, the *Blasons anatomiques du corps femenin: Ensemble les Contreblasons* (1543, 1550, 1554, 1568). In spite of Marot's injunction to avoid offending words or body parts, many blasons from that collection fall under the category of the obscene, in the satirical trad. of the paradoxical eulogy. The genre of the *contreblason,* also initiated by Marot, turns the genre upside down, either by deriding ugly objects or by criticizing the very enterprise of praising the human body (Charles de La Hueterie, *Le Contreblason de la beauté des membres du corps humain,* 1537).

The poetics of the blason has been connected to its heraldic origin (a description of a coat of arms); to the emblem, where woodcut, poetic description, and interpretation are similarly linked; to mannerism (Saunders, Vickers 1997, Giordano); and to *ekphrasis* and epideixis.

Frequently used devices include *anaphora, enumeratio,* and *hyperbole. According to Sébillet, a good blason should be brief, set in octo- or decasyllabic verses, in couplets, and have an epigrammatic conclusion. However, blasons have from the start been of various lengths: they are less defined by a specific format than by their descriptive and epideictic mode. The Pléiade expanded the genre with *sonnets-blasons* and *hymnes-blasons*; Paul Éluard, René Étiemble, and Régine Detambel revived it in prose and *free verse in the 20th c.

In studies of early mod. Eur. poetry, the blason has been discussed in the 1980s and 1990s as an instance of appropriation and control. From the perspective of feminist poetics, the blason is a male inventory of the female body; from that of postcolonial studies, a way of mapping and taking control of the Other.

See CATALOG, SATIRE.

■ J. Vianey, *Le Pétrarquisme en France au XVIe siècle* (1909); R. E. Pike, "The Blasons in French Literature of the 16th Century," *RR* 27 (1936); K. Kazimierz, "Des Recherches sur l'évolution du blason au XVIe siècle," *Zagadnienia Rodzajow Literarick* (1967); D. B. Wilson, *Descriptive Poetry in France from Blason to Baroque* (1967); A. Tomarken and E. Tomarken, "The Rise and Fall of the Sixteenth-Century French *Blason,*" *Symposium* 29 (1975); N. J. Vickers, "Diana Described: Scattered Woman and Scattered Rhyme," *CritI* 8 (1981); A. Saunders, *The Sixteenth-Century Blason Poétique* (1982); N. J. Vickers, " 'The Blazon of Sweet Beauty's Best': Shakespeare's *Lucrece,*" *Shakespeare and the Question of Theory,* ed. P. Parker and G. Hartman (1985); P. Parker, "Rhetorics of Property: Exploration, Inventory, Blazon," *Literary Fat Ladies* (1987); N. J. Vickers, "Members Only: Marot's Anatomical Blazons," *The Body in Parts,* ed. D. Hillman and C. Mazzio (1997); M. J. Giordano, "The *Blason anatomique* and Related Fields: Emblematics, Nominalism, Mannerism, and Descriptive Anatomy as Illustrated by M. Scève's *Blason de la Gorge,*" *An Interregnum of the Sign,* ed. D. Graham (2001).

I. SILVER; T.V.F. BROGAN; C. ALDUY

BLUES. Originating in Af. Am. folk culture, the blues has developed into a central inspiration for a great deal of Am. poetry. The music is distinguished thematically and philosophically by its posture of direct confrontation with the melancholy psychological state also called *blues* that is produced by unfortunate circumstances of lost love or unjust circumstances of racism and poverty. Ralph Ellison describes this motivation behind the music: "The blues is an impulse to keep the painful details and episodes of a brutal experience alive in one's aching consciousness, to finger its jagged grain, and to transcend it, not by the consolation of philosophy but by squeezing from it a near-tragic, near-comic lyricism." In other words, the blues transcends the pain by keeping it alive in the music itself.

This lyricism took many forms, though it has come to be associated most directly with the 12-bar blues. This form consists of three lines with an *aab* rhyme scheme, with the first line repeated in the second, often with slight variation in syntax or intonation, and with the third providing either ironic commentary or some resolution or both, as in the following lines from "The Backwater Blues": "Backwater blues done call me to pack my things and go / Backwater blues done call me to pack my things and go. / 'Cause my house fell down and I can't live there no more." These lines also convey the typical sense of loss and isolation that permeates the blues and that is reinforced by the repetition, as well as the understatement and ironic humor with which the singer confronts that loss, since her house "fell down" in the third line not of its own volition but because of the dramatic and destructive Mississippi flood of 1927. Indeed, clichés about the blues are sometimes true, as many songs mourn lost loves, castigate two-timing lovers, lament loneliness, and confess melancholy, though occasionally with a similarly understated tongue in cheek, leading Langston Hughes famously to characterize the blues as sometimes laughing to keep from crying. This tone of sadness is also expressed by what is sometimes called the "blue note," notes in the music scale distinctively flattened to melancholic effect. Simultaneously, a call-and-response interaction between voice and instrument, and between singer and audience, expresses at least the hope for unity and sympathy in the isolation. Through this complex leavening of melancholy with ironic humor, the blues exemplifies a defining tragic-comic humor and subtle emotional affirmation of Af. Am. folk culture.

Its own kind of verse, the blues inspired a great number of Af. Am. poets with this formal enactment of its psychological state, its stoic sensibility, and its existential philosophy,

allowing the poet to extend into verse the central ideas and practices of black oral trads. First, the blues derives from spirituals, slave work songs and field hollers, cultural forms of communal unity, spiritual renewal, and, at times, political resistance developed by enslaved Afs. and by Af. Ams. enduring segregation. Second, blues singers often adapt folk ballads, using such folk heroes as John Henry, High John the Conqueror, and Stagolee as subjects and even as personae. Also, like those *ballads, blues songs use *rhyme and *repetition to create possibilities for humor, irony, and *lament that would be familiar to the almost exclusively black original audiences for the music. In addition, blues musicians often sing personalized versions of the same songs—called standards—and improvise on several standard *tropes, incl. the train and its whistle as symbols of mobility, moments of decision on the crossroads, and the flood of 1927, as well as the well-known themes of lost or cheating loves. Improvisation itself—the ability to "riff" on common themes and to change songs in every performance—was part of this stoic assertion of self by offering personal versions of common problems. In these ways, the blues fosters the creation of a distinctive Af. Am. communal culture as a bulwark against social oppression and existential angst.

From these common themes and cultural roots emerged varied modes of song that, in their various ways, would come to characterize blues poetry. There is the so-called classic blues like "Backwater Blues" sung in recordings by such well-known artists as Ma Rainey and Bessie Smith, women who complicated the music's traditionally masculine themes with their female perspectives and who helped to establish the 12-bar blues as the music's most identifiable form. There are also several regional subgenres, including the originating, acoustic Mississippi delta blues, which produced Robert Johnson and Muddy Waters, among others; the urban, electric guitar-based Chicago blues; and the later, jazz-influenced Kansas City blues. New Orleans boasts Dr. John, while Eric Clapton is celebrated for his mod. versions of the music.

Langston Hughes initiated the now-prevalent practice of adapting this empowering existential self-assertion of the blues and its variegated musical forms and trads. to literary poetry. In one of his best-known poems, "The Weary Blues," Hughes describes a blues musician whose singing was inspiring and who eased his own pain so that he could sleep. Hughes also included lyrics from an actual song called "The Weary Blues." Moreover, in many other poems, Hughes translated the 12-bar blues into six-line stanzas, both by adapting actual lyrics of the urban blues he heard in Harlem and by creating his own. His contemporary in the 1920s, Sterling A. Brown, likewise adapted rural blues songs from his folklore research into poetry. This turn to folk culture for poetic sources was characteristic of the Harlem Renaissance, the cultural flourishing of Af. Ams. in and around Harlem in the 1920s in which Hughes and Brown participated. Since then, Gwendolyn Brooks, Melvin B. Tolson, Robert Hayden, Honoree Fannonne Jeffers, and Kevin Young are among the many poets who found in the wit, sarcasm, and existentialism of the music an approach amenable to portraying black people realistically and complexly, eliciting call-and-response relations between poet and poem analogous to that of blues musician and audience. The posture of self-affirmation in the face of a rigid society also appealed to Beat poets.

Indeed, the blues has come to be understood not only as one of the defining practices and sensibilities of Af. Am. popular and literary culture but as a distinctive Af. Am. contribution to Am. culture, literary and otherwise. E.g., Houston A. Baker suggested that the critic of Af. Am. lit. was much like a blues musician sitting at the crossroads whose imagination constitutes what Baker called a "blues matrix." Tony Bolden went further, implying that even such cultural forms as the spiritual were actually blues-inflected. Moreover, most scholars of music in poetry acknowledge that jazz not only emerged from the blues but constitutes a musical and thematic continuum from the saddest, most stoic blues to a joyful, improvisational jazz celebration. As scholars such as Sascha Feinstein, Meta DuEwa Jones, T. J. Anderson, and Kimberly Benston have pointed out, there is a jazz-blues aesthetic in Am. poetry, ranging from Jack Kerouac to Yusef Komunyakaa. There are also now folk festivals dedicated to the blues and many of its figures—Robert Johnson, B.B. King, Bessie Smith, Ma Rainey—have become cultural icons, clarifying the powerful influence of the blues.

■ P. Oliver, *The Meaning of the Blues* (1963); R. Ellison, *Shadow and Act* (1965); A. Murray, *Stomping the Blues* (1976); H. A. Baker Jr., *Blues,*

Ideology and Afro-American Literature (1984); S. Tracy, *Langston Hughes and the Blues* (1988); *The Jazz Poetry Anthology*, ed. S. Feinstein and Y. Komunyakaa (1996); T. Gioia, *The History of Jazz* (1997); A. Davis, *Blues Legacies and Black Feminism: Gertrude "Ma" Rainey, Bessie Smith and Billie Holiday* (1998); K. Benston, *Performing Blackness: Enactments of African American Modernism* (2000); M. Jones, "Jazz Prosodies: Orality and Texuality," *Callaloo* 25 (2002); T. J. Anderson, *Notes to Make the Sound Come Right: Four Innovations of Jazz Poetry* (2004); T. Bolden, *Afro-Blue: Improvisations in African American Poetry and Culture* (2004).

K. D. Leonard

BROKEN RHYME. *Broken rhyme* usually designates the division by hyphenation of a word at the end of a line in order to isolate the portion of that word that produces a rhyme with a word at the end of a subsequent line: e.g., "As prone to all ill, and of good as for-*get*- / ful, as proud, lustfull, and as much in *debt*" (Alexander Pope), or "Winter and summer, night and *morn*, / I languish at this table dark; / My office window has a *corn*- / er looks into St. James's Park" (William Thackeray). In Eng. poetry, poets from Shakespeare to Ogden Nash have used broken rhyme to comic and satiric effect. G. M. Hopkins uses it as a resource for serious poetry, e.g., in "The Windhover" and "To What Serves Mortal Beauty?," going so far as to link the final portion of one line with an isolated phoneme in the next ("at the door / Drowned" rhymes with "reward"); this he called the *rove over* rhyme. Broken rhymes have also been used by John Donne (*Satyres* 3 and 4) and e. e. cummings. Yet broken rhyme is more frequent still in non-Eng. trads.; it was developed extensively in Rus. poetry, particularly in the work of 20th-c. poets Vladimir Mayakovsky, Velimir Khlebnikov, and Joseph Brodsky.

Broken rhyme's counterpart in unrhymed verse is *enjambment. Both rely on visual form: for all the "breaking," the binding of the syllables within the broken word is, in fact, stronger than the line end, generating the tension that characterizes each technique.

In Lord Byron, some instances of broken rhyme also meet the criteria for mosaic rhyme or split rhyme, in that the rhyme is achieved not by pairing two words but rather by pairing one word with multiple words: "Start not! Still chaster reader—she'll be *nice hence-* / Forward, and there is no great cause to quake; / This liberty is a poetic *licence*"; elsewhere in *Don Juan*, we see pure examples of mosaic rhyme, though this is also now referred to as broken rhyme by numerous sources: "But—Oh! ye lords and ladies intel*lectual*, / Inform us truly, have they not hen-*pecked you all*"?

See CHAIN RHYME.

T.V.F. BROGAN; J. CROFT

BURLESQUE. *See* PARODY.

CAESURA

I. Caesura vs. Pause
II. Position
III. Extra Syllables

A term that derives from the Lat. verb *caedere*, "to cut off," and refers to the place in a line of verse where the metrical flow is temporarily "cut off." When this "cut" occurs at the beginning of a line, it is called an "initial caesura"; when it occurs in the middle of a line, it is called a "medial caesura"; and when it occurs at the end of a line, it is called a "terminal caesura." In OE poems such as *Beowulf*, caesuras occur predictably between the two half-lines (*hemistich) that are linked by *alliteration. Chaucer used caesuras with greater variety in his *iambic pentameter, and William Shakespeare used them with even more variety in his *blank verse. Poets during and after the Eng. Ren. often placed several caesuras in a line—or no caesuras in a line—to alter the rhythm of the meter, which would otherwise be as monotonous as the ticking of a metronome. 18th-c. poets such as Alexander Pope used caesuras to create a sense of balance or symmetry. In Pope's famous couplet "True wit is nature to advantage dressed, / What oft was thought, but ne'er so well expressed" (*An Essay on Criticism*, 297–98), the caesura in the second line allows the reader to pause before balancing the traditional contraries of wit and nature, thought and speech. 19th- and 20th-c. poets who broke away from metrical verse to write *free verse used caesuras in unexpected places in an attempt to represent more accurately the spontaneous way people thought and spoke. When Ezra Pound and e. e. cummings composed poems by arranging words—or even syllables—in unconventional patterns on the page and when poets such as Charles Olson and Allen Ginsberg declared that poetic lines should be units of breath, caesuras were often indicated by spaces between phrases. In contemp. writing, the poetic term *caesura* is frequently used metaphorically to mean any space, break, or pause in a sequence. Thus, Stephen Melville titles a chapter "Caesura" in *AIDS and the National Body* to refer to a pause in the long "sentence" of dying caused by AIDS. Other contemp. scholars write of "the caesura of the Holocaust" or "the caesura of religion."

I. Caesura vs. Pause. In every sentence, a syntactic juncture or pause between phrases or clauses is usually signaled by punctuation. Traditionally, a caesura is the metrical phenomenon in verse that corresponds to this break in syntax. Often these "breaks" are not carefully distinguished in *prosody and lit. crit. Some critics use *pause, rest*, and *caesura* interchangeably. Strict constructionists argue that performative pauses and individual speech tempos have nothing to do with caesuras in a traditional metrical design. Nor do so-called metrical pauses (missing syllables in accentual verse and other verse systems whose time is filled by a rest) have anything to do with a caesura. According to the traditional view, a poet deliberately places a caesura in a line to break up the metrical flow of verse and to prevent monotony. By contrast, a reader can break up the flow any way he or she deems appropriate. Although some prosodists have claimed that, strictly speaking, a caesura is not a component of a metrical pattern or is only realized in performance, these are minority views.

II. Position. The position and number of caesuras in a line vary from one verse system to another. In cl. prosody, a caesura referred specifically to a pause within a foot of metrical verse. A diaeresis referred to a pause at the end of a foot. The semantic shift from caesura to diaeresis may have occurred in Pierre de Ronsard's *Abrégé de l'art poétique françois* (1565). During the Ren., the mod. concept of caesura as a pause at the end of a metrical foot first surfaced in the prosody manuals of the *Séconde Rhétorique* of early 16th-c. France. A rule forbidding an extra syllable before the caesura was set forth in the *Pleine rhétorique* (1521) of Pierre Fabri and in the *Art poétique* (1555) of Jacques Peletier du Mans, who seems to have been the first to use the term *césure* in Fr.

In Gr. and Lat. poetry, caesuras were regulated more as to position than as to number, and technical terms have been developed to designate the most common placements in the *hexameter line. The term *penthemimeral* refers to a caesura appearing after the first long syllable of the third foot (i.e., after the fifth half-foot), and *hephthemimeral* refers to a caesura after the seventh half-foot. Cl. poets avoided dividing the hexameter line into two equal halves with a caesura. Fixed caesura placement was a major criterion in romance prosodies, esp. Fr. prosody. Indeed, when Victor Hugo moved the caesura in his Fr. *alexandrine lines to create the *trimètre*, it was considered one of the most revolutionary moments in Fr. romanticism. In Eng. verse, caesura placement varies considerably according to metrical subgenre (dramatic verse vs. narrative and lyric; rhymed couplets vs. blank verse). At the end of the 19th c., Jakob Schipper promoted the doctrine that the caesura was essential to the structure of iambic pentameter (fully half of the 50 pps. devoted to Chaucerian meter in his *Englische Metrik* treated the caesura) and that variation in caesura placement was a deliberate strategy to combat the tedium of perfectly metered lines of verse.

III. Extra Syllables. The conventional terminology for line endings, *masculine* and *feminine*, is sometimes still applied to caesuras. Thus, a caesura that follows a stressed syllable is called masculine, and one that follows an unstressed syllable is called feminine. Romance philologists and prosodists of the later 19th c. developed the terms *epic* and *lyric* to refer to two types of feminine caesuras that followed, respectively, an unstressed syllable that is not counted as part of the metrical pattern and an unstressed syllable that is counted. This system of classification arose from speculations about OF epics and lyric poems of troubadours and trouvères. In 1903, L. E. Kastner showed that the notion of epic caesuras was "not justified by facts." Unfortunately, these terms were taken up by scholars to describe caesural variation in Chaucer, with the implication that Eng. patterns of syllabic variation around the caesura "strictly correspond to their French models" (Schipper, *History*, 133). Further studies have shown that caesura placement in Eng. verse—esp. Chaucer's and Shakespeare's—is not strictly regulated.

■ L. E. Kastner, "The Epic Caesura in the Poetry of the Trouvères and Troubadours," *MLQ* 6 (1903); Schipper, *History* (1910); A. L. F. Snell, *Pause* (1918); A. Oras, *Pause Patterns in Elizabethan and Jacobean Drama* (1960); J. Malof, *A Manual of English Meters* (1970); Allen; J. P. Poe,

Caesurae in the Hexameter Line of Latin Elegiac Verse (1974); R. Tsur, *A Perception-Oriented Theory of Metre* (1977); G. Wright, *Shakespeare's Metrical Art* (1988); *A Dictionary of Literary Terms and Literary Theory*, ed. J. A. Cuddon (1998); S. Fry, *The Ode Less Travelled* (2006); *A New Handbook of Literary Terms*, ed. D. Mikics (2007).

T.V.F. BROGAN; H. HART

CANON. *Canon* developed in Eng. as a religious term with two primary designations: ecclesiastical rule, law, or decree; and the collection of books of the Bible validated by the Christian Church, a criterion that excluded other scriptural writings. In literary studies, the term *canon* typically indicates a real or notional list of great works, those discussed in the major studies of lit. hist. and crit. and taught in schools and colleges as elements of proper education. In the last two decades of the 20th c., the idea of the canon moved to the center of Anglo-Am. and other areas of Western literary study and attracted energetic mainstream political debate. At the core of this ferment was the concept of literary value, in particular the question of how and by whom such value has been defined in the past. Scholars began to explore through what historical processes the canon of great books and authors had come into being and through what processes of exclusion other authors and works had been defined as other than "great." Was it the case that the best works, with "best" defined in aesthetic terms, had simply withstood the test of time and been passed from one generation to the next? Or had forces of political and social exclusion, forces whose criteria might now be usefully questioned, elevated some works and diminished others of theoretically equal value? These kinds of questions had a special currency in the Anglo-Am. and postcolonial fields, while they were generally less relevant in many Eur. lits. Scholars debated the content of the current canon, "recovered" unknown writers (often women and people of color), and rewrote literary anthols. They also began to write the hist. of "canon formation," i.e., the hist. of how the canon came into being.

The long hist. of canon-making is inseparable from the hist. of poetics. In Chinese culture of the 6th c. (which saw the appearance of significant comprehensive anthols.) and after, the condition of poetry's being (or becoming) canonical—often called "canonicity"—became an important social and cultural criterion, esp.

from the Song dynasty (ca. 960–1279) on. The growth of a class of literati united by their shared education in preparing for the civil-service exams and the spread of inexpensive printed books gave the criterion social force. Canonicity existed in Japan as well, though until the Edo period (1600), the concept of the canon was largely limited to a fairly small aristocratic population. Perhaps the more important issue surrounding canonicity in Japan occurs with the Meiji era (1868–1912), when attempts at rapid Westernization and modernization led to the establishment of a "national canon" for largely patriotic and pedagogic purposes.

In Eng., as in many langs., poetry was the first canonical genre. The mod. canon was born in the 18th c., at a time when men of letters understood their literary heritage as consisting almost exclusively of poets. While the value of poetry was unquestioned, the relative value of ancient and mod. writings was a subject of heated debate. Used in this context, the word *modern* simply means nonclassical, i.e., written in vernacular or native langs. such as Eng. rather than in the "educated" ancient langs. of Gr. and Lat. While the value of the ancient classics in Gr. and Lat. was assumed, the value of writing in the Eng. lang. had been contested for centuries. Through the middle of the 18th c., common conceptions held that mod. poets like Edmund Waller and John Dryden had improved on writers from the past through their eloquence and smooth, regular verses. They brought the lang. to a stage of devel. superior to where it stood in the poetry of such past figures as Chaucer. In the 1740s and 1750s, the idea that the present improved on the past gave way. Now the idea that ancient texts were valuable was redefined to include not only Gr. and Roman ancients, but the Eng. past and the Eng. lang. as well. The high canonical figures who emerged from this revaluation of the poetic past were the poets Edmund Spenser, Shakespeare, and John Milton. Thus, the Eng. "classics" came into being.

This shift in focus entailed a revision of criteria for judgment. Poetry was now prized not for its smoothness, its regularity, and its ling. improvements over the rough lang. of the past but for its formidable difficulties, historical remoteness, and craggy sublimity. Engaging the Eng. classics was now comparable to interpreting great texts in cl. tongues; only those with special skill would be able to apprehend these texts properly. This new vision of the Eng. past

marked it as fundamentally distinct from the realm of the merely popular. Such a distinction was pressing in an era when revolutionary social changes included rising literacy rates; increased access for women to education, reading, and writing; destabilization of class distinctions; and the rise of the novel, all of which created new social and class pressures.

The definitions of both *poetry* and *lit.* were thrown into uncertainty by these changes. *Poetry* had once been a more general term for all imaginative lit., incl. verse but not limited to it; now the term *lit.* increasingly assumed this more general function, and *poetry* moved to a position more elevated than the prose works that were popular with readers. Shakespeare emerged in the 1750s as *the* national poet, a figure who represented both "literary" qualities antithetical to the market and, simultaneously, enthusiastic popularity. He represented a resolution to the era's tensions over literary valuation.

A century later, the concept of Eng. "classics" endured, although the terms for defining a classic continued to evolve. In 1879–80, the poet, critic, professor, and literary arbiter Matthew Arnold still identified Shakespeare and Milton as "our poetical classics," ranking the recent poet William Wordsworth in third position. No longer hindered by the need to justify the value of writing in the Eng. lang., Arnold in "The Study of Poetry" saw "the true and right meaning of the word *classic, classical*" as "the class of the very best." Our object in studying poetry, according to Arnold, is that of "clearly feeling and of deeply enjoying the really excellent." Arnold's concept of "classics"—works that withstand a test of timeless excellence—would survive well into the 20th c. esp. in popular usage, but in professional settings, it was overtaken by what came to be called "the canon." As Guillory (1993) observes, "The word 'canon' displaces the expressly honorific term 'classic' precisely in order to isolate the 'classics' as the object of critique."

Canon crit. made its first mark in curricula in the wake of the social upheavals of the 1960s. Socially engaged academics carried their politics into the classroom, teaching what came to be called "noncanonical" materials, often by or about people socially disfranchised based on race, class, or gender. Af. Am. poets such as Frances Harper and Paul Laurence Dunbar and women poets such as Alice Cary, Phoebe Cary, Lucy Larcom, and Celia Thaxter, who had been minimized or entirely neglected in 20th-c. textbooks, were now reclaimed by canon-conscious teachers and literary historians. One recurrent question at the core of debate was whether previously noncanonical texts were "as good" as traditionally canonical ones, putting new pressure on the criteria for assessing textual value. Gradually, challenges to the canon began to affect the margins of publishing and scholarship and eventually to alter mainstream publishing and teaching, generating the wide public debate of the 1980s and 1990s in particular. From these interrogations of the idea of the canon (no longer the "classics"), canon scholarship emerged as a new field in its own right, concerned not only with the politics of the current canon but with developing a precise hist. of canon formation at different times and places.

Such scholarship has focused in particular on how canons are formed and disseminated through institutions such as literary anthols. and the school system, esp. the university. The case of one of the most canonical Am. poets, Walt Whitman, provides a useful example of how the poetry canon changes over time. Literary textbooks published since 1919, the centennial of Whitman's birth, vary in how they define his stature. Early textbooks preferred his more conventional verse, such as "O Captain! My Captain!" and did not categorize him as a major poet. By the 1930s, the climate of appreciation for literary modernism and its radical formal experiments, and the growth of American literature as a professional field and a subject for higher study, had cultivated a new appreciation for Whitman's technical innovations. This change in poetic culture led to a revaluation of Whitman's poetic contributions and to a dramatic change in his stature. By 1950, he had become one of the major Am. writers.

The canon debates of the last two decades of the 20th c. often centered on putatively conservative and liberal positions about whether and how the canon replicated historical exclusions based on race, class, and gender. Guillory redefined the fundamental terms of the debate in 1993, arguing that the actual nature of the problem underlying the canon debates was a crisis in the cultural capital of literary study itself, a form of study "increasingly marginal to the social function of the present educational system." Canon scholarship has dismantled the idea of "the canon" as a single monolithic entity; the term is now more likely to be used in plural or more historically restricted senses.

■ M. Arnold, "The Study of Poetry" and "Wordsworth," *Matthew Arnold's Essays in Criticism*, ed. G.K. Chesterton (1964); E. Miner, "On the Genesis and Development of Literary Systems," *CritI* 5.2–3 (1978–79); B. M. Metzger, *The Canon of the New Testament* (1988); P. Yu, "Poems in Their Place: Collections and Canons in Early Chinese Literature," *HJAS* 50 (1990); P. Lauter, *Canons and Contexts* (1991); J. Guillory, *Cultural Capital* (1993) and "Canon," *Critical Terms for Literary Study*, ed. F. Lentricchia and T. McLaughlin, 2d ed. (1995); A. Golding, *From Outlaw to Classic* (1995); J. Kramnick, *Making the English Canon* (1998); T. Ross, *The Making of the English Literary Canon* (1998); *Inventing the Classics: Modernity, National Identity, and Japanese Literature*, ed. H. Shirane and T. Suzuki (2000); R. Terry, *Poetry and the Making of the English Literary Past* (2001); J. Csicsila, *Canons by Consensus* (2004); W. J. T. Mitchell, "Canon," *New Keywords*, ed. T. Bennett et al. (2005); E. Renker, *The Origins of American Literature Studies: An Institutional History* (2007).

E. RENKER

CARPE DIEM (Lat., "pluck [enjoy] the day"). A phrase from Horace, *Odes* 1.11, that enjoins full enjoyment of the present time. The hedonistic form of the motif ("eat, drink, and be merry . . .") is already fully developed in the Egyptian "Song of the Harper" and in the advice of Siduri to Gilgamesh (Pritchard). Typically, the *carpe diem* injunction is pronounced amid warnings about the transience of life, the uncertainty of the future, and the inevitability and finality of death (". . . for tomorrow we die"). The motif occurs in many genres of Gr. poetry: *lyric (Alcaeus, frag. 38a; *Anacreontea* 32), *elegy (Theognis 973–78), drama (Aeschylus, *Persians* 840–42; Euripides, *Alcestis* 780–802), and *epigrams (*Anthologia Palatina* 5.79, 5.118, 11.38). The advice to enjoy the present can range from eating (*Iliad* 24.618–19) and drinking (Alcaeus, frag. 38a) to love (Catullus 5: "Let us live, my Lesbia, and let us love"). The Roman master of the motif was Horace, many of whose poems urge a refined, Epicurean enjoyment of the day (e.g., *Odes* 1.4, 1.9, 1.11, 2.14, 3.29, 4.7). To stress the urgency of enjoying the present in the face of fleeting time, the speaker often draws analogies from nature; consequently, the subgenre is full of references to rising and setting suns, seasonal changes, and flowers.

The late Lat. poem "De rosis nascentibus" attributed to Ausonius (ca. 400 CE), which describes roses blooming at Paestum and concludes with the advice "Gather, maiden, roses, while the bloom is fresh and youth is fresh," established the rose as one of the emblems of the carpe diem poem (e.g., Pierre de Ronsard, "Mignonne, allons voir si la rose"; Edmund Spenser, *The Faerie Queene* 2.12.74–75; Robert Herrick, "Gather ye rosebuds while ye may"; and Edmund Waller, "Go, lovely Rose"). In Ren. poetry, the carpe diem theme often serves as the basis of "persuasions" to seduce coy young women, as in Samuel Daniel (*Delia* 31), Thomas Carew ("To A. L. Perswasions to love"), and John Milton (*Comus* 736–54); but the best-known example in Eng. is Andrew Marvell's "To His Coy Mistress," which prominently exhibits the syllogistic form implicit in many carpe diem poems. In the 19th c., Edward FitzGerald's versions of *The Rubáiyát of Omar Khayyám* popularized the hedonistic carpe diem theme. Twentieth-c. examples include A. E. Housman's "Loveliest of Trees, the Cherry Now" and John Crowe Ransom's "Blue Girls."

■ F. Bruser, "*Comus* and the Rose Song," *SP* 44 (1947); H. Weber, *La Création poétique au XVIe siècle en France* (1956); J. B. Pritchard, *Ancient Near-Eastern Texts* (1969); R.G.M. Nisbet and M. Hubbard, *A Commentary on Horace, Odes Book I* (1970); C. Yandell, "*Carpe Diem*, Poetic Immortality, and the Gendered Ideology of Time," *Renaissance Women Writers*, ed. A. R. Larsen and C. Winn (1994); and "*Carpe Diem* Revisited: Ronsard's Temporal Ploys," *Sixteenth-Century Journal* 28 (1997); E. H. Sagaser, "Sporting the While: *Carpe Diem* and the Cruel Fair in Samuel Daniel's *Delia* and the *Complaint of Rosamond*," *Exemplaria* 10 (1998).

W. H. RACE

CATACHRESIS (Gr., "abuse"). The tidiest definition of this *trope dates back, it has been argued, to the Stoic grammarians: *catachresis* is the use of a borrowed word for something that does not have a name of its own. We speak thus of the "legs" of a table or the "foot" of a bed. Augustine gives the example of *piscina*: the word denotes a swimming pool or tank, despite the complete absence of fish (*piscis*; *De doctrina christiana* 3.29). According to this most straightforward analysis, catachresis functions like a *metaphor, implying the comparison of two objects. However, unlike a metaphor—which enacts a lexical transfer by establishing the equivalence of two terms—catachresis performs its transfers in the face of a *missing* term,

thus without anchoring its meaning in the logic of equivalence. For instance, "thunderbolts of eloquence" (*eloquentiae fulmina*)—one of Quintilian's examples of metaphor—describes particularly effective discourse by equating *eloquence* with a *lightning flash* (cf. 8.6.7). In contrast, *piscina* uses the name of fish to describe something that otherwise has no name. A metaphor has, as it were, taken up residence as a proper name. As one mod. theorist explains, "[T]here is no other possible word to denote the 'wings' of a house, or the 'arms' of a chair, and yet 'wings' and 'arms' are *instantly, already* metaphorical" (Barthes). Following this line of thought, writers have often defined *catachresis* as a so-called dead metaphor: a metaphor so fundamental to expression that no distinction from literal use is possible.

According to this logic, catachresis operates under the pressure of necessity: a catachrestic transfer takes place when a "proper" proper name is lacking. "[I]f for lacke of naturall and proper terme or worde we take another, neither naturall nor proper," writes George Puttenham in his 1589 *Arte of English Poesie*, "and do vntruly applie it to the thing which we would seeme to expresse . . . it is not then spoken by this figure *Metaphore* . . . but by plaine abuse" (3.17). Catachresis borders on *malapropism* (mistaking one word for another) or *paradiastole* (euphemistic redescription); its "abuse" entails a misapplication of terms. But with catachresis, such misapplications are seemingly unavoidable. Impropriety is built into the trope irreducibly, from the ground up.

The figure's irreducible impropriety has led postmod. and poststructuralist observers to privilege catachresis as "the common denominator of rhetoricity as such" (Laclau). For such theorists, *catachresis* becomes the name for the inescapable metaphorical or rhetorical function of lang. The trope then bespeaks our general inability to trace human meaning back to the bedrock, "literal" reality on which it presumably rests. Giving the lie to our handy philological narratives, catachresis instead reveals the ways in which lang. is "always already" figurative. Moreover, thanks to the way it generates new meanings and uses from a semantic void (i.e., the "lack" that Puttenham notes in his definition), catachresis can then be taken to characterize the originary gap at the heart of all systems of meaning. *Catachresis* names the origin of lang.—or indeed of any symbolic system—as "rupture" or "doubling" rather than as singular presence. This general rhetorical analysis of the trope has been deployed in disciplines as diverse as political science, media and cultural studies, anthropology, and psychoanalysis. Some notable examples include Spivak's use of the trope to characterize postcolonial discourse; Laclau's view of social hegemony as catachrestic; Barthes's investigation of the figure of beauty in 19th-c. realism; and Derrida's critique of metaphoricity in Western philosophy.

The postmod. treatment of the trope is exceptionally powerful and holds great explanatory force. Such readings have tended to focus on only one aspect of the trope's hist., however: namely, the preoccupation with the problem of a primitive semantic lack. It could be argued that another, related thread is equally important: the question of what we might call semantic "place." Here Quintilian's characterization of the trope is paradigmatic. Like many writers before and since, Quintilian defines *catachresis* as a species or version of metaphor. Indeed, his account in many ways anticipates postmod. thought, celebrating catachresis not as the *abuse* of metaphor but rather as metaphor so elemental as to be *necessary*—as when we speak of crops being "thirsty" although they have no throats (8.6.5–6). At the same time, however, the 1st-c. rhetor explains that the trope functions by adapting whatever term is closest at hand: "By [*catachresis*] . . . is meant the practice of adapting the nearest [*proximo*] available term to describe something for which no actual term exists" (8.6.34).

To privilege catachresis as Quintilian does is to foreground the problem of semantic place. A criterion of proximity—of neighboring place—undergirds his understanding of the trope. Indeed, at stake here is the cl. definition of *trope* itself, with its strongly spatialized conception of ling. property: i.e., the "place" where a word "properly" belongs. Once again, we turn to Quintilian for his influential definition: "[*trope* is] the transference of words and phrases from the place which is strictly theirs to another to which they do not properly belong" (9.1.4). Thus understood, trope maps out an entire lexical geography, where each word or phrase finds its accepted coordinates in relation not only to a world of things but to the world of other words and phrases. Moreover, as far back as Aristotle, metaphor has been understood to organize these places through the ability "to see the same" (*to homoion therein estin*): i.e., the ability to recognize analogies, resemblances, and hierarchies (*Poetics* 1459a18). Catachresis, however, unsettles our ability to determine such resemblance.

Simply put, a judgment of similarity requires at least two terms for comparison; with catachresis, however, one of these terms is missing. A word is transferred from one place to another—to a place that lacks any name of its own. Where metaphor anchors its transfers on the basis of resemblance, catachresis functions on the basis of sheer proximity. In place of no name, we adapt the nearest available term. We grab what is closest to hand. But what is nearness in lang., proximity of terminology, if it is not a judgment of resemblance? What is semantic place *tout court*? What is a place without a name? Indeed, catachresis raises the uncomfortable notion of an *empty* ling. place: of a place held open *in* lang. but not inhabited *by* lang. Catachresis thus invokes a world whose contours and contents are already shaped, but not yet named, by lang. This is a world that comes to us already articulated and processed by trope, a world chewed up by lang. before we meaning-makers even arrive on the scene.

According to this thread of its hist., the abuse of catachresis is not that it misapplies a name but rather that it violates our sense of place. This violation has lead to a common alternate definition of the trope as a "mixed," "extravagant," or (most tellingly) "far-fetched" metaphor (Lanham). According to this understanding, catachresis disrupts the reassurances and taxonomic ordering of resemblance, offering instead a world where semantics has lost its bearings, where the foreign and far away has collapsed in on the near and the neighborly. It is perhaps the catachrestic oddity of the trope that its hist. reveals two such seemingly opposed interpretations: on the one hand, catachresis as metaphor that is "far-fetched" or "extravagant" (literally: *wandering out of bounds*); on the other hand, catachresis as metaphor so familiar and domesticated as to be considered quite "dead."

■ Augustine, *On Christian Doctrine*, trans. D. W. Robertson (1958); Quintilian, *Institutio oratoria*, trans. H. E. Butler (1958); R. Barthes, *S/Z*, trans. R. Miller (1974); P. de Man, "The Epistemology of Metaphor," *CritI* 5.1 (1978)—spec. iss. on metaphor; D. A. Russell, "Theories of Style," *Criticism in Antiquity* (1981); J. Derrida, "White Mythology: Metaphor in the Text of Philosophy," *Margins of Philosophy*, trans. A. Bass (1982); P. Parker, "Metaphorical Plot," *Literary Fat Ladies* (1987), and "Metaphor and

Catachresis," *The Ends of Rhetoric*, ed. J. Bender and D. E. Wellbery (1990); Lanham; E. Laclau, *On Populist Reason* (2005).

L. Freinkel

CATALEXIS (Gr., "coming to an abrupt end"). The process by which a metrical *colon or line is shortened on the end. The adjectival form, *catalectic*, describes omission of one syllable, the final one; the older, technical term for double catalectic forms is *brachycatalectic*. The normal form, where no syllable is lacking, is sometimes called *acatalectic*; and when extra syllables appear at the end, the colon or line is said to be *hypermetric*. Catalexis applies only to ends; shortening at the beginning is normally treated separately since the metrical environment differs.

Catalexis is evident in both cl. Gr. and Sanskrit prosody and seems to have derived in part from IE prosody, though it would have appeared indigenously as a normal linguistic process. In cl. Gr., all the most common metrical cola (*dactylic, *anapestic, *iambic, *trochaic, aeolic) have catalectic forms, in which the last two syllables are shortened to one heavy syllable (longum). But the precise mechanism of catalexis in classical prosody is complex and varies from meter to meter. More important, the catalexis often appears at the end of a metrical period or stanza—esp. in dactylic, trochaic, and anapestic verse—so that the principle of shortening or blunting has double effect.

In the mod. poetries, catalexis is not common at all in iambic verse but is frequent in trochaic and ternary meters, where the unexpectedly sudden and forceful close (on a stress) gives bite. In Eng., the trochaic *tetrameter of eight syllables is often found together with a catalectic line of seven, both forms meshing smoothly. Why catalexis should operate well in some meters but not others still awaits definitive explanation; temporal metrists would say that in *accentual verse and other meters that retain a close association with music and song, the missing weak syllable at the end is filled by a pause. In any event, it is manifest that catalexis is one of the fundamental principles of *rhythm, and provision must be made for it in any theory of meter.

■ L.P.E. Parker, "Catalexis," *CQ* 26 (1976); Morier; M. L. West, "Three Topics in Greek Metre," *CQ* 32 (1982).

T.V.F. Brogan

CATALOG. An enumeration of persons, places, things, or ideas in poetry that often displays some common referent or context such as power, heroism, or beauty. The catalog differs from the simple list or inventory by incl. more descriptive information and by affording the writer more opportunity for digression or thematic devel. The catalog is of ancient origin and is found in almost all lits. of the world. In antiquity, the catalog plays a didactic or mnemonic role, e.g., in the Bible (Gen. 10 and Matt. 1). More frequently, however, the catalog has a clearly aesthetic function. In epic lit., e.g., it conveys the size and power of armies, as in Homer's list of ships and heroes in *Iliad* 2, and the technique creates the effect of vastness and panoramic sweep, both in geographical space and in narrative time. Similar effects of epic expansions occur in Virgil's catalog of heroes in *Aeneid* 7 and Milton's catalog of fallen angels in *Paradise Lost* 2.

Med. and Ren. poetry developed catalog techniques based on cl. models to produce an encyclopedic variety of topics and forms. Ovid's catalog of trees drawn to Orpheus in *Metamorphoses* 10 serves that purpose for similar lists in Virgil, Chaucer, and Edmund Spenser. In Spenser's *Faerie Queene* book 1, the catalog of trees places the action of the poem within the epic trad. and marks the poet's position within what Ferry calls a "subliminal catalog of immortal names." A second major form, the *ubi sunt* poem, features a catalog of absences in order to meditate on mortality and the transience of life, asking where the dead are now. Med. Lat. poems feature the phrase itself, as in the hymn "De Brevitate Vitae," and OE poems of the Exeter Book, such as "The Wanderer," call out the individual dead in order to meditate on the common fate of all. A third rich trad. features the catalog of beautiful attributes in order to praise a beloved (see BLASON). The catalog of women is a related type, deriving in the Western trad. from Hesiod and Homer and developing into the catalog of the "good woman" type in Boccaccio and Chaucer. Although the catalog of feminine beauty may preserve gender stereotypes, it can function in other ways in a poem like Shakespeare's sonnet 130, "My mistress' eyes are nothing like the sun."

In 19th- and 20th-c. Eur. and Am. poetry, other functions of catalog and catalog rhet. have emerged. Writers in antebellum America featured catalog rhet. in both poetry and prose, notably in R. W. Emerson's and H. D. Thoreau's essays, in Herman Melville's encyclopedic fictions, and, most important, in Walt Whitman's long poems. While Whitman's catalog rhet. creates an effect of potentially endless and random multiplicity, it can also combine with effects of thematic or dramatic unity. Whitman's catalog rhet. takes parataxis as a basic organizing principle in order to develop coordinating techniques of syntactic parallelism such as *polysyndeton and asyndeton. Catalog rhet. also features pronounced forms of repetition, such as *anaphora and epistrophe, in order to create effects of nonmetrical rhythm and rhetorical power. Despite formal restrictions of line length, metrical pattern, and generic limitation, catalog enacts a principle of nearly infinite expandability.

■ J. W. Bright, "The 'ubi sunt' Formula," *MLN* 8 (1893); T. W. Allen, "The Homeric Catalogue," *JHS* 30 (1910); D. W. Schumann, "Observations on Enumerative Style in Modern German Poetry," *PMLA* 59 (1944); S. K. Coffman, " 'Crossing Brooklyn Ferry': A Note on the Catalogue Technique in Whitman's Poetry," *MP* 51 (1954); L. Spitzer, "La enumeración caótica en la poesía moderna," *Lingüística e historia literaria* (1955); H. E. Wedeck, "The Catalogue in Latin and Medieval Latin Poetry," *M&H* 13 (1960); L. Buell, "Transcendentalist Catalogue Rhetoric: Vision versus Form," *AL* 40 (1968); S. A. Barney, "Chaucer's Lists," *The Wisdom of Poetry*, ed. L. D. Benson and S. Wenzel (1982); N. Howe, *The Old English Catalogue Poems* (1985); M. L. West, *The Hesiodic Catalogue of Women* (1985); A. Ferry, *The Art of Naming* (1988); J. P. Warren, *Walt Whitman's Language Experiment* (1990); G. McLeod, *Virtue and Venom: Catalogues of Women from Antiquity to the Renaissance* (1991); R. E. Belknap, *The List: The Uses and Pleasures of Cataloguing* (2004).

R. A. HORNSBY; T.V.F. BROGAN; J. P. WARREN

CHAIN RHYME (Ger. *Kettenreim, äusserer Reim, verschr, änkter Reim*). Interlocking or interlaced rhyme that refers to any rhyme scheme in which one line or stanza links to the next line or stanza, forming a pattern of alternating rhymes. *Terza rima is one form: here the medial rhyme in each *tercet becomes the enclosing ones of the next, *aba bcb cdc*, and so on. Robert Frost extends this scheme to the quatrain in "Stopping by Woods on a Snowy Evening." Examples of chain rhyme range widely, from Af. folk forms and Eng. nursery rhymes to Edmund Spenser's *Amoretti*. According to

Myers and Wukasch, the *villanelle also employs chain rhyme, since the first and third lines of the initial tercet alternately recur as the third line of subsequent tercets, *A1bA2 abA1 abA2*, and so forth. Chain rhyme, like *cross rhyme, has recently been used by scholars to refer to the *abab* pattern. Historically, though, chain rhyme, also identified as linked rhyme by Turco, rhymes the last word of one line to the first word of the next line, creating a chiming effect. In Fr. prosody, the *Grands Rhétoriqueurs* of the late 15th and early 16th cs. developed the terms *rime fratrisée, entrelacée, enchaînée,* and *annexxée* for a rhyme sound or syllable at line end repeated at the beginning of the next line. The repeated syllable, however, must carry a different meaning. Recent scholars (Alim, Bradley) have noted the abundant use of chain rhyme in Am. rap and hip-hop, which not only serves to effect a technique of generative improvisation but creates an incantatory effect; the sound repetition is typically amplified by the addition of *internal rhyme. Rapper Talib Kweli, with Pharaohe Monch and Common, employs chain rhyme in "The Truth." Chain rhyme extended to repetition of entire words becomes the rhetorical figure *anadiplosis, a type of concatenation.

■ Patterson; L. Turco, *The Book of Forms: A Handbook of Poetics,* 3d ed. (2000); H. S. Alim, "On Some Serious Next Millennium Rap Ishhh," *Journal of English Linguistics* 31 (2003); J. Myers and D. Wukasch, *A Dictionary of Poetic Terms* (2003); A. Bradley, *Book of Rhymes: The Poetics of Hip Hop* (2009).

T.V.F. BROGAN; J. CHANG

CHIASMUS (Gr., "a placing crosswise," from the Gr. letter X, "chi," and the verb *chiazein*, "to mark with diagonal lines like an X"). The repetition of a pair of sounds, words, phrases, or ideas in the reverse order, producing an *abba* structure, as in Satan's attempt to rally the rebel angels: "The mind is its own place, and in itself / Can make a Heav'n of Hell, a Hell of Heav'n" (*Paradise Lost* 1.254–55). Although the term *chiasmus* appears in Eng. in 1871, its mod. hist. is closely bound up with that of *antimetabole,* the Eng. usage of which dates to George Puttenham's *Arte of English Poesie* in 1589 (*OED*). The earliest attestations of *antimetabole* can be found in Cousin, who cites definitions by Quintilian (9.3.85) and Alexander Numenius (3.37.23) and synonymous terms in Phoebammon (3.55.2). Quintilian gives two examples of antimetabole: "Non, ut edam, vivo; sed, ut vivam, edo" (I do not live that I may eat, but eat that I may live) and, from Cicero, "Ut et sine invidia culpa plectatur, et sine culpa invidia ponatur" (That both guilt may be punished without odium, and odium may be laid aside without guilt). While *antimetabole* (and its Lat. term *commutatio*) once covered all such reciprocal exchanges, regardless of alterations in case or tense, *chiasmus* now appears to be the more capacious term and antimetabole a species of chiasmus (Miller and Mermall). In recent literary theory, and esp. work influenced by deconstruction, *chiasmus* has enjoyed wide currency as a critical term. The trope has been esp. important for Derrida, since *chiasmus* lays bare the "natural invertability" of a hierarchy of two terms—a description that could apply just as easily to deconstruction (Beidler). Deconstructionists have employed *chiasmus* in specific instances to describe the tension between "theological thought and its linguistic underthought" in G. M. Hopkins (Miller) and "the reversal of the figural order" in R. M. Rilke (de Man).

Some of the most ancient examples of chiasmus are found in Ugaritic texts (1400–1200 BCE), which may have influenced the composition of the OT. Biblical exegetes have indeed revealed chiasmus in verse (Gen. 9:6: "Whoso sheds the blood of man, / By man his blood shall be shed") and chapter (the Gospels of Matthew and John, the letters of Paul) (Breck, Thomson). Although *chiasmus* frequently describes the repetition of particular phonemes or the inversion of clauses, it is not uncommon to find that an entire poem or novel has a chiastic structure or that several kinds of chiasmus are at work simultaneously. In *Eunoia* (2009), Christian Bök's clever "The scented dessert smells even sweeter when served ere the sweetness melts" features chiasmus of sound and syntax ("smells," "sweeter," "sweetness," "melts"). Affecting both semantics and syntax, Hopkins's line "This seeing the sick endears them to us, us too it endears" ("Felix Randal," 9) concludes with an *ellipsis* of the grammatical object. If, as Thomson prefers, we construe *chiasmus* more broadly as the bilateral symmetry "of four or more elements around a central axis," the *Epic of Gilgamesh*, Chaucer's *Parliament of Fowls*, John Dryden's "A Song for St. Cecilia's Day," S. T. Coleridge's "Frost at Midnight" (Nänny), Alfred, Lord Tennyson's *In Memoriam*, and Raymond Roussel's *Nouvelles Impressions d'Afrique* might all be considered to

have chiastic patterns. E. M. Forster famously attributes the "triumph" of Henry James's *The Ambassadors* to the chiastic, or "hourglass," shape of its plot. Quinn defines *chiasmus* by comparing it to other repetitive figures like *epanodos*, the amplification or expansion of a series, and *palindrome*, a sentence that shows the same syntax and meaning forward or backward. The elliptical approach of chiasmus can sometimes be seen as an elegant *periphrasis* of those emotions for which bald statement is impossible: "Grief has become the pain only pain erases" (Agha Shahid Ali, "Not All, Only a Few Return").

■ C. Walz, *Rhetores Graeci*, 9 v. (1832–36); *Allen and Greenough's New Latin Grammar*, ed. J. B. Greenough et al. (1903); E. M. Forster, *Aspects of the Novel* (1927); J. Cousin, *Études sur Quintilien* (1936); M. Joseph, *Shakespeare's Use of the Arts of Language* (1947); M. M. Mahood, *Shakespeare's Wordplay* (1957); A. Di Marco, "Der Chiasmus in der Bibel," *Linguistica Biblica* 37–39 (1976); P. de Man, *Allegories of Reading* (1979); *Chiasmus in Antiquity*, ed. W. Welch (1981); Group μ; A. Quinn, *Figures of Speech* (1982); H. Horvei, *The Chev'ril Glove* (1984); J. Derrida, *Glas*, trans. J. P. Leavey Jr. and R. Rand (1986); J. H. Miller, "The Linguistic Moment," *Gerard Manley Hopkins: Modern Critical Views*, ed. H. Bloom (1986); R. Norman, *Samuel Butler and the Meaning of Chiasmus* (1986); W. Shea, "Chiasmus and the Structure of David's Lament," *Journal of Biblical Literature* 105 (1986); J. Derrida, *The Truth in Painting*, trans. G. Bennington and I. McLeod (1987); M. Nänny, "Chiasmus in Literature: Ornament or Function?" *Word and Image* 4 (1988); T. Mermall, "The Chiasmus: Unamuno's Master Trope," and J. W. Miller and T. Mermall, "Antimetabole and Chiasmus," *PMLA* 105 (1990); J. Veitch, " 'Moondust in the Prowling Eye': The History Poems of Robert Lowell," *Contemporary Literature* 33 (1992); J. Breck, *The Shape of Biblical Language* (1994); I. Thomson, *Chiasmus in the Pauline Letters* (1995); Lausberg; E.P.J. Corbett, *Classical Rhetoric for the Modern Student*, 4th ed. (1999); P. G. Beidler, "Chiastic Strands in *The Wreck of the Deutschland*," *VP* 38 (2000); S. Adams, *Poetic Designs* (2003); B. Costello, *Shifting Ground* (2003); H. Vendler, *Poets Thinking* (2006); M. Garber, *Shakespeare and Modern Culture* (2008); W. Engel, *Chiastic Designs in English Literature from Sidney to Shakespeare* (2009).

T.V.F. BROGAN; A. W. HALSALL; W. HUNTER

CHRISTABEL METER. Term for the verse form of S. T. Coleridge's "Christabel" (1797–1800, pub. 1816), believed by Coleridge to be a species of *accentual verse. In the preface to the poem, he writes that "the meter of *Christabel* is not, properly speaking, irregular, though it may seem so from its being founded on . . . counting in each line the accents, not the syllables." The number of syllables in the poem "may vary from seven to twelve," but "in each line the accents will be found to be only four." He calls this a "new principle" in Eng. poetry and claims that variations in syllable count are made intentionally: "occasional variation in number of syllables is not introduced wantonly . . . but in correspondence with some transition in the nature of the imagery or passion." Up to the turn of the 20th c., Coleridge was generally believed in his assertions, and "Christabel" was considered an important example of accentual verse in Eng.

Upon closer inspection, however, numerous scholars have found Coleridge's claims to be false. Robert Bridges showed in 1901 (rev. ed. 1921) that Coleridge is actually writing *accentual-syllabic verse. And Snell showed in 1929 that "four-fifths of the lines of *Christabel* are perfectly regular; that is, they are the conventional four-stress iambic verse usually in couplet form, with only such variations in general as are found in this sort of meter. If [the remaining one-fifth of the poem's lines] is scanned according to the principle that 'light syllables may occasionally be added or subtracted without altering the normal verse meter' . . . the entire poem is iambic with monosyllabic and anapestic substitutions." In short, the poem is heavily iambic and effectively octosyllabic: of the 655 lines of the poem, 523 (80%) are perfectly regular octosyllables, and 92% vary by only one syllable one way or the other. And Coleridge's implication, in the preface, that he is the first to use syllabic variation for purposes of metrical expressiveness seems an unreasonable slight to earlier poets, such as Shakespeare, John Donne, and John Milton.

■ Bridges; A.L.F. Snell, "The Meter of 'Christabel,'" *Fred Newton Scott Anniversary Papers* (1929); Brogan; B. O'Driscoll, "The 'Invention' of a Meter: 'Christabel' Meter as Fact and Fiction," *JEGP* 100.4 (2001); M. Russett, "Meter, Identity, Voice: Untranslating 'Christabel,'" *SEL* 43.4 (2003).

T.V.F. BROGAN; M. WEINSTEIN

CLOSURE. Refers most broadly to the manner in which texts end or the qualities characterizing their conclusions. More specifically, the term "poetic closure" is used to refer to the achievement of an effect of finality, resolution, and stability at the end of a poem. In the latter sense, closure appears to be a generally valued quality, the achievement of which is not confined to the poetry of any particular period or nation. Its modes and the techniques by which it is secured do, however, vary in accord with stylistic, particularly structural, variables.

Closural effects are primarily a function of the reader's perception of a poem's total structure; i.e., they involve his or her experience of the relation of the concluding portion of a poem to the entire composition. The generating principles that constitute a poem's formal and thematic structure arouse continuously changing sets of expectations, which elicit various hypotheses from a reader concerning the poem's immediate direction and ultimate design. Successful closure occurs when, at the end of a poem, the reader is left without residual expectations: his or her developing hypotheses have been confirmed and validated (or, in the case of "surprise" endings, the unexpected turn has been accommodated and justified retrospectively), and he or she is left with a sense of the poem's completeness, which is to say of the integrity of his or her own experience of it and the appropriateness of its cessation at that point.

Closure may be strengthened by specifically *terminal* features in a poem, i.e., things that happen at the end of it. These include the repetition and balance of formal elements (as in *alliteration and *parallelism), explicit allusions to finality and repose, and the terminal return, after a deviation, to a previously established structural "norm" (e.g., a metrical norm). Closural failures (e.g., anticlimax) usually involve factors that leave the reader with residual expectations. They may also arise from weak or incompatible structural principles or from a stylistic discrepancy between the structure of the poem and its mode of closure. Weak closure may, however, be deliberately cultivated: much modernist poetry shares with modernist works in other genres and art forms a tendency toward apparent anticlosure, rejecting strong closural effects in favor of irresolution, incompleteness, and a quality of "openness." *Language poet Lyn Hejinian, e.g., advocates a "rejection of closure" and the creation of "open text" that "emphasizes or foregrounds process" and actively engages the reader. One can profitably compare and contrast the self-consciously disruptive rejection of closure as it operates in mod. Western poetry with a long-standing Chinese poetics of incompleteness and suggestiveness.

■ B. H. Smith, *Poetic Closure: A Study of How Poems End* (1968); P. Hamon, "Clausules," *Poétique* 24 (1975); *Concepts of Closure*, spec. iss. of *YFS* 67 (1984); L. Hejinian, "The Rejection of Closure," *Poetics Jour.* 4 (1985); Y. Ye, *Chinese Poetic Closure* (1996); J. E. Vincent, *Queer Lyrics: Difficulty and Closure in American Poetry* (2002).

B. H. SMITH; A. WATSON

COLON (Gr., "limb, member"). As a metrical term, colon may refer to at least three different things: (1) a metrical or rhythmical unit sometimes divisible into two or three equivalent metra but also capable of functioning alongside cola of a similar or different character as a means of articulating rhythmical sequences that resist division into such metra; (2) a syntactical or rhetorical phrase, usually marked off by punctuation, that combines with comparable phrases to articulate the meaning of a sentence; and (3) the portions of a rhythmical pattern that intervene between any two positions at which word end is significantly more frequent in instantiations of the pattern than its absence. Type 1 cola are *rhythmical*: basic components of a verse design; type 2 cola are *rhetorical*: a way of articulating the text of a given instantiation of the design; type 3 cola are *verbal-rhythmical*: a means of achieving a compromise between the constancy of a given rhythmical design and the large variety of verbal patterns theoretically capable of appearing in its instantiations.

Rhythmical cola are usually what a writer has in mind in discussing those forms in which the colon rather than the metron is felt to be the basic rhythmical unit. Verbal-rhythmical cola appear frequently in discussions of the structure of metric forms such as the Gr. *trimeter, which, in the earliest stages of its devel., is a variable dicolon: either $x - \cup - x + - \cup - x - \cup -$ or $x - \cup - x - \cup + - x - \cup -$, depending on whether the penthemimeral or hephthemimeral *caesura, one or the other of which was obligatory, appears in the particular line under consideration. It is perfectly possible, however, for this verbal-rhythmical dicolon to be a rhetorical tricolon as well—as in Menander's "*O dystyches! O dystyches! O dystyches!*" ("Woe! Woe! Woe!" [*Dyskolos* 574]). Here the first verbal-rhythmical colon ends after the second "*O*,"

the first rhetorical one after the first "*dystyches*." (Compare the structure of the *alexandrin ternaire*, which shows a rhetorical 4–4–4 grouping of syllables but usually retains the word end after the sixth syllable that allows it to be, like the cl. *alexandrine, a verbal-rhythmical dicolon.)

As the number of attested instances of any given design decreases, it becomes increasingly difficult to distinguish rhetorical from verbal-rhythmical cola, and when regular metric structure is absent, the two tend to merge or become confused with rhythmical cola as well. In such situations, the overall verse design may be so irregular that identification of rhythmical units is possible only if one assumes that rhetorical boundaries or recurring verbal boundaries coincide with the boundaries of basic rhythmical units. Proceeding on this assumption, perfectly justified in many instances, has been standard practice, at least since Aristophanes of Byzantium (ca. 250–185 BCE) established his "measuring into cola" (*colometria*) for the lyric poets and the lyric portions of drama and began the custom of allotting to each colon its separate line of text. It is not valid in all instances, however, and one must reckon with the possibility, first raised by A. M. Dale, that the whole notion of the colon as a basic structural unit analogous to the foot or metron is inappropriate in dealing with certain types of rhythm.

■ J. Irigoin, *Recherches sur les mètres de la lyrique chorale grecque* (1953), with the review by L.P.E. Parker, *Bulletin of the Institute of Classical Studies* 5 (1958); G. S. Kirk, "The Structure of the Homeric Hexameter," *Yale Classical Studies* 20 (1966); Dale, "Classification and Terminology" (1968), and "The Metrical Units of Greek Lyric Verse," *Collected Papers* (1969); West, "Units of Analysis," sec. IB; L. E. Rossi, "Estensione e valore del *colon* nell' esametro omerico," *Struttura e storia dell esametro Greco*, ed. M. Fantuzzi and R. Pretagostini (1996); N. Baechle, *Metrical Constraint and the Interpretation of Style in the Tragic Trimeter* (2007).

A. T. COLE

COMPLAINT (Gr. *schetliasmos*, Lat. *plangere*). An established rhetorical term by the time of Aristotle's *Rhetoric* (1395a9), complaint is a varied mode that crosses numerous generic boundaries. Usually, it is a dramatic, highly emotional *lament that reveals the complainant's specific grievances against a public or private injustice. The most influential complaints from antiquity are found in Ovid's *Heroides*, a collection of epistolary complaints in which abandoned lovers narrate their stories in hope of receiving recognition for their suffering (Farrell). The mode also borrows from the Heb. trad. of lamentation in the books of Job and Jeremiah and the med. *planctus* that were central to mourning in the med. church. In the Middle Ages and Ren., three sometimes coinciding strains of complaint are evident: (1) satiric complaints that expose the evil ways of the world (*contemptus mundi*, e.g., Alan de Lille, *De planctu naturae*, and Edmund Spenser's collection *Complaints, Containing Sundrie Small Poems of the Worlds Vanitie* [1591]); (2) didactic complaints that relate the fall of great persons, often called "fall of princes" or "*de casibus*" narratives (e.g., Giovanni Boccaccio, *De casibus virorum illustrium*; Chaucer, "The Monk's Tale"; and the Ren. collection *A Mirror for Magistrates* [1559]); and (3) lover's complaints, including both short poems written in the Petrarchan mode (e.g., by Thomas Wyatt and Henry Howard, the Earl of Surrey, in *Tottel's Miscellany* [1557]) and more ambitious monologues that are frequently voiced by female speakers but have male complaints embedded within the "female" complaint framework (e.g., Samuel Daniel, *The Complaint of Rosamond* [1592]; and Shakespeare, *A Lover's Complaint* [1609]). Ren. complaints employ legal rhet. in the *ballads and broadsides of public executions (Craik) and in revenge tragedies (Thomas Kyd, *The Spanish Tragedy* [1592]; and Shakespeare, *Titus Andronicus* [1594]). Other prominent examples of complaint include Chaucer, "A Complaint unto Pity" (Chaucer has many experimental complaints, on the model of Fr. and It., as ballades or in *ottava rima); Abraham Cowley, "The Complaint" (1663); and Edward Young's long discursive poem *Complaint, or Night Thoughts* (1742–45). In Occitan poetry, the complaint takes the form of the *enueg*, which inspired the 36th of Ezra Pound's *Cantos*. In the 20th and 21st cs., the complaint frequently appears in *blues lyrics and hip-hop poetics (Berlant).

■ H. Stein, *Studies in Spenser's Complaints* (1934); *The Mirror for Magistrates*, ed. L. B. Campbell (1938); J. Peter, *Complaint and Satire in Early English Literature* (1956); W. A. Davenport, *Chaucer* (1988); L. Berlant, "The Female Complaint," *Social Text* 19–20 (1988); J. Kerrigan, *Motives of Woe* (1991); J. Farrell, "Reading and Writing the *Heroides*," *Harvard Studies in Classical Philology* 98 (1998); K. A. Craik, "Shakespeare's *A Lover's Complaint* and Early Modern Criminal Confession," *ShQ* 53 (2002).

W. H. Race; J. Díaz

COMPOSITION. *See* poet; versification.

COMPOSITION BY FIELD is a phrase by Charles Olson (1910–70) in his seminal essay "Projective Verse" (1950). The phrase evokes at once a poetics (or a philosophy of writing), a mode of practice (or heuristic activity that discovers its own order), and a kind of poem that is recognizable both visually and aurally. In the latter sense, the page space features loosely configured lines, white space in integral relation to the text, interlineal *caesurae, and fragments following the pulse of thinking and feeling as it occurs. The mode of practice rests on engagement with one's compositional and ontological energies (physical being, breath) in the absolute present of writing. And in the poetics of projective verse, *form in any particular work emerges from the multiple pressures of content. These verbal constellations relate to several artistic modes of the time, incl. action painting (Jackson Pollock), gestural dance performances using casual movement (Merce Cunningham), and improvisatory modes of jazz (Charlie Parker). Projective verse posits writing as made of existential choices defined by desire and act and as seeing, feeling, and understanding in the present—a kind of phenomenology out of conformity with that of traditional or even *free-verse prosodies. In this lightning-strike poetics, the page (called here *the field*) becomes a zone of "energy transfer." However, there is a tension between two senses of the poet: as the channel of organic energies (*participation mystique*) and as master, constructing the poem.

The polemical feeling of the essay, typical of the rhets. of manifesto (here featuring a masculinist diction), began in a fervent resistance to the influence of T. S. Eliot. Olson saw the *Four Quartets* in particular as confining, both for its adherence to a traditional religious ideology and for the repetitive architectonics of its "closed" form. Composition by field produced open form and, therefore, resisted conventional poetic markers (such as *rhyme and metrical *repetition) and featured paratactic organization in syntax (see hypotaxis and parataxis).

In bringing the prosodic and experiential radicalism of the avant-garde into the contemp. period, Olson influenced several poets whose work appeared in Donald Allen's important anthol. of 1960 (e.g., Robert Creeley, Robert Duncan, Robin Blaser, Denise Levertov). While a new phrase in 1950, *composition by field* as concept has analogues to modernist poetic practice, such as the phrasal lobes and white space of Stéphane Mallarmé's *Un coup de dés* (1897; see VISUAL POETRY); the erasure of syntactic connection as a way of freeing words from inherited connotations, described in F. T. Marinetti's 1914 manifesto as *parole in libertà* (words in freedom); and the productive misunderstanding of the ideogram in Ezra Pound's manifesto-compilation from the notes of Ernest Fenollosa, *The Chinese Written Character as a Medium for Poetry* (1919).

■ M. Perloff, "Charles Olson and the 'Inferior Predecessors': 'Projective Verse' Revisited," *ELH* 40 (1973); G. Hutchinson, "The Pleistocene in the Projective: Some of Olson's Sources," *AL* 54 (1982); B. Hatlen, "Pound's Pisan Cantos and the Origins of Projective Verse," *Ezra Pound and Poetic Influence*, ed. H. M. Dennis (2000); J. Osborne, "Black Mountain and Projective Verse," *A Companion to Twentieth-Century Poetry*, ed. N. Roberts (2001).

R. B. DuPlessis

CONCEIT. Three meanings are commonly found: (1) the "idea" informing a poem or play (cf. Philip Sidney's *Defence of Poesy*, George Puttenham's *Arte of English Poesie*, and *Hamlet* [2.2.530]); (2) an esp. elaborate metaphor or simile like those in Petrarch's *Canzoniere*; (3) a figure of thought, typical of baroque and metaphysical poetry and prose, which ingeniously compares dissimilar things and ideas, cultivating thereby surprise, followed, ideally, by admiration and insight. While all three kinds stress poetic invention, only the third, rooted largely in 17th-c. theory and practice, ascribes both aesthetic and epistemological value to the conceit. Based on but not limited to *metaphor, the baroque conceit aims wittily to engage both imagination and intellect without acknowledging either's sovereignty. As Gardner writes, "A conceit is a comparison whose ingenuity is more striking than its justness, or, at least, is more immediately striking. . . . [A] comparison becomes a conceit when we are made to concede likeness while being strongly conscious of unlikeness." Such is the case with John Donne's 12-line conceit in "A Valediction: Forbidding Mourning" comparing the souls of separated lovers to the legs of a compass. Cast as a proposition needing proof, the conceit yields images

at once more abstract and precise than those typical of Petrarchan conceits.

Often structured like a paralogism or abbreviated syllogism, the baroque or metaphysical conceit exploits literary and cultural commonplaces as well as tropes. Unlike a *simile or strong metaphor, its terms are frequently allusive or qualified by argument, thus its perceived artificiality. When Luis de Góngora in the *Soledades* (1.481–90) compares Ferdinand Magellan's sight of coral islands in the Pacific to Actaeon's gazing on the white limbs of Diana bathing in the Eurotas river, the wit of the *concepto* lies in realizing the common peril for both men; but it also depends on the commonplace of forbidden beauty, as well as the simile that cupidity is like eros. The conceit also typically tries to marry the concrete and abstract, without, though, becoming allegorical. As Donne implores in "A nocturnall upon S. Lucies day":

> Study me then, you, who shall lovers bee
> At the next world, that is, at the next Spring:
> For I am every dead thing,
> In whom love wrought new Alchimie.
> For his art did expresse
> A quintessence even from nothingnesse,
> From dull privations, and leane emptinesse:
> He ruin'd mee, and I am re-begot
> Of absence, darknesse, death; things which
> are not.

The paradoxical image of the speaker as "every dead thing" is distilled from two premises: first, the notion that alchemy produces "quintessence" from "nothingnesse"; second, the analogy that the "art" of "love" is like alchemy's. Further, the lover's hyperbolic transformation is striking and worth studying, Donne suggests, because his own poetic "art" is able to unite hitherto irreconcilable extremes.

As the finest product of "wit" (Lat. *ingenium*, It. *ingegno*, Sp. *ingenio*, Fr. *esprit*, Ger. *Witz*), the baroque conceit underscores the subjective aspects of poetic invention. Yet to interpret it, the reader's ingenuity must partly mimic the poet's. As a contemporary, Jasper Mayne, writes of Donne's verse: "[W]e are thought wits, when 'tis understood."

The baroque conceit has various origins. The epigrammatic wit of Martial and the *Greek Anthology*, avidly imitated by J. C. Scaliger, Clément Marot, Ben Jonson, Martin Opitz, and others, encourages its devel. Alternately, Petrarch and his lyric successors refine a sophisticated metaphoric discourse commonly labeled "conceited." In *Canzoniere* 127, Petrarch takes the terms in a simile comparing love's effect on him to the sun melting snow ("come 'l sol neve mi governa Amore") and then elaborates each of them in a complex series of metaphoric images. Pierre de Ronsard's *Amours*, Francisco de Quevedo's *Canta sola a Lisi* (*Poems to Lisi*), and Shakespeare's sonnets exemplify the many ways that the rich array of Petrarchan conceits are later imitated. But Shakespeare's ironic *blason in sonnet 130 ("My mistress' eyes . . .") also indicates how belated Petrarchans seek to find ever more ingenious, extravagant conceits that might still surprise and move. (Such "outdoing" persists into the 19th c.; Charles Baudelaire, e.g., compares his beloved to a rotting carcass in "Une charogne.")

During the mid-17th c., the conceit becomes the focus of a novel, theoretically rich poetics that, borrowing its terms from faculty psychology and scholastic logic, tries to account for the new conceited styles of Giambattista Marino and Góngora, the revival of Senecan and other "pointed" prose styles, and the period's fascination with emblems, aphorisms, and other forms of wit.

Baltasar Gracián's *Agudeza y arte de ingenio* (1648) defines the concepto as "an act of the understanding" that "consists of an excellent concordance, a harmonic correlation, between two or three knowable extremes." A figure either of "proportion" or "disproportion," the conceit is the chief means by which the ingenio "finds" and then "expresses" the "correspondence" between objects in a manner "that not only is content with the truth, as is judgment, but aspires to the beautiful." The finished product of such invention aims to be more than what is typically called a poetic conceit in Eng. For though Gracián equivocates whether such correspondences exist outside the witty mind, he unambiguously casts the concepto as the most discerning way to express new ideas.

Emanuele Tesauro's *Il cannocchiale aristotelico* (1654) describes the *concetto* as the acme of poetic creation. Comparing its "wonders" (*meraviglie*) to scripture's symbolic, parabolic effects, Tesauro also regards the new science's epistemological novelties as justifying *concetti*. Adapting Aristotle's notion of *asteia* (urbanity), he makes metaphor's "mental flight" and the poet's ingenio the basis for the conceit. Initially compared to an enthymeme, the conceit is later described as a "metaphorical argument"

or "caviling fiction." Celebrating how conceits produce new knowledge from old categories of thought, Tesauro dubs them "urbanely fallacious arguments" (*argomenti urbanamente fallici*).

In *Life of Cowley* (1781), however, Samuel Johnson regrets how in metaphysical poetry "the most heterogeneous ideas are yoked by violence together." He blames its overly "analytic" style and "slender conceits and laboured particularities." Yet his perceptive critique of Donne and Abraham Cowley's penchant for *discordia concors*, or "combination of dissimilar images or discovery of occult resemblances in things apparently unlike" neatly defines the conceit. Responding to Johnson and heralding his own poetics, T. S. Eliot (1921, 1926) celebrates the metaphysical conceit as uniquely suited to uniting thought and feeling. Tuve reads conceited imagery as emerging from the dialectics of Peter Ramus and his followers and as a "stylistically very striking" form of judgment. Leaning on Gracián's treatise, 20th-c. Sp. crit. treats the style of Quevedo and Góngora as *conceptista*. Gilman sees similarities between the conceit and anamorphosis. Proctor, Brodsky, and Van Hook analyze the conceit's illogic. Blanco and Vuilleumier regard the conceit as the culmination of Ren. poetics. Rousset and Hallyn stress how the dissolution of the Ren. analogical worldview encourages the conceit's devel.

Further afield, the surrealist emphasis on startling *imagery recalls the aesthetic claims of the baroque conceit but ignores its epistemological promise. Comte de Lautréamont's image of "a boy as beautiful as a chance meeting on a dissecting table of a sewing machine and an umbrella" (from his prose poem *Les Chants de Maldoror*, 1869) is analyzed in André Breton's *Manifesto of Surrealism* (1924): "The value of the image depends upon the beauty of the spark obtained; it is, consequently, a function of the difference of potential between the two conductors. When the difference exists only slightly, as in a comparison, the spark is lacking."

Finally, forms akin to the Petrarchan conceit occur outside the Eur. trad. The *kāvya* (cl.) style of Sanskrit poetry often favors extended, complex metaphors (cf. Kālidāsa's "Cloud Messenger"). In med. Persian and Urdu poetry, the *ghazal* is fueled by elaborate, symbolic comparisons; Ḥāfiẓ's fusion of earthly and divine love yields many strikingly conceited images.

■ M. Praz, *Studi sul concettismo* (1934); F. Yates, "The Emblematic Conceit in Giordano Bruno's

De Gli Eroici Furori and in the Elizabethan Sonnet Sequences," *Journal of the Warburg and Courtauld Institutes* 6 (1943); R. Tuve, *Elizabethan and Metaphysical Imagery* (1947); A. Parker, "La 'Agudeza' en algunos sonetos de Quevedo," *Estudios dedicados a Menéndez Pidal*, v. 3 (1952); G. Watson, "Hobbes and the Metaphysical Conceit," *Journal of the History of Ideas* 16 (1955); *The Metaphysical Poets*, ed. H. Gardner (1957); A. Terry, "Quevedo and the Metaphysical Conceit," *BHS* 35 (1958); E. Donato, "Tesauro's Poetics: Through the Looking Glass," *MLN* 78 (1963); J. Rousset, *L'intérieur et l'extérieur* (1968); K.K. Ruthven, *The Conceit* (1969); G. Conte, *La Metafora barocca* (1972); R. E. Proctor, "Emanuele Tesauro: A Theory of the Conceit," *MLN* 88 (1973); E. Gilman, *The Curious Perspective: Literary and Pictorial Wit in the Seventeenth Century* (1978); C. Brodsky, "The Imaging of the Logical Conceit," *ELH* 49 (1982); A. Parker, "'Concept' and 'Conceit': An Aspect of Comparative Literary History," *MLR* 77 (1982); J. W. Van Hook, "'Concupiscence of Witt': The Metaphysical Conceit in Baroque Poetics," *MP* 84 (1986); T. E. May, *Wit of the Golden Age* (1986); J. Tilakasiri, *Kalidasa's Imagery and Theory of Poetics* (1988); M. Blanco, *Les rhétoriques de la pointe: Baltasar Gracián et le conceptisme en Europe* (1992); A. Schimmel, *A Two-Colored Brocade: The Imagery of Persian Poetry* (1992); T. S. Eliot, "The Metaphysical Poets" (1921), "The Conceit in Donne" (1926), *The Varieties of Metaphysical Poetry*, ed. R. Schuchard (1993); T. Althaus, *Epigrammatisches Barock* (1996); A. Zárate Ruiz, *Gracián, Wit, and the Baroque Age* (1996); F. Vuilleumier, "Les conceptismes," *Histoire de la rhétorique dans l'Europe moderne, 1450–1950* (1999); F. Hallyn, "Cosmography and Poetics," *CHLC*, v. 3, ed. G. P. Norton (1999); P. Frare, *"Per istra-foro di perspettiva": Il "Cannocchiale Aristotelico" el a poesia del seicento* (2000); H. Meyer, "Jesuit Concedes Jesuit Conceits: A Hit on Sarbievius' Head," *Gedächtnis und Phantasma*, ed. S. Frank et al. (2001); Y. Hersant, *La métaphore baroque: d'Aristote á Tesauro* (2001); R. Rambuss, "Sacred Subjects and the Aversive Metaphysical Conceit: Crashaw, Serrano, Ofili," *ELH* 71 (2004).

C. JOHNSON

CONCRETE POETRY. Although used in a general way to refer to work that has been composed with specific attention to graphic features such as typography, layout, shape, or distribution on the page, concrete poetry properly understood has a more specific definition

created in the mid-1950s by the Swiss-Bolivian poet Eugen Gomringer and the Brazilian poets Décio Pignatari and Haroldo and Augusto de Campos. The original tenets of concrete poetry are clear in the early writings of the latter group. Their 1958 "Pilot Plan for Concrete Poetry" outlines a distinct approach in which form and meaning (material expression and reference field) would be as close to each other as possible. Thus, *concrete* suggests a unification of the word with its presentation. The poets derived certain ideas from the work of Ezra Pound, in particular his adoption of Ernest Fenollosa's productive misunderstanding of the Chinese ideogram as a self-identical verbal-visual expression. The concrete poets recast this notion into an idea of isomorphism (identity of shape and meaning) that they believed embodied an ideal of structure as content. This attempt to eliminate extraneous associations or ambiguities comports with the aesthetics of "specific objects" expressed by minimalist artists of the 1960s, who sought to strip art objects of all superfluous elements.

Gomringer's poem "silencio" (1953) exemplifies the concretists' aim of creating a total integration of word as image in a single aesthetic expression. By repeating the word "silence" eight times to frame an empty "quiet" space, Gomringer's poem is self-defining and self-referential. Gomringer had been the secretary to Max Bill, a visual artist and graphic designer affiliated with the New Bauhaus, a post–World War II Swiss movement with a highly formalist orientation. Bill used the term *concrete* to identify his own functionalist, analytical methodology, which had an influence on the devel. of Swiss-style graphic design. Though committed to principles of self-identical work, concrete poets were profoundly interested in and attracted by mass culture and the graphic langs. of signage and advertising. Pignatari's famous "beba coca cola" (1957) reworks commercial lang. to critique corporate colonialism.

Concrete poets embraced the concept of intermedia works that could operate simultaneously in verbal-to-visual and acoustic modes. The use of sans serif typefaces, particularly Helvetica and Univers, lent the concrete poets an air of cool modernity that separated their work typographically from trads. of humanist poetry and *lyric voice. Many concrete poets distanced themselves from earlier 20th-c. avant-garde movements by their less explicit political content and absence of inflammatory rhet. But they continued the trad. of writing manifestos to state their aesthetic positions.

Concrete poetry found many adherents, and the poets who identified themselves with the term quickly expanded to include major figures in Europe, the Brit. Isles, the U.S., Japan, and South America. With increased distance and time, the work of these groups and individuals expanded beyond the strict orthodoxy outlined in the pilot plan. Thus, many poets who experimented with visual forms and typographic features are loosely associated with concrete poetry, even though their work is only pictorial, composed as a field or a score, rather than conforming to the strictly self-referential guidelines of concretism. By the time the first three major anthols. of concrete poetry appeared, ed. by E. Williams (1967), S. Bann (1967), and M. E. Solt (1968), their editorial range included poets from around the globe.

Precedents for concrete poetry can be traced to cl. antiquity and followed into the Middle Ages when poems shaped as religious icons carried theological meaning. Similar shaped works appeared in printed form in the Ren. and after as part of a contemplative trad. and then in a secular era as novelties and poetic amusements. Few visually shaped works follow the intellectual rigor of concrete poetry's self-identical reduction. Important later 20th-c. devels. brought concrete poetry into dialogue with procedural work, visual arts, installation, film, *sound poetry, typewriter poetry, critical theories of deconstruction and performance, and later digital works using animation and graphic means. *See* VISUAL POETRY.

■ *Concrete Poetry: An International Anthology*, ed. S. Bann (1967); *An Anthology of Concrete Poetry*, ed. E. Williams (1967); *Concrete Poetry: A World View*, ed. M. E. Solt (1968); D. Judd, "Specific Objects," *Donald Judd: Complete Writings 1959–1975* (1975); D. Seaman, *Concrete Poetry in France* (1981); W. Bohn, *The Aesthetics of Visual Poetry 1914–1928* (1986); J. Drucker, *The Visible Word* (1994); *Experimental-Visual-Concrete*, ed. K. D. Jackson, J. Drucker (1996); *Poesure et Peintrie*, ed. B. Blistène, V. Legrand (1998); W. Bohn, *Modern Visual Poetry* (2000).

J. DRUCKER

CONFESSIONAL POETRY. *Confession* in religious, psychoanalytic, criminal, and legal settings refers to the revelation of a shameful secret, as in a sin, crime, moral failing, social transgression, or neurosis. In an Am. literary context, confessional poetry refers to a group of poets writing during the 1950s and 1960s (Robert Lowell, W. D. Snodgrass, John Berryman, Sylvia Plath, Anne Sexton), who often employed the first-person *voice to explore transgressive autobiographical subjects incl. mental illness, familial trauma, gender and sexuality, and moral and political iconoclasm. M. L. Rosenthal originated the term in a review of Robert Lowell's *Life Studies* in 1959: "Because of the way Lowell brought his private humiliations, sufferings, and psychological problems into the poems of *Life Studies*, the word 'confessional' seemed appropriate." Confessional poetry is formally diverse, employing narrative, lyric, and dramatic modes and both free and metrical forms, while stylistically it often follows conventions of 19th-c. realist prose in its presentation of autobiographical material (Perloff). For example, Lowell's *Life Studies* originated in his prose memoir *91 Revere Street*, and he stated in an interview with Ian Hamilton that he wanted the poems to be as "single-surfaced as a photograph." The confessional poets' debts to modernism are also evident in uses of surrealist imagery (Plath) and multivocality (Berryman).

Confession in postwar Am. poetry can be seen as part of a more general resurgence of neoromantic poetics and a turn to autobiographical practices after World War II. Allen Ginsberg's effort in *Howl* to "stand before you speechless and intelligent and shaking with shame, rejected yet confessing out the soul" spelled an end to poetic impersonality (Eliot) and the New Critical bias against intention and affect. A variety of postwar poets sought forms of "naked," honest expression; cultivated spontaneity, immediacy, and a conversational style; privileged process over product; explored the Freudian unconscious and taboo desires; and initiated new methods of conjoining poetry and everyday life. Ginsberg's *Howl*, Frank O'Hara's personism, Amiri Baraka's "Black Art," Adrienne Rich's feminist poetics, and Robert Bly's Deep Image all share an interest in the poet's person as the ground for varied explorations of self, politics, nation, and aesthetics. Despite the specific connotations of *confessional poetry*, then, it emerges from and converses with trads. of romantic lyric, autobiography, and the poetry of witness. Contemp. poets who explore confession, incl. Sharon Olds, Frank Bidart, and Susan Hahn, indicate its enduring interest.

Judgments of confessional poetry have hinged on interpretations of the poem's relationship to the biographical poet. Detractors have read the poems as naïve autobiographical utterances and often as literal forms of therapeutic catharsis unmediated by aesthetic considerations, or conversely, as exhibitionist, sensationalist, self-serving performances (e.g., Lerner, Bawer, Gullans). Defenders have emphasized the problems with biographical readings, pointing out that judgments of the poetry often rest on moral evaluation of the poet's conduct (Travisano) and that pejorative responses are often feminized. Confessional poets and their sympathetic critics have pointed out the artful, fictive nature of confessional representation and performance, incl. the use of dramatic personae and dramatic *monologue (Lowell, Sexton, Berryman), while feminist scholars have emphasized Sexton's and Plath's performance and interrogation of the gendered self as a critical commentary on cold-war culture and an important influence on feminist poetry and performance art.

Given the pejorative connotations of *confessional poetry*, Travisano has called for its demise as a "critical paradigm," while others argue that the concept of confession can usefully elucidate poetry's truth claims. In that the confessant unveils secrets despite the stigma of shame, this revelation against societal resistance contributes to the expectation of the liberation of truth. As de Man writes, to confess is "to overcome guilt and shame in the name of truth: it is an epistemological use of language in which ethical values . . . are superseded by values of truth and falsehood." Gilmore argues that "as a mode of truth production the confession in both its oral and its written forms grants the autobiographer a kind of authority derived from the confessor's proximity to 'truth.'" Critics influenced by poststructuralism have found in confessional poetry not liberating, therapeutic expression but complex challenges to ideals of the coherent subject, referential lang., truth, and sincerity. Foucault's understanding of confession has proven particularly influential. Counter to the belief that confession "unburdens" or "liberates," Foucault argues that confession is "the effect of a power that constrains us." As "a ritual that unfolds within a power relationship," the confession is shaped by the "authority who requires the confession, prescribes and appreciates it, and intervenes in order to judge,

punish, forgive, console, and reconcile." Critics have drawn attention to confessional poetry's foregrounding of these power relationships and to the poetry's negotiation of its reader as a potential judge, analyst, jailer, or confessor. From this perspective, confessional poetry reveals the moral problem of judgment and explores the epistemological problems of truth and the relation of life and lit.

If one reads confessional poetry in the context of the longer trad. of confessional lit., Augustine and Jean-Jacques Rousseau provide two important models. For Augustine, self-conscious reflection on and repentance for sin lead to conversion and incorporation within a Christian community, whereas, for Rousseau, confession enacts individual difference rather than moral conformity, permitting the painting of a "portrait in every way true to nature." In Rousseau's text, confession of "sin" allows him to indict an inherently unjust society rather than take responsibility for error; de Man argues that confession-cum-excuse allows Rousseau to take pleasure in the exhibition of shame. Both models are evident in the poetic trad.; as Davie argues, there are poets who confess virtue (William Wordsworth) and those who confess vice (Lord Byron, Charles Baudelaire), poets who seek accommodation within a moral community and others who transgress moral community to critical ends. In mid-20th c. America, although the influence of Augustinian confession persists (New), Rousseau's example dominates; Rosenthal influentially argued that the confessional poet's alienation from society embodies a nation and culture in crisis. Successive critics often treat the confessional poet as "representative victim" (Breslin) and the confessional poem as an instrument that mirrors and critically diagnoses the culture. Hence, Middlebrook argues that "the images of the confessional poem encode the whole culture's shame-making machinery," while others have demonstrated confessional poetry's critical engagements with specific contexts, incl. Freudian psychoanalysis, McCarthyism, surveillance, privacy law, television, commercial culture, and gendered codes.

■ R. Langbaum, *The Poetry of Experience: The Dramatic Monologue in Modern Literary Tradition* (1957); M. L. Rosenthal, *The New Poets: American and British Poetry since World War II* (1967); D. Davie, "On Sincerity: From Wordsworth to Ginsberg," *Encounter* 31 (1968); L. Trilling, *Sincerity and Authenticity* (1972); M. Perloff, *The Poetic Art of Robert Lowell*

(1973); M. Foucault, *The History of Sexuality, Volume 1: An Introduction*, trans. R. Hurley (1978); P. de Man, *Allegories of Reading* (1979); P. Breslin, *The Psycho-Political Muse: American Poetry since the 1950s* (1987); L. Lerner, "What Is Confessional Poetry?" *Critical Quarterly* 29 (1987); C. Gullans, "Review of *Live or Die*," *Anne Sexton: Telling the Tale*, ed. S. E. Colburn (1988); I. Hamilton, "A Conversation with Robert Lowell," *Robert Lowell, Interviews and Memoirs*, ed. J. Meyers (1988); B. Bawer, "Sylvia Plath and the Poetry of Confession," *The New Criterion* 9 (1991); M. Perloff, *Radical Artifice* (1991); J. Rose, *The Haunting of Sylvia Plath* (1991); C. Forché, *Against Forgetting: Twentieth-Century Poetry of Witness* (1993); K. Lant, "The Big Strip Tease: Female Bodies and Male Power in the Poetry of Sylvia Plath," *Contemporary Literature* 34 (1993); D. Middlebrook, "What Was Confessional Poetry?" and G. Orr, "The Postconfessional Lyric," *The Columbia History of American Poetry*, ed. J. Parini (1993); L. Gilmore, "Policing Truth: Confession, Gender, and Autobiographical Authority," *Autobiography and Postmodernism*, ed. K. Ashley, L. Gilmore, G. Peters (1994); R. Felski, "On Confession," *Women, Autobiography, Theory: A Reader*, ed. S. Smith and J. Watson (1998); C. Britzolakis, *Sylvia Plath and the Theatre of Mourning* (1999); I. Gammel, *Confessional Politics: Women's Sexual Self-Representations in Life Writing and Popular Media* (1999); T. Travisano, *Midcentury Quartet: Bishop, Lowell, Jarrell, Berryman, and the Making of a Postmodern Aesthetic* (1999); D. H. Blake, "Public Dreams: Berryman, Celebrity, and the Culture of Confession," *American Literary History* 13 (2001); M. Bryant, "Plath, Domesticity, and the Art of Advertising," *College Literature* 29 (2002); D. Nelson, *Pursuing Privacy in Cold War America* (2002); J. Rose, *On Not Being Able to Sleep: Psychoanalysis and the Modern World* (2003); T. Brain, "Dangerous Confessions: The Problem of Reading Sylvia Plath Biographically," J. Gill, "Introduction," and E. Gregory, "Confessing the Body: Plath, Sexton, Berryman, Lowell, Ginsberg, and the Gendered Poetics of the 'Real,'" *Modern Confessional Writing*, ed. J. Gill (2006); E. New, "Confession, Reformation, and Counter-Reformation in the Career of Robert Lowell," and S. Burt, "My Name Is Henri: Contemporary Poets Discover John Berryman," *Reading the Middle Generation Anew*, ed. E. L. Haralson (2006); S. Rosenbaum, *Professing Sincerity: Modern Lyric Poetry, Commercial Culture, and the Crisis in Reading* (2007);

J. Badia, *Sylvia Plath and the Mythology of Women Readers* (2011).

S. ROSENBAUM

CONSONANCE. In *prosody, *consonance* refers most strictly to the repetition of the sound of a final consonant or consonant cluster in stressed, unrhymed syllables near enough to be heard together, as in Robert Lowell's "iro*nic* rai*n*bow" and "Go*bb*ets of blu*bb*er" or Robert Browning's "Rebu*ck*led the chee*k*-strap, chained sla*ck*er the bit," where three final *k* sounds emphasize the stressed syllables bu*ck*-chee*k*-sla*ck*. Consonance parallels the repetitions in *alliteration (initial consonant) and *assonance (vowel) and can be combined either within a syllable to produce other effects, such as *rhyme (assonance + consonance) or pararhyme (alliteration + consonance). Critics have sometimes used the terms *consonance, assonance,* and *alliteration* interchangeably with some loss of precision. *Consonance* also sometimes specifically denotes cases of pararhyme, an effect commonly found in early Celtic, Germanic, and Icelandic poetry, and in W. H. Auden's "*reader* to *rider*" or in early Ren. verse such as Luigi Pulci's "Stille le stelle ch'a tetto era tutta." This effect has been referred to alternately as *bracket rhyme, bracket alliteration, bracket consonance,* or *rich consonance,* though it may be useful to distinguish this double echo from the single echo of final consonant repetition. This would allow one to say that "rider" both alliterates and consonates with "reader," while in *fur-fair, f* alliterates and *r* consonates. Consonance has often fallen loosely under the terms *half rhyme, near rhyme,* or *slant rhyme,* which may blur the distinction between differing vowel and consonant echoes. Combinations that appear to rhyme to the eye, such as lo*ve*-mo*ve,* may only consonate, though some such pairs are accepted by convention as rhyme. Several critics have identified other instances of "partial" or "semi" consonance when, e.g., one or more echoes involve slightly differing clusters, as in Dylan Thomas's pairing pla*tes*-hea*rts,* which differs by the *r* in hearts but retains the *t-s* echo in both. Likewise, one may find "close" consonance between voiced and unvoiced final consonant echoes, as in the *f* and *v* of wi*f*e-lo*v*e or *s* and *z* of hea*rs*e-wa*r*es. Consonance becomes more subtle, and harder to hear, between complex vowel or glide endings, as in the *y* of day-lie, also sometimes called *semiconsonance,* while "zero-consonance" has been used to describe repeating vowels without the final consonant echo. There is little agreement, however, on the use of these more narrowly defined terms. There is no consensus either about how to notate consonantal echoes across stressed and unstressed syllables or in ambiguous rhythms, though most critics take a pragmatic approach to capturing such effects.

Though occasionally criticized as "imperfect" rhyme, consonance has been used with great frequency as ornamentation; as a substitute for or contrast with rhyme; as a device to create *parallelism, to amplify rhythmic effects, or to forestall closure; and as a structuring device in its own right. Lucretius has many lines such as "Cernere adorari licet et sentire sonare," with four final *r*'s in stressed syllables. Though final written consonants are not often pronounced in Fr., Nicolas Boileau echos final *s* and *r* in "Changer Narcisse en fleur, couvrir Daphné d'écorce." Shakespeare normally preferred other phonic echoes, but his couplet from *Romeo and Juliet* (2.3.3–4) is far from unique: "And flecked darkness like a drunkard reels / From forth day's path and Titan's fiery wheels," where six of ten stressed peaks consonate with *k* or *th*. John Dryden used it for parallelism, often with other echoes ("piercing wi*t* and pregnant though*t*); for joining adjective to noun ("o*d*ious ai*d*," "exten*d*ed wa*nd*"); and for *onomatopoeia ("A buzzing noise of bees his ears alarms," where the *z* of buzz ends every stressed syllable). Emily Dickinson and R. W. Emerson employed consonance often in place of end rhyme, as in Dickinson's "I like to see it lap the miles," with lines ending u*p*-ste*p*, pee*r*-pa*re*, whi*le*-hi*ll*, and sta*re*-doo*r*. G. M. Hopkins is known for a variety of phonic echoes, including pairs such as Gho*st*-brea*st*, ye*ll*ow-sa*ll*ows.

In the 20th c., dozens of poets showed an interest in consonance as an anchor for various formal schema. W. B. Yeats's "Meditations in Time of Civil War" sometimes prefers consonance over end rhyme, as in the *d-r-d-r* pattern of woo*d*, wa*r*, roa*d*, bloo*d*, sta*re*. Consonance dominates Dylan Thomas's "And Death Shall Have No Dominion," inverting the usual proportion of end consonance to end rhyme. Ted Hughes combines rhyme and consonance, as in frozen-eyes-snows-rows-snail*s*. Wilfred Owen has more consonance by itself (shri*ll*-wai*l*ing-ca*ll*), as do Theodore Roethke and Hart Crane, who lets the consonance of *r* dominate a whole stanza of "Voyages II."

■ K. Burke, "On Musicality in Verse," *The Philosophy of Literary Form* (1941); J. Travis,

"Intralinear Rhyme and Consonance in Early Celtic and Early Germanic Poetry," *Germanic Review* 18 (1943); A. Oras, "Surry's Technique of Phonetic Echoes," *JEGP* 50 (1951), and "Lyrical Instrumentation in Marlowe," *Studies in Shakespeare*, ed. A. D. Matthews (1953); D. Masson, "Vowel and Consonant Patterns in Poetry" and "Thematic Analyses of Sounds in Poetry," and A. Oras, "Spenser and Milton: Some Parallels and Contrasts in the Handling of Sound," *Essays on the Language of Literature*, ed. S. Chatman and S. R. Levin (1967); R. Astley, "Stations of the Breath," *PMLA* 84 (1969); G. N. Leech, *A Linguistic Guide to English Poetry* (1969); P. G. Adams, *Graces of Harmony: Alliteration, Assonance, and Consonance in Eighteenth-Century British Poetry* (1977); M. Williams, *Patterns of Poetry* (1986); J. J. Small, *Positive as Sound* (1990); P. G. Adams, "Edward Taylor's Love Affair with Sounding Language," *Order in Variety*, ed. R. W. Crump (1991); D. Robey, *Sound and Structure in the Divine Comedy* (2000); M. W. Edwards, *Sound, Sense, and Rhythm* (2002); S. Heaney, *Finders Keepers* (2002); M. Tyler, *A Singing Contest* (2005); B. Devine, *Yeats, the Master of Sound* (2006); W. Harmon, "A Game of Feet," *SR* 116 (2008); L. Wheeler, *Voicing American Poetry* (2008).

P. G. ADAMS; R. S. STILLING

CONVENTION. Any rule that by implicit agreement between a writer and some of his or her readers (or of the audience) allows the writer certain freedoms in, and imposes certain restrictions on, his or her treatment of style, structure, genre, or theme and enables these readers to interpret the work correctly. Combining social and objective functions, literary conventions are intersubjective; they hold (like ling. conventions) the normative force that underlies the possibility of communication at all.

Unlike users of ling. conventions, readers who are party to literary conventions may be very few indeed, else a writer could never create a new convention (e.g., *free verse or *sprung rhythm), revive an old convention (such as *alliterative meters in mod. langs.), or abandon an old convention (the pastoral *elegy). Readers who are ignorant of—or at least out of sympathy with—the convention must to some extent misinterpret a work that exemplifies it; and when the number of such readers becomes large, writers may abandon the convention—though, of course, works that exemplify it remain to be interpreted. Samuel Johnson in his judgment of "Lycidas" is an instance of a reader who misinterprets a work because he is out of sympathy with its conventions (*Life of Milton*).

Conventions govern the relations of matter to form, means to ends, and parts to wholes. Some examples of conventions of style are the rhyme scheme of the *sonnet and the diction of the *ballad; of structure, beginning an *epic in medias res and the strophic structure of the *ode; of genre, representing the subject of a pastoral elegy as a shepherd; of theme, attitudes toward love in the Cavalier lyric and toward death in the Elizabethan lyric. The function of any particular convention is determined by its relation to the other conventions that together form the literary system. At any point in the hist. of its transmission, this system provides for the finite articulation of infinite literary possibilities.

Conventions both liberate and restrict the writer. Because conventions usually form sets and are motivated by traditional acceptance, a writer's decision to use a certain convention obliges him or her to use certain others or risk misleading the reader. The conventions of the epic, e.g., allow a writer to achieve effects of scale but compel him or her to forgo the conversational idiom of the metaphysical lyric.

To break with conventions (or "rules") is sometimes thought a merit, sometimes a defect; but such a break is never abandonment of all conventions, merely replacement of an old set with a new. William Wordsworth condemns 18th-c. poetry for using poetic diction (Preface to the 1800 *Lyrical Ballads*); Leavis condemns Georgian poetry for adhering to "19th-century conventions of 'the poetical'." The institutional character of convention supports theories of literary change based on the dialectic of trad. and innovation. In New Criticism, "conventional 'materials'" are "rendered dramatic and moving" by the individual work (Brooks), while in Russian formalism, dominant conventions change in function as they are displaced by the nascent ones they potentially contain.

Innovation results in new conventions. While established conventions may become, like ling. conventions, unconscious and apparently arbitrary, their reliance on implicit social agreement suggests that new conventions arise through nonexplicit cooperation, in the manner of social games of coordination (Lewis, Pavel). Genre theorists hold that when the "traits" of individual works of lit. no longer conform to the "type" specified by an established convention, they may begin to form the "type" of a new convention and thus set a new "horizon of expectation" for writers and readers (Hirsch, Jauss).

The social nature of conventions also distinguishes them from universals; hence, e.g., neo-Aristotelian restrictions of the term *convention* to denote "any characteristic of the matter or technique of a poem the reason for the presence of which cannot be inferred from the necessities of the form envisaged but must be sought in the historical circumstances of its composition" (Crane). Structuralism concedes the conventionality of all norms but seeks to identify the universal laws of relation by which they are organized. The pervasiveness of convention accounts in poststructuralism for the absorption of subjectivity and authorial intention into *écriture*, the autonomous productivity of writing as an institution (Barthes 1953), and for the concept of a plural, "writable" text whose meaning is unintelligible in traditional, "readerly" terms and must be written or invented by its readers (Barthes 1970). In New Historicism, the social basis of literary conventions allows for their resituation in relation to the conventions of nonliterary discourse and of nondiscursive practices and institutions.

Because conventions mediate between nature and its representation, as well as between authors and readers, different theories of convention (and different historical periods) will lay differing stress on their relation to universals, natural imperatives, trad., society, or the individual.

■ J. L. Lowes, *Convention and Revolt in Poetry* (1922); F. R. Leavis, *New Bearings in English Poetry* (1932); Brooks; R. S. Crane, *The Languages of Criticism and the Structure of Poetry* (1953); R. Barthes, *Writing Degree Zero*, trans. A. Lavers and C. Smith (1968); R. M. Browne, *Theories of Convention in Contemporary American Criticism* (1956); E. D. Hirsch Jr., *Validity in Interpretation* (1967); D. K. Lewis, *Convention* (1969); R. Barthes, *S/Z*, trans. R. Miller (1974); S. R. Levin, "The Conventions of Poetry," *Literary Style: A Symposium*, ed. S. Chatman (1971); V. Forrest-Thomson, "Levels in Poetic Convention," *Journal of European Studies* 2 (1972); J. Culler, *Structuralist Poetics* (1976), and "Convention and Meaning: Derrida and Austin," *NLH* 13 (1981); L. Manley, *Convention, 1500–1750* (1980), and "Concepts of Convention and Models of Critical Discourse," *NLH* 13.1 (1981)—spec. iss. "On Convention:

I"; M. Steinmann, "Superordinate Genre Conventions," *Poetics* 10 (1981); H. R. Jauss, *Toward an Aesthetic of Reception*, trans. T. Bahti (1982); *NLH* 14.2 (1983)—spec. iss. "On Convention: II"; C. E. Reeves, "The Languages of Convention," *PoT* 7 (1986), and "'Conveniency to Nature': Literary Art and Arbitrariness," *PMLA* 101 (1986); T. Pavel, "Literary Conventions," in *Rules and Conventions*, ed. M. Hjort (1992); J. Wood, "Truth, Convention, Realism," *How Fiction Works* (2009).

M. STEINMANN; L. MANLEY

COUPLET (from Lat. *copula*). Two contiguous lines of verse that function as a metrical unit and are so marked either by (usually) rhyme or syntax or both. This two-line unit appears in many poetries, incl. Sanskrit (e.g., the *śloka* of cl. epic; see G. Thompson), Chinese (the couplet appeared in the *Shijing*, composed during the Zhou dynasty [1046–256 BCE]), Ar., and Persian. Since the advent of rhymed verse in the Eur. vernaculars in the 12th c., the couplet has counted as one of the principal units of versification in Western poetry, whether as an independent poem of a gnomic or epigrammatic nature (see EPIGRAM), as a subordinate element in other stanzaic forms—two of the principal stanzaic forms of the later Middle Ages and the Ren., *ottava rima* and *rhyme royal*, both conclude with a couplet, as does the Shakespearean *sonnet*—or as a stanzaic form for extended verse composition, narrative or philosophical. In each of these modes, the tightness of the couplet and closeness of its rhyme make it esp. suited for purposes of formal conclusion, summation, or epigrammatic comment. In dramatic verse, the couplet occurs in the cl. Fr. drama, the older Ger. and Dutch drama, and the "heroic plays" of Restoration England. It also fills an important function in Elizabethan and Jacobean drama as a variation from the standard *blank verse*, its principal use being to mark for the audience, aurally, the conclusion of a scene or a climax in dramatic action. The couplet occupies a unique and interesting position in the typology of verse forms. Standing midway between stichic verse and strophic, it permits the fluidity of the former while also taking advantage of some of the effects of the latter.

In the med. Fr. epic, the older assonanted *laisse* gives way to rhyme in couplets around the 12th c. The earliest examples, such as the *Cantilène de Sainte Eulalie* and the *Vie de Saint Léger*, are in closed couplets (Meyer). Chrétien de Troyes (fl. after 1150) seems to have introduced *enjambement*, which by the 13th c. is common (e.g., Raoul de Houdenc). After the *Chanson de Roland* (early 12th c.), first the decasyllabic, then the *alexandrine* couplet is the dominant form of OF narrative and dramatic poetry (see DECASYLLABLE). In the hands of the masters of Fr. classicism— Pierre Corneille, Molière, Jean Racine, Jean de La Fontaine—the couplet is end-stopped and relatively self-contained, but a freer use of enjambment is found among the romantics. Under Fr. influence, the alexandrine couplet became the dominant metrical form of Ger. and Dutch narrative and dramatic verse of the 17th and 18th cs. Subsequently, a more indigenous Ger. couplet, the tetrameter couplet called *Knittelvers*, was revived by J. W. Goethe and Friedrich Schiller. The term *couplet* is sometimes used in Fr. prosody with the meaning of stanza, as in the *couplet carré* (square couplet), an octave composed of octosyllables.

In Eng. poetry, though the octosyllabic or iambic tetrameter couplet has been used well (see OCTOSYLLABLE), by far the most important couplet form has been isometric and composed of two lines of iambic pentameter. As perfected by John Dryden and Alexander Pope, the so-called *heroic couplet* is "closed"—syntax and thought fit perfectly into the envelope of rhyme and meter sealed at the end of the couplet— and in this form dominates the poetry of the neoclassical period: "Know then thyself, presume not God to scan," says Pope in the *Essay on Man*, "The proper study of Mankind is Man." When meter and syntax thus conclude together, the couplet is said to be end-stopped.

The couplet is "open" when enjambed, i.e., when the syntactic and metrical frames do not close together at the end of the couplet, the sentence being carried forward into subsequent couplets to any length desired and ending at any point in the line. This form of the couplet is historically older and not much less common than the closed form in Eng. poetry as a whole. It was introduced by Chaucer and continued to be produced (e.g., Edmund Spenser, "Mother Hubberd's Tale" [1591]; Nicholas Breton, *The Uncasing of Machivils Instructions to His Sonne* [1613]) well into the 17th c. during the very time when the closed or "heroical" couplet was being established. George Puttenham and other Ren. critics labeled this older form "riding rhyme." It was further explored in the

19th c. (e.g., Robert Browning), proving then as ever esp. suited for continuous narrative and didactic verse. Long sentences in enjambed couplets constitute the rhymed equivalent of the *"verse paragraph" in blank verse. In a medial form between closed and open, each two-line sentence ends at the end of the *first* line of the couplet, making for systematic counterpointing of syntax against meter.

Not all Eng. couplets are isometric, however. Poets as diverse as George Herbert and Browning have developed couplet forms that rhyme lines of unequal length: "With their triumphs and their glories and the rest. / Love is best!" (Browning, "Love among the Ruins"). A related heterometric form of couplet that developed in Gr. and Lat., a hexameter followed by a pentameter, came to be known for its generic usage as the *elegiac distich*. Passed down through the Middle Ages as a semipopular form (e.g., the *Distichs of Cato*), it survived into mod. times, often as a vestigial visual format with alternate lines indented, as in W. H. Auden's "In Praise of Limestone" or the first section of "The Sea and the Mirror." In the late 20th and early 21st cs., a two-line, couplet-like stanza established itself as the common visual format of much unrhymed, nonmetrical verse, e.g., A. R. Ammons's *Garbage*.

■ Schipper; P. Meyer, "Le Couplet de deux vers," *Romania* 23 (1894); C.H.G. Helm, *Zur Rhythmik der kurzen Reimpaare des XVI Jahrhunderten* (1895); C. C. Spiker, "The Ten-Syllable Rhyming Couplet," *West Virginia University Philological Papers* 1 (1929); P. Verrier, *Le Vers français*, v. 2 (1931–32); G. Wehowsky, *Schmuckformen und Formbruch in der deutschen Reimpaardichtung des Mittelalters* (1936); E.N.S. Thompson, "The Octosyllabic Couplet," *PQ* 18 (1939); F. W. Ness, *The Use of Rhyme in Shakespeare's Plays* (1941), esp. ch. 5, App. C; B. H. Smith, *Poetic Closure* (1968); J. A. Jones, *Pope's Couplet Art* (1969); W. B. Piper, *The Heroic Couplet* (1969); Brogan, 389 ff.; Gasparov, *History*; J. P. Hunter, "Formalism and History: Binarism and the Anglophone Couplet," *MLQ* 61 (2000); *The Bhagavad Gita*, trans. G. Thompson (2008)—intro. note on the trans.

T.V.F. BROGAN; W. B. PIPER; S. CUSHMAN

CROSS RHYME (Ger. *Kreuzreim, überschlagender Reim*; Fr. *rime brisée, rime croisée*). Also known as envelope rhyme or enclosed rhyme, cross rhyme is now commonly used to refer to the *abab* pattern of end words in a quatrain (Perloff, Scott, Adams). But as Schipper has pointed out, when two long lines of a rhyming *couplet are connected by a rhyme before the *caesura as well as by a rhyme at the end of the line (interlaced rhyme, *rime entrelacée*), they will seem to be broken up into four short lines of cross rhyme, and some overlap between the terms is understandable. Most common in long-line verse, such as the med. Lat. hexameter, cross rhyme also features prominently in certain Ir. stanza forms, such as the *droighneach* and the *rannaigheacht mhor*, both of which have at least two cross rhymes in each couplet (Turco).

■ Schipper, *History*; M. Perloff, *Rhyme and Meaning in the Poetry of Yeats* (1970); C. Scott, *The Riches of Rhyme* (1988); L. Turco, *The Book of Forms* (2000); S. Adams, *Poetic Designs* (2003).

W. HUNTER

D

DACTYL (Gr., "finger"). In cl. prosody, a metrical foot consisting of one long syllable followed by two short ones. In the mod. prosodies based on *accent, an accented syllable followed by two unaccented ones (e.g., *suddenly, ominous*). Dactyl is the metrical basis of much of cl. Gr. and Lat. poetry: in narrative verse, it is used particularly for the *hexameter and *elegiac distich, and in lyric, it is used alone and with other cola, esp. the epitrite, in various combinations known collectively as *dactylo-epitrite*. These latter did not survive the cl. age, though the dactylic hexameter remained the meter for much Lat. art verse through most of the Middle Ages. In the transition from Lat. to the vernaculars, however, it lost place to iambic—which even in antiquity had been the meter felt to be closest to common (Gr.) speech and had been used for recitation meters such as dialogue in drama—as the staple meter of art verse and *epic. Dactylic verse was, however, revived in Ger. by August Buchner in his opera *Orpheus* (1638), arousing a brief vogue, evidenced in Simon Dach and Friedrich von Logau.

The dactyl is usually mentioned in handbooks of Eng. metrics along with the *anapest and perhaps the amphibrach as the three mod. ternary meters, but in running series, these are almost impossible to differentiate, esp. if the line ends are ambiguous. If dactylic meter was suited to Gr., it was less suited to Lat., with its stress accent, and even less suited to the mod. langs. Hence, the status of this metrical foot in mod. times is completely the reverse of its cl. prestige: it is now used mostly for light verse and humorous subgenres, such as the recent "double dactyls."

■ A. Köster, "Deutsche Daktylen," *Zeitschrift für Deutsches Altertum und Deutsche Literatur* 46 (1901); Wilamowitz, pt. 2, ch. 10; Koster, ch. 4; Dale, ch. 3; Halporn et al.; Snell; West; C. Golston and T. Riad, "The Phonology of Classical Greek Meter," *Linguistics* 38 (2000).

T.V.F. BROGAN

DECASYLLABLE. A line of ten syllables; metrical structures built on it vary, but normally the term refers to the Fr. *décasyllabe* and the Eng. *iambic pentameter. In Fr. verse, the decasyllable appeared about the middle of the 11th c., in *La Vie de St. Alexis* and *Le Boèce*, with a *caesura after the fourth syllable and two fixed accents on the fourth and tenth syllables: so 4//6, with 6//4 as a possible variant form; 5//5, perhaps the oldest version of the decasyllable, also occurs both in the med. period and among poets of the 19th c. The classic 4//6 form leads one to expect a line of three rhythmic measures, one in the 4 and two in the 6; the description of the 5//5 alternative by Bonaventure des Périers (early 16th c.) as "taratantara" (2 + 3) suggests the expectation of two measures in each *hemistich of 5. With the appearance of the *Chanson de Roland* (early 12th c.), the decasyllable became the standard line of Fr. epic and narrative verse, i.e. the *chansons de geste*, until the appearance of the *alexandrine at the beginning of the 12th c., which gradually supplanted it. In OF lyric verse, it is more common than the *octosyllable, making it the principal Fr. meter from the 14th c. to the mid-16th c., when the poets of the Pléiade appropriated the alexandrine for the lyric, too (Joachim du Bellay referred to the decasyllable as the *vers héroïque*; Pierre de Ronsard dubbed it the *vers commun* and employed it in his *Franciade* [1572], albeit against his better judgment). Thereafter, the alexandrine became the standard line for most serious poetry in Fr., though the decasyllable continued to play an important role: in the 17th and 18th cs., it served the ballade, the *epigram, the *ode, the *mock epic, (e.g., Jean-Baptiste-Louis Gresset's *Ver-Vert* [1734]), the *verse epistle (Jean-Baptiste Rousseau), and comedy (Voltaire) and appeared among the *vers mêlés* of the fable; the intermittent use of the 5//5 version, alongside 4//6, in the 19th c. (Pierre de Béranger, Alfred de Musset, Marceline Desbordes-Valmore, Victor Hugo, Théophile Gautier, Charles Baudelaire, Théodore de Banville, Charles-Marie Leconte de Lisle) often harked back to its med. origins in song (e.g., *chansons de toile*) but was susceptible to other modalities, while in the hands of Paul Verlaine, Arthur Rimbaud, and Jules Laforgue, the line also became a site of metrico-rhythmic polymorphousness; in the 20th c., Paul Valéry was prompted by the decasyllable's insistent rhythmic shape to adopt it for "Le Cimetière marin" (1922), although he acknowledged its lack of popularity, characterized it as "poor and monotonous," and recognized the need to "raise this *Ten* to the power of *Twelve*." Ironically, it is in *vers libre* that the decasyllabic line recovered much of its lost status, whether as an "authentic" decasyllable, metrically constituted, or as a nonce string of ten syllables.

In Italy, the *endecasillabo* (11 syllables but with a feminine ending) appeared early in the 12th c. and was used by Dante, Petrarch, and Boccaccio. Chaucer may have discovered the line in their work (the last syllable would have been dropped in Eng. pronunciation), if he had not already become acquainted with the corresponding Fr. meter. In any case, the decasyllabic line in Chaucer's hands took on the five-stress alternating pattern later to be called *iambic*, a form that, regardless of whether one counts syllables or stresses or both, and despite the considerable variation it enjoyed in the 15th c., as Chaucer's successors tried to imitate a meter they imperfectly understood, was secured by the authority of Chaucer's reputation until "rediscovered"—i.e., reconstructed—by Thomas Wyatt and Henry Howard, the Earl of Surrey, in the early 16th c. In the hands of Philip Sidney, Edmund Spenser, and William Shakespeare, the Eng. decasyllable—given the Latinate name *pentameter* by the classicizing Ren.—became the great staple meter of Eng. poetry and the foundation of *blank verse, the *heroic couplet, the *sonnet, and many other stanzaic forms; it has been estimated that some 70% of Eng. poetry of the high art-verse trad. has been written in the iambic pentameter line.

■ Bridges; P. Valéry, "Au sujet du *Cimetière marin*," *Oeuvres I*, ed. J. Hytier (1957); G. T. Wright, *Shakespeare's Metrical Art* (1988); J.-P. Bobillot, "Entre mètre et non-mètre: le « décasyllabe » chez Rimbaud," *Parade Sauvage* 10 (1994); B. de Cornulier, *Art poétique* (1995); M. J. Duffell, " 'The Craft So Long to Lerne': Chaucer's Invention of Iambic Pentameter," *Chaucer Review* 34 (2000); A. English, *Verlaine, poète de l'indécidable* (2005).

T.V.F. BROGAN; C. SCOTT

DECORUM (Gr. *to prepon*, "what is decorous"). The cl. term *decorum* refers to one of the criteria for judging those things whose excellence lends itself more appropriately to qualitative than to quantitative measurement. This definition depends on the ancient distinction between two types of measure posited by Plato in *The Statesman* (283d–85a) and adopted by Aristotle in his ethical, political, rhetorical, and literary treatises. Excess and deficiency, Plato says, are measurable in terms of not only the quantitative largeness or smallness of objects in relation to each other but each object's approximation to a norm of "due measure." All the arts owe the effectiveness and beauty of their products to this norm, *to metron*, whose criteria of what is commensurate (*to metrion*), decorous (*to prepon*), timely (*to kairon*), and needful (*to deon*), all address themselves to the "mean" (*to meson*) rather than to the fixed, arithmetically defined extremes. This distinction is central to literary decorum, because lit. shares its subject matter and certain principles of stylistic representation with the disciplines of law, ethics, and rhet., which also are concerned with the qualitative analysis and judgment of human experience.

With respect to subject matter, Aristotle says that poetry treats human actions (*Poetics* 2, 4, 6–9) by revealing their universal significance in terms of the "kinds of things a certain kind of person will say or do in accordance with probability or necessity" (Else trans., 9.4). The kinds of things said or done will indicate certain moral qualities (*poious*) of character that, in turn, confer certain qualities (*poias*) on the actions themselves (6.5–6). Extending the terms of Plato's *Statesman* (283d–85b, 294a–97e) to ethics, law, and rhet., Aristotle defines the concept of virtue necessary to evaluate such qualities of character as a balanced "disposition" (*hexis*) of the emotions achieved by the observation of the "mean" (*mesotes*) relative to each situation (*Nicomachean Ethics* [*EN*] 2.6). Likewise in law, equity is a "disposition" achieved through the individual application of a "quantitatively" invariable code of statutes for (amounts of) rewards and penalties to "qualitatively" variable and unpredictable human actions. As the builder of Lesbos bent his leaden ruler to a particular stone, so the judge, in drawing upon the universal law of nature (*to katholou*), might rectify the particular application of civil law by making a special ordinance to fit the discrete case (*EN* 5.7, 10). Equity brings these universal considerations to bear by looking to the qualitative questions of the legislator's intentions and of the kind (*poios*) of person the accused has generally or always been in order to mitigate his present act (*Rhetoric* 1.13.13–19).

With respect to stylistic representation, all verbal (as opposed to arithmetical) expression is qualitative and rests content if it can establish a likely similarity (rather than an exact equivalence) between things (Plato, *Cratylus* 432ab, *Timaeus* 29cd). *Diction achieves decorum by a proper balance between "distinctive" words, which contribute dignity while avoiding obtrusiveness, and "familiar" words, which, while avoiding meanness, contribute clarity (Aristotle, *Rhetoric* 3.2–3, *Poetics* 21–22). Lang. in general achieves decorum if the style expresses the degree of emotion proper to the importance of the subject and makes the speaker appear to have the kind of character proper to the occasion and audience. The greater the subject, the more powerful the emotions the speaker or writer may decorously solicit. The more shrewdly he estimates the "disposition" that informs the character of his listeners, the more he can achieve the "timely" (*eukairos*) degree of sophistication appropriate to the occasion (*Rhetoric* 3.7; cf. Plato, *Phaedrus* 277bc).

Influenced by the Middle Stoicism of Panaetius and Posidonius, Cicero did most to define and transmit the relation of literary decorum to ethics and law, suggested by such words as *decor* and *decet*, in his philosophical and rhetorical treatises (*De officiis* 1.14, 93–161; *De oratore* 69–74, 123–25). From his reformulation of Platonic, Aristotelian, and Isocratean attitudes, there flowed an immense variety of literary and artistic applications of the concept by grammarians, poets, rhetoricians, historians, philosophers, theologians, and encyclopedic writers on specialized disciplines. Most exemplary, perhaps, of the vitality and versatility of this trad. is Augustine's adaptation of it to Christian oratory and exegesis in *De doctrina christiana*, where, while virtually rejecting the cl. *doctrine* of "levels of style"—to which decorum was often reduced—he gave the cl. *principle* of decorum new life and applications (see Auerbach).

Like the "mean" and "disposition" of ethics and equity, decorum is an activity rather than a set of specific characteristics of style or content to be discovered, preserved, and reproduced. It is a fluid corrective process that must achieve and maintain, instant by instant, the delicate balance among the formal, cognitive, and judicative intentions of literary discourse. Its constant resistance to imbalance, taking different forms in different periods, never offers a "solution" to be found or expressed by literary "rules" with which later neoclassical theorists often try to identify it. As soon as they reduce it to a doctrine concerning either a given kind of subject or a given kind of style or a fixed relation of the one to the other, decorum ceases to exist, because its activity is a continuous negotiation between the two. For the forms that particular reductions or recoveries have taken, the reader must look to those literary controversies endemic to the period, genre, or issue of interest.

■ E. M. Cope and J. E. Sandys, *The Rhetoric of Aristotle*, 3 v. (1877); G. L. Hendrickson, "The Peripatetic Mean of Style and the Three Stylistic Characters," *AJP* 25 (1904); and "The Origin and Meaning of the Ancient Characters of Style," *AJP* 26 (1905); J.W.H. Atkins, *Literary Criticism in Antiquity*, 2 v. (1934); W. Jaeger, *Paideia*, 3 v. (1943)—cultural background; E. De Bruyne, *Études d'esthétique médiévale*, 3 v. (1946)—med. background; M. T. Herrick, *The Fusion of Horatian and Aristotelian Literary Criticism, 1531–1555* (1946); Curtius, ch. 10; Norden; H. I. Marrou, *Histoire de l'éducation dans l'antiquité*, 5th ed. (1960)—cultural background; Weinberg; F. Quadlbauer, *Die antike Theorie der Genera Dicendi im lateinischen Mittelalter* (1962); C. O. Brink, *Horace on Poetry*, 3 v. (1963–82); G. F. Else, *Aristotle's Poetics: The Argument* (1963); E. Auerbach, *Literary Language and Its Public in Late Latin Antiquity and in the Middle Ages*, trans. R. Manheim (1965), ch. 1; T. A. Kranidas, *The Fierce Equation* (1965); M. Pohlenz, "*To prepon*," *Kleine Schriften*, ed. H. Dorrie (1965); A. Patterson, *Hermogenes and the Renaissance* (1970); T. McAlindon, *Shakespeare and Decorum* (1973); Murphy; W. Edinger, *Samuel Johnson and Poetic Style* (1977)—18th-c. background; W. Trimpi, *Muses of One Mind* (1983)—see index; K. Eden, *Poetic and Legal Fiction in the Aristotelian Tradition* (1986); J. Mueller, "The Mastery of Decorum: Politics as Poetry in Milton's Sonnets," *CritI* 3 (1987); T. Krier, *Gazing on Secret Sights: Spenser, Classical Imitation and the Decorum of Vision* (1990), chs. 3–5; S. D. Troyan, *Textual Decorum: A Rhetoric of Attitudes in Medieval Literature* (1994); W. V. Clausen, *Virgil's "Aeneid": Decorum, Allusion, and Ideology* (2002); R. Sowerby, "The Decorum of Pope's *Iliad*," *Translation and Literature* 13 (2004); A. Paternoster, "Decorum and Indecorum in the '*Seconda redazione*' of B. Castiglione's '*Libro del Cortegiano*,'" *MLR* 99 (2004); L. Kurke, *Aesopic Conversations* (2011).

W. Trimpi; F. L. Blumberg

DEIXIS. *Deictics* (or shifters, *embrayeurs*) are features of lang. involving a reference to a specific act of communication in which they are used; *deixis* is the process of deictic speech. Deictic terms refer to a present situation of utterance and its speaker rather than to a fixed object, concept, or reality. Common deictics are those of time (e.g., *now*, *today*), space (e.g., *here*, *this town*), person (*I*, *you*), and social position (e.g., formal and informal address); but many ling. elements such as demonstratives, verb tenses, and anaphoric articles are potentially deictics, depending on how they refer to the situation of utterance. In each case, the reality to which the deictic term refers is solely a "reality of discourse" (Benveniste): the instance of deixis can be identified only within the discourse that contains it and, therefore, has no meaning except in the context in which it is produced. In lit., and esp. in poetic lang., deictics function as important interpretive devices. By alluding to a real or hypothetical situation of utterance (such as the present moment from which a poem is spoken within its fiction) and relating it to other situations (e.g., a past event that informs that present) or by collapsing such distinctions (as Walt Whitman and Language poetry often do), deictics are factors in the establishment of a poetic *persona, temporality, and relation to hist.

■ U. Weinreich, "On the Semantic Structure of Language," *Universals of Language*, ed. J. Greenberg (1966); E. Benveniste, *Problems in General Linguistics*, trans. M. E. Meek (1971); R. Jakobson, "Shifters and Verbal Categories," Jakobson, v. 2; Culler; O. Ducrot and T. Todorov, *Encyclopedic Dictionary of the Sciences of Language*, trans. C. Porter (1979); R. Greene, *Post-Petrarchism* (1991).

N. PINES

DEMOTION. In Eng. versification, when three consecutive syllables or single-syllable words are stressed in a line whose metrical pattern has been securely established—by preceding lines or by a reader/performer's sense of its trad. ("this is a tetrameter stanza"; "these are pentameter lines")—the middle syllable is experienced as "demoted," although it may have exactly the same stress, emphasis, or loudness as the adjacent words or syllables. Derek Attridge states a rule for this demotion thus: "A stressed syllable may realise an offbeat when it occurs between two stressed syllables." The reader/performer recognizes that to maintain the metricality of the work, only the first and third emphasized syllables will "carry the *beat."

E.g., when Thomas Hardy speaks about being undistressed "By hearts grown cold to me," an established expectation of a *trimeter line will demote "grown" between "hearts" and "cold." When Emily Dickinson, writing of agony, says that "The eyes glaze once, and that is Death," the four-beat expectation is realized by the demotion of "glaze."

Demotion can also occur in a second metrical circumstance that Attridge defines as being "after a line-boundary and before a stressed syllable." In Shakespeare's song beginning with the tetrameters "Full fathom five thy father lies; / Of his bones are coral made," the initial stressed word, "Full," is demoted.

Both "after a line-boundary" and "between two stressed syllables" conditions are in play when Alexander Pope's pentameter states that "True ease in writing comes from art, not chance," where a performer can experience demotions of both "True" and "not."

Demotion thus allows these additionally stressed lines better to convey, within the alternations of familiar patterns, Hardy's and Dickinson's heightened emotions, the depth of a father's drowning, and the strength of Pope's conviction about artful writing.

■ Attridge, *Rhythms*; Carper and Attridge.

T. CARPER

DEVOTIONAL POETRY. Although the distinction between religious poetry in general and devotional poetry in particular is never absolute, devotional poetry is often recognizable for its tendency to address a divinity, a sacred thing, or a religious figure. Poetic addresses with religious meaning constitute part of the sacred lit. of many religions, and they often influence later trads. in devotional poetry. Because of its reliance on poetic address, devotional poetry shows a close kinship with *lyric poetry, and it often uses an intimate, first-person voice. Yet this first person may stand for a community rather than an individual, and devotional poetry, esp. when sung or chanted, may serve liturgical functions. This article concentrates on devotional poetry in Hinduism, Judaism, Christianity, and Islam. In general and in this article, the term excludes polemical and homiletic poetry, as well as *epics and other long narrative forms, though these may include devotional forms and serve devotional purposes.

Much devotional poetry portrays the relation to the divine in terms of wonder and praise, but some concerns painful experiences of affliction, guilt, unfulfilled longing, estrangement, and doubt. Its most common forms are prayer, meditation, and *hymn; and its purposes include praise, supplication, *complaint, *lament, consolation, self-examination, and confession. How the divine is experienced and understood—whether as master, parent, lover, judge, king, confessor, creator, teacher, savior, or friend—often determines the poetic mode by which it is addressed, and this mode in turn determines the classes of thoughts and feelings that the poetry expresses.

Many devotional trads. employ a highly metaphorical lang. to describe experiences of the unseen. In general, such lang. reflects the representational challenge posed by devotional poetry's central concern with the relationship between human and divine, body and soul. Specific metaphors, esp. those drawn from erotic experience and from human governmental and disciplinary structures, suggest links between devotion and these areas of experience, though the significance of these links varies.

The Hindu devotional trad. begins with the *Rig Veda*, a collection of Sanskrit hymns, prayers, and supplications possibly dating to the 15th c. BCE. The *Rig Veda* is one of the four Vedas, the most sacred texts of the Hindu religion, and it is thought that its verses were recited by Vedic priests during ritual sacrifices. The most important influence on Indian devotional poetry since antiquity was the *Bhakti* movement, which began around the 6th c. CE in the Tamil-speaking south and spread through northern India over the next thousand years, enriching lit. in many langs. The movement emphasized inner experience over external forms, and universal access to God over control by a priestly hierarchy. Bhakti poet-saints incl. Kabīr (15th c.) and Sūrdās (16th c.) have influenced such mod. writers as Rabindranath Tagore and Robert Bly.

The Heb. Bible also contains important poetic texts, incl. the Song of Solomon, which trad. has taken to license the erotic expression of devotional feeling; the book of Job, an important source for later poetry of affliction; and, above all, the Psalms, which mix confession with praise, supplication with thanksgiving, and fear with love, sometimes in a tone of bold familiarity (see PSALMS). Later Heb. devotional poetry, such as that of Solomon Ibn Gabirol (ca.

1021–55) and Jehudah Halevi (ca. 1074–1141), the two greatest poets of the Heb. Golden Age in Spain, remains deeply biblical. Gabirol's *Keter Malkhut* (Kingly Crown) combines numerous themes of the Psalms: praise for God's attributes and the work of creation, the contrast between God's magnificence and the speaker's sin and insignificance, the hope of mercy, the recognition of God's wrath, and gratitude for God's goodness in saving the speaker.

Christian devotional poetry is also greatly indebted to biblical models such as the Psalms, esp. the seven penitential psalms, as well as to early Christian hymns such as those of Prudentius and Ambrose (both 4th c.). To the themes of the psalter, Christian poetry adds an emphasis on absolution and redemption through the Incarnation, Passion, and Resurrection of Jesus Christ; Roman Catholic poetry also meditates on the lives of the saints and the Virgin Mary. The doctrinal controversies and spiritual intensity of the Reformation and Counter-Reformation reinvigorated Christian verse. Biblical forms and themes mixed with new devotional practices and with courtly forms such as the *sonnet and the Ren. lyric to produce, in the vernacular lits. of Europe, many of Christian poetry's highest achievements. These include the stirring hymns of Martin Luther in Germany; the mystic journey of St. John of the Cross's *Noche oscura del alma* (*Dark Night of the Soul*) in Spain; the metrical psalters composed by Clément Marot and Théodore de Beza in France and by Philip Sidney and Mary Sidney in England; the spiritual sonnets and religious lyrics of John Donne, George Herbert, and many others in England; and the late metaphysical poetry of Edward Taylor's *Preparatory Meditations* in colonial New England. Victorian poets such as G. M. Hopkins also wrote distinguished devotional verse.

Although several verses in the Qur'an criticize poets (26:224–26), the following verse (26:227) allows for exceptions; and in the 9th and again in the 13th c., Sufi mystics developed an exceptional body of poetry expressing a personal, loving relationship to Allah. Thirteenth-c. Sufi poets include Ibn al-Arabī, Ibn al-Fāriḍ (both Arabic), and Rūmī (Persian), whose central theme is perhaps the power of divine love to transcend cultural and religious differences. Also important in Islam is the *qaṣīda*, or praise poem, which was adapted to express devotion to the Prophet Muhammad, typically celebrating his birth, attributes, exploits, and powers.

The most famous example is the "Qaṣīdat al-Burdah" (The Mantle) of the Egyptian Sufi poet al-Būṣīrī (ca. 1212–96), itself modeled on the 7th-c. poem of the same name said to have been presented to Muhammad by Ka'b ibn Zuhayr.

Devotional poetry has traditionally been one of the literary forms most available to women, and female poets have made important contributions to most of its trads. Rābi'ah al-'Adawīyah (d. 801) profoundly influenced the devel. of Sufi devotional poetry by introducing its emphasis on love and mystic union. Kāraikkāl Ammaiyār (6th c.), a devotee of Śiva, was an early Tamil *Bhakti* poet-saint. Mīrābāī (15th c.) remains one of the most beloved poet-saints of the later Bhakti trad.; her emphasis on Krishna's physical beauty and her desire to share his bridal bed with him raise questions about the gender of devotion. The Christian devotional revival of the 16th and 17th cs. drew notable contributions from St. Teresa of Ávila in Spain; Gabrielle de Coignard and Anne de Marquets in France; Sor Juana Inés de la Cruz in Mexico; and Aemilia Lanyer, An Collins, and Hester Pulter in England. Christina Rossetti is second in reputation only to Hopkins among practitioners of the Victorian devotional lyric. Emily Dickinson treats many devotional themes while tending more toward uncertainty than to the comforts of faith.

Dickinson anticipates an important trend in 20th-c. devotional poetry. Some poets have reacted to the modernist themes of the crisis of civilization and the death of God by amplifying the elements of complaint and doubt already present in many devotional trads. Wallace Stevens's "Sunday Morning," T. S. Eliot's *Four Quartets*, Anthony Hecht's "Rites and Ceremonies," and Louise Glück's *The Wild Iris* ask more questions than they answer, showing that devotional poetry can be written in the interrogative mood.

■ H. Brémond, *Prière et Poésie* (1926); L. Martz, *The Poetry of Meditation* (1954); W. T. Noon, *Poetry and Prayer* (1967); R. Woolf, *The English Religious Lyric in the Middle Ages* (1968); T. Cave, *Devotional Poetry in France, c. 1570–1613* (1969); B. K. Lewalski, *Protestant Poetics and the Seventeenth-Century Religious Lyric* (1979); G. B. Tennyson, *Victorian Devotional Poetry* (1981); A. Schimmel, *Mystical Poetry in Islam* (1982); R. Strier, *Love Known* (1983); R. Alter, *The Art of Biblical Poetry* (1985); P. S. Diehl, *The Medieval European Religious Lyric: An Ars Poetica* (1985); N. Cutler, *The Poetics of Tamil Devotion* (1987);

J. N. Wall, *Transformations of the Word: Spenser, Herbert, Vaughan* (1988); M. Schoenfeldt, *Prayer and Power* (1991); R. Rambuss, *Closet Devotions* (1998); R. Targoff, *Common Prayer: The Language of Public Devotion in Early Modern England* (2001); F. B. Brown et al., "Poetry," *The Encyclopedia of Religion*, ed. L. Jones, 2d ed. (2005); J. S. Hawley, *Three Bhakti Voices* (2005).

K.J.E. GRAHAM

DIALOGUE. Denotes an exchange of words between or among dramatized speakers in lit., whether or not their speeches are written with a view to theatrical representation. Dialogue has characterized writing for the stage at least since the first actor stepped out from a chorus, although there are also important uses of *monologue in the drama. In poetic as in theatrical dialogue, a responsive conversation expresses diverse viewpoints, which are thereby opened to possible change. The device allows a wider range of ideas, emotions, and perspectives than is readily available to a single voice and reliably generates dramatic conflict of a kind that a collection of discrepant monologues, such as Edgar Lee Masters's *Spoon River Anthology* or even Robert Browning's *The Ring and the Book*, does not. Monologues tacitly interrupted and poems in which one framing voice introduces another main voice are not legitimate examples of dialogue, which demands interactive response. Dialogue impels all forms in which it appears toward dramatic confrontation, even as it tends to favor the rhythms and nuances of speech.

The best known cl. examples are the Socratic dialogues of Plato, written in prose but apparently based on 5th-c. BCE dramatic mimes by Sophron and Epicharmus. Cl. authors included verse dialogue in satiric, *pastoral, and philosophical poems. Lucian modeled his prose *Dialogues of the Dead* on Plato but used the form primarily for satiric and comic purposes. Numerous satires of Horace became models of vivid colloquial exchange between poetic speakers. Virgil's *eclogues presented short pastoral dialogues in verse. Dialogue in poetry often remained purely literary, although it also encouraged recitation, as in formal philosophical disputation and such musical developments as the love duet, liturgical antiphony, and oratorio.

Verse dialogue flourished in the Middle Ages in debates and flyting. The dualistic philosophical temper of the age fostered dialogue, as in *The Owl and the Nightingale*. A typical subject was the debate between the soul and the body. Med. romances and allegories used dialogue in ways that raise a doubt as to whether they were solely for reading or were also meant to be staged. Many Asian poems fit this description as well. The 13th-c. *Roman de la Rose* employed multiple speakers for satiric and dramatic purposes, while the Fr. *débat* and *parlement* were forms of poetic contest that influenced the med. devel. of the drama, François Villon's dialogue between heart and body being a notable example. Popular ballads often included more than one speaker to heighten dramatic tension or suspense, as in "Lord Randall" and "Edward."

The Ren. revived specifically philosophical dialogue in verse, related to the devel. of prose dialogues by Thomas Elyot, Thomas More, and Roger Ascham. Torquato Tasso called the dialogue *imitazione di ragionamento* (imitation of reasoning), claiming that it reconciled drama and (its cognate and companion since Plato) dialectic. In the 16th and 17th cs., John Heywood's "Dialogue of Proverbs" and Margaret Cavendish's dialogue poems were effective examples of the form. Songs in question-and-answer format by Shakespeare and Philip Sidney emphasized the link between dialogue and the interrogative mode. Multiple voices in Edmund Spenser's *Shepheardes Calender* recalled the dialogue trad. of Virgil's *Eclogues*. Notable Ren. examples of dialogue poems include Samuel Daniel's "Ulysses and the Siren" and Andrew Marvell's "Dialogue between the Soul and the Body." Courtly masques (Ben Jonson, John Milton) prominently combined dialogue with music and lyrics, a combination that was also adapted for interludes within stage comedy and romance. Allegorical poems like John Dryden's *The Hind and the Panther* provided an occasion for dialogue, as did 18th-c. direct-speech poems like Alexander Pope's "Epilogue to the *Satires*." The adoption of multiple speakers in the Scots ballads of Robert Burns and the Dorset eclogues of William Barnes suggests some affinity between dialogue and dialect.

The romantic predilection for lyrical solo did not prevent the deployment of dialogue in poetic experiments by Lord Byron, John Keats, and esp. P. B. Shelley. Ger. and Scandinavian writers of songs and ballads made widespread use of the device. Victorian efforts to contextualize the romantic lyric chiefly took form in the dramatic monologue, but Alfred, Lord Tennyson; Browning; Matthew Arnold; and Thomas Hardy all used dialogue in poems as well as verse dramas. Revived interest in prose dialogue appears in Oscar Wilde and later, in France, in the dialogue experiments of Paul Valéry.

Twentieth-c. poetry exhibits further blurring of generic distinctions pertinent to this topic. "A Dialogue of Self and Soul" is only the clearest example of W. B. Yeats's frequent reliance on traditional verse dialogue. Writings by Samuel Beckett, Dylan Thomas, and Robert Frost suggest the role of poetic dialogue in a wider variety of dramatic and nondramatic forms. Polyphonic, juxtapositive, and commentatorial modes in T. S. Eliot and esp. Ezra Pound often read like dialogue by other means. Call-and-response conventions have revitalized dialogue in poetry from the Af. diaspora. Implied dialogue in lyrics by Geoffrey Hill and Ted Hughes objectifies the subject and produces heightened dramatic tension. In all these ways, as in the Victorian dramatization of the monologue, dialogue poems deemphasize the autonomy of the poetic word, stressing instead the conditional aspects of utterance. Dialogue thus retains an important place, even as traditional distinctions between verse and poetry, lit. and performance, are questioned and explored.

The historically recurrent overlap among dialogue, dialectics, and dialect finds its major mod. theorist in the Rus. critic Mikhail Bakhtin. Although Bakhtin's writings emphasize the novel, his analysis of the role of the "dialogic" has implications for understanding all literary meaning. On Bakhtin's showing, even ostensible monologues always harbor a conditioning dialogic element. This view implicitly decenters the authority often claimed for first-person lyric or poetic narrative. For Bakhtin, the unsaid, the partially said, and the equivocally said are as potentially meaningful as the clearly said; and these moreover, like all lang. uses, result from social forces, whose contending interplay it remains the privilege, and accordingly the ethical duty, of dialogue to play out.

■ E. Merrill, *The Dialogue in English Literature* (1911); E. R. Purpus, "The Dialogue in English Literature, 1660–1725," *ELH* 17 (1950); W. J. Ong, *Ramus, Method, and the Decay of Dialogue* (1958); F. M. Keener, *English Dialogues of the Dead* (1973); J. Mukarovskij, *The Word and Verbal Art*, trans. and ed. J. Burbank and T. Steiner (1977), ch. 2; M. E. Brown, *Double Lyric* (1980); D. Marsh, *The Quattrocento Dialogue* (1980); M. M. Bakhtin, *The Dialogic Imagination*, ed. M. Holquist, trans. C. Emerson and

M. Holquist (1981); A. K. Kennedy, *Dramatic Dialogue* (1983); T. Todorov and M. M. Bakhtin, *The Dialogical Principle*, trans. W. Godzich (1984); *Bakhtin*, ed. G. S. Morson (1986); J. R. Snyder, *Writing the Scene of Speaking* (1989); *The Interpretation of Dialogue*, ed. T. Maranhão (1989); G. S. Morson and C. Emerson, *Mikhail Bakhtin* (1990); D. H. Bialostosky, *Wordsworth, Dialogics, and the Practice of Criticism* (1992); M. S. Macovski, *Dialogue and Literature* (1992); M. Eskin, *Ethics and Dialogue* (2000); K. Njogu, *Reading Poetry as Dialogue* (2004).

B. A. NICHOLS; H. F. TUCKER

DICTION. Diction signifies the words or phrases chosen for a piece of writing. It is the Latinate equivalent of Gr. *lexis*, which was accepted as Eng. usage by the *OED* in the second ed. (first citations in 1950 [citing *MP*]; Frye [1957]). *Lexis* is a more useful term than *diction* because more neutral, but it is still chiefly used in ling. (*OED*, sense 1.2), not in poetics. It is important to distinguish "the diction of poetry" from "poetic diction" (esp. in the 18th-c. sense). "Poetic diction" or even just "diction" may elicit only the question of unusual lang. rather than questions concerning all the lang. of poetry.

The primary rule for thinking about diction is that words in a poem always exist in relation, never in isolation: "there are no bad words or good words; there are only words in bad or good places" (Nowottny). Otherwise, classifying diction can be a barren exercise, just as concentrating on isolated words can be barren for a beginning poet. Consistency within the chosen area of diction is necessary for a well-made poem, and consistency is not always easy to achieve. Listening for a poem's range of diction enables the reader to hear moves outside that range. Great skill in diction implies that a poet knows words as he or she knows people (Hollander 1988), knows how "words have a stubborn life of their own" (Elton), and knows that words need to be "at home" (Eliot, *Little Gidding*, the best mod. poetic description of diction "that is right").

Some useful categories for studying diction may be drawn from the *OED*'s introductory matter (now also online), where vocabulary may be examined as follows: (1) *identification*, incl. usual spelling, pronunciation, grammatical part of speech, whether specialized, and status (e.g., rare, obsolete, archaic, colloquial, dialectal); (2) *etymology*, incl. subsequent word formation and cognates in other langs.; (3)

signification, which builds on other dictionaries and on quotations; and (4) *illustrative quotations*, which show forms and uses, particular senses, earliest use (or, for obsolete words, latest use), and connotations. Studies of diction might test these categories for any given poem. In common usage, *meaning* refers to definition under category (3), but *meaning* as defined by the *OED* incl. all four categories. And *meaning* in poetry, fully defined, includes all functions of a word.

Diction includes all parts of speech, not simply nouns, adjectives, and verbs. Emphasis on what is striking tends to isolate main parts of speech and imposes a dubious standard of vividness. Even articles matter (cf. Walt Whitman and E. M. Forster on passages to India). Verb forms matter (see Merrill, 21, on first-person present active indicative). Prepositions can have metaphorical force or double possibilities (e.g., "of," a favorite device of Wallace Stevens; see Hollander 1997). The grammatical structures of different langs. offer other possibilities for plurisignation and ambiguity (see SYNTAX, POETIC).

Discussions of diction often pull more toward polemics than poetics. It may be impossible to separate the two, but the effort is essential (Nowottny is exemplary). S. T. Coleridge's dictum should be remembered: every great and original author "has had the task of creating the taste by which he is to be enjoyed" (cited by Wordsworth 1815), a task that perforce includes polemics. Thus, T. S. Eliot's attacks on the Keats–Tennyson line of diction, esp. as developed by A. C. Swinburne, are better read generically in terms of charm and *riddle, as Frye does (1976). Similarly, it is important not to read mod. assumptions about diction back into older poetry. (See Strang, on reading Edmund Spenser's work in Spenser's lang., not "as if he were writing mod. Eng. with intermittent lapses into strange expressions.") Critics need to pay attention to historical scholarship on the contemporaneity or archaism of words—often difficult to assess.

There are only a few general questions concerning diction, and they have remained for centuries. The most fruitful may be the more particular ones. One long-standing general issue is whether a special diction for poetry exists or should exist. This, in turn, depends on how poetry is defined or what type of poetry is in question. Of discussions in antiquity, those by Aristotle, Dionysius of Halicarnassus,

Horace, and Longinus are the most important. Aristotle's few remarks remain pertinent: poetic diction should be both clear and striking: "ordinary words" give clarity; "strange words, metaphors" should be judiciously used to give surprising effects, to make diction shine and to avoid diction that is inappropriately "mean." In the Middle Ages and early Ren., the issue of diction became important as med. Lat. gave way to the vernaculars. Dante's *De vulgari eloquentia* (*On Vernacular Eloquence*, ca. 1304) is the central text in the *questione della lingua*. Dante classifies diction according to various contexts. E.g., in *DVE* 2.7, he gives detailed criteria for words suitable for "the highest style." Some are as specific as in Paul Valéry's well-known search for "a word that is feminine, disyllabic, includes P or F, ends in a mute syllable, and is a synonym for break or disintegration, and not learned, not rare. Six conditions—at least!" (Nowottny). Dante sees that the main question, as so often, is appropriateness or *decorum. He also stresses appropriateness for the person using a given lexis (e.g., sufficient natural talent, art, and learning), a criterion largely unfamiliar today.

The term *poetic diction* is strongly associated with 18th-c. poetry, largely because of William Wordsworth's attacks on it in the Preface to *Lyrical Ballads*. Wordsworth notes that *Lyrical Ballads* includes "little of what is usually called poetic diction," by which he means the *epithets, *periphrases, *personifications, archaisms, and other conventionalized phrases too often used unthinkingly in Augustan poetry. As against Thomas Gray, e.g., who wrote that "the language of the age is never the language of poetry" (letter to R. West, April 1742), Wordsworth advocated using the "real language of men," esp. those in humble circumstances and rustic life. But Wordsworth laid down many conditions governing such "real language" in poetry (e.g., men "in a state of vivid sensation," the lang. adapted and purified, a selection only).

Coleridge (1817), with his superior critical mind, saw that "the language of real life" was an "equivocal expression" applying only to some poetry, and there in ways never denied (chs. 14–22). He rejected the argument of rusticity, asserting that the lang. of Wordsworth's rustics derives from a strong grounding in the lang. of the Eng. Bible (authorized version, 1611) and the liturgy or hymn-book. In any case, the best part of lang., says Coleridge, is derived not from objects but from "reflection on the acts of the mind itself." By "real,"

Wordsworth actually means "ordinary" lang., the *lingua communis* (cf. *OED*, Pref., 2d ed.), and even this needs cultivation to become truly *communis* (Coleridge cites Dante). Wordsworth's real object, Coleridge saw, was to attack assumptions about a supposedly necessary poetic diction. The debate is of great importance for diction. It marks the shift from what Frye calls a high mimetic mode to a low mimetic one, a shift still governing the diction of poetry today. (In Fr. poetry, the shift comes a little later and is associated with Victor Hugo [Preface to *Cromwell*, 1827].)

Coleridge disagreed with Wordsworth's contention that "there neither is, nor can be any *essential* difference between the lang. of prose and metrical composition." Though there is a "neutral style" common to prose and poetry, Coleridge finds it notable that such a theory "should have proceeded from a poet, whose diction, next to that of Shakespeare and Milton, appears to me of all others the most *individualized* and characteristic." Some words in a poem may well be in everyday use; but "are those words *in those places* commonly employed in real life to express the same thought or outward thing? . . . No! nor are the modes of connections; and still less the breaks and transitions" (ch. 20). In Coleridge's modification of Wordsworth's well-intentioned arguments, readers may still find essential principles applicable to questions of poetic diction.

The 20th c., in one sense, took up Wordsworth's argument, steadily removing virtually every restriction on diction. The 21st c. now generally bars no word whatever from the diction of poetry, at least in the Germanic and Romance langs. Struggles over appropriate diction in the 19th c. included attacks on the romantics, Robert Browning, and Whitman. Attempts by Robert Bridges and others to domesticate G. M. Hopkins's extraordinary diction are well known. In the early 20th c., Edwardian critics with genteel notions of poetry objected to Rupert Brooke's writing about seasickness and to Wilfred Owen's disgust at the horrors of World War I (Stead). Wordsworth's "real language of men" was twisted by some into attacks on any unusual diction whatsoever—difficult, local, learned—a problem to this day, though now less from genteel notions than egalitarian ones inappropriately extended to the diction of all poetry. Yet the diction of poetry may still be associated with the lang. of a certain class—see Tony Harrison's poems playing standard Eng.

against working-class Eng. But if poetry now generally admits all types of diction, it remains true that the diction of poetry—of the Bible, Shakespeare, and the ballads, e.g.—needs to be learned. Otherwise, most older poetry, as well as much contemp., cannot be well read at all (Vendler). The diction of the authorized version of the Bible and of the Gr. and Lat. classics has influenced Eng. poetry for centuries. Virgil's diction in *eclogue, *georgic, and *epic was admired and imitated well past the Ren. The strategies and effects of allusion should not be overlooked.

Historical changes in the lang. make the use of good dictionaries mandatory. In Eng., the OED is the most generous and its quotations invaluable, but other dictionaries are also needed (e.g., of U.S. Eng., for etymology). The elementary philological categories of widening and narrowing and raising and lowering in meaning are useful. (Cf. wanton, where solely mod. senses must not be applied to John Milton's use, or even as late as Bridges's "Wanton with long delay the gay spring leaping cometh" ["April, 1885"]; gay is well known.) Hidden semantic and connotative changes must be esp. watched, along with favorite words in a given time (Miles). The diction of some mod. poets pays attention to historical ling., while that of others is largely synchronic; readers should test.

Etymologies are stories of origins. The etymologist cares whether they are true or false, but a poet need not (Ruthven); mythologies are for the poet as useful as hists. Philology may include certain assumptions about poetic diction (see Barfield against Max Müller). Etymologies may include hists. of war and struggle (for nationalism involves lang. just as class does). Poets may exploit the riches of etymology (see Geoffrey Hill's Mystery of the Charity of Charles Péguy on Eng. and Fr. diction). Etymology may function as a "mode of thought" (Curtius) or as a specific "frame for trope" (see Hollander 1988, on Hopkins) or both. Invented or implied etymologies can also be useful (silva through Dante's well-known selva links by sound and sense with salveo, salvatio, etc.). Milton plays earlier etymological meaning against later meaning, such play functioning as a trope for the fallen state of lang. (Cook). Eng. is unusually accommodating, combining as it does both Latinate and Germanic words. Other important word roots should also be noted (cf.

the etymological appropriateness of sherbet in Eliot's "Journey of the Magi").

Diction may be considered along an axis of old to new, with archaism at one end and innovation (incl. neologism) at the other. Archaism may be introduced to enlarge the diction of poetry, sometimes through native terms (Spenser, Hopkins). Or it may be used for certain genres (e.g., literary imitations of oral ballads) or for specific effects, ironic, allusive, or other. Innovation may remain peculiar to one poet or may enlarge the poetic lexicon. Neologisms (new-coined words) tend now to be associated with novelty more than freshness and sometimes with strained effects. The very word indicates they are not common currency. Some periods are conducive to expanding diction in general (the mid-14th c., the late 16th c.) or to expanding diction in some areas (the lang. of digital technology, nowadays, though not yet in general poetic diction). Where poets do not invent or resuscitate terms, they draw on vocabulary from different contemporaneous sources (see the OED categories). Foreign, local, and dialectal words, as well as slang, are noted below. The precision of terms drawn from such areas as theology, philosophy, or the Bible must not be underestimated, for controversy can center on one word. Studies working outward from single words (e.g. Empson; Lewis; Barfield on ruin) are valuable reminders of historical and conceptual significance in diction.

Shakespeare has contributed most to the enlargement of our stock of words; critics regularly note how often he provides the first example of a given word in the OED. He adapts words from the stock of both Eng. (e.g., lonely, presumably from Sidney's loneliness) and other langs. (monumental, from Lat.); he apparently invents words (bump); he shifts their grammatical function (control as a verb rather than a noun), and more. He possesses the largest known vocabulary of any poet, but it is his extraordinary use of so large a word hoard (as against ordinary recognition) that is so remarkable.

Most new words are now generally drawn from scientific or technical sources, though poetry makes comparatively little use of them. In the 18th c., poets could say that "Newton demands the Muse" (see M. H. Nicholson's title), but poets today do not generally say that "Einstein demands the Muse." A. R. Ammons is one of the few mod. poets exploiting the possibilities of new scientific diction: e.g., zygote

(1891, *OED*) rhymed with *goat*; *white dwarf* (1924, *OED* 2d ed.); and *black hole* (1969). Of the large stock of colloquial and slang expressions, many are evanescent or inert, though special uses may be effective. Shakespeare's gift for introducing colloquial diction is a salutary reminder not to reject colloquialisms per se. Or see Stevens (*Shucks, Pfft* in "Add This to Rhetoric") or Merrill (*slush* [funds] in "Snow Jobs"). The same may be said of slang, a vernacular speech below colloquial on a three-part scale of (1) standard or formal Eng., (2) colloquial Eng., and (3) slang. (See *The New Partridge Dictionary of Slang and Unconventional English*, 8th ed. rev. [2006].) Slang may come from the lingo of specialized trades or professions, schools, sports, etc., and may move up through colloquial to standard Eng. It appears more often in prose than in poetry. But poetry can make effective use of it from François Villon's underworld slang of the 15th c. to T. S. Eliot's *demobbed* in *The Waste Land*. For a brief telling discussion of the question, see George Eliot, *Middlemarch*, ch. 11.

Along the axis of old to new, the most interesting question is why and how some diction begins to sound dated. Archaisms and innovations alike are easy to hear. So also is the diction we designate as, say, 18th-c. or Tennysonian or Whitmanian. But what is it that distinguishes the poetic diction of a generation ago, and why do amateur poets tend to use the diction of their poetic grandparents? The aging of words or the passing of their claim on our allegiance is of continuing interest to poets as part of the diachronic aspect of their art.

Different types of poetry require different lexical practice, though such requirements vary according to time and place. Oral poetry makes use of stock phrases or epithets cast into formulas. Some of Homer's epithets became renowned, e.g., *poluphloisbos* (loud-roaring) for the sea (see Amy Clampitt's echo of this). Compound epithets in OE poetry are known by the ON term *kenning and sometimes take the form of a riddle. Different genres also require different practice (Fowler), a requirement much relaxed today. Epic required a high-style diction, as did the *sublime (see Monk). Genres of the middle and low style drew from a different register. *Satire usually works in the middle style but allows much leeway, esp. in Juvenalian as against Horatian satire. Any diction may become banal—e.g., that of the 16th-c. sonneteers or that of some *pastoral writers

(cf. Coleridge, *Letters*, 9 Oct. 1794: "The word 'swain' . . . conveys too much of the Cant of Pastoral"). Connotation or association is governed partly by genre and is all-important for diction.

Diction also depends partly on place. The largest division in Eng. is between Great Britain and the U.S., but poetry from elsewhere (Africa, Asia, Australasia, Canada, the Caribbean, Ireland) also shows important differences. Establishing a distinctive poetic style in a new country with an old lang. presents peculiar problems that novelty in itself will not solve. Within a country, diction will vary locally, and poets can make memorable uses of local terms (Yeats of *perne* in "Sailing to Byzantium," Eliot of *rote* in *The Dry Salvages*; Whitman uses native Amerindian terms). The question of dialect shades into this. Robert Burns and Thomas Hardy draw on local and dialectal words. Hopkins's remarkable diction derives from current lang., dialectal and other, as well as older words; some (e.g., *pitch*) have specific usage for Hopkins (see Milroy). The use of Af. Am. vernacular Eng. is familiar (Paul Laurence Dunbar, Langston Hughes, James Weldon Johnson); Derek Walcott includes the Creole of St. Lucia. Foreign diction or xenoglossia, a special case, works along a scale of assimilation, for standard diction includes many words originally considered foreign. Considerable use of foreign diction (apart from novelties like macaronic verse) implies a special contract with the reader, at least in societies unaccustomed to hearing more than one lang. Diction may also vary according to class (see above). It is doubtful if it varies in a general way according to gender.

Interpretive categories are numerous, and readers should be aware of them as such; even taxonomies are interpretive. Beyond the categories already mentioned, diction may be judged according to the degree of "smoothness" (Tennyson as against Browning is a standard example; see Frye 1957), centering on the large and important question of sound in lexis (cf. Seamus Heaney on W. H. Auden: "the gnomic clunk of Anglo-Saxon phrasing . . ." [*The Government of the Tongue* (1989), 124]). Or diction may be judged by the degree of difficulty (Browning, Hopkins, Eliot, Stevens), though once-difficult diction can become familiar. Strangeness in diction can contribute to the strangeness sometimes thought necessary for aesthetic effect (Barfield) or for poetry itself (Genette, arguing with Jean Cohen, also compares the *ostranenie* [defamiliarization] of the Rus. formalists and the lang. of a state of dreaming). Some poets are known for difficult or strange diction (e.g., Spenser, the metaphysical poets, Whitman, Browning), but readers should also note consummate skill in quieter effects of diction (e.g., Robert Frost, Philip Larkin, Elizabeth Bishop).

Distinctive diction is part of what makes a poet familiar, and the diction of a poet may be studied in itself (see Fowler). The discipline of the art of diction is still best understood by studying the comments and revisions of good poets.

■ **General Studies:** W. Wordsworth, "Preface, *Lyrical Ballads*, 3d ed. (1802), incl. "Appendix on . . . Poetic Diction"; and Wordsworth, "Essay, Supplementary to the Preface" (1815); S. T. Coleridge, *Biographia Literaria* (1817); Aristotle, *Poetics*, trans. I. Bywater (1909); O. Elton, "The Poet's Dictionary," *E&S* 14 (1929); W. Empson, *The Structure of Complex Words* (1951); D. Davie, *Purity of Diction in English Verse* (1952); Curtius; Frye; C. S. Lewis, *Studies in Words* (1960); W. Nowottny, *The Language Poets Use* (1962)—essential reading; J. Miles, *Eras and Modes in English Poetry*, 2d ed. (1964); K. K. Ruthven, "The Poet as Etymologist," *CQ* 11 (1969); O. Barfield, *Poetic Diction*, 3d ed. (1973)—important reading; F. W. Bateson, *English Poetry and the English Language*, 3d ed. (1973); A. Sherbo, *English Poetic Diction from Chaucer to Wordsworth* (1975); N. Frye, "Charms and Riddles," *Spiritus Mundi* (1976); Fowler—excellent on diction and genre; G. Genette, *Figures of Literary Discourse* (trans. 1982), esp. 75–102; J. Merrill, *Recitative: Prose* (1986); J. Boase-Beier, *Poetic Compounds* (1987); C. Ricks, *The Force of Poetry* (1987); A. Ferry, *The Art of Naming* (1988); J. Hollander, *Melodious Guile* (1988); H. Vendler, *The Music of What Happens* (1988); S. Adamson, "Literary Language," *CHEL* (1992), v. 3, 539–653; v. 4, 589–692; J. Hollander, *The Work of Poetry* (1997).
■ **Specialized Studies:** S. H. Monk, *The Sublime* (1935); V. L. Rubel, *Poetic Diction in the English Renaissance* (1941); J. Arthos, *The Language of Natural Description in 18th-Century Poetry* (1949); M. M. Mahood, *Shakespeare's Wordplay* (1957); Wimsatt and Brooks, ch. 16; A. Ewert, "Dante's Theory of Diction," *MHRA* 31 (1959); C. K. Stead, *The New Poetic* (1964); G. Tillotson, *Augustan Poetic Diction* (1964); W.J.B. Owen, *Wordsworth as Critic* (1969); H. Kenner, *The Pound Era* (1971), esp. 94–191;

D. Alighieri, *Literary Criticism of Dante Alighieri*, ed. and trans. R. S. Haller (1973); J. Milroy, *The Language of G. M. Hopkins* (1977); N. Hilton, *Literal Imagination: Blake's Vision of Words* (1983); M. H. Abrams, "Wordsworth and Coleridge on Diction and Figures," *The Correspondent Breeze* (1984); R.W.V. Elliott, *Thomas Hardy's English* (1984); C. Ricks, *T. S. Eliot and Prejudice* (1988); R.O.A.M. Lyne, *Words and the Poet* (1989)—Virgil; B.M.H. Strang, "Language," *Spenser Encyclopedia*, ed. A. C. Hamilton et al. (1990); E. Cook, *Against Coercion: Games Poets Play* (1998); C. Miller, *The Invention of Evening* (2006).

E. Cook

DIMETER (Gr., "of two measures"). A line consisting of two measures. In classical prosody, the metron in *iambic, *trochaic, and *anapestic verse is a dipody (pair of feet); hence, the cl. iambic dimeter contains two metra or four feet. But in mod. prosodies, the concept of the metron was never established: here *-meter* is synonymous with foot. The Eng. iambic dimeter, therefore, consists of two feet, the trimeter of three feet, etc. This terminology applies only to *accentual-syllabic verse, which is regular: *accentual verse—e.g., a line of two stresses but a variable number of syllables—is not, properly speaking, a dimeter. Short-lined verse in Eng., such as the *Skeltonic, is rarely regular enough to be called dimeter, though dimeter lines feature in the Burns stanza and the *limerick. More regular examples do occur, particularly in the 16th- and 17th-c. lyric, e.g., Michael Drayton's "An Amouret Anacreontic" and Robert Herrick's "To a Lark." More recent approximations include W. H. Auden's "This Lunar Beauty" and Donald Justice's "Dreams of Water."

T.V.F. Brogan; J. M. Cocola

DOZENS. A game of exchanging, in contest form, ritualized verbal insults, which are usually in rhymed *couplets and often profane. The term is probably a literate corruption of the vernacular *doesn'ts*, relating to forbidden lang. activity. The game is practiced now mostly among adolescent Af. Am. males, though its origin is thought to lie in the verbal insult contests of West Africa. The dozens is a subcategory of *signifying. Sometimes referred to as *woofing, sounding, cutting, capping,* or *chopping,* the ritual is most often called *playing the dozens.* The subjects of the insults are frequently the relatives of the verbal opponent, esp. his mother, and the insults are frequently sexual. A mildly phrased example of the dozens technique and style would be "I don't play the dozens, the dozens ain't my game, / But the way I loved your mama is a crying shame."

The players of the dozens must display great skill with *rhyme, wit, and *rhythm to win the approval of their audience. The dozens is partly an initiation ritual that teaches a player how to hold his equilibrium by learning to master the power of words and humor. The exchange takes place as a verbal duel in which words and humor are chosen to sting, so that the opponent will be goaded to either greater lexical creativity or defeat. Langston Hughes draws on the trad. of the dozens, particularly in his long poetic work *Ask Your Mama* (1961), as do Richard Wright and Ralph Ellison. Several genres of popular music, most recently hip-hop, have maintained the visibility of the dozens in mass culture.

See INVECTIVE.

■ R. D. Abrahams, *Deep Down in the Jungle* (1970); *Rappin' and Stylin' Out*, ed. T. Kochman (1972); W. Labov, *Language in the Inner City* (1972); L. W. Levine, *Black Culture and Black Consciousness* (1977); G. Smitherman, *Talkin and Testifyin* (1977); H. L. Gates Jr., *The Signifying Monkey* (1988); M. Morgan, "The Africanness of Counterlanguage among Afro-Americans," *Africanisms in Afro-American Language Varieties*, ed. S. Mufwene (1993); J. R. Rickford and R. J. Rickford, *Spoken Soul* (2000); E. Wald, *The Dozens* (2012).

E. A. PETERS

DRAMATIC MONOLOGUE. *See* MONOLOGUE.

DRAMATIC POETRY

I. Definition
II. Dramatic Poetry and Drama in Verse
III. Dramatic Poetry and Performance Theory
IV. Dramatic Poetry in the Theater

I. Definition. Dramatic poetry is at best an intrinsically contestable critical category and at worst a violent oxymoron, sparking the theoretical and historical friction between performance and poetry, theater and writing, action and lang. For Aristotle, drama is one kind of *poesis*, but within his analysis of drama, lang.—the verbal, *poetic* dimension of plays—is subordinate to plot, character, and thought. In the context of the *Poetics*, this hierarchy makes sense because dramatic *mimesis is composed

not of words but of deeds (the "imitation of action"). Dramatic poetry implies that words are defined in relation to the work of the theater's other instruments of mimesis—the temporal structure of the event, its plot; the practices of acting and the projection of character, or *ethos*; the design of music and spectacle—principally conveyed not by lang. but by actors, "with all the people engaged in the *mimesis* actually doing things" (*Poetics* 1448a). Nonetheless, drama has a persistent association with formally inventive lang., from the range of verse forms encompassed by tragedy and comedy in Aristotle's era to the verbal richness of much contemp. drama, even when that drama is written in prose. Cohn pointed out in the previous ed., "Western critics have interpreted the phrase dramatic poetry in three main ways: (1) lyrics or short poems that imply a scene; (2) plays that are valorized with the adjective 'poetic'; and (3) dramas whose dialogue is calculatingly rhythmed—in rhythms that are often regularized into meters and that are usually presented as discrete lines on the page." As Cohn recognized, resigned to treat dramatic poetry as synonymous with "verse drama," these definitions are inadequate. The first embraces lyric poems written from the perspective of individual characters and so understands *drama*—as a mode of cultural production involving *performance as well as scripted lang.—in metaphorical terms: for all their "drama," Robert Browning's "My Last Duchess" or T. S. Eliot's "The Love Song of J. Alfred Prufrock" are not conceived for embodied mimesis. The second turns the word *poetic* into a term of approbation, without critical purchase on the function or purpose of lang. in performance. The third—verse drama—segregates a class of drama according to the accidents of culture and hist.: emphasizing the use of verse rather than the distinctive contribution that verbal design makes to the conception of dramatic action. Although verse has had a complex impact on drama and its performance, "dramatic poetry" points toward a more searching problem, having to do with the functioning of writing in the making of drama, a form of *poiēsis* extending beyond words, in which—to recall Austin's discussion of *performative* speech—scripted words are expected to *do things* well beyond what the words themselves *say*. More than verse drama, dramatic poetry is a term of theoretical inquiry, pointing to the troubled interface where writing meets performance in the definition of drama.

II. Dramatic Poetry and Drama in Verse. Dramatic writing has a longstanding historical connection with verse. The reciprocity between drama and ritual is often marked in the ceremonial character of dramatic performances staged in connection with religious or civic events or with the formalities of an aristocratic court reflected by patterned and often elevated lang. In Eur. drama, the lineage of scripted dramatic performance originates in the 6th- and 5th-c. BCE Gr. civic festivals sponsoring competitions in the performance of dithyrambs (large choruses of men or boys), tragedy (a trilogy of three tragedies composed by a single playwright, followed by a satyr play), and eventually comedy; the major festival, which sponsored the plays of the surviving dramatists Aeschylus, Sophocles, Euripides, and Aristophanes, was the Athenian City Dionysia, held annually in March–April. Cl. Gr. tragedy used a variety of verse meters for the chorus, while individual roles (like the chorus, all played by men) were assigned iambic trimeter and developed a characteristic structure: a *prologue*, in which a single character—the Watchman in Aeschylus's *Agamemnon*, Dionysus in Euripides' *Bacchae*—opens the play; the *parodos*, or singing/dancing entrance of the chorus; a series of *episodes* in *dialogue between individual characters, punctuated by choral *odes*, with their characteristic verbal (and, logically, physical) movements of *strophe, *antistrophe, and *epode; and, after the stunning *catastrophe*, the *exodos* of the chorus. In comedy, Aristophanes deployed a wider range of metrical forms both for choruses and for individual speeches. Roman drama, initially based on Gr. models, was first performed in the 3d c. BCE and quickly developed its own formal and thematic identity; the verse meter of Plautus's comedies was generally based on the trochaic septenarius, though with considerable latitude, while Terence consistently favored the iambic senarius and Seneca scrupulously employed the iambic trimeter.

The decline of the Roman Empire brought the decline of its institutions, incl. theater; while popular performance surely persisted, formal, written drama emerges—uneasily—as an instrument of the Church, in the versified *tropes that minimally illustrated and enacted portions of the Roman Catholic Mass, beginning in the 9th or 10th c. CE. The Lat. tropes were very occasionally adapted into vernacular langs.—as in the 12th-c. Anglo-Norman *Jeu d'Adam*—but the energetic vernacular drama of 14th- and 15th-c. Europe was also typically based on religious themes, either in the scriptural narratives of the great Corpus Christi cycles or the theological debate of the morality plays, and developed indigenous verse forms as well. Though the verse of the anonymous Wakefield Master, involving the deft balance of assonance and rhyme in a complex nine-line stanza form, is best known, the Eng. cycles (Wakefield, York, Chester, and N-Town) generally make fine use of the metrical trads. and alliterative verse of the period, echoed in the surprisingly fluid use of a basic octosyllabic line in the 15th-c. Fr. farce *Master Pathelin*.

In Europe, then, verse plays an important role at the origin and devel. of dramatic writing from Athenian tragedy through both the Lat. and vernacular forms of med. drama to the two principal venues of dramatic performance in the early mod. period: the commercial public theater and the more stylized theater of the aristocratic courts. Verse coordinates with elevated subject matter and the elite social world of a specific audience in other early dramatic trads., linking aesthetic to social functions in cl. Sanskrit drama and in the Nō theater of the med. Japanese court, much as in the Stuart court masque and the neoclassical Fr. drama of the 17th c. In some theatrical genres, however, the elaborate verbal script is held apart from the sphere of enactment. In the South Asian dance drama *Kathakali*, the performers are accompanied by song and narration, but they do not speak themselves; in the *Ramlila*—a ten-day enactment of Ram's battle with Ravan in the *Rāmāyaṇa*—the actors improvise their performance, coordinating it with the simultaneous recitation of the Hindu epic.

The pervasive devel. of two institutions—print publishing and the secular commercial theater—redefined the practices of dramatic writing and performance in 16th- and 17th-c. Europe. Though most of the printed drama in the period was propelled by the theater's need for new material, a developing notion of "lit." as a distinct, valuable genre of writing coordinated with the perception of dramatic poetry's signifying a special class of drama, in which an elaborate verbal structure has a value independent from its utility in instigating or sustaining stage performance. And yet, segregating the complexities of dramatic composition in verse from the intricacies of dramatic writing in prose miscasts the literary and theatrical hist. of Western drama. Many of the early mod. masters of dramatic verse—Shakespeare and Ben Jonson among them—were masters of dramatic prose and masters of stagecraft as well, shaping verse or prose and various dramatic genres to meet the demand of specific theaters and their audiences. A richly pointed prose sustains the hist. of comic drama, from Niccolò Machiavelli's satiric *Mandragola* (1518) through Jonson's *Bartholomew Fair* (1614) to the plays of William Wycherley, George Etherege, William Congreve, George Farquhar, Oliver Goldsmith, and R. B. Sheridan in the 17th and 18th cs.; and to mods. like Oscar Wilde, G. B. Shaw, and Tom Stoppard, much as comedy from Shakespeare to Molière to Caryl Churchill has also been written in a fluent and supple verse.

Verse is undeniably associated with social class in Eur. drama, the privileged mode of courtly works like the masque and the plays of Fr. neoclassicism; it is also associated with aristocratic characters in the plays of the early mod. Eng. commercial theater and sustains related notions of dramatic *decorum. In his *Defence of Poesy* (written ca. 1580, pub. 1595), Philip Sidney complains about the mingling of verse and prose, which implies a "mongrel" blending of tragedy and comedy; and Félix Lope de Vega's *El arte nuevo de hacer comedias* (1609) similarly encourages Sp. poets to avoid blending high and low subjects, suggesting different verse forms as appropriate to different events: décimas for complaints, *sonnets for those waiting in expectation, *tercets for serious matters, and redondillas for love. Expanding Lope's principles, a typical role in one of Pedro Calderón de la Barca's plays moves through a range of verse forms, each appropriate to the ethical and dramatic situation of the moment. Rather than multiplying verse forms, 17th-c. Fr. theater relies on the poet's mastery of the *alexandrine couplet, the vehicle of heroic clamor in Pierre Corneille, of balanced wit in Molière, and of probing ethical dilemma in Jean Racine, while Eng.-lang. verse drama typically relies on the more fluid informality of *blank verse.

The association between verse and high, serious, "tragic" drama in early mod. Europe is a matter of convention, regardless of whether writers like Christopher Marlowe, Shakespeare, Jonson, or Racine considered themselves part of a "poetic" heritage. The rising prestige of Shakespeare as a poet in the later 18th and 19th cs., alongside the democratization of literacy and lit., lends dramatic poetry its mod. inflection, the sense that the value of a play's

verbal composition, its *poetry*, is independent of its functioning in theatrical representation. The great Eur. poets of the romantic period succeeded in some measure in writing a theatrically ambitious verse drama, notably G. E. Lessing's *Nathan der Weise* (1779), Friedrich Schiller's *Maria Stuart* (1800), Heinrich von Kleist's durable comedy *The Broken Jug* (1808) and his scarifying tragedy *Penthesilea* (1808), S. T. Coleridge's *Remorse* (1813), Lord Byron's *Manfred* (1819), P. B. Shelley's *The Cenci* (1819, staged at the Théâtre Alfred Jarry by Antonin Artaud in 1935), Alexander Pushkin's *Boris Godunov* (1825), Alfred de Musset's *Lorenzaccio* (1834), Robert Browning's *A Blot in the 'Scutcheon* (1843), and Alfred, Lord Tennyson's *Becket* (1895).

In 1881, Émile Zola called for poets to recognize "that poetry is everywhere, in everything": poetic lang. appeared, by the late 19th c., incapable of addressing the dramatic situations of mod. life. After a brilliant and theatrically successful career as a verse dramatist culminating in *Brand* (1866) and *Peer Gynt* (1867), Henrik Ibsen, e.g., decided to address a broader contemp. audience about mod. social life with plays written in prose. And yet, while some contemporaries complained about the unpoetic superficiality of Ibsen's lang., his prose—rigorously impoverished of decoration—enables the slightest nuance to gain richly "poetic" depth: the icy, black water of Nora's imagined suicide, Hedda's "vine leaves in his hair," the secret demons of will and desire that flay Solness's flesh. Indeed, the attraction of verse remained strong: Ibsen's great rival August Strindberg wrote and verse dramas throughout his career, as did other playwrights now sometimes remembered for their naturalistic plays, such as Gerhart Hauptmann. Maurice Maeterlinck wrote symbolic dramas in an image-laden prose; and, without resorting directly to verse, Frank Wedekind frequently experimented with lang. in ways that resisted a strict division between naturalistic prose and more evocative poetry.

Foregrounding the artifice of the play's verbal dimension, mod. verse drama resists the subordination of its lang. to the representational "surface" characteristic of naturalism's attention to everyday life. For this reason, in the 20th c. dramatic poetry becomes increasingly cognate with a deeply antitheatrical impulse visible in the work of a range of playwrights largely continuing the trad. linking verse to elevated subject matter and philosophical introspection:

Edmond Rostand's durable *Cyrano de Bergerac* (1897) and the plays of Stephen Phillips, Maxwell Anderson, Christopher Fry, and Paul Claudel, among many others. Dramatic poetry, though, also provided an alternative means of using lang. to impel the potential innovation of theatrical experience; here, the varied use of verse and prose in the plays of W. B. Yeats, Eliot, W. H. Auden, and Auden's collaborations with Christopher Isherwood, as well as the more experimental work of Gertrude Stein and Samuel Beckett, charts an effort not to withdraw dramatic poetry from theatricality but to use lang. to explore new means of articulating writing with stage action. The intercalation of different verse forms, or of verse with prose, also jibes with the critical disorientation at the heart of Bertolt Brecht's *Verfremdungseffekt* (usually translated as "alienation effect" or "distancing effect"), visible in his own plays like *Saint Joan of the Stockyards* (1931) and *The Resistible Rise of Arturo Ui* (1941) and in the function of *song throughout his plays. The use of verse as a means of emphasizing the theatrical work of dramatic lang. sustains much of Peter Weiss's work (incl. his best known play, *The Persecution and Assassination of Jean-Paul Marat as Performed by the Inmates of the Asylum of Charenton under the Direction of the Marquis de Sade,* widely known as *Marat/Sade* [1963]), as well as embodying a postcolonial concern for the politics of lang. and performance genres in several of Wole Soyinka's plays, notably *The Lion and the Jewel* (1963); in Aimé Césaire's adaptation of Shakespeare, *A Tempest* (1969), and often in the plays of Derek Walcott. Verbal experiment sustains much contemp. dramatic writing, often writing conceived to generate political or social friction in performance: Caryl Churchill's satiric *Serious Money* (1987), John Arden's drama, the brilliant use of verse and song alongside the prose of Edward Bond's plays. Several playwrights whose lang. is formally inventive yet not restricted either to formal or *free verse—Thomas Bernhard, Heiner Müller, María Irene Fornes, Suzan-Lori Parks—are precisely engaged in the problem of dramatic poetry.

III. Dramatic Poetry and Performance Theory.
Given that different performance conventions construct the force of lang. in and as performance, what does *poetic* writing contribute to drama? In one sense, poetry lends its distinctive verbal density to the dramatic event, creating an opportunity for form, imagery, and meter

to be woven into the conceptual practices of performance. Yet while mod. poets sometimes assume that poetry should govern the practices of the stage, the most enduring experiments in dramatic poetry tend in a different direction. Yeats's *Plays for Dancers* coordinates an imagistic moment of intense, verbalized perception against the parallel, speechless, physical expression of dance to music. Rather than taking the physical expression of theater merely to illustrate the verbal "meanings" of the poetry, Yeats's plays provoke a rich reciprocity between the ultimately incompatible discourses of lang. and movement, poetry and embodiment in the theater.

Among playwrights, Eliot most searchingly attempted to chart the extent to which it was possible for dramatic composition to alter, even revivify, the circumstances of performance. Although Eliot's writing about dramatic poetry spans his career—from "The Possibility of a Poetic Drama" and "Rhetoric and Poetic Drama," both of which appeared in *The Sacred Wood* (1920), to *Poetry and Drama* (1951)—his obituary for the music-hall star Marie Lloyd expresses his canniest vision of theater, the sense that the "working man" who saw Lloyd in the music hall and "joined in the chorus was himself performing part of the act; he was engaged in that collaboration of the audience with the artist which is necessary in all art and most obviously in dramatic art" (*Selected Essays*). From his early dramatic monologues onward, Eliot's poetic imagination engaged with drama; turning to the writing of plays, he explored how writing might galvanize the social ritual of theatrical performance, might provide a means to shape that collaboration among poet, performers, and participating audience through the process of playing.

But while Eliot typically takes dramatic poetry as synonymous with verse drama, his most experimental play, *Murder in the Cathedral* (1935), demonstrates that it is not the difference between verse and prose that identifies the force of poetic drama but the ways lang. engages with the means of theater. *Murder in the Cathedral* is largely written in prose, using different modes of written discourse—the Chorus' rhythmically chanted verse, Thomas's prose sermon, the Knights' Shavian apology—to afford different opportunities for collaboration in the dramatic event. In *Poetry and Drama*, Eliot confessed that he may have been chasing a "mirage," a verse drama at once composed "of human action and of words, such as to present at once the two aspects of dramatic and of musical order." New forms of verbal composition (here limited to verse drama) might afford powerful, innovative forms of human action, which would—taking up the distinction between drama and music—use representation, the dramatic fiction, to render the present, transitory harmonies of the performance itself significant. Eliot imagined that this design of theatrical experience could take shape only through verse, rather than through a systematic use of verbal/oral genres to reposition the work of lang. on the stage. Perhaps he was looking in the wrong direction: the play that would transform the Western theater's sense of the overlapping of lang. and event, dramatic poetry and the music of experience, the represented fiction and the ephemeral *thereness* of performance, took the stage the following 1952–53 season, at an obscure Parisian theater, written in Fr. by an Ir. expatriate named Samuel Beckett, its lyrical prose betrayed by its prosaic title, *En Attendant Godot.*

That is, as opposed to verse drama, dramatic poetry seizes the theoretical function of lang. in theatrical performance. In the middle decades of the 20th c., dramatic poetry provided a critical code for imagining the work of dramatic writing as instigating new forms of performance, action not subordinated to the rhet., politics, or sociology of theatrical verisimilitude (see Bentley, Fergusson, R. Williams). In the U.S., the Living Theatre—which would become notorious for its participatory spectacles in the late 1960s and 70s—charted the consequences of using poetry to instigate new performance, staging Paul Goodman's plays, Gertrude Stein's *Doctor Faustus Lights the Lights* (1938), Eliot's *Sweeney Agonistes* (1932), John Ashbery's *The Heroes* (1950), W. H. Auden's *The Age of Anxiety* (1947), W. C. Williams's *Many Loves* (1961), and Jackson Mac Low's *The Marrying Maiden* (1961). What this drama and many of the most innovative plays since Beckett—Sam Shepard's *Tooth of Crime* (1972), Peter Barnes's *The Bewitched* (1974), Müller's *Hamletmachine* (1977), Parks's *The Death of the Last Black Man in the Whole Entire World* (1990), Sarah Kane's *4.48 Psychosis* (1999)—suggest is that, while some forms of dramatic innovation arise in theatrical practice (the opportunities afforded by the box set, electric lighting, simultaneous video, V. E. Meyerhold's biomechanics, Artaud's theater of cruelty, Brecht's epic theater), others are summoned by new forms of writing, writing

that demands a different accommodation to, and often the invention of, new performance practices. And while that writing is not always in verse, what defines it as dramatic poetry is an original imagination both for the interplay between words and for the interplay among words and the material signification they will inevitably impel, mediate, and be absorbed into in the process of dramatic performance.

How should we understand the function of scripted lang. in the Western trads. of drama and its performance? Dramatic poetry imagines a recalibration of the *agency* of writing in the process of theater; it implies a significant role in dramatic *poesis* for its verbal element, lang. In Western theater—esp. since the rise of print and the incorporation of printed plays into lit. as books—this role has sometimes been imagined as determinative, as though the poet created the play in lang. and theatrical performance has a secondary ministerial function merely to execute the poet's completed work in the medium of performance. But the words on the page cannot determine their performance. As Austin discovered, in "performative" speech, words do not make statements; sometimes—as in the sentence "I promise" or the "I do" of a marriage ceremony—they "do things": to speak the words is to act within a sustaining context of performance *convention, convention that limits what, how, and whether the performance *performs*. In this sense, the notion of theater as executing the text's direction might form one paradigm of performance but is hardly essential to dramatic performance, nor is it illustrated by the hist. of theatrical practice, the unfolding narrative of changing ways to make writing do work as theater in the changing performative conventions of the stage.

While one line of critique has attempted to restrict dramatic performance to the appropriate "stage presentation" of a literary work fixed and complete as dramatic poetry (see Brooks and Heilman; see also Lehmann), the real challenge of understanding dramatic poetry is to model its contribution to the performance process, a process that arises outside and beyond the control of the text. Dramatic poetry animates the dual scene of performance, the fictive play and its theatrical playing, where lang. is the instrument of the actor's work, what he or she has to work with in the creation of something that is *not* poetry, not even principally verbal: theatrical and dramatic action. Recalling Burke's "dramatistic" model for the analysis of actions—any action can be conceived in terms of the ratio between the *act, agent, agency, purpose,* and *scene* of performance—dramatic performance foregrounds an inherently duplicitous event, in which the represented acts, agents, purposes, and scene of the dramatic fiction can be created (and known to the audience) only through their implication by the material grammar of theatrical practice, the *acts* we understand as theatrical performance, the actors as *agents* of stage action, the leading *purposes* of the production, the *scene* of the theater itself. Dramatic poetry occupies a dual *agency*, at once the fictive dialogue between characters—the *agency* of their actions—and the actor's *agency*, i.e., his or her instrument for embodied mimesis, for making play. In performance, dramatic poetry may or may not be privileged among a given theater's various *agencies*—visual design, movement vocabulary, vocal production—for articulating dramatic action through the theatrical event. Although Yeats based his *Plays for Dancers* on an understanding of the Japanese Nō, Nō performance clearly situates its writing within a highly conventionalized performance trad.: the actors are masked, follow a generally prescribed trajectory around the stage, adopt patterned gestures, and give voice to the text (singing it) in largely determined ways (some of the characters' lines are spoken by the seated musicians as well). Rather than seeming subordinate to the structure and meaning of the script, performance seems to govern how the densely ornate, "literary" script will be incorporated as an event.

IV. Dramatic Poetry in the Theater. The study of dramatic poetry is often undertaken in purely literary terms, considering *prosody and *meter, *imagery and *metaphor, structure and theme. These elements are important and may well bear on performance. The meter of Shakespeare's plays creates a range of opportunities for actors: Romeo's sudden monosyllables when he first sees Juliet; the tension between the intensification and evacuation of meaning in King Lear's "Never, never, never, never, never." But while purely verbal structures may provide opportunities, how or whether they are seized and transformed into action, depends on the behavioral conventions of contemp. performance. Dramatic poetry is always altered by its theatrical use, even when those uses are seen as scrupulously "faithful" to the play: the heavily built "realistic" Shakespeare of the 19th c. necessitated the reordering of scenes and extensive cutting of the text for the play to be staged in a reasonable duration; despite his elegant delivery of Hamlet's verse, Laurence Olivier cut roughly half the text and the roles of Rosencrantz, Guildenstern, and Fortinbras from his 1948 Oscar-winning film; most Eng.-lang. productions of Molière's plays today substitute blank verse or heroic couplets for the Fr. alexandrines.

While dramatic poetry is changed by performance, it also makes demands on performance that the contemp. theater struggles to engage: in the 1880s and 1890s, Ibsen's leading female roles—Nora Helmer in *A Doll's House* or Hedda Gabler—were difficult for actors to perform because they violated generic (and gender) performance conventions; Master Builder Solness, with his deeply disorienting discourse of demonic wish fulfillment, seemed nearly impossible to accommodate to the demands of the contemp. framing of dramatic character. Ibsen's lang. required a new approach to making dramatic poetry signify in the register of stage "character." Later, the inaction of Beckett's *Waiting for Godot* seemed, perhaps purposely, both undramatic and untheatrical, at least until Beckett's peculiar poetry was seen to invoke and transform a familiar performance discourse: the fractured coupling of vaudevillians, Gogo and Didi, as an eternal, poignant, even allegorical Laurel and Hardy. Some plays—Djuna Barnes's *Antiphon* (1958); nearly all of Stein's drama; Adrienne Kennedy's *Funnyhouse of a Negro* (1962); the "synthetic fragments" of Müller's *Germania Death in Berlin* (1978), *Despoiled Shore Medea-material Landscape with Argonauts* (1982), and various "performance texts"; Parks's *America Play* (1994), *Venus* (1996), *Fucking A* (2000), with their strikingly idiosyncratic typographic design on the page—illustrate how dramatic poetry puts pressure on theatrical practice, enforcing a search for new modes of articulation, enunciation, and embodiment.

Perhaps the most familiar example of this problem is the notion of the animating "subtext" of desire, a through-line of psychological action trending toward a distinctive "objective" that the director Konstantin Stanislavski devised in his work on Anton Chekhov's refractory plays. Chekhov's poetry is elusive and indirect; the writing did not conform to conventional notions of dramatic action at the turn of the 20th c. and so seemed not to provide an appropriate agency for acting. Harmonizing each actor/character's objective into the overall purpose of the production, Stanislavski developed the notion of the emotional subtext, the act that the actor/character was attempting to perform *through* the often-elliptical script. The subtext implies the essential fungibility of the words on the page: the words may say one thing, but they enable the actors to do something else with them, to seduce, challenge, insult, rebuke, flatter. As Eliot knew, words fail; for Stanislavski, dramatic action is falsified by what the words say, even as it is enabled by what the words can be made to do (the script's "I love you" might be sustained in performance as "I really dislike you" or "I am trying to hurt you by telling you 'I love you'" or "I hate myself"). Stanislavski found a means to transform Chekhov's dramatic poetry into dramatic performance by framing lang. as agency, a means to use the poetry to perform a legible, significant act. It is a measure of Stanislavski's theatrical imagination—and, perhaps, of the compromised place of poetry in mod. theater—that his terms are now essential to any discussion of Chekhov, of mod. drama, and of a significant range of mod. performance training.

Although Stanislavski's invention of the theatrical means for Chekhov in the theater is a specific case, it suggests that drama is always performed in cultural and theatrical circumstances redefining its poetry (it is notable, but not surprising, that Chekhov was not impressed with all of Stanislavski's decisions as a director). Classic drama, now incl. Chekhov, of course, inevitably provides the agency for performances unimaginable to the poet. *The Taming of the Shrew*, *The Merchant of Venice*, *Othello* today are animated by contemp. attitudes about gender, religion, race; words such as *woman*, *Jew*, *black* signify differently from the way they did on the early mod. stage, implicating the speaker (both actor and character) in different ethical terms, as a different kind of agent; and their performance also implicates us, as agents of contemp. theater and society. Even lines that seem to describe the action they perform—Herod's "I stamp! I stare! I look all about!" from the Coventry nativity play—clearly provide the actor with the instigation to action, an action that will gain its specific force and meaning from the way the actor uses the lines (esp. given the ms.'s stage direction that Herod "rages in the street").

Dramatic writing is writing for use, and even writing that seems to direct its performance evinces this truth: Beckett's *Quad* (1981)—a play that exists entirely in stage directions, which command actors to circumnavigate and bisect a square-shaped pattern in a specific sequence—has given rise to an arresting range of productions. Indeed, one of the most surprising turns of mod. literary and theater hist. has to do with Beckett's plays in the theater. Although dramatic poetry has generally been equated with the dialogue, taking stage directions as merely theatrical instruments extrinsic to the play's literary identity, in the 1980s Beckett's stage directions became the center of an important critical controversy, as several productions—JoAnne Akalaitis's *Endgame* at the American Repertory Theatre in 1984, Gildas Bourget's pink-set *Fin de partie* at the Comédie Française in 1988, an all-women *Waiting for Godot* by De Haarlemse Toneelschuur the same year, Deborah Warner's environmental *Footfalls* in London in 1994, the casting of twin sisters as Didi and Gogo in a 2006 *Godot* in Pontadera, Italy—drew legal attention for changing the theatrical scene imaged in the text. What this controversy illustrates is the fact that the propriety of dramatic poetry is determined not on the page but by the social, theatrical, and (here) legal structures through which poetry and performance are defined.

Indeed, George Tabori's idiosyncratic productions of *Waiting for Godot* usefully refract this question. In his 1984 *Godot* at the Munich Kammerspiele, the actors playing Didi and Gogo sat at a table, text in hand, apparently rehearsing the play, reading stage directions aloud, working themselves deeply into "performance," and then pulling back to examine the script: the production allegorized the ways writing, rather than governing stage practice, is an instrument in the actors' hands, used to create something else, a performance. In Tabori's 2006 *Godot* at the Berliner Ensemble, the actors frequently extemporized with the audience and—more to the point—had an ongoing conversation with the prompter, seated at her table just outside the circular playing area. Rather than staging the "performance" as an objectified image, derived from the text and situated frontally before the audience, this production conceived dramatic performance as transactional, dramatic poetry sustaining a collaboration between the institutionalized conventions of performance (the prompter) and the individual temperament of the actors, and between the actors—who, in any production, are always available to us, speaking for themselves as well as "in character"—and the audience, collaboration sustained by the actors' ongoing ironic byplay about the play and their performance of it. For some audiences, no doubt, Tabori's *Godot* approached travesty, epitomized by the moment when Didi and Gogo knocked over the tree in Act 2, perhaps confirming Beckett's withering remark to his biographer Deirdre Bair that, in his ideal drama, there would be "no actors, only the text." And yet, as Tabori's productions suggest, dramatic poetry is an important but not necessarily *the* governing instrument of theater: dramatic performance will locate dramatic poetry as poetry in a Burkean ratio to the other elements of theatrical action, an event in which the poetry is recomposed in the immediate bodily and spatial discourse devised by actors and audiences.

Dramatic poetry summons a poetics of duplicity, suggesting that while lang. might have a range of function in the dramatic fiction, it will be remade by the process of production into specific actions that cannot be anticipated from the words alone. What does the actor do on Othello's line "And smote him, thus," the line in which he executes the terrible justice of Venice—the justice he once exercised on the turbaned Turk who "traduced the state"—on himself? In the late 19th c., the It. actor Tommaso Salvini created a sensation by seeming to hack away at his sinewy throat with a small knife. Other actors have opted for different gestures: Anthony Hopkins grinning ironically as he plunges a silver poniard into his abdomen; Laurence Fishburne, strangling himself with his necklace as he takes the "circumcised dog" by the "throat," before finishing his work with a knife to the heart. If how this gesture is performed frames our sense of the event—how Othello acts shaping what Othello means, what the experience and so the content of this justice is—then how much more significant is every nuance and shading of the actor's transformation of words into deeds. What does the actress perform with Cordelia's "Nothing": a repudiation of Lear's inappropriate question? Insolence directed toward her sisters? Fearful self-protection? Punctilious coolness? Posture and movement, vocal tone, the production's general conventions of address, the entire corporeal armature of social behavior—rendered esp. significant through the marked conventions of stage acting—will operate with this single word to make it work, do significant work here, work that must say and do much more than "Nothing."

Finally, dramatic poetry is both material to be reshaped (words made into acts) and an instrument, an agency of theatrical labor, something the agents of the production both work on and work with to fashion the performance. A specific performance is neither implicit in nor derivable from the text alone. Since poetry is the dual agency of both dramatic (fictional) and theatrical (actual) activity onstage, can we finally distinguish meaningfully between presence and representation in performance? In any fully dramatic performance, even those most insistent on a scrupulous "fidelity" to "the text," presentational immediacy is the principal node of our engagement in the play. Echoing S. T. Coleridge, this effect has been seized as a "willing suspension of disbelief," but the reference to "belief" is a distraction: belief in the dramatic fiction is never significantly in play in the theater—we are always aware that Olivier is not murdering anyone, even though Othello is. Yet Othello cannot be distinguished from Olivier; Othello is what Olivier is doing, making there with us, an enacted poetry that disappears the moment the actor loses his bearings or we our concentration. To swing into action, leap to the stage, and save Desdemona is not merely to mistake the role of the audience but to mistake the event entirely and so destroy it: Desdemona will not be saved; she will simply stop being there as the actress stops working and calls for the police.

Dramatic performance refuses a strict opposition between word and deed, speech and action, representation and presentation, the drama and its performance. Although the poet's work is completed with the framing of the dramatic poem, we may well feel that *Antigone* or *Phèdre* or *Hamletmachine* have a semantic identity richer than the other tools and materials of theatrical performance. While dramatic poetry will be actualized in means that lie outside the script, specific opportunities for using dramatic poetry emerge in clearer outline when the text is conceived in relation to the performance practices of its original theater, esp. when—as is the case with Shakespeare or Chekhov—the playwright worked within a specific stage architecture, system of production conventions, and with a given acting company. For all the character's famous seductiveness, the Cleopatra of Shakespeare's *Antony and Cleopatra* is a considerably ironic role, availing itself of the verbal japes typical of the cross-dressing boy actor and drawing our attention to the convention as well: Cleopatra, after all, commits suicide in order to avoid seeing "some squeaking Cleopatra boy my greatness," exactly what Shakespeare's original audiences saw. Chekhov wanted Stanislavski—drawn to serious, sentimental roles—to play the part of Lopakhin in *The Cherry Orchard*; though Stanislavski chose to play Gaev, perhaps Chekhov wanted the performance to resist framing Lopakhin as a stereotypically comic peasant. So, too, some playwrights have been closely involved in staging their work, leaving a record of their intentions with regard to theatrical production. Beckett came to direct many of his plays and (perhaps surprisingly) often revised his own texts to accommodate an altered sense of the work the text could do as performance. For stage productions of *Not I* (1972), he came to prefer dropping the silent Auditor, nonetheless insisting that this role be retained in published scripts of the play.

Beyond that, dramatic poetry sometimes appears to allegorize thematic aspects of the animating ethical dynamics of its originating theater, particularly if we seize the role as an instrument for doing, rather than as the representation of a fixed character. The potentially incoherent seriality of the role of Hamlet, demanding a strikingly distinct temperament in every scene, speaks to an early mod. anxiety about the stability of the ethical subject, one perhaps recorded in the poetry, too, in Hamlet's *or*, his tendency to multiply adjectives— "Remorseless, treacherous, lecherous, kindless villain!"—in an ultimately vain attempt to fix the nature of human character (and much else) in words. The harrowing exploration of a tormented psychological inscape in Ibsen's Rosmer similarly engages with the instability of the mod. "self"; the repetitive expressionless movement of Parks's Black Man with Watermelon in *Death of the Last Black Man in the Whole Entire World* signifies within an embodied, and alienated, historical discourse for the evocation of "race" in performance.

And yet plays are limited neither to their original theaters nor to their original circumstances of production. One of the lessons of the reconstructed Globe Theatre in London is that its productions articulate a complex historical ambivalence, enabling us to see some of the working elements of Shakespeare's poetry in an open-air platform theater, but with the constant recognition that, despite the authentic timbers, hand-made costumes, and even reconstructed accents and performance techniques, we are participating in a specific form of *mod.* performance—the living-hist. historical reconstruction—taking its place along other mod. performance genres, the living-hist. museum, the theme park, performance art, and contemp. Shakespeare production, for that matter.

Along similar lines, critics sometimes imply that dramatic performance is a special genre of performance, one in which theatrical meaning *should* be determined by the aims of the poet, that the rhetorical purpose of dramatic performance is precisely to evince the *poet's* work. Some dramatic trads. have been notably conservative in this regard, often by massively restricting the repertoire, and strictly codifying legitimate training and performance practice so as to establish a relatively unchanging relation between poetry and its performance: Japanese Nō is a familiar case in point, as is the Comédie Française. Yet while this understanding appears to subordinate stage to page, it actually suggests just the opposite. It is the practice of the stage that encodes the signs of proper "fidelity" to the poetry: rhythmic utterance, for instance, or a pause at line endings. Whether it is speaking the verse emphatically without motion or gesture (Yeats rehearsed his actors in barrels), wearing doublet and hose for mod. Shakespeare, or adopting the Method "crouch" to express an emotional volatility ready to spring into being: to the extent that these behaviors signify fidelity to a specific play, they do so by encoding the poetry in a specific regime of performance, one both outside and beyond the imagination of the text.

The hist. of Western theater is a hist. of change: the workable practices for transforming dramatic poetry into theatrical play dynamically reciprocate with forms of social behavior, with ideas about identity and society, with notions of the purposes of art. To see Shakespeare's *The Winter's Tale* in a regional summer Shakespeare festival in the U.S. or directed by Sam Mendes at the Old Vic in London or directed by Robert Wilson at the Berliner Ensemble is more than seeing three "versions" of one "play" (let alone an event directly cognate with the play that might have taken place in Shakespeare's London). It is to see three distinct articulations of the purpose and agency of dramatic poetry, the materialization—with all that the word implies for the resources of time, talent, space, audience—of three distinct ideas of what dramatic performance is and is for and how its poetry might be forcefully configured as something else, dramatic action. Much as the self-evident "meanings" of poems change as they are read in new locations, with new purposes, and as part of changing systems of social and cultural understanding, so dramatic poetry—performed in a more extraverted, embodied, public fashion, through articulate but changing conventions of signification—will inevitably provide the instrument for new, unanticipated action and experience in the theater. Lang. and narrative are embedded in the world as well as in lit., and plays—whether classics like *Medea* and *King Lear* or more recent work like Kane's *Blasted* (1995) or Gao Xingjian's *The Other Shore* (1986)—seem, in a given time and place, to afford certain possibilities of performance, some familiar and conventional, some surprising and unexpectedly effective, some so controversial as to raise the question of whether they work, perform theatrical *work* with the poetry at all. While it may appear to compromise the poetic integrity of the text, the transformation of words into legibly embodied acts—acts that necessarily exceed, qualify, remake the text as our understanding of its theatrical agency changes—is what enables the continued vitality, the performative force, of dramatic poetry and dramatic performance.

See GENRE, MONOLOGUE, POETICS.

■ **Literary Criticism and History:** L. Abercrombie, "The Function of Poetry in the Drama," *Poetry Review* 1 (1912); M. E. Prior, *The Language of Tragedy* (1947); C. Brooks and R. B. Heilman, *Understanding Drama* (1948); G. F. Else, *Aristotle's Poetics* (1957); R. Lattimore, *Poetry of Greek Tragedy* (1958); D. Donoghue, *The Third Voice* (1959); M. Bieber, *History of the Greek and Roman Theater*, 2d ed. (1961); M. C. Bradbrook, *English Dramatic Form* (1965); V. A. Kolve, *The Play Called Corpus Christi* (1966); J. Scherer, *La Dramaturgie classique en France* (1968); J. Barish, *Ben Jonson and the Language of Prose Comedy* (1970); R. Williams, *Drama from Ibsen to Genet* (1971); H.H.A. Gowda, *Dramatic Poetry from Medieval to Modern Times* (1972); K. J. Worth, *Revolutions in Modern English Drama* (1972); A. P. Hinchcliffe, *Modern Verse Drama* (1977); O. Taplin, *Greek Tragedy in Action* (1978); J. Baxter, *Shakespeare's Poetic Styles* (1980); D. Breuer, *Deutsche Metrik und Vergeschichte* (1981); C. Freer, *The Poetics of Jacobean*

Drama (1981); G. R. Hibbard, *The Making of Shakespeare's Dramatic Poetry* (1981); E. Havelock, *Preface to Plato* (1982); T. Rosenmeyer, *The Art of Aeschylus* (1982); A. Brown, *A New Companion to Greek Tragedy* (1983); G. Hoffmanm, "Das moderne amerikanische Versdrama," *Das amerikanische Drama,* ed. G. Hoffman (1984); G. T. Wright, *Shakespeare's Metrical Art* (1988); J. W. Flannery, *W. B. Yeats and the Idea of a Theatre* (1989); D. Bair, *Samuel Beckett* (1990); W. B. Worthen, *Modern Drama and the Rhetoric of Theater* (1992); R. Cohn, "Dramatic Poetry," *New Princeton Encyclopedia of Poetry and Poetics,* ed. A. Preminger et al. (1993); M. Bristol, *Big-Time Shakespeare* (1996); F. Zeitlin, *Playing the Other* (1996); Aristotle, *Poetics,* trans. M. E. Hubbard (1998); J. S. Peters, *Theatre of the Book* (2000); R. McDonald, *Shakespeare and the Arts of Language* (2001); T. Eagleton, *Sweet Violence* (2002); J. Enders, *The Medieval Theater of Cruelty* (2002); S. Orgel, *The Authentic Shakespeare* (2002); N. Slater, *Spectator Politics* (2002); J. Enders, *Death by Drama and Other Medieval Urban Legends* (2005).

■ **Theater History:** N. Díaz de Escovar and F. de P. Lasso de la Vega, *Historia del teatro español,* 2 v. (1924); H. C. Lancaster, *History of French Dramatic Literature in the 17th Century,* 9 v. (1929–42); A. Nicoll, *A History of English Drama, 1660–1900,* 6 v. (1952–59); A. Nicoll, *English Drama 1900–1930* (1973); F. H. Sandbach, *The Comic Theatre of Greece and Rome* (1977); J. Barish, *The Antitheatrical Prejudice* (1981); W. B. Worthen, *The Idea of the Actor* (1984); J. R. Roach, *The Player's Passion* (1985); A. W. Pickard-Cambridge, *The Dramatic Festivals of Athens,* 2d ed. (1989); *Nothing to Do with Dionysos?,* ed. J. Winkler and F. Zeitlin (1990); M. McKendrick, *Theatre in Spain, 1490–1700* (1992); *A New History of Early English Drama,* ed. J. D. Cox and D. S. Kastan (1997); T. Hauptfleisch, *Theatre and Society in South Africa* (1997); *Cambridge History of American Theatre,* ed. D. Wilmeth et al., 3 v. (1998); S. Chatterjee, *The Colonial Staged* (1998); *World Encyclopedia of Contemporary Theatre,* ed. D. Rubin et al., 5 v. (2000); *Encyclopedia of Latin American Theater,* ed. E. Cortés and M. Barrea-Marlys (2003); M. Banham, *A History of Theatre in Africa* (2004); N. Bhathia, *Acts of Authority/Acts of Resistance* (2004); *Cambridge History of British Theatre,* ed. P. Thomson et al. (2004); *Contemporary Theatres in Europe,* ed. J. Kelleher and N. Ridout (2006); P. Zarrilli, B. McConachie,

G. J. Williams, C. F. Sorgenfrei, *Theatre Histories* (2006); J. Hollander, *Indian Folk Theatres* (2007); O. Okagbue, *African Theatres and Performance* (2007); A. Versenyi, *Theatre in Latin America* (2009).
■ **Theory and Performance Studies:** S. T. Coleridge, *Biographia Literaria* (1817); É. Zola, *Le naturalisme au théâtre* (1881); T. S. Eliot, *The Sacred Wood* (1920); W. B. Yeats, *Essays* (1924); H. Granville-Barker, *On Poetry in Drama* (1937); K. Burke, *A Grammar of Motives* (1945); E. Bentley, *The Playwright as Thinker* (1946); Eliot, *Essays*; J. L. Barrault, *Reflections on the Theatre* (1951); T. S. Eliot, *Poetry and Drama* (1951); F. Fergusson, *Idea of a Theater* (1953); A. Artaud, *The Theater and Its Double*, trans. M. C. Richards (1958); W. H. Auden, *The Dyer's Hand* (1962); R. Barthes, *On Racine*, trans. R. Howard (1963); P. Brook, *The Empty Space* (1968); J. Cocteau, "Préface de 1922," *Les Mariés de la Tour Eiffel* (1969); M. Goldman, *Shakespeare and the Energies of Drama* (1972), and *The Actor's Freedom* (1975); B. Brecht, *Brecht on Theatre*, ed. and trans. John Willett (1977); J. L. Styan, *The Shakespeare Revolution* (1977); B. Beckerman, *Dynamics of Drama* (1979); H. Blau, *Take up the Bodies* (1982); O. Mandel, "Poetry and Excessive Poetry in the Theatre," *Centennial Review* 26 (1982); M. Carlson, *Theories of the Theatre* (1984); C. J. Herington, *Poetry into Drama* (1985); C. W. Meister, *Dramatic Criticism* (1985); B. O. States, *Great Reckonings in Little Rooms* (1985); M. Esslin, *The Field of Drama* (1987); H. Berger Jr., *Imaginary Audition* (1989); E. Fischer-Lichte, *Semiotics of Theatre* (1992); S. B. Garner Jr., *Bodied Spaces* (1994); U. Chaudhuri, *Staging Place* (1995); S-L. Parks, "From Elements of Style," *The America Play and Other Works* (1995); J. L. Austin, *How to Do Things with Words*, 2d ed., ed. J. O. Urmson and M. Sbisá (1997); J. Wise, *Dionysus Writes* (1999); M. Puchner, *Stage Fright* (2002); B. Bennett, *All Theater Is Revolutionary Theater* (2005); H.-T. Lehmann, *Postdramatic Theatre* (2006); W. B. Worthen, *Print and the Poetics of Modern Drama* (2006); R. Weimann and D. Bruster, *Shakespeare and the Power of Performance* (2008); E. Fischer-Lichte, *Transformative Power of Performance* (2008); *Companion to Shakespeare and Performance*, ed. B. Hodgdon and W. B. Worthen (2008); K. Stanislavski, *An Actor's Work*, ed. and trans. J. Benedetti (2008); W. B. Worthen, *Drama: Between Poetry and Performance* (2010).

W. B. WORTHEN

DREAM VISION. A literary work describing the dream(s) of a first-person narrator identified with the author. Although religious and apocalyptic visions were composed from late antiquity on, the literary genre flourished in Europe from the 12th through the early 16th c. Its major antecedents included biblical dreams and revelations, Macrobius's commentary on Cicero's *Somnium Scipionis* (ca. 5th c.), and Boethius's *De consolatione philosophiae* (early 6th c.). Significant themes included erotic desire, religious or philosophical questions, and social critique, subgenres that could be combined in a single work. The genre is defined by a frame that sets the narrator's actual circumstances against the dream, but many influential works borrowed its conventions for waking visions (as in *De consolatione philosophiae*, Alain de Lille's *De planctu naturae*, Dante's *Divina commedia*, John Gower's *Confessio amantis*, and Christine de Pizan's *Livre de la cité des dames*). Dream visions were frequently allegorical and had close ties to debate lit., emphasizing a sequence of reported speeches. The narrator often wanders in a field or garden on a spring morning before falling asleep and dreams of a densely symbolic landscape in which he converses with various *personifications, is instructed by an otherworldly mentor, or overhears debates among nonhuman interlocutors such as birds or the body and soul. The dreamer is typically distressed by love or melancholy in waking life and is characterized as isolated, naïve, or awkward; the vision develops the tension between his ignorance at the time of the dream and the wisdom of the poet writing with the benefit of experience. This double consciousness underscores the self-conscious quality of the dream vision, calling attention to the author and the artifice of his *persona. Debates over the interpretation of dreams and their supernatural, psychological, or somatic origins inform the genre's epistemological and hermeneutic concerns, allowing it to explore the truthfulness of literary fictions, the relationship between natural and divine knowledge, and the limits of human reason. Many visions associate the ephemeral and multivalent dream form with irresolvable debates and unanswered questions rather than with fully revealed truth, and the vision may or may not provide a remedy for the dreamer's initial suffering.

The dream vision first attained popularity in France with the genre-defining *Roman de la Rose* (ca. 1230, ca. 1270–80) and the philosophical *De* *planctu naturae* (composed mid-12th c.), which were followed by the courtly amatory poems of Guillaume de Machaut and Jean Froissart. The form was embraced by the major poets of late 14th-c. England, notably in Chaucer's four long dream-vision poems, which inspired many imitations, and in the alliterative trad. best exemplified by *Pearl* and by William Langland's *Piers Plowman*. Dream visions maintained their popularity throughout the 15th c. in works by John Lydgate, John Skelton, and several Scottish poets but declined ca. 1500, esp. with the resurgence of *lyric as a vehicle for poetic introspection. Dreams remained a popular literary device, however, and later analogues to the framed narrative vision appear in John Bunyan's *Pilgrim's Progress* and in works by John Keats and James Joyce.

■ H. R. Jauss, *La Génèse de la poésie allégorique française au moyen âge* (1962); C. Hieatt, *The Realism of Dream Visions* (1967); E. Kirk, *The Dream Thought of "Piers Plowman"* (1972); A. C. Spearing, *Medieval Dream Poetry* (1976); K. L. Lynch, *The High Medieval Dream Vision* (1988); J. S. Russell, *The English Dream Vision* (1988); S. F. Kruger, *Dreaming in the Middle Ages* (1992); *Reading Dreams*, ed. P. Brown (1999); K. L. Lynch, *Chaucer's Philosophical Visions* (2000).

A. WALLING

E

ECLOGUE (Gr. *ek* + *leg-*, "to pick from"). As a noun, *ekloge* was used to describe harvesting crops, drafting soldiers, electing leaders, reckoning accounts, and sampling texts; then in Lat. as *ecloga*, its meaning was specialized to, e.g., part of a poetry book (Statius, *Silvae*, 3 Pref. 20: *summa est ecloga*, "is the last component"). The term was similarly used by commentators for Horace's *Epistles* 2.1 and book of *Epodes*, also for the ten components of Virgil's *Bucolics* (or *Eclogues*), perhaps by the poet himself defining them as parts of a designed book (Hutchinson, Van Sickle). The Virgilian example focused *eclogue* to mean short dialogue or monologue with more or less oblique allegory of politics, erotics, and poetics, all presented in dramatic form (enabling their early and recurrent theatrical success) as speech by herdsmen (*pastores*), from which later came the name *pastoral* for a *genre featuring shepherds.

At his book's climax, Virgil also invented the mytheme of Arcadia as song's origin and ideal, challenging the Sicily of Gr. Theocritus, whose *idylls* (little forms), were collected as *Boukolika* (about cowherds). They featured herders of cattle, sheep, and goats, dramatizing an old Gr. cognitive *metaphor*, to herd thoughts (*boukolein*; Gutzwiller). Deploying herdsmen in heroic meter (epos), Theocritus prefigured the tension between bucolic and heroic themes, characters, and plots that was to animate Virgil and later trad., with recurrent contrasts between slight and great.

Eclogue as pastoral allegory in the manner inaugurated by Virgil recurs in subsequent Lat. *Bucolics* (Calpurnius, Nemesianus) and served Dante to defend his *Divine Comedy* in a programmatic eclogue to Giovanni di Virgilio. Outdoing Virgil's ten, Petrarch assembles 12 eclogues into a bucolic book, declaring himself moved by "lonely woods" to write something "pastoral" (*Epistolae familiares* 10.4). Emulative eclogue books proliferate, among them Giovanni Boccaccio's miscellany of 16 (*Bucolicum carmen . . . distinctum eglogis*, following Petrarch with allegorical meaning "beneath the bark"); 12 Christian eclogues of Antonio Geraldini; six of Jacopo Sannazaro featuring fishermen (*piscatores*); ten of Mantuan's pious *Adulescentia* (mentioned with affection

by Shakespeare); and 12 in Edmund Spenser's *Shepheardes Calender* (1579), programmatically mingling erotics and metapoetics with court flattery and religious satire, also turning *ekloge*, *ecloga* (Gr., Lat.), *egloga* (Italianate Lat., It.), *égloga* (Sp.), *eclog* (Eng.), and *eclogue* (Fr., Eng.) into "aeglogue," explained as "Goteheards tales" by Spenser in the appended commentary he attributes to the otherwise unidentified E. K. (cf. Gr. *aiges* + *logos*). Affirming the allegorical and cognitive heritage of eclogues, George Puttenham's *Arte of English Poesie* (1589) says that an eclogue is written "not of purpose to counterfeit or represent the rusticall manner of loves and communication, but under the vaile of homely persons and in rude speeches to insinuate and glaunce at greater matters."

As such, the eclogue prompted remarkable diversity of cognitive applications apart from books, e.g., in Fr., Pierre de Ronsard's *Bergeries, eclogues et mascarades* (which was acted at court); in Sp., Garcilaso de la Vega's *Églogas*; and in Eng., Alexander Barclay's *Eclogues* and Barnabe Googe's *Eglogs*. The cognitive outreach spread to produce, e.g., town eclogues (John Gay, Jonathan Swift, Mary Wortley Montagu, Royall Tyler) and still prompts scattered pieces, e.g., from W. H. Auden and Seamus Heaney; and sequences or books, e.g., from W. Antony, Derek Walcott, and David Baker, extending too the pastoral realm of "green thought" (Andrew Marvell) to mod. ecology in the widespread coinage *ecologue*.

■ W. W. Greg, *Pastoral Poetry and Pastoral Drama* (1906); R. F. Jones, "Eclogue Types in English Poetry of the Eighteenth Century," *Journal of English and Germanic Philology* 24 (1925); A. Hulubei, *L'Églogue en France au XVIe Siècle, Époque Des Valois (1515–1589)* (1938); D. Lessig, *Ursprung und Entwicklung der Spanischen Ekloge Bis 1650; mit Anhang Eines Eklogenkataloges* (1962); E. Bolisani and M. Valgimigli, *La Corrispondenza Poetica di Dante Alighieri e Giovanni di Virgilio* (1963); W. L. Grant, *Neo-Latin Literature and the Pastoral* (1965); W. Antony, *The Arminarm Eclogues* (1971); G. Otto, *Ode, Ekloge und Elegie Im 18. Jahrhundert Zur Theorie und Praxis Französischer Lyrik Nach Boileau* (1973); D. Walcott, "Italian Eclogues [for Joseph Brodsky]," *The Bounty* (1997);

85

D. Baker, *Midwest Eclogue* (2005); K. Belford, *Ecologue* (2005); K. Gutzwiller, "The Herdsman in Greek Thought," *Brill's Companion to Greek and Latin Pastoral*, ed. M. Fantuzzi and T. Papanghelis (2006); P. McDonald, *Pastorals* (2006); I. Twiddy, "Seamus Heaney's Versions of Pastoral," *Essays in Criticism* 56 (2006); G. O. Hutchinson, *Talking Books: Readings in Hellenistic and Roman Books of Poetry* (2008); J. Van Sickle, *Virgil's "Book of Bucolics": The Ten Eclogues Translated into English Verse* (2011).

J. VAN SICKLE

EKPHRASIS (pl. *ekphraseis*). Detailed description of an image, primarily visual; in specialized form, limited to description of a work of visual art. *Ekphrasis* is a term proper first to cl. rhet. but becomes a key part of the art of description in poetry, historiography, romance, and novels. As Hagstrum contends, ekphrasis probably entered mod. poetry from Gr. romance. While mod. ekphrasis has never belonged exclusively to a single genre, certain kinds of ekphraseis have become associated with particular styles and forms—the *blason and the Petrarchan lyric, e.g.

Ekphrasis in rhet. was used to focus and amplify emotions, with the rhetor lingering over key aspects of an image in order to persuade his audience (Cicero, *De oratore*; Quintilian, *Institutio oratoria*). *Ekphrasis* in this regard is often conflated with *enargeia*, Aristotle's term not just for visual detail, but for *tropes of animation (*Rhetoric* 3.11.2). Ekphraseis were also a crucial part of the rhetor's method for memorizing a speech. All a rhetor's examples or major points of argument could be "placed" in imagination in a particular part of a mental image—the 12 houses of the zodiac, imagined in a wheel, were often used for this purpose. The rhetor then needed to recall only the image to have access to the items stored there. Detailed mental images were a crucial part of this art of memory from Gorgias (*Encomium of Helen*) forward, and in this context, emotionally powerful images were particularly important. The formative example here is of the poet Simonides of Ceos, who was able to identify the victims of a building collapse by remembering exactly where they had been seated during dinner (Cicero, *De oratore*). In the med. period, the *ars memoria* have a rich hist., with several texts devoted to describing and understanding the *imagery deemed necessary to remembering (Thomas Bradwardine, *De memoria artificiali adquirenda*, among others).

The poetic representation of works of visual art was promoted by the trad. most often identified with Horace of *ut pictura poesis* (as is painting, so is poetry). Theories of the sister arts held not only that poetry and painting (as well as music) would present the same subject matter but that their moral content, instructional value, and affective potential were parallel. While the sister-arts trad. has never disappeared, the status of the poetic image has undergone significant shifts. During the Reformation, as Gilman shows, iconoclastic approaches to worship made ekphraseis both dangerous and desirable. Poetic ekphraseis took a reader's attention from exterior, potentially idolatrous imagery and pointed inward to the mind and soul; however, the images of poetry were understood to be deeply powerful and thus required great care in their use. In the 20th c., the imagist poets sought to renew the power of poetry to set objects before the reader's eyes and used stripped-down forms of description to attempt to create a sense of visual immediacy.

The most famous ancient examples of ekphrastic descriptions of art were frequently imitated in med. and Ren. writing and include Homer's description of Achilles' shield in the *Iliad*, the shield of Aeneas in Virgil's *Aeneid*, and the tapestries of Arachne and Minerva in Ovid's *Metamorphoses*. Buildings have also been important subjects, as with John Milton's description of Pandaemonium in *Paradise Lost* or with the Ren. trad. of the country house poem. More rarely, ekphraseis may also represent music, as in Thomas Mann's *Magic Mountain* or John Dryden's "Alexander's Feast."

There is a rich variety of ekphrastic description beyond those of works of art, as may be seen in the med. *dream vision, the Petrarchan blason of a woman's beauty, or in emblem poems. Landscape description is one of the more common forms of ekphrasis, and gardens are also a rich subject (Andrew Marvell's "The Garden" is a particularly powerful example, where the last stanza pictures a parterre with a sundial and zodiac). *Georgic poetry, with its representations of labor, is also home to ekphrastic description of landscape and its alterations.

Ekphraseis serve many (nonexclusive) purposes. Some are virtuoso displays of poetic skill intended to align the author with the cl. trad., esp. with Virgil (as part of the poetic apprenticeship identified with Virgil's movement from *pastoral to georgic and then *epic). With the med. *ars memoria*, images were understood to have mental power, allowing vast amounts of information to be collated and stored in the mind; detailed description was essential to this function. Some images have almost magical meanings, as with elements of dream visions or with Gnostic writings. Other ekphraseis, as with emblem poems, are offered as subjects of religious meditation (George Herbert, Richard Crashaw, John Donne). Religious iconography may also determine which visual elements in a poem receive detailed description (as with the pentangle in *Sir Gawain and the Green Knight*); other objects or places may be carefully drawn in order to emphasize allegorical meaning (Gawain's armor) or ritual (Gawain's hunt—some ekphraseis in *Gawain* serve multiple purposes). Some ekphraseis are used to emphasize cultural norms or exemplary kinds of virtue; in the country house poem, e.g., the landowner's hospitality, power, taste, and lineage are made manifest by descriptions of his property (Andrew Marvell's "Appleton House" or Ben Jonson's "To Penshurst"). At times, ekphraseis are hidden, used as puzzles or to indicate esoteric knowledge, as in Donne's "A Valediction: Forbidding Mourning," where a compass sketches out a circle with a pinpoint at its center—the alchemical symbol for gold—while the poem evokes gold "to airy thinness beat." While ekphraseis perhaps most often are of objects of beauty, the grotesque and ugly are represented as well (the contents of London's gutters in Jonathan Swift's "A Description of a City Shower" or the decayed face of the prostitute in his "A Beautiful Young Nymph Going to Bed").

Ekphraseis play important roles in novels, too. They may be used in many of the ways listed above, but they also come into new prominence with the realist novel. The proliferating objects of the mod. world populate the 19th-c. novel, and the details of 19th-c. interiors or the clutter of the city form the backbone of realism. In novels as well as in poetry, ekphrastic descriptions also may be used to create foci that bring subjective experience into play, so that the emotions of a character emerge through description of the external world. This is often the case in epistolary fiction, as with Belford's description of Clarissa's prison in Samuel Richardson's *Clarissa* or the landscapes of Charlotte Smith's *Desmond*.

The psychological and neurological mechanisms underlying ekphraseis are becoming better understood, as cognitive science has begun to explore imagery across the senses. While most investigations have focused on visual imagery, there have also been investigations of the imagery of sound, taste, touch, and smell, as well as on effects, like those of motion, that involve combinations of imagery from across the five senses (Scarry, Starr).

See IMAGERY.

■ Curtius; F. Yates, *The Art of Memory* (1965); M. Krieger, "Ekphrasis and the Still Movement of Poetry; or *Laokoön* Revisited," *The Poet as Critic*, ed. F. McDowell (1967); E. Gilman, *Iconoclasm and Poetry in the English Reformation* (1986); J. Hagstrum, *The Sister Arts* (1987); W.J.T. Mitchell, *Iconology* (1987); J. Hollander "The Poetics of Ekphrasis," *Word and Image* 4 (1988); M. Carruthers, *The Book of Memory* (1990); J.A.W. Heffernan, *Museum of Words: The Poetics of Ekphrasis from Homer to Ashbery* (1993); M. Doody, *The True Story of the Novel* (1996); M. Carruthers, *The Craft of Thought* (1998); E. Scarry, *Dreaming by the Book* (1999); *The Medieval Craft of Memory*, ed. M. Carruthers and J. Ziolkowski (2002); E. Freedgood, *The Ideas in Things* (2006); C. Wall, *The Prose of Things* (2006); G. G. Starr, "Multisensory Imagery," *The Johns Hopkins Handbook of Cognitive Cultural Studies*, ed. L. Zunshine (2010).

G. G. STARR

ELEGIAC DISTICH, elegiac couplet (Gr., *elegeion*). In Gr. poetry, a distinctive meter consisting of a *hexameter followed by an asynartete combination of two end-shortened dactylic tripodies (– ∪ ∪ – ∪ ∪ – + – ∪ ∪ – ∪ ∪ –). It is, thus, a species of *epode (sense 2), in which the second line (later analyzed as a *pentameter consisting of a central *spondee between pairs of *dactyls and *anapests) gives the distinctive and satisfying effect of medial and final shortening (*catalexis). Originally used by the 6th- and 7th-c. BCE writers Archilochus, Callinus, Tyrtaeus, Theognis, and Mimnermus for a variety of topics and occasions—flute songs, symposiastic and poetic competitions, war songs, dedications, *epitaphs, inscriptions, *laments on love or death—it came to be associated thereafter with only one, i.e., loss or mourning—hence, *elegy in the mod. sense. It seems to embody reflection, advice, and exhortation—essentially "sharing one's thoughts." Threnodies, ritual laments, or cries uttered by professional poets at funerals may also have used the meter.

Outside the "elegiac" context, whether on love or death, the distich was specifically the meter of *epigrams, esp. after the 4th c., when literary imitations of verse inscriptions were cultivated by the Alexandrian poets. This fixation of meter to genre lasts the longest. Ennius introduced it into Lat. and later the skill of Martial ensured its passage into the Middle Ages. In Lat., the love elegy emerges as a major genre, characterized in the Augustans (Tibullus, Propertius, Ovid) by a preference, not noticeable in Catullus and his Gr. predecessors, for sense pause at the end of each couplet. A further refinement, esp. evident in Ovid and his successors, was the requirement that the final word in the pentameter be disyllabic. In the opening lines of the *Amores*, Ovid jokes that, though he intended to write of things epic—hence, in *hexameters—Cupid first stole a foot from his second line, then supplied the poet with suitable subject matter for the resulting combination of hexameter and pentameter by shooting him with one of his arrows.

In the Middle Ages, the elegiac distich was associated with *leonine verse, where it acquired rhyme. In the Ren., it was imitated, along with other Gr. quantitative meters, and such efforts were revived in the 18th and 19th cs. Examples are found in Eng. in works by Edmund Spenser, Philip Sidney, S. T. Coleridge, Arthur Clough, Charles Kingsley, and A. C. Swinburne; in Ger., by F. G. Klopstock, Friedrich Schiller, J. W. Goethe, and Friedrich Hölderlin; and in It., by Gabriele D'Annunzio. Coleridge's trans. of Schiller's elegiac distich is well known: "In the hexameter rises the fountain's silvery column, / In the pentameter aye falling in melody back." Naturalized into the accentually based prosodies of the vernacular meters, it was imitated in isometric couplets, as in Christopher Marlowe's Ovid, whence it exerted influence on the devel. of the *heroic couplet.

■ R. Reitzenstein, "Epigramm," Pauly-Wissowa, 6.1 (1907); K. Strecker, "Leoninische Hexameter und Pentameter in 9. Jahrhundert," *Neues Archiv für ältere deutsche Geschichtskunde* 44 (1922); C. M. Bowra, *Early Greek Elegists*, 2d ed. (1938); P. Friedländer, *Epigrammata: Greek Inscriptions in Verse from the Beginnings to the Persian Wars* (1948); M. Platnauer, *Latin Elegiac Verse* (1951); L. P. Wilkinson, *Golden Latin Artistry* (1963); T. G. Rosenmeyer, "Elegiac and Elegos," *California Studies in Classical Antiquity* 1 (1968); D. Ross, *Style and Tradition in Catullus* (1969); M. L. West, *Studies in Greek Elegy and Iambus* (1974); A.W.H. Adkins, *Poetic Craft in the Early Greek Elegists* (1984); R. M. Marina Sáez, *La métrica de los epigramas de Marcial* (1998).

T.V.F. BROGAN; A. T. COLE

ELEGIAC STANZA, elegiac quatrain, heroic quatrain. In Eng., the iambic pentameter quatrain rhymed *abab*. While it had been frequently employed without elegiac feeling or intention by other poets, e.g., Shakespeare in his sonnets and John Dryden in his *Annus Mirabilis,* the term *elegiac stanza* was apparently made popular by its use in Thomas Gray's "Elegy Written in a Country Churchyard" (1750), though, in fact, the association of the *quatrain with *elegy in Eng. appears at least as early as James Hammond's *Love Elegies* (1743) and was employed "almost invariably" for elegiac verse for about a century thereafter (Bate)—cf. William Wordsworth's "Elegiac Stanzas Suggested by Peele Castle."

■ W. J. Bate, *The Stylistic Development of Keats* (1945).

T.V.F. BROGAN; S. F. FOGLE

ELEGY

I. History
II. Criticism

I. History. In mod. usage, an *elegy* is a poem of loss or mourning. The term is Gr., its initial significance metrical: *elegeia* designates a poem in elegiac *couplets. In antiquity, the meter is used for a range of subjects and styles, incl. the kind of combative, promiscuous love presented in the poetry of Propertius, Tibullus, and Ovid. The popularity and prestige of what is still called Roman love elegy make *elegy* a loose synonym for "love poem" in early mod. usage, though the cl. exemplars are not generally "elegiac" in what becomes the dominant sense of the term. The meter, however, was also popular for *epitaphs, both literal and literary; all the Roman elegists also wrote elegies in the mod. sense, and in antiquity, the metrical term also becomes a synonym for *"lament." Neo-Lat. poets from the 15th c. on compose new works in elegiac couplets, and attempts are made to transfer the meter to the vernaculars. Among the most successful is J. W. Goethe's, incl. a collection of *Römische Elegien* (1795), scandalously sensual love poems, defiantly unmournful. Some critics (such as J. C. Scaliger in the 16th c.) try to theorize a common ground between Roman love elegy and lament for the dead (both involve *complaints); the popularity of Petrarchism in the Ren. strengthens a feeling that absence and frustration are central themes in *love poetry; and along these lines, "dire-lamenting elegies" (Shakespeare, *Two Gentlemen of Verona*) can be recommended to a would-be seducer. This composite understanding of the genre, however, is never fully worked out and gradually fades.

The most important cl. models for the later devel. of elegy are *pastoral: the lament for Daphnis (who died of love) by Theocritus, the elegy for Adonis attributed to Bion, the elegy on Bion attributed to Moschus, and another lament for Daphnis in the fifth *eclogue of Virgil. All are stylized and mythic, with hints of ritual; the first three are punctuated by incantatory *refrains. The elegies on Daphnis are staged performances within an otherwise casual setting. Nonhuman elements of the pastoral world are enlisted in the mourning: nymphs, satyrs, the landscape itself. In Virgil, the song of grief is paired with one celebrating the dead man's apotheosis; the poem is usually read as an allegory on the death and deification of Julius Caesar. Virgil's poem becomes particularly influential and adaptable. In the 9th c., Paschasius Radbertus composes an imitation in which the nuns Galathea and Phyllis sing of a deceased shepherd monk as a figure for Christ. At the prompting of humanism, Ren. poets experiment with the pastoral elegy and use it for a range of personal, political, and symbolic reference. Few collections of pastorals in the Ren. are without at least one elegy, and there are important stand-alone examples, such as Clément Marot's "Eglogue" on the death of Louise of Savoy (1531). John Milton composes two full-fledged pastoral elegies: *Epitaphium Damonis* in Lat., on a close friend (1639), and "Lycidas" in Eng., on a schoolmate (1637). The latter is widely regarded as Milton's first major poetic achievement and the most successful vernacular instance of the genre. It was, nevertheless, sharply criticized in the next century by Samuel Johnson for its artificiality; he speaks for a growing disenchantment with the genre. Major poets, however, can return to it in full dress: P. B. Shelley in "Adonais" (1821) on the shockingly early death of John Keats, W. B. Yeats in "Shepherd and Goatherd" (1918) on an unnamed shepherd who "died in the great war beyond the sea." The presence of the genre can also be felt in less-adorned poems, in the general sense that the countryside is the right place for

elegiac feeling (Thomas Gray's "Elegy Written in a Country Churchyard," 1750) or in the arch affirmation of natural sympathy with which W. H. Auden opens his elegy on Yeats (1939).

Pastoral, however, is only a specialized trad. within the wider field of poetic treatments of death and loss. Such poems (which may or may not call themselves elegies) show an immense diversity, within which filiations can be complex. Some important examples are really *sui generis*; among the few unforgettable Eng. poems of the first decade of the 16th c. is John Skelton's *Philip Sparrow*, 1,400 unpredictable lines on the death of a young girl's pet bird. The object in question is usually another person, often specifically identified: an important public figure or someone with a close personal connection to the poet, such as a spouse, lover, parent, child, or friend. Elegies on other poets are particularly common; elegies for oneself are at least as old as Ovid's exile poems. Elegies for groups or classes of people (esp. those killed in war) date back to the Greeks but become a particular feature of the 20th c. (such as Anna Akhmatova's *Requiem* (1935, pub. 1963) on the "nameless friends" lost in the Stalinist terror of 1935–40). Poems can present themselves as epitaphs or as containing epitaphs, sometimes addressing a visitor to the cemetery (*siste viator*). Even in times that value poetic artifice at its most elaborate, poems of personal grief—such as Henry King's "Exequy" on the dead wife he calls "his matchless never to be forgotten friend" (1634)—can be strikingly direct in their effect. In 20th-c. writing, the appetite for directness becomes conspicuous, at times brutal ("he's dead / the old bastard"; W. C. Williams, "Death" [1930]). It is, however, an equally famous resource of elegies to proceed by complicated indirection. In Chaucer's *The Book of the Duchess* (ca. 1368), occasioned by the death of his patron's wife, the dreaming narrator cannot acknowledge that occasion until the last of the poem's 1,300 lines, long after the reader has divined it. The mourning in Keats's ode "To Autumn" (1819) is almost entirely subliminal and inexplicit, but strong enough to make three stanzas of seasonal description one of the touchstone lyrics in the lang.

Some important elegies are expansive in their reach. In Walt Whitman's "Out of the Cradle Endlessly Rocking" (1860), a child (as in *Philip Sparrow* reacting to the death of a bird) hears from the sea a message of "Death, death, death, death, death" that is also the start of a visionary poetic calling. Paul Valéry's "Le Cimitière marin" (1922) sets an individual attempt at spiritual and intellectual transcendence amid the felt presence of the dead in a seaside graveyard at noon (its text is appropriated by Krzysztof Penderecki for "Dies irae" [1967], an oratorio on Auschwitz). Perhaps the most distinguished 20th-c. poems to call themselves elegies are R. M. Rilke's *Duineser Elegien* (written 1912–22), which move between a sense of insufficiency and loss basic to human consciousness—"And so we live, and are always taking leave"—and a higher order of awareness among beings whom the poet calls "Angels."

II. Criticism. Critical thought about elegy has been an attempt to come to grips with this diversity, sometimes inadvertently amplifying it. Despite, e.g., current acknowledgment that they have little claim to the term, a number of poignant OE poems have for 200 years been called *elegies* in a move so closely associated with a sense of their value that the designation is unlikely to change. The prestige and longevity of the genre have increased its variety, and it has often splintered and become unrecognizable to itself; an important "school of elegy," for instance, in early 19th-c. Rus. poetry produced poems that share emotional intimacy and style but little topical focus. A mountain setting is required by the trad. of cl. Ger. elegy identified in Ziolkowski's study of Friedrich Schiller's originary "Der Spaziergang" (1795). Yet wherever we draw the boundaries of kind, some version of elegy is pervasively written about in every lang.

Critics writing in Eng. seem to agree that the topics of loss and death and the speech act of lament characterize the genre; that its mode is primarily *lyric, with certain characteristic generic markers (*apostrophe, exclamation, *pathetic fallacy, epideixis, pastoral topoi, allusion, *epitaph); and that its indigenous moods are sorrow, shock, rage, longing, melancholy, and resolution—often in quick succession. Most literary historians have understood elegy as closely linked to the hist., theory, and decorum of cultural practices of mourning. Pigman's *Grief and Renaissance Elegy* and Sacks's *The English Elegy* are two particularly influential studies, both pub. in 1985, that continue to set questions and topics for later scholars. While studies vary in the extent of their embrace of psychoanalysis or cultural hist., they concur in describing the elegy as, in Pigman's phrase, "a process of mourning." Pigman identifies a shift in Reformation views and

practices of mourning with consequences for elegy; Sacks sees the conventions of the genre from Edmund Spenser to Yeats as answerable to psychological needs. Later critics weigh in with some mix of social hist., psychology, and aesthetic analysis. Ramazani registers a protest by mod. elegy against normative cultural models of mourning; Zeiger, Kennedy, and others explore the importance of elegy as a resource for traumatic collective grief over breast cancer, AIDS, and the events of September 11, 2001; Spargo explores the psychological dimension of the form with philosophical attention.

Other puzzles invite attention. Why, if elegy is "a process of mourning," are so many elegies lyrics with little narrative or processional content? Standard definitions of *elegy* can strain against the temporality of lyric. Elegy's recourse to emotion seems incompletely explained by psychological or social models of grief or even by a notion of the poem as expressive. The emotions represented by the poem and the emotional experience that the poem offers to the reader are distinct; their trajectories need not coincide. They can, of course—as when, in a practice shared by other contemp. readers, Queen Victoria and George Eliot annotated the text of Alfred, Lord Tennyson's *In Memoriam* (1850) so that it referred to their own lost loves. Such evidence suggests that elegy is a kind of manual or liturgy for personal use; this function of the genre encouraged criteria such as sincerity or Johnson's "passion" to dominate critical evaluation of it. Yet such criteria seem ill suited to the power of poems such as "Lycidas," Spenser's "Daphnaida," Whitman's "When Lilacs Last in the Dooryard Bloom'd," and Auden's "In Memory of Sigmund Freud," which lament the deaths of persons who were not, in the standard sense of the term, "mourned" by the authors. Neither do current theories about the genre's purposes, collective or private, account for the numerous elegies of animals, objects, and so forth or for the peculiar ludic uses of the form by poets like Skelton, Emily Dickinson, Robert Burns, and the anonymous author of "Groanes from Newgate, or, An elegy upon Edvvard Dun, Esq. the cities common hangman, who dyed naturally in his bed the 11th of September, 1663."

The publication of elegy awaits further study. Chaucer's ms. *Book of the Duchess* is thought to have been produced for and performed at anniversary memorial events continuing long after the death of the duchess. With the advent of print, volumes of elegy were collected and printed to honor particular deaths (such as the famous volumes for Philip Sidney and the one containing "Lycidas"). Print also facilitated the voluminous appearance of elegy in broadside, and in the 17th c., the form developed what now seems like an incongruous affinity for acrostics and anagrams. Cavitch (2002) describes the publication of elegy in early New England with a traveler's report that there was not "one Country House in fifty which has not its Walls garnished with half a Score of these Sort of Poems." The changing forms of publication suggest a different hist. of elegy from what crit. might lead us to expect and also disabuse us of the sense that that hist. has reached any kind of conclusion.

See BLUES, ELEGIAC DISTICH, ELEGIAC STANZA.

■ E. Z. Lambert, *Placing Sorrow: A Study of the Pastoral Elegy Convention from Theocritus to Milton* (1976); T. Ziolkowski, *The Classical German Elegy 1795–1950* (1980); G. W. Pigman III, *Grief and English Renaissance Elegy* (1985); P. Sacks, *The English Elegy* (1985); C. M. Schenck, *Mourning and Panegyric* (1988); D. Kay, *Melodious Tears: The English Funeral Elegy from Spenser to Milton* (1990); J. Ramazani, *Poetry of Mourning: The Modern Elegy from Hardy to Heaney* (1994); E. Schor, *Bearing the Dead: The British Culture of Mourning from the Enlightenment to Victoria* (1994); W. D. Shaw, *Elegy and Paradox* (1994); M. F. Zeiger, *Beyond Consolation: Death, Sexuality, and the Changing Shapes of Elegy* (1997); M. Homans, *Royal Representations: Queen Victoria and British Culture 1837–1876* (1998); J. Hammond, *The American Puritan Elegy* (2000); M. Cavitch, "Interiority and Artifact: Death and Self-Inscription in Thomas Smith's *Self-Portrait*," *Early American Literature* 37 (2002); R. C. Spargo, *The Ethics of Mourning* (2004); M. Cavitch, *American Elegy* (2007); D. Kennedy, *Elegy* (2007); *The Oxford Handbook of the Elegy*, ed. K. A. Weisman (2010).

G. BRADEN; E. FOWLER

ELISION (Lat., "striking out"; Gr., *synaloepha*). In *prosody, the general term for several devices of contraction whereby two syllables are reduced to one. The Gr. term *synaloepha* nowadays tends to be restricted to only one form; other terms formerly used for elision in cl. prosody include *crasis* and *synizesis*. The forms of elision are: (1) *aphaeresis*: dropping of a word-initial syllable (vowel); (2) *syncope*: dropping of

a word-internal syllable; (3) *apocope*: dropping of a word-final syllable (vowel); (4) *synaeresis*: coalescing of two vowels within a word; and (5) *synaloepha*: coalescing of two vowels across a word boundary, i.e., ending one word and beginning the next. (The corresponding terms for addition of a syllable to the beginning, middle, or end of a word are *prosthesis, epenthesis,* and *proparalepsis,* respectively.)

Collectively, these are sometimes called, on the analogy of rhet., the "metric figures" (Elwert); Johann Susenbrotus, e.g., gives a taxonomy, calling the types of elision *metaplasms,* i.e., the class of figures for adding or subtracting a letter or syllable. Elision of whole words or phrases is *ellipsis. Probably at least some of the older terminology is confused, and certainly many prosodists over the centuries have failed to grasp that the reductive processes at work here are normal linguistic ones, not "poetical" devices peculiar to metrical verse. The shortening of words and smoothing out of the alternation of vowels and consonants are both common processes in speech. The opposite of elision is *hiatus.

In Gr., elision, variable in prose but more regular in poetry, is indicated by an apostrophe (') to mark the disappearance of the elided vowel (generally short *alpha, epsilon,* and *omikron* as well as the diphthong *ai* occasionally in Homer and in comedy); but when elision occurs in Gr. compound words, the apostrophe is not used. In Lat., a final vowel or a vowel followed by final *m* was not omitted from the written lang.; but as a rule, it was ignored metrically when the next word in the same measure began with a vowel, diphthong, or the aspirate *h*. In the mod. vernaculars, the apostrophe was retained to indicate graphically certain types of elision, but outside these, there is a larger case of words that have syllabically alternate forms in ordinary speech, e.g., *heaven,* which some speakers pronounce as a disyllable, some as a monosyllable. This syllabic variance is, of course, useful to poets who write in syllable-counting meters; thus, Sipe shows that in the overwhelming number of cases, Shakespeare chooses the one or other form of such words, which she terms "doublets," so as to conform to the meter.

There is some presumption that the number of syllables in the word that fits the *scansion of the line will be the number uttered in *performance (reading aloud) of the line. Robert Bridges, however, who has one of the seminal mod. discussions, uses the term *elision* in a special sense, to denote syllables that should be elided for purposes of scansion but not in pronunciation, a theory that divides scansion from performance. Ramsey has termed this "semi-elision," in his crit. of Bridges's position. The problem of poets' alteration of the syllabic structure of their lang. for metrical purposes is far more complex than is usually assumed; indeed, the very problem of determining what was ordinary speech practice at various times in the past itself is very difficult. Most of the hist. of Eng. metrical theory from ca. 1650 to 1925 could be framed in terms of dispute about elision, i.e., syllabic regularity.

■ T. S. Omond and W. Thomas, "Milton and Syllabism," *MLR* 4–5 (1909–10); Bridges; Omond; W. J. Bate, *The Stylistic Development of Keats* (1945); P. Fussell Jr., "The Theory of Poetic Contractions," *Theory of Prosody in 18th-Century England* (1954); A. C. Partridge, *Orthography in Shakespeare and Elizabethan Drama* (1964); Chatman; R. O. Evans, *Milton's Elisions* (1966); J. Soubiran, *L'elision dans la poésie latine* (1966); D. L. Sipe, *Shakespeare's Metrics* (1968); Allen; P. Ramsey, *The Fickle Glass* (1979), appendix; West; Elwert, *Italienische*.

T.V.F. BROGAN

ELLIPSIS (or *eclipsis*; Gr., "leaving out," "defect"; Lat. *detractio*). The most common term for the class of figures of syntactic omission (deletion). (Omission or deletion of syllables for metrical purposes is treated as *elision.) Ellipsis as a genus includes several species: ellipsis of conjunctions between words is brachylogia, between clauses, *asyndeton; ellipsis of a verb (in a different sense) is *zeugma; ellipsis of a clause, particularly the main clause (B) after a subordinate (Y) in a construction such as "If X, then A; if Y then B"—e.g. "If you will do it, all will be well; if not, . . ."—is anapodoton. These differ from figures such as aposiopesis, the dropping of the end of a sentence, leaving it incomplete, in that, in ellipsis, the thought is complete; it is only that a word or words ordinarily called for in the full construction but not strictly necessary are omitted (since obvious). This obviousness that makes the omission possible is, therefore, much facilitated by the use of *parallelism of syntactic members in the construction, which explains the importance of such parallelism for achieving that effect of compression, the hallmark of the closed *heroic couplet. So Alexander Pope has "Where wigs [strive] with wigs, // [where]

with sword-knots sword-knots strive" (*The Rape of the Lock* 1.101).

Gr. rhetoricians permitted omission of substantives, pronouns, objects, finite verbs, main clauses, and (more rarely) clauses; poets since the Ren. have allowed omission of almost any member so long as the meaning remains clear (Quintilian, *Institutio oratoria* 9.3.58). Shakespeare has "And he to England shall along with you" (*Hamlet* 3.3.4) and "when he's old, cashiered" (*Othello* 1.1.48). Mod. poets (e.g., Ezra Pound, T. S. Eliot, W. H. Auden, W. C. Williams) have found ellipsis esp. useful for conveying the speed and clipped form of colloquial speech and for expressing emotion.

See SYNTAX, POETIC.

■ E. A. Abbott, *A Shakespearean Grammar* (1886), 279–94—extensive lists of examples; Group μ, 69 ff.; Corbett—prose examples; E. Rozik, "Ellipsis and the Surface Structures of Verbal and Nonverbal Metaphor," *Semiotica* 119 (1998); J. Merchant, "Fragments and Ellipsis," *Linguistics and Philosophy* 27 (2004); *The Syntax of Nonsententials*, ed. L. Progovac et al. (2006).

T.V.F. BROGAN

ENCOMIUM. Strictly, a Gr. choral lyric performed "in the revel" (*komos*) to celebrate a person's achievements. More generally, the name is applied to any poem praising a human rather than a god (Plato, *Republic* 607a; Aristotle, *Poetics* 4), and it coincides with other designations such as *panegyric and epinikion. In the generic categories devised by the Alexandrian librarians to classify Gr. choral lyric, *encomium* referred to poems that were less formal than epinikia and that were probably, like the skolion, performed at banquets. Simonides brought the genre to its maturity, but no examples of his encomia are extant; only fragments remain of the encomia of the two most important subsequent authors, Pindar (fr. 118–28) and Bacchylides (fr. 20Aa–g). In its broadest application, *encomium* becomes indistinguishable from *praise* as a subdivision of epideictic oratory (Aristotle, *Rhetoric* 1358b18 ff.). Both the first Sophistic movement (5th c. BCE) and the second (2d c. CE) produced prose encomia of frivolous and paradoxical subjects (Pease), forerunners of Erasmus's *Moriae encomium* (*The Praise of Folly*).

Although encomiastic passages can be found throughout Greco-Roman poetry (Burgess), salient examples include Theocritus, *Idylls* 16 and 17; Horace, *Odes* 4.4 and 4.14; (Tibullus) 3.7; and the anonymous *Laus pisonis*. Encomia continue to be written in the Byzantine period (Viljamaa), the Middle Ages (Baldwin), and the Ren. (Hardison, Garrison).

■ Pauly-Wissowa; T. Burgess, *Epideictic Literature* (1902); G. Fraustadt, *Encomiorum in litteris Graecis usque ad Romanam aetatem historia* (1909); A. S. Pease, "Things without Honor," *CP* 21 (1926); C. S. Baldwin, *Medieval Rhetoric and Poetic* (1928); A. E. Harvey, "The Classification of Greek Lyric Poetry," *CQ* 5 (1955); H. K. Miller, "The Paradoxical Encomium with Special Reference to Its Vogue in England, 1600–1800" *MP* 53 (1956); O. B. Hardison Jr., *The Enduring Monument* (1962); W. Meinke, *Untersuchungen zu den Enkomiastischen Gedichten Theokrits* (1965); T. Viljamaa, *Studies in Greek Encomiastic Poetry of the Early Byzantine Period* (1968); J. D. Garrison, *Dryden and the Tradition of Panegyric* (1975); A. W. Nightingale, "The Folly of Praise: Plato's Critique of Encomiastic Discourse in the *Lysis* and *Symposium*," *CQ* n.s. 43 (1993).

W. H. RACE

ENGLISH PROSODY

I. Old English
II. Middle English
III. Modern English

I. Old English (ca. 500–1100 CE). OE verse, like that of the other early Germanic langs. (Old Saxon, OHG, ON), is composed in hemistichs or verses linked by *alliteration into long lines. Despite some technical differences between the strict metrical style of *Beowulf* or *Exodus* and the freer style of the late poem "The Battle of Maldon" (ca. 991), the extant trad. during the four centuries from Cædmon's "Hymn" (ca. 670) to the Norman Conquest (1066) is remarkably homogeneous. The main variation from this normal *meter is the infrequent hypermetric verse (Ger. *Schwellvers*). Of the 30,000 lines of OE poetry, there are fewer than 950 hypermetric verses, which usually occur in clusters and exceed the normal metrical limit by several heavy syllables.

It has sometimes been said that OE poetry is in the "strong-stress" trad. along with mod. *accentual verse on the assumption that each hemistich contains two main stresses and an indeterminate number of unstressed syllables. Although it is obvious that word stress is an important element of OE meter (alliteration depends on it), it has also become clear in studies of the past

four decades that OE meter is a complex mix of at least three elements that are usually assigned to different metrical typologies: stress, quantity, and syllable count. At present, there is no agreement on which element is most basic and which two are derivative. In addition to these phonological determinants, some studies posit word shape as a prime (Russom, Bredehoft).

It has always been known that quantity was an element of OE meter, although its position was considered secondary: in summaries of OE meter for handbooks and anthols., it was often omitted altogether. The technicalities involve resolution (whereby a short stressed syllable is grouped with the following syllable into a unit) and suspension of resolution. Renewed attention to Kaluza's Law has highlighted the importance of syllable quantity in the formulation of an adequate theory (Fulk).

Syllable counting is the least obvious of the elements to figure into a statement of OE meter. A glance down a page of OE poetry in a mod. ed. confirms the variable length of lines that seem far from being "syllabic." However, the accordion-like expansion of the OE line is permitted only in certain specified parts of the verse. Elsewhere, there is a close matching of syllable or "syllable equivalent" with the abstract metrical unit, the "position" or "member." Because a pattern of four members was posited in the most influential study of OE meter (Sievers), there is nothing radical in beginning with a one-to-one mapping of syllable (or syllable equivalent) and metrical unit. A syllable-count pattern is generally accepted for a reconstructed IE meter (manifested in Avestan and, with secondary quantitative patterns, in Vedic). Just as Gr. meter seems to have developed by expanding the syllable count through quantitative equivalences, esp. in the dactylic hexameter, so possibly did Germanic meter (although distinguishing historical derivation from convergent innovation within a limited repertoire of possible elements is beyond reach). ON meter reflects syllable count even better than OE, the meters of Old Saxon and OHG much less so.

If Sievers's system invites these speculations in its "four members," this aspect has been completely displaced by his simultaneous but more tangible reification of the "five types," the most common patterns of syllables bearing full stress, secondary stress, and weak stress. The five types (labeled A through E) appear in every intro. to OE poetry of the past c., and the scheme serves as a convenient taxonomy for mnemonic, peda-gogical, and classificatory purposes:

A	/ x / x	gomban gyldan
B	x / x /	þenden wordum wēold
C	x / / x	ofer hronrāde
D	/ / \ x	cwēn Hrōðgāres
E	/ \ x /	flōdȳþum feor

Still, one may question whether Sievers's types are the cause (the paradigm) or the effect (epiphenomena of a more basic pattern) and in any event whether the types are compatible with the two-stress idea. Types D and E regularly have three stresses (with the lightest falling on a syllable that elsewhere counts as a full ictus), and many types A and C appear to have only one stress.

The most obvious feature of the earliest poetry in the Germanic langs. is alliteration. As with *rhyme in later accentual-syllabic verse, alliteration does not determine metrical structure, which is easily discoverable without this cue. This superficial feature survived the rupture in the trad. caused by the Norman Conquest.

II. Middle English. ME prosody, a highly controverted field, has achieved little consensus as to the exact nature and origin of forms or even basic terminology. What is beyond dispute is that between the late 10th and late 14th cs., metrical innovation in ME verse flourished, encouraged by complex influences both foreign and native.

A. *Evolution of the Native Tradition.* Alliterative poetry of the cl. OE type continued to be written up to the Norman Conquest, the last poem in the strict meter arguably being *The Death of Edward* in 1066, on the event that brought about William's invasion. By the time of *The Description of Durham*, ca. 1104–9, only superficial elements of the meter remain, and the early ME verse that followed (e.g., *The Departing Soul's Address to the Body, The First Worcester Fragment*, Layamon's *Brut*) is clearly "looser" than OE alliterative verse. Whether it was modernized in lang. and meter from the cl. OE trad. or descended from a "popular" oral trad. or developed from the "rhythmical alliteration" of Wulfstan's and Ælfric's prose, early ME verse does share some features of OE verse. Lines are composed of two half lines usually linked by alliteration. However, half lines carry a greater number of unstressed syllables than in OE meter, and the rising and falling rhythm (x

/ x / x) predominates. Rhythmic patterns are irregular and cannot usefully be categorized on the basis of Sievers's five types (see sect. 1 above). Both alliteration and *leonine rhyme are treated as ornaments, but often neither alliteration nor rhyme occurs.

B. *Middle English Accentual-Syllabic Verse.* By the early 12th c., rhyme comes into use as a structural principle, borrowed probably from med. Lat. (e.g., Godric's *Hymns*, ca. 1170) but also under the influence of Fr., particularly the Anglo-Norman *vers décasyllabe*. Finally, it supplants alliteration altogether. The adaptation of Anglo-Norman and Fr. models to Eng. phonology leads to the octosyllabic couplet in contours of alternating stress, a staple of ME verse, as in John Gower's *Confessio amantis* and Chaucer's *House of Fame*. Octosyllabic verse in a variety of forms—couplets, the ballade stanza, cross-rhymed quatrains, and octaves—continues through the 15th c. (see OCTOSYLLABLE).

A number of other forms indebted to both med. Lat. and Anglo-Norman models come into play at the end of the 12th c.: a long line in mixed lengths of 12 and 14 syllables rhyming in couplets, quatrains, or octaves; the Burns stanza; and the ballade. It is believed that couplets of the 14-syllable line, by adding internal rhyme and breaking at the half lines into short-line quatrains, produced "8s and 6s," a form isomorphic to *ballad meter. The same internal rhyme breaks the alliterative long line into a short alliterative complex that persists from Layamon through the late tail-rhyme stanzas (e.g., *Sir Degrevaunt*). Tail rhyme, also derived from med. Lat. and Anglo-Norman exemplars, becomes the characteristic stanza of the Eng. metrical romances, usually in six- or 12-line stanzas. The addition of rhyme to the ornamental alliterative line produces a wide range of stanzas, as in the celebrated Harley lyrics. Generally speaking, the addition of rhyme coincides with a shift from accentual to accentual-syllabic verse, so that the number of syllables and the number and position of stresses in the line become relatively fixed. ME verse normally imitates the simple binary meters characteristic of med. Lat. verse, e.g., the *Poema morale* (ca. 1170), which imitates the Lat. septenarius.

C. *The Alliterative Long Line.* Alliterative composition in prose and rhymed verse continues throughout the 13th and 14th cs. in a broad continuum of styles derived from both the native trad. and from Lat. and Fr. The Harley lyrics (ms. composed ca. 1340–50) beautifully illustrate the difficulty of sorting out the separate strands. Of the 18 alliterative lyrics, 15 are arguably in a mixed iambic-anapestic meter more akin to meters found in Alfred, Lord Tennyson; Robert Browning; A. C. Swinburne; and Robert Frost than to anything in OE or early ME (hence, the apparent familiarity of the rhythms of these poems). For the rhythm of early 14th-c. lyrics, studies of "strict stress-meter" in Eng. by Tarlinskaja (cf. Rus. *dol'nik*) are more revealing than comparisons with OE meter.

For the so-called Alliterative Revival of the mid- 14th c., no substantial recent scholarship has examined the old problem of the external reasons for this remarkable flowering in the West Midlands. However, much progress has been made in understanding the metrical structure. These discoveries make it more difficult to trace a natural evolution, as Oakden did, from late OE through Layamon at the turn of the 13th c. to the Alliterative Revival of the late 14th and early 15th cs. Meanwhile, the term Alliterative Revival has been questioned in recent scholarship for ignoring much poetry of the 13th and 14th cs. that would show a more continuous trad. if our records were more complete.

It is not clear that our fuller understanding of the metrical structure can be tied to datable cultural and intellectual trends or the influence of other langs. It is equally unclear how the similarities with OE meter can be established as derivative from the earlier stage: e.g., both trads. have a highly specified element of syllable count, but it is hard to know whether this element was handed down as a metrical artifice or if the syllable count and departures from it in extra unstressed syllables are to be expected in a *stress-timed* language: in both OE and ME, the intervals between stresses appear to be regulated, as opposed to a *syllable-timed* language like Fr., in which the intervals between syllables are.

What can be specified precisely for poems like *Sir Gawain and the Green Knight* is the metrical structure of the second half of the long line (the b-verse) in terms of syllables that receive a metrical beat and syllables that do not. For the most part, the syllables that receive a beat are the stressed syllables of lexical words (esp. nouns and adjectives) and syllables that do not receive a metrical beat (thus forming an offbeat) are syllables of function words

and unstressed syllables of lexical words. The requirements are technical but crucial for any generalization about Eng. metrical typology in the Middle Ages: the b-verse must contain two beats and exactly one "strong dip" or "long dip" (two or more metrically unstressed syllables— Duggan, Cable); furthermore, the verse must end with exactly one unstressed syllable (Putter et al.), and the vowel of that syllable must be a schwa (Yakovlev). Having stated all these prescriptions for the b-verse, one can hypothesize that the a-verse is "otherwise, anything," i.e., any combination of long and short dips and of schwa and nonschwa vowels that does not meet the requirements for the b-verse. The two halves of the long line would then be "heteromorphic" (a term introduced by McIntosh but used only at the level of the foot); efforts to confirm or falsify this hypothesis are part of the ongoing scholarship in ME metrics. Meanwhile, there are exceptions to all the "rules" stated above (and resulting disagreements among metrists), and William Langland's *Piers Plowman* has more exceptions than most.

D. *Chaucer and the 15th Century.* The declining fortunes of Anglo-Norman in the mid-14th c. seem to have encouraged a shifting of attention to strict Fr. forms, and Chaucer's indebtedness to native ME prosody has proved increasingly difficult to demonstrate. Chaucer can certainly use ornamental alliteration, particularly in battle scenes (e.g., "The Knight's Tale," 2601 ff.), but his clearest adaptation of native ME prosody, in the tail rhyme and bob lines of "Tale of Sir Thopas," is satiric. In *The Parliament of Fowls*, Chaucer abandons the octosyllabic couplet for *rhyme royal, his staple stanza for formal poems (*Troilus and Criseyde*), and a form related to the monk's tale stanza. Chaucer also imitates the Fr. triple ballade ("Complaint of Venus") and rondel and the It. *terza rima ("A Complaint to His Lady"); *Anelida and Arcite* contains much prosodic experimentation.

But Chaucer's most significant technical achievement is the heroic or decasyllabic line (see DECASYLLABLE) in couplets, derived perhaps by expanding the octosyllabic couplet, perhaps from the rhyme royal stanza; its origin is disputed, so the very terms used to refer to it have never been settled. Chaucer is the first to use the five-beat or iambic pentameter couplet in Eng. (either in the prologue to the *Legend of Good Women* or in an early version of the "Knight's Tale"). Most prosodists agree that Chaucer's line has a predominantly "iambic" rhythm with variations: line-initial trochaic substitution (occasionally after the caesura), secondary stress on polysyllables, elision, and occasional weak stresses. Chaucer's greatness as a metrical artist lies in his skill at tensing rhetorical and syntactic accent against the basic metrical pattern.

Chaucer's enormous influence after his death in 1400 preserved his verse forms through the 15th c. It is not clear that his disciples understood what they imitated, although part of the problem may be gaps in our mod. understanding analogous to faulty readings of Chaucer before mod. texts were edited and the phonology of final e was established. John Lydgate's prosody, which influenced nearly every 15th-c. poet, is known especially for the "broken-backed" line, in which only a caesura appears to separate two strong stresses. However, an assumption of Chaucerian phonology will often justify a final e even if it is not written in the ms., and many lines become smoother. In fact, some of the undeniable badness of Lydgate's verse may result from an insistent, artificial regularity rather than from the stumbling rhythms that have usually been perceived. The 15th c.'s main contribution is the carol, though the pentameter couplet and rhyme royal are its staple forms.

III. Modern (after 1500)

A. *16th and Early 17th Centuries.* Early mod. Eng. verse represents competing trads.: (1) cl. quantitative verse, from Gr. and Lat. models (both strophic and hexameter lines), which proved incompatible with the accentual structure of Eng.; (2) "old-fashioned" accentual and alliterative poetry favored by John Skelton and others, a native form surviving until midcentury in the tumbling verse of the popular stage; and (3) the decasyllabic line, originating with Chaucer, sustained by his successors, and modified by the Eng. imitators of Petrarch and his It. and Fr. followers. Losing interest in quantitative schemes, Tudor poets and dramatists taught themselves to convert the *patterns* of cl. meters, especially iambic, to an accentual verse system in which accent or stress, not length, determines the measure. Early forms employed until almost the 17th c. include *fourteeners and poulter's measure, but the iambic pentameter line soon began to show its flexibility and expressive powers in various tonal registers. Favored by Thomas Wyatt in some of his most successful sonnets, the form was taken up without rhyme

by Henry Howard, the Earl of Surrey, for his trans. of part of the *Aeneid* and then used by Thomas Sackville and Thomas Norton for their political tragedy *Gorboduc* (1561). In the hands of Philip Sidney, Christopher Marlowe, Edmund Spenser, Shakespeare, and Ben Jonson, the iambic pentameter line revealed qualities that transformed lyric verse, helped usher in the greatest period of Brit. drama, and determined the future of Eng. poetry.

The virtues of the blank verse line derive from its moderate length, the ten syllables avoiding the liability of the longer line to split in half and of the short line to sound childish. The particular dynamic of *blank verse, especially for drama, dwells in the tension between, on the one hand, the semantic energies and grammatical claims of the sentence and, on the other, the rhythmic regularity of sequential pentameter lines (Wright). Poets exploited the variety of blank verse by finding that (1) the midline phrasal break could be variously located, (2) stressed syllables might be unequal in strength (and unstressed ones, too), (3) variations in the placement of stressing in the line could confer grace and energy, and (4) with occasional, even frequent, *enjambment, a passage could flow smoothly through unequal grammatical segments and seem as much speech as verse.

Discovering the malleability of the line, some poets developed its capacity for variation so thoroughly as to threaten the security of the pentameter frame. The later Shakespeare, John Webster, Thomas Middleton (in dramatic verse), and especially John Donne (in his *Satyres, Elegies,* and letters) exaggerate such features as enjambment, elision, inversion and other accentual variations, line length (both abbreviated and extended), and multiple pauses within the line. In achieving a speech-like immediacy, they vastly expanded the tonal possibilities of the form. Donne also pursued such variety in his *Songs and Sonnets,* leading Jonson to complain that he should be hanged for not keeping the accent. This vigorous period of innovation was contemporaneous with the less extreme prosodic experiments of Jonson and his followers. Their commitment to cl. forms and balanced lines gave rise to less radical but equally significant creativity with rhythm, rhyme, and length of line.

B. *Later 17th and 18th Centuries.* Spenser, Jonson, and George Herbert became the models for much lyric verse of the 17th c., with most poets endorsing Samuel Daniel's conservative view about the value of rhyme (*A Defence of Ryme*, 1603). Donne's successors, down through Andrew Marvell, John Milton, and Jonathan Swift, employ the tetrameter couplet as a balanced form for conveying subtle and sometimes ironic argument. The multiplicity of the blank verse line attracted an unparalleled voice in Milton, who chose it for *Paradise Lost* and explicitly defended it in a prefatory note to the poem. Prosodically correct (though in accordance with rules that are apparently his own—see Bridges, Sprott, and Weismiller) and extraordinarily resourceful, his epic verse, audaciously blank, keeps the grand grammatical sentence boldly diverging from yet counterpoised with the equally heroic line.

But it is the *heroic couplet, deriving from the decasyllables of Chaucer and Jonson and usurping the rhythmic possibilities of the blank-verse line, that becomes the sovereign form in Eng. poetry for over a c. It invited Edmund Waller, John Denham, John Dryden, and eventually Alexander Pope to exploit its hospitality to antithetical words and phrases: they built oppositions into the line or set line against line in a seemingly inexhaustible display of verbal balance, polish, ingenuity, and "bite." *Odes, Pindaric or Horatian, afforded the resourceful poet a different variety of challenging formal (and cl.) structures. Augustan prosodists (Edward Bysshe, Richard Bentley, and Henry Pemberton) and critics (Samuel Johnson) condemn departures from metrical norms, but toward the end of the c., monotony and desire for change eventually hastened the return of blank verse, esp. as a medium for reflection. At the same time, the rediscovery of the ballad stimulated the writing of lyric poems in looser forms and encouraged other variation in poems with an iambic base.

C. 19th Century. Liberated from the couplet, romantic poetry explores rich veins of blank and stanzaic verse of various shapes and dimensions (Curran). But the century's poets soon divide into opposing distinct prosodic camps: one moves toward accentual verse, with its strong recurrent pattern of regular beats, the other toward free verse and its highlighting of the rhythmical phrase. The first group tries on various modes: triple meters (E. A. Poe and H. W. Longfellow), anapestic variation in iambic verse (Browning, Swinburne, Thomas Hardy), the

accentually *sprung rhythm of the *"Christabel" meter and G. M. Hopkins, and dipodic rhythms (Browning, George Meredith, Rudyard Kipling), all of which, as they strengthen both the equality and the isochronism of the beat, diminish the role of expressive variation within the line. Tennyson and Browning are exceptional in their ability still to write compelling blank verse. The second party prefers early types of free verse, expressive (as in Walt Whitman) of loosely measured sequences of self-reliant perceptions. The ordered lines of Ren. and Augustan verse, apparently representing some combination of natural order, the forces of authority, and social and political hierarchies, begin increasingly to lose their appeal as the century proceeds. They yield to the romantic and postromantic quest for a vehicle appropriate to the inner experience of a human subject deprived of religious and social certainty.

D. 20th Century. The most influential voices soon make free verse the chief metrical mode. Ezra Pound and W. C. Williams embrace Whitman's elevation of the rhythmic phrase, apparently imitating ordinary speech but often introducing such effects as unexpected rhyme and audacious rhythmic play. Certain modernist poets mix familiar forms, including blank verse, with a freer prosody, as in T. S. Eliot's *The Waste Land*, where disintegration is a principal motif. Some of Whitman's self-proclaimed followers (e.g., Allen Ginsberg and the Beat poets) eschew conventional forms almost entirely. Poets who often retain traditional meters (e.g., Wallace Stevens, Robert Lowell, John Berryman) adapt them freely, as if they represented some order of reality, sanity, or conduct only dimly and intermittently descried; and in many major poets, traditional forms recur, sometimes brilliantly redeemed (W. B. Yeats, Robert Frost, W. H. Auden, Richard Wilbur, Philip Larkin, Anthony Hecht, and several contemp. Eng. poets). Other forms explored by 20th-c. poets (esp. Marianne Moore and Auden) include *syllabic verse, which furnishes a concealed formal structure, and *concrete poetry. Late in the c., many Language poets consciously represent their subversion of form as an attack on the social conventions and practices of capitalism; and Af. Am., Caribbean, and postcolonial writers, grown increasingly accomplished and prominent, promote their own cultural forms, often in combination with the conventions of the Eng. trad. Fed by all these strains,

Eng. poetry at the beginning of the 21st c. has contrived a truce between the surety of familiar forms and the liberty of the individual voice, with poets adjusting the emphasis according to their bent.

Analysis of poetic modes comes generally after the fact, but in every period, prosodic crit. has a moralistic flavor, with many critics and poets disdaining their predecessors: e.g., 19th-c. poets, such as John Keats and Matthew Arnold, sometimes dismissed their Augustan precursors as writers of mere prose. Inconclusive debate has always attended the effort to relate prosody to meaning. Pope's famous dictum that "the sound should seem an echo to the sense," illustrated with his lines about "swift Camilla," represents one side of the case; the other is taken by Johnson, who (also famously) dismisses the general applicability of the contention. In various periods, poets, critics, and readers have sensed a semiotic function of prosody without being able to generalize persuasively about it. The regular pentameter line and the internal aural challenges to it represent a wider contest between order and individuality, and in the 20th c., the failure of traditional forms often signifies personal and social collapse. Some feminist critics have identified traditional meter with the restrictions of patriarchal control: Emily Dickinson, e.g., is said to have mostly avoided iambic pentameter as connoting the forces of Father and Christianity. But there is little agreement on such an iconic function of prosody.

See ALLITERATION; FREE VERSE; HEROIC VERSE; RHYTHM; SOUND; STANZA; VERSIFICATION.

■ **Old English:** Sievers; M. Kaluza, *A Short History of English Versification* (1911); J. C. Pope, *The Rhythm of "Beowulf,"* 2d ed. (1966); A. J. Bliss, *The Metre of "Beowulf,"* 2d ed. (1967); T. Cable, *The Meter and Melody of "Beowulf"* (1974); Brogan, sect. K; G. Russom, *Old English Meter and Linguistic Theory* (1987); W. Obst, *Der Rhythmus des "Beowulf"* (1987); R. D. Fulk, *A History of Old English Meter* (1992); B. R. Hutcheson, *Old English Poetic Metre* (1995); S. Suzuki, *The Metrical Organization of "Beowulf"* (1996); T. A. Bredehoft, *Early English Metre* (2005).

■ **Middle English:** *General:* Schipper; K. Luick *Englische Metrik* (1893); B. Ten Brink, *The Language and Metre of Chaucer* (1920); J. P. Oakden, *Alliterative Poetry in Middle English,* 2 v. (1930–35); A. McI. Trounce, "The English Tail-Rhyme Romances," *Medium Ævum* 1–2

(1932–34); F. Pyle, "The Place of Anglo-Norman in the History of English Versification," *Hermathena* 49 (1935); P. F. Baum, *Chaucer's Verse* (1961); M. Borroff, *"Sir Gawain and the Green Knight": A Metrical and Stylistic Study* (1962); M. D. Legge, *Anglo-Norman Literature and Its Background* (1963); Pearsall; Brogan, sect. K; U. Fries, *Einführung in die Sprache Chaucers* (1985); A.V. C. Schmidt, *The Clerkly Maker* (1987); M. Tarlinskaja, *Strict Stress-Meter in English Poetry* (1993). *Alliterative Revival:* J. R. Hulbert, "A Hypothesis Concerning the Alliterative Revival," *MP* 28 (1930); R. A. Waldron, "Oral-Formulaic Technique and Middle English Alliterative Poetry," *Speculum* 32 (1957); E. Salter, "The Alliterative Revival," *MP* 64 (1966–67); T. Turville-Petre, *The Alliterative Revival* (1977); A. McIntosh, "Early Middle English Alliterative Verse," and D. Pearsall, "The Alliterative Revival," *Middle English Alliterative Poetry,* ed. D. A. Lawton (1982); H. Duggan, "The Shape of the B-Verse in Middle English Alliterative Poetry," *Speculum* 61 (1986); T. Cable, *The English Alliterative Tradition* (1991); R. Hanna, "Alliterative Poetry," *Cambridge History of Medieval English Literature,* ed. D. Wallace (1999); C. Chism, *Alliterative Revivals* (2002); H. Zimmerman, "Continuity and Innovation: Scholarship on the Middle English Alliterative Revival," *Jahrbuch für Internationale Germanistik* 35 (2003); A. Putter, J. Jefferson, and M. Stokes, *Studies in the Metre of Alliterative Verse* (2007); N. Yakovlev, "Prosodic Restrictions on the Short Dip in Late Middle English Alliterative Verse," *YLS* 23 (2009).

■ **Modern:** Schipper; Smith—texts of Ren. prosodists; Schipper, *History*; Bridges; Omond; O. Jespersen, "Notes on Metre," rpt. in his *Linguistica* (1933); G. W. Allen, *American Prosody* (1934)—dated but not yet replaced; S. E. Sprott, *Milton's Art of Prosody* (1953); P. Fussell, *Theory of Prosody in Eighteenth-Century England* (1954); Wimsatt and Beardsley; Saintsbury, *Prosody*—eccentric theoretically; J. Thompson, *The Founding of English Metre* (1961); M. Halpern, "On the Two Chief Metrical Modes in English," *PMLA* 77 (1962)—fundamental; Chatman; K. Shapiro and R. Beum, *A Prosody Handbook* (1965); W. B. Piper, *The Heroic Couplet* (1969); J. Malof, *A Manual of English Meters* (1970); D. Attridge, *Well-Weighed Syllables* (1974); D. Crystal, "Intonation and Metrical Theory," *The English Tone of Voice* (1975);

Tarlinskaja; E. Weismiller, "Blank Verse," *A Milton Encyclopedia*, ed. W. B. Hunter et al. (1978); H. Gross, ed., *The Structure of Verse*, 2d ed. (1979); C. O. Hartman, *Free Verse* (1980); Brogan—full list of references with annotations; Hollander; D. Wesling, *The New Poetries* (1985); S. Woods, *Natural Emphasis* (1985); S. Curran, *Poetic Form and British Romanticism* (1986); G. T. Wright, *Shakespeare's Metrical Art* (1988); O. B. Hardison Jr., *Prosody and Purpose in the English Renaissance* (1989); A. Finch, *The Ghost of Meter* (1993); H. Gross and R. Mc-Dowell, *Sound and Form in Modern Poetry*, 2d ed. (1996); R. McDonald, *Shakespeare's Late Style* (2006); J. Longenbach, *The Art of the Poetic Line* (2007).

T. CABLE (OE); R. H.OSBERG
AND T. CABLE (ME); G. T. WRIGHT
AND R. McDONALD (MOD.)

ENJAMBMENT (Fr., *enjamber*, "to straddle or encroach"). The continuation of a syntactic unit from one line to the next without a major juncture or pause; the opposite of an end-stopped line. While enjambment can refer to any verse that is not end-stopped, it is generally reserved for instances in which the "not stopping" of the verse is felt as overflow, esp. in relation to some poetic effect, as in the opening lines of Shakespeare's sonnet 116: "Let me not to the marriage of true minds / Admit impediments." In these lines, the desire not to admit impediments to the marriage of true minds is enacted poetically because the sentence "refuses" to stop at the line's end. One way to emphasize enjambment is to combine the use of enjambment with *cae-sura* (mid-line pause), as demonstrated in the following passage from *Hamlet*: "[The world is] an unweeded garden / That goes to seed; things rank and gross in nature / Possess it merely. That it should come to this!" (1.2.135–7). The enjambments and caesuras in these lines reinforce the image of a weedy garden outgrowing its proper boundaries, as well as the jumps in Hamlet's thoughts.

Enjambment can give the reader mixed messages: the closure of the metrical pattern at line end implies a pause, while the incompletion of the phrase says to go on. These conflicting signals can heighten tension or temporarily suggest one meaning only to adjust that meaning when the phrase is completed. To some degree, enjambment has been associated with freedom and transgression since romanticism; such

associations are predicated on a norm of end-stopped verse and sparing use of enjambment, in relation to which the enjambment appears liberating. Enjambment ultimately depends on expectation of a pause at line's end; if verses are enjambed routinely, readers may perceive the text as something like prose.

Cl. *hexameter is mainly end-stopped, as is Sanskrit verse. Though Homer's hexameters are more frequently enjambed than, say, those of the Hellenistic writers, it is often hard to discern poetic motivation behind the enjambments (the effect of enjambment in oral poetry and in *song may be different from that of written verse). Virgil uses enjambment in ways that sometimes seem poetically motivated and sometimes not. Enjambment can be found in biblical Heb. and cl. Ar. verse, but it is not the norm. Enjambment is the norm in Old Germanic alliterative verse, incl. OE, where rhyme is unknown and lines are bound together by *alliteration used to mark the meter. Prior to the 12th c., enjambment is rare in OF poetry: the *trouvère* Chrétien de Troyes (fl. after 1150) seems to have been the first poet in the Eur. vernaculars to break his verses systematically. By the 15th c., enjambment is widely used, and even more so in the 16th, esp. by Pierre de Ronsard (who coined the term) and the poets of the Pléiade. In the 17th c., enjambment was impugned by François de Malherbe and later Nicolas Boileau. These neoclassical authorities, however, allowed its use in certain circumstances—in decasyllabic poetry (see DECASYLLABLE) and in the less "noble" genres such as comedy and fable. Occasionally, enjambment occurs even in tragedy.

Since André Chénier (1762–94), enjambment has been accepted in all genres in Fr. The device was exploited to the full by Victor Hugo, whose famous enjambment at the beginning of *Hernani*—"Serait-ce déjà lui? C'est bien à l'escalier / Dérobé" (Is he already here? It must be by the secret staircase)—had the force of a manifesto (because adjectives generally follow nouns in Fr., Hugo is able to place *dérobé* [secret] on the other side of the line break). Enjambment was a fundamental characteristic of the *vers libéré* of the later 19th c. and the *vers libre* that emerged from it. In French prosody, enjambment has been a subject of controversy: since Fr. rhythms are in essence phrasal, line-terminal accents tend to coincide with significant syntactic junctures. Consequently, the terminology for analyzing types of constructions in enjambment is more developed in Fr. prosody than in Eng.

In Eng., enjambment was used widely by the Elizabethans for dramatic and narrative verse. The neoclassical *couplet drove most enjambment from the scene in the 18th c., but the example of John Milton revived it for the romantics, who saw it as the metrical emblem for liberation from neoclassical rules. (In Milton, enjambment is sometimes used to thwart readers' expectations—to provide a momentary shock of error that may be likened to a recognition of living in a fallen world.) William Wordsworth makes frequent use of enjambment in his *blank verse poems ("Tintern Abbey," *The Prelude*), as does John Keats (*Endymion*). G. M. Hopkins's *"sprung rhythm" introduces "roving over" (metrical and syntactic enjambment) so that "the scanning runs on without a break from the beginning . . . of a stanza to the end." 20th-c. poets like W. C. Williams and e. e. cummings use enjambment so frequently that it is the rule rather than the exception in many of their poems.

Since at least the mid-19th c., poets have made increased use of what is sometimes called "hard enjambment"—enjambment so striking it cannot help but be felt. Enjambment of this sort might include enjambment across stanzas (as when Charles Baudelaire, speaking of how the "belly and breasts" of his mistress "advanced" toward him in "Les Bijoux" ["Jewels"], places the verb advanced at the beginning of a stanza); enjambment separating articles or adjectives from their nouns (as in Williams's *Spring and All*: "under the surge of the blue / mottled clouds driven from the / northeast— a cold wind."); and enjambment that splits a word across a line (as in Hopkins's opening to "The Windhover": "I caught this morning morning's minion, king- / dom of daylight's dauphin"). Perception of hard enjambment, like the perception of enjambment in general, depends on such factors as the reader's experience and literary-historical context. No comprehensive taxonomy of types or effects of enjambment exists.

See LINE.

■ M. Parry, "The Distinctive Character of Enjambment in Homeric Verse" (1929), rpt. in Parry (1971); Hollander, "'Sense Variously Drawn Out: Some Observations on English Enjambment"; H. Golomb, *Enjambment in Poetry* (1979); S. Cushman, *William Carlos Williams and the Meanings of Measure*, ch. 1 (1985); R. Silliman, "Terms of Enjambment," *The Line*

in Postmodern Poetry, ed. R. Frank and H. Sayre (1988); A. Sanni, "On *tadmin* (Enjambment) and Structural Coherence in Classical Arabic Poetry," *Bulletin of the School of Oriental and African Studies* 52, no. 3 (1989); C. Higbie, *Measure and Music: Enjambment and Sentence Structure in the "Iliad"* (1991); M. E. Clark, "Enjambment and Binding in Homeric Hexameter," *Phoenix* 48 (1994); M. L. Shaw, "Verse and Prose," *The Cambridge Introduction to French Poetry* (2003).

T.V.F. BROGAN; C. SCOTT; S. MONTE

ENVOI, envoy (Fr., "a sending on the way"). A short concluding stanza, often addressed to a noble patron (frequently "Prince") and summarizing the argument of a lyric. In the *sestina, the envoi normally consists of three lines, in the ballade of four, and in the *chant royal* of either five or seven, thus repeating the metrical pattern as well as the *rhyme scheme of the half stanza that precedes it. During the great period of the OF fixed forms, it restates the poem's major theme, serving as an interpretive gloss within the poem itself. For this reason, the Occitan troubadours called their envois *tornadas* (returns).

Among the Eng. poets, Walter Scott, Robert Southey, and A. C. Swinburne employed envois. Chaucer wrote a number of ballades in which he departs from the customary form by closing with an envoi that is equal in length to a regular stanza of the poem, usually his favorite *rhyme royal. In mod. imitations, the envoi is often ironic or satirical and may be addressed to any entity related to the poem, e.g., "birds" (N. E. Tyerman's "Ballad: Before My Bookshelves"), "bookmen" (Lionel Johnson's "Ballade of the *Caxton Head*"), "moralists" (Brander Matthews's still humorous "The Ballade of Fact and Fiction"), and so on.

■ H. L. Cohen, *Lyric Forms from France* (1922); R. Dragonetti, *La Technique poétique des trouvères dans la chanson courtoise* (1960), pt. 1, ch. 4; Tarlinskaja, ch. 7; Gasparov, *History*.

A. PREMINGER; D. J. ROTHMAN

EPIC

I. History
II. Theory

I. History

A. Definitions. An epic is a long narrative poem of heroic action: "narrative," in that it tells a story; "poem," in that it is written in verse rather than prose; "heroic action," while reinterpreted by each major epic poet, in that, broadly defined, it recounts deeds of great valor that bear consequence for the community to which the hero belongs. An epic plot is typically focused on the deeds of a single person or hero, mortal though exceptionally strong, intelligent, or brave, and often assisted or opposed by gods. Epic is set in a remote or legendary past represented as an age of greater heroism than the present. Its style is elevated and rhetorical. To compose an epic has often been viewed as the foremost challenge a poet can undertake, and the enduringly successful epics are a small and select group.

A distinction is commonly drawn between oral or "primary" epic, which has its origins in oral *performance, and literary or "secondary" epic, composed as a written text. Oral poetry is performed by a skilled singer who improvises on familiar material, drawing on a stock of formulas, fixed phrases in particular metrical patterns, like an improvising musician's repertory of riffs. The oral poet also employs formulaic type-scenes, such as the feast, assembly, arming of the hero, or single combat, which can be varied as the context requires. In the 1920s, a young Am. scholar, Milman Parry, demonstrated that the *Iliad* and the *Odyssey* bear traces of oral composition. The Homeric epithets, or characterizing phrases—"strong-greaved Achaians," "Agamemnon, lord of men"—vary, Parry noted, according to grammatical case and position in the line, a phenomenon best accounted for by origins in oral performance. Parry subsequently tested his hypothesis by recording living oral poets in the Balkans, who improvised using formulaic lines, phrases, and scenes in similar fashion. Trads. of oral heroic poetry exist in Egypt, Arabia, Kirghistan, Mali, and elsewhere.

The distinction between oral and literary epic is not absolute and can mislead if treated too rigidly. Poems that have been passed down unwritten into recent times can be considered oral in a straightforward sense, but, in cases such as the *Iliad*, we are necessarily dealing with written texts, whose proximity to a prior oral trad. is a matter of conjecture. The *Iliad* contains traces of oral composition, but the text we have is not itself an oral poem, nor should we assume that it was the first version to be transcribed. Primary epic is sometimes described as "traditional," but, in fact, both primary and secondary epic are traditional forms of art; the

process of *traditio* or handing down takes place directly in primary epic, at a distance in secondary epic. In oral poetry, the matter of the song and the art of recitation are handed down from bard to bard, presumably through sustained personal contact. In literary epic, the new poet signals participation in the epic trad. by imitating formal, thematic, and stylistic elements of previous epics, so that an informed reader may readily sense the relation between old and new. While all genres contain such imitative gestures, they are esp. prominent in epic, where the presence of the old in the new is strongly felt.

To define *epic* broadly as any long narrative poem of heroic action has the advantage of inclusiveness. It recognizes the artistry of heroic narrative poems around the world and allows for cross-cultural comparisons such as the studies carried out by Parry and his student Albert Lord. The disadvantage of applying the term *epic* to poems around the world is that to do so effaces the trads. to which each poem belongs. The Babylonian *Epic of Gilgamesh*, the Sanskrit *Mahābhārata*, the OF *Chanson de Roland*, the OE *Beowulf*, and the South Slavic oral poems recorded by Parry and Lord in the 1930s—not to mention the *Odyssey* and the *Iliad*—all qualify as narrative poems of heroic action, but to call them all epics is to subsume them within a category that would have been unrecognizable to their authors and first audiences. They are most accurately understood within their own cultural contexts, on their own generic terms.

The term *epic* has a long hist. of usage in a narrower sense, to refer to the trad. of heroic narrative poetry written in conscious descent from the *Iliad* and the *Odyssey* by way of Virgil's *Aeneid*. That the two Homeric poems were the source of this trad. was taken as fact in antiquity and never forgotten; but while the prestige of Homer's name endured, the texts themselves became, in most of Europe, lost poems in a lost lang. from late antiquity into the Ren., known only in fragments and redactions. The *Aeneid* was received as a classic virtually from the moment of its appearance; since it was written in Lat., it never lost its familiarity, and it retained its status as the paradigmatic epic even after the 16th c. when the Homeric poems became more widely known in Europe. More than any other poem, the *Aeneid* established the conventions of epic as they were understood by later poets; while many of these conventions originate in Homer, their Virgilian versions would become the most widely imitated. These conventions, described in greater detail below, include stylistic elements such as extended *similes, elevated *diction, and *epithets; formal elements such as the proem, bringing the audience *in medias res*, digression, and prophecy; recurrent scenes such as the celestial descent, the earthly paradise, the *catalog, the *locus amoenus*, *ekphrasis, and *katabasis*. No epic poem contains every conventional feature, and no feature is present in every poem. The unity of the genre is best understood in terms of Ludwig Wittgenstein's concept of family resemblance, "a complicated network of similarities overlapping and criss-crossing: sometimes overall similarities, sometimes similarities of detail" (*Philosophical Investigations*). Thinking of generic unity in this way releases the critic from the fruitless task of distinguishing between essential and accidental features of epic and from the equally fruitless task of determining which poems deserve inclusion; as Greene saw it, poems participate in the epic mode to different degrees.

B. *Conventions.* (i) Proem. An epic poem conventionally begins with an introductory passage or proem (Lat. *proemium*, "preface" or "introduction"). The proem includes a proposition or brief statement of the poem's subject. The choice of words in the proposition is of special significance since it indicates the poem's major themes and emphases, frequently with a revisionary gesture toward previous epics. As so often, the paradigmatic instance is Virgilian. The first words of the *Aeneid*, "arma virumque cano" (I sing of arms and a man) allude, in "arms," to the martial subject matter of the *Iliad* and, in "man," to the lone voyaging hero of the *Odyssey*, thus indicating Virgil's aim to encompass the subjects of both Homeric poems within his own. The proem also includes an invocation, where the poet invokes the assistance of the Muse to inspire his song. In Gr. mythology, the Muses are the nine daughters of Zeus and Mnemosyne, goddess of memory; the Muse associated with epic poetry is named Calliope. The convention of invoking the Muse derives from epic's origins in oral performance. In Gr. oral trad., the invocation was a prayer, overheard by the audience, offered at the start of each performance to the Muse or Muses, patron deities of the professional singer. The convention was retained in literary epic, with postclassical poets understanding it in symbolic or Christian terms. A third element commonly found within the epic proem is a dedication,

or expression of homage by the poet toward an earthly patron or head of state. Thus, e.g., Statius addresses the Roman emperor Domitian at the beginning of the *Thebiad*: "And you, glory added to Latium's fame, whom, as you take on your aged / father's enterprises anew, Rome wishes hers for eternity . . ." (1.22–4).

Secondary proems and invocations are sometimes to be found within a poem, typically preceding heightened moments or major changes of scene.

(ii) In medias res. The Lat. phrase *in medias res* means "into the midst of things" and refers to the epic convention of beginning not at the earliest point of the story but with the action already under way. The phrase derives from Horace's *Ars poetica*. A poet telling of the Trojan War, Horace writes, should not begin with Helen's birth from an egg:

> He gets right to the point and carries the reader
> Into the midst of things, as if known already . . .
>
> ("To the Pisos," 147–49)

In this passage, Horace is discussing the skill, necessary to all narrative poets, of capturing the interest of the audience from the outset. It is the reader or listener (Lat. *auditor*), not the poem, who is to be carried into the middle of events. While Horace's example is taken from the epic subject of Troy, he is not making a point about epic specifically. The phrase *in medias res* came to be understood and applied, however, as prescribing a particular nonlinear shape for epic narrative: the poem was to start at the heart of the story, usually with a burst of action, and fill in the chronologically prior events at a later point. This understanding probably came about through the combination of Horatian precept with Virgilian example. The *Aeneid* begins not with the fall of Troy but with the Trojan exiles approaching their destination, when the goddess Juno drives them off course with a violent storm; once on shore, Aeneas recounts earlier events in a flashback. Among numerous later examples, Marco Girolamo Vida's *Christiad* (1535), a Neo-Lat. epic on the passion of Christ, begins not with Christ's birth but with his entry into Jerusalem; Luís de Camões's *Lusiads* (1572), which tells of Vasco da Gama's voyage from Portugal to India, begins with the Port. mariners already past the Cape of Good Hope and approaching Mozambique.

(iii) Forms of digression. The nonlinear shape of epic narrative has other conventional features. If the poem begins by bringing the reader in medias res, prior events must be filled in subsequently. One standard way of doing so is through an embedded narrative told by a guest to a host after a meal, when the host, having fulfilled the first obligations of hospitality, may with courtesy put questions, and the refreshed guest may answer at leisure. Thus, Odysseus relates his famous "wanderings" to the Phaeacian king Alcinous and his court; Aeneas tells of the fall of Troy and the Trojans' subsequent journey to Dido and her court at Carthage; and in John Milton's *Paradise Lost*, the angel Raphael descends to Adam and Eve, is welcomed as their guest, and thereafter tells them of the war in heaven and the creation of the world.

Another form of digression is the epic prophecy, in which a seer furnishes the hero with an account or vision of future events. Through prophecy, the legendary past in which the epic is set can be linked to the historical present from which it is told. Typically, the prophet is a supernatural character or prophesies by supernatural means. The prophecy takes place in a special setting reached by a guided journey: in the underworld (see katabasis, below) or the heavens or during a sea voyage. A distinctive subcategory is the dynastic prophecy, in which the seer tells or shows the hero a genealogy of glorious descendants. Prophetic digression can also be expressed by the narrative voice, as in this succinct Miltonic example: "So clomb this first grand thief into God's fold: / So since into his church lewd hirelings climb" (*Paradise Lost* 4.192–93).

A third form of epic digression is the episode or incident loosely connected to the primary epic plot. The tale of Olindo and Sofronia in Torquato Tasso's *Gerusalemme liberata*, book 2, is an example. Heroic poems in the chivalric romance trad., such as Ludovico Ariosto's *Orlando furioso* and Alonso de Ercilla's *La Araucana*, are highly episodic. In the *Poetics*, book 9, Aristotle deprecates episodic plot, which he defines as a structure in which "the episodes or acts succeed one another without probable or necessary sequence"; the *Odyssey*, he felt, was properly unified, because Odysseus's various adventures were sufficiently connected to one another. In the early mod. period, after Aristotle's *Poetics* gained renewed influence in the 16th c., the subject of episodes received considerable

attention from literary critics. Some authors criticized *Orlando furioso* and other romances for violating Aristotelian unity of action; others praised their episodic plots for their variety; others such as Torquato Tasso sought a middle way, attempting to reconcile the pleasures of romance with Aristotelian principles.

(iv) Katabasis. Among the most distinctive of epic conventions is the katabasis (Gr., "descent") or descent to the underworld. As so often, Virgil's treatment is inspired by Homer, and it is Virgil's that becomes paradigmatic. Odysseus's visit to the land of the dead in the *Odyssey*, book 11, is not, strictly speaking, a katabasis but a *nekuia*, or summoning of ghosts, though the place's location is indistinct, Odysseus reaches it by ship. The journey of Aeneas to the underworld in the *Aeneid*, book 6, is a heightened supernatural episode rich in symbolic detail, through which Aeneas gains a fuller understanding of his mission and its fated consequences. Aeneas's journey involves several parts: first, elaborate ritual preparation for the descent, guided by the Cumaean Sibyl, priestess of Apollo; second, passage through the various regions of the underworld, encountering familiar ghosts; last, Aeneas's meeting with his father Anchises in Elysium, abode of the blessed. Anchises explains to his son the progress of the soul from death to rebirth and shows him a spiritual pageant of famous Romans culminating in Virgil's own time. The episode has proven among the most influential in Western lit. The whole of Dante's *Divine Comedy* could be described as a Christianized expansion of the *Aeneid*, book 6. In *Orlando furioso*, Ariosto includes a katabasis touched with travesty; the dynastic heroine Bradamante is treacherously dropped down a hole and happens to land at the tomb of Merlin, who shows her a dynastic pageant of her glorious descendants, enacted by conjured demons. The Mammon episode in Edmund Spenser's *Faerie Queene* is a form of katabasis.

(v) Celestial vision. Epic narrative moves between heaven and earth, juxtaposing the earth-bound perspectives of mortal characters with the exalted viewpoint of gods. On rare occasions, a mortal hero is allowed to see from a higher perspective, either by means of a vision or a literal ascent. Like the katabasis, such episodes involve a supernatural guide and show exceptional divine favor to the recipient; they provide the hero with higher knowledge, often prophetic or metaphysical, with which he returns enlightened to his earthly endeavor. Where the katabasis provides knowledge from below, the celestial vision provides knowledge from above. In ancient epic, certain heroes are granted brief moments of privileged sight, in which a god removes the film from their vision (Diomedes at *Iliad* 5.127–28, Aeneas at *Aeneid* 2.604–6). The more sustained form of celestial vision, however, is a postclassical convention, incorporating elements of the *dream vision and the genre of apocalypse or revelation, whose best-known instance is the last book of the NT. Dante's *Paradiso* is the most extended example of an epic celestial vision; others include Astolfo's voyage to the moon in *Orlando furioso*; Goffredo's dream vision in *Gerusalemme liberata*, book 14; Redcrosse Knight's vision of the New Jerusalem in *The Faerie Queene*; and Michael's instruction of Adam in the last two books of *Paradise Lost*.

(vi) Ekphrasis. An ekphrasis (Gr., "description") is a verbal account of a work of visual art. The description of Achilles' shield in the *Iliad*, book 18, is the epic prototype. Made for the hero by the god Hephaestus, the shield is decorated with images of the heavenly bodies, scenes of a city at peace, and scenes of a city at war; its imagery has been subject to a wide range of interpretation. Virgil uses ekphrasis to describe legendary events prior to the poem's main narrative and historical events posterior to it: the doors of Juno's temple in Carthage are decorated with scenes from the Trojan War, and Aeneas's divinely wrought shield is decorated with scenes of future Roman triumphs. Later poets would follow Virgil in using ekphrasis to link epic past with historical present. Thus, in *Orlando furioso*, the walls of Tristan's castle show the deeds of Frankish kings from Sigibert to Francis I, while in *The Lusiads*, the painted flags of Vasco da Gama's ship depict Port. heroes from the legendary founding of the nation to the 15th c.

(vii) *Aristeia*. The aristeia (Gr., "prowess") is an episode in which a warrior performs great exploits on the battlefield. The model here is the *Iliad*, which contains five major aristeiai whose characteristic elements were widely imitated by later poets. These elements include the arming of the hero; his killing of enemy champions; his driving the enemy before him in a rout; an initial setback (a wound or removal from battle), followed by prayer to the gods, reinvigoration, and return to combat. An aristeia

does not necessarily end in victory, even in the short term; often the episode concludes with the hero driven back, wounded, or even killed. The aristeia provides one means of introducing variety into battle scenes. By exalting secondary warriors earlier in the poem with their own aristeiai, the poet can amplify the deeds of the primary hero; to do so, however, requires of the poet sufficient skill to describe gradations of extraordinary valor. In the *Iliad*, the first four aristeiai of Diomedes, Agamemnon, Hector, and Patroclus are genuinely impressive; when Achilles finally enters the fighting, however, his irresistible accomplishment in killing exceeds anything that has come before.

(viii) *Locus amoenus*. The locus amoenus (Lat., "delightful place") is an earthly paradise, a place of bliss and repose. It features lush gardens, splashing fountains, tame creatures, clement weather, fruit-bearing trees, and often the promise of sexual pleasures. Its mythological antecedents include the Elysian fields of cl. trad. and the Garden of Eden in Genesis; its representation in epic owes much to the *pastoral trad. In Ren. epics such as *The Faerie Queene* and *Gerusalemme liberata*, earthly paradises frequently prove false; their pleasures are created by enchantment, and they are inhabited by temptresses who would lure the hero from his duties. Benign versions include Dante's earthly paradise atop Mt. Purgatory, Venus's isle of love in the *Lusiads*, and, above all, Milton's Paradise, a representation of the Garden of Eden itself.

C. Style. Epic is written in an elevated *style, befitting its subject matter. Archaisms and poetic diction are accepted in epic to a greater extent than in genres dealing with subjects closer to their readers' quotidian experience. In poems written in Eng. or mod. Romance langs., Latinisms and Latinate forms are common. Stylistic features include the epithet or characterizing phrase, such as "swift-footed Achilles" or "Hector, breaker of horses." Also common is *periphrasis, an indirect expression used in place of a direct one, as in "Cytherea's son" for Aeneas (*Paradise Lost* 9.19). Of special note is the epic simile, an extended comparison in which the vehicle (the term used to describe) is developed beyond its ground of analogy with the tenor (the term described), so that the simile becomes a miniature tale unto itself. Here, for instance, Milton's Satan is described lying on the fiery lake of hell:

```
         . . . in bulk as huge
As whom the Fables name of monstrous
    size,
Titanian, or Earth-born, that warr'd on
    Jove,
Briareos or Typhon, whom the Den
By ancient Tarsus held, or that Sea-beast
Leviathan, which God of all his works
Created hugest that swim th' Ocean
    stream:
Him haply slumbring on the Norway foam
The Pilot of some small night-founder'd
    Skiff,
Deeming some Island, oft, as Sea-men tell,
With fixed Anchor in his skaly rind
Moors by his side under the Lee, while
    Night
Invests the Sea, and wished Morn delayes:
So stretcht out huge in length the
    Arch-fiend lay
Chain'd on the burning Lake.
```

The difficulty of maintaining an appropriately high style over the course of a long poem, without lapses into grandiosity on the one hand or bathos on the other, is one reason that successful epics have been rare.

Epic's marriage of high style and heroic matter makes possible the parodic subgenre of *mock epic, where the high epic style is applied to low, everyday, or absurd subject matter, creating a humorous mismatch.

D. Women in Epic. There is a long trad. of women warriors in epic. A lost epic, the *Aethiopis* of Arctinus of Miletus, recounted the story of Penthesileia the Amazon queen, who was an ally of the Trojans. The most influential example of the type is Virgil's Camilla, leader of the Volscians, who fights against the Trojans in an impressive aristeia until she is killed by a javelin. Her successors include Bradamante and Marfisa in *Orlando furioso*, Clorinda in *Gerusalemme liberata*, and Britomart in *The Faerie Queene*. Ariosto's Bradamante combines the figures of woman warrior and dynastic spouse; formidable with sword or lance, she is also the legendary progenitrix of the House of Este, Dukes of Ferrara and Ariosto's patrons. Spenser follows Ariosto in this combination; his Britomart is a female knight who allegorically embodies the virtue of chastity and the mythical ancestor of Queen Elizabeth. Tasso's Clorinda is both warrior and tragic lover. Raised a Muslim,

she is beloved of the Christian knight Tancredi, who mortally wounds her in an eroticized duel and baptizes her as she dies.

Another recurrent female character type impedes the hero's progress, keeping him from his path through seduction or constraint until he breaks free and abandons her. The prototypes here are Calypso and Circe in the *Odyssey*. Calypso is an immortal nymph who keeps Odysseus for herself on her island until commanded by the Olympian gods to let him go. Circe, also an island nymph, lures men into her house and, by witchcraft, transforms them into beasts; once Odysseus, with divine assistance, breaks her spell, she becomes his lover and assists him. In the *Aeneid*, the woman with whom the hero dallies and delays becomes a tragic figure. Virgil's Dido is a mortal woman, the widowed queen of Carthage; when Aeneas and his Trojans are shipwrecked on her shores, she falls in love with him, and they live as a couple until the gods intervene, commanding Aeneas to depart—whereupon she kills herself. Virgil leaves no doubt that Aeneas must leave Dido to fulfill his destiny, and Roman readers would note her association with Carthage, Rome's old enemy; but the queen is portrayed sympathetically as a victim of circumstance, an unfortunate (*infelix*) casualty in the founding of Rome. Many readers have shared the reaction of the young Augustine, who shed tears for Dido's death. Ren. versions of these figures include Alcina in the *Orlando furioso*, Armida in the *Gerusalemme liberata*, and Acrasia in *The Faerie Queene*; these similarly named characters are ill-intentioned temptresses from whose clutches seduced knights must be rescued. Although the epic trad. generally represents such female characters as a temptation that the male hero must overcome to carry out his mission, they appeal powerfully to hero and readers alike; these episodes have often been recognized as among the most memorable in their respective poems. An intriguing version of Dido appears in *La Araucana* and belongs to a robust "Defense of Dido" trad. that was esp. popular in Spain.

Discussion of the right relation between the sexes becomes a major theme in at least two epics of the Ren. The marriage of Adam and Eve, companionate yet hierarchical, is an important focus of *Paradise Lost*. *Orlando furioso* carries on a running discussion about women's virtue, sometimes ironically and sometimes in earnest, with Ariosto frequently giving voice to what in 16th-c. terms would have been a pro-feminist position.

Epics written by women include *Enrico ou-vero Bisancio acquistato* (*Enrico, or Byzantium Conquered*, 1635), by the Venetian Lucrezia Marinella; the biblical epic *Iudith* by the Fr. woman of letters Marie de Calages (1660); and the creation poem *Order and Disorder* (1679; first complete ed. 2001), identified in 2001 as the work of Lucy Hutchinson.

E. Divine Action. Epic is primarily concerned with the deeds of mortals, but its most powerful characters are gods. In the *Iliad,* the *Odyssey,* and the *Aeneid* the Olympian gods intervene frequently in human affairs, assisting some and destroying others. Sometimes the gods act in the interest of justice as they see it; sometimes they act on their own prerogative or even whim. Their enormous power is neither good nor evil; it simply is. The supreme Olympian god (Zeus in Gr., Jupiter in Lat.) holds final authority, but he allows wide latitude to his fellow Olympians to act as they see fit, and so they do. This latitude allows for factions or competing interests among the gods, which play a major structural role in cl. epic plot. The quarrelsome, anthropomorphized gods of epic scandalized some readers even in antiquity, Plato among them, but since they figured so prominently in the most prestigious poems of the age, they were too important to ignore.

How to Christianize divine action was one of the enduring problems of postclassical epic. Christian poets who sought to imitate Homer and Virgil assumed that a mod. epic that would rival the ancients required a supernatural element of some kind; they also knew that, in this respect, their cl. models could not be followed too closely. The pagan gods were no longer acceptable, but what could be put in their place? One approach, derived from the long herme-neutic trad. of reading the gods of cl. epic allegorically, was to introduce allegorized divine characters. These might be *personifications, like Milton's Sin and Death; they might be the Olympian gods themselves in allegorical guise, as in the *Lusiads*, Petrarch's *Africa*, or Spenser's "Mutability Cantos." Another approach, derived from the chivalric trad., was to replace intervening gods with magic: enchanted woods, mythical beasts, sorcerers, demons, and the like. A third approach, the most distinctively Christian, was to substitute God and Satan for the community of Olympian gods, as in Vida,

Tasso, or Milton. None of these approaches was without its difficulties.

II. Theory

A. Classical and Alexandrian Greek. The rich epic trad. of the Greeks (Homer, Hesiod, Arctinus, Antimachus) was at first criticized more from an ethical than a literary standpoint. Xenophanes (frag. 11, Diels-Kranz), e.g., objected to Homer and Hesiod's depiction of gods as thieves, adulterers, and deceivers. In the *Republic*, Plato combines the ethical and literary when he attacks Homer for teaching the young morally pernicious ideas by the method of imitation. Since, for Plato, Homer is also the founder of tragedy, both genres stand condemned.

For Aristotle, too, poetry is imitation, but from this, he draws a radically different conclusion. Not only is imitation natural to humans, but, as intensified by tragedy, it can produce, by means of pity and fear, a *katharsis ton pathematon*. That for Aristotle this puzzling but evidently drastic effect is also valid for epic follows from his acceptance of another Platonic insight, that epic is inherently dramatic. Since, unlike Plato, Aristotle argues that drama is the superior genre, the best epic must be Homer's because it is already "dramatic" (an adjective that Aristotle may have coined). Since Aristotle believes that drama (Gr., "that which is done") is important, it follows that the action has primacy. Not the soul of the hero but the mythic interaction of personae is the soul of the play, and indeed Aristotle criticizes epics that assert their unity merely by hanging a collection of disparate adventures onto a well-known name. Aristotle demands organic unity from the epic and requires that it be *eusynopton* (easily grasped in its totality) and that it not exceed the length of dramas shown at one sitting, a period of time usually calculated at 6,000 or 7,000 lines. Apollonius of Rhodes's *Argonautica*, written in Alexandria (3d c. BCE), exactly meets the criterion.

Aristotle objects to the confusion of epic and historical narrative, perhaps because he has a strict notion of the historian's duty to record. He ignores the fact that already Thucydides, e.g., had used mythical models to interpret events. He disapproves of the versification of Herodotus, but in allowing for "poetic" or imaginative prose, Aristotle opened the door to the mod. epic novel. The definition of *epic* attributed to his pupil and successor as head of the Lyceum in Athens, Theophrastus, as "that which embraces divine, heroic, and human affairs," shifts the emphasis from form to content. Aristotle's modification in the *Rhetoric* of his views on vocabulary is related. The *Poetics* had laid down that epic vocabulary should be clear but elevated, marked by the use of poetic words or "glosses." The later *Rhetoric*, however, under the impulse of Euripides, permits the use of words from the lang. of everyday life. He accepts as Homeric the comic *Margites* (The Crazy Man; cf. *Orlando furioso*), now lost, a silly account in mixed meters of a bumpkin who is not even sure how to proceed on his wedding night. Such openness contradicts Plato's severity and that of many later "Aristotelians."

The scholia or interpretive comments written in the margins of Homeric mss. prove that, after Aristotle, a practical crit. was worked out that preserved and extended his insights. Here, the *Iliad* and the *Odyssey* are regarded as tragedies, though the notion was not lost that Homer was also the founder of comedy. The contrast between epic and hist. is maintained. "Fantasy" is praised (cf. Dante, *Paradiso* 33.142) both as pure imagination and as graphic visualization of detail. Nonlinear presentation of the story may be made and at a variety of ling. levels.

The *Certamen*, also called the *Contest of Homer and Hesiod*, is extant in a text from the 2d c. CE but is believed to stem from an earlier work by Alcidamas (4th c. BCE). From antiquity, the question of which poet wrote first, and therefore had greater claim to legitimacy, existed, as did the idea that a poetic contest had taken place between the two. In the *Certamen*, which expands on a brief mention of a competition in the *Works and Days* (8th c. BCE), Hesiod wins because his works deal with the domestic and agricultural, rather than the martial. This issue of the domestic as an appropriate focus for epic will appear again in Milton's *Paradise Lost* and in later explorations of the relationship between novel and epic.

Callimachus in Alexandria (3d c. BCE) shared Aristotle's objections to the versification of Herodotus. In rejecting the eulogistic epic, he worked out, in his own epic *Hecale*, a different kind of Homer-*imitatio* from the straight comparison of the mod. champion to a Homeric counterpart, a type apparently sought by Alexander the Great from the poetaster Choirilos of Iasos. Too little of Callimachus's epic *Galateia* now survives to make judgment possible, but his *Deification of Arsinoe* in lyric meter set the precedent for the appeal by a junior deity to

a senior for elucidation that would become a *topos* of the Lat. eulogy (e.g., in Claudian and Sidonius Apollinaris) and even be adapted by Dante in the first canzone of the *Vita nuova*. Since this topos had Homeric precedent (*Iliad* 1.493 ff.), Callimachus was indicating which parts of the Homeric legacy were imitable and how. In his elegiac *Aetia*, Callimachus advanced Hesiod as the figurehead of his new approach to epic.

The *Argonautica* is a further demonstration of the Alexandrian theory of epic. Out of their element in the heroic ambience, the characters collectively and Jason individually are often gripped by *amekhanie* (helplessness). Unified by verbal echoes of the red-gold icon of the fleece, the poem underplays the conventionally heroic in showing both the futility of war and the degradation of the hero who, dependent on a witch's Promethean magic, eventually becomes the cowardly murderer of Apsyrtus. Homeric allusions point the lesson, and the reader knows from Euripides that eventually the marriage of Jason and Medea will end not in triumph but in disaster.

B. Classical and Medieval Latin. The Callimachean and Apollonian epic, i.e., the kind written by scholar-poets, treated the lit. of the past by allusion and reminiscence in a polyphonic way. Catullus, the bitter foe of historical epic, also uses this technique in his poem 64. Similarly, in the *Aeneid*, Virgil uses Homer as a sounding board rarely for simple harmony but to secure extra and discordant resonance for his mod. symphony. Thus, Dido is at once the *Odyssey*'s Calypso, Circe, Nausicaa, and Arete, and the *Iliad*'s Helen and Andromache. Aeneas is Odysseus, Ajax, Paris, Agamemnon, Hector, and Achilles. There is no end to the sliding identities and exchanges (*metamorphoses*) of the characters. The poet who had quoted from Callimachus in *Eclogue* 6 in order to introduce an Ovidian poetic program and had progressed to epic through the Hesiodic *Georgics*, may, therefore, be properly regarded as Callimachean. But he is also Aristotelian, both in the dramatic nature of his poem and in its tragic affinities. In Italy, Aeneas gropes toward victory over the bodies of friend and foe alike. Vengeful Dido, by the technique of verbal reminiscence and recurrent imagery, is never absent from the poem. And although the epic exalts the origins of Rome, "umbrae" (shadows) is characteristically its last word.

The first Alexandrians were scholar-poets, and the third head of the library, Eratosthenes, still exemplified this ideal. But the early divergence of the two vocations led to a split between creative and critical sensibilities. Horace's *Ars poetica* (1st c. BCE), described by an ancient commentator as a versification of the prose treatise of the Alexandrian scholar Neoptolemus of Parium, though clearly in its emphasis on the *vates* more than this, recommends by its form a musicality in which arrangement and correspondence, interlace and arabesque, will replace the pedestrian logic of prose. A Roman and an Augustan, Horace moves beyond Callimachus when he urges that the poet, without in any way betraying Gr. refinement, must also be a *vates*, engaged with his society and with the reform of public morals. This is an aspect of cl. epic subsumed by Dante in his allusion to *Orazio satiro* (*Inferno* 4.89).

Finally, Horace, who spoke of Homer's "auditor" (listener), took for granted a feature of ancient epic theory now often overlooked. Epic did not cease to be oral with Homer. The power of Virgil's "hypocrisis" (acting ability), the "sweetness and marvelous harlotries" of his voice, are attested in the *Life* written by Donatus (4th c. CE). This Aristotelian closeness to drama again implies polyphonic composition. According to this understanding of Virgil, there cannot be a single, univocal, "right" interpretation of the action.

However, with Virgil, epic, generally concerned with reflecting and establishing the self-identity of the culture that produces it, becomes heavily invested in the political. Virgil casts Aeneas as the first of a line of rulers culminating in the emperor Augustus, thus tying the foundation of Rome to the Trojan War and rewriting Aeneas's adventures as a myth of imperial foundation. He reinvents the crafty hero of the *Odyssey* as the ideal Roman character: Aeneas is an extraordinary warrior, but he is *pius* and obedient, qualities that were more valued by imperial Rome, and are, in the *Aeneid*, responsible for its founding. If Virgil's dramatic qualities are polyphonic, his narrative is nonetheless what M. Bakhtin, writing about epic in the mid-20th c., would term "monologic": the *Aeneid*'s story is told in the inimitable and defined voice of a national identity that, as Quint argues, accepts its own version of events as absolute and ignores the possibility of another, outside voice. While the voices of marginalized figures—the abandoned Dido, the defeated

Rutulians—continually intrude, Virgil's epic is nonetheless the act of a civilization writing its own self-contained and victorious hist.

The crit. by Agrippa of the *Aeneid* for its *communia verba*, recorded by Donatus in his *Life of Virgil*, shows that there had developed even under Augustus the theory that epic, as the most sublime of genres, demanded the most sublime lang. Petronius's implied crits. of Lucan in the *Satyricon* prove the persistence of this notion. At the end of cl. antiquity, the same theory received a fatally deceptive application. *Rhetorica ad Herennium* (ca. 86–82 BCE), influential in the Middle Ages, distinguished three styles, high, middle, and low; and, conveniently, Virgil had written three major poems: obviously, the *Eclogues* must exemplify the low style, the *Georgics* the middle, and the *Aeneid* the high. This was the doctrine that eventually found its med. canonization in the *rota virgiliana* (Virgilian wheel) devised by John of Garland. By this, names, weapons, even trees that could be mentioned in the different styles were carefully prescribed. One part of the deadly consequences of this doctrine was that the opening toward comedy in the epic (the *Margites*) was lost. Yet even the late antique commentator Servius had remarked of the *Aeneid*, book 4, "paene comicus stilus est: nec mirum, ubi de amore tractatur" (the style is almost comic, and no surprise, considering the theme is love), and the trad. of Virgilian epic practice does not reject the comic.

Stung by Platonic crit. of Homer's "lying," Gr. Stoic philosophers in particular had developed a method of interpreting the Homeric narrative in symbolic terms intended to rescue its moral and theological credibility. In his efforts to reclaim all the genres for the new religion, the Christian Lat. poet Prudentius (ca. 348–405) wrote the epic *Psychomachia*, in which the contending champions were no longer flesh-and-blood heroes but abstract qualities of the soul. It was only a short step from this to allegorizing Virgil's *Aeneid*, the most important example of this being Fulgentius (late 5th–early 6th c.). Highly praised allegorical epics have been written, of which the most important is probably Spenser's incomplete *Faerie Queene* (1590, 1596).

The critical failure of later antiquity meant, in effect, that any epic theory that was to make sense had to be recoverable from the practice of major poets. This fact lent even greater significance to the already towering figure of Dante, since it was he who, as the author of the epic

Divine Comedy in the vernacular, broke decisively with both med. prescription and practice. He acknowledges the influence of Virgil's style (*Inferno* 1.85–87), and invokes in reference to his own journey that of Aeneas to the underworld, during which the future hist. of Rome is revealed to him (2.13–27). However, even as Dante is influenced by Virgil's political vision of epic, the epic journey is here recast as a personal and internal process, the struggle of the Christian soul to find God; the grandeur of conquest becomes the humility of spiritual seeking.

C. Renaissance to Modern. The Ren. critics (Marco Girolamo Vida, *De arte poetica*, 1527; Francesco Robortello, *In librum Aristotelis de arte poetica explicationes*, 1548; Antonio Minturno, *De poeta*, 1559; *L'arte poetica*, 1563) were often prescriptive rather than descriptive. Armed with the *Poetics* (trans. into Lat. by Giorgio Valla in 1498, 1536; Gr. text 1508; It. trans. 1549) and eventually with an amalgam of Aristotle and Horace, they advanced to wear down the "unclassical" in epic but were largely the unconscious victims of old ideas. J. C. Scaliger, the most gifted scholar among them (*Poetices libri septem*, 1561), uses the evidence of lang. to decry Homer and exalt Virgil: the display by Homer of *humilitas, simplicitas, loquacitas*, and *ruditas* in his style must make him inferior to the Roman. If Virgil echoes Homer's description of Strife in his picture of Fama in book 4 of the *Aeneid*, that is an excuse for loading Homer with abuse. And just as ruthlessly as Agrippa with Virgil, these critics set about Dante, Ariosto, and Tasso for their unclassical backsliding.

In particular, because of the runaway popularity of Ariosto's *Orlando furioso* (1516), the issue of what kinds of subject matter, lang., and formal structure could be considered legitimately epic was of great interest in Italy in the mid-16th c. A number of critics objected to Ariosto (often in the strongest terms) because of his lack of moral purpose and, more significant, his failure to adhere to Aristotle's requirements for both a single, unified story and "probability" (which for Aristotle meant persuasiveness rather than, as for these critics, the absence of the fantastic). Attempting to rescue Ariosto from his detractors, Giambattista Giraldi Cinthio (*Discorso intorno al comporre dei romanzi*, 1554) and Giambattista Pigna (*I romanzi*, 1554) wrote that Ariosto's text was not a bad epic, but of a distinct

genre with its own narrative conventions and subject matter: the romance. Cinthio argued against the stultifying classicism of his contemporaries, suggesting that, as cultures and tastes develop, so too do literary forms, which should be judged by practical example rather than by abstract theory. According to the precept set by Ariosto and his predecessor Matteo Maria Boiardo, epic tells the story of one man, romance the story of many; thus, the latter has a more episodic, less unified structure than epic. The publication of Tasso's *Gerusalemme liberata* (1581) brought the discussion to near-fever pitch: his work was frequently pitted against Ariosto's, and both were praised as an example of Aristotelian unity (Camillo Pellegrino, *Il Carrafa*, 1584) and dismissed as a work of inferior artistry. Tasso, responding to the debate (*Discorsi dell'arte poetica*, 1587, although composed 1567–70), takes the part of the Aristotelians, insisting that romance and epic are not discrete genres and that, instead, Ariosto's loose structure and multiplicity of action make for a highly flawed epic.

The political nature of Virgilian epic continues in the Ren. Camões's *Lusiads* builds on an ostensibly prosaic story—the trading expedition of da Gama—to write a glorious and elaborate Port. hist. Tasso's portrayal of the First Crusade as the rightful liberation of Jerusalem by an army of virtuous Christians is intended to stir up support for the Catholic ambition, during the Counter-Reformation, of capturing Jerusalem from Ottoman control. Spenser's layered allegory is a celebration of Queen Elizabeth I in the figure of the "Faerie Queene" Gloriana, while it simultaneously casts her as the direct descendant of Gloriana and King Arthur. The poem, moreover, deals with a number of contemp. political issues, incl. the trial of Mary, Queen of Scots; anxieties about Catholicism and the empire of Philip II; and England's colonial interest in Ireland.

In Eng., Milton (*Paradise Lost*, 1667, 1674; *Paradise Regained*, 1671) was greatly influenced by both It. example and precept. He knew Giacopo Mazzoni's *Difesa della Commedia di Dante* (1587) and the theoretical work of Tasso, whose old patron, Count Manso, he had met during his travels in Italy (1637–39). He quotes from the *Orlando furioso* at the beginning of *Paradise Lost* (1.16, cf. *Orlando furioso* 1.2.2). And yet *Paradise Lost* is a self-consciously Eng. work, employing a traditionally Eng. meter and thoroughly Protestant in its theology. Milton's

Epitaphium Damonis (1639) toys with the idea of a historical epic on Arthurian legends, and his notebooks, preserved in Cambridge, show that he considered a dramatic treatment of the same topics and of the story of Adam. In returning to epic, he fixed on this theological theme, to which the closest cl. parallel would be Hesiod's *Theogony*. It enabled him to set out his profoundest beliefs in the origin of the moral order of the universe, the human condition, and the Christian promise of atonement. Like Hesiod, moreover, Milton moves away from the subject matter of the Virgilian trad., the "Warrs, hitherto the onely Argument / Heroic deem'd" (*Paradise Lost* 9.28–29). His epic contains an extended martial episode—the war in heaven, in which Satan's followers rebel against divine authority—but the work is largely domestic in its focus, portraying the relationship between Adam and Eve as one of shared work, untainted sexuality, and great mutual love, thus prefiguring the domestic focus of the novel. Milton's assumption in the poem of a difficult lang., criticized by Samuel Johnson, is part of the struggle to convey truths larger than life. His *Paradise Regained* uses a simpler style to depict Christ's rebuttal of the temptations of Satan, emphasizing his humanity rather than divinity and, in Dantean fashion, his humility rather than glory.

In the 17th c., Fr. critics adapted and propagated the It. recension of Aristotle's rules, emphasizing unity, *decorum, and verisimilitude, although the first trans. of the *Poetics* into Fr. did not appear until 1671. André Dacier's ed. and commentary (*La Poétique d'Aristote contenant les règles les plus exactes pour juger du poème héroique et des pièces de théâtre, la tragédie et la comédie*, 1692) became standard. This and other critical works (René Rapin, *Réflexions sur la poétique d'Aristote*, 1674; René le Bossu, *Traité du poème épique*, 1675) were regarded as normative throughout Europe. The epics they inspired have been universally regarded as failures.

By the late 17th. c., in Eng., epic was both a major influence and a source of anxiety. It was impossible to write epic in the straightforward manner of the Ren. poets; the genre was no longer part of current literary practice, and any attempt to produce it was to self-consciously and artificially to delve backward into the archaic. The poets of the Restoration and 18th c. wrote mock epic, which both parodied, portraying the trivial or the ridiculous in lofty style (John Dryden, "MacFlecknoe,"

1682; Alexander Pope, *The Rape of the Lock*, 1714; and *The Dunciad*, 1743) or mocking lofty lang. (Samuel Butler, *Hudibras*, 1663–78), and reverenced the original epic form. Both Dryden and Pope produced trans. of cl. epics. The continued public interest in early epic is likewise reflected in James Macpherson's 1760–62 publication of *Ossian*, which he claimed to have trans. from an ancient Gaelic text and which sparked controversy between those who insisted on its inauthenticity (Samuel Johnson among them) and those who argued for its antiquity and formal unity. In an argument that proved enormously influential even into the 20th c., G.W.F. Hegel theorized that epic, as a primitive form, was the expression of a nation's unified character, system of values, and worldview; the age of technological modernity cannot produce epic because people no longer engage vitally with the world around them (*Lectures on Aesthetics*, compiled 1835–38).

Conflict with France and increasing status as an imperial power helped to spur a resurgence of epics or works with significant epic characteristics in 19th c. Eng. (Dentith, Tucker). The romantics admired the vast cultural and poetic scope of the epic but were less intimidated by it than their predecessors: P. B. Shelley is as quick to criticize what he sees as the derivative efforts of Virgil as he is to praise Homer, Dante, and Milton (*Defence of Poetry*, 1821). However, poets who addressed martial, political, or national themes confronted the same potential archaism that had troubled writers in the previous century and a half, with widely varying results (Walter Scott, *Marmion*, 1808; Alfred, Lord Tennyson, *Idylls of the King*, 1859–85; William Morris, *Sigurd the Volsung*, 1876). At the same time, another kind of epic emerged, which dealt with nonmartial, contemp. subject matter and which was largely unhampered by issues of archaism because it addressed directly the values and concerns—here, primarily issues of selfhood and individual experience—of the age that produced it. In *The Prelude* (1805, pub. 1850), William Wordsworth adapts the traditional proem to declare human intellect and emotion, as well as a few intangibles (e.g. Truth, Beauty, Love) his epic subjects; Lord Byron's worldly and satirical *Don Juan* (1819–24), through the adventures of an oft-seduced innocent, reinscribes the epic conventions into a world-weary and ironic voice; Elizabeth Barrett Browning's *Aurora Leigh* (1856) uses a lofty and heroic style to narrate the adventures of an intellectually gifted young woman, who, in turn, insists that epic heroism is possible in any age.

But it is the novel that has proven the most resilient and productive descendant of the epic trad. Two 20th.-c. studies, Georg Lukács's *Theory of the Novel* (1916) and Bakhtin's essay "Epic and Novel" (written 1941, pub. 1970), have been influential in examining the relation between the two genres, which, following Hegel, they see as an issue of antiquity versus modernity. For Lukács, epic expresses a "totality" of collective experience that precludes individualism because the society that produces epic is utterly unified; the novel is the mod. attempt to recover that sense of totality, now lost, by reshaping the world through a process of individual experience. Bakhtin argues that epic deals with a founding hist. that exists before any sense of a transitory present and that, therefore, its perspective is absolute: there is no possibility of reinterpretation because there are no outside voices. The novel, by contrast, consists of many voices in a world of mutable time. For both, epic is the product of an absolute totality: Lukács sees the novel as heralding the loss of this totality, while for Bakhtin, it signals its triumphant overthrow. In addition, novels frequently address similar questions of modernity, often casting themselves as a derivation of or departure from antiquity (Scott, *Ivanhoe*, 1819; Gustave Flaubert, *Madame Bovary*, 1856–57]). Perhaps most famously, George Eliot's *Middlemarch* (1871–72) draws on St. Theresa's "epic life" as a symbol to explore the frustration that passionate and inspired young women encounter in an age that allows them few opportunities for greatness. The novel ends on a domestic note, as its heroine redirects her potentially epic nature to marriage and private life.

This is not to say that the cl. epic was effaced by modernity or the birth of the novel. On the contrary, literary modernism of the early 20th c., which was deeply influenced by the unprecedented violence of World War I, brought with it an interest in reviving and reincorporating the trad. T. S. Eliot's *The Waste Land* (1922), Ezra Pound's many publications of the *Cantos* (1925–72), and James Joyce's *Ulysses* (1922) reinvent the stories and themes of cl. epic to reflect a new kind of consciousness, marked by disillusionment, fragmentation, and discontinuity. *Ulysses* translates the vast scope of the Homeric epic to a novel spanning only one day and dealing with ordinary, middle-class characters and concerns; far from the monologic epic spirit or the polyphony of Virgil's style, Joyce's novel is

a cacophony of voices and thoughts, and it is often impossible to distinguish the thoughts of one character from the voice of another or from the narrator.

The creation of epic continues in recent years; the most prominent example is Derek Walcott's *Omeros* (1990), which translates Homeric elements into a story dealing with African hist. and working-class protagonists on a Caribbean island. *Omeros* is, like the epics of the Virgilian trad., explicitly political, bringing to light the effects of colonialism and slavery and imbuing the lives of its disenfranchised characters, as Dentith observes, with epic importance and dignity.

See NARRATIVE POETRY.

■ **Criticism and History**: H. T. Swedenberg, *The Theory of the Epic in England, 1650–1800* (1944); C. M. Bowra, *From Virgil to Milton* (1945), and *Heroic Poetry* (1952); E.M.W. Tillyard, *The English Epic and Its Background* (1954); R. A. Sayce, *The French Biblical Epic in the Seventeenth Century* (1955); T. M. Greene, *The Descent from Heaven: A Study in Epic Continuity* (1963); R. Durling, *The Figure of the Poet in Renaissance Epic* (1965); J. M. Steadman, *Milton and the Renaissance Hero* (1967); A. B. Giamatti, *The Earthly Paradise and the Renaissance Epic* (1966); M. R. Lida de Malkiel, *Dido en la literatura española* (1974)–on the *Defense of Dido*; L. Ariosto, *Orlando Furioso*, trans. B. Reynolds (1977); Parry; F. Blessington, *"Paradise Lost" and the Classical Epic* (1979); G. Nagy, *The Best of the Achaeans* (1979); M. Murrin, *The Allegorical Epic* (1980); M. M. Bahktin, "Epic and the Novel," *The Dialogic Imagination*, ed. M. Holquist, trans. C. Emerson and M. Holquist (1981); S. Revard, *The War in Heaven* (1980); A. Fichter, *Poets Historical: Dynastic Epic in the Renaissance* (1982); J. Kates, *Tasso and Milton: The Problem of Christian Epic* (1983); L. Robinson, *Monstrous Regiment: The Lady Knight in Sixteenth-century Epic* (1985); C. Martindale, *John Milton and the Transformation of Ancient Epic* (1986); R. Martin, *The Language of Heroes* (1989); A. Parry, *The Language of Achilles and Other Papers* (1989); D. C. Feeney, *The Gods in Epic* (1991); J. B. Hainsworth, *The Idea of Epic* (1991); A. Lord, *Epic Singers and Oral Tradition* (1991); A. Ford, *Homer: The Poetry of the Past* (1992); S. Wofford, *The Choice of Achilles: The Ideology of Figure in the Epic* (1992); C. Burrow, *Epic Romance: Homer to Milton* (1993); P. Hardie, *The Epic Successors of Virgil* (1993); D. Quint, *Epic and Empire*

(1993); M. Desmond, *Reading Dido* (1994); M. Murrin, *History and Warfare in Renaissance Epic* (1994); J. Watkins, *The Specter of Dido: Spenser and Virgilian Epic* (1995); F. Moretti, *Modern Epic* (1996); G. Teskey, *Allegory and Violence* (1996); *Epic Traditions in the Contemporary World: The Poetics of Community*, ed. M. Beissinger, J. Tylus, S. Wofford (1999); Lord; J. Everson, *The Italian Romance Epic in the Age of Humanism* (2001); Horace, *The Epistles of Horace*, trans. D. Ferry (2001); Statius, *Silvae*, ed. and trans. D. R. Shackleton Bailey (2003); R. Padrón, *The Spacious Word: Cartography, Literature, and Empire in Early Modern Spain* (2004); *A Companion to Ancient Epic*, ed. J. M. Foley (2005); J. C. Warner, *The Augustinian Epic, Petrarch to Milton* (2005); T. Gregory, *From Many Gods to One: Divine Action in Renaissance Epic* (2006); S. Zatti, *The Quest for Epic: From Ariosto to Tasso* (2006).

■ **Theory:** D. Comparetti, *Vergil in the Middle Ages*, trans. E.F.M. Benecke (1895); Faral; J. E. Spingarn, *History of Literary Criticism in the Renaissance*, 2d ed. (1925); H. Strecker, "Theorie des Epos," *Reallexikon I* 4.28–38; E. Reitzenstein, "Zur Stiltheorie des Kallimachos," *Festschrift Richard Reitzenstein* (1931); Lewis; M.-L. von Franz, *Die aesthetischen Anschauungen der Iliasscholien* (1943); M. T. Herrick, *The Fusion of Horatian and Aristotelian Literary Criticism, 1531–1555* (1946); Auerbach; Curtius; Frye; Weinberg; D. M. Foerster, *The Fortunes of Epic Poetry: A Study in English and American Criticism 1750–1950* (1962); F. J. Worstbrock, *Elemente einer Poetik der Aeneis* (1963); G. N. Knauer, *Die Aeneis und Homer* (1964); A. Lesky, *A History of Greek Literature*, trans. J. Willis and C. de Heer (1966); K. Ziegler, *Das hellenistische Epos*, 2d ed. (1966); J. K. Newman, *Augustus and the New Poetry* (1967); E. Fränkel, *Noten zu den Argonautika des Apollonios* (1968); S. Koster, *Antike Epostheorien* (1970); *Classical and Medieval Literary Criticism*, ed. A. Preminger et al. (1974); *Homer to Brecht: The European Epic and Dramatic Tradition*, ed. M. Seidel and E. Mendelson (1976); R. Häussler, *Das historische Epos der Griechen und Römer bis Vergil* (1976); G. S. Kirk, *Homer and the Oral Tradition* (1976); R. Häussler, *Das historische Epos von Lucan bis Silius und seine Theorie* (1978); J. K. Newman, *The Classical Epic Tradition* (1986); S. M. Eisenstein, *Nonindifferent Nature* [1964], trans. H. Marshall (1987); R.O.A.M. Lyne, *Further Voices in Vergil's "Aeneid"* (1987); D. Shive, *Naming Achilles* (1987); B. Graziosi, *Inventing Homer: The Early Reception of Epic* (2002); S. Dentith, *Epic and Empire in Nineteenth-Century Britain* (2006); H. F. Tucker, *Epic, Britain's Historic Muse 1790–1910* (2008).

T. B. Gregory (hist.); J. K. Newman; T. Meyers (theory)

EPIGRAM (Gr. *epigramma*, "inscription"). An ancient form, first carved on gravestones, statuary, and buildings. Epigrams encompass an almost infinite variety of tone and subject, but they are defined by concision (relatively speaking: while many epigrams are two to four lines long, others are considerably longer). Many but certainly not all epigrams aim for a point or turn. Alone and as part of other forms, the epigram has many formal affiliations. Longer epigrams can shade into *elegy or *verse epistle. Poetic *epitaphs are a subgenre of epigram, and emblems, *proverbs, aphorisms, maxims, and adages have often been shaped into epigrams. The *sonnet, particularly the Eng. sonnet, with its structure of three *quatrains and a concluding *couplet, has strong roots in the epigram.

Epigrams influenced Western poetry through two cl. sources: the *Greek Anthology* and Roman epigrammatists, esp. Catullus and Martial. The *Greek Anthology* is additive, incl. poems written over the course of more than a thousand years, a gathering first begun by Meleager around 90 BCE. It originates the concept of anthology itself (literally, "garland or gathering of flowers"), a collection arranged by some kind of ordering principle. *Greek Anthology* epigrams range from epitaphic to erotic, from invitations to thank-you notes, from satiric to polemical to moral; most are in *elegiac distichs. In the 10th c. CE, Constantine Cephalas, a Byzantine Greek, compiled a 15-part anthol., combining and rearranging earlier collections. In 1301, Maximus Planudes compiled an expurgated version, the first to appear in print (in 1494; called the *Planudean Anthology*). It had a profound effect on subsequent Neo-Lat. and developing vernacular poetry. In 1606, Claudius Salmasius (Claude Saumaise) discovered a copy of Cephalas's version of the anthol. in the Elector Palatine's library in Heidelberg. This full version, known as the *Palatine Anthology*, was finally published between 1794 and 1814 in 13 vols.

Roman devels. of the epigram trad. bear the stamp of particular authors. Especially influential are Catullus and Martial, who arranged epigrams in groups unified by the presence of a witty, observant persona. Catullus's epigrams of everyday life and intimate social relationships demonstrate the form's lyric potential. Martial explicitly modeled his epigrams on Catullus's but developed a much sharper degree of social *satire, underscored by the strong closure effected by a point or turn.

Ren. poetry embraced the epigram: from anthol.-influenced collections incl. sonnet sequences (e.g., Clément Marot in France), to incisive satiric epigrams influenced by Martial (e.g., Baltasar Alcázar and Juan de Mal Lara in Spain), to aphoristic commonplaces. The extensive treatment of the epigram by important theorists such as J. C. Scaliger (*Poetices libri septem* [Seven Books of Poetics], 1561) and George Puttenham (*The Arte of English Poesie*, 1589) established it as a core cl. genre. Because of its antiquity and brevity, the epigram was central to humanist education, trans. and imitated by pupils throughout Europe. Thomas More's and Étienne Pasquier's Neo-Lat. epigrams exemplify the international humanist culture that remained vibrant through the 17th c.

In Eng., notable 16th-c. epigrammatists include John Heywood, John Harington, and John Davies. The mature flowering of the Eng. epigram came in the 17th c. with Ben Jonson, Martial's most influential Eng. imitator. His epigrams combine cl. learning with dramatic accuracy; they range from miniature portraits of city and court denizens ("To My Lord Ignorant": "Thou call'st me Poet, as a terme of shame: / But I have my revenge made, in thy name"), to epideictic epigrams of named personages and touching epitaphs such as "On My First Son." Emblems, most famously Francis Quarles's, yoked epigrams with images. George Herbert wrote Lat. epigrams, and not only his Eng. poetry but his very conception of *The Temple* as a linked poetic book is indebted to the epigram trad. Richard Crashaw's divine epigrams are shockingly physical performances of baroque compression. Robert Herrick experimented with *tone and subject; *Hesperides* includes hundreds of epigrams ranging from versified maxims to social satire, Catullan love lyrics, and epitaphs for flowers, pets, and himself. While Andrew Marvell also wrote discrete epigrams, "Upon Appleton House," with its tight, allusive stanzas, is one of the great achievements of the epigram trad.

At different historical moments, the two epigrammatic strains (brief lyrics, on the one hand, pointed aphorisms or satires, on the other) can coexist, or one can dominate. In a sense, the epigram was most pervasive in the long 18th c. John Dryden, Nicolas Boileau, Alexander Pope, Voltaire, J. W. Goethe, and Friedrich Schiller wrote epigrams; and, more generally, the centrality of the couplet to neoclassical poetics is an epigrammatic devel. By the late 18th c., however, many poets reacted against pointed wit and turned to epigram's lyric potential. Thomas Gray's "Elegy Written in a Country Churchyard" combines aphoristic formulations with elegiac reverie; and William Wordsworth, while explicitly rejecting epigrammatic wit, worked extensively with epigram's subgenre, epitaph. Nevertheless, the pointed epigram remained important. William Blake returned to epigram's origins, engraving poetry with image. The proverbs embedded in Blake's *Marriage of Heaven and Hell* ("The road of excess leads to the palace of wisdom") foreshadow the strongly turned, witty aphorisms of Oscar Wilde, Mark Twain, and Dorothy Parker. W. S. Landor is a notable epigrammatist, and epigram is the building block of Lord Byron's mock epic *Don Juan*. Antonio Machado and Fernando Pessoa make an epigrammatic mode available as a stance or perspective.

American poetry has fostered a brilliant epigram trad. Emily Dickinson's aphoristic, gathered poems are epigrams. Ezra Pound's imagistic "In a Station of the Metro" attempts to fuse epigram and haiku; H.D., Wallace Stevens, and W. C. Williams used the epigrammatic mode to capture direct address and strong imagery; J. V. Cunningham's epigrams are explicitly cl. Because of its ling. compression, strong turn, and use of rhyme for point, epigram continues to be a dominant form in contemp. lyric poetry.

■ T. K. Whipple, *Martial and the English Epigram from Sir Thomas Wyatt to Ben Jonson* (1925); J. Hutton, *The Greek Anthology in Italy* (1935) and *The Greek Anthology in France and the Latin Writers in the Netherlands* (1946); H. H. Hudson, *The Epigram in the English Renaissance* (1947); I. P. Rothberg, "Hurtado de Mendoza and the Greek Epigrams," *Hispanic Review* 26 (1958); B. H. Smith, *Poetic Closure* (1968); G. Hartman, *Beyond Formalism* (1970); R. L. Colie, *The Resources of Kind: Genre-Theory in the Renaissance* (1973); A. Fowler, *Kinds of Literature* (1982); A. Cameron, *The Greek Anthology: From Meleager to Planudes* (1993); D. Russell, "The Genres of Epigram and Emblem," *CHLC*, v. 3, ed. G. P. Norton (1999); *Oxford Classical Dictionary*, ed. S. Hornblower and A. Spawforth, 3d ed. (2003); A. W. Taylor, "Between Surrey and

Marot: Nicolas Bourbon and the Artful Translation of the Epigram," *Translation and Literature* 15 (2006); W. Fitzgerald, *Martial: The World of the Epigram* (2007); *Brill's Companion to Hellenistic Epigram*, ed. P. Bing and J. Bruss (2007).

A. B. COIRO

EPITAPH (Gr., "writing on a tomb"). A funerary inscription or a literary composition imitating such an inscription. Literate cultures have often commemorated the dead in artful epitaphs: e.g., laudatory epitaphs combining ornate prose and verse were an important premod. Chinese literary genre, while cl. Ar. inscriptions combined prose biography with verse warnings of divine judgment.

In the West, pithy Gr. verse grave inscriptions, most influentially in elegiac couplets, arose in the 7th c. BCE. Epigrammatists through the Hellenistic period composed both inscriptional and pseudoinscriptional epitaphs, some ribald and satiric. Many appear in book 7 of the *Greek Anthology*. With expressive brevity epitaphs lament, beg remembrance, proclaim fame, warn of death's inevitability, and bid the passerby enjoy life or imitate the deceased. The dead sometimes "speak" (imperiously or imploringly) to the visitor, as in Simonides' famous *elegiac distich on the Spartans at Thermopylae ("Go, stranger, tell the Spartans / That here obedient to their laws we lie").

Poets of Augustan Rome adapt the epitaphic voice of the dead for highly original fictional epitaphs (e.g., Horace's *Odes* 1.28, Propertius's *Elegies* 1.21). They also influentially provide pithy epitaphic self-descriptions: an elegiac distich ancient biographers ascribe to Virgil encapsulates his life and achievement, Propertius and Tibullus incorporate two-line epitaphs on themselves in their love elegies, and Ovid provides a two-couplet epitaph imploring fellow lovers to wish his bones lie soft (a traditional formula) in *Tristia* 3.3. Virgil's *Eclogues* 5 and Ovid's *Amores* 2.6 also influentially conclude lengthy *laments with brief panegyric epitaphs providing forceful closure and the consolation of fame. The Silver Lat. epigrammatist Martial writes much-admired satiric epitaphs and tender ones on beloved slave boys and pets.

Early Christian and med. epitaphs combined commemoration with *memento mori* verses, proclamations of the afterlife, and requests for prayers. Lat. and then vernacular formulas like the grimly chiastic "As you are now, so once was I, / As I am now, soon you must be" appear

on med. to 19th-c. gravestones. Numerous Ren. epigrammatists, by contrast, recall cl. accents of restrained grief or praise of individual achievement, such as the 15th-c. Neo-Lat. poet Michele Marullo: "Here I, Alcino, lie: my mourning parents buried me. / That is life's and childbirth's reward"; "His ancestry if you are told, you will feel contempt, but you will admire his deeds. / The former derives from fortune, the latter from character." Giovanni Pontano's *De tumulis* (Of Grave Mounds, 1505) combines cl. and Christian motifs in epitaphs on family and friends. Seventeenth-c. Eng. epigrammatists produce memorable epitaphs. Ben Jonson's "On My First Daughter" describes the mourning parents with third-person restraint; depicts the daughter Mary in a feminized heaven; tenderly plays (as is common in epitaphs) with her name; and closes with Roman solicitude for her earthly remains. "On My First Son" laments before deploying epitaphic formulas and a Martial echo to express Jonson's paternal pride tempered by a wish henceforth not to be attached "too much" to what he loves. Jonson's disciple Robert Herrick writes self-consciously modest epitaphic tributes to humble creatures (infants, his maid, his dog) as well as to himself.

Eighteenth- and 19th-c. inscriptions for the social elite were often verbose, bombastic panegyrics; critics lambasted "sepulchral lies" (Alexander Pope). In his essay on epitaphs, Samuel Johnson warned against falsehood but approved omitting faults. Yet poets continued to write epigrammatic epitaphs both for panegyric, as in Pope's heroic couplet on Isaac Newton ("Nature, and Nature's Laws lay hid in Night. / God said, *Let Newton be*! And all was *Light*"), and *satire. Alexis Piron mocked the Fr. Academy that had rejected him: "Ci-gît Piron, qui ne fut rien, / Pas même académicien" (Here lies Piron, who was nothing, / Not even a member of the Academy). With a terse somberness recalling Gr. epitaphs, by contrast, Herman Melville's Civil War epitaphs commemorate unnamed soldiers' tragic honor.

Late 18th- and 19th-c. poets also treat the epitaph as spur to *lyric. Thomas Gray's "Elegy Written in a Country Churchyard" influentially meditates on people's desire for remembrance, exemplified by humble churchyard epitaphs, before concluding with the poet's own epitaph. William Wordsworth, the author of three essays on the genre, composed epitaphs, lyrical responses to epitaphs, and poems such as "The Solitary Reaper" adapting motifs such as the address to the passerby. Walt Whitman's "As Toilsome I Wander'd Virginia's Woods" incorporates a "rude" one-line Civil War inscription as its insistent refrain.

In the 20th-c. West, grave inscriptions largely disappeared as a serious poetic form with the decline of the living's contact with the buried dead. Poets have continued to write comic, satiric, and fictional epitaphs (such as Thomas Hardy's Gr.-indebted epitaphs on cynics and pessimists and those on an imaginary Midwestern town's inhabitants in Edgar Lee Masters's *Spoon River Anthology*, 1915). Poetic epitaphs on soldiers and victims of war have been the most common type of serious epitaph, such as Rudyard Kipling's and A. E. Housman's World War I compositions. Otherwise, poets composing epitaphs have self-consciously revised the tropes of a genre whose anachronism is part of the point. R. M. Rilke's epitaph on himself, "Rose, oh pure contradiction, delight / in being nobody's sleep under so many / eyelids," hermetically addresses the rose, a symbol of poetry itself, rather than the reader. W. B. Yeats's self-epitaph from "Under Ben Bulben," "Cast a cold eye / On life, on death. / Horseman, pass by," substitutes for the cl. pedestrian wayfarer an equestrian evoking antiquated Ir. nobility and deploys cl. pithiness to demand not respect or pity for the dead but heroic disdain for the mortal. Anne Carson's *Men in the Off Hours* (2000) contains pithy, highly enigmatic "Epitaphs" on "Evil," "Europe," and "Thaw," evoking cl. epitaphs' elegiac couplets but written as if they were partially comprehensible fragments from bygone civilizations. Carson also discovers in ms. crossouts a new form of epitaph, where "all is lost, yet still there."

See ELEGY, EPIGRAM.

■ P. Friedländer, *Epigrammata: Greek Inscriptions in Verse from the Beginnings to the Persian War* (1948); W. Peek, *Griechische Grabgedichte* (1960); R. Lattimore, *Themes in Greek and Latin Epitaphs* (1962); E. Bernhardt-Kabisch, "Wordsworth: The Monumental Poet," *PQ* 44 (1965); G. Hartman, "Wordsworth, Inscriptions, and Romantic Nature Poetry," *From Sensibility to Romanticism*, ed. F. W. Hilles and H. Bloom (1965); *L'Epigramme Grecque*, ed. A. E. Raubitschek (1968); G. Grigson, *The Faber Book of Epigrams and Epitaphs* (1977); E. Bernhardt-Kabisch, "The Epitaph and the Romantic Poets: A Survey," *Huntington Library Quarterly* 30 (1978); P. Ariès, *The Hour of Our Death*, trans. H. Weaver (1981); D. Fried, "Repetition, Refrain, and Epitaph," *ELH* 53 (1986); K. Mills-Court, *Poetry as Epitaph: Representation and Poetic Language* (1990); J. Scodel, *The English Poetic Epitaph: Commemoration and Conflict from Jonson to Wordsworth* (1991); A. Schottenhammer, "Characteristics of Song Epitaphs," *Burial in Song China*, ed. D. Kuhn (1994); A. Petrucci, *Writing the Dead: Death and Writing Strategies in the Western Tradition*, trans. M. Sullivan (1998); K. S. Guthke, *Epitaph Culture in the West* (2003); W. Waters, *Poetry's Touch: On Lyric Address* (2003); W. Diem and M. Schöller, *The Living and the Dead in Islam: Studies in Arabic Epitaphs*, 3 v. (2004).

J. SCODEL

EPITHALAMIUM (Gr., "in front of the wedding chamber"). The term *epithalamion* (Lat. *epithalamium*) categorizes texts concerning marriage, but epithalamia are as varied in their structures and tonalities as the occasions they commemorate. They range from poems that sedulously engage with norms established by earlier participants in the genre to ones linked to their predecessors merely by their subject matter. Some are unambiguously and joyously celebratory; others, such as John Suckling's "Ballade, Upon a Wedding," parody the participants, the event, and the convention, while yet other texts uneasily occupy shifting positions on that spectrum. Similarly, the genre encompasses everything from poems erotic enough to court the label of pornography, notably the work of the Neo-Lat. writer Johannes Secundus, to some that virtually ignore sex. Different though epithalamia are in these and other ways, they typically offer a particularly valuable occasion for studying the interaction of literary conventions and social practices and pressures on issues ranging from gender to politics to spatiality.

Reflected in the name of the genre, the folk practice of singing outside the room where the marriage is consummated lies behind later versions of the epithalamium. The Song of Solomon and Psalm 45 offer scriptural antecedents. Many Gr. and Lat. poems, notably Theocritus's *Idyll* 18, describe weddings; but by far the most influential cl. contributions are three poems by the Roman poet Catullus: 61, 62, and 64. The imitation of these earlier models common in later poems mirrors the concern for lineage thematized in the poems themselves.

Although the Middle Ages witnessed the use of epithalamic lang. in descriptions of mystical spiritual marriages, the genre did not enjoy a vogue until the Ren. That period saw numerous Neo-Lat. epithalamia, as well as an extensive discussion of both literary and folk versions of this mode in the monumental Lat. text by J. C. Scaliger, *Poetices libri septem* (Seven Books of Poetics, 1561). The Fr. poets participating in the genre include Clément Marot and Pierre de Ronsard. Contributions from the Sp. Golden Age often incorporate the allegorical figure of Fame; indeed, many epithalamia in the early mod. era, incl. Edmund Spenser's *Prothalamion* (1596), court patronage through eulogistic tributes to the participants in a royal or aristocratic wedding. By far the most influential Eng. instance, however, is Spenser's *Epithalamion* (1595), written for his own wedding. The popularity of the genre soared in the 17th c., with John Donne, Ben Jonson, and Robert Herrick, among others, writing such lyrics. Epithalamia also appeared in 16th- and 17th-c. plays and in masques.

Versions arise in many other cultures and eras as well. Asian trads., e.g., include ancient poems praising members of the couple. Alfred, Lord Tennyson's *In Memoriam* (1850) ends on verses about a wedding, an example of the elegiac elements so common in wedding poetry (perhaps encouraged by the tale of the fatal events at the marriage of the mythological poet Orpheus). Among the many 20th-c. epithalamia are wedding poetry by W. H. Auden, James Merrill, and Gertrude Stein.

Common conventions of the Eng. and continental trads. include praise of the couple; invocations of the mythological figure associated with marriages, Hymen; prayers for children; allusions to dangers that must be avoided; and references to houses and thresholds. Often the poet assumes the role of master of ceremonies. *Refrains frequently appear, as do images of nature and warfare, as well as references to political events, the latter exemplifying the social and public orientation of many epithalamia. Critics often divide the genre into two types: the so-called lyric epithalamium, which generally describes the events of the wedding day in chronological form, as Catullus 61 does; and the epic epithalamium, exemplified by Catullus 64, which recounts a mythological story connected with a marriage. Other scholars have, however, challenged this binary categorization, stressing that some poems fit imperfectly and many others not at all.

In addition to the elegiac propensities exemplified by the work of Tennyson and many other poets, the genre of marriage often effects its own flirtations or marriages with and divorces from many other poetic genres. *Pastoral elements are common. The epithalamium borrows from Petrarchan love poetry and often also offers a countervailing vision in which conjugal happiness replaces the frustrations often though not invariably associated with Petrarchism. Epithalamia within masques, a number of which celebrate weddings, gesture toward an affinity between those modes that encapsulate recurrent characteristics of wedding poetry: both that genre and masques are concerned to acknowledge but contain threats, esp. to communal order, and both emphasize the relationship between individuals and the community. Esp. intriguing is the link between the *paraclausithyron*, a convention that portrays a lover attempting to gain admission to the house of the beloved, and the epithalamium: on one level, the wedding poem is a potential sequel or alternative to this sort of "closed-door poem," while spatially it reverses positions, placing the lover within an enclosed space suggested by its title and the rest of the community outside.

See BLASON.

■ *English Epithalamies*, ed. R. Case (1896); J. McPeek, *Catullus in Strange and Distant Britain* (1939); T. M. Greene, "Spenser and the Epithalamic Convention," *CL* 9 (1957); A. Hieatt, *Short Time's Endless Monument* (1960); V. Tufte, *The Poetry of Marriage* (1970); *High Wedlock Then Be Honored*, ed. V. Tufte (1970); J. Loewenstein, "Echo's Ring: Orpheus and Spenser's Career," *English Literary Renaissance* 16 (1986); C. Schenck, *Mourning and Panegyric* (1988); T. Deveny, "Poets and Patrons: Literary Adulation in the Epithalamium of the Spanish Golden Age," *South Atlantic Review* 53 (1988); H. Dubrow, *A Happier Eden* (1990); J. Owens, "The Poetics of Accommodation in Spenser's 'Epithalamion,'" *SEL* 40 (2000); B. Boehrer, "'Lycidas': The Pastoral Elegy as Same-Sex Epithalamium," *PMLA* 117 (2002).

H. DUBROW

EPITHET. A modifier specifying an essential characteristic and appearing with a noun or a proper name to form a phrase. The word derives from the Gr. *epitheton* (attributed, added), which Lat. grammarians considered to be equivalent to "adjective." Isidore of Seville writes that epithets "are called either adjectives (*adiectivus*) or additions, because they are 'added to' (*adicere*, ppl. *adiectus*) nouns to complete the meaning." In mod. scholarship, the term designates a rhetorical device whose best known examples come from Homer, such as the first elements of "wine-dark sea" and "swift-footed Achilles." They appear in formulaic constructions, i.e., each phrase follows a metrical pattern and conveys an essential idea. In this rhetorical sense, epithets are not restricted to single adjectives; they may include nouns or phrases. Conveying what is essential to the noun continues to characterize epithet even in later centuries when the phrase is not formulaic. George Herbert's "quick ey'd love," which resembles the Homeric "gray-eyed Athena," and John Milton's "all-ruling heaven," which William Wordsworth later adopted, illustrate this defining characteristic. The distinction between epithet and adjective, however, is not always clear.

The formulaic nature of older epithets is not limited to Gr. and Lat., which inherited them as a feature indigenous to IE verse, as with the Homeric phrase for "imperishable fame" (κλέος ἄφθιτον), which has an exact analog in the ancient *Rig Veda* (*śrávas ákṣitam*). Still other formulaic epithets find parallels among various IE poetic trads. However, the device extends beyond IE languages. Epithets or constructions very like them can be found, e.g., in med. Ar. love poetry, Twi literature of Ghana, and early Japanese court poetry known as *waka*, which calls them *makura-kotoba* (pillow words).

In Eng. lit., the device has an older hist. than, for instance, the Homeric imitation in Edmund Spenser's "rosy-fingred Morning." *Beowulf* and other OE poems made frequent use of formulas like *æþeling ær-god*, "preeminent prince," and kennings like *lyft-floga*, "air-flier, dragon" and *freoðu-webbe*, "peace-weaver, lady." The appositive syntax allowed multiple epithets in lines like *he on ræste geseah / guð-werigne Grendel licgan, / aldor-leasne*, "he saw Grendel lying in rest, battle-weary, lifeless." Another influence in Eng. and elsewhere, though difficult to measure, may be the litanies in Christian liturgy, which include sequences such as *Jesu potentissime, Jesu patientissime, Jesu obedientissime, Jesu mitis et humilis corde*. Not limited to Christianity, the repetition of epithet-like names for the divine is a feature of religious trads. throughout history.

The device can be extended. Once it becomes well established, an epithet can stand alone, such as "The Philosopher," meaning "The Philosopher Aristotle." This omission of the noun was known in cl. rhet. as *antonomasia. In a "transferred epithet," the modifier typically specifies a human attribute and applies it to an inanimate noun (e.g., "angry crown," "condemned cell"). A colloquial use since the 19th c., which owes little to the rhetorical device, applies to any offensive or abusive term, e.g., "racial epithet."

■ B. Groom, *The Formation and Use of Compound Epithets in English Poetry from 1579* (1937); L. H. Ofosu-Appiah, "On Translating the Homeric Epithet and Simile into Twi," *Africa* 30 (1960); F. C. Robinson, *"Beowulf" and the Appositive Style* (1985); *A Waka Anthology*, trans. E. A. Cranston (1993); *The Etymologies of Isidore of Seville*, trans. S. A. Barney et al. (2006); M. L. West, *Indo-European Poetry and Myth* (2007).

D. G. Donoghue

EPODE (Gr., "after-song"). (1) Gr. lyric *odes of the archaic and cl. periods often consisted of three parts: the *strophe and *antistrophe, which were metrically identical, i.e., in responsion, and the concluding epode, which differed in meter. Ben Jonson called them, usefully, "turn," "counter-turn," and "stand." Collectively, they are called a "triad." Stesichorus used extended sets of such triads for lyric narrative, Pindar and Bacchylides composed epinikion odes in triads, and the choral songs of Attic drama often contain an epode after one or more sets of responding strophes and antistrophes. The Gr. noun *epōidos* (Lat. *epodos*), which was originally an adjective, was feminine in gender when used to designate the last part of a triad (*epōidos strophē*). (2) When masculine (*epōidos stichos*), it denoted the second (and occasionally third), shorter *colon of a brief strophe, consisting in most cases of a *hexameter or an *iambic *trimeter followed by a colon in *dactylic or iambic meter. The poems composed of strophes with such alternating meters in their two (or three) cola are also called epodes. The archaic poets Archilochus and Hipponax used this kind of composition, often for personal *invective, e.g., Archilochus's "Cologne Epode," recounting a seduction. In the Hellenistic age, epodic composition was adapted to book poetry, as in Callimachus's *Iambi* 5, 6, and 7 and in some *epigrams. Horace introduced the form into Lat. in his epodes, which he called *Iambi*.

■ Dale; Maas; West.

R. J. Getty; J. W. Halporn;
K. J. Gutzwiller

EUPHONY (Gr., "good sound"). Euphony, particularly in dramatic works and poetry, is a smoothness and harmony of sounds that are agreeable to the ear and pleasing in the physical act of pronouncing them or in the mental act of their unvoiced performance.

John Milton begins his elegiac "Lycidas" with euphony's engaging calmness, "Yet once more, O ye Laurels, and once more, / Ye Myrtles brown, with ivy never sere," before turning to the more rugged sounds of cacophony, the opposite of euphony, as he speaks of his own poetry's unmellowed maturity: "I come to pluck your berries harsh and crude."

Sometimes it is difficult to determine the part played by such sound effects. Reader/performers of the final line of Elizabeth Barrett Browning's sonnet that begins "How do I love thee? Let me count the ways" are unlikely to experience cacophony in "I shall but love thee better after death"—even though the line contains the same *sh, b, d,* and *r* sounds as Milton's dissonant line about plucking "berries harsh and crude." What the line says is likely to suppress possible perceptions of discordance.

Euphony is evident in W. B. Yeats's poem "Adam's Curse" when the poet praises labor "to articulate sweet sounds together," bringing the result of his own effort to our attention by means of euphonious harmonies of sound and meaning in a memorable phrase. His concluding line for "The Lake Isle of Innisfree," about "lake water lapping," is a study in the soothing lowering of vowel sounds from *e* to *a* to *o*: "I hear it in the deep heart's core."

Alexander Pope, in his *Essay on Criticism*, demonstrates that "The Sound must seem an Echo to the Sense" with his own euphonious lines: "Soft is the Strain when Zephyr gently blows, / And the smooth Stream in smoother numbers flows" (365–67). However, Pope also notes that euphony can be overdone by "tuneful Fools," who "Equal syllables alone require, / Tho' oft the Ear the open Vowels tire" (340, 344–45).

See SOUND.

■ L. Bishop, "Euphony," *Lang&S* 18 (1986).

T. CARPER

EYE RHYME (sight rhyme, visual rhyme). Two or more words that seem to rhyme visually, in that their spelling is nearly identical (they begin differently but end alike), but in pronunciation do not. Example: *rough/cough/through/though/plough.* Eye rhymes must be discriminated with care, for, although their quantity is greater than is often thought, they are a relative rarity. Many words that are spelled similarly but do not now seem to rhyme in the aural sense did rhyme in earlier stages of the lang. or do or did so in other dialects than our own; none of these is a genuine eye rhyme.

Still, poets have always been conscious of the visual dimension of poetry (Hollander's "poem in the eye"). This consciousness extends from larger effects—e.g., conceiving of the poem as a purely visual entity, in forms of *visual poetry such as pattern poetry and *concrete poetry—to smaller—e.g., playing with the visual shapes of words, chiefly in eye rhyme. Though eye rhymes certainly exist in cl. and med. Lat., the invention of printing in the West intensified interest. Poets of the past two centuries particularly have seen the correspondence of visual forms as an important strategy for expanding the domains and resources of poetry beyond those of traditional prosody.

Strictly speaking, eye rhyme is not a rhyme at all. But genuine instances of eye rhyme address the relations of sound to spelling in lang. and poetry. E.g., spelling differences in aural rhyme are invisible, whereas spelling similarities in eye rhyme are opaque: they are the marked form. *Rhyme is by definition sound correspondence, but insofar as spelling is meant to denote sound, we must both ignore it and, when necessary, pay attention to it. Hence, accurate knowledge not only of historical phonology and dialectology but of the spelling conventions of the lang. (the idea of a "correct" spelling scarcely exists before the 19th c.) is key to understanding rhyme in both the aural and visual senses. Eye rhyme thus raises the very question of the aural and (or versus) the visual modes of poetry.

■ Schipper, *History*; H. C. Wyld, *Studies in English Rhymes from Surrey to Pope* (1923); Hollander; K. Hanson, "Vowel Variation in English Rhyme," *Studies in the History of the English Language*, ed. D. Minkova and R. Stockwell (2002).

T.V.F. BROGAN; S. S. BILL

F

FABLIAU. A comic tale in verse that flourished in the 12th and 13th cs., principally in the north of France. While the name, which means "little fable" in the Picard dialect, suggests a short story, some fabliaux run over a thousand lines. Most are short, however, and share an unabashedly bawdy humor, focusing mainly on the body and its functions. From sexual excitation to excretory humiliation to gastronomic satisfaction, fabliaux focus on the materiality of everyday embodiment. Although cartoonish violence separates the fabliau from realism, the attention to food, sex, and feces presents an unadorned view of bodily experience. Nearly all of the approximately 150 tales that can be called fabliaux were written in octosyllabic couplets, and although a few names, such as Rutebeuf, Philippe de Beaumanoir, Jean Bodel, and Gautier le Leu, have been associated with the fabliau, most examples remain anonymous.

Much debate surrounds the criteria for defining the genre itself, incl. audience and purpose of the fabliau. First proposed in 1883, Bédier's argument for the genre's bourgeois origins remained unquestioned until Nykrog's analysis, which pointed to the predominance of noble and lyrical sentiments in the fabliaux as proof of their courtly aims. Mod. scholars tend to favor the view that authors as well as audiences were not limited to any one social class, which means that fabliaux are not united by a single thematic purpose. Despite acknowledging greater thematic diversity, Noomen and Boogaard posit a more limited stylistic range for the fabliau (they accept only 127 tales, as opposed to Nykrog's 160).

More recent crit. has focused on the fabliau's challenge to systems of bodily order, incl. gender, status, and religion. Though many tales are antifeminist in their association of women with voracious sexual desire, the same narratives illustrate female ingenuity and superiority, often over foolish or arrogant husbands. If there is a prevailing theme in the plots of the fabliaux, it is that of "the trickster tricked." Besides gender, hierarchies of social status and religious authority are frequently subject to upheaval. Priests are humiliated, merchants are bilked, and husbands are fooled. Yet this emphasis on instability extends even further: scholarship of late has investigated the impact of fabliaux on the med. written lang., with some critics arguing that the vulgar lang. of the genre called for a new literary vocabulary. Other scholars have examined narrative presence in the poems, which is often marked by idiosyncratic asides suggesting an improvised oral performance. Since many of the tale's tellers are identified with the shiftless, scheming characters of the tales, poetic production is also associated with bodily disorder, primarily through the tales' impetus to laughter.

In the 14th c., the vogue of the fabliau spread to Italy and England, where Chaucer borrowed freely from the genre for several of his *Canterbury Tales*, most notably "The Miller's Tale" and "The Reeve's Tale." Fabliau trad. continued in the prose *nouvelle*, but the influence of the older form may be seen centuries later in the poetry of Jean de La Fontaine in France, C. F. Gellert in Germany, and I. A. Krylov in Russia.

■ W. M. Hart, "The Fabliau and Popular Literature," *PMLA* 23 (1908), and "The Narrative Art of the Old French Fabliau," *Kittredge Anniversary Papers* (1913); J. Bédier, *Les Fabliaux*, 5th ed. (1925); J. Rychner, *Contribution à l'étude des fabliaux*, 2 v. (1960); *The Literary Context of Chaucer's Fabliaux*, ed. L. D. Benson and T. M. Andersson (1971); P. Dronke, "The Rise of the Medieval Fabliau," *Romanische Forschungen* 85 (1973); P. Nykrog, *Les Fabliaux*, rpt. with a "Post-scriptum 1973" (1973); *Gallic Salt*, trans. R. L. Harrison (1974); *The Humor of the Fabliaux*, ed. T. D. Cooke and B. L. Honeycutt (1974); T. Cooke, *The Old French and Chaucerian Fabliaux* (1978); *Cuckolds, Clerics, and Countrymen*, trans. J. Duval (1982); R. E. Lewis, "The English Fabliau Tradition and Chaucer's 'Miller's Tale,'" *MP* 79 (1982); P. Ménard, *Les Fabliaux* (1983); *Nouveau recueil complet des fabliaux*, ed. W. Noomen and N. van den Boogaard, 10 v. (1983–98); R. H. Bloch, *The Scandal of the Fabliaux* (1986); C. Muscatine, *The Old French Fabliaux* (1986); J. Hines, *The Fabliau in English* (1993); L. Rossi, *Fabliaux Érotiques* (1993); S. Gaunt, *Gender and Genre in Medieval French Literature* (1995); N. J. Lacy, *Reading Fabliaux* (1999); B. J. Levy, *The Comic Text* (2000); J. A. Dane, "The Wife of Bath's Shipman's Tale and the Invention of

Chaucerian Fabliaux," *MLR* 99 (2004); H. A. Crocker, *Comic Provocations* (2006).

A. Preminger; R. L. Harrison; H. Crocker

FOOT (MODERN). Ren. prosodists and critics, in reaction against medievalism, looked back to cl. antiquity for doctrine on the making of poetry. Many speak of verse's being organized only by syllable count "with some regard of the accent" (Philip Sidney, *Defence of Poesy*), but Brit. schoolchildren from Shakespeare through S. T. Coleridge learned to scan and write the forms of the Lat. feet at school, and John Donne in "A Litanie" speaks of "rhythmique Feete." As George T. Wright shows, in the early Tudor poets, one finds lines that are clearly composed by feet: they have disyllabic segmentation to excess. But the better poets soon discovered that the verse paradigms they learned at school could be manipulated at a higher level of sophistication; gradually, they began to write lines that could be composed, and understood, without such mechanistic rules yet that could still be scanned—though less simply—by such rules. Scholarly treatises on prosody continued for centuries to teach the doctrine of feet.

Further, from about 1550 to at least 1900, most Western metrical theories derived from cl. prosody, as that was reinterpreted in successive eras—particularly in the 19th c., which saw the rise of cl. philology in Germany. Common to all these theories was the presumption that, in metrical lines, syllables are to be taken together in groups, as metrical units; such units occupy a position in the theory midway between the metrical position (or syllable) and the *line. Both the concept of the metrical foot itself and the particular names and forms of the feet were taken directly from Gr., all of them being redefined as the accentual equivalents of the identical patterns in the quantitative prosody of cl. Gr. Thus, the Gr. iamb, short + long ($\cup$ –), was reformulated as unstressed + stressed (x /). The Gr. notion of the metron in certain meters was ignored (as were, by and large, other cl. concepts such as the colon, the anceps syllable, and *brevis in longo*). Many prosodists continued to talk of longs and shorts—indeed, for centuries—but, in fact, stress and/or syllable count was the basis for most Western meters by about the 4th c. CE. Whether the foot was an element of poetic composition or merely of analysis—i.e., *scansion—remained an issue of dispute.

Classicizing prosodists in the 19th and early 20th cs., such as J. M. Schipper and G. Saintsbury, tried to map the forms and rules of cl. prosody directly onto Eng., resulting in the foot-substitution model, in which variations from a basic meter are described as substitutions of alternative feet, such as *"trochaic substitutions" in the *iambic line. Thus, highly complex patterns can be made by stringing together various feet. It is apparently this model that T. S. Eliot refers to in "Reflections on Vers Libre" (1917) when he writes, "Any line can be divided into feet and accents. The simpler metres are a repetition of one combination, perhaps a long and a short, or a short and a long syllable, five times repeated. There is, however, no reason why, within the single line, there should be any repetition; why there should not be lines (as there are) divisible only into feet of different types." Versions of this model—sometimes more linguistically sophisticated—are still widely used in poetry handbooks and textbooks.

Assuming we call our units feet, the next question is how many types of feet there are, which entails the question of what principles are used to construct the foot. Even well into the 20th c., classicizing prosodists were inclined to admit nearly as many feet in Eng. poetry as in Gr.: Saintsbury lists 21 feet; as late as 1979, Paul Fussell admits six but thinks "it does no harm to be acquainted with" 11 others. But the great majority recognized, by the late 19th c., only four to six types: these included the two commonest binary feet—iambs (x /) and trochees (/ x)—and ternary feet—dactyls (/ x x) and anapests (x x /)—with the ternary feet far less common than the binary; and some metrists added spondees (/ /) and *pyrrhics (x x). The nature of Eng. phonology makes verse forms based primarily on spondees and pyrrhics impossible, but these units sometimes play a role in foot-substitution approaches to meter. A few other feet, such as amphibrachs (x / x), have been used as the basis of metrical composition, but more rarely. Some mid-20th-c. structural linguists admitted dozens or even thousands more types of feet by making distinctions on the basis of linguistic features such as whether the stresses fall in mono- or polysyllables, whether the stresses are natural or promoted-demoted, or other features (see DEMOTION). But these schemes complicated the analysis unnecessarily by mixing various levels of structure. E.g., there is good evidence that metrical rules distinguish between stress in polysyllables and in monosyllables (lexical stress in polysyllables is often more strictly constrained in what positions in the line it can occupy), but this fact can be handled more elegantly by keeping the levels separate and adding simple rules stating where each type of stress can go or at what level of stress particular rules apply. Most current theories number the foot types in Eng. poetry somewhere between two and five, depending on the principles and criteria applied.

See ACCENT, QUANTITY, VARIABLE FOOT.

■ G. Saintsbury, *A History of English Prosody* (1906–10), and *Historical Manual of English Prosody* (1910); Schipper, *History*; G. Stewart, *The Technique of English Verse* (1958); M. Halpern, "On the Two Chief Metrical Modes in English," *PMLA* 77 (1962); Chatman; C. L. Stevenson, "The Rhythm of English Verse," *JAAC* 28 (1970); W. S. Allen, *Accent and Rhythm* (1973); M. Shapiro, *Asymmetry* (1976); R. Jakobson, "Linguistics and Poetics" (1960), rpt. in *Selected Writings*, v. 5 (1988); P. Fussell, *Poetic Meter and Poetic Form* (1979); Scott; Brogan, sect. E; D. Attridge, *The Rhythms of English Poetry* (1982); G. T. Wright, *Shakespeare's Metrical Art* (1988); J. A. Goldsmith, *Autosegmental and Metrical Phonology* (1990); Cureton; B. Hayes, *Metrical Stress Theory* (1995); K. Hanson and P. Kiparsky, "A Parametric Theory of Poetic Meter," *Language* 72.2 (1996); G. Russom, *"Beowulf" and Old Germanic Meter* (1998); M. Kinzie, *A Poet's Guide to Poetry* (1999); T. Steele, *All the Fun's in How You Say a Thing* (1999); N. Fabb, *Language and Literary Structure* (2002); N. Fabb and M. Halle, *Meter in Poetry* (2008).

A. M. DEVINE; L. D. STEPHENS;
T.V.F. BROGAN; G. B. COOPER

FORM. As a term for the multiple systems that shape as well as convey information, *form* is a dynamic subject in philosophy and metaphysics, linguistic theory, literary analysis, visual and material arts, and culture at large. The *OED* gives 22 definitions, with subcategory refinements and variations. Even with a focus on poetry and poetics, coherent definition is difficult. Poetic form used to be binary: what was not content or context; the shape rather than the substance; any element or event of lang. not translatable, paraphrasable, or reducible to information. The binary entails a distinction between preexisting origin and material result, between determination and effect, between idea

or feeling and its realization. Yet lang. theory from the 18th c. on (and poetic practice well before) has been challenging these binaries, most forcefully with the notion of constitutive form—form as active producer, not just passive register, of meaning.

To appeal to the Lat. root *forma* is suggestive but inconclusive, for it reproduces the question, indicating both an ideal abstraction (correlative to the Gr. *eidos*, "primary idea") and a material appearance or shape. Plato and Aristotle often stand for this difference: form as the unchanging, structuring principle; form as the structure of a particular instance. In the Platonic view, famously articulated in *The Republic*, book 10, form is a transcendent idea and essential ideal, distinct from merely suggestive material instantiations. For Aristotle, form is immanent, emergent, and coactive with its expressive materials—the several cases from which a general typology may be deduced. Platonic form is authorized by transcendent origin; Aristotelian form is realized in process, devel., and achievement.

Prose form may refer to macrostructures of argument, narrative, plot, or schemes of fictive organization; to the length and array of its composite units (chapters, paragraphs, sentences); or to the formation of the sentence by patterns of syntax, rhythm and sound, image and figure. Prose can be "poetic" in these aspects (and there is a genre of *prose poem); conversely, poetry may sound prosaic (as some complain about *blank verse), relaxing formal definition to evoke conversation or a pre-formal flux of consciousness. There are, moreover, composite forms: interplays of prose and verse, of visual and verbal forms. William Blake's pages show all this, as well as a visual poetics of verbal forms: the sublime walls of words, the semiotics of block letters and free-flowing script. Another form is the shaped poem (see VISUAL POETRY), such as George Herbert's "Altar" and "Easter Wings," with the poetic lines organized into a visual shape, to signify a close connection of informing subject and expressive form.

What distinguishes *poetic* form is the *line that is a poet's determination, not a compositor's. Line-forms may involve the suspense of *enjambment and the punctuation of blank space at the line's end—as in William Wordsworth's "There was a Boy": "in that silence, while he hung / Listening." While the compositor of the 2d ed. of *Lyrical Ballads* (in which this verse was first published) set the lines of its new

Preface, the poet shaped this line and decided where to end it (here, to recruit the pause and cut to the suspense of "hung."). Blake is among those poets for whom even hyphenation can be poetic form, springing semantically pertinent syllables at a line's end, sometimes flouting standard practice ("Here alone I in books formd of me-/-tals")—this cut set to spring "me" from the medium. The form of a poetic line can follow, press against, or overturn metrical forms and trads.; it can be arranged in stanzas (regular or not, traditional or innovative), and play across end-rhyme patterns and rhyme fields. In all its events, poetic form signals a relation to trad.—whether using or refusing it, whether honoring or violating decorum, whether endorsing standards or applying a new signature. There is a trad. of auto-referential poetic forms, such as sonnets on the *sonnet.

Mindful of cl. theories, and with immediate debts to A. W. Schlegel, S. T. Coleridge distinguishes "mechanic form" from "organic form": "mechanic form" is the impression of "a pre-determined form, not necessarily arising out of the properties of the material," while "organic form" is "innate; it shapes, as it develops itself from within, and the fullness of its devel. is one and the same with the perfection of its outward form. Such as the life is, such is the form" (*Lectures on Shakespeare*). G. M. Hopkins's poetics of inscape and instress evolve from this distinction. Like Hopkins, Coleridge reflects, even dramatizes, organic poetics in his practice. He may work a received form against the emotional and dramatic demands of the event at hand (his sonnet "To Asra" plays its "overflowing" passion across enjambments that challenge the orders of rhyme); or he may make the mechanics part of the meaning: the poetic forms of repetition that plague *The Rime of the Ancient Mariner* correlate the endless repetitions of the mariner's existential fate. Or he may use shifts in meter for dramatic effects, as in the leveling of a curse in "Christabel" (see CHRISTABEL METER).

Lang. itself is both a received form and material for transformation. Invoking the complexities of *forma*, Coleridge correlates outward shape with shaping principle, contingency with determinate forces, to theorize a living process materially realizing itself: "'*Forma formans per formam formatam translucens*' [forming form through formed form shining] is the definition and perfection of *ideal* art" (*Biographia Literaria*); "Something there must be to realize the form, something in and by which the *forma informans* reveals itself" ("Principles of Genial Criticism"). Formal practices are also contextually charged. In the era of the Fr. Revolution, a discourse of "organic form"—seemingly liberated from prescription to follow the pulse of nature—could be invoked for principles of liberal education or could be harnessed to conservative ideology, to defend a system of unequal but complementary subjects on the model of nature. Thus, Edmund Burke on the hierarchy of classes, of rank and servitude stated in *Reflections on the Revolution in France* (1790): "Our political system is placed in a just correspondence and symmetry with the order of the world ... moulding together the great mysterious incorporation of the human race ... preserving the method of nature in the conduct of the state"; "The characteristic essence of property, formed out of the combined principles of its acquisition and conservation, is to be *unequal*."

Choices of poetic form signify, too. To write in *ballad form is to evoke an alliance, desired or ironized, with oral and popular culture; a *Spenserian stanza conjures Spenserian "romance." The difficulty of this last form, moreover, flaunts a poet's skill, as do other famously intricate forms, such as *terza rima or the *sestina and its multiples. A first-person blank-verse lyric recalls the soliloquies of William Shakespeare's tragic heroes, as John Milton knew when he dictated the great, anguished meditation on his blindness at the head of *Paradise Lost*, book 3. Milton's epic blank verse also bears a politics of form, which he advertised in 1674 as a recovery of "ancient liberty" from "the troublesom and modern bondage of Rimeing" for the sake of "apt Numbers, fit quantity of Syllables, and the sense variously drawn out from one Verse into another." To write a blank-verse *epic in the 19th c. is to declare not only a release from the regime of 18th-c. *couplets but an affection (with aesthetic or political prestige) for Miltonic poetics. When Wordsworth wrote about shepherd Michael in epic blank verse (rather than in a ballad), his challenge to decorum struck some contemporaries as unpoetic, ludicrous, or worse: the poetic wing of the Fr. Revolution in advancing the lower classes to higher forms. But the quiet dignity brought tears to Matthew Arnold's Victorian eyes.

In 1818, William Hazlitt took a satiric perspective on the patent politics of mod. poetics: "rhyme was looked upon as a relic of the feudal system, and regular metre was abolished along with regular government" ("Living Poets"). Even so, such allegories are slippery. By 1814, Tory Wordsworth was writing a blank-verse epic (*The Excursion*), and Liberal Lord Byron was hewing to rhyme: "Prose poets like blank-verse, I'm fond of rhyme, / Good workmen never quarrel with their tools," he wrote in *ottava rima (Don Juan,* 1819). In 1816, political liberals such as Leigh Hunt were wielding couplets with cheeky avant-garde flash. Even the affection in the 18th c. for orderly heroic couplets is no clear signifier: it may convey a neoclassical ethos (aesthetic, political, social) of balance and symmetry; or it may pose a highly wrought artificial contrast to the messiness of material life in its economic turmoil, political intrigues and perils, and unrelenting urban filth. A dramatic *monologue arrayed in *pentameter couplets, yet with rhythms and enjambments that mute meter and rhyme, stages an artifice of subtly crafted casual conversation—the canny form that Robert Browning devised for a duke speaking with affable condescension to a count's envoy about his last and (he hopes) next duchess.

When, in 1951, Cleanth Brooks contended that "form is meaning," he was holding faith with "the primary concern of criticism": "the problem of unity—the kind of whole which the literary work forms or fails to form, and the relation of the various parts to each other in building up this whole" ("Formalist Critic"). Yet Paul de Man saw in this "problem" a blind but incipient theorizing of form as indeterminacy, a "rhetoric of temporality" in which form can never achieve organic completion or totality ("Temporality"). As the dynamic register and producer of tensions, ironies, and contradictions, form, to de Man, necessarily subverts the "totalizing principle" in the mind of the poet and reader to open into a field of active, ceaseless negotiation ("Form and Intent").

Even critics such as Terry Eagleton, who in 1976 tended to indict the stabilizing allure of literary forms for recasting "historical contradictions into ideologically resolvable form," have been rethinking the charge. By 1986, Eagleton was admitting that while a literary text is "constrained" by formal principles, it can also put these into question—a dynamic "most

evident in a poem, which deploys words usually to be found in the lexicon, but by combining and condensing them generates an irreducible specificity of force and meaning." By 2007, he was writing about poetic form in terms with which Brooks (though with different social poetics) might concur:

> Form and content are inseparable in this sense—that literary criticism typically involves grasping *what* is said in terms of *how* it is said. . . . this seems true above all in poetry—a literary genre which could almost be defined as one in which form and content are intimately interwoven. It is as though poetry above all discloses the secret truth of literary writing: that form is *constitutive* of content and not just a reflection of it. Tone, rhythm, rhyme, syntax, assonance, grammar, punctuation, and so on, are actually generators of meaning, not just containers of it. To modify any of them is to modify meaning itself.

In theory, crit., and poetic practice, distillations of form from contexts, contents, and contingencies of event are difficult to manage because form is meaningful and meanings are formed. Lang. shaped in poetic form resists conscription as information for other frameworks of analysis; the forms are performative, informative, a context, a content, and an activity in reading. Our bibliographies are rife with titles that begin "*Form and . . .*" or "*Forms of . . .*" (often with the deconstructive pressure of a sequel, ". . . *of Forms*") or that pun into cognates of *reform, deform, perform, inform, formal.* Far from supplying a stable referent, form shapes the question, restlessly in play as a barometer of critical and theoretical investments. Form, poetry, and poetics seem destined to versatile, volatile, unpredictable transformations.

See METER, RHYME, STANZA.

■ C. Brooks, *The Well Wrought Urn* (1947), and "The Formalist Critic," *KR* (1951); E. Cassirer, *Philosophy of Symbolic Forms,* trans. R. Manheim (1953); S. Langer, *Feeling and Form* (1953); K. Burke, *Philosophy of Literary Form* (1957); G. Hartman, *Beyond Formalism* (1970); P. de Man, "The Rhetoric of Temporality" (1969) and essays in *Blindness and Insight* (1971); C. Ricks, "A pure organic pleasure from the lines," *Essays in Criticism* (1971); Hollander; T. Eagleton, *Criticism and Ideology*

(1976); P. Fussell, *Poetic Meter and Poetic Form* (1979); M. Perloff, *The Poetics of Indeterminacy* (1981); R. Barthes, *The Responsibility of Forms*, trans. R. Howard (1982); W. Keach, *Shelley's Style* (1984); J. H. Miller, *The Linguistic Moment* (1985); T. Eagleton, *William Shakespeare* (1986); D. Attridge, *Peculiar Language* (1988); J. Hollander, *Melodious Guile* (1988), and *Rhyme's Reason* (1989); *The Politics of Poetic Form*, ed. C. Bernstein (1990); M. Jay, *Force Fields* (1993); D. Attridge, "Literary Form and the Demands of Politics," in *Aesthetics and Ideology*, ed. G. Levine (1994)—also essays therein by Keach and Wolfson; P. Hobsbaum, *Metre, Rhythm and Verse Form* (1996); S. Wolfson, *Formal Charges* (1997); I. Armstrong, *The Radical Aesthetic* (2000); R. Strier, "How Formalism Became a Dirty Word, and Why We Can't Do without It," in *Renaissance Literature and Its Formal Engagements* (2002); D. Donoghue, *Speaking of Beauty* (2003); W. Keach, *Arbitrary Power* (2004); P. Alpers, "Renaissance Lyrics and Their Situations," *NLH* 38 (2007); T. Eagleton, *How to Read a Poem* (2007); A. Leighton, *On Form: Poetry, Aestheticism, and the Legacy of a Word* (2007); M. Levinson, "What is New Formalism?" *PMLA* 122 (2007); *Reading for Form*, ed. S. Wolfson and M. Brown (2007); C. Levine, *Forms: Whole, Rhythm, Hierarchy, Network* (2015).

S. J. WOLFSON

FOURTEENER. In Eng., a metrical line of 14 syllables, usually comprising seven *iambs, which since the Middle Ages has taken two distinct forms used for various kinds of poetry and thus exhibiting widely differing characteristics. When a pair of fourteeners are broken by *hemistichs to form a quatrain of lines stressed 4-3-4-3 and rhyming *abab*, they become the familiar "eight-and-six" form of *ballad meter called common meter or common measure. S. T. Coleridge imitated the looser form of this meter in "Kubla Khan," as did many other 19th-c. poets attempting literary imitations of "folk poetry." William Blake often used an unbroken fourteener in his "prophetic books," possibly in imitation of the biblical style from various Eng. trans.

The eight-and-six pattern was used widely in the 16th c. for hymns; indeed, Thomas Sternhold and John Hopkins adapted it from contemp. song specifically to take advantage of its popularity and energy for their metrical psalter. It was also used for polished lyrics such as Robert Herrick's "Gather ye rosebuds while ye may." Shakespeare uses it for comic effect in the "Pyramus and Thisbe" play performed by the "rude mechanicals" in *A Midsummer Night's Dream*. Closely related is poulter's measure, a line of 12 syllables followed by a fourteener, which when broken into a quatrain gives the 3-3-4-3 pattern of short meter. But the fourteener was also used extensively in the 16th c. for the elevated genres, in particular for translating Lat. tragedy and epic. It is used for trans. of Seneca's tragedies by Jasper Heywood and others published by Thomas Newton in the *Tenne Tragedies* (1581) and by Arthur Golding for his trans. of Ovid's *Metamorphoses* (1567). The most famous and impressive use of fourteeners in Eng. is probably George Chapman's trans. of Homer's *Iliad* (1616). The contrast between the effect of fourteeners in popular and learned genres is striking:

> The king sits in Dumferline town
> Drinking the blood-red wine;
> "O whare will I get a skeely skipper
> To sail this new ship of mine?"
> ("Sir Patrick Spens")

> Achilles' banefull wrath resound, O
>   Goddesse, that impos'd
> Infinite sorrowes on the Greekes, and many
>   brave soules los'd
> From breasts Heroique—sent them farre, to
>   that invisible cave
> That no light comforts; and their lims to
>   dogs and vultures gave.
> (Chapman's Homer)

Opinions differ about the origins of the fourteener. Schipper calls it a septenarius—more precisely, the trochaic tetrameter brachycatalectic—implying that it was derived from imitation of med. Lat. poems in that meter. The native influence of ballad meter is also obvious. But another explanation is equally likely: the great cl. epic meter, the dactylic hexameter, contains on average about 16 "times," and it may be that early Eng. translators thought the fourteener was the closest vernacular equivalent.

■ Schipper, *History*; P. Verrier, *Le Vers français*, v. 2–3 (1931–32); J. Thompson, *The Founding of English Metre*, 2d ed. (1989); O. B. Hardison Jr., *Prosody and Purpose in the English Renaissance* (1988); M. Hunt, "Fourteeners in Shakespeare's *Cymbeline*," *N & Q* 47 (2000).

O. B. HARDISON; T.V.F. BROGAN; S. S. BILL

FREE VERSE

I. History
II. Form

Free verse is poetry without a combination of a regular metrical pattern and a consistent line length. The exact denotation of the term has long been disputed, and usage varies in whether other organizing principles such as rhyme scheme, syllable count, or count of strong stresses are excluded. Because most definitions are negative and/or metaphorical, the positive features characteristic of free verse are somewhat undefined. Free verse is normally divided into poet-determined lines (not dependent on page width, like prose or *prose poems); beyond that aspect, certain formal structures such as syntactic *parallelism, heavy *enjambment, conspicuous use of white space, or stress clash are frequently seen, but none is definitive. Some writers have argued that free verse is not, properly speaking, a verse form at all; yet, whether one calls it a verse form, a set of verse forms, or one end of a formal continuum, it has been common in Eng. and many other langs. since the 20th c.

I. History. The origins of free verse predate the 20th c. Scholars have pointed to possible predecessors such as ancient Heb. lit. and its mod. trans., esp. the King James Bible; the *Epic of Gilgamesh*; very early Gr. poetry; relatively loose *blank verse from the Ren.; the choruses of John Milton's *Samson Agonistes;* Fr. *vers libres classiques* or *vers libéré* of the 17th and 18th cs.; late 18th- and early 19th-cs. innovations such as Christopher Smart's *catalogs in *Jubilate Agno*, William Blake's prophetic books, James Macpherson's Ossianic poems, and S. T. Coleridge's "Christabel"; J. W. Goethe's and Friedrich Hölderlin's poetry in Ger., Alexander Pushkin's in Rus., other romantic-era poets, and rhythmical prose from various periods. Some of these antecedents influenced mod. free verse, while others may have merely anticipated it, just as some include arguably nonmetrical verse while others are simply innovations within constrained metrical trads. The more immediate ancestors of mod. free verse in Eng. come from the mid-to-late 19th c.: Walt Whitman most important among them, but also other innovators in Eng. and other langs., esp. the Fr. symbolists. From a formal point of view, 20th-c. poetry merely extends trends that were already in process.

But self-proclaimed "free verse" in Eng. has implied not only a set of formal practices or procedures but, at various times, a movement, a group-identity marker, and a political statement. Most important, it has marked a poet as "modern." Influenced by the *vers libre* movement in Fr., which began in the 1880s, the free verse movement in Eng. began in the first two decades of the 1900s with T. E. Hulme, Ezra Pound, T. S. Eliot, W. C. Williams, H. D., D. H. Lawrence, Amy Lowell, and others. From the earliest days of the movement, poets and groups periodically published polemics arguing in favor of a line that "follows the contours of [the poet's] thought and is free rather than regular" (Hulme), "compos[ing] in the sequence of the musical phrase, not in the sequence of the metronome" (Pound), "composition by field, as opposed to the old line, stanza . . ." (Charles Olson; see COMPOSITION BY FIELD), "undisturbed flow from the mind of personal secret idea-words, *blowing* (as per jazz musician) on subject of image" (Jack Kerouac), etc. Prescriptions are often justified in terms of a desire for more direct expression of thought or for lang. that naturally or organically matches the form of its referent. Although the adoption of free verse has often been seen as part of a rebellion against some decadent prior order, the specific political engagement of that rebellion could range from Fascist sympathies to conservative Anglicanism to mild populism to open hedonism to mystical spiritualism to New Left activism to anarchism. All of these attitudes could also be found in metrically regular poetry of the same periods, though free verse may lend itself esp. easily to direct political statement. And free verse has always been marked by sharp differences among its practitioners over matters of both form and content. Free verse has continued to evolve, and new schools and movements (e.g., the Beat poets, the Black Mountain school, the New York school, Language poetry) have arisen periodically.

II. Form. Free verse allows immense formal diversity. Lines may be as short as a syllable (or even a typographical letter) or too long to fit within the margins of a printed page. Stress patterns may be as random as the lang. allows, or they may show notable parallelism. Line breaks range from emphatically end-stopped to heavily enjambed. The visual arrangement of lines on the page may be exploited in various ways, from extra white spaces (to show pauses, create emphasis, or show different voices), to arrangement in concrete shapes, to serious derangement of syntactic structure such that the reader must piece the parts together like shards of a clay tablet (see VISUAL POETRY). The syntax may be similar to that of everyday speech or that of formal prose, or it may be a specialized poetic grammar that would be considered telegraphic, ill-formed, or even incoherent in other contexts. The register may be learned and literary, colloquial and vulgar, or (often) conspicuously mixed (see DICTION). The poem may avoid traditional sound patterns such as *rhyme and *alliteration, or it may make extensive use of them. Poems may be densely rhythmic, casually conversational, or prosaically expository.

Various writers have proposed to divide free verse into categories. Many list types or schools based on a confluence of key formal features, usually identified with a particularly influential poet. Chris Beyers's *A History of Free Verse* is fairly typical in listing four such types: (1) the long line (e.g., in Whitman), (2) the short line (e.g., in Williams and H. D.), (3) verse "haunted by meter" (e.g., in Eliot), and (4) verse that "avoids tradition" (e.g., in Lawrence). Individual poets are undoubtedly influential on the practice of other poets. Furthermore, "schools" of poetry may cohere as much by ideologies, guiding metaphors about form, or social networks as by their actual poetic practice, so these relationships are important from a literary-historical point of view; however, basing a theory of formal types on particular poets is problematic: there is no one-to-one match between poets and forms.

An alternative approach to listing a finite number of types or schools is to explore the formal features exploited to varying degrees and in various combinations by most free-verse poets. Eleanor Berry's "The Free Verse Spectrum," e.g., proposes a five-dimensional descriptive matrix based on continuous axes rather than binary divisions. Implicit in this exploration of features is often the question of what, in the absence of regular meter or rhyme, makes this lang. poetic. An exhaustive list is not possible, but some prominent features follow:

A. Lineation. Division into lines is the one feature shared by all free verse (excluding prose poetry). Different poets and theorists handle line structure quite differently, but some important aspects include *rhythm, both in terms of timing and of salience; phrasing or grouping; segmentation of attention; and visual effects.

The line is generally considered a unit of rhythm. Some writers have claimed that all the lines in a poem take approximately equal amounts of time to say or read, but this position can be defended empirically only for a limited number of free-verse poems. Similarly, the claim that each line is one breath is plausible for some poems but not for most. Poets do not even agree, in theory or in actual oral *performance, as to whether there is or should be a pause at the end of each line. Instead, the lines may signal a more abstract kind of equivalence, segmenting the text into comparable units of attention, emphasis, or weight. A word, image, or phrase occupying a line by itself, or ending a line, tends to receive more focus than the same item buried in a long line.

Still, we probably do tend to read or speak longer lines faster than shorter lines and to slow down, at least slightly, at line breaks, bringing unequal lines closer to temporal equivalence. This tendency helps explain why some poets and critics say shorter lines speed a poem up, while others say they slow it down: word by word, they slow it down, but line by line, they speed it up.

Line length is the most commonly cited feature distinguishing one type of free verse from another. The distinction between the long, mostly end-stopped, often parallel, oratorical long lines of Whitman and the short, often enjambed, colloquial, imagistic lines of Williams is seen as basic. Again, free-verse lines can be virtually any length, and even Williams and Whitman vary their own lines, but this long/short distinction can be a useful starting point.

In most free verse, lines tend to correspond to phrases or clauses: as a default, line breaks will coincide with the more important phrase boundaries. Where line and phrase boundaries do not correspond, the lines are enjambed, and "tension" may result. Most free verse has some enjambment, and in some poems, it is the norm rather than the exception. Critics disagree on their evaluation of this as on so many issues; some denigrate line divisions that do not reflect the "natural" units of lang.; others criticize poems for a lack of tension between line and phrase, which they find flat or boring. In either case, the decision of where to break lines is a key element of free-verse *versification.

B. Stanzas. Another grouping effect happens not within the line but between lines: some free verse is basically stichic, with no obvious grouping of lines or grouping only into long verse paragraphs. Other free verse is stanzaic or strophic, with lines grouped into units of similar numbers of lines (see STROPHE). Sometimes the grouping of lines is largely a visual device, in which the stanzas do not correspond to whole units of syntax, phonology, argument, or image; in other poems, the groupings are tightly linked and structural despite not being joined by predictable patterns of meter or rhyme. In other words, just as lines may be end-stopped or enjambed, stanzas may reinforce or undercut syntactic, phonological, and semantic units.

C. Parallelism. A common feature of verbal art worldwide is parallelism: the recurrence of similar units. This is true of metrically regular verse as well as free verse, but because free verse avoids the pervasive parallel structures of meter and rhyme, other kinds, esp. syntactic parallelism, tend to become more important. Syntactic parallelism frequently occurs in combination with rhetorical figures involving repetition of words or phrases. The best known of these devices is *anaphora, the repetition of words at the beginnings of lines, sentences, clauses, or phrases. (N.B.: *anaphora* is used differently in ling.) A well-known example is Allen Ginsberg's *Howl*: in pt. 1, over 60 lines are parallel relative clauses beginning with "who." Syntactic parallelism is easiest to recognize in combination with anaphora or similar devices, but quite possible without them. An example of parallelism with only minimal repetition of words is James Wright's "Spring Images," in which each stanza is a sentence of almost identical syntax:

> Two athletes
> Are dancing in the cathedral
> Of the wind.
>
> A butterfly lights on the branch
> Of your green voice.
>
> Small antelopes
> Fall asleep in the ashes
> Of the moon.

D. Rhyme and Meter. Free verse generally avoids strict rhyme schemes, as in *sonnets or *ballads, and strict alliteration patterns, as in OE verse; however, free verse may include extensive sound patterning on an unpredictable basis. Virtually every possible type of sound repetition may occur: not only alliteration, *assonance, and rhyme but also more complex combinations of sounds. In some free-verse poems such effects are woven densely throughout, while in other poems, they are occasional ornaments (see SOUND).

Similarly, since free verse, by definition, avoids regular meter, there is no predictable pattern of recurrent feet (or of strong and weak positions) combined with a consistent line length; however, this statement does not mean that meter, in the sense of recurring patterns of stressed and unstressed syllables, or of rhythmic beats and offbeats, is irrelevant. First, some verse is explicitly composed in lines of a given number of strong stresses, with the total number of syllables unspecified. This patterning might qualify as an *"accentual" meter, but poems patterned this way are often called free verse. Second, recognizable metrical lines or line fragments occur prominently in some free verse; it remains free verse because these sequences are not consistent or predictable. Some critics link these flashes of metrical regularity to moments of heightened intensity in the poem or to iconic emotional values of different meters. Although the most-discussed sequences match well-known verse forms such as *iambic pentameter or *tetrameter, one also finds ad hoc metrical patterns that are repeated enough within a poem to be noticeable, but do not fit traditional metrical terminology.

On a more general, statistical level, there seem to be prosodic differences between the free verse and prose of a given poet even where no "ghosts of meter" are obvious. Some recent research suggests that free verse on average has more stress density, more stress clashes, more binary alternation of stressed and unstressed syllables, and more rhythmic units of a given number of syllables (e.g., four or six) than general prose. Certain grammatical and lexical differences correspond to these prosodic ones.

E. Intonation. Recent research has increasingly focused on intonation (pitch patterns) in free verse. Intonation is a factor in all speech, incl. poetry, but because it is not shown in writing, it has been underappreciated. Renewed interest has been buoyed by improved sound technology, by more sophisticated theories of intonation, and by the increased popularity of oral poetry performance—from traditional poetry readings to poetry slams and other formats. Intonation is esp. important in free verse because, in the absence of meter and rhyme, intonation plays a primary role in signaling line ends, grouping of lines, parallelism, and other structural relationships. It also forms coherent rhythmic structures in itself, e.g., in sequences of alternating rising and falling tones, or in repeated complex contours.

F. *Content.* Subject matter is not necessarily different in free verse from metrically regular verse. Free verse appears to facilitate more "transparent" lang. in some poems, in which the form is hardly noticed, and this facility may have implications for the emotional effects that can be achieved. Also, the relation of form to content can be different for different types of free verse, although one can find exceptions to virtually any form–content pairing. Where lines are short, the reader's attention is drawn to individual words or short phrases, and this tendency lends itself to a focus on images or on words as words. Where lines are long, the attention is drawn more to the sweep of ideas and to larger rhythmic structures; this attraction may lend itself to a grander scale of arguments and comparisons, among other differences.

See LINE, METER, RHYME, SPRUNG RHYTHM, STANZA, SYLLABIC VERSE, VARIABLE FOOT.

■ T. S. Eliot, "Reflections on *Vers Libre*," *New Statesman* 8 (1917); E. Pound, "A Retrospect," *Pavannes and Divisions* (1918); H. Monroe, "The Free Verse Movement in America," *English Journal* 3 (1924); T. E. Hulme, "A Lecture on Modern Poetry," *Further Speculations* (1936); Olson; D. Levertov, "Notes on Organic Form," *Poetry* 106 (1965); P. Ramsey, "Free Verse: Some Steps toward Definition," *SP* 65 (1968); C. Hartman, *Free Verse: An Essay on Prosody* (1980); R. Hass, *Twentieth-Century Pleasures* (1984); T. Steele, *Missing Measures: Modern Poetry and the Revolt against Meter* (1990); Cureton; J. Kerouac, "Essentials of Spontaneous Prose," *The Portable Beat Reader*, ed. A. Charters (1992); S. Cushman, *Fictions of Form in American Poetry* (1993); A. Finch, *The Ghost of Meter* (1993); H. Gross and R. McDowell, *Sound and Form in Modern Poetry*, 2d ed. (1996); H. T. Kirby-Smith, *The Origins of Free Verse* (1996); D. Wesling, *The Scissors of Meter* (1996); E. Berry, "The Free Verse Spectrum," *CE* 59 (1997); G. B. Cooper, *Mysterious Music: Rhythm and Free Verse* (1998); C. Beyers, *A History of Free Verse* (2001).

G. B. COOPER

G

GENRE. Most broadly, the term *genre* desig- nates the long and controversial hist. of liter- ary classification from antiquity to the present. The practice of grouping individual texts into distinct categories, called *genres*, is common to writers and readers of all periods. But these genres are themselves contingent, historical. Writers' tendencies and readers' expectations regarding the identifying features of a particu- lar genre—theme, *style, *form, vocabulary, *syntax, address, allusion, morphology, me- dium, and so forth—are highly variable, both synchronically and diachronically. While de- bate over the nature and attributes of particu- lar genres sometimes devolves into a chicken- or-egg squabble (which comes first, the generic category or the individual work?), it is also one of the chief engines of lit. hist. Thinking about lit. in terms of genre both piques and gratifies the human appetite for classification—the urge to identify unidentical things. But the dyna- mism of generic change also drives powerful narratives of difference and autonomy. We may think of a text as an expressive (authorial) or communicative (textual) intention endowed with a form that makes its meaning intelli- gible to others, even across great distances of time and space. At the same time, we recog- nize it to be a set of discursive effects not fully reducible to recognizable intentions or formal rules. Genres insist on horizons of meaning and expectation (Jauss), but they also give rise, through each act of reading, to dialectics and questions (Conte 1986).

Genre means "kind" or "sort" and is etymo- logically related to words such as *gender, genus*, and *beget*. Not surprisingly, texts in generic groupings are often understood to possess a kin-like relation to one another. Texts in the grouping known as "epic," e.g., are commonly said to "belong" to that genre, very much as if it were a family or clan. There has been a wide variety of genealogical and biological models of generic change, from J. W. Goethe's organicism, to Ferdinand Brunetière's speciation, to Franco Moretti's stemmatism. Some—Brunetière is the chief example—have rightly been faulted for thinking too strictly in terms of naturalis- tic categories. But the work of recent critics as different from one another in kind as Fowler,

Kristeva, and McKeon attests to the continu- ing viability of biological analogies for a wide variety of rhetorical, discursive, historicist, and materialist theorizations of genre that are all diachronic and antiessentialist. Even a genre theorist as profoundly skeptical of communica- tive intention as Jacques Derrida nevertheless speaks of genres in terms of a more generalized sociality. Like him, many readers prefer to think of a text as "participating in" rather than "be- longing to" a particular genre.

Belonging, participation, and other anthro- pomorphisms of genre, such as miscegenation, locomotion, sterility, and even death, find a precursor in Aristotle, who, in his *Poetics* (4th c. BCE), credits the differentiation of poetic genres to differences not only in poetic objects but in poets' own characters: the kind of person you are (e.g., superior, serious, noble vs. inferior, base, vulgar) dictates, Aristotle (following Plato) reasoned, the kind of poem you will write. This characterological determinism did not uni- formly dictate cl. poetic practice, which reflects more freely and self-consciously made decisions about what and how to write. But such associa- tions between genre and human nature, behav- ior, and relationship nevertheless abounded in antiquity and persist in much later expressivist thinking about genre and its implications for literary studies. The mod. aestheticization of the sapphic fragment as *"lyric," for instance, has its origins in the ancient reification of the emotional timbre of the poet Sappho's voice.

What postromantics habitually call Sappho's "lyrics," however, do not find their original the- orization in either Plato or Aristotle, to whom centuries of trad., as we will see, have confus- ingly attributed the critical establishment of a trio of "major" or "basic" genres: *epic, *dra- matic, and lyric (cf. Hegel). The lyric—when characterized as poetry that is neither chiefly narrative (epic) nor chiefly imitative (dramatic), but rather directly expressive of the poet's own thoughts and feelings—is, in fact, precisely that which is absent or excluded from Aristotle's sys- tem. The genre system proper to Aristotle com- prises the object (either the actions of superior characters or the actions of inferior characters) and mode (either narrative or dramatic) of po- etic address. The four possible combinations are tragedy (superior-dramatic), epic (superior-narrative), comedy (inferior-dramatic), and parody (inferior-narrative). The two genres that matter most to Aristotle are epic and, above all, tragedy. He gives comedy and *parody short shrift, and what later theorists call "lyric" is nowhere to be found in the *Poetics*. The lit. of antiquity is full of types of poems—incl. *elegies, *odes, *epigrams, *epithalamia, and epinikia—that, since the 16th c., have generally been classified as lyric genres. But this is a mod. classification, not an Aristotelian or aboriginal or "natural" one.

Many mod. inheritors of the *Poetics*, incl. major poets and theorists of the Ren. who got their Aristotle channeled largely through Horace's *Ars poetica* (1st c. BCE), were intensely devoted to further, more accurately construed fundamentals of Aristotelian genre theory, which included an emphasis on structural unity and *mimesis, as well as a sense of literary kinds as both fixed in their rules and finite in their number. This devotion persisted through, and even beyond, the neoclassical era. Yet from Dante and Ludovico Ariosto to Ben Jonson (himself one of Horace's many Ren. trans.), John Dryden, Alexander Pope, and, much later, Matthew Arnold, some of the strongest advocates of cl. *decorum nevertheless insisted on maintaining a critical relation to it—reevaluating received rules and deviating from them in keeping with specific aesthetic or social goals, with the perception of a generally advancing understanding of the world, the object of poetic mimesis. As Pope puts it in his *Essay on Criticism* (1711),

> Learn hence for Ancient *Rules* a just
>   Esteem;
> To copy *Nature* is to copy *Them*.
> Some Beauties yet, no Precepts can declare,
> For there's a *Happiness* as well as *Care*.
> *Musick* resembles *Poetry*, in each
> Are *nameless Graces* which no Methods
>   teach,
> And which a *Master-Hand* alone can reach.
> If, where the *Rules* not far enough extend,
> (Since Rules were made but to promote
>   their End)
> Some Lucky LICENCE answers to the full
> Th' Intent propos'd, *that License* is a *Rule*.

Pope's "lucky license" seems to anticipate later flowerings of arguments against inflexible and prescriptive concepts of genre—e.g., the individualistic arguments closely associated

with the rise of continental and Brit. romanticism. The late 18th and early 19th cs. saw an expansion and liberalization of genre theory and crit., an influential positing of open rather than closed generic systems. Many romantic writers felt that any historically determined set of fixed categories imposed on fresh poetic production was inadequate to new, dynamic theories of consciousness and growing confidence in the autonomy of aesthetic judgment. As human consciousness changed, they reasoned, new genres would continue to emerge. Other poets and theorists went even further, strongly resisting generic systematization of any kind (cf. Curran, Rajan). Although the idea that there exist only certain fixed, transhistorical genres has *never* been accepted without controversy, these romantic, post-Kantian devels. would be esp. consequential in the ongoing, contentious shifts in genre theory—shifts esp. visible beginning in the late 18th c.—away from taxonomics and toward hermeneutics. Static taxonomics was largely rejected in favor of various competing historical models of generic devel. and transformation. And the principles of generic decorum that Aristotle and esp. Horace insisted on as normative standards linking the qualitative evaluation of poetry to the realm of human conduct would never regain their former influence.

This historical change is more comprehensively reflected, in part, in the transition from prescriptive models of genre (how poetry *ought* to be written) to descriptive-prospective models (how poetry *has been* and *may yet be* written). But this transition is not simply diachronic, no straightforward triumph of the mod. over the ancient. For, although it was Horace, and not Derrida, who coined the term "the law of genre" and although he insisted in his *Ars poetica* that mixed genres were monstrous violations of generic purity, yet Horace's own poetic practice, as Farrell demonstrates, is a thick forest of generic hybridization. Cl. poetry itself, as the example of Horace makes plain, frequently destabilizes cl. norms of genre. Indeed, the lack of congruence between theory and practice is the energizing, often conflicted condition of emergence for authors' individual works and for the historical appearance and transformation, in every period, of generic norms and expectations.

Still, for the sprawling Lat. and vernacular lits. of the Middle Ages, there were little anxious reflection and debate on the priorities of cl. poetics, such as would ensue from the rediscovery of Aristotle's *Poetics* in the early 16th c. Cl. terms persisted, but without much normative force; and they were supplemented by new terms, such as *vision, legend,* and *romance.* Yet there was no free-for-all. Many aspects of ancient rhet. and poetics were transmitted and adapted as schemata. And by the 13th c., the med. obsession with classification had focused its concentrated attention on Aristotle's recently translated works on logic, politics, ethics, and zoology. Moreover, both Christian dogma and Christian discourse entailed complex thematic and structural links across late Lat. Christian antiquity and the Middle Ages. Fowler, e.g., points to the extensive modulation of allegory at the crossings of Christian and non-Christian canons. And Jauss provides a general warning against the retrospective imposition of a distinction between "spiritual" and "worldly" genres, pointing to the extraordinary range of models for med. literary genres found in the Bible, incl. *hymns, *laments, sagas, legends, genealogy, letters, contracts, biographies, *proverbs, *riddles, parables, epistles, and sermons. Jauss also finds in med. genres, such as the courtly lyric, signs of the coming great shifts in the perceived purposiveness and autonomy of literary genres.

Indeed, with the later rediscovery of Aristotle's *Poetics* came not only a rededication to perceived cl. norms and a consequent sense of the impropriety and even alterity of med. "mixed" genres but a radical reinterpretation—really, as we have seen, a misreading—of the *Poetics* itself. The nonrepresentational genres—Genette calls them "a cloud of small forms"—that were effectively ignored by Aristotle as neither narrative nor dramatic became an increasingly important aggregate in Ren. genre theory and beyond. They were, as Genette observes, assimilated or promoted in two ways: first, by reclassifying nonimitative genres (those that imitate no action but merely express the poet's thoughts and feelings) as being in their own way imitative of the activities of thinking and feeling; second, and more radically, by rejecting the devaluation of the nonimitative genres and by elevating the status of their aggregate identity as "lyric" to the level of "epic" and "dramatic."

The hist. of the revaluation of genres, such as that of the ascendancy of lyric, is also a hist. of the recategorization of individual works and the reconfiguration of generic categories themselves. Lucretius's *De rerum natura* (1st c. BCE),

e.g., has been variously classified as didactic epic, scientific poem, and verse sermon. Lucretius himself takes pains to justify his setting forth of Epicurean doctrine in "Pierian song," and Ren. theorists debated whether *De rerum natura* counted as "poesy" at all. Yet John Milton, like Virgil before him, found it to be an essential model for his own transformation of cosmological epic. In the late 18th c., it inspired the "poeticized science" of Erasmus Darwin. In the 19th c., Karl Marx simply classed *De rerum natura* with other philosophical treatises in his Jena diss., while Alfred, Lord Tennyson made Lucretius the subject of a dramatic *monologue discrediting his materialism. And Lionel Johnson's *lyric sequence, "Lucretius" (1895), opens with what one could call a Lucretian *sonnet, written, like *De rerum natura,* in hexameters.

As Johnson's sonnet helps to illustrate, the conventions of a genre may include formal, thematic, stylistic, and mimetic features: like many sonnets, it has 14 lines, it is about death, its language is elevated and meditative, and it seems to avoid direct address. Most commonly, a genre is constituted and recognized through shifting combinations, or ensembles, of such features. Deviations from the conventions of a given genre are often, as in Johnson's "Lucretius," small enough or self-conscious enough to highlight, rather than obscure, a particular text's generic resemblance to other texts. And while, generally speaking, the greater the deviation, the more attenuated the resemblance, sometimes it is, in fact, the more radical deviations—such as G. M. Hopkins's curtal sonnets and Alexander Pushkin's Onegin stanzas (also known as "Pushkin sonnets")—that are most effective at drawing fresh attention to the durability of received conventions.

Identifying such variations, though it may sometimes seem like a very specialized, even trivial, technical matter, has significant consequences for literary hist., crit., and theory. Shakespeare's sonnet 126, e.g., quite self-consciously stops two lines short of the conventional 14, signaling, among other things, the action of the "sickle hour" of death, referred to in line two, which cuts all love—and lovers—short. In the 1609 quarto, two pairs of italic brackets stand in for the missing (if this is a sonnet, we expect them to be there) 13th and 14th lines. But many later printings do not reproduce them. Is this sonnet unfinished? Does the typographically marked absence of the final two lines finish it? Does the absence of the brackets undo it? Either way, the perception of a gap between text and generic convention is a condition of interpretation, not only of the poem but of the published sequence of Shakespeare's *Sonnets*, to which it belongs. There are methodological consequences as well. Ignoring the typographic element means rejecting the interpretive significance of the 1609 text's nonverbal graphic elements—something to which materialist scholars would object. Accepting as a sonnet a 12-line poem embedded within a sequence of 14-line poems may call into question the integrity of the sequence. Refusing to accept a 12-line poem as a sonnet may call into question the sequence's stability and completeness.

By 1609, the sonnet was ubiquitous, and the popular *sonnet sequence was already well established as much more than a mere collection of individual poems. From their Dantean and Petrarchan models, both Philip Sidney and Shakespeare had learned a self-conscious style that begged—and sometimes beggared—the question of the relation between text-sequence and event-sequence. Structural ambiguity also helped blur the distinction between factual and fictional accounts, between author and persona. Later sonnet sequences, from John Donne's to Marilyn Hacker's, have continued to be written and read as implicit or explicit meditations, not only on autobiography but on narrative as such, and on the possible relation of nonnarrative or counternarrative poetry to themes of religious devotion, erotic love, and psychological interiority. Vikram Seth's *The Golden Gate* (1986), a book composed entirely of Pushkin sonnets, was very successfully marketed as a novel, prompting some to lament the further narrativization of all lit., while others celebrated the way novelistic discourse disseminated this traditional poetic form among new communities of readers.

Narratives may come in all sorts of genres, from the cl. epic and the Ren. sonnet sequence to the existential drama and the psychoanalytic case study. However, most theories of narrative and narrativity focus chiefly on literary fiction, esp. the novel. From the perspective of the present, the novel has become for many a *synecdoche for genre as such (cf. McKeon). When students in contemp. lit. classrooms refer to *Hamlet* or *The Waste Land* as a "novel," they are not necessarily making a simple category error but rather reflecting a broad cultural and critical shift toward treating the novel as paradigmatic of

all that is interesting and dynamic in what Bourdieu calls the "literary field." Bakhtin's theory of the novel's exceptionality among other genres prompts his claim that lit. in the mod. era has undergone a process of "novelization." Not that other genres have grown to resemble novels in their features but that the nature of the novel— its status as the only "uncompleted" genre, its distinctive structural relation to the present, its fundamental plasticity, and its devotion to public autocritique—"sparks the renovation of all other genres . . . infects them with its spirit of process and inconclusiveness . . . implies their liberation from all that serves as a brake on their unique development" (Bakhtin 1981).

This remedial prescription for further generic devel. finds its counterpart in the wish to dispense altogether with the genre concept in literary analysis—a wish that had been gaining critical force since the 18th c. (cf. Schlegel) but that reached its furthest extreme in Croce's insistence that genre is a useless and even dangerous abstraction that draws attention away from each individual text's notable singularity, on which its aesthetic value, in Croce's view, depends. But Jauss and many others have given the lie to Croce's impossibly absolutist view of expressive singularity. For to be even minimally intelligible, any text, any expressive act, must refer to some set of conventions or norms against which its singularity can be noted and its novelty measured.

Post-Crocean reassertions and refutations of the meaningfulness and utility of the concept of genre are extremely diverse, ranging from Crane's neo-Aristotelianism, to Jakobson's emphasis on ling. structures and Bakhtin's on "speech genres," to Burke's posing of genres as frames of symbolic adjustment, to the competing anthropological structuralisms of Frye and Todorov, to Jauss's historical-systems model, to Miller's situational pragmatics, to Jameson's historical materialism, to Kristeva's intertextuality, to Nelson's psychoanalytic reflections on genre as repetition compulsion, to Altman's work on film genres and Holt's on genre and popular music, to the reflexive questioning of critical genres in Stewart, Jackson, and Poovey. The diversity, sophistication, and ongoingness of such work testify to the stickiness of genre, not just as a concept that will not be shaken off but as that which provides the necessary traction for the mediation of literary and social discourse.

See CONVENTION.

■ K.W.F. Schlegel, *Gespräch über die Poesie* (1800); J. W. Goethe, "Naturformen der Dichtung," *Noten und Abhandlungen zu besserem Verständnis des west-östlichen Divans* (1819); F. Brunetière, *L'évolution des genres dans l'histoire de la littérature* (1890); B. Croce, *Estetica come scienza dell'espressione e linguistica generale* (1902); K. Viëtor, "Probleme der literarischen Gattungsgeschichte," *Deutsche Vierteljahrschrift für literaturwissenschaft und Geistesgeschichte* 9 (1931); *Critics and Criticism*, ed. R. S. Crane (1952); Frye; K. Burke, *Attitudes Toward History* (1959); R. Jakobson, "Linguistics and Poetics," Jakobson, v. 3; E. D. Hirsch, *Validity in Interpretation* (1967); C. Guillén, *Literature as System* (1971); P. Hernadi, *Beyond Genre* (1972); R. L. Colie, *The Resources of Kind: Genre-Theory in the Renaissance* (1973); Culler; G.W.F. Hegel, *Aesthetics*, trans. T. M. Knox, 2 v. (1975); T. Todorov, *The Fantastic*, trans. R. Howard (1975); J. Derrida, "La loi du genre / The Law of Genre," *Glyph* 7 (1980); M. M. Bakhtin, *The Dialogic Imagination*, ed. M. Holquist, trans. C. Emerson and M. Holquist (1981); F. Jameson, *The Political Unconscious* (1981); "Genre," spec. iss., *Poetics* 10.2–3, ed. M.-L. Ryan (1981); H. Dubrow, *Genre* (1982); H. R. Jauss, *Toward an Aesthetic of Reception*, trans. T. Bahti (1982); Fowler; J. Kristeva, *Revolution in Poetic Language*, trans. M. Waller (1984); C. R. Miller, "Genre as Social Action," *QJS* 70 (1984); A. Rosmarin, *The Power of Genre* (1985); M. M. Bakhtin, *Speech Genres and Other Late Essays*, trans. V. W. McGee (1986); R. Cohen, "History and Genre," *NLH* 17 (1986); G. B. Conte, *The Rhetoric of Imitation*, trans. C. Segal (1986); S. Curran, *Poetic Form and British Romanticism* (1986); *Renaissance Genres*, ed. B. K. Lewalski (1986); T. Todorov, *Genres in Discourse*, trans. C. Porter (1990); S. Stewart, *Crimes of Writing* (1991); G. Genette, *The Architext*, trans. J. E. Lewin (1992); T. O. Beebee, *The Ideology of Genre* (1994); C. B. Conte, *Genres and Readers*, trans. G. W. Most (1994); P. Bourdieu, *The Rules of Art*, trans. S. Emanuel (1996); R. Altman, *Film/Genre* (1999); *Modern Genre Theory*, ed. D. Duff (2000); *Theory of the Novel*, ed. M. McKeon (2000); T. Rajan, "Theories of Genre," *CHLC*, v. 5, ed. M. Brown (2000); V. Nelson, *The Secret Life of Puppets* (2001); "Theorizing Genres," spec. iss., *NLH* 34.2–3, ed. R. Cohen (2003); J. Farrell, "Classical Genre in Theory and Practice," *NLH* 34 (2003); V. Jackson, *Dickinson's Misery* (2005); F. Moretti, *Graphs, Maps, Trees* (2005); J. Frow,

Genre (2006); "Remapping *Genre*," spec. iss., *PMLA* 122.5, ed. W. C. Dimock and B. Robbins (2007); F. Holt, *Genre in Popular Music* (2007); M. Poovey, *Genres of the Credit Economy* (2008).

M. CAVITCH

GEORGIC. A type of poetry that takes its name from Virgil's *Georgics* (29 BCE), the middle work in Virgil's career between his *pastorals (Eclogues, 39 BCE) and his *epic (Aeneid, 29–19 BCE). Sometimes earlier didactic verse, such as Hesiod's *Works and Days* or Lucretius's *De rerum natura*, which influenced Virgil's poem, are named as prototypes. The four books of Virgil's *Georgics* present themselves as a set of instructions or precepts (*praecepta*) for the tending (*cultus*) of crops, vines, cattle, and bees. They mix their precepts with myth, meteorological lore, philosophy, and narrative digression in order to represent the dignity—but also the difficulty and daily care—of rural labor. However, while Virgil's poem drew carefully from Greek and Roman agricultural and scientific treatises (Aratus, Varro, and others), it would not have served the practical needs of a real farmer; its audience was learned and urban, located largely in the circle of Augustus in Rome. As Virgil's central pun on *vertere* (to turn) and *versus* (the furrow in the field and a line of written verse) emphasizes, the *Georgics* are just as much about the poet's careful labor of representation within a larger field of cultivating activities. Highlighting and reflecting on its own medium, in other words, the poem offers a complex meditation on the affinities and differences between the tending of words and the culture of the ground. It is no accident, therefore, that the *Georgics* are the most carefully wrought and densely allusive of Virgil's works or that John Dryden's 1697 Eng. rendition promoted them as the "best poem by the best poet."

Instances of georgic before Dryden include Poliziano's *Rusticus* (1489), Luigi Alamanni's *La Colitivazione* (1546), and Thomas Tusser's *Five Hundred Points of Husbandry* (1573). In 17th-c. England, however, georgic is present more often as a mode or set of themes than as strict formal imitation. In *The Advancement of Learning*, Francis Bacon promoted his new science as a "georgics of the mind, concerning the husbandry and tillage thereof," and the georgic appealed widely to Bacon's followers later in the century (Abraham Cowley, Samuel Hartlib, John Evelyn, and others), who were interested in experiment, education, and estate management. It took Dryden's version, prefaced by an influential essay on the poem by Joseph Addison, to touch off a series of marked imitations, serious and mock, and to establish the georgic as a distinctive genre during the 18th c. Examples included John Philips's *Cyder* (1708), John Gay's *Rural Sports* (1713), William Somervile's *The Chace* (1735), Christopher Smart's *The Hop Garden* (1753), John Dyer's *The Fleece* (1757), and James Grainger's *The Sugar Cane* (1764). Among the several reasons for this proliferation was the appeal of Virgil's ambivalent and plangent celebration of empire to Britons whose awareness of their own nation's territorial ambitions and liabilities was similarly vexed, esp. after the Act of Union joining Scotland to England and Wales in 1707. Less imitative but far more influential, James Thomson's *The Seasons* (1730) and William Cowper's *The Task* (1785) merged georgic elements with other descriptive genres to produce long topographical poems that were the most popular verse of the century. These shaped the meditative, descriptive verse of the first generation of romantic poets, including Charlotte Smith, S. T. Coleridge, and William Wordsworth (see esp. Wordsworth's long philosophical poem *The Excursion* [1815]). After Wordsworth, in part because of the growing prominence of the novel and other prose genres dedicated to the tasks of daily life, georgic once again appears more often as a mode; its attitudes and concerns persisted, but informing a range of poetic and prose genres. Georgic verse maintained a foothold in 19th- and early 20th-c. America, where agrarian improvement and national expansion came later than in Britain. Its presence is more or less marked in the work of Joel Barlow, Walt Whitman, Robert Frost, Lorine Niedecker, Muriel Rukeyser, and others. In mid-20th-c. Brazil, one of the definitive poems of the Noigandres school, Décio Pignatari's "terra" (1956, pub. 1962) was called

by Haroldo de Campos a "concrete 'georgic'" for the way it retrieves the notion of the line of verse as a furrow (see CONCRETE POETRY).

Addison's "Essay on the Georgics" distinguished its subject sharply from pastoral, but as the aristocratic figure of the Ren. courtier receded behind the models of the working landowner and small independent proprietor, in practice these adjacent genres overlapped. For verse written from the mid-17th c. on, pastoral and georgic mark the ends of a spectrum of possibilities for writing about the countryside, as well as for representing the vocation of the poet. If pastoral's emphasis inclines toward the sympathy of nature, the spontaneity of production, and the leisure of the singer, the attention of georgic falls on the necessity of skill and effort to counteract the wayward tendencies of nature and civilization alike.

See ECLOGUE.

■ D. Durling, *The Georgic Tradition in English Poetry* (1934); *An Anthology of Concrete Poetry*, ed. E. Williams (1967); J. Chalker, *The English Georgic* (1969); R. Cohen, "Innovation and Variation," *Literature and History*, ed. R. Cohen and M. Krieger (1974); R. Feingold, *Nature and Society* (1978); J. Barrell, *English Literature in History* (1984); A. Low, *The Georgic Revolution* (1985); A. Fowler, "The Beginnings of English Georgic," *Renaissance Genres*, ed. B. K. Lewalski (1986); K. Heinzelman, "Roman Georgic in a Georgian Age, *TSLL* 33 (1991); F. de Bruyn, "From Virgilian Georgic to Agricultural Science," *Augustan Subjects*, ed. A. Rivero (1997); K. O'Brien, "Imperial Georgic," *The Country and the City Revisited*, ed. G. Maclean, D. Landry, and J. P. Ward (1999); R. F. Thomas, *Reading Virgil and His Texts* (1999); T. Sweet, *American Georgics* (2001); R. Thomas, *Virgil and the Augustan Reception* (2001); K. Goodman, *Georgic Modernity and British Romanticism* (2004).

K. GOODMAN

HAIKU, WESTERN

I. Before 1910
II. Through the Two World Wars
III. Resurgence in the 1950s

From the time of *Japonisme* in painting (1850–1910), Japanese arts began to exert an unprecedented influence on Western art and artists. In the exchange between Japan and the West, the verse practice known as *haiku*—the term was coined by Masaoka Shiki about 1900—would come to exert great influence over the entirety of the 20th c. and after. In Western langs., haiku is commonly arranged into three lines, a rendition of the Japanese syllabic pattern of five, seven, and five moras, although, in Japanese, these often appear in a single line. An alternate designation is *hokku* (first verse), which implies a longer string of linked verses known as *renga*. Haiku practice in the West typically presents verses rich in *imagery, often juxtaposed in startling combinations. Furthermore, "stepping stones" of images running through longer verses (as Allen Ginsberg called Ezra Pound's practice) bring Western haiku into resemblance to traditional Japanese renga, the collaborative linked verse form of which *haikai* was a subgenre—albeit the Western adaptations are typically the product of a single poet rather than a group. The following article outlines some prominent adaptations of haiku into Fr., Am., Sp., and Lat. Am. poetry.

I. Before 1910. The Western adoption of haiku poetry began in 1905 when Paul-Louis Couchoud (1879–1959), who was also among the first translators of haiku, composed poems in Fr. in the fashion of haiku (pub. in 1905 in a booklet titled *Au fil de l'eau*). Other minor poets in France followed Couchoud's lead, copying and modifying his Fr.-lang. haiku poems and trans. A 1902 ms. of José Juan Tablada (1871–1945) of Mexico, *Nao de China,* reportedly included Sp.-lang. haiku, which would make him the first to adapt haiku to another lang. It is referred to as if it had been pub., although it seems never to have been. Nonetheless, Tablada trans. and pub. original haiku in the second decade of the

1900s, and, by the following decade, he had developed into an energetic promoter of the practice. Antonio Machado (1875–1939) of Spain was another early participant in haiku. His 1907 *Soledades, Galerías, Otros poemas* contains poems that were most likely haiku-inspired, although there is speculation that they derive from Sp. folk genres. The early imagists in London, encouraged by T. E. Hulme (1883–1917), adapted the extremely brief Japanese poetic forms of *tanka* and haiku to their experimental poetry.

II. Through the Two World Wars. From 1910 to 1919, many imagist poets produced poems with haiku-like juxtapositions. Imagist experimentation included Amy Lowell's (1874–1925) visual Japonisme in *Pictures of the Floating World* and Ezra Pound's (1885–1972) "hokku-like" "In a Station of the Metro." The depth of imagist engagement with haiku was indicated by Fletcher (1946): "I should say that the influence of haiku on the Imagists was more considerable than almost anyone has suspected." After imagist experiments, two Fr. poets, Julien Vocance (1878–1954) and Paul Éluard (1895–1952), became prominent. Both contributed haiku to the 1920 issue of *Nouvelle Revue Française* that declared 1920 "the year of haikai in France." Éluard's hybrids have elements of Dada and nascent surrealism. Publications in Spain and Mexico carried Tablada's haiku starting in 1919. Also in Spain, haiku found its way into the brevity of line and image formation of many of the Generation of 1927, incl. Federico García Lorca (1898–1936), and the poet at the forefront of avant-gardism in Spain, Guillermo de Torre (1900–71). De Torre's haiku was hybrid with *visual poetry, bringing his accomplishments beyond what others had achieved. While the years of World War I and between the wars were very fertile times for the spread of haiku, from the mid-1930s and the Sp. Civil War, and to the end of World War II, the atmosphere that had fostered such international activities turned inhospitable; the activities of vanguard artists were viewed with distrust; and rather than risk the same fate as Lorca, many artists abandoned their avant-garde activities.

III. Resurgence in the 1950s. The 1950s saw a resurgence of avant-garde activity that generally included the writing of haiku. There was renewed interest in Japanese culture, Zen Buddhism, trans. of Japanese lit., and scholarly tracts on Japan. Among those in the Beat movement, Jack Kerouac (1922–69), Allen Ginsberg (1926–97), and Gary Snyder (b. 1930), who resided in Kyoto for years, demonstrated great interest in Asia and Buddhism. Kerouac put haiku to jazz accompaniment in the late 1950s, but his haiku were collected and published only in 2003. Ginsberg discussed his connection to haiku as a connection between what he called "ellipsis" and condensed images. Snyder had been a student of East Asian langs.; his engagement with East Asian poetry is perhaps the greatest among all Western poets. However, it was not only North Americans who were haiku transformers in the 1950s. The concrete poets of Brazil, in particular Haroldo de Campos (1929–2003) and Pedro Xisto (1901–87), wrote haiku and engaged Asian poetics in their practice and theoretical writings (see CONCRETE POETRY). Furthermore, literary giants such as Jorge Luis Borges (1899–1986) wrote haiku in both the 1920s and the 1950s. In Mexico, Octavio Paz (1914–98) picked up the thread of avant-gardism as well as the haiku torch from his countryman Tablada. Paz's "Bashō An" contains the lines "vowels, consonants: / the house of the world" that, like the entire poem, self-consciously oscillate among ling. construct (haiku), its architectural, physical counterpart (Bashō's hut), and the phenomenological world. In so doing, they raise the Buddhist question of the relationship among conjurer-poet, poetic product, and constructing the greater world, a question that has long been at the heart of East Asian poetry. "Bashō An" simultaneously constitutes a tribute to and an enactment of haiku poetics and stands as a bridge between East and West of haiku image-pillars supporting poetics suspended across space-time.

■ A. Neuville, *Haïkaï et Tankas: Epigrammes à la japonaise* (1908); *Anthologie de la littérature japonaise des origines au XXe siècle*, ed. M. Revon (1910); E. Pound, "Vorticism," *Fortnightly Review* 571 (1914); J. Vocance, "Cent Visions de Guerre," *Grande Revue* 5 (1916); and "Haïkaïs," *Nouvelle Revue Française* 15 (1920); W. L. Schwartz, *The Imaginative Interpretation of the Far East in Modern French Literature, 1800–1925* (1927); J. G. Fletcher, "The Orient and Contemporary Poetry," *Asian Legacy in American Life*, ed. A. Christy (1945); K. Yasuda, *A Pepper Pod: Classic Japanese Poems Together with Original Haiku*, trans. A. Neuville (1946)—foreword by J. G. Fletcher; R. H. Blyth, *Haiku* (1949); *Breve Antologia Brasileira de Haikai*, ed. E. Martins (1954); E. Miner, "Pound, Haiku, and the Image," *HudR* 9 (1956–57); G. Brower, *Haiku in Western Languages* (1972); J. R. Jiménez, "La difusión del *haiku*: Díez Canedo y la revista *España*," *Cuadernos de Investigación Filológica* 12–13 (1987); J. Johnson, *Haiku Poetics in Twentieth-Century Avant-Garde Poetry* (2011).

J. JOHNSON

HEMISTICH (Gr., "half line"). A half line of verse; the two hemistichs are divided by the *caesura. In Gr., it usually forms an independent *colon. The device is used in Gr. and subsequent drama whenever characters exchange half lines of dialogue rapidly, giving the effect of sharp argument; in Gr., such a series is called *hemistichomythia* (see STICHOMYTHIA, SPLIT LINES). In other types of poetry, an isolated hemistich may give the effect of great emotional or physical disturbance, e.g., Virgil's isolated half lines in the *Aeneid* (1.534, 2.233), whence Shakespeare may have learned the device, but John Dryden eschews isolated hemistichs as "the imperfect products of a hasty Muse" (dedication to the *Aeneid*).

In Old Germanic poetry—i.e., in OE, OHG, and ON—the hemistich is the primary structural unit of the meter (see ENGLISH PROSODY). The first hemistich is technically called the a-verse (or on-verse), the second hemistich the b-verse (or off-verse). In the definitive typology of OE meter, Sievers showed that all the hemistichs in *Beowulf* could be reduced to orderly variations of only five types (A-E). Further, although each half line in *Beowulf* generally contains metrical patterns that could occur in the other half (disregarding *alliteration), hemistichs are by no means metrically interchangeable. A few hemistichs are exclusively first half-line types (e.g., type A with a light first lift and the expanded type D), and studies have shown that certain combinations of first and second half lines, while not prohibited, are avoided (e.g., two type As or two type Bs); consequently, the structure of the long line is far from being a random mixture of self-contained hemistichs. All this seems to imply that the poet put together hemistichs according to some definite principles as yet undiscovered. Recent studies have also shown the ME alliterative line to have a clearer hemistichic structure than was assumed by most 19th- and 20th-c. scholars.

■ Sievers; J. L. Hancock, *Studies in Stichomythia* (1917); A. J. Bliss, *The Metre of "Beowulf,"* 2d ed. (1967); T. Cable, "Middle English Meter and Its Theoretical Implications," *YLS* 2 (1988).

T.V.F. BROGAN; R. A. HORNSBY; T. CABLE

HENDECASYLLABLE. A line of 11 syllables, the hendecasyllable is significant in both the quantitative verse of Gr. and Lat. and in the accentual and syllabic prosodies of the mod. Romance langs., though as different meters. In cl. prosody, the hendecasyllable is the phalaecean, which has the pattern ∪ ∪ (or ∪ ∪ –; – ∪; – –) – ∪ ∪ – ∪ – ∪ – ∪ and is chiefly associated with Catullus. But in the Middle Ages, as the quantitative or "metrical" Lat. verse was transformed into the accentually based "rhythmic" verse of the vernaculars, the It. *endecasillabo* seems to have evolved from the cl. *sapphic or iambic *trimeter; its relation to the Fr. *décasyllabe* in the earliest stages is disputed. In *De vulgari eloquentia* (*On Vernacular Eloquence*, 2.5, 2.12; ca. 1304), Dante defined the hendecasyllable as the most noble line of It. prosody, the one most suitable for the highest forms of poetic expression in the vernacular and, as such, the preferred line for the *canzone*, the most illustrious of *lyric forms; the hendecasyllable has been the staple line of It. poetry since the 13th c. The names of the line forms in It. prosody are established by the place of the principal accent; thus, the normal hendecasyllable has 11 syllables, with a fixed stress falling on the tenth (the *endecasillabo piano*); normally in this form of the meter, the final word in the line is paroxytonic. Occasionally, lines of ten syllables occur; these are the analogues of the Romance *decasyllables and, in their unrhymed form and more distantly, the Eng. *iambic pentameter. Lines of 12 syllables also occur, the final word then being proparoxytonic. In addition to the major stress on the tenth syllable, the It. hendecasyllable is divided by a variable *caesura into two *hemistiches of unequal length, one a *settenario* and the other a *quinario*—with a corresponding secondary stress on either the sixth syllable (*endecasillabo a maiore*: "nel mezzo del cammín / di nostra vita") or the fourth (*endecasillabo a minore*: "mi ritrovái /; per una selva oscùra"). In the former, the settenario comprises the first hemistich, followed by the quinario, and vice

versa in the latter. Given the large number of dispositions of the secondary stresses in the line, the hendecasyllable is the most versatile meter in It. prosody, being used in virtually every genre (canzone, *ballata*, *sonnet, *terza rima*, *ottava rima*, *madrigal, and others) and for all subjects by most It. poets. A distinctive feature of many It. stanza forms is "the harmony of eleven and seven" (Ker), a mixing of hendecasyllables and *heptasyllables that carried over into Sp. prosody as well.

The Marqués de Santillana adapted the hendecasyllable to the Sp. sonnet form in 1444, and in general, the devel. of the hendecasyllable in Spain followed the same pattern as that in Italy. Heinrich Heine and J. W. Goethe imitated the It. hendecasyllable in Germany. In England, the iambic pentameter was influenced in its early stages (i.e., in both Chaucer and Thomas Wyatt) by the It. endecasillabo, but 11-syllable lines in Eng. are usually simply pentameters with an (extrametrical) feminine ending (see MASCULINE AND FEMININE): true hendecasyllables in Eng. after the Ren. are usually trans. or imitations of Catullus.

■ W. Thomas, *Le Décasyllabe roman et sa fortune en Europe* (1904); F. D'Ovidio, *Versificazione italiana e arte poetica medievale* (1910); W. P. Ker, "De superbia carminum," *Form and Style in Poetry* (1928); M. Serretta, *Endecasillabi crescenti* (1938); A. Monteverdi, "I primi endecasillabi italiani," *Studi romanzi* 28 (1939); V. Pernicone, "Storia e svolgimento della metrica," *Tecnica e teoria letteraria*, ed. M. Fubini, 2d ed. (1951); M. Burger, *Recherches sur la structure et l'origine des vers romans* (1957); D. S. Avalle, *Preistoria dell'endecasillabo* (1963); G. E. Sansone, "Per un'analisi strutturale dell'endecasillabo," *Lingua e Stile* 2 (1967); A. D. Scaglione, "Periodic Syntax and Flexible Meter in the *Divina Commedia*," *RPh* 21 (1967); I. Baldelli, "Endecasillabo," *Enciclopedia Dantesca*, ed. U. Bosco, v. 2 (1970); P. Boyde, "The Hendecasyllable," *Dante's Style in his Lyric Poetry* (1971); A. B. Giamatti, "Italian," in Wimsatt; F. Caliri, *Tecnica e poesia* (1974); Spongano; Wilkins; P. G. Beltrami, *Metrica, poetica, metrica dantesca* (1981); Elwert, *Italienische*; A. Menichetti, *Metrica italiana* (1993); S. Orlando, *Manuale di metrica italiana* (1994).

T.V.F. BROGAN; R. A. SWANSON; C. KLEINHENZ

HENDIADYS (Gr., "one through two"). The use of two substantives (occasionally two adjectives or two verbs), joined by a conjunction, to express a single but complex idea: one of the elements is logically subordinate to the other, as in "sound and fury" (*Macbeth* 5.5.27) for "furious sound." The figure appears in the Bible and in Gr. verse and prose but is not referred to before Servius (4th c. CE), who notes it in Virgil (e.g., *pateris libamus et auro*: we pour our libations from cups and gold = from golden cups—*Georgics* 2.192). In Gr., according to Sansone, hendiadys typically shows a "reciprocal" (21) relation between its two elements, "*either of which* could be logically and grammatically subordinated to the other" (19): thus *pros haima kai stalagmon* (A. *Eumenides* 247) may mean both "the dripping of the blood" and "the dripping blood" (20).

Virgil's hendiadys sometimes involves two distinct ideas (Hahn)—from cups and from gold—as well as a third that fuses them. The sum is elusive and complex. Shakespeare, mining the figure's mysterious and antilogical overtones, uses hendiadys far more than any other Eng. writer, often in conjunction with other kinds of doublets, to cast doubt on the authenticity of linguistic and social unions (couplings, contracts, marriages) and to provide a linguistic mirror for the internal agitation and ambivalence of troubled characters and plays. See esp. *Hamlet* (Wright, Kermode). Vickers, citing Kerl and Empson, disputes this view. Housman parodies Gr. hendiadys in "I go into the house with *heels and speed*"(emphasis added).

■ A. E. Housman, "Fragment of a Greek Tragedy," *Bromsgrovian* (1893), rpt. in *Parodies*, ed. D. Macdonald (1960); H. Poutsma, "Hendiadys in English . . . ," *Neophilologus* 2, no. 1 (1917); E. A. Hahn, "Hendiadys: Is There Such a Thing?" *CW* 15 (1921–22); E. Kerl, "Das Hendiadyoin bei Shakespeare," diss., U. of Marburg (1922); Empson; G. T. Wright, "Hendiadys and *Hamlet*," *PMLA* 96 (1981); K. T. Loesch and G. T. Wright, "Forum: Hendiadys," *PMLA* 97 (1982); D. Sansone, "On Hendiadys in Greek," *Glotta* 62 (1984); F. Kermode, "Cornelius and Voltimand," *Forms of Attention* (1985), and *Shakespeare's Language* (2000); B. Vickers, "*Counterfeiting*" *Shakespeare* (2002).

G. T. WRIGHT

HEPTAMETER. This term means a line of seven feet, but metrists have at times termed *heptameters* meters that have little resemblance to each other beyond syllable count, so the term is perhaps better avoided. It is occasionally used to refer to cl. meters such as the Lat. *septenarius*, which is a brachycatalectic line of seven *trochaic feet, and it has been used by some prosodists for mod. meters such as the Ren. *fourteener, as in George Chapman's trans. of Homer, but this is not the same type of meter, has a different rhythm, and is used in radically different contexts. Still less is it an appropriate term for Eng. *ballad meter, which in its most common form is set in *quatrains of lines of 4-3-4-3 *accentual verse. Schipper uses this term more or less synonymously with *septenary* for ME poems in 14–15 syllables such as the *Poema morale* and *Ormulum*, but here too terminology implies a derivation and structure that now seem problematic. In mod. Eng. verse, the term is applicable mainly to the long line of William Blake's later prophetic books, a line that Blake said "avoided a monotonous cadence like that of Milton and Shakespeare" by achieving "a variety in every line, both in cadence and number of syllables." Syllable count actually ranges as high as 21. Blake's sources would seem to be the Bible, James Macpherson, and late 18th-c. Ger. experiments in long-lined verse such as those in Friedrich Hölderlin's *Hyperion*, but Blake himself claimed that the form was given him in automatic writing. Other 19th-c. instances are William Wordsworth's "The Norman Boy" and "The Poet's Dream" (coupleted quatrains); Lord Byron's "Stanzas for Music"; Walter Scott's "The Noble Moringer"; Elizabeth Barrett Browning's "Cowper's Grave"; and J. G. Whittier's "Massachusetts to Virginia."

■ Schipper; A. Ostriker, *Vision and Verse in William Blake* (1965); K. Raine, "A Note on Blake's 'Unfettered Verse,'" *William Blake: Essays for S. Foster Damon*, ed. A. H. Rosenfeld (1969).

T.V.F. BROGAN

HEROIC COUPLET. A rhyming pair of Eng. heroic (that is, *iambic *pentameter) lines, most often used for *epigrams, verse essays, *satires, and narrative verse and the dominant form for Eng. poetry from ca. 1640 to ca. 1790. The Eng. created the heroic couplet in the 16th c. by imposing a regular iambic stress pattern and a regular *caesura (falling normally after the fourth, fifth, or sixth syllable) on the old Chaucerian decasyllabic line (see DECASYLLABLE) and by imposing on the Chaucerian couplet (called "riding rhyme" by George Puttenham and George Gascoigne) a regular hierarchy of pauses—respectively, caesural, first-line, and end-of-couplet—adapted from the Lat. *elegiac distich. This form, in which the end of the couplet regularly coincides with the end of a sentence, would later be called "closed," as opposed to the "open" type, in which there is no such coincidence of line and syntax.

The transformation of the Chaucerian line into what Puttenham and John Dryden called the "heroic" line was evolutionary, spanning the 16th c. from ca. 1520 to 1600 (Thompson). But the imposition of the hierarchy of pauses on the loose couplet inherited from Chaucer was more dramatic, taking place almost explosively between 1590 and 1600, when numbers of Eng. poets translated and adapted Lat. poems in elegiac distichs—chiefly the *Amores* and *Heroides* of Ovid and the *Epigrammaton* of Martial—achieving or approximating a correspondence of couplet to distich. Christopher Marlowe's trans. of the *Amores* accomplishes a virtually unexceptionable equivalence:

> sive es docta, places raras dotata per artes;
> sive rudis, placita es simplicitate tua.
> est, quae Callimachi prae nostris rustica dicat
> carmina—cui placeo, protinus ipsa placet.
> est etiam, quae me vatem et mea carmina culpet—
> culpantis cupiam sustinuisse femur.
> molliter incedit—motu capit; altera dur est—
> at poterit tacto mollior esse viro.

> (If she be learn'd, then for her skill I crave her,
> If not, because shees simple I would have her.
> Before *Callimachus* one preferres me farre,
> Seeing she likes my bookes why should we jarre?
> An other railes at me and that I write
> Yet would I lie with her if that I might.
> Trips she, it likes me well, plods she, what then?
> Shee would be nimbler, lying with a man.)

Other poets significant for the devel. of the form were Nicholas Grimald (who preceded the wave), John Harington, John Marston, Thomas Heywood, Joseph Hall, Michael Drayton, Ben Jonson, and John Donne.

The immediate result of this structural imitation was the affixing onto Eng. couplets of the Lat. distich's hierarchy of pauses and of a correspondingly balanced rhet. Note the balances above between the sharply demarcated lines of single couplets—"If . . . / If not . . ."—and the sharply divided halves of single lines—"If . . . then"; "Trips . . . plods." Eng. rhyme, which had the same closural power as the recurrent half-line pattern in the *pentameter of the Lat. distich, allowed the Eng. measure, once it outgrew its dependence on the Lat. model, to become much more flexible and thus absorb the modifications by which successive Eng. poets from Donne to George Crabbe transformed it into a medium of great expressive power.

At the same time, the heroic couplet also underwent a second major devel., beginning with Marlowe's *Hero and Leander* (1593) and extending until about 1660, in which the formal elements, the rhyme, and all the pauses were subsumed and all but concealed. This process, which Marlowe himself practiced cautiously, was carried further by George Chapman in his trans. of the *Odyssey* (1614) and in William Chamberlayne's long romance *Pharonnida* (1659). This "romance" or "open" couplet pointedly rejected the emphasis and definition established by the closed couplet; here, rhyme and syntax do not parallel and reinforce each other, and the formal elements work against sense, creating mystery and remoteness instead of clarity and precision. But the romance couplet vanished from Eng. poetry before the Restoration, to be revived—briefly, and appropriately—by such romantic poets as John Keats (*Endymion*), Leigh Hunt (*The Story of Rimini*), and Thomas Moore (*Lalla Rookh*).

Meanwhile, the closed couplet was refined and extended in the 17th c. by such poets as Francis Beaumont and George Sandys, then Edmund Waller, John Denham, and Abraham Cowley, and thus handed on to Dryden (practicing 1660–1700) and Alexander Pope (practicing ca. 1700–45). The heroic couplet as all these poets understood it is both described and exemplified in the famous lines from "Cooper's Hill" (1642) that Denham addressed to the Thames:

> O could I flow like thee, and make thy stream
> My great example, as it is my theme!
> Though deep, yet clear, though gentle, yet not dull,
> Strong without rage, without ore-flowing full.

As this widely known and widely imitated little passage illustrates, the closed couplet provides continuous support in its half line, line, and couplet spans for certain rhetorical devices and corresponding intellectual procedures, particularly *parallelism ("deep . . . gentle . . . / Strong . . . full"), with which poets enforced systems of induction, and *antithesis ("gentle . . . not dull"), with which they determined comparisons and refined analyses. They often intensified such patterns with the elliptical figures *zeugma and syllepsis ("O could I flow like thee, and [could I] make thy stream") and with inversion ("Strong without rage, without ore-flowing full"). The argumentative and persuasive implications of such practices were esp. pertinent to an age empirical in intellectual tendency and social in cultural orientation.

Dryden chiefly developed the oratorical possibilities of the heroic couplet, addressing large, potentially turbulent groups: in theatrical prologues, men and women, or fops and gentlemen; in satires, Whigs and Tories, or Puritans and Anglicans. He projected himself not as an individual but as a spokesman, a representative of one faction or, if possible (as in the opening of *Astraea Redux*), of sensible Englishmen in general. In *Religio Laici*, he concludes his exposition of how Catholics and Protestants both in their own way abuse the Bible:

So all we make of Heavens discover'd Will
Is not to have it, or to use it ill.
The Danger's much the same; on several
    Shelves
If *others* wreck *us*, or *we* wreck our *selves*.

Notice, first, Dryden's use of the formal aspects of the closed couplet—the definitive use of caesura in the second and fourth lines and the emphasis of the rhymes—and, second, the way he unifies the two sides, partially by using plural pronouns, himself taking the position of spokesman for both.

Pope developed the heroic couplet into a primarily social—as opposed to Dryden's political—instrument. He presented himself as a sensible gentleman addressing either an intimate friend—as in the opening lines of the *Essay on Man*—or an attentive society—as in the *Essay on Criticism*—or, as in his mature essays and epistles, both at once. In this conversational exchange with his friend Dr. John Arbuthnot, the sensible (if sensibly exasperated) gentleman asks who has been hurt by his social satire:

Does not one Table *Bavius* still admit?
Still to one Bishop *Philips* seems a Wit?

Still *Sappho*—'Hold! for God-sake—you'll offend:
No Names—be calm—learn Prudence of
    a Friend:
I too could write, and I am twice as tall,
But Foes like these!'—One Flatt'rer's worse
    than all;
Of all mad Creatures, if the Learn'd are
    right,
It is the Slaver kills, and not the Bite.

Notice, first, the caesura-defined parallel in line 5, and the formally illuminated antithesis, dividing both "Foes . . . [and] Flatt'rer" and the two conversationalists, in line 6; and, second, Pope's and his friend's awareness, although they are in intimate talk, that the walls have ears. Dryden in his most characteristic achievements aimed at political harmony or what he called "common quiet." Pope aimed, rather, at generally shared understanding or what he called "common sense."

The heroic couplet, modified in various ways, supported the generation of great poets who followed Pope, esp. Samuel Johnson, Charles Churchill, Oliver Goldsmith, and Crabbe. And even when Eng. culture shifted its focus from general understanding to individual expression—and quite properly revived the open couplet—several poets, chief among them Lord Byron, still found the closed couplet useful for public satire. Robert Browning ("My Last Duchess") and Matthew Arnold used the heroic couplet in the Victorian period; T. S. Eliot composed a heroic couplet section for *The Waste Land*, which he wisely excised when Ezra Pound made him see that he could not compete with Pope; and Robert Frost produced several exemplary heroic couplet poems (e.g., "The Tuft of Flowers"). Among more recent examples (see Steele, Caplan), A. D. Hope's extended use of the heroic couplet in *Dunciad Minor* stands out.

See BLANK VERSE, HEROIC VERSE.

■ Schipper; F. E. Schelling, "Ben Jonson and the Classical School," *PMLA* 13 (1898); G. P. Shannon, "Nicholas Grimald's Heroic Couplet and the Latin Elegiac Distich," *PMLA* 45 (1930); R. C. Wallerstein, "The Development of the Rhetoric and Metre of the Heroic Couplet," *PMLA* 50 (1935); G. Williamson, "The Rhetorical Pattern of Neo-classical Wit," *MP* 33 (1935–36); E. R. Wasserman, "The Return of the Enjambed Couplet," *ELH* 7 (1940); Y. Winters, "The Heroic Couplet and Its

Recent Revivals," *In Defense of Reason* (1943); W. C. Brown, *The Triumph of Form* (1948); W. K. Wimsatt, "One Relation of Rhyme to Reason," *The Verbal Icon* (1954); J. H. Adler, *The Reach of Art* (1964); J. A. Jones, *Pope's Couplet Art* (1969); W. B. Piper, *The Heroic Couplet* (1969); G. T. Amis, "The Structure of the Augustan Couplet," *Genre* 9 (1976); H. Carruth, "Three Notes on the Versewriting of Alexander Pope," *Michigan Quarterly Review* 15 (1976); *An Heroic Couplet Anthology*, ed. W. B. Piper (1977); Thompson; Brogan, 389 ff.; P. Deane, *At Home in Time: Forms of Neo-Augustanism in Modern English Verse* (1994); T. Steele, "'The Bravest Sort of Verses': The Heroic Couplet," Finch and Varnes; D. Caplan, *Questions of Possibility* (2005), ch. 4.

W. B. Piper; S. Cushman

HEROIC VERSE, heroic meter, heroic poetry. The term came to be used for *epic in the Middle Ages and after. Isidore of Seville in his *Etymologiae* (7th c. CE) defines *heroic poetry* (*carmen heroicum*) as being so named "because in it the affairs and deeds of brave men are narrated (for heroes are spoken of as men practically supernatural and worthy of Heaven on account of their wisdom and bravery); and this meter precedes others in status." In the Ren., Marco Girolamo Vida proclaims the subject of his *De arte poetica* (On Poetic Art, 1527) to be heroic poetry, though, in fact, it consists mainly of practical advice for poets derived from Horace and Quintilian. Torquato Tasso in his *Discorsi del poema eroico* (Discourses on the Heroic Poem, 1594) advocated a more romantic conception of epic but also insisted on accurate depiction of historical reality; he also wrote "heroic sonnets" celebrating great men and events of the past. John Dryden opens the Preface to his trans. of Virgil (1697) with the statement that "a heroick Poem, truly such, is undoubtedly the greatest Work which the Soul of Man is capable to perform."

Heroic meter is the *meter characteristic of heroic poetry: in cl. Gr. and Lat., this was, of course, the (dactylic) *hexameter. With the emergence of the Romance vernaculars from low Lat., however, poets in each lang. sought a line form that would represent the equivalent or analogue of the noblest meter of antiquity, the hexameter, the canonical meter of the epic trad. These were the *hendecasyllable (*versi sciolti*) in It.; first the *alexandrine, then the *décasyllabe* in Fr.; and first the *fourteener, then *blank verse

in Eng. Thomas Sébillet and Joachim du Bellay brought into Fr. use the term *vers héroique* for the décasyllabe, but Pierre de Ronsard, opposing the *decasyllable, used it rather for the alexandrine.

Heroic verse is still today the most neutral term for the ten-syllable, five-stress line in Eng. otherwise called *iambic pentameter* or *decasyllable*. Each of the latter two terms, while acceptable for general usage, carries with it connotations that are not historically accurate in every age and, hence, should be used with care. The former implies associations with classical prosody that many now feel inappropriate ("feet"), while the latter implies ones with Romance prosody that are equally inappropriate (syllabism as the chief criterion). It is certainly true that, in the first half of the 16th c., when Eng. poets were rediscovering or simply constructing the line that was to become the great staple of Eng. poetry, most of them had been given training at school in Lat. metrics. Others, however, were very familiar with continental verse models, chiefly It. and Fr., that offered a line of 10 to 12 syllables with variable stressing equally available for adaptation into Eng. The point is that all the Romance models were isomorphs of the cl. line that adapted itself to the varying ling. constraints of each new lang. into which it was imported.

■ R. C. Williams, *The Theory of the Heroic Epic in Italian Criticism of the 16th Century* (1921); Curtius, ch. 9; Weinberg; *Concepts of the Hero in the Middle Ages and Renaissance*, ed. N. T. Burns and C. J. Reagan (1975); J. M. Steadman, *Milton and the Paradoxes of Renaissance Heroism* (1987); *Heroic Epic and Saga*, ed. F. J. Oinas (1978)—surveys 15 national lits.; G. T. Wright, *Shakespeare's Metrical Art* (1988); O. B. Hardison Jr., *Prosody and Purpose in the English Renaissance* (1989); W. J. Kennedy, "Heroic Poem before Spenser," and M. A. Radzinowicz, "Heroic Poem since Spenser," *The Spenser Encyclopedia*, ed. A. C. Hamilton et al. (1990); B. Murdoch, "Heroic Verse," *Camden House History of German Literature, Vol. 2: German Literature of the Early Middle Ages*, ed. B. Murdoch (2004).

T.V.F. Brogan

HEXAMETER. Strictly speaking, any line of verse composed of six metrical feet. The only such line with a major role in lit. hist. is dactylic hexameter, for which *hexameter* is usually shorthand. It was the meter of the earliest and most prestigious poetry of cl. antiquity and became the dominant meter for nondramatic verse in cl. Gr. and Lat. lit. The basic template is a 17-syllable line of five *dactyls (– ᴗ ᴗ) and a concluding *spondee (– –); individual lines occasionally show that pattern: "quadrupedante putrem sonitu quatit ungula campum" (*Aeneid* 8.596). For individual dactyls, spondees can be substituted, though never for all five and seldom in the fifth foot; a line can, in fact, be as short as 13 syllables: "monstrum horrendum, informe, ingens, cui lumen ademptum" (*Aeneid* 3.658, with vowels elided in the first three feet). Most lines are from 14 to 16 syllables, and variation of dactyls and spondees is part of the craft: "aurea subnectens exsertae cingula mammae" (*Aeneid* 1.492: – ᴗ ᴗ | – | – – | – ᴗ ᴗ | – – | – –). In most cases the conclusion of the line is marked by the regular cadence – ᴗ ᴗ | – x (the so-called adonean *colon), though a spondee in the penultimate foot is occasionally used for special effect. Rhythmic pacing is also managed by shifting the location of a *caesura. It usually occurs within the third, less often within the fourth foot; a caesura between the third and fourth feet, which would divide the line in two, is avoided. A caesura bisecting the third foot is called penthemimeral, one bisecting the fourth is called hephthimeral. The portion of a line preceding a penthemimeral caesura (the pattern – ᴗ ᴗ – ᴗ ᴗ –) is known as a hemiepes (half-epic) and is used as a building block in other cl. meters. A word break between the fourth and fifth feet, rare in Homeric epic, is associated with *pastoral poetry and is known as the bucolic diaeresis.

At some times and places, stricter rules are also observed; a particularly stringent set is employed for one of the last great effusions of cl. Gr. poetry, the 48-book *Dionysiaca* of Nonnus from the 5th c. CE. The meter in its basic form, however, appears fully developed no later than 700 BCE as the meter of the Homeric epics; Hesiod also uses it exclusively. By the 6th c. BCE, it has been adapted to a couplet form, the so-called *elegiac distich, which consists of a dactylic hexameter and a truncated version of itself that is called a *pentameter (in effect, a double hemiepes); this meter has its own hist. as the meter of epigram and love poetry. Both meters are used in Lat. by Ennius in the early 2nd c. BCE. Throughout cl. antiquity, dactylic hexameter proper remains the almost exclusive meter of narrative verse, as well as pastoral and didactic poetry and, in Lat., *satire. As Lat.

shifts over to qualitative rhymed verse in the Middle Ages, a hybrid known as *leonine verse becomes popular, though its regular use of internal rhyme has the significant effect of breaking the august long line into smaller units: "Orpheus Eurydice sociatur, amicus amice, / matre canente dea, dum rite colunt hymenea" (Hugh Primas). Unrhymed quantitative hexameter poems such as Virgil's *Aeneid* and Ovid's *Metamorphoses* nevertheless continue to be read as major embodiments of the prestige of cl. civilization, and new poems in the meter continue to be written. It is still the main vehicle for Lat. verse composition (some productions by the young Arthur Rimbaud were his first pub. works).

With the Ren. come both a revived use of the hexameter in Neo-Lat. poetry and attempts to transfer it in some form into the vernaculars: as a vehicle for translating cl. poetry and potentially as an authoritative verse form for the developing national lits. *Esametri italiani* are debuted in the *Certame Coronario*, a public literary contest staged by Leon Battista Alberti and Leonardo Dati in 1441 to promote poetry in the vernacular; there is some follow-up by other It. poets into the next century. An ambitious attempt is mounted by the Pléiade poet Jean-Antoine de Baïf, who founds an Académie de Poésie et de Musique (1567–73) expressly to develop and promulgate rules for truly quantitative Fr. verse on the cl. model (*vers mesurés à l'antique*); the results are modest but still command respect. In England, the linguistic change from ME to mod. Eng. seems to open the possibility of a comparable shift in *Eng. prosody. The hexameter, as it happens, falls exactly between the two indigenous claimants to Eng. poetry's dominant meter: the *iambic pentameter that is Chaucer's principal medium and a seven-beat iambic line—the *fourteener—that is a typographical rearrangement from the traditional 4-3 *ballad stanza. Both were used for trans. of the *Aeneid* published in the course of the century—the former by Gavin Douglas (1553) and (without rhyme) Henry Howard, the Earl of Surrey (1554–57), the latter by Thomas Phaer (1562) and Thomas Twynne (1573)—but in humanist circles, there was influential opinion that an appropriately anglicized dactylic hexameter was needed. Roger Ascham quotes in his *Scholemaster* (1570) from an Eng. *Odyssey* in purportedly quantitative hexameters; in 1582, Richard Stanyhurst publishes four books of the *Aeneid* in his version of the original meter, together with his own detailed rules for determining Eng. *quantity. The eccentricity of those rules and the bizarreness of Stanyhurst's diction ("Lyke bandog grinning, with gnash tusk greedelye snarring") attract a good deal of mockery, but better poets—Philip Sidney and Thomas Campion most notably—are also drawn to the possibility of Eng. quantitative verse and experiment with it in various meters, with varying degrees of success. Two of the embedded poems in the first version of Sidney's prose romance *Arcadia* (1590, 1593) are in hexameters written to his own quantitative rules, though quantity has a way of coinciding with stress: "When that noble toppe doth nodd, I beleeve she salutes me; / When by the winde it maketh a noyse, I do thinke she doth answer." By the 17th c., however, the effort has run its course, and the accentual-syllabic iambic pentameter is firmly established as the touchstone meter for Eng. poetry.

More straightforwardly qualitative but unrhymed dactylic hexameters (with an accentual trochee generally acceptable as the equivalent of a spondee) make a place for themselves in later periods. The publication of the first three cantos of F. G. Klopstock's *Der Messias* in 1748 establishes the meter as a viable one in mod. Ger. J. W. Goethe uses it successfully for his epic *Hermann und Dorothea* (1797), where part of the effect is the way in which the classicizing form plays off against the contemp. setting of the French Revolution. The unrhymed elegiac distich also takes root in Ger. Goethe employs it for some of his most personal poems; at one point in his *Römische Elegien*, he represents the composition of dactylic hexameters as love play: "Oftmals hab ich auch schon in ihren Armen gedichtet / Und des Hexameters Mass leise mit fingernder Hand / Ihr auf den Rücken gezählt" (even in her arms I have often composed poetry and, tapping with my hand, softly counted out the beat of the hexameter on her back; 5.15–17). A trans. of the *Iliad* into hexameters by Nikolai Gnedich, completed after 20 years of work in 1829, made a big impression in Rus. literary circles. Alexander Pushkin praised it extravagantly and was moved to experiments of his own in unrhymed hexameters and elegiacs. Both meters are used in Rus. poetry into the 20th c., esp. for trans.; Valery Bryusov, a leader of the symbolist movement, produced an esp. striking hexameter trans. of the *Aeneid* (pub. posthumously in 1933). Robert Southey's *Vision of Judgment* (1821; famously parodied by Lord Byron the next year in a poem of the same name) is the first of a line of 19th-c. Eng. poems in unrhymed hexameters. The best known is H. W. Longfellow's *Evangeline* (1847), a love story set in mod. hist., somewhat on the model of *Hermann und Dorothea*. The effect of the meter there is largely one of solemnity: "This is the forest primeval. The murmuring pines and the hemlocks, / Bearded with moss, and in garments green, indistinct in the twilight, / Stand like Druids of eld, with voices sad and prophetic." Alfred, Lord Tennyson, on the other hand, decided that hexameters in Eng. are "only fit for comic subjects"; his mockery of some attempts to have it otherwise became famous: "These lame hexameters the strong wing'd music of Homer! / No—but a most burlesque barbarous experiment" ("On Translations of Homer"). Tennyson's distaste is related to the seriousness with which he regarded quantity. The late 19th and early 20th cs. saw renewed attempts, by Robert Bridges and others, to reestablish Eng. verse, and with it the Eng. hexameter, on a quantitative basis, but they proved infertile. Cecil Day-Lewis was more influential in using a loosely defined six-stress line, suggesting the cl. meter but not attempting any strict observance of its rules, for his trans. of Virgil (1952): "I tell about war and the hero who first from Troy's frontier, / Displaced by destiny, came to the Lavinian shores." Such a form has proved very popular for trans. from cl. epic and continues to be used. The unacknowledged contours of the ancient meter can at times be sensed beneath the verse and prose of mod. writers, esp. those with cl. training. James Joyce's *Ulysses* (1922) opens with 14 syllables cadenced as a dactylic hexameter, spondaic in the fifth foot.

■ Omond; R. Burgi, *A History of the Russian Hexameter* (1954); Maas; W. Bennett, *German Verse in Classical Metres* (1963); J. Thompson, *The Founding of English Metre* (1961); D. Attridge, *Well-weighed Syllables* (1974); West; Gasparov, *History*.

G. Braden

HIATUS. The grammatical and metrical term for the gap that is created by pronunciation of contiguous vowels, either within a word or (more commonly) word-terminal and following word-initial. The effect of the juncture is a slight catch or pause in delivery. The alternative is to remove one vowel via *elision. In Eng. like other langs., the indefinite article (*a*) has an alternate form (*an*) that exists specifically to prevent hiatus. In both prose and poetry, hiatus has been deemed a fault since at least the time of Gorgias and Isocrates; Cicero and Quintilian (*Institutio oratoria* 9.4.34 ff.) discuss it at length. In the cl. langs., hiatus was common in Gr. epic poetry, with and without shortening of the first vowel, but rarer in Lat. Occitan had no strict rules about elision and hiatus; in OF, hiatus was generally tolerated until the 14th c.: there is no elision to prevent hiatus in the *Saint Alexis* (about 1040), but in Jean Froissart, there are 132 cases of elision against five of hiatus (Lote). In Fr. prosody since François de Malherbe (17th c.), the use of hiatus was proscribed. In It., hiatus is generally avoided, as it is in Sp., though in Sp. it was the rule into the late 14th c., after which time its frequency waned. Richter summarizes the cl., Ren., and Fr. views; distinguishes nine types of hiatus; and gives statistics and examples for each type. Pope's mimetic example, "Though oft the ear the open vowels tire" (*Essay on Criticism* 2.345), is more famous than it is offensive, and indeed the strict censuring of hiatus in Fr. and Eng. neoclassical crit. seems mainly genuflection to the ancients, for elision is common in speech.

Debra San classifies two other types of hiatus: narrative and grammatical. Narrative hiatus is the logical or chronological interruption of story line by flashbacks, tangents, and authorial commentary. Grammatical hiatus varies from the insertion of an adjective between an article and the following noun to the more noticeable tmesis. Subject-verb hiatus, a form of grammatical hiatus, is the syntactical interruption between the subject and verb in a sentence over a number of poetic lines by subordinate clauses, parenthetical insertions, and other phrases.

■ A. Braam, *Malherbes Hiatus Verbot* (1884); A. Pleines, *Hiat und Elision im Provenzalischen* (1886); J. Franck, "Aus der Gesch. des Hiat im Verse," *ZDA* 48 (1906); Thieme, 370—cites 12 Fr. studies; Bridges; J. Pelz, *Der prosodische Hiat* (1930); W.J.H. Richter, *Der Hiat im englischen Klassizismus (Milton, Dryden, Pope)* (1934); Lote 3.87; A. Stene, *Hiatus in English* (1954); P. Habermann and W. Mohr, "Hiat," *Reallexikon II*; Maas, sect. 141; Elwert, 62–67; Morier; D. San, "Hiatus of Subject and Verb in Poetic Language" *Style* 39 (2005).

T.V.F. BROGAN; D. VERALDI

HOMOEOTELEUTON (or *homoioteleuton,* Gr.; "similar endings"; cf. *homoioptoton*). This term first occurs in Aristotle (*Rhetoric* 5.9.9;

1410b2) but (though the phenomenon may be found in Gorgias) is normally applied to cl. Lat. (see Quintilian 9.3.77–80). It describes identical or similar inflectional case endings on words in proximity, whether in prose or verse, as in Cicero's famous "Abiit, abscessit, evasit, erupit"; most often the words are at the ends of cola (in prose) or lines (in verse). Aristotle distinguishes three types of sound similarity in endings. When homoeoteleuton occurs at the end of two or more lines in succession, it becomes "case rhyme"—as when Cicero ends three consecutive *hexameters with *monebant, ferebant,* and *iubebant.* But it should be understood that homoeoteleuton is not an instance of *rhyme, strictly speaking, for, in inflectional langs., similarity of word ending is the rule rather than the exception, so often can scarcely be avoided. In noninflected, positional langs., such as Eng., by contrast, the poet must labor for the phonic echo. Word endings in homoeoteleuton bear grammatical information, but that is all. In a system where these do not exist, rhyme poses phonic similarity precisely to point up the semantic difference of the roots. Homoeoteleuton is chosen by the lang.; rhyme is chosen by the poet. True rhyme first appears in the Christian Lat. hymns of the 3rd to 4th cs. CE. Still, it is clear that homoeoteleuton was a distinct and intentional stylistic device and was capable of some range of effect. It is more common by far in Lat. than in Gr. By a curious turn, something of the same effect was later achieved in *rime grammaticale* as practiced in 15th- and 16th.-c. Fr. poetry by the *rhétoriqueurs.* The general association of homoeoteleuton with grammatical necessity (i.e., similarity) and rhyme with intentional artfulness (i.e., semantic difference) is evident in the problematic proposition by W. K. Wimsatt, a proponent of New Criticism, of the difference between homoeoteleuton and rhyme as a figure for the difference between prose and poetry.

■ P. Rasi, *Dell'omoeoteleuto latino* (1891); W. K. Wimsatt, "One Relation of Rhyme to Reason," *MLQ* 5, no. 3 (1944); N. I. Herescu, *La Poésie latine* (1960); E. H. Guggenheimer, *Rhyme Effects and Rhyming Figures* (1972); Lausberg, 360–63; L. Håkanson, "Homoeoteleuton in Latin Dactylic Verse," *Harvard Studies in Classical Philology* 86 (1982); Lanham; Norden; D. R. Shackleton Bailey, *Homoeoteleuton in Latin Dactylic Verse* (1994); S. Friedberg, "Prose and Poetry," *PoT* 26 (2005).

T.V.F. BROGAN; N. GERBER

HYMN. An ancient Gr. liturgical and literary genre that assimilates Near-Eastern and specifically Heb. trad. in the Septuagint trans. (LXX) of the OT, the hymn was introduced into Christian trad. in the Gr. NT and the Lat. Vulgate Bible and by the Gr. and Lat. fathers, and has continued to flourish in Western culture in both liturgical and literary trads. down to the 21st c. Other trads. represented in Asian and in early Am. cultures, as well as in those of ancient Akkad, Sumer, and Egypt that influenced Heb. trad., are important but lie beyond the scope of this entry.

The Gr. noun *hymnos* refers to a song, poem, or speech that praises gods and sometimes heroes and abstractions. Hymns are in lyric measures, *hexameters, elegiac couplets, and even prose in late antiquity; the longest critical discussion of the hymn by the rhetorician Menander, *Peri Epideiktikon* (3d c. CE), makes no distinction between prose and verse. Most of the Gr. lyric hymns (mainly fragments by Alcaeus, Simonides, Bacchylides, Timotheus, and Pindar) were probably sung in religious worship. Similarly, the hexameter *Orphic Hymns* with their markedly theurgic emphasis may have been designed for religious purposes, although such abstractions as Justice, Equity, Law, and Fortune, as well as the Stars, Death, and Sleep, are subjects of praise. Thucydides refers to one of the hexameter *Homeric Hymns* as a prelude or preface; these presumably were literary introductions to epic recitations. The famous philosophic hymn by the Stoic Cleanthes (4th–3d c. BCE) is probably literary rather than liturgical in intention, as are the *Hymns* by the Neoplatonic philosopher Proclus (5th c. CE), although there is a significant theurgic element in the latter. The six extant *Hymns* of the Gr. poet Callimachus, in hexameters and elegiac couplets, are certainly literary emulations of the *Homeric Hymns*, and the long prose hymns of the apostate Emperor Julian (4th c. CE) could not have been used in worship.

When the LXX translators came to the Heb. OT, they used the nouns *hymnos, psalmos* (song or tune played to a stringed instrument), *ode* (song), and *ainesis* (praise), and the related verbs (*hymneo*, etc.) to translate a variety of Heb. words for praise, song, music, thanksgiving, speech, beauty, and joy. Several psalms are identified in their titles as hymns (e.g., 53, 60), incl. sometimes the explicit use of both words, *psalmos* and *hymnos* (6, 75; see PSALM). The psalms are also identified with odes or songs in

several titles (e.g., 51), sometimes in the expression "a song of a psalm" (*ode psalmou*, 65), at others as "a psalm of a song" (*psalmos odes*, 67 and 74). Psalm 136.3 connects *ode* and *hymnos*; and, in two similar NT passages, all three terms are mentioned together with the implication of rough equivalence (Eph. 5:19, Col. 3:16).

While literary hymns were not a popular or important genre in pagan Roman adaptations of Gr. literary forms, Lat. Christians of the 4th c., influenced by the hymn singing of the Eastern Church, revived and introduced both literary and liturgical hymns into the Lat. West. This revival is also reflected in Jerome's Vulgate trans. of the Bible, where the transliterations *hymnus* and *psalmus* are regularly employed (along with a more accurate and consistent trans. of the OT Heb.). In his *Confessions* (9.7), Augustine remarks on the introduction of the singing of hymns and psalms in Milan by Ambrose. Isidore's influential *Etymologiae* (7th c.) identifies the Psalms of David as hymns (1.39.17) and asserts that, properly speaking, they must praise God and be sung, although in another work he notes that Hilary of Poitiers (also 4th c.) first composed hymns in celebrations of saints and martyrs (*De ecclesiacis officiis* 1.7).

Ambrose's short hymns (eight quatrains of iambic dimeter) are explicitly trinitarian and were intended to counteract Arian doctrine, which had itself apparently been fostered by hymns of an Arian bent. Considerable suspicion remained in the 6th and 7th cs. over the liturgical use of hymns composed by men as opposed to the divinely inspired Psalms of the Bible. But the unquestioned orthodoxy of Ambrose himself probably helped the hymn become accepted as a regular part of the liturgy along with the psalmody. As the Middle Ages progressed, many brilliant new hymns were added to the Lat. hymnody, from the great passion hymn "Vexilla regis prodeunt" by Fortunatus (7th c.) and the "Veni, Creator Spiritus" (trans. by John Dryden) to Thomas Aquinas's hymns for Corpus Christi day and the Franciscan "Stabat mater." Closely related to the hymn is the med. "prose" or sequence. Noteworthy are the works of Notker Balbulus (9th–10th cs.) and of Adam of St. Victor (12th c.), and the magnificent Franciscan "Dies irae."

The Reformation renewed the suspicion of hymns among many Protestants. Although Martin Luther composed hymns from paraphrases of the Psalms and other portions of the Bible, he also translated hymns from the

Roman breviary and wrote original ones. John Calvin, on the other hand, who opposed the use of man-made hymns in congregational worship, retained the poet Clément Marot to create a metrical psalmody or psalter in Fr., and the Calvinistic position strongly influenced the Anglican and Presbyterian churches in Great Britain in the 16th and 17th cs. The renderings of the Anglican psalmody by Thomas Sternhold and John Hopkins (2d ed., 1549), generally infelicitous but set in *ballad meter, may have prompted many Eng. poets of the Elizabethan and Jacobean periods to experiment with trans. of the Psalms (Philip and Mary Sidney produced an entire psalter, while John Milton translated 17 psalms in a variety of verse forms); but in popular terms, the Sternhold-Hopkins psalter was enormously successful.

The Roman Catholic Church experienced a different problem. The great influence of Ren. humanism led to a succession of more or less unfortunate revisions of the hymnody beginning with that by Leo X in 1525 and ending with Urban VIII's in the early 17th c. The motive was to turn the late cl. and med. Lat. of the hymns and sequences into good cl. Lat.

It remained for the Eng. nonconformist minister Isaac Watts to revive the writing of original hymns in the 18th c. and turn the primary focus of hymns away from literary artistry back to the rugged emotional expression of strong religious beliefs (*Hymns and Spiritual Songs*, 1707–9). As the 18th c. progressed, there occurred an enormous outpouring of hymns, along with new metrical versions of psalms, in the works of John and Charles Wesley, John Newton, Augustus Montague Toplady, Edward Perronet, the poet William Cowper, and many others, some of which (e.g., those by Charles Wesley) have great lyric power.

This outpouring continued in the 19th c. The works of Fanny Crosby and Katherine Hankey and the musical arrangements of W. H. Doane are preeminent among those of literally hundreds of writers and composers. New hymns were composed to the end of the 20th c. (e.g., by Doris Akers and Stuart Hamblen) and continue to this day (e.g., by Andraé Crouch and Ralph Carmichael). New and revised hymnals are still being arranged.

At about the same time that Ambrose introduced congregational hymn singing to the Christian church in Milan, the Christian poet Prudentius (ca. 348–405) wrote Christian literary hymns in the manner of the pagan poets of antiquity. Although some of Prudentius's creations are brief enough to be sung congregationally, many of his hymns are much too long for worship, and all have obvious literary and poetic pretensions. The fine lyric measures in two of his collections (*Peristephanon* and *Cathemerinon*) celebrate mainly saints and martyrs.

The cl. literary hymn was revived during the Ren. in both its Prudentian and secular forms. Pope Paul II's 140-line *sapphic "Hymnus de passione" (15th c.) could have been written by Prudentius, but Giovanni Pontano's (1426–1503) sapphic "Hymnus in noctem" (from his *Parthenopei*) imitates Catullus's lyric celebration of Diana. Pontano also wrote Christian literary hymns in Lat. elegiacs. Another Neo-Lat. poet, Marcantonio Flaminio (1498–1550), who wrote probably the best liturgical hymns of the Ren. (in Ambrosian dimeters), also composed a celebrated literary lyric, "Hymnus in Auroram."

Michele Marullo's 15th-c. *Hymni naturales* were found by many in the Ren. to be too thoroughly pagan in subject and tone as well as form. There were other celebrated Christian literary hymns in the Ren., esp. those by Marco Girolamo Vida in the early 16th c. (*Hymni*, 1536). The later vernacular poets follow the lead of the Neo-Latinists. Pierre de Ronsard, along with Marullo the most prolific writer of literary hymns, composes both explicitly Christian and secular, philosophical hymns along with mythological celebrations. The first two of Edmund Spenser's *Four Hymns* celebrate love and beauty in a cl. philosophical (and Petrarchan) way, while the latter two celebrate heavenly (i.e., Christian) love and beauty.

These two trads. continue in Neo-Lat. and the vernacular lits., most notably in George Chapman's two long hymns in *The Shadow of Night* (1594), in Raphael Thorius's celebrated *Hymnus tabaci* (1625), in several of Richard Crashaw's long Christian literary hymns, James Thomson's "A Hymn on the Seasons," John Keats's "Hymn to Apollo," and P. B. Shelley's "Hymn to Intellectual Beauty," "Hymn of Apollo," and "Hymn of Pan."

While liturgical hymns tend simply to start and stop, the literary hymn frequently has an Aristotelian coherence—a beginning, middle, and end. Typically, it begins with an invocation and *apostrophe. The main body will narrate an important story or describe some moral, philosophic, or scientific attribute. A prayer and farewell provide the conclusion. The hist. of literary hymns is marked by great stylistic variation and rhetorical elaboration, depending on the writer's object of praise and his conception of the relation of style to content. The definitive survey of this trad. remains to be written.

■ **Anthologies and Primary Texts**: *Analecta hymnica medii aevi* (1886–1922); *Early Latin Hymns*, ed. A. Walpole (1922); *Mystical Hymns of Orpheus*, trans. T. Taylor (1896); *Lyra Graeca*, ed. and trans. J. Edmonds, 3 v. (1922); *Proclus's Biography, Hymns, and Works*, trans. K. Guthrie (1925); *Poeti Latini del Quattrocento*, ed. F. Arnaldi et al. (1964); *Hymni latini antiquissimi XXV*, ed. W. Bulst (1975); *Hymns for the Family of God*, ed. F. Bock (1976); *New Oxford Book of Christian Verse*, ed. D. Davie (1981); *English Hymns of the Nineteenth Century*, ed. R. Arnold (2004).

■ **Criticism and History**: G. M. Dreves, *Aurelius Ambrosius* (1893); R. Wünsch, "Hymnos," Pauly-Wissowa, esp. 2.119, 3.145 ff.; Manitius; "Psalters," *Dictionary of Hymnology*, ed. J. Julian, 2d ed., 2 v. (1907); L. Benson, *Hymnody of the Christian Church* (1927); P. Von Rohr-Sauer, *English Metrical Psalms from 1600 to 1660* (1938); O. A. Beckerlegge, "An Attempt at a Classification of Charles Wesley's Metres," *London Quarterly Review* 169 (1944); H. Smith, "English Metrical Psalms in the Sixteenth Century and Their Literary Significance," *Huntington Library Quarterly* 9 (1946); R. E. Messenger, *The Medieval Latin Hymn* (1953); Raby, *Christian*; *Reallexikon II* 1.736–41; Bowra; L. Benson, *The English Hymn* (1962); J. Szövérffy, *Die Annalen der lateinischen Hymnendichtung*, 2 v. (1964–65); C. Maddison, *Marcantonio Flaminio* (1966); H. Gneuss, *Hymnar und Hymnen im englischen Mittelalter* (1968); P. Rollinson, "Renaissance of the Literary Hymn," *Renaissance Papers* (1968); C. Freer, *Music for a King* (1971); J. Szövérffy, *Iberian Hymnody: Survey and Problems* (1971); J. Ijsewijn, *Companion to Neo-Latin Studies* (1977); J. Szövérffy, *Guide to Byzantine Hymnography* (1978); *Menander Rhetor*, ed. and trans. D. Russell and N. Wilson (1981); J. Szövérffy, *Religious Lyrics of the Middle Ages: Hymnological Studies and Collected Essays* (1983); P. S. Diehl, *The Medieval European Religious Lyric* (1985); J. Szövérffy, *Concise History of Medieval Latin Hymnody* (1985); and *Latin Hymns* (1989); W. D. Furley, "Praise and Persuasion in Greek Hymns," *JHS* 115 (1995); D. Sheerin, "Hymns," *Medieval Latin*, ed. F.A.C. Mantello and A. G. Rigg (1996); M. Depew, "Enacted and Represented Dedications: Genre and Greek Hymn," *Matrices of Genre*, ed. M. Depew and D. D. Obbink (2000); C. Léglu, *Between Sequence and Sirventes* (2000); J. R. Watson, "Hymn," *A Companion to Victorian Poetry*, ed. R. Cronin, A. Chapman, A. H. Harrison (2002); *Sapientia et Eloquentia*, ed. G. Iversen and N. Bell (2009).

P. ROLLINSON

HYPERBATON. A technical term from the cl. art of rhet., hyperbaton is a generic name for a variety of figures of speech that transpose words within a sentence. Figures contained under the umbrella of hyperbaton include anastrophe (transposition of two words in a sentence); hysteron proteron (syntax or sense placed out of logical or temporal order); hypallage (transposition of the natural relationship between two elements in a proposition); tmesis (separation of a compound word by the insertion of another word); and parenthesis (insertion of a word, phrase, or sentence into an already complete sentence), among others. These figures deviate from ordinary word order by means of reversal, transposition, and interruption; together they constitute some of the most widely used rhetorical devices in poetry. Although hyperbaton is more common in Gr. and Lat. writing than in noninflected langs. that depend on word order for sense, poets writing in the Eur. vernaculars have nevertheless made frequent use of its constructions. Through syntactical displacements, hyperbaton may emphasize a particular word or idea, convey an emotional state, or fulfill the demands of poetic meter. The result may be humorous—as in Shakespeare's *A Midsummer Night's Dream*, when Bottom cries, "I see a voice. Now will I to the chink, / To spy and I can hear my Thisby's face"—as well as lyrical—as in Emily Dickinson's poem, "From cocoon forth a butterfly / As lady from her door / Emerged—."

Longinus offers the most extensive ancient discussion of hyperbaton, calling the figure "the truest mark of vehement emotion." According to this view, the figure imitates the speech of a person who has been carried away by a violent feeling: "while under the stress of their excitement, like a ship before a veering wind, they lay their words and thoughts first on one tack then another, and keep altering the natural order of sequence into innumerable variations" (*Peri hypsous* [*On the Sublime*]). Such a conception of hyperbaton indicates how the figure could be included in the list of syntactical displacements through which psychoanalytic crit. reads the unconscious intentions of the subject (Lacan). However, although hyperbaton may imitate the natural speech of a person afflicted with great emotion, cl. theory understands it to be the product of rhetorical technique. Quintilian claims that, without figures such as hyperbaton, lang. would be "rough, harsh, limp, or disjointed," with words "constrained as their natural order demands" (*Institutio oratoria*).

Like other rhetorical figures, definitions of hyperbaton rely upon an idea of ordinary, natural, or normal lang. against which its lexical transpositions can become legible. The Gr. word literally means "to overstep," and Lat. and Eng. trans. of hyperbaton—such as *transgressio* and "the trespasser"—convey its association with acts of transgression (Quintilian, *Institutio oratoria*; George Puttenham, *Arte of English Poesie*). This thematic of transgression can become a part of the figure's meaning in a poetic context, as when Edmund Spenser uses hyperbaton to describe the actions of a deceitful man in book 6 of *The Faerie Queene*:

> For to maligne, t'envie, t'use shifting slight,
> Be arguments of a vile donghill mind,
> Which what it dare not doe by open might,
> To worke by wicked treason wayes doth find,
> By such discourteous deeds discovering his base kind.

The grammatical disorders of hyperbaton may also imply a corresponding social disorder, as suggested in Winston Churchill's reputed comment to an officious newspaper editor: "This is the kind of impertinence up with which I will not put." Hyperbaton is rarely used today as a term of literary analysis, as deviations in word order now seem coincident with poetic lang. itself, rather than a particular form of figuration.

See SCHEME.

■ J. Lacan, "The Insistence of the Letter in the Unconscious," *YFS* 36–37 (1966); H. Weil, *The Order of Words in the Ancient Languages Compared With That of the Modern Languages* (1978); B. Vickers, *In Defense of Rhetoric* (1988); B. Dupriez, *A Dictionary of Literary Devices* (1991); Lanham; G. Burton, "Silva Rhetoricae" (http://rhetoric.byu.edu).

J. C. MANN

HYPERBOLE (Gr., "throwing beyond"). Hyperbole is a figure of speech marked by flagrant exaggeration. From Deut. 1:28 where "cities are fortified to heaven" to Virgil's "Twin rocks that threaten heaven" (*Aeneid* 1.162) to Shakespeare's "it smells to heaven" (*Hamlet* 3.3), hyperbole is common across all lits. Isocrates invokes the trope by name, calling his subject "a god among men" (*Evagoras* 72). Aristotle recognized it as a type of metaphor and suggested it demonstrates a vehemence associated with youth or anger (*Rhetoric* 1413a). Quintilian identifies it with comic wit as "an elegant straining of the truth" (*Institutio oratoria* 8.6.67).

Because hyperbole pushes comparison past simple credibility, the Ren. critic George Puttenham designated it as a figure of "immoderate excesse" and dubbed it the "over reacher" (*The Arte of English Poesie* 3.7). Though the suitability of diction to subject matter has been a primary topic among critics from antiquity to today, the distortion of truth in hyperbole is instantly recognizable. Hyperbole succeeds by making propositions that are either impossible—"What is he . . . whose phrase of sorrow / Conjures the wandering stars, and makes them stand / Like wonder-wounded hearers?" (*Ham.* 5.1)—or that are linked to a "comparative absolute": "Zenocrate, the loveliest maid alive, / Fairer than rocks of pearl and precious stone" (Christopher Marlowe's *Tamburlaine*, 1.1.3). The use of hyperbole in drama produces different effects from those it produces in poetry; overextension may be less tolerable in a poetic speaker than a tragic protagonist, for whom the added dimension of action may be measured against expression in ways unavailable to the poet.

Hyperbole achieves its end by a seeming contradiction, as a truth is nonetheless understood somewhere short of the false mark. Beyond speech, it is considered a "figure of thought" and is related to the forms of understatement *litotes and meiosis.

■ G. Genette, "Hyperboles," *Figures I* (1966); G. V. Stanivukovic, "'Mounting above the Truthe': On Hyperbole in English Renaissance Literature," *Forum for Modern Language Studies* 43 (2007).

K. MCFADDEN

HYPOTAXIS AND PARATAXIS. Contrasting ways of connecting clauses or phrases, whether in prose or in verse. In a hypotactic style, one specifies the logical relationships among elements, rendering the entailments and dependencies among them explicit by placing them in a hierarchy of levels of grammatical subordination. The main clause is connected to the dependent elements by subordinating conjunctions (*while, because, if,* etc.) or by relative pronouns (*who, which, that,* etc.). Hypotaxis also may extend beyond the sentence boundary, in which case the term refers to a style in which the logical relationships among sentences are explicitly rendered.

In a paratactic style, the logical relationships among elements are not specified but are left to be inferred by the reader. Within the sentence, a paratactic style may connect clauses or phrases at the same grammatical level with coordinating conjunctions (employing *polysyndeton) or without coordinating conjunctions (employing *asyndeton). The relationships among sentences can be paratactic as well, as in Caesar's famous claim, *"veni, vidi, vici."*

Hypotaxis and parataxis are each capable of varied poetic uses. Because hypotactic styles specify the logical connections among their elements, they lend themselves to establishing the sense that the main poetic idea has been meditated upon and seen from all its angles. Hypotaxis can also suggest that the speaker is somewhat detached from the immediacy of the action, perhaps to enable a deeper purchase upon its nature or a more reflective account of its meaning. Finally, a hypotactic style lends itself to registering qualifications, hesitations, and mixed feelings since it provides the grammatical means of weighing conflicting moments against each other.

Parataxis, by contrast, is esp. suited to rendering thoughts and actions from the urgent perspective of a participant caught in the immediate flow of events. As a hypotactic style lends itself naturally to an analytical point of view, so a paratactic style lends itself naturally to the rush and chaos of life as it is lived in the immediate first-person. A hypotactic style sometimes indicates the desire to evaluate the subject of the poem with a this-worldly intellect; a paratactic style sometimes indicates the desire to gain poetic access to the otherworldly power readers associated with archaic or primitive texts.

Because it leaves the logical relationship among terms unspecified, a paratactic style is useful in circumstances where the meaning of an event or the nature of its connections should be suggested by the author or inferred by the reader, as in the "subverted metaphors" frequently employed in haiku or in *pantun*, where the relationship between two observations (in the first form) or between two couplets (in the second) is implied but unstated. The tendency to leave the connections implicit also makes possible a slightly different relationship between author and reader since the author does not so much explain a thought as require the reader to achieve that thought by a leap of imagination. Thus, parataxis is particularly useful when a meaning is designed to be shown rather than said, as in the famous example of Ezra Pound's "In a Station of the Metro." That the connections must be suggested rather than defined makes a paratactic style also capable of implying that the poem registers a power beyond its ability to articulate, that it sees its elements as brightly lit particulars that direct the attention into a fraught and unspeakable background where the power of the narration is, as in the Abraham episode in Genesis (in Auerbach's famous reading of that episode in *Mimesis*), a function of the disparity between the terseness of the narration and the immensity and obscurity of the ultimate subject of that narration. Auerbach says of this kind of parataxis that "it is precisely the absence of causal connective, the naked statement of what happens—the statement which replaces deduction and comprehension by an amazed beholding that does not even seek to comprehend—which gives this sentence its grandeur."

Many interesting effects can be achieved by playing the tone against the grain of the syntax. In a letter to Sidney Cox in 1915, Robert Frost jeered at "Solway Ford" by Wilfred Gibson, noting that if one were to "look at the way the sentences run on," one would discover that "they are not sentences at all in my sense of the word." Clearly, Frost did not mean that the sentences were ungrammatical but that they did not have what he calls the "sentence sound," the unmistakable syntactic tang of living utterance. Part of the problem seems to be the unintentionally comic disparity between the syntax of the passage and its intended tone. The poem turns on a moment of violence in which the protagonist's horse rears and breaks free, overturning his wagon upon him and leaving him pinned beneath it, to await the incoming tide by which he will be drowned. Gibson is horrified by the scene and wishes us to feel that horror. But the sentence in which this violent action is rendered is a stately, complexly hypotactic word temple. The effect of adopting a hypotactic rather than a paratactic syntax is to distance the observer and the poet from the action. One might imagine wishing to do so for purposes of irony, but it is hard to see irony in the long sentence that Gibson actually wrote, which begins, "The empty wain made slowly over the sand." Compare, for instance, the syntax in the moment of violent action in Wilfred Owen's "Dulce et Decorum Est," in which a column of retreating British soldiers during World War I is suddenly caught up in a barrage of gas shells. In the passage beginning "Gas! GAS! Quick, boys!" the sentences are long, but the syntax is intensely paratactic. Later in the poem, Owen adopts a pointedly hypotactic syntax, meant to reflect bitterly not only upon the distance between the civilian's point of view and the soldier's but also upon the meaning of the heritage of cl. eloquence summed up in Horace's motto that it is sweet and fitting to die for one's country. Frost himself renders the chainsaw accident in "Out, Out—" in surprisingly hypotactic lang.; but in that poem, the tension between the syntax and the meaning is meant to capture the speaker's inability to come to terms with the violence of the scene. Unlike Gibson, Frost is well aware of the strangeness of the syntax he uses, and he exploits it to give a nightmarish unreality to the moment of the accident. Although the sentences are quite short, they all seem to be fragments of a longer hypotactic sentence the speaker cannot get straight.

Paratactic styles are often underlined by anaphora (repeated words or phrases at the beginning of sentences or verses). Anaphora is particularly characteristic of folk or archaic styles of narration—the Bible, say, or the Child ballads. Anaphora often places events in a flow of rhapsody where the coherence of the passage is provided not by articulating the logical connections among the events but by tapping into the sense that this story has been retold so often that its inevitabilities go without saying. Anaphora initiates a flow of eloquence that presumably can just keep on going—it may not articulate the relationships among the successive objects, but it places them in a context of unending rhetorical abundance. Walt Whitman's anaphoric *catalogs are a good example of the alliance between parataxis and anaphora.

See ANAPHORA, CATALOG.

■ Auerbach; T. W. Adorno, "Parataxis: Zur späten Lyrik Hölderlins," *Gesammelte Schriften*, ed. R. Tiedemann and H. Schweppenhäuser, v. 11 (1974); R. Alter, *The Art of Biblical Narrative* (1981); J. L. Jugel, *The Idea of Biblical Poetry* (1981); A. Easthope, *Poetry as Discourse* (1983); R. Silliman, *The New Sentence* (1987); F. Jameson, *Postmodernism, or, The Cultural Logic of Late Capitalism* (1991); B. Perelman, *The Marginalization of Poetry* (1996); L. Hejinian, *The Language of Inquiry* (2000); Lord.

J. Burt

IAMBIC (Gr. *iambos*; Ger. *Jambus*). The chief meter in most cl. and mod. prosody. Iambic meter is based on the iamb, a metrical *foot consisting of a short or unstressed syllable followed by a long or stressed syllable. In Lat. poetry, the iamb was comprised of this short and long syllable pair; in Gr. it was a metron consisting of this plus a preceding anceps and long syllable: x – ◡ –. The word *iambos* (pl. *iamboi*) first appears in Archilochus and is used for a distinct genre of poetry, namely, *invective; this generic association was carried into Roman times. The name for the meter thus derived from the genre with which it was originally associated, not vice versa. Originally, the word *iambic* may have arisen from occasions on which ritual songs (some of them lampoons) were sung and danced. Archilochus uses iambic metra in *trimeters, *tetrameters, and *epodes; and the Ionian poets who preferred it have come to be known as "iambographers."

Iambic was thought in antiquity to be the rhythm nearest to common speech. Throughout Gr. and Lat. poetry, iambic in trimeter and tetrameter is the standard meter for recitation forms, esp. dramatic *dialogue. The Lat. iambic dimeter became, with Augustine, Ambrose, and Hilary of Poitiers, the standard line for the early Christian *hymn, making it perhaps the chief meter of the Middle Ages and the ancestor of the mod. tetrameter, very important in Rus., and second only to the pentameter in Eng. and Ger. The same claim has been made in mod. times about Eng. as was made by the ancients about Gr. (Aristotle, *Rhetoric*, book 3)—namely, that iambic is the rhythm of common speech.

This view—that much poetry is iambic because lang. is iambic—may be bolstered by the recognition that iambic rhythm is, more simply, an alternating pattern and that, given any system of two values (on-off, long-short, stressed-unstressed), alternation is the simplest pattern capable of being generated. On the other hand, alternation clearly describes *trochaic meters just as well as it does iambic. Several important psychological experiments in the 20th c. showed that when auditors are presented with an alternating series of weak and strong tones that are perfectly isochronous (equidistant), they invariably *hear* them as grouped into binary units—i.e., iambic or trochaic, most often trochaic. When the intensity of the stress is increased, the units are perceived as trochaic. When the stress, or the interval after the stress, is lengthened, the units are perceived as iambic. In general, when intervals are irregular, the series will be heard as trochaic. More recently, Hayes has claimed that the apparent asymmetry between iambs and trochees is based on an extralinguistic principle of rhythmic grouping called the iambic/trochaic law. According to this model, the basic properties of rhythmic structure may determine ling. stress.

All these experiments report on only primary (simple) rhythmic series and not on lang. In contrast, it has also been argued that lang. itself is in fact a secondary rhythmic series where multiple rhythms are enacted, and interact, across the same space simultaneously. When the events are words, lang. imposes a secondary or counterrhythm on top of the phonological rhythm of stresses and unstresses that is morphological and syntactic; here, word types and word boundaries matter. Morphological factors have been shown to be real and important forces in cl. meters. We must realize that readers' and auditors' perceptions of lines as "iambic" or "trochaic" depend on both phonotactics and morphotactics within the metrical frame. Trochaic rhythms are sensitive to (1) the word shapes used to fill the pattern (trochaic words are needed frequently) and (2) alteration of the beginnings or ends of the sequences (*catalexis is important), whereas iambic rhythms seem not to be sensitive to either. Anacrusis is common in iambic verse but virtually impossible in trochaic, catalexis is unusual, and word shapes are largely immaterial—iambic verse accepts virtually any. Halpern argues persuasively that iambic meter is a more complex and subtle meter because it is capable of effects of modulation not possible in any other meter, whether trochaic, ternary, or purely accentual. Iambic meter, i.e., is not the reverse of trochaic but rather in its own class altogether.

Disruption of an iambic meter might seem attainable in several ways: extra stresses in the line, missing stresses in the line, or extra unstressed syllables without loss of stresses (extra syllables). But iambic generally tolerates occasional extra syllables and dislocations of stress placement very well, esp. at major syntactic boundaries such as the beginning of the line and the *caesura. In general, contiguous stresses are the most serious problem for iambic meters. The general principles of rhythm apply: as long as the reader's perceptual frame, the "metrical set," is not broken, considerable variation is possible. Further, the lang. has an efficient mechanism for demoting heavy contiguous stresses and for promoting weak stresses in runs of unstressed syllables so as to even out the rhythm. Older prosodists who advocated the notion of trochaic "substitutions" in iambic verse perhaps failed to grasp that such feet are not trochaic; so long as the iambic metrical set is preserved, they are perceived as complications, not violations. This suggests that the terms *iambic* and *trochaic* should be applied only to meters, not units of meters.

Several important poets have felt that iambic rhythm is tyrannous: Ezra Pound observed that "the god damn iamb magnetizes certain verbal sequences" (*Letters* 1950); for the *vers-librists* and imagists, then, "to break the pentameter, that was the first heave" (Canto 81), and the means were "to compose in the sequence of the musical phrase, not in sequence of a metronome" ("A Few Dont's by an Imagiste" [1913]), means Pound claimed to have found in Occitan poetry and Chinese. Breaking the iambic rhythm is precisely the effect G. M. Hopkins sought to achieve with *"sprung rhythm."

Various iambic meters have now been identified both in poetry and in common speech patterns (by literary scholars and linguists, respectively) across a diverse range of lang. contexts, incl. Korean, Somali, Paumari, and Hungarian. *See* PYRRHIC, SPONDEE.

■ J. M. Edmonds, *Elegy and Iambus* (1931); A. D. Knox, "The Early Iambus," *Philologus* 87 (1932); E. Pound, "Treatise on Metre," *ABC of Reading* (1934); H. Woodrow, "Time Perception," *Handbook of Experimental Psychology*, ed. S. Stevens (1951); J. Thompson, "Sir Philip and the Forsaken Iamb," *KR* 20 (1958); Maas; M. Halpern, "On the Two Chief Metrical Modes in English," *PMLA* 77 (1962); D. W. Cummings and J. Herum, "Metrical Boundaries and Rhythm-Phrases," *MLQ* 28 (1967); Dale; M. L. West, *Studies in Greek Elegy and Iambus* (1974); P. Fraisse, *Psychologie du rythme* (1974); G. Nagy, "Iambos: Typologies of Invective and Praise," *Arethusa* 9 (1976); Halporn et al.; Brogan; M. L. West, *Introduction to Greek Metre* (1987);

J. Thompson, *The Founding of English Metre*, 2d ed. (1989); B. Hayes, *Metrical Stress Theory* (1995); G. Powell, "The Two Paradigms for Iambic Pentameter and Twentieth-Century Metrical Experimentation," *MLR* 91 (1996); M. J. Duffell, "'The Craft So Long to Lerne': Chaucer's Invention of the Iambic Pentameter," *Chaucer Review* 34 (2000); *Iambic Ideas*, ed. A. Cavarzere, A. Aloni, and A. Barchiesi (2001); *Formal Approaches to Poetry*, ed. B. E. Dresher and N. Friedberg (2006); Duffell.

T.V.F. BROGAN; S. S. BILL

IDYLL, idyl (Gr. *eidyllion* [diminutive of *eidos*, "form"], "short separate poem"; in Gr., a pastoral poem or idyll is *eidyllion Boukolikon*). One of the several synonyms used by the Gr. grammarians for the poems of Theocritus, Bion, and Moschus, which at other times are called *bucolic*, *eclogue*, and *pastoral*. Theocritus's ten pastoral poems, no doubt because of their superiority, became the prototype of the idyll. In the 16th and 17th cs., esp. in France, there was frequent insistence that pastorals in dialogue be called *eclogues*, those in narrative, *idylls*. In Ger., *Idylle* is the ordinary term for pastoral. Two biblical books—Ruth and Song of Songs—are sometimes called *idylls*, which may be taken to illustrate the latitude of the term. Note that Alfred, Lord Tennyson's *Idylls of the King* (1859) is hardly pastoral. Perhaps Tennyson thought that the use of the term was appropriate: each idyll contains an incident in the matter of Arthur and his knights that is separate (or framed) but at the same time connected with the central theme; the contents treat the Christian virtues in an ideal manner and in a remote setting. But there is very little in Robert Browning's *Dramatic Idylls* (1879–80), which mainly explore psychological crises, to place them in the pastoral trad. The adjectival form, *idyllic*, is more regularly and conventionally applied to works or scenes that present picturesque rural scenery and a life of innocence and tranquillity, but this has little specific relation to any poetic genre. *See* GEORGIC.

■ M. H. Shackford, "A Definition of the Pastoral Idyll," *PMLA* 19 (1904); P. van Tieghem, "Les Idylls de Gessner et le rêve pastoral," *Le Préromantisme*, v. 2 (1930); P. Merker, *Deutsche Idyllendichtung* (1934); E. Merker, "Idylle," *Reallexikon II* 1.742–49; J. Tismar, *Gestörte Idyllen* (1973); T. Lange, *Idyll und exotische Sehnsucht* (1976); K. Bernhard, *Idylle* (1977); R. Böschenstein-Schäfer, *Idylle*, 2d ed. (1977);

V. Nemoianu, *Micro-Harmony: Growth and Uses of the Idyllic Model in Literature* (1977); J. B. Pearce, "Theocritus and Oral Tradition," *Oral Tradition* 8 (1993); S. Halse, "The Literary Idyll in Germany, England, and Scandinavia, 1770–1848," *Romantic Prose Fiction*, ed. G. Gillespie (2008).

T.V.F. BROGAN; J. E. CONGLETON

IMAGE. *Image* and **imagery* are among the most widely used and poorly understood terms in poetic theory, occurring in so many different contexts that it may well be impossible to provide any rational, systematic account of their usage. A poetic image is, variously, a *metaphor, *simile, or figure of speech; a concrete verbal reference; a recurrent motif; a psychological event in the reader's mind; the vehicle or second term of a metaphor; a *symbol or symbolic pattern; the global impression of a poem as a unified structure.

The term's meaning and use have also varied radically depending on time and place. While the concept has been at the center of Chinese poetics for centuries, for instance, its prominence in Western criticism is a relatively mod. phenomenon. Frazer argues that the term first becomes important to Eng. crit. in the 17th c., perhaps under the influence of empiricist models of the mind. Thomas Hobbes and John Locke use the term as a key element in their accounts of sensation, perception, memory, imagination, and lang., developing a "picture-theory" of consciousness as a system of receiving, storing, and retrieving mental images. The term continues to play an important role in neoclassical poetics, usually in accounts of description. Joseph Addison, in the *Spectator* papers on the "Pleasures of the Imagination" (nos. 411–21, 1712), argues that images are what allow the poet to "get the better of nature": "the reader finds a scene drawn in stronger colors and painted more to the life in his imagination by the help of words than by an actual survey of the scene which they describe."

In romantic and postromantic poetry and poetics, the image persists in a sublimated and refined form and is often defined in opposition to "mental pictures" (Edmund Burke) or to the "merely descriptive" or "painted," ornamental images of 18th-c. poetry. S. T. Coleridge's distinctions between symbol and allegory ("living educts" versus a mere "picture language") and imagination and fancy (creative versus remembered images) consistently appeal to a difference between a "higher," inward, intellectual image and a lower, outward, sensuous one. The notion of the poetic symbol, along with the poetic process as an expressive rather than mimetic endeavor, helps to articulate the notion of the romantic image as something more refined, subtle, and active than its neoclassical predecessor. Modernist poetics often combines (while claiming to transcend) the neoclassical and romantic concepts of the image, urging poets to make their lang. concrete and sensuous while articulating a theory of poetic structure that regards the entire poem as a kind of matrix or crystallized form of energy, as if the poem were an abstract image. Thus, Ezra Pound stresses the importance of both the psychological and structural features of the image when he famously defines it as "that which presents an intellectual and emotional complex in an instant of time." In part because of the powerful influence of imagism as propounded by Pound and others, *image*, however ambiguously defined, is treated in much 20th-c. crit. as though it were synonymous with poetry itself. Day-Lewis offers a declaration that could stand in for any number of mod. and contemp. poets: "the image is the constant in all poetry, and every poem is an image."

Understandings of *image* shifted through the 20th c. and into the 21st as critics grappled with the increasing prominence of visual media. Whereas at the beginning of the century, modernists turned to the visual image as a source of immediacy and presence, an increased sensitivity to forms of mechanical and later digital reproduction made it seem inevitable that the image would offer a different lesson: that images do not offer direct access to reality but point always instead to other images. Like words, they are governed by their own grammars and rhets. and must be interpreted according to specific conventions. Rather than strive for the iconicity of the image, then, postmodern critics stress the etymological relation between *image* and *imitation*. Words and images share the common condition of all representation, woven together into a mediated web of signs and simulations.

A critique of the concept of the poetic image would probably begin by noting that it tends to blur a distinction that underlies a large tract of poetics, namely, the difference between literal and figurative lang. An image is, on the one hand, "the only available word to cover every kind of simile [and] metaphor" (Spurgeon); on the other hand, it is simply "what the words actually name" (Kenner), the literal referents of lang., concrete objects. Pound's treatment of the concept is again illustrative. One of his instructions for would-be imagists is that a poem should offer a "direct treatment of the 'thing' whether subjective or objective." Emphasizing at once its immediacy and, by putting "thing" in quotation marks, calling that directness into question, Pound suggests that the image can reconcile the subjective and objective character of representation. The image, in other words, designates both metaphor and description, both a purely ling. relation between words and a referential relation to a nonlinguistic reality, both a rhetorical device and a psychological event. This confusion is most evident in theories of metaphor that follow Richards's influential distinction between *tenor* and *vehicle*. Is Shakespeare's metaphor "Juliet is the sun" to be understood as an image because "sun" is a concrete noun that evokes a sensuous picture in the reader's mind? Or is the whole expression an image because it insists on a "likeness" between two unlike things? Is an image, in short, a bearer of sensuous immediacy and presence or a relationship formed by the conjunction of two different words and their associated vocabularies? Is it a mode of apprehension or a rhetorical device? Whatever we may understand as the meaning of the term *image* in any particular context, it seems clear that the general function of the term has been to make this distinction difficult, if not impossible.

What could be at stake in perpetuating confusion between metaphor and description or between figurative and literal lang.? One possibility is that the figurative-versus-literal-lang. distinction is itself untenable, and the ambiguous use of the term *image* is simply a symptom of this fact. *Image*, understood in its narrow and literal sense as a picture or statue, is a metaphor for metaphor itself (a sign by similitude or resemblance) and for mimetic representation or iconicity. Since literary representation does not represent by likeness the way pictorial images do, literary representation is itself only and always metaphorical, whether or not it employs particular figures. (Goodman argues, for instance, that representation, properly speaking, only occurs in dense, analogical systems like pictures and that a verbal description, no matter how detailed, never amounts to a depiction.) The literal-figurative distinction itself appeals to an implicit distinction between "letters" (writing) and "figures" (images, pictures, designs, or bodies in space). The concept of

"poetic imagery" is, thus, a kind of oxymoron, installing an alien medium (painting, sculpture, visual art) at the heart of verbal expression. The motives for this incorporation of the visual arts are usually clear enough: the whole panoply of values that go with painting—presence, immediacy, vividness—are appropriated for poetry. But there are equally powerful motives for keeping the incorporation of the visual under control, for seeing the visual arts as a dangerous rival as well as a helpful ally. G. E. Lessing, in *Laokoön* (1766), thought that the emulation of the visual arts by lit. would lead to static, lifeless description, while Burke (*A Philosophical Enquiry into the Origin of Our Ideas of the Sublime and the Beautiful*, 1757) argued that visual imaging was a vastly overrated aspect of literary response, incompatible with the opacity he associated with true literary sublimity. Within this trad., the rivalry between word and image is frequently animated by anxieties about other forms of difference, chiefly those related to race, gender, and sexuality. Thus, as both Mitchell and Heffernan demonstrate, *ekphrasis* is often understood as a struggle between masculine poet and feminized image. The recurrent figure of the blind poet, whose blindness is a crucial condition of his insight and freedom from merely "external" visual images, reminds us that the boundaries between images and texts, figures and letters, the visual and the verbal are not so easily breached in Western poetics.

Another place where the contradictory tendencies of poetic imagery may be glimpsed is in the area of reader response. Here the image plays the role of a supplement to the poetic text (Derrida). It opens an empty space to be filled by the activity of the reader's imagination. Ideally, it completes the text in the reader's mind, in the world it projects, in the "spaces" between its words, bringing the "vision" of the poem sensuously, perceptually alive; but it may equally well open a threatening space of indeterminacy. Thus, the voice and sound—aural "images" such as *rhyme, *rhythm, *onomatopoeia, and *tone—are the first place to look for perfect iconicity in poetry. But what of the imperfect, secondary icons—the "mental pictures" that voice and sound produce, the imaginary spaces—theater, dream vision, movie, map, or diagram—that arise out of the reading experience? Poetics discloses a certain ambivalence toward these phenomena. While visualization, for instance, is universally acknowledged as an aspect of reader response, there is still considerable resistance to treating it as a legitimate object of literary study. The supposed "privacy" and "inaccessibility" of mental images seem to preclude empirical investigation, and the supposed randomness of visual associations with verbal cues seems to rule out any systematic account. But mental imagery has taken on a whole new life in the work of postbehavioral cognitive psychology. Literary critics who want to talk about poetic imagery in the sense of readers' visual response would do well to consult the work of philosophers and psychologists such as Jerry Fodor, Nelson Goodman, Ned Block, and Stephen Kosslyn, who have conducted experimental studies of visualization and mental imaging. Ludwig Wittgenstein's critique of the "picture theory" of meaning (*Philosophical Investigations*, 1957) also ought to be required reading for those who think of images as private. If mental images are an essential part of the reading experience, why should it be any more difficult to describe or interpret them than the images offered in Sigmund Freud's *The Interpretation of Dreams*?

At the same time, psychologists experimenting in the field of mental imaging might attend to poets and critics who have dealt with this question. It seems obvious, for instance, that mental imaging cannot be a subject of laboratory investigation alone but must be understood in the context of cultural hist. Some cultures and ages have encouraged reader visualization far more extensively than others: "quick poetic eyes" and the "test of the pencil," e.g., were the slogans of 18th-c. poetics, which urged the reader to match his or her experience with conventional, public models from painting and sculpture. We might ask why Shakespeare seems to have been singled out as the principal object of traditional image studies in Eng. crit. One answer may be that the study of imagery is part of the transformation of each Shakespearean play from a prompt-book for the theater into a printed text for private reading. The first such study, Walter Whiter's *A Specimen of a Commentary on Shakespeare* (1794), was pub. in the same era that saw Shakespeare move from the playhouse to the study and heard Charles Lamb's famous argument that "the plays of Shakespeare are less calculated for performance on a stage, than those of almost any other dramatist whatever" ("On the Tragedies of Shakespeare," 1811). For Lamb, the inadequate visual and aural presence of mere actors on stage was to be replaced with "the sublime images, the poetry alone . . . which is present to our minds in the reading." Whatever its merits, Lamb's argument makes it clear that the issue of mental imaging is not solely a matter for experimental investigation but entails deeply disputed cultural values—the rivalry of visual and aural media (incl. the "breach" or "hinge" between written and spoken lang. explored by Derrida); the contest between art understood as a public, performative mode and its role as a private, subjective refuge; the notion of authorial intention as a mental representation ("vision" or "design") that stands before or behind the poem.

The very idea of the mental image seems inextricably connected with the notion of reading as the entry into a private space (the Lockean metaphor of the mind as a *camera obscura* or "dark room" into which ideas are admitted through sensory apertures reinforces, with a kind of metaimage, this picture of mental solitude in an interior space filled with representations). It is not surprising, then, that the concept of the poetic image in all its ambivalence holds part of the central ground of poetics, serving as both the mechanism of reference to and deferral of an external, imitated or projected reality; as the projection of authorial intention (but also of unauthorized "unconscious" meaning); as the ling. ligature that composes figures of speech and thought and decomposes them into a general condition of lang. and consciousness; as the realm of freedom and dangerous uncertainty in reader response. Future crit. of the poetic image must, at minimum, take account of the historical variability of the concept and resist the temptation to dissolve poetic expression into the universal solvent of "the image."

See MIMESIS, UT PICTURA POESIS.

■ E. Pound, *Pavannes and Divisions* (1918); H. W. Wells, *Poetic Imagery* (1924); S. J. Brown, *The World of Imagery* (1927); O. Barfield, *Poetic Diction* (1928); J. Dewey, "The Common Substance of All the Arts," *Art as Experience* (1934); C. Spurgeon, *Shakespeare's Imagery and What It Tells Us* (1935); I. A. Richards, *The Philosophy of Rhetoric* (1936); C. Brooks, "Metaphor and the Tradition," *Modern Poetry and the Tradition* (1939); L. H. Hornstein, "Analysis of Imagery: A Critique of Literary Method," *PMLA* 57 (1942); C. D. Day-Lewis, *The Poetic Image* (1947); R. B. Heilman, *This Great Stage: Image and Structure in "King Lear"* (1948); R. H. Fogle, *The Imagery of Keats and Shelley* (1949);

W. Clemen, *The Development of Shakespeare's Image* (1951); Abrams; Wellek and Warren, ch. 15; Frye; F. Kermode, *The Romantic Image* (1957); H. Kenner, *The Art of Poetry* (1959); R. Frazer, "The Origin of the Term *Image*," *ELH* 27 (1960); M. Hardt, *Das Bild in der Dichtung* (1966); P. N. Furbank, *Reflections on the Word "Image"* (1970); J. Derrida, *Of Grammatology*, trans. G. C. Spivak (1974); N. Goodman, *Languages of Art* (1976); S. Kosslyn, *Image and Mind* (1980); T. Ziolkowski, *Disenchanted Images* (1977); *The Language of Images*, spec. iss. of *CritI* 6.3 (1980); N. Block, *Imagery* (1981); M. A. Caws, *The Eye in the Text* (1981); *Image and Code*, ed. W. Steiner (1981); W. Steiner, *The Colors of Rhetoric* (1982); *Articulate Images*, ed. R. Wendorf (1983); P. de Man, "Intentional Structure of the Romantic Image," *The Rhetoric of Romanticism* (1984); *Image/Imago/Imagination*, spec. iss. of *NLH* 15.3 (1984); W.J.T. Mitchell, *Iconology* (1987); P. Yu, *The Reading of Imagery in the Chinese Poetic Tradition* (1987); J. Heffernan, *Museum of Words* (1993); H. Belting, *Likeness and Presence*, trans. E. Jephcott (1994); W.J.T. Mitchell, *Picture Theory* (1994); S. Durham, *Phantom Communities* (1997); K. Jacobs, *The Eye's Mind* (2001); J. Rancière, *The Future of the Image*, trans. G. Elliott (2007); E. B. Loizeaux, *Twentieth-Century Poetry and the Visual Arts* (2008).

W.J.T. MITCHELL; B. GLAVEY

IMAGERY

  I. Culture and Criticism
 II. Sense, Mind, and Language
III. Imagery and Discourse

I. Culture and Criticism. *Imagery*, like the related word *imitate*, invokes the power of imagination, the cultural uses and dangers of likeness, and the baffling confluence of concrete and abstract, literal and figurative, body and mind, matter and spirit. One index of the cultural volatility of imagery is its place in religions. Religious trads. such as Judaism oppose the worship of images as false; Islam avoids the representation of all divinely created forms, although Islamic exegesis addresses the uses and limits of inner and outer meaning; Hinduism and Buddhism embrace imagery; and many shamanistic religions employ totemic images. Rich Christian trads. of sacramental imagery are accompanied by strong countercurrents of iconoclasm, as in the Iconoclastic Controversy

of the 8th and 9th cs. in the Eastern Church and the Protestant Reformation. Problems of imagery are implicit in Midrash and in patristic and med. biblical exegesis, esp. in the devel. of the four senses of scripture.

Images occupy a critical place in the Gr. philosophical mediation of the material and the ideal. Plato distinguishes true ideas from false likenesses, images being at a double remove from reality, and he credits neither painting nor poetry as knowledge. Aristotle recognized the central role of imagery in the formation of thought, and by identifying structures of representation, he legitimized the arts as forms of truth. Roman commentators such as Horace, Longinus, and Quintilian spoke of imagery and its uses in poetry and rhetoric. Horace coined the formula *ut pictura poesis (as is painting, so is poetry), drawing upon an aphorism attributed to Simonides of Ceos by Plutarch, who praised the historians whose lively prose made readers see actions described in words. The rhetorical figure *ekphrasis was widely used by Gr. and Roman writers for imagery that makes something appear in poetry as if present, "laying it out before the eyes," in the words of Cicero's De oratore.

The genre of the *dream vision and med. descriptive formulas like the *blason or laisses similaires are rich sources for imagery in theory and practice. In the widely disseminated Ren. convention of Petrarchism, description of the *imago vera* of the beloved object erects a symbolic infrastructure embodying subject and object, and the theoretical structure of Petrarchan imagery is a major source of Renaissance poetics. But the consideration of imagery as a category in literary theory and practice begins with early mod. lit. crit., Frazer argues, in the 16th and 17th cs. (also Furbank, Legouis [in Miner], and Mitchell [1986]).

The functions of the term during the Ren. were still largely fulfilled by the figures of rhetorical *copia*, a persuasive writing style marked by abundant *schemes and *tropes. Figurative lang. was viewed as both an ornament and a means of embodiment. Erasmus and other Ren. practitioners promoted *enargeia*, vivid, pictorial imagery that achieves copia through its sheer quantity and detail.

Philip Sidney's *Defence of Poesy* (1595) makes a paradoxical claim for the excellence of poetry among the rival arts: he contends that the poet "nothing affirms, and therefore never lieth," for poets work through the senses to move a will infected by the passions away from vice through images of virtue. For Sidney, the delightful instruction of imagery fuses the abstraction of philosophy and the concrete example of hist. Nicolas Boileau similarly calls on the animation and warmth of imagery as a source of poetic power.

II. Sense, Mind, and Language. With the growth of skepticism and empiricism in the late 17th and early 18th cs., interest turned to the cognitive function of imagery. The epistemology of Thomas Hobbes and the associationist psychology of John Locke led to a way of looking at poetry in which the image was the connecting link between experience (object) and knowledge (subject). An image was reproduced in the mind as an initial sensation was produced in bodily perception. Thus, when the eye perceives a certain color, a person will register an image of that color in the mind—"image" because the subjective sensation experienced will be a copy of the objective phenomenon of color.

Of course, the mind may also produce images when remembering something once perceived but no longer present or reflecting on remembered experience or combining perceptions and the products of imagination or hallucinating out of dreams and fever. In literary usage, *imagery* thus comes to refer to images produced in the mind by words that refer to sense perceptions and to the many artistic permutations of sense impression, memory, and fabrication.

G. E. Lessing's *Laokoön* (1766), an influential critique of the arts as systems of signs, argues against the equation of imagery in the visual and verbal arts, distinguishing time and space as the proper places of poetry and painting. The descriptive poetry of the 18th c. often dwelt on imagery of landscape in the memory and words of the observing subject. Creative power was assumed to reside in the "imagination," a volume of images entering and circulating in the mind. With romantic transcendentalism, the world appeared as the garment of God, the abstract and general residing in the concrete and particular, and Spirit was felt to be immanent in Matter. Nature was itself divine, and nature poetry, a way to body forth the sacred. Imagery, therefore, was elevated to the level of *symbol, to become an embodiment of truth and a central issue of poetry and crit. In "Tintern Abbey," William Wordsworth claims to find in the

contemplation of sensual experience a source of conscious life: "While with an eye made quiet by the power / Of harmony, and the deep power of joy, / We see into the life of things."

Science and lit. shared an interest in the powers of imagery during the latter 19th c. The philologist Max Müller accounted for metaphorical imagery as an organic part of the growth of lang., rather than as an ornament. To conceive of immaterial things, human beings must express them as images of material things because human lang. lags behind conceptual needs. So lang. grows through *metaphor, from image to idea. The word *spirit*, e.g., has as its root meaning "breath"; as the need to express an immaterial conception of soul or deity emerged, an existent concrete word stood for the new abstract meaning.

Francis Galton's experiments in the psychology of perception (1880) suggested that people differ in their image making. While one person may reveal a predominant tendency to visualize his or her reading, memories, and ruminations, another may favor the mind's "ear," another the mind's "nose," and yet another may have little imagery at all. Other psychologists, such as the Am. Joseph Jastrow, became interested in ambiguous images, suggesting that perception was not just the result of external sense data but also a product of the mind.

Symbolist poets frequently turned to *synaesthesia* to confound the separate senses of experience and to expose the richness of the poet's soul, as in Charles Baudelaire's poem "Correspondances," which evokes forests of symbols that have powers of infinite expansion; exotic and unfathomable things, like amber, musk, and incense, enrapture the soul and senses. Arthur Rimbaud's "Voyelles" ("Vowels") seeks an arbitrary dislocation of perceptions and understanding: "A black, E white, I red, U green, O blue."

Psychology often categorizes images through the senses: visual (sight, brightness, clarity, color, and motion), auditory (hearing), olfactory (smell), gustatory (taste), tactile (touch, temperature, texture), organic (awareness of heartbeat, pulse, breathing, digestion), and kinesthetic (awareness of muscle tension and movement). The role of different senses emerged as one way of categorizing poetic imagery early in the last century of crit. A line of John Keats's poetry might be tactile and organic—e.g., "For ever warm and still to be enjoy'd, / For ever panting, and for ever young" ("Ode on a

Grecian Urn"). Themes such as behavior, location, and time may also classify imagery in relation to such matters as warfare, eating, hair, the domestic, the urban, birds, mountains, morning, or summer.

Critics in the early 20th c. cataloged images and identified dominant sets or clusters of images within a poem or a poet's oeuvre, a *genre, or a literary period or style, drawing analogies to themes, authorship, historical or biographical origins, organic form, or the symbolic organization of cultural forms like myth or archetype. When the meaning and function of imagery were adapted as markers of the literary in theories about poetic lang. and creation, imagery became one of the key terms of the New Criticism. Knight (1930) found in imagery a pattern below the level of plot and character that is an index of the intellectual content of Shakespeare's plays. Warren (1946) saw in the *Rime of the Ancient Mariner* a symbol of the artist-archetype, embodied in the figure of the Mariner, torn between the conflicting and ambiguous claims of reason (symbolized by the sun) and the imagination (symbolized by the moon). Burke (1941) compared S. T. Coleridge's letters with image-clusters in the *Ancient Mariner* and concluded that the albatross symbolizes the poet's guilt over his addiction to opium, thus illuminating the motivational structure of the poem. But I. A. Richards in *Principles of Literary Criticism*, like Galton, found that the sensual perception of images in poetry differed radically from one reader to another and excluded visual imagery from crit., focusing instead largely on the semantic operations at work in imagery.

Sensory imagery, however concrete or referential, comes to be seen in many forms of 20th-c. crit. as exercising complex figurative functions. Freudian and Jungian theories of mind look toward the complex function of images in personality and culture. Structuralist ling. theory defines lang. as an arbitrary system of signs through which reference is always mediated, and the understanding of imagery as a system of signs is similarly transformed. Verbal and visual imagery in ling. and philosophical theory offered famous illustrations of the function of the sign. Ferdinand de Saussure, e.g., produces a diagram of the tree, and Ludwig Wittgenstein borrows from Jastrow the image of the duck-rabbit to explore the roles of mind, lang., and sense.

Richards introduced terms such as *tenor* and *vehicle* that often came to be used to explain the structure of imagery not as purely sensual but as figurative lang., and similar terms may be found in structuralist poetics. In Robert Burns's *simile "my love is like a red, red rose," images like the color, texture, or odor of a rose are figures for a lady's blush, her delicate skin, her fragrance. Burns's speaker is saying that his lady is to him as June is to the world, bringing rebirth and joy. The lady makes him feel as spring makes him feel: the ground of comparison is a set of feelings and associations. The imagery of the vehicle (the rose) and of the tenor (my love) are discrete objects related by thinking and feeling and writing and reading human subjects. Those associations are the ground of the simile that connects vehicle and tenor. The poem presents imagery of rose and of lady, and the qualities attributed to these objects intersect. But the rose and the lady are not images of one another. As Gertrude Stein observed, a rose is a rose is a rose.

Yet powerful imagery invites us to forget that distinction. An image involving *synecdoche, e.g., blurs the distinction of part and whole or container and thing contained—as in a ruby-red glass of wine. Just which object is ruby red, the glass or the wine? Where is the ruby if one cannot drink or taste it and it will not hold liquid? Or would a red object that has a taste, like a cherry, create likewise illogical imagery?

The mixing of images can be comical when it produces a material absurdity, as in the line "I smell a rat, Mr. Speaker; I see him floating in the air, but I will yet nip him in the bud." But Quintilian (see CATACHRESIS) argued that such imagery may be effective when it borrows an available term for one that does not exist, and such fused images easily enter the canon of poetry, as in Hamlet's "to take arms against a sea of troubles." Here if we do not imagine from the lang. of the character a demented warrior slashing at the sea with his sword, we may imagine two separate sets of images related in metaphor—feeling overwhelmed by troubles as by the inundation of the sea and doing something about them as when a warrior arms himself and marches out to meet the enemy.

Such understanding of imagery reflects a social and historical understanding of lang. Even decorous poetic imagery may violate the norms of sense perception, as when poetry flattens images into the merely picturesque, a danger Wordsworth contemplates in the lines "hedgerows hardly hedge-rows, little lines / Of sportive wood run wild: these pastoral farms, / Green to the very door" ("Tintern Abbey").

Precious imagery eclipses the role of the senses in description, as in Belinda's awakening in Alexander Pope's *Rape of the Lock*: "Sol thro' white curtains shot a tim'rous ray." In satiric or grotesque poetry (see SATIRE), imagery often conjoins visual objects incongruously, piling them up, or exposing shame or weakness for comic or absurd effect and challenging norms of *decorum and belief, as in the gutters of Jonathan Swift's "Description of a City Shower," where "dead cats and turnip-tops come tumbling down the flood."

In some imagery like the metaphysical *conceit, a trope that marks one of the major interests of early 20th-c. crit. (Wells, Rugoff, Tuve, Miller), poets are licensed to challenge the reader with an image that reveals a significance that first appearances would make seem unlikely.

Similar interest in overlapping imagery may be seen in the imagist movement of the early 20th c., where one image may be defined through another distinctly apart from it as an "intellectual and emotional complex" perceived through lang. "in an instant of time." In Ezra Pound's "In a Station of the Metro," for instance, faces in a crowd are seen as petals on a bough. According to Pound, a poem of this sort tries to record the precise instant in which a thing outward and objective transforms itself or darts into a thing inward and subjective.

Critics such as Roman Jakobson working in the school of Russian formalism approached lit. as organized violence committed on ordinary speech. Lit. deviates from and thus empowers speech through devices such as *meter or imagery—these deviations make it lit.

III. Imagery and Discourse. Mid-20th-c. devels. in speculative and experimental psychology, involving phenomenology, epistemology, and cognitive psychology, questioned what mental imagery is. Block, e.g., argued against the objection that internal pictures are nonexistent because we do not have pictures in the brain and an inner eye with which to see them. Images are verbal and conceptual to Block, who proposed that there are two kinds of imagery, one that represents perception in roughly the same way pictures do, the other that represents as lang. does, i.e., conceptually. Block also contended that some images combine pictorial and verbal elements and that the real question is what types of representation are possible. Furbank, on the other hand, after giving a very

useful hist. of the term *image* to the imagists, reveals the ambiguities and confusions involved in using the terms *image* and *concrete* to describe qualities of the verbal medium. We should not confuse *abstract* with *general* or *concrete* with *specific*. *Concrete*, e.g., does not necessarily mean "sensuous," and that which is *specific* may very well also be *abstract*. The only actual physical element of poetry is found in the subvocal or silent actions of tongue and larynx as a poem is recited or read. Furbank has suggested that we drop the term *imagery* altogether. Cognitive psychologists and neuroscientists over the second half of the 20th c. revived interest in imagery and gathered empirical evidence about the status of sense imagery and mental imagery, looking at the interference of motor and visual perception, e.g., or at examples of mental rotation or analogue images.

Mitchell (1986) places the entire issue of imagery within the broad historical context of knowledge as a cultural product. He has provided a chart of the "family of images" to indicate the different meanings of *imagery*: graphic images (pictures, statues, designs) are found in art hist.; optical images (mirrors, projections) in physics; perceptual images (sense data, "species," appearances) in philosophy and theology; mental images (dreams, memories, ideas, phantasmata) in psychology and epistemology; and verbal images (metaphors, descriptions, writing) in lit. crit.

Imagery frequently enters into deconstructive philosophy and crit. as an occurrence of false origins or priority. Images may be the necessary supplements of originals (like the Platonic "Form of the Good") that cannot be otherwise known. Images involving binaries (such as black and white) include their opposites as a black or white object does not. In work such as "Plato's Pharmacy," Jacques Derrida offers a critique of the logic of Plato's imagery; Derrida's own work often relies on playful images to unsettle received ideas, as in the image of Plato dictating to a writing Socrates in *The Post Card*. P. de Man's work deconstructs the unity of the figural icon or the notion of dominant figures and looks to ways in which critical insight depends on blindness to assertion and yielding to the knots of lang.

One feature of postmod. Language poetry of recent decades is an emphasis on the materiality of the signifier rather than its reference to a prior material object or experience; here, imagery is not the product of a material sense perception but a material function of lang., as in Lyn Hejinian's claim in "Happily" (2000) to write with inexact straightness in a place between phrases of the imagination.

Mitchell (1986) has promoted the study of iconology across the media and of the relations of visual and verbal representations in the context of social and political issues. His argument concerning the nature and function of imagery averts a mere binary between the empiricist positivism and deconstruction. Both our signs and the world they signify are a product of human action and understanding, and although our modes of knowledge and representation may be arbitrary and conventional, they are the constituents of the forms of life—the practices and trads. within which we make epistemological, ethical, and political choices. The question is, therefore, not simply "what is an image?" but more "how do we transfer images into powers worthy of trust and respect?" Discourse, Mitchell concludes, projects worlds and states of affairs that can be pictured concretely and tested against other representations.

Approaching the problem from a sociopolitical-historical perspective, Weimann would remind us that, while for mod. critics the meaning of a poem is secondary to its figures, for Ren. and metaphysical poets the meaning was primary. Here he agrees with Tuve that mod. interpretations fail to do justice to the intentions and structures of earlier works. Metaphor, he says, is neither autonomous nor decorative; rather, it relates human and universe, and the link or interaction between tenor and vehicle is the core. Hist. is part of the meaning of a metaphor. Shakespeare's freedom of ling. transference reflects the social mobility of his era, an age of transitions and contradictions. That neoclassical critics did not value Shakespeare's rich imagery but preferred plot over diction reflects their own view of the person in society. This valuation was reversed during the romantic age, but even the romantics did not place form over meaning. Modernist poets and critics, Weimann argues, emphasizing the autonomy of a literary work and its spatial patterns, have removed lit. from both hist. and its audience. In seeking liberation from time and space and from hist. into myth, this trad. has rejected the mimetic function of lit. in cl. crit. (see MIMESIS), as well as the expressive principle of romanticism. Metaphor is now seen as an escape from reality and has become severed from its social meaning. In reply, Weimann calls for

an integration of the study of imagery within a more comprehensive vision of lit. hist.

Yu's analysis of Chinese imagery suggests ways in which the study of poetic imagery can be enriched further by means of comparative studies. She sees a fundamental difference between "attitudes toward poetic imagery in classical China" and "those commonly taken for granted in the West." Western conceptions are based on the dualism of matter and spirit and on the twin assumptions of mimesis and fictionality: poetry embodies concretely a transcendent reality, and the *poet is a creator of hitherto unapprehended relations between these two disparate realms. The Chinese assumption, by contrast, is nondualistic: there are indeed different categories of existence—personal, familial, social, political, natural—but they all belong to the same earthly realm, and the poet represents reality both in a literal sense and by joining various images that have already been molded for him by his culture. Thus, the Chinese poetic and critical trads. reveal the conventional correspondences used by the poets in their efforts to juxtapose images so as to suggest rather than explain meaning.

■ **Criticism and History**: W. Whiter, *A Specimen of a Commentary on Shakespeare* (1794); W. Spaulding, *A Letter on Shakespeare's Authorship of "The Two Noble Kinsmen"* (1876); Richards; S. J. Brown, *The World of Imagery* (1927); G. W. Knight, *The Wheel of Fire* (1930); F. C. Kolbe, *Shakespeare's Way* (1930); C. Spurgeon, *Shakespeare's Imagery and What It Tells Us* (1935); U. Ellis-Fermor, *Some Recent Research in Shakespeare's Imagery* (1937); K. Burke, *Attitudes toward History* (1937); G. W. Knight, *The Burning Oracle* (1939); M. B. Smith, *Marlowe's Imagery and the Marlowe Canon* (1940); K. Burke, *The Philosophy of Literary Form* (1941); L. H. Hornstein, "Analysis of Imagery," *PMLA* 57 (1942); G. W. Knight, *The Chariot of Wrath* (1942); E. A. Armstrong, *Shakespeare's Imagination* (1946); Brooks; R. B. Heilman, *This Great Stage* (1948); D. A. Stauffer, *Shakespeare's World of Images* (1949); T. H. Banks, *Milton's Imagery* (1950); W. H. Clemen, *The Development of Shakespeare's Imagery* (1951); F. Marsh, *Wordsworth's Imagery* (1952); J. E. Hankins, *Shakespeare's Derived Imagery* (1953); Frye; J. W. Beach, *Obsessive Images* (1960); R. Frazer, "The Origin of the Term 'Image'," *ELH* 27 (1960); G. W. Knight, *The Crown of Life* (1961); G. W. Williams, *Image and Symbol in the Sacred Poetry of Richard Crashaw* (1963); D. A. West, *The Imagery and Poetry of*

Lucretius (1969); P. N. Furbank, *Reflections on the Word "Image"* (1970); S. A. Barlow, *The Imagery of Euripides* (1971); *Seventeenth-Century Imagery*, ed. E. Miner (1971); W. E. Rogers, *Image and Abstraction* (1972); J. Doebler, *Shakespeare's Speaking Pictures* (1974); R. Weimann, *Structure and Society in Literary History* (1976); J. H. Matthews, *The Imagery of Surrealism* (1977); V. N. Sinha, *The Imagery and Language of Keats's Odes* (1978); R. Berry, *Shakespearean Metaphor* (1978); T. Cave, *The Cornucopian Text* (1979); de Man; V. S. Kolve, *Chaucer and the Imagery of Narrative* (1984); J. Steadman, *Milton's Biblical and Classical Imagery* (1984); J. Dundas, *The Spider and the Bee* (1985); W.J.T. Mitchell, *Iconology* (1986), *Art and the Public Sphere* (1993), and *Picture Theory* (1994); V. A. Kolve, *Telling Images* (2009).

■ **Figurative Language**: M. Müller, *Lectures on the Science of Language*, 2d ser. (1894); F. I. Carpenter, *Metaphor and Simile in Minor Elizabethan Drama* (1895); G. Buck, *The Metaphor* (1899); J. G. Jennings, *An Essay on Metaphor in Poetry* (1915); H. W. Wells, *Poetic Imagery* (1924); O. Barfield, *Poetic Diction* (1928); E. Holmes, *Aspects of Elizabethan Imagery* (1929); I. A. Richards, *The Philosophy of Rhetoric* (1936), and *Interpretation in Teaching* (1938); M. A. Rugoff, *Donne's Imagery* (1939); C. Brooks, *Modern Poetry and the Tradition* (1939); R. Tuve, *Elizabethan and Metaphysical Imagery* (1947); C. D. Lewis, *The Poetic Image* (1947); H. Coombs, *Literature and Criticism* (1953); W. K. Wimsatt, *The Verbal Icon* (1954); F. Kermode, *The Romantic Image* (1957); C. Brooke-Rose, *A Grammar of Metaphor* (1958); O. Barfield, "The Meaning of the Word 'Literal'," *Metaphor and Symbol*, ed. L. C. Knights and B. Cottle (1960); M. Peckham, "Metaphor," *The Triumph of Romanticism* (1970); E. E. Ericson, "A Structural Approach to Imagery," *Style* 3 (1969); G. Lakoff and M. Johnson, *Metaphors We Live By* (1980); R. J. Fogelin, *Figuratively Speaking* (1988); J. Witherow, "Anger and Heat: A Study of Figurative Language," *Journal of Literary Semantics* 33 (2004).

■ **Journals**: *Journal of Mental Imagery; The Literary Image; Word & Image.*

■ **Mental Imagery**: F. Galton, "Statistics of Mental Imagery," *Mind* 5 (1880); G. H. Betts, *The Distributions and Functions of Mental Imagery* (1909); J. K. Bonnell, "Touch Images in the Poetry of Robert Browning," *PMLA* 37 (1922); E. Rickert, *New Methods for the Study of Literature* (1927); J. E. Downey, *Creative Imagination* (1929); R. H. Fogle, *The Imagery of Keats and*

Shelley (1949); R. A. Brower, *The Fields of Light* (1951); Wellek and Warren, ch. 15; *The Language of Images*, ed. W. T. J. Mitchell (1980); *Imagery*, ed. N. Block (1981); P. Yu, *The Reading of Imagery in the Chinese Poetic Tradition* (1987); W.J.T. Mitchell, "The Pictorial Turn," *Artforum* 30.7 (1992); M. Tye, *The Imagery Debate* (1992); W.J.T. Mitchell, "What Do Pictures Want?" *October* 77 (1996); N.J.T. Thomas, "Mental Imagery," *Stanford Encyclopedia of Philosophy*, ed. E. N. Zalta, http://plato.stanford.edu/archives/fall2010/entries/mental-imagery.

■ **Symbol and Myth**: O. Rank, *Art and Artist*, trans. C. F. Atkinson (1932); R. P. Warren, "A Poem of Pure Imagination," *The Rime of the Ancient Mariner by Samuel Taylor Coleridge* (1946); Crane; P. Wheelwright, *The Burning Fountain* (1954); H. Musurillo, *Symbol and Myth in Ancient Poetry* (1961); P. Wheelwright, *Metaphor and Reality* (1962); K. Burke, *Language as Symbolic Action* (1966); A. Cook, *Figural Choice in Poetry and Art* (1985).

S. FOLEY

INDETERMINACY. Denotes a lingering state of indecision with regard to the meaning of a given sign, statement, or text, marking the lack of a stable context for interpretation. Indeterminacy tends to be an exclusive category that implies an irresolvable conflict between discrete meanings and interpretations (i.e., the four irreconcilable meanings that Miller finds in William Wordsworth's "Resolution and Independence"), as opposed to polysemy, which is often an inclusive category that implies a plurality of meanings and contexts for interpretation where their sheer proliferation, not their irresolvability, is the central issue. Indeterminate texts are composed of terms that do not cohere in a consistent interpretation and, therefore, remain obscure and enigmatic, leading to a suspension of meaning. As a critical term, *indeterminacy* gained currency in poststructuralist lit. crit., which emphasized what Hartman called "a hermeneutics of indeterminacy" or "a type of analysis that has renounced the ambition to master or demystify its subject (text, psyche) by technocratic, predictive, or authoritarian formulas."

Indeterminacy is brought about when no single meaning or interpretation may be adequately fixed around a given text, because of a radical separation of signifiers from their signifieds. Indeterminate texts are, thus, characterized not by the "depth" of complex intertextual relations and different associative and metaphoric connections but by disjunctive metonymic relations that give rise to a peculiar "surface tension." In indeterminate texts, the symbolic evocations generated by words on the page are no longer grounded in a coherent discourse, so that it becomes impossible to decide which of these associations are relevant and which are not. This displacement of meaning corresponds to the basic situation of Saussurean ling. in which "there are only differences without positive terms." The ling. sign is reduced to an ultimate differential unit, which is then combined with other differential units in a signifying chain according to the laws of a closed system. Lacan has termed this phenomenon "the sliding of the signified under the signifier" and claimed that it is the outcome of the nature of the signifier, which "always anticipates meaning by deploying its dimension in some sense before it." Thus, e.g., at the level of the sentence, one might consider a chain of signifiers that is interrupted before the significant term is introduced (in such combinations as "The fact remains . . . ," "For example . . . ," "Still perhaps . . . ," etc.). According to Lacan, these chains of signifiers, supposedly meaningless, make sense, despite lacking an explicit reference, and that sense becomes all the more oppressive for having been denied. Similarly, in indeterminate texts, signifiers cease to be "signifiers of something" and become "signifiers to someone"; while they may have no clear referential function, they retain emotive and conative functions. The definitive discussion of indeterminacy in mod. poetry is that of Perloff.

See APORIA.

■ M. Perloff, *The Poetics of Indeterminacy* (1981); F. de Saussure, *Course in General Linguistics*, ed. C. Bally and A. Sechehaye, trans. R. Harris (1983); J. H. Miller, *The Linguistic Moment* (1985); B. J. Martine, *Indeterminacy and Intelligibility* (1992); G. Graff, "Determinacy/Indeterminacy," *Critical Terms for Literary Study*, ed. F. Lentricchia and T. McLaughlin, 2d ed. (1995); *Artifice and Indeterminacy: An Anthology of New Poetics*, ed. C. Beach (1998); J. Ashton, "'Rose Is a Rose': Gertrude Stein and the Critique of Indeterminacy," *Modernism/Modernity* 9 (2002); U. Wirth, "Derrida and Peirce on Indeterminacy, Iteration, and Replication," *Semiotica* 143 (2003); J. Lacan, "The Instance of the Letter in the Unconscious," *Écrits: A Selection*, trans. B. Fink (2004); J. Medina, "Anthropologism, Naturalism, and

the Pragmatic Study of Lan-guage," *Journal of Pragmatics* 36 (2004); G. Hartman, *Criticism in the Wilderness*, 2d ed. (2007); J. Lezra, "The Indecisive Muse: Ethics in Translation and the Idea of History," *CL* 60 (2008).

N. PINES

IN MEMORIAM STANZA. A four-line stanza in iambic tetrameter, rhyming *abba*; so called from its use in Alfred, Lord Tennyson's *In Memoriam* (1850):

I hold it true, whate'er befall;
I feel it, when I sorrow most;
'Tis better to have loved and lost
Than never to have loved at all.

Although Tennyson believed himself the originator of the stanza, it may be found in 17th-c. poetry, notably Ben Jonson ("An Elegy": "Though beauty be the mark of praise") and Lord Herbert of Cherbury ("An Ode upon a Question moved, whether Love should continue for ever?"). Before *In Memoriam*, Tennyson used the stanza in a few political poems. Early fragments of *In Memoriam* employ an *abab* stanza.

The *abba* form evokes traditional love poetry by recalling the octave of the Petrarchan *sonnet. The "measured" lang. of the tetrameter line, in contrast to the pentameter line of sonnets, produces a sense of something lost; the line's curtness suggests the poet's skepticism about the efficacy of lang. to express feeling and meaning, and implies an effort toward self-control.

Later uses of the stanza are rare; they include Oscar Wilde's "Symphony in Yellow" and Philip Larkin's "The Trees."

■ Schipper, *History*; E. P. Morton, "The Stanza of *In Memoriam*," *MLN* 21 (1906), and "Poems in the Stanza of *In Memoriam*," *MLN* 24 (1909); Saintsbury, *Prosody*; S. Gates, "Poetics, Metaphysics, Genre: The Stanza Form of *In Memoriam*," *VP* 37 (1999).

A. PREMINGER, E. T. JOHNSTON

INTERNAL RHYME (Ger. *Inreim, Binnenreim*; It. *rimalmezzo*). Refers to the Eng. cover term for a variety of rhymes that occur not at the end of the line but within the line. Internal rhyme, therefore, shifts emphasis away from line endings and often away from the interplay between lines to the interplay between words. While the terminology is not standardized across prosodies, the typology of forms includes

(1) rhyming (a) a word at line end with a word or words in the same line or (b) in another; or (2) rhyming (a) words within a line with each other but not with a word at line end or (b) a word or words within one line with a word or words in another but not with a word at line end. E.g., G. M. Hopkins uses types (1a) and (2a) in "Carrion Comfort": "That my chaff might fly; my grain lie, sheer and clear. / Nay in all that toil, that coil." Charlotte Smith employs internal rhyme more subtly with type (2b) in "Ode to Death":

> Friend of the wretched! wherefore should
>   the eye
> Of blank Despair, whence tears have ceased
>   to flow,
> Be turned from thee?—Ah! wherefore fears
>   to die
> He, who compelled each poignant grief to
>   know,
> Drains to its lowest dregs the cup of woe?

Types (1a) and (2a) occur within a single line, types (1b) and (2b) usually in two consecutive lines. Type (1a), Ger. *Inreim* or *Mittelreim*, Fr. *rime léonine* or *renforcée*, most often rhymes the word at line end with the word at the *caesura: this form developed in the Middle Ages and is known as *leonine rhyme and the form that in English prosody is usually meant by the phrase *internal rhyme*. Type (2a), Ger. *Binnenreim*, most often rhymes two words inside the same line and is sometimes in Eng. called *sectional rhyme*; if the rhyming in a long-line couplet is ——*a* ——*a* ——*b* / ——*a* ——*a* ——*b*, splitting into short-line verse will give tail rhyme. Type (1b), Ger. *Kettenreim* or *Mittenreim*, Fr. *rime batelée*, most often rhymes the line-end word of one line with the caesural word of the next or vice versa; Eng. prosodists sometimes call this *caesura rhyme*. In the Fr. *rime brisée*, caesura rhymes with caesura and end with end; this was already developed in leonine verse and is treated here as *cross rhyme. Both Fr. and Ger. forms developed from med. Lat.; Meyer gives a full taxonomy of types. The Fr. terms for these elaborately interlaced sound patterns were developed mainly by the *Grands Rhétoriqueurs* of the late 15th and early 16th cs. Internal rhyme has also been an important structuring agent in non-Western oral poetries. Lao and Thai poetries, e.g., feature yoked-word rhyme, which strings together rhyme after rhyme to heighten musical-performative aspects of lang. and which has been difficult to replicate in Eng. trans. Internal rhyme is also a chief characteristic of hip-hop poetics.

■ K. Bartsch, "Der innere Reim in der höfischen Lyrik," *Germania* 12 (1867); Meyer; Patterson; W. Vogt, "Binnenreime in der Edda," *Acta Philologica Scandinavica* 12 (1938); H. Forster, "Der Binnenreim (Reimformel)," *Sprachspiegel* 37 (1981); Brogan; C. Compton, "Lao Poetics: Internal Rhyme in the Text of a *Lam Sithandone* Performance," *Papers on Tai Languages, Linguistics, and Literatures*, ed. C. J. Compton and J. F. Hartmann (1992); A. Bradley, *Book of Rhymes: The Poetics of Hip Hop* (2009).
T.V.F. Brogan; J. Chang

INVECTIVE. A personal attack or *satire, often scurrilous, formerly written mainly in verse. Invective is to be differentiated from satire on the grounds that it is personal, motivated by malice, and unjust; thus, John Dennis remarks that satire "can never exist where the censures are not just. In that case the Versifyer, instead of a Satirist, is a Lampooner, and infamous Libeller." Invective is as old as poetry and as widespread; in the West, it appears (if not in the Homeric *Margites*) at least as early as Archilochus, who wrote an invective against Lycambes; other notable Gr. examples include those by Hipponax against Bupalus, by Anacreon against Artemon, and others by Xenophanes, Timon of Phlius, Sotades, Menippus, and (less virulently) Callimachus. Indeed, iambic verse itself (see IAMBIC) is in its earliest, Ionian form so called specifically because of its association with invective, which has the specific characteristics both of a speaker giving vent to personal hatred and of common speech for its vehicle, to which iambic meter was thought by the ancients to conform. In Lat., invective is written, though in a wider variety of meters, chiefly by Catullus, Ovid (*Ibis*), Martial, and Varro. In the Middle Ages, Petrarch's invective against doctors, *Invective contra medicum*, is notable; in the Ren., the scope of personal invective was expanded considerably by the invention of printing, which provided broadsides, bills, and *ballads particularly well suited for rapid and wide dispersal of political invective and satire. Eng. invective of this sort abounds particularly in the Restoration and 18th c.; indeed, the Eng. word *lampoon* (from the Fr. slang term *lamper*, "to guzzle, swill down") dates only from the mid-17th c. John Wilmot, the Earl of Rochester's *History of Insipids, a Lampoon* (1680) is but one of many of his and of others. John Dryden, a master of invective, nevertheless deplores it in his "Discourse concerning the Original and Progress of Satire" (1693) as both illegal and dangerous. After 1750, however, verse invective, like other verse genres such as *narrative poetry, rapidly gave ground to prose as the medium of choice, except in the (remarkably durable) trad. of the *epigram, incl. scurrilous and vindictive epigrams, which were produced in the 20th c., notably by J. V. Cunningham.

See DOZENS.

■ J. Addison, *Spectator*, no. 23; *An Anthology of Invective and Abuse* (1929) and *More Invective* (1930), both ed. H. Kingsmill; J. C. Manning, *Blue Invective* (1973); *The Book of Insults, Ancient and Modern*, ed. N. McPhee (1978); *Tygers of Wrath: Poems of Hate, Anger, and Invective*, ed. X. J. Kennedy (1981); A. Richlin, *The Garden of Priapus* (1983); *The Devil's Book of Verse*, ed. R. Conniff (1983); *The Blasted Pine: An Anthology*, ed. F. R. Scott and A. J. M. Smith (1965)—Canadian; R. M. Rosen, *Old Comedy and the Iambographic Tradition* (1988); H. Rawson, *Wicked Words* (1989); G. J. van Gelder, *The Bad and the Ugly: Attitudes towards Invective Poetry (Hija') in Classical Arabic Literature* (1989); K. Swenson, *Performing Definitions* (1991); L. Watson, *Arae: Curse Poetry in Antiquity* (1991); A. Sáenz-Badillos, "Hebrew Invective Poetry: The Debate between Todros Abulafia and Phinehas Halevi," *Prooftexts* 16 (1996); G. Nagy, *The Best of the Achaeans*, 2d ed. (1999)—chs. 12–13; P. M. Thornton, "Insinuation, Insult, and Invective: The Threshold of Power and Protest in Modern China," *Comparative Studies in Society and History* 44 (2002); I. Ruffell, "Beyond Satire: Horace, Popular Invective and the Segregation of Literature," *Journal of Roman Studies* 93 (2003); M.-H. Larochelle, "L'Invective ou le rapprochement conflictuel," *Dalhousie French Studies* 74 (2006).

T.V.F. BROGAN

IRONY. According to the Roman rhetorician Quintilian (ca. 35–100 CE), *irony* is saying something other than what is understood. By the time Quintilian offered this definition, there were already two intertwined philosophical and rhetorical trads. considering the scope and definition of *irony*, and this twin hist. continues to this day. Irony is at once a general attitude and a localized figure of speech; it can be as broad as the Socratic commitment to knowing that one does not know and as specific as substituting one word for its opposite.

Irony can be considered philosophically as a mode of life or a general relation to knowledge and understanding. It is usually accepted that this philosophical trad. begins with Plato's Socrates, whose mode of questioning in Plato's dialogues is to accept the terms of his interlocutors' definitions and then to push those definitions (occasionally) to the point where the meaning of the discussed term either dissolves completely, leaving only a gap (*aporia*), or at least points to the need to create a definition that is more adequate than the common acceptance of a term's use. Socrates is described in the dialogues as deploying *eironeia*, which in the Gr. tragedies prior to Plato had designated deception or lying but which in the dialogues comes to refer to a strategy for attaining truth, a strategy that *appears* to accept the terms of common sense and received wisdom but ultimately exposes ordinary lang. to be inadequate. When Socrates asks Thrasymachus, in Plato's *Republic* (ca. 380 BCE), for a definition of "justice" and Thrasymachus replies that "justice is the advantage of the powerful" or "justice is paying back what one owes," Socrates accepts these definitions and then goes on to ask whether one would still call "just" actions undertaken by those in power who were mistaken about their own interests or whether returning an ax to a madman could still be a case of justice. Thrasymachus is baffled and *accuses* Socrates of irony, suggesting that (for Thrasymachus, at least) there is something pernicious about Socrates' undermining of everyday lang. and accepted usage. This sense that irony is undermining and linguistically and socially pernicious begins with Plato and continues into the 21st c. Aristotle (384–322 BCE), in his *Ethics* and *Rhetoric*, after Plato, suggested that the responsible citizen of good character should not remain distant and detached from everyday truth claims, norms, and conventions. Irony is socially irresponsible in its undermining of shared political conventions. Cicero (106–43 BCE) also claimed in *De oratore* that the active and engaged participant in a polity would use rhetorical strategies within his own context but would not, as Socrates seemed to do, have such a distanced attitude to the entire lang. that no engagement or meaning would ever be possible or secure. In the 19th c., both philosophers (Søren Kierkegaard, 1813–55) and literary critics (such as the Ger. romantics associated with the *Athenaeum* jour.) celebrated Socrates as the only "true" character insofar as he lived his life aware of the impossibility of coinciding completely with everyday lang. In the 21st c., both celebrations and denunciations of Socratic irony remain in force. The Am. pragmatist Richard Rorty (1931–2007) suggested that, given the necessary impossibility of establishing an absolute truth on which a society might establish its norms, all we can do is adopt our norms and political vocabularies, remaining aware that there is a certain provisional and contingent nature to all truth claims. We may be publicly sincere but privately ironic. Rorty endorses a Socratic mode of irony as a general attitude toward life and knowledge, and an acceptance that everyday definitions and conventions can never be adequate to some putative universal and final sense. Rorty's irony has been criticized as an abandonment of philosophical responsibility and as an overly postmod. failure to consider the difficult questions of truth, legitimation, and justification (just as Socrates was ultimately deemed by the court of Athens to have corrupted the youth). Yet Rorty himself criticizes one of the more complex aspects of Socrates' irony: by suggesting that everyday definitions are inadequate to define or establish a final sense for concepts such as justice, truth, beauty, or the good, Socratic irony assumes that, when one uses irony to negate or distance oneself from everyday understanding, there will emerge some other, better, universal meaning.

Rorty is in keeping with post-20th-c. refusals to consider that a meaning or sense might transcend ordinary usage and conventions. There has been a widespread rejection of any such "Platonism," any idea that there might be a universal meaning for concepts, such as "justice," and that ordinary lang. ought to be corrected by an appeal to some proper and essential sense. For this reason, many of the 20th-c. and contemp. readings of the two modes of irony, either as a limited rhetorical device or as a style of living whereby one distances oneself from conventions, have been negative. That is, it is not assumed that when one "says something other than what is understood," there is some proper or universal sense that lies outside common sense. For Rorty, this attempt to "'eff' the ineffable" is a mistake that irony ought to cure. Irony should destroy rather than encourage the demands for universal truth claims. Accordingly, Socratic irony was reinterpreted in the 20th c., with philosophers and literary critics arguing that Socrates indicates a specific way of life, an awareness that there is no ultimate truth or

essence of humanity and that one must simply form oneself as a literary character.

In addition to being a general attitude or point of view whereby one might characterize entire texts as ironic—such as Jonathan Swift's *Modest Proposal* of 1729 and its "logical" argument for cannibalism as a means of solving the problem of hunger and poverty—irony is also a *trope. Socrates' use of irony was wide ranging, sometimes encompassing a critical attitude toward knowledge—accepting that one uses a lang. even if it remains inadequate to capture the higher and essential truths of concepts such as truth and beauty—but sometimes restricted to specifically rhetorical cases of irony. Here, rather than the mode of a character or way of life, there is the substitution of one term for its opposite, so that Socrates will hail a sophist as "wise" when the context of the dialogue and its devel. suggest otherwise. One way in which this contrariness of meaning—Quintilian's "saying something other than is understood"—can be explained is through a theory of tropes. If other figures, such as *metaphor, substitute like for like, irony substitutes opposites. Irony differs from other tropes or figures in its capacity to work differently according to context and differently within context, depending on who is reading or listening and how one is situated in relation to the speaker. Jane Austen's opening of *Pride and Prejudice* (1813)—"It is a truth universally acknowledged, that a single man in possession of a good fortune, must be in want of a wife"—is read as irony only if one does not accept the economic norms of the bourgeois marriage market. James Joyce's opening sentence of "The Dead" (1914)—"Lily, the caretaker's daughter, was literally run off her feet"—is marked as ironic only if one has the ling. resources to know that one cannot *literally* run off one's feet. Irony has a hierarchical dimension, excluding some members of the audience from its "other" or implied sense.

That "other sense" remains difficult to secure and accounts for the multiple senses and levels of irony. These could be summarized as the following:

1. Simple rhetorical irony, the substitution of one sense for another. (Samuel Johnson's example from the dictionary of 1755 was "Bolingbroke was a holy man," an example that demonstrates that the implied sense would always depend on context and assumed values.)

2. Dramatic irony, where a character speaks in such a manner that the audience or reader

recognizes the limited or contradictory nature of his or her speech. This occurs in Shakespeare's *Julius Caesar* when Marc Antony repeatedly declares that "Brutus is an honorable man" while detailing Brutus's duplicity. In this case, a character is *using* irony as a figure within his own context. More complex dramatic irony occurs in *Macbeth* where the audience hears the witches' predictions in one sense, Macbeth in another; and this is compounded if we anticipate the tragic course of events to follow. Dramatic irony is not confined to on-stage drama. It includes cases in which the audience or reader understands something quite different from the speaker's intended sense and can include nonfictional cases. We can perceive an irony in Martin Luther King's famous "I have a dream" speech, e.g., if we know that, for all his hope, events would run entirely contrary to his envisioned and expected future. In cases of fictional texts, characters such as those in Robert Browning's dramatic monologues can express extreme religious propriety or love, while the events narrated by that very character reveal the opposite. In "My Last Duchess," the character declaring his love reveals himself to be violently controlling, while "In the Spanish Cloister" is spoken from the point of view of a morally zealous monk whose accusations of his fellow monastery inhabitants disclose his own envy and malevolence.

3. Tragic irony, where events follow a course despite, and often because of, characters' attempts to control their own fate. The audience sees a course of events unfolding, despite the characters' efforts to command their own destiny. It is Oedipus's attempt to avoid the predicted killing of his own father, e.g., that leads him to pursue the course of events that he has sought to avoid.

4. Cosmic irony occurs when the universe or cosmos appears to correct, or fly in the face of, our expectations. This has a literary mode, as in Thomas Hardy's novel *Tess of the D'Urbervilles* (1891), in which the peasant family's attempt to regain its honorable lineage results in the ruin of the well-meaning and noble Tess. This sense of cosmic contrariness captures one of the dominant popular uses of the word *irony*, when sports commentators, newscasters, or popular songwriters use *ironic* to signal that, despite our intentions, life plays itself out in a contrary direction.

5. Romantic irony is defined by the Ger. literary theorists of Jena in the *Athenaeum* jour.

and taken up by 20th-c. theorists such as Paul de Man, Philippe Lacoue-Labarthe, and Jean-Luc Nancy, defines *irony* as the "permanent parabasis of tropes," suggesting that irony is not limited to a figure of speech within a text but opens a point of view outside the text's own frame—parabasis—in which the reader or audience gains a sense of the text *as text,* not as a sign referring to some proper sense or meaning.

6. Postmod. irony is generally diagnosed or celebrated as the recognition of a loss of stable or shared meaning. Those like Rorty or (in different ways) de Man regard irony as a liberation from the idea that words are direct markers of some underlying meaning or natural referent. Others regard postmod. irony as nihilistic, as evidence for a loss of faith in public legitimation and shared understanding.

7. Irony as a trope or the substitution of a word for its opposite can range from sarcasm, the aim of which is usually to wound, such as John Searle's "That was a brilliant thing to do," to a negation without a secure opposed sense as in W. H. Auden's use of the word "clever" in his poem "September 1, 1939": "as the clever hopes expire / Of a low dishonest decade."

■ *Institutio oratoria of Quintilian,* trans. H. Butler (1921); D. Muecke, *Irony* (1970); W. C. Booth, *A Rhetoric of Irony* (1974); A. Mellor, *English Romantic Irony* (1980); D. Muecke, *Irony and the Ironic,* 2d ed. (1982); P. de Man, *The Rhetoric of Romanticism* (1984); J. Searle, *Expression and Meaning* (1985); P. Lacoue-Labarthe and J. Nancy, *The Literary Absolute,* trans. P. Barnard and C. Lester (1988); C. Lang, *Irony/Humor: Critical Paradigms* (1988); S. Kierkegaard, *The Concept of Irony, with Continual Reference to Socrates,* trans. L. M. Capel (1989); R. Rorty, *Contingency, Irony, and Solidarity* (1989); E. Behler, *Irony and the Discourse of Modernity* (1990); G. Vlastos, *Socrates, Ironist and Moral Philosopher* (1991); C. Colebrook, *Irony* (2004).

C. COLEBROOK

ISOCOLON AND PARISON. *Parison* (Gr., "almost equal") describes syntactic members (phrases, clauses, sentences or lines of verse) showing *parallelism of structure. In short, they are identical in grammar or form. *Isocolon* (Gr., "equal length") denotes members that are identical in number of syllables or in *scansion. Two members could show parison without isocolon: the number and types of words would match identically, but the words themselves would not match in number of syllables. Conversely, two members could be isosyllabic and even identical rhythmically without having exact correspondence of members. But normally *parison* implies *isocolon* as well. Sometimes an obvious word is elided in the second member: "The ox hath known his owner, and the ass his master's crib." Isocolon is particularly of interest because Aristotle mentions it in the *Rhetoric* as the figure that produces symmetry and balance in speech and, thus, creates rhythmical prose or even measures in verse; cf. Quintilian 9.3.76. In rhythmical prose, it is important for estab-

lishing the various forms of the cursus. Vickers gives examples of parison: "As Caesar lov'd me, I weep for him; as he was fortunate, I rejoice at it; as he was valiant, I honour him; but as he was ambitious, I slew him" (*Julius Caesar* 3.1.24); and of isocolon: "Was ever woman in this humour woo'd? / Was ever woman in this humour won?" (*Richard III* 1.2.227). The parison by Nathaniel in *Love's Labour's Lost* (5.1.2) is famous.

■ Norden; A. Quinn, *Figures of Speech* (1982)—esp. 77–79; Vickers.

T.V.F. BROGAN

KENNING (pl. *kenningar*). A multinoun substitution for a single noun, e.g. "din of spears" for battle. Although found in many poetries, the kenning is best known from Old Germanic verse. Kennings are common in West Germanic poetry, and scholars have recognized a kenning in the expression of "corpse-sea," i.e., "blood," on the Eggjum runic inscription from western Norway, ca. 700 CE. ON eddic poetry also makes use of kennings, but their greatest importance was in skaldic poetry.

In med. Icelandic rhet., the verb *kenna* (*við*), "make known (by)," was used to explain these expressions: "din" (the base word in mod. analysis) is "made known" as battle by "of spears" (the determinant). The determinant may be in the genitive case, as here, or may attach to the base word to form a compound (spear-din); the base word takes the morphological and syntactic form of the concept the kenning replaces. In skaldic poetry, the determinant could, in turn, be replaced by another determinant; if "flame of battle" means "sword," then "flame of the din of spears" makes an acceptable kenning. Snorri Sturluson, the 13th-c. poet and man of letters and the first to attempt a rhet. of kennings, called this example *tvíkennt* (twice-determined) in the commentary to *Háttatal* in his *Edda*. If another determinant were added, to make a four-part kenning, he would call it *rekit*, "driven." Snorri cautioned against "driven" kennings with more than six parts.

The relationship between the base word and determinant(s) could be essentially metonymic, as in "Baldr's father" for Odin, or metaphoric, as in the examples above. The kennings of West Germanic poetry, frequently used in connection with variation, tend toward the first category, those of skaldic poetry toward the second. Many skaldic kennings rely on Norse mythology or heroic legend for the links between the parts; thus, poetry is the "theft of Odin" because he stole it from the giants. In skaldic poetry, the number of concepts for which kennings may substitute is limited to about 100, among which warrior, woman, weapons, and battle are well represented. Since the base words tend to be fairly stereotyped (kennings for "woman" often have the name of a goddess as base word, e.g.), the system is relatively closed, but kennings make up nearly all the nouns in skaldic poetry, and the verbs are not important. Having imposed on themselves this closed system, the skalds exploited it brilliantly. In skaldic poetry, the sum of the kennings is, to be sure, greater than their parts, but the best skalds made every word count.

■ R. Meissner, *Die Kenningar der Skalden* (1921); H. van der Merwe Scholtz, *The Kenning in Anglo-Saxon and Old Norse Poetry* (1927); H. Lie, *"Natur" og "unatur" i skaldekunsten* (1957); R. Frank, *Old Norse Court Poetry* (1978); *Snorri Sturluson, Edda,* ed. A. Faulkes (1982–98); E. Marold, *Kenningkunst* (1983); M. Clunies Ross, *Skáldskaparmál* (1986); F. Amory, "Kennings, Referentiality, and Metaphors," *Arkiv för nordisk filologi* (1988); G. Holland, "Kennings, Metaphors, and Semantic Formulae in Old Norse dróttkvætt," *Arkiv för nordisk filologi* (2005).

J. LINDOW

LAMENT. A poem or song of grief, frequently accompanied by instrumental music and by ritualized vocal gestures and symbolic movements such as wailing and breast-beating. As an element of ritual practices such as funerals, cultic worship, and formal rites of passage and leave-taking, and in representations of these practices in literary forms incl. epic, tragedy, and *elegy, lament reaches back to the beginnings of recorded culture: in the Mesopotamian city-laments of the 3d millennium BCE, in Homer's *Iliad* and *Odyssey* (8th c. BCE), in the *Epic of Gilgamesh* (7th c. BCE), in the Heb. Psalms (13th–6th c. BCE) and book of Lamentations (6th c. BCE), and throughout the tragedies and pastorals of Gr. and Roman antiquity. From the Judaic trad., lament was carried over into the Christic (e.g., Christ's lament for Jerusalem in the 1st-c. gospels of Matthew and Luke) and the Islamic (e.g., in the "Lament" from Rūmī's 13th-c. poem *Masnavi*). In Sanskrit lit., "The Lament of Rati" is a celebrated passage from Kālidāsa's 5th-c. epic *Kumārasambhava*. In the Middle Ages, lament took shape in the Lat. *planctus* and in the melancholy vernacular poems of the Exeter Book poets (Anglo-Saxon), the *kharja* of Spain (Mozarabic), and the *planh* of the troubadours (Occitan). Med. *chansons de geste* and Ren. epic poems abound in stylized laments for fallen heroes, and innumerable mod. poets have imitated the bucolic laments of Theocritus (3d c. BCE) and Virgil (1st c. BCE) and the plangent refrain of Bion's famous "Lament for Adonis" (ca. 100 BCE). In 17th-c. Italy, the dramatic lament was popularized by Claudio Monteverdi and other composers and became an essential element of opera. Ritualized lament, with or without instrumental music, remains an important part of the mourning cultures of many societies, incl. the Druze *nabd* of Lebanon, the Irish keen, the *k'u-ko* of southern China, the Ga *adowa* of Ghana, the Setu laments of Estonia, and Af. Am. *blues.

Laments commonly figure collective as well as individual losses. They may protest the status quo, as in Tahmina's lament in Firdawsī's 10th-c. Iranian epic *Shāhnāma*, or foster powerful identifications across sociopolitical divides, as in the many laments in Aeschylus's *The Persians*

(472 BCE), which is as much about Athenian identification with the Persians they have destroyed as it is about Athenian joy at their defeat of the Persians at Salamis. Lament may give form to impulses of compunction, reconciliation, and forgiveness as well as despair, melancholy, and resentment. Although correspondence between representation and social practice is often obscure, archeological evidence (e.g., of Mycenaean funerary practices) and comparative anthropological evidence (e.g., of mod. Gr. ritual customs and beliefs) help supplement and clarify the literary record.

The suffering of captive women and the destruction of cities are prominent and frequently intertwined themes in ancient laments. Such laments may spur, even as they seek to manage, communal grief. The lamentations of women esp. are often marked as both dangerous and necessary—dangerous, because their public indulgence could give way to women's unchecked erotic passion or rage or exacerbate the grief of men, possibly inciting vengeance and other social disruption; necessary, because a community's potentially disabling grief requires an expressive channel, such as might be forbidden or stigmatized among men. Male lamentation abounds in ancient and mod. lits., sometimes celebrated as a masculine duty and achievement, sometimes criticized or interdicted as a feminizing practice. But in many societies, ancient and mod., women are thought to have a privileged relation to grief, and lamentation is often one of the few permissible, if constrained, forms of political expression available to them. Women tend to be the generic subjects of literary laments, even—or perhaps esp.—where the losses sustained by men and the genres (such as epic and tragedy) owned by men are thought to matter most, as in the *kommoi* shared with tragic choruses by lamenting heroines such as Electra, and in mod. instances like Britomart's Petrarchan lament in book 3 of Edmund Spenser's *The Faerie Queene* (1590, 1596). Women's losses are brought to the fore in other genres as well, incl. dramatic adaptations of Antigone's lament, from Sophocles' *Antigone* (5th c. BCE) to Griselda Gambaro's *Antígona Furiosa* (1986), and Irish poet Eileen O'Connell's (Eibhlín Dubh Ní Chonaill) literary transformation of folk mourning practices in her *Lament for Art O'Leary* (1773).

In mod. works like O'Connell's and Gambaro's, lament distinguishes itself from other poetic mourning genres, such as elegy and *epitaph, through its closer connection with ritual incantation and remains audible in Jewish and Christian psalms and in the Islamic *marthiya*. As one moves beyond poetry's religious domain, the term loses much of its distinguishing force—except in the musical trad., where lament has continued to receive distinctive formal treatment, esp. in oratorio and opera, from Monteverdi's *Lamento d'Arianna* (composed 1608) to Giacomo Carissimi's *Jephte* (ca. 1649), Henry Purcell's *Dido and Aeneas* (1689), G. F. Handel's *Agrippina* (1709) and *Saul* (1738), Modest Mussorgsky's *Boris Godunov* (1874), and Benjamin Britten's *Turn of the Screw* (1954). Mod. poems without musical settings that call themselves laments—from the late med. Scots "Lament for the Makaris" by William Dunbar to the many *soi-disant* laments by Robert Burns, John Clare, Thomas Hardy, Felicia Hemans, Langston Hughes, Katharine Tynan, and W. C. Williams—may do so to reactivate the association not just with music as such but with sung or chanted lang. as collective and communal expression, sometimes harkening back to the trads. of antiquity, sometimes using popular forms like the ballad.

See COMPLAINT.

■ S. Girard, *Funeral Music and Customs in Venezuela* (1980); S. Feld, *Sound and Sentiment*, 2d ed. (1990); C. N. Seremetakis, *The Last Word* (1991); P. W. Ferris Jr., *The Genre of Communal Lament in the Bible and the Ancient Near East* (1992); G. Holst-Warhaft, *Dangerous Voices* (1992); "Lament," spec. iss., *Early Music* 27.3 (1999); M. Alexiou, *The Ritual Lament in Greek Tradition*, 2d ed. (2002); N. Loraux, *The Mourning Voice* (2002); C. Dué, *The Captive Woman's Lament in Greek Tragedy* (2006); M. G. McGeachy, *Lonesome Words* (2006); R. Saunders, *Lamentation and Modernity in Literature, Philosophy, and Culture* (2007); C. Lansing, *Passion and Order* (2008); *Lament*, ed. A. Suter (2008).

M. CAVITCH

LEONINE RHYME, VERSE. "Once rhyme invaded the hexameter," John Addington Symonds remarked, "the best verses of the medieval period in that measure are leonine." Also the worst (Raby). Ordinarily, the term refers to internal rhyme in the med. Lat. *hexameter

(i.e., the word at line end rhyming with the word preceding the *caesura); technically, it denotes an oxytonic word ending (a "feminine" rhyme; see MASCULINE AND FEMININE). Though there are examples in cl. Lat. poetry (e.g., Ovid, *Ars amatoria*) and *epitaph verse, leonine rhyme flourished in med. Lat. after the 9th c., being so popular it was imitated in Ir., Eng. (the OE "Rhyming Poem"), Ger., and (esp.) Fr. It is regularly mentioned in the med. prosody manuals of *ars metrica* and *séconde rhétorique*. Presumably the device came into verse from one of the clausulae of rhythmical prose, the *cursus leoninus*, though the origin of the term is uncertain: some trace it to Pope Leo the Great, others to Leoninus, a 12th-c. Benedictine canon of Paris (fl. 1135; see Erdmann).

Leonine verse refers to a hexameter-pentameter *couplet (not always rhymed), as in Eberhard's *Laborintus*—the meter known to antiquity as the *elegiac distich. Both in these couplets and in hexameter couplets, more elaborate schemes of internal rhyming quickly developed both in Occitan and OF such as rhyming the lines' first two *hemistichs together and last two together (Lat. *versus interlaqueati*, Fr. *rime enterlacée*, "interwoven rhyme"); or a double rhyme in the first line, a second double rhyme in the second, and a third binding the ends of the two lines—which by breaking gives the *aabccb* scheme of Fr. *rime couée*, "tail rhyme." Thus, the partitioning of long-line Lat. verse via internal rhyme paved the way for a multitude of short-line lyric stanzas in the vernaculars.

■ W. Wackernagel, "Gesch. des deutschen Hexameters und Pentameters bis auf Klopstock," *Kleinere Schriften*, v. 2 (1873); E. Freymond, "Über den reichen Reim bei altfranzösischen Dichtern," *ZRP* 6 (1882); Schipper 1.305 ff; Kastner; Meyer, 2.267; K. Strecker, "Leoninische Hexameter und Pentameter im 9. Jahrhundert," *Neues Archiv für ältere deutsche Geschichteskunde* 44 (1922), 213 ff.; C. Erdmann, "Leonitas," *Corona Quernea: Festgabe Karl Strecker* (1941); Lote, 2.141 ff.; Curtius, 8.2–3; Raby, *Secular*, 1.228, 2.1; Norden.

T.V.F. BROGAN

LETTER, VERSE. *See* VERSE EPISTLE.

LIMERICK. The limerick is the most popular form of comic or light verse in Eng., often nonsensical and frequently bawdy, but this exacting verse form existed long before it got its name in the late 19th c.

The limerick form consists of five lines of *accentual verse rhyming *aabba,* the first, second, and fifth lines having 3 stresses, the third and fourth 2; the rhythm is effectually anapestic or amphibrachic. The first syllables of each line (and unstressed syllables elsewhere in the lines, though less frequently so) may be omitted. Although the fifth line typically provides a clinching statement or twist, in the early hist. of the form and until the late 19th c., the final line simply repeated the first. A good example of this earlier pattern is the popular nursery rhyme "Hickere, Dickere Dock" (1744), a poem that shares the limerick's structure but not its traditionally bawdy subject matter.

The earliest examples of the use of this short verse form date back to the 13th c.; however, the limerick form is associated in the popular imagination with Edward Lear (*A Book of Nonsense,* 1846). J. H. Murray, writing in 1898, deemed it an error to term Lear's nonsense verse "limericks," as his use of the form did not conform to the strict pattern outlined above, and indeed the term was not used by Lear himself to describe his own verse. Undoubtedly, however, the success of Lear's variations on this form led to its widespread and enduring popularity, and it was even adopted by such authors as Alfred, Lord Tennyson, A. C. Swinburne, Rudyard Kipling, R. L. Stevenson, and W. S. Gilbert, until, by the beginning of the 20th c., it had become a fashion. The tendency in the mod. limerick of using the final line for surprise or witty reversal in place of a repeated last line has now become the norm.

The most common theory regarding the origin of the name is the form's adoption as a parlor game in which party-goers were invited to extemporize a song that ended with the line "Will you come up to Limerick?" Other theories range from the belief that it was an old Fr. form brought to the Ir. town of Limerick in 1700 by returning veterans of the Fr. war to the idea that it originated in the nursery rhymes published as *Mother Goose's Melodies* (1791).

See NONSENSE VERSE.

■ J. H. Murray, *Notes and Queries* (1898); L. Reed, *The Complete Limerick Book* (1925); *Oxford Book of Nursery Rhymes,* ed. I. and P. Opie (1951); A. Liede, *Dichtung als Spiel,* v. 2 (1963); G. Legman, *The Limerick* (1964, 1988); W. S. Baring-Gould, *The Lure of the Limerick* (1972); *The Limerick: 1700 Examples* (1970, 1974), *The New Limerick* (1977), both ed. G.

Legman; C. Bibby, *The Art of the Limerick* (1978); G. N. Belknap, "History of the Limerick," *The Papers of the Bibliographical Society of America* 75 (1981); *Penguin Book of Limericks,* ed. E. O. Parrott (1984).

T.V.F. BROGAN; A. PREMINGER;
I. D. COPESTAKE

LINE (Sanskrit, *pāda*; Gr., *stichos,* Lat. *versus* "verse"). The line is fundamental to poetry itself, for the line differentiates verse from prose: throughout most of recorded history, poetry has been cast in verse, and verse is set in lines. That is, verse is cast in sentences and lines, prose in sentences and paragraphs. The sense in prose flows continuously, while in verse it is segmented to increase the density of information and the awareness of structure. It is impossible that there could be verse not set in lines. It is possible there could be poetry not set in lines, if one defines poetry as verbal composition marked by a comparatively high degree of memorability, beauty, sublimity, delightfulness, instructiveness, figurativeness, ellipticality, intensity, uncanniness, linguistic patterning, or some combination of these or other qualities. Hybrid forms such as rhythmical prose and the *prose poem demonstrate the poetic possibilities of prose, as do many moments in short stories, novels, essays, and longer nonfictional forms throughout the world. But we must assume that the preponderance of the world's poetry has been cast in lines, whether they read from left to right (e.g., Eng., Fr., Ger.), right to left (e.g., Heb. and Ar.), or top to bottom (e.g., cl. Chinese), precisely to take advantage of those resources which verse has to offer (see PROSODY). In Eng., usage of "line" (etymologically descended from Lat., *linum* "flax") to signify the "portion of a metrical composition which is usually written in one line: a verse" (*OED*) dates from the second half of the 16th c. and reflects the growth of print culture (see below).

A. Structure. Readers and auditors of poetry perceive the line as a rhythmical unit and a unit of structure. As a unit of measure, it is linked to its neighbors to form higher-level structures, and as a structure itself, it is built of lower-level units. In metrical verse the line is usually segmented into elements—*hemistichs, measures or metra, or feet (see FOOT, MODERN)—but it is the line which generates these intralinear units and not vice versa. Lines are not made simply by defining some unit of measure such as a foot and then stringing units together, because the units are susceptible of differential constraint at differing points in the line. The line, that is, has a shape or contour, and a structure as a whole, over and above the sum of its constituent elements. In various verse systems these elements are bound together in differing ways, such as structural alliteration in OE. It is true that, in the handbooks, meters are usually specified by the type of foot and number of feet per line—i.e. monometer (a line of 1 foot), *dimeter (2 feet), *trimeter (3 feet), *tetrameter (4 feet), *pentameter (5 feet), *hexameter (6 feet), *heptameter (7 feet). But these simplistic descriptors do not capture the internal dynamics of a line, such as the Gr. hexameter.

How do readers and auditors recognize the line as a rhythmical unit? In isometric verse, meter measures out a constant spacing, either of a certain number of events or a certain span of time (depending on one's theory of meter) which the mind's internal counter tracks in cognition; meter also provides predictable internal structure. The line can also be bound together by syntactic and rhetorical structures such as *parallelism and *antithesis which have their own internal logic of completion; these structures may or may not be threaded into meter: in biblical Heb. verse they are, in Whitman they are not.

B. Line End. Probably the most common strategy is to mark the *end* of the line, since without some sort of signal, we would not know where one line ended and a second one began. Traditionally the signal has been thought to be a "pause," though not a metrical (line-internal) one but rather some kind of rhetorical or performative one. But this claim derives not from prosody (verse theory), or from claims about the nature or ontological status of poetry as *sound, but rather from assumptions put in play about *performance, about the reading aloud of verse. On this account, performers of poetry recognize the line as a unit (by seeing it as such when read from the page, for example) and mark its end in delivery with a linguistic pause or paralinguistic cue such as elongation of the final syllable. Auditors hear these cues, which cross or ignore syntax, as boundary markers.

An alternative conception of the signal, which depends rather on assumptions about the visual formatting of poetry on a page, is the stretch of empty space beyond the line,

a stretch usually not aligned with the empty stretches beyond other lines, producing an appearance of jagged margining. This signal is perceived in reading and *may* be taken not only as a terminal marker but even as a part of structure (see below).

But both these answers specify phenomena *after* the line ends. A more powerful conception of the signal, not committed to any doctrine about either performance or format, would be, "some kind of marker," not after the final syllable of the line but *in* the final syllables of the line. In Gr. and Lat. poetry, where the meter is quantitative, auditors could recognize the ends of lines because they were marked by an alteration in the meter, either an increase in the formality in its closing syllables, a *cadence*, or unexpected shortening at line end, *catalexis*. In the hexameter, for example, the line closes on a spondee—two heavy syllables in succession—rather than a dactyl, a closural pattern which is obligatory. In post-cl. verse, line ends have been most often marked by some distinctive sound echo, chiefly *rhyme, though important also are the several other strategies of sound-repetition that are rhyme-like or exceed rhyme: *homoeoteleuton, *assonance, identical rhyme. Short lines in particular seem to demand the support of rhyme, or else they will be mistaken for the cola that are parts of longer lines; this is a major factor in the devel. of the *lyric. Also important are strategies for end-of-line semantic emphasis: Richard Wilbur, for example, sometimes employs the strategy of putting important words at line end, words that may offer an elliptical synopsis or ironic commentary on the argument of the poem. All these strategies, taken together as devices for end-fixing, i.e., *marking* or *weighting* line ends to foreground them perceptually, constitute one of the most distinctive categories of metrical universals, conspicuous in a wide range of verse systems.

The phenomenon of extra syllables at line end is fairly extensive and a feature of several prosodies: line endings are classified depending on whether the last stress falls on the final syllable of the line (a "masculine" ending) or the penultimate one (a "feminine" one; see MASCULINE AND FEMININE). The distinction dates from at least Occitan poetry, and may date from ancient Gr. Classifying types of line endings was also one of the central "metrical tests" that several Brit. and Ger. Shakespeare scholars of the later 19th c. hoped would yield a definitive chronology of the plays. Spedding in 1847 suggested the "pause test," which tabulated frequencies of stopped vs. enjambed lines. Bathurst (1857), Craik, and Hertzberg discussed "weak endings"; Ingram (1874) distinguished types of these as "light" endings (enjambed lines ending on a pronoun, verb, or relative bearing only secondary stress, plus a slight pause) and "weak" (enjambment on a proclitic, esp. a conjunction or preposition, allowing no pause at all—see Brogan for citations).

C. Line and Syntax. The syllables of the line are the arena for deploying meter or rhythm; they are also the ground of syntax and sense: these two structures, line and syntax, overwrite the same space. Some verse forms regularly align line units with sense units; such lines are known as *end-stopped*. The ("closed") *heroic couplet, for example, ends the first line at a major syntactic break and the second at a full stop (sentence end). But few forms do so *every* line. Systematic contrast or opposition of line units and sense units (line end and sentence flow) is the complex phenomenon known as *enjambment*. In enjambed verse, syntax pulls the reader through line end into the next line, while the prosodic boundary suggests a pause if not a stop. In reading, the mind makes projections, in that pause, based on what has come before, about what word is most likely to appear at the beginning of the next line, expectations which a masterful poet will deliberately thwart, forcing rapid rereading: in Milton such error is the emblem of man's postlapsarian state. Certainly in modern times, at least, it has been thought that one of the chief functions of line division is to stand in tension with or counterpoint to the divisions of grammar and sense, effecting, in the reader's processing of the poem, multiple simultaneous pattern recognition. Even in enjambed verse, the word at line end, which the French call the *contre-rejet*, receives some sort of momentary foregrounding or emphasis. This is not a matter of the word marking the end but of the end marking the word.

D. Aural Line and Visual Line. Since the advent of writing in Gr., ca. 750 BCE, and certainly since the advent of printing in the West, ca. 1450 CE, the line has had a visual reality in poetry, but long before that time and without interruption throughout print culture it has had an auditory one. This history gives the line—poetry itself—a fundamental duality, in the eye and ear, as both seen and heard

(Hollander), a duality complicated, especially in the twentieth century and after by the ascendance of *free verse. Instances such as the ms. of the OE epic *Beowulf* (Cotton Vitellius A.xv), in which the alliterating four-stress metrical segments do not appear as individual lines, or a ms. of a Japanese haiku in which the seventeen-mora form appears as a single vertical line, though usually represented by three lines in translation, raise interesting questions about the nature and integrity of lineation. But arguments about the historical or ontological precedence of the aural over the visual line miss the point: these forms are, for us now, both realities; the important question is how they affect each other—whether, for example, the break at line end demands a pause, performed or imagined. Two phenomena complicating discussion of the line as a visible entity are the *split line and the typographic runover. Both these phenomena force a distinction between the line as a concrete unit of printing and the line as an abstract unit of composition, which may not correspond to a single printed unit. In most modern printings of a Shakespeare play, for example, the two parts of a single iambic pentameter line split between two speakers appear on different lines on the page, the second indented to begin after the end of the one set above it. Meanwhile, in the first section of Allen Ginsberg's *Howl*, an abstract "line," which begins with the repeated, left-justified pronoun "who," may run over to many lines of print, making it unlikely that that line could ever be contained by a single line of print, even in a very large book. With the advent of electronic poetry new possibilities arise for representing lines visually, and one can image even Ginsberg's longest line running horizontally unbroken across a screen, but the defiance of his gesture, setting two notions of "line" against one another, would be lost.

E. Line Forms. Up to the advent of free verse, line forms and line lengths are mainly determined by genre specification, so that poets who wish to write, say, in *elegiac distichs (hexameter plus pentameter), know or learn, by reading their predecessors, what forms have already been tried, for what kinds of subjects, with what kinds of tone, and with what success. In metrical verse, that is, line forms were mainly determined by history and convention, by the interplay of tradition and the individual talent; and the prosody which generated them was aurally based. Free verse, by contrast, foregrounded visual space and posited the line within a two-dimensional matrix where blanks, white spaces, drops, gaps, and other dislocations became possible. This is not to say that free verse abandoned aurality, for some poets, such as the Beats, Charles Olson with his "projective verse," and the proponents of *sound poetry and "text-sound," continued to speak programmatically of the line as based on the energy of the breath. It is only to say that visual prosody was made central to free verse at least in claim, and if aural prosody was at the same time not dispensed with, no poet seemed to wish or prosodist to be able, at least for the first century of free-verse practice, to give a definitive account of the relations of the one to the other.

To think, however, that the free-verse line can function solely as visual prosody, without the resources of aural prosody to aid it, is to commit what Perloff calls the "linear fallacy," making some free verse indistinguishable from prose chopped up into lines. The sonic and rhythmic devices of aural prosody offer poetry effects *not available* to prose: and if these are to be discarded, visual prosody must provide others, or else the distinction between prose and verse collapses. One might respond that several Eng. poets—Ben Jonson and Alexander Pope, to name but two—wrote out drafts of their poems first in prose before versifying them; and verse translators routinely work through intermediary prose versions. But this practice shows simply that they wished to clarify the argumentative or narrative structure first to get it out of the way, so as to concentrate on *poetic* effects.

See FREE VERSE, METER, PROSODY, STANZA, VERSIFICATION, VISUAL POETRY.

■ C. A. Langworthy, "Verse-Sentence Patterns in English Poetry," *PQ* 7 (1928); J. S. Diekhoff, "Terminal Pause in Milton's Verse," *SP* 32 (1935); A. Oras, "Echoing Verse Endings in Paradise Lost," *South Atlantic Studies for Sturgis E. Leavitt* (1953); C. L. Stevenson, "The Rhythm of English Verse," *JAAC* 28 (1970); D. Crystal, "Intonation and Metrical Theory," *TPS* (1971); C. Ricks, "Wordsworth," *Essays in Criticism* 21 (1971); B. Stáblein, "Versus," *MGG*, v. 13; H. McCord, "Breaking and Entering," and D. Laferrière, "Free and Non-Free Verse," *Lang&S* 10 (1977); J. Lotman, *The Structure of the Artistic Text*, trans. G. Lenhoff and R. Vroon (1977); D. Levertov, "On the Function of the Line," *Chicago Review* 30 (1979), *Epoch* 29 (1980)—symposium; M. Perloff, "The Linear Fallacy," *Georgia Review* 35 (1981), response in 36 (1982); Brogan; J. C. Stalker, "Reader Expectations and the Poetic Line," *Lang&S* 15 (1982); P. P. Byers, "The Auditory Reality of the Verse Line," *Style* 17 (1983); R. Bradford, "'Verse Only to the Eye'?: Line Endings in Paradise Lost," *EIC* 33 (1983); S. A. Keenan, "Effects of Chunking and Line Length on Reading Efficiency," *Visual Language* 18 (1984); *The Line in Postmodern Poetry*, ed. R. Frank and H. Sayre (1988); R. Pinsky, *The Sounds of Poetry* (1998); J.173Longenbach, *The Art of the Poetic Line* (2008); E. B. Voigt, *The Art of Syntax* (2009); *A Broken Thing: Poets on the Line*, ed. E. Rosko and A. Vander Zee (2011).

T.V.F. BROGAN; S. CUSHMAN

LITOTES (Gr., "plainness," "simplicity"). A form of meiosis, employing (1) affirmation by the negative of the contrary ("Not half bad"; "I'll bet you won't" meaning "I'm certain you will") or (2) deliberate understatement for purposes of intensification ("He was a good soldier; say no more" for a hero). Servius, commenting on Virgil's *Georgics* 2.125, says, "non tarda, id est, strenuissima: nam litotes figura est" (not slow, that is, most brisk: for the figure is litotes). Litotes is used so frequently in *Beowulf* and other OE, ON, and Old Germanic poetry that it has become (with the *kenning) one of its distinguishing features, e.g., "ðæt wæs god cyning" (that was a good king), following a passage telling how the king flourished on earth, prospered in honors, and brought neighboring realms to pay him tribute. Chaucer's cook is described as "nat pale as a forpyned goost. / A fat swan loved he best of any roost" ("General Prologue," 205–6). John Milton has "Nor are thy lips ungraceful, Sire of men, / Nor tongue ineloquent" (*Paradise Lost* 8.18–19). Alexander Pope uses litotes as an effective satiric instrument.

Like meiosis, *hyperbole, *irony, and *paradox, litotes requires that the reader refer to the ostensive situation, i.e., to the utterance's pragmatic context, in order to perceive the disparity between the words taken literally and their intended sense. Group μ distinguishes litotes from meiosis, or "arithmetical" understatement ("one says less so as to say more") by restricting litotes to the "double" negation of a grammatical and lexical contrary. So Chimène's conciliatory remark to her lover, "Go, I do not hate you" (Pierre Corneille, *Le Cid* 3.4), negates the lexeme *hatred*, while at the same time the negative assertion posits the opposite series of statements referring to the degrees between loving and not hating. Thus, the seemingly negative construction of the litotes not only suppresses a positive seme, replacing it with the corresponding negative one, but replaces any one of a series of negative semes. Corbett illustrates how litotes may function in forensic rhet. with an example of the lawyer who assists his client "by referring to a case of vandalism as 'boyish highjinks.' A rose by any other name will smell as sweet, but a crime, if referred to by a name that is not too patently disproportionate, may lose some of its heinousness." Litotes in this instance functions like euphemism by reducing the resistance of the audience. In logic, the device corresponding to litotes is obversion.

The distinction between litotes and meiosis is that, in the former, calling a thing less than it is makes evident that it is actually larger, whereas in the latter, calling it less is meant to make it less.

■ K. Weyman, *Studien Über die Figur der Litotes* (1886); O. Jespersen, *Negation in English and Other Languages* (1917); A. Hübner, *Die "Mhd. Ironie" oder die Litotes im Altdeutschen* (1930); F. Bracher, "Understatement in Old English Poetry," *PMLA* 52 (1937); L. M. Hollander, "Litotes in Old Norse," *PMLA* 53 (1938); M. Joseph, *Shakespeare's Use of the Arts of Language* (1947); C. Perelman and L. Olbrechts-Tyteca, *The New Rhetoric*, trans. J. Wilkinson and P. Weaver (1969); Lausberg; Morier; Group μ; Corbett.

R. O. Evans; A. W. Halsall; T.V.F. Brogan

LOVE POETRY

  I. Issues and Assumptions
  II. Thematic Overview
  III. Conventions and Personae

I. Issues and Assumptions. Love poetry is one of the oldest and most widespread types of *lyric. It has come down to us from ancient Egyptian times, been authored by male and female poets, projected through and upon different sexual personae, and developed a host of striking and sometimes globally itinerant conventions. It has etched episodes in compelling plotlines and provided an imaginative space in which to articulate and contemplate the human emotions of affection, sexual passion, and idealism as these join in what we call *love*.

Though most anthologists would acknowledge love poetry's ongoing importance in the lyric trad., it was not always so recognized by 20th-c. Eur. and Am. critics. This had to do largely with reigning theoretical and historical assumptions, as Hancock points out in "Unworthy of a Serious Song?" For instance, the notion of poetic "impersonality" often made love poetry into something of an oxymoron. T. S. Eliot, whose *Waste Land* and individual lyrics seldom engaged with the theme of love unless to describe its impossibility, also wrote in his critical essays of the poet's necessary "impersonality." And though many of the most appreciated mod. love poets could not easily be accommodated within this view, the position was taken up by a number of influential critics (particularly Wimsatt and Beardsley, and, more polemically, Barthes). In a commendable eagerness to emphasize poetry as lang. and text, such a critical assumption made it difficult to embrace love poetry when it dwelt, as was often the case, on seemingly "personal" themes.

Historical assumptions also hampered our understanding of love poetry. For instance, many Am. and Eur. critics of the 20th c. saw the subject of love poetry largely through the historical lens of courtly love—a view that places the beginnings of love poetry with the 11th-c. Occitan poets. Authors such as Lewis and Rougemont provided influential hists. of Eur. love lyric, all stemming from this source. Though Dronke early pointed out the much more complex and variegated hist. of courtly love, situating it within a wider set of influences and themes, this broader view was not as often accepted as the one that saw the trad. in its more limited guise, thereby excluding a fuller hist. of love poetry.

A third problem for the study of love poetry has been the limited availability of texts from other parts of the globe. New anthols. of trans. poems have begun to remedy this gap, broadening our sense of what love poetry can be in different ling., geographical, and cultural settings. Thanks largely to this growing range of anthols., as well as fuller critical descriptions of poetry from around the world, we are beginning to gain a greater awareness of love poetry's diversity, from the earliest Egyptian love songs to the present. This article gestures toward some of this diversity, though it would be impossible to explore it fully. The list of readings included should amplify this brief discussion.

The continuing popularity of anthols. of love poetry itself bears comment. Readers have always appreciated the love lyric, even when critics have been more reticent. Perhaps readers read love poetry to reenvision their own understanding of love and, to some extent, their own sense of identity. This need not be a simple mirroring. Reading love poetry from different geographic, ling., and historical contexts expands our sense of love's possible meanings in our own lives and those of others. In this sense, love poetry is not only one of the most common types of poetry written but a type with particular audience appeal.

II. Thematic Overview. Love poetry imaginatively presents the vicissitudes of that human emotion we call *love*. But what is love? Is it sexual pleasure, passionate desire, religious enlightenment, joyful connection to another, a painful disruption and reconstruction of self, or a cherishing of another human being? Is it idealized or sexual, public or private, a sickness unto death or an exhilarating rebirth of the mind and the senses? If we are to believe the poets, it is all these and more. According to lang., culture, time, and individual poetic insight, love is constructed in an endless variety of ways. For love itself, as well as the poetry that represents it, is, at least in part, an imaginative construction. It may be performed in a variety of ways and with differing results.

Of the themes that have characterized love poetry across the centuries and in many cultures across the globe, the tension between ideal and earthly passion is one of the most pervasive. This is a theme sometimes supported by religious and philosophical thought and by popular poetic practice—and has varied in importance according to historical and cultural context. To generalize greatly, the love lyric in its earliest forms seems to embrace a more earthly love, while med. and early mod. poetry explore more idealizing strains. The enormously diverse love poetry of the late 19th, 20th, and 21st cs. tends again toward less idealized themes.

Our oldest known love poems from ancient Egypt reveal a frank appreciation of the earthly nature of love. Sensual themes drawn from popular song celebrate youth, nature, and the sheer pleasures—and at times, the pains—of love. These poems, existing in the oral as well as written trad., are believed to have directly influenced the Heb. Song of Songs composed centuries later. Their themes and their reliance on female as well as male speakers have persisted in African poetry to this day and assert themselves

with renewed vigor in the mod. and contemp. love lyric of many cultures.

From Sappho's great love lyrics focused on erotic longing to other Gr. texts, there is a complex legacy of poetic meditations on love. Much Roman poetry—particularly that of Ovid and Catullus—while in many ways emulating the Gr. heritage, present a love poetry that is often playful and even cynical. Here, love is entertaining and sometimes dangerous—a passion to be controlled and, at times, purposely extinguished. Examples from this trad. continue over the centuries, turning to homosexual as well as heterosexual themes and later flourishing in parallel with idealizing strands.

It is not in these very early love lyrics but rather in Plato's *Phaedrus* and *Symposium* that we find the most idealizing demands of eros, as the desire for transcendence of the human for the divine. Erotic desire, often described in homoerotic or clearly homosexual terms, animates a view of love that seeks not mere earthly satisfaction so much as the continuation of passion, often until the self can fuse with the divine. It is such erotic love that Rougemont claims stands behind the courtly love trad. Death has an inevitable role to play here, often presented in love poetry through the death of the beloved (as in Dante's *Vita nuova* and *Divina commedia*), making consummation of love impossible and endless desire inevitable. But at times the death of the lover is suggested also as the outcome of ceaseless passion.

Centuries of Eur. love poetry beginning with the troubadours in the 11th c. celebrate a love that reaches beyond the material alone to ennoble lover and beloved. But as Hamill suggests, an idealizing spirit, with its aspiration to move from the human to a more transcendent love, is celebrated in many cultures and from very early times. In the Persian and the Ar. trads., e.g., where earthly love has a specific role in the ascent to the love of God, we find a rich vein of idealizing love poetry. Often laced with humor and irony, playing on complex ambiguities, such poetry is well known from the 9th c. onward, and its mystical aspirations reach us today through the love poetry of Andalusia as well as the powerful verses of Jalāl al-Dīn Rūmī and the *ghazals* of Ḥāfiẓ. Indian poetry from the earliest Sanskrit and *Bhakti* has made sensual love at times the figure for spiritual yearning, as well as of sexual, courtly pleasure. Poetry by figures such as the 15th-c. Kabīr and Vidyāpati have inspired generations of poets around the world. In yet another context, we find the writing of Sor Juana Inés de la Cruz, where a unique rendering of religious and earthly love emerges in a Mexico recently transformed through violent cultural encounters.

Over the centuries, these two strains of poetry have persisted and often joined forces. Later centuries mark a few thematic junctures of particular interest. The luxuries of court settings and noble rank have, for instance, often contributed to the idealizing refinement of love poetry. This occurs in a good deal of med. and Ren. Eur. court poetry, where the social status of lover and beloved itself contributes to an expected lyric decorum.

One sees very different aristocratic poetries in the long, complex hist. of both Chinese and Japanese love lyric. Associated with the courts and often with royal figures, love poetry reveals sophisticated devels. in verse forms as well as themes. Each trad. stands alone and in some ways at odds with Eur. examples, though similar in its strong dependence on an aristocratic court culture for conventions of great poetic refinement, for a poetic play within stylized themes—as well as for material survival.

In the later Eur. romantic trad., the ideal and earthly produce a very different synthesis as poets depict a love both sexual and ennobling. But unlike their med. and Ren. precursors, and corresponding to different philosophical and religious expectations, these poets did not seek a divine goal outside earthly love but rather love's innate creativity. As Singer suggests in *The Nature of Love*, the lovers become ideal because they *are* lovers, filled with the creative spirit conveyed by the joining of sensuous and spiritual aspects of love—and the expectations of 19th-c. philosophy. Its themes often depict love as a path to death and destruction, but at other times more positive views prevail. With the romantic love lyric, courtly poetry's reliance on high social station gives way to a new openness to all social ranks, and women gain greater prominence as poets and as personae (see PERSONA).

Following in the wake of these more democratic and dialogical themes, love poets of the late 19th and 20th cs. begin to describe not only the experience of "falling in love" but what Singer describes as "being in love" and "staying in love." Though the theme of death also plays a role in this more mod. poetry, it tends to quicken the senses, making present pleasures and appreciations more intense, as it amplifies

the importance of memory. An awareness of the transitory infiltrates amatory experience with heightened intensity.

Of course, the 19th c. brings not only a transformed love poetry to Europe: Europe brings the political and cultural context of colonial expansion, oppression, empire, and postcolonial response to much of the world. With colonial educational systems in Africa and India, e.g., came the invasion of cultures not only with guns and tools of commercial exploitation but with the insistent contact of different literary and poetic trads. Rich legacies of original-lang. poetry experienced an often violent encounter with the lyrics of Europe. What has emerged from this impact includes waves of trans., adaptations, new verse forms, and original inspirations, as well as reactions against the poetry of the colonizing nations. The ling., formal, and thematic effects of these encounters on the poetries of all trads. deserve ongoing study. For a genre as wide-ranging and diverse as the love lyric, such study has only begun.

Partly for this reason, it is hard to generalize about the themes of 20th- and 21st-c. love poetry across many cultures. However, a few salient qualities may be noted. First, in much if not most mod. love poetry, there is a muting of interest in highly idealizing themes and a greater acceptance of sexuality and sensuality. In many cultures, though hardly all, homosexual and lesbian themes become more frequent, as does poetry composed by women. Second, there is often a turn away from universal or stylized themes to the particulars of the individual love experience. The details of everyday life and sometimes the seemingly autobiographical elements connecting lover and beloved replace the earlier, more universal themes of yearning leading to transcendence. Third, a situated, particularized memory often replaces stylized imagery with cultural, historical, stylistic, and other thematic returns to the past. Fourth, mod. and contemp. love poetry is increasingly aware of its many poetic encounters over time and geographic space. These affect both themes and formal conventions.

III. Conventions and Personae. The conventions of love poetry include agreed-upon elements of style, genre, and structure that restrict the poet's work yet allow him or her to communicate with the audience or reader. A few have played a role in several different cultural and historical contexts. Some of love poetry's conventions relate to its themes, outlined above, but others deal in verse forms, imagery, and personae. Who do we imagine is speaking in a poem? How private does the lang. seem—or how public and rhetorical? Though a love poem may sometimes, through its particularity and detail, give the impression of a straightforward rendition of personal experience, it is always a fashioned, indirect expression, an imaginative performance in the medium of words. It is, in short, always art. Lang., with its constructions of *diction, figuration, and *sound, intensifies the imaginative dimensions of the poem as it mediates any direct perception of sincerity.

A. The Secular Love Lyric: Ancient Egyptian and Hebrew. Our earliest love songs from ancient Egypt (1305–1080 BCE) provide examples of male and female personae, in each case imagining and/or addressing lovers of the opposite sex. Some humorous, some serious in tone—all offer the earliest known love songs, still a pleasure to read. They include poems of ecstasy, despair, a listing of the beloved's qualities, and descriptions of the more physical aspects of love. The openness and variety of these poems, their oral as well as written trad., remain ongoing traits, particularly evident, e.g., in later Swahili song. Female personae reappear in many African folk trads., inspiring later poets as well.

Scholars generally believe that the early Egyptian songs, very likely used for entertainment purposes, were popular in origin, though hardly naïve. The diction remains unpretentious, not stylized, and at times humorous and ironic. Imagery evokes the pastoral with its flowers, birds, and gardens. Highly crafted poems, they were likely sung as well as written. Their lines are not metered or rhymed but have a clear rhythm. Each song has a marked end point and most belong to larger cycles.

These early Egyptian songs were part of a trad. that seems to have influenced the best-known love poem in the world: the Song of Songs. Scholars now mostly agree that this poem, long read allegorically, is a secular love lyric—or collection of them—that was created by a sophisticated poet and was likely appreciated in popular recitation as well as elite writing. The many parts (or poems) of the Song offer different personae—incl. a woman, a man, and even groups. A young woman speaker dominates much of the poem, describing her desire and pleasure in love. These are fully

reciprocated in the words spoken by the man. At times, a dialogue structure of alternating voices and matching images appears, creating a sense of mutuality between male and female personae. Nature imagery, some of it conventional, some of it astonishing in its metaphorical leaps, characterizes the poem, along with imagery from art and architecture. Though the verses are not metrical or rhymed, *parallelism and, at times, direct *repetitions, shape the text. The Song as a whole celebrates young love of a joyful, openly sexual nature but also includes references to death and to separation. With its *pastoral grace and delicate shading of love with death, the poem stands alone in the Heb. and indeed in subsequent trads.

B. Classical Greek and Latin Love Poetry. Fundamental to the Eur. trad. of love poetry are the cl. Greeks and Romans. Most famous among them is Sappho, a woman poet from Lesbos, whose texts are spoken in a woman's voice and most often concern affection, or passion, for other women. Whether Sappho herself was lesbian is something we cannot know—neither from the fragmentary corpus of her poetry nor from biographical data. But that her poetry often spoke through and about female personae and about erotic love we do know.

Derived from a long hist. of oral poetry, the aeolic meter Sappho used may well go back to an IE base. With its self-conscious meditation and description of the lover's inner state, her verse may be the most famous love poetry in the Eur. trad. Bringing to the reader an interior world of love's suffering and reflection, Sappho along with Archilochus and Alcaeus ushered in the era of cl. poetry, with its quest for internal reflection. Anacreon followed. A lyric poet of great skill, whose rhythmic verse patterns were imitated by later writers, he often turned to humor rather than yearning—as he addressed both male and female lovers (see ANACREONTIC).

When the Romans overcame the Greeks, the Lat. writers began to gain poetic hegemony. Yet these poets were keenly aware of their debts to the stunning Gr. trad. that came before. Catullus, whose learned and witty love poetry was addressed to Lesbia, evoking Sappho, was a case in point. Developing the Roman *elegy, based on Gr. models of alternating lines of dactylic hexameter and pentameter, Catullus's witty lyrics were followed by those of Tibullus and Propertius, with their own amatory elegies to beloved women. A poetry of high society, theirs was not a lyric of longing but of lively love affairs. But of all the Lat. love poets, Ovid was the master. His love elegies—incl. the *Heroides*, written through the personae of famous women from the cl. past—were particularly influential, as was his imagery with its martial motifs. In his *Ars amatoria* and the *Remedia amoris*, he satirically presented a view of love that influenced poets and readers for centuries to come, one in which male and female were each given new stature.

C. *"Religions of Love."* In the med. period, Eur. love poetry takes on a very different shape and distinctive set of forms as well as themes. Lewis, who in his *Allegory of Love* describes courtly love in terms of "Humility, Courtesy, Adultery and the Religion of Love," assigns its beginnings to 11th-c. Languedoc. The beloved woman, an idealized figure of high social status, inspires her male lover with a passion that ennobles him. Engaging in a sort of quest myth for union with her—but also for his own moral excellence—her lover begins a spiritual journey. A view of love shared by the troubadour poets of Occitania, then by the *trouvères* in northern France and eventually by poets throughout Europe, the convention often depended on the imagery of Ovid but joined this to an idealization of the beloved, suggesting a religion of love, reminiscent of the cult of the Virgin Mary. In this courtly context, homosexual love was rarely voiced. Apart from the trobairitz, women seldom were poetic speakers. The early, aristocratic cult of Eur. courtly love reached its pinnacle in the *Dolce stil nuovo* and the poetry of Dante, though it continued, with important thematic variations, in Petrarch's *sonnet sequence and subsequent renditions of the Ren. love lyric. In later centuries, homosexual motifs reappeared in the works of Shakespeare and Michelangelo, for instance, and the early idealism of love was also often challenged. But these early mod. versions remained largely aristocratic, attached to court life, with its refined lang. of the developing vernaculars. Throughout, many fixed verse forms emerged, such as the *villanelle, the *sestina, and the canzone, though the 14-line *sonnet held the greatest appeal.

Ar. love poetry of the 7th to 10th c. developed the genre to an exquisite art form—comparable in some ways to the Eur. courtly love trad. Generally voiced by a male persona, it often described a service of love to a capricious lady. In the 9th c., such love service could take by turns idealizing and highly physical descriptions and at times included homosexual motifs. In the hands of some writers, such love poetry transformed into the fully mystical, with the poet expressing desire for a divine beloved.

Influenced by early Ar. forms and conventions, Persian poets produced similarly idealized personae and love songs. In the ghazal form, based on linked *couplets with associated imagery, a courtly love very like that of the Occitan poets appears. But in spite of its similarities to the Eur. versions, distinct differences remain. One was the greater weight given to the sensual elements of love, for earthly love was deemed a necessary step in the ladder of love. Another was the absence of adulterous love. A third difference was the acceptance of homoerotic motifs.

Throughout the Persian and much of the Ar. trad., the mystical love song remains an important form for centuries. Turning to an earthly or divine beloved, the eroticism of Rūmī and Ḥāfiz produced distinctive personae and a powerful, if highly ambiguous erotic trad.

The Indian lyric of idealized love was more varied than the Eur., Ar., or Persian, given the many langs.—such as Sanskrit, Prakrit, Tamil, Hindi, and Bengali, to mention a few—and religious motifs it expressed. Whether described as love in consummation or in separation and longing, the ancient Indian love lyric was often part of religious devotion. Poets such as Kālidāsa and Bhartṛhari address the god Śiva. In Indian religious belief, the gods can at times reciprocate. At others, the emphasis falls on the lover's continued yearning. In the Indian trad., female desire is as often celebrated as male. The 12th-c. female poet Mahādēviyakka, for instance, reveals her intense yearning and praise for Śiva, often described in very sensual terms. In more secular visions, a lover's memory may shuttle between moments of separation and consummation. Though the sensual may open out to a more mystical knowledge, it may also simply be addressed as one of the many aspects of love. The ambiguity and beauty of the verse of 15th- and 17th-c. love poetry offered by Kabīr, Bihārī Lal, and Mīrābāī remain part of the trad. in India and beyond.

D. *Court Poetries.* In Chinese and Japanese poetry of the cl. period, refined court poetries flourished. In China, early popular love poetry was widely appreciated, though sometimes later read allegorically by elite audiences. But already in the Southern Dynasties (420–589), love poetry held an important place in court culture. These poems of love were written according to specific conventions. For instance, though the poets were usually male, they took the persona of a woman in love. For the most part, these were songs of sadness, longing, and nostalgia, written from the viewpoint of the woman, left alone in her boudoir, awaiting her wandering lover. Written in series of five- or seven-character lines, the poems reveal subtle parallelisms of image and tone that unify them. The later Tang dynasty poets (618–907), particularly Li Bai and Du Fu, reached pinnacles of fame in an era when poetry had become an essential ingredient in court and professional culture. The achievement of the Tang was its establishment of regulated tone patterns within verse forms and, in terms of love poetry's themes, its exploration of the ambiguities of love. The Song dynasty (960–1295) often used a style of poetry called *ci* that was tied to musical forms and particular melodies and revolved around courtesan culture. Topics of the lover's desire were often expressed in this versatile form. Late in the Ming dynasty (1368–1644), the ci was used again by the poet Chen Zilong, who exchanged lyrics with his courtesan lover Liu Shi. Their equally passionate and talented verse reveals the devel. of female as well as male voices in poetry, one that continues into the contemp. period.

Japanese court poetry was likewise highly refined in its use of poetic form and lang. Collections of poems early presented a version of courtly love. Often a poetry of yearning, it could also at times celebrate consummation. Erotic images of tangled hair or wetness were frequently employed. And the theme of laments by passionate women was a long-lasting convention in Japanese love poetry all the way to the 20th c.

Poetry before the 13th c. was almost always associated with the courts. Compilers, who were also poets, joined short *waka* poems together in long sequences. At other times, poets gathered for poetic contests, Some of the most famous poets of the Japanese waka period are female— incl. Ono no Komachi and Izumi Shikibu.

Renga, or linked poetry, existed early in the trad. but gained popularity in the Japanese Middle Ages and later in the 13th, 14th, and 15th cs. Poetry was, among other things, an art of communication—with other poets as well as the audience. Joint writing of renga was a frequent court event. When renga was composed

there, women poets participated. From renga, the haikai and eventually the *haiku developed. The 17-syllable haiku originated as the first links of renga sequences but eventually became separated for discrete appreciation. The haiku grew popular in Europe and the Americas, thanks largely to Ezra Pound. Often confined to a seasonal image from nature, it could also reflect upon love.

E. *European Romantic Poetry.* In Eur. romanticism, when a merging of ideal and real was supported by philosophical views of the aesthetic in figures such as Immanuel Kant, Friedrich Schiller, S. T. Coleridge, and G.W.F. Hegel, the poetry of erotic love flourished. Through the work of the imagination, feeling joined intellect as it engaged the reader with new, more "organic" (as opposed to "mechanical" and fixed) poetic form. Shakespeare, with his manifold sensibility and playful use of lang. and verse, was particularly admired. Nineteenth-c. figures such as William Wordsworth joined love with nature—and poetry with more colloquial diction. In a turn to more democratic themes, folk motifs arose. The *ballad soon finds a central place, as does the *ode, though *blank verse is often cultivated as a means to organic form. In the work of John Keats and Coleridge, the poet addresses a female beloved, though Lord Byron's poetry evokes both homosexual and heterosexual themes. Women began writing in greater number than before, and poets such as Christina Rossetti and Elizabeth Barrett Browning effectively transformed traditional forms and personae for their own purposes.

In Ger. poetry, J. W. Goethe turns to the ballad to evoke the folkloric past, as he also experiments with a number of other Eur. verse forms and the Persian ghazal. He writes *Roman Elegies* to describe a sexual awakening. At times addressing love songs to women as a source of creativity and pleasure, at others he explores homosexual themes. Schiller, in his idealizing mode, praises his beloved Laura, evoking the Petrarchan past.

In Fr. lit., the works of Jean-Jacques Rousseau sometimes inspired utopian versions of love based in marriage and virtue. But Fr. romantic poets were better known for their descriptions of the agony of love, a theme well described in Praz's book on the topic. Charles Baudelaire, with his impersonal persona and visions of sexuality and urban love, guided the love lyric toward a new realism invoking lesbians, prostitutes, and cadavers, all the while sculpting verses in traditional fixed verse forms. Arthur Rimbaud and Paul Verlaine would follow.

F. *Modern Love Poetries*. Love poetry has grown only more popular since the mid-19th c. Web sites as well as printed anthols. allow us to read lyrics from around the world and over the centuries. Poets continue to explore the genre, regularly registering its importance in the very titles of their works, as Hancock notes: Adrienne Rich ("Twenty-One Love Poems"), Anne Sexton (*Love Poems*), Pablo Neruda (*Twenty Love Poems and a Song of Despair*), Anna Akhmatova (*Forty-Seven Love Poems*), W. C. Williams (*Journey to Love*), Yehuda Amichai (*Love Poems*), Robert Graves (*Poems about Love*).

Vigorous in its production, the genre has again changed. Many poets of the 20th and 21st cs. welcome a greater openness to sexuality, while constructing a more particularized, seemingly "personal" articulation of amatory experience. Many also write with keener attention to historical, ling., and cultural situation.

More than at any time since the cl. period, the love poem embraces a new sexual frankness. Since the late 19th c., there has been an increasing inclusion of gay and lesbian poetries, as well as a less inhibited rendition of sensual love. This is clear enough in the anglophone trad. Walt Whitman, for instance, engages multitudes in his single "I," at times suggesting loves homosexual and heterosexual. Emily Dickinson brings a powerful female perspective to the erotic, Amy Lowell describes an ongoing lesbian relationship, and H.D. employs mythic figures to depict her love. W. H. Auden keeps gender uncertain in his poems.

If various renditions of earthly love have been welcome in Eur. and North Am. cultures, they have not been absent elsewhere. Latin Am. love poetry has long embraced a warmly sensual experience of love—not only in the lyrics of Pablo Neruda, often considered the greatest love poet of the 20th c., but in those of many others as well. Gabriela Mistral, Carlos Drummond de Andrade, Octavio Paz, and younger poets such as Roberto Sosa and Coral Bracho have transformed the mod. love lyric through memory and reflection on the moment. Mod. Indian love poetry, known best through the writing of Rabindranath Tagore, imagines love in more than 20 Indian langs., often in productive exchange with Eur. and Am. styles. African poets, building on an ancient trad. of sensual love, popular song, and strong female voices, write texts in a wide variety of langs. and postcolonial contexts. From Léopold Sédar Senghor and Christopher Okigbo to Ifi Amadiume, poets join powerful imagery from Af. cultures to distinctive reflections on love. In contemp. Ar. and Persian poetry, love continues to thrive. Adūnis, writing in Ar., is one of the world's best-known poets. The astonishing poet Furūgh Farrukhzād had a transformative effect on Persian poetry, treating themes of love from a female perspective in an innovative and sometimes explicit manner. In China, love lyrics come to us from an array of male and female poets. The 19th-c. poet Wu Tsao included descriptions of lesbian love and sexual explicitness that shocked but prepared the way for later poets. Similarly, it was a woman who most transformed Japanese love poetry of the 20th c. Yosano Akiko's collection *Midaregami* changed conventional views of women's sexuality as it opened new veins of love poetry to men as well as women poets in the 20th c. Mod. Heb. showed renewed interest in secular love poetry in the 20th c., most famously in the work of Yehuda Amichai, but in later poets as well.

Exploring more earthly passions, mod. poetry also constructs more earthly, particularized descriptions—and with them a new imagination of love. No longer a vague desire for erotic fusion, love in contemp. poetry often prefers a cherishing of self and other over a longer term. Here, individual memory rather than fixed themes lends the poem depth and coherence.

Memory may invoke an image that illuminates an aspect of love, as happens, for instance, through the rural metaphors in Seamus Heaney's love lyrics addressed to his wife. But memory also inheres in poetic form and lang. The poet's very choice of such a form—Neruda's sonnets or Adrienne Rich's ghazals—elicits a conversation with poets and readers over time and space.

Other memories inhere in the lang. in which a poet writes. Lang. can evoke a postcolonial experience, or socioeconomic context, or nostalgia for a past, or an address to a particular audience. Available on the Web as well as in print form, contemp. love poetry in many cultures often turns to music for full expression, reminding us of its beginnings in the Egyptian love song. Thanks to the creativity of poets in different cultural sites, writing in varied langs. and drawing on a complex but increasingly accessible hist. of themes and conventions, fresh and exciting love poetry awaits the reader today.

Anthologies and Primary Texts: *A Choice of Flowers: Chaguo la Maua; An Anthology of Swahili Love Poetry,* trans. J. Knappert (1972); *A Book of Love Poetry,* ed. J. Stallworthy (1973); *Love Songs of the New Kingdom,* trans. J. L. Foster (1974—ancient Egypt); *Sanskrit Love Poetry,* trans. W. Merwin and J. Moussaieff Masson (1977); *An Anthology of Modern Persian Poetry,* trans. A. Karini-Hakkak (1978); *The Penguin Book of Hebrew Verse,* ed. T. Carmi (1981); *Chinese Love Poetry,* trans. A Birrell (1982); *Love Poems by Women,* ed. W. Mulford (1990); *The Song of Songs,* trans. M. Falk (1990); *Greek Lyric Poetry,* trans. M. West (1993); *The Arc of Love,* ed. C. Coss (1996)—lesbian love poetry; *The Erotic Spirit,* ed. S. Hamill (1996); *Gay Love Poetry,* ed. N. Powell (1997); *What Sappho Would Have Said,* ed. E. Donoghue (1997); *Love Speaks Its Name,* ed. J. D. McClatchy (2001)—gay and lesbian love poetry; *Music of a Distant Drum,* trans. B. Lewis (2001)—Ar., Persian, Turkish, Heb.; *The Anchor Book of Chinese Poetry,* ed. T. Barnstone and C. Ping (2005); *Indian Love Poems,* ed. M. Alexander (2005); *Shambhala Anthology of Chinese Poetry,* ed. and trans. J. P. Seaton (2006); *Bending the Bow,* ed. F. M. Chipasula (2009)—African love poetry; *Islamic Mystical Poetry,* ed. and trans. M. Jamal (2009); *The Oxford Book of Latin American Poetry,* ed. C. Vicuña and E. Livón-Grosman (2009); *Love Haiku,* ed. and trans. P. Donegan and Y. Ishibashi (2010).

■ **Criticism and History:** Lewis; W. K. Wimsatt and M. C. Beardsley, "The Intentional Fallacy," *The Verbal Icon* (1954); M. Valency, *In Praise of Love* (1958)—Ren. love lyric; H. Bloom, *The Visionary Company* (1961); R. H. Brower and E. Miner, *Japanese Court Poetry* (1961); Dronke; M. Praz, *The Romantic Agony,* trans. A. Davidson (1970); J. Scott, *Love and Protest* (1972)—Chinese love lyric; R. Barthes, "The Death of the Author," *Image, Music, Text,* trans. S. Heath (1977); E. Miner, *Japanese Linked Poetry* (1979); J. Walker, "Conventions of Love Poetry in Japan and the West," *Journal of the Association of Teachers of Japanese* 14 (1979); J. Hagstrum, *Sex and Sensibility* (1980)—early mod. love; A. Perry, *Erotic Spirituality* (1980); A. Schimmel, *As Through a Veil: Mystical Poetry in Islam* (1982); D. de Rougemont, *Love in the Western World,* trans. M. Belgion, rev. ed. (1983); M. Fox, *The Song of Songs and the Ancient Egyptian Love Songs* (1985); J. Hagstrum,

The Romantic Body (1985); R. Scheindlin, *Wine, Women and Death* (1986); G. Woods, *Articulate Flesh: Male Homo-Eroticism and Modern Poetry* (1987); P. Veyne, *Roman Erotic Elegy,* trans. D. Pellauer (1988); A. R. Jones, *The Currency of Eros* (1990)—Ren. women poets; C. Paglia, *Sexual Personae* (1991); E. Selinger, *What Is It Then between Us?* (1998)—mod. Amer. love lyric; R. Greene, *Unrequited Conquests* (1999); T. Hancock, "Unworthy of a Serious Song?" *CQ* 32 (2003); and "The Chemistry of Love Poetry," *CQ* 36 (2007); C. Petievich, *When Men Speak as Women* (2007)—Islamic poetry; I. Singer, *The Nature of Love,* 3 v. (2009).

S. L. BERMANN

LYRIC (Gr. *lyra,* "lyre"). In Western *poetics, almost all poetry is now characterized as *lyric,* but this has not always been the case. Over the last three centuries, *lyric* has shifted its meaning from adjective to noun, from a quality in poetry to a category that can seem to include nearly all verse. The ancient, med., and early mod. verse we now think of as lyric was made up of a variety of *songs or short occasional poems. Since the 18th c., brevity, subjectivity, passion, and sensuality have been the qualities associated with poems called *lyric;* thus, in modernity, the term is used for a kind of poetry that expresses personal feeling (G.W.F. Hegel) in a concentrated and harmoniously arranged form (E. A. Poe, S. T. Coleridge) and that is indirectly addressed to the private reader (William Wordsworth, John Stuart Mill). A mod. invention, this idea of lyric has profoundly influenced how we understand the hist. of all poetic genres.

In the early romantic period, lit. began to be divided into three large categories, culminating in J. W. Goethe's idea of the three "natural forms of poetry": lyric, *epic, and drama. The categories were then cast as ancient distinctions, but, in fact, *lyric* was a third term added to literary description by 18th- and 19th-c. lit. crit. (Genette). This is not to say that there were no ancient or med. or early mod. or 17th- or 18th-c. lyric poems, but that these poems were not understood as *lyric* in our current sense of the term. Fowler puts the situation most succinctly when he warns that *lyric* in literary theory from Cicero through John Dryden is "not to be confused with the modern term." A persistent confusion—among verse *genres, between historical genres and natural "forms," between adjective and noun, between cognitive and affective registers, between grammar and rhet., between privacy and publicity, and among various ideas about poetry—may be the best way to define our current sense of the lyric. It is a confusion that has proven enormously generative for both poets and critics.

The etymology of *lyric* is derived from the Gr. musical instrument used to accompany the songs of poets. In the Alexandrian period, when the texts taken from Gr. songs were collected in the library, the poems once sung in *performance were grouped together and called *lyrics* (Most). Thus, *lyric* was from its inception a term used to describe a music that could no longer be heard, an idea of poetry characterized by a lost collective experience. Most of the ancient poets we refer to as the earliest lyric poets (such as Sappho, Alcaeus, Anacreon, and Pindar) would not have understood this description. Plato and Aristotle did not use the term *lyrikos* in the *Republic* and the *Poetics*; before *lyrikos* began to be used as a term for songs once sung to the lyre, the key terms were *melos* (song) and *melikos* (song-like or melodic). Johnson (1982) has argued that "one thing about the nature of poetry that moderns have steadily recognized and that ancients could not recognize is the significance, the importance, of the inner stories that personal lyric imitates." If we think of the personal lyric not as a mod. invention but rather as a kind of poetry that modernity has come to recognize even retrospectively, then the absence of terms and concepts to describe ancient lyrics did not mean that ancient lyrics did not exist; on the other hand, there is abundant evidence to suggest that the reason for the absence of lyric as an important category in ancient poetics is that our notion of subjectivity, emotion, and compression in poetry—in sum, the personal lyric—did not match ideas about poetry (or persons) in antiquity.

The notion that the lyric was an ideal poetic form that no poet had yet achieved actually proved a generative model for poetics in the 19th c. In "Thoughts on Poetry and Its Varieties" (1833), Mill proclaimed that "lyric poetry, as it was the earliest kind, is also . . . more imminently and peculiarly poetry than any other: it is the poetry most natural to a really poetic temperament, and least capable of being successfully imitated by one not so endowed by nature." Here, Mill gathers the 18th-c. attribution of original or primal expression (already evident in Trapp and in Jones's antimimetic argument about "Asiatick" lyric) into the 19th-c. idealization of the lyric as subjective representation. Yet

according to Mill, not even Wordsworth and P. B. Shelley, "the two English authors of our own day who have produced the greatest quantity of true and enduring poetry," could actually write lyric poetry that partook of both these qualities at once. While great, Mill laments that "the genius of Wordsworth is essentially unlyrical," and Shelley "is the reverse" in the sense that he had immense lyrical gifts but "had not, at the period of his deplorably early death, reached sufficiently far that intellectual progression of which he was capable." If for Hegel the ideal lyric poet would move civilization forward in his perfect self-expression, for Mill the ideal lyric poet would have to do two things no one had yet perfectly done: be the representative of both original nature and acquired culture. In "The Poet" (1844), R. W. Emerson echoed Mill's and Hegel's impossibly ideal characterizations of the lyric poet, casting that ideal as culturally democratic and Am., and lamenting that "I look in vain for the poet I describe." A young Walt Whitman was in the audience when Emerson gave his lecture in Brooklyn, and several years later claimed to be the poet of "lyric utterances" Emerson and Mill and Hegel and America had been looking for. To call the heroic poet of 19th-c. philosophy and Whitman's bravado *lyric* is to stretch the term very far indeed, but that is what happened to the definition of *lyric* in the second half of the 19th c. In the world of ideas, the lyric became "more imminently and peculiarly poetry than any other" verse genre, indeed, so much so that *lyric* and *poetry* began to be synonymous terms.

While the lyricization of all verse genres meant the creation of a lyric ideal in lit. crit., in the 19th-c. culture of mass print, *lyric* became a synonym for *poetry* in another sense by becoming a default term for short poems, a practical name for verse that did not obey the protocols of neoclassical genres such as the Pindaric ode or conform to the popular standards of ballads or hymns. While both neoclassical and popular genres persisted within the new print lyric, as Rowlinson has remarked, in the 19th c. "lyric appears as a genre newly totalized in print." In the titles of popular poetry volumes, *lyric* became the name for a generic alternative, as in *Lays and Lyrics* by Charles Gray (1841) or *Legends and Lyrics* by Adelaide Proctor (1863). These print uses of *lyric* shifted the sense of *Lyrical Ballads* (1798) or even of Alfred, Lord Tennyson's *Poems, Chiefly Lyrical* (1830) toward a simple noun that readers came to recognize.

Both the expansion of *lyric* to describe all poetry in its ideal state and the shrinking of the term to fit print conventions and popular taste irked Poe, a writer always early to sense shifts or conflicts in the hist. of ideas. Before Whitman's "lyric utterances" stretched poetry beyond form, Poe declared in "The Philosophy of Composition" (1846) that "what we term a long poem is, in fact, merely a succession of brief ones," since "a poem is such, only inasmuch as it intensely excites, by elevating, the soul; and all intense excitements are, through a psychal necessity, brief." Poe's emphasis on an affective definition of form reached back to Longinus and echoed Coleridge, but it also proved influential for later 19th-c. theories of lyricism. To define the lyric not as the perfection of subjective representation or as primal cultural expression but as momentary sensation again made the lyric a mobile concept, adaptable to various kinds of poetry.

In practice, while there were all sorts of poems labeled *lyrics* in print and many gestures toward the lyricism associated with musical performance, there were also all sorts of self-conscious departures from "the lyric" in the poetry of the second half of the 19th c.—so much so that there were few poems critics would call purely *lyric*. Tucker has suggested that Robert Browning's dramatic *monologues have become models of what we now think of as lyric, since they represent fictional speakers, but he also suggests that the dramatic monologues "began as a dramatic response to lyric isolationism." Almost as soon as an ideal of personal lyric expression emerged in the 19th c., then, it was honored more often in the exception than as a rule.

In the first decades of the 20th c., as in the previous century when *lyric* became an umbrella term for many different kinds of poetry, there was not one verse genre one could call *the modern lyric*; rather, there were various verse experiments in what later 20th-c. crit. increasingly cast as the alienation of the mod. lyric subject. Ezra Pound and T. S. Eliot, Robert Frost, W. C. Williams, and Wallace Stevens all wrote short poems we now call *lyric*, though they tended not to use that description of their work. As Eliot wrote in "The Three Voices of Poetry" (1957),

> The term "lyric" itself is unsatisfactory. We think first of verse intended to be sung . . . But we apply it also to poetry that was

never intended for a musical setting, or which we dissociate from its music . . The very definition of "lyric," in the Oxford *Dictionary*, indicates that the word cannot be satisfactorily defined: "*Lyric:* Now the name for short poems, usually divided into stanzas or strophes, and directly expressing the poet's own thoughts and sentiments."

How short does a poem have to be, to be called a "lyric"? The emphasis on brevity, and the suggestion of division into stanzas, seem residual from the association of the voice with music. But there is no necessary relation between brevity and the expression of the poet's own thoughts and feelings.

Eliot goes on to define *lyric* in Mill's terms, as "the voice of the poet talking to himself," but his impatience with older definitions signals another shift in the mod. sense of the term, from Mill's impossible ideal of lyricism to the normal condition of each individual's fractured private thoughts. That shift was influential for the mid-century "confessional" poets (see CONFESSIONAL POETRY), who might be thought of as pure lyric poets in Eliot's sense; but, again, by that point in the century, the term *lyric* had become very broad, as it began to be used to describe all first-person poetry.

If, in the first part of the 20th c., the notion of the lyric was still in flux, how did it become such a normative term by the middle of the century? In the hist. we have traced here, the idea of lyric began to do the work of a genre as early as the late 16th c., but it took 400 years before the lyric became synonymous with one poetic genre—or rather, 400 years before poetry was thought of as one lyricized genre. As the idea of genre itself changed in the 18th c., that shift advanced dramatically, but the discourses of poets and critics were not fully aligned in the 19th c., and the lyricization of poetry proceeded by fits and starts. It was only in the consolidation of 20th-c. lit. crit. that the process of lyricization was accomplished, and a broad idea of the lyric became exemplary for the reading of all poetry. That example emerged from and was reflected in the predominance of the New Criticism, which took up a model of the personal lyric close to Eliot's as the object of literary close reading. In different ways, Am. critics such as Cleanth Brooks and Robert Penn Warren in the late 1930s, W. K. Wimsatt and M. C. Beardsley in the 1940s, and Reuben Brower in the

1950s assumed Eliot's definition of the personal lyric and used I. A. Richards's focus on individual poems in his "practical criticism" to forge a model of all poems as essentially lyric. That model was primarily pedagogical, but it became a way of reading that, in turn, influenced the way poems were written, and it remains the normative model for the production and reception of most poetry. Perhaps the most influential contemp. representative of this influential way of reading is Helen Vendler, who strongly advocates a definition of lyric as the personal expression of a fictional speaker, as "the genre that directs its *mimesis* toward the performance of the mind in solitary speech" (1997). Vendler believes that this "solitary" model of the lyric should be used to read all poetic genres at all moments in hist.

That model, while still assumed in much teaching of poetry, has since given way to post-structuralist critiques of lyric reading such as that of Paul de Man (like Vendler, a student of Brower, the New Critic who coined the phrase *close reading*), and to postmodernism and avant-garde poetics. When de Man wrote in "Anthropomorphism and Trope" in the late 20th c. that "the lyric is not a genre, but one name among several to designate the defensive motion of the understanding, the possibility of a future hermeneutics," he raised the question of how the lyric had become a matter of interpretation, a way of reading. The hist. of the lyric is the hist. of the ways an idea has become a genre and the ways in which that genre has been manipulated by poets and critics alike. As in earlier centuries, the late 20th-c. reaction to the elevation of the lyric as a mode of professional reading (what Poovey has called "the lyricization of literary criticism") became a reaction-formation for and against a version of the lyric that could exist only in theory. In the 21st c., that purely theoretical sense of all postromantic personal poems as consistently lyric has prompted a critical and poetic turn away from a version of lit. hist. now retrospectively cast as consistent. In his intro. to the *Ubuweb Anthology of Conceptual Writing* (http://www.ubu.com/concept/), e.g., the poet and critic Craig Dworkin begins,

> Poetry expresses the emotional truth of the self. A craft honed by especially sensitive individuals, it puts metaphor and image in the service of song.
> Or at least that's the story we've inherited from Romanticism, handed down

for over 200 years in a caricatured and mummified ethos—and as if it still made sense after two centuries of radical social change. . . . But what would a non-expressive poetry look like?

As we have seen, the story of the lyric has hardly been "caricatured and mummified" during its long hist., nor has the hist. of the lyric precluded many "non-expressive" elements in poetry—not even, or perhaps not esp., for the last 200 years. Instead, the story of the lyric charts the hist. of poetics. The lesson of that hist. is that *lyric* has not always named the same thing, but neither has one kind of poem simply changed its name many times over the course of the many centuries the term has been in use. As of this writing, there is still an active debate in lit. crit. over the definition of the lyric. Culler has recently suggested that we try to "prevent a certain narrowing of conception of the lyric and a tendency, understandable given the realities of literary education today, to treat lyric on the model of narrative, so that the dramatic monologue becomes the model of all lyric." Instead, he urges that we retain a transhistorical definition of the lyric because "thinking of lyric as transnational and broadly historical opens up critical possibilities," particularly the possibility of comparative lit. crit. Both Dworkin and Culler tell only partial accounts of lyric as a concept. A sense of either "a caricatured and mummified ethos" or of historical and cultural continuity will not render the intricate turns in the hist. of the lyric or of ideas associated with lyric. When that hist. becomes visible behind or beneath critical and poetic fictions, it testifies to the tremendous malleability of the term, to the ways in which the lyric persists as an idea of poetry fixed at points by lit. hist., often frozen by lit. crit., but as subject to change as the definition of poetry itself.

See POEM, POETRY.

■ S. T. Coleridge, *Biographia Literaria* (1817); G. Saintsbury, *Seventeenth-Century Lyrics* (1892); K. Burke, "On Musicality in Verse," *The Philosophy of Literary Form* (1941); Brooks; Abrams, "The Lyric as Poetic Norm"; Frye; C. Guillén, *Literature as System* (1971); M. Foucault, *The Archaeology of Knowledge* [1969], trans. A. M. Sheridan Smith (1972); H. Gardner, *The Metaphysical Poets* (1972); W. Benjamin, *Charles Baudelaire*, trans. H. Zohn (1973); H. Friedrich, *The Structure of Modern Poetry*, trans. J. Neugroschel (1974);

A. Welsh, *Roots of Lyric* (1978); S. Cameron, *Lyric Time: Dickinson and the Limits of Genre* (1979); J. Culler, "Apostrophe," *The Pursuit of Signs* (1981); A. Fowler, *Kinds of Literature* (1982); D. A. Campbell, *Greek Lyric, Volume I: Sappho and Alcaeus* (1982); W. R. Johnson, *The Idea of Lyric* (1982); G. Most, "Greek Lyric Poets," *Ancient Writers: Greece and Rome* (1982); P. de Man, *The Rhetoric of Romanticism* (1984); Hollander; *Lyric Poetry: Beyond New Criticism*, ed. C. Hošek and P. Parker (1985)—esp. H. Tucker, "Dramatic Monologue and the Overhearing of Lyric," and J. Culler, "Changes in the Study of the Lyric"; J. Fineman, *Shakespeare's Perjured Eye* (1986); J. Culler, "The Modern Lyric: Generic Continuity and Critical Practice," *Comparative Perspective on Literature*, ed. C. Koelb and S. Noakes (1988); C. Siskin, *The Historicity of Romantic Discourse* (1988); R. Greene, *Post-Petrarchism* (1991)—esp. the intro.; G. Genette, *The Architext*, trans. J. E. Lewin (1992); A. Grossman, "Summa Lyrica," *The Sighted Singer* (1992); P. Zumthor, *Toward a Medieval Poetics*, trans. P. Bennett (1992); C. Siskin, "The Lyric Mix: Romanticism, Genre, and the Fate of Literature," *Wordsworth Circle* 25 (1994); A. Marotti, *Manuscript, Print, and the English Renaissance Lyric* (1995); M. Perloff, *Wittgenstein's Ladder: Poetic Language and the Strangeness of the Ordinary* (1996); H. Vendler, *The Art of Shakespeare's Sonnets* (1997); R. Greene, "The Lyric," *CHLC* v. 3, ed. G. P. Norton (1999); Y. Prins, *Victorian Sap-pho* (1999); "The System of Genres in Troubadour Lyric," *Medieval Lyric*, ed. W. D. Paden (2000); M. Poovey, "The Model System of Contemporary Literary Criticism," *CritI* 27 (2001); M. Rowlinson, "Lyric," *A Companion to Victorian Poetry*, ed. R. Cronin, A. Chapman, H. A. Harrison (2002); S. Stewart, *Poetry and the Fate of the Senses* (2002); H. Vendler, *Poets Thinking: Pope, Whitman, Dickinson, Yeats* (2004); V. Jackson, *Dickinson's Misery: A Theory of Lyric Reading* (2005); H. Vendler, *Invisible Listeners: Lyric Intimacy in Herbert, Whitman, and Ashbery* (2005); M. Blasing, *Lyric Poetry* (2007); J. Culler, "Why Lyric?" *PMLA* 123 (2008); H. Dubrow, *The Challenges of Orpheus* (2008); R. von Hallberg, *Lyric Powers* (2008); R. Terada, "After the Critique of Lyric," *PMLA* 123 (2008); F. Budelmann, "Introducing Greek Lyric," *Cambridge Companion to Greek Lyric* (2009); M. Lowrie, "Lyric," *Oxford Encyclopedia of Ancient Greece and Rome*, ed. M. Gargarin and E. Fantham (2010); J. Culler, "Genre: Lyric," *Genre: Collected Essays from the English Institute*, ed. R. Warhol (2011).

V. JACKSON

LYRIC SEQUENCE. A collocation of lyrics, the lyric sequence is generally thought to have gained its vernacular identity in the Ren. and after from Petrarch (1304–74), who wrote and arranged his sequence called *Rime sparse* (Scattered Rhymes) or, alternatively, *Canzoniere* (Songbook) over 40 years. Both titles ironically point away from the rigorous ordering of Petrarch's 366 amatory and devotional lyrics, which manifests several patterns at once (formal, fictional, calendrical) to establish a continuum—or discontinuum, considering the newfound structural importance of the white space between the lyrics—that greatly exceeds the unities of earlier lyric collections. Petrarch's diverse models included the book of Psalms; the lyric volumes of Catullus, Propertius, and other Augustan poets; Dante's prosimetric *Vita nuova* (ca. 1292–93) and his short sequence *Rime petrose* (ca. 1296); and the 13th-c. chansonniers of the Occitan troubadours.

For two centuries after Petrarch's death, the possibilities opened by the lyric sequence—to write lyric *in extenso*, allowing each poetic integer to hold its autonomy as it participates in a larger unity—attracted the efforts of poets in all the countries of Europe; Wilkins lists most of these, an astonishing array. The lyric sequence effectively became to *lyric what tragedy was to drama or what the novel would be to narrative—not merely a "form" but a complex of generic capacities. Some particularly interesting lyric sequences are written at the margins or in the hiatuses of the convention: the 24-*sonnet sequence (1555) by the Fr. poet Louise Labé dissents from the sexual politics of Petrarchism; the Italians Giovanni Salvatorino and Girolamo Malipiero, believing Petrarch's speaker insufficiently Christian, adapt the forms and much of the lang. of the *Rime sparse* to purely devotional experience in their respective works *Thesoro de sacra scrittura* (ca. 1540) and *Il Petrarca spirituale* (1536); and, near the end of the century, after most Eur. cultures had temporarily exhausted the sequence, a generation of Eng. sonneteers between Thomas Watson's *Hekatompathia* (1582) and Michael Drayton's *Idea* (1600) undertook a frenzy of experimentation, refinement, and superstitious imitation of Petrarch (see SONNET). While a number of poets essentially non-Petrarchan in topics and ideology are attracted by the lyric sequence (e.g., George Gascoigne, the first to use the term *sequence* in Eng., in *Alexander Nevile* [1575], and Ben Jonson in *The Forest* [1616]), nearly every sequence in this period interprets some aspect of Petrarch's rich achievement. Even such monuments of their vernaculars as Pierre de Ronsard's *Sonnets pour Hélène* (1578, enl. 1584), Luís de Camões's *Rimas* (pub. posthumously 1595, though written as early as the 1540s), and Shakespeare's sonnets (ca. 1593–99, pub. 1609) are, in the first analysis, responses to the *Rime sparse* as a compendium of organizational strategies—formal, characterological, devotional, political, speculative.

The principal trend in the 17th-c. lyric sequence develops its religious dimensions. Virtuoso events include Jean de La Ceppède's *Théorèmes* (1613, 1622), George Herbert's *The Temple* (1633), and John Donne's *Holy Sonnets*, incl. "La Corona," a seven-unit crown of sonnets (1633). The first major North Am. lyric sequence, Edward Taylor's *Preparatory Meditations* (written 1682–1725), arrives near the end of this line. The 18th and 19th cs., perhaps because of an attenuation of the formal resources of Petrarchism, perhaps from ineluctable shifts in Eur. poetics and ideologies, produce little of compelling interest in the form of the lyric sequence itself (though much important poetry within the form). The romantics composed numerous lyric sequences, but the unities of these works are generally looser than those of earlier specimens; one notices the tendency, as in Novalis and William Wordsworth, e.g., to announce a lyric sequence to be, in effect, a single poem, thus affirming the idea of its unity but waiving the actual tensions generated between strong integers and an equally strong unifying structure.

The most successful 19th-c. Eur. and Am. lyric sequences tend to be like Alfred, Lord Tennyson's *In Memoriam* (1850) in that they do not imitate Petrarch's outward forms and gestures but find contemp. analogues for his inventions—which perhaps inevitably means discarding the sonnet in favor of other constituents. Noteworthy and influential examples include Charles Baudelaire's *Petits poèmes en prose* (1869) and the hand-sewn fascicles of Emily Dickinson. While in earlier eds., Dickinson's lyrics were often arranged as suited the editor's fancy (i.e., in thematic groupings), work by scholars such as R. W. Franklin, Susan Howe, and Virginia Jackson has shed light on the sequential nature of Dickinson's poems and

considered the relationships among poem, fascicle page, bound fascicle, and poetic oeuvre. Walt Whitman's *Leaves of Grass* (1855 et seq.) is the most visionary of 19th-c. lyric sequences; his influence on the lyric sequence is virtually that of a New World Petrarch and has led to an extraordinary abundance of works in the mod. period, esp. in the U.S. and in Latin America. Whitman's legacy is particularly legible in Juan Ramón Jiménez's *Diario de un poeta reciéncasado* (1916), Pablo Neruda's *Veinte poemas de amor y una canción desesperada* (1924), Hart Crane's *The Bridge* (1930), Federico García Lorca's *Poeta en Nueva York* (1930), Wallace Stevens's "Notes toward a Supreme Fiction" (1942), and Frank O'Hara's *Lunch Poems* (1964), among others.

Modernist upheavals included a reinvestment in the long poem, creating certain challenges in attempting to distinguish between long poem and lyric sequence, but the term *lyric sequence* is most accurately applied to works that maintain a sense of tension between the unity or interrelation of the whole and the independent workings of each part. The term is particularly apt when individual integers in a sequence demonstrate some level of engagement with the lyric, be this understood as subject position, level of musicality, or aim toward brevity. Some, like Conte, have insisted on a further division between the lyric sequence and the postmod. poetic series, claiming for "serial form" a deliberate absence of the arc, progress, or devel. they deem necessary for a lyric sequence and citing projects like Robert Duncan's *Passages* (1968–87) or Robert Creeley's *Pieces* (1968) as examples. Others, like Rosenthal and Gall, speak of "poetic sequence" rather than lyric sequence and include modernist epics such as Ezra Pound's *Cantos* and W. C. Williams's *Paterson* in this category.

Mod. and contemp. poets have invented a wide range of means of sustaining continuity throughout a sequence. Pablo Neruda's *Veinte poemas* explores *persona through the use of direct address and the creation of a distinct poetic voice, while John Berryman's *77 Dream Songs* (1964) are held together by the character Henry, who both is and is not Berryman himself. O'Hara's *Lunch Poems* benefits from the conceit of the poems' spontaneous composition during his daily lunch breaks and his walks through Manhattan. The unity of Eugenio Montale's *Ossi di Seppia* (1925) derives from Montale's deep engagement with the Ligurian landscape, and that of Francis Ponge's

Le parti pris des choses (1942) from sustained attention to commonplace objects. In *The Sonnets* (1964), Ted Berrigan breathes new life into the trad. of the sonnet sequence by combining surrealist techniques such as collage and aleatory procedures with epistolary address and fragmented narrative. Rosmarie Waldrop's *prose-poem sequence *The Reproduction of Profiles* (1987) derives unity from the syntactic patterning of Waldrop's intertextual engagement with Ludwig Wittgenstein, while the skillful use of repetition, the autobiographical tone, and the formal constraint of a set number of poems with a set number of sentences make Lyn Hejinian's *My Life* (1980–87) an exemplary postmod. lyric sequence.

■ E. H. Wilkins, "A General Survey of Renaissance Petrarchism," *Studies in the Life and Works of Petrarch* (1955); C. T. Neely, "The Structure of Renaissance Sonnet Sequences," *ELH* 45 (1977)—limited to Eng.; *Arethusa* 13 (1980)—five essays and bibl. on the Augustan volumes; M. L. Rosenthal and S. M. Gall, *The Modern Poetic Sequence* (1983); H. Vendler, *The Odes of John Keats* (1983)—the odes as a lyric sequence; N. Fraistat, *The Poem and the Book* (1985); *Poems in Their Place*, ed. N. Fraistat (1986)—on Eng. romantic collections; J. Freccero, "The Fig Tree and the Laurel," *Literary Theory/Renaissance Texts*, ed. P. Parker and D. Quint (1986); Hollier; T. P. Roche Jr., *Petrarch and the English Sonnet Sequences* (1989)—esp. on the religious elements of the early mod. sequence; J. M. Conte, *Unending Design: The Forms of Postmodern Poetry* (1991); R. Greene, *Post-Petrarchism* (1991); V. Jackson, *Dickinson's Misery: A Theory of Lyric Reading* (2005).

R. Greene; B. Tate

MADRIGAL. A name given to an It. poetic and musical form in the 14th c. and to a different form in the 16th c. and later. The early madrigal, of which Petrarch's "Nova angeletta" (*Canzoniere* 106) is an example, consisted typically of two or three three-line stanzas with no set rhyme scheme followed by a couplet or *ritornello*. The lines often comprised eleven syllables, sometimes seven. Musical settings used two or three voices, the lower of which may have been performed on an instrument. The same music was repeated for the stanzas, with different music for the ritornello.

In the 16th c., the musical madrigal used various kinds of poetic forms—the *canzone*, the *ballata*, the *sonnet—as well as the madrigal proper, which had become a very free monostrophic verse form of about a dozen seven- and eleven-syllable lines with no fixed order or rhyme scheme, although they usually ended in a *couplet. The musical settings varied considerably but usually consisted of three to six voices in a mixture of polyphonic and homophonic textures. Many 16th-c. musical madrigals, notably those by Luca Marenzio, made a point of illustrating the sense or emotion of the text by means of musical conventions, so each phrase of the text was set to its own music. The subjects tended to be pastoral and amatory. Many of these texts are anonymous, but madrigal verses by Giovanni Battista Guarini, Pietro Bembo, Antonio Alamanni, and Jacopo Sannazaro were set, as well as sonnets from Petrarch and stanzas from the narrative poems of Ludovico Ariosto and Torquato Tasso.

This later style of madrigal influenced the Sp. *villancico* and was adopted by composers in Germany, Poland, Denmark, and the Netherlands. Italianate madrigals flourished esp. in England. Although madrigals were imported as early as the 1530s, the Eng. seem not to have begun composing their own until after the publication in 1588 of *Musica Transalpina*, an anthol. of It. music with words in Eng. trans. The It. models made feminine rhyme a consistent feature of these trans. The earliest Eng. poem called a madrigal appears in book 3 of Philip Sidney's *Old Arcadia* (written ca. 1577–80), a 15-line poem of mixed six- and ten-syllable lines with masculine rhymes. Some later Eng. writers such as Barnabe Barnes use the term *madrigal* loosely to designate lyrics in various forms (see *Englands Helicon*, 1600). Eng. madrigal composers set verses in many forms, some of which did resemble the It. madrigal.

By the middle of the 17th c., the musical madrigal was dead in England and, in Italy, had been transformed by Caccini, Monteverdi, and others into *concertato*-style pieces with instrumental continuo that would rapidly evolve into the baroque aria. But amateur singers in England revived some madrigals as early as the mid-18th c. They have been performed ever since.

■ K. Vossler, *Das deutsche Madrigal* (1898); *The English Madrigalists*, ed. E. H. Fellowes, rev. ed. (1956–76); E. H. Fellowes, *English Madrigal Composers*, 2d ed. (1948); A. Einstein, *The Italian Madrigal*, 3 v. (1949); A. Obertello, *Madrigali Italiani in Inghilterra* (1949); N. Pirrotta et al., "Madrigal," *MGG*; J. Kerman, *The Elizabethan Madrigal* (1962); *English Madrigal Verse*, ed. E. H. Fellowes, F. W. Sternfeld, D. Greer, 3d ed. (1967); B. Pattison, *Music and Poetry of the English Renaissance*, 2d ed. (1970); J. Roche, *The Madrigal* (1972); Wilkins; P. Ledger, *The Oxford Book of English Madrigals* (1978); A. Newcomb, *The Madrigal at Ferrara, 1579–1597*, 2 v. (1980); K. von Fischer et al., "Madrigal," *New Grove*; J. Chater, *Luca Marenzio and the Italian Madrigal*, 2 v. (1981); E. Doughtie, *English Renaissance Song* (1986); J. Haar, *Essays on Italian Poetry and Music in the Renaissance* (1986); W. Maynard, *Elizabethan Lyric Poetry and Its Music* (1986); I. Fenlon and J. Haar, *The Italian Madrigal in the Early Sixteenth Century* (1988); M. Feldman, *City Culture and the Madrigal at Venice* (1995); P. F. Cutter, "The Renaissance Madrigal: An Overview," *Recapturing the Renaissance*, ed. D. S. Wood and P. A. Miller (1995).

E. Doughtie

MASCULINE AND FEMININE. The terms *masculine* and *feminine* have to do with how prosodic units end: a masculine ending has an accented syllable at the end, while a feminine ending has an unaccented syllable at the end. The distinction is applied to how lines end, as

189

well as to rhymes and *caesuras. The rhyme between *fount* and *mount*, e.g., is said to be masculine, that between *fountain* and *mountain* feminine.

With ordinary feminine rhyme, the accented rhyming syllable is followed by an undifferentiated unaccented syllable, so that the rhyme in both cases is between *fount* and *mount*, with the unaccented -*ain* syllable being the same in both words. In some cases, the additional syllable is some sort of functional suffix, as with *walking/talking* and *truly/duly*.

Confusingly, the feminine rhyme is sometimes called *double*, even though the actual rhyme remains an affair of single accented syllables. An authentic double rhyme, such as that between *childhood* and *wildwood*, must now be called *compound*. That sort of rhyme seems to be feminine also, except that the less-accented syllables are differentiated. Use of *double* for *feminine* does facilitate the extension of terminology to triple (*medicate/dedicate*), quadruple (*medicated/dedicated*), quintuple (*medicatedly/dedicatedly*), and so forth.

Since most Eng. verse is *iambic, most Eng. verse lines, whether rhymed or not, end with an accented syllable. Lines that happen to end with an unaccented syllable are said to have a feminine ending, but the point is hardly worth making unless such endings occur in unusual abundance, as in Hamlet's soliloquy:

To be or not to be—that is the question:
Whether 'tis nobler in the mind to suffer
The slings and arrows of outrageous
    fortune,
Or to take arms against a sea of troubles
And, by opposing, end them. To die, to
    sleep. . . .

Some have suggested that the feminine ending is less definite, resolute, decisive, or forcible, and some likewise account for the term *feminine* on the basis of an attribution of certain qualities to women; but all that is entirely subjective, impressionistic, and conditional. With Hamlet's meditation, however, the unusual number of successive feminine endings may contribute to a slower pace and more deliberate movement.

Because of the so-called *e* feminine in older Fr. and in ME, many lines in Chaucer end with an unaccented syllable, which later became mute:

As lene was his hors as is a rake,
And he nas nat right fat, I undertake. . . .

For Chaucer, that rhyme is feminine; for us, masculine.

The commonest sort of feminine rhyme places an unaccented syllable after an accented rhyming syllable, as in *headed/breaded*. In an uncommon sort, the second syllable is undifferentiated but does carry a level of secondary stress, as with *headline/breadline*.

The distinction between masculine and feminine also applies to a midline pause or caesura. The masculine caesura falls after an accented syllable:

Let Rome in Tiber melt, || and the wide
    arch
Of the ranged empire fall. || Here is my
    space.
Kingdoms are clay; || our dungy earth alike
Feeds beast as man; || the nobleness of life
Is to do thus; || when such a mutual pair
And such a twain can do't.
                    (*Antony and Cleopatra* 1.1.34)

The barge she sat in, || like a burnished
    throne,
Burned on the water: || the poop was
    beaten gold. . . .
                              (*Ant.* 2.2.200)

Although much depends on a subjective response to a variable performance, the former may seem more definite and resolute, the latter indefinite and irresolute, with the possibility of a "dying fall."

Frequently in rhymed verse, a feminine rhyme will appear in an environment of mostly masculine rhymes, which are much commoner in Eng. There are very few poems that employ nothing but multiple rhymes, and all of them are humorous in one way or another. (Some suggest that the feminine rhyme is inherently paradoxical, since rhyme is defined by how a syllable ends; something after the end may seem contradictory.) Thomas Hardy's "A Refusal," on the denial of a memorial place in Westminster Abbey to Lord Byron, has no masculine rhymes. A few, such as "charity"/"clarity," are triple, but most are feminine in a variety of types. Many are ordinary ("dinner"/"sinner"); some involve mosaic rhyme, in which one word rhymes with two ("stonework"/"own work"). A few are of the compound variety ("name mere"/"fame here").

Many poems place masculine and feminine endings in a recurrent pattern. The commonest pattern alternates feminine and masculine, as in A. E. Housman's "Epitaph on an Army of Mercenaries":

> These, in the day when heaven was falling,
> The hour when Earth's foundations fled,
> Followed their mercenary calling
> And took their wages and are dead.

Alternation of masculine and feminine is rarer and may be associated with comic syncopation:

> Yankee Doodle went to town
> A-riding on a pony
> Stuck a feather in his hat
> And called it macaroni.
>
> Yankee Doodle keep it up
> Yankee Doodle dandy
> Mind the music and the step
> And with the girls be handy.

G. M. Hopkins's It. *sonnet "The Windhover," with a rhyme scheme of *abbaabba cdcdcd*, uses masculine rhymes in the *a* and *c* positions, feminine in the *b* and *d*. In a small bonus, the accented syllable in the *a* rhyme ("wing," "thing," and so forth) is echoed by the unaccented syllable in the *b* ("riding"/"hiding"). A similar effect may be heard in "Epitaph on an Army of Mercenaries," where the masculine rhymes in the first stanza ("fled"/"dead") are echoed by the feminine rhymes in the second ("suspended"/"defended").

■ G. Saintsbury, *Historical Manual of English Prosody* (1919); P. W. Timberlake, *The Feminine Ending in English Blank Verse* (1931); F. Manning Smith, "Mrs. Browning's Rhymes," *PMLA* 54 (1939); Saintsbury, *Prosody*; P. Fussell, *Poetic Meter and Poetic Form*, rev. ed. (1979); W. Harmon, "Rhyme in English Verse: History, Structures, Functions," *SP* 84 (1987); P. Hobsbaum, *Metre, Rhythm and Verse Form* (1996); W. Harmon, "English Versification: Fifteen Hundred Years of Continuity and Change," *SP* 94 (1997); J. Hollander, *Rhyme's Reason* (2001).

W. HARMON

METAPHOR (Gr., "transference").

I. Critical Views
II. History
III. Recent Views
IV. Current Debates
V. Summary

A trope, or figurative expression, in which a word or phrase is shifted from its normal uses to a context where it evokes new meanings. When the ordinary meaning of a word is at odds with the context, we tend to seek relevant features of the word and the situation that will reveal the intended meaning. If there is a conceptual or material connection between the word and what it denotes—e.g., using cause for effect ("I read Shakespeare," meaning his works) or part for whole ("give me a hand," meaning physical help)—the figure usually has another name (in these examples, *metonymy and *synecdoche, respectively). To understand metaphors, one must find meanings not predetermined by lang., logic, or experience. In the terminology of traditional rhet., these figures are "tropes of a word," appearing in a literal context; in "tropes of a sentence," the entire context is figurative, as in allegory, fable, and (according to some) *irony.

Following Richards, we can call a word or phrase that seems anomalous the "vehicle" of the trope and refer to the underlying idea that it seems to designate as the "tenor." An extended metaphor, as the name implies, is one that the poet develops in some detail. A *conceit is an intricate, intellectual, or far-fetched metaphor; a diminishing metaphor, one of its types, uses a pejorative vehicle with reference to an esteemed tenor. An extreme or exaggerated conceit is a *catachresis. Mixed metaphor, traditionally derided because it jumbles disparate vehicles together, has recently found some critical acceptance. Dead metaphor presents fossilized metaphors in ordinary usage (e.g., "he *missed* the *point*").

What Quintilian said of tropes remains true today: "This is a subject which has given rise to interminable disputes among the teachers of literature, who have quarreled no less violently with the philosophers than among themselves over the problem of the genera and species into which tropes may be divided, their number and their correct classification." To say that metaphor is any trope that cannot be classified as metonymy, *hyperbole, etc., is to provide only a negative definition. Any attempt to define metaphor positively—e.g., "the application of a word or phrase to something it does not literally denote, on the basis of a similarity between the objects or ideas involved"—will inevitably apply to other tropes.

Some critics accept this consequence and call all tropes metaphors. But even this definition begs the question of how to distinguish the figurative from the literal or at best relegates it to accepted usage. If two species are members of the same genus on the basis of similarity, are they not "like" the genus and, therefore, like each other? Extension of this argument leads to the conclusion that all figures should be understood literally. On the other hand, every object is unique: "it is only the roughness of the eye that makes any two persons, things, situations seem alike" (Walter Pater). Perfect literalness might be achieved by giving each object a unique name. In relation to that standard, a common noun is a metaphor because it provides a name that can be applied to different entities on the basis of a likeness between them. Hence, "literal" lang. can be considered metaphorical. Some argue that metaphor can result from grammar alone, without change of word meaning (see *Grammatical Metaphor* in biblio.). For advocates of conceptual metaphor theory, metaphors are representations of mental processes that are not revealed by ling. analysis. Others claim that metaphor is neither a ling. nor a cognitive issue but one based on the intentions of people using lang. for practical purposes. Concise treatment of the burgeoning field must exclude dozens of theories; Rolf and Leezenberg treat many that are not discussed below.

Despite these arguments and attempts to create a more satisfactory classification of figures, the definitions of the major tropes have remained unchanged since the cl. period. The most innovative attempts to clarify the status of metaphor have come from philosophers, linguists, and historians, who have explored metaphor's relation to propositional truth and meaning, to the origins of lang. and myth, to worldviews, scientific models, social attitudes, and ordinary usage. For their purposes, conventional and dead metaphors provide adequate examples for analysis. Scholars and literary critics, less concerned with theory than with practice, have usually accepted the imprecise accounts of metaphor handed down by trad. and focused their attention on its effects in particular poems. To say this is not to claim that the uses of metaphor in poetry are categorically different from those in other domains of lang. use but simply to call attention to the institutionalized character of poetry. The expectations in place when one starts reading a poem differ from those active in reading a newspaper or in conversing.

Emphasis in this discussion will be on poetics and the disciplines historically associated with that topic: rhet., philosophy, and lings. Discussion of metaphor has come full circle, reviving issues forgotten for centuries, while creating possibilities for further devels. A summary of what critics have usually said about metaphor, with some account of objections to traditional views, will provide a context for a brief discussion of historically important theories of metaphor and contemp. treatments of the subject.

I. Critical Views. Aristotle's discussion of *simile in the *Rhetoric* was until recently the starting point of most treatments of metaphor. In saying that Achilles "sprang at the foe as a lion," Homer used a simile; had he said "the lion sprang at them," it would have been a metaphor. In one case, according to Aristotle, the comparison is explicit (using *like* or *as*); in the other, the word *lion* is "transferred" to Achilles, but the meaning is the same. Quintilian endorsed Aristotle's view of metaphor as a condensed simile: "in the latter we compare some object to the thing which we wish to describe, whereas in the former the object is actually substituted for the thing." What Black has called the "comparison view" of metaphor is based on the grammatical form "A is B"; metaphor is seen as a condensed simile, meaning that A is (like) B. The "substitution view," as Black says, takes "the lion sprang" as the paradigmatic form of metaphor: rather than predicating a likeness, metaphor uses a figurative word in place of a literal one. Both these views are compatible with the reductive conception of metaphor as "saying one thing and meaning another," thus implying that the poet has gone out of the way to say something other than what was meant (perhaps in the interests of decorating an ordinary thought) and suggesting that, in reading poetry, one must dismantle metaphors to find out what the poem "really means."

A different conception of metaphor is necessary to sustain Aristotle's claim, endorsed through the centuries, that metaphor is the most significant feature of poetic style: "that alone cannot be learnt; it is the token of genius. For the right use of metaphor means an eye for resemblances." New metaphors are said to spring from the poet's heightened emotion, keen perception, or intellectual acuity; their functions are aesthetic (making expression more vivid or interesting), pragmatic (conveying meanings concisely), and cognitive (providing words to describe things that have no literal name or rendering complex abstractions easy to understand through concrete analogies). Emphasis on the value of concreteness and sensory appeal in metaphor is frequent. Some mod. critics treat metaphor under the general rubric *imagery (*Bild* has a corresponding importance in Ger. crit., as does *image* in Fr. crit.).

Opposing the comparison and substitution views, 20th-c. critics and philosophers developed more intricate accounts of the verbal and cognitive processes involved in metaphoric usage. Despite their differences, the "interaction" view (Richards, Black), "controversion theory" (Beardsley), and "fusion" view (espoused by New Critics) all hold that metaphor creates meanings not readily accessible through literal lang. Rather than simply substituting one word for another or comparing two things, metaphor invokes a transaction between words and things, after which the words, things, and thoughts are not quite the same. Metaphor, from these perspectives, is not a decorative figure but a transformed literalism, meaning precisely what it says. Fusion theorists argue that it unifies the concrete and abstract, the sensual and the conceptual in a *concrete universal or symbol. An entire poem, if it is organically unified, can, therefore, be called a metaphor.

A less audacious explanation of the uniqueness of metaphor is discussed in the next section; at present, let us simply note what problems this view solves and what ones it creates. Treating all tropes as metaphors, the fusion theory frees crit. from the inconsistent classification systems handed down from antiquity. Synecdoche, as a species-genus or part-whole relation, can be imputed to any comparison whatever (everything being "like" everything else in some generic respect, or part of it, if the level of abstraction is high enough). Metonymy can be an empirically observed association (cause-effect), an entailment (attribute for subject), or a contingent relation (object for possessor). Since no single principle of classification governs these distinctions, one figurative expression can exemplify two or more tropes, as Antoine Foquelin observed (*La Rhétorique françoise* [1555]). Fusion theorists eliminate this problem and seek the new meanings released by metaphor, rather than reducing them to uninformative categories.

This freedom from pedantry can, however, entail a loss of precision leading to the neglect, if not the dismissal or misperception, of many tropes. The blurring of traditional distinctions leads to changes in the ways figures are construed. *Pale death*, which would now be considered a trite metaphor involving personification, was in the Ren. a metonymy (death, not personified, is the cause of the effect paleness). The verbal vitality created by tropes other than metaphor is categorized as imagery if it is sensory and *style if it is not. Similes, otherwise identical to metaphors, are automatically accorded a lower status merely because they use the word *like* or *as*—a sign of timidity in the eyes of the fusion theorist, who may see in simile new possibilities for describing the nature of lang.

Single-minded emphasis on the meaning of metaphor, apart from the semantic and grammatical details of its realization, can lead both mod. theorists and traditionalists to questionable interpretive practices. In most textbooks, the only examples of metaphor provided are in the form "A is B," despite the fact that this is not the most common grammatical form, "the A of B" ("th' expense of spirit") and "the A B" ("the dying year") being more frequent (see Brooke-Rose). When they encounter metaphorical verbs, adjectives, and adverbs, critics who seek new meanings in poetry are tempted to transfer the figuration of these word classes over to the nouns with which they are associated. If a speaker snarls a reply or has a green thought, the critic concludes that the poet has said that the speaker is a dog or wolf and that the thought is a plant. Samuel Johnson's line in *The Vanity of Human Wishes* describing those who gain preferment—"They mount, they shine, evaporate, and fall"—may be clarified through reference to fireworks or fog and mayflies (living for a day), but its power and meaning evaporate if one concludes that the metaphoric verbs are a roundabout way of saying that the rich and famous are like insects.

The alternative assumption would be that the poet wanted to connect figurative attributes to a noun that remains literal; the nominal "A is B" equation was, after all, available to the poet, along with the other grammatical forms that create identity (apposition, demonstrative reference) and presumably would be used if that were the meaning. The tendency to think that metaphors always equate or fuse entities (nouns) reduces the varied effects of metaphor in poetry to a single register. Poets may intend their figurative renderings of process, attribute, and attitude to evoke a range of relations, from suggestiveness to total fusion. If so, they are not well served by theorists who translate every figurative inclination into a declaration of equivalence. The affective and aesthetic functions of metaphor, usually mentioned in traditional accounts, have been emphasized by a few mod. critics who oppose the assumption that the purpose of metaphor is to convey meanings. Forrest-Thomson argues that "the worst disservice criticism can do to poetry is to understand it too soon." Mod. poets in particular try to forestall this haste by using metaphors that do not lend themselves to assimilation by the discursive elements of the text. Thus, they try to preserve poetry from reduction to paraphrastic statement. Shklovsky goes further, asserting that the purpose of new metaphors is not to create meaning but to renew perception by "defamiliarizing" the world: unlikely comparisons retard reading and force us to reconceive objects that ordinary words allow us to pass over in haste.

II. History. Four approaches have dominated all attempts to improve on the account of metaphor provided by the cl. trad. Some writers propose more logical classifications of the tropes. Others undertake semantic analysis of the ways in which features of a word's meaning are activated or repressed in figurative usage. These two modes of analysis blend into each other, but they can be distinguished from treatments of metaphor that emphasize its existential entailments—its relation to reality and to hist. rather than to logic and lang. The crudity of this fourfold classification must justify the brevity of the following discussion, which touches on only those treatments of metaphor that, from a contemp. perspective, seem crucial.

For Aristotle, metaphor has two functions and two structures. In the *Poetics*, its function is to lend dignity to style, by creating an enigma that reveals a likeness or by giving a name to something that had been nameless ("the ship *plowed* the sea"). But in the *Rhetoric*, metaphor appears as a technique of persuasion, used to make a case appear better or worse than it is. Mod. critics would say that *kill*, *murder*, and *execute* have the same denotation but differ in connotation; for Aristotle, one of the three words would be proper in relation to a particular act, and the other two would be metaphors. From its rhetorical uses, metaphor acquires its reputation as a dangerous deviation from the truth, being for that reason castigated by Thomas Hobbes, John Locke, and other Enlightenment philosophers.

The four kinds of metaphor distinguished by Aristotle in the *Poetics* are of two structural types. One results from substitution (of species for genus, genus for species, or species for species), the two terms having a logical or "natural" relation to each other. The other type has an analogical or equational structure: A is to B as C is to D. Although only two of the four terms need be mentioned (A and D, or B and C), we must infer the other two in order to derive the meaning: "the evening of life" enables us to reconstruct "evening is to day as X is to life." Here we find the bifurcation that will henceforth characterize discussions of tropes: one type is based on accepted conceptual relationships (here, genus-species), and the other type includes all tropes that cannot be so defined. Species-genus and species-species relations are part of common knowledge; to cross from genus to genus, we need four terms that create what might be called a hypothetical likeness, one not given by logic or nature.

The species-genus relation is one of many that make it possible to infer the tenor from the vehicle. Identification of other such relations (e.g., cause for effect, container for contents) led to the proliferation of names for the tropes in rhet. Once they separated themselves from Aristotle's generic metaphor, it was necessary to define metaphor in such a way that it would not include the other tropes. Quintilian's solution—to say that metaphor is a substitution involving any permutation of the terms "animate" and "inanimate"—is not as unreasonable as it first appears. The dividing line between these two domains, which is a fundamental feature of lang. and culture, cannot easily be crossed by species-genus, part-whole, or subject-adjunct relations. Furthermore, animate-inanimate metaphors are strikingly frequent in poetry, as are animate-animate metaphors involving humans and nature. Analysis based on meaning later gave prominence to *personification and the *pathetic fallacy, appearance and reality, or inner and outer as the quintessential forms of metaphor.

Looking back on Quintilian from the perspectives provided by Giambattista Vico, the romantic poets, and semioticians, we can see that his untidy classification (which defines metaphor by reference to its subject matter, the other tropes by reference to "categorical" relationships) reveals something about the role of metaphor that escapes notice in any purely formal analysis. But when subject matter becomes the primary basis of classification, as it is in 19th- and 20th-c. studies such as those of Brinkmann, Konrad, and Spurgeon, the specificity of the tropes dissolves in the all-embracing category "imagery."

For the Ren., Quintilian's *Institutio oratoria* (pub. 1470) provided an orderly exposition of rhet. in place of the patchwork syntheses inferrable from other cl. texts; Quintilian's renown made him one target of Peter Ramus's campaign to reform the curriculum. Ramus concluded that there were four basic tropes: metonymy (connection through cause, effect, or adjunct), irony ("a change in meaning from opposites to opposites"), metaphor ("a change in meaning from comparisons to comparisons"), and synecdoche (species and genus). In Vico's *Scienza nuova* (*New Science,* 1725), these four become the basis of a hist. of lang. and civilization. In the age of the gods, metonymy ruled: lightning and thunder were a great effect of unknown origin, and humankind imagined the agent Jove as the cause. The age of heroes was one of synecdoche: men who held themselves to be sons of Jove embodied his abstract attributes. The age of men is the age of metaphor, in which likenesses are taken from bodies "to signify the operation of abstract minds"; and philosophy gives rise to what we call "literal" meaning.

Ramus is the precursor of mod. attempts to reduce tropes to a rationale, and Vico occupies the same position in relation to mod. discussions of metaphor's importance in the devel. of lang., though their successors are not always aware of this lineage. That lang. was originally metaphorical, mythic, and poetic is a common theme in romanticism—e.g., in Jean-Jacques Rousseau, J. G. Herder, F.W.J. Schelling, and P. B. Shelley—but there is little evidence that Vico was their source (the idea can be found in Lucretius, among others). Müller, Werner, and Cassirer exemplify the Ger. thinkers who have developed this theory; Langer and Wheelwright contributed to its popularity in Am. crit. Nietzsche's contrary thesis—that lang. was originally concrete and literal in reference and that the abstract vocabulary now considered literal is, in fact, metaphorical—has recently attracted critical attention (de Man). But as Vico pointed out, it makes little sense to speak of lang. as either literal or metaphorical before it incorporates a distinction between the two. Even Gadamer's carefully worded claims about the historical and conceptual primacy of metaphor cannot escape Vico's objection.

The theories of metaphor proposed by Richards, Black, and Beardsley, which incorporate insights into the workings of lang. and meaning derived from 20th-c. analytic philosophy, provide an alternative to traditional accounts of metaphor as a substitution, comparison, or fusion of meanings. Sentences, Richards says, are neither created nor interpreted by putting together words with unique meanings. Any ordinary word has several meanings and a number of loosely associated characteristics; often it will be both noun and verb or noun and adjective. The varied traits or semes of a word's meaning are sometimes sorted into two groups—denotations (characteristics essential to a distinct sense of the word) and connotations—but in practice, this distinction is hard to maintain. (In his precise and revealing analysis of this issue, MacCormac describes words as "fuzzy sets.") Only when placed in a context does a word take on one or more meanings, at which time some of its traits become salient and others are suppressed. It is often difficult to decide when we have crossed the line between literal and figurative usage. In the series "green dress" (dyed), "green field" (growing), "green shoot" (alive, despite color), and "green thought," connotations shift before becoming clearly metaphorical.

Richards looked on metaphor as a "transaction between contexts," in which tenor and vehicle combine in varied ways to produce meanings. Beardsley argues persuasively that metaphor is intentional: we find it in words, not in the objects to which they refer. Black's "interaction theory" contains an important distinction between the "focus" and "frame" of a metaphor (the figurative expression and the sentence in which it occurs). The focus brings with it not just connotations but a "system of associated commonplaces"—what Eco will later call "encyclopedic knowledge"—that interact with the frame to evoke knowledge shared by a speech community. To say "the lion sprang at them," meaning Achilles sprang, makes sense only because of common lore about the lion (a hunter, not an herbivore; sociable with its own kind, unlike the tiger, but not a herd animal; monogamous; a lone hunter, unlike the wolf). The lion cannot represent courage until, through a prior mapping of culture on nature, he is the king of beasts. Black emphasizes the *"extensions* of meaning" that novel metaphors bring to lang., but his theory has proved most useful in understanding the inherited and dead metaphors that structure a society's way of thinking and talking about itself.

III. Recent Views. Every innovative critical theory of the later 20th c. generated a new delineation of metaphor—either as the "other" of its own conceptual domain or as the very ground of its new insights. One of the most influential innovations has been Jakobson's opposition of metaphor to metonymy. In his view, metaphor results from the substitution of one term for another; it is characteristic of poetry and some literary movements, such as romanticism and symbolism. Metonymy, based on contiguity, appears more frequently in prose and typifies realism. Though they often cross disciplinary boundaries, these theories of metaphor can be classified as (1) ling. or semiotic (based on intralinguistic relationships or relations between signs of any sort); (2) rhetorical or pragmatic (involving a difference between sentence meaning and speaker meaning); (3) philosophical (emphasizing relations between words and reality or sense and reference); and (4) extended (treating nonlinguistic relationships in other disciplines).

The most ambitious semiotic attempt to identify ling. features of metaphor appears in *A General Rhetoric*, produced by Group μ of the University of Liège. They treat all unexpected suppressions, additions, repetitions, or permutations of ling. elements, from phonemes to phrases, as figures, the nonfigurative being a hypothetical "degree zero" discourse from which rhet. deviates. Metaphor results from an implicit decomposition of words into their semes (lexical features), some of which will be cancelled and others added when one word is substituted for another. The natural route for such substitutions is through species and genus, as Aristotle observed, and Group μ concludes that a metaphor consists of two synecdoches, the progression being either species-genus-species (the intermediate term being a class that includes the first and last terms) or whole-part-whole (here the central term is a class formed where the first and last overlap). Levin, using a more flexible scheme for the transfer and deletion of semantic features, shows that there are six ways to interpret a metaphor (his example is "the stone died"). He points out that the grammatical structure of many metaphors allows for the transfer of features in two directions: "the brook smiled" can either humanize the brook or add sparkle and liquidity to the idea of smiling. Although he analyzes metaphor as an intralinguistic phenomenon, Levin recognizes that Aristotle's fourth type, analogy, often depends upon reference to reality—a fact that Group μ overlooked. Thus, metaphor appears to escape formalization within a system. Eco's semiotic solution to this problem is to imagine an encyclopedia that describes all the features of reality not included in the semanticist's dictionary. For Riffaterre (1978), mimetic reference is only a feint that the literary text makes before refocusing itself in a network of semiotic commonplaces.

Proponents of speech act theory are the most important representatives of rhetorical and pragmatic theories. They hold that metaphor cannot be explained through reference to relationships between words and their ling. contexts. They make a categorical distinction between "word or sentence meaning" and "speaker's utterance meaning." Metaphor, in their view, arises from a disparity between the literal meaning of the words used and what is intended by the speaker or writer. Words always retain their invariant "locutionary" definitions, but when used to make metaphors, there is something odd about them and the hearer infers unstated suggestions or meanings. Grice's theory of "conversational implicature" provides a set of rules and maxims for normal talk that, when violated, may alert us to the fact that someone is speaking figuratively. His theory, like Searle's, locates metaphor in a difference between utterance meaning and speaker meaning—the domain of pragmatics—and is subject to the same sorts of crit. that speech act theory has elicited (see Sadock in Ortony).

Searle and Grice are philosophers, but their theories entail empirical claims of relevance to linguists. In the work of Davidson and of Goodman, one finds more strictly philosophic treatments of metaphor. Meaning, in Davidson's view, involves only the relation between lang. and reality. He is willing to accept the pragmatic "distinction between what words mean and what they are used to do," but he denies the existence of metaphoric meaning: "metaphors mean what the words, in their most literal interpretation, mean, and nothing more." To this one might reply that if we did not realize they were patently false, we would not know they were figurative. Recognizing them as such, we may discover truths about the world, but this is not a consequence of some meaning inherent in the words. Goodman disagrees. In *Languages of Art*, he conceives of metaphor, like many other activities, as exemplification. Rather than applying a label to a thing, we use the thing as an example of the label, as when the lively appearance of the literal brook is seen as an instance of smiling. This reverses the direction of denotation: the example refers to the word, rather than vice versa, and the word may bring with it a whole schema of relationships that will be sorted anew in the metaphorical context. Goodman concludes that metaphor is "no more independent of truth or falsity than literal use."

Postponing discussion of deeper philosophical differences that divide theorists, one cannot help but note that they tend to privilege different moments in the interpretive process. At first glance, or outside time, metaphor is false (Davidson). Realizing that the creator of a metaphor means something else, one might create a theory of the difference between sentence and speaker meaning (Searle, Grice). When engaged in deciphering, a reader enacts the interaction theory—discovering new meanings—and the falsity of metaphor is forgotten. Truth usually results from testing many examples to find one rule; in metaphor, meaning emerges from repeated consideration of a single example, uncovering all its possibilities; and a hypothesis or generalization is the product of the process, not its inception. In accordance with information theory, the low probability of a word or phrase in a particular context implies that it carries a great deal of meaning.

IV. Current Debates. Through the work of Lakoff and Johnson, understanding of dead metaphors has been transformed. Most commonplace metaphors express a connection between a concept and a realm of experience. Among their examples of these conceptual metaphors are "argument is war" and "time is money." In their terminology, the conceptual term is the target, and the concrete term is the source. Each such "A is B" is a generic schema that can generate dozens of specific tropes, based on connections between the two domains. Their examples serve as reminders that not only nouns but adjectives, verbs, adverbs, and prepositions abound in tropes. As Searle remarked, conventional metaphors spring back to life when new aspects of the analogy are evoked (e.g., "he torpedoed my argument," "his refutation was a dud"). For Lakoff and Johnson, such interactions of the abstract and concrete are not simply analogies, and "conceptual metaphors" are not

provisional aspects of lang. use. They exemplify the ways that we conceptually organize experience. War and argument cannot be separated from each other.

Poetics can certainly benefit from attention to conventional metaphors, long neglected in discussions of poetry. As Turner (1987) showed, a single domain such as kinship can generate hundreds of analogies that differ in interesting ways. He and Lakoff provide examples of how basic conceptual metaphors concerning life, time, and death occur in a wide range of traditional and contemp. poems. When metaphor is seen as a form of conceptual mapping rather than verbal expression, it has implications for psychology, anthropology, neurology, and cognitive science. If rooted in bodily experience, metaphor may reveal universal conceptual patterns; those specific to particular cultures might then be correlated with different langs. or modes of understanding (Kövecses). The cohesion of specific groups within a society may be strengthened by shared conceptual metaphors. If so, the topic is important for sociology, politics, and rhetorical studies of public relations and advertising.

When these devels. are connected with neurology and cognitive science, the scope and significance of the project become clear. What is at stake is nothing less than a unified theory of human behavior, mapping a progression from embodied experience, inscribed in neural pathways, to action, thought, and expression. This change has confirmed the relevance of earlier con-ceptions of metaphor. Jakobson's association of metaphor and metonymy with the right and left hemispheres of the brain, mentioned earlier, has led to numerous experiments that make use of neural imaging. The idea that abstract thought emerged from metaphor, as suggested by Vico, Rousseau, and Herder, gained support through two centuries during which philologists traced the evolution of word meanings. Metaphor is now a topic of discussion in many disciplines, treated in hundreds of articles annually. Following the ling. turn of the 20th c., the paradigmatic shift of the 21st c. may be a tropical turn.

For poetics, the emphasis on conceptual metaphor has been immensely valuable. In both crit. and pedagogy, poetry has been rescued from the modernist overemphasis on originality and recognized as dependent on conventional cultural codes that it shares with the lyrics of popular music. The hist. of poetry suggests that innovative metaphor may be even less common than conceptual metaphor theorists suggest. They have frequently treated three examples as innovative: "man is a wolf," "that surgeon is a butcher," and "my lawyer is a shark." Dicts. and poetry anthols. confirm the impression that these have existed for cs. The human and animal kingdoms, with the lion as the king of beasts, were mapped onto each other long ago. The names of many species—rats, snakes, skunks, foxes, weasels—have literalized meanings referring to humans. Even condensed dicts. list two literal meanings for the humans known as wolves or as sharks; a "butcher," as noun or verb, literally means a botcher or a bungler. The elaborate schemas produced to account for how we understand such usage seem beside the point, unless they are hypotheses about the neural activity of those encountering such usage for the first time or hypotheses about how we understand literal statements.

The conceptual metaphor theory of Lakoff, Johnson, Turner, and their followers treats metaphor as a cognitive, not a ling., phenomenon. The theory has prompted empirical studies of figurative lang., based on data banks such as the British National Corpus (100,000,000 words from 20th-c. pubs.). One important result of such work is evidence that metaphors commonly used in conversation and prose are quite different from those produced by theorists as examples. Often the meaning is clear even when the literal "tenor" or "target domain" is indeterminate: when a man is "gaining ground" with a woman, should we think of war, affection, or territorial encroachment? Corpus analysts conclude that there is no clear-cut boundary between literal and figurative usage. Phrases and word couplings that were once either literal or figurative are now usually or always figurative—making them, in effect, literal. E.g., "heavy blow" and "pay a high price" are rarely used literally; a search for the phrase "old fox" turns up only the (literalized) metaphorical meaning. Those who construct examples for experimental purposes sometimes mistake commonplace for original metaphors, and vice versa (Stefanowitsch, Hanks, Deignan, Hilpert). Given the lack of agreement about the difference between figurative, literalized, and literal expressions, the gap between theory and empirical studies has not been bridged.

The antithetical view of metaphor—as uncommon insight rather than an oddity reducible to literal thought and expression—has long lacked a persuasive justification. Those who have proposed this view, from Aristotle to Davidson, have not supported it with convincing arguments. Fauconnier and Turner provide the best explanation we have of connections between metaphor, insight, and ling. innovation. Each of the two entities in the traditional "A is B" metaphor has a number of features (connotations or semes). We can list the features together in a hypothetical "generic space." The traits that they share and the context will usually indicate the implied meaning. The novel or emergent metaphor does not yield its meaning through that procedure; no revealing correspondence in the generic space is evident. That leads to reconsideration of traits not shared and the creation of what Fauconnier and Turner call a "blended space," from which unanticipated meanings may emerge.

The title of Turner's book *Death Is the Mother of Beauty* (a phrase taken from a poem by Wallace Stevens) provides an example of creative metaphor. Death ends life; how can it give birth? The traditional Grim Reaper and his scythe are replaced by a maternal force that "strews the leaves / of sure obliteration on our paths." The leaves are not cut down by an untimely scythe but fall when their time has come. The lines call attention to the natural, inevitable death that makes urgent the fulfillment of desire. Paradoxically, consciousness of death gives birth—to awareness of beauty's transience. An entire stanza prompts us to make these inferences and others concerning procreation; it directs but also multiplies the potential insights. Turner and Fauconnier are sensitive to the interaction of metaphor and other tropes in contexts that limit the possible meanings in some directions but thereby expand them in others.

V. Summary. The figural use of "metaphor" in mod. theory, through which it assimilates not only all other tropes (as in Aristotle) but models, analogies, and narrative methods as well, leads back to the question of whether the literal and figurative can be distinguished from one another. The simplest and in some ways most logical answers are that ling. meaning is all literal (Davidson) or all figural (Nietzsche). Children do not discriminate between the two in lang. acquisition, and there is little evidence that adult comprehension of literal and metaphorical usage involves different psychological processes (Rummelhart). Some argue that tropes can be entirely literal (see *Grammatical Metaphor*). Rather than attempting to identify rules capable of accounting for literal usage and then explaining figures as transformations or deviations from this set, one can treat literalness "as a limiting case rather than a norm" and develop a pragmatic theory of meaning in which metaphors need not be considered different from other usage (Sperber and Wilson).

Figurative indirectness also seems prevalent in Chinese and Japanese poetry. Varieties of parallel structure, the Chinese stylistic figures of *bi* (comparison) and *xing* (incitation, affective image), and the tendency to imply without asserting a relation between mood and scene imply a reticence at odds with propositional assertion (Owen, Cheng, Cai). The 20th-c. confrontation of truth and metaphor, based on the assumption that metaphor is an assertive predication, may have been misguided.

The analogies and metaphors that prompt insight do not have to appear in poetry. Many have emerged from our interactions with technology. Fauconnier and Turner call attention to the consequences of comparing a disruptive program in a computer to a virus in an organism. The analogy itself comes to life when one pursues its implications. Antibiotics will prove useless; the first line of defense would be to identify sources of the infection and methods of preventing it from entering the system. Determining the molecular structure (code) of the virus would be useful for the creation of feedback mechanisms that could neutralize its effects. Through the same kind of reasoning, the models used in scientific theories serve heuristic functions when familiar structures are used to map uncharted phenomena. Hesse and Kuhn extended Black's discussion of the subject in *Models and Metaphors*. Citing the work of Bachelard and Canguilhem, Derrida (1972) suggested that the function of metaphor in science is not merely heuristic. Hesse endorses Boyd's claim (in Ortony) that "metaphors are *constitutive* of the theories they express, rather than merely exegetical."

As the hists. of science and poetry show, metaphors and models are tools for thought that may or may not prove productive. When productive, they implant thoughts that become part of a society and culture—what we (unconsciously) think with, rather than think about. Pepper's *World Hypotheses* claims that different ways of life are based on "root metaphors" that affect every aspect of experience.

For Blumenberg's philosophical anthropology, such a metaphor constitutes a worldview, a "set of institutions, customs, and expectations that maintain a life-world" and constitute its "selves" (Pavesich). The difference between creative and commonplace metaphors may be a function of the amount of consciousness they evoke.

While contributing to an understanding of its ling. features and conceptual implications, theories of metaphor show that it is not simply one critical problem among others, notable only for the number of disagreements it causes. Ricoeur finds in philosophic metaphor a potential for revealing the nature of being. But as that which lies outside the literal, normal, proper, or systematic, metaphor serves as a topic through which each theory and philosophy defines itself. Metaphor is not simply true or false but that which marks the limits of the distinctions between the two or between meaning and nonsense. As Derrida says, "Each time that a rhetoric defines metaphor, not only is *a* philosophy implied, but also a conceptual network in which philosophy *itself* has been constituted." Thus, agreement about the status of metaphor will be deferred until all other ling. and philosophic disputes have been resolved.

See TROPE.

■ **Anthologies:** *Philosophical Perspectives on Metaphor*, ed. M. Johnson (1981); *Metaphor and Thought*, ed. A. Ortony (1993); *Aspects of Metaphor*, ed. J. Hintikka (1994); *Grammatical Metaphor*, ed. A.-M. Simon-Vandenbergen, M. Taverniers, and L. Ravelli (2003); *Cognitive Linguistics*, ed. D. Geerarts (2006); *Corpus-Based Approaches to Metaphor and Metonymy*, ed. A. Stefanowitsch and S. Gries (2006); *The Cambridge Handbook of Metaphor and Thought*, ed. R. W. Gibbs Jr. (2008).

■ **History:** M. Müller, *Lectures on the Science of Language* (1862, 1865); F. Brinkmann, *Die Metaphern* (1878); H. Werner, *Die Ursprünge der Metapher* (1919); W. B. Stanford, *Greek Metaphor* (1936); H. Konrad, *Étude sur la métaphore* (1939); E. Cassirer, *Language and Myth*, trans. S. Langer (1946); F. Nietzsche, "On Truth and Lies in a Nonmoral Sense" [1873], *Philosophy and Truth*, ed. D. Breazeale (1979); L. Doležel, *Occidental Poetics* (1990); K.W.F. Schlegel, "Dialogue on Poesy" [1799], *Theory as Practice*, ed. J. Schulte-Sasse (1997); G. Bergounioux, "La sémantique dans le champ de la linguistique francophone jusqu'à 1916" and B. Nerlich, "La métaphore et la métonymie," *Sémiotiques* 14 (1998); B. Nerlich and D. D. Clarke, "Mind,

Meaning and Metaphor," *History of the Human Sciences* 14 (2001).

■ **Texts:** C. K. Ogden and I. A. Richards, *The Meaning of Meaning* (1923); C. Spurgeon, *Shakespeare's Imagery* (1935); G. Bachelard, *La Formation de l'esprit scientifique* (1938); S. K. Langer, *Philosophy in a New Key* (1942); S. Pepper, *World Hypotheses* (1942); C. Brooke-Rose, *A Grammar of Metaphor* (1958); M. Black, *Models and Metaphors* (1962); P. Wheelwright, *Myth and Reality* (1962); I. A. Richards, *The Philosophy of Rhetoric* ([1936] 1965); V. Shklovsky, "Art as Technique" [1917], *Russian Formalist Criticism*, ed. and trans. L. Lemon and M. J. Reis (1965); M. Hesse, *Models and Analogies in Science* (1966); H. Weinreich, "Explorations in Semantic Theory," *Current Trends in Linguistics* 3 (1966): G. Canguilhem, *Études d'histoire et de philosophie des sciences* (1968); N. Goodman, *Languages of Art* (1968); K. Burke, "Four Master Tropes," *A Grammar of Motives* ([1945] 1969); M. C. Beardsley, "The Metaphorical Twist," *Philosophy and Phenomenological Research* 22 (1962); G. Vico, *The New Science*, ed. and trans. T. G. Bergin and M. H. Fisch ([1744] 1970); H. White, *Metahistory* (1973); H. Bloom, *A Map of Misreading* (1975); H.-G. Gadamer, *Truth and Method*, trans. J. Weinsheimer and D. Marshall ([1960] 1989); H. Bloom, *Wallace Stevens* (1977); P. Ricoeur, *The Rule of Metaphor*, trans. R. Czerny ([1975] 1977); D. Davidson, "What Metaphors Mean," and P. de Man, "The Epistemology of Metaphor," *CritI* 5 (1978); V. Forrest-Thomson, *Poetic Artifice* (1978); M. Riffaterre, *Semiotics of Poetry* (1978); M. Black, "How Metaphors Work," and N. Goodman, "Metaphor as Moonlighting," *CritI* 6 (1979); J. Derrida, *The Archeology of the Frivolous*, trans. J. Leavey ([1973] 1980); G. Lakoff and M. Johnson, *Metaphors We Live By* (1980); Group μ, "White Mythology," *Margins of Philosophy*, trans. A. Bass, ([1972] 1982); U. Eco, "The Scandal of Metaphor," *PoT* 4 (1983); M. Riffaterre, *Text Production*, trans. T. Lyons (1983); U. Eco, "Metaphor, Dictionary, and Encyclopedia," *NLH* 15 (1984); E. R. Mac-Cormac, *A Cognitive Theory of Metaphor* (1985); S. Owen, *Traditional Chinese Poetry and Poetics* (1985); D. Sperber and D. Wilson, *Relevance* (1986); R. Jakobson, "Two Aspects of Language and Two Types of Aphasic Disturbances," 1956, rpt. in Jakobson, v. 2; E. F. Kittay, *Metaphor* (1987); M. Turner, *Death Is the Mother of Beauty* (1987); F. Cheng, "The Reciprocity of Subject and Object in Chinese Poetic Language," *Poetics East and West*, ed. M. Doleželová-Velingerová

(1988–89); H. P. Grice, "Logic and Conversation," 1975, *Studies in the Ways of Words* (1989); G. Lakoff and M. Turner, *More than Cool Reason* (1989); *Metaphor and Thought*, ed. A. Ortony (1993)—see esp. M. Black, "More about Metaphor" (1977), R. Boyd, "Metaphor and Theory Change," T. Kuhn, "Metaphor in Science," S. Levin, "Standard Approaches to Metaphor," D. Rummelhart, "Some Problems with the Notion of Literal Meanings," J. Sadock, "Figurative Speech and Linguistics," and J. Searle, "Metaphor"; B. Indurkhya, "Metaphor as Change of Representation," and E. Steinhart and E. Kittay, "Generating Metaphors from Networks," in *Aspects of Metaphor*, ed. J. Hintikka (1994); R. M. White, *The Structure of Metaphor* (1996); G. Fauconnier, *Mappings in Thought and Language* (1997); S. Glucksberg, *Understanding Figurative Language* (2001); M. Leezenberg, *Contexts of Metaphor* (2001); G. Fauconnier and M. Turner, *The Way We Think* (2002); Z. Kövecses, *Metaphor* (2002); A.-M. Simon-Vandenbergen, "Lexical Metaphor and Interpersonal Meaning," *Grammatical Metaphor*, ed. A.-M. Simon-Vandenbergen et al. (2003); Z. Kövecses, *Metaphor in Culture* (2005); E. Rolf, *Metaphertheorien* (2005); E. Romero and B. Soria, "Cognitive Metaphor Theory Revisited," *Journal of Literary Semantics* 34 (2005); *Corpus-based Approaches to Metaphor and Metonymy*, ed. A. Stefanowitsch and S. T. Gries (2006); G. Fauconnier and M. Turner, "Conceptual Integration Networks," *Cognitive Linguistics*, ed. D. Geeraerts (2006); J. Derrida, "The Retrait of Metaphor," 1978, *Psyche*, ed. P. Kamuf and E. Rottenberg (2007); *The Cambridge Handbook of Metaphor and Thought*, ed. R. W. Gibbs Jr. (2008); V. Pavesich, "Hans Blumenberg's Philosophical Anthropology," *Journal of the History of Philosophy* 46 (2008); Z.-Q. Cai, "Introduction," *How to Read Chinese Poetry*, ed. Z.-Q. Cai (2008).

W. MARTIN

METER (Gr. *metron*).

I. Four Categories
II. Debates About Meter
III. Functions

Meter is the measure of sound patterning in verse, occurring when a *rhythm is repeated throughout a passage of lang. with such regularity that a base unit (such as a *foot) becomes a norm and governs poetic composition. Meter is an idealized pattern, a cultural construct understood as artistic shaping of the sound pattern of a lang. All langs. possess the makings of metrical systems. Metrical verse works the basic properties of a given lang. to a more highly regularized level. When studying meters, one focuses on their historical changes, on their cultural associations, and on describing and analyzing specific meters shaped by individual poets into metrical styles. As cultural constructs, meters are a major part of verse design. While design, like rhythm, is innate for humans desiring a sense of order, designs are made, learned, and passed on in a culture. They are open to innovation and transcend the linguistic material of which they are made (Hollander; Cushman). As a regularized organization of *sound, metrical design both uses and pulls against the speech patterning of lang. The ordinary rhythms of a lang. must rise to an unusual degree of prominence to become a meter. As a result, meter can heighten emotion and compete with sense. Aristotle noticed that a too-heightened rhythm could override sense and persuade, an effect Roman Jakobson regarded as the basis of the poetic function (Sebeok). Julia Kristeva sees in this poetic function the argument between the rhythmic (the feminine) and the rational (the law, the masculine) dimensions of lang. (Cook).

Cultures develop particular verse trads. based on normative meters that are recognized tacitly as well formed or not, indicating that the rules are made by cultures and learned in the same way lang. competence is acquired. For this reason, meters also change; "rules" restrict what may count as metrical for a particular time and place, i.e., what linguistic situations in the verse may occur when exceptions to the norm appear in a verse meter (see individual entries for specific langs. and lit. hists.). Measurement of verse in a given lang. may depend primarily on *quantity, *accent (stress), syllable, tone (pitch), or *syntax. One of these will be the dominant component of a meter, and one or more of the others may affect it, but full descriptions of the influence on metrical patterning of secondary features, such as *rhyme and sound (in all langs.; see Crystal), are still being developed by linguists.

In a stress-based lang. like Eng., two levels of stress—strong and weak—define the normative pattern that forms the idealized metrical base. Identifying the meter of a poem or part of a poem is accomplished by a process of marking stresses, called *scanning*, and yields a *scansion. In actuality, the idealized pattern is realized at three or four perceptual levels of stress. The term *scansion* has been traditionally reserved for marking the idealized pattern, but since the 1950s, theories using ling. have marked three or four levels in order to develop descriptive and explanatory "rules" (see below). Within these relative perceptual levels, the basic pattern can be perceived because the adjacent stresses remain weak or strong relative to each other (Chatman; Halle and Keyser). The actual levels of stress compose the rhythm of the passage and create sound, meaning, and expressive qualities specific to a poem. The idealized pattern gains flexibility or rigidity depending on "allowable" departures that have been built up (and continue to be built up) as a trad. of metrical composition by poets' adding new variations on the metrical base. The numbers and location of weak and strong stresses that comprise a unit define the type of meter. New meters that are devised may enter the metrical code of a literary trad. with sufficient use by poets and recognition by readers.

Four metrical categories are traditionally recognized in Eng. poetry, named for the distinguishing factor that establishes the unit of measure: accentual, accentual-syllabic (also known as accentual isosyllabic), syllabic (also known as isosyllabic), and quantitative (though this category is controversial; see below). The name of a metrical type (e.g., *ballad, *iambic *pentameter) refers variously to the poetic trad. of that meter, to an entire poem, to a section of a poem, or to the line pattern. Meter inhabits a context, as is demonstrated by lines that might be scanned as more than one meter if they occurred in different metrical contexts. E.g., this line from W. B. Yeats's "The Second Coming"—"Turning and turning in the widening gyre"—might be scanned as dactylic, except that the remainder of the poem is iambic pentameter. But the line is a quite traditional iambic pentameter, engaging an initial strong onset (*Turn*-), a strong fourth syllable, a strong (relative to the surrounding syllables) sixth syllable (*in*), and an elided weak stress (-*ening*) on the ninth syllable, which gives the line an extra-metrical eleventh syllable that is weak.

The concept of measuring verse into units, called feet, and units into lines with a specified number of feet is an analytic one, originally imposed by the Greeks on poetic compositions as a way of describing the disciplining of rhythmic repetition into lines of verse when verse was written down. (Gr. prosodists were divided between the *rhythmikoi*, who measured by rhythm, as in music, and the *metrikoi*, who measured by foot.) Measuring meter in feet is known as the classical approach to meter; it was imported into Eng. during the Ren. and has prevailed as a guide to verse composition and prosodic study as influenced by Romance verse. Other approaches have been developed in the 20th c., thanks to mod. ling., scientific methods and goals of investigation, and the explosion of nonmetrical poetry. The most important of these have been systems grounded in generative metrics, linguistic theories of the sound patterning of the Eng. phrase, and the iambic-only theory of Eng. meter. While the cl. approach is the least adequate for describing and explaining the linguistic basis of metrical occurrence and function, it is the one used in common parlance, by the majority of poets, critics, and teachers.

Although actual sound can be measured with instruments, what counts in meter, as in all *prosody, is the perception of sound pattern. Sound in poetry has physical, mental, and psychological importance. It is heard and trans. by the brain into rhythm and meaning. It is felt as vibration in the areas that produce sound, from the chest up to the mouth and nasal cavity. The psychological recognition and importance of rhythmic repetition are probably as old as human beings, a physical order felt, heard, and understood in such universal experiences as the heartbeat, walking, breathing, dance, and ritual performances, some to music and some not (Hollander, Tsur). Poets throughout hist. have asserted that they write to the paces of these rhythmic repetitions. In most meters, one measuring feature must be principal, but others may exert some constraint. The name of the unit and the number of units per line are the characteristic ways of defining metrical type.

I. Four Categories.

A. *Accentual Meter* is the oldest meter in Eng., beginning with Anglo-Saxon verse; continuing into the devel. of the ballad across Great Britain, northern Europe, and Russia; and regaining prominence in the 19th and 20th cs. (see ACCENTUAL VERSE). In accentual meter, each accent (or *stress*) is felt as a strong pulse or *beat. Lines of verse typically repeat a set number of beats, but counting beats alone is not sufficient to make patterning felt with the regularity of meter, since accents are distributed over speech

and prose as well. OE strong-stress meter is organized as half-lines, with two beats per half-line (*hemistich) on either side of a strong *caesura and various patterns of *alliteration governing the stresses. Over the course of the 20th c., theorists have attempted to describe OE meter, a difficult task since the nature of the Anglo-Saxon sound system must be understood from existing verse itself. Anglo-Saxon is not amenable to the cl. approach, so other systems have been developed to describe and explain the meter (see ENGLISH PROSODY). Anglo-Saxon strong-stress meter is not possible in mod. Eng. because its prosody does not have the structural patterning of the older lang. Nevertheless, poets since the Ren. have taken the four-beat alliterative characteristics of the form for verse cohesion, disregarding the other metrical restrictions. The Alliterative Revival in the late 19th and early 20th cs. saw many poets attempting alliterative accentual meter. G. M. Hopkins was inspired to write a strong accentual line with frequent alliteration, which he called *sprung rhythm. Poets such as Robert Bridges, Ezra Pound, T. S. Eliot, Wallace Stevens, W. H. Auden, Richard Wilbur, Robert Pinsky, and Seamus Heaney composed poems on the model and, on occasion, incorporated allusive, alliterative four-stress lines in free verse accentual-syllabic poems (see ALLITERATION).

The most common type of accentual poetry in Eng. is *ballad meter. The form appears to have developed from the strong-stress Anglo-Saxon meter and, in its oldest forms before the meter also developed accentual-syllabic regularity, is characterized by number of accents per line with a mid-line caesura and a variable number of syllables around accented syllables. In lines one and three of a ballad stanza, there are four stresses, two and two, on each side of a midline caesura. Lines two and four bear three stresses or, alternatively, pairings of two and two. Some argue that the number of syllables bearing weak stress and accompanying each strongly stressed syllable is restricted by a durational aspect. This restriction is likely due to musical bar-time—what can be sung or said within an isochronic perception of time (see Lehiste)—as the ballad developed as an oral form composed to music. Ballad meter is thus not a pure accentual meter for metrists who consider the pure form to be a measuring of accents only.

A pure accentual meter is rare since some regularity must be built up in order for the rhythm to be experienced as recurring with a high measure of regularity; however, the expectation trained into the ear by cultural codes for poetry may be expanded, as it has been in contemp. verse, which makes up for cohesion lost in metrical patterning with qualitative sound patterning. The five-beat line in the work of some poets (e.g., Stanley Plumly) is exemplary: positioning and grouping of units are not regular; only a norm of accents per line is. But there is leeway; some lines may bear four, six, or seven or even more beats. *Consonance and *assonance are relied on for repetition of sound. This style of metrical practice results in a "loose" accentual verse, analogous to the loose style of iambic pentameter; other critics regard this accentual style as a type of *free verse, since it only recalls, but is freed from, the accentual-syllabic constraints of traditional meters. The ten-beat line developed by C. K. Williams is another such meter: it can be viewed as a ten-beat accentual, a loose double iambic pentameter, or a free verse composition.

B. *Syllabic Meter* is defined by the number of syllables per line (see SYLLABIC VERSE). Simple or "pure" syllabism constitutes the basic meter of, e.g., Japanese poetry and Hungarian folk poetry. At various moments in their respective literary histories, it has also governed Polish poetry (as well as the Rus. verse based on Polish models), Slovak poetry, and Mordvinian folk songs. Complex or mixed syllabism, which combines syllabic patterning with some other obligatory linguistic feature, appears, for example, in Chinese poetry, which combines syllabism with tonal patterns, and Welsh poetry, which combines it with intricate rhyming. Sitting between these two categories, Fr. poetry presents an interesting borderline case: though usually considered syllabic, like Japanese, Fr. poetry depends heavily on rhyme to strengthen its syllabic frame in a way that Japanese poetry does not, although occasional alliteration, assonance, and consonance certainly enrich the latter. It. and Sp. versification are syllabic in their own complex ways, with a role for stress in determining the abstract pattern of the line—in general, stressed syllables must occupy certain positions—as well as rules governing the computation of syllables within and between words (see ELISION, HIATUS, SYNAERESIS); all of these factors figure in reckoning for metrical purposes the number of syllables in the line. In Eng., there is no traditional form that uses pure

syllabic meter because in Eng. and other Germanic langs., accentual contour overrides the perception of syllable count. The mora-timed Japanese haiku has been adapted to Eng., as three lines in a pattern of five, seven, and five syllables of any stress level; but what is heard foremost in Eng. are stresses, not syllables.

The limited perceptibility of the syllable in the inevitable presence of accents, however, does not mean that poets writing in Eng. do not use syllabic count as a basis for verse composition. A poet may decide to use the syllable as the compositional unit, establishing a certain number of syllables per line—either all lines having the same number of syllables or a pattern of syllables of different count for each stanza that may be quite idiosyncratic and different for each poem, such as the poems for which Marianne Moore is best known. Moore read her poems across line ends, without pause; on her printed copies, she marked the accents. Well-crafted syllabic verse may achieve a high degree of cohesion from repetition of syllable number and pattern, qualitative sound patterning, and spatial organization. As in Moore's poems, artful use of shape and space on the page, combined with repetition of phones, creates wonderful dramatic, semantic, emotional, and iconic effects (see VISUAL POETRY). On the one hand, by itself syllabic meter in poetry in a stress-based lang. is a weak device for cohesion, being aurally imperceptible or nearly so; the verse will sound rhythmic at best. On the other hand, syllabic patterning can make for strong cohesion in visual form. While some theorists maintain there can be no syllabic meter in Eng. (R. Wallace in Baker), others maintain that meter merely means measure, and the syllable-counting is one way of measuring a line, perceptible or not (Gioia in Baker). The debate about syllabic meter in Eng. turns on how meter is defined—as compositional or perceptual.

C. *Accentual-Syllabic Meter* is the most common by far in mod. Eng. poetry because of its synthetic devel. from Germanic and Romance langs. and poetries (see ACCENTUAL-SYLLABIC VERSE). The meter shares the structuring principles of syllabic meter and accentual meter, patterning a set number of strong and weak syllables in an idealized base. Thus, e.g., according to a cl. description, a line of iambic pentameter has five *iambs (weak/strong, weak/strong, weak/strong, weak/strong, weak/strong). Iambic pentameter is the most common Eng. meter because of the flexibility with which it can be worked for rhythmic variety. The meter began as a synthesis when med. Eng. poets adapted Fr. verse forms to the accentual system of Eng. and to established Eng. verse forms. Russom's description of Anglo-Saxon metrics suggests that Chaucer may at least in part, have been writing OE metrical patterns to a syllabic base count, as he employed a ten-syllable line with stresses that follow the Romance rule of alternating stress (see Halle and Keyser; Chomsky and Halle; Russom). Although iambic pentameter has a long trad., the meter cannot be said to have been in Chaucer's time or Thomas Wyatt's or John Milton's or Alexander Pope's what it has become today. To make definition and description of the meter even more complex, what poets and critics count as "acceptable" variations on the idealized pentameter pattern is not constant, even among those within a literary period. Disagreement abounds, as it did in the Ren. with *Tottel's Miscellany* (1557), as to whether some verse is iambic pentameter if it strays too far from the idealized base. In descriptive terms, though not always in prescriptive, iambic pentameter is regarded as occurring along a range, with *strict* at one end, where the stresses fall mostly on the stressed positions of the idealized pattern, and *loose* at the other end, allowing more leeway in stress placement and in the numbers of unstressed syllables between stresses. In terms of the meter's devel., describing the line's idealized meter as five feet of iambs may be inaccurate: as Marina Tarlinskaja's statistical analysis on a large corpus of Shakespeare's verse drama shows, only the last two "feet"—the final seventh through tenth syllables—consistently take the idealized pattern of a string of weak-strong units. According to her data, the first syllable is stressed in over 42% of Shakespeare's lines. The cl. approach to meter calls this stressed onset a *trochaic substitution*. While this may be a convenient term, the concept is inconsistent with the reality of how the meter developed or was thought of by early versifiers, since cl. scansion was imported from Lat. after iambic pentameter came into existence. What this means is that versifiers did not write by "rules" devised in the cl. poetry; rather the "rules" were a later attempt begun in the mid-Ren. to regulate the verse meter by limiting variation. The restriction on numbers of syllables per line and positions allowable for stressed syllables encouraged a stricter metrical practice, and by the 18th c., the strictest form

of the meter was being written, exemplified with the greatest flexibility in the verse practice of Pope. In the early 20th c., the meter achieved its loosest form, as developed and exemplified in the loose meter used in Robert Frost's poems to sound like conversation.

D. *Quantitative Meter* measures syllabic length or duration and is the basis of ancient Gr. and Lat. prosody (see QUANTITY). In the Ren., poets experimented with quantitative meter in imitation of cl. models, but these experiments do not sound metrical to Eng. ears. No true quantitative meter is possible in Eng. because of its accent-based system; the Romance langs. exhibit an alternating rhythm, like mod. Eng., but rhythm based on duration, not the relative pitch-height that is the chief component of Eng. stress.

II. Debates About Meter. Disagreements over meter tend to be contentious and entrenched, pitting the cl. approach against mod. ling., and linguists themselves divide over basic issues such as what is the motivation for prominence assignment; whether meter involves only measurable sound features of the foot or whether meter cannot be separated from the rhythmic influence of higher level systems and nontemporal sound structures; whether musical theory applies to meter; whether actual readers' perceptions are relevant to meter; and whether a universal theory of meter is possible.

At the opposite extreme from the cl. approach are theories that admit only one type of meter in Eng. Some theorists have asserted that meter in Eng. is trochaic, citing the pronunciations of Germanic words and compounds, which stress the onset syllable, whereas others argue that Eng. is iambic, with line onset stresses adjusted to iambs by postulating a silent uptake before the stressed onset (Wallace and essays on this debate in Baker). Latinate words, by contrast, prefer an iambic rhythm, with the two heritages mixing to comprise the two basic meters, as well as the variety seen in iambic pentameter. In the iambic-only view, *anapests are expanded iambs, *dactyls are expanded trochees, and *spondees are iambs as their relative stress assignments show. Debates over these issues indicate that meter in mod. Eng. combines accentual and syllabic features. From the oldest existing poetry in Eng. to mod. free verse, units are built of stressed syllables with a varying *but always limited* number of relatively weaker syllables surrounding them. This character is perhaps inevitable given the alternating stress pattern of Eng. and the regularity of repetition that makes for perception of meter.

III. Functions. Meter signals *genre, elicits the pleasures of musicality in expectation and surprise, imitates meaning in the content (see MIMESIS), contributes to *tone (e.g., ironic, satiric, oracular, conversational), and bears social and cultural meanings. The first three of these functions were much studied by New Criticism and structuralism (essays in Sebeok and in Chatman and Levin). The last two of these functions have been most neglected despite their analytic potential with respect to critical and cultural studies (Hurley). Because the definitions and limits of meters are preferences of a group or a time, what is called a meter can change, and the theories and functions of meter will also change over time.

■ Saintsbury, *Prosody*; Sebeok; Chatman; M. Halle and S. Keyser, "Chaucer and the Study of Prosody," *CE* 28 (1966): 187–219; Chomsky and Halle; Wimsatt; *Essays on the Language of Literature*, ed. S. Chatman and S. Levin (1975)—historical; P. Kiparsky, "Stress, Syntax, and Meter," *Lang* 51 (1975): 576–616; M.A.K. Halliday, *Halliday: System and Function in Language*, ed. G. Kress (1976); I. Lehiste, "Isochrony Reconsidered," *JPhon* 5 (1977): 253–63; Attridge, *Rhythms*; C. Hollis, *Language and Style in "Leaves of Grass"* (1983); S. Cushman, *William Carlos Williams and the Meanings of Measure* (1985); P. Kiparsky, "On Theory and Interpretation," Fabb et al.; G. Russom, *Old English Meter and Linguistic Theory* (1987); M. Tarlinskaja, *Shakespeare's Verse* (1987); Hollander; P. Kiparsky and G. Youmans, *Rhythm and Meter* (1989); T. Steele, *Missing Measures: Modern Poetry and the Revolt against Meter* (1990); R. Tsur, *Toward a Theory of Cognitive Poetics* (1992); C. Hartman, *English Metrics: A Hypertext Tutorial and Reference* (1995); *English Historical Metrics*, ed. J. Anderson and C. McCully (1996); *Meter in English: A Critical Engagement*, ed. D. Baker (1996); C. Hasty, *Meter as Rhythm* (1997); D. Crystal, *Language and Play* (1998); R. Pinsky, *The Sounds of Poetry* (1998); J. Wimsatt, "Alliteration and Hopkins' Sprung Rhythm," *PoT* 19 (1998); T. Steele, *All the Fun's in How You Say a Thing* (1999); V. Shemtov, "Metrical Hybridization: Prosodic Ambiguities as a Form of Social Dialogue," *PoT* 22, no. 1 (2001): 165–87; Carper and Attridge;

M. Russett, "Meter, Identity, Voice: Untranslating 'Christabel'," *SEL* 43 (2003); J. Cook, *Poetry in Theory* (2004); Y. Moriya, "Alliteration versus Natural Speech Rhythm in Determining the Meter of ME Alliterative Verse," *English Studies* 85 (2004); M. Hurley, "The Pragmatics of Prosody," *Style* 41 (2007).

R. WINSLOW

METONYMY (Gr., "change of name"; Lat. *denominatio*). A trope in which one expression is substituted for another on the basis of some material, causal, or conceptual relation. Quintilian lists the kinds traditionally distinguished: container for thing contained ("I'll have a glass"); agent for act, product, or object possessed ("reading Wordsworth"); cause for effect; time or place for their characteristics or products ("a bloody decade," "I'll have Burgundy"); associated object for its possessor or user ("the crown" for the king). Other kinds, previously considered *synecdoche, are now often included in metonymy: parts of the body for states of consciousness associated with them (head and heart for thought and feeling), material for object made of it (ivories for piano keys), and attributes or abstract features for concrete entities.

Because metonymy involves some literal or referential connection between tenor and vehicle, it is often contrasted with *metaphor, in which no such relationship exists. When the effect of metonymy is to create a sense of vividness or particularity—as in Thomas Gray's "drowsy tinklings" of sheep (the sound of their bells) or John Keats's "beaker full of the warm South"—the figure is often treated as an instance of *imagery. But the metonymies "drowsy tinklings" and "South" are not concrete images. Metonymic reference can evoke entire realms of meaning concisely, as in Ezra Pound's evocation of journalism and religion: "We have the press for wafer." W. H. Auden's "the clever *hopes expire* / Of a *low* dishonest *decade*" shows that a clear surface meaning can arise from metonymic associations of cause, attribute, and effect that are far from simple. Conversely, metonymy can create riddles, as in Dylan Thomas's "Altarwise by owl-light," which suggests facing east in the dark.

Ruwet points out that some metonymies result from verbal deletions that reduce redundancy. "A glass of Burgundy wine" becomes "a glass of Burgundy" or simply "Burgundy" or "a glass" when the sentence or context implies the rest. In "I just read [a novel by] Balzac," the phrase in brackets can be deleted because the context conveys its sense. Corpus-based studies of figurative lang. show that metonymy is often part of a ling. "collocation" in which several words always appear together. The phrase "provide [name of a country] with" produces a country-for-its-people metonymy, whereas "in [country]" is always interpreted literally. The word "heart," when preceded by a quantifier (some, few, many, all), is almost always metonymic (Hilpert).

Attempts to produce a definition of metonymy that would show what generic features its different types have in common have been part of the larger project of deriving a systematic rationale underlying *tropes. The meaning assigned to metonymy in such cases is determined by the number of tropes identified and the categorical features used to define them (ling., logical, semiotic, and/or psychological). Peter Ramus, Giambattista Vico, and their mod. followers hold that there are four basic tropes, the other three being metaphor, synecdoche, and *irony. Bloom retains six; Jakobson treats two, metonymy and metaphor. The meaning of metonymy expands as the number of tropes decreases. Among mod. adherents of fourfold classification, Burke would limit metonymy to "reduction" (incorporeal and corporeal); White defines it as part-whole reduction; Bloom treats it as a change from full to empty. In these three definitions, metonymy is not reversible: to substitute incorporeal for corporeal or empty for full would be another trope (synecdoche, for Burke and Bloom). These critics use the names of the tropes figuratively, applying them to passages or to entire texts.

In practice, it is often difficult to distinguish metonymy from the basic forms of synecdoche (part for whole, genus for species, or the reverse). Some hold that synecdoche entails a "one-many" substitution, or, in logical terms, a change of extension, whereas metonymy is a one-for-one replacement involving a change of intension (Henry). Rejecting that proposal, many critics use the term *metonymy* for both.

The opposition of metonymy to metaphor, treating these as the primary tropes, originated in Fr. structuralism and Russian formalism. Saussure held that there are two sorts of relationships between words: linear (syntagmatic) connections when they are used and associative (paradigmatic) connections of meaning in our minds. The Fr. psychologist Roudet referred to the linear connections as "contiguity," which sometimes evince metonymy. Paradigmatic changes, resulting from conceptual resemblance or similarity, were in his view metaphoric (Blank). Eichenbaum held that metaphor operates at a "supra-linguistic" level, that of the idea: a word is pulled from its semantic field to superimpose a second level of meaning on the literal level. Metonymy, he said, is a displacement, or lateral semantic shift, that lends words new meanings without leaving the literal plane. In "Marginal Notes on the Prose of the Poet Pasternak" (1935), Jakobson extended the dichotomy, suggesting that frequent use of metaphor unites the poet's mythology and being, separated from the world. Poets who prefer metonymy, on the other hand, project their being on an outer reality that their emotion and perception displace from the normal. The shifting, sequential character of metonymy, he said, was more common in prose than in poetry. Like Eichenbaum, Jakobson associated metaphor with poetry and metonymy with prose (Lodge).

Reworking the distinction in "Two Aspects of Language and Two Types of Aphasic Disturbances" (1956), Jakobson described metaphor as a metalinguistic operation—roughly speaking, a process through which an idea or theme is actualized in words. Metonymy, he said, was a change that operated on the hierarchy of ling. units, either affecting their order or substituting part of a word's meaning, or one associated with it, for the word itself. Both tropes can result from substitution of one word for another or from combination (the succession of words on the syntagmatic axis). In metaphor, e.g., a single word can be substituted for another, or the two can be successive ("A is B"). A series of metaphors may point toward a single theme, as in Shakespeare's sonnet that successively likens old age to autumn, sunset, and a dying fire. Metonymy does not produce a metalinguistic idea unifying the chain. Jakobson held that these two tropes could be used to classify mental disorders (e.g., aphasia), literary movements (romanticism and symbolism being based on metaphor, realism on metonymy), styles in painting and cinematography, operations of the unconscious (Sigmund Freud's "identification and symbolism" being metaphor, whereas "displacement" and "condensation" are metonymy), and cultural practices (such as the two types of magic identified by J. G. Frazer—one based on similarity, the other on contiguity). Adapting Jakobson's taxonomy to his own psychoanalytic theory, Lacan treated discourse as a continuous metonymy, displaced from the real, in which metaphoric, unconscious signifiers sometimes appear (Ruegg, Vergote).

Attempts to revise or simplify the metonymy-metaphor opposition as conceived by Jakobson and Lacan have taken several forms. Henry defines metonymy as the result of a psychological focus that substitutes the name of one of a word's semantic elements (semes) for the word itself. Metaphor, in his view, is a combination of two metonymies. Le Guern argues that the "contiguity" of Jakobson's metonymy involves reference to reality, whereas metaphor is the product of a purely ling. or conceptual operation. De Man pushes this difference further, seeing metonymy not only as referential but as contingent or accidental, in opposition to the pull toward unification of essences that underlies most uses of metaphor. Bredin agrees that metonymy refers to the world and sees its "extrinsic relations" as "a kind of ontological cement holding the world together," not as contingencies. Metaphor is also referential in his view, both figures being opposed to the "structural" or intralinguistic relations underlying synecdoche.

The reliance of metonymy on reference to experience may account for the difficulty theorists have in defining it. To say that it depends on contiguity or the transfer of features in a single domain, scheme, or model is to admit metaphorically that it cannot be delimited. Traditional sources list 23 types of metonymy (Peirsman and Geeraerts); Radden and Kövecses identify 49. The inadequacy of referential, pragmatic, and semantic definitions has led to an analysis of tropes based on the mental operations underlying their ling. expression. For conceptual-metaphor theorists, metonymical connections between physical reality and ideas support the thesis that lang. emerged from bodily experience. Physical warmth, a red face, and high blood pressure generate metonymies related to anger; hand, heart, and head signify action, feeling, and thought. In cognitive linguistics, one finds simple verbal patterns explained as intricate configurations of metonymy. "I can see your point" becomes a metonymy for "I see your point" (potential for actual). Corporations become metonymic wholes, parts of which (company, executives, workers) are activated in different statements. Metonymy gives actions and actors the names of objects (a ski; to ski; skier). The complexity of this view, inadequately represented here, becomes apparent

in the anthols. listed in the bibl. The discussion of metonymy produced by cognitive linguists and conceptual-metaphor theorists dwarfs that of the preceding two millennia. The objects of analysis are commonplace expressions that may make us aware of verbal intricacies but not of interesting variations. Poetry shares with everyday conversation a creative production of metonymy that sometimes attracts scholarly attention (Nerlich and Clarke).

Those who seek a logic underlying metonymy and other tropes are forced to redefine them, shifting some traditional meanings to other tropes and positing new conceptual entities that include the features that remain. In so doing, they often seek an explanation of tropes as rule-governed transformations of a posited conceptual literalism. The theoretical clarity thus obtained results from attempting to make the terminology of rhet. and poetics useful for philosophy, ling., and cognitive science.

See TROPE.

■ **Primary Texts**: L. Roudet, "Sur la classification psychologique des changements sémantiques," *Journal de psychologie* 18 (1921); B. Eichenbaum, *Anna Akhmatova* (1923); K. Burke, *A Grammar of Motives* ([1945] 1969); Jakobson: v. 2 for "Two Aspects of Language" and v. 5 for essay on Pasternak (in Ger.); J. Lacan, *Écrits,* trans. B. Fink ([1966] 2006); A. Henry, *Métonymie et métaphore* (1971); M. Le Guern, *Sémantique de la métaphore et de la métonymie* (1973); H. White, *Metahistory* (1973); F. de Saussure, *Course in General Linguistics,* ed. C. Bally and A. Sechehaye, trans. W. Baskin (1974); H. Bloom, *A Map of Misreading* (1975); N. Ruwet, "Synecdoches et métonymies," *Poétique* 6 (1975); H. Bloom, *Wallace Stevens* (1977); D. Lodge, *The Modes of Modern Writing* (1977); P. Ricoeur, *The Rule of Metaphor,* trans. R. Czerny (1977); P. de Man, *Allegories of Reading* (1979); M. Ruegg, "Metaphor and Metonymy," *Glyph* 6 (1979); G. Lakoff and M. Johnson, *Metaphors We Live By* (1980); J. Culler, *The Pursuit of Signs* (1981); G. Genette, *Figures of Literary Discourse,* trans. A. Sheridan (1982); U. Eco, *Semiotics and the Philosophy of Language* (1984); R. Jakobson, *Language in Literature,* ed. K. Pomorska (1987); M. Hilpert, "Keeping an Eye on the Data," in *Corpus-based Approaches to Metaphor and Metonymy,* ed. A. Stefanowitsch and S. Gries (2006).

■ **Criticism**: A. Vergote, "From Freud's 'Other Scene' to Lacan's 'Other,'" *Interpreting Lacan,* ed. J. Smith and W. Kerrigan (1983); H. Bredin,

"Metonymy," *PoT* 5 (1984); W. Bohn, "Jakobson's Theory of Metaphor and Metonymy, An Annotated Bibliography," *Style* 18 (1984); J. Hedley, *Powers in Verse* (1988); Lausberg; G. Radden and Z. Kövecses, "Towards a Theory of Metonymy," in *Metonymy in Language and Thought*, ed. K.-U. Panther and G. Radden (1999); A. Blank, "Co-presence and Succession," in *Metaphor and Metonymy at the Crossroads*, ed. A. Barcelona (2000); B. Nerlich and D. Clarke, "Ambiguities We Live By," *Journal of Pragmatics* 33 (2001); A. Barcelona, "Clarifying and Applying the Notions of Metaphor and Metonymy within Cognitive Linguistics," *Metaphor and Metonymy in Comparison and Contrast*, ed. R. Dirven and R. Pörings (2002); *Metonymy and Pragmatic Inferencing*, ed. K.-U. Panther and L. Thornburg (2003); A. Al-Sharafi, *Textual Metonymy* (2004); G. Steen, "Metonymy Goes Cognitive-Linguistic," *Style* 39 (2005); Y. Peirsman and D. Geeraerts, "Metonymy as a Prototypical Category," *Cognitive Linguistics* 17 (2006); K. Allan, *Metaphor and Metonymy* (2008).

W. MARTIN

MIMESIS

I. Beginnings
II. Plato
III. Aristotle
IV. Later Greek Views
V. Legacy

I. Beginnings. Gr. *mimesis* is related to the noun *mimos*, which denotes both an actor of mime (in its ancient form, a subliterary dramatic genre with spoken text) and the genre itself. Performative vividness is accordingly one stratum of the semantics of *mimesis*. The cognate verb first occurs in connection with some kind of role playing by a chorus at Homeric *Hymn to Apollo* 162–64. Other early usage connects the *mimesis* word group with various kinds of depiction and expressive evocation in song, music, dance, and visual art.

In the 5th c. BCE, a trad. of poetics started to attach itself to this terminology. In Aristophanes' *Thesmophoriazusae* the tragedian Agathon, propounding a principle of creative identification between poets and their characters, says that "the qualities we do not possess ourselves must be found by mimesis" (155–56). The context here reduces to comic parody (Agathon is composing in female dress) a model of imaginative and dramatic simulation. By this date, as subsequent evidence confirms, mimesis was becoming embroiled in theoretical debates about the workings of poetic representation and expression. Although mimesis terms are also used of behavioral imitation and emulation, *imitation* is generally an inadequate trans. for the critical and aesthetic ideas associated with this vocabulary. From the cl. period onward, mimesis is a standard Gr. way of denoting the "second life" of poetry (and other artistic media). But the word itself does not automatically bring with it any specific suppositions about the sources or ontological status of the kinds of "life" to which poetry gives form.

II. Plato. The lang. of mimesis has a wide range of reference in the Platonic corpus; even the cosmos itself counts as the Creator's mimetic work of art (*Timaeus*, e.g., 39e). The most concentrated account of poetic mimesis, but with important shifts of perspective, occurs in books 2–3 and 10 of the *Republic*. At *Republic* 2.373b, Socrates treats mimesis as a broad cultural category embracing poetry, visual art, music, dance, and more besides: i.e., something like a general concept of artistic representation and figuration. Later, however, at 3.392d, he limits the term (in a typology that has influenced mod. narratologists) to the dramatic, first-person mode of narrative discourse (*diegesis*), as opposed to the descriptive, third-person mode. Socrates maintains that the inward focus of poetic mimesis in this restricted sense engenders a corresponding intensity of experience for actors and readers (reading aloud is pertinent here), encouraging a kind of psychic multiplicity: an extension of the kind of theory parodied in Aristophanes' *Thesmophoriazusae* is visible here. This part of the *Republic* belongs within a larger framework that judges poetry principally in terms of ethical "truthfulness," while nonetheless allowing for elements of invention/fiction in narrative details (e.g., 2.382d). Neither here nor elsewhere does Plato treat poetic mimesis as standing in a simple relationship to the world.

In *Republic* book 10, Socrates returns to a broader concept of mimesis, notoriously using an analogy with mirrors to set up a provocative comparison of poetry with painting. But even the mirror *simile itself (10.596d–e) is far from straightforward. Socrates applies it to the representation of objects some of which ("everything in the sky and in Hades," 596c) are *not* accessible to actual mirrors. Elsewhere in the *Republic* (e.g., 5.472d), moreover, Socrates clearly acknowledges the existence of idealized, nonrealist painting. So the critique of poetic "appearances" and "simulacra" is principally directed at the phenomenology and ethical psychology of poetic experience, not at the literal truth or otherwise of poetry's materials. Mimesis functions here as a concept with which to analyze (and question) the ways in which poetry molds its own versions of the world. It does not in itself impose a uniform paradigm of poetic representation or expression, let alone any simple notion of imitation.

Crucial to book 10's critique is the affective process by which poetry seduces its audiences into internalizing its implicit values. At the climax of the critique, Socrates highlights the art form tragedy (incl. Homer, "teacher" of the tragedians), whose pessimistic force poses a peculiar challenge to a positive philosophical vision of reality. "Even the best of us," he says (605c–d), "surrender" to the intense emotions of such poetry: temporarily at least, tragedy makes the soul assimilate a worldview in its response to images of irremediable suffering and annihilation. The most significant aspect of mimesis, on this account, is not its use of naturalistic surfaces but its capacity to shape and imprint a whole sensibility.

Outside the *Republic*, there are many references to poetic/artistic mimesis that bear out the complexity of Plato's reflections on the subject. *Cratylus* 432a–d, e.g., advances a conception of (visual) mimesis as having a "qualitative" rather than replicatory relationship to what it represents. The *Sophist* distinguishes between two types of mimesis, "eicastic" (reliant on objective accuracy) and "phantastic" (involving a viewer-dependent perspectivism): the implications for poetry are not developed, though there are links with parts of *Republic* 10. Finally, the *Laws* contains many thoughts on mimesis, incl. an intricate analysis of the plural criteria (truth/fidelity, benefit, pleasure, beauty) by which the success of mimetic works might be judged (2.653–71). Contrary to many mod. summaries, there is no such thing as a fixed Platonic paradigm of mimesis, whether in poetry or elsewhere, only a series of attempts to define the triangular relationship between artistic expression, reality, and the minds of readers/viewers.

III. Aristotle. Aristotle's treatment of mimesis picks up from Plato's but gives the concept a

role within a positive anthropology of human culture, whereas Plato had tended to freight it with philosophical doubts and problems. The first chapter of the *Poetics* adopts the premise, clearly assumed as familiar, that (most forms of) poetry, music, dance, and visual art are species of mimesis. Contrary to a common misunderstanding, Aristotle never says that those arts as such "imitate nature." That phrase (better translated as "follow the principles of nature") is found at, e.g., *Physics* 2.2, 194a21, referring not to artistic representations but to the teleology of human craftsmanship in imposing form on matter.

Aristotle nowhere defines mimesis. But in *Poetics* 3, he diverges from *Republic* book 3 by using mimesis rather than "narrative discourse" as the master category within which different modes of poetic representation can be distinguished. Since Aristotle distinguishes poetry, *qua* mimesis, sharply from factual discourse such as philosophy/science (*Poetics* 1) and hist. (*Poetics* 9), his notion of mimesis has affinities with later ideas of fiction. This certainly does not mean, however, that he disconnects poetic imagination from reality. In *Poetics* 25, he states that poets, like other mimetic artists such as painters, can depict three kinds of world: actuality ("things as they are or were"), an amalgam of culturally accepted beliefs ("what people say and think"), or an ideal ("things as they ought to be"). This might seem to give poetry practically unlimited scope. Yet Aristotle's schema, while open to the operations of creative imagination (cf. *Poetics* 17), has no room for free fantasy. It presupposes that poets produce images of experience that can be grasped (both cognitively and emotionally) with implicit reference to consistent standards of human significance.

Throughout his discussion of tragedy and epic, Aristotle equates such standards with "probability and/or necessity." That formula, however, does not entail strict adherence to quotidian reality: how could it, where heroic characters and events are concerned? But it does require compelling dramatic coherence in the causality and psychology of the action portrayed. Mimesis, therefore, does not track particular features of the world. It is an exercise of emotionally engaged imagination in picturing things that "*might* happen" (*Poetics* 9). This produces a paradox in Aristotle's position: in *Poetics* 6, he calls tragedy "(a) mimesis of life," but in chs. 7–8, he stresses that the unity of a tragic/epic plot depends on narrative conditions far more rigorous than the diffuseness of life itself. Aristotelian mimesis is an artistic process that selectively reconfigures the "raw materials" of life. As such, it possesses a quasi-philosophical value: an ability to see beyond contingent particulars to a grasp of underlying structures of meaning. *Poetics* 4, which posits a human instinct for mimesis (as manifested in children's imaginative play), regards the desire to understand as a link between poetry and philosophy. *Poetics* 9 calls poetry "more philosophical" than hist., basing this judgment on poetry's capacity to convey an awareness of "universals." Unlike philosophy itself, mimesis makes this possible not through analysis and abstraction but through vivid concentration of narrative and expressive form.

IV. Later Greek Views. Mimesis remained a foundational concept of Gr. poetics (and philosophy of art more generally) throughout antiquity. While it always involves interpretation of the relationship between art and life/nature, its implications and nuances vary with the presuppositions of different critics and schools of thought. Broadly speaking, ideas of mimesis were divided between emphasis on fidelity (world-reflecting truthfulness) and the prioritizing of fiction (world-simulating inventiveness).

Of the two major Hellenistic schools of philosophy, the Stoics saw good poetry (like the life of Stoic virtue itself) as standing in mimetic conformity with the rational unity of the cosmos. This meant that they typically treated poetic mimesis as a medium in which philosophical ideas could be encapsulated in narrative and dramatic form: we find this, e.g., in Strabo's reading of Homer as a protophilosopher (*Geography* 1.1–2). On this account, mimesis entails true correspondence to the divine structure of reality, even if the correspondence is sometimes taken as allegorically encoded. For Epicureanism, by contrast, mimesis is more like a superficial reflection of all the different views of life (incl. deluded beliefs) that poets and their audiences are capable of producing. This understanding of the concept makes it easy for Epicureans to see poetry as standing in no fixed relationship to truth and, accordingly, as containing space for fiction: Philodemus, in his (now fragmentary) treatise *On Poems*, appears to have occupied such a position.

Mimesis remained not only adaptable but problematic. Plutarch, in "How the Young Man Should Study Poetry," attempts to elaborate a moderate Platonism while also admitting some Aristotelian formulations. He blocks a more radical Platonic critique by equating mimesis with invention and contrasting it sharply with (philosophical) truth. But by retaining a canon of "likeness to the truth," he struggles to reconcile the competing demands of fiction and ethical reliability in his model of poetry. A different kind of tension emerges at Philostratus's *Life of Apollonius* 6.19 (3d c. CE), where Apollonius, speaking of images of deities, contrasts mimesis as representation of "what has been seen" with *phantasia* as representation of what the artist has *not* seen but only creatively imagined. It is exaggerated, however, to claim evidence here for an entirely antimimetic aesthetic: sect. 2.22 shows that mimesis is still a basic tenet and can indeed be extended to the imaginative processes of the *recipients* of art.

Further ambiguities in the status of mimesis arise in Neoplatonism. Proclus's commentary on Plato's *Republic* fluctuates in its understanding of the concept. But it finally equates the mimetic with all poetry that works through an anthropocentric imagination and its emotions. Higher intellectual truths, according to Proclus, require poetic symbolism and allegory—or a hermeneutic that can discover these properties beneath the mimetic surface of a text. By philosophizing Homer, but also reading Plato himself as a partly mimetic writer, Proclus shows how ancient arguments over mimesis lead to deep perplexities about the resources and uses of poetry.

V. Legacy. Because of the variations and debates outlined above, mimesis should count not as a unitary concept but a "family" of ideas in poetic (and aesthetic) theory. Its legacy is far more complex than often suggested. Rendered by Lat. *imitatio* and vernacular equivalents, mimetic assumptions were a source of poetic theory from Ren. humanism to 19th-c. naturalism. But behind such slogans as the "imitation of nature" lurked plural conceptions of literary representation and expression. When romanticism reacted against neoclassical canons, it did not abandon all mimetic premises, esp. since the latter could encompass (as we have seen) forms of idealism. Even in the 20th c., modified versions of mimesis remained detectable, partly in popular expectations of "truth to life" and the like, partly in more abstract theorizing. The results can be paradoxical: Bertolt Brecht, e.g., spurns the mimesis of bourgeois "illusionism" yet develops techniques for a new type of truth-ful realism; Roland Barthes discards belief in veridical representation but retains a "reality ef-fect" whose credentials seem remarkably close to mimetic image-making. Despite a waning use of the older vocabulary of mimesis, many concerns associated with it have survived tena-ciously in mod. poetics.

See EPIC.

■ G. Sörbom, *Mimesis and Art* (1966); P. Ricoeur, "Mimesis and Representation," *Annals of Scholarship* 2 (1981); R. Lamberton, *Homer the Theologian* (1986); C. Prendergast, *The Order of Mimesis* (1986); G. Gebauer and C. Wulf, *Mimesis: Culture, Art, Society,* trans. D. Reneau (1995); F. Burwick, *Mimesis and Its Romantic Reflections* (2001); S. Halliwell, *The Aesthetics of Mimesis* (2002), and "The Theory and Practice of Narrative in Plato," *Narratology and Interpretation,* ed. J. Grethlein and A. Ren-gakos (2009).

S. HALLIWELL

MOCK EPIC, MOCK HEROIC. The mock heroic is a literary mode, primarily satiric, in which present realities are juxtaposed to a noble and heroic past, only to be found wanting. Au-thors sometimes evoke the heroic past by men-tioning figures or events (as in Jonathan Swift's "Battle of the Books"), but more often they do so allusively, by imitating heroic style, charac-terizations, actions, and so forth. Mock epic draws its heroic precedents specifically from the standard repertoire of the epic: invocations, dedications, celestial interventions, epic similes, canto divisions, and battles.

Although the mock heroic has ancient roots in the Homeric *Batrachomyomachia* (*Battle of the Frogs and Mice*) and instances can be found up to the present, the heyday of the form was the neoclassical movement of the 17th and 18th cs. Nicolas Boileau's 1674 *Le Lutrin* (*The Lectern*) is commonly cited as the first neoclas-sical mock epic. The mock heroic was com-mon in prose (as in Henry Fielding's *Joseph Andrews* and *Tom Jones*). This period also saw other mock forms (mock odes, elegies, pasto-rals, romances, and others), but the mock he-roic/epic most fully exemplified the tenor of the time.

In tone, neoclassical mock-heroic/epic satire is sometimes light, as in the amiable raillery of Alexander Pope's *Rape of the Lock*; in such cases, the present reality is seen as trivial, so that the contrast with the heroic point of reference is more amusing than dangerous. But more often, the satire ranges toward ridicule and humilia-tion of its victims (as in John Dryden's "Mac-Flecknoe" and Pope's *Dunciad*). In these cases, the present reality is a matter not of amusement but of cultural, social, and moral threat. Typi-cally, the derision is grounded in class prejudice, juxtaposing high literary form (and its noble values) and low persons pretending or, worse, acting above their station to demean the com-monweal. High-born miscreants are not ex-empt, however, esp. when they act below their station. Less commonly, gender roles also pro-vide a basis for mock-heroic satire.

■ R. P. Bond, *English Burlesque Poetry, 1700–1750* (1932); G. deF. Lord, *Heroic Mockery* (1977); U. Broich, *The 18th-Century Mock-Heroic Poem* (1990); G. G. Colomb, *Designs on Truth: The Poetics of Augustan Mock Heroic* (1992); R. G. Terry, *Mock-Heroic from Butler to Cowper* (2005).

G. G. COLOMB

MONOLOGUE. In the widest sense, a sustained first-person utterance for which, whether or not an audience is expressly evoked, rhetorical mo-tives outweigh meditative or deliberative ones. Orations, petitionary prayers, and *laments are often monologues; so are many *lyric poems. Thus, monologue is less a genre than a device many genres employ. Arising from the implied circumstances that shape it, monologue has a clearly dramatic element: it characteristically defines elements of subjectivity and personality against pressures—destiny, hist., other people—whose resistance gives those elements shape. The term may refer to sections within a longer work that privilege a single voice and unitary stand-point. The technical, literary sense of monologue is not inconsistent with more ordinary usage: speech that monopolizes conversation, or the patter of a stand-up comic.

In poetry, monologue has clear connections to drama. *Soliloquy* refers to a form of mono-logue in which an actor speaks alone on stage, whether overheard in the act of formulating private thoughts and feelings (Hamlet) or ad-dressing the audience directly (Iago). Some-times a work opens like Christopher Marlowe's *Doctor Faustus* or Lord Byron's *Manfred* with a soliloquy by the main character. Heard or over-heard, monologue invites complex interplay between character and audience. Some of the most powerful passages in dramatic poetry are written as monologue.

The technique is ancient and so entwined with the ritual roots of drama that no distinct origin may be specified. Significant biblical examples occur in the Psalms and the prophets, where utterances cast in monologic form riveted the connection between vatic inspiration and impassioned verse. Lengthy speeches couched in refined rhet. and articulating an individual position appear in cl. epics and odes as well as dramas. Some miming included single-voiced speech, although dialogue was preferred there.

The cultivation of first-person speakers in Theocritus's idylls produced admirable examples of monologue, as did elegiac poems by Propertius. Elegies, diatribes, and comic harangues often display strong monologic elements; philosophical poems seldom do; verse epistles, while meant to be read rather than declaimed, still are monologic in their emphasis on the written performance of character. *Prosopopoeia, a cl. rhetorical form feigning speech by a personage of note (Athena, Hector), held an important place within pedagogy. It also influenced the female impersonations comprised by Ovid's *Heroides*, a work strikingly analogous to the independent Chinese trad. wherein courtiers sought preferment by addressing to the emperor poems in the guise of an abandoned woman.

Monologue like other devices stemming from drama remains open to ironies of context, although in some historical phases these may lie dormant. Germanic lit., incl. OE derivatives like "The Wanderer" and "The Wife's Lament," employs the monologue to valorize subjectivity. Devotional poetry tends to canonize monologue: in the later Middle Ages, e.g., speeches addressed by the Virgin to the Cross became a fixed subgenre. The dramatic element incubated within med. religious verse emerged in early mod. variations on the cl. epistle and *complaint. Poets from William Dunbar to Thomas Wyatt bred out of Chaucer's stock, with grafts from Ovid and Horace, a precedent emulated throughout the later 16th c. by George Gascoigne, Walter Ralegh, and others. These Elizabethans, like their dramatist counterparts, exploited monologic effects ranging from uncompromising rhetorical directness to the self-anatomy of a divided mind. Satan's monologue at the start of John Milton's *Paradise Lost*, book 4, culminates this development; Milton's complementary "L'Allegro" and "Il Penseroso" point up the tendency for monologue to solicit, or preempt, response.

Retreating in the face of socially preoccupied Restoration and Augustan verse, monologue remained essential to Alexander Pope's self-fashioning, most subtly in "Eloisa to Abelard," a poem that inspired many successors during the sensibility era. In the romantic period, the normative identity of poet with speaker elevated monologue to stardom as a vehicle for heroic recuperations of creative selfhood as performed in elegy and ode. Yet, at the same time, the ironic potential suppressed under high romanticism flourished in the comedy routine that was Byron's *Don Juan*. Even in more sober productions like William Wordsworth's "Tintern Abbey," monologue so winnowed consciousness as to render the confessing mind an object of curiosity to itself. S. T. Coleridge's term for the lyric genre thus produced, *conversation poem*, expresses a paradox that resided within monologue all along.

Lineally descended from this romantic genre, the Victorian dramatic monologue represents the most significant generic flowering of the device in postromantic poetry. Robert Browning called "My Last Duchess" and its congeners "dramatic lyrics," a name that emphasizes the genre's hybridity. Browning preeminently, but in tandem with Alfred, Lord Tennyson and Elizabeth Barrett, drove to new intensity monologue's constitutive tension between speakers' psychological complexity and the web of ambient circumstance in which they are enmeshed. Formally, the Victorian dramatic monologue embraced both the legacy of stage monologue in blank verse and also the trad. of the *ballad, with adapted stanzaic forms whose artifice figures the genre's oblique but persistent link to narrative. In *Maud: A Monodrama*, Tennyson took monologue where a prosopopoeia like his "Ulysses" had pointed, toward a serial tableau portraying mercurial moods of a single mind rather than a dramatic situation powerfully conceived. Later Victorian and Edwardian poets developed these overtures, most notably William Morris, D. G. Rossetti, Christina Rossetti, A. C. Swinburne, and Augusta Webster.

Affinities between these 19th-c. devels. and closet drama show the dramatic monologue anticipating modernist playwriting by August Strindberg, Luigi Pirandello, and Samuel Beckett. Browning's conception flows through modernist poetry via Ezra Pound, Tennyson's via T. S. Eliot, whose doctrine of impersonality adjoined W. B. Yeats's doctrine of the mask or *persona to provide the mod. poetic monologue with theoretical support. Among Am. poets E. A. Robinson, Edgar Lee Masters, Robert Frost, and Langston Hughes worked regional or ethnic variations on monologue's capacity to project a representative identity, while in later generations Robert Lowell, Sylvia Plath, Elizabeth Bishop, and John Ashbery renewed the discrepancy between poet and speaker by spinning the psychological thread of monologue to a virtually clinical fineness. To rehistoricize this trad. and highlight its political subtexts has been the achievement of such contemp. poets as Richard Howard, Frank Bidart, Ai, and Carol Ann Duffy.

See DIALOGUE, DRAMATIC POETRY.

■ F. Leo, *Der Monolog im Drama* (1908); E. W. Roessler, *The Soliloquy in German Drama* (1915); I. B. Sessions, "The Dramatic Monologue," *PMLA* 62 (1947); H. Schauer and F. W. Wodtke, "Monolog," *Reallexikon II*, v. 2; R. Langbaum, *The Poetry of Experience* (1957); A. D. Culler, "Monodrama and the Dramatic Monologue," *PMLA* 90 (1975); R. W. Rader, "The Dramatic Monologue and Related Lyric Forms," *CritI* 3 (1976); A. Sinfield, *Dramatic Monologue* (1977); J. Blundell, *Menander and the Monologue* (1980); K. Frieden, *Genius and Monologue* (1985); L. D. Martin, *Browning's Dramatic Monologues and the Post-Romantic Subject* (1985); A. Rosmarin, *The Power of Genre* (1985); W. Clemen, *Shakespeare's Soliloquies* (1987); J. T. Mayer, *T. S. Eliot's Silent Voices* (1989); W. D. Shaw, *Origins of the Monologue* (1999); G. Byron, *Dramatic Monologue* (2003).

B. A. NICHOLS; H. F. TUCKER

N

NARRATIVE POETRY

I. History
II. Poetic Form and Narrative Poetry
III. Criticism

Narrative turns the raw material of story—the "telling" of a concatenation of events unfolding in linear time—into a (more or less) artful organization of those events that may complicate their chronology, suggest their significance, emphasize their affect, or invite their interpretation. Narrative *poetry* heightens this process by framing the act of telling in the rhythmically and sonically constructed lang. of verse. Although particularly monumental and foundational works from many cultures (e.g., the Mesopotamian *Epic of Gilgamesh*, the Sanskrit *Mahābhārata* and *Rāmāyaṇa*, the Homeric epics, the OE *Beowulf*, the MHG *Nibelungenlied*) and certain poetic genres (e.g., *epic, metrical romance, *ballad) are particularly associated with narrative poetry, poetic narrative is a capacious category and also embraces beast fable, *satire, the dramatic *monologue, reflective spiritual autobiography (e.g., William Wordsworth's *The Prelude*), allegorical anatomy (*Roman de la Rose*, *Piers Plowman*), some elegies (e.g., Walt Whitman's "When Lilacs Last in the Dooryard Bloom'd" and G. M. Hopkins's "The Wreck of the Deutschland"), and, albeit in fragmented or subverted form, the modernist *lyric sequences of Hart Crane, T. S. Eliot, Ezra Pound, and W. C. Williams. Furthermore, the boundaries between narrative and lyric verse are always fungible: poems usually classified as *lyric may supply a significant amount of narrative context for an act of reflection unfolding in arrested time (as in the work of Elizabeth Bishop, Robert Lowell, and Seamus Heaney).

Although theories of narrative tend to focus primarily, if not exclusively, on the novel, narrative poems vigorously exploit and in many cases anticipate the literary practices we find in sophisticated prose fictions. Traditional ballads like "Tam Lin" often make telling use of *ellipsis and parataxis (see HYPOTAXIS AND PARATAXIS). The late 14th-c. alliterative romance *Sir Gawain and the Green Knight* interlaces and eventually fuses its multiple plot motifs with great elegance and power. Chaucer's *Troilus and Criseyde* presents its characters with a degree of verisimilitude and a detailed attention to their physical surroundings and speech that has provoked some readers to praise its "novelistic" qualities. The epic narrative of John Milton's *Paradise Lost* elaborately reorders linear chronology and interrupts narrative sequence with prolepsis and flashback. Robert Browning's well-known dramatic monologue "My Last Duchess" makes use of a framed narration and an unreliable narrator. Many of Robert Frost's narrative poems advance action and develop character through the careful unfolding of dialogue.

The heightened, ordered lang. of pre-20th-c. narrative poetry does mean, however, that the illusion of transparent representation of experience so valued in the realist novel will be adumbrated by the visible and sometimes elaborate artifice of poetic form. Indeed, major narrative poems become the occasion for the invention of new stanzaic vehicles, fresh rooms for the creation of a particular imaginative universe (e.g., the nine-line stanza developed by Edmund Spenser for *The Faerie Queene*, the *terza rima* of Dante's *Divina commedia*, and the sonnet-like stanzas of Alexander Pushkin's *Evgenij Onegin*). Complex internal patterning can produce its own order of *mimesis: the evocation of a particular kind of experience may be achieved through metrical design or the structures of rhyme (as we see in the use of *enjambment and *caesura to organize meaning across Milton's blank verse paragraphs or in the deployment of Chaucer's hypnotic repetition and recontextualization of semantically loaded rhyme pairs—*routhe/trouthe*, *herte/ smerte*, *Troye/joye*—across the narrative arc of *Troilus and Criseyde*). Poetic fictions can, moreover, draw on the dynamics of lyric to interrupt linear narrative drive, sometimes offering pauses, reflection, and dilation by way of a shift in the genre of represented utterance (e.g., the elegiac digressions within the later stages of *Beowulf*), sometimes embedding songs within the action (as in Alfred, Lord Tennyson's *The Princess*), sometimes by way of a larger hybridization produced by the fusion of "lyric" and "narrative" (or synchronic and diachronic) possibility.

I. History. The hist. of narrative poetry suggests that different poetic modes speak to the needs of particular historical moments; at the same time, it is one of perpetual return as genres are reclaimed and revised. In preliterate cultures, the protocols of orally composed poetry—formulaic diction, the rhythmic patterning of elevated utterance, the deployment of traditional themes and episodes—help to bind and fix important narratives: stories of origin (etiologies, theodicies, genealogies), cultural hists., hero tales, national myth. Homeric epic also foregrounds, in the *Odyssey*, the narrative capacity of the individual as well as the tale of the tribe: Odysseus, the man of many turns and many stories, repeatedly refashions himself in narrative. The later hist. of epic reveals that monumental poetic acts of storytelling are always in dialogue with other narrative poems. Virgil's *Aeneid* (29–19 BCE) adapts Homeric epic to celebrate the values of Augustan Rome; his appropriation of Homer's characters and his repositioning of Trojan refugees as the founders of his own city fuse the wars of the *Iliad* and the wanderings of the *Odyssey* within a single work that translates the Homeric warrior code into the civic duty and stoicism of the virtuous Aeneas. The *Aeneid* discloses, furthermore, the time-bending capacity of poetic narrative: the Trojan past and the events of Virgil's own historical moment are folded into the struggles of his hero.

Ovid's *Metamorphoses* (1–8 CE) reimagines epic, inserting idiosyncratic and selective coverage of events from the *Iliad*, *Odyssey*, and *Aeneid* in books 12–14 of its ambitious compendium of myth and hist. The work's narrative technique is strikingly inventive and even experimental, incl. complex framings of embedded episodes and acts of internal storytelling, formal virtuosity (as in the phrases reflecting across line endings in book 3's account of Narcissus at the pond), and stylistic play (extending at times into *parody, as in the hyperbolic pastoral lyric of the giant Polyphemus).

The vernacular long poems of the Eur. Middle Ages include heroic narratives (e.g., the *Chanson de Roland* and the *Poema del Cid*) but more notably fuse chivalric and courtly ideals in the romances that flourished in the wake of Chrétien de Troyes's 12th-c. Arthurian narratives, whose octosyllabic rhymed *couplets frame courtly dialogue and explorations of interiority as well as knightly adventure. Romance slides toward lyric in the *Lais* of Chrétien's near-contemporary, Marie de France, whose tales include short evocative mood pieces (e.g., *Chevrefoil*). In Eng., the author of *Sir Gawain and the Green Knight* demonstrates the power of sophisticated alliterative verse to frame a quest narrative that is also a moral journey, although it is metrical romance (*King Horn*, *Sir Orfeo*, *The Squire of Low Degree*) that constitutes the predominant popular narrative mode. Chaucer's late 14th-c. narrative poems are remarkable for their modal range (they include *fabliaux, *dream visions, saint's lives, beast fables, Ovidian adaptations, the sophisticated romance of the aforementioned *Troilus and Criseyde*), and the lively frame of the storytelling competition between the pilgrims of the *Canterbury Tales* embraces numerous carefully imagined alternative narrators who variously present their tales in protoheroic couplets or formal stanzas.

The most ambitious experiments of med. narrative poetry are notably evident in Italy. Dante's *Commedia* (written 1307–21) offers religious epic focused through a first-person narrator; his introduction of Virgil as the narrator's guide through hell and purgatory puts his work in quite literal conversation with cl. epic. The recursive rhymes of the *Commedia*'s terza rima afford a particularly striking medium for the descriptive, meditative, and visionary passages that interweave its protagonist's three-part journey. The innovative lyric sequence of Dante's near-contemporary, Petrarch, the *Canzoniere*, while not strictly a narrative project, demonstrates the potential for a congeries of lyric moments to provoke or suggest a narrative dynamic; subsequent lyric sequences (most notoriously Shakespeare's *Sonnets*) have continued to provoke narrative interpretation.

The great narrative poems of the Ren. fuse multiple genres even as they stake their claims for vernacular national poetries. Ludovico Ariosto's *Orlando furioso* (1516) and Torquato Tasso's *Gerusalemme liberata* (1581) interlace erotic quests with heroic matter, and Ariosto marshals a striking mixture of tones in his cheerfully errant and digressive storytelling. Both use the intricate *ottava rima* stanza developed by Giovanni Boccaccio in his *Teseida* and *Il Filostrato* two centuries previously. Spenser's *The Faerie Queene* (1590, 1596) complicates epic-romance with sophisticated allegorical anatomy; although influenced by Ariosto, the author replaces ottava rima with his own nine-line stanza. *The Faerie Queene*'s mythopoesis often draws on and revises the *Metamorphoses*;

lighter ventures into Ovidianism appear in the shorter epyllion (or "short epic") form, most notably Christopher Marlowe's *Hero and Leander* (1593) and Shakespeare's *Venus and Adonis* (1593). Marlowe's poem offers a striking example of the narrative possibilities of the *heroic couplet, not only in its passages of rapid action but in elaborate rhetorical set pieces and ekphrastic digressions.

Milton's *Paradise Lost* (1667, 1674) breaks with what he termed the "bondage" of rhyme and offers the first Eng. blank-verse epic. In the poet's ambitious retelling of the origins of the human condition, lengthy *verse paragraphs elaborate meaning and complicate the sequential unfolding of thought through sustained enjambment, mirroring on the small scale the work's challenging representation of a timeline that encompasses both genesis and apocalypse. In the century after Milton, the long satirical narratives and *mock epics of John Dryden and Alexander Pope eschew *blank verse in favor of the more aphoristic possibilities of the heroic couplet; in the later 18th c., George Crabbe discloses the quieter and more naturalistic capacities of that particular form in the rural narratives of *The Village* (1783).

The romantics appropriate and revise the blank-verse epic (most obviously in the spiritual autobiography of Wordsworth's *The Prelude* [1805, pub. 1850], although Wordsworth also employs blank verse in shorter narrative works such as "Michael"). Their poetry also reworks other narrative forms. The traditional ballad's effective use of simple, charged diction, minimalist but telling description, and a narrative dynamic heavily reliant on repetition with variation had attracted more literary treatments in earlier centuries (e.g., in Walter Ralegh's "Walsingham"); the very title of Wordsworth and S. T. Coleridge's *Lyrical Ballads* (1798) suggests an interest in appropriating the form in a more reflective manner (both Wordsworth and Coleridge experiment with a more dilatory six-line stanza in, e.g., the former's "The Idiot Boy" and the latter's *The Rime of the Ancient Mariner*). Elsewhere, John Keats's use of an abbreviated final line in the quatrains of "La Belle Dame sans Merci" (1820) modifies the conventional ballad stanza to create a powerful sense of loss, diminishment, and melancholy.

Keats borrows the recursive *Spenserian stanza for the leisurely sensuous romance narrative of "The Eve of St. Agnes" (1820); Lord Byron deploys its capacity for digression and

interruption to very different effect in his satirical epic *Don Juan* (1819–24). As the 19th c. unfolds, a continuing interest in the long narrative poem diverges, on the one hand, into nostalgia and neomedievalism (Tennyson's *Idylls of the King*, the poems of D. G. Rossetti, and, eventually, W. B. Yeats's Celtic mythologies) and, on the other, into something not dissimilar to the verisimilitude of the realist novel. Pushkin's *Evgenij Onegin* (1825–32) makes a complex and artful stanzaic form the vehicle for representing colloquial description and dialogue and reflections on contemp. life. Robert Browning's multipart blank-verse narrative *The Ring and the Book* (1868–69) brings together a sequence of idiosyncratic dramatic monologues retracing the same set of events in Ren. Italy; Elizabeth Barrett Browning's account of the travails of a female artist in *Aurora Leigh* (1856) offers a contemp. blank-verse Bildungsroman. George Meredith's *Modern Love* (1862) co-opts the lyric sequence for quasi-novelistic purposes. Moving into the 20th c., one finds a sparser, starker version of romantic blank-verse narrative in the snapshot rural narratives (e.g., "The Death of the Hired Man," "Home Burial") of Robert Frost's *North of Boston* collection (1914).

With the particular valorization of the lyric (and the lyric sequence) in the 20th c., poetic storytelling tends to fall out of favor and becomes associated with middlebrow "parlor poetry" (like some of the highly recitable works of Rudyard Kipling and H. W. Longfellow) or with the Victorian light verse of Lewis Carroll and W. S. Gilbert. Its early 20th-c. exponents are little read, although they too can revisit older modes, as in John Masefield's beast fable *Reynard the Fox* (1919) or G. K. Chesterton's melodramatic take on Ren. heroic poetry in "Lepanto" (1911). Narrative poetry does not, however, disappear. The accessible vignettes of Edgar Lee Masters's *Spoon River Anthology* (1916) have a more sophisticated modernist counterpart in Melvin B. Tolson's lyric sequence *Harlem Gallery* (1965). T. S. Eliot's structural use of the Grail quest myth and his fragmentary and fragmented quotation of earlier narrative poetry and familiar forms (dramatic blank verse, the narrative quatrain) in *The Waste Land* (1922) work in tension with the ellipses and discontinuities of a poem that keeps entertaining narrative possibilities only to frustrate them. The ballad has continued to attract mod. and contemp. practitioners (see, e.g., W. H. Auden's "As I Walked Out One Evening" and Dudley Randall's "Ballad of Birmingham"). An almost Ovidian interest in rewriting old stories in new terms characterizes the work of Carol Ann Duffy ("Mrs. Midas," "Little Red Cap"). The Caribbean poet Derek Walcott's expansive postcolonial epic *Omeros* (1990), composed in a modified version of terza rima, embraces extended allusions to Homeric and Dantean journeyings (and exiles) as it both retraces the horrors of the middle passage and slides into metapoetic reflections. Rather less monumentally, Vikram Seth's *The Golden Gate* (1986) attempts a Pushkinesque narrative in tetrameter sonnets set in contemp. California. Narrative poetry has been championed by some New Formalists (such as Annie Finch and Mark Jarman), but less conservative artists have also worked in this territory. The experimentalist Ronald Johnson creates a new story by selectively erasing much of the text of the first four books of *Paradise Lost* in *RADIOS OI-OIV* (1976); the classicist Anne Carson offers a postmod. spin on the Geryon/Hercules myth in *Autobiography of Red* (1998); Lyn Hejinian's at once highly structured and paratactic sequence of prose poems *My Life* (1980–87) might be seen as a contemp. (and differently gendered) response to *The Prelude*.

II. Poetic Form and Narrative Poetry.

In narrative poetry, the resources of poetic form have always been thoroughly entangled with the fiction-making process. At the conclusion of each long stanza of alliterating lines in *Sir Gawain and the Green Knight*, an isolated line with a single stress is followed by a rhymed quatrain, and this five-line bob and wheel presents new information in a particularly emphatic manner. A stanza detailing the hero's lonely quest is followed by the miniature line "al one" (all alone), whose very isolation emphasizes the protagonist's condition; after an extended description of the alien warrior who invades King Arthur's court, the information that he is not only mysterious but entirely *green* is delayed to the final emphatic rhyme word of the quatrain. The wandering romance narratives and perpetual self-complication of Spenser's *Faerie Queene* are complemented by its stanzaic design whose *ababbcbcc* rhyme scheme encourages recapitulation, a small-scale doubling back that augments or reexamines what has already been said; at the same time, Spenser's switch from iambic pentameter to a longer *alexandrine in the ninth lines of each stanza produces repeated (and repeatedly superseded) moments of summary, gloss, or provisional closure that complement

the larger narrative's own insistent swerves from any final ending. Spenser's additional predilection for allowing sonic effects to heighten narrative action is evident in the following description of his Red Cross Knight's encounter with the female monster Errour:

> Yet kindling rage, her selfe she gathered round,
> And all attonce her beastly body raizd
> With doubled forces high above the ground:
> Tho wrapping up her wrethéd sterne arownd,
> Lept fierce upon his shield, and her huge traine
> All suddenly about his body wound

The repeated rhymes on "wound" encourage the stanza to wind about the reader even as the monster entangles the knight.

Repetition with variation, a favorite strategy of both the traditional and the literary ballad, can be deployed with powerful narrative force. In "She Moved through the Fair," a poignant folk lyric collected by the Ir. poet Padraic Colum, the words of the narrator's lost beloved, "It will not be long, love, / 'Til our wedding day," take on a quite different meaning when, as a ghost, she reiterates her promise in the work's concluding stanza. In *The Rime of the Ancient Mariner*, Coleridge's occasional expansion of the traditional four-line stanza into six lines, repeating with minimal variation the fourth line in the sixth, enhances the obsessive and incantatory nature of the tale told by the Mariner to the Wedding Guest. Meter can also powerfully shape narrative tone and mood: in Christina Rossetti's *Goblin Market* (1862), the steady accretion of lines beginning with trochaic and dactylic feet not only emphasizes the feverish quality of the fable but heightens, in its climactic stanzas, the assault on all the senses endured by its heroine. G. M. Hopkins's innovative *sprung rhythm in "The Wreck of the Deutschland" (1918) evokes the turbulence and uncertainty of tempest and shipwreck.

Narrative poems in rhymed couplets offer in each rhyme's completion temporary gestures toward containment and *closure that may operate in tension with the forward drive of plot and foster the witty and epigrammatic quality of poets as disparate as Chaucer, Marlowe, and Pope. In satiric narrative, they can also offer exquisitely controlled moments of comic anticlimax, as in the following from

Pope's *Rape of the Lock* (1714): "The skil-
ful nymph reviews her force with care / 'Let
spades be trumps!' she said, and trumps they
were." (Wilfred Owen's World War I dream
narrative "Strange Meeting" [1918] poignantly
unbalances the confident pace of couplet narrative in its employment of half- and slant
rhymes throughout.) Blank-verse narrative
removes sonic closure, and its enjambments
can open up line endings to a powerful sense
of semantic uncertainty, vigorously exploited
by Milton in *Paradise Lost*, whose extended
and flexible verse paragraphs regularly qualify
meaning and create surprise, as in the retrospective reinflection of the word "merit" by
the enjambed line that follows in the poet's
description of how, in imperial splendor,

Satan exalted sat, by merit raised
To that bad eminence.

The mere absence of rhyme does not preclude,
of course, the heightened effects of poetic diction and meter: in the following description of
Satan's voyage through Chaos, the accumulation of monosyllables and *spondees in the second and third lines and the pounding *iambs
that place strong stress on verbs of movement in
the fourth powerfully evoke a laborious, scrab-
bling, almost animal journeying:

. . .the Fiend
O'er bog or steep, through strait, rough,
dense, or rare,
With head, hands, wings, or feet pursues
his way,
And swims or sinks, or wades or creeps or
flies.

The deployment of strong caesurae in both
blank and rhymed verse also contributes to
strong narrative effects; a metrical pause can
allow discourse to change direction or create a
space for the reader to fill. Browning uses these
tactics simultaneously when the murderous
narrator of "My Last Duchess" offers self-reve-
lation at the very moment that he swerves from
full confession:

I gave commands;
Then all smiles stopped together. There she
stands
As if alive. Will't please you rise? We'll meet
The company below.

Narrative poetry can, furthermore, deploy
the resources of typography to reinforce the
work of form in shaping the unfolding of a

fiction. In Frost's "Death of the Hired Man," a
final *split line packs a climactic punch:

"Warren?" she questioned.
          "Dead," was all he answered.

In Eliot's *The Waste Land*, by contrast, typography repeatedly shatters the formal containment
of putative plot: teasing fragments of narrative
are interrupted by white space; new beginnings
or fruitless returns erupt out of nowhere.

III. Criticism. Little critical work has focused
specifically on narrative poetry, although the
critical taxonomies and terminologies developed by narrative theorists such as Chatman,
Genette, and Ricoeur may be usefully applied
to narrative in verse. This is, to a large extent,
the result of a critical tendency to rely on a po-
etry/prose binary that reduces poetry to lyric
and elides the presence and work of poetic narrative; the influential stylistic poetics of Jakobson, e.g., associates epic with the "metonymical" capacity of prose fiction as opposed to the
"metaphoric" nature of lyric. Scholes, Kellogg,
and Phelan's *The Nature of Narrative* pays more
sustained attention to narrative poetry than any
other work in this field, although the authors'
interest in the historical develop. of narratives
allows relatively little space for discussion of
the particular shaping capacities of poetic form.
Among crit. not strictly aimed at narrative poetry, McHugh's rich essay on the linear unfolding of meaning in lyric and the pivotal force of
the line ending in "making and breaking" sense
might be equally well applied to the workings
of narrative poetry. Among works on particular
narrative poets or particular narrative genres,
the crit. of Boitani (on med. poetic narrative),
Greene (on the epic trad.), Berger (on Spenser's
Faerie Queene), Crosman (on Milton's *Paradise
Lost*), Fischer (on romantic verse narratives),
and Tucker (on the Victorian long poem) offer
particularly useful insights.

See DRAMATIC POETRY.

■ R. Jakobson, "Linguistics and Poetics," in
Sebeok; T. M. Greene, *The Descent from Heaven:
A Study in Epic Continuity* (1963); F. Kermode,
The Sense of an Ending (1967); S. Chatman, *Story
and Discourse: Narrative Structure in Fiction and
Film* (1978); R. Crosman, *Reading "Paradise
Lost"* (1980); G. Genette, *Narrative Discourse*,
trans. J. Lewin (1980); F. G. Andersen, O. Holzapfel, and T. Pettitt, *The Ballad as Narrative*
(1982); P. Boitani, *English Medieval Narrative in
the Thirteenth and Fourteenth Centuries*, trans.

J. K. Hall (1982); *The Oxford Book of Narrative Verse*, ed. I. Opie and P. Opie (1983); P. Ricoeur, *Time and Narrative*, trans. K. McLaughlin and D. Pellauer (1984); H. Berger Jr., *Revisionary Play: Studies in the Spenserian Dynamic* (1988) P. Zumthor, *Oral Poetry*, trans. K. Murphy-Judy (1990); H. Fischer, *Romantic Verse Narrative* (1991); C. R. Kinney, *Strategies of Poetic Narrative: Chaucer, Spenser, Milton, Eliot* (1992); H. McHugh, "Moving Means, Meaning Moves: Notes on Lyric Destination," *Poets Teaching Poets*, ed. G. Orr and E. B. Voigt (1996); *After New Formalism: Poets on Form, Narrative and Tradition*, ed. A. Finch (1999); N. Roberts, *Narrative and Voice in Postwar Poetry* (1999); P. Cobley, *Narrative* (2001); R. Scholes, R. Kellogg, and J. Phelan, *The Nature of Narrative*, 2d ed. (2006); H. F. Tucker, *Epic: Britain's Heroic Muse, 1790–1910* (2008).

C. R. KINNEY

NARRATOR. *See* PERSONA; VOICE.

NEAR RHYME, generic rhyme, half rhyme, imperfect rhyme, oblique rhyme, off-rhyme, pararhyme, partial rhyme, slant rhyme. There is no standard term in Eng.; *near rhyme* will be used here as a cover term for several varieties of rhyming practice that are related to yet do not fulfill the canonical definition of *rhyme nor exceed it, as in *rich rhyme. Judgmental adjectives were better avoided, for they carry the pejorative implication that a near rhyme is a failure to achieve true rhyme, either on account of deficiency of lang. resources or incompetence of the poet—equally dubious assumptions, both. *Near* must be taken, therefore, not in the sense of "imperfect" but rather of "approximate," i.e., close to the narrow band of instances qualifying as canonical end rhyme but outside it, in the wider field of "related or alternative forms of sound correspondence" (Scherr). Within the Eng. taxonomy, most forms of near rhyme, of which there are several, amount to various complex types of *consonance and produce such rhymes as "justice"/"hostess" (Jonathan Swift), "port"/"chart" (Emily Dickinson), or word such as *grope/cup, maze/coze, drunkard/conquered.* Žirmunskij distinguishes the forms of rhyme as "exact," "augmented" (by deletion or addition), and "altered" (by both, meaning substitution), a typology accepted and extended by Gasparov.

In judging rhymes, it is important not to be misled by shifts in historical phonology, whereby rhymes that now seem only near were actually true rhymes in their day, e.g., Alexander Pope's "obey" / "tea." Further, it is important that near rhyme be conceived not solely in terms of Eng. practice; for since the early 20th c., the status of near rhyme in Eng. has been problematized, while in Rus., e.g., prosodists since Žirmunskij have recognized both "approximate" and "inexact" rhyme as part of the standard definition of *rhyme* (see Scherr). In Celtic prosody, too, esp. Ir. and Welsh, near rhyme has been recognized and approved as an important and constructive element of rhyming technique since the Middle Ages under the rubric of *generic rhyme*; and indeed, near rhyme first appears in Eng. deliberately in Henry Vaughan, in imitation of Welsh prosody. In Fr. prosody of the early 20th c., the term *accord* was proposed by Jules Romains (pseud. of Louis Farigoule, 1885–1972) and Georges Chennevière (1884–1927), poets and theorists of the movement known as unanimism, for a variety of forms of consonance and near rhyme. The accords of Romains were attacked by Maurice Grammont but may have influenced the *pararhyme* of Wilfred Owen.

In fact, near rhyme has played an important role in most of the major Western prosodies of the late 19th and early 20th cs.—not only Brit. (G. M. Hopkins, W. B. Yeats, Owen, W. H. Auden, Cecil Day-Lewis, Stephen Spender, Louis MacNeice, Dylan Thomas) and Am. (Dickinson—from whom much of the later Am. practice derives), but Rus. (Alexander Blok, Valery Bryusov, Vladimir Mayakovsky, Boris Pasternak). In Eng., the trad. of canonical rhyme was old but not deeply established, having always had to contend with the enormous force of Shakespearean and Miltonic *blank verse and, after 1855, *free verse. But Rus. never developed extensive trads. of either blank or free verse, so that, in the 20th c., Rus. modernist poets experimented extensively with new and variant rhyme forms—as many as 50% of Mayakovsky's rhymes are noncanonical. In the West, the avant-garde prosodies sought to dispense with both meter and rhyme, but, in Russia, it was only the former: rhyme practice was not abandoned but expanded. Experiments with the one went hand in hand with experiments with the other, but renunciation of the one did not necessarily entail the other as well. In Eng., free verse, of course, dropped rhyme, but several major poets who retained traditional verse forms and meters, e.g., Yeats and Auden, also chose to explore near rhyme: Yeats's practice includes rhymes such as "push"/"rush" and "up"/"drop" in a sonnet, e.g., ("Leda and the Swan"). Owen developed what he called *pararhyme*, a kind of frame rhyme in which the initial and final consonants are repeated while the vowel is varied—e.g. "killed"/"cold," "mystery"/"mastery," "friend"/"frowned"—deliberately to express the wrenching sensation of war. This sort of effect is explored also by Dickinson and Hopkins, as it had been by Vaughan.

In much late Victorian and Edwardian crit., one finds frequent attacks by reactionary prosodists on all less-than-correct rhyming as decadent, degenerate, and incompetent, attacks epitomized in George Saintsbury and Brander Matthews. But in retrospect, such practice is to be seen not as a falling away from a standard but as a redefinition of that standard. In a radical age, the breaking of conventions is an expansive and creative act. Near rhyme is, in this sense, not an abandonment of rhyme in defeat but an opening up of possibilities, not supplanting rhyme but enriching it.

There is evidence from Rus., if any were needed, that each poet develops his or her own distinctive idiolect in near rhyme, preferring to explore not the entire range of possibilities but rather only certain types. But no extensive and reliable set of data on rhyme has yet been collected. The practice of near rhyme in art verse is, of course, the primary interest, but it has also been used extensively and probably for much longer in light verse, *satire, and (perhaps) dialect poetry.

■ K. Meyer, *Primer of Irish Metrics* (1909); V. Žirmunskij, *Rifma* (1923), ch. 3; J. Romains and G. Chennevière, *Petit traité de versif* (1923); J. Hytier, *Les techniques modernes du vers français* (1923), reviewed by M. Grammont in *Revue des langues romanes* 62 (1923); T. W. Herbert, "Near-Rimes and Paraphones," *SR* 14 (1937); L. Pszczołowska, *Rym* (1972); B. P. Goncarov, *Zvukovaja organizatsija stixa i problemy rifmy* (1973); M. Shapiro, *Asymmetry* (1976), ch. 4; W. E. Rickert, "Rhyme Terms," *Style* 12 (1978); M. L. Gasparov, "Towards an Analysis of Russian Inexact Rhyme," *Metre, Rhythm, Stanza, Rhyme*, ed. G. S. Smith (1980); Scott, 233–36; W. Frawley, "A Note on the Phonology of Slant Rhyme," *Lang&S* 17 (1984); Scherr, ch. 4; B. J. Small, *Positive as Sound* (1990)—Dickinson.

T.V.F. BROGAN

NONSENSE VERSE. Some consider *nonsense* a wide category that includes almost any verse that creates a fantastical world with its own rules, while others consider it a narrow category that includes only verse that disrupts the operations of lang., typically by employing an abnormal syntax or invented words. Both these formulations describe many aspects of *nonsense*, and the two often overlap. E.g., Lewis Carroll's "Jabberwocky," an instance of nonsense verse that uses a largely invented vocabulary, is introduced in the context of Carroll's fantastical Looking-Glass world:

> 'Twas brillig, and the slithy toves
>   Did gyre and gimble in the wabe:
> All mimsy were the borogoves,
>   And the mome raths outgrabe.

Neither of these formulations, however, suffices to describe the broad scope of what authors, anthologizers, and critics have called *nonsense verse*. Nonsense verse is the versified instance of nonsense lit., a category of writing that transforms into virtues the vices associated with the pejorative term *nonsense*: silliness, incomprehensibility, childishness, pointlessness, and triviality, among others.

Critics have disagreed over whether nonsense is a genre, as Tigges believes, or something more nebulous, "less a genre than a possibility, a dimension, a boundary which poetry touches more frequently than we usually imagine," as Haughton does. In either approach, critics treat the works of Edward Lear and Carroll as the foremost exemplars of the category in Eng. Nevertheless, Malcolm has found the origins of Eng. nonsense not in the mid-19th c. but earlier, in the 17th. A Fr. nonsense trad. dates to the Middle Ages. While some critics warn against tendencies to universalize nonsense, it exists in a wide spectrum of trads., whether Eur., Chinese, Indian, or Ar.

Despite its name, nonsense does not wholly escape sense, and critics draw a sharp distinction between nonsense and mere gibberish. Nonsense remains rule-based, even if the rules are different from those of our world, and Lecercle has urged readers to dispel the notion that nonsense "presents us with the charming disorder of freedom." Rather, nonsense deals in a complex interplay of order and disorder, of meaning and nonmeaning. Even the most gibberish-like instances of verse engage a reader's impulse toward meaning, "the mind's force toward order" (Sewell). Tigges argues that such interplay is the central characteristic of nonsense, which he considers "a genre of narrative literature which balances a multiplicity of meanings with a simultaneous absence of meaning."

Nonsense is not just light but willfully unserious: its very point often seems to be pointlessness. Nevertheless, some critics have rejected a connection between nonsense and the comic, arguing that much of what happens in nonsense is serious indeed. Even when deeply serious or troubling events happen in nonsense, however, they tend to be deployed for comic effect. Lear's *limericks, e.g., feature heinous acts of violence and tragedy, but the reader is meant to delight in those acts:

There was an Old Man of Peru,
Who watched his wife making a stew;
But once, by mistake, in a stove she did
 bake
That unfortunate Man of Peru.

Understood realistically, this event would be tragic. In the context of nonsense, it is funny and even silly, as the prominent grin on the face of the woman in Lear's accompanying illustration confirms.

Writers of nonsense often adopt a poetics of formal excess that values improbability more than precision. Nonsense rhymes, often polysyllabic, jarring, and repeated over and over again, are regularly played for laughs. Like Lear's limericks, most instances of nonsense verse feature four- and three-beat rhythms.

Critics have identified a number of characteristic devices through which nonsense disrupts common sense. Sewell, Stewart, and Tigges catalog many of these devices, incl. mirroring, reversals, and inversions, as in Carroll's Looking-Glass world; the simultaneous juxtaposition of improbable elements; and the adoption of and strict adherence to seemingly arbitrary rules. These devices create an alternative to the ordinary world, but they also reflect it. By creating a nonsensical alternative world order, they reveal the rules of the ordinary world to be arbitrary as well. As Wittgenstein once wrote, "[T]he negation of nonsense is nonsense" rather than normative sense.

Even when nonsense does not disrupt syntax or vocabulary, it tends to have a special relationship to lang. in which the metaphorical mechanisms of lang. are taken literally or in which lang. is treated as a tangible material object. Stewart cites the expression "he thought that the sun rose and set on her," noting that in nonsense "the person is likely to get very hot or, at least, very tired from such a burden."

The relationship of nonsense to satire and parody has been a source of significant critical disagreement. Some, like Chesterton, Cammaerts, and Sewell, argue that nonsense should be disconnected from real-world concerns, that satire and parody would taint "that state of security, freedom, and purely mental delight that is proper to the [nonsense] game" (Sewell). Others, incl. Amis and Lecercle, associate parody and satire closely with nonsense, arguing that "a great deal of what passes for nonsense is or was generic parody" (Amis), that "parodies . . . are very frequent in nonsense texts, . . . and they are the privileged locus for the dialogue between the author and his child readers" (Lecercle).

The assumption that the audience of nonsense is children, however, proves equally vexed. While much nonsense is aimed directly at children, much is intended for the delight of adults, incl. the 17th-c. examples explored by Malcolm. These poems do not aim for a juvenile readership at all but instead take the adult lang. of reason to hyperbolic extremes, so forcefully embracing the sophistication of academic lang. as to render it utterly silly.

Though nonsense verse includes a great deal of verse that does not disrupt the operations of lang., Carroll's archetypal example of nonsense verse remains the best of what does. Many of the words in "Jabberwocky" are Carroll's inventions, and ling. textbooks regularly cite the stanza as an example of the power of ling. structure to produce meaning despite the absence of stable meanings for much of its vocabulary. As important to what makes "Jabberwocky" nonsense as the lang. itself, however, is the context in which the poem appears, in *Through the Looking-Glass*. Alice encounters the poem and is baffled by it, and Humpty Dumpty later confidently but dubiously explains the meanings of various of Carroll's invented words: " 'Well, 'TOVES' are something like badgers—they're something like lizards—and they're like corkscrews.' " Humpty Dumpty, it becomes clear, provides few actual solutions to the problems of meaning in the poem. In part, readers are meant to laugh at his confident analysis. The silliness of these reactions to the poem, and not just its disruption of lang., makes it fit into the same category of nonsense verse as Lear's limericks. Carroll's original version of the first stanza of the poem falsely posited it as a newly discovered "Stanza of Anglo-Saxon Verse" and glossed every single unfamiliar term in a straight-faced mockery of academic discourse, suggesting that the joke was in place all along. It is not just that "Jabberwocky" is written in invented lang. but that we understand it as invented and are in on Carroll's joke that allows us to categorize it as nonsense.

■ G. K. Chesterton, *The Defendant* (1902); *A Nonsense Anthology*, ed. C. Wells (1902); E. Cammaerts, *The Poetry of Nonsense* (1926); L. E. Arnaud, *French Nonsense Literature in the Middle Ages* (1942); E. Partridge, *Here, There and Everywhere* (1950); E. Sewell, *The Field of Nonsense* (1952); G. Orwell, *Shooting an Elephant* (1954); *Anthologie du nonsense*, ed. R. Benayoun (1957); W. Forster, *Poetry of Significant Nonsense* (1962); A. Liede, *Dichtung als Spiel*, 2 v. (1963); G. Deleuze, *Logique du sens* (1969); R. Hildebrandt, *Nonsense* (1970); *The Nonsense Book*, ed. D. Emrich (1970); A. Schöne, *Englische Nonsense und Gruselballaden* (1970); D. Petzolt, *Formen und Funktionen der englischen Nonsense Dichtung im 19* (1972); K. Amis, "Introduction," *The New Oxford Book of Light Verse*, ed. K. Amis (1978); S. Stewart, *Nonsense: Aspects of Intertextuality in Folklore and Literature* (1979); P. Cachia, "An Uncommon Use of Nonsense Verse in Colloquial Arabic," *Journal of Arabic Literature* 14 (1983); H. Haughton, "Introduction," *The Chatto Book of Nonsense Poetry*, ed. H. Haughton (1988); W. Tigges, *An Anatomy of Literary Nonsense* (1988); J.-J. Lecercle, *Philosophy of Nonsense* (1994); M. Parsons, *Touch Monkeys* (1994); L. Wittgenstein, *Cambridge Letters*, ed. B. McGuinness and G. H. von Wright (1995); N. Malcolm, *The Origins of English Nonsense* (1997); *The Penguin Book of Nonsense Verse*, ed. Q. Blake (2001); E. Lear, *The Complete Verse and Other Nonsense*, ed. V. Noakes (2002); R. McGillis, "Nonsense," *A Companion to Victorian Poetry*, ed. R. Cronin, A. Chapman, and A. H. Harrison (2002); *The Everyman Book of Nonsense Verse*, ed. L. Guinness (2005); *The Tenth Rasa: An Anthology of Indian Nonsense*, ed. Michael Heyman (2008).

E. RETTBERG

O

OCTAVE (rarely, octet). A *stanza of eight lines. Octaves appear as isolable stanzas, such as the It. *ottava rima* (rhyming *abababcc*) and the Fr. *ballade* (*ababbcbc*), as well as the single octave in Fr. called the *huitain* and the single *ballade* stanza in Eng. called the monk's tale stanza after Chaucer's usage. The octave is the stanza of the first rank in Occitan poetry, a favorite of the troubadours; and although the *trouvères* of northern France are less exclusive, they still show a preference for the octave: roughly a third of all extant OF lyrics are set in one form or another of octave. In Sp., the octave of octosyllables rhyming *abbaacca*, less often *ababbccb* or *abbaacac*, is called the *copla de arte menor*; that of 12-syllable lines, the *copla de arte mayor*. In It., the Sicilian octave in hendecasyllables rhyming *abababab* first appears in the 13th c. In ON skaldic poetry, the most important stanzas are *drottkvætt* and *hrynhent*, octaves of six- and eight-syllable lines, respectively. In Rus. poetry, which favors *quatrains, poets frequently connect two quatrains to form octaves, as in Alexander Pushkin, or vary rhyme schemes; e.g., Fyodor Tiutchev and Marina Tsvetaeva formed their own octaves with uneven rhyme schemes (*aabccbba* and *ababacac*, respectively).

Octaves are also important components of larger stanzas: the first eight lines of the *sonnet are called the octave. P. B. Shelley uses octaves for "The Witch of Atlas," as does John Keats for "Isabella." "I have finished the First Canto, a long one, of about 180 octaves," says Lord Byron in a letter apropos of *Don Juan*. G. M. Hopkins uses the scheme *ababcbca* for "The Wreck of the Deutschland." Osip Mandelstam composed a famous set of varying octaves in the early 1930s, the "Vos'mistishiia." John Berryman uses heterometrical octaves in *abcbddba* for "Homage to Mistress Bradstreet." Louis Zukofsky's *80 Flowers* is a sequence of 81 octaves.

■ Schipper; R. Beum, "Yeats's Octaves," *TSLL* 3 (1961); R. Moran, "The Octaves of E. A. Robinson," *Colby Quarterly* 7 (1969).

T.V.F. Brogan; K. M. Campbell

OCTOSYLLABLE. A line of eight syllables, one of the two most popular line forms in the Eur. vernaculars: the chief line form in Sp.

poetry, the oldest in Fr., and the second most important in Eng. It derives presumably from the iambic *dimeter line of med. Lat. hymnody, established by Ambrose in the 4th c. and pervasive in the later Middle Ages. In Fr., the octosyllable first appears in the 10th c. in the *Vie de Saint Léger* (40 sixains in *couplets) and is the most popular meter of OF and Anglo-Norman narrative poetry (excluding the *chansons de geste*, which adopted first the *decasyllable, then the *alexandrine) of the 12th through 15th c.—i.e., chronicles, romances (e.g., Wace), saints' lives, *lais*, *fabliaux*, and dits—and was esp. favored (along with the decasyllable) for the courtly love lyric (esp. ballades and *rondeaux) and popular lyric genres (*chansons de toile, pastourelles*) from the 14th to the mid-16th c. It is also common in med. drama. Finally, it is the staple meter of folk verse, of poetry of the oral trad., as in the late med. ballads. In succeeding centuries, the octosyllable never lost the close connections thus established to hymnody, song, and orality, and (esp. in couplets) to narrative.

After 1500, Pierre de Ronsard and François de Malherbe made it the meter of the *ode, but in post-Ren. Fr. poetry, the octosyllable became associated with light verse: even as late as the 18th c., Alain René Le Sage, Alexis Piron, and Voltaire used it for popular appeal. Its lability and the swift return of its rhymes have given it a reputation for alertness, impertinence, and zest. In rhythmical structure, the *octosyllabe* is mercurial and often ambiguous: it has only one fixed accent, on the eighth syllable, either one or two secondary accents, and no *caesura. This ambiguity derives from the fact that it is caught uneasily between the three-accent norm of the decasyllable and the two-accent norm of the hexasyllable, thus frequently inviting both a two-accent and a three-accent reading, e.g., Théodore de Banville: "Quand je baise, pâle de fièvre" (3 + 5 syllables or 3 + 2 + 3). Whereas the alexandrine is the line of sustained discourse, usually enjoying a certain syntactic completeness, the octosyllable parcels syntax into a series of fragmentary tableaux or near-autonomous images that can stand in a variety of potential relationships with each other. These are the qualities that attracted

Théophile Gautier (*Émaux et camées*, 1852) and the symbolist poets to octosyllabic verse.

Spain received octosyllables (normally in varied *rhyme schemes rather than couplets) in the 14th c. (Juan Ruiz, *Libro de buen amor*) from the Occitan troubadours by way of Galician-Port. sources; these reinforced a native tendency toward the octosyllable in earlier Sp. poetry. By the 15th c., the Sp. *octosílabo* was firmly established through collections of courtly lyrics (e.g., the *Cancionero de Baena*) and since that time has come to be the national meter par excellence in Spain. There is no set rhythmical pattern: the only requirement is that the line contain from seven to nine syllables (endings vary) with stress on the seventh.

In Eng., the octosyllable is, in the Latinate terminology of foot metrics, commonly called iambic *tetrameter; in Ger., it is called the *Kurzzeile* or *Kurzvers*. Occasionally, it is trochaic, and when so, often catalectic (see CATALEXIS), the "8s and 7s" giving a special (and powerful) effect, as in the stanzas of W. H. Auden's elegy to W. B. Yeats beginning "Earth receive an honored guest." It forms the staple line of several stanzas, such as the long meter of the ballads (see BALLAD METER) and the *In Memoriam stanza but is more commonly associated with couplets. Lord Byron's reference to "the fatal facility of the octo-syllabic meter" alludes to the danger of singsong monotony, a danger offset, however, by the rapid movement of the line, which makes it an excellent medium for narrative verse. But in the hands of a skilled craftsman, monotony is not difficult to avoid, as evidenced by John Milton's "Il Penseroso" and J. W. Goethe's "Selige Sehnsucht."

In England, the influence of the Fr. octosyllable in the 12th and 13th cs. through Anglo-Norman poets such as Geoffrey Gaimar, Wace, and Benoît de Sainte-Maure led to a refinement in the syllabic regularity of the indigenous ME four-stress line used for narrative verse (Layamon; *The Owl and the Nightingale*; *Sir Orfeo*; John Barbour's *Bruce*). Chaucer translated part of the *Roman de la Rose*, which is in octosyllabic couplets, from which, according to the received theory, he learned to adapt, *mutatis mutandis*, the metrical structures of the OF line to the exigencies of the Eng. lang. The octosyllables of *The Book of the Duchess* and *The House of Fame* yield to the decasyllables of the *Canterbury Tales*. Chaucer's successors, esp. John Gower (*Confessio amantis*), could

not equal his flexibility. The octosyllable finds heavy use in the miracle and morality plays but a lessening use in the 16th c. (chiefly songs). After 1600, the tetrameter becomes the vehicle of shorter poems, descriptive or philosophical, by Ben Jonson, Milton ("L'Allegro" and "Il Penseroso"), Andrew Marvell ("To His Coy Mistress"), John Gay, Matthew Prior, Jonathan Swift (his favorite meter, e.g., "Verses on the Death of Dr. Swift"), William Collins, and others; the jogging, satiric octosyllables and polysyllabic rhymes of Samuel Butler's *Hudibras* (1663–78) canonized the name—hudibrastic verse. In the 19th c., narrative verse both serious and whimsical was again written in the "8s" as Robert Burns, William Wordsworth, and S. T. Coleridge ("Christabel," in couplets), but esp. Lord Byron, Walter Scott, John Keats, and William Morris ("The Earthly Paradise") brought the tetrameter couplet to a height it had not seen since ME.

However, it is dangerous to treat all eight-syllable lines as a class, without due adjustment for the differences in metrical systems of each national poetry. One cannot treat the Sp. *octosílabo*, the Fr. *octosyllabe*, the Lat. *octonarius*, and the Eng. iambic tetrameter, e.g., as necessary equivalents—i.e., as having the same structure or effects. Each resides within a distinctive verse system dependent in part on the lang. in which it operates. As Michel Grimaud has put it, "eight is a different number" in langs. such as Fr. and Eng.

■ C. M. Lewis, *The Foreign Sources of Modern English Versification* (1898); E. P. Shannon, "Chaucer's Use of the Octosyllabic Verse," *JEGP* 12 (1913); Thieme, 373 ff.; P. Verrier, *Le Vers français*, 3 v. (1931–32); P.-A. Becker, *Der gepaarte Achtsilber in der französischen Dichtung* (1934); E.N.S. Thompson, "The Octosyllabic Couplet," *PQ* 18 (1939); D. C. Clarke, "The Spanish Octosyllable," *HR* 10 (1942); Lote; J. Saavedra Molina, *El octosílabo castellano* (1945); M. D. Legge, *Anglo-Norman Literature and Its Background* (1963); F. Deloffre, *Le Vers français* (1969); Elwert; Navarro; C. Scott, *A Question of Syllables* (1986); E. B. Vitz, "Rethinking Old French Literature: The Orality of the Octosyllabic Couplet," *RR* 77 (1986); J. Kittay, "On Octo," *RR* 78 (1987); S. R. Guthrie, "Machaut and the Octosyllabe," *Chaucer's French Contemporaries*, ed. R. B. Palmer (1999); R. Noyer, "Generative Metrics and Old French Octosyllabic Verse," *Language Variation and Change* 14 (2002).

T.V.F. BROGAN; C. SCOTT

ODE (Gr. *aeidein*, "to sing," "to chant"). In mod. usage, the term for the most formal, ceremonious, and complexly organized form of *lyric poetry, usually of considerable length. It is frequently the vehicle for public utterance on state occasions, e.g., a ruler's birthday, accession, or funeral, or the dedication of some imposing public monument. The ode as it has evolved in contemp. lits. generally shows a dual inheritance from cl. sources, variously combining the measured, recurrent stanza of the Horatian ode, with its attendant balance of *tone and sentiment (sometimes amounting to a controlled ambiguity, as in Andrew Marvell's "Horatian Ode" on Oliver Cromwell), and the regular or irregular stanzaic triad of Pindar, with its elevated, vertiginously changeable tone (as in William Collins's "Ode on the Poetical Character"), in interesting manifestations as late as Robert Bridges and Paul Claudel. Both forms have frequently been used for poems celebrating public events, but both have just as frequently eschewed such events, sometimes pointedly, in favor of private occasions of crisis or joy. Nonetheless, of all poetic forms, the ode has continued since Pindar to be the mostly likely choice of poets reimbursed as laureates or other spokespersons. The serious tone of the ode calls for the use of a heightened diction and enrichment by poetic device, but this lays it open, more readily than any other lyric form, to burlesque.

In Gr. lit., the odes of Pindar (ca. 522–443 BCE) were designed for choric song and dance. The words, the sole surviving element of the integral experience, reflect the demands of the other two arts. A *strophe, a complex metrical structure whose length and pattern of heterometrical lines vary from one ode to another, reflects a dance pattern, which is then repeated exactly in an *antistrophe (the dancers repeating the steps but in the opposite direction), the pattern being closed by an *epode, or third section, of differing length and structure. The ode as a whole (surviving examples range from fragments to nearly 300 lines) is built up by exact metrical repetition of the original triadic pattern. These odes, written for performance in a Dionysiac theater or perhaps in the Agora to celebrate athletic victories, frequently appear incoherent in their brilliance of imagery, abrupt shifts in subject matter, and apparent disorder of form within the individual sections. But mod. crit. has answered such objections, which date from the time of Pindar himself, by discerning

dominating images, emotional relationships between subjects, and complex metrical organization. The tone of the odes is emotional, exalted, and intense; the subject matter, whatever divine myths can be adduced to the occasion.

Apart from Pindar, another pervasive source of the mod. ode in Gr. lit. is the cult *hymn, which derived from the *Homeric Hymns* and flourished during the Alexandrian period in the work of Callimachus and others. This sort of poem is notable not for its form but for its structure of argument: an invocation of a deity (later of a personified natural or psychological entity), followed by a narrative genealogy establishing the antiquity and authenticity of the deity, followed by a petition for some special favor, and concluding with a vow of future service. A complete mod. instance of this structure is John Keats's "Ode to Psyche." Yet another source of the mod. ode's structure of prayerful petition is the Psalms and other poems of the Heb. Bible (see PSALM), which increasingly influenced Eng. poetry by way of John Milton, the crit. of John Dennis, the original and translated hymns of Isaac Watts, and Robert Lowth's *De sacra poesi Hebraeorum* (*Sacred Poetry of the Hebrews*, 1753).

In Lat. lit., the characteristic ode is associated with Horace (65–8 BCE), who derived his forms not from Pindar but from less elaborate Gr. lyrics, through Alcaeus and Sappho. The Horatian ode is tranquil rather than intense, contemplative rather than brilliant, and intended for the reader in private rather than for the spectator in the theater. Horace also wrote commissioned odes, most notably the "Carmen saeculare" for Augustus, all of which more closely approximated the Pindaric form and voice; but his influence on mod. poetry is felt more directly in the trad. of what might be called the sustained *epigram, esp. in the period between Ben Jonson and Matthew Prior. Among the Eng. poets of note, only Mark Akenside habitually wrote odes in the Horatian vein, but in the 17th c. poets as diverse as Robert Herrick, Thomas Randolph, and—most important among them—Marvell with his Cromwell ode wrote urbane Horatians.

The third form of the mod. ode, the *anacreontic, is descended from the 16th-c. discovery of a group of some 60 poems, all credited to Anacreon, although the Gr. originals now appear to span a full thousand years. In general, the lines are short and, in comparison with the Pindaric ode, the forms simple, the subjects being love or drinking, as in the 18th-c. song "To Anacreon in Heaven," whose tune was appropriated for "The Star-Spangled Banner."

Throughout Europe, the hist. of the ode commences with the rediscovery of the cl. forms. The humanistic ode of the 15th and earlier 16th c. shows the adaptation of old meters to new subjects by Francesco Filelfo, in both Gr. and Lat., and by Giannantonio Campano, Giovanni Pontano, and Marcantonio Flaminio in Neo-Lat. The example of the humanistic ode and the publication in 1513 of the Aldine edition of Pindar were the strongest influences on the vernacular ode in Italy; tentative Pindaric experiments were made by Giangiorgio Trissino, Luigi Alamanni, and Antonio Minturno but without establishing the ode as a new genre. More successful were the attempts in France by members of the Pléiade: after minor trials of the new form by others, Pierre de Ronsard in 1550 published *The First Four Books of the Odes*, stylistic imitations of Horace, Anacreon, and (in the first book) Pindar. Influenced by Ronsard, Bernardo Tasso and Gabriello Chiabrera later in the century succeeded in popularizing the form in Italy, where it has been used successfully by, among others, Alessandro Manzoni, Giacomo Leopardi (in his *Di canzone*, 1824), Giosuè Carducci (*Odi barbare*, 1877), and Gabriele D'Annunzio (*Odi navale*, 1892). In France, the example of Ronsard was widely followed, notably by Nicolas Boileau in the 17th c. and by Voltaire and others in formal occasional verse in the 18th. The romantic period lent a more personal note to both form and subject matter, notably in the work of Alphonse de Lamartine, Alfred de Musset, and Victor Hugo. Later, highly personal treatments of the genre may be found in Paul Verlaine's *Odes en son honneur* (1893) and Paul Valéry's *Odes* (1920). Claudel's *Cinq grandes odes* (1907), finally, shows a tendency in many odes of the 20th c. to explore traditional forms of experience, in this case Catholic devotion. In Sp., odes have figured in the work of Pablo Neruda (1904–73), who wrote three volumes of them: *Odas elementales* (1954), *Nuevas odas elementales* (1956), and *Tercer libro de las odas* (1957).

The ode became characteristically Ger. only with the work of G. R. Weckherlin (*Oden und Gesänge*, 1618–19), who, as court poet at Stuttgart, attempted to purify and refashion Ger. letters according to foreign models. In the mid-18th c., F. G. Klopstock modified the cl. models by use of free rhythms, grand abstract subjects, and a heavy influence from the Lutheran psalms. Later, J. W. Goethe and Friedrich Schiller returned to cl. models and feeling, as in Schiller's "Ode to Joy," used in the final movement of Ludwig van Beethoven's Ninth Symphony. At the turn of the 19th c., Friedrich Hölderlin in his complex, mystical, unrhymed odes united cl. themes with the characteristic resources of the Ger. lang. Since Hölderlin, few noteworthy odes have been written in Ger., with the possible exception of those of Rudolph Alexander Schröder (*Deutsche Oden*, 1912).

The few attempts at domesticating the ode in 16th-c. England were largely unsuccessful, although there is probably some influence of the cl. ode on Edmund Spenser's *Fowre Hymnes*, *Prothalamion*, and *Epithalamion*. In 1629 appeared the first great imitation of Pindar in Eng., Jonson's "Ode on the Death of Sir Lucius Cary and Sir H. Morison," with the strophe, antistrophe, and epode of the cl. model indicated by the Eng. terms "turn," "counter-turn," and "stand." In the same year, Milton began the composition of his great ode, "On the Morning of Christ's Nativity," in regular stanzaic form. The genre, however, attained great popularity in Eng. only with the publication of Abraham Cowley's *Pindarique Odes* in 1656, in which he attempted, like Ronsard and Weckherlin before him, to make available to his own lang. the spirit and tone of Pindar rather than to furnish an exact transcription of his manner. Cowley was uncertain whether Pindar's odes were regular, and the matter was not settled until 1706, when the playwright William Congreve published with an ode of his own a "Discourse" showing that they were indeed regular. With the appearance in 1749 of a scholarly trans. of Pindar by Gilbert West, the fashion for Cowleyan Pindarics died away. With John Dryden begin the great formal odes of the 18th c.: first the "Ode to the Memory of Mrs. Anne Killigrew" and then, marking the reunion of formal verse and music, the "Song for St. Cecilia's Day" and "Alexander's Feast." St. Cecilia's Day odes by many authors had long been written, but the trad. ended with "Alexander's Feast." For the 18th c., the ode was the perfect means of expressing the *sublime. Using *personification and other devices of allegory, Thomas Gray and William Collins in the mid-18th c. marshal emotions ranging from anxiety to terror in the service of their central theme, the "progress of poetry," making the ode a crisis poem that reflects the rivalry of mod. lyric with the great poets and genres of the past. The romantic ode in Eng. lit. is a poem written on the occasion of a vocational or existential crisis in order to reassert the power and range of the poet's voice. It is the romantic ode that best suits the remark of Susan Stewart that "odes give birth to poets." The Eng. romantic ode begins with S. T. Coleridge's "Dejection: An Ode" (1802) and William Wordsworth's pseudo-Pindaric "Ode: Intimations of Immortality" (1804, pub. 1807). Wordsworth's "Intimations" ode, with its varied line lengths, complex rhyme scheme, and stanzas of varying length and pattern, has been called the greatest Eng. Pindaric ode. Of the other major romantic poets, P. B. Shelley wrote the "Ode to the West Wind" and Keats the "Ode on a Grecian Urn," "Ode to a Nightingale," and "To Autumn," arguably the finest odes in the lang. These odes were written in regular stanzas derived not from Horace but from Keats's own experiments with the *sonnet form. Since the romantic period, with the exception of a few brilliant but isolated examples such as Alfred, Lord Tennyson's "Ode on the Death of the Duke of Wellington" and G. M. Hopkins's "The Wreck of the Deutschland," the ode has been neither a popular nor a really successful genre in Eng. Among mod. poets, the personal ode in the Horatian manner has been revived with some success, notably by Allen Tate ("Ode to the Confederate Dead") and W. H. Auden ("In Memory of W. B. Yeats," "In Praise of Limestone").

■ Schipper, v. 2, sects. 516–25, and *History*, 366 ff.—on the Pindaric; G. Carducci, "Dello svolgimento dell'ode in Italia," *Opere*, v. 16 (1905); E. R. Keppeler, *Die Pindarische Ode in der dt. Poesie des XVII und XVIII Jhs.* (1911); R. Shafer, *The English Ode to 1660* (1918); I. Silver, *The Pindaric Odes of Ronsard* (1937); G. N. Shuster, *The English Ode from Milton to Keats* (1940); G. Highet, *The Classical Tradition* (1949); N. Maclean, "From Action to Image: Theories of the Lyric in the Eighteenth Century," in Crane; C. Maddison, *Apollo and the Nine: A History of the Ode* (1960); Bowra; K. Viëtor, *Gesch. der deutschen Ode*, 2d ed. (1961); A. W. Pickard-Cambridge, *Dithyramb, Tragedy and Comedy*, 2d ed. (1962); S. Commager, *The Odes of Horace* (1962); K. Schlüter, *Die englische Ode* (1964); H. D. Goldstein, "Anglorum Pindarus: Model and Milieu," *CL* 17 (1965); P. Habermann, "Antike Versmasse und Strophen-(Oden-) formen im Deutschen," and J. Wiegand and W. Kohlschmidt, "Ode," *Reallexikon II*; J. Heath-Stubbs, *The Ode* (1969);

G. Hartman, "Blake and the Progress of Poetry," *Beyond Formalism* (1970); G. Otto, *Ode, Ekloge und Elegie im 18. Jahrhundert* (1973); J. D. Jump, *The Ode* (1974); Wilkins; M. R. Lefkowitz, *The Victory Ode* (1976); P. H. Fry, *The Poet's Calling in the English Ode* (1980); J. Culler, *The Pursuit of Signs* (1981), ch. 7; K. Crotty, *Song and Action: The Victory Odes of Pindar* (1982); W. Mullen, *Choreia* (1982); H. Vendler, *The Odes of John Keats* (1983); M. H. Abrams, *The Correspondent Breeze* (1984), ch. 4; J. W. Rhodes, *Keats's Major Odes: An Annotated Bibliography of Criticism* (1984); A. P. Burnett, *The Art of Bacchylides* (1985); D. S. Carne-Ross, *Pindar* (1985); N. Teich, "The Ode in English Literary History," *Papers on Language and Literature* 21 (1985); Terras; S. Curran, *Poetic Form and British Romanticism* (1986), ch. 4; W. Fitzgerald, *Agonistic Poetry: The Pindaric Mode in Pindar, Horace, Hölderlin, and the English Ode* (1987); Hollier, 198 ff.; *Selected Odes of Pablo Neruda*, ed. and trans. M. S. Peden (1990); G. Davis, *Polyhymnia* (1991); J. D. Kneale, "Romantic Aversions: Apostrophe Reconsidered," *ELH* 58 (1991); L. Kurke, *The Traffic in Praise: Pindar and the Poetics of Social Economy* (1991); J. Ygaunin, *Pindare et les poètes de la celebration*, 8 v. (1997); S. P. Revard, *Pindar and the Reniassance Hymn-Ode, 1450–1700* (2001); S. Stewart, "What Praise Poems Are For," *PMLA* 120 (2005); N. Dauvois, *Renaissance de l'ode: l'ode française au tournant de l'année 1550* (2007); M. Koehler, "Odes of Absorption in the Restoration and Early Eighteenth Century," *SEL* 47 (2007).

S. F. FOGLE; P. H. FRY

ONOMATOPOEIA (Ger. *Klangmalerei, Lautsymbolik*). The traditional term for words that seem to imitate their referents. In the strict sense, onomatopoeia refers to words that imitate sounds (e.g., *dingdong, roar, swish, murmur, susurrus*), but other qualities such as size, motion, and even color may be suggested; the term is often used to denote any word whose sound is felt to have a "natural" or direct relation with its sense. Since their phonetic shapes seem motivated rather than arbitrary, onomatopoeic words exert significant limitations on Ferdinand de Saussure's doctrine of the arbitrariness of the sign. Both Otto Jespersen and Edward Sapir showed evidence that Saussure greatly overstated his case.

Onomatopoeia is one of four verbal effects often called "expressive" or "mimetic" but known in ling. as "phonetic symbolism" or "sound symbolism." None of these descriptors is wholly satisfactory, and, in fact, onomatopoeic words are, per the terminology of Charles S. Peirce, *icons* rather than *symbols*; they are not symbolic in the way ordinary words are, for their semiotic approach to representation is a highly motivated attempt at direct identity, rather than an arbitrary or relatively motivated form of indirect analogy. Beyond (1) onomatopoeia itself (words that imitate sounds in nature), three other interrelated iconic verbal effects include (2) articulatory gestures or kinesthesia (predicated on movements of the vocal or facial muscles; see SOUND); (3) *synaesthesia, phonesthemes, and other associative phenomena (wherein heard sounds trigger other sensory impressions); and (4) morphosymbolism and iconic syntax (see below).

It has long been fashionable among literary critics to disparage onomatopoeia as a crude and over-obvious poetic device, but there is considerable ling. evidence for iconicity as an important process in lang.; indeed, certain iconic effects operate across a wide spectrum of langs. and so may be linguistic universals. Jespersen's astonishingly long list of words having the unrounded high front vowel /i/, with all connoting "small, slight, insignificant, or weak," is famous; in Eng., this phoneme is used almost universally as a suffix for small, familiar, or comforting things (e.g., *mommy, daddy, baby, doggie, kitty*). Woodworth's analysis of *deixis in 26 langs. revealed a "systematic relationship between vowel quality and distance," namely, that a word having proximal meaning has a vowel of higher pitch than one having distal meaning.

Furthermore, iconic effects in lang. are not merely phonological but morphological and syntactic. Onomatopoeia is, therefore, simply the most conspicuous instance of a broad range of natural linguistic effects, not a merely "poetic" device. In ordinary speech, sound is motivated by sense: once sense is selected, sound follows. But in iconic speech, sense is motivated by sound: words are chosen for their sound, which itself determines meaning. In the case of onomatopoeia, the sound of the word may imitate a natural phenomenon in the world, but the sound of the word is not often precisely the sound of the thing. As Seymour Chatman shows, the connection is not exact, and most onomatopoeic words are only approximations of the natural sounds. Even words for animal

sounds are highly conventionalized in every lang.: the Eng. speaker styles the dog's bark as *bow wow* or *arf arf* or *woof*, whereas the Mandarin Chinese speaker has it as *wang wang*. Meanwhile, in Eng., the pig's grunt is styled *oink, oink*, whereas the Brazilian Port. speaker has it as *croinh croinh*.

All of this suggests that sound-symbolic effects do not operate without words to trigger them: words that are primary in establishing the semantic field. Sounds can never precede meaning: they can only operate on meanings already lexically created. Nevertheless, onomatopoeia generally aims to approximate the physical properties of its sounds to the physical properties of its real objects. From the wider perspective of sound symbolism or iconicity, onomatopoeia is part of a much larger set of associative relations between word-sounds and meanings. Associative processes operate extensively among words themselves, particularly in morphology, though also in syntax. The sound shape of a word is almost never created from nothing: it is usually formed in relation to some existing word. After it comes into existence, it is continuously subject to diachronic and synchronic influence from other words in the lang. system. Any entity, no matter how arbitrary upon its entry into the system, is thereafter subject to continuous accommodation to and influence by other entities in the system.

It should be noted that many writers use the term *onomatopoeia* for something that amounts to what Dwight Bolinger has termed "reverse onomatopoeia": here "not only is the word assimilated to the sound, but the sound is also assimilated to the 'wordness' of the word." Bolinger identifies a series of morphosemantic processes based mainly on association whereby the form influences the meaning or the meaning influences the form of words. In this way, constellations of words form over time, all having similar meanings and similar sounds: one example is the series of Eng. words beginning with *gl-* which have to do with light; another is the set of words ending in *-ash*. Consequently, as Bolinger explains, "when we speak of sound-suggestiveness, we speak of the entire lang., not just of a few imitative or self-sufficient forms."

The subject of iconicity in lang. has always been a significant issue for linguists and stood as a topic of lively interest to the ancients. It is central to Plato's *Cratylus*, and also appears in Aristotle (*Rhet.* 3.9), Demetrius (*On Style*), Dionysius of Halicarnassus (*On Literary*

Composition), and Quintilian (*Institutio oratoria* 9.3, 9.4). Saussure impressed indelibly upon the mind of the 20th c. the idea that the relation between word and thing is arbitrary. But of course, desire cuts so much deeper than fact. Poets continually desire to make lang. appropriate, so that words partake of the nature of things. And the agency is the fact that words *are* things, have physical bodies with extension in space and duration in time. For fuller discussion of the several types of expressive sound in poetry, see EUPHONY.

■ O. Jespersen, "Sound Symbolism," *Language* (1922); J. R. Firth, *Speech* (1930); C. S. Peirce, *Collected Papers*, ed. C. Hartshorne and P. Weiss, 8 v. (1931–58); O. Jespersen, "Symbolic Value of the Vowel *I*," *Linguistica* (1933); E. Sapir, *Selected Writings* (1949); J. R. Firth, "Modes of Meaning," *E&S* 4 (1951); D. T. Mace, "The Doctrine of Sound and Sense in Augustan Poetic Theory," *RES* 2 (1951); Wellek and Warren, ch. 13; W. T. Moynihan, "The Auditory Correlative," *JAAC* 17 (1958); Z. Wittoch, "Les Onomatopées forment-elles une système dans la langue?" *AION-SL* 4 (1962); D. Bolinger, *Forms of English* (1965), esp. "The Sign Is Not Arbitrary," "Word Affinities," and "Rime, Assonance, and Morpheme Analysis"; Chatman; M. B. Emeneau, "Onomatopoetics in the Indian Linguistic Area," *Lang* 45 (1969); J. D. Sadler, "Onomatopoeia," *CJ* 67 (1972); J. A. Barish, "Yvor Winters and the Antimimetic Prejudice," *NLH* 2 (1970); G. L. Anderson, "Phonetic Symbolism and Phonological Style," *Current Trends in Stylistics* (1972); W. K. Wimsatt, "In Search of Verbal Mimesis," *Day of the Leopards* (1976); P. L. French, "Toward an Explanation of Phonetic Symbolism," *Word* 28 (1977); Y. Malkiel, "From Phonosymbolism to Morphosymbolism," *Fourth LACUS Forum* (1978), supp. by D. B. Justice, "Iconicity and Association," *RPh* 33 (1980); R. Jakobson and L. Waugh, "The Spell of Speech Sounds," *The Sound Shape of Language* (1979), also rpt. in Jakobson, v. 8; L. I. Weinstock, "Onomatopoeia and Related Phenomena in Biblical Hebrew," *DAI* 40 (1979): 3268A; D. A. Pharies, "Sound Symbolism in the Romance Languages," *DAI* 41 (1980): 231A; R. A. Wescott, *Sound and Sense: Essays on Phonosemic Subjects* (1980); M. Borroff, "Sound Symbolism as Drama in the Poetry of Wallace Stevens," *ELH* 48 (1981); Brogan, 97–108—survey of studies; Morier; R. Lewis, *On Reading French Verse* (1982), ch. 7; N. L. Woodworth, "Sound Symbolism in Proximal and Distal Forms," *Linguistics* 29 (1991); M. Borroff, "Sound Symbolism as Drama in the Poetry of Robert Frost," *PMLA* 107 (1992); H. Bredin, "Onomatopoeia as a Figure and a Linguistic Principle" *NLH* 27 (1996); E. R. Anderson, *A Grammar of Iconism* (1998).

T.V.F. BROGAN; J. M. COCOLA

OTTAVA RIMA. Though now widely dispersed in various Western langs., largely because of the fame of Lord Byron's masterpiece *Don Juan*, ottava rima (or *ottava toscana*; Ger. *stanze*; Rus. *oktava*) originated as an Italian prosody, an *octave stanza in *hendecasyllables rhyming *abababcc*. Though its origin is obscure, it is clearly a form that evolved in an oral poetic culture. Scholars relate the form to the stanza of the *canzone* or the *sirventes*, perhaps in imitation of the Sicilian *strambotto* that emerged in the 14th c. for long poems (*cantari*) of less than epic length. It was in use in religious verse of late 13th-c. Italy, but only received definitive artistic form in Giovanni Boccaccio's *Filostrato* (1335?) and *Teseida* (1340–42?). It soon became the dominant form of It. narrative verse, being developed in the 15th c. by Politian, Luigi Pulci, and Matteo Maria Boiardo and reaching its apotheosis in the *Orlando furioso* (1516) of Ludovico Ariosto, where its potentialities for richness, complexity, and variety of effect are brilliantly exploited. Torquato Tasso (*Gerusalemme liberata*) showed his mastery of the form later in the century, and it was subsequently employed in Italy by Giambattista Marino (*Adone*), Alessandro Tassoni (*La secchia rapita*), Vittorio Alfieri (*Etruria vendicata*), Niccoló Tommaseo (*Una serva, La Contessa Matilde*), and Giovanni Marradi (*Sinfonia del bosco*).

In the broader Eur. context, the poets of Ren. Spain and Portugal followed the It. example in adopting the form for narrative purposes. Notable *epics in ottava rima are Alonso de Ercilla's *La Araucana* in Sp. and Luís de Camões's *The Lusíads* in Port. The form was explored by Eng. Ren. poets like Thomas Wyatt (some 15 poems, most monostrophic), Philip Sidney (*Old Arcadia*), Edmund Spenser, Samuel Daniel (*Civil Wars*), Michael Drayton, and Fulke Greville; and it was followed as well in the great trans. by John Harington (Ariosto) and Edward Fairfax (Tasso). John Milton uses it for the coda of "Lycidas."

The form did not find its true non-It. master until Byron, whose trans. of a portion of Pulci's *Morgante Maggiore* (inspired by J. H. Frere's

The Monks and the Giants) launched him into a deep exploration of the stanza's poetic resources. After a brief use of the form in an epistle to his sister in 1816, he began using the stanza extensively in 1817, first in *Beppo* and then, with astonishing panache, in *Don Juan* and *The Vision of Judgment*. P. B. Shelley used it after 1820, chiefly for "The Witch of Atlas," and John Keats uses it earlier for "Isabella." It was popularized in Rus. poetry by Alexander Pushkin on the model of Byron.

The work of the great masters of the stanza—Boccaccio, Pulci, Ariosto, Byron—suggests that ottava rima is most suited to work of a varied nature, blending serious, comic, and satiric attitudes and mingling narrative and discursive modes. Referring to Pulci, Byron calls it "the half-serious rhyme" (*Don Juan* 4.6). Its accumulation of rhyme, reaching a precarious crescendo with the third repetition, prepares the reader for the neat summation, the acute observation, or the epigrammatic twist that comes with the final couplet:

> And Julia's voice was lost, except in sighs,
> > Until too late for useful conversation;
> The tears were gushing from her gentle eyes,
> > I wish, indeed, they had not had
> > > occasion;
> But who, alas! can love, and then be wise?
> > Not that remorse did not oppose
> > > temptation:
> A little still she strove, and much repented,
> And whispering "I will ne'er consent"—
> > > consented.
> > > > (*Don Juan* 1.117)

At eight lines (cf. the Spenserian of nine), the ottava rima stanza is long enough to carry the thread of narrative but not so long that it becomes unmanageable, and it allows much greater room for exposition and elaboration than do *quatrains.

Although A. C. Swinburne remarked that Byron's achievement had spoiled the chances for later poets, he himself employed the form to wonderful effect in his seriocomic narrative "Arthur's Flogging." W. B. Yeats, a mod. master of the form, uses it for some 15 of his poems, incl. "Sailing to Byzantium," "Among School Children," and "The Circus Animals' Desertion." Significantly, Yeats develops the form precisely at the same time (1910–19) that the dreamy style of his early period is evolving into the more realistic, colloquial style of the great poems of his middle period. After Yeats, the form is brilliantly used by A. D. Hope, James Merrill, Kenneth Koch (*The Duplications*, 1975), Anthony Burgess (*Byrne*, pub. posthumously in 1995), Alan Wearne (*The Lovemakers*, 2001), and by various other late 20th-c. Eng.-lang. poets.

■ Schipper; P. Habermann, "Stanze," *Reallexikon I*; G. Bunte, *Zur Verskunst der deutschen Stanze* (1928); V. Pernicone, "Storia e svolgimento della metrica," *Problemi ed orientamenti critici di lingua e di letteratura italiana*, ed. A. Momigliano, v. 2 (1948); G. M. Ridenour, *The Style of "Don Juan"* (1960); A. Limentani, "Storia e struttura dell'ottava rima," *Lettere italiane* 13 (1961); A. Roncaglia, "Per la storia dell'ottava rima," *CN* 25 (1965); R. Beum, *The Poetic Art of W. B. Yeats* (1969), ch. 10; E. G. Etkind, *Russkie poety-perevodchiki ot Trediakovskogo do Pushkina* (1973), 155–201; Spongano; Wilkins; Elwert, *Italienische*; I. K. Lilly, "Some Structural Invariants in Russian and German Ottava Rima," *Style* 21 (1987); F. Calitti, "L'ottava rima: stile pedestre, umile, moderno," *Anticomoderno* (1996); L. Bartoli, "Considerazioni attorno ad una questione metricologica. Il Boccaccio e le origini dell'ottava rima," *Quaderns d'Italià* 4–5 (1999–2000); C. Addison, "*Ottava Rima* and Novelistic Discourse," *Journal of Narrative Theory* 34.2 (2004).

A. PREMINGER; C. KLEINHENZ; T.V.F. BROGAN.; J. McGANN

P

PALINODE. A poem or song of retraction; originally a term applied to a lyric by Stesichorus (early 6th c. BCE) in which he recanted his earlier attack upon Helen as the cause of the Trojan War. The palinode became common after Ovid's *Remedia amoris,* supposedly written to retract his *Ars amatoria.* It is a frequent device in med. and Ren. love poetry, incl. the *Roman de la Rose.* Chaucer's *Legend of Good Women* is a palinode retracting *Troilus and Criseyde,* and a character called Palinode appears in Edmund Spenser's *The Shepheardes Calender.* Any ritualistic recantation may loosely be called a palinode, even one in prose, but the term *palinodic form* denotes a particular pattern in which two metrically corresponding elements are interrupted by another pair of similarly corresponding elements. The palinodic form may be represented as *a b b' a'* where the letters refer to lines, stanzas, or strophes, and where *a b* makes a statement that *b' a'* recants.

■ U. von Wilamowitz-Moellendorff, *Sappho und Simonides* (1913); P. Philippy, *Love's Remedies* (1995); M. Demos, "Stesichorus' Palinode in the 'Phaedrus,'" *CW* 90.4 (1997); C. Gutleben, "Palinodes, Palindromes and Palimpsests: Strategies of Deliberate Self-Contradiction in Postmodern British Fiction," *Miscelánea* 26 (2002).

R. A. HORNSBY; A. L. FRENCH

PANEGYRIC (Gr. *panegyricos,* "for a festival assembly") originally denoted an oration delivered at one of the Gr. festivals; later it came to designate a speech or poem in praise of some person, object, or event. As such, panegyric is rhetorically classed as a type of epideictic poetry or oratory, the major branches of which are praise and *invective. Panegyrics praising heroes, athletes, armies, and dynasties are present in most cultures, incl. in oral poetry, though Western scholarship generally borrows the terminology for panegyric and its particular subgenres and specific occasions from the Gr., such as *epinikion,* a victory *ode; *epithalamium,* a marriage song; *encomium,* presumably praise of the host at the *komos* revel; and eulogy, a speech or poem in praise of the dead. In med. China, however, panegyric, for which a technical term is lacking, was not conceived as a separate genre but rather as poetry (*shi*) "written at imperial command" (*yingzhao* or *yingzhi*), an effect of the commission by or dedication to a reigning monarch. With its morphological elasticity, the Ar. root for "praise," *m-d-ḥ,* produces an extensive terminology for the relations involved in panegyric: praise or a mode of poetry (*madḥ*), the praised one or patron (*mamdūḥ*), the panegyrist (*mādiḥ*), a panegyrical poem or section of a poem (*madīḥ, midḥa*), and self-glorification (*tamadduḥ*).

The cl. rules of panegyric are given in the rhetorical works of Menander and Hermogenes; famous examples include the *Panegyricus* of Isocrates, the panegyric of Pliny the Younger on Trajan, and the 11 other *XII Panegyrici latini* (4th c. CE). Pindar's odes have sometimes been described as panegyrics. After the 3d c. BCE, when much of rhetorical theory was appropriated for poetics, panegyric was accepted as a formal poetic type, and its rules were given in handbooks of poetry. Significant Western examples of panegyrics include Sidonius Apollinaris's poems on the Emperors Avitus, Majorian, and Anthemius; Claudian's on the consulships of Honorius, Stilicho, Probinus, and Olybrius; the panegyric on the death of Celsus by Paulinus of Nola; Aldhelm's *De laudibus virginitatis*; and innumerable Christian Lat. poems in praise of Mary, the Cross, and the martyrs, though hagiographical or devotional praise might well constitute a distinctly different type of praise from panegyric, since the author is not engaged with the social exchange inherent in a patron-poet relationship. J. C. Scaliger (*Poetices libri septem,* 1561) distinguishes, e.g., between panegyric, which tends to deal with present men and deeds, and encomium, which deals with those of the past; but, in general, the two are indistinguishable. Menander, however, categorizes epideictic according to the object of praise, incl. praise of the gods (*hymnos*), praise of countries or cities, and praise of people or animals.

In Ar. and early Persian trads., the *qaṣīda* was the primary verse form for panegyric, though it contained other sections, as well. In later centuries, esp. in Persian, the *ghazal* and *rubāʿī* forms were sometimes used as vehicles of panegyric. In addition to praising the justice, wisdom, power, and victories of the ruler, a Persian panegyric often closes with two lines of prayer for him. Most Persian works of *epic and romance open with a section of praise, sometimes several hundred lines long and organized hierarchically, first to God, then the Prophet, possibly the caliphs or saints, followed by the ruling patron, and often the crown prince. The basic system of patronage that developed for Ar. at the caliphal court in Damascus, Baghdad, and Cordoba was replicated throughout the Middle East, South and Central Asia, North Africa and Andalusia, and for other lits., Persian, Turkish, and Urdu, etc. Kings, sultans, and military potentates, whether of local dynasties or major empires (Timurid, Safavid, Ottoman, Mughal) felt the need to retain poets, one of whom often served as poet laureate, and to encourage recitation of panegyric poems on state, religious, and other ceremonial occasions. Al-Mutanabbī (d. 965), e.g., made Sayf al-Dawla and his court in Aleppo famous through his successful panegyrics. Persian poetry reemerged as a literate trad. in the 10th and 11th cs. largely because the Samanid and Ghaznavid courts decided actively to patronize and encourage Persian poets. Maḥmūd of Ghazna (d. 1030), the Maeceneas of Persian poetry, gathered major panegyric poets around his court (e.g., Farrukhī and 'Unṣurī) and established the expectation that other sultans and shahs would do likewise. Panegyric poets at the Arabo-Persian courts frequently served as courtiers and boon companions, occasionally coming under political suspicion and suffering imprisonment or execution. The inherent threat of revenge in verse, however, balanced the power relation to some extent; some patrons' reputations were forever tarnished by satires from disgruntled former panegyric poets, e.g., al-Mutanabbī's wicked invective on Kāfūr in the 10th c.; and Firdawsī's satire on Maḥmūd of Ghazna in the 11th c. The complex dynamics of these patronage relationships led rhetoricians to analyze the poetics of sincerity under rubrics like "praise that sounds like blame" and "blame that sounds like praise."

Panegyric remained popular through the Eur. Middle Ages both as an independent poetic form and as an important *topos* in longer narrative poems, esp. epic and, like other such forms, it persisted into the Ren., with perhaps more emphasis on the praise of secular figures and institutions. The panegyric underwent a brief revival in 17th-c. encomiastic occasional verse, e.g., Edmund Waller's "Panegyrick to My Lord Protector" (1655). The Eng. subgenre

known as the country house poem is a variety of panegyric.

■ Pauly-Wissowa 5.2581–83, 18.2340–62; T. Burgess, *Epideictic Literature* (1902); Curtius; R. Haller, "Lobgedichte," *Reallexikon II*; *XII Panegyrici latini*, ed. R.A.B. Mynors (1964); T. Viljamaa, *Studies in Greek Encomiastic Poetry of the Early Byzantine Period* (1968); J. Stuart, *Izibongo: Zulu Praise-Poems*, ed. T. Cope (1968); A. Georgi, *Das lateinische und deutsche Preisgedicht des Mittelalters* (1969); F. Cairns, *Generic Composition in Greek and Roman Poetry* (1972); B. K. Lewalski, *Donne's "Anniversaries" and the Poetry of Praise* (1973); J. D. Garrison, *Dryden and the Tradition of Panegyric* (1975); S. Sperl, "Islamic Kingship and Arabic Panegyric Poetry in the Early Ninth Century," *Journal of Arabic Literature* 8 (1977); A. C. Hodza, *Shona Praise Poetry*, ed. G. Fortune (1979); J. O'Donnell, *Cassiodorus* (1979); *Leaf and Bone: African Praise-Poems*, ed. J. Gleason (1980); S. MacCormack, *Art and Ceremony in Late Antiquity* (1981); R. S. Peterson, *Imitation and Praise in the Poems of Ben Jonson* (1981); A. Hardie, *Statius and the Silvae* (1983); R. Helgerson, *Self-Crowned Laureates: Spenser, Jonson, Milton and the Literary System* (1983); G. W. Most, *The Measures of Praise* (1985); J. Altieri, *The Theatre of Praise: The Panegyric Tradition in Seventeenth-Century English Drama* (1986); B. Gold, *Literary Patronage in Greece and Rome* (1987); J. S. Meisami, *Medieval Persian Court Poetry* (1987); W. Portmann, *Geschichte in der spätantiken Panegyrik* (1988); *Patronage in Ancient Society*, ed. A. Wallace-Hadrill (1989); L. Kurke, *The Traffic in Praise* (1991); S. P. Stetkevych, *Abū Tammām and the Poetics of the Abbasid Age* (1991); A. Hamori, *The Composition of Mutanabbī's Panegyrics to Sayf al-Dawla* (1992); J. T. Rowland, *Faint Praise and Civil Leer: The "Decline" of Eighteenth-Century Panegyric* (1994); *Reorientations: Arabic and Persian Poetry*, ed. S. P. Stetkevych (1994); *Qasida Poetry in Islamic Asia and Africa*, ed. S. Sperl and C. Shackle, 2 v. (1996); *The Propaganda of Power: The Role of Panegyric in Late Antiquity*, ed. M. Whitby (1998); *Greek Biography and Panegyric in Late Antiquity*, ed. T. Hägg and P. Rousseau (2000); P. L. Bowditch, *Horace and the Gift Economy of Patronage* (2001); S. P. Stetkevych, *The Poetics of Islamic Legitimacy* (2002); B. Gruendler, *Medieval Arabic Praise Poetry: Ibn al-Rūmī and the Patron's Redemption* (2003); H. Mackie, *Graceful Errors: Pindar and the Performance of Praise* (2003); D. Fearn,

Bacchylides: Politics, Performance, Poetic Tradition (2007); *Pindar's Poetry, Patrons, and Festivals*, ed. S. Hornblower and C. Morgan (2007); F. Wu, *Written at Imperial Command: Panegyric Poetry in Early Medieval China* (2008); *A Companion to Horace*, ed. G. Davis (2010). F. Lewis, "Sincerely Flattering Panegyrics: The Shrinking Ghaznavid Qasida," *Necklace of the Pleiades*, ed. F. D. Lewis and S. Sharma (2010).

O. B. Hardison; T.V.F. Brogan; F. Lewis

PARADOX. A daring statement that unites seemingly contradictory words but that on closer examination proves to have unexpected meaning and truth ("The longest way round is the shortest way home"; "Life is death and death is life"). The structure of paradox is similar to the oxymoron, which unites two contradictory concepts into a third ("heavy lightness"), a favorite strategy of Petrarchism. Paradoxes are esp. suited to an expression of the unspeakable in religion, mysticism, and poetry. First discussed in its formal elements in Stoic philosophy and cl. rhet., the paradox became more widely used after Sebastian Frank (*280 Paradoxa from the Holy Scriptures*, 1534) and has always retained an appeal to the Christian mode of expression, as in Martin Luther and Blaise Pascal. In the *Concluding Scientific Postscript* (1846), Søren Kierkegaard considered God's becoming man the greatest paradox for human existence.

The most famous literary example of sustained paradox is *The Praise of Folly* by Erasmus (1511). In the baroque period, paradox became a central figure; it is particularly important in metaphysical poetry, esp. the poetry and prose of John Donne, who makes frequent use of paradox and paradoxical lang. in the *Paradoxes and Problems* and *Songs and Sonnets* (both 1633). The paradox is manifest in the lit. of the 17th and 18th cs. in its antithetical verbal structure rather than as argument. Denis Diderot in his late dialogue *Le Paradoxe sur le comédien* (1778)—on the art of acting but with far-reaching implications for poetry—holds that an actor should not feel the passion he expresses but should transcend direct imitation and rise to the conception of an intellectual model. Everything in him should become a controlled work of art, and the emotional state should be left to the spectator. In the romantic period, Friedrich Schlegel (*Fragments*, 1797) called the paradox a basic form of human experience and linked it closely with poetry and *irony. Thomas De Quincey in his *Autobiographical Sketches* (1834–53) argued

that the paradox is a vital element in poetry, reflecting the paradoxical nature of the world that poetry imitates. Friedrich Nietzsche made paradox a key term of human experience and of his own literary expression. In the lit. of the 20th c., paradox often fuses with the absurd, which can be interpreted as an intensified, often existential expression of the paradox.

The term *paradox* is widely employed in 20th-c. crit., esp. in the work of the New Criticism. Cleanth Brooks discusses it in *The Well Wrought Urn* (esp. ch. 1) as a form of indirection that is distinctively characteristic of poetic lang. and structure. As his example from William Wordsworth ("Composed Upon Westminster Bridge") illustrates, Brooks does not use paradox in the strict antithetical sense but gives it an unusually broad range by showing that good poems are written from insights that enlarge or startlingly modify our commonplace conceptions and understandings, esp. those residing in overly simplistic distinctions; this disruptive function of poetic lang. is precisely what Brooks calls paradoxical. Since the degree of paradoxical disruption is an index of poetic meaning, paradox and poetry assume a very close affinity with one another. Subsequently, this New Critical emphasis on paradox was taken up in deconstruction. Paul de Man argued that the insistence by the New Critics on the unity, harmony, and identity of a poetic work was irreconcilable with their insistence on irony, paradox, and ambiguity—or, rather, that the insistence on unity was the "blindness" of the New Criticism, whereas the insistence on irony and paradox was its "insight."

See ANTITHESIS.

■ Brooks; A. E. Malloch, "Techniques and Function of the Renaissance Paradox," *SP* 53 (1956); W. V. Quine, *The Ways of Paradox and Other Essays* (1966); R. L. Colie, *Paradoxia Epidemica: The Renaissance Tradition of Paradox* (1966), "Literary Paradox," *DHI*; de Man; *Le Paradoxe au temps de la Renaissance*, ed. M. T. Jones-Davies (1982); J.J.Y. Liu, *Language—Paradox—Poetics: A Chinese Perspective*, ed. R. J. Lynn (1988); W. D. Shaw, *Elegy and Paradox* (1994).

E. H. Behler

PARALIPSIS (Gr. *paraleipsis*, "a leaving aside"). The device by which a speaker draws attention to a topic by claiming not to speak of that very same topic (e.g., "I'm not going to tell you what I heard, but . . ."). A narrower term than *apophasis* (*OED*: Gr. "denial," from "to speak off"), which includes other methods of argument or representation by denial (such as the apophatic or negative theology of denying or negating positive statements about what God is), paralipsis should not be confused with *occupatio,* the anticipating and answering of an opponent's arguments (Kelly). Paralipsis is also known as preterition (Lat. *praeteritio*). Paralipsis has been used as synonymous with *paralepsis* (Gr., "a taking aside"), though the precision of this use is questionable. *Aposiopesis* (Gr., "a becoming silent") is different from paralipsis since it refers to the speaker's coming to an abrupt halt in speech, as if overwhelmed with emotion by the unexpressed thought. The Lat. *occultatio* is also related to paralipsis because *occultatio* is used to present evidence that is exaggerated, cannot be proved, or does not stand up against scrutiny by passing over such information as if it were unimportant to the argument. In narrative theory, paralipsis refers to a homodiegetic narrator's omitting or suppressing information that he or she is fully cognizant of from the temporal point of narration; *paralepsis* is the opposite of paralipsis. Paralipsis is related to—but should not be confused with—*analepsis* (a flashback) and *prolepsis* (a flash-forward). James Phelan identifies some examples of paralipsis as paradoxical (e.g., when a narrator unselfconsciously appears to be as naïve as his or her narrated self). Alison Case suggests that Phelan's vision of paralipsis is a convention of 20th-c. fiction rather than a perennial aesthetic.

■ *Rhetores Graeci,* ed. C. Walz, 9 v. (1832–36); S. Usher, "*Occultatio* in Cicero's Speeches," *AJP* 86 (1965); H. A. Kelly, "*Occupatio* as Negative Narration," *MP* 74 (1977); J. Phelan, *Narrative as Rhetoric* (1996); *A Companion to Narrative Theory,* ed. J. Phelan and P. J. Rabinowitz (2005)—ch. 20 and glossary.

D. VERALDI; S. CUSHMAN

PARALLELISM (Gr., "side by side"). Parallelism is widely understood as a repetition of structure or pattern in adjacent phrases, clauses, or sentences within discourse in general and poetry in particular, e.g., "When the eye is cleared of obstacles, it sees sharply. When the ear is cleared of obstacles, it hears well" (*Wisdom of Lao-Tse*). The repeating structure is often syntactic in nature, as in the present example and in general in Chinese poetry (Plaks). However, the repetition may entail other ling. components such as lexicon, phonology, morphology, and rhythm (Jakobson, Hrushovski). A repetition in structural form serves, like rhyme, to associate the semantic content of the phrases or lines that share the common feature. Sometimes formally parallel propositions are roughly synonymous, e.g., "I will knock a boy into their wombs, / a baby into their embrace" (*Kalevala*; Finnish); but sometimes the coupled lines express different, though related, notions, e.g., "He wept evenings, he wept mornings, / most of all he wept nights" (*Kalevala*). Here the contrast between daytime and nocturnal behavior is crucial. Psycholinguistic investigations suggest it is natural, or at least conventional, to correlate similarity of structure and similarity of meaning. Thus, a subject in an experiment, when presented with the stimulus sentence "The lazy student failed the exam," responded with "The smart girl passed the test," a sentence parallel in structure and related in meaning.

Parallelism is characteristic of popular and formal poetry in many cultures, from ancient to mod. times, but it may function as an only occasional *trope within a work. The Babylonian creation myth *Enuma Elish* (ca. 1200 BCE) begins with a couplet in parallelism: "When on high the heaven was not yet named, / [and] below the earth was not called by name [i.e., created]" (trans. Greenstein; cf. Foster 439). Although parallelism frequently recurs in this lengthy text, it is not continuous. In such works as biblical Heb. poetry and the *Kalevala*, most couplets exhibit parallelism. Consider, e.g., this typical sequence from the prebiblical epic poetry of North Syria (Ugarit):

> Pour wine into a silver basin, / Into a gold basin, honey.
> Ascend to the top of the lookout; / Mount the city-wall's shoulder.
> Raise your hands toward the sky. / Sacrifice to Bull El, your Father.
> Adore Baal with your sacrifice, / Dagon's Son with your offering.
>   (*Kirta*; trans. Greenstein in Parker 14)

In each couplet, the second line essentially elaborates the content of the first. Kugel and Alter in their studies of biblical parallelism indicate that the second line in parallelism often intensifies or extends the sense of the first; compare:

The new-wed groom will go forth;
To another man he'll drive his wife; / To a
stranger his own true love.
　　　(*Kirta*; trans. Greenstein in Parker 15)

In this example, as in many others, the syntax of the parallel line is identical in the underlying pattern, in the deep structure, while there are variations, such as deleting (gapping) the verb ("he'll drive") in the surface structure. Parallelism in syntactic structure must accordingly be sought in the deep structure as well as in the surface form (Kiparsky, Greenstein). In the Heb. Psalm 105:17, the line "He [God] sent ahead of them a man" is followed by "Joseph was sold as a slave." Though on the surface the syntax of each line seems different, in generative theory the second line, formulated in the passive voice, is underlyingly active—"[Someone] sold Joseph as a slave." The sentence in the deep structure is transformed in the surface structure into a concrete passive sentence. On the deep or abstract level, the syntactic structures are identical (subject noun-phrase, verb-phrase, adverbial phrase). The fact that parallelism obtains fundamentally on the abstract level is clear from instances in which a word or phrase in the surface structure of the first line is gapped in the second line, even when it lacks grammatical agreement. E.g., in the following Ugaritic (N. Syrian, 13th c. BCE) couplet—"Her father sets the stand of the balance, / Her mother the trays of the balance" (*Nikkal and Yarikh*)—the verb "sets" is masculine; if it were to appear in the surface structure of the second line, it would have to be feminine in form (trans. Greenstein; cf. D. Marcus in Parker 217).

When a word or phrase is deleted in the parallel line, it is routine to compensate for the syllables lost by expanding one of the parallel elements, e.g., "I will certainly stop the women's laughter, / the daughters' peals of laughter" (*Kalevala*). In the Heb. couplet, "Why is light given to one-who-suffers, / and life to those-bitter-of spirit?" (Job 3:20), the verb "is given" is gapped in the second line and the single word "one-who-suffers" is paralleled by the two-word phrase "those-bitter-of spirit," which is an extension in sense as well as form, as Job extrapolates from his own instance of suffering to that of others, perhaps even all others, as well.

In biblical Heb. verse, the first line of a couplet nearly always comprises a complete clause, if not a complete sentence, and the second line ordinarily reiterates it in parallelism, at least in part. The second line, however, may extend the first line without repeating any of its syntactic structure. The result is a sort of *enjambment, e.g., "He called up against me a holiday / for breaking down my young men!" (Lam. 1:15; see Dobbs-Allsopp). In such cases, we may either understand the entire first line to be repeated in the deep structure of the second line—and deleted; or we may understand that, in this parallelism, balance of line length, rather than repetition of syntactic structure, is determinative (see below).

Biblical Heb. is the best-known system of parallelism, first described in depth by Bishop Robert Lowth in 1753. Jewish exegetes of the Middle Ages had expressed a less elaborate understanding of parallelism according to which "it is a doubling of the meaning using different words" (David Kimḥi, Provence, ca. 1200). Lowth, too, laid emphasis on semantic reiteration alongside syntactic repetition: "When a Proposition is delivered, and a second is subjoined to it, or drawn under it, equivalent, or contrasted with it in Sense; or similar to it in the form of Grammatical Construction; these I call Parallel lines; and the words, or phrases, answering one to another in the corresponding Lines, Parallel Terms" (*Isaiah: A New Translation*, 1778).

In the 1980s, both O'Connor and Greenstein suggested that parallelism be regarded as the rhetorical structuration of propositions, whose meanings are brought into conjunction by their formal similarities. Consider Psalm 23:1: "The Lord is my shepherd, / I shall not want." The two propositions have no inherent link semantically. Bringing the two clauses together through parallelism, however, establishes a meaningful connection: the speaker will lack nothing because the Lord is, metaphorically, a shepherd who protects, guides, and cares for him or her. Note as well that the two lines of the couplet have different syntactic structures. They display above all a quasi-metrical balance. A minority view holds that there is a strictly recoverable metrical component to the poetry of the Heb. Bible (e.g., Sievers), but in the absence of any convincing theory, it is more generally maintained that there is an unrecoverable or vague metrical element in the verse.

Biblical parallelism, as J. G. Herder first observed in 1783, is primarily characterized by a balance of line length. Secondarily, it may feature a repetition of syntactic structure and the distribution of conventionally paired words (silver-gold, heaven-earth, father-mother, slave-son of a maidservant, wine-blood of grapes, listen-give ear, etc.) between the parallel lines. Accordingly, the couplet immediately following Psalm 23:1 is "In grassy meadows he lays me down (*yarbitséni*), / By still waters he leads me (*yenahaléni*)." Here we find a quasi-metrical balance, full repetition of syntactic structure, the distribution of the word pair "meadow-waters" (cf. Joel 1:20) between the two members of the parallelism, and on top of that a phonetic echo of the verb from line to line.

In Chinese verse and rhet., as was said, it is typical to formulate full lines in complete syntactic parallelism, e.g., "In the vast desert a solitary column of smoke rises straight, / Over the long river the setting sun looms round" (Wang Wei; quoted in Plaks 536). In Eng. Ren. poetry, by contrast, it is common to pattern phrases in sequence in parallelism, e.g., "Light of my life, and life of my desire"; "Oft with true sighes, oft with uncalled teares, / Now with slow words, now with dumbe eloquence" (Philip Sidney, *Astrophil and Stella* 68, 61). Such sequences can be extended, e.g., "My mouth doth water, and my breast doth swell, / My tongue doth itch, my thoughts in labour be" (37). In more complex structures, the individual entities are themselves likely to be more complex, forming full sentences in parallelism:

Let Fortune lay on me her worst disgrace,
Let folke orecharg'd with braine against
    me crie,
Let clouds bedimme my face, breake in
    mine eye,
Let me no steps but of lost labour trace,
Let all the earth with scorne recount my
    case.

(*Astrophil and Stella*, 64)

In Eur. poetry since the Ren., biblical influence has reinforced the use of parallelism to the point that few major verse texts are without some parallelism. William Blake and Christopher Smart both use quasi-biblical parallelism extensively. This tendency reaches a turning point when Walt Whitman makes use of biblical structures to supplant the metrical basis of Eng. prosody itself:

The prairie-grass accepting its own special
    odor breathing,
I demand of it the spiritual corresponding,

Demand the most copious and close companionship of men,
Demand the blades to rise of words, acts,
    beings.

("Calamus," *Leaves of Grass*)

Full, indeed extraordinarily long, lines can be formulated in parallelism, as in Dylan Thomas's opening affirmation, "The force that through the green fuse drives the flower / Drives my green age" and its (nonadjacent) parallel, "The force that drives the water through the rocks / Drives my red blood." Similarly in the well-known opening of Allen Ginsberg's *Howl* (1955), the second line refers back to the syntax of the latter part of the first line (beginning "I saw the best minds of my generation . . ."), re-duplicating and elaborating it. The underlying structure of the second line is, accordingly, "[I saw the best minds of my generation . . .], dragging themselves through the negro streets at dawn looking for an angry fix." Essentially, the form we find here is the same as that of ancient Ugaritic and Heb. verse, in which the deletion of an element in the second line is accompanied by an extension of an ungapped element.

Ginsberg's poem captures the cadences of oral discourse, bringing the historical trajectory of parallelism full circle, for while parallelism becomes a convention of formal, literate composition, its beginnings are unquestionably in an oral context. Many poetries featuring parallelism tend to be either oral or early literate. The later typological category is important: the poetry of the Heb. Bible began to be written down over two and a half millennia ago, while Finnish folk poetry has been recorded for only a century and a half, but cl. Heb. and Finnish poetry are comparably close to the oral poetic situation and comparably far from the literate setting.

Parallelism is well represented in traditional poetry in Chinese (and its literary offspring, Vietnamese), in Toda (but not in the other Dravidian tongues), in the Semitic langs. (see above and cf. several types of "parallel prose" in Ar.), in the Uralic langs. (incl. Finnish), in the Austronesian langs. (Rotinese is the best known), and in the Mayan langs. Both med. and mod. Rus. folk poetry is parallelistic, as is some Altaic (Mongol and Turkic) verse.

See HYPOTAXIS AND PARATAXIS.

■ R. Lowth, *De sacra poesi Hebraeorum, Lectures on the Sacred Poetry of the Hebrews*, trans. G. Gregory (1753); J. G. Herder, *Vom Geist* der hebräischen Poesie (1753), trans. *The Spirit of Hebrew Poetry* (1833); E. Sievers, *Metrische Studien I–II* (1901–7); *The Wisdom of Laotse*, trans. and ed. Lin Yutang (1948); Jakobson, esp. v. 3; *The Kalevala*, trans. F. P. Magoun Jr. (1963); B. Hrushovski, "Prosody, Hebrew," *Encyclopedia Judaica* (1971); P. Kiparsky, "The Role of Linguistics in a Theory of Poetry," *Daedalus* 102 (1973); J. J. Fox, "Roman Jakobson and the Comparative Study of Parallelism," *Roman Jakobson*, ed. D. Armstrong and C. H. Van Schooneveld (1977); J. M. Lotman, *The Structure of the Artistic Text*, trans. G. Lenhoff and R. Vroon (1977); S. A. Geller, *Parallelism in Early Biblical Poetry* (1979); M. O'Connor, *Hebrew Verse Structure* (1980); J. L. Kugel, *The Idea of Biblical Poetry* (1981); E. L. Greenstein, "How Does Parallelism Mean?" *A Sense of Text* (1983); R. Alter, *The Art of Biblical Poetry* (1985); A. Berlin, *The Dynamics of Biblical Parallelism* (1985); Terras; M. R. Lichtmann, *The Contemplative Poetry of G. M. Hopkins* (1989); A. H. Plaks, "Where the Lines Meet: Parallelism in Chinese and Western Literature," *PoT* 11 (1990); *Ugaritic Narrative Poetry*, ed. S. B. Parker (1997); F. W. Dobbs-Allsopp, "The Enjambing Line in Lamentations: A Taxonomy (Part 1)," *Zeitschrift für die alttestamentliche Wissenschaft* 113 (2001); B. R. Foster, *Before the Muses* (2005)—anthol. of Akkadian lit.

M. P. O'Connor; E. L. Greenstein

PARODY. Derived from the Gr. roots *para* (alongside, counter) and *odos* (song), parody as a form of ironic imitation has been with us since ancient times. It changes with the culture, however, so no transhistorical definition is possible: its forms, its relations to the parodied text, and its intentions are not the same in North America today as they were in 18th-c. England or Aristotle's Greece. Theories of parody have changed along with the form's aesthetic manifestations, but two major views have emerged, both derived, though in different ways, from the word's etymology. In the age of Alexander Pope and John Dryden, e.g., parody was seen as a "countersong"—a biting, often satiric, imitation intended to wittily "counter" (i.e., to mock or ridicule) what really was an intended "target." In our mod. and postmod. times, parody has come to mean more of an intimate "song beside"—an ironic but not necessarily disrespectful revisiting and recontextualizing of an earlier work.

In formal terms, parody is a doubled structure, incorporating backgrounded aspects of the parodied text of the past into the foreground of its present self. The two texts neither merge nor cancel each other out; they work together, while remaining distinct. From either of its historically defined perspectives, parody involves opposition or contrast: it is a form of repetition with ironic critical difference, marking difference rather than similarity (Gilman 1974, 1976; Hutcheon). Therein lies the difference between parody and pastiche. Though both are forms of acknowledged borrowing (and in that acknowledging, they differ from the hoax, the plagiarism, or the forgery), pastiche does not aim at ironic inversion leading to difference. Neither does allusion or quotation in itself, though both can be used ironically. To continue with distinctions, both burlesque and travesty by definition involve ridiculing humor, but parody does not necessarily—neither now nor in its cl. uses (Householder). It can range in its tones and moods from the seriously respectful to the playful to the scathingly critical because that is the range of *irony, its major rhetorical strategy.

But it is parody's defining critical distance that has always permitted *satire to be so effectively deployed through parodic textual forms. From Catullus to Wendy Cope, satirists have used and continue to use the pointed and effective doubling of parody's textual voices as a vehicle to unmask the duplicities of human society. Pope's *mock epics *The Rape of the Lock* and *The Dunciad*, the latter with its ironic use of Virgil's *Eclogues*, stand as fine examples of the complexity of the interrelationship of parody and satire: the mock epic did not mock the epic but satirized the pretensions of the contemporary as set against the ideal norms implied by the parodied text or set of conventions. This is not to say that the literary forms themselves could not be critiqued: John Milton's *Paradise Lost* uses epic conventions but also critically parodies those conventions and the whole cl. heroic ethos, by consistently associating them with Satan and his legions; and Chaucer's "The Tale of Sir Thopas" ridicules the clichés of med. verse romance.

A form of what has been called intertextuality (Kristeva, Genette) or interart discourse, parody can also involve a self-reflexive (Rose 1979) and critical act of reassessment and acclimatization. But there is often a tension between the potentially conservative effect of repetition and the potentially revolutionary impact of difference. These contradictory ideological implications of parody took center stage in the postmod. 1980s and the years after, in both the lit. itself and the critical theorizing. And yet despite the complicity that postmod. parody implied, it was the more critical dimension that would come to dominate because of changes in political contexts. Parody's echoing repetition has always implicitly contested romantic concepts of creative originality and singularity, as well as capitalist notions of individual ownership and copyright, but it clearly was seen to challenge (or, more accurately, to be *used* to challenge) many other dominant political positions. Parody came to be reinterpreted through what Rich called women's "revisioning," a looking back with new eyes on a literary trad. dominated by male perspectives and a subsequent rewriting of it in a differently gendered key. This echoing contestation was mirrored in what Gates and others historicized as Af. Am. *"signifying"—another kind of double-voiced repetition and inversion, but this time one that responds to both dominant and vernacular discourses. Postcolonial crit.'s focus on how formerly colonized writers could "write back" to empire through critically rewriting or even (in Bhabha's refigured sense of the word) mimicking its canonical texts coincided with the work of indigenous writers in the Americas to adapt dominant discourses to create new and highly critical hybrid forms (Powell). Queer writing and theory politicized Sontag's notion of "camp" to make ironic repetition the device of choice for challenging homophobia.

In short, whatever the political contestation, parody proved a useful rhetorical strategy, a counter-discourse (Terdiman), to confront the past and potentially to move beyond it. For example, Thylias Moss's various parodies that recode poems racially ("Interpretation of a Poem by Frost" or "A Reconsideration of the Blackbird") are typical of all these manifestations, in both theory and practice, in that the parodies' situation in the world, so to speak, becomes the focus of attention: the time and the place, the ideological frame of reference, the personal and social context—not only of parodist but also of readers of the work. What has also become clear through this new politicized context, however, is that parody is fundamentally ambivalent or paradoxical; it is doubled and divided because of that defining mix of repetition and difference. If it is transgressive, it is only as a form of authorized transgression, like Bakhtin's carnivalesque (1973). It cannot help inscribing and granting authority to what it parodies, even if it aims to challenge it. Parody enacts both continuity and change.

That unavoidable ambivalence may help explain why, depending on the time and place, parody has been either prized or derided, called both noble and vile. On the negative end of the evaluation scale, it has beencalled parasitic and derivative, esp. within a romantic aesthetic. With the inauguration of copyright laws came defamation suits against parodists. Yet, early in the 20th c., the Russian formalists prized works like Lord Byron's *Don Juan* because their parodic form coincided with their own theory of the essential conventionality of literary form and the role of parody in its denuding or laying bare (Erlich). Read in contexts ranging from T. S. Eliot's valorizing of what he called the historical sense to Bakhtin's privileging of dialogism or double voicing, parody has been welcomed as a form of textual appropriation that self-reflexively foregrounds both the formal and the ideological dimensions of lit. It has become one mode of coming to terms with the texts of that rich and, for some, intimidating legacy of the past (Bate), offering a model, however ironized, for the process of transfer and reorganization of that past—whether such recycling be of literary conventions or individual works.

Parodies must be recognized as double-voiced discourses in order for their ironic inversion to function; if they are not, they will simply be naturalized and their doubling ignored. That is why some parodists resort to overtly revealing titles: Anthony Hecht's famous ironic take on Matthew Arnold is dubbed "The Dover Bitch"; P. B. Shelley's parody of William Wordsworth is titled "Peter Bell the Third," while William Maginn's of S. T. Coleridge is called "The Rime of the Auncient Waggonere." For parody to be recognized and interpreted, there must be (cultural, ling., literary) codes shared between the encoder and the decoder, the parodist and the reader, or the structural superimposition of texts will be missed. The potential for elitism inherent in the need for shared codes has been frequently pointed out, but less attention has been paid to the didactic value of parody in teaching or in positively co-opting the art of the past by textual incorporation and ironic commentary. Forrest-Thomson has argued that the mod. poet manages to mediate between the ling. codes we normally recognize and use and those that emerge from an assimilation and transformation of those codes. Parodic poetry in particular can function overtly as this kind of link. Parody is a way to preserve continuity in discontinuity—without the Bloomian anxiety of influence.

■ **Anthologies:** *A Book of Parodies*, ed. A. Symons (1908); *A Century of Parody and Imitation*, ed. W. Jerrold and R. M. Leonard (1913); *A Parody Anthology*, ed. C. Wells (1919); *Apes and Parrots*, ed. J. Collings Squire (1928); *American Literature in Parody*, ed. R. P. Falk (1955); *Parodies*, ed. D. Macdonald (1960); *The Brand X Anthology of Poetry*, ed. W. Zaranka (1981); *The Faber Book of Parodies*, ed. S. Brett (1984); *Unauthorized Versions*, ed. K. Baker (1990); *Romantic Parodies, 1797–1831*, ed. D. A. Kent and D. R. Ewen (1992).

■ **Criticism and History:** S. Martin, *On Parody* (1896); C. Stone, *Parody* (1914); G. Kitchin, *A Survey of Burlesque and Parody in English* (1931); F. W. Householder, "Parodia," *CP* 39 (1944); F. J. Lelièvre, "The Basis of Ancient Parody," *Greece and Rome* 1 (1954); E. Courtney, "Parody and Literary Allusion in Menippean Satire," *Philologus* 106 (1962); G. Highet, *Anatomy of Satire* (1962); V. Erlich, *Russian Formalism*, 2d ed. (1965); J. G. Riewald, "Parody as Criticism," *Neophilologus* 50 (1966); U. Weisstein, "Parody, Travesty, and Burlesque," *Proceedings of the 4th Congress of the ICLA* (1966); S. Sontag, "Notes on Camp," *Against Interpretation* (1967); S. Golopentia-Eretescu, "Grammaire de la parodie," *Cahiers de linguistique théorique et appliquée* 6 (1969); G. D. Kiremidjian, "The Aesthetics of Parody," *JAAC* 28 (1969); W. J. Bate, *The Burden of the Past and the English Poet* (1970); G. Lee, *Allusion, Parody and Imitation* (1971); M. M. Bakhtin, *Rabelais and His World*, trans. H. Iswolsky (1973); H. Bloom, *The Anxiety of Influence* (1973); T. Verweyen, *Eine Theorie der Parodie* (1973); O. M. Friedenberg, "The Origin of Parody," *Semiotics and Structuralism*, ed. H. Baran (1974); S. L. Gilman, *The Parodic Sermon in European Perspective* (1974); L. Dällenbach, "Intertexte et autotexte," *Poétique* 27 (1976); S. L. Gilman, *Nietzschean Parody* (1976); W. Karrer, *Parodie, Travestie, Pastiche* (1977); V. Forrest-Thomson, *Poetic Artifice* (1978); Z. Ben-Porat, "The Poetics of Literary Allusion," *PTL: A Journal for Descriptive Poetics and Theory of Literature* 1 (1979); A. Rich, *On Lies, Secrets, and Silence* (1979); M. A. Rose, *Parody//Meta-Fiction* (1979); M. M. Bakhtin, *The Dialogic Imagination*, ed. M. Holquist, trans. C. Emerson and M. Holquist (1981); W. Freund, *Die literarische Parodie* (1981); H. Bhabha, "Of Mimicry and Man," *October* 28 (1984); E. Cobley, "Sameness and Difference in Literary Repetition," *Semiotic Inquiry* 4 (1984); R. Terdiman, *Discourse/Counter Discourse* (1985); J. Kristeva, "Word, Dialogue and Novel," *The Kristeva Reader*, ed. T. Moi (1986); J. A. Dane, *Parody* (1988); H. L. Gates Jr., *The Signifying Monkey* (1988); M. A. Rose, *Parody* (1993); G. Genette, *Palimpsests*, trans. C. Newman and C. Doubinsky (1997); *Parody*, ed. B. Müller (1997); S. Dentith, *Parody* (2000); L. Hutcheon, *A Theory of Parody*, 2d ed. (2000); M. Powell, "Rhetorics of Survivance: How American Indians *Use* Writing," *CCC* 53.3 (2002), http://www.inventio.us/ccc/; R. L. Mack, *The Genius of Parody* (2007).

L. HUTCHEON AND M. WOODLAND

PARONOMASIA (Gr., occasionally in Lat. [pure Lat. *agnominatio*], Eng. from 1577, *OED*). Wordplay based on like-sounding words, e.g., a pun. In rhet., often one type of pun only, as against, e.g., *antanaclasis* (Lanham). *Pun*, a later word (from 1644, *OED*), has come to include earlier rhetorical figures for wordplay (Spitzer).

Rhetoricians from Aristotle onward are mostly cautious about paronomasia, chiefly about its overuse, while noting its effectiveness when used appropriately (*Rhetorica ad Herennium*, early 1st c. BCE; Geoffrey of Vinsauf, *Poetria nova*, ca. 1210). Some stress its low status (Henry Peacham, *The Garden of Eloquence*, 1593; Ben Jonson, *Timber*, 1641; César Chesneau Dumarsais, *Traité des tropes*, 1730). Overuse is a question of competence, but status is simply a question of taste and fashion, which may vary from one era to another. From cl. through med. to Ren. writing, the functions of paronomasia were not confined to comic, let alone trivial, purposes. But 18th-c. neoclassical writers disliked it (Joseph Addison, *Spectator* no. 61, 1711, where it is called "false wit"; Alexander Pope, *Peri Bathous* [Bathos], 1727). Poets in the 19th c. made little use of paronomasia compared with their 17th-c. predecessors, though some enjoyed it in prose writing (S. T. Coleridge, Charles Lamb). Among major poets, Emily Dickinson and G. M. Hopkins are exceptions. In general, the 19th c. assigned it to comic verse (Thomas Hood, Lewis Carroll, Edward Lear, W. S. Gilbert). Modernist poets (e.g., T. S. Eliot, Wallace Stevens) used paronomasia for serious effects, reviving the concept of *serio ludere*. But it is still a question whether paronomasia has regained its earlier status as a figure, lost when 18th-c. rhet. downgraded the pun.

Paronomasia may occur in all types of poetry, from comic to sublime. The Heb. Bible uses it (*Moses* means both one "drawn out" of the water [Heb. *mosheh*] and one who "draws out" Israel from bondage [Heb. *mashah*]; Marks); so does the Christian Bible (Jesus puns on the name *Peter* and *petra*, rock, Matt. 16:18). Cl. Gr. writers enjoyed it (Stanford), as did some Lat. writers, such as Virgil (Ahl, Spence). Augustine records the delight of contemp. North African congregations in *hilaritas*, incl. wordplay (Brown). Shakespeare is fertile in the deployment of paronomasia for both comic and serious effects. Mercutio's dying pun is well known: tomorrow he will be "a grave man" (*Romeo and Juliet* 3.1.98); Hamlet puns on "sun" and "son" (*Hamlet* 1.2.64 and 67), a pun sometimes extended to Christ, as in George Herbert's "The Son." John Milton puns in the first line of *Paradise Lost* on "fruit" of a tree and "fruit" as result. *Limericks delight in outrageous witty puns.

Paronomasia runs from *piano* to *forte* effects. Edmund Spenser's is quiet and often builds slowly, as does the paronomasia in poetry by Herbert through Elizabeth Bishop and beyond. John Donne's likes to display itself ("A Hymn to God the Father," 1633: "done" and "Donne").

In the analysis of puns, the most familiar division is between homophonic puns (like-sounding, as in "done" and "Donne") and homonymic or semantic puns (different meanings in one word, as in railroad "ties" and "ties" of the heart in Bishop's "Chemin de Fer"). In poetry, it is useful to distinguish paronomasia as a *scheme and paronomasia as a *trope. A simple homophonic pun without further reverberation beyond sheer pleasure would be classified as a scheme (Hood's "Faithless Sally Brown": "They went and told the sexton / And the sexton tolled the bell.") But puns can move toward trope, when they begin to generate fables about themselves (Fried), as seen with Virgil or Stevens above.

Multilingual puns also flourished over the centuries, esp. when Lat. was commonly known. Ludovico Ariosto used an ancient one, newly rediscovered, in his hippogryph or horse-griffin (*gryphus* puns on the griffin and a type of playful riddle, *griphos*, a pun that Carroll also used for his Gryphon in *Alice in Wonderland* [Cook 2006]). James Joyce's *Finnegans Wake* is rich in such puns, and the art is not lost in

poetry: witness Stevens's brilliant paronomasia on "selvages / salvages" in "Esthétique du Mal," sect. 5, echoing Dante's *selva oscura* and Eliot's "The Dry Salvages."

Most paronomasia in poetry is verbal, but visual puns are possible, as in James Merrill's "The owlet umlaut peeps and hoots / Above the open vowel" ("Lost in Translation") or Tony Harrison's "blank printer's ems" that duly appear in the next line, resulting in a justified right margin ("Self-Justification"). So are oral puns, as in "Crows in Winter" by Anthony Hecht: "the wind, a voiceless thorn" (punning on the OE letter *thorn*, the unvoiced *th*).

A few words have a hist. of paronomasia in poetry and invite special attention, e.g., *turn*, *leaves*, *room*. *Turn* is the root meaning of Gr. *trope* and may also refer to the turning of the end of a poetic line (cf. Fr. *verser*). Seamus Heaney, following an old trad., extends this to the lines made by a ploughman (*Preoccupations*). *Leaves* is a longstanding trope for the souls of the dead, from Homer through Virgil, Milton, P. B. Shelley, Stevens, and others; a pun on the Eng. verb *leave* is a given. *Stanza* means "room."

As with *riddle and charm, the pun is associated with very early writing. Possibly it gave birth to Western writing itself in the Sumerian alphabet of pre-3000 BCE Mesopotamia, to follow Jared Diamond in *Guns, Germs and Steel* (1997): *ti* as "life" and as "arrow." As Frye says, "Paronomasia is one of the essential elements of verbal creation."

■ S. Freud, "The Technique of Jokes," *The Standard Edition of the Complete Psychological Works*, ed. and trans. J. Strachey, v. 8 (1905); W. B. Stanford, *Ambiguity in Greek Literature* (1939); L. Spitzer, "Puns," *JEGP* 49 (1950); Frye; M. M. Mahood, *Shakespeare's Wordplay* (1957); P. Brown, *Augustine of Hippo* (1967); F. Ahl, *Metaformations: Soundplay and Wordplay in Ovid and Other Classical Poets* (1985); E. Cook, *Poetry, Word-Play and Word-War in Wallace Stevens* (1988); J. Culler, "The Call of the Phoneme: Introduction," and D. Fried, "Rhyme Puns," *On Puns: The Foundation of Letters*, ed. J. Culler (1988); Lanham; *Connotations* 2.1–3 (1992) and 3.1–2 (1993–94)—largely on paronomasia; H. Marks, "Biblical Naming and Poetic Etymology," *Journal of Bible Literature* 114 (1995); E. Cook, *Enigmas and Riddles in Literature* (2006); S. Spence, "Avian Ways: Influence and Innovationin Lucretius and Vergil," *L'Esprit Créateur* 49 (2009).

E. COOK

PASTORAL

I. Ancient
II. Modern

I. Ancient. Ancient pastorals are poems in *hexameters, either dramatic in form or with minimal narrative framing, in which fictional herdsmen sing songs to one another or to an absent beloved, in a stylized natural setting. The poems are short, typically less than 150 lines long, and plot and character devel. are minimal: pastoral's major innovation is to make the performance of an internal poetic event—the pastoral song—and the fictional world in which this performance takes place—a *locus amoenus*, or peaceful rural location with flowing water and shady trees—the chief attractions of a literary genre.

Models for the centrality of performance and the herdsman as a poetic subject can be found in earlier lit.: the songs of the fictional bard Demodocus and the pastoral life of the Cyclops in Homer's *Odyssey* are esp. important. However, pastoral owes its existence as a genre to Theocritus, a Sicilian Greek of the early 3d c. BCE who synthesized these elements of Panhellenic literary myth with mythical and performance trads. of his native country, making the legendary herdsman Daphnis the prototypical pastoral singer and adapting the mime trad. known to us through the fragments of the Syracusan Sophron (late 5th to early 4th c. BCE) to his own poetic purposes.

The fictional world Theocritus fashioned from these diverse materials is highly resistant to epistemological reduction: mythical trads. are blatantly contradicted, mimetic and mythical registers are superimposed, and characters with the same name do not resemble one another from one poem to the next. The herdsmen speak hexameters, but in a Doric dialect—a strange conflation of rusticity and heroic *epic—and there is no attempt to distinguish metrically between the spoken and sung portions of the poems (unlike in, e.g., Edmund Spenser's *Shepheardes Calender*). The unifying *trope is the pastoral singer's self-identification with an imagined predecessor: a would-be herdsman-singer proves his mastery by merging with his own archetype in performance (*Idyll* 1, 5, 7) or fails conspicuously in his attempt to do so (*Idyll* 3).

Imitation of Theocritus began early, and the collections of Gr. pastoral poetry that have survived contain spurious poems that expand the genre's formal and characterological range: the songs of *Idyll* 8 are set off as elegiacs, *Idyll* 21 is about fishermen, and the consummated teen romance of *Idyll* 27 contrasts with the unrequited desire that defines the Theocritean lover. More ambitious devels. can be seen in two poems that marry the setting of Theocritean pastoral with Near Eastern *lament trads.: the "Lament for Adonis" of Bion (probably late 2d c. BCE) and the "Lament for Bion," erroneously ascribed to Moschus (mid-2d c. BCE). The former is distinguished by an affective intensity, particularly in its use of *pathetic fallacy, alien to Theocritus; the latter portrays a historical poet lamented by his own characters, boldly foregrounding the possibility that the poet might include himself within his pastoral fiction that is merely hinted at in Theocritus's *Idyll* 7.

The supreme achievement of ancient pastoral and the one that ensured the genre's survival in later Eur. lit. is Virgil's *Eclogues* (between 42 and 35 BCE). Virgil had no literary dialects to play with, and what distinguishes his herdsmen as speakers and singers is an exquisitely wrought *diction that exploits all the resources of Lat. phonology, word order, and verbal *rhythm to create a richly textured art lang., inviting recognition as the first great achievement of an ambitious young poet. Virgil himself moves in and out of his collection as he merges with and withdraws from his fictional singers: in *Eclogue* 5 and 9, Menalcas is closely identified with the authorial voice, while the narrator of *Eclogue* 6 cites words of Apollo that refer to him as Tityrus, an identification of poet and character that gains additional credence from the argument of Virgil's 4th-c. commentator Servius, that Tityrus represents the poet in *Eclogue* 1 because he too had his land saved from appropriation by military veterans through the intervention of a powerful figure at Rome.

No single identification of poet and character can be easily maintained over the entirety of the *Eclogues*. However, the possibility of such an identification, which is adopted intermittently as an interpretive possibility by ancient commentators on Theocritus's *Idylls*, in Virgil's book becomes pastoral's founding fiction: authorial self-disguising is what allows the pastoral world to be recognized as contemp. hist. in herdsman's clothing. Conversely, as the *Idylls* stage the emergence of consolatory forms of fictional self-projection, the *Eclogues* show how such self-projection is constrained by historical circumstance. The songs of the *Eclogues* are sung in a cultural landscape, and the transactions of pastoral identity that occur in them are subject to cancellation from without.

The *Eclogues* of Calpurnius Siculus (mid-1st c. CE) make the conditions of pastoral dependence an occasion of praise for the Emperor Nero. Reading Virgil's Tityrus as a figure of poetic gratitude, Calpurnius presents himself as Corydon, a cowherd who has seen the wonders of Rome and returned to proclaim a new Golden Age to his fellow herdsmen. Calpurnius dispenses with the ambiguities of Virgil's identifications, using a single herdsman to develop a sustained vision of poetry's dependence on imperial patronage, and of the pastoral fiction in which this dependency is figured. Calpurnius is a master of court pastoral; the same cannot be said of the author of the two Einsiedeln Eclogues, named after the Swiss monastery in which their ms. was discovered: even in their incomplete state, the turgidity of their poetic lang. and the poverty of invention with which they attempt to emulate Calpurnius's courtly dramas are painfully apparent.

The final flowers of the ancient pastoral trad. are the four *Eclogues* of the 3d-c. Carthaginian Nemesianus, the last of which provided the epigraph to Ezra Pound's *Hugh Selwyn Mauberley.* Nemesianus evinces no interest in the metapoetic potential of the herdsman-singer, fashioning instead a sequence of brief bucolic dramas that, while classicizing in their lang., are innovative in landscape and character. *Eclogue* 2 is particularly noteworthy: two adolescent shepherd boys recall the intensity of the desire that led them to rape a young girl as she was gathering flowers in the countryside. In its mixture of erotic violence, mythic depth, and social realism, the poem points to the continuing vitality of the genre of which Nemesianus's *Eclogues* are our last ancient example.

II. Modern. From the Ren. to romanticism, Europe and its overseas territories hosted a great flowering of pastoral lit., accompanied by ubiquitous representations of idyllic nature in the visual arts and music. Propelled by humanism and increasing secularization, mod. pastorals rehearse the kind's signature themes of natural harmony, love, friendship, virtue, and poetry itself, using a coded set of names, locales, and poetic commonplaces associated with ancient literary shepherds. Its predictable

artifice notwithstanding, the resilient convention proved an apt mirror for dramatic changes in early mod. experience—rising nations, growing cities and courts, rural depopulation, religious tensions, territorial expansion, new human encounters—as trans-Atlantic Edens and New Arcadias attest. Naturally capacious in form and subject, mod. pastorals experiment energetically with hybridity and polyphony, recombining inherited materials while reaching into new discursive territories.

In the early 14th c., eclogues modeled on Virgil appear first in Italy, where Dante, Petrarch, and Giovanni Boccaccio prepare the way for more Lat. eclogues by Mateo Boiardo, Baptista Spagnuoli (known as Mantuan), Jacopo Sannazaro, and numerous other Eur. poets. Widespread trans. of Virgil, among them those of Bernardino Pulci in 1482 and Luis de León, ca. 1580, parallel cultivation of vernacular eclogues by leading 16th-c. poets, incl. Garcilaso de la Vega, Fernando de Herrera, Francisco de Figueroa, Luís de Camões, Clément Marot, Pierre de Ronsard, and Edmund Spenser. Some prove enormously influential for the course of national poetry: Garcilaso's three eclogues (1543) reinvent *lyric lang. in Sp.; Spenser's *Shepheardes Calender* (1579), composed of 12 eclogues, is often considered the first great Eng. Ren. poem (Kermode). As an umbrella for diverse prosodic and rhetorical types, vernacular eclogues welcome *panegyrics, poetic contests and disputes, *elegies, laments and quarrels, *songs, *epithalamia, narrative anecdotes, *satires, and philosophical meditations. Verse on pastoral themes is ubiquitous: virtually every significant early mod. poet (among them John Milton, Luis de Góngora, and Giambattista Marino) uses the mode to treat themes of love and loss, often borrowing *tropes and sentimental postures from troubadour lyric, Petrarch's *Canzoniere*, oral lyric and *ballad trads., and rustic vernacular dialects. But the kind makes room for Christian themes, as in Sannazaro's short Lat. epic *De partu virginis* (On the Virgin Birth, 1526), Luis de León's contemplative vernacular odes, and the mystical *Cántico espiritual* (*Spiritual Canticle*, 1584; 1586–91) of St. John of the Cross.

Pastoral dramas offer imaginary rustic diversions to audiences in cities and aristocratic courts, using the kind's stylized settings as backdrop for staging such concerns as the workings of affect, temperament, passions, virtues, and good government. With precedent in Boccaccio's allegorical *Ameto* (1341–42),

Giambattista Giraldi Cinthio's satyr play *Egle* (1545), Torquato Tasso's *Aminta* (1581), and Giovanni Battista Guarini's *Il pastor fido* (written 1583, pub. 1590) dramatize for court audiences at Ferrara period debates about the nature of virtuous love. A vogue of pastoral-mythological plays (30 in 1580s Italy alone) established pastoral tragicomedy as a legitimate third dramatic genre along with comedy and tragedy and made It. plays models for international imitation. In France, Honorat de Bueil, seigneur de Racan's *Les Bergeries* (1625) spawned a school of courtly shepherds' plays; John Lyly's *Gallathea* (1592), George Peele's *Arraignment of Paris* (1584), John Fletcher's *Faithful Shepherdess* (1610), Ben Jonson's *Sad Shepherd* (1641), and Allan Ramsay's *Gentle Shepherd* (1725, in lowland Scots dialect), parallel pastoral scenes in Shakespeare and other Eng. dramatists. In Spain, building on med. trads. (oral lyric, *pastorela*), early 16th-c. performable eclogues by Gil Vicente, Juan del Encina, and Lucas Fernández treat secular and sacred subjects, perfecting the comic type of the rustic shepherd. Pastoral episodes, courtly and rustic, are common in 17th-c. historical comedies, mythological palace dramas, and *autos sacramentales* on eucharistic themes, notably in Sor Juana Inés de la Cruz's *Auto del divino Narciso* (1590).

Anticipated in Boccaccio's *Ameto,* the hybrid pastoral romance takes hold in Eur. imagination following publication of Sannazaro's *Arcadia* (1502, 1504), which frames 12 eclogues in prose narrative, and Jorge de Montemayor's *Diana* (1559), whose looser alternation of verse and prose subsequently prevails. Both inspire many imitations, incl. Gaspar Gil Polo's *Diana enamorada* (1564), Miguel de Cervantes's *La Galatea* (1585), Philip Sidney's *Arcadia* (1590, 1593), Félix Lope de Vega's *La Arcadia* (1598) and the sacred *Pastores de Belén* (Shepherds of Bethlehem, 1612), and Honoré d'Urfé's *L'Astrée* (1607–28). In contrast with much ancient and early mod. pastoral verse, these romances accord central roles and the privilege of lyric expression to their female characters. By displacing refined courtiers into edenic settings where they meet savages (as in Montemayor, Cervantes, and Spenser's *Faerie Queene*, [1590, 1596]), their fictions resonate with experiences of exile (Sephardic diaspora, forced conversions), utopian dreaming, and New World wanderings. Ties to epic, court masque, early mod. opera, the long mythological poem, and dialogues such as Luis de León's *De los nombres de Cristo* (*The Names of Christ*, 1583) bespeak pastoral romance's seminal importance in early mod. generic experiments. Pastoral material (idyllic interludes, poems, dialogues) turns up regularly in Ren. romance (chivalric, Moorish, sentimental, Gr., historical), fostering mergers among those kinds and creating a laboratory for the representation of subjectivity in prose. Though gradually stripped of conventional trappings, pastoral's motifs and sentimental discourses are steadily integrated into the central business of prose fiction, making it a fundamental building block of the mod. novel.

Emphasis on lang. and place makes pastoral a natural home for discussions on the role of vernaculars and lit. in mod. civilizations. The simple, rustic diction that purist decorum assigns to shepherds is redefined as an aesthetic of melodic eloquence, an ethics of truthful speech, and the badge of cultural distinction. Numerous pastoral poets (Dante, Pietro Bembo, Joachim du Bellay, Fernando de Herrera, Cervantes, Sidney) publish defenses of mod. langs. and poetry. Foundational in discourses of nationhood as verbal incarnation of place, cultivated lang. elevates pastoral's historical geographies and precious verbal artifacts to the status of national treasure.

Although courtly pastoral, exhausted by overuse and the extreme stylizations of *préciosité* and rococo, went the way of Europe's absolutist courts and aristocratic estates, the kind's humanistic engagement with philosophical and political questions gave it a long hold on the literary imagination. Antonio de Guevara's double-edged satire and international best seller *Menosprecio de corte y alabanza de aldea* (Dispraise of the Court and Praise of the Village, 1539) earned cs. of trans., imitations, and adaptations. The mode's strategy, suggestive of its links to neo-Stoic thought, of apparently retreating from the world, then reflecting on it, has made it useful in very diverse contexts. In the face of absolutist and ecclesiastical censorship, as in late 16th-c. Spain, pastoral's affinity for masking, displacement, and allegory provides a vehicle for political and cultural critiques certain to be suppressed in more direct discourses. Pastoral's interest in the relation of humans to the natural world and to each other accounts for its tendency to surface in contexts like anticonquest discourse (Bartolomé de Las Casas's vision of wolves, sheep, and good shepherds in the Americas), Enlightenment philosophy (Jean-Jacques Rousseau's natural man), and romantic poetry (the "precious boon" of nature that William Wordsworth accused humans of giving away). Giamatti finds ubiquitous earthly paradises in early mod. Eur. epics; New World sagas such as Alonso de Ercilla's *Araucana* (3 parts: 1569, 1578, 1589) make frequent political use of the same trope and particularly of the feminine voices of pastoral romance.

See DRAMATIC POETRY, ECLOGUE, IDYLL.

■ **Ancient:** P.-E. Legrand, *Etude sur Théocrite* (1898); U. von. Wilamowitz-Moellendorf, *Hellenistische Dichtung in der Zeit des Kallimachos.* 2 v. (1924); W. Arland, *Nachtheokritische Bukolik* (1937); B. Otis, *Virgil: A Study in Civilized Poetry* (1963); M.C.J. Putnam, *Virgil's Pastoral Art* (1970); E. A. Schmidt, *Poetische Reflexion: Vergils Bukolik* (1972); W. Elliger, *Die Darstellung der Landschaft in der griechischen Dichtung* (1975); J. Van Sickle, *The Design of Virgil's Bucolics* (1978); P. Alpers, *The Singer of the Eclogues* (1979); C. Segal, *Poetry and Myth in Ancient Pastoral* (1981); D. M. Halperin, *Before Pastoral* (1983); E. Bowie, "Theocritus' Seventh *Idyll*, Philetas and Longus," *CQ* 35 (1985); C. Newlands, "Urban Pastoral: The Seventh Eclogue of Calpurnius Siculus," *Classical Antiquity* 6 (1987); A. Patterson, *Pastoral and Ideology* (1987); K. J. Gutzwiller, *Theocritus' Pastoral Analogies* (1991); *Theocritus*, ed. M. A. Harder, R. F. Regtuit, G. C. Wakker (1996); *Cambridge Companion to Virgil*, ed. C. Martindale (1997); T. K. Hubbard, *The Pipes of Pan* (1998); M. Fantuzzi, "Theocritus and the Bucolic Genre," *Tradition and Innovation in Hellenistic Poetry*, ed. M. Fantuzzi and R. L. Hunter (2004); B. Breed, *Pastoral Inscriptions: Reading and Writing Virgil's "Eclogues"* (2006); *Brill's Companion to Greek and Latin Pastoral*, ed. M. Fantuzzi and T. D. Papanghelis (2006); *Pastoral Palimpsests*, ed. M. Paschalis (2007); M. Payne, *Theocritus and the Invention of Fiction* (2007).

■ **Modern:** W. Empson, *Some Versions of Pastoral* (1935); M. I. Gerhardt, *La Pastorale* (1950); *English Pastoral Poetry from the Beginnings to Marvell*, ed. F. Kermode (1952); R. Poggioli, *The Oaten Flute* (1957); J.-B. Avalle-Arce, *La novela pastoril española* (1959); A. B. Giamatti, *The Earthly Paradise and the Renaissance Epic* (1960); E. L. Rivers, "The Pastoral Paradox of Natural Art," *MLN* 77 (1962); T. G. Rosenmeyer, *The Green Cabinet: Theocritus and the European Pastoral Lyric* (1969); P. V. Marinelli, *Pastoral* (1971); C. McDonald Vance, *The Extravagant Shepherd* (1973); F. López-Estrada,

Los libros de pastores en la literatura española (1974); A. Solé-Leris, *The Spanish Pastoral Novel* (1980); M. Y. Jehenson, *The Golden World of the Pastoral* (1981); P. Fernández-Cañadas de Greenwood, *Pastoral Poetics: The Uses of Conventions in Renaissance Pastoral Romance* (1983); W. J. Kennedy, *Jacopo Sannazaro and the Uses of Pastoral* (1983); P. Alpers, *What Is Pastoral?* (1996); *Cambridge History of Italian Literature*, ed. P. Brand and L. Pertile, 2d ed. (1999); L. Sampson, *Pastoral Drama in Early Modern Italy* (2006).

M. PAYNE (ANCIENT); M. M. GAYLORD (MOD.)

PATHETIC FALLACY. A phrase coined by John Ruskin in v. 3, ch. 12 of *Modern Painters* (1856) to denote an enduring practice in Western lit.: the tendency of poets and painters to imbue the natural world with human feeling. For Ruskin, it becomes an important criterion of artistic excellence. The fallacy, due to "an excited state of the feelings, making us, for the time, more or less irrational," creates "a falseness in all our impressions of external things." The offending example is taken from a poem in Charles Kingsley's novel *Alton Locke*: "They rowed her in across the rolling foam— / The cruel, crawling foam." Ruskin declares that "the foam is not cruel, neither does it crawl," the author's state of mind being "one in which the reason is unhinged by grief."

For Ruskin, there are two classes of poets, "the Creative (Shakspere [*sic*], Homer, Dante), and Reflective or Perceptive (Wordsworth, Keats, Tennyson)"; it is one of the faults of the latter group that it admits the pathetic fallacy. But Ruskin was unconcerned with the psychological origins of the pathetic fallacy, and his ideas should not be applied indiscriminately to other lits. B. F. Dick contends that the "origins of the pathetic fallacy probably lie in a primitive homeopathy . . . wherein man regarded himself as part of his natural surroundings." In older lits., the pathetic fallacy does not always have the pejorative implications that Ruskin's definition established. Dick considers the Babylonian *Epic of Gilgamesh* an early and important source of the pathetic fallacy: in a climactic passage, all of nature weeps for the death of the warrior Enkidu; since Enkidu embodies the ideals of the natural man, nature as the universal parent must reflect the joys and sorrows of her children. Homer, for Ruskin one of the first order of poets, occasionally employs the pathetic fallacy, but he characteristically attributes human feelings to weapons instead of the natural world—a standard convention of the war epic. It is generally agreed that in the *Iliad* Homer falls prey to Ruskin's censures only once, when the sea rejoices as Poseidon passes overhead in his chariot (13.27–29). Yet even in this case, Homer strictly curtails the passage, avoiding the indulgences Ruskin would later criticize.

Based on various cl. models, the *pastoral elegies of the 16th and 17th cs. provided Eng. poetry with a natural arena for the pathetic fallacy. The early Eng. translators—e.g., Sir William Drummond, who trans. the sonnets of the It. poet Jacopo Sannazaro in 1616—were among the first poets to provide the Eng. trad. with flowers, lilies, and columbine that would bow their heads in sympathetic response to the poet's grief; the pathetic fallacy's earliest appearance is, thus, not the result of native invention but of the preservation of a pastoral convention.

Although he was unconcerned to invent a name for it, Samuel Johnson recognized the phenomenon in the 18th c. and complained 100 years earlier than Ruskin that the phrase "pastoral verse" referred simply to poetry in which, among other things, "the clouds weep." Johnson was reacting to the excesses of sentimentality in 18th-c. verse, but the device continued to be employed: it appears with varying frequency throughout the work of William Collins, William Cowper, Robert Burns, William Blake, William Wordsworth, P. B. Shelley, John Keats, Alfred, Lord Tennyson, and G. M. Hopkins. Wordsworth, justifying its usage, argued that "objects . . . derive their influence not from properties inherent in them . . . , but from such as are bestowed upon them by the minds of those who are conversant with or affected by these objects." Tennyson, on the other hand, was well schooled in the scientific issues of his day, and his descriptions of natural objects are often clinically precise: after 1842, his verse reveals a markedly less frequent usage of pathetic fallacy (Miles), and *In Memoriam* offers a striking revision of the device by evoking its essential effect without indulging its excesses ("Calm is the morn without a sound. / Calm as to suit a calmer grief" [11.1–2]).

During the 20th c., the most vigorous applications of the pathetic fallacy have been self-consciously designed to explore the epistemological issues implied by the technique. Mod. usage of the pathetic fallacy ironically emphasizes the loss of communion between the individual and the natural world; and in its implied envy of an older world where such communion once existed, it resurrects yet another remnant of its ancient origin, pastoral nostalgia. Recent attempts to deploy the concept have not advanced the discussion in significant ways; at best, the pathetic fallacy has migrated into more subjective renderings of individual perception that privilege a kind of "middle ground" between the object we perceive and the act of perception itself. Mervyn Sprung argues in his discussion of the pathetic fallacy in *After Truth* that "to treat outer objects either as possessing nothing but their spatial properties . . . or as naturally possessing all qualities we give them in the everyday . . . is to fail to grasp the symbiosis of the inner and outer." Clearly, Ruskin was not concerned about achieving the "symbiosis of inner and outer"; the central confusion here speaks, among other things, to the overall weariness of the concept in contemp. usage.

See PERSONIFICATION.

■ F. O. Copley, "The Pathetic Fallacy in Early Greek Poetry," *AJP* 58 (1937); J. Miles, *Pathetic Fallacy in the 19th Century* (1942); B. F. Dick, "Ancient Pastoral and the Pathetic Fallacy," *CL* 20 (1968); J. Bump, "Stevens and Lawrence: The Poetry of Nature and the Spirit of the Age," *Southern Review* 18 (1982); D. Hesla, "Singing in Chaos: Wallace Stevens and Three or Four Ideas," *AL* 57 (1985); A. Hecht, "The Pathetic Fallacy," *Yale Review* 74 (1985), M. Sprung, *After Truth* (1994).

S. BURRIS

PATTERN POETRY. *See* CONCRETE POETRY; VISUAL POETRY.

PENTAMETER. In cl. prosody, this term should denote a meter of five measures or feet, as its name says, but, in fact, the Gr. pentameter, which is dactylic, does not contain five of any metra: it consists of two hemiepes with an invariable *caesura: – ◡ ◡ – ◡ ◡ – | – ◡ ◡ – ◡ ◡ – . Contraction of the shorts in the first half of the line is common; the second half runs as shown. It is the conventional name for the second verse in the couplet form called the *elegiac distich, though this is probably a hexameter shortened internally. The cl. Gr. and Lat. pentameter should not be confused with the Eng. "iambic pentameter," despite the fact that the Ren. prosodists derived that name from cl. precedent, for the Eng. line had been written in great numbers for two cs. (since Chaucer)

before it was given any cl. name, and the internal metrical structures of the two meters are quite distinct—this follows from the deeper and more systematic differences between quantitative and accentual verse-systems (see ACCENTUAL VERSE, METER, QUANTITY). Other terms lacking cl. connotations that were formerly and are sometimes still used for the staple line of Eng. dramatic and narrative verse include *heroic verse and *decasyllable (see BLANK VERSE, HEROIC COUPLET); which term of these three one chooses depends on what genealogy one assumes for the Eng. line (cl., native, Romance, mixed) and what features of the line one takes as constitutive—feet, stress count, syllable count, or the latter two, or the latter two as creating the first one (feet). Despite the fact that trochaic tetrameters (see TETRAMETER) are fairly frequent in Eng., trochaic pentameters are extremely rare—Shakespeare's line "Never, never, never, never, never" (*King Lear* 5.3.365) notwithstanding; virtually the only sustained example is Robert Browning's "One Word More."
■ Wilamowitz; Crusius; Halporn et al.; Snell; West; P. Groves, *Strange Music* (1998); D. Keppel-Jones, *The Strict Metrical Tradition* (2001).

J. W. HALPORN; T.V.F. BROGAN

PERFORMANCE (Lat. *recitatio*; Ger. *Vortrag*, *Rezitation*).

I. Theory
II. History
III. Practice

I. Theory. Performance refers to the recitation of poetry by its author, a professional performer, or any other reader either alone or before an audience; the term normally implies the latter. The performance of poetry also entails a setting and a performance style. Though poets naturally seem the most likely performers, from ancient times to at least the Ren., a class of professional performers or singers has usually been available for performance. The setting for performance may be a literary salon, a ceremonial civic or state occasion, or a quasi-theatrical performance at which a poet, poets, or performers address a public. By extension to electronic audio and visual media, performances also have been disseminated via radio or television broadcasts; phonograph records, audio tapes, or compact disks; and videotapes, DVDs, and films. A distinction should be made here between performances that are live and static recordings

thereof: the latter are fixed copies of but a single performance reduced in form and recoded into some machine lang.

It is also essential to distinguish between the performance of a poem and its composition. These two processes may or may not coincide. In the first case, the poetry presented in performance has already been transcribed as a written text, whether ms., scribal copy, or pub. book. This is the condition of nearly all mod., literary poetry: composition has been completed, and the work has passed into textuality. Here performance and composition are separated in temporal sequence.

In the second case, namely, oral poetry, no distinction is made between composition and performance: the "text" is spontaneously composed during performance by illiterate bards. Such a "text" is unique in every performance. Successive recitations by even the same bard may draw upon the same story pattern, but the construction of scenes and selection of verbal details are different in every case; the choice of wording and phrasing is both controlled by, and assists, a stock of relatively fixed "formulas." These are at once both narrative and metrical building blocks, serving to construct metrical lines and a coherent story. It should be noted that, in historical terms, the second class preceded the first—i.e., orality preceded the invention of writing, print technology, and the spread of literacy (reading). But even in mod. literate cultures where written texts are widely pub., spontaneous composition has reemerged as a species of what Walter Ong terms "secondary orality."

The audience is one of the least understood components of all performative arts: Western poetics has taken virtually no interest in this subject. It is obvious, however, that audiences often bring with them significant sets of expectations about subject, diction, tone, and versification. As William Wordsworth remarked, the poet who would write in a new style must create the audience by which it will be appreciated—or perish. Some audiences are trained, but most are not. Audience comprehension of oral texts is unknown: some verse trads., such as OE, apparently helped auditors recognize meter with musical chords, e.g. In general, it would seem reasonable to assume that audiences cannot quickly process archaisms or unusual words, complex meters or heterometric stanza forms, or distanced rhymes or elaborate sonal interlace. On the other hand, sound patterns are very much obscured by orthography, particularly in a lang. such as Eng. Sound patterning can certainly be recognized *as* elaborate in performance even when it is not evident *how*, exactly, the sounds are structured. It is a question just how much of poetic form is perceived in oral transmission.

In one respect, however, audiences have an easier time with the recognition of meaning in oral texts. Seymour Chatman isolates a central difference between the reading and *scansion of poems on the one hand and their performance on the other: in the former two activities, ambiguities of interpretation can be preserved and do not have to be settled one way or the other ("disambiguated"). But in performance, all ambiguities have to be resolved before or during delivery. Since the nature of performance is linear and temporal, sentences can be read aloud only once and must be given a specific intonational pattern. Hence, in performance, the performer is forced to choose between alternative intonational patterns and their associated meanings.

Performance styles are one of the most interesting subjects in *prosody and have direct connections to acting and articulation in the theater. Jakobson has distinguished between "delivery design" and "delivery instance," the former set by verse form, the latter representing the features that are specific to each performance. But between these lies the realm of expressive style. The two general classes of styles are realistic (naturalistic) and oratorical (declamatory, dramatic, rhapsodic, incantatory). C. S. Lewis once identified two types of performers of metrical verse: "minstrels" (who recite in a singsong voice, letting scansion override sense) and "actors" (who give a flamboyantly expressive recitation, ignoring meter altogether). And early in the 20th c., Robert Bridges argued that verses should be scanned in one way but read aloud in another, tilting toward minstrelsy.

The triumph of naturalistic technique in mod. drama has obscured the fact that artificial modes of delivery are well attested in antiquity, as reported by the grammarian Sacerdos (Keil 6.448). The evidence adduced by W. S. Allen for "scanning pronunciation" and the demonstration of Ren. pedagogy by Attridge suggest that the practice of reciting verses aloud in an artificial manner has been more the rule than the exception in the West. E.g., the romantic poets usually chanted their poetic texts when reading aloud, differentiating their lang. from natural speech by moving it closer to music

(Perkins). For dramatic verse that is metrical, particularly Shakespeare's, actors learn that attention to scansion will elucidate nuances of meaning in lines that a literal or natural delivery style will not manifest (Hardison). Consequently, great actors learn how to convey both sense and meter together, so that each supports the other.

II. History. In Asian poetry, the trad. of poetry presentation is esp. important in Chinese and Japanese poetry and continues in 20th-c. Japan. Western poetry readings from the Greeks to the 19th c. have mainly favored invitational performances in courtly settings. It is likely that performances of poetry took place at the Alexandrian court of the Ptolemies (ca. 325–30 BCE) and, at Rome, in the aristocratic residences of Gaius Cilnius Maecenas (d. 8 BCE), who encouraged the work of Virgil, Horace, and Propertius. In Petronius's *Satyricon*, Trimalchio first writes, then recites, his own "poetry" to the guests at his banquet.

The fifth of the five great divisions of cl. rhet.—after *inventio* (discovery), *dispositio* (arrangement), *elocutio* (style), and *memoria* (memorization)—was *pronuntiatio* or delivery. This was less developed in antiquity than the first four subjects, though Aristotle discusses it, as do Cicero (*De Inventione* 1.9) and the *Rhetorica ad Herennium* (3.9), treating, like most subsequent rhetoricians, voice control and gesture. Quintilian devotes a lengthy chapter to the subject (*Institutio oratoria* 11.3). The practice of reciting Lat. verses was encouraged by all the med. Lat. grammarians and central to Ren. education.

The Occitan troubadours retained professional performers, *joglars,* to recite their verses, though the poets of the Minnesang did not; other itinerant minstrels maintained themselves by recitation throughout the Middle Ages. Written poetry was recited at the 13th-c. court of Frederick II, in the Florentine circle of Lorenzo de' Medici (late 15th c.), and in the late 17th-c. *salons* of the Princes de Condé. In the 18th c., however, the patronage system gave way to one of public consumption of published books, and performance accordingly changed from a courtly to a public function. As a young poet of the late 1770s, J. W. Goethe read his work at the Weimar court; on the occasion of a production of *Faust* to commemorate his 80th birthday in 1829, he personally coached the actors in the delivery of their lines. The 18th c. also witnessed the emergence of elocution as an important part of the theory of rhet. In the U.S., before the flourishing of printing presses, the typical mode of disseminating poetry was through handwritten ms. and oral performance, increasingly in forums such as clubs and literary circles.

In the 19th c., public recitations by both poets and their admirers became commonplace. The work of Robert Browning was recited in meetings of the Browning Society (founded 1881), an organization that produced hundreds of offshoots in the U.S. in the 1880s and 1890s. A *Goethe Gesellschaft* (founded 1885) held readings in places as distant as St. Petersburg and New York. Elocution was even further popularized in the 19th c.; the practice of reading aloud from lit. after dinner in Victorian households was widespread. The work of treasured poets was memorized and declaimed regularly in schools and churches, and some famous late 19th-c. poets, incl. Alfred, Lord Tennyson and a reader believed to be Walt Whitman, were recorded on wax cylinder. Elocution led to the emergence in the 20th c. of "oral interpretation" as a formal activity in Am. university departments of speech.

The performance of poetry is central to symbolist poetics. Stéphane Mallarmé read his poetry to a select audience on designated Tuesdays at which the poet himself played both host and reader in oracular style. While Mallarmé's poetry was anything but spontaneously written, his performances both personalized and socialized the work. Stefan George's mode of delivery was consciously influenced by Mallarmé: the audience was restricted to the poet's disciples (*Kreis*), and the occasion was perceived as cultic and sacral. George read from ms. in a strictly rhapsodic style that disciples were required to follow.

In the 20th c., naturalistic or realistic delivery styles gradually have gained the upper hand over a more artificial, vatic performance style. W. B. Yeats was much concerned with having his work sound spontaneous and natural, though his delivery style, like Ezra Pound's, was dramatic and incantatory. By contrast, T. S. Eliot's performances were aristocratic in style and tonally flat. The Wagnerian prescription of having the performer seem spontaneous in expression but personally remote had its best 20th-c. exemplar in Dylan Thomas, whose dramatic, incantatory style contrasted sharply with the plain, conversational style of Robert Frost and W. H. Auden. Frost's "sentence sounds" are the intonational patterns of colloquial speech, esp. as frozen into idioms—precisely the kind of speech effects that would be likely to come across well to audiences on Frost's frequent reading tours.

Politically motivated poetry readings early in the 20th c. served as models for others to come in the second half of the century. In post-revolutionary Russia, Vladimir Mayakovsky sang the praises of the October Revolution in lyrics written to be read aloud; his dramatic performances attracted mass audiences both in western Europe and the U.S. avant-garde movements of the 1920s and 1930s such as Dada and surrealism generated performances of poetry staged simultaneously with music, dance, and film, and so anticipated the intermedia performances later in the century. Poetry readings of the 1950s and 1960s often took the form of multimedia presentations and random artistic "happenings." Prominent innovators of the poetry performance in the 1950s were the Beat poets, notably Allen Ginsberg, Gregory Corso, and Lawrence Ferlinghetti, all instrumental figures in the movement now known as the San Francisco Renaissance. Orality and performance were foregrounded in the poetics of Charles Olson, who conceived of the poem as a "field of action" (see COMPOSITION BY FIELD) and made his unit of measure the "breath group." Olson's "projective verse" found followers in Robert Duncan, Robert Creeley, and Denise Levertov. Af. Caribbean dub poetry, a form that originated in Jamaica in the 1970s where poetry is spoken over reggae rhythms, has been important to a range of diasporic artists, like Linton Kwesi Johnson, who intervene in an evolving cultural politics through performance.

Since 1960, New York, Chicago, and San Francisco have been the major Am. poetry performance centers, with London, Amsterdam, and West Berlin their Eur. counterparts. In New York, the poetry reading movement of the 1960s generally associated with the name of Paul Blackburn served as a stimulus for a new vogue of poetry readings in other parts of the country, esp. in Chicago and on the West Coast. Further experimentation with elements of recitation, music, song, digitized or synthesized sound, drama, mime, dance, and video, which are mixed, merged, altered, choreographed, or improvised in seriatim, simultaneous, random, or collage order, characterized the phenomena variously called *sound poetry, multimedia, or sometimes "performance art" of the 1970s and 1980s. David Antin called his improvisations "talk poems." Jerome Rothenberg's interest in tribal poetry led to his reconstruction in print of sound poetry along with notation of the ritual contexts that surround it. The anthropologist Dell Hymes, with Rothenberg a proponent of ethnopoetics, devised a method of transcribing and analyzing folklore and oral narrative that pays attention to poetic structures within speech.

Since the 1950s, then, the performance of poetry in America has undergone a resurgence, becoming a standard element in the practice of poetry in the Eng.-speaking world. Its tone ranges from conversational idioms to street lang. Jazz or rock music, electronic audio and visual effects, and spontaneous dramatic presentations sometimes accompany recitation, esp. outside of universities, where, it has been argued, an aesthetic narrowness prevails (Lazer). The ethos in intermedia events such as these is one of experimentation, liberation, and spontaneity. Like other contemp. literary genres, postmod. poetry maintains a strong interest in performance as a reaction to academic interpretation and its fixation on the text.

Dana Gioia has noted the decline of print culture in the late 20th and 21st cs. and the rise of a new oral poetry, encompassing rap, cowboy poetry, and poetry slams, that recalls poetry's origins in preliterate cultures and is overwhelmingly formalist and populist. While some of the new performance poetry is performed live and subsequently disseminated in traditional print form, other work is delivered to audiences through electronic media, incl. radio, recordings, and television, as in the PBS series *The United States of Poetry*, HBO's *Def Poetry Jam*, and MTV's *Spoken Word Unplugged*. Sound files on the Internet, through such archival sites as UbuWeb and PennSound, enable anyone with access to a computer to hear the voice of mod. and contemp. poets reading aloud from their work. Former U.S. Poet Laureate Robert Pinsky's Internet-based Favorite Poem Project, launched in 1998, includes videos of ordinary Americans reading their favorite poems.

The heritage of all the various forms of postmodernism in America has been a turning away from the autonomy of the text and the presumption that a text presents one determinate meaning or its author's intended meaning toward the more fluid, less determinate, free play of readerly responses to texts. Hence, critical interest has shifted from written documents to performances as experiences. Many audiences still consider the performance of poetry a communal, nearly sacral event for heightened speech, investing the poet with the transformative powers of the *vates*. And many readers and teachers of poetry continue to believe that poetry achieves its body only when given material form, as sound, in the air, aloud.

III. Practice. Discussions of poetic performance from earliest times to the present focus mainly on bards', actors', and poets' oral presentations, rather than the inner performances that precede and shape our vocalizations. But before a person recites a poem, particularly a metrical poem, he or she has already made decisions about which words in the lines invite special emphasis. Largely the decisions are determined by characteristics of the lang. being spoken and the meter, if any, being used: these will lead the reader familiar with the lang. and its poetic forms to observe mid- and end-line pauses and to emphasize particular syllables. But further refinements and judgments are personal.

The notion that there is, or should be, an entirely "correct" performance of any given line is put in doubt when highly regarded scholars insist on differing rhythmic performances of well-known lines from esteemed poets. Every reader/performer of Shakespeare's sonnet 116, which begins "Let me not to the marriage of true minds / Admit impediments," must come to a conclusion about how to respond to and produce that opening line either in mind or out loud. George T. Wright hears the poem opening with the "quiet, confidential tones" he finds characteristic of the sonnet as a whole, so he begins his commentary by suggesting that "Let" is the line's first emphasized word and that while "not" carries the second beat, it is relatively unemphasized: "*Let* me not." Helen Vendler hears the sonnet's opening differently. Experiencing the poem as a rebuttal of another's claims (the young man's), she feels that "the iambic prosody" brings "the pressure of rhetorical refutation" into the poem's first line, requiring an emphasis on "me": "Let *me* not."

However much one may insist on the correctness of either performance, each is right in its own way and worthy of consideration. And it is by adding one's own experience with the line to such efforts of judgment that a deeper involvement with Shakespeare's memorable sonnet can be achieved.

Lines in many poems have a variety of linguistically and metrically permissible emphases, but there are instances when established metrical patterns limit the possibilities of alternative performances. E.g., John Donne, in "The Canonization," creates metaphors for his love in five stanzas whose second lines can be felt as four beats, even though the third stanza's second line could be experienced as having three beats ("Call her *one*, mee another *flye*") or even five beats ("*Call* her *one*, mee another *flye*"). However, the performance that gives emphasis to both "her" and "mee" not only satisfies metrical expectation ("Call *her* one, *mee* another *flye*") but heightens the sense of the lovers' unity. Likewise, in the same poet's "The Sun Rising," the fifth lines in the poem's three stanzas ("Sawcy pedantique wretch, goe chide," "If her eyes have not blinded thine," and "Thou sunne art halfe as happy'as wee") are easily experienced as having four beats. Although a prose-like performance of the second-stanza line is possible ("If her *eyes* have not *blind*ed *thine*"), it is the four-beat performance ("If *her* eyes *have* not *blind*ed *thine*") that both realizes the metrical norm and dramatizes the loved one's eyes whose brightness challenges the sun's.

Performing the various rhythmical possibilities of even the most familiar poems can extend their ranges of implication and meaning. Two quite different notions about the personalities of the speaker in Robert Frost's "Stopping by Woods on a Snowy Evening" and the landowner whose "house is in the village" can emerge from slightly different choices among the permissible emphases of the poem's third line, "He will not see me stopping here." One likely performance of the line would follow the steady iambic, or offbeat-beat, pattern clearly established at the poem's opening: "He *will* not *see* me *stop*ping *here*." But on reimagining, and reperforming, a linguistically permissible emphasis on "He" would more strongly evoke a sense of difference that is central to the poem—the difference between a villager who regards his woods as a possession and the poet-speaker who regards them as a place for experiencing things "lovely, dark and deep." And with the new performance taken into account, other words take on new significance: "He will not see me stopping here" becomes more apprehensive, perhaps even threatening, than something like "He will not mind my stopping here." An alternate performance again enlarges possibilities of feeling and the poem's pleasures.

■ **Theory and History:** JOURNALS: *Literature in Performance* (1980–88) and continued as *Text*

and Performance Quarterly (1989–); *Oral Tradition* (1986–). STUDIES: Bridges; R. C. Crosby, "Oral Delivery in the Middle Ages," *Speculum* 11 (1936); W. B. Nichols, *The Speaking of Poetry* (1937); R. C. Crosby, "Chaucer and the Custom of Oral Delivery," *Speculum* 13 (1938); S. F. Bonner, *Roman Declamation* (1950); D. Whitelock, *The Audience of* Beowulf (1951); K. Wais, *Mallarmé*, 2d ed. (1952); E. Salin, *Um Stefan George*, 2d ed. (1954); F. Trojan, *Die Kunst der Rezitation* (1954); S. Chatman, "Linguistics, Poetics, and Interpretation," *QJS* 43 (1957); Y. Winters, "The Audible Reading of Poetry," *The Function of Criticism* (1957); C. S. Lewis, "Metre," *REL* 1 (1960); Jakobson, "Linguistics and Poetics," in Sebeok; F. Berry, *Poetry and the Physical Voice* (1962); S. Chatman, "Linguistic Style, Literary Style, and Performance," *Monograph Series Languages & Linguistics* 13 (1962); S. Levin, "Suprasegmentals and the Performance of Poetry," *QJS* 48 (1962); D. Levertov, "Approach to Public Poetry Listenings," *VQR* 41 (1965); K. T. Loesch, "Literary Ambiguity and Oral Performance," *QJS* 51 (1965); D. Norberg, "La Récitation du vers latin," *NM* 66 (1965); *The New Russian Poets, 1953–1968*, ed. G. Reavey (1966); W. C. Forrest, "The Poem as a Summons to Performance," *BJA* 9 (1969); G. Poulet, "Phenomenology of Reading," *NLH* 1 (1969); H. Hein, "Performance as an Aesthetic Category," *JAAC* 28 (1970); P. Dickinson, "Spoken Words," *Encounter* 34 (1970); *The East Side Scene*, ed. A. De Loach (1972); S. Massie, *The Living Mirror: Five Young Poets from Leningrad* (1972); Allen; D. Attridge, *Well-Weighed Syllables* (1974); *Performance in Postmodern Culture*, ed. M. Benamou et al. (1977); Ruth Finnegan, *Oral Poetry* (1977); M. C. Beardsley, "Right Readings and Good Readings," *Literature in Performance* 1 (1980); D. Hymes, *"In Vain I Tried to Tell You"* (1981); M. L. West, "The Singing of Homer," *JHS* 101 (1981); W. Ong, *Orality and Literacy* (1982); *The Poetry Reading*, ed. S. Vincent and E. Zweig (1981); B. Rowland, "*Pronuntiatio* and its Effect on Chaucer's Audience," *SAC* 4 (1982); O. B. Hardison, "Speaking the Speech," *ShQ* 34 (1983); D. A. Russell, *Greek Declamation* (1983); W. G. Thalmann, *Conventions of Form and Thought in Early Greek Epic Poetry* (1984), ch. 4; D. Wojahn, "Appraising the Age of the Poetry Reading," *NER/ BLQ* 8 (1985); J.-C. Milner and F. Regnault, *Dire le vers* (1987); E. Griffiths, *The Printed Voice of Victorian Poetry* (1988); R. Schechner,

Performance Theory, 2d ed. (1988); G. Danek, "Singing Homer," *WHB* 31 (1989); M. Davidson, *The San Francisco Renaissance* (1989); D. Oliver, *Poetry and Narrative in Performance* (1989); H. M. Sayre, *The Object of Performance* (1989); "Performance," *Critical Terms for Literary Study*, ed. F. Lentricchia and T. McLaughlin (1990); D. Cusic, *The Poet as Performer* (1991); S. G. Daitz, "On Reading Homer Aloud," *AJP* 112 (1991); D. Perkins, "How the Romantics Recited Poetry," *SEL* 4 (1991); *Performance*, spec. iss. of *PMLA* 107.3 (1992); H. Lazer, "Poetry Readings and the Contemporary Canon," *Opposing Poetries: Volume One* (1996); M. Morrisson, "Performing the Pure Voice: Elocution, Verse Recitation, and Modernist Poetry in Pre-War London," *Modernism/Modernity* 3 (1996); *Sound States*, ed. A. Morris (1997); *Close Listening*, ed. C. Bernstein (1998); Lord; J. M. Foley, *How to Read an Oral Poem* (2002); D. Gioia, *Disappearing Ink* (1994), ch. 1; M. Loeffelholz, *From School to Salon* (2004); P. Middleton, *Distant Reading* (2005); J. S. Rubin, *Songs of Ourselves* (2007).

■ **Practice**: Attridge, *Rhythms*; G. Wright, *Shakespeare's Metrical Art* (1988); Attridge, *Poetic Rhythm*; H. Vendler, *The Art of Shakespeare's Sonnets* (1997); Carper and Attridge.

T.V.F. Brogan, W. B. Fleischmann, T. Hoffman (theory and history); T. Carper (practice)

PERIPHRASIS. A circumlocution, a roundabout expression that avoids naming something by its most direct term. Since it is constituted through a culturally perceived relationship to a word or phrase that it is *not*, periphrasis has no distinctive form of its own but articulates itself variously through other figures, esp. *metaphor. Quintilian (*Institutio oratoria* 8.6.59) subdivides it by function into two types: the euphemistic or "necessary," as in the avoidance of obscenity or other unpleasant matters (Plato's "the fated journey" for "death"—cf. the mod. "passing away"); and the decorative, used for stylistic embellishment (Virgil's "Aurora sprinkled the earth with new light" for "day broke"). The descriptive kind includes most periphrases that approximate a two-word definition by combining a specific with a general term ("the finny tribe" to signify fish). Longinus considered it productive of sublimity but, like Quintilian, warned against its excesses, such as preciosity or pleonasm (28–29). Later writers have characterized it as representing a term by its (whole or partial) definition, as in the expression "pressed milk" for "cheese." Periphrasis also appears in poetry that tries to translate culture-specific concepts from one lang. to another without neologism.

Though it is unlikely that any movement or era in poetry has succeeded in suppressing periphrasis altogether, some styles favor it more than others. Curtius associates it, like other rhetorical ornaments, with mannerism and marks stages in its use and abuse. Oral traditions frequently build formulas around periphrases, as in the patronymic "son of Tydeus" for "Diomedes"; these have important metrical functions and are not ornament.

While widely used in biblical and Homeric lit. and by Hesiod, the devel. of periphrasis as an important feature of poetic style begins with Lucretius and Virgil, and through their influence, it became a staple device of *epic and descriptive poetry throughout the Middle Ages and into the Ren. Classified by med. rhetoricians as a trope of *amplification, periphrasis suited the conception of style that emphasized *copia* and invention. The OE poetic device of variation typically employs multiple periphrastic constructions, as does the *kenning, the characteristic device of Old Germanic and ON poetry, which, in its more elaborate forms, illustrates the connection between periphrasis and *riddle.

Given new impetus through the work of the Pléiade, periphrasis proliferated in 17th-c. diction, particularly as influenced by the scientific spirit of the age, and even more so in the stock poetic diction of the 18th c., where descriptive poetry often shows periphrastic constructions (Arthos). Since the 18th c., the form has lost much of its prestige in the romantic and mod. reaction against rhetorical artifice; more often than not, it survives only in inflated uses for humorous effect, as in Charles Dickens. Yet its occasional appearance in the work of modernists such as T. S. Eliot ("white hair of the waves blown back" for "foam") suggests that, insofar as directness of locution is not always the preferable route (direct speech being, most often, shorn of semantic density and allusive richness), periphrasis has an enduring poetic usefulness.

See DICTION.

■ P. Aronstein, "Die periphrastische Form im Englischen," *Anglia* 42 (1918); J. Arthos, *The Language of Natural Description in Eighteenth-Century Poetry* (1949); Curtius; D. S. McCoy,

Tradition and Convention: A Study of Periphrasis in English Pastoral Poetry from 1557–1715 (1965); Lausberg—compendium of citations; A. Quinn, *Figures of Speech* (1982); J. P. Blevins, "Periphrasis as Syntactic Exponence," *Patterns in Paradigms*, ed. F. Ackerman, J. P. Blevins, and G. S. Stump (2008).

W. W. PARKS; J. ARTHOS

PERSONA. Denotes the speaker (or more generally, the source) of any poem that is imagined to be spoken in a distinctive *voice or narrated from a determinate vantage—whether that speaker is presumed to be the poet, a fictional character, or even an inanimate object. But the *idea* of persona carries in it all the complexity of the hist. of the word. Originally used to denote the mask worn by an actor in Roman drama, *persona* has been offered as a trans. of the Gr. *prosopon* (face), though the idea of their synonymy antedates both terms; and also (suggestively but mistakenly) as a derivation from *per sonare* (to sound through). This pair of false etymologies recapitulates a tension apparent in the term's use: in Cicero's theory of *personae*, the public roles that an adult is called on to play were understood to be aspects, rather than concealments, of the self. For Seneca, the performance of a public persona represented a falsification of the true self that lies beneath. Early in its hist., then, we find *persona* referring to both performance and actor, to the public trapping and suits of feeling, and also to that within that passes show.

Persona becomes an important term for poetry precisely because so much of it speaks in the first person—seemingly disclosing private or hidden aspects of self and subjective experience—but does so in highly shaped and mediated ways, in lang. that bears the stamp of artifice and form. Thus, persona is a conceptual peg on which to hang the distinction between the idea that poems are the sincere expression of the person who makes them and the idea that poems are constructions that use lang. in some other, estranging or objectifying way. Accounts of what that way is—and what function it serves—vary; a poetic persona may be a transparent impersonation, as in dramatic *monologue. Creating a morally compromised or troubling speaker like Robert Browning's Duke of Ferrara or Ai's Joseph McCarthy puts the poet in an ironic relation to his or her own words and places readers in a critical relationship to the idea of sincere expression and literal

lang. But the use of a persona need not identify a poem as a "mere" fiction. A poetic persona may stand in a complex rhetorical and performative relation to the poet, as in Juvenal's satires or Jonathan Swift's, making the identification of propositions and attitudes into a puzzle or a hall of mirrors (in John Berryman's *Dream Songs,* Henry, the poet's alter ego, has his own alter ego and interlocutor, Mr. Bones). Persona may function in a universal or representative capacity, as does Dante's questing protagonist ("Dante") in the *Divine Comedy. Persona* may also refer to the idea that a poem puts forward beliefs, attitudes, or feelings in hypothetical form—as a way of inquiring into what it is to be a self or as a means of operating on oneself. This sense may be in operation when a speaker is obviously an invention (as in Frank Bidart's "Herbert White," which refracts the poet's desperate desire to animate the world outside the self with sense through the persona of a child-murdering necrophiliac); but even "I" may be a persona in this sense, as Emily Dickinson suggests: "When I state myself, as the Representative of the Verse—it does not mean—me—but a supposed person."

The recent hist. of the concept of persona focuses on the tension between person and supposition and exacerbates it. If persona becomes a *theoretical* issue in the wake of the explicit articulation of the idea that the poet speaks *in propria persona*, and speaks so truly and sincerely, then the theoretical *problem* of persona is a postromantic one—and even more acutely, a modernist one. Paul Valéry's "sieved" and "filtered" inspiration, W. B. Yeats's daemons and masks, T. S. Eliot's doctrine of "impersonality," Ezra Pound's *Personae*, and Fernando Pessoa's heteronyms all in their various ways cultivate persona as a reaction against the idea of romantic poetics.

Translating these modernist experiments into interpretive principles, the New Critics theorized the gap between a thought or feeling and its objectification. The idea of a poem as a "verbal icon" (Wimsatt) or "a dramatic fiction" (Brower) may have been initially intended to block inquiry into the poet's expressive intention in order to focus attention on the dynamics of lang. and form; its effect was to make persona seem an entailment of the very idea of verbal art. Thus, the *obligation* to treat poetic speakers as personae carries over into postmodernity in ever more extreme forms, both as a theory of poetry (Berryman, speaking even of Robert Lowell's ostensibly *confessional "Skunk Hour": ("The necessity for the artist of selection opens inevitably an abyss between his person and his persona") and as a general problematic for life in lang. (Paul de Man's claim that autobiography is both a characteristic of every text and "a defacement of the mind" is, in effect, an argument for the inescapability of persona, as is Barthes's notion that "all writing" partakes of a "special voice" of which lit. "is precisely the invention").

■ R. P. Blackmur, "The Masks of Ezra Pound," *The Double Agent* (1935); Richard Ellmann, *W. B. Yeats: The Man and the Masks* (1948); R. Brower, *Fields of Light* (1951); M. Mack, "The Muse of Satire." *Yale Review* 41 (1951); W. K. Wimsatt and M. C. Beardsley, "The Intentional Fallacy" and "The Affective Fallacy," *The Verbal Icon* (1954); T. S. Eliot, "The Three Voices of Poetry," *On Poetry and Poets* (1957); G. Wright, *The Poet in the Poem* (1960); I. Ehrenpreis, "Personae," *Restoration and Eighteenth-Century*, ed. C. Camden (1963); L. Trilling, *Sincerity and Authenticity* (1971); *The Author in His Work*, ed. L. L. Martz and A. Williams (1978); R. Elliott, *The Literary Persona* (1982); C. Altieri, *Self and Sensibility in Contemporary Poetry* (1984); P. de Man, "Autobiography as De-facement," *The Rhetoric of Romanticism* (1984); R. Barthes, "The Death of the Author," *The Rustle of Language*, trans. R. Howard (1989); C. Park, "Talking Back to the Speaker," *Rejoining the Common Reader* (1991); M. Perloff, "Language Poetry and the Lyric Subject: Ron Silliman's Albany, Susan Howe's Buffalo," *CritI* 25 (1999); S. Bartsch, *The Mirror of the Self* (2006); O. Izenberg, *Being Numerous: Poetry and the Ground of Social Life* (2011).

O. IZENBERG

PERSONIFICATION. A device that brings to life, in a human figure, something abstract, collective, inanimate, dead, nonreasoning, or epitomizing: Oiseuse, the porter at the gate of the walled garden of the *Roman de la Rose*, and her porter-colleagues—both named Genius— in two gardens of *The Faerie Queene*; Mankind in his morality play; Love, Lady Mary Wroth's ever-crying child; Honour, William Collins's gray pilgrim; Autumn at the cider-press in John Keats's *ode; W. B. Yeats's Quiet, who "wanders laughing and eating her wild heart"; Patrick Pearse's lonely mother Ireland; and Clumsy, Mrs. Clumsy, and No-No in Gjertrud

Schnackenberg's parlor allegory. A prominent strategy for poets, personification also appears in ordinary speech, prose, painting, sculpture, architecture, cartoons, film, and other media.

Familiar in antiquity, personification becomes esp. important and complex in the aesthetic programs of the Eur. Middle Ages and Ren., which exploited its capacity for philosophy and enlisted its predilection for hiding the arcane or even dangerous proposition in plain sight. Though often instigated by something as simple as grammatical gender, personification is a way of thought that can generate a wide range of effects and consequences: from folkloric characters such as Jack Frost to the "persons" accorded rights in the medical, civil-rights, and corporate-law decisions of contemp. high courts. Thus, it can act as a figure of speech and as a form of social or political acknowledgment.

In lit., personification is a mode of characterization that, when pervasive, may grow into personification allegory (e.g., Prudentius's *Psychomachia*, William Langland's *Piers Plowman*, John Bunyan's *The Pilgrim's Progress*). Yet it may also make an isolated appearance as a person when a character becomes symbolic in a nonallegorical work. Allegorical personifications are notable for their slippery qualities. In a psychologically revealing yet not naturalistic canto by Edmund Spenser, the beleaguered husband Malbecco transforms into Jealousy itself. Rarely do personifications remain static; even the deadly sins of *Piers Plowman* repent, belying their nomination. Personification is sometimes unjustly regarded as a badly wrought or primitive kind of characterization because of its abstraction. Such a view fails to notice that the purpose of literary character is not always to render an individual person one might wish to be or to love. In its abstraction, personification is capable of considering personhood over the scope of the entire fiction, past the bounds of character. In this role, personification should be seen as a device for distributing agency, emotion, cognition, gender, and the like.

The notions of quintessence and epitome are conveyed by the ordinary expression "to personify": when we say, "she personifies grace and beauty," for instance, we take an already human figure and regard it as a personification. The canonical personifications Christian (the hero of *Pilgrim's Progress*) and Everyman (he of the 15th-c. morality play) suggest that fiction does personify humans (the Christian, the ordinary man), though definitions have specified the nonhuman as the material of personification. Similarly, it is profitable to see the conventional persons that dominate the thought of disciplines (legal person, economic man, the reasonable person, the soul, the object of figurative painting, and so forth) as personifications too, in that they embody notions of personhood that entail complex argument. Considered in this way, all characterization involves a degree of personification. But it must be understood that to say so is to apply personification as an analytic tool (in a way analogous to the practice of allegoresis on a work that is not allegorical) without regard to whether we have received cues from the lang. that fit the work to the primary definition of *personification*. Such a move should not be allowed to erode *personification*'s specificity as a technical term that can identify examples of a poetic device.

Like other devices, personification has many near neighbors and collaborators that help to distinguish it. *Apostrophe is closely associated with personification because address can be part of the process, conjuring presence and agency. Personification appears frequently in dialogue and debate: for instance, Boethius's *De consolatione philosophiae* (*Consolation of Philosophy*) fashions its complaints and inquiries in the form of a conversation between the author and Lady Philosophy; and, in *Piers Plowman*, Will's interlocutors are often drawn from faculty psychology—Conscience, Imagynatif, Kynde Wyt, and so forth. Similarly, the late med. morality play involves its protagonist in dialogue with a series of allegorical personifications. When a poet gives speech to an animal or object (such as the speaking Cross in the OE "Dream of the Rood"), the resulting personification may be called *prosopopoeia. In practice, this term is nearly synonymous with personification, though *prosopopoeia* is more a term of rhet. than of lit. crit. *Personification* is best reserved for personhood: in cases like Emily Dickinson's "I like to see it lap the miles," where a train acts like a horse, perhaps we need a word like "beastification." Such a term might also cover beast fables, in which animals are given human motivations and capacities without becoming human figures. Are they humans turned into beasts or beasts into part-humans? A glimmer of personification that does not develop into a recognizably human figure (like Katherine Philips's "courteous Tree") is better identified as an example of *pathetic fallacy.

William Wordsworth abjured personification. Ernst Cassirer saw personification as a regime in the hist. of human intellectual devel., a mode of thought that replaced myth when, with the waning of the premod. era, human consciousness became more skeptical and less primitive. These mod. slights seem to underestimate the sophisticated ontological theses of ancient and med. personification and falsely to impute a mature rationality to mod. thought. When in "The Knight's Tale" Chaucer moves with subtlety among the many possible shapes of Venus, it is exquisitely effective, amounting to a psychology, an astronomy, a theology, an anthropology, a literary feat, and a theory of art, by turns. She is a personification of love and of the influence of the planet Venus; she is a goddess worshiped by Palamon and his culture; she is a literary character, an allusion, and part of the epic machinery; she is feminine beauty and its abstract force. Personification is influentially discussed by the cognitive linguists Lakoff and Johnson as "entity" *metaphor, a species of ontological metaphor; yet personification's epistemological functions can be comically overstated, as is suggested by the voyeuristic glimpse of Venus disporting with Riches, her porter, in the back corner of the temple in Chaucer's *Parliament of Fowls*. That the device has important, noncognitive appeals to sensual response is made esp. clear there and in the many erotic portraits of personified love produced by artists in words, paint, and other media over the centuries.

■ R. W. Frank, "The Art of Reading Mediaeval Personification Allegory" *ELH* 20 (1953); A. Fletcher, *Allegory* (1964); R. Tuve, *Allegorical Imagery* (1966); N. D. Isaacs, "The Convention of Personification in *Beowulf*," *Old English Poetry*, ed. R. P. Creed (1967); A. D. Nuttall, *Two Concepts of Allegory* (1967); M. W. Bloomfield, "Allegory as Interpretation" *NLH* 3 (1972); M. Quilligan, *The Language of Allegory* (1979); S. Barney, *Allegories of History, Allegories of Love* (1979); G. Lakoff and M. Johnson, *Metaphors We Live By* (1980); D. Davie, "Personification," *Essays in Criticism* 31 (1981); P. de Man, *The Rhetoric of Romanticism* (1984); L. Griffiths, *Personification in "Piers Plowman"* (1985); S. Knapp, *Personification and the Sublime* (1985); D. A. Harris, *Tennyson and Personification* (1986); J. Whitman, *Allegory* (1987); J. H. Miller, *Versions of Pygmalion* (1990); J. J. Paxson, *The Poetics of Personification* (1994); F. Ferguson, "Canons, Poetics, and Social

Value: Jeremy Bentham and How to Do Things with People" *MLN* 110 (1995); G. Teskey, *Allegory and Violence* (1996); M. Loeffelholz, "Poetry, Slavery, Personification," *SIR* 38 (1999); E. Fowler, *Literary Character* (2003); A. Hungerford, *The Holocaust of Texts* (2003); F. Kiefer, *Shakespeare's Visual Theater* (2003); S. Tolmie, "Langland, Wittgenstein, and the End of Language," *YLS* 20 (2006); A. Escobedo, "Allegorical Agency and the Sins of Angels," *ELH* 75 (2008); H. Keenleyside, "Personification for the People: On James Thomson's *The Seasons*" *ELH* 76 (2009).

E. FOWLER

POEM. A composition, often in *lines, that draws on some or all of the following common features: *rhythm, *meter, figuration (incl. rhetorical *schemes and *tropes), and artifice (incl. *diction and *syntax). Poems of different times and places do not necessarily resemble one another so much as they share a recognition from their respective cultures that they embody poeticity or what the Rus. linguist Roman Jakobson called the *poetic function*: "Poeticity is present when the word is felt as a word and not a mere representation of the object being named or an outburst of emotion, when words and their composition, their meaning, their external and inner form acquire a weight and value of their own instead of referring indifferently to reality." The poem comes into existence when an actual set of elements such as those named above is attached to the relevant cultural category (e.g., Fr. *poème*, Ger. *Gedicht*, Hungarian *vers*, Polish *wiersz*, or Chinese *shi*). Not only is a poem both made and recognized as such by its maker or others, but the network of related concepts, most manifestly *poetry and *poet, is potentially modified by the admission of the new poem. *Poem* is not a universal concept: sometimes, as in the Occitan *vers*, the relevant term means "verse" (in the sense of a single line or several lines, a strictly technical meaning) and only implies *poem* (in the culturally recognized sense).

As the integer or complete constitutive unit of poetry, the poem displays some of the generative principles theorized in poetics such as equivalence, unity, intertextuality, or defamiliarization. In principle, it is often a statement in little of a poetics (derived from, e.g., cl. poetics, futurism, objectivism, or other established or ad hoc principles). However, in practice—i.e, under reading or interpretation—the character of the poem, like that of any work of lit., is

often autonomous, equivocal, or ambiguous. If poems are made by their creators, they are often remade in interpretation by each generation of readers.

Theorists, poets, and observers have more often defined *poetry* than the term *poem*. Unlike the *genre or medium we call *poetry*, which maintains a theoretical and practical discourse going back to Plato, the object into which poetry is usually resolved, the poem, is notoriously hard to isolate and discuss. Theories of poetry may be classified in a number of ways, notably according to the scheme advanced by M. H. Abrams in the 1950s and developed since, which considers four kinds of theories: mimetic, expressive, pragmatic, and objective.

The first two categories, which are concerned with *mimesis and expression, respectively, and thus are associated with cl. and romantic doctrines, while they often address the nature of the poem, tend to give more attention to other factors, such as the nature of poetry or the power of the poet; in contrast, theories of the latter two categories often have a great deal to say about the poem in the context of their propositions about poetry. Pragmatic theories in the West, as Abrams shows, derive from ancient rhetorical theory and esp. from Horace's *Ars poetica* (1st c. BCE), which emphasizes the effects produced in the reader who is taught and moved. Much poetic theory of the Ren. and the Enlightenment is largely pragmatic, but this approach belongs to no age; it may appear in any time or place in which the ends or effects of poetry are in focus. Abrams argues that, in Europe, objective theories develop in the 18th c. out of two models for the poem: the "heterocosmic model," which grants each poem the status of a "unique, coherent, and autonomous world," and the "contemplation model," which emphasizes the disinterested study of the poem. Notions of the poem as world are esp. prevalent in the work of Ren. thinkers such as Torquato Tasso, J. C. Scaliger, and Philip Sidney; but one might argue that they proceed from a certain understanding of poetry as world-making and the poet as a godlike creator rather than from a speculative attention to the nature of the poem per se. Alexander Baumgarten's dictum in *Meditationes Philosophicae de Nonnullis ad Poema Pertinentibus* (*Reflections on Poetry*, 1735)—"the poet is like a maker or creator, so the poem ought to be like a world"—indicates his prior assumptions about the poem. Likewise, the contemplative approach often has more to do with valorizing the role of the perceiver or reader—augmenting his or her office with a moral and even theological dimension—than with a new idea of the poem itself as somehow suitable for contemplation.

Romantic and decadent thinkers such as John Keats and E. A. Poe bring a new measure of concern to the nature of the poem as such: any hist. of ideas about the poem must take account of Poe's famous statement that "a poem is such, only inasmuch as it intensely excites, by elevating, the soul, and all intense excitements are through a psychal necessity, brief" ("The Philosophy of Composition," 1849). Charles Baudelaire repeats this observation: "anything that exceeds the period of attention which a human being can give to the poetic form is no longer a poem." But it is really under the auspices of *modernism—when poems were very long as often as very short—that a concentration of speculative power attaches to the poem itself, perhaps through an exhaustion with general and idealist theories of poetry, perhaps through a new awareness of the social and cultural lives of poems as objects in the world, like paintings and sculptures.

Observations about the nature of the poem by poets and critics of the 1900s and after tend to be not only object- rather than genre-oriented but openly prescriptive and empirical rather than theoretical, and may be nakedly ideological as well: after all, this is a question that lends itself to pronouncements and dicta more readily than does the nature of the genre. For instance, Ezra Pound's famous "A Retrospect" about imagism (1918) is a set of prescriptions at the level of the poem rather than of poetry (e.g., "to use absolutely no word that does not contribute to the presentation"); in Pound's assessment of the preceding six years of imagism, "perhaps a few good poems have come from the new method, and if so it is justified." Emphasizing craft, procedure, and values, many such modernist observations seem intended to shed the idealisms and mystifications that had accumulated around the idea of poetry since at least the Ren. Even the gnomic "Ars Poetica" (1926) by Archibald MacLeish, composed during his sojourn in the community of Am. expatriates in Paris, restates these premises while perhaps inadvertently reintroducing mystification: "A poem should not mean / But be."

To be precise, notions about the poem are articulated on a different plane than theories about poetry itself. The assumptions and practices of a reader confronted with an actual poem are often ideological and experiential rather than theoretical; practical and object-oriented instead of abstract. The question "How do I go about understanding this poem?" is not fully answered by Abrams's four doctrines, which provide broad principles for the nature of poetry; operating within those doctrines, readers in empirical practice tend to follow procedures that reflect their education, interests, or inclinations. These reading and writing practices belong to at least four categories: the assimilationist, the integrationist, the artifactualist, and the irreducibilist. While any of these may coincide with the kinds of theories of poetry that Abrams and others describe, they are more ad hoc than those theories, often more assumed or felt than reasoned. Moreover, they are not radically separate from one another; rather, these positions are often in conversation with one another, so that traces of one become visible even in what appears to be an uncompromising statement of the other.

Assimilationist accounts of the poem emphasize its continuity with other literary and cultural *genres and forms. From this standpoint, poetry may be close to narrative and drama (for instance, it may be fundamentally dramatic, as in Kenneth Burke's theory of dramatism), or the poem may deeply resemble other sorts of art objects or events such as painting, sculpture, or dance. Perhaps Horace, with his dictum *ut pictura poesis*, is the original assimilationist, but many other critics and readers of the postclassical era, from Sidney to Ezra Pound to the textual artist Kenneth Goldsmith, subscribe to this notion.

Integrationists take seriously the notion that poems rarely exist in isolation from other poems and, thus, seek to absorb them into larger wholes such as anthol., books, songbooks, *lyric sequences, genres, schools, and movements. Implicitly or directly, they may challenge the premise that the poem is the relevant integer of analysis. Much scholarship on med. poetry, of Asia as well as Europe, is of this sort, reflecting the conditions in which many premod. poems were performed or written, with little or no investment in the idea of the individual poem; likewise, a great deal of crit. concerning Ren. sonneteers from Petrarch through the early 17th c. The genre crit. of Eur. poetry that was current from the late 1950s (prompted by Northrop Frye's "Theory of Genres" in *Anatomy of Criticism*,

1957) to about 1980 followed an integrationist paradigm.

The artifactualist position does not always entail an understanding of the poem's nature different from that of the two categories already mentioned; in fact, it may serve as the adjunct to any of the other positions, relating to any and all of them in some measure. An artifactualist statement describes a poem as the expression of some abstract principle—*form, structure, texture, artifice, hist.—and describes or narrates how such a principle becomes manifest in the poem we have. It is tempting to think of artifactualism as the default position of mod. poetics because its reliance on formal description in the service of various possible ends strikes many contemp. readers as natural and inevitable. To put it another way, from the mid-20th c. on, nearly any other position from historicism to formalism to personalism (the construal of poems according to one's own poetic practice) may compromise with artifactualism without incurring the charge of inconsistency; on the contrary, the neglect of artifactualism may be reproached as insufficiently attentive to the poem itself. Many poets who do not articulate an explicit poetics but discuss the making of their and others' poems are loosely artifactualist (e.g.,W. B. Yeats, Pablo Neruda, Cid Corman), as are many critics who give their attention to the sources, genesis, and reception of particular poems (e.g., Hugh Kenner on Pound's career) and many critics who are also poets, such as Veronica Forrest-Thomson. Readers of Anglo-Am. poetry who are accustomed to thinking of historicism and formalism as opposed positions may think it odd to find both standpoints in the same category. Nonetheless, it is the nature of a default position to stand invisibly behind views that ostentatiously stage a competition even as they agree in fundamental matters.

Finally, the irreducibilist view is that every poem is a unique event unassimilable to genres and the other arts and only minimally responsive to general values such as form, craft, or period. Octavio Paz asks, "How can we lay hold on poetry if each poem reveals itself as something different and irreducible? . . . Poetry is not the sum of all poems. Each poetic creation is a self-sufficient unit. The part is the whole." Irreducibilists may be at once the ultimate historicists (not only every period but every poem—its own period—must be read on its terms) and the ultimate formalists (each poem generates a unique formal protocol that

must be recovered and explained); and while irreducibilism may accept something like an artifactualist position in practice, its logical outcome is properly spoken by Paz when he asserts that "each poem is a unique object, created by a 'technique' that dies at the very moment of creation." A strict irreducibilism would hold that, when poems are susceptible to analysis under rubrics such as genre or form, they have failed as poems ("when a poet acquires a style, a manner, he stops being a poet and becomes a constructor of literary artifacts"). A further step in this doctrine notes that most critics and readers, fixated on constants in poetry such as form or style, are unable to recognize what is properly poetic in the objects they address or the creators who made them. While the irreducibilist strain runs through a great deal of historical and contemp. discourse on poetry, uncompromising (as opposed to merely nominal or superstitious) irreducibilists are rare. The It. philosopher Benedetto Croce was one. The kind of experimental poet who produces poems and perhaps manifestos but not crit. or who is uninterested in formulating an explicit poetics is often an irreducibilist; the Brazilian modernist Oswald de Andrade sometimes expresses such views, and several well-known poems of the later modernist era in Brazil (Manuel Bandeira's "O Último Poema" ["The Last Poem," 1968] and Carlos Drummond de Andrade's "Procura da Poesia" [Search for Poetry, 1945]) take this stance. Some of the less discursive, more atomistic work associated with the era of Language poetry in the U.S. belongs to an irreducibilist impulse (e.g., Bruce Andrews, P. Inman). Paz is among the most prominent poet-critics to embrace the position without equivocation; it does not impede but curiously enlivens his most important work of crit., concerning the Mexican baroque poet Sor Juana Inés de la Cruz.

As object and event, an inalienable element of lives and societies, the poem responds as much to cultural and personal notions as to theories and doctrines of poetry. It may seem so ubiquitous as to be invisible, so firmly possessed as to be ours alone, so natural as to resist abstraction. To take these conditions into account while explaining the poem in principle is one of the continual challenges of poetics.

■ C. Brooks, "The Poem as Organism," *English Institute Annual* 1940 (1941); Abrams; A. Baumgarten, *Reflections on Poetry*, trans. K. Aschenbrenner and W. B. Holther (1954); W. K. Wimsatt, "The Concrete Universal" (1947) and with M. C. Beardsley, "The Intentional Fallacy" (1946), both in *The Verbal Icon* (1954); Jakobson, "What Is Poetry?" v. 3; O. Paz, *The Bow and the Lyre*, trans. R.L.C. Simms (1973); C. Baudelaire, *Oeuvres complètes*, ed. C. Pichois, 2 v. (1975–76); B. Croce, *Poetry and Literature*, trans. G. Gullace (1981); M. H. Abrams, "Poetry, Theories of (Western)," *New Princeton Encyclopedia of Poetry and Poetics*, ed. A. Preminger and T.V.F. Brogan (1993).

R. Greene

POET. The Greeks called the poet a "maker"— *poiētēs* or *poētēs*—and that word took hold in Lat. and other Eur. langs., incl. It., Fr., and Eng. But what precisely does the poet make? The obvious answer is *poems, the arrangements of words that he or she composes. Yet poets have often been given credit for bolder kinds of making. According to ancient Gr. fables, Amphion built Thebes from stones his songs called into place, and Orpheus's songs drew trees and beasts and stones to follow him. Ren. critics allegorized these stories as the harmonious beginning of civilization: poets had tamed the wilderness and softened the hearts of men. In the *Defence of Poesy*, Philip Sidney thought that the poet delivered a golden world, "in making things either better than Nature bringeth forth, or, quite anew, forms such as never were in Nature." Potentially that power of creation resembles, at one remove, the power of the Creator who first made the world. Other cultures have also regarded poets as godlike. Vyasa, who is both the putative author of the Indian *Mahābhārata* and a character in the epic, sometimes seems to be an avatar of the god Krishna. And even those who find such exalted views of the poet presumptuous or absurd concede that poets are capable of making fabulous fictions or myths. Historically, most nations and societies have preserved poems, usually attributed to a specific maker, that embody their trads. and values. The works of Homer were so revered in ancient Greece that they supplied the basis of education. In this way, the poet can represent a whole community bound by a common lang. and stories that everyone knows.

The ideal of the poet as maker of golden worlds and founding myths tends to lose sight of the maker of poems, however, who dwindles to a mere name or legend. No one knows with any certainty who Homer was or where or when he lived or whether he was blind or even whether any one person composed the works attributed to him. Thus, "Homer" signifies a stamp of authenticity, a name that certifies the greatness of the poems. The effort to trace a particular person seems incidental to the aura of the maker. The first poet recorded by hist., Enheduanna of Ur (ca. 2400 BCE), was the daughter of King Sargon and priestess of Inanna (Ishtar), whom she magnifies in *hymns that also refer to herself. Yet the goddess, the historical figure, the poet, and the legend are hard to separate, esp. since mss. of these poems date from centuries later. Similar problems veil the identities of virtually all early poets. In works preserved through oral trads. or scattered tablets, it is generally impossible to single out the original maker or to determine whether such an individual ever existed. Often the title of author falls to the scholar who first put a standard text together or wrote it down. Thus, the Mesopotamian *Epic of Gilgamesh* is supposed to have been revised and codified by Sîn-liqe-unninni (ca. 1200 BCE), a priest and scribe who lived more than a millennium after the work began and who inherited the honor of being its poet. Mod. ideas of authorship are challenged by these attributions. Nevertheless, the name of the poet casts a spell, as "Sappho" lends luster to every scrap or fragment of verse ascribed to her. It is as if the power of wonderful poems compelled their audiences to imagine the wonder-workers or divine spirits who made them. In the Heb. Bible, great hymns and songs are traditionally associated with inspired leaders and kings such as Moses (Deut. 32, 33), David (Ps.), and Solomon (Song of Sol.). Here the maker of nations absorbs the maker of verses; only someone anointed by God seems worthy of this sublime lang.

From this point of view, the poet is someone chosen, not someone who willfully tries to make poems. Hesiod, the poet of the *Theogony* (ca. 700 BCE), introduces himself as a shepherd tending his flock on Helicon when the Muses descended on him, gave him a staff of bay, breathed a voice into him, and instructed him to spend his life singing their praises. Variations on this theme recur in many other times and places. In a prologue attached to some versions of the *Rāmāyana*, when the illiterate Vālmīki sees a hunter shoot a crane, the cries of its grieving mate inspire him to invent the meter (*sloka*) in which, at the bidding of Brahma, he will compose the epic that follows. Another illiterate, Cædmon, was sleeping in a cowshed, according to the Venerable Bede (ca. 731 CE), when a mysterious voice taught him to sing in praise of God. Sophisticated poets of later eras have also felt themselves to be chosen—sometimes, as with Friedrich Hölderlin, almost against their will. John Keats's *Fall of Hyperion* (1856) begins with a vision in which the narrator, in mortal peril, confronts the possibility that he might be an idle dreamer rather than a chosen poet; the issue was unresolved, and the poem remained unfinished. But many lovers of poetry still contend that no one can resolve to be a poet or learn the trade because poets are born—or chosen—not made.

To call someone a true poet, therefore, is frequently less a description than a glorification. The word itself implies a superior talent, if not a touch of genius. In many fields, as Horace famously advised, mediocrity is quite acceptable—a second-rate lawyer can still do useful work—but neither men nor gods nor booksellers can abide a would-be poet. A number of terms distinguish poets from pretenders, who are called versemongers and versifiers, poetasters and rhymers. Even in mod. times, when canonizing a chosen few might be regarded as judgmental or elitist, it seems important to decide who qualifies as a poet and who does not. Verdicts like these apply to every kind of verse maker, to lyricists and troubadours as well as poets laureate; not every candidate can be the real thing. Perhaps a lingering sense of the role of those poets who once functioned as priests and prophets or as the living memory of their people accounts for the claims still made for poets, even in societies that do not award them much status or financial support. Yet secular eras have also reserved a special place for those who seem to be born to the calling. Cædmon's story set a pattern that has been often repeated. A fascination with "natural," uneducated makers of verse grew esp. strong in 18th- and 19th-c. Britain, when working-class or peasant geniuses appealed to the reading public; and at least two, Robert Burns and John Clare, eventually came to be recognized as major poets. Nature, not art, was supposed to have formed them and blessed them with inspiration. More recently, in 1955, Minou Drouet, just eight years old, became a best-selling Fr. poet (despite suspicions that her mother had written the poems). Apparently, children too can be struck by the muse.

A rival view of the poet, however, would stress the importance of learning a craft. From that perspective, poets are made, not born. As a demanding vocation, poetry requires unceasing study, a knowledge of what other poets have done, a mastery of *prosody and all the tools of verse, and lifelong practice. Such study is needed still more as the poet ages. Almost everyone is capable of writing one heartfelt poem, it is sometimes said, but only someone devoted to the craft of poetry can continue to write and to grow (Drouet stopped writing poems when she was 14). Moreover, the poet must understand the world in order to write well about it. Through much of hist., poetry was considered a type of learning, and "the learned poet" furnished an example to be followed. Scholars and critics often looked down on writers who were unacquainted with cl. texts. In *The Wisdom of the Ancients* (1609), Francis Bacon interpreted Orpheus as "a representation of universal Philosophy"; the archetypal poet was also the archetypal sage. The association of poetry with wisdom spans many cultures. It has been esp. powerful in early societies around the world, from the Americas to Africa to Iceland to Java, where native poets have supplied some basic models of how to live. But cl. trads. in the West have asked the poet for supreme craftsmanship as well as universal knowledge. In this respect, the exemplary figure is Virgil, who in late Roman times and in the Middle Ages came to be known simply as "the Poet." Virgil excelled in each of the genres most admired in his time: *eclogues, *georgics, *epic; he absorbed and improved on the best poems of the past; in search of perfection, he wrote only a few lines a day and constantly revised them; he created not only individual poems but the pattern of a full poetic career, in which the poet progresses through stages until each work seems part of one great whole, the lifework of the poet. Yet, in addition, Virgil was renowned as a *vates* or seer who had foreseen the coming of Christ and learned the secrets of the dead and whose works could be consulted to divine the future (the *sortes Virgilianæ*). Hence, "the Poet," both craftsman and magus, guides Dante through hell and purgatory in the *Divine Comedy* until, at the earthly paradise, they reach the limits of pagan and earthly knowledge. The poet Dante acknowledges his master and at the same time asserts the superiority of a Christian worldview. But together the two great poets affirm the value of their vocation, a craft that, pursued through a lifetime, culminates in understanding and bringing word of first and last things through art.

In such works, the master craftsman mounts above any mere human being. "The Poet" may take the name of Virgil, but he has gone far beyond the particular person who once lived and behaved as other people do. As characters in the *Divine Comedy*, both "Virgil" and "Dante" are useful fictions, filling the roles they play in the grand scheme of the poem. To be sure, the fictional Dante does draw on the memories and opinions of the poet who has created him and whose name he shares. But the relation between the character and his creator can never be taken for granted. In the past few centuries, many poets have tried to close that gap; they insist that the voice that speaks in a poem should be the same as that of the man or woman who made it. The romantics often regarded a capacity for deep feeling as the mark of a poet and direct expression of feeling as the mark of a good or authentic poem. In *The Prelude*, William Wordsworth gave epic scope to the story of how he had realized himself as a poet; and later poets, such as Walt Whitman and Vladimir Mayakovsky, liked to imply that their work had exposed the naked truth of who they were. Rhetorically, that open self-presentation can help to establish a sense of intimacy between writer and reader. Older poets had also recognized its power. Sappho seems to hold nothing back; Catullus and Ovid seem adept at revealing themselves; Petrarch and Dante confess their personal faults and obsessions. Moreover, even those who are ordinarily more reserved can flash forth at crucial moments. Many readers cherish the passages in *Paradise Lost* when John Milton, in the first person, thrusts his own struggles and feelings into the story.

It is tempting to view such disclosures as a transparent kind of autobiography, encompassing not only the situation of the poet but his or her inner life. Yet the image of the poet within the poem, like a painter's self-portrait, reveals only as much as will serve an artistic effect. Quite often a glimpse of the person behind the lines may function to tease or intrigue the reader, provoking a curiosity forever invited and yet evaded. T. S. Eliot, for instance, mastered that art, despite his advocacy of "impersonality." Good craftsmen know what to withhold as well as what to divulge. These strategies can be very complex. Hence, self-portraits of poets cover a wide range of forms and purposes, from Li Ch'ing-chao's *tz'u* to Allen Ginsberg's *Howl*. In the Japanese genre of the poetic diary (*uta nikki*), prose and verse combine in a personal journal enriched by an anthol. of poems. Thus, Matsuo Bashō's *Narrow Road to the Interior*

(1689) offers a travelogue sprinkled with haiku in which exquisite descriptions of nature convey the inner landscape of the poet. The diary documents spontaneous impressions of a historical journey into perilous regions. Yet it was carefully revised to accommodate both the facts and the person to a series of moods woven together, as if the writer himself were a work of art. Other poetic genres also insinuate that they are revealing the private life of the poet. The *sonnet sequences of Petrarch, Pierre de Ronsard, and Shakespeare, e.g., have often been combed like diaries for evidence of whom and how the poet loved. But such evidence is untrustworthy at best. The sonnets of Louise Labé offer a famous, searing case hist. of a passionate woman in love; but lately some scholars have argued that Labé never existed and that a group of men concocted those sonnets. Whatever the truth may be, it cannot be determined solely by the testimony of the poems, whose personal voice often echoes the voices of many earlier works. In this way, the poet seems constructed or pieced together from expectations about what a poet should be.

Those expectations also keep changing over time. Perhaps, in the distant past, poets knew just what societies wanted from them. The shaman, the bard, the court poet all were rewarded for doing their duty, whether as oracles, entertainers, or eulogists of their patrons. Even in those days, they tended to complain about the difficulty of making verses to make a living. Yet their way of life was accepted. In some societies, everyone recognized the value of poetry, which seemed as indispensable as breathing. During most of Chinese hist., from the earliest emperors until the era of Mao Zedong, all educated people could and did write verse, catching fleeting emotions or memorializing special occasions. The practice was so familiar that Chinese has no word that designates "the poet," although great writers like Li Po and Tu Fu were honored as masters or "teachers." In lesser hands, a skillful piece of verse might function to impress superiors or advance a career; a courtier who could not ask a favor from the emperor directly could appeal to him with a poem. But in most mod. societies, poets can seldom rely on being valued or noticed. Since the rise of print culture and the decline of patronage, they have largely depended on selling their wares to the public, and very few have found that profitable. Nor does poetry seem quite respectable as a profession or job description. The vast majority of poets earn their keep by doing other kinds of work, most often (in the U.S.) by teaching. There is little agreement, moreover, about what they contribute to society or about what society owes them. Poets and lovers of poetry continue to feel that poems provide something essential, whether by revitalizing lang., by noticing things that daily routines pass over, or by reminding readers of what it means to be alive. But much of the public seems content with a world in which the poet has no place at all.

The lack of any well-defined social role might be regarded, even so, as a peculiar advantage. If poets are outsiders, they are free to examine and challenge all the assumptions that other people usually take for granted. One model of the poet was put forward in the 15th c. by François Villon, whose popular ballads traded on his exploits as a ruffian and thief. Four centuries later Charles Baudelaire explored the creative possibilities of evil, Paul Verlaine and Arthur Rimbaud devoted themselves to breaking rules and laws in poems, and Oscar Wilde linked criminals and other performing rebels still make the most of. But the freedom of poets from social constraints and conventions can also inspire a more positive mission, a resistance to the empty formulas of those in power. When others are afraid to speak, the poet sometimes bears a special burden. In the former Soviet Union, when the government brooked no opposition and suppressed any unauthorized publication—"Poets, we are—and that rhymes with pariahs," Marina Tsvetaeva wrote in "Poets"—a small core of outcast writers, whose poems circulated in secret or by word of mouth, seemed to represent the conscience of the nation. Osip Mandelstam paid with his life for "anti-Soviet" verse, and Anna Akhmatova bore witness to the suffering of her people. Such poetry broke a terrible silence; many readers knew those poems by heart. And poets have seldom been more revered. (In the relative freedom of Russia today, some writers complain, poetry matters less.) Yet the mandate to serve as watchman and witness has not lost its force. Amid the troubles of times and places where free speech is throttled, dissident poets around the world have managed to defy authority and scorn injustice. That social or antisocial role has honored the name of the poet.

Yet most countries tolerate poets. Insofar as the mod. poet does have a voice, it tends to be the still, small voice that lingers in the mind when someone has turned off the busy hum of mass-market diversions. A memorable phrase or two—"the still small voice," "the busy hum"—can alter perceptions. Hence, poets take on the special task of ministering to lang., refining its rhythms, preserving or transforming its stock of words and expressions. Ever since Stéphane Mallarmé, some theorists have claimed that the poet is foremost a maker of lang., giving "a purer sense to the words of the tribe" ("The Tomb of Edgar Poe"). The power of poetic lang. to mold ideas, or even to inspire fresh ways of thinking, had earlier moved P. B. Shelley to declare that "poets are the unacknowledged legislators of the World"; they create the words and ideals that will govern the future. Lately, more skeptical theorists have sometimes reduced the poet to a captive or special effect of lang., a medium in which all human beings are submerged and that dissolves any illusion of a unique personality. Yet somehow that special effect of lang. has survived long after the tongues that first gave rise to it have passed away. The maker of golden worlds and the maker of poems still represent the possibility of making something new. The poet, as R. W. Emerson said, is "the Namer, or Language-maker" who converts the world into words, and that process links the distant past to those who make poems today.

■ Curtius; T. S. Eliot, *On Poetry and Poets* (1957); W. H. Auden, *The Dyer's Hand* (1962); *Japanese Poetic Diaries*, trans. E. Miner (1969); W. J. Bate, *The Burden of the Past and the English Poet* (1970); M. Heidegger, *Poetry, Language, Thought*, trans. A. Hofstadter (1971); M. Foucault, *Language, Counter-Memory, Practice*, trans. D. F. Bouchard and S. Simon (1977); R. Hingley, *Nightingale Fever: Russian Poets in Revolution* (1981); L. Lipking, *The Life of the Poet* (1981); R. Helgerson, *Self-Crowned Laureates* (1983); R. Alter, *The Art of Biblical Poetry* (1985); M. W. Bloomfield and C. W. Dunn, *The Role of the Poet in Early Societies* (1989); C. Bernstein, *A Poetics* (1992); C. Watkins, *How to Kill a Dragon: Aspects of Indo-European Poetics* (1995); P. Bourdieu, *The Rules of Art*, trans. S. Emanuel (1996); J. Brockington, *The Sanskrit Epics* (1998); J. Black, *Reading Sumerian Poetry* (1998); A. Hiltebeitel, *Rethinking the Mahābhārata* (2001); M. Huchon, *Louise Labé* (2006); G. M. Sanders, *Words Well Put: Visions of Poetic Competence in the Chinese Tradition* (2006); A. R. Ascoli, *Dante and the*

Making of a Modern Author (2008); J. Ramazani, *A Transnational Poetics* (2009).

L. LIPKING

POETICS, WESTERN

I. Classical
II. Medieval and Early Modern
III. Romanticism to Modernism
IV. Postmodernism and Beyond

Poetics is the branch of lit. crit. devoted to
poetry, esp. to the study of its characteristic
techniques, conventions, and strategies. The
word can also refer to theoretical texts on the
topic, above all to Aristotle's famous philosophical treatise. Sometimes *poetics* is used in
both a narrower and a more expansive sense.
On the one hand, it can designate the compositional principles to which a particular *poet
subscribes. These principles may remain implicit, or they may be made overt in a variety
of ways, ranging from the occasional and casual, such as John Keats's famous discussion of
"negative capability" in a letter to his brother
on December 21, 1817, to the serious and scholarly, such as Czesław Miłosz's Charles Eliot
Norton Lectures, published as *The Witness of
Poetry* (1984). On the other hand, *poetics* may
be used as a label for any formal or informal
survey of the structures, devices, and norms
that enable a discourse, genre, or cultural system to produce particular effects. Prominent
examples would include Gaston Bachelard's *La
Poétique de l'espace* (1958; trans. as *The Poetics
of Space*, 1964), Linda Hutcheon's *A Poetics of
Postmodernism* (1988), and Tzvetan Todorov's
Poétique de la prose (1971; trans. as *The Poetics
of Prose*, 1977), none of which places poetry at
the center of its argument. When employed in
this expanded sense, *poetics* is often implicitly
opposed to *hermeneutics*, i.e., the practice of interpretation. In other words, one explains how
something works, not what it means.

I. Classical. In the West, the discipline of poetics has its origins in Gr. antiquity. Although he
never wrote a single extended work on the subject, Plato's scattered comments on poetry have
served as a standard starting point for understanding the art form. His dialogue *Ion*, for instance, argues that poetry is written in a state of
divinely inspired madness. The thesis that poetry comes to a poet from outside, from some
higher or alien authority, has had a long and
surprising hist. in the millennia since, down to

20th- and 21st-c. experiments with automatic
writing, computational poetry, cybertext, and
found poetry.

Plato is best known for a set of related arguments made in the *Republic*. He maintains
that poetry addresses itself to the emotions. Instead of encouraging rational thought, it stirs
the passions of its audience. Such manipulation
may be acceptable in a few limited cases, such
as *hymns to the gods or *encomia celebrating
illustrious heroes, which encourage people to
live better lives. Otherwise, poetry is an inferior art. It is no more than a crude attempt to
reproduce in words ideas that transcend lang.
(see MIMESIS).

Again, these propositions have cast a long
shadow. Statements on poetics have conventionally taken a stand on whether poetry's
propensity to provoke strong feelings is to be
celebrated, as Longinus (see SUBLIME for the author and dating controversy) does in *Peri hypsous* (*On the Sublime*, 1st c. CE), or to be handled
carefully, as in William Wordsworth's Preface to
the 2d ed. of *Lyrical Ballads* (1800), which advocates tempering emotion through the use of
regular *rhyme and *meter. Similarly, the question of poetry's relation to truth has been a leit-
motif in writings on poetics, with fascinating
consequences, such as Pierre de Ronsard's insistence in *Abrégé de l'art poétique françois* (A Summary of the French Art of Poetry, 1565) that
poets must study as many occupations as possible, incl. blacksmithing, falconry, and sailing,
if they are to gain the experiential knowledge
necessary for fine writing—or W. H. Auden's
public confession in "Dichtung and Wahrheit"
(1959) that he was sexually attracted to someone other than his long-term companion Chester Kallman.

Aristotle's *Poetics* made the problems of affect and representation fundamental to Western
discussions of poetry. In response to Plato, he
maintains that imitation is not the same thing
as producing a flawed, degraded copy. Children,
he notes, spontaneously enjoy imitating others;
it is a natural human faculty, as well as a technique fundamental to all learning. Moreover,
poets do not slavishly repeat what they witness,
know, or have heard. When they compose poetry they invent scenes, characters, and actions.
Historians might find themselves constrained
by the arbitrariness of actual events; poets, in
contrast, present their audiences with pretend
but "probable" scenarios that are better suited
to moving them in appropriate ways. Tragedy,

for instance, relies on the spectacle of heroic men and women undergoing apt suffering to cause people to feel intense fear and pity. After being "purged" of these troublesome emotions (catharsis), they will then, presumably, be prepared to act more rationally and hence make better decisions in the future.

It can be surprising to encounter mention of tragedy in the middle of a broader discussion of poetics. In the course of his rebuttal of Plato, Aristotle pursues his usual strategy of argument by classification. He identifies and differentiates two poetic *genres, *epic and tragedy (with a third genre, comedy, apparently covered in the lost second half of the *Poetics*). This taxonomic project stands at the head of a long series of similar endeavors with great influence on later writers. E.g., Pierre Corneille's *Trois Discours sur le poème dramatique* (Three Discourses on Dramatic Poetry, 1660) formalizes the Aristotelian doctrine of the three unities of place, time, and action that later governed not only neoclassical drama but modernist works such as James Joyce's *Ulysses* (1922). Torquato Tasso reverses Aristotle by elevating epic above tragedy in *Discorsi del poema eroico* (*Discourses on the Heroic Poem*, 1594), an argument that had a profound effect on John Milton as he mulled his literary future. Northrop Frye's *Anatomy of Criticism* (1957) takes Aristotle's arguments about genre and uses them as a starting point for proposing a sweeping model for understanding all of literary hist.

For many, a second surprising aspect of Aristotle's *Poetics* is its relative lack of attention to *prosody. Although he does twice discuss meter (books 4.14 and 24.5–6), he does not directly and intimately connect the act of making (*poiēsis*) that defines poetry with the patterning of *sound. Like Plato, he can often appear more concerned with what a poem relates—its content—than the specific words, and the specific word ordering, that a poet selects. There are instances of such analysis in antiquity—above all Dionysius of Halicarnassus's *Peri syntheseos onomaton* (On the Arrangement of Words, 1st c. BCE), but already one can begin to see the possibility of what later critics will consider to be a distinction between *verse* and *poetry*. Francis Bacon's *The Advancement of Learning* (1605), for instance, acknowledges that some critics might consider poetry distinguishable by its *style but rejects such a definition as superficial and prefers the argument

that poetry is "feigned history." By the time of P. B. Shelley's *Defence of Poetry* (1840), it was possible to argue that, as long as they display Aristotelian virtues such as harmony, order, and unity, artworks of any kind (music, sculpture, dance) deserve the label *poetry*.

II. Medieval and Early Modern. In general, cl., med., and early mod. authors worry less about *form and more about poetry's ability to educate readers, esp. young people. Plato's *Protagoras* and Aristotle's *Politics* both argue that the purpose of poetry is to edify its audience, and Plutarch's "Quomodo adolescens poetas audire debeat" ("How the Young Man Should Study Poetry," 1st c. CE) goes so far as to recommend that one should emend poets' writings to guarantee their probity. Often treatments of poetry's instructional potential also contemplate its seductive qualities. Horace's *Ars poetica* (1st c. BCE) famously asserts that poets are "those who mix the useful with the sweet," and he prescribes such a mixture as the best means of "mold[ing] a child's young lips." While in later centuries there are dissenters such as Lodovico Castelvetro—whose *Poetica d'Aristotele vulgarizzata e sposta* (Aristotle's *Poetics* Translated and Expounded; 1570, 1576) endorses pleasure as the primary motivation for reading or writing poetry—until the 19th c. it remained conventional to defend poetry's capacity for moral instruction, as well as to justify any by-the-by enjoyment as a means of enticing the weak and impressionable to start on the path toward virtue and goodness. Indeed, given that the primary text on poetics available during the Middle Ages, a commentary on Aristotle's *Poetics* by the Ar. philosopher Ibn Rushd (Averroës), emphasizes poetry's moral purpose and civic-mindedness, one could track an unbroken lineage in the West of moralizing statements on poetics from Plutarch to late 20th-c. works such as Adrienne Rich's "When We Dead Awaken: Writing as Re-Vision" (1971) and Cary Nelson's *Repression and Recovery* (1989).

Significantly, this trad. rarely embraces straightforward didacticism. Dante's *Convivio* (ca. 1304–7), e.g., argues that, in a good poem, the literal, denotative meaning is supplemented by other, "allegorical" strata that touch on matters such as ethics and theology. In his *Difesa della Commedia di Dante* (*On the Defense of the Comedy of Dante*, 1587), Giacopo Mazzoni further explains that allegory is necessary because poets must use concrete and credible images to communicate with a wide audience, many of whom are ill-suited to abstract thought. Poetry might, therefore, resemble a game in certain respects; but as long as poets play such word games in the service of public virtue, then, *contra* Plato, they perform a useful function in society. Such gaming could, in fact, Giambattista Giraldi Cinthio contends in his *Discorso intorno al comporre dei romanzi* (Discourse on the Composition of Romances, 1554), lead poets to innovate boldly, even creating entirely new and unprecedented kinds of poetry, such as Ludovico Ariosto's long, self-interrupting narrative poem *Orlando furioso* (1516), which departs from Aristotelian prescriptions on almost every count. Even if the purpose of poetry remains constant across the ages—to praise the good and condemn the bad—to remain effective, poets must vary the means by which they pursue those ends.

The republication of Aristotle's *Poetics* in 1508 and its trans. into Lat. in 1536, plus the ready availability of Horace's *Ars poetica* in significant eds. such as the one pub. in Paris in 1500, ensured that the questions of seeming, pleasure, truth, and utility remained central to Western discussions of poetics during the Ren. and into the Enlightenment. Landmark works such as Philip Sidney's *Defence of Poesy* (1595), John Dryden's *Essay of Dramatic Poesy* (1668), and Alexander Pope's *Essay on Criticism* (1711) devote themselves to reprising and revising cl. stands on these subjects. When Samuel Johnson states that "the greatest excellency of art" is to "imitate nature; but it is necessary to distinguish those parts of nature, which are most proper for imitation" (*Rambler*, no. 4), or when Matthew Arnold claims that "truth and seriousness" are the *sine qua non* of good verse ("The Study of Poetry," 1880), one can hear echoes of Aristotle on *mimesis as well as two millennia of debates concerning the most compelling, improving, and expedient means of representing humans and the world. Even treatises such as Baltasar Gracián's *Agudeza y arte de ingenio* (*Cleverness and the Art of Wit*, 1642, rev. ed. 1648) that defend what might appear to be disruptively antimimetic devices—in particular, wild punning and exaggerated uses of figurative lang.—nevertheless continue to justify such obstructive artifice by crediting pyrotechnic displays of wit with the power to render poetry's lessons more sensuously and intellectually appealing.

Variations within this overall pattern do exist. E.g., George Puttenham's *Arte of English Poesie* (1589) distinguishes itself by blurring the boundaries between rhetoric and poetics. He borrows terms pell-mell from rhetorical manuals in the trad. of Cicero's *De inventione* (ca. 86 BCE), the *Rhetorica ad Herennium* (early 1st c. BCE), and Quintilian's *Institutio oratoria* (ca. 93–95 CE) to anatomize Eng. verse. Surprisingly, he also attends closely to sound, distinguishing Elizabethan stress-based meters from cl. quantitative prosody. Puttenham's emphasis on poetry as, first, a discursive system susceptible of formal analysis and, second, a means of stirring an audience can make him sound unusually contemporary. In fact, New Historicists in the 1980s and 1990s such as Jonathan Goldberg, Stephen Greenblatt, and Patricia Parker looked to Puttenham as a touchstone and precursor, someone who pioneered the exploration of the dynamic relationship between literary texts and cultural contexts. One could also, however, construe Puttenham as engaged in a variant on the *querelle des anciens et des modernes* (quarrel of ancients and moderns), seeking to prove that a vernacular lang. and lit. can achieve excellences similar to but distinct from Lat. and Gr. precursors. In this regard, the *Arte of English Poesie* deserves comparison to works such as Vasily Trediakovsky's *Novyi i kratkii sposob k slozheniiu rossiiskikh stikhov* (New and Brief Method for Composing Russian Verse, 1735) and Mikhail Lomonosov's *Pis'mo o pravilakh rossiiskogo stikhotvorstva* (Letter on the Rules of Russian Prosody, 1739), which similarly turn to the study of rhet. to help codify the *conventions, devices, and forms characteristic of an emergent *canon of vernacular poetry.

Another prominent strand within early mod. and Enlightenment poetics concerns comparisons between poetry and the other arts. Sometimes this discussion takes the form of a *paragone*, a mock-combat reminiscent of the duels between singing shepherds in the cl. *pastoral, as in the first act of Shakespeare's *Timon of Athens* (1623). At other times, the exercise leads to an extended philosophical reflection, as in Leonardo da Vinci's jours., or most famously in G. E. Lessing's *Laokoön* (*Laocoön*, 1766). Lessing maintains that Horace's injunction *ut pictura poesis*—that a poem should resemble a painting—was mistaken. Poetry, he believes, unfolds over time, whereas painting extends across space but can be taken in by the eye in an instant. Devices suitable to one art simply cannot be transposed effectively into the other. These arguments concerning what might now be called *medium specificity* have haunted poetics ever since. Is poetry distinguished from other art forms simply because it uses lang. to communicate, as Clement Greenberg contends in "Towards a Newer Laocoön" (1940)? Or is it at its core something more precise, as Nathaniel Mackey argues in *Paracritical Hinge* (2005), an art that showcases the "occult clamor" audible in speech and song?

III. Romanticism to Modernism. Around the year 1800, poets, literary critics, and philosophers began not simply to question or revise but to break with the Aristotelian legacy. As M. H. Abrams recounts in *The Mirror and the Lamp* (1953), mimetic theories of poetry started to give way to an emphasis on expression. In the West, people took to describing and evaluating poetry based on its success or failure in eloquently and accurately communicating a writer's innermost thoughts, feelings, experiences, fantasies, and dreams, esp. as they touch on abstractions, spiritual matters, and historical causes that transcend the merely personal and arbitrary. From this vantage point, fidelity in representation and seriousness of moral purpose matter less than a given writer's intensity, sincerity, passion, and ingenuity. Indecorous or lowly content and mannered or otherwise distorted depictions of the external world are excusable as long as poets obey the dictates of their imagination and conscience. In doing so, moreover, they are free to dispense with received guidelines and models concerning proper poetic form. A poem's structure, *diction, *rhythm, and other organizing traits should arise *organically*, i.e., in tight, close conjunction with the unfolding of its denotative meaning and its connotative associations.

These precepts are all well known, of course, as aspects of romantic poetics. Key texts include A.W. and Friedrich Schlegel's jour. the *Athenaeum* (1798–1800), S. T. Coleridge's *Biographia Literaria* (1817), Wordsworth's Preface, and Shelley's *Defence*. Philosophically, the most important contributions were by Immanuel Kant and G.W.F. Hegel. In different but complementary ways, they assert that the mind plays an active role in the constitution of the external world. Later writers and thinkers became enamored of the power and the possibilities that this idea makes available. In the extreme formulation of this argument, poets do not reflect existing realities. Through the agency of the imagination, they, in fact, can create new ones ex nihilo—and might even be responsible for generating and sustaining the current actuality that they inhabit. Wallace Stevens's *The Necessary Angel* (1951) represents perhaps the most rigorous, sober, yet also far-reaching formulation of this romantic doctrine.

Kant deserves mention here for a second, additional reason. His *Kritik der Urteilskraft* (*Critique of Judgment*, 1790) holds that aesthetic judgments belong to a category independent of moral judgments and judgments that convey information or knowledge. To read a poem and expect to come away with moral instruction or other kinds of useful data is to make a logical mistake, i.e., to treat it as something other than a work of art. (As Ludwig Wittgenstein's *Zettel* [1967] puts it, "Do not forget that a poem, although it is composed in the language of information, is not used in the language-game of giving information.") Kant, in effect, makes the first sustained case for art's autonomy, its separation from other spheres of human activity; the next two centuries would see many restatements and revisions of this thesis. Friedrich Schiller's *Ästhetische Erziehung des Menschen* (*On the Aesthetic Education of Man*, 1795), e.g., stakes out a position that would later be summed up as "art for art's sake." Theodor Adorno's "Rede über Lyrik und Gesellschaft" ("Lyric Poetry and Society," 1957) claims that, insofar as Western aesthetics from Kant onward has provided poets an illusion of refuge from hist. and politics, they are thereby granted an opportunity to imaginatively negate the world they inhabit and dream of living free of capitalist necessity.

The expressive school of poetics found its last great expositor in Benedetto Croce. In *Ariosto, Corneille e Shakespeare* (1919), he states that "style is nothing other than the expression of the poet and his very soul." He believes that one should approach a poem as an aesthetic whole and trace its tone and other formal features in order to elucidate the mind and spirit that prompted its composition. Of course, such an approach presupposes that a given author's internal life is worth reconstructing and appreciating, an assumption that would come under attack from many quarters over the course of the 20th c. One set of writers expressed strong reservations regarding whose subjectivities and experiences are presumed to be normative within Western expressive poetics. They also questioned whether poetry could or should address a generic reader. These opponents of unreflective universalism include Gloria Anzaldúa, Amiri Baraka, Audre Lorde, M. NourbeSe Philip, and Denise Riley.

Other critics wondered whether poetry ought to place any priority at all on individual expression. In *Toward the Decolonization of African Literature* (1980), Chinweizu, Onwuchekwa Jemie, and Ihechukwu Madubuike argue that the anglophone poetic canon is excessively inward-directed and protective of privacy. They contrast it to the "public language" exemplified by oral Af. poetries, which emphasize direct, performative connections between poet and audience. Léopold Sédar Senghor, in his *Dialogue sur la poésie francophone* (Dialogue on Francophone Poetry, 1979), goes further, suggesting that the mod. Eur. has entirely lost touch with myth, the shared collective system of stories and symbols that elevate poetry above self-indulgent coos and complaints. On the other side of the Atlantic, Édouard Glissant, in *L'intention poétique* (Poetic Intention, 1969), makes a parallel argument, disparaging Crocean creative genius in the name of a poetry that could embody and perpetuate a healthy group consciousness.

Early in the 20th c., the Rus. formalists proposed a fundamental reorientation of poetics away from expression altogether. Beginning with Viktor Shklovsky's "Voskreshenie slova" ("Resurrection of the Word," 1914), they polemically minimized the status of the author in favor of attending to the *priemy* (devices) in a work of lit. A poem does not convey a message; it draws attention to itself, more specifically, to its construction and function. Poetry in the aggregate, too, is not a gallery of brilliant achievements. It is a self-generating system of texts. New poems are not the product of inspiration and brilliant execution. Rather, as Yuri Tynianov says in "Literaturnyi fakt" (Literary Fact, 1924), they are "mutations" that receive attention (instead of vanishing into historical oblivion unnoticed) because they depart in unusually striking ways from once-popular but now overly familiar, commonplace ways of assembling poetic devices.

Anglo-Am. New Criticism also sharply differentiated between poet and poem. E.g., even when written in the first person and offering seemingly autobiographical details, a *lyric, New Critics such as John Crowe Ransom, Allen Tate, and Robert Penn Warren would assert, remains a thing apart, voiced by an implied "speaker" who, whatever overlap might exist with the poet, never coincides entirely. Studies

such as Cleanth Brooks's *The Well Wrought Urn* (1947) and William Empson's *Seven Types of Ambiguity* (1930) demonstrate the virtues of close reading, the intensive scrutiny of a poem's lang. and prosody that proceeds with limited or no reference to the original historical context in which it was written or to its poet's biography or psychology. If a poem is worthwhile, close reading can proceed almost indefinitely, since its paradoxes, convoluted figures of speech, and many levels of meaning reward intense prolonged interpretation. As promoted via arguments such as W. K. Wimsatt and M. C. Beardsley's essays "The Intentional Fallacy" (1946) and "The Affective Fallacy" (1946), close reading amounts to a somewhat peculiar variant on cl. rhet. that limits itself to the formal analysis of texts while neglecting their intended or observed effects on readers.

IV. Postmodernism and Beyond. Although strong pedagogically, New Criticism did not happen to offer a consistent theory of poetry as a literary system. It preferred to examine poems, not to generalize about poetry as a whole. Structuralism, as developed and practiced in France in the decades after World War II, reverses this privileging of texts over textuality—i.e., instead of focusing on the appreciation of singular artworks, it seeks to elucidate cultural sign systems in toto. As Gérard Genette explains in "Structuralisme et critique littéraire" ("Structuralism and Literary Criticism," 1966), discrete literary objects should be conceived not as unitary and stand-alone but as relational entities, explicable only with reference to the larger system of themes, motifs, and keywords that constitute the literary system out of which the work has been assembled. Michael Riffaterre's *Semiotics of Poetry* (1978) asserts that, as a consequence, it is a mistake to read literary works such as poems as if they were primarily referential or mimetic. A poem's sentences, images, themes, and rhetorical devices signify—convey meaning—only insofar as they participate in *semiotic structures*, the sign configurations that make up poetry as a system that readers have learned to recognize. Jonathan Culler's *Structuralist Poetics* (1975) summarizes this approach to reading by stating that it privileges poetics over interpretation. In other words, instead of seeking to restate a poem's meaning in new words, it engages in description intended to locate a poem within an array of relevant categories. E.g., if a critic recognizes that Jan Kochanowski's *Treny* (Threnodies, 1580) is a collection of elegies for his daughter Urszula, she cannot straight away begin by pondering whether the poet is being overly sentimental, nor can she start expounding on the blend of Ren. humanism and staunch Catholicism that the lyrics exhibit. She must first ask what is an *elegy, how *Treny* relates to other elegies, and where elegy fits within literary production as a whole in the early mod. Polish-Lithuanian Commonwealth.

Structuralism quickly gave way to a variety of poststructuralisms that then had widespread impact in Western academies during the 1970s and 1980s. Structuralism, critics quickly discovered, has a fatal flaw. It requires people to agree that it is possible to create ling. descriptions that can analytically stand in for actual cultural systems. Roland Barthes's book *Système de la mode* (*The Fashion System*, 1967), for instance, has to be understood as offering *in words* a sufficient mapping and explanation of how fashion itself operates in Fr. society. Poststructuralists attack this assumption from many different angles. Can any use of lang. ever accurately depict what happens in the ever- and swiftly changing external world? Are systems ever intelligible in their entirety? Do they even exist as wholes, or are they, in fact, made up of myriad competing interlinked ephemeral partial systems?

One philosopher who helped poststructuralists address these issues is Martin Heidegger, whose later essays such as "Der Ursprung des Kunstwerkes" ("The Origin of the Work of Art," 1935) and ". . . dichterisch wohnet der Mensch . . ." ("Poetically Man Dwells," 1951) propose that Truth and Being never entirely reveal themselves. They can be approached only sidelong, and each revelation, by spotlighting one aspect of what people seek to know, often distracts them from or even blinds them to other facets. What is one to do? Poetry, Heidegger contends, is the art in which lang. most overtly stages its own emergence from nothingness, thus making it the best vehicle for pondering how and why the world exists.

The intellectual ferment in poststructuralist circles gave rise to numerous provocative arguments about poetics. The Yale School—which includes Harold Bloom, Paul de Man, Barbara Johnson, Geoffrey Hartman, and J. Hillis Miller—concentrated on showing that poetry always resorts to misnaming and misrecognition in its perpetual quest to affirm truths and essences that, in reality, are never self-evident or fully apprehensible. In essays such as "Shibboleth. Pour Paul Celan" (1986),

Jacques Derrida suggests that a poem can best be read by launching off from particular details (such as an appended date of composition) and exploring its many ramifications as far as one may go. On this view, a poem is neither a self-enclosed artifact nor a gateway to systemic verities but a starting and ending point for a voyage into ling. possibility. Marjorie Perloff's *The Poetics of Indeterminacy* (1978) agrees that poems open outward into vertiginous anarchic free play and speculation, but she also underscores that such moments of indeterminacy remain constricted or counterbalanced by convention, context, and what else appears in a text. A poem cannot mean "just anything." Julia Kristeva's *La révolution du langage poétique* (1974, trans. as *Revolution in Poetic Language*, 1984) associates the infinite suggestiveness in good poetry with its nonsemantic components, esp. its rhythm and sound play, which she believes are traces of the profound, embodied communicative ties between child and mother that precede the forced imposition of patriarchal grammar and logic.

Poststructuralism's near-exclusive focus on lang., texts, and intertextuality quickly produced its own countermovement, a push toward relocating poetry's meaning in social, cultural, economic, and political institutions and discursive practices. Indispensable have been philosophers such as Michel Foucault, whose *Surveiller et punir* (1975, trans. as *Discipline and Punish*, 1979) presents all texts as implicated in networks of power and knowledge, and Antonio Gramsci, whose *Quaderni del carcere* (1964, trans. as *Prison Notebooks*, 1971) maintains that texts acquire meaning and social significance not so much through what they say but through the links made between different spheres of activity. (An antiwar poem, for instance, can have no impact on a nation's war effort unless poetry is "articulated with," considered vitally connected to, other forms of effective political speech. Otherwise, it might as well celebrate May flowers or the *Mayflower*.)

New Historicists present poetry as a mode of cultural production that has unacknowledged connections to other varieties. It can, Stephen Greenblatt argues in *Renaissance Self-Fashioning* (1980), serve as a means of drawing attention from patrons and heightening one's social status. Louis Montrose's *The Purpose of Playing* (1996) isolates "theatricality" as a shared attribute and value in Ren. Eng. religion, courtly society, and verse drama. More recent cultural studies approaches to poetics—as Maria Damon and Ira Livingston recount in their introduction to *Poetry and Cultural Studies* (2009)—define themselves by setting aside any conventional distinctions between high/elite and low/mass/popular culture, by suspending evaluative distinctions between good/bad, and by denying the autonomy of aesthetics. The composition and the interpretation of poetry are often related to, and grounded in, contemp. activist projects, and a critic should not prejudge which humanities, social sciences, or other disciplines will prove best suited to illuminating a poem's "cultural work," its particular contribution to society, economics, and politics on behalf of what particular constituency.

Dissatisfaction with disciplinary limits characterizes other continuing conversations within the field of poetics. Many scholars have grown uneasy with the national, geographic, and ling. divisions that all too often artificially seal off different corpora of poetry from one other. In response, they have started surveying ways in which poetry takes shape and operates *transnationally*, i.e., across and despite nation-state boundaries. Indeed, studies such as Yunte Huang's *Transpacific Displacements* (2002) trouble the East/West divide. Another set of boundary-crossing scholars have attempted to supplement the humanistic analysis of poetry with methods and insights drawn from ling., psychology, neuroscience, and philosophy of mind. In *Toward a Theory of Cognitive Poetics* (1992), Reuven Tsur describes the enterprise of cognitive poetics as an inquiry into how mental processes shape and constrain literary response and poetic structure. Crit. in this vein meticulously examines patterns in texts while simultaneously paying close attention to the cognitive states and dynamics involved in acts of interpretation.

A final important point: one should not assume from this overview that, by the year 2000, poetics had become solely an academic or university-based pursuit. As the new millennium approached, poets, too, continued to show themselves as capable as ever of making pioneering provocative arguments about the nature and function of their chosen art form. One recurrent ambition was to define poetry as a special kind of rhet. whose antimimetic and nonsemantic aspects enable it to serve liberatory political ends. The Moscow Conceptualists, e.g., among them Andrei Monastyrsky, Vsevolod Nekrasov, and Lev Rubinshtein,

hold that poetry can provide an escape from oppressive ideologies and state surveillance. They believe that attending to the empty unmeaning clichés, errors, repetitions, and other verbal "junk" pervasive in everyday lang. use grants access to a blissful nothingness external to officially sanctioned truths and values. Halfway around the globe, another literary movement, Language poetry, challenged the liberal democratic faith in the autonomy of the individual in the name of alternative, revolutionary modes of being in the world and being with others. Am. and Canadian writers affiliated with the movement such as Charles Bernstein, Lyn Hejinian, and Steve McCaffery frequently characterize their readers as "co-creators" of a poem, completing or continuing the process of meaning production initiated by its author. In Latin America, the publication of Haroldo de Campos's *Galáxias* (1984) helped to catalyze the emergence of a self-consciously neobaroque poetics that is assertively, foundationally "postcolonial" and "antimodern." Coral Bracho, Eduardo Milán, Néstor Perlongher, and Raúl Zurita celebrate archaism, ornament, excess, inconsistency, asymmetry, and other disruptive, striking, and fanciful devices as means of seducing readers away from what they perceive as the misleading clarity and unearned rectitude of Western rationalist thought. They seek, as John Beverley puts it in "Nuevas vacilaciones sobre el barroco" (New Vacillations on the Baroque, 1988), a "possible culture and society starting from the mutilation that imperialism has inflicted on its people."

While all these figures might polemically oppose the centrality that mimesis has played in Western poetics since the days of Plato and Aristotle, they nonetheless recognizably operate within that same trad.: i.e., they focus their attention on whether and how lang. touches on the world, and they inquire into poetry's capacity to improve human behavior. And these concerns, too, more broadly typify the best contemp. writing on poetry by poets, whether represented by, say, the exilic musings of Agha Shahid Ali, the affirming feminism of Nicole Brossard, or the probing postapartheid meditations on justice and ethics by Ingrid de Kok. In the 21st c., the word *poetics* will surely continue its curious ambiguity, signifying, on the one hand, something institutional and perduring—a branch of lit. crit.—and, on the other hand, something altogether more changeable, porous, and unpredictable, namely, the compositional principles that poets themselves discover and apply during the writing process.

See POEM, POETRY.

■ T.S. Eliot, *The Sacred Wood* (1920); E. Pound, *ABC of Reading* (1930); E. Drew, *Discovering Poetry* (1933); J. C. Ransom, "Criticism, Inc.," *Virginia Quarterly Review* 13 (1937); A. Tate, "Tension in Poetry," *Southern Review* 4 (1938); Y. Winters, *In Defense of Reason* (1947); R. P. Blackmur, *Language as Gesture* (1952); J. Lezama Lima, *La expresión americana* (1957); Weinberg; B. Hathaway, *The Age of Criticism* (1962); G. Stein, "Composition as Explanation" [1926], *What Are Masterpieces?* (1970); F. Kermode, *Renaissance Essays* (1971); H. Bloom, *The Anxiety of Influence* (1973); R. Barthes, *The Pleasure of the Text*, trans. R. Miller (1975); J. M. Lotman, *The Structure of the Artistic Text*, trans. G. Lenhoff and R. Vroon (1977); V. Forrest-Thomson, *Poetic Artifice* (1978); P. N. Medvedev and M. M. Bakhtin, *The Formal Method of Literary Scholarship*, trans. A. Wehrle (1978); de Man; A. Easthope, *Poetry as Discourse* (1983); J. J. McGann, *The Romantic Ideology* (1983); T. Todorov, *Introduction to Poetics*, trans. R. Howard (1983); *Lyric Poetry*, ed. C. Hošek and P. Parker (1985); A. Carson, *Eros the Bittersweet* (1986); S. McCaffery, *North of Intention* (1986); C. Bernstein, *Artifice of Absorption* (1987); B. Johnson, "Apostrophe, Animation, and Abortion," *A World of Difference* (1987); R. B. DuPlessis, *The Pink Guitar* (1990); M. Brown, *Preromanticism* (1994); H. de Campos, *Ideograma* (1994); H. Meschonnic, *Politique du rythme, politique du sujet* (1995); J.-L. Nancy, *The Muses*, trans. P. Kamuf (1996); G. Agamben, *The End of the Poem*, trans. D. Heller-Roazen (1999); R. Jakobson, "The Newest Russian Poetry" ("Noveishaia russkaia poeziia," 1921), *My Futurist Years*, ed. B. Jangfeldt and S. Rudy, trans. S. Rudy (1999); P. Lacoue-Labarthe, *Poetry as Experience*, trans. A. Tarnowski (1999); M. Perloff, *Wittgenstein's Ladder* (1999); L. Hejinian, *The Language of Inquiry* (2000); S. Stewart, *Poetry and the Fate of the Senses* (2002); *Poetry in Theory*, ed. J. Cook (2004); M.A.R. Habib, *A History of Literary Criticism from Plato to the Present* (2005); R. von Hallberg, *Lyric Powers* (2008); B. Groys, *History Becomes Form* (2010).

B. M. REED

POETRY. Accounts of *poetry* as a category tend to outline essential features in an argument that might claim general assent. The range of past and present usage of the word,

however, eludes such unifying accounts and invites us to think of *poetry* as a word of ancient Gr. origin, with a long and rich hist. One part of that hist. is the assumption that the word refers to something that transcends its hist. or has a conceptual core that runs through all the variations in its use. That hist. has been driven by acts of calling certain representations or classes of representation *poetry*.

The hist. begins with a set of Gr. terms: *poiēsis, making; *poiēma*, a thing made, a work; *poiētēs*, a maker, *poet; *poiētike* (*technē*), the making (art/technique), *poetics. None of these words quite corresponds to the later categorical term *poetry*. The first attempt to give a comprehensive account, Aristotle's *Poetics*, set this hist. of change in motion by incl. the Socratic dialogues in prose but excluding Empedocles' versified natural philosophy. Prior to Aristotle, the Greeks had roughly assumed that *poetry*, when applied to discourse, referred to making verse. By excluding metrical composition as the defining criterion, Aristotle turned the object of "making" into a problem. Combined with Plato's critique of the conceptual value of poetry (for which Aristotle had an answer), Aristotle's question of what poetry "is" and, no less important, what poetry "is not" initiated a process of redefining and extending the categorical term. That process had a weight that was lacking in more specific questions: what is a *sonnet or a play or even a debated term like *epic?

Aristotle, thinking primarily of drama and epic, answered the question he posed with the claim that the object of "making" was a plot (*muthos*), an old term redefined and transformed into a set of internally necessary relations by the logic of Aristotle's argument. Although we now identify poetry primarily with *lyric, it is not at all clear how well Gr. lyric would have satisfied Aristotle's definition. Thereafter, poetry, in its mutations through various Eur. langs., was destabilized, in natural lang. referring to a set of metrical genres and in theory referring to some idea realized in only a subset of texts.

In the wholesale borrowing of Gr. literary vocabulary by the Romans, the conceptual morphology of *poiēsis* was Latinized and used for general terms covering a range of metrical discursive forms more commonly referred to by specific genre names, some borrowed from Gr. but others such as *carmina* (oddly trans. as *odes) from native Lat. We will call these Latinized and later vernacularized variations of the Gr. *poiēsis* "poetry words," the borrowed terms that helped create the impression of a universal concept that transcended its instantiation in any particular lang. Until the late Middle Ages, *poema, poetica* (*ars*), and *poeta* remained Lat. terms. The bards, *scops*, and *skalds, troubadours, trouvères, rimatori,* and *Minnesänger* came to be called *poets* in the vernacular only later. If such rhymers were referred to in Lat., the poetry words were sometimes used. In Dante, the poetry words were firmly established for vernacular composition. Indeed, in the *Vita nuova* and the *Convivio,* we have *poetria,* a categorical term roughly corresponding to *poetry.* The term was borrowed from med. Lat. but used in an apparently new way. Petrarch, who so profoundly aspired to be a "poet" in the Lat. sense, still termed his vernacular verse *Rime sparse* (or *Rerum vulgarium fragmenta*)—even though he calls what he does in the vernacular lyrics *poetando,* "making poems." The term *poetry,* in its variations, gradually came into use in the Eur. vernaculars; there it appears as a general term, covering a wide range of metrical discourses in the vernacular and implicitly linking recent vernacular metrical writing to Gr. and Lat. trads.

On a certain level of theoretical discourse, the vernacular derivatives of the Lat. continued to carry the full range of the Aristotelian usage, referring to epic (and verse *narrative), drama (in verse), and even lyric (although Ren. It. critics rarely considered lyric in their treatises on poetics). This range continued well into the 19th c., esp. in Germany, which came to favor the native term *Dichtung* for metrical composition, as opposed to the general term (derived from Fr.), *Poesie,* for lit. in a larger sense, incl. the novel. In popular usage, however, *epic* and *drama* increasingly appeared as marked terms (such as John Dryden's *An Essay of Dramatic Poesy*), while the unmarked term *poetry* came to refer primarily to lyric. In the 19th c., variations on the term *literature* eventually supplanted this larger sense of "poetry."

As the meaning of *poetry* was becoming increasingly centered on lyric and shorter *narrative verse, the range of discursive forms called *poetry* was broadening in the late 18th and 19th cs. In part, this broadening followed from renewed interest in and the recovery of earlier lit. from the Middle Ages, whose vernacular lyrics were now conventionally called *poetry.* Anonymous oral verse such as *ballads and folk songs became *poetry. Poetry* was also used to describe a variety of metrical genres from the old, literate cultures of Asia, genres that were sometimes very far from the sense of the term that we find in Aristotle. *Shi'ir,* the categorical term for strict metrical lyric genres in the Islamic world, was called *poetry. Kāvya,* with a range that included prose and was centered, like Aristotle, on epic and drama, was called *poetry.* The lyric form *shi,* in its East Asian variations, was, like *poetry,* a concept going beyond formal definition (by this period in Chinese one could say that there was no "shi" in something that was formally a "shi"); this too was called *poetry.* In the latter part of the 19th c., protoanthropologists found *poetry* in the verse of preliterate societies. Eventually in the 20th c., Homer, once the prime example of the poet as maker, became the name attached to the record of a collective practice of oral composition, which was called *oral poetry.* Such a radically extended corpus of what might be considered poetry, combined with the evolving practice of Eur. writers who called themselves *poets,* required a new and far broader understanding of the term.

Some basic transformations in the idea of poetry occurred in the early 19th c. These transformations have come to be so taken for granted that they are now seen as essential to poetry rather than as historical phenomena.

Aristotle's claim that a poet made "plots" was no longer appropriate for the new ways in which the word *poetry* was used. G.W.F. Hegel proposed in the *Aesthetics* that the material of poetry was "inner representations" (*innere Vorstellen*) to which the poet gave form and that lang. was merely an accidental means of manifestation. From this, Hegel concluded that poetry could be translated from one lang. to another without essential loss. Only a few decades separated Hegel's lectures on aesthetics from P. B. Shelley's memorable comparison of translating poetry to casting a violet into a crucible (*A Defence of Poetry*). The differences among discursive forms called *poetry* were the companion of the nationalization of poetry. Even Hegel insists that there are different poetries of different nations or areas, each distinct in "spirit, feeling, outlook, expression." The idea that poetry appears through particular words in a unique national lang. and is thus untranslatable was very much a product of the 19th c. It went with the idea of a distinctly national culture, the unprecedented dissemination of a normalized national lang. and the suppression of regional variation through a new school system based on the authorized vernacular. It was an idea that served the mythology of the ethnic unity of the nation-state.

We see yet another important transformation in poetry in Hegel's *Aesthetics*: the rejection of occasional poetry, which is made to answer social needs and demands. Through much of its hist., lyric poetry in particular was socially grounded—it served to praise, blame, petition, insult, and seduce. Such contingency in poetry violated the freedom that Hegel saw at the heart of poetry. The idea that poetry should be an end in itself was to have profound consequences later in the century.

In the 19th c., a few poets could still make a living by writing poetry (Victor Hugo may have been the last), but by and large, poetry came to be seen as an exercise of pure art detached from any pragmatic social ground. Mod. theorists from Theodor Adorno to Pierre Bourdieu have argued that valorizing poetry's disengagement from social utility was itself socially grounded. The putative social autonomy of the poet has remained, however, the general assumption, with the only serious exception being the subordination of poetry to the needs of socialist revolution. Nonsocialist critics consider such poetry potentially propaganda, thus, not true poetry.

Like other cultural products of Europe, this new version of poetry traveled with colonialism and the display of Eur. technological power. The Eur. diasporic cultures of the New World, Africa, and the Pacific kept up by reading and sometimes sending aspiring young poets back to Europe—most often to Paris. From the mid-19th through the early 20th c., Fr. and Eng. poetry was exported to the literate cultures of Asia. In Asia, these imported Eur. trads. competed with and sometimes entirely replaced established literary trads. There was usually a stage during which writers tried to accommodate new Eur. ways of writing in traditional forms, beginning with Tanzimat (Transformation) in Ottoman Turkey in the 1840s. Similar phases came later in Japan, China, South Asia, and the Persian and Ar. world. In some cases, as with the destruction of the culture of Mughal Dehli following the Sepoy Rebellion, political upheaval destroyed the community on which continuity depended. In other cases, the dissatisfaction of young writers with traditional poetic forms led to what was often termed *new poetry*, essentially on a Eur. model (ranging from romanticism to the avant-gardes of the early 20th c.).

In Japan, China, South Asia, and the Islamic world, these versions of *new poetry* entered a tense relationship with the existing older poetry.

The later represented cultural trad., a conservatism that, through the course of the 20th c., increasingly represented nationalism. The former began with its eyes fixed firmly on Western Europe but gradually saw itself as representing an international community of poetry. Both the *new poetry* and the various forms of older poetry were, however, understood as different versions of some universal thing now called *poetry*. Although the terms used for *poetry* were regional and thus asserted continuity with older trads., the semantic range of such terms expanded to accommodate the vague universalism of *poetry*, as used in the various Eur. vernaculars.

Through the 19th c. and early 20th c., Western Eur. poetry was being diffused through the Eur. diaspora, through Eastern Europe and Russia and through the colonies and independent states feeling the weight of Eur. technological power. During this same period, poetry was changing rapidly, primarily in France. One could easily argue that the technology of distribution had become so rapid that, in order to retain their cultural advantage, Fr. poets had continuously to supersede their recent predecessors; they had, in effect, entered a mod., self-conscious fashion system.

It is important to understand the differences in cultural power at this long moment in hist. The Rus. elite visited and stayed in Paris; the Fr. elite by and large did not stay in Moscow or St. Petersburg. If Rus. books were imported to France, they were purchased by Russians; if Fr. books were imported to St. Petersburg, they were purchased by Russians. Rubén Darío went to Paris and brought back a new poetry that began a transformation of Lat. Am. poetry; although the Fr. would eventually become interested in the new Latin Am. poetry, they did not go to Mexico City at the turn of the 20th c.—much less to León, Nicaragua, where Darío became a poet—to get literary inspiration. Orientalists in England, France, and Germany studied cl. Ar., Persian, and Ottoman poetry; their trans. were widely read and appreciated, giving us J. W. Goethe's *West-östlicher Divan* (*West-Eastern Divan*) and Edward FitzGerald's trans. of ʿUmar Khayyām. But (somewhat later), young Ar. and Turkish intellectuals frequented the Fr. bookstores in Alexandria and Istanbul for the latest shipments from Paris. In Alexandria (and often in Paris), C. P. Cavafy was arguably not a "Greek poet," but a very innovative "Western European poet" who wrote in Gr.

An essay by the Am. poet E. A. Poe, "The Poetic Principle," had an immense impact in France. Poetry was to aspire to the condition of music, a pure aesthetic experience of concentrated intensity. Although still tied to the ideology of national lang. in its untranslatability, the lang. of pure poetry was distinct from lang. elsewhere, which was seen as based on utility and social engagement.

From the middle of the 19th c., there was an ever-increasing diversity in the kinds of discourse that were called *poetry*. Paris attempted to assert hegemony in successive versions of an avant-garde and, for much of the world, succeeded until World War II. Such hegemony, however, could be contested from the very beginning of poetic modernity in figures such as Walt Whitman and Emily Dickinson.

Changes in technology and the structures of cultural authority in the second half of the 20th c. and into the 21st c. have profoundly changed the world of poetry. Improvements in the technology of printing and dissemination made the production of poetry less dependent on large publishers with established structures of distribution. The shrinking readership for contemp. poetry simultaneously made publishing poetry less desirable for large publishers. By the end of the 20th c., the Web became an important venue for poetry, with communities of readers no longer in any common physical location but able to communicate with each other—and sometimes with the poets—with great ease.

The literary reviews of an earlier era, in which the judgment of established cultural figures exerted a profound influence on the careers of younger poets, became less important. The rapid expansion of the university system in the second half of the 20th c. made the academy a central force in the evolution of poetry, with a proliferation of critics recovering and publicizing older poetry, passing judgment on contemp. poetry, offering venues for poets giving readings and lectures, and often providing regular employment for poets. The sheer number of such colleges and universities in the New World, Europe, and much of Asia has led to a radically decentered world of poetry. The poetry communities on the Web have increasingly offered challenges to such academic authority.

What is the understanding of poetry that unites diverse practices from *concrete poetry to computer-generated poems to *waka* that follow the sentiments and rules of propriety from a millennium earlier to a traditional Chinese poem in which a father admonishes his son who has asked for money to buy a tape recorder? In each case, a cultural authority of one sort or another can step in and say, "That is *not* poetry." Yet each of the diverse practices of poetry in the early 21st c. derives from some moment in the hist. of the word, and each stakes a claim that excludes some practice of poetry elsewhere.

See POEM.

■ J. W. Mackail, "The Definition of Poetry," *Lectures on Poetry* (1911); J. C. Ransom, "Poetry: A Note in Ontology," *The World's Body* (1938), and "Wanted: An Ontological Critic," *The New Criticism* (1941); M. T. Herrick, *The Fusion of Horatian and Aristotelian Literary Criticism, 1531–1555* (1946), esp. ch. 4; J. J. Donohue, *The Theory of Literary Kinds*, v. 2 (1949); E. C. Pettet, "Shakespeare's Conception of Poetry," *E&S* 3 (1950); Abrams; Curtius, 152–53; R. Wellek, "The Mode of Existence of the Literary Work of Art," Wellek and Warren; C. L. Stevenson, "On 'What Is a Poem?'" *Philosophical Review* 66 (1957); S. Hynes, "Poetry, Poetic, Poem," *CE* 19 (1958); R. Jakobson, "Linguistics and Poetics," Sebeok, rpt. in Jakobson, v. 2; N. A. Greenberg, "The Use of *Poiēma* and *Poiēsis*," *Harvard Studies in Classical Philology* 65 (1961); V. M. Hamm, "The Ontology of the Literary Work of Art," *The Critical Matrix*, ed. P. R. Sullivan (1961)—trans. and paraphrase of Ingarden, continued in *CE* 32 (1970); R. Fowler, "Linguistic Theory and the Study of Literature," *Essays on Style and Language* (1966); J. Levy, "The Meanings of Form and the Forms of Meaning," *Poetics—Poetyka—Poetika*, ed. R. Jakobson et al. (1966); E. M. Zemach, "The Ontological Status of Art Objects," *JAAC* 25 (1966–67); J. A. Davison, *From Archilochus to Pindar* (1968); R. Harriott, *Poetry and Criticism before Plato* (1969); R. Häussler, "Poiema und Poiesis," *Forschungen zur römischen Literatur*, ed. W. Wimmel (1970); D. M. Miller, "The Location of Verbal Art," *Lang&S* 3 (1970); R. Ingarden, *The Literary Work of Art*, trans. G. G. Grabowicz (1973), and *The Cognition of the Literary Work of Art*, trans. R. A. Crowley and K. R. Olson (1973); T. McFarland, "Poetry and the Poem," *Literary Theory and Structure*, ed. F. Brady et al. (1973); J. Buchler, *The Main of Light* (1974); E. Miner, "The Objective Fallacy and the Real Existence of Literature," *PTL* 1 (1976); M. P. Battin, "Plato on True and False Poetry," *JAAC* 36 (1977); J. Margolis, "The Ontological Peculiarity of Works of Art," *JAAC* 36 (1977); Fish, "How to Recognize a Poem When

You See One"; E. H. Falk, *The Poetics of Roman Ingarden* (1981); A. L. Ford, "A Study of Early Greek Terms for Poetry: 'Aoide,' 'Epos,' and 'Poesis,'" *DAI* 42 (1981); J. J. McGann, "The Text, the Poem, and the Problem of Historical Method," *NLH* 12 (1981); W. J. Verdenius, "The Principles of Greek Literary Criticism," *Mnemosyne* 4 (1983); R. Shusterman, *The Object of Literary Criticism* (1984), ch. 3; G. B. Walsh, *The Varieties of Enchantment: Early Greek Views of the Nature of Poetry* (1984); Hollander; T. Clark, "Being in Mime," *MLN* 101 (1986); P. Fry, *A Defense of Poetry: Reflections on the Occasion of Writing* (1995); G. Agamben, *The End of the Poem*, trans. D. Heller-Roazen (1999); D. Heller-Roazen, *Echolalias: On the Forgetting of Language* (2008); A. Grossman, *True-Love: Essays on Poetry and Valuing* (2009).

S. OWEN

POIĒSIS (from the Gr. verb *poieō*, infinitive *poiein*, "to make form"). The verb, not the noun, was prominent in usage first. In the context of poetry, the substantive *poiētēs* (*poet) was long more common than the abstract noun *poiēsis*. Indeed, the art of poetry as such was often denoted as *poiētikē*, from which the discipline of *poetics obtains its name.

In general usage, the verb form *poiein* retained as primary meaning an act of formation and transformation of matter in the cosmic sphere in relation to time. Though ultimately, as a social practice, it involves *technē* (art) and thus belongs to the world of art, *poiēsis* in the sense of making form is still present in the lang. of biology and cybernetics (as in *autopoiesis*, the self-generation of living organisms) or medicine (as in *hematopoiesis*, the process by which bone marrow produces red blood cells).

It is important to observe this primary sense of making form when discussing the term *poiēsis* in the context of poetry and poetics. The poet as *homo faber* (man, the maker) and the poem as the made thing are commonplaces that persist throughout the hist. of Western poetics, often in tension with other formulations that identify the poet as prophet or seer (Lat. *vates*), as a vessel of divine inspiration, or as the transcendent voice of the age.

Esp. when the complement or alternative has been an idealist program for poetry—for instance, the Aristotelian notion of poetry as *mimesis as adapted in the Eur. Ren.—the notion of poetry as poiēsis has held an undiminished power, perhaps because it explains what other programs often cannot: how we encounter a poem as object, how a poem radically alters reality, how a poem is actually made. The hist. of Western poetics includes many episodes in which idealist or even metaphysical claims for poetry are answered (and not necessarily contradicted) by corresponding claims that proceed from poiēsis: e.g., Philip Sidney's fusion of Platonism and Aristotelianism in his *Defence of Poesy* (written ca. 1580, pub. 1595) meets its counterpart in George Puttenham's contemporaneous *Arte of English Poesie* (1589), which begins with this statement: "a poet is as much to say as a maker." A reductive but not inaccurate thesis would have it that this tension between idealist creating and materialist making permeates the entire hist. of signification of the term *poiēsis*.

In the 20th c., renewed attention to poiēsis was the outcome of a modernist aspiration to shake off the burden of the romantic genius. Modernist poetry and crit. often named the poem not as fiction, ideation, or reflection but as new reality in itself; described the poetic act as the making of a new thing; and—in the spirit of Dante's praise of Arnaut Daniel as "miglior fabbro del parlar materno" (a better craftsman of the mother tongue; *Purgatorio* 26.117), echoed in T. S. Eliot's dedication to *The Waste Land* (1922)—celebrated the poet as agent of creation rather than instrument of representation. Crucial here would be the early theoretical texts of Paul Valéry: "The Introduction to the Method of Leonardo da Vinci" (1894) and "Poetry and Abstract Thought" (1939).

In this specific sense, one might discern in modernist thinking something of the emergent notional frame of *poiēsis*. Its most ancient appearance in Homeric Gr. (as *poiein*) pertains primarily to working on matter, shape, or form and only secondarily to abstraction, whereby it might suggest availing or producing forms. As philosophy takes over in the cl. Gr. imaginary, this primary materialist notion of *poiēsis* becomes degraded relative to *praxis* (action) or *dēmiourgia* (creation). Yet it is interesting to note that, in strict etymology, the root reference of *dēmiourgia* bears a sort of communal instrumentalism. As opposed to poiētēs, who encounters form as object, dēmiourgos is one whose work derives its primary meaning from the public sphere, as the word itself shows: *dēmos + ergon*. This ergon (work) covers a range of action: a dēmiourgos can be a seer as much as a doctor.

Arguably because of the Christian invest-ment in the notion of creation out of the absolute, but no doubt also because of the epistemological permutations of Platonism from the Hellenistic era onward, the referential framework that comes to measure the genius of a poet is drawn not from *poiēsis* but from *dēmiourgia*. In Plato, one might say (though in *Timaeus* both notions are intertwined) that dēmiourgos is still in effect a worker who commits an ergon, even if this ergon is the universe itself, while the poet is a shaper who shapes forms. But for Plato, shaping forms is, in the last instance, inevitably misshaping, de-forming—hence, his alarm for the poet as a shaper who *transforms* morals, essentially a po-litical, not ethical, act that leaves no place for the poet but exile from the city. Plato's concern is warranted from the standpoint of what will become the philosophical (and later, theologi-cal) desire to harness an unalterable, inalienable truth. This is because shaping is always altering; thus, to form is always to *transform*, conceived, in a materialist way, as the process of bringing otherness to bear on the world, as opposed to receiving otherness as external authority. In this respect, inherent in the infinitive *poiein* is also an element of destruction, and there is no ex-ternal guarantee that would absolve any poiēsis of the destructive elements of the alteration it performs.

The mod. viewpoint sustains this creative and destructive action in *poiein*. The struggle between what we can abusively call "private" and "public" poetics has not resolved, histori-cally, the social demands posed by the idea of the poet as a shaper of forms. Astonishingly long lasting, the force of Plato's political prejudice has been crucial in the formation of modernity. Discussions of the Platonic dimensions of the term *poiēsis* often restrict themselves to its central invocation in the *Symposium*, where the notion is infused with various permutations of eros. There too, how-ever, the ultimate power of poiēsis consists not in the shaping of form or even the erotic creation and production of life but in the transformation of the soul by virtue of philo-sophical practice. In the usurpation of poiēsis, philosophy defeats poetry yet again.

It is no surprise that, in the long preces-sion of Western thought, whereby the quarrel between poetry and philosophy is relentlessly conducted, the advocates of poiēsis as mate-rial (trans)formation are those who resist the seductions of Platonism and its derivatives. Few, however, explicitly name poiēsis as such to be the matrix of their philosophical pursuit. One such thinker would surely be Giambat-tista Vico, whose *Scienza nuova* (*New Science*, 1725) extends the Ren. rendition of poiēsis beyond the task of *imitatio natura* and indeed inaugurates thinking of hist. as a poetic proj-ect. While it is difficult to speak of Vico's direct philosophical descendants, in retrospect a vast trajectory of strains of thought either in avant-garde poetics (from the 19th c. on) or political aesthetics (esp. heterodox tendencies unfolding out of Hegelian Marxism) engages with similar views of hist. as poiēsis.

However, of all mod. philosophical en-counters with poiēsis specifically, Martin Hei-degger's engagement remains most influential. Although Heidegger's claim to discover the originary meaning of *poiēsis* should be taken lightly, nonetheless his explicit decision to out-maneuver the vast Platonic legacy by turning to the pre-Socratics lends a new aspect to the notion. In Heidegger's texts, poiēsis is invoked as the overcoming of the ancient quarrel be-tween poetry and philosophy by standing for the disclosure (*a-lētheia*) of Being. Already in the *Einführung in die Metaphysik* (*Introduction to Metaphysics*, 1936), Heidegger forwards what will eventually become the central focus of his work: poetry is thought itself (*dichten ist den-ken*), and thereby all philosophical thinking is truly poetic and vice versa. Even if one can trace theological elements in Heidegger's invocation of poiēsis as radical creation, his gesture does, in part, return to the Gr. *poiein* its radical forma-tive force.

This force resonates in discourses of mo-dernity, both aesthetic and political. An en-tire society can be said to engage in poiēsis in its radical moments of self-determination. In this sense, and bearing reference to Vico, poiēsis can be linked to hist. in the making. This making cannot be said to have a precise temporality; hence, traditional methods of historiography cannot grasp it. Its working is a perpetual reworking that would not spare even itself as an object of that work. (The common-place notion of a poem always being at work on itself, on making itself into a poem, should be understood here as an elemental force of poiēsis.) The duration of shaping matter into form, as Henri Bergson would have it, occurs in (or as) a radical present. This is a paradoxi-cal condition, which is why its boundaries exceed the capacity of both narration and symbolization and can only be grasped in a performative vein. The energy of poiēsis is dramatic: literally, to form is to make form happen, to change form—incl. one's own. The social and political substance of poiēsis is thus signified not only by its constitutively transformative power, which would be a mere abstraction, but by the fact that, since its ancient Gr. meaning, it pertains to humanity's immanent (even if perpetually self-altering) encounter with the world.

■ H. Bergson, *The Creative Mind*, trans. M.L.C. Addison (1946); M. Heidegger, *Introduction to Metaphysics* (1936), trans. R. Manheim (1959); H. Maturana and F. Varela, *Autopoiesis and Cognition* (1974); M. Heidegger, *Poetry, Language, Thought*, trans. A. Hofstadter (1976); H.R. Jauss, "Poiesis," trans. M. Shaw, *CritI* 8 (1982); D. W. Price, *History Made, History Imagined: Contemporary Literature, Poiesis, and the Past* (1999); W. V. Spanos, "The Question of Philosophy and Poiesis in the Posthistorical Age: Thinking/Imagining the Shadow of Metaphysics," *Boundary 2* 27 (2000); T. Martin, *Poiesis and Possible Worlds: A Study in Modality and Literary Theory* (2004); J. Hölzl, *Transience: A Poiesis, of Dis/appearance* (2010); S. K. Levine, *Poiesis: The Language of Psychology and the Speech of the Soul* (2011).

S. GOURGOURIS

POINT OF VIEW. *See* PERSONA; VOICE.

POLYPTOTON (Gr., "word in many cases"; Lat. *traductio*). Related to the varieties of simple word repetition or iteration, which in cl. rhet. are treated under the genus of ploce, is another class of figures that repeat a word or words by varying their word class (part of speech) or by giving different forms of the same root or stem. Shakespeare takes great interest in this device; it increases patterning without wearying the ear, and it takes advantage of the differing functions, energies, and positionings that different word classes are permitted in speech. Schaar says that Shakespeare uses polyptoton "almost to excess," "using derivatives of more than a hundred stems" in the sonnets. Some of these are but natural in the amplification of any theme, e.g., *love—lov'st—beloved—loving—love's—lovers*, though it is obvious in other cases that the figuration is intentional, as in sonnet 43:

And darkly bright, are bright in dark directed.
Then thou, whose shadow shadows doth make bright—
How would thy shadow's form form happy show
To the clear day with thy much clearer light.

To Shakespeare's hundred forms in 154 sonnets, compare Philip Sidney's 45 in the 108 of *Astrophil and Stella*, Edmund Spenser's 27 in the 89 *Amoretti*, and Pierre de Ronsard's 63 in the 218 of *Amours* I.

Transferred to *prosody, polyptoton at line end becomes, mutatis mutandis, a type of rhyme that also avails itself of grammatical categories, which was known to the *rhétoriqueurs* as *rime grammaticale*. To us now, this does not seem true rhyme, but standards for acceptability in rhyming have varied from age to age.

Very similar to polyptoton is antanaclasis, repetition of a word with a shift in meaning. By using two forms of a word, antanaclasis can play on two senses of it and thereby generate homonymic puns. Shifting the meaning of the word without repeating it, the shift being entailed by a second predicate or modifier, is the function of the elusive syllepsis. Recognition of all these forms suggests that we should construct a taxonomy of the varieties of word repetition as given (albeit often confusedly) in cl. and Ren. rhet. Four types seem distinguishable: repetition of the same word, in the same grammatical form, with the same meaning (ploce and epizeuxis); same word, same form, different meaning (antanaclasis); same word, different form, same meaning (polyptoton); same word, different form, different meaning (sometimes called antanaclasis, sometimes polyptoton). Here, however, one must define *word* and *form* carefully. Also related is anthimeria—another favorite of Shakespeare's—the turning of one part of speech into another, particularly the making of verbs out of nouns.

Some rhetoricians have used *traductio* in the sense not of polyptoton but of ploce, or direct word repetition (see Quintilian, *Institutio oratoria* 9.3.68–73); one should, therefore, be explicit about definitions when using any of these terms.

■ M. Joseph, *Shakespeare's Use of the Arts of Language* (1947); C. Schaar, *An Elizabethan Sonnet Problem* (1960); L. A. Sonnino, *Handbook to Sixteenth-Century Rhetoric* (1968); Group μ, 124–26; A. Quinn, *Figures of Speech* (1982);

Vickers; B. Vickers, *Classical Rhetoric in English Poetry*, 2d ed. (1989)—esp. 129–30, 146–48; Corbett; M. E. Auer, "'Und eine Freiheit macht uns alle Frei!' Das Polyptoton in Schillers Freiheitsdenken," *Monatshefte für Deutschsprachige Literatur und Kultur* 100 (2008); V. Langer, "De la métamorphose," *Esprit généreux, esprit pantagruélique*, ed. R. Leushuis and Z. Zalloua (2008).

T.V.F. BROGAN

POLYSYNDETON (Gr., "much compounded"). The repetition of conjunctions, normally *and*; the opposite of *asyndeton, which is the omission of conjunctions; common in all kinds of poetry. Quintilian (*Institutio oratoria* 9.3.51–54) remarks, however, that "the source of [both figures] is the same, as they render what we say more vivacious and energetic, exhibiting an appearance of vehemence, and of passion bursting forth as it were time after time," citing, as an illustration, "Both house, and household gods, and arms, and Amyclaean dog, and quiver formed of Cretan make" (Virgil, *Georgics* 3.344–45). Longinus discusses both figures, differentiating them. Mod. rhetorical theorists point out that, in addition to a sense of breathlessness, polysyndeton may add emphasis to the items in an enumeration or may represent the "flow and continuity of experience" (Corbett). Conversely, Quinn observes that by slowing down a sentence, polysyndeton may add "dignity" to it or produce an incantatory effect. The latter usage may explain the numerous examples of polysyndeton often cited in the Bible (e.g., Gen. 1:24–25; Rev. 13:1). Examples may be found in Horace, *Odes* 15; in Petrarch, *Canzoniere* 61 (polysyndeton is a major structuring device in Petrarch's poetry); in Shakespeare, sonnet 66; in Walt Whitman; and in T. S. Eliot's "Journey of the Magi" (11–15). Group μ, which classifies polysyndeton among metataxes, i.e., as a figure of repetitive addition affecting syntax, explains the effect in the Eliot passage as "responsible for the harmony of the sentence and the metrical scheme of the verse. This is not by chance, since . . . harmony and metrics are systematic groups of practices and rules, two vast syntactic figures that proceed by addition and repetition." In some cases, then, the polysyndeton may contribute to rhythm. Although polysyndeton in Eng. poetry mainly involves the repetition of *and*, examples occur in which other conjunctions repeat, as in Eliot's "The Love Song of J. Alfred Prufrock"

(101–2), though these are disputed, since they do not give the same effect; cf. Milton, whose Satan "pursues his way/And swims or sinks, or wades, or creeps, or flies" (*Paradise Lost* 2.949–50) or *Othello* 3.3.77–80, where a series of *ors* offer logical alternatives.

See HYPOTAXIS AND PARATAXIS.

■ Group μ; A. Quinn, *Figures of Speech* (1982); J. P. Houston, *Shakespearean Sentences* (1988); Corbett.

T.V.F. BROGAN; A. W. HALSALL

PROSE POEM. The extreme conventions of 18th-c. Fr. neoclassicism, with its strict rules for the differentiation of poetry from prose, are to be blamed—or, depending on one's point of view, thanked—for the controversially hybrid and (aesthetically and politically) revolutionary genre of the prose poem. With its oxymoronic title and its form based on contradiction, the prose poem is suitable to an extraordinary range of perception and expression, from the ambivalent (in content as in form) to the mimetic and the narrative or anecdotal. Let's come down clearly on the side of gratefulness, since the prose poem occasions a rapidly increasing interest. Its principal characteristics are those that would ensure unity even in brevity and poetic quality even without the line breaks of *free verse: high patterning, rhythmic and figural repetition, sustained intensity, and compactness. The short form is a sure model here; otherwise, the prose poem merges with the essay.

Generally speaking, the prose poem represents a field of vision, only to be, on occasion, cut off abruptly. Emotion is contracted under the force of ellipsis, so deepened and made dense. The rhapsodic mode and what Charles Baudelaire called the "prickings of the unconscious" are, in the most interesting examples, combined with the metaphoric and the ontological. So the prose poem aims at knowing or finding out something not accessible under the more restrictive conventions of verse (Beaujour). It is frequently the manifestation of a willfully self-sufficient form characterized above all by its brevity. It is often spatially interesting (D. Scott). For some critics, it is necessarily intertextual (Riffaterre); for others, politically oriented (Monroe). It is, in any case, not necessarily "poetic" in the traditional sense of the *lyric and can even indulge in an engaging wit.

The prose poem is usually considered to date from Aloysius Bertrand's *Gaspard de la*

Nuit (1842), though he was writing prose poems earlier, and to be marked by heavy traces of Fr. symbolism and conditioned by the stringency of the Fr. separation of genres. Among its antecedents are the poeticized prose verses of the Bible, of cl. and folk lyrics, and of other foreign verse; the poeticized prose of such romantics as Chateaubriand and the prose passages of William Wordsworth's *Lyrical Ballads*; as well as the intermixtures of verse and prose in Maurice de Guérin's "Le Centaure," Ludwig Tieck's *Reisegedichte eines Kranken*, and Charles Augustin Sainte-Beuve's *Alexandrin familier*. Characteristically, it was the romantics who came to the defense of this hybrid form: Victor Hugo's plea for the *mélange des genres* (mixture of genres) in his preface to *Cromwell* is the natural counterpart to Jules-Amédée Barbey d'Aurevilly's apology for the prose poem. A case could be made for certain manifestos as the natural extension of the prose poem into a form fitted for display.

Perhaps the most celebrated example of the prose poem is Baudelaire's *Petits Poèmes en prose*, or *Le Spleen de Paris* (begun 1855, pub. 1869), in which he pays tribute to Bertrand for originating the genre. Baudelaire's texts can complicate figuration to the point of "figuring us" as reader (Johnson, in Caws and Riffaterre). His "Thyrse" offers female poetic windings and arabesques around an upright male prose pole as the highly eroticized primary metaphor of mixing, while the *Petits poèmes* themselves are at once anecdotal and intimate, to the point of mixing the self with the subject. Arthur Rimbaud's *Illuminations* (written 1872–76) celebrate with extraordinary intensity the emergence of poems from less intimate matter, a newness dynamic in its instantaneity, yet the precursor of the aesthetic of suddenness practiced by Hugo von Hofmannsthal in his *Philosophie des Metaphorischen*—the speed of the metaphor is an "illumination in which, for just a moment, we catch a glimpse of the universal analogy"—and by imagists such as Ezra Pound. Rimbaldian confusion of first- and third-person perspective ("the lyric process of undergoing oneself and the more properly novelistic business of mapping out a behavior," according to C. Scott) sets up, together with his notational rapidity, a kind of vibratory instant. Stéphane Mallarmé's *Divagations* (begun 1864, pub. 1897) with their intricate inwindings of metaphor, Comte de Lautréamont's *Chants de Maldoror* (the first canto in 1868, the rest pub. posthumously in

1879), lush with a sort of fruity violence, André Gide's *Nourritures terrestres* (Earthy eats, 1897), and Paul Claudel's *Connaissance de l'est* (Knowing the East, 1900), nostalgic and suggestively pictorial, lead to Paul Valéry's *Alphabet* (1912), whose form has been compared to what Valéry later calls, speaking of the dual function of discourse, "the coming and going between two worlds" (Lawler).

Elsewhere, the prose poem flourishes with a different cast: early on, in Switzerland, with Salomon Gessner (*Idylls*, 1756); in Germany, with Novalis and Friedrich Hölderlin, then Stefan George, R. M. Rilke, Franz Kafka, Ernst Bloch, and recently, in former East Germany, Helga Novak; in Austria, Hofmannsthal, Peter Altenberg, and Alfred Polgar; in Belgium, Emile Verhaeren; in England, Thomas De Quincey, Thomas Lovell Beddoes, Oscar Wilde, and the imagists; in Russia, Ivan Turgeynev and the Rus. futurists, esp. Velimir Khlebnikov; in Italy, the cubo-futurists such as F. T. Marinetti; in Spain, Gustavo Adolfo Bécquer, Juan Ramón Jiménez, and Luis Cernuda; in Latin America, recently, Jorge Luis Borges, Pablo Neruda, and Octavio Paz; and in Denmark, J. P. Jacobsen.

Modernist writing as practiced in France after symbolism and postsymbolism increasingly problematized the genre; the so-called cubist poets Max Jacob, Pierre Reverdy, and Blaise Cendrars each gave a particular slant to the prose poem, emphasizing respectively its "situation," its strangely reticent irresolution, and its simultaneous perceptions. The Fr. surrealists Paul Éluard, André Breton, and Robert Desnos provide a rich nostalgia and revelatory illumination by means of a startling juxtaposition of images; Gertrude Stein's *Tender Buttons* reaches a height of the lyric and the everyday held in tension, taking its energy from the androgynous. Among recent 20th- and 21st-c. Fr. poets, René Char, Saint-John Perse, and Francis Ponge, and then Yves Bonnefoy, Jacques Dupin, and Michel Deguy prove the sustained vigor of the genre, proved equally in the U.S. (after Walt Whitman, of course), by such prose poets as James Wright, Robert Bly, W. S. Merwin, Russell Edson, John Ashbery, and John Hollander, and such Language poets (after Stein and W. C. Williams) as Charles Bernstein.

See VERS LIBRE.

■ V. Clayton, *The Prose Poem in French Literature of the Eighteenth Century* (1936);

G. Díaz-Plaja, *El poema en prosa en España* (1956); S. Bernard, *Le Poème en prose de Baudelaire jusqu'á nos jours* (1959); M. Parent, *Saint-John Perse et quelques devanciers* (1960); U. Fülleborn, *Das deutsche Prosagedicht* (1970); D. Katz, "The Contemporary Prose Poem in French: An Anthology with English Translations and an Essay on the Prose Poem," *DAI* 31 (1970), 2921A; R. Edson, "The Prose Poem in America," *Parnassus* 5 (1976); U. Fülleborn, *Deutsche Prosagedichte des 20. Jahrhunderts* (1976); *The Prose Poem: An International Anthology*, ed. M. Benedikt (1976); C. Scott, "The Prose Poem and Free Verse," *Modernism*, ed. M. Bradbury and J. McFarlane (1976); D. Lehman, "The Marriage of Poetry and Prose," *DAI* 39, 8A (1979): 4938; K. Slott, "Poetics of the 19th-Century French Prose Poem," *DAI* 41, 3A (1980): 1075; J. Holden, "The Prose Lyric," *Ohio Review* 24 (1980); D. Keene, *The Modern Japanese Prose Poem* (1980); B. Johnson, *The Critical Difference* (1981), ch. 3; S. H. Miller, "The Poetics of the Postmodern American Prose Poem," *DAI* 42 (1981): 2132; R. E. Alexander, "The American Prose Poem, 1890–1980," *DAI* 44, 2A (1983): 489; *The Prose Poem in France: Theory and Practice*, ed. M. A. Caws and H. Riffaterre (1983)—13 essays on Fr. and Eng.; D. Scott, "La structure spatiale du poème en prose," *Poètique* 59 (1984); U. Fülleborn, *Deutsche Prosagedichte vom 18. Jahrhundert bis zur letzten Jahrhundertwende* (1985); S. H. Miller, "John Ashbery's Prose Poem," *American Poetry* 3 (1985); M. Perloff, *The Dance of the Intellect* (1985); D. Wesling, *The New Poetries* (1985), ch. 6; M. S. Murphy, "Genre as Subversion: The Prose Poem in England and America," *DAI* 46 (1986): 1932A; R. G. Cohn, *Mallarmé's Prose Poems* (1987); J. Kittay and W. Godzich, *The Emergence of Prose* (1987); J. Monroe, *A Poverty of Objects: The Prose Poem and the Politics of Genre* (1987); R. Silliman, *The New Sentence* (1987); J. Simon, *The Prose Poem as a Genre in 19th-Century European Literature* (1987); S. Fredman, *Poet's Prose*, 2nd ed. (1990); M. Delville, *The American Prose Poem: Poetic Form and the Boundaries of Genre* (1998); *Great American Prose Poems: From Poe to the Present*, ed. D. Lehman (2003).

M. A. CAWS

PROSODY (Gr. *prosodia*, originally the musical part of a song, "tune"; later, the marking of accents; Lat. *accentus*, "song added to speech").

I. Introduction
II. Elements, Structure, System
III. Analysis
IV. Prose and Free Verse
V. Linguistic Prosody and Literary Studies

I. Introduction. Traditionally, prosody is the study of measurable structures of *sound in language and in poetry. Linguistic prosody is concerned with describing and explaining the structure and function of the suprasegmentals in lang., those aspects—pitch, duration, loudness, and juncture—that produce the contoured streams of sound by which the *segments* are voiced. Literary prosody was traditionally the study of prose rhythm and *versification. From the 19th c., prosody began a slow expansion toward inclusion of other levels of organization, as verse experimentation, reactions to metricality, and the rise of *free verse shifted importance to qualitative sound (see below), which increasingly performed many of the binding functions of verse design formerly associated solely with *meter. In addition, the visual patterning of verse joined prosody, as the visible aspects of printed poems also performed prosodic functions (see VISUAL POETRY). With generative and functional ling., prosody has now come to include the hierarchy of structures, up to the *stanza, built from nonphonological elements affected by the phonological system (see Ross 2008). Since poetry is a verbal design using linguistic material, literary prosody has benefited enormously from the concepts, categories, and analytic approaches of ling. An objective attention to the lang. object, detailed and overarching, enriches the literary critic's apprehension and understanding of aesthetic elements, forms, and processes that work with and on lang. and form.

II. Elements, Structure, System. Prosody belongs to the phonological system, the lowest order system interacting with and affecting the morphological, syntactical, and semantic systems. An influential theory, articulated by Paul Kiparsky (in Fabb et al.), regards prosody in all langs. as characterized by four interactive systems: (1) periodicity, or repetitive patterning in alternating stresses by a set of processes that maintains the periodic return; (2) constituency, or grouping of stresses into feet—strong/weak or weak/strong—depending on the lang.; (3) maximal articulation, or hierarchical grouping into several levels of larger groups, each comprised of smaller bundles, e.g., syllables into words, words into phrases, and (in poetry) feet into half lines, half lines into lines, lines into couplets, and so on; and (4) even distribution, or balancing the phrase or line, by regulating where heavy and light units may be positioned to maintain a sense of equal order (see Lerdahl and Jakendoff for an opposing theory based on a musical metaphor instead of on the constituency metaphor). These systems include the lang. of poetry. Ross (2008) has recently combined these four systems to yield two prosodic structuring systems: sectioning and arraying. The first includes the first three of Kiparsky's systems, and the second speaks to the fourth, wherein the entire system of a poem contains an array of prosodies (elements functioning in and as patterns) distributed in an organized fashion for aesthetic texture and effects. Recalling earlier critics' metaphor for poetic texture as woven tapestry, Ross includes the qualitative structures (segmentals) and sees these as a set of overlays the analyst can look at one by one, group by group, as he or she lays them down over others. Boundaries are then the intersections, the "cusps" of rhythmic shape where the features relevant to poetic meaning and effect are made prominent. These are the areas of density that rise into prominence in the reader's perception to become salient features for interpretation (see Ross). In addition, Gil and Shoshany and others regard pragmatic and rhetorical features as part of the prosodic system at the higher hierarchical levels.

Sound is produced by the breathing and vocal apparatus of the physical body and is felt as vibration and resonance for semantic, emotive, and aesthetic effects. Temporal and measurable, sound is energy in the form of waves. It becomes meaningful in lang. when perceived by users as consisting of elements and structures of the phonological system. As temporal, the structural units (e.g., feet, phrases) have perceptual isochrony (though not actual isochrony) and *rhythm. The more rhythmic a passage of lang., the greater the tendency toward isochrony, with metered verse bearing the closest perceptual equivalence among units and groupings of units. The tendency toward isochrony is a feature of lang., but in poetry, the more highly regular the recurrence of units from which a pattern is built, the closer the tendency toward approximation. While some theorists disagree that isochrony operates in lang. testing of perception by actual hearers gives evidence that

perception counts as much as actual phonic measurement. What is important is the perception of isochrony, the felt equivalence of time, as in music. Similarly, with sound in written texts, what counts is the perceptual experience of sound "heard" by readers of poetry and rhythmic prose as an approximate equivalence of timing with which a performance's phrasing works as the baseline for expansive expression (Lehiste; Bolinger).

Segmentals are the smallest units of lang., the *phones* or actual sounds represented somewhat inaccurately in Eng. by the letters or *graphemes* (though the *graph* is important in some visual prosody). Phones are the important elements of the segmental patterns in poetry; they make up the figures of speech that are repetitions of sound for the sake of sound (e.g., *alliteration, *assonance, *rhyme), permitting a range of rhythmic expressivity. Suprasegmentals are the components that comprise the measurable production of sound, because they exist in time: loudness (intensity, volume), duration (length), pitch (tone or fundamental frequency), and juncture (markers of boundary and linkage among segments and groupings). They are the phonological components of lang., working together in various ways in the different langs. to give shape—contour, grouping, and boundary. They are said to be *over* (*supra*) the segments because they are the sound occurring when the various groupings of linguistic segments are spoken. They produce coherence, make meaningful distinctions, foreground information, and indicate where emotional interest lies. The three components of temporal sound—pitch, loudness, and duration—are most often found in combination, but in varying degrees in the different langs. and situations. One of these three components is characteristically dominant in a lang.: e.g., Japanese keeps syllabic length even and the pitch range narrow so as not to be an influence over the syllable, but tonic pitch, as in Chinese, may distinguish the words that otherwise sound and are written the same. By contrast in Eng. a different aspect of pitch—relative change in frequency—is meaningful. Sound prominence in langs. like Eng. is also called *accent or stress. Syllables in the nonprominent range are called *unaccented* or *unstressed*. Stress, still the term most frequently used in common parlance, is perhaps the least accurate because of its more general meaning as emphasis or prominence and because of its long association with loudness, which was mistakenly thought until

50 years ago to be the most important factor in realizing prominence. Instead, pitch change (not *a* pitch) is the most frequent and reliable indicator of prosodic prominence, occurring in 99% of cases of prominent syllables, with loudness and/or length also a factor though not always both (see Fry 1955; Ladefoged). Like musical notes, pitch change in lang. can be heard as rises and falls from the pitch level on which nonprominent syllables occur within the range of the specific speaking voice. Loudness and length also change relative to the nonprominent level of voicing, but these can be artificially produced in such a way as to throw the perception off, without a true change in prominence.

When distributed among nonprominent syllables, prominence shapes the sound of lang. The more regular the distribution of peaks, the more rhythmic the lang., with meter defining the extreme of greatest regularity. The suprasegmental system places some syllables into a nonprominent range and thrusts other syllables onto peaks, but a highly rhythmic system will tend to draw the linguistic prominence system into the overlaid poetic system, causing prominence peaks to be promoted or demoted in level. This is the reason meter, which counts only two levels of prominence (strong and weak), and rhythm, which counts more, are distinguished by literary analysts. Most agree that there are four perceptual levels of stress in Eng.: primary, secondary, tertiary, and nonprominent (see Chomsky and Halle; Halliday; see Bolinger on three-level perceptual system; Gates 1987 on why a three-level system is not always adequate). The prosodic shape that is spread over groupings is called either an accentual, a stress, a prominence, or an intonation *contour*, depending on what aspects of the prosodic system are under consideration. Chomsky and Halle termed the contour unit the *phonological phrase*, aligning it with the syntactic phrase, which they believed motivated prominence. The "phrase" is now often thought of as akin to the musical phrase, which distributes the tonal shape of an information unit (Halliday), or as a unit of emotional interest as recognized by the speaker (Bolinger). More recently, there is agreement that information is sectioned into "chunks" because the brain appears to process it that way, in both the making and receiving modes (Ross 2008). The chunks present the way the speaker is thinking about the information's importance as foreground and background. A chunk may have up to five or six prominence peaks,

a number which appears to correspond to the brain's processing limit. This limit matches that noticed by Chomsky and Halle, and it matches the upper number of peaks in poetic lines in the world's langs.—besides the pentameter, the line has a strong tendency to group into three and three (*hexameter), three and four (*fourteener), etc. But in poetry, these chunked linguistic groupings coexist with the rhythmic groupings, working sometimes within, sometimes across the established rhythmical set of a poem. The cross-structuring creates potentials for vocal realizations that open up a multivalent, polysemantic verbal design. The dual systems' additional key functions are to indicate poetic *genre; give pleasure; provide cohesion; compose structure; and support, undercut, inflect, and reflect meaning (see TONE).

The fourth suprasegmental—juncture—gives boundary to syllables, words, phrases, "chunks" and at the same time indicates how they are to be joined. Silence is the aspect of juncture most relevant to poetic analysis, emerging, for instance, in and around *caesura, line ending (pause, *enjambment), and word boundaries that cut across the perception of foot boundaries (e.g., *The form was steady*, in iambic pentameter, where *steady* crosses the fourth into the fifth iambic foot). In visual prosody, juncture is often the most prominent of the suprasegmentals, with spacing indicating silence, lack, drama; appearing instead of punctuation; and functioning in all manner of expressive, rhetorical, and semantic ways.

Qualitative prosody refers to phonic (vs. phonemic) cohesion: e.g., repetition of consonantal sounds, vowel sounds, and groupings of sounds from two phones to syntactic units (e.g., *br, str, I saw the, out of the, down from the, Turning and turning*). Qualitative sound patterning is rhyming in its broadest sense (Kiparsky in Fabb, et al., for a componential view of rhyme). Whereas quantitative sound patterns are paralinguistic, operating to organize meaning for coherence *over* a segment of lang., qualitative sound patterns function to provide cohesion among units and groups *within* a text. Ross (1999) views these two types as "interpenetrating" prosodies. And while linguistic sound systems function largely to gather and focus meaning and tone for communication, when density of features is high enough to foreground lang. itself (Jakobson's poetic function), rhythm works to restrain linear forward progression, thrusting the mind back on repetition, drawing the reader/auditor away from sense into the flow that is rhythm itself. It is the nature of poetic lang. to move against and counteract the semantic system, and it is the principal characteristic, function, and effect of poetry (Jakobson; Kristeva—both in Cook).

III. Analysis. What literary prosody keeps to the fore is the dialectic between rhythm and code (i.e., between semiotic and symbolic, felt and rational modes). When prosody is left out of poetic analysis and interpretation, what is left is impoverished as aesthetic crit.

The tension created by the pull of a lang. system's features and functions against the way a verbal artist uses, exploits, and pressures the system has been regarded for the past 100 years as the main subject of the study of literature *as literature.* Variety in prominence levels that pressures the ideal metrical pattern, along with other pressuring features, has been valued since New Criticism and other varieties of formalism described and privileged tensive forces in its valuations. While the theory wars and debates over the *canon in the postmod. period gave pause to aesthetic study in the U.S., cognitive stylistics, which studies the way poetic elements, structures, and functions are processed in the mind, has generated a body of research from data on actual readers' understanding that demonstrates how the tensions are created by the semantic associations that all words carry. Words with similar sound features and similar sets of semantic features will create convergence, while words with similar sound features and very different semantic features will create divergence, with a range of lower to higher between these extremes (Tsur). Tension results from aggregates of features that possess varying degrees of sound, semantic, and/or syntactic clash: e.g., in W. B. Yeats's "The Wild Swans at Coole" the rhyming words "rings" and "wings" converge in terms of their grammatical status as nouns, but the shapes of the two objects are divergent: rings are circular and stable, wings are blade-shaped and associated with motion. So there is a satisfaction of similarity in sound and grammar, but also an emotional intensity in the small dissimilarity of the initial phones and the greater clash of the two objects drawn into semantic relation. The lines are thereby texturally entwined, so that they produce an emotional intensity higher than the normative emotional interest a prominence word acquires in the normative intonation/information system of the Eng. lang. (Hollander on "mounting" prominence; Gates

1987 on "surmounting" prominence; Bolinger on the heightening of emotion when the normal pitch range is exceeded).

It could be said that Yeats is making "rings" (in two senses, phonic and semantic) of qualitative sound in end and internal rhymes:

> And scatter wheeling in great broken rings
>   Upon their clamorous wings.

The *-ing* of *rings* circles back and also chimes with *wheeling*, and again with *wings. And, scat-*, and *clam-* make another cohesive pattern, and *Up-* and *-ous* yet another, holding the lines in close relation through assonance, creating the beauty and pleasure of ordering, as in music, while also, some might argue, imitating the repetitive circling of which the lines speak. There is, however, tension as well, in that only some of the syllables rhyme; and in the differing parts of speech drawn together in rhyme. The open vowels, *a* in *great* and *o* in *open* and *clamorous,* work contrastively, in tension, with the *e* and short *i* sounds to round and open out the sonorous quality of the lines, giving an expansiveness to accompany the repeated closing in of circularity. Morphological, syntactic, and semantic features brought into sound cohesion both unify and clash, initiating perceptual experiences that serve to signal the poetic function of play, of genre, of pleasure, of tension, of meaning (see Tsur; Ross 1999).

IV. Prose and Free Verse. Since lang. has prosody, prosody may be artistically shaped in prose as well as in verse. Ancient Gr. and Rom. orators elaborated at length on how to use rhythm for persuasion in grammar, music, and rhet. (Cicero, Quintilian, Augustine; Aristotle cautioned against too much rhythm). The marks of punctuation, capitalization, and paragraphing originated as a graphic system to mark writing for oral performance. Med. writers continued to develop prose rhythm as part of rhet. (e.g., *cursus in ars dictaminis* and *ars praedicandi*); rhetorical handbooks included prosody through the 19th c.; and prosodic patterning continues to be taught in some schools as part of prose composition, though without the elaborations of the earlier centuries. Mod. free verse makes use of prose rhythm, beginning with Walt Whitman's 1855 ed. of *Leaves of Grass,* which, according to one theory, marked breath pauses with dots in the manner recommended by 19th-c. rhetorical manuals (Hollis). In the eds. following the first, Whitman dropped the dot-marking system and used the standard system of punctuation to mark off rhythmic units (Gates 1985). Emily Dickinson used the dash for many junctures in lieu of standard punctuation early on. Stéphane Mallarmé, follower of Whitman's practice and an inventor of the *prose poem, declared that prose did not exist—"There is alphabet, and then there are verses which are more or less closely knit, more or less diffuse. So long as there is a straining toward style, there is versification." Some 20th-c. poets created systems of punctuation for distinctive prosodic styles, in some cases omitting it entirely (e.g., e. e. cummings, W. S. Merwin in some of his work). W. C. Williams wrote in a system of the prose unit he called at first the *variable foot*, later revised to the *relative measure*, which produced cultural, social, and poetic meanings and effects (Cushman 1985; Steele; Gates). The prosodies of dramatists and fiction writers have also been examined as part of their prose styles (e.g., G. B. Shaw, Henry James, Ernest Hemingway, Thomas Wolfe, Annie Dillard). Varieties of free verse range from highly cadenced prose to mixed meters (the majority of free verse today) to prosodies made of the appearance or sounds of graphs and phonemes. The prose poem is without the highly regular prosody of meter, but its qualitative and rhythmic qualities provide the cohesion that meter and narrative give in other genres. The resources of mod. ling. make intensive analysis of these forms possible. As in poetry but in lesser degree, the regularity of prosodic styling in prose and free verse promotes attention to the qualitative and quantitative sound systems, enhancing perceptual attention, heightening emotion, and working the felt experience to some effect.

V. Linguistic Prosody and Literary Studies.
Ling. continues to develop highly sophisticated understandings of prosody. The structuralists' failed attempt to discover a universal system has been recuperated by a somewhat different inquiry into the possibility of constructing a universal prosody in the form of a set of obligatory and optional rules for poetries in all langs. As with the structuralist project, the effort is yielding detailed knowledge about lang. and poetic systems, whether or not the end goal can be reached. While the literary historian and critic need not know ling. prosody

theory, drawing from the systematic knowledge of linguists changes what can be analyzed, and so greatly assists interpretation. To ignore the functions and effects of the sound system is to risk less complete, less insightful understanding.
■ D. Fry, "Experiments in the Reception of Stress," and "Duration and Intensity as Physical Correlates," *Journal of the Acoustical Society of America* 28 (1955); P. Ladefoged, *Elements of Acoustic Phonetics* (1962); Chatman; Chomsky and Halle; M. K. Halliday, *Halliday: System and Function in Language*, ed. G. Kress (1976); I. Lehiste, "Isochrony Reconsidered," *Journal of Acoustics* 5 (1977); C. Hartman, *Free Verse: An Essay on Prosody* (1980); Attridge, *Rhythms*; C. Hollis, *Language and Style in "Leaves of Grass"* (1983); F. Lerdahl and R. Jackendoff, *A Generative Theory of Tonal Music* (1983); D. Gil and R. Shoshany, "On the Scope of Prosodic Theory," *Discussion Papers, Fifth International Phonology Meeting*, ed. W. Pfeiffer and J. Rennison (1984); Hollander; S. Cushman, *William Carlos Williams and the Meanings of Measure* (1985); R. Gates, "The Identity of American Free Verse: The Prosodic Study of Whitman's 'Lilacs'," *Lang&S* 18 (1985); D. Bolinger, *Intonation and Its Parts* (1986); *The Linguistics of Writing: Arguments between Language and Literature*, ed. N. Fabb, D. Attridge, A. Durant, C. Mac-Cabe (1987); R. Gates, "Forging an American Poetry from Speech Rhythms: Williams after Whitman," *PoT* 8.3–4 (1987); T. Steele, *Missing Measures* (1990); R. Gates, "T.S. Eliot's Prosody and the Free Verse Tradition: Restricting Whitman's 'Free Growth of Metrical Laws'," *PoT* 11.3 (1991); R. Tsur, *Toward a Theory of Cognitive Poetics* (1992); S. Cushman, *Fictions of Form in American Poetry* (1993); D. Gil, "'Il pleut doucement sur la ville': The Rhythm of a Metaphor," *PoT* 14.1 (1993); H. Gross, *Sound and Form in Modern Poetry*, 2d ed. (1996); G. Cooper, *Mysterious Music: Rhythm and Free Verse* (1998); C. Scott, *The Poetics of French Verse: Studies in Reading* (1998); H. Ross, "Beauty—How Hopkins Pied It," *Language Sciences* 21 (1999); V. Shemtov, "Metrical Hybridization: Prosodic Ambiguities As a Form of Social Dialogue," *PoT* 22.1 (2001); J. Cook, *Poetry in Theory* (2004); T. Wharton and D. Wilson, "Relevance and Prosody," *Journal of Pragmatics* 38, no. 10 (2006); M. Hurley, "The Pragmatics of Prosody," *Style* 41.1 (2007); H. Ross, "Structural Prosody," *Cognitive Poetics* 1.2 (2008).

R. WINSLOW

PROSOPOPOEIA (Gr. *prosopon*, "face," "person," and *poiein* "to make"). The speech of an imaginary person. A term still used for *personification—the attribution of human qualities to animals or inanimate objects—to which it is closely allied. Pierre Fontanier, however, argues, prosopopoeia "must not be confused with personification, apostrophe or dialogism . . . [since it] consists in staging, as it were, absent, dead, supernatural or even inanimate beings. These are made to act, speak, answer as is our wont" (Riffaterre 1985). As a means of making a speech "vivid" or lively, Fontanier's definition agrees with that of the Tudor rhetoricians, who placed prosopopoeia in the list of figures that included *prosopographia, characterismus, ethopoeia* (which together give us our notions of fictional portraiture); mimesis of gesture, pronunciation, and utterance; and *dialogismus* or *sermocinatio*, by which an imaginary person is given the ability to speak. In antiquity, *prosopopoeiae* were school exercises in which writers took on the persona of a famous historical or mythological figure in a composition with the end of exhibiting his character (cf. Quintilian 3.8.49). At times, however, both rhetorical and poetic theoreticians use prosopopoeia far more expansively to indicate the vivid presentation of something absent or imaginary before the eye and ear. The example given by Quintilian (9.3.89), "Avarice is the mother of cruelty," shows that prosopopoeia exists as a *trope at the basic levels of *metaphor or axiom. Likewise, P. de Man calls prosopopoeia "the master trope of poetic discourse" (1986), because it posits "voice or face by means of language" (1984). Thus, prosopopoeia operates like a mask and is analogous to any adoption of *persona. To address an imaginary person as if present engages the figure of *apostrophe; however, J. Douglas Kneale insists that prosopopoeia is the more appropriate term. Historically, apostrophe is defined as a "turning away" from the primary audience; thus, Kneale argues, unified addresses, such as William Blake's "The Sick Rose," P. B. Shelley's "Ode to the West Wind," and John Keats's "Ode on a Grecian Urn," are all prosopopoeiae because they infer the possibility of reply.

■ Fontanier; P. de Man, "Autobiography as De-Facement," *The Rhetoric of Romanticism* (1984); P. de Man, "Hypogram and Inscription," *The Resistance to Theory* (1986); M. Riffaterre, "Prosopopoeia," *YFS* 69 (1985); J. D. Kneale, "Romantic Aversions: Apostrophe Reconsidered," *ELH* 58 (1991).

T.V.F. BROGAN; A. W. HALSALL; J. S. SYCHTERZ

PROVERB. A traditional saying, pithily or wittily expressed. Proverbial expression is traditionally given to customs and legal and ethical maxims, *blasons populaires*, superstitions, weather and medical lore, prophecies, and other categories of conventional wisdom. Proverbs are among the oldest poetic expressions in Sanskrit, Heb., Germanic, and Scandinavian lits. "Learned" proverbs are those long current in lit., as distinct from "popular" trad. The former come into Western Eur. lit. both from the Bible and the Church fathers and from such cl. sources as Aristophanes, Theophrastus, Lucian, and Plautus. Erasmus's *Adagia* (1500) was instrumental in spreading cl. proverb lore among the Eur. vernaculars. The first Eng. collection was John Heywood's *Dialogue conteining . . . All the Proverbs in the English Language* (1546). But proverbs had been commonly used by OE and ME writers, particularly Chaucer. The Elizabethan delight in proverbs is evident in John Lyly's *Euphues* (1580) and in countless plays—as it is in Shakespeare. The genres of lit. in which proverbs frequently occur are the didactic (e.g., Chaucer's "Tale of Melibeus," Ben Franklin's *Way to Wealth*, and J. W. Goethe's "Sprichwörtliches"); the satirical (Alexander Pope); works depicting folk characters (Miguel de Cervantes's *Don Quixote*, J. R. Lowell's *The Biglow Papers*); works reproducing local or national characteristics (E. A. Robinson's "New England"); and literary tours de force (François Villon's "Ballade des proverbes").

What distinguishes proverbs from other figures such as idioms or *metaphors, Milner proposes, is their structure of "four quarters" in a "balanced relationship . . . both in their form and content." This configuration, evident in *Waste / not, / Want / not* or *Qui seme / le vent / Recolte / la tempete* (He who sows the wind shall reap the whirlwind), appears in ancient and non-Eur. as well as in mod. langs. Milner associates this balanced four-part form with Carl Jung's paradigm of the structure of the mind. Milner's analysis, however, is found inadequate by Dundes, who proposes the proverb as "a traditional propositional statement consisting of at least one descriptive element" that consists of "a topic and a comment." Proverbs that contain "a single descriptive element are non-oppositional," while those with two or more "may be either oppositional or non-oppositional." Dundes relates proverbial structures to that of *riddles; however, "proverbs only state problems in contrast to riddles which solve them." Dundes calls for empirical testing of his hypothesis with proverbs from various cultures.

See EPIGRAM.

■ G. Bebermeyer, "Sprichwort," *Reallexikon* 4.132–51; W. Bonser and T. A. Stephens, *Proverb Literature: A Bibliography* (1930); A. Taylor, *The Proverb* (1931; reissued with index, 1962); B. J. Whiting, *Chaucer's Use of Proverbs* (1934); W. Gottschalk, *Sprichwörter des Romanen*, 3 v. (1935–38); G. Frank, "Proverbs in Medieval Literature," *MLN* 58 (1943); S. Singer, *Sprichwörter des Mittelalters*, 3 v. (1944–47); W. G. Smith and P. Harvey, *Oxford Dictionary of English Proverbs*, 2d ed., rev. (1948); M. P. Tilley, *Dictionary of the Proverbs in England in the Sixteenth and Seventeenth Centuries* (1950); O.E.E. Moll, *Sprichwörterbibliographie* (1958); D. MacDonald, "Proverbs, *Sententiae*, and *Exempla* in Chaucer's Comic Tales," *Speculum* 41 (1966); H. Weinstock, *Die Funktion elisabethanischer Sprichwörter und Pseudosprichwörter bei Shakespeare* (1966); F. Seiler, *Deutsche Sprichwortkunde*, 2d ed. (1967); C. G. Smith, *Shakespeare's Proverb Lore*, 2d ed. (1968); G. B. Milner, "What Is a Proverb?" *New Society* (Feb. 6, 1969); and "De l'Armature des Locutions Proverbiales: Essai de Taxonomie Semantique," *L'Homme* 9 (1969); F. A. de Caro and W. K. McNeil, *American Proverb Literature: A Bibliography* (1970); *Oxford Classical Dictionary*, "Paroemiographers" (1970); M. I. Kuusi, *Towards an International Type-System of Proverbs* (1972); W. R. Herzenstiel, *Erziehungserfahrung im deutschen Sprichwort* (1973); P. Zumthor, "L'épiphonème proverbial," *Revue des sciences humaines* 163 (1976); A. Dundes, "On the Structure of the Proverb," *The Wisdom of Many: Essays on the Proverb*, ed. W. Mieder and A. Dundes (1981); R. W. Dent, *Shakespeare's Proverbial Language: An Index* (1981); W. Mieder, *International Pro-verb Scholarship: An Annotated Bibliography* (1982), *Supplement 1* (1990), *Supplement 2* (1992); R. W. Dent, *Proverbial Language in English Drama Exclusive of Shakespeare, 1495–1616: An Index* (1984); H. and A. Beyer, *Sprichwörterlexikon* (1985); *Prentice-Hall Encyclopedia of World Proverbs*, ed. W. Mieder (1986); W. Mieder, *American Proverbs: A Study of Texts and Contexts* (1989);

B. J. Whiting, *Modern Proverbs and Proverbial Sayings* (1989); C. Cannon, "Proverbs and the Wisdom of Literature," *Textual Practice* 24 (2010).

D. HOFFMAN

PSALM (Gr. *psalmos*, "sacred song," "hymn"). A *psalm* is a sacred song or poem, conventionally describing the chapters of verse comprising the book of Psalms in the Heb. Bible. There are 150 psalms in the Heb. canon, with several more appearing in postbiblical sources such as the Dead Sea Scrolls. Several poems of the psalm type appear throughout the Bible, placed in the mouths of individual or collective prayers.

The poetic form of the psalm, at least as it has come down in the Western literary trad., is an invention of the ancient Near East. Often associated with ritual, the psalm was an important literary medium in Mesopotamia, Egypt, Hatti (Asia Minor), Ugarit (northern Syria), and, one may assume, despite the lack of surviving texts, in Canaan. The psalmists of ancient Israel took over forms from the surrounding cultures, adapting images, phrases, and even whole sequences of lines, but often with an evident polemical purpose: to attribute to the God of Israel those powers and beneficences that others claimed for their gods.

The book of Psalms as we have it is a product of the Second Temple (Hellenistic) period, when various, occasionally overlapping, collections of poems were assembled into a single anthol. The included psalms were composed over a period of several hundred years, the earliest going back to the beginning of the first millennium BCE. While certain diachronic shifts in lang. and poetics are discernible, far more striking are the continuities of *style and *convention. A parade example is the adaptation in Psalms 96 and 98 of an invocation of the "sons of the gods" to render homage to the Lord in the archaic Psalm 29: first, the mythological cohort is replaced by the peoples of the earth; then, the sacrifices they are bidden to offer are replaced by a musical fanfare.

The most common Heb. term for psalm—*mizmor*—denotes a song sung to musical accompaniment. The earliest Heb. name of the book is "The Book of Praisings," although the word for *praise*—*tehillah*—is used only intermittently and serves as the title of only one psalm. Other psalm headings ascribe the poem to King David, the legendary singer of Israelite trad., or to another figure; or they describe the occasion giving rise to the psalm; or they describe the musical mode in which the psalm is to be chanted. In spite of shared terminology, the psalter includes a wide variety of song types. The two predominant genres are praise and supplication, the latter of which features a complaint in need of remediation. Together these make up more than two-thirds of the book of Psalms. Many psalms, however, are of mixed genre and treat diverse situations. Even within one subgenre, there are striking differences in emphasis: a supplication may stress sin and contrition, the speaker's terror in a moment of acute distress, a reflective meditation on human transience, and much else. Among the other genres, such as wisdom meditations and historical reviews, most unusual are royal psalms, which are addressed not to the deity but to the king.

Some of the Heb. psalms are marked for liturgical performance on specified occasions or at specified moments in the temple rite. A view promulgated by Mowinckel and others holds that many psalms were used at an annual New Year festival, when the God YHWH was enthroned as king. There is both internal and external support for this hypothesis. Other psalms seem designed for individual recitation in moments of anguish or exaltation. The double nature of the psalms, alternately collective and personal, thankful and remonstrative, has been a source of their relevance both to the institutional and the individual lives of Jews and Christians ever since.

Poetically, the psalms exhibit a higher degree of convention, cliché, and patterning than other genres of biblical poetry. A few psalms are cast as alphabetic acrostics. The reader encounters *refrains or refrain-like *repetitions, antiphonal voices, and *inclusio* or envelope structures, in which the ending echoes images, motifs, or even whole phrases from the beginning. The rich *imagery and other sophisticated tropes of Psalm 23 ("The Lord is my shepherd; / I shall not want" . . .) are not characteristic of the psalter as a whole.

Yet the beautifully arranged movements and the archetypal simplicity of style of the biblical psalms have made them a recurrent source of inspiration to later poets. With the resurgence of interest in the Bible after the Reformation, adaptations of psalms became widespread. In France, the versions of Clément Marot are particularly noteworthy. The apogee of psalmodic verse in Western langs. was reached in Ren.

England, where the Bible in its new vernacular version became central to the culture. A variety of Eng. poets, from Thomas Wyatt and Philip Sidney to George Herbert and John Milton, tried their hand at metrical versions of psalms. In the signal instance of Herbert, the poet's original production owes something abiding in its *diction, imagery, and sense of *form to the model of the biblical psalms. Mod. Eng. poetry continues to evince a deep interest in psalms, as in the work of Dylan Thomas and in Donald Davie's *To Scorch or Freeze* (1988).

See HYMN.

■ J. Julian, *A Dictionary of Hymnology* (1925); H. Smith, "English Metrical Psalms in the Sixteenth Century and Their Literary Significance," *Huntington Library Quarterly* 9 (1946); S. Mowinckel, *The Psalms in Israel's Worship*, trans. R. Ap-Thomas, 2 v. (1962); R. C. Culley, *Oral-Formulaic Language in the Biblical Psalms* (1967); H. L. Ginsberg, "A Strand in the Cord of Hebraic Hymnody," *Eretz-Israel* 9 (1969); A. L. Strauss, *Bedarkhei hasifrut* (1970); C. Freer, *Music for a King* (1972)—Herbert and metrical psalms; L. Sabourin, *The Psalms*, rev. ed. (1974); C. Westermann, *Praise and Lament in the Psalms*, trans. K. R. Crim and R. N. Soulen (1981); C. Bloch, *Spelling the Word: George Herbert and the Bible* (1985); G. H. Wilson, *The Editing of the Hebrew Psalter* (1985); J. L. Kugel, "Topics in the History of the Spirituality of the Psalms," *Jewish Spirituality from the Bible through the Middle Ages,* ed. A. Green (1986); R. Alter, "Psalms," *Literary Guide to the Bible,* ed. R. Alter and F. Kermode (1987); E. L. Greenstein, "Psalms," *Encyclopedia of Religion,* ed. M. Eliade, v. 12 (1987); E. S. Gerstenberger, *Psalms, Part I, with an Introduction to Cultic Poetry* (1988); W. L. Holladay, *The Psalms through Three Thousand Years* (1993); N. M. Sarna, *Songs of the Heart: An Introduction to the Book of Psalms* (1993); Y. Avishur, *Studies in Hebrew and Ugaritic Psalms* (1994); S. E. Gillingham, *The Poems and Psalms of the Hebrew Bible* (1994); P. D. Miller, *They Cried to the Lord: The Form and Theology of Biblical Prayer* (1994); B. Nitzan, *Qumran Prayer and Religious Poetry* (1994); H. J. Levine, *Sing unto God a New Song: A Contemporary Reading of the Psalms* (1995); S. Weitzman, *Song and Story in Biblical Narrative* (1997); H. Gunkel and J. Begrich, *An Introduction to the Psalms,* trans. J. D. Nogalski (1998); E. S. Gerstenberger, *Psalms, Part 2, and Lamentations* (2001); *The Book of Psalms: Composition and Reception,* ed. P. W. Flint and P. D.

Miller (2005); K. L. Sparks, "Hymns, Prayers, and Laments," *Ancient Texts for the Study of the Hebrew Bible* (2005)—survey of extrabiblical parallels to Psalms with bibl.

R. ALTER; E. L. GREENSTEIN

PUN. *See* PARONOMASIA.

PYRRHIC (Gr., "used in the *pyrriche* or war dance"). In cl. prosody, a metrical foot of two short syllables. This may be said to have been the shortest metrical foot in Gr. and Lat. verse, although its admissibility was denied by the ancient *rhythmici* such as Aristoxenus, who felt that feet must be of at least three *chronoi* (temporal elements). In the mod. prosodies based on *accent, such as Eng., the existence of pyrrhic feet is disputed: several important metrists (e.g., J. B. Mayor, Robert Bridges, Joseph Malof, G. T. Wright) have recognized them as legitimate variations or substitutions in iambic verse; others deny them (J. M. Schipper, George Saintsbury). The dispute between the two camps turns on the issue of whether gradations of stress in the line are to be treated relatively or absolutely. In a line such as Andrew Marvell's "To a green thought in a green shade," the stress pattern (using notation of four levels of stress numbered 1 through 4, 1 being strongest, 4 weakest) might be said to be 3-4-2-1-3-4-2-1. Since Otto Jespersen's seminal 1903 article "Notes on Metre," many prosodists have accepted his claim that stress is perceived only in relation to its surroundings; and if one

asks about each pair of syllables in the line from Marvell's "The Garden," 3s outweigh 4s, as 1s do 2s, so that the *scansion is properly trochee + iamb + trochee + iamb. There are, additionally, some theoretical grounds for thinking that feet composed of homogeneous members should not be recognized; for further discussion of this issue, with bibl., see FOOT and SPONDEE.

Other metrists, however, would say that, in Marvell's line, 2s and 1s are both stronger than 3s and 4s and that readerly distinctions of stressing are made in absolute terms, not relative—giving the scansion pyrrhic + spondee + pyrrhic + spondee. Absolutists thus view the pyrrhic as a foot of two weakly stressed syllables; precisely how weak the one syllable is in relation to the other is unimportant. Historically, this approach has appealed to classicizing metrists, and it has a certain direct appeal; Saintsbury is eccentric (here as in much else) in accepting spondees but not pyrrhics. The sequence weaker-weaker-stronger-stronger is reasonably common in Eng. iambic pentameter verse; Wright gives many examples from Shakespeare. What one calls it—some classicizing metrists once liked to call it an ionic foot, while Attridge calls it "stress-final pairing"—is, however, less important than whether one hears relatively or absolutely.

■ Crusius; F. Pyle, "Pyrrhic and Spondee," *Hermathena* 107 (1968); J. Malof, *A Manual of English Meters* (1970); Attridge, *Rhythms*; West; G. T. Wright, *Shakespeare's Metrical Art* (1988).

T.V.F. BROGAN; R. J. GETTY

Q

QUANTITY

I. Concepts Ancient and Modern
II. Linguistic Basis

I. Concepts Ancient and Modern. Quantity is a property of syllables and forms the basis of the metrical *prosody of some langs. Quantitative verse is contrasted with verse based on syllable count or on word accent. Terminology and concepts of quantity in Western poetics descend from practice and description in cl. Gr. and Lat. In ancient and in many mod. theories, quantity is closely connected with vowel length—also called vowel quantity—and the same terms, *long* and *short*, are used to describe both vowels and syllables. So, "durationalists" have assumed that the elapsed time of the entire syllable is the criterion of difference, and some have made a point of variation within the two categories (ancient *rhythmici*, unlike *metrici*, focused on the varied realizations of quantity in performance). Most scholars now treat the distinction as an opposition of structures; W. S. Allen (1973) recommends following the ancient Indian trad. in calling syllables either "heavy" or "light" in weight.

A separate distinction, between "open" and "closed" syllables, is often part of the definition of quantity; open syllables end in a vowel, closed in a consonant. Gr. and Lat. syllabification rules allow closed syllables only when a vowel is followed by at least two consonants (VC-CV). Open syllables with a short vowel are short; closed syllables and syllables with a long vowel are long. So: *ar-mă vĭ-rŭm-que* ˘ . . . (vowel quantity above the line, syllable quantity below; in *ar-* the actual vowel quantity is "hidden" since the internal closed syllable is necessarily long). A syllable is long "by nature" if it has a long vowel; if it has a short vowel but is closed, it is long "by position" (Gr. *thesei*; Lat. *positione*, meaning either "by convention" or "by placement"; the distinction reflects the confusion of vowel and syllable quantities). Since the combination of a plosive + liquid was sometimes treated as a single consonant (Gr. *pat-ros* vs. *pa-tros*), the preceding syllable was said to be "common"—long or short. Syllables were reckoned across a line of verse without regard to word end, although word-final syllables might be subject to special treatment (in particular, *elision). The details of practice, incl. interaction with word stress and the permissibility of ad hoc adjustments to quantity, varied between langs., over time, and with degree of stylization (*epic is freest, while comedy, in particular, respects spoken norms), but they do not affect the fundamental categorization of long and short syllables. In Eng., efforts to apply the cl. quantitative system to analysis or composition have foundered on the difficulty of defining long and short (Attridge; cf. Stone and various experiments by Robert Bridges).

The metrical patterns of quantitative poetry comprise long or short "elements" (Maas) or "positions" (West) in which a particular syllable quantity is required, but patterns often incorporate alternatives (the distinction between pattern and instance, never entirely absent, was formalized by Maas). An element where either a short or long may be used is anceps (a post-classical term); the final element of a verse is always "indifferent" to short or long (anceps, "common," and "indifferent" have had multiple and overlapping usages; "neutralization" is the mod. technical term). By "contraction," one long may replace the positions for two short syllables, and by "resolution," two shorts replace a long syllable. Both are restricted in application. Contraction is very familiar from the epic dactylic; resolution is common in comic *iambic; much *lyric excludes both. But the 2:1 replacements (not unique to Gr. and Lat.) are understood in durational terms to mean that a long quantity temporally equals twice a short; the short is the minimal time unit, Gr., *chronos* or *sema*; Lat. and mod. technical term, *mora*. A "triseme" and "tetraseme" are each a further prolongation of a long syllable. Surviving Hellenistic and later musical settings incorporate these ratios. For most 19th- to mid-20th-c. scholars, anceps was identified with what ancient rhythmicians recognized as an *alogos* (irrational) duration, between long and short, and so was taken to require a third quantity whose intermediate length was satisfied by altered performance of either syllable structure (the possibility of a third quantity was refuted in Devine and Stephens [1975]).

Quantitative rhythm may inhere in a pattern, since most patterns require a long element after every anceps or one or two short ones; a sequence of more than two shorts is taken to imply underlying resolution and of two or more longs to involve anceps, contraction, or syncopation (the omission of a short; never in this context for rhythmic reversal). Scholars differ on whether syncopation implies prolongation. Nonetheless, patterns have traditionally been analyzed into quantitative feet formed by combinations of long and short syllables, with *rhythm determined by the internal ratios and usually with allowed substitutions among feet providing the variations in pattern. Some scholars have held that quantitative feet are only the verbal representation of nonverbal rhythms incorporating a metrical ictus (i.e., stress) or a musical beat and ratios other than 2:1 between long and short; some durationalists even adjusted unequal feet to equal "bars." Quantitative feet have allowed more opportunity than syllable quantity to confound separate systems of prosody (so Lanier, Kitto).

II. Linguistic Basis. In phonology, quantity, also known as syllable weight, is measured in moras, also known as weight units (Hyman). A light (or short) syllable has one mora, a heavy (or long) syllable has two moras, and a superheavy (or overlong) syllable has three moras. Quantity is a property of the *rhyme of a syllable (in phonology "rhyme" means the part of the syllable that excludes the onset); that is, initial consonants never count for weight (though see Gordon 2005 for possible exceptions). The quantity of a syllable is determined by how many moras constitute the rhyme of that syllable.

In a quantity-insensitive lang., coda consonants do not contribute to weight; rather they share a mora with the vowel. Such langs. also lack long vowels, by definition. Quantity-insensitive langs. include Fr. and Polish. In a typical quantity-sensitive lang., a syllable is heavy either by having a long vowel or being closed by a coda consonant—this is also called weight by position—or both. Eng., Lat., Sanskrit, and Ar. are examples of quantity-sensitive langs. Some quantity-sensitive langs. (e.g., Khalkha Mongolian) have nonmoraic codas, meaning that syllable weight is determined only by vowel length, not by the number of consonants. Still other langs. (e.g., Kwakw'ala [Gordon 2004]) show a pattern where sonorant consonants,

such as m, n, r, and l, are moraic, while obstruent consonants such as t, d, p, and k are not. While it may seem arbitrary that a consonant may add weight in one lang. but not in another, recent work has shown that these patterns reflect subtle differences in the way these sounds are pronounced across langs. (Broselow, Chen, and Huffman).

The relationship between quantity sensitivity and quantitative verse is not a simple one. Quantity-sensitive langs. do not necessarily have quantitative verse. Lat. and It., e.g., are both quantity-sensitive, stress-accent langs.; yet Lat. verse is largely quantitative, while It. verse is based on stress and syllable count. Furthermore, the distinction between quantitative verse and *accentual verse is not black and white. There is a statistical tendency in both Lat. and Gr. verse to align word stress with metrical ictus (Allen 1965, 1968), while in several Eng. meters, the phenomenon of resolution is sensitive to syllable weight (Kiparsky and Hanson; Kiparsky). Thus the sequence of vowels and consonants in a syllable does not automatically determine whether that syllable will count as light or heavy in verse; rather, this is a product of the interplay among the quantity sensitivity of the lang., metrical conventions, and ultimately the stylistic preferences of particular poets.

See FOOT, MODERN.

■ **Concepts Ancient and Modern:** S. Lanier, *The Science of English Verse* (1880); W. J. Stone, *On the Use of Classical Metres in English* (1899)—describes, critiques and prescribes; H.D.F. Kitto, "Rhythm, Metre, and Black Magic," *Classical Review* 56 (1942); Maas, 1–25; W. S. Allen, *Accent and Rhythm* (1973); T. Georgiades, *Greek Music, Verse, and Dance*, trans. E. Benedict and M. L. Martinez (1973); D. Attridge, *Well-Weighed Syllables* (1974); A. M. Devine and L. D. Stephens, "Anceps," *Greek Roman and Byzantine Studies* 16: 197–215 (1975); West, 7–25—a compromise between durationalist and structuralist approaches; T. Cole, *Epiploke* (1988)—proposes quantitative patterns as temporal designs; L. Pearson, *Aristoxenus: Elementa Rhythmica* (1990); A. M. Devine and L. D. Stephens, *The Prosody of Greek Speech* (1994), ch. 2.

■ **Linguistic Basis:** W. S. Allen, *Vox Latina* (1965), and *Vox Graeca* (1968); P. Kiparsky, "Sprung Rhythm," *Phonetics and Phonology, Volume 1: Rhythm and Meter* (1989); B. Hayes,

Metrical Stress Theory (1995); K. Hanson and P. Kiparsky, "A Parametric Theory of Poetic Meter," *Lang* 72.2 (1996); E. Broselow, S. Chen, and M. Huffman, "Syllable Weight: Convergence of Phonology and Phonetics," *Phonology* 14 (1997); L. Hyman, *A Theory of Phonological Weight* ([1984] 2003); M. Gordon, "Syllable Weight," *Phonetic Bases for Phonological Markedness*, ed. B. Hayes, R. Kirchner, and D. Steriade (2004); M. Gordon, "A Perceptually-driven Account of Onset-sensitive Stress," *Natural Language and Linguistic Theory* 23 (2005); M. Gordon, *Syllable Weight* (2006).

J. Lidov (ancient/modern);
A. Jaker (linguistics)

QUATRAIN. A stanza of four lines, usually rhymed. The quatrain, with its many variations, is the most common stanza form in Eur. poetry. Established as the meter of the *hymn in the 3d c. CE (after the Lat. iambic dimeter or two-foot line), it became a conventional meter in the Middle Ages as iambic tetrameter (alone or mixed with trimeter). These four- and three-foot lines correspond to the four-beat line, which is the basis for several forms of the *ballad meter, also a vernacular staple in the Middle Ages. Since then, the "four by four" (a quatrain with lines of four "feet" or "stresses") has been a common stanza for hymns, *ballads, and nursery rhymes. The quatrain is the form of the Sp. *cópula*, the Rus. *chastushka*, the Georgian *shairi*, the Malay *pantun*, the Ger. *Schnaderhüpfel*, the Chinese and Japanese *shichigon-zekku*, the Iranian *rubāʿī*, and the Welsh *englyn*. In 1834, August Meineke argued that Horace's *Odes* exhibit quatrain structure.

Irrespective of length, most rhyming quatrains adhere to one of the following rhyme patterns: *abab* or *xbyb*, called *"cross rhyme" (in which *x* and *y* represent unrhymed lines), which includes ballad meter, the elegiac stanza, the heroic quatrain (as in Thomas Gray's "Elegy Written in a Country Churchyard") and is the rhyme scheme of most Fr. quatrains; *abba* called "envelope rhyme" or the envelope stanza of which Alfred, Lord Tennyson's *In Memoriam stanza is a type. Theses two rhyme schemes have been the most popular forms in Western poetry since the 12th c., used primarily as a unit of composition in longer poems and forming the two components of the octave of the *sonnet. Other rhyme schemes include *aabb*, in which internal balance or *antithesis is achieved through opposed *couplets, as in P. B. Shelley's "The Sensitive Plant"; *aaaa* or *aaxa*, a monorhymed or nearly monorhymed stanza, such as Gottfried Keller's "Abendlied" or the *Rubaiyat* stanza. There are also interlinking rhyming quatrains that alternate *masculine and feminine rhymes, as in the most common Rus. stanza form (*AbAb* or *aBaB*, in which the capitals denote feminine rhymes). As a complete poem, the quatrain is often epigrammatic (see EPIGRAM). In hymn meter, common quatrain variations are common meter or common measure (alternating iambic tetrameter and trimeter rhyming *abab*), long meter (four iambic tetrameter lines, rhyming the second and fourth lines and sometimes the first and third), and short meter (two iambic trimeter lines, followed by a third line of iambic tetramter and ending with another trimeter line, rhyming the second and fourth lines and sometimes the first and third).

■ P. Martinon, *Les Strophes* (1912); Meyer; Carper and Attridge.

T.V.F. Brogan; M. Martin

R

REFRAIN (Ger. *Kehrreim*). A line, lines, or the final part of a line repeated verbatim within a poem, esp. at ends of stanzas; in song, a burden or chorus (through the 16th c., also called *refreit*); a structurally significant repetend separated by at least one line of nonrepeating material (hence distinguished, in Eur. poetics, from rime riche, *anaphora, and epistrophe). Refrains may be as short as one word or longer than the longest nonrepeated stanza. They may dispense with paraphrasable meaning entirely or become units of independent sense whose changing implications comment on the rest of a poem; most refrains fall somewhere in between.

A frequent (though by no means universal) feature of oral poetry, refrain may give a solo performer time to remember the next verse or encourage communal recitation. Refrains appear in sacred writings of antiquity, incl. the Egyptian *Book of the Dead*, the Heb. Psalms (e.g., 24, 67), and the *Rig Veda* (e.g., 10:121), as well as in early Gr. *pastoral poetry, Lat. *epithalamia of Catullus (61, 64), and the OE *Deor*.

Refrain and forms based on refrain take on unparalleled frequency and importance in med. Europe: refrains appear in med. Lat. hymnody and antiphonal responsion, in almost all ME carols, and in OF from ca. 1147. Refrains then become required components of such med. and Ren. forms as ballade and roundeau, ME tail rhyme, Dutch *refrein*, It. *ballata*, Sp. *villancico*, and Port. *cantiga*. Later poets (esp. in the 19th c.) can hence use refrain and forms requiring refrain to signal med. inheritance.

In ms. cultures and in oral transmission, otherwise differing poems may share a refrain, or the "same" poem may exist with various refrains. A refrain may separate itself on ling. grounds from the rest of a poem, preserving other (almost always older) vocabulary and grammar or using another lang. altogether (e.g., Lat. refrain in ME and Ren. Eng.; Ar. refrain in Sp.; Mozarabic in 9th-c. Andalusian Heb. and Ar.). The text of a poem set down to be sung or recited often records a refrain only once: where performance trad. is lost or unclear, mod. scholars may remain unsure (as in Andalusian *muwashshah*) whether or when a certain segment (in *muwashshah*, the *kharja*) constitutes a refrain or stands apart in some other (nonrepeated) way.

Analogous to refrain in Eur. and Eur.-derived poetics is the Persian and Persian-derived *radif*, a word or short phrase repeated at each line end after a given rhyme in Persian poetry from the 10th c. on, and in later poetry with Persian models, esp. Urdu and Turkish (but never Ar.). Persian and Persian-derived monorhymed forms *ghazal*, *qaṣīda*, and *rubāʿī* (quatrain) use the same radif (if any) throughout a given poem. The radif becomes most important (and most like refrain in Eur. poetry) in the ghazal from the 12th c. (e.g., in the Persian poet Sanā'ī on, when the ghazal in Persian becomes a fixed form. Wholly apart from Persian-influenced forms, longer refrains (of full sentences or complete ideas) occur in postclassical poetry of the Indian subcontinent, incl. Kannada *vacanas* (from 10th to 12th c.) and the Hindi *Bhakti* poetry of, e.g., Kabīr (15th c.).

Refrains in Ren. and later written poems link them to oral trads., to "folk" poetry and to song, esp. to such popular or participatory sung genres as work songs, dance songs, *ballads, lullabies, and children's games. A mod. poet's frequent recourse to refrain (as in W. B. Yeats or Okot p'Bitek) often pays homage to oral or "folk" culture generally. Some refrains with musical settings include *nonsense, as in Shakespeare's songs, or consist entirely of it, as in Korean *Koryo sogyo* songs (11th c.), whose otherwise senseless refrain not only fits but imitates accompanying music.

Refrain promises regularity (even when the promise is violated or fulfilled in some nonliteral way) and implies a distinction (of speaker, *tone, subject, or audience) between repeated and nonrepeated parts. Refrain risks monotony within a long work but can bind together a short one; most poems organized around refrains are relatively short, either narrative (as ballads) or lyric. Within long works, refrain may distinguish inset lyric or odic passages from the narrative or dramatic verse that surrounds them. In mod. poems not otherwise songlike, refrain can suggest self-division, haunting, or obsession, hence mortality (E. A. Poe, "The Raven"; M.-L. Halpern, "Memento Mori") or else a congregation's call-and-response (Sterling

Brown, "Old Lem"). Refrain in freestanding poems may also comment on the passage of time (Edmund Spenser, *Prothalamion*; Federico García Lorca, "Llanto por Ignacio Sánchez Mejías") or interrupt narrative and argument with the stronger emotion of song.

See BALLAD, REPETITION, SONG.

■ F. Gummere, *The Beginnings of Poetry* (1908) but also L. Pound, *Poetic Origins and the Ballad* (1921) and P. Gainer, *The Refrain in the English and Scottish Popular Ballads* (1933); N. van den Boogaard, *Rondeaux et refrains du XIIe au début de XIVe siècle* (1969); T. Newcombe, "The Refrain in Troubadour Lyric Poetry," *Nottingham Medieval Studies* 19 (1975); J. Hollander, *The Figure of Echo* (1981), and *Melodious Guile* (1988), ch. 7; L. Magnus, *The Track of the Repetend* (1989); F. D. Lewis, "The Rise and Fall of a Persian Refrain," *Reorientations*, ed. S. P. Stetkevych (1994); L. A. Garner, "Contexts of Interpretation in the Burdens of Middle English Carols," *Neophilologus* 84 (2000); *Literature of Al-Andalus*, ed. M. R. Menocal and M. Sells (2000), ch. 7; J. M. Foley, *How to Read an Oral Poem* (2002); G. Alkon, "Refrain and the Limits of Poetic Power in Spenser, Herbert, Hardy and Stevens," *Western Humanities Review* 58 (2004).

S. BURT

REPETITION. The structure of repetition underlies the majority of poetic devices, and it is possible to argue that repetition defines the poetic use of lang. The effects of repetition are, however, multivalent and range from lending unity and coherence to exposing the fundamental difference between the repeated elements. Even as repetition may effect poetic closure and provide the poem with a regular pattern, exact repetition is impossible: the simple fact of temporal discontinuity between repeated elements leads to a difference in their functions, via the accumulation of significance and recontextualization (as demonstrated, e.g., by Edgar Allan Poe's "The Raven" in the radically unstable meaning of the repeated word "nevermore"). That is why Gertrude Stein, famous for her highly repetitive texts, claims "there is no repetition." At the same time, the poem's repetitions set up expectations and guide interpretation.

Repetition structures poetic forms at all levels, as in the repetition of sounds (*alliteration, *assonance, *consonance, *rhyme, homonym, or *paronomasia); repetition of syllables (*syllabic verse, *rich rhyme); repetition of words (*anaphora, *anadiplosis, parechesis, traductio, ploce); identical rhyme, repetend, *catalog, list, and the pattern of word repetitions in traditional *lyric forms, such as, e.g., the end words in a *sestina; repetition of lines (*refrain, incremental repetition, envelope stanza pattern, used also in verse forms such as *pantun* and *villanelle); repetition of measure (*rhythm; *meter); repetition of syntactical patterns (*parallelism, *hypotaxis and parataxis); repetition of the line break (*free verse); semantic repetition (pleonasm, synonymy, and repetitions of figures, images, concepts, themes); and intertextual repetition (allusion or pastiche).

Repetition not only patterns (as the examples above demonstrate) but parallels and reinforces those poetic devices that distinguish verse from prose. Similarly to the line break, it disrupts the linearity of lang., creating a counterpoint rather than continuity of narrative logic. Repetition of the same element in different contexts may also perform a metaphorical function. As readers often observe, repetition draws attention to itself and tends to denaturalize lang.: the more repetitions there are in a poem, the more we are conscious of the poem's artifice and the less able to come up with the poem's paraphrasable meaning. In fact, intense repetition may lead to the loss of meaning (the signifier entirely replaces the signified). It has been observed also that repetition marks the collective in lang., revealing a polyphony and taking poetic expression beyond a single voice.

A poem's various repetitions interact, creating a complex effect. E.g., in the final couplet of Shakespeare's sonnet 18, a pattern of alliteration, assonance, paronomasia, and syntactic parallelism creates a series of echoes: "So long as men can breathe, or eyes can see / So long lives this, and this gives life to thee." W. C. Williams's "To a Poor Old Woman" is an example of *free verse exploiting the counterpoint between syntax and line break. The sentence/line that begins the second stanza, "They taste good to her," is repeated twice but broken into three lines. Apart from revealing an ambiguity or plurality of meanings inherent in a simple sentence, because of the mismatch between syntax and lineation, the repetitions create a pronounced, syncopated rhythm.

In ritual poetries, repetition has a performative function and lends them illocutionary power. Prayers, mantras, Santería or voodoo rituals, and various liturgies all rely on verbal repetition that supplants logic with emotive effect. Repetition is the basis of prosody in the Heb. Bible; its syntactical parallelism has exerted an influence on Anglo-Am. poetry of such dissimilar poets as Christopher Smart (*Jubilate Agno*), William Blake ("The Garden of Love"), Walt Whitman ("Song of Myself"), and Allen Ginsberg (*Howl*).

Oral poems are repeated by being passed from generation to generation as well as structured by repetition that serves as a mnemonic device. Scholars of orality point to various degrees of balance between the repetition of formulas, themes and story patterns, and improvisation. Needless to say, the function of repetition in oral texts is different from that in written poetry, and oral trad. demonstrate a wide range of practices, thus varying among themselves in their use of repetition.

In Native Am. poetics, because of the traditional connection between the sacred and the verbal, often much importance has been placed on exact repetition of an oral text. Embedded in a specific occasion (where many other elements, such as music, dance, and gesture actively produce meaning, comparably to contemp. intermedia art) a *song, chant, spell, prayer, or oration has a performative function and may be repeated several times, depending on the specificity of the event (e.g., a healing prayer repeated line by line after the shaman by the patient). Native Am. songs and chants employ repetition as a structural device (often said to echo natural cycles, as well as tribal inheritance), where grammatical and semantic repetition is said to increase the incantatory (as opposed to narrative) qualities of a given performance. Considering the Native Am. concept of authorship (and audience), a "poem" is always a type of repetition entailing a source larger than the speaker (communal, natural, or sacred), rather than an expression of a unique voice. Western poetics has less patience for repetition: ethnocentric critics reveal that Native Am. repetitions are often expurgated in trans. into Eng. because considered untranslatable, redundant, or meaningless.

Rhythm and repetition (sometimes engaged in chiastic reversals) are said to be the defining elements of black culture. James A. Snead juxtaposes this feature of black "non-progressive" culture with Western tendency (present in Eur. and Eurocentric cultures from the late 16th c. up until the modernist revolution in the 20th) to "cover up" its repetitions for the sake of the ideology of progress, realism, and faithful representation of reality in art. Repetition lies at the core of Af. verbal trad. (e.g., call-and-response patterns) that informs much of black art: it shapes Af. and Af. Am. music and its lyrics (slave songs, spirituals, gospel, *blues, and rap); it grounds improvisation in jazz (which needs an established pattern to diverge from); it is a pronounced feature in black folk sermons. All of these models find their way into Af. Am. poetry. Snead refers to the repeated beat as "social," i.e., available to be played with by new voices. *Signifying, defined by Henry Louis Gates Jr. as the "black trope of tropes," depends on repetition with a difference. As a play of signifiers, this "figure for black rhetorical figures" (Gates) consistently draws attention to its repetitions, a feature often explored by Af. Am. poets. Harryette Mullen's *Muse & Drudge* signifies, among others, on W.E.B. Du Bois's concept of "double consciousness" (Huehls); Michael Harper's "Dear John, Dear Coltrane" signifies on Coltrane's "Love Supreme"; Langston Hughes's *Ask Your Mama* is, according to Gates, the most representative Af. Am. poem based on signifying as a mode of discourse.

Repetition in poetry has been studied from a number of perspectives and with tools from various fields. Mod. philosophers (from Søren Kierkegaard and Friedrich Nietzsche to Gilles Deleuze and Jacques Derrida) make a distinction between two forms or competing effects of repetition that can be provisionally defined as repetition-as-unity and repetition-as-difference. The former, sometimes referred to as "Platonic repetition" or "recollection," is based on the principle of identity or original similitude that is recovered by repetition (e.g., by *mimesis); the latter is a disclosure or production of difference. This binary definition of repetition often extends to other binary oppositions, such as hierarchy vs. nonhierarchical difference; theological grounding vs. lack of ground; order vs. disorder; stasis vs. movement; habit vs. creativity; trad. vs. individual talent; codification vs. dissent; authority of the text vs. surrender of authorial control; and linearity vs. rupture. An example of the former model is found by Mircea Eliade in archaic societies' belief in the possibility of recovering an ideal past, of repeating the original act performed by the gods, heroes, or ancestors. Transformational grammar (Noam Chomsky) aims at recovering the "deep structure" of lang. from which all "surface structures" may be generated. The later model, of repetition without an original, is present, e.g., in Baudrillard's concept of the simulacrum. Structuralism in anthropology (Claude Lévi-Strauss)—but also in ling. (Ferdinand de Saussure) and literary studies (Roman Jakobson); see the poetic function as a type of repetition—posits the existence of a system that underlies all concrete manifestations of social (also linguistic) phenomena. (Were one to apply the Saussurean structuralist linguistic model directly to poetic repetition, repetition of the sign would be realized by repeated words and phrases; repetition of the signifier by rhyme and alliteration; repetition of the signified by, e.g., synonymy.) In a Freudian psychoanalytic definition of the repetition compulsion, repetition is seen as both symptom (mechanical reenactment of the repressed) and cure (repetition in the transferential context of therapy). The cure consists in the move from unconscious, mechanical reenactment to conscious remembering: paradoxically, one needs to remember in order to forget, i.e., to free oneself of the past. Some readers argue that, through its various repetitions, poetry speaks to the irrational side of our brains (Finch). Conceptions of the historical (also in literary and poetic hist.) similarly rely on alternative uses of repetition. Edward Said's critique of Giambattista Vico's model of hist., e.g., works along the common binary: in place of the "filiative" or genealogical model of repetition embraced by Vico, Said proposes a model that is "affiliative." Said emphasizes those forces in hist. that counter generative continuity and are based on affiliation. Obviously, the very tendency to account for repetition via binary oppositions is itself structuralist in its provenance, and, arguably, the two types of repetition always coexist, one always calling up the other, even as the tendency of a text and/or interpretation leans toward one more than the other.

The multivalence of poetic repetition is reflected in the variety of theoretical approaches to it. Those, again, tend to fall into two recognizable types: a grounded repetition that recovers an original and an ungrounded repetition that reveals difference. Thus, e.g., the notion of "organic form" in poetry is usually grounded in the first type of repetition (and tends to be less explicitly repetitive or "covers up" its repetitions), while highly crafted poetic forms seem more of a "mechanical" exercise in which form produces content. In literary theory,

Harold Bloom's *Anxiety of Influence* uses the genealogical model of repetition (critiqued by Said) to set the stage for his theory of poetic influence. Barbara Johnson discusses two types of repetition used, respectively, by William Wordsworth and E. A. Poe, arguing that the distinction between the two gives the study of poetry the key to "articulating authenticity with conventionality, originality and continuity, freshness with what is recognizably 'fit' to be called poetic." Wordsworth's and Poe's models of poetic creativity may seem incompatible, as Wordsworth's is based on "emotion recollected in tranquility" and aims at the recovery of an original moment, while Poe's rests on mechanical repetition of words and sounds; one is based on the signified, the other on the signifier. Johnson, however, deconstructs the opposition demonstrating that the two types of repetition and, consequently, the two definitions of poetic lang. are inextricable, even if one is the text's explicit argument and the other its "subversive ghost" (see also J. Hillis Miller). The confusion between the two types of repetition, argues Johnson, is not an error but the condition of poetic lang. itself.

■ M. Eliade, *The Myth of the Eternal Return*, trans. W. R. Trask (1954); Jakobson, v. 3; B. H. Smith, *Poetic Closure* (1968); D. Tedlock, "Introduction," *Finding the Center* (1972); "Tradition and the Individual Talent," Eliot, *Essays*; E. Said, "On Repetition," *Literature of Fact* (1976); J. Hollander, *The Figure of Echo* (1981); J. A. Snead, "Repetition as a Figure of Black Culture," *Black American Literature Forum* 15 (1981); J. H. Miller, *Fiction and Repetition* (1982); S. Kierkegaard, *Fear and Trembling*, trans. H. V. Hong and E. H. Hong (1983); D. Fried, "Repetition, Refrain and Epitaph," *ELH* 53 (1986); H. L. Gates Jr., *The Signifying Monkey* (1988); B. Johnson, *A World of Difference* (1989); J. Baudrillard, *Simulacra and Simulation*, trans. S. F. Glaser (1994); G. Deleuze, *Difference and Repetition*, trans. P. Patton (1994); G. Stein, "Portraits and Repetition," *Gertrude Stein: Writings 1932–1946* (1998); S. Freud, *The Complete Psychological Works of Sigmund Freud: Beyond the Pleasure Principle, Group Psychology and Other Works*, v. 18 (2001); M. Huehls, "Spun Puns (and Anagrams): Exchange Economies, Subjectivity and History in Harryette Mullen's *Muse & Drudge*," *Contemporary Literature* 44 (2004); A. Finch, *The Body of Poetry* (2005); K. Mazur, *Poetry and Repetition* (2005).

K. Mazur

RHYME

I. Origin and History of Rhyme
II. Rhyme in Western Poetries, Particularly in English

I. Origin and History of Rhyme in World Poetries. There have been two chief views on the origin and devel. of rhyme. The derivationist position is that rhyme originated in one locus and was disseminated to all others. Turner argued as early as 1808 that rhyme originated in Chinese or Sanskrit (but not Ar.; for Ren. arguments about the Ar. origin of rhyme, see Dainotto), whence it spread via the trade routes to Europe. Draper claimed China as the single point of origin (according to him, the earliest attested rhymes in Chinese date from ca. 1000 BCE; according to Kenner, 1200 BCE), from which it spread to ancient Iran by means of Mongol hordes and westward to Rome with Persian mystery cults; but, as McKie has argued, Draper's ambiguous evidence suggests dual sources in Iran and China. The alternate view, set forth as early as 1803 by Swift, is that rhyme does not take its origin exclusively in any one lang. but is a natural ling. structure that can arise in any lang. having the right set of features. The fact that rhyme originated once shows that it can originate at any time. It is a simple ling. fact that the number of sounds available in any lang. is limited, and its many words must, therefore, be combinations of only a few sounds. There is considerable evidence that children manufacture rhymes spontaneously as one basic form of sound permutation; also conspicuous is rhyme in the chants and charms of many primitive cultures. Systematic rhyming has appeared in such widely separated langs. that its spontaneous devel. in more than one of them seems a reasonable assumption. We should not seek to find the ultimate "origin" of rhyme in Western poetry by tracing rhyme forms back through langs. to some common source. Still, it is a thundering fact that most of the world's 4,000 langs. lack or avoid rhyme in their poetries altogether (Whitehall).

In the hist. of the world's poetries, those cultures that have most extensively developed rhyme have been Chinese in the East and in the West, Ar., Ir., Occitan, Fr., Ger., Eng., and Rus. Note that rhyme is not originally native to any Eur. lang. or even IE. Regardless of whether rhyme had one source or several, it is indisputable that, both in ancient and med. lits., there are several discernible routes of transmission, the tracing of which is neither impossible nor unimportant, merely difficult. It is obvious that specific rhyme forms, like meters and stanzas, have been imported into langs. via trans. or imitation of famous poets and canonical works in another lang. (Homer, Virgil, Dante, Petrarch, Shakespeare), even where rhyme was already indigenous.

II. Rhyme in Western Poetries, Particularly in English. Philip Sidney in the *Defence of Poesy* calls rhyme "the chiefe life" of mod. versifying; indeed, so it must still seem, despite the advent of the great trad. of Eng. *blank verse from Shakespeare to Alfred, Lord Tennyson, and even the advent of the several free-verse prosodies after 1850: the 1st ed. of the *Oxford Book of English Verse* (1900) contains 883 poems of which only 16 lack rhyme. And what is true of Eng. is even more true of Rus., where the trad. of rhyme is more extensively developed, and esp. Fr., where rhyme is truly fundamental to the whole system of versification. Rhyme is, as Oscar Wilde said, "the one chord we have added to the Greek lyre."

A. *Definition.* In the specific sense of the term as used in Eng., *rhyme* is the linkage in poetry of two syllables at line end (for internal rhyming, see below) that have identical stressed vowels and subsequent phonemes but differ in initial consonant(s) if any are present—syllables that, in short, begin differently and end alike. This is the paradigmatic case for Eng.; but in the half-dozen other langs. where rhyme has been developed as a major poetic device, many other varieties have been developed, resulting in more expansive definitions admitting any one of several kinds of sound echo in verse. More broadly, however, we must say that *rhyme* is the phonological correlation of differing semantic units at distinctive points in verse. It is essential that the definition not be framed solely in terms of sound, for that would exclude the cognitive function.

Rhyme calls into prominence simultaneously a complex set of responses based on identity and difference. On the phonic level, the likeness of the rhyming syllables (at their ends) points up their difference (at their beginnings). The phonic semblance (and difference) then points up semantic semblance or difference: the equivalence of the rhyme syllables or words on the phonic level implies a relation or likeness or difference on the semantic level. Rhyme in this sense, i.e., *end rhyme*, is, with *meter, a primary form of sound patterning in mod. verse and deploys sound similarity as the means to semantic and structural ends.

Crucial to these ends, as with all others in *prosody, is segmentation. As with the clausulae of late antique prose rhythm, rhyme marks the ends of runs of syllables in speech and thereby segments the sound stream into equal or per-ceived-equal units or sections: this segmentation, in turn, establishes equivalence, which is essential to *repetition and the effects it is capable of. Lotman says that, if all equivalences in the poetic line are classed as either positional (rhythmic) or euphonic (sonal), then rhyme is created at the intersection of the two sets.

From the usual sense of the term *rhyme*—i.e., the sound common to two or more words or a word that echoes another word—other senses derive by *synecdoche, i.e., (1) a poem in rhymed verse or (2) rhymed verse in general; or by *metonymy, i.e., (3) any kind of sound echo between words (e.g., alliteration, assonance, *consonance) or (4) more generally, any kind of correspondence, congruence, or accord (cf. J. R. Lowell's "of which he was as unaware as the blue river is of its rhyme with the blue sky" from *The English Poets*, 1888).

The spelling *r-h-y-m-e* became common in Eng. in the 17th c.; the earlier Ren. and ME spelling, *r-i-m-e*, derives from OF *rime*, *ritme* (< Med Lat. *rithmi* < Lat. *rithmus*, *rhythmus* < Gr. *rhythmos*). The OF form gave the Occitan, Sp., Catalan, Port., and It. cognates *rima* and MHG, ON, and Old Icelandic *rim*, later *rima* (rhymed poem, ballad). This form of *rim* is not to be confused with (though it is related to) OHG, OE *rim* (number) or with OE, ON *hrim* (hoar-frost, rime-frost). The term *rim* in the mod. sense of *rhyme* first appears in an Anglo-Norman rhymed sermon of the early 12th c.; in this c., rhyme became a central feature of short-lined lyric poetry in Occitan and came to replace assonance in the *laisses* of the OF *chansons de geste*. In Eng., the spelling *r-i-m-e* / *r-y-m-e* for vernacular, accentual, rhymed verse was preserved to ca. 1560, when spelling reform based on the classics brought in *r-i-t-h-m-e* / *r-y-t-h-m-e* (pronounced to rhyme with *crime* and spelled *r-i-'-m-e* by Ben Jonson), current to 1700, after which time *r-h-y-t-h-m* became the spelling for that concept in the mod. sense. About 1600, however, *rhime*/*rhyme* appears, presumably to distinguish rhyming from rhythmical/metrical

effects; *r-h-y-m-e* subsequently won out, though the (historically correct) spelling *r-i-m-e* has never entirely disappeared.

In med. Lat., *rithmus*/*rythmus* denotes *versus rithmici* (rhythmical verse), meaning verse whose meter is based on *accent, not *quantity (*versus metrici*) and that employs end-rhyme. Lat. rhythmical verse, appears as early as the 3d to 4th cs. CE and reaches its culmination in the 12th c., though verse written on quantitative principles continued to be written throughout the Middle Ages. This fact—two metrical systems side by side in med. Lat.—is responsible for the mod. phrase "without rhyme or reason," meaning neither *rhythmus* nor *ratio*, i.e., not any kind of verse at all. In short, the word for accentually based and rhymed verse in med. Lat. vacillated between an *i* and *y* spelling for its vowel; the Ren. distinguished these two criteria and, hence, terms for them. Ren. spelling reform affected the visual shapes of the words; pronunciation diverged later. *Rhythm* and *rhyme* are, thus, intimately related not only etymologically but conceptually.

There are two final points about definition. First, the definition of what counts as rhyme is conventional and cultural: it expands and contracts from one national poetry, age, verse trad., and genre to another. Hence, definition must shortly give way to a taxonomy of types (below). Second, there is the issue of positing rhyme at line end itself (see LINE). Žirmunskij, looking at rhyme as not only sound echo but the marker of line end, sees that function as having an effect on the rhythmic organization of the line. Indeed, it is commonly assumed that rhyme exerts a metrical function in marking the ends of the lines. But, of course, rhyme is not restricted to line end, suggesting that "any sound repetition that has an organizing function in the metrical composition of the poem should be included in the concept of rhyme" (1923). Further, as de Cornulier argues, rhyme does not exactly reside at line end: its positioning shapes the entire structure of the line, so that we should more accurately say that the rhyme resides in the entire line. Removing rhymes from lines does not merely render them rhymeless; it alters their lexical-semantic structure altogether.

B. Taxonomy. Rhyme correlates syllables by sound. We may describe the structure of the syllable as initial consonant or consonant cluster (the so-called support or prop consonant [Fr.

consonne d'appui]; this may be in the zero state, i.e., absent) + medial vowel (or diphthong) + final consonant (or cluster, if present), which we may schematize as CVC. If we ask which elements of a syllable can be repeated in a second syllable in correspondence with the first, letting underlining denote a sound repeated identically, then seven configurations are possible (the eighth possibility is null; these are simply the permutations of a set of three elements), having these forms and Eng. names:

1. C̲V C alliteration (*bad / boy*)
2. C V̲ C assonance (*back / rat*)
3. C V C̲ consonance (*back / neck*)
4. C̲V̲ C reverse rhyme (*back / bat*)
5. C̲V C̲ [no standard term] frame rhyme, pararhyme (*back / buck*)
6. C V̲ C̲ rhyme strictly speaking (*back / rack*)
7. C̲V̲ C̲ Rich rhyme, rime riche, or identical rhyme (*bat* [wooden cylinder] / *bat* [flying creature])

This schema presumes that both syllables are identical in all other respects, i.e., their phonological and morphological characteristics—e.g., that both syllables are stressed monosyllables. But, of course, this is not usually the case, certainly not for Fr. or It. or Rus., not even for Eng. A more elaborate taxonomy would subsume all such variants. To date, no such inventory of rhyme structures has yet been given. When it is, it will explain a number of effects as yet unaccounted for, clarify relations between forms in the same or different langs. hitherto thought unrelated or remote, and provide a comprehensive and synthetic overview of the structure of the system, showing how rhyme processes function as an integral system. It will also, presumably, correlate with the schema of rhetorical figures and processes given by Group μ.

C. Analogues. Inside poetry, there are a number of structures that have rhyme-like effects or functions or exceed the domain of rhyme, verging into repetition. The *sestina, e.g., repeats a sequence of whole words rather than rhyme sounds. Several rhetorical devices generate comparable effects to those of rhyme even in unrhymed verse: in the 10,000 lines of *Paradise Lost*, there are over 100 cases of epistrophe, nearly 100 of *anaphora, 60 of *anadiplosis, 50 of epanalepsis, and 40 of epizeuxis, all of them, as Broadbent says, "iterative schemes tending to the effect of rhyme." Milton also weights

words at line end (Broadbent calls this "anti-rhyme"), counterposing semantically heavy and contrastive terms at *Paradise Lost* 4.561–62, e.g.: "Tempt not the Lord thy God, he said and stood. / But Satan smitten with amazement fell"—an effect reinforced all the more by reiteration of these two terms via ploce ten more times in the following 21 lines, and echoed thereafter at 4.590–91 (cf. 9.832–33). In American Sign Language poetry, poets achieve rhyme-like effects using hand shapes.

Outside poetry, rhyme is commonly thought of as a "poetical" device, but, in fact, it is a broadly attested ling. structure used for marking the ends of important words and phrases to make them memorable. Rhyme is widely used not only for ludic and didactic purposes, as in rhymed and rhythmical calendrical mnemonics, children's counting-out and jump-rope rhymes, and jingles for ads (see Chasar) but for other types of memorable speech such as *proverbs, *epigrams, inscriptions, mottoes, *riddles, puns, and jokes (Brogan). Children seem to be able to manufacture rhymes not only spontaneously and happily but more readily than the other six forms cited at the top of section II.B above, suggesting that the closural or "final-fixed" structure that is rhyme is somehow more salient for cognitive processing (see Rayman and Zaidel), as the vast lit. on the role of rhyme in promoting children's phonemic awareness, lang. acquisition, and literacy suggests. Perhaps the most common form of rhyming in lang. is seen in mnemonic formulas, catch phrases that rhyme, e.g., *true blue, ill will, fender bender, double trouble, high and dry*. The list of such popular and proverbial phrases is astonishingly long, and the device is also used in poetry (Donne, "Song (Go and Catch a Falling Star)"; Eliot, *Four Quartets*).

In an important study, Bolinger has shown that in every lang., words that begin or end alike in sound come to be perceived as related even when they have no etymological connection. This sort of paradigmatic or synchronic associativity is even stronger than the historical kinship of words, which is often concealed by spelling and pronunciation changes, and is extended naturally into poetry as rhyme without any alteration of form or function. The inevitability of rhyme suggested by this study becomes harder to deny in light of evidence that rhyme-like structures apparently exist even in nonhuman langs., such as that of whales (Guinee and Payne), challenging those who think of rhyme as more artificial than natural to reconsider.

■ J. S. Schütze, *Versuch einer Theorie des Reims nach Inhalt und Form* (1802)—Kantian semantic theory; T. Swift, "Essay on the Rise and Progress of Rhime," *Transactions of the Royal Irish Academy* 9 (1803); S. Turner, "An Inquiry Respecting the Early Use of Rhyme," *Archaeologia* 14 (1808); A. Croke, *Essay on the Origin, Progress, and Decline of Rhyming Latin Verse* (1828); F. Wolf, *Über die Lais, Sequenzen, und Leiche* (1841), 161 ff.; W. Masing, *Über Ursprung und Verbreitung des Reims* (1866); T. de Banville, *Petit traité de poésie française* (1872); Schipper, 1.1.7, 1.4.1; E. Freymond, "Über den reichen Reim bei altfranzösischen Dichtern," *ZRP* 6 (1882); W. Grimm, "Zur Gesch. des Reims" (1852), rpt. in *Kleinere Schriften* (1887)—still the best Ger. survey; A. Ehrenfeld, *Studien zur Theorie des Reims*, 2 v. (1897–1904); P. Delaporte, *De la rime française* (1898); G. Mari, *Riassunto e dizionarietto di ritmica italiana* (1901); Kastner, ch. 3; Meyer, v. 1, ch. 2—med. Lat.; A. Gabrielson, *Rhyme as a Criterion of the Pronunciation of Spenser, Pope, Byron, and Swinburne* (1909); Schipper, *History* 270 ff.; Thieme, ch. 8 and 376, 379–80—full list of Fr. work to 1914; W. Braune, "Reim und Vers," *Sitzungsb. der Heidelberger Akad. der Wiss., phil.-hist. Klasse* (1916)—etymology; F. Zschech, *Die Kritik des Reims in England* (1917); O. Brik, "Zvukovie povtory," *Poetika* (1919); E. Sapir, "The Heuristic Value of Rhyme," *Queen's Quarterly* 27 (1920); B. de Selincourt, "Rhyme in English Poetry," *E&S* 7 (1921); H. C. Wyld, *Studies in English Rhymes from Surrey to Pope* (1923); V. M. Žirmunskij, *Rifma, ee istoriia i teoriia* (1923); W. B. Sedgwick, "The Origin of Rhyme," *Revue Benedictine* 36 (1924); Morris-Jones—Celtic; K. Wesle, *Frühmittelhochdeutsche Reimstudien* (1925); P. Habermann, "Reim," etc., *Reallexikon I* 3.25–44; J. W. Rankin, "Rime and Reason," *PMLA* 44 (1929); H. Lanz, *The Physical Basis of Rhyme* (1931); N. Törnqvist, "Zur Gesch. des Wortes Reim," *Humanistika Vetenskapssamfundet i Lund, Årsberättelse* (1934–35), v. 3—Celtic, Germanic, and Romance; Patterson—fullest source for the Rhétoriqueurs; K. Stryjewski, *Reimform und Reimfunktion* (1940)—near rhyme in Eng.; K. Burke, "On Musicality in Verse," *The Philosophy of Literary Form* (1941); F. W. Ness, *The Use of Rhyme in Shakespeare's Plays* (1941); U. Pretzel, *Frühgesch. des deutschen Reims* (1941); A. M. Clark, *Studies in Literary Modes* (1945); Le Gentil, v. 1, bk. 2; A. Oras, "Echoing Verse Endings in Paradise Lost," *South Atlantic Studies for S. E. Leavitt*, ed. S. A. Stoudemire (1953); Raby, *Christian*; W. K. Wimsatt, "One Relation of Rhyme to Reason" and "Rhetoric and Poems," *The Verbal Icon* (1954)—classic studies of semantics; J. W. Draper, "The Origin of Rhyme," *RLC* 31 (1957), 39 (1965); Beare—broad scope for Western; Raby, *Secular*; J. B. Broadbent, "Milton's Rhetoric," *MP* 56 (1959); Saintsbury, *Prosody*, v. 1, App. 8, and v. 3, App. 4; F. G. Ryder, "How Rhymed Is a Poem?" *Word* 19 (1963); M. Masui, *The Structure of Chaucer's Rime Words* (1964); D. L. Bolinger, "Rime, Assonance, and Morpheme Analysis," *Forms of English* (1965); J. Cohen, *Structure du langage poétique* (1966); C. A. Owen Jr., "'Thy Drasty Ryming,'" *SP* 63 (1966)—Chaucer; R. Abernathy, "Rhymes, Non-Rhymes, and Antirhyme," *To Honor Roman Jakobson*, v. 1 (1967); E. J. Dobson, *English Pronunciation 1500–1700*, 2d ed., 2 v. (1968); H. Whitehall, "Rhyme: Sources and Diffusion," *Ibadan* 25 (1968); M. Perloff, *Rhyme and Meaning in the Poetry of Yeats* (1970); L. Pszczołowska, *Rym* (1970)—Polish; V. Nemoianu, "Levels of Study in the Semantics of Rhyme," *Style* 5 (1971); E. H. Guggenheimer, *Rhyme Effects and Rhyming Figures* (1972)—cl.; T. Eekman, *The Realm of Rhyme* (1974)—comparative Slavic; V. F. Markov, "V zaščitu raznoudarnoi rifmy (informativnyi obzor)," *Russian Poetics*, ed. T. Eekman and D. S. Worth (1975); L. P. Elwell-Sutton, *The Persian Metres* (1976), App. 1; M. Shapiro, *Asymmetry* (1976), ch. 4; *Die Genese der europäischen Endreimdichtung*, ed. U. Ernst and P.-E. Neuser (1977); J. M. Lotman, *The Structure of the Artistic Text*, trans. G. Lenhoff and R. Vroon (1977); D. S. Worth, "Roman Jakobson and the Study of Rhyme," *Roman Jakobson: Echoes of His Scholarship*, ed. D. Armstrong (1977); W. E. Rickert, "Rhyme Terms," *Style* 12 (1978); G. Schweikle, "Reim," etc., *Reallexikon II* 3.403–31; D. Wesling, *The Chances of Rhyme* (1980); Scott; Brogan, 77 ff.—full bibl. for Eng. to 1981, with coverage of other langs. in appendices, extended in *Verseform* (1989); B. de Cornulier, "La rime n'est pas une marque de fin de vers," *Poétique* 46 (1981); Group μ; Mazaleyrat; J. Molino and J. Tamine, "Des rimes, et quelques raisons," *Poétique* 52 (1982); D. S. Samoilov, *Kniga o russkoi rifme*, 2d ed. (1982)—fullest study of Rus.; R. Birkenhauer, *Reimpoetik am*

Beispiel Stefan Georges (1983); B. de Cornulier, "Sur les groupements de vers classiques
et la rime," *Cahiers de grammaire* 6 (1983);
F. P. Memmo, *Dizionario di metrica italiana*
(1983); Navarro—Sp.; Norden, 2.810 ff.; *The
Old English Riming Poem*, ed. O. Macrae-
Gibson (1983); D. Billy, "La nomenclature
des rimes," *Poétique* 57 (1984); M. T. Ikegami,
Rhyme and Pronunciation (1984)—ME; W. E.
Rickert, "Semantic Consequences of Rhyme,"
Literature in Performance 4 (1984); Cham-
bers—Occitan; "Rhyme and the True Call-
ing of Words," in Hollander; W. E. Rickert,
"B. de Cornulier, "Rime 'riche' et fonction
de la rime," *Littérature* 59 (1985); B. Nagel,
*Das Reimproblem in der deutschen Dichtung
vom Otfridvers zum freien Vers* (1985); Scherr,
ch. 4; W. Harmon, "Rhyme in English Verse:
History, Structures, Functions," *SP* 84 (1987);
L. M. Guinee and K. B. Payne, "Rhyme-Like
Repetitions in Songs of Humpback Whales,"
Ethology 79 (1988); C. Scott, *The Riches of
Rhyme* (1988); J. J. Small, *Positive as Sound*
(1990); G. Stewart, *Reading Voices* (1990), ch.
2; B.M.H. Strang, "Language, General," *The
Spenser Encyclopedia*, ed. A. C. Hamilton et
al. (1990); L. Mugglestone, "The Fallacy of
the Cockney Rhyme," *RES* 42 (1991); J. Ray-
man and E. Zaidel, "Rhyming and the Right
Hemisphere," *Brain and Language* 40 (1991);
Gasparov, *History*; M. McKie, "The Origins
and Early Development of Rhyme in English Verse," *MLR* (1997); Morier; W. Flesch,
"The Conjuror's Trick, or How to Rhyme,"
Literary Imagination 3 (2001); K. Hanson,
"Vowel Variation in English Rhyme," *Studies
in the History of the English Language*, ed. D.
Minkova and R. Stockwell (2002); H. Kenner,
"Rhyme: An Unfinished Monograph," *Common Knowledge* 10 (2004); R. Dainotto, "Of
the Arab Origin of Modern Europe: Giam-
maria Barbieri, Juan Andrés, and the Origin
of Rhyme," *CL* 58 (2006); J. P. Hunter, "Seven
Reasons for Rhyme," *Ritual, Routine, and Regime*, ed. L. Clymer (2006); K. Árnason, "On
the Principles of Nordic Rhyme and Alliteration," *Arkiv for Nordisk Filologi/Archives for
Scandinavian Philology* 122 (2007); A. Bradley,
Book of Rhymes: The Poetics of Hip Hop (2009);
S. Stewart, "Rhyme and Freedom," *The Sound
of Poetry/The Poetry of Sound*, ed. M. Perloff
and C. Dworkin (2009); M. Chasar, "The
Business of Rhyming: Burma-Shave Poetry
and Popular Culture," *PMLA* 125 (2010).

T.V.F. Brogan, S. Cushman

RHYME ROYAL. A seven-line *pentameter
*stanza rhyming *ababbcc*, one of many complex stanzas developed in the late Middle Ages;
sometimes called the Troilus stanza, after Chaucer's use of it in *Troilus and Criseyde*. The name
has speculatively been associated with the stanzaic form of the Scottish King James I's "The
Kingis Quair" (c. 1425) but is more likely to
have emerged from late med. Fr. forms of ceremonial and festive addresses to royalty; these
trads. underlie the vigor of rhyme royal in John
Skelton's Eng. *Magnyfycence*, Thomas Sackville's
induction to *A Mirror for Magistrates*, and other
works of drama, pageantry, and rhetorical address in Eng.

Chaucer's devel. of rhyme royal emerges
from his familiarity with Fr. courtly poetry, esp.
the ballade stanzas of Guillaume de Machaut
and Eustache Deschamps, and with the *ottava
rima* of Giovanni Boccaccio. Chaucer adapted
and shortened by one line each of these forms
while amplifying the stanza's syntactic spacious-
ness. He uses rhyme royal in a ballade-like way
for reflection, philosophizing, and emotional
expressiveness, as does his contemporary John
Gower, who favors rhyme royal for philosophical love poetry. Chaucer also uses rhyme royal
for narrative, a brilliant innovation, in the
Troilus and *The Parliament of Fowls, Anelida
and Arcite*, and certain *Canterbury Tales*. In
the *Troilus*, it is agile and flexible: enjambed
or end-stopped at any point, enjambing even
across stanza breaks, it accommodates dialogue,
action, or reflection; it moves swiftly or slowly,
in tones exalted, rough, or colloquial. When
Shakespeare used rhyme royal in *The Rape of
Lucrece*, he tested its capacities for violent action and violent reflection at once.

The rhyme scheme of rhyme royal, with its
medial *bb* *couplet, means that the first *quatrain, in alternating rhymes, ends with a line
(line 4) which is also the first line of that medial couplet (lines 4–5). Readers might experience this overlap as a unifying ligature or as
a gradual disruption or surprise in the move
from quatrain to couplet; the third *b*-rhyme
(line 5) as a dilation or amplification that
slows narrative momentum. These potentialities create a sense of amplitude and openness
within the stanza, lending it to delineation of
elusive temporal experiences: reverie, dream,
vision, thresholds between waking and sleeping, dawns and dusks. Chaucer explores rhyme
royal's temporal capacities in the directions of
dream vision and comedy in *The Parliament of*

Fowls, in the direction of philosophical love narrative and tragedy in the *Troilus*. Thomas Wyatt develops temporal bemusement in other directions through rhyme royal in "They Flee from Me"; Edmund Spenser in "An Hymne of Heavenly Beauty"; John Milton in "On the Death of a Fair Infant Dying of a Cough" and in the proem of "On the Morning of Christ's Nativity." In this latter poem, the rhyme royal stanza has been expanded and its historical argument deepened by augmenting its seventh line to a Spenserian *alexandrine, a move that would influence the rhyme royal practices of Thomas Chatterton, S. T. Coleridge, and William Wordsworth when they revived med. forms and genres (e.g., Wordsworth's "Resolution and Independence"). In mod. times, the most powerful poem in this line is W. B. Yeats's "A Bronze Head."

The rhyme royal stanza has been decreed solemn at least since the 16th c., when George Gascoigne considered it "serving best for grave discourses"; this could fairly be said of some rhyme royal works by 15th- and early 16th-c. Chaucerians like John Lydgate, Thomas Hoccleve, William Dunbar, Robert Henryson, Stephen Hawes, and Alexander Barclay. But it could not be said of the range of Chaucerian work in the form, much less of W.H. Auden's use of it for tonal juxtapositions in the 1955 poem "The Shield of Achilles," or his 1937 tour de force *Letter to Lord Byron*, which impersonates a light poem by achieving a long rhyme royal poem with abundant feminine rhymes and a wittering air. It is a bravura, unique performance—as is Francis Kinaston's 1635 achievement of translating a full two books of Chaucer's *Troilus* into perfect Lat. rhyme royal stanzas, published as *Amorum Troili et Creseidae libri duo priores Anglico-Latini*.

See SEPTET.

T. KRIER

RHYME SCHEME (Ger. *Reimfolge*). An ideal pattern of rhyme in strophic or stichic verse or the written representation of the same. Usually, the term *rhyme scheme* refers to end rhymes, but variants of the conventional representation can refer also to *internal rhyme. Poets may undertake significant departures from the model rhyme scheme suggested by a poem, and the variability of *rhyme itself leads to further variability of actual rhyme patterns. A standardized notation for rhyme scheme uses lowercase letters of the alphabet to represent patterns:

the first rhyme sound is represented as *a* at its first and every subsequent occurrence, the second *b*, and so on, with *x* (and sometimes *y*, *z*, etc., in sequence) for lines that do not rhyme. Thus, *couplets rhyme *aa bb cc dd*, etc., *rhyme royal *ababbcc*, and the Shakespearean *sonnet *ababcdcdefefgg*. This system of notation was employed as early as the Ren., when Antonio Minturno used it in his *L'arte Poetica* (1563). No standardized notation exists for the *refrains of forms in which entire words or lines are repeated, e.g., the *sestina, the *villanelle, and the ghazal, but critics generally use the capital *R* or a superscript diacritical mark or number. Rhyme schemes bind constellations of sound and meaning as they link poems to formal trads. Just as the rhyme scheme of a Shakespearean sonnet divides the poem sonically into three quatrains and a couplet, e.g., the thought in the poem typically progresses in three parts toward the proposition of the closing couplet. Even as it binds internally, the rhyme scheme of a sonnet can connect it to the larger hist. of all sonnets and, by means of that connection, generate a range of figurative meanings. Not all rhyme schemes bind sound, meaning, and poetic trad. as tightly as the typical Shakespearean sonnet, however, and various rhyme schemes have greater and lesser degrees of complexity and bond force (Ger. *Reimzwang*).

See STANZA.

■ A. Minturno, *L'arte poetica* (1563); J. Hollander, *Melodious Guile* (1988), ch. 5—how particular sonnets allegorize their own rhyme schemes; S. Adams, *Poetic Designs* (1997); M. N. Carminati et al., "Readers' Responses to Sub-genre and Rhyme Scheme in Poetry," *Poetics* 34 (2006).

T.V.F. BROGAN; E. RETTBERG

RHYTHM (Gr. *rhythmos*; Lat. *rhythmus*).

  I. Features of Rhythm
  II. Rhythm versus Meter
  III. Analysis of Rhythm

Although when it was first used in Eng., in the 16th and 17th cs., the word *rhythm* was not clearly distinguished from the word *rhyme* (both words being spelled in a variety of ways), by the 18th c. it was being consistently employed to refer to the durational qualities of poetry and music, and soon extended to analogous properties of the visual arts. In the 19th c., it was generalized to movement of a regular kind—most often the alternation of strong and weak elements—in any sphere, and appropriated by the physical sciences for periodicities and patterns in a range of natural phenomena. The word has retained throughout its hist. an aesthetic aspect, suggesting a movement or spatial arrangement that exhibits some degree of regularity without being mechanical. In poetry and music, it is often opposed to *meter, understood as a more precisely structured, quantifiable movement.

One cannot understand rhythm without considering its realization in human psychology and physiology; as readers of poetry, it is the *experience* of rhythm that is important to us, and this experience is both mental and bodily. At its most basic, rhythm is a patterning of energy, of tension and release, movement and countermovement that we both perceive and produce—or reproduce—in our own brains and muscles. The most powerful stimuli in producing a sense of rhythm are those that can be interpreted as bursts of energy, the drum being an obvious example. There is a distinction to be made between the noun *rhythm* and the adjective *rhythmic*: the latter usually implies a fairly strong regularity, so that we can say, "This is not a particularly rhythmic line," whereas the former can embrace both movements that are metronomic in character and those that are far from metronomic. In their use of rhythm, poetry and music are most closely allied—which does not mean that poetry can be adequately analyzed by means of musical notation (though the many attempts to do so are not without interest), but that both arts draw on the same human rhythmic faculty and thus can gain insights from one another.

Every spoken lang. has its own rhythm, which is to say a distinctive movement of sound, and the pulses of energy that produce it, in a temporal dimension. Linguistic rhythm is a product of the particular language's deployment of volume, duration, timbre, and pitch in reflecting lexical and syntactic structures as well as particular emphases. As the use of the term *rhythm* suggests, there is a degree of periodicity in this use of sound, although different langs. achieve it in different ways. The most common classification of langs. is threefold: stress-timed langs., such as Eng., Ger., and Dutch; syllable-timed langs., such as Fr., It., and Sp.; and mora-timed langs., such as Japanese and Tamil (where the speech rhythm is based on subsyllabic elements). This does not mean that in spoken Eng., e.g., the durations between stresses are objectively equal, nor that in spoken Fr., all syllables are of the same length. Phonetic evidence shows that isochronism is not a matter of equal duration but of a tendency in this direction, evident, for instance, in the relative durations of vowels to consonants, which are proportionally higher in stress-timed languages (see Ramus et al.). Speakers of Eng. perceive stresses as the dominant element in the language's tendency toward regular rhythm, whereas the syllables—although they too play a part in creating the rhythmic quality of Eng. speech—are felt to be subsidiary. In Fr., by contrast, the syllables are felt to be the carriers of rhythm, with stress a secondary feature.

The characteristic verse forms of a lang. reflect its rhythm; thus, traditional Fr. verse is based on a syllable count, while traditional Eng. verse is based on the disposition of stresses. However, in Fr. and in Eng., the rhythmic subtlety of which metrical poetry is capable arises from the interplay between syllabic and stress rhythms, both of which are produced by the operation of the body's musculature in sequences of tension and release. In the most strongly regular verse, the different sources of rhythmic movement in a lang. are aligned, and the resulting movement conforms to the general properties of rhythmic organization.

*Free verse does not organize the features of the lang. in such a way as to produce a regular rhythm, but due to the inherently rhythmic character of every lang. and the structuring devices used by the poet (which can include lineation, syntactic arrangement, and rhyme), rhythm remains an important element in the reader's experience.

I. Features of Rhythm. Rhythm as a psychophysiological phenomenon possesses certain properties, irrespective of the medium in which it is realized. Stable rhythms characteristically display five features: regularity, repetition, variety, hierarchy, and grouping.

A. *Regularity*. Rhythmic series consist of perceived signals occurring at intervals that are either regular or are close enough to being regular to create and constantly reinforce the expectation of regularity. In reading a text, the mind is continually making rapid predictions about what is likely to be perceived on the basis of what it has just perceived (and still holds in short-term memory); if the expected signal is delayed or missing, the mind will often supply it. An experience of rhythm will not arise if the time lapse between signals is too great; this, however, is not likely to happen in the case of poetry, except in a very unusual style of performance. When regularity is marked, and the expectation of regularity strong, the signals are perceived as *beats. (It has been argued, e.g. by Couper-Kuhlen, that this happens in spoken Eng. as well as in verse.)

B. *Repetition.* In order for a rhythm to be perceived, the successive stimuli must be experienced as *the same* stimulus occurring over and over again. In poetry, the rhythm is based on identifiable linguistic units: stressed syllables, syllables, or mora (irrespective of the phonetic differences that occur as these units are repeated). Again, expectation plays a large role in the perception of rhythmic stimuli: having heard a number of repeated signals, we are likely to interpret further stimuli as more of the same.

C. *Variation.* Exact repetition is usually felt to be monotonous, however, though the precise point at which pleasurable repetition becomes tedious is not easily specifiable. Variation is thus crucial to the enjoyment of rhythm, but if the signal varies too greatly from what is expected, the pattern will be perceived as unrhythmical—or as the beginning of a new rhythmic series.

D. *Hierarchy.* The repeated stimuli that create a regular rhythm are usually perceived as possessing some further organization, rather than being understood as a simple series. The fact that we hear a clock's "tick-tick-tick-tick" as "tick-tock-tick-tock" is one of the most familiar examples of this tendency: in this case, an exactly repeated stimulus is interpreted as an alternation between a stronger and weaker signal. This interpretation produces a hierarchy: over and above the rhythm of the repeated sounds, we hear a more widely spaced rhythm made up of the "stronger" sounds. If we were asked to tap on one out of every two sounds, we would find ourselves tapping on those we hear as "ticks" rather than those we hear as "tocks."

The hierarchical nature of regular rhythm is very clear in music, where the fundamental rhythmic units, the beats, are perceived in patterns of strong and weak, or strong, less strong, and weak, and so on. Thus a *measure of four beats will begin (according to convention) with the strongest beat, followed

by a weak beat, then a somewhat strong beat, then another weak beat. Once this pattern is established (something that can be achieved in a number of ways, incl. variations in pitch, timbre, or loudness), it will continue to be heard unless an alternative organization imposes itself on the hearer. In verse, a four-beat line will tend to follow the same pattern, although other factors such as emphasis and syntax can obscure it. The common stanza in *accentual-syllabic verse consisting of 4 four-beat, or *tetrameter, lines can be thought of as having an underlying rhythm in which the initial beats of the first and third lines are the strongest (the "highest" level of the hierarchy, where each unit is two lines), the next strongest beats are at the start of the second and last lines, then the third beats of each line, then the second and final beats of each line. The first stanza of William Blake's "London" will illustrate, using **B**, B, **b**, b to indicate beats of descending strength:

I wander thro' each charter'd street.
B   b   **b**   b

Near where the charter'd Thames does flow
B   b   **b**   b

And mark in every face I meet
B   b   **b**   b

Marks of weakness, marks of woe
B   b   **b**   b

This tendency is particularly marked in dipodic verse, in which the lang. of the lines induces a strong alternation between the beats; alternatively, it can be obscured by the establishment of a contrary rhythm by the lang.

Rhythmic hierarchies are based on twos and threes; series of four or more are perceived as having stronger and weaker beats, and therefore a hierarchical structure. At the lowest level of the hierarchy, this gives rise to duple and triple rhythms; above this level, arrangements of threes are less common. By far the commonest rhythm is the duple rhythm, that is, one based on simple alternation between stronger and weaker stimuli, beat and offbeat; and in popular verse in many langs., this alternation is repeated at higher levels to produce the familiar four-beat rhythm—also a staple of med. verse, Lat. and vernacular, sacred and profane, and many trads. of art verse.

At a certain point in the hierarchy that cannot be defined precisely (and no doubt varies from reader to reader), rhythm fades, to be replaced by what might be called balance. Thus, the relation between 2 four-line tetrameter stanzas is unlikely to be perceived as a matter of rhythm—which is to say, it is unlikely to be registered somatically—though it may be intellectually understood as a strong-weak, or weak-strong, relation. Some analysts, however, incl. Cureton, use the word *rhythm* for relations over these much longer spans.

E. Grouping. As a result of rhythm's hierarchical nature, mora, syllables, or stresses (depending on the lang.) are perceived in groups of two or three or combinations thereof. Grouping is achieved not by the insertion of dividers between the groups, although the use of bar lines and foot divisions may seem to suggest this, but rather by a number of factors working together to encourage the perception of a closer link between some elements than between others. The use of a strict meter is one such factor: accentual-syllabic verse in a duple meter that begins regularly with an unstressed syllable or offbeat will encourage the perception of groups of two syllables, unstressed then stressed; this is *iambic meter, each unit of which is an iambic *foot. The reverse arrangement produces *trochaic feet. If, as in the former, weaker elements are grouped before stronger elements, the result is a rising rhythm; if, as in the latter, stronger elements are grouped before weaker elements, the result is a falling rhythm. Tetrameter lines exhibit a tendency to divide into two groups of four syllables; in *pentameter lines, there is less pressure to fall into a regular grouping (though 4:6 and 6:4 are the most common groups). *Alexandrines most often fall into two groups of six syllables. However, word, phrase, clause, and sentence divisions may cut across these metrically induced groupings to produce a more complex, less clear-cut pattern of groups. And if the meter does not generate particular expectations of grouping—for instance, if the openings of lines vary freely between beats and offbeats—these linguistic divisions, together with line divisions, play the dominant role in determining the perception of groups.

II. Rhythm versus Meter. The distinction between rhythm and meter is old, dating to at least the 4th c. BCE. The disagreement between the *metrici* and the *rhythmici* in ancient Greece reflected two approaches to verse, one strictly quantitative, the other musical, and the two terms have retained these connotations. Meter is that aspect of regular rhythm that can be labeled and counted. It is sometimes conceptualized as an abstract pattern coexisting with the actual, varied rhythm of the poem's lang., and most systems of *scansion are designed to provide a graphic representation of this pattern, though there is no psychological evidence for the simultaneous perception of two different levels in our apprehension of metrical verse. The evidence of Ren. attempts to write vernacular verse in cl. meters, however, suggests that the intellectual apprehension of complex metrical patterns can coexist with the aural appreciation of rhythm.

When the rhythm-bearing features of a lang. are arranged in such a way as to produce marked regularity, and thus the perception of beats, the basis for metrical organization exists. And when the series of beats and intervening offbeats are themselves organized into patterns, a meter is perceived, usually in conformity with a set of numerical constraints that has developed in the linguistic trad. in question. Meter can thus be understood as a particular form of rhythm, but it must be remembered that even the strictest metrical verse will retain some of the variety and unpredictability of the language's native rhythm. The establishment of a metrical pattern will also have an effect on the perception of rhythm, for instance, in the promotion or *demotion of certain syllables. Any verse allows for a variety of individual *performances, within the parameters set by the norms of the lang., and, in the case of regular verse, the demands of the meter.

III. Analysis of Rhythm. The task of rhythmic analysis is to reflect the movement of lang.—words, phrases, clauses, and sentences—in verse, as perceived by the reader. In free verse, this movement does not induce the experience of a regular pattern and its accompanying expectations, although with some free verse, it is appropriate to include an indication of its movement toward and away from such a pattern. In metrical verse, a full rhythmic analysis will include scrutiny of the movement that both creates and varies a metrical pattern.

One approach to rhythmic analysis is to examine phonetic records of performances of verse, using techniques developed for the phonetic analysis of speech (see, e.g., Chatman and Tsur, *Poetic Rhythm*). This approach is esp.

useful for illuminating the different performance styles of different readers and periods, less useful in understanding the rhythmic properties common to a number of readings. The use of musical symbols to represent the rhythmic features of spoken lang. in verse, as proposed, for instance, by Joshua Steele in *Prosodia Rationalis* (1775) and Sidney Lanier in *The Science of English Verse* (1880), has proved less successful, since musical rhythm is determined by specified pitches and durations, whereas linguistic rhythm depends on relations among units.

Phonological investigations of lang. rhythms may utilize terminology that overlaps with that of poetic analysis, thanks to the close connection between natural speech rhythm and verse trad., thus providing tools for rhythmic analysis in poetry (see Hanson and Kiparsky; Hayes 1984 and 1989). Whereas earlier phonological accounts of stress in Eng. relied on the apportioning of numbered levels to syllables, often influencing studies of poetic rhythm, generative phonology and subsequent devels. in linguistic science have demonstrated the importance of lexical and syntactic structures, as well as the operation of general rules of rhythm, in establishing rhythmic hierarchies.

Another approach draws on studies of rhythm in music to scrutinize the complex hierarchies created by the phonological, morphological, and syntactic properties of the lang. used in verse. Cureton, for instance, exploits the influential theory of musical rhythm propounded by Lerdahl and Jackendoff (itself owing much to generative studies of lang.) to develop an account of rhythmic phrasing in verse (see also Attridge, *Poetic Rhythm*, ch. 8). Discussions of folk songs by Hayes and MacEachern and by Kiparsky using optimality theory have provided insights into the relation among the rhythm of the spoken lang., the rhythm established by the meter, and the rhythm of the musical setting. Approaches within the field of cognitive poetics make use of studies of brain functions, such as the operation of short-term or working memory, and build on older studies of perception such as Gestalt theory (see Tsur 1977). There is still much that is not fully understood about the operation of rhythm in verse, and its relation to the rhythms of lang. and of music, and to rhythm itself as a perceptual phenomenon.

■ **Rhythm and Music:** D. Tovey, "Rhythm," *Encyclopaedia Britannica*, 11th ed. (1910–11); G. W. Cooper and L. B. Meyer, *The Rhythmic Structure of Music* (1960); F. Lerdahl and R. Jackendoff, *A Generative Theory of Tonal Music* (1983); J. London, "Rhythm," *Grove Music Online*, http://www.grovemusic.com/shared/views/article.html?from=az&section=music.45963.

■ **Rhythm and Speech:** K. L. Pike, *The Intonation of American English* (1945); D. Abercrombie, *Studies in Phonetics and Linguistics* (1965); D. L. Bolinger, *Forms of English* (1965); Chomsky and Halle; D. Crystal, *Prosodic Systems and Intonation in English* (1969); J. G. Martin, "Rhythmic (Hierarchical) versus Serial Structure in Speech and Other Behavior," *PsychologR* 79 (1972); Allen—Part I on general questions; G. D. Allen, "Speech Rhythm," *JPhon* 3 (1975); M. Liberman and A. Prince, "On Stress and Linguistic Rhythm," *LingI* 8 (1977); I. Lehiste, "Isochrony Reconsidered," *JPhon* 7 (1979); H. J. Giegerich, "On Stress-Timing in English Phonology," *Lingua* 51 (1980); B. Hayes, "The Phonology of Rhythm in English," *LingI* 15 (1984); E. Couper-Kuhlen, *English Speech Rhythm* (1993); F. Ramus, M. Nespor, and J. Mehler, "Correlates of Linguistic Rhythm in the Speech Signal," *Cognition* 73 (1999).

■ **Rhythm and Verse:** Chatman; M. W. Croll, *Style, Rhetoric and Rhythm*, ed. J. M. Patrick et al. (1966); W. Mohr, "Rhythmus," *Reallexikon II* v. 3 (1971); D. W. Harding, *Words into Rhythm* (1976); P. Kiparsky, "The Rhythmic Structure of English Verse," *LingI* 8 (1977); R. Tsur, *A Perception-Oriented Theory of Metre* (1977); T.V.F. Brogan, *English Versification, 1570–1980* (1981)—bibl.; Attridge, *Rhythms*; Scherr; C. Scott, *A Question of Syllables* (1986)—rhythm in Fr. verse; B. Hayes, "The Prosodic Hierarchy in Meter," *Phonetics and Phonology I*, ed. P. Kiparsky and G. Youmans (1989); Cureton; Attridge, *Poetic Rhythm*; K. Hanson and P. Kiparsky, "A Parametric Theory of Poetic Meter," *Lang* 72 (1996); B. Hayes and M. MacEachern, "Quatrain Form in English Folk Verse," *Lang* 74 (1998); R. Tsur, *Poetic Rhythm* (1998); E. Arndt and H. Fricke, "Rhythmus," *Reallexikon III*, v. 3 (2003); P. Kiparsky, "A Modular Metrics for Folk Verse," *Formal Approaches to Poetry*, ed. B. E. Dresher and N. Friedberg (2006).

D. ATTRIDGE

RICH RHYME (Fr. *rime riche*, Ger. *reicher Reim*, It. *rima cara*). Definitions of "exact" or "true" rhyme tend to require a difference in sound along with the similarity: the final vowel and all following phonemes sound the same, but the preceding consonant or consonants differ, if any are present (e.g., *may/day*). In accentual langs. such as Eng., exact rhyme will entail the sameness of the final stressed vowel and all following phonemes (see RHYME). Rich rhyme extends sonic similarity back to the preceding consonant, e.g., *may/dismay* or even *may/May*.

The consonant-vowel-consonant likenesses of rich rhyme suggest three general possibilities. First, the rhymed terms may be homophones, with like sound but different spelling and meaning, e.g., *night/knight, foul/fowl, stare/stair*, or Fr. *violence/balance*. Homographs, with differing sound but like spelling, as in *read / read* (present tense, past tense) or *conflict/conflict* (verb, noun), have affinities with rich rhyme but can be more accurately labeled eye rhyme since they feature differing vowel sounds. The most extreme case of rich rhyme is the homonym, in which both spelling and sound are alike but meaning significantly differs, e.g., Eng. *want/want* (lack, desire), *port/port* (harbor, wine) or Fr. *été/été* (summer, been).

The term *rich rhyme* derives from a Fr. spectrum of rhyming, from the poor rhyme of *assonance through sufficient and rich rhyme to the even richer *leonine rhyme, which extends rhyming backward over two full syllables (and must be distinguished from the homonymous med. verse form). The Fr. origin of the term suggests its frequency in the lang. The technique appears in quantity in the 15th c. as one of the devices of the *rhétoriqueurs*, and Thomas Sébillet gave it the name *rime riche* in 1490. Pierre de Ronsard, Joachim du Bellay, and other poets of the Pléiade allowed it in moderation. After 1600, rich rhyme fell out of favor in Fr. but was later revived by the romantics, particularly Victor Hugo. Championed subsequently by Théodore de Banville, it was used even more by the Parnassians.

Chaucer and John Gower, whose Eng. owes much to Fr., employ rich rhyme regularly: *heere/heere* (here /hear), e.g., and *herte/herte* (hurt/heart). However, since the Ren., in which Thomas Wyatt and Edmund Spenser used rich rhyme regularly, the practice has been quite rare. Many *prosody manuals insist that rich rhyme is impermissible in Eng., to the extent that some give rich rhyme the name "false rhyme." Hollander argues that rich rhyme in Eng. "always must fall ridiculously flat, underlined as the like syllables are by their stressed position. In English *rime très*

riche is always in a sense, *rime pauvre*." Small has argued that Eng. resistance to rich rhyme arises more from convention than from actual qualities of the lang., and she finds a surprising prevalence of rich rhyme in Emily Dickinson's verse. Because of its rarity, rich rhyme in Eng. offers an element of surprise that can be used to accentuate semantic meaning. The two rhymed words may be alike in sound, but they can differ with respect to local meaning or usage while also contrasting with the more typical rhymes around them.

Rich rhyme occurs in many other lits., incl. It., Sp., and cl. Ar. Identical rhyme extends the similitude of rich rhyme to the level of meaning, e.g., *may/may*, where both are the verb. The echo device is one species of rich rhyme. Ger. *rührende Reim* is a type of mosaic rich or identical rhyme popular in MHG in which one of the rhyming words is a compound of the other, e.g., Ger. *zeigen/erzeigen*, Fr. *aroi/a roi*, Eng. *mortal/immortal*.

■ T. de Banville, *Petit traité de poésie française* (1872); P. Delaporte, *De la rime française* (1898); Kastner; Schipper, *History*, 273; C. von Kraus, "Der rührende Reim im Mittelhochdeutschen," *ZDA* 56 (1918); Patterson; M. Ito, *John Gower the Medieval Poet* (1976); C. Smith, "On Sound-Patterning in the *Poema de mio Cid*," *Hispanic Review* 44 (1976); Scott; Mazaleyrat; D. Billy, "La Nomenclature des Rimes," *Poétique* 15 (1984); B. de Cornulier, "Rime 'riche' et fonction de la rime," *Littérature* 59 (1985); Hollander; Scherr; C. Scott, *The Riches of Rhyme* (1988); J. J. Small, *Positive as Sound* (1990), ch. 4; G.J. van Gelder, "Rhyme in Maqāmāt," *Journal of Semitic Studies* 44 (1999).

T.V.F. BROGAN; E. RETTBERG

RIDDLE. Ancient and worldwide phenomena in both oral trad. (the "folk riddle") and written lit. (the "literary riddle"), riddles take the form of question and answer. Typically, an intentionally misleading question presents an enigma that can be resolved only by a clever "right" answer. The impulse to dismiss riddle as "a sort of trick question which, once answered, has no further interest—a silly puzzle which, once clarified, self-destructs" (Wilbur) has been refuted by a long trad. of scholarship that treats riddle as a site for central aspects of poetry and poetics, incl. *metaphor, wordplay, *paradox, and *imagery.

In a "true riddle," the question presents a description, which usually describes something in terms of something else, and a "block element," a contradiction or confusion that disrupts the initial description. E.g., the riddle "What plows and plows, but no furrow remains" first appears to describe a plow, then blocks that answer by eliminating the effect of a plow. The implicit answer to this riddle—a ship—arises only after the listener or reader suppresses the initial response and thinks of another object to which the verb *plow* might apply. Such riddles are essentially metaphors with one term concealed, pointing out both similarities and differences between the terms. Some metaphorical riddles leave the block element implicit: "Back of the village sit those who have donned white kerchiefs" (fence posts, each with a cap of snow). Other kinds of riddles rely on puns—"What turns without moving" (milk)—or on anomalies in the laws of nature—"I tremble at each breath of air, / And yet can heaviest burdens bear" (water).

The folk riddle tends to appear in structured social occasions, from children's games to adult rituals like courtship in tribal South Africa and funeral wakes in the West Indies. A number of other kinds of enigmatic questions associated with riddle also occur in social ritual: e.g., biblical riddles, which describe a character in the Bible; the joking questions known as "conundrums," e.g., "How is a duck like an icicle? Both grow down"; wisdom questions, as in a catechism; charades, which describe a word syllable by syllable; and parody forms such as the catch-riddle, which tricks the answerer into an embarrassing answer.

Literary riddle brings literary ambitions to the basic form of folk riddle, tending toward longer and more elaborate expression. In contrast to folk riddles, literary riddles may use abstractions as topics (e.g., creation, humility, death, wisdom), exploit the device of *prosopopoeia*, delight in obscene suggestions, and even give away the answer in the text or title.

The literary riddle has a long hist., appearing in Sanskrit, in which the cosmological riddles of the *Rig Veda* go back to the early first millennium BCE; in Heb., where a trad. of literary riddles runs from the OT and Talmud through the Heb. poetry of med. Spain, incl. the poetry of Dunash Ibn Labrat (10th c.) and Jehudah Halevi (ca. 1074–1141); in Gr., esp. in the *Greek Anthology* and in Byzantine lit.; in Ar., from the 10th c. to the present, the most famous Ar. riddlemaster being Al-Ḥarīrī (ca. 1050–1120); in Persian lit. extending from the 10th and 11th

cs. through the 16th, incl. the epic *Shāhnāma* of Firdawsī (b. 940); and perhaps in Chinese, where evidence, though no discovered text, suggests literary riddling in the 12th and 13th cs. A rich med. trad. began in Europe with 100 Lat. riddles by Symphosius (5th c.). In England, Aldhelm (640–709) wrote 100 riddles in Anglo-Lat. hexameters (*Enigmata*), contributing to the genre of the etymological riddle, which uses the text of the riddle to explore the Lat. name of the answer. The riddles of the OE Exeter Book (ca. 10th c.), which feature involved riddling descriptions of everyday things, are exemplary and have been the focus of much critical consideration. The Ren. was another productive period for the literary riddle, particularly in Italy. Later writers attracted to riddles include Miguel de Cervantes, Jonathan Swift, Friedrich Schiller, Heinrich Heine, and Emily Dickinson.

These instances of the riddle genre can be distinguished from a pervasive literary mode of riddling at work in a bevy of other genres incl. "sacred writing, . . . tragedy, comedy, romance, lyric kinds, even the novel," as Cook has noted. Indeed, the conjunction and disjunction of implicitly compared terms in riddle suggest poetic *metaphor, as Aristotle argued in the *Rhetoric*: "metaphors imply riddles, and therefore a good riddle can furnish a good metaphor." Frye, in *Anatomy of Criticism*, associates riddle with visual imagery, arguing that "the radical of *opsis* in the lyric is *riddle*," and Welsh treats the visual imagery of riddles as the basis for a theory of the roots of *lyric poetry. Wilbur observes that the visual suggestions in the question of a riddle imprint themselves on readers' minds, a mental quirk that gives the metaphoric pairings of riddles more impact: "If someone says to me, *think of a white bird*, a white bird appears in my mind's eye; if I am then told to forget about the bird, I find that its image will not go away."

The dialogic structure of even literary riddle suggests social interaction, "a competition between the riddler and the riddlees" (Pagis). As such, a riddle holds in social and literary tension the meaning it conceals and the meaning it reveals. "The deliberate obscurity of riddles," Tiffany argues, "does not imply the absence of disclosure or sociability." The process of mental concentration and play that riddles demand, in fact, can instruct: children, e.g., explore the ling. and cognitive systems of their cultures through riddle contests (McDowell).

Riddles, in fact, model defamiliarization, the poetic process of making the world strange that Viktor Shklovsky treated as central to the literary imagination. The first term of the question is made strange by the block element, and once an answer arrives, both terms are made strange in relation to each other. As Tiffany has argued, a riddle "withholds the name of a thing, so that the thing may appear as what it is not, in order to be revealed for what it is." The figurative operations of riddle, then, have suggested compressed instances of the operations of poetic imagery and wordplay. The task of discerning the connections and disjunctions of lang. and meaning that the interpreter of riddles undertakes, far from a passing triviality or a forgettable joke, mirrors the process of literary interpretation itself.

See KENNING.

■ *The Demaundes Joyous* (1511; rpt. 1971)— first mod. Eng. riddle book; J. B. Friedreich, *Geschichte des Räthsels* (1860); K. Ohlert, *Rätsel und Gesellschaftsspiel der alten Griechen*, 2d ed. (1886); W. Schultz, "Rätsel," Pauly-Wissowa; W. Schultz, *Rätsel aus dem hellenischen Kulturkreise* (1909–12); *The Riddles of Aldhelm*, trans. J. H. Pitman (1925); M. De Filippis, *The Literary Riddle in Italy to the End of the Sixteenth Century* (1948); A. Taylor, *The Literary Riddle before 1600* (1948), and *English Riddles from Oral Tradition* (1951); M. De Filippis, *The Literary Riddle in Italy in the Seventeenth Century* (1953); V. Hull and A. Taylor, *A Collection of Irish Riddles* (1955); Frye; K. Wagner, "Rätsel," *Reallexikon II*; J. F. Adams, "The Anglo-Saxon Riddle as Lyric Mode," *Criticism* 7 (1965); D. Bhagwat, *The Riddle in Indian Life, Lore and Literature* (1965); C. T. Scott, *Persian and Arabic Riddles* (1965); A. Hacikyan, *A Linguistic and Literary Analysis of Old English Riddles* (1966); M. De Filippis, *The Literary Riddle in Italy in the Eighteenth Century* (1967); D. D. Lucas, *Emily Dickinson and Riddle* (1969); C. T. Scott, "On Defining the Riddle," *Genre* 2 (1969); R. Finnegan, *Oral Literature in Africa* (1970), ch. 15; R. D. Abrahams and A. Dundes, "Riddles," *Folklore and Folklife*, ed. R. M. Dorson (1972); *Deutsches Rätselbuch*, ed. V. Schupp (1972); I. Basgöz and A. Tietze, *Bilmece: A Corpus of Turkish Riddles* (1973); J. Lindow, "Riddles, Kennings, and the Complexity of Skaldic Poetry," *Scandinavian Studies* 47 (1975); N. Frye, "Charms and Riddles," *Spiritus Mundi* (1976); *JAF* 89.352 (1976)—special

iss. on riddles and riddling; *The Old English Riddles of the Exeter Book*, ed. C. Williamson (1977); Welsh; J. H. McDowell, *Children's Riddling* (1979); C. Williamson, *A Feast of Creatures* (1982); *Riddles Ancient and Modern*, ed. M. Bryant (1983); W. J. Pepicello and T. A. Green, *The Language of Riddles* (1984); D. Sadovnikov, *Riddles of the Russian People* (1986); R. Wilbur, "The Persistence of Riddles," *Yale Review* 78 (1989); D. Pagis, "Toward a Theory of the Literary Riddle," *Untying the Knot*, ed. G. Hasan-Rokem and D. Shulman (1996)— useful ed. collection; R. Wehlau, *The Riddle of Creation* (1997); E. Cook, *Enigmas and Riddles in Literature* (2006); D. Tiffany, *Infidel Poetics* (2009).

A. WELSH; E. RETTBERG

RIME RICHE. *See* RHYME; RICH RHYME.

RONDEAU. Originally the generic term for all Fr. forms derived from dance-rounds (*rondes* or *rondels*) with singing accompaniment: the refrain was sung by the chorus—the general body of dancers—and the variable section by the leader. The written forebears of the rondeau are generally thought to be the *rondets* or *rondets de carole* from 13th-c. romances.

The form by which we know the rondeau today emerged in the 15th c. and by the beginning of the 16th c. had displaced all competitors. The poem is constructed on two rhymes only with lines of eight or ten syllables, and the first word or phrase of the first line is used as a *refrain; this curtailed, repeating line, called the *rentrement*, usually does not rhyme. As a type of truncated refrain, the *rentrement* may have derived from copyists' habits of abbreviation, common in the Middle Ages. In Fr. prosody, *rentrements* are usually associated with the rondeau, but whenever the refrains of any poem are an abbreviated version of the first line either of the poem or of each stanza (e.g., Thomas Wyatt, "In *aeternum*," "Forget not yet," "*Quondam* was I"), then the term *rentrement* can be justifiably applied.

Traditional lengths for the rondeau are 12 or 15 lines (if the two brief *rentrements* are not considered lines, 10 or 13) printed in two or three stanzas. In the 15th c., both lengths appear: François Villon's "Mort, j'appelle de ta rigueur" is 12 lines in length, while Clément Marot's "Au bon vieux temps" is 15, and both poems have been lineated with two and three stanzas. If we let *R* stand for the *rentrement*, the 12-line rondeau is *abbaabR abbaR* in two stanzas or *abba abR abbaR* in three, while the 15-line rondeau is *aabbaaabR aabbaR* in two stanzas or *aabba aabR aabbaR* in three.

During the course of the 16th c., the rondeau gradually disappeared. It was restored to fashion at the beginning of the 17th c. by the *précieux* poets, esp. Vincent Voiture, on whose 15-line example Théodore de Banville based his 19th-c. revival of the form. Although Alfred de Musset had experimented with the form earlier in the 19th c., taking some liberties with the rhymes, it was Banville's practice that provided the model for the later 19th- and 20th-c. explorations of the form. In England, aside from 16th-c. examples (Wyatt in particular), the rondeau did not really flourish until the end of the 19th c., when under Banville's influence, Fr. forms attracted the enthusiasm of light verse poets such as Austin Dobson, Edmund Gosse, W. E. Henley, Ernest Dowson, Thomas Hardy, and Robert Bridges. Their influence was felt in America: the Af. Am. poet Paul Laurence Dunbar's most well-known poem may be the 1896 rondeau "We Wear the Mask," whose title is also its *rentrement*. In Germany, where it has also been called *Ringelgedicht*, *Ringelreim*, and *Rundreim*, the rondeau was used by Georg Rudolf Weckherlin, Johann Nikolaus Götz, Johann Fischart, and later Otto Eric Hartleben.

In the 20th c., an immensely famous rondeau was Canadian doctor John McCrae's "In Flanders Fields" (1915), a poem frequently recited and rp. both during and long after World War I. "In Flanders fields the poppies blow," begins the lyric, ending with a stern call to the public to "keep faith" with the battlefield dead. Through the efforts of the Royal Legion of Canada, the YMCA, the National American Legion, the American and French Childrens' League, and the British Legion, McCrae's Flanders poppy became an instantly recognizable symbol worn in Canada and Britain annually on November 11, Remembrance Day, to commemorate the Great War dead. When the poem first appeared, few of these literal legions may have recognized its form: even the best-selling posthumous collection of McCrae's poetry published in 1919 referred to it as a highly original kind of *sonnet. In 2001, the first stanza of "In Flanders Fields" was printed on the Canadian ten-dollar bill.

The management of the *rentrement* is the key to the rondeau's expressive capabilities. Banville says that the *rentrement* is "both more and less than a line, for it plays the major role in the rondeau's overall design. It is at once the rondeau's subject, its *raison d'être* and its means of expression." Fr. poets, wishing to keep the *rentrement* unrhymed, yet fatally drawn to rhyme, found a solution in the punning *rentrement*, which rhymes with itself rather than merely repeating itself (e.g., "son or," "sonore," "s'honore"). Consequently, in the Fr. rondeau, the *rentrement* tends to remain unassimilated, full of wit, buoyancy, and semantic fireworks. The Eng. poets, on the other hand, sought to integrate the *rentrement* more fully, both by frequently allowing it to rhyme with either the *a* or *b* lines, thus pushing the rondeau in the direction of that exclusively Eng. form, the roundel, and by exploiting its metrical continuity with the rest of the stanza. The Eng. *rentrement* is also usually longer than the Fr., four syllables rather than one or two. In short, the Eng. rondeau is altogether graver and more meditative than the Fr., its *rentrement* more clearly a lyric destination, a focus of self-recollection, intimate knowledge, and haunting memory.

The *rondeau redoublé*, similar in form, was rare even at the time of Jean Marot, who is known to have composed one in 1526. In the 17th c., a few isolated examples occur in the works of Mme. Deshoulières and Jean de La Fontaine; Banville uses the form in the 19th c. Marot's *rondeau redoublé*, 24 lines in six *quatrains plus the *rentrement*, may be schematized as follows (R signifying the *rentrement* and capitals and primes denoting whole-line refrains): *ABA'B' babA abaB babA' abaB' babaR*. Each line of stanza 1 is employed in turn as the last line of each of the following four stanzas, which thus serve to develop the content of stanza 1; the final stanza then makes a comment or summation. Dorothy Parker's "Rondeau Redoublé (And Scarcely Worth the Trouble, At That)" of 1926 follows the four-century-old scheme of Marot exactly.

■ T. de Banville, *Petit traité de poésie française* (1872); Patterson; M. Françon, "La pratique et la théorie du rondeau et du rondel chez Théodore de Banville," *MLN* 52 (1937); F. Gennrich, "Deutsche Rondeaux," *BGDSL(H)* 72 (1950), and *Das altfranzösische Rondeau und Virelai im 12. und 13. Jahrhundert* (1963); N.H.J. van den Boogaard, *Rondeaux et Refrains du XIIe siècle au début du XIVe* (1969)—prints all known rondeaux ca. 1228–1332, but must be used with caution; F. Deloffre, *Le Vers français* (1969); M. Françon, "Wyatt et le rondeau," *RQ* 24 (1971); F. M. Tierney, "The Causes of the Revival of the Rondeau," *Revue de l'Université d'Ottawa* 43 (1973); Elwert; C. Scott, "The Revival of the Rondeau in France and England 1860–1920," *RLC* 213 (1980), and *French Verse-Art* (1980); Morier; J. Britnell, "'Clore et rentrer': The Decline of the Rondeau," *FS* 37 (1983); J.F.W. Vance, *Death So Noble* (1997).

C. SCOTT; T.V.F. BROGAN; A. L. FRENCH

S

SAPPHIC. In early Gr. poetry, an important aeolic verse form named after Sappho, a Gr. poet from the island of Lesbos of the 7th–6th c. BCE. Prosodically, this form has been of interest to poets throughout most of the hist. of Western poetry; generically, it has evoked ever-increasing interest in the subjects of gender and love vis-à-vis poetry, most recently poetry written by women.

The term *sapphic* refers to both a meter and a stanza form. The sapphic line, called the *lesser sapphic*, is a *hendecasyllable of the pattern – ∪ – x – ∪ ∪ – ∪ – – . The sapphic stanza consists of two lesser sapphic lines followed by a 16-syllable line that is an extended form of the other two: – ∪ – x – ∪ ∪ – ∪ – x + – ∪ ∪ – – . This latter has been analyzed in several ways; one traditional account sees the last *colon as an adonic colon (– ∪ ∪ – –) and treats it as a separate line, giving the sapphic stanza four lines in all. Sappho's contemporary Alcaeus also used the stanza and may have been its inventor. Catullus composed two *odes in sapphics (11 and 51), the second of which is a trans. and adaptation of Sappho frag. 31 (Lobel-Page); with these poems, he probably introduced the sapphic into Lat. poetry, but it is not certain. It is Horace, however, who provided the sapphic model for subsequent Roman and Eur. poets; in his *Odes*, he uses the form 27 times, second in frequency only to alcaics. Horace also makes a single use (*Odes* 1.8) of the greater sapphic *strophe, i.e., an Aristophaneus (– ∪ ∪ – ∪ – –) followed by a greater sapphic line of 15 syllables (– ∪ – – – | ∪ ∪ – | – ∪ ∪ – ∪ – –), which can be analyzed as a sapphic hendecasyllable with an inserted choriamb. His treatment of the sapphic as a four-line stanza canonized that form for posterity. Seneca sometimes uses the separate elements in a different order, e.g., by arranging a continuous series of longer lines with an adonic clausula.

In the Middle Ages, the sapphic acquired rhyme and was instrumental in the transition from metrical (quantitative) to rhythmical (accentual) meter (Norberg). After the hexameter and the iambic dimeter quatrain (for *hymns), it is the most popular verse form of the med. period: there are 127 examples in *Analecta hymnica* (Selected Hymns). In the Ren. and after, accentual versions of the sapphic became three lines of 11 syllables followed by a fourth line of five, the whole in trochees and *dactyls. The fourth line instances the phenomenon of tailing or end shortening well attested in other stanza forms.

The revival of Horatian influence on poetics evoked wide interest in the sapphic stanza among poets and prosodists in Italy, France, Germany, England, and Spain. Leonardo Dati used it for the first time in It. (1441), followed by Galeotto del Carretto, Claudio Tolomei, and others; in the 19th c., experiments were made by Felice Cavallotti and by Giosuè Carducci (*Odi barbare*). Estéban de Villegas is the chief practitioner in Spain. In the 18th-c. Ger. revival of interest in quantitative verse, F. G. Klopstock varied an unrhymed stanza with regular positional changes of the trisyllabic foot in the lesser sapphic lines; later, August von Platen and others essayed the strict Horatian form. In Eng., sapphics have been written by Philip Sidney (*Old Arcadia*; *Certain Sonnets* 25); Isaac Watts (*Horae lyricae*); Alexander Pope ("Ode on Solitude"); William Cowper ("Lines under the Influence of Delirium"); Robert Southey ("The Widow"); Alfred, Lord Tennyson; A. C. Swinburne (*Poems and Ballads*); Thomas Hardy (the first poem in *Wessex Poems*); Ezra Pound ("Apparuit"), and John Frederick Nims (*Sappho to Valéry*, 2d ed., 1990). The sapphic has been the longest lived of the cl. lyric strophes in the West. But full studies of its hist. in several vernaculars still remain to be written.

See LOVE POETRY.

■ G. Mazzoni, "Per la storia della saffica in Italia," *Atti dell' Acc. Scienze lett. arti* 10 (1894); E. Hjaerne, "Das sapfiska strofen i svensk verskonst," *Sprak och Stil* 13 (1913); Pauly-Wissowa, Supp., 11.1222 ff.; Hardie, pt. 2, ch. 3; Omond; H. Rüdiger, *Geschichte der deutschen Sappho-Übersetzungen* (1934); D. L. Page, *Sappho and Alcaeus* (1955); Norberg; Bowra; W. Bennett, *German Verse in Classical Metres* (1963); L. P. Wilkinson, *Golden Latin Artistry* (1963); Koster; H. Kenner, "The Muse in Tatters," *Agenda* 6 (1968); N. A. Bonavia-Hunt, *Horace the Minstrel* (1969); R.G.M. Nisbet and M. Hubbard, *A Commentary on Horace, Odes Book 1* (1970); R. Paulin, "Six Sapphic Odes 1753–1934," *Seminar* 10 (1974); E. Schäfer,

Deutscher Horaz (1976); E. Weber, "Prosodie verbale et prosodie musicale: La Strophe sapphique au Moyen Age et à la Renaissance," *Le Moyen Français* 5 (1979); Halporn et al.; P. Stotz, *Sonderformen der sapphischen Dichtung* (1982); Navarro; West, 32 ff.; J. Crawford, "Sidney's Sapphics and the Role of Interpretive Communities," *ELH* 69 (2002).

R. A. SWANSON; T.V.F. BROGAN; J. W. HALPORN

SATIRE. Satire is both a mode and a genre of verse and prose lit. that adopts a critical attitude toward its target with the goal of censuring human folly. Satire is an eminently versatile form whose structure, style, tone, and subjects vary across a wide spectrum, but generally intends, as Jonathan Swift states, "to mend the world" ("A Vindication of Mr. Gay and *The Beggar's Opera*").

In terms of its purpose, satire is polemical, contentiously attacking its victims with the hope of dissuading readers from vice and persuading them (to greater and lesser degrees) toward virtue. In terms of structure, satire is primarily a borrower of literary and rhetorical forms, using other genres to support its didactic agenda (see Guilhamet). As Paulson describes it, satire explores the lowest range of potential human actions within a framework or fiction that best serves its ridiculing function (*Fictions of Satire*). Some of satire's favorite housing fictions include diatribe (the outraged declamations of Lucilius and Juvenal); Socratic-style dialogue (the *sermones* or conversations of Horace and the more cynical dialogues of Lucian); epic (Lucian's *True History*, which parodies the works of Homer and Herodotus; Nicolas Boileau's *mock epic Le Lutrin* and Alexander Pope's *The Dunciad* and *The Rape of the Lock*, which parody the works of Virgil and John Milton); romance (Petronius's *Satyricon*, Voltaire's *Candide*, Samuel Butler's *Hudibras*, Lord Byron's *Don Juan*); burlesque (e.g., the ridiculing of Homer in the *Battle of the Frogs and Mice*); the *encomium (the ironic praises of Erasmus's *Praise of Folly* and John Dryden's "MacFlecknoe"); beast fable (Apuleius's *The Golden Ass* [or *Metamorphoses*], the med. tales of Reynard the Fox, Edmund Spenser's "Mother Hubberds Tale"); epistle (Pope's "To a Lady" and "To Dr. Arbuthnot"; Mary Wortley Montagu's "An Epistle from Mrs. Yonge to Her Husband"); religious complaint (cf. the parodies of the med. Goliard poets); the *dream vision of William Langland's *Piers Plowman*, Chaucer's "Pardoner's Tale," T. S. Eliot's "The Hippopotamus"); *pastoral (Aphra Behn's "The Disappointment," Swift's "A Description of the Morning" and "A Pastoral Dialogue"); civic poetry (Samuel Johnson's *London*, W. H. Auden's "The Unknown Citizen," e. e. cummings's "next to of course god america"); treatise (Swift's deeply ironic *A Modest Proposal* and *A Tale of a Tub*, and Pope's *Peri Bathous*); travel narrative (e.g., Swift's *Gulliver's Travels*); and drama (the Gr. Old Comedy of Aristophanes, the humor plays of Ben Jonson, John Gay's *The Beggar's Opera*). In fact, there are few if any genres that the satiric mode cannot adopt with effects that range from the richly comic to the devastatingly tragic. Similarly, there are few if any media that satire cannot inhabit, including mod. favorites such as film (*Dr. Strangelove*), television, and the Internet. Since the focus of the present article is on poetry and poetics, many major artistic, dramatic, and novelistic satires are beyond its scope, such as the paintings of William Hogarth; select dramas of Molière, Henry Fielding, William Congreve, W. S. Gilbert, G. B. Shaw, Oscar Wilde, and Caryl Churchill; the novels of George Orwell (*Animal Farm*, *1984*), Charlotte Gilman (*Herland*), and Joseph Heller (*Catch-22*); the satiric writings of Mark Twain and Ambrose Bierce; the satiric cartoons and essays of the magazine *Punch*; and so on.

Although satire can call upon a long hist. of formal conventions and rhetorical tropes such as *irony, *personification, and *hyperbole, satire is distinctive for its overt engagement (at varying levels of critical distance) with its immediate historical context ("all the things which men do . . . is the hodge-podge of my little book"; Juvenal, *Satires* 1.85–86), a fact that often makes the colloquial lang. and topical subjects of satiric verse obscure. Because satire criticizes the contemp. world, the satirist is frequently compelled to employ an array of self-protective structures, including a range of personae, apology, allegory, and claims of innocent comedic intent; however, such gestures are belied by the satirist's bold assertion that his work alone offers "antidotes to [the] pestilential sins" of a morally diseased society (Everard Guilpin's *Skialetheia*, Prelud. 70). The satirist serves as self-appointed prosecutor, judge, and jury, exposing and condemning the worst excesses of human behavior, sometimes, like Horace, with the intention of improving the wicked through humorous moral instruction, and sometimes, like Juvenal, with the object of provoking the wicked to guilt, shame, rage, and tears (Horace, *Satires* 1.4.103–29 and Juvenal, *Satires* 1.166–68). Despite satire's standard defensive claim to employ only "feigned [i.e., fictitious] private names to note general vices" (John Marston's "To Him"; *The Scourge of Villanie* 8–9), the perception of libelous lampoons in satire has often drawn the attention of the authorities and has frequently provoked censorship, from the Roman Twelve Tables outlawing libelous verses (Cicero, *De republica* 4.12; Horace, *Epistles* 2.1.152–54) to Emperor Augustus's edict against "defamatory little books" (in Suetonius, *Life of Augustus* 55) to England's 1599 prohibition against the publication of satire, as well as the Theatrical Licensing Act of 1737.

As described by Kernan in *The Cankered Muse*, satire demonstrates a tension between the comic and the tragic strains; however, satire employs both as strategies in the service of its didactic and apotropaic agendas. Horace prefers his ironic mode of satire "to speak the truth with a laugh" (*Satires* 1.1.24), and Persius admires the comic ability of the "sly rogue" Horace to "touch every fault while his friend stands and laughs" (*Satires* 1.116–17). Anderson (1982) characterizes the Horatian comic mode as not merely witty but socially "constructive" and "humane" (39), and many Ren., Restoration, and Augustan-era imitators have been drawn to Horace's apparent benevolence and erudition. In his prefatory epistle to *The Praise of Folly*, Erasmus states his preference for the Horatian principle of delightful instruction and his dislike of Juvenal's "cesspool of secret vice"; in *The Defence of Poesy* (1595), Philip Sidney, citing Persius's praise of Horace, says satire "sportingly never leaveth until he make a man laugh at folly"; and in *An Essay on Criticism*, Pope writes that Horace "charms with graceful Negligence, / And without method, talks us into sense" (653–54). The Juvenalian approach is more severe, denouncing the crimes rather than mocking the follies of a society where depravity is the norm. Anderson (1982) identifies the "tragic" character of the Juvenalian mode in its symbolic depiction of Roman degeneracy. Milton claims that true satire is "borne out of a Tragedy, so ought to resemble his parentage, to strike high" (*An Apology* 6.12–13), a vision shared by the banned group of Eng. Ren. satirists who preferred the Juvenalian tragic mode as a means to expose the moral excesses common at the end of the reign of Elizabeth I:

"Satire hath a nobler vein / He's a Strappado, rack, and some such pain / To base lewd vice" (Guilpin). Where the comic satiric strategy employs fools as types of ridiculous behavior that are more instructive than threatening (like "the terrible people" of Ogden Nash's comic poem), the tragic strategy presents a hopeless world inhabited entirely by the wicked, which often includes the satiric speaker himself.

Although both the etymology of the word *satire* and the historical origin of the concept are equivocal, many of satire's defining characteristics can be traced back to a number of related trads. The word itself is derived from the Lat. *satura*, meaning a "mixture," and is related to the Lat. *satur*, meaning "full." The Lat. grammarian Diomedes (late 4th c. CE) contends that *satura* may have derived from the *satura lanx*, the ritual plate overflowing with offerings to the gods; or from the word for a kind of stuffing made from various ingredients; or from the *lex satura*, a single legal proposition composed of a number of smaller issues. Diomedes links these separate roots: all, in one way or another, refer to the structure of satire as a miscellany poem, an array of different kinds of verse united by their common intent to ridicule a range of subjects, such as the miscellanies produced by the Roman poets Ennius and Pacuvius (see Keil). As an individual poetic genre, the Roman grammarian Quintilian (ca. 35–100 CE) claimed verse satire as a wholly Roman invention devoid of Gr. influence, with Lucilius as the first Roman to advance the genre (*Institutio oratoria* 10.1.96–97).

While it is true that the etymology of the word *satire* is not related to the Gr. word for satyrs (σατυρος; Lat. *satyrus*), as demonstrated by Isaac Causabon in 1605 (see *De satyrica Graecorum poesi et Romanorum satira*), the form and style of Roman verse satire owe much to the trad. of Gr. *invective poetry; Dryden explains in his 1693 work "A Discourse Concerning the Original and Progress of Satire," "And thus far 'tis allowed that the Grecians had such poems; but that they were wholly different *in specie* from that to which the Romans gave the name of Satire." Horace himself admits to the complementary nature of Gr. and Roman invective poetry, noting that Lucilius modeled his keen and witty satiric style on the Gr. playwrights of Old Comedy, Aristophanes, Eupolis, and Cratinus, changing only their meter while maintaining their freedom to assault the vicious in society by name (*Satires* 1.4.1–8). Diomedes' position is similar, claiming that Roman verse satire may have been named for the goat-legged companions of Dionysus because Roman satire discusses the same kind of laughable and shameful behaviors practiced by the Gr. satyrs. This idea of complementary stylistic trads. continued well into the Ren., as suggested by the conscious conflation of the two trads. in the spelling of the word as *Satyre*. Thomas Drant's 1566 definition of satire, e.g., claims that it was named either for the Satyrs or for the "waspish" god, Saturn. Intriguingly, Drant also wonders if the word might have the same origin as the Ar. word for "spear," referring to the satirist's method of skewering his targets. Similarly, Elliott claims the satiric poems of ancient Arabia (the *hija'*) as an early example of satire's conventional use as a magical weapon intended to destroy one's enemies.

Other ancient rituals cited by Elliott as conceptual influences on satire include the Gr. phallic songs (*iambic verses intended to cleanse society as part of the fertility rites), the invective poetic curses of Archilochus (7th c. BCE), and the *glám dícind* satiric poems used by ancient Ir. bards to bring infamy and death upon those who displeased them. Dryden mentions two other influential Gr. trads.: the parody-rich *silloi* poems, perhaps derived from Silenus, foster-father of Dionysus, and the Gr. satyr play (the only remaining example of which is Euripides' *Cyclops*), a play performed after three tragedies in which satyrs act as chorus in order to mock issues taken seriously in the preceding plays. Horace describes one other decidedly Roman poetic trad. underlying the conception of satire: the Fescennine ritual. As part of the harvest festivals, participants would hurl humorous rustic abuse at each other in alternating verses. Such liberal verbal freedom was made illegal, states Horace, only after its "cruel tooth" offended honorable families (*Epistles* 2.1.139–56).

Philosophically, cl. satire owes much to the Cynic and Stoic schools. Much of Juvenal's style is cynical in its iconoclastic perspective, angry tone, and declamatory rhet. Other cynic satirists of note include Menippus and his Roman imitator Varro, as well as Petronius, Lucian, John Marston, and John Wilmot, the Earl of Rochester. Shakespeare's railing satirists Thersites (*Troilus and Cressida*) and Apemantus (*Timon of Athens*) exemplify the Cynic trad. with their incessant barking at fools and hypocrites. Elements of Stoic philosophy, a softened version of Cynicism, are present in the satires of Persius and Juvenal, as when, e.g., Juvenal

asserts in Satire 10 the virtues of wishing for a "healthy mind in a healthy body" (356) or as Johnson writes in his imitation titled *The Vanity of Human Wishes* (1749), "Pour forth thy fervors for a healthful mind, / Obedient passions, and a will resign'd" (359–60). However, one should not confuse a satirist's engagement with the institutions of his era with adherence to them; Highet (*Juvenal*, 93) argues that Juvenal rejected Stoic teachings (as suggested in Satire 13.120–24), a position supported by Coffey. Satirists conventionally present themselves as staunch individualists, the lone voice of reason driven to mock or to decry the wealth of abuses that surround them. With so much evil in the world, writes Juvenal, "it is difficult *not* to write satire" (1.30).

Structurally, the kind of Roman verse satire practiced by Lucilius, Horace, Juvenal, and later imitators such as John Donne and Pope, has elements in common with dramatic forms such as Gr. Old Comedy and Roman New Comedy. Roman verse satire is often framed as a rhetorical/dramatic debate between the satirist's speaking persona and an adversary, the former taking the position of *vituperatio* (blame) and the latter taking the position of *laus* (praise). The vice in question is then, as Randolph describes it, thoroughly examined in the first sect. of the poem, and the opposing virtue is recommended in the final sect. However, even within the confines of this generic structure, formal verse satire is rarely a stable form, flowing easily into congenial genres such as comedy, beast fable, and prose narrative. Horace, e.g., inserts the Aesopian beast fable of the town mouse and the country mouse into book 2, Satire 6, and Juvenal inserts an allegorical tale of a giant fish into Satire 4.

In addition to formal verse satire, Quintilian mentions another "older type of satire" practiced by Menippus's Roman imitator Varro, in which verse satire is mixed with prose (10.1.95–96). Dryden also mentions the influence of the cynical satires of Menippus and their manner of mixing several sorts of verse with prose, as well as their paradoxical tone of *spoudogeloioi*, or serious-laughter (64–67). In this category, Dryden places the works of Petronius, Apuleius, and Lucian, as well as John Barclay's picaresque novel *Euphormionis Satyricon* and his own *Absalom and Achitophel* and "MacFlecknoe." Given their cynical and unorthodox perspectives and despite their heavy reliance on prose, one could also place works such as Thomas More's *Utopia*,

Miguel de Cervantes's *Don Quixote*, and Aldous Huxley's *Brave New World* under the Menippean umbrella.

The critical hist. of satire in the 20th and early 21st cs. is an uneasy stalemate between formalist and historicist perspectives. From the mid-1950s through the 1960s, the formalist or New Critical methodology recommended a mode of inquiry that rejected the historicists' concerns with literary origins in favor of exploring the conscious "artifice" of the poetry, i.e., the recurrent rhetorical and dramatic conventions of satire. One particularly innovative formalist study of the period is Frye's *Anatomy of Criticism*, in which satire is categorized among the four interrelated pregeneric *mythoi* (specifically, the mythos of winter). Frye argues that satire is a kind of "militant irony" whose structural scheme is the ironic application of romantic conventions to realistic contents. Some half-century later, the debate over the "historicity" of satire, meaning the nature and extent of satire's contact with its social context, continued, with scholars such as Bogel, Griffin, and Knight attempting to find a balance between historical conditions and formal traditions. In this context, the sociolinguistic theories of Mikhail Bakhtin are especially relevant for their ability to reconcile the dialogue between form and context in satire. Bakhtin argues that cl. "serio-comical" lit., which includes both formal verse and Menippean satire, is a precursor to the mod. novel, a form intended to provoke "the permanent corrective of laughter" that familiarizes and debases the loftier genres. Another of Bakhtin's contributions is his conception of "carnivalistic literature," a humorously profane remnant of folk culture and ritual that is deliberately contrasted against the usual hierarchical relationships of everyday life; another is his exploration of the ideological nature of Menippean satire as a carnivalized genre that combines topical and fantastic situations in order to test conventional truths, the effect of which is a challenge to all forms of orthodoxy.

See PARODY.

■ **Anthologies**: *A Treasury of Satire*, ed. E. Johnson (1945); *Poems on Affairs of State*, ed. G. deF. Lord et al., 7 v. (1963–75)—Eng. satirical verse, 1660–1714; *English Poetic Satire*, G. Rousseau and N. Rudenstine (1972); *Oxford Book of Satirical Verse*, ed. G. Grigson (1980); *An Anthology of 18th-Century Satire*, ed. P. Heaney (1994); *The Malcontents*, ed. J. Queenan (2002).

■ **Criticism and History**: J. Dryden, "A Discourse concerning the Original and Progress of Satire" (1693); *Essays of John Dryden*, ed. W. P. Kerr, 2 v. (1926); M. C. Randolph, "The Structural Design of the Formal Verse Satire," *PQ* 21 (1942); M. Mack, "The Muse of Satire," *Yale Review* 41 (1951); I. Jack, *Augustan Satire* (1952); G. Highet, *Juvenal the Satirist* (1954); J. Peter, *Complaint and Satire in Early English Literature* (1956); Frye; A. Kernan, *The Cankered Muse* (1959); R. Elliott, *The Power of Satire* (1960); G. Highet, *The Anatomy of Satire* (1962); J. P. Sullivan, *Satire* (1963)—Roman lit.; W. S. Anderson, *Anger in Juvenal and Seneca* (1964); A. Kernan, *The Plot of Satire* (1965); R. Paulson, *The Fictions of Satire* (1967), and *Satire and the Novel in 18th-Century England* (1967); H. D. Weinbrot, *The Formal Strain* (1969); *Tudor Verse Satire*, ed. K. W. Gransden (1970); R. Paulson, *Satire* (1971); W. Booth, *A Rhetoric of Irony* (1974); R. Seldon, *English Verse Satire 1590–1767* (1978); E. A. Bloom and L. D. Bloom, *Satire's Persuasive Voice* (1979); T. Lockwood, *Post-Augustan Satire* (1979); M. Seidel, *The Satiric Inheritance* (1979); M. M. Bakhtin, *The Dialogic Imagination*, ed. M. Holquist, trans. C. Emerson and M. Holquist (1981); W. S. Anderson, *Essays on Roman Satire* (1982); N. Rudd, *The Satires of Horace*, 2d ed. (1982); H. D. Weinbrot, *Alexander Pope and the Traditions of Formal Verse Satire* (1982); V. Carretta, *The Snarling Muse* (1983); M. M. Bakhtin, *Problems of Dostoevsky's Poetics*, ed. and trans. C. Emerson (1984), and *Rabelais and His World*, trans. H. Iswolsky (1984); F. Nussbaum, *The Brink of All We Hate: English Satires on Women, 1660–1750* (1984); L. Hutcheon, *A Theory of Parody* (1985); E. Pollack, *The Poetics of Sexual Myth* (1985)—Swift and Pope; L. Guilhamet, *Satire and the Transformation of Genre* (1987); H. Javadi, *Satire in Persian Literature* (1988); *Eighteenth-Century Satire*, ed. H. D. Weinbrot (1988); K. Freudenburg, *The Walking Muse* (1992); *Horace Made New*, ed. C. Martindale and D. Hopkins (1993); J. Relihan, *Ancient Menippean Satire* (1993); D. Griffin, *Satire* (1994); L. Hutcheon, *Irony's Edge* (1994); C. Rawson, *Satire and Sentiment 1660–1830* (1994); M. Wood, *Radical Satire and Print Culture, 1790–1822* (1994); *Cutting Edges*, ed. J. Gill (1995)—postmod. crit. on 18th-c. satire; R. Zimbardo, *At Zero Point* (1998); F. Bogel, *The Difference Satire Makes* (2001)—from Jonson to Byron; K. Freudenburg, *Satires of Rome* (2001); J. Ogborn and

P. Buckroyd, *Satire* (2001); C. Knight, *The Literature of Satire* (2004); *The Cambridge Companion to Roman Satire*, ed. K. Freudenburg (2005); J. Scott, *Satire* (2005); H. D. Weinbrot, *Menippean Satire Reconsidered* (2005); C. Keane, *Figuring Genre in Roman Satire* (2006); R. Rosen, *Making Mockery* (2007).

W. R. JONES

SCANSION

I. Definition and History
II. Notation
III. Meter, Rhythm, and Scansion
IV. Pros and Cons of Scansion

I. Definition and History. Scansion describes the structure of verse lines by breaking them down into their component feet and identifying the metrical character of the individual syllables. The word comes from the Lat. *scandere*, "to climb," and *scansio*, "a climbing." Charlton T. Lewis and Charles Short, in their *Latin Dictionary*, suggest that figurative uses of the verb in Roman poetry (e.g., Lucretius's comment that living things climb step by step to maturity [*On the Universe* 2.1123] and Horace's remark that care climbs aboard a ship with the restless traveler [*Odes* 2.16.21]) led Late Lat. grammarians to adopt the idiom *scandere versus*—"to climb up, i.e., *to measure* or *read* [verse] by its feet." Other authorities (e.g., *The American Heritage Dictionary of the English Language*, 4th ed., and *The New Oxford American Dictionary*, 2d ed.) speculate that the term originates in the custom of lifting and lowering the foot to keep time with a piece of music or poetry. Both hypotheses associate the human foot with the metrical foot (Gr. *pous*, Lat. *pes*) and involve the concept of verse as measure or count (Gr. *metron*, Lat. *numerus*). Terentianus Maurus, who toward the end of the 2d c. CE composed a verse essay about metrics, appears to be one of the earliest writers to speak of scanning poetry (*On Letters, Syllables, and Meters* 547, 1753). Though one might suspect that *scansion* etymologically connects with *scan* in the sense of "examine closely," this latter denotation does not appear until the 16th c. and is an extension of the prosodic usage rather than an influence upon it.

Scansion and metrical analysis are almost as old as poetry. No sooner do poets start composing in meter than they begin exploring ways in which it can enhance meaning. When, for instance, at *Iliad* 23.221, Achilles is "calling to the spirit of poor Patroclus" and pouring out wine to the gods in honor of his dead friend, Homer contracts all the *dactyls of the *hexameter into *spondees, which create a solemn, heavy movement appropriate to his hero's act. Indeed, in Greek, *sponde* means "libation," and the prosodic spondee (*spondeios*) is so named because the foot, consisting of two long syllables, suits the slow rhythms of libational songs and chants. Further, the wine that mortals present the gods is unwatered—Homer himself speaks at *Iliad* 2.341 and 4.159 of the "unmixed libations," *spondai akretoi*, that conclude a truce or treaty—and this purely spondaic line about Achilles' devotions not only suggests their ceremonial gravity but also perhaps points to the undiluted nature of his offering and his grief:

ψυχην κικλησκων Πατροκληος δειλοιο

‾ ‿ ‿ | ‾ ‿ ‿ | ‾ ‾ | ‾ ‿ ‿ | ‾ ‿ ‿ | ‾ ‾

psuchen | kikles | kon Pat | rokle | os dei | loio

(Ancient poets always treat the final syllable of the hexameter as long, even when it is short, as it is here, where it consists simply of an omicron—the theory being that the pause at the line end compensates for the syllable's brevity.)

By the cl. age, metrical analysis has become a subject of general literary interest and study, as we can infer from the amusing scene in Aristophanes' *Clouds* in which Socrates proposes to teach the ignorant farmer Strepsiades about trimeters and tetrameters and the dactyl. The very nature of the jokes—Strepsiades mistakes the meters for measures of commercial exchange and can understand *daktulos* only with respect to its common meaning of "finger," as in giving somebody the finger—indicates that the playwright trusts that his large and miscellaneous audience knows something about versification and the vocabulary employed to discuss it. By the same token, Gr. and Lat. writers on rhet., incl. Isocrates, Aristotle, Cicero, and Quintilian, discuss rhythmical arrangement in terms of short (Gr. *brachus*, Lat. *brevis*) and long (Gr. *makros*, Lat. *longus*) syllables and consider various prosodic topics as they relate to the composition of both verse and prose.

Metrical analysis, moreover, plays a critical role in the trad. of textual scholarship inaugurated in the Hellenistic period at the library in Alexandria. Prior to this time, Gr. lyric poetry seems to have been written out consecutively in the manner of prose; but Aristophanes of Byzantium (3d–2d c. BCE), in his eds. of lyric writers, divides their poems into metrical *cola* in order to clarify the poems' linear and strophic structures (see COLON). Similarly, in part to facilitate the accurate reading of poems and the understanding of their meters, Hellenistic scholars develop various diacritical and punctuation marks; and as M. L. West indicates, the macron and breve signs we still use in scanning cl. verse appear as early as the 2d c. BCE in papyri of scholarly copies of the poets "over vowels about whose quantity the reader might be uncertain because the words or forms were archaic or poetic." In addition, in Hephaestion's *Guide to Meter* (mid-2d c. CE), we have a prototype of the student manual of prosody that lists different feet and rhythms and illustrates them with apposite passages of poetry.

Yet, as the word's relatively late appearance suggests, scansion seems most notably to reflect or respond to the linguistic conditions and educational needs of the postclassical world. In late antiquity, accent replaces length as the central prosodic element in Gr. and Lat.; and in the Middle Ages, Gr. falls into disuse throughout much of Europe, while the vernaculars supplant Lat. in everyday speech. Though Lat. remains, in the Middle Ages and beyond, a lingua franca for the intellectual community, it is no longer native to those who use it, nor do they speak it as the ancients did. Knowledge of metrics is essential for those wishing to comprehend the lang. and its lit. This situation grows even more critical during the revival of ancient learning in the Ren., when the humanists make the study of cl. Lat. the basis of elementary education and when the composition of quantitative Lat. verse becomes both a measure of scholastic achievement and a serious pursuit for many major poets from Petrarch to John Milton.

Scansion figures throughout Eng. lit. crit., which adopts the exercise from cl. studies. Both George Gascoigne, in his pioneering "Certain Notes of Instruction concerning the Making of Verse or Rhyme in English" (1575), and George Puttenham, in his *Arte of English Poesie* (1589), refer to scanning by name and supply sample scansions to illustrate their ideas about Eng. metrical structure. (Gascoigne uses an acute accent to register what we would call metrically accented syllables and a grave accent to mark metrically unaccented ones, while Puttenham scans with breves and macrons.) In the 17th, 18th, and 19th cs., the study of Eng. prosody is advanced by, among others, Ben Jonson, John Dryden, Thomas Warton,

Thomas Sheridan, Samuel Johnson, Thomas Jefferson (whose underappreciated "Thoughts on English Prosody" anticipates, in its differentiation of degrees of accent, approaches to scansion adopted by 20th-c. linguists like Otto Jespersen), William Wordsworth, S. T. Coleridge, and Edwin Guest. Further, beginning with Nicholas Rowe, Shakespeare's editors apply metrical analysis to the texts of his plays, with a view to correcting mislineations in the folio eds. These mislineations had occurred for various reasons, including the practice, among the original compositors, of splitting verse lines in two, or of breaking up a prose passage into shorter lines as if it were verse, when there was too little text to fill a column or page. (Conversely, when the compositors needed to conserve space, they sometimes ran verse lines together in prose fashion.) During this time, metrical analysis also continues to figure in cl. scholarship, as is shown by Richard Bentley's celebrated discovery of the digamma. Bentley postulates that this consonant existed in archaic Gr. but had disappeared by the cl. age, when he realizes that its absence explains many apparent metrical glitches in the eds. of Homer from the Alexandrian period forward—particularly those cases where a word-ending short vowel followed by a word beginning with a vowel still receives full metrical value rather than being elided. Gr. verse generally avoids such hiatuses, and Bentley perceives that their occurrences in Homer often reflect the loss of the digamma that originally began the second word and separated the two vowels. Scansion becomes even more prominent in Eng. literary studies in the second half of the 19th c., when Eng. lit. enters school curricula as a formal discipline. This period launches a vogue for handbooks on Eng. meter that has continued ever since.

This period also witnesses the beginning of what will eventually become a widespread misapprehension that to write in a meter is to limit oneself to a single, rigid formula rather than to adopt a general pattern susceptible to various internal modulations; and several developments in scansion contribute to this misapprehension. For one thing, in the second half of the 19th c., Eng. prosodists increasingly use, in scanning, vertical bars to separate feet from one another, a practice relatively rare prior to this time. Since Eng. meters customarily entail a succession of metrically identical feet, the practice gives scanned lines a strong visual impression of uniformity that deflects attention from the rhythmical shadings the lines may possess when spoken. (Foot division does not produce this effect so markedly in cl. verse because its quantitative metric allows that a long syllable may at points replace two short syllables and that two shorts may replace one long. Hence, though the hexameters of Homer and Virgil, to take two obvious cases, are strictly isosyllabic in a durational sense, they usually contain a mix of dactyls and spondees.)

Another practice that emerges in this period and that emphasizes the structural regularity of metrical poetry at the expense of its tonal variety is the schoolroom exercise of having students verbally scan verse by sing-songing it in unison:

I *wan*dered *lone*ly *as* a *cloud*

or

This is the *fo*rest pri*mev*al. The *mur*muring *pines* and the *hem*locks

Though this exercise highlights basic prosodic structures, it drains metered verse of its human inflections and natural rhythms.

A final and related factor that focuses awareness on the simplicity of metrical description and slights the complexity of metrical practice is Sidney Lanier's *Science of English Verse* (1880). In this work, which exerts considerable influence on prosodic thinking in the late 19th and early 20th cs., Lanier suggests that iambic verse is written in 3/8 time, involves an alternation of verbal eighth notes and quarter notes, and follows the sequence of tick-*tack*, tick-*tack*. This theory contributes to the notion, in Ezra Pound and others, that the rhythms of traditional versification are those of the metronome, itself an invention of the 19th c.

Overall, these developments serve as a warning that scansion and metrical analysis may, if misunderstood or misapplied, muddle the subject they aim to illuminate.

II. Notation. Most literary cultures devise notation to register the rhythmic or phonological properties of their lang. and poetry, and students of Eng. verse have explored many systems of scansion, incl. those involving letters, musical notes, numbers, and graphic representations. However, a simple group of symbols has generally held sway. Prior to the 20th c., Eng. prosodists usually signify metrically unaccented syllables with the breve (˘) cl. prosodists use to register short syllables. When signifying metrically accented syllables, they employ the macron

(–) cl. prosodists apply to long ones. During the 20th c., the breve and macron give way to an x for metrically unaccented syllables and an acute accent (´) for metrically accented ones. This shift reflects a growing consensus that xs and acute accents better indicate that Eng. metric weighs syllabic stress and not, as the breve and macron might suggest, syllabic length. (Be it noted, however, that breves and macrons persist in some discussions of Eng. versification; and in other discussions, the two systems mix—the most common blend assigning breves to metrically unaccented syllables and acute accents to metrically accented ones.)

Another mark that often figures in scansion (esp., as has been noted, in the last century and a half) is a vertical bar to divide the individual feet of the line from one another; and here it is important to remember two points. First, scansion treats verse lines merely as rows of syllables. *It concerns units of rhythm, not units of sense.* Hence, as the line already cited from Homer demonstrates—and as some of the lines cited below testify—divisions between feet do not necessarily correspond to divisions between words, phrases, and clauses. Second, in scanning Eng. verse, we determine whether a syllable is metrically accented solely by comparing it with the other syllable or syllables of the foot in which it appears. We do not weigh it against all the other syllables in the line or poem. Nor do we concern ourselves with whether the foot's accented syllable is much heavier than its unaccented syllable or syllables or only a little heavier. Though such nuances will affect and enliven the specific rhythm of the spoken line, scansion cannot, with its simple descriptive tools, register their continual and shifting complexities.

With regard to more specialized aspects of notation, there exist wide and confusing variations of practice—sadly, no metrical Moses has ever climbed Parnassus and received an authoritative Ten Commandments of Scansion from Apollo—yet several devices appear with some frequency. In particular, when prosodists mark a feminine ending (i.e., an extra, metrically unaccented syllable at the end of a line), most place the x in parentheses to indicate that the syllable is, literally, "hypermetrical"—beyond the measure and having no effect on its identity. For the same reason, they usually do not place, in front of the syllable, a vertical foot-division bar, a procedure that might mislead the casual observer into thinking that the syllable comprised an additional foot.

Conventional notation, then, renders as follows these lines from E. A. Robinson's "Eros Turannos" and Louise Bogan's "Cassandra." (Bogan's line has a feminine ending.)

```
  x  /  x    /   x   /   x  /
Tra di | tion, touch | ing all | he sees
  x   /  x    /  x /  x  /   x  / (x)
To me, | one sil | ly task | is like | another
```

Scansion thus demonstrates that Robinson's line is an iambic tetrameter, a line consisting of four iambic feet, and that Bogan's line an iambic pentameter, a line consisting of five iambic feet. Moreover, since any type of foot can be "substituted" for another, as long as such substitutions are not so frequent or so placed as to dissolve the meter, scansion can enable us to locate metrical variants and appreciate their effect in those cases where they serve an expressive purpose.

Occasionally, feet admit of different scansions, as is illustrated by the famous line from Shakespeare's *Hamlet*:

To be, or not to be: | that is | the question

Probably, most actors treat the fourth foot as trochaic: *that* is the question. Such a reading stresses the crux of Hamlet's situation: should he live and suffer the corruption he sees about him, or should he oppose it and thereby almost surely bring on his death? Yet an actor might speak the fourth foot as an iamb—that *is* the question—to emphasize the immediacy of Hamlet's predicament and the urgency of resolving it. (Either reading is metrically conventional. Historically, along with the feminine ending, the most common variants in Eng. iambic verse are a trochaic substitution at the beginning of the line and a trochaic substitution after a midline pause.)

III. Meter, Rhythm, and Scansion. One can steer clear of the confusions that sometimes plague scansion by bearing in mind that versification involves the concurrent but distinguishable phenomena of meter and rhythm. A meter is an analytic abstraction, a norm or basic pattern. For instance, the norm of the iambic pentameter is

weak *strong*, weak *strong*, weak *strong*, weak
strong, weak *strong*

Rhythm, on the other hand, concerns the realization of this pattern in living speech.

On rare occasions, as in this line from Thomas Traherne's "The Salutation," the poet's rhythm may replicate the normative pattern and consist of five successive two-syllable, rear-stressed phrases or words:

The earth, the seas, the light, the day, the skies

More frequently, the rhythm may entail an alternation of weak and strong syllables that tracks the norm fairly closely, as in this line from John Keats's "To Autumn":

And touch the stubble-plains with rosy hue

However, most iambic pentameters do not feature uniform fluctuation. Rather, the alternation between weak and strong syllables will be relatively emphatic at some points and less so at others. Poets compose not only in feet but also in larger words, phrases, clauses, and sentences whose tones are not limited to minimal and maximal accent but incorporate innumerable gradations of stress.

In this respect, we might compare iambic pentameters to mountain ranges. Valleys and peaks alternate. But not every peak is an Everest, nor is every valley a Grand Canyon. For example, this line from Thom Gunn's "In Santa Maria del Popolo" features two peaks that are not very high:

Resisting, by embracing, nothingness

And this line from Wallace Stevens's "Sunday Morning" has a valley that is not very deep:

She causes boys to pile new plums and pears

Further, because the iambic line requires only the maintenance of the lighter-to-heavier fluctuation—and because the only requirement of an iamb is that its second syllable be weightier than its first—a metrically unaccented syllable at one point in the line may carry more speech stress than a metrically accented syllable at another point. This occurs in this line from Philip Larkin's "Vers de Société":

Beyond the light stand failure and remorse

"Stand" (the metrically unaccented syllable of foot three) has more speech stress than "and" (the metrically accented syllable of foot four). Even so, the line maintains the fluctuation of lighter to heavier syllables and scans conventionally:

x /   x /   x /   x /   x /
Beyond | the light | stand fail | ure and | remorse

Sometimes, a poet follows an iamb of two relatively light syllables with an iamb of two relatively heavy ones. When this occurs, the fluctuation in stress is suspended in favor of an ascent over four syllables. Philip Sidney, in the opening line of his sonnet to the moon, employs this scheme to reinforce sonically the image he presents:

With how sad steps, O moon, thou climb'st the sky

Some authorities scan feet like "new plums," "stand fail-," and "sad steps" as spondees and feet like "-ing by," "-ure and," and "With how" as *pyrrhics, in the belief that such feet are analogous to ancient spondees, which, as we observed earlier, consist of two long syllables, and ancient pyrrhics, which consist of two short ones. However, it is doubtful whether pyrrhics and spondees are generally helpful or necessary to the analysis of Eng. verse. Ancient metrics measure syllabic quantity, and long and short syllables can be identified by phonetic rules; hence, cl. pyrrhics and spondees are immediately recognizable metrical phenomena. In contrast, mod. Eng. meter measures syllabic stress, and this cannot be consistently determined by external principle but is often affected by verbal environment, grammatical function, rhetorical sense, or some combination of these factors. In particular, any of the lang.'s many monosyllabic words can serve, given the right context, as metrically accented or unaccented. Because of such variabilities and because successive syllables in Eng. rarely feature equal degrees of stress, Eng. pyrrhics and spondees are not so much objective metrical facts as rhythmical effects, the perception and identification of which must be to some extent subjective. Each reader must decide for him- or herself when two syllables are close enough in their stress properties to be treated as equal. More specifically, introducing routinely spondees and pyrrhics into the

scansion of Eng. iambic verse misconstrues its nature, insofar as the practice implies that feet whose syllables are relatively close in weight are metrical variants, whereas such feet occur all the time in any naturally and competently written iambic poem.

IV. Pros and Cons of Scansion. Because scansion has at times contributed to confusions of metrical description with metrical practice, some have wondered whether we should scrap the exercise in favor of prosodic studies that more broadly address ways in which meters cooperate with the lexical and syntactical elements of lang. Might it be wiser, some have asked, to direct attention to phrasal and clausal arrangements in verse lines rather than focusing on little two- and three-syllable units? As Cunningham puts it, we might be better off "regarding a meter, not as a schematic diagram of scansions, but as a collection of syllabic-syntactic types . . . [for] this is the way we perceive meter when we read without hesitation or analysis, that is, poetically. We do not hear diagrams."

The approach Cunningham suggests merits the most serious consideration, holding out the prospect of engaging the actual process by which poets compose poems and readers experience them; still, there remains a strong case for retaining traditional scansion. To be sure, it construes words, phrases, and clauses merely as abstract feet, and this procedure sometimes appears peculiar and unnatural. Yet we should remember, again, that scansion concerns rhythmical organization, not verbal sense. And it is only reasonable, when discussing a type of rhythm, to speak of its most fundamental component, such as (in the case of iambic rhythm) a weak syllable followed by a strong one. Moreover, scansion provides a compact and comprehensive method for examining metrical structure. And though we would in theory benefit greatly from an account of all the syllabic-syntactic types relevant to a particular meter, compiling such a compendium would probably prove in many cases a practical impossibility. The Eng. pentameter, even when self-contained and end-stopped, can accommodate any number of syntactical forms. If we add arrangements that involve run-over lines—arrangements that traverse as well as interact with metrical units—the possibilities seem boundless.

Further, scansion does not exclude other kinds of analysis. Scanning by feet does not prevent our considering ways in which

SCHEME   319

grammar and meter cooperate, any more than it precludes our appreciation of how the stress a syllable carries may be influenced by its verbal environment, grammatical function, or rhetorical sense. Ultimately, negative feelings about scansion mostly result from misunderstandings of it. And instead of jettisoning a system that has, whatever its quirks and deficiencies, fruitfully served centuries of poets and readers, we should try, as patiently as possible, to correct the misunderstandings. More specifically, whenever we discuss prosody, we should be careful to distinguish between meter and rhythm—between the comprehensive pattern of the norm and the many particular ways it can be realized in living speech.

Scansion and metrical analysis have served literary scholarship and education in the past and can continue to do so in the future. They may also encourage and support versification in an age when much imaginative lit. has gravitated to prose or to forms of free verse that, though valuable and interesting in themselves, explore concepts and cadences outside the registers of traditional metrics. Perhaps most important of all, metrical analysis and scansion may help us keep poetry, even as we acknowledge its grandeurs and mysteries, connected with the modest but nourishing disciplines of rhet., grammar, logic, and phonetics.

See ENGLISH PROSODY, METER, RHYTHM.

■ **History:** Bridges; G. L. Trager and H. L. Smith Jr., *An Outline of English Structure* (1951); Saintsbury, *Prosody*; Chomsky and Halle; R. Pfeiffer, *History of Classical Scholarship from the Beginnings to the End of the Hellenistic Age* (1968); Brogan; West; P. Werstine, "Line Division in Shakespeare's Dramatic Verse: An Editorial Problem," *Analytical and Enumerative Bibliography* 8 (1984); S. Woods, *Natural Emphasis* (1985); G. T. Wright, *Shakespeare's Metrical Art* (1988); J. Thompson, *The Founding of English Metre*, 2d ed. (1989); T. Cable, *The English Alliterative Tradition* (1991); L. D. Reynolds and N. G. Wilson, *Scribes and Scholars*, 3d ed. (1991); B. O'Donnell, *The Passion of Meter* (1995); *English Historical Metrics*, ed. C. B. McCully and J. J. Anderson (1996); *Twentieth-Century American Poetics*, D. Gioia, D. Mason, and M. Schoerke, with D. C. Stone (2004).

■ **Criticism:** O. Jespersen, "Notes on Metre," *Linguistica* (1933); E. Pound, "A Retrospect," *Literary Essays of Ezra Pound*, ed. T. S. Eliot (1954); Y. Winters, "The Audible Reading of Poetry," *The Function of Criticism* (1957);

M. Halpern, "On the Two Chief Metrical Modes in English," *PMLA* 77 (1962); V. Nabokov, *Notes on Prosody* (1964); W. K. Wimsatt and M. C. Beardsley, "The Concept of Meter," *Hateful Contraries* (1965); J. McAuley, *Versification* (1966); R. A. Hornsby, *Reading Latin Poetry* (1967); J. V. Cunningham, "How Shall the Poem Be Written?" *Collected Essays* (1976); *The Structure of Verse*, ed. H. Gross, rev. ed. (1979); P. Fussell, *Poetic Meter and Poetic Form*, rev. ed. (1979); Attridge, *Rhythms*; T. Jefferson, "Thoughts on English Prosody," *Writings*, ed. M. D. Peterson (1984); J. Hollander, *Rhyme's Reason*, 2d ed. (1989); *Rhythm and Meter*, ed. P. Kiparsky and G. Youmans (1989); *Meter in English*, ed. D. Baker (1996); A. Corn, *The Poem's Heartbeat* (1997); R. Pinsky, *The Sounds of Poetry* (1998); T. Steele, *All the Fun's in How You Say a Thing* (1999); Finch and Varnes; S. Fry, *The Ode Less Travelled* (2005); D. Caplan, *Poetic Form* (2007); R. Frost, "The Figure a Poem Makes," *The Collected Prose of Robert Frost*, ed. M. Richardson (2007); M. D. Hurley, "The Pragmatics of Prosody," *Style* 41 (2007).

T. STEELE

SCHEME. A technical term from the cl. art of rhet., a *scheme* is a general category of figurative lang. that includes any artful deviation from the ordinary arrangement of words. Unlike *tropes, which work on the signification of words, schemes involve only their arrangement, as in this *chiasmus: "I do not live to eat, but eat to live." This syntactical rearrangement may take a variety of forms, incl. changes in word order (anastrophe), the omission or repetition of words (*asyndeton, antimetabole), or the use of parallel or antithetical grammatical structures (*isocolon, *antithesis). The term derives from *schēma*, one of many Gr. words for outward "form" or "shape," which was used to name a general concept of perceptible form in the arts of rhet., grammar, logic, mathematics, and music (Auerbach). In antiquity, schemes were often divided into schemes of words and of thought (*schēmata lexeos* and *dianoias*), although rhetors rarely agreed on a list of schemes that alter verbal expression without altering thought as well. Cicero (*De oratore*) and the anonymous *Rhetorica ad Herennium* use *schēmata* to refer to the three levels of *style (grand, middle, simple), while Quintilian translates the term as *figura*, meaning "a configuration of language distinct from the common and immediately obvious form" (*Institutio oratoria*). In Lat. and vernacular rhets. after Quintilian, *scheme* becomes differentiated from its Lat. trans. (figura), becoming instead the term for a *kind* of rhetorical figure. Along with its counterpart *trope*, *scheme* persists as a subclassification of *figure* well into the 17th c., when it begins to fade from regular use in writing on rhet. and lit. Although structuralist ling. and deconstruction resuscitated rhet. as a hermeneutical code in the 20th c., *scheme* was not restored to regular use as a term of art, and it is now rarely used to speak about figurative lang. in rhet. or lit.

In distinguishing schēma from trope, Quintilian calls it "a purposeful deviation in sense or language from the ordinary simple form; the analogy is now with sitting, bending forwards, or looking back" (*Institutio oratoria*). Later analogies reinforce this distinction between inward meaning and outward form by comparing schemes to costume, clothing, and ornament. Cl. definitions of *scheme* thus rely on an idea of ordinary (naked, natural, or plain) speech that is then clothed by the figures of rhet. The discursive force of such ornament varies throughout rhet.'s long hist., with schemes swelling in number and acquiring greater currency in courtly cultures that emphasize fashion, performance, or external show as constitutive of identity. In theories of rhet. and poetics informed by mod. ling., there is considerable skepticism toward the notion that there exists an "ordinary" lang. to be ornamented by figures of speech. Such theory concludes that rhetorical figures are not supplementary decorations but rather fundamental structures of lang. and thought (Jakobson, Derrida, de Man). Although this theory of figures as constitutive of, and coextensive with, lang. makes its exemplary arguments with reference to tropes such as *metaphor and *metonymy, it has resulted in a generalized critical method inclined to discover substantive meaning in the lexical patterns and shapes of what used to be called rhetorical schemes.

■ Jakobson and Halle, "Two Aspects of Language and Two Types of Aphasic Disturbances"; E. Auerbach, "Figura," trans. R. Manheim, *Scenes from the Drama of European Literature* (1959); O. Ducrot and T. Todorov, *Encyclopedic Dictionary of the Sciences of Language*, trans. C. Porter (1979); G. Genette, *Figures of Literary Discourse*, trans. A. Sheridan (1981); T. Todorov, *Introduction to Poetics*, trans. R. Howard (1981); de Man, "The Rhetoric of Temporality" and "The Rhetoric of Blindness"; P. de Man,

"Anthropomorphism and Trope in the Lyric," *The Rhetoric of Romanticism* (1984), and "Hypogram and Inscription" and "The Resistance to Theory," *The Resistance to Theory* (1986); J. Derrida, "White Mythology," *Margins of Philosophy*, trans. A. Bass (1986); Vickers, *Defence*; B. Dupriez, *A Dictionary of Literary Devices* (1991); Lanham; *Renaissance Figures of Speech*, ed. G. Alexander, S. Anderson, and K. Ettenhuber (2007); G. Burton, "Silva Rhetoricae," http://rhetoric.byu.edu.

J. C. MANN

SEPTET. A seven-line stanza in one of a large number of metrical and *rhyme schemes. Isometric forms include the Sicilian septet, rhyming *ababab*, and the Sp. septet or septilla, traditionally octosyllabic, presently octosyllabic or pentameter and rhyming *aabccba* or *abbacca*. Heterometric forms include the roundelet, a med. Fr. seven-line stanza with *refrain, in which lines 1, 3, and 7 are identical, and with syllable counts of 4-8-4-8-8-4. These tight forms are marked by the play of a strict two-rhyme pattern and/or verbal repetitions; these schemes are adapted freely in ambitious poems like Eustache Deschamps' "Vous qui vivez à présent en ce monde" (14th c.), and, earlier, in troubadour song. Septets are found in the poetries of Eur., East Asian, and West Asian lang. families. In Eng., septets are developed with subtlety and syntactic expansiveness by Mary Sidney Herbert in her dedicatory poem to her brother, "To the Angel Spirit of the Most Excellent Philip Sidney" in 13 stanzas of *iambic *pentameter septets; by John Donne in "The Good-morrow," and by John Milton in "On the Death of a Fair Infant Dying of a Cough," both of whom end their septets with an *alexandrine in the Spenserian mode. The richest septet form in Eng. is *rhyme royal, developed brilliantly by Chaucer and used as well by John Gower, Thomas Wyatt, Milton, and W. H. Auden.
■ Le Gentil.

T. KRIER

SESTET (It. *sestette, sestetto*). According to the *OED*, the term first appeared in Eng. in 1867, when Leigh Hunt and S. Adams Lee used it to signify the minor division or last six lines of a *sonnet, preceded by an *octave. Sometimes the octave states a proposition or situation and the sestet a conclusion, but no fast rules for content can be formulated. The rhyme scheme of the sestet varies: in an It. sonnet, it is usually *cdecde*, in an Eng., *efefgg*, but there are others. The term *sestet* is not generally used for a six-line stanza apart from a sonnet. The older term *sexain* is still used for such stanzas, which may be patterned in various ways.

■ *The Book of the Sonnet*, ed. L. Hunt and S. Adams Lee, 1:10–11 (1867).

R. O. EVANS; S. CUSHMAN

SESTINA (It. *sestine*, *sesta rima*). The most complicated of the verse forms initiated by the troubadours, the sestina is composed of six stanzas of six lines each, followed by an *envoi of three lines, all of which are unrhymed, and all decasyllabic (Eng.), hendecasyllabic (It.), or *alexandrine (Fr.). The same six end words occur in each stanza, but in a shifting order that follows a fixed pattern: each successive stanza takes its pattern from a reversed (bottom-up) pairing of the lines of the preceding stanza (i.e., last and first, then next to last and second, then third from last and third). If we let the numbers 1 through 6 stand for the end words, we may schematize the pattern as follows:

stanza 1	:	123456
stanza 2	:	615243
stanza 3	:	364125
stanza 4	:	532614
stanza 5	:	451362
stanza 6	:	246531
envoi	:	531 or 135

More commonly, the envoi, or *tornada*, is further complicated by the fact that the remaining three end words, 246, must also occur in the course of its three lines, so that it gathers up all six together.

The invention of the sestina is usually attributed to Arnaut Daniel (fl. 1180–95), and the form was widely cultivated both by his Occitan followers in Italy (Dante, Petrarch, Gaspara Stampa), Spain, and Portugal (Luís de Camões, Bernardim Ribeiro). A rhymed version (*abcbca* in the first stanza) was introduced into France by Pontus de Tyard (*Erreurs amoureuses*, 1549), a member of the Pléiade; Philip Sidney dispenses with rhyme for "Ye Goatherd Gods," a double sestina in the *Arcadia* (1590, 1593). In Germany, the poets of the 17th c. were attracted to the sestina (Martin Opitz, Andreas Gryphius, G. R. Weckherlin). In France and England, the sestina enjoyed a revival in the 19th c., thanks to the Comte de Gramont and to A. C. Swinburne, both of whom developed rhymed versions, Gramont's all on the same two-rhyme model

(*abaabb* in the first stanza), Swinburne's not surprisingly more variable, given that he also composed a double sestina of twelve 12-line stanzas ("The Complaint of Lisa"). Gramont prefaced his collection with a hist. of the sestina, in which he describes it as "a reverie in which the same ideas, the same objects, occur to the mind in a succession of different aspects, which nonetheless resemble one another, fluid and changing shape like the clouds in the sky." The sestina interested the Fr. and Eng. Parnassians less than the other Romance fixed forms, but it has enjoyed a growing popularity in the 20th and 21st cs. Ezra Pound called the sestina "a form like a thin sheet of flame, folding and infolding upon itself," and his "Sestina: Altaforte" and "Sestina for Isolt" reintroduced the form to readers. Following W. H. Auden's "Paysage moralisé" and Louis Zukofsky's "Mantis," Am. poets have shown a remarkable interest in the form. Anthony Hecht's "The Book of Yolek," Elizabeth Bishop's "Sestina" and "A Miracle for Breakfast," and John Ashbery's "Farm Implements and Rutabagas in a Landscape" suggest the form's flexibility, as the repetitions evoke states as different as uncanny menace, claustrophobic containment, and comic playfulness. Indeed, from the mid-20th c. to the present, the sestina has enjoyed a great popularity in Am. poetry, at least partly because it serves the poetic culture's needs. A favorite exercise in creative writing classes, it allows poets to demonstrate a professional skill while exploring its limits. The form's repetitions also inspire poets interested in word games, as lang. forms the material of composition.

■ F. de Gramont, *Sestines, précédés de l'histoire de la sextine* (1872); Kastner; F. Davidson, "The Origin of Sestina," *MLN* 25 (1910); A. Jeanroy, "La 'sestina doppia' de Dante et les origines de la sestine," *Romania* 42 (1912); H. L. Cohen, *Lyric Forms from France* (1922); E. Pound, *The Spirit of Romance* (1952); L. Fiedler, "Green Thoughts in a Green Shade," *KR* 18 (1956); J. Riesz, *Die Sestine* (1971); I. Baldelli, "Sestina," *Enciclopedia Dantesca*, ed. G. Petrocchi et al., 5 v. (1970–78); M. Shapiro, *Hieroglyph of Time: The Petrarchan Sestina* (1980); Morier; A. Roncaglia, "L'invenzione della sestina," *Metrica* 2 (1981); Elwert, *Italienische*, sect. 82; J. F. Nims, *A Local Habitation* (1985); D. Caplan, *Questions of Possibility: Contemporary Poetry and Poetic Form* (2004); S. Burt, "Sestina! or, The Fate of the Idea of Form," *MP* 105 (2007).

A. PREMINGER; C. SCOTT; D. CAPLAN

SIGNIFYING is a dominant satiric form in Af. Am. verbal expression that provides a basis for both poetry and literary reception, a procedure for speakers and poets and a program by which Af. Am. writers read and interpret one another (Gates). Signifying subsumes many other tropes (e.g., *metaphor, *metonymy, *catachresis) and has many tones, often ironic. It was nurtured significantly in Af. Am. vernacular poetic forms such as toasts, sagas, and *blues. There is a toast trad. known specifically as the *signifying monkey poem*, which treats all kinds of subjects satirically. Among the sagas, "Titanic Shine" is perhaps the best known. The blues is replete with signifying lines such as "Ain't a baker in town / Can bake a sweet jelly roll like mine" and "Take this hammer and carry it to my captain: / Tell him I'm gone." Although not restricted to poetry, the use of the signifying trad. in Af. Am. writing can be traced from the earliest poets such as Jupiter Hammon (b. 1711) through Paul Laurence Dunbar (1872–1906), Langston Hughes (1902–67), then to poets of the 1960s and after such as Haki Madhubuti (Don L. Lee; b. 1942), Sonia Sanchez (b. 1934), Nikki Giovanni (b. 1943), and June Jordan (1936–2002).

See SATIRE.

■ C. Mitchell-Kernan, "Signifying," *Motherwit from the Laughing Barrel: Readings in the Interpretation of Afro-American Folklore*, ed. A. Dundes (1973); G. Smitherman, *Talkin and Testifyin* (1977); H. L. Gates Jr., "The Blackness of Blackness: A Critique on the Sign and the Signifying Monkey," *Figures in Black* (1987), and *The Signifying Monkey* (1988); K. Euell, "Signifyin(g) Ritual: Subverting Stereotypes, Salvaging Icons," *African American Review* 31 (1997); M. Marrouchi, *Signifying with a Vengeance* (2002)—postcolonial culture; A. Smith, "Blues, Criticism, and the Signifying Trickster," *Popular Music* 24 (2005).

E. A. PETERS

SIMILE. A figure of speech most conservatively defined as an explicit comparison using *like* or *as*—e.g., "black, naked women with necks / wound round and round with wire / like the necks of light bulbs" (Elizabeth Bishop, "In the Waiting Room"). The function of the comparison is to reveal an unexpected likeness between two seemingly disparate things—in this case, the necks of tribal women and light bulbs. Simile is probably the "oldest readily identifiable poetic artifice in European litera-

ture" (Holoka), stretching back through Homer and Mycenaean epic poetry to Sumerian, Sanskrit, and Chinese.

Critics and theorists disagree over what distinguishes simile from factual comparisons on the one hand and *metaphor on the other. While some theorists argue that factual comparisons ("My eyes are like yours") and similes (such as Chaucer's "hir eyen greye as glas") differ only in degree, others argue that they differ in kind (a confusion that William Wordsworth successfully exploits in "Tintern Abbey" when he follows the "wreaths of smoke / Sent up, in silence" with "as might seem / Of vagrant dwellers in the houseless woods"). Similarly, some critics adhere to the traditional view that metaphor is a compressed simile, distinguishable from simile only in being an implicit rather than an explicit comparison (Miller), whereas others conclude that not all metaphors and similes are interchangeable, that metaphor is a "use of language," whereas comparison itself is a "psychological process" (Ortony). These questions have entered the domain of ling., where at least one theorist has argued in favor of a single "deep structure" of comparison, variously realized as either simile or metaphor, that is capable of distinguishing both similes from factual comparisons and also metaphors from mere copulative equations such as "My car is a Ford" (Mack). The latter solution supports a growing sense that simile may be marked not only by *like* or *as* but also by many other comparative markers, incl. verbs such as *resemble*, *echo*, and *seem*; connectives such as *as if* and *as though*; and phrases such as *the way that* (Darian). From this perspective, it seems likely that simile encompasses analogy, rather than being a discrete form of comparison. At the very least, the current exploration into the range of simile suggests that it may be a far more pervasive aspect of both lang. and perception than has previously been thought.

In Western culture, there has been a traditional prejudice against simile in favor of metaphor. Wheelwright suggests that this trad. begins with Aristotle, who judges simile inferior for two reasons: since it is longer than metaphor, it is "less pleasing" and since simile "does not affirm that this *is* that, the mind does not inquire into the matter" (*Rhetoric* 3.4.1406b). As Derrida has noted, "[T]here is no more classical theory of metaphor than treating it as an 'economical' way of avoiding 'extended explanations': and . . . of avoiding simile." The 20th

c. was esp. rigid in privileging metaphor over simile. At least prior to poststructuralist crit., many 20th-c. critics and theorists heralded metaphor as a model for understanding lang., thought, and philosophy. Frye, e.g., regards simile as a "displaced" metaphor, which, for him, corresponds to the displacement of mythic identity into naturalism. Only recently have a few critics begun to regard simile not just as "literary embellishment" but as "a tool for serious thinking, scientific and otherwise" that "transcribes a paradigm of the creative act itself, whether in poetry or physics" (Darian).

Despite the long denigration of simile by critics, poets have consistently used the simile. The earliest recorded Western lit., Sumerian, uses similes in virtually every genre (Kramer). Among them are similes that seem uncannily familiar, such as "as wide as the earth" and "as everlasting as the earth." Similes are used throughout the *Rig Veda*—e.g., "In the East the brilliant dawns have stood / Like posts set up at sacrifices" (Cook). Certainly, Homer uses similes, though his nearly formulaic ones (such as Thetis's rising out of the sea like a mist) hover somewhere between *epithet and metaphor; and in this regard, it is provocative that Aristotle allies "proportional metaphor, which contains an epithet" with comparisons (McCall). As Green has pointed out, Virgil's "characteristic trope" is the simile. Chaucer frequently turns to simile, esp. for humor, as when describing "hende Nicholas" as being "as sweete as is the roote / Of lycorys, or any cetewale." Shakespeare achieves *irony by negating conventional similes in "My mistress' eyes are nothing like the sun."

Despite the prevailing 19th-c. emphasis on the *symbol, P. B. Shelley habitually turns to simile. In the "Hymn to Intellectual Beauty," the "unseen Power" visits

> with as inconstant wing
> As summer winds that creep from flower
>   to flower,—
> Like moonbeams that behind some piny
>   mountain shower,
> It visits with inconstant glance
> Each human heart and countenance;
> Like hues and harmonies of evening,—
> Like clouds in starlight widely spread,—
> Like memory of music fled—

Equally curious—given the early 20th-c. bias in favor of imagism that followed Ezra Pound's injunction to "use no unnecessary word" (and that encouraged the excision of similes)—is the

Wallace Stevens's increasing use of the simile in key passages of his poetry. He concludes his *Collected Poems* with "It was like / A new knowledge of reality," a simile that calls attention to the problematic relation between poetry and what it represents.

The most revered form of simile is the epic simile, a lengthy comparison between two highly complex objects, actions, or relations. Homer is credited with inaugurating the epic simile, there being no known simile before the *Iliad* of such length or sophistication as the following:

> As is the generation of leaves, so is that of
>   humanity.
> The wind scatters the leaves on the ground,
>   but the live timber
> burgeons with leaves again in the season of
>   spring returning.
> So one generation of men will grow while
>   another dies.

While the epic simile may be used by Homer for contrast, digression, or thematic amplification, subsequent poets such as Virgil, Dante, Ludovico Ariosto, Edmund Spenser, and John Milton refine the device, making it integral to the structure of the epic. Later poets frequently resuscitate specific Homeric similes (Holoka), as does Virgil when comparing the "whole crowd" to the "forest leaves that flutter down / at the first autumn frost" (*Aeneid* 6.305–10), or as does Milton when describing Lucifer's "Legions" that "lay intrans't / Thick as Autumnal Leaves that strow the Brooks / In *Vallombrosa*" (*Paradise Lost* 1.301–3).

■ H. Fränkel, *Die homerischen Gleichnisse* (1921); W. P. Ker, *Form and Style in Poetry* (1928); C. M. Bowra, *Tradition and Design in the "Iliad"* (1930); J. Whaler, "The Miltonic Simile," *PMLA* 46 (1931); Z. E. Green, "Observations on the Epic Simile in the *Faerie Queene*," *PQ* 14 (1935); Frye; K. Widmer, "The Iconography of Renunciation: The Miltonic Simile," *ELH* 25 (1958); C. S. Lewis, "Dante's Simile," *Nottingham Medieval Studies* 9 (1965); P. Wheelwright, *The Burning Fountain*, rev. ed. (1968); M. H. McCall, *Ancient Rhetorical Theories of Simile and Comparison* (1969); S. N. Kramer, "Sumerian Simile," *JAOS* 89 (1969); S. G. Darian, "Simile and the Creative Process," *Lang&S* 6 (1973); D. Mack, "Metaphoring as Speech Act," *Poetics* 4 (1975); J. Derrida, "White Mythology," *NLH* 6 (1975); J. P. Holoka, "'Thick as Autumnal Leaves,'" *Milton*

Quarterly 10 (1976); R. H. Lansing, *From Image to Idea: The Simile in Dante's "Divine Comedy"* (1977); G. A. Miller, "Images and Models, Simile and Metaphors," and A. Ortony, "The Role of Similarity in Simile and Metaphors," *Metaphor and Thought*, ed. A. Ortony (1979); J. N. Swift, "Simile of Disguise and the Reader of *Paradise Lost*," *South Atlantic Quarterly* 79 (1980); K. O. Murtaugh, *Ariosto and the Classical Simile* (1980); A. Cook, *Figural Choice in Poetry and Art* (1985); J. V. Brogan, *Stevens and Simile: A Theory of Language* (1986); S. A. Nimis, *Narrative Semiotics in the Epic Tradition: The Simile* (1987); S. J. Wolfson, "'Comparing Power': Coleridge and Simile," *Coleridge's Theory of Imagination Today*, ed. C. Gallant (1989); W. Prunty, *Fallen from the Symboled World* (1989); S. Glucksberg, *Understanding Figurative Language* (2001).

J. V. BROGAN; H. SMITH RICHMOND

SKELTONIC. A kind of poem named after its originator, the Eng. poet laureate John Skelton (ca. 1460–1529). Skeltonic poems are distinguished by short lines and long stretches of monorhyme, called *leashes*. End *rhymes are not crossed. Lines have between two and five stresses, although three-stress lines occur most frequently. *Alliteration abounds, and although he writes primarily in Eng., Skelton includes scraps of Lat. and Fr. occasionally as well. The rhymes continue "as long as the resources of the language hold out," in Lewis's phrase; rhyme, rather than meaning, seems to drive the poems forward.

A vigorous vernacular form, Skeltonics served Skelton primarily for his *satires, which ranged in *tone from the lighter humor of *The Book of Philip Sparrow* to the fierce misogyny of *The Tunning of Elinor Rumming* to the moral strains of *Colin Clout* to the vicious ad hominem attacks of *Why Come Ye Not to Court?*, to name the works most pub. in the 16th c. and most anthologized now. Although involved in the courts of both Henry VII and VIII; laureated by Oxford, Cambridge, and Louvain; and a Catholic priest, Skelton was long linked with popular or even vulgar verse. George Puttenham in *The Arte of English Poesie* (1589) dismissed him as a "rude rayling rimer," part of which critique is in reaction to his use of "short distances and short measures, pleasing only the popular ear."

Scholars have not yet achieved a consensus on the origin of Skeltonics: they have been seen as deriving from various med. trads., incl. Lat. verse,

Lat. rhyming prose, and the Catholic liturgy, among others. Scholars and critics since Skelton's time also dispute the value of the Skeltonic. Many, following Puttenham, have seen it simply as doggerel. Mod. poets such as Robert Graves and W. H. Auden held the Skeltonic in higher esteem. Among mod. critics, Lewis sees it as fitting only when representing "immature or disorganized states of consciousness," while Fish sees it as a choice of blunt moral content over false eloquence.

Other than Skelton himself, poets have rarely used Skeltonics, although some Protestant reformers employed them soon after his death. Although Skelton was a Catholic priest hired by Cardinal Thomas Wolsey to write an anti-Protestant propaganda poem (*Replycacion*), his attacks on the Church made his poetry easily assimilable to the Protestant cause, and several Protestant satires were written in Skeltonics, incl. *The Image of Hypocrisy* (1534) and *Vox Populi Vox Dei* (1547).

■ W. Nelson, *John Skelton, Laureate* (1939); C. S. Lewis, *English Literature in the Sixteenth Century, Excluding Drama* (1954); S. Fish, *John Skelton's Poetry* (1965); A. Kinney, *John Skelton: Priest as Poet* (1987); G. Walker, *John Skelton and the Politics of the 1520s* (1988); J. Griffiths, *John Skelton and Poetic Authority* (2006).

R. KAPLAN

SLANG. *See* DICTION.

SONG (Lat. *carmen*, Fr. *chanson*, Ger. *Lied*). *Song* refers broadly to the combined effect of music and words in a composition meant to be heard as music rather than read silently. Music, in addition to being the vehicle of transmission, frequently reinforces or enhances the emotional force of the text as perceived by the composer of the musical setting. While some songs are dramatic, song is distinguished from extended compositions involving music and text (such as opera) by its relative brevity. Since most songs are poems set to music, by extension any poem that is suitable for combination with music or is expressive in ways that might be construed as musical may also be referred to as song, and occasionally *song* is used to designate a strictly musical composition without text, deemed "poetic" in its expressivity or featuring markedly "vocal" melodic writing for instruments. From the musical standpoint, *song* has been restricted almost exclusively to musical settings of verse; experiments in setting prose have been very limited. Further, *song* has usually been reserved for compositions for solo voice or a small group of voices (typically one or two voices to a part) rather than a full choir and for voice(s) alone or in combination with one or two instruments rather than a full orchestra. In any case, the resulting balance, favoring the audibility of the text and thus appreciation of the nuances of its combination with music, is a defining characteristic of the genre; for literary purposes, these characteristics have also fostered perception of *song* as personal utterance projecting a limited emotional stance experienced by a single *persona.

As a literary term, *song* is related to *lyric, originally a text or poem sung to the accompaniment of the lyre and eventually used in lit. in divergent senses to refer, on the one hand, to any poem actually set or intended to be set to music (ditty), and, on the other, to any poem focusing on the arousal of emotion as would be characteristic of the kind of poem typically sung to the lyre (or to any other musical accompaniment) as song. *Lyric*, however, has attained much wider currency than has *song* and is the commonly accepted term today for both these meanings, whereas *song*, as a literary term, means an utterance partaking in some way of the condition of music. The musicality of a poem may be thought of in relation to the ways a text might be interpreted by a musical setting. Some songs correspond closely to the formal properties of the text (incl. metrical, linear, and strophic form), while others emphasize the semantic properties (rendering the meaning of individual words or phrases or expressing the tone or mood of the poem). They need not, of course, exclude each other; indeed, it is frequently difficult if not impossible to separate what may be a metrical rendering from its expressive function. The distinction is useful, however, as some songs favor one or the other, in turn influencing what are considered songlike elements or effects in poetry. The association of poetry with music in the songs of the late Ren. in England offers examples of both types of correspondence. In some (as in songs by Thomas Campion, who wrote both words and music), the rendering of the formal dimensions of poetry is precise: musical meter is aligned with poetic *meter, lines of verse are of uniform length and set to musical phrases of the same length (words are not repeated or extended by musical means), and the strophic *repetition of the poem is rendered through repetition of music (as in traditional hymn singing). Poetry

that lends itself to settings of this sort is typically predictable in all these dimensions; hence, such a poem may be designated *song*. In the *madrigal and in some lute songs, by contrast, such formal properties are likely to be ignored and musical devices instead correlated with individual words to enhance meaning. This might mean repetition of words of special poignancy ("weep, weep") or highlighting of such words through exaggerated duration or unusually high or low pitch; frequently such representation is accomplished through a technique called *word-painting*, which aligns individual words with musical figures that can be said to depict their meaning (a descending scale for the word *down*; a dissonance for the word *grief*). Such practices also lead to predictability, in this case, in *diction. In the poetic miscellanies of the period, *song* and *sonnet sometimes seem to be used interchangeably and often refer to poems with one or more of these characteristics. At worst, they are poems filled with cliché and cloyingly regular in formal properties; at best, they achieve a delicate balance between the demands of successful musical rendition and fresh invention.

Songs featuring more general expressivity of mood or tone in music appear less frequently in this period, although the lutenist-composer John Dowland achieved some remarkable successes in this mode. Perhaps most famous is his "Lachrimae," which existed as an instrumental composition before being provided with its now-famous text, "Flow, my tears." The pervasively doleful mood of the piece is created musically in the accompaniment through its preponderance of descending melodic lines, its minor harmonies, its low register, and the slow, deliberate pace of its phrasing; the poem seems, in effect, to make verbal what the musical rhet. of emotion suggests. The role of music, then, in this type of song is less specifically text-dependent than in other types, and the required balance between music and poetry depends to a greater extent on the availability of appropriate instrumental resources to combine with the voice.

The *lied* of 19th-c. Ger. lit. best exemplifies the fully developed expressive setting. In the hands of Franz Schubert, and to a great extent of those who followed him (Robert Schumann, Johannes Brahms, Hugo Wolf), the role of the accompanying instrument was enhanced to create a highly emotional song evocative of the overall tone or mood of the poem. Many give credit to the devel. of the mod. grand piano for the success of the lied. Although the notion of expressive setting was not new, as the role of the instrumental accompaniment in Claudio Monteverdi's "Combattimento di Tancredi e Clorinda" demonstrates, such pieces violated the required intimacy of voice and single instrument characteristic of song, and it was not until the devel. of a single instrument with the expressive range of the piano that this mode of song could flourish. The genre also depended on—and stimulated—a poetry that provided the appropriate moods, expressed in terms that could be adequately mimicked by music. This is found in the poetry of Ger. romanticism, with its frequent evocation of nature or of ordinary human activity as the locus of emotion. For Schubert, the presence in the poem of a running brook or a woman spinning wool as the background to an emotion-filled reverie provided a means for music to enhance what the poem could only suggest. In this context, poetry can be said to be song-like if it presents an intense, sustained, clear, emotional stance, called forth by an activity that takes place in time. Typically, such poems feature only one such stance or a decided shift from one to another; striking *ambiguity or *paradox is less song-like insofar as these conditions are less readily imitated in music.

Curiously, poems that depend extensively on the so-called musicality of words (e.g., Edith Sitwell's "abstract poetry" and the later experiments in *sound poetry) are not necessarily song-like, because the sounds of the words draw attention to themselves and thereby detract from the poem's ability to evoke an emotional state.

The most extended use of *song* to refer to a kind of poetry takes the connection well beyond any mechanical representation or concurrence to questions of intent or of the relation to strains of creativity. Thus, Maritain uses *song* to designate the entire genre of lyric poetry, as distinct from narrative or dramatic, referring to "the Poem or the Song as the poetry of internal music . . . the immediate expression of creative intuition, the meaning whose intentional content is purely a recess of the subjectivity awakened to itself and things—perceived through an obscure, simple, and totally nonconceptual apperception." Such conceptions of the nature of song center on the ability of music to tap some source of understanding or sympathy that is not touched by lang. Kramer speaks of "the mythical union of a lower reality embodied in language

and a higher one embodied in music," stating that "through song, usually the song of a disincarnate voice or of a figure touched by divinity, lang. is represented as broaching the ineffable"; this is the sense implied in the use of music to evoke the supernatural, whether through strictly instrumental means or through charms, as is common in drama. Music has traditionally been associated with magic and with religious experience (despite the objections at various times of both Catholic and Puritan), and it is commonly thought of as the lang. of love. The fusion, therefore, of music and poetry in song has been thought to bring about the most perfect communication possible, combining the ineffable expressivity of music with the rational capabilities of words. And by derivation, poems that are perceived as visionary, conjuring some understanding beyond the normal capacities of words, may be called songs. Edmund Spenser's *Epithalamion* and *Prothalamion*, William Blake's *Songs of Innocence and Experience*, and Walt Whitman's "Song of Myself" come to mind.

Scholarship on song as music and text frequently focuses on function and social context. Vernacular song and folk song, for instance, have generated a huge independent lit. (not represented in the biblio. below). Although the distinctions between these and the many types of so-called art song are not always clear, the popular genres are less likely to have strong literary connections. Similarly, the literary connection is clearest with secular song, though the relations between music and text in sacred song run the same gamut as in secular. All song types, however, lend themselves well to critical methodologies of recent prominence (such as feminism or New Historicism) and a growing number of comparative explorations of song lit. of other cultures has emerged.

Song has also come to designate certain purely musical compositions, presumably those, like poems called "song," that partake in some measure of the shared experience of music and poetry. Most frequent in this usage are such 19th-c. compositions as Felix Mendelssohn's "Songs without Words" for piano—short, expressive pieces, typically with a striking, singable melody and the sense that one could describe in words a suitable emotional frame of reference. Their proximity to the lied is probably not coincidence; *song*, or *lied*, in that context describes that combination of words and music producing a compressed and intense expression of the rhet. of emotion, and if words are merely implied, the effect is nevertheless present and the composition known as "song."

Several specialized types of song, established by use, have similarly given their names to poetic types, esp. *elegy, *lament, *hymn, lay or *lai*, *ballad, carol, *rondeau, and canzonet.

See AIR, ALBA, BLUES, RHYTHM, SOUND.

■ **Song as Music**: F. Gennrich, *Grundriss einer Formenlehre des mittelalterlichen Liedes* (1932); J. Maritain, *Creative Intuition in Art and Poetry* (1953); R. Lebègue, "Ronsard et la musique," *Musique et poésie au XVI siècle* (1954); G. Müller and G. Reichert, "Lied," *Reallexikon II* 2.42–62; D. Cooke, *The Language of Music* (1959); A. Sydow, *Das Lied* (1962); C. M. Bowra, *Primitive Song* (1962); R. H. Thomas, *Poetry and Song in the German Baroque* (1963); *The Penguin Book of Lieder*, ed. S. S. Prawer (1964); R. Taylor, *The Art of the Minnesinger* (1968); B. H. Bronson, *The Ballad as Song* (1969); D. Ivey, *Song* (1970)—on musical settings of Eng., Fr., Ger., and It. poetry, 17th–20th cs.; E. Brody and R. A. Fowkes, *The German Lied and Its Poetry* (1971); J. M. Stein, *Poem and Music in the German Lied* (1971); M. C. Beardsley, "Verse and Music," Wimsatt; H. van der Werf, *The Chansons of the Troubadours and Trouvères* (1972); D. Fischer-Dieskau, *Schubert's Songs: A Biographical Study* (1977); *Medieval English Songs*, ed. E. J. Dobson and F. Ll. Harrison (1979); "Song" and "Lied," *New Grove*; M. Booth, *The Experience of Songs* (1981); R. C. Friedberg, *American Art Song and American Poetry*, 2 v. (1981); S. Ratcliffe, *Campion: On Song* (1981); J. A. Winn, *Unsuspected Eloquence: A History of the Relations between Poetry and Music* (1981); E. B. Jorgens, *The Well-Tun'd Word: Musical Interpretations of English Poetry, 1597–1651* (1982); L. Kramer, *Music and Poetry: The Nineteenth Century and After* (1984); S. Banfield, *Sensibility and English Song: Critical Studies of the Early Twentieth Century*, 2 v. (1985); M. M. Stoljar, *Poetry and Song in Late Eighteenth-Century Germany* (1985); E. Doughtie, *English Renaissance Song* (1986); W. Maynard, *Elizabethan Lyric Poetry and Its Music* (1986); J. Stevens, *Words and Music in the Middle Ages* (1986); D. Seaton, *The Art Song: A Research and Information Guide* (1987)—esp. "Aesthetics, Analysis, Criticism"; J. W. Smeed, *German Song and Its Poetry, 1740–1900* (1987); D. M. Hertz, *The Tuning of the Word* (1988); *Lyrics of the Middle Ages*, ed. J. J. Wilhelm (1990); L. E. Auld, "Text as Pre-Text: French Court Airs and Their Ditties," *Literature and the Other Arts* (1993); S. Hart, "Masking the

Violence in Melody: Songs of World War II," *The Image of Violence in Literature, the Media, and Society*, ed. W. Wright and S. Kaplan (1995); M. L. Switten, *Music and Poetry in the Middle Ages* (1995); S. Zheng, "Female Heroes and Moonish Lovers: Women's Paradoxical Identities in Modern Chinese Songs," *Journal of Women's History* 8 (1997); D. Fischlin, *In Small Proportions: A Poetics of the English Ayre, 1596–1622* (1998); D. Schaberg, "Song and the Historical Imagination in Early China," *HJAS* 59 (1999); P. Coren, "Singing and Silence: Female Personae in the English Ayre," *Renaissance Studies* 16 (2002).

■ **Song in Literature**: T. S. Eliot, *The Music of Poetry* (1942); W. R. Bowden, *The English Dramatic Lyric, 1603–42* (1951); J. Hollander, *The Untuning of the Sky: Ideas of Music in English Poetry, 1500–1700* (1961); P. J. Seng, *The Vocal Songs in the Plays of Shakespeare* (1967); E. Garke, *The Use of Songs in Elizabethan Prose Fiction* (1972); J. H. Long, *Shakespeare's Use of Music* (1972); C. Ericson-Roos, *The Songs of Robert Burns* (1977); B. H. Fairchild, *Such Holy Song: Music as Idea, Form, and Image in the Poetry of William Blake* (1980); W. R. Johnson, *The Idea of Lyric* (1982); L. Schleiner, *The Living Lyre in English Verse from Elizabeth through the Restoration* (1984); E. H. Winkler, *The Function of Song in Contemporary British Drama* (1990).

E. B. JORGENS

SONNET (from It. *sonetto*, "a little sound or song"). A 14-line line poem normally in *hendecasyllables (It.), iambic pentameter (Eng.), or *alexandrines (Fr.), whose rhyme scheme varies despite the assumption that the sonnet form is fixed. The three most widely recognized versions of the sonnet, with their traditional rhyme schemes, are the It. or Petrarchan (octave: *abbaabba*; sestet: *cdecde* or *cdcdcd* or a similar combination that avoids the closing couplet), the Spenserian (*ababbcbccdcdee*), and the Eng. or Shakespearean (*ababcdcdefefgg*). Weeks showed in a sample of just under 6,000 Eng. sonnets that 60% used the *abbaabba* pattern for the octaves and 22% *ababcdcd*.

The It. pattern (the most widely used) invites a two-part division of thought: the octave's unified pattern leads to the *volta or "turn" in the more varied sestet. The *abbaabba* octave is a blend of three brace-rhyme quatrains: the middle four lines, whose sounds overlap the others, reiterate the identical envelope pattern but with the sounds reversed, i.e., *baab*. The sestet, with its element of unpredictability, its usually more intense rhyme activity (three rhymes in six lines coming after two in eight), and the structural interdependence of the tercets, implies acceleration in thought and feeling.

The Spenserian and Shakespearean patterns offer relief to the difficulty of rhyming in Eng. and invite a division of thought into three quatrains and a closing or summarizing couplet; even though such arbitrary divisions are frequently ignored by the poet, the more open rhyme schemes tend to impress the fourfold structure on the reader's ear and to suggest a stepped progression toward the closing couplet.

Most deviations from the foregoing patterns have resulted from liberties taken in rhyming, but a few innovations of the sonnet are the following: *alternating*, where the tercets alternate with the quatrains (Catulle Mendès); *caudate*, with "tails" of added lines (G. M. Hopkins, Albert Samain, R. M. Rilke); *chained* or *linked*, each line beginning with the last word of the previous line; *continuous*, *iterating*, or *monorhymed* on one or two rhyme sounds throughout (Giacomo da Lentini, Stéphane Mallarmé, Edmund Gosse); *corona*, a series joined together by theme (It.) or rhyme or repeated lines (Sp. and Eng., e.g., John Donne) for *panegyric; *curtal*, a sonnet of ten lines with a halfline tailpiece, divided 6 + 4½ (Hopkins); *dialogue*, a sonnet distributed between two speakers and usually *pastoral in inspiration (Cecco Angiolieri, Austin Dobson); *double*, a sonnet of 28 lines (Monte Andrea); *enclosed*, in which the tercets are sandwiched between the quatrains (Charles Baudelaire, Jean Pierre Rambosson); *interwoven*, with medial as well as end rhyme; *retrograde*, reading the same backward as forward; *reversed* (also called *sonettessa*), in which the sestet precedes the octave (Baudelaire, Paul Verlaine, Ricarda Huch)—for a reversed Shakespearean sonnet, see Rupert Brooke's "Sonnet Reversed"; *rinterzato*, a sonnet with eight short lines interspersed, making a whole of 22 lines (Guittone d'Arezzo); *terza rima*, with the linked-tercets *aba bcb* rhyme scheme; *unrhymed*, where the division into quatrains and tercets is still observed, but the lines are blank (Joachim du Bellay, J. R. Becher). In Eng., the 16-line poems of George Meredith's sequence *Modern Love* (1862) are clearly related to the sonnet in their themes and *abbacddcef-feghhg* rhyme scheme.

Historically, the sonnet began as some variant of the It. pattern; it is probable that the form resulted either from the addition of a double refrain of six lines (two tercets) to the two-quatrain Sicilian *strambotto* or from conscious modeling on the form of the *canzone*. The current form of the sonnet originated in the Sicilian court of Frederick II (1205–50), with 60 of the Sicilian school's sonnets in existence today. The sonnets of Giacomo da Lentini (fl. 1215–33) were followed by those of Guido Guinizzelli and Guido Cavalcanti. Although others of Lentini's contemporaries (the Abbot of Tivoli, Jacopo Mostacci, Pier delle Vigne, Rinaldo d'Aquino) used the form and established the octave-sestet divisions (with quatrain-tercet subdivisions), it remained for d'Arezzo (1230–94) to invent the *abbaabba* octave, which became traditional through its use by Dante (*Vita nuova, Rime*) and Petrarch (*Canzoniere*); Antonio da Tempo, in his *Summa artis rithmici* (1332), is the first to enunciate theoretical discussion of the sonnet as a type. The sonnets of Dante to Beatrice and of Petrarch to Laura normally opened with a strong statement that was then developed; but they were not unmarked by the artificiality of treatment that stemmed from variations on the Platonic love themes, an artificiality that was to be exported with the form in the 15th and 16th cs. as the sonnet moved to Spain, Portugal, the Netherlands, Poland, and England, and later to Germany, Scandinavia, and Russia, until its use was pan-Eur. and the number of poets not attempting it negligible. The sonnet entered the Heb. lang. (in hendecasyllables) in Italy and Spain, as a primary form in which rhyme entered its poetry, esp. in sonnets by Immanuel of Rome at the end of the 13th to the beginning of the 14th c. Following Petrarch, there was in Italy some diminution of dignity in use of the form (as in Serafino dall'Aquila [1466–1500]), but with the work of Michelangelo, Pietro Bembo, Baldassare Castiglione, Gaspara Stampa, Vittoria Colonna, and Torquato Tasso, the sonnet was reaffirmed as a structure admirably suited to the expression of emotion in lyrical mood, adaptable to a wide range of subject matter (e.g., love, politics, religion), and employed with skill by many writers in the centuries to follow (Vittorio Alfieri, Ugo Foscolo, Giosuè Carducci, Gabriele D'Annunzio).

It was the Marqués de Santillana (1398–1458), who introduced the sonnet form (in hendecasyllables, even) to Spain, although it was not established there until the 16th c., the time of Juan Boscán (ca. 1490–1542) and esp. Garcilaso de la Vega (1503–36), Félix Lope de Vega (1562–1635), and other dramatists of the *siglo de oro*. Francisco Sá de Miranda (1481–1558) and his disciple António Ferreira brought the sonnet to Portugal, where it is better known in the *Rimas* of Luís de Camões (1524–80) and in the exquisite work of Antero de Quental (1842–91). Clément Marot (1496–1544) and Mellin de Saint Gelais (1491–1558) introduced it to France, but du Bellay (ca. 1522–60) was most active, writing (in the Petrarchan pattern) the first non-Italian cycle, *L'Olive*, as well as *Les Regrets* and *Les Antiquités de Rome* (trans. by Edmund Spenser as *The Ruins of Rome*, a source for Shakespeare's sonnets). Pierre de Ronsard (1524–85), who experimented with the form in alexandrines, Philippe Desportes (1546–1606), and Louise Labé (1522–66) wrote many sonnets, while François de Malherbe (1555–1628) put his authority behind the *abbaabbaccdede* pattern in alexandrines, which became the accepted line length. After an era of decline in Europe in the 18th c., Théophile Gautier (1811–72), Gérard de Nerval (1808–55), and Baudelaire (1821–67) revived the form, as did Verlaine, Mallarmé, Arthur Rimbaud, J.-M. de Heredia (1842–1905), and Paul Valéry (1871–1945). Germany received the form relatively late, in the writings of G. R. Weckherlin (1584–1653) and, esp. insofar as creative achievement is concerned, Andreas Gryphius (1616–64). A period of disuse followed until Gottfried Bürger (1747–94) revived the form and anticipated its use by A. W. Schlegel, J. F. Eichendorff, Ludwig Tieck, and other romantic writers. The sonnets of August Graf von Platen (1796–1835), *Sonette aus Venedig*, rank among the best in mod. times, while in more recent years the mystical sequence *Sonette an Orpheus* (1923) of Rilke and the writings of R. A. Schröder have brought the Ger. sonnet to another high point.

The sonnet arrived in England from Italy via Thomas Wyatt (1503–42), who preferred the sestet's closing couplet. Wyatt adhered to the Petrarchan octave; Henry Howard, the Earl of Surrey (1517–47), established the *ababcdcdefefgg* rhyme scheme, a pattern more congenial to the comparatively rhyme-poor Eng. lang. in that it filled the 14 lines by seven rhymes, not five. This pattern was popular in the Ren. Wide variation existed in rhyme schemes and line lengths; Shakespeare was its best practitioner. A rhyme scheme more attractive to Spenser (and in its first nine lines paralleling his *Spenserian stanza) was *ababbcbccdcdee*, a compromise between It. and Eng. patterns. The period also saw many *sonnet sequences, including those of Philip Sidney (*Astrophil and Stella*, pub. 1591), Samuel Daniel (*Delia*), Michael Drayton (*Idea*), Spenser (*Amoretti*), Lady Mary Wroth (*Pamphilia to Amphilanthus*), and Shakespeare. It remained for John Milton to introduce the true It. pattern, to break from sequences to occasional sonnets, to have a wider sense of content, to give greater unity to the form by frequently permitting octave to run into sestet (the "Miltonic" sonnet anticipated by the Elizabethans), and to give a greater richness to the texture by employing *enjambment. And sonnet-like structures of 14 lines have even been discerned in the stichic verse of *Paradise Lost*, a practice later echoed by William Wordsworth and Thomas Hardy (Johnson 1982). Milton's was the strongest influence when, after a century of disuse, the sonnet was revived in the late 18th c. by Thomas Gray, Thomas Warton, William Cowper, and William Lisle Bowles and reestablished in the early 19th by Wordsworth (who eased rhyme demands by use of an *abbaacca* octave in nearly half of his more than 500 sonnets), by Anna Seward, and by John Keats, whose frequent use of the Shakespearean pattern reaffirmed its worthiness. By this time, the scope of sonnet themes had broadened widely; in Leigh Hunt and Keats, it even embraced an unaccustomed humor. Sonnet theory was also developing tentatively during this period (as in Hunt's "Essay on the Sonnet") to eventuate in an unrealistic purism in T.W.H. Crosland's *The English Sonnet* (1917) before it was later more temperately approached. Since the impetus of the romantic revival, the form has had a continuing and at times distinguished use, as in D. G. Rossetti (*The House of Life*), Christina Rossetti, Elizabeth Barrett Browning (*Sonnets from the Portuguese*), and A. C. Swinburne. Few poets of the 20th c. (W. H. Auden, Dylan Thomas, Geoffrey Hill, and Seamus Heaney might be named) matched the consistent level of production found in the earlier work, although an occasional single sonnet, such as W. B. Yeats's "Leda and the Swan," has rare beauty.

While sonnets were ubiquitous in the colonial Americas, the form did not appear in New England until the last quarter of the 18th c., in the work of Col. David Humphreys, but once introduced, the form spread rapidly if not distinctively until H. W. Longfellow (1807–82), using the It. pattern, lifted it in dignity and lyric tone (esp. in the *Divina commedia* sequence) to a level easily equal to its counterpart in England. Subsequently, E. A. Robinson, Robert Frost, Claude McKay (born in Jamaica), Edna St. Vincent Millay, e. e. cummings, and Robert Lowell, among others, produced memorable sonnets, as have more recent Am. and Eng.-lang. poets such as Ted Berrigan, James K. Baxter (New Zealand), Rafael Campo, Anne Carson (Canada), Tony Harrison (England), Marilyn Hacker, John Hollander, Edwin Morgan (Scotland), and Bernadette Mayer.

In the 20th and early 21st cs., sonnets have continued to broaden to include almost any subject and mood. Structurally, even within the traditional patterns, the sonnet has reflected the principal influences evident in mod. poetry as a whole: *free-verse innovations have frequently led to less metronomic movement within the iambic norm; alternatives to exact rhymes have replenished the stock of rhyme pairs and have sophisticated acoustic relationships; and a more natural idiom has removed much of a burdensome artificiality. Such adaptability suggests continued interest in and use of the form.

■ H. Welti, *Gesch. des Sonettes in der deutschen Dichtung* (1884); Schipper, 2.835 ff; L. Biadene, *Morfologia del sonetto nei secoli XIII e XIV* (1889); *Sonnets on the Sonnet*, ed. M. Russell (1898); M. Jasinski, *Histoire du sonnet en France* (1903); L. T. Weeks, "The Order of Rimes of the English Sonnet," *MLN* 25 (1910)—data; Thieme, 381 ff—lists 17 Fr. works, 1548–1903; F. Villey, "Marot et le premier sonnet français," *Revue d'Histoire Littéraire de la France* 20 (1920); R. D. Havens, *The Influence of Milton on English Poetry* (1922)—surveys 18th- and 19th-c. Eng. sonnets; W. L. Bullock, "The Genesis of the English Sonnet Form," *PMLA* 38 (1923); L. G. Sterner, *The Sonnet in American Literature* (1930); L. Zillman, *John Keats and the Sonnet Tradition* (1939); W. Mönch, *Das Sonett* (1955)—most comprehensive study to date, with extended bibl.; E. Rivers, "Certain Formal Characteristics of the Primitive Love Sonnet," *Speculum* 33 (1958); E. H. Wilkins, *The Invention of the Sonnet and Other Studies in Italian Literature* (1959); E. Núñez Mata, *Historia y origen del soneto* (1967); S. Booth, *An Essay on Shakespeare's Sonnets* (1969); *Das deutsche Sonett*, ed. J. U. Fechner (1969); J. Levy, "The Development of Rhyme-Scheme and of Syntactic Pattern in the English Renaissance Sonnet," "On the Relations of Language and Stanza

Pattern in the English Sonnet," rpt. in his *Paralipomena* (1971); M. Françon, "L'Introduction du sonnet en France," *RPh* 26 (1972); J. Fuller, *The Sonnet* (1972); L. M. Johnson, *Wordsworth and the Sonnet* (1973); F. Jost, "The Sonnet in its European Context," *Introduction to Comparative Literature* (1974); Wilkins; R. L. Colie, *Shakespeare's Living Art* (1974); C. Scott, "The Limits of the Sonnet," *RLC* 50 (1976); F. Kimmich, "Sonnets before Opitz," *German Quarterly* 49 (1976); D. H. Scott, *Sonnet Theory and Practice in Nineteenth-Century France* (1977); H.-J. Schlütter, *Sonett* (1979); S. Hornsby and J. R. Bennett, "The Sonnet: An Annotated Bibliography from 1940 to the Present," *Style* 13 (1979); J. Geninasca, "Forme fixe et forme discursive dans quelques sonnets de Baudelaire," *Cahiers de l'Association internationale des études françaises* 32 (1980); Brogan, 455 ff.; Fowler; L. M. Johnson, *Wordsworth's Metaphysical Verse* (1982)—blank-verse sonnets; *Russkij sonet*, ed. B. Romanov, and *Russkij sonet*, ed. V. S. Sovalin (both 1983)—anthols.; Elwert, *Italienische*, sect. 83; F. Rigolot, "Qu'est-ce qu'un sonnet?" *Revue d'Histoire Littéraire de la France* 84 (1984) C. Kleinhenz, *The Early Italian Sonnet* (1986); Hollier; S. L. Bermann, *The Sonnet over Time* (1989)—Petrarch, Shakespeare, and Baudelaire; P. Oppenheimer, *The Birth of the Modern Mind* (1989); G. Warkentin, "Sonnet, Sonnet Sequence," *The Spenser Encyclopedia*, ed. A. C. Hamilton et al. (1990); A. L. Martin, *Cervantes and the Burlesque Sonnet* (1991); *Six Masters of the Spanish Sonnet*, ed. and trans. W. Barnstone (1992); M.R.G. Spiller, *The Development of the Sonnet* (1992); D. Bregman, *The Golden Way* (1995)—Heb. sonnet; Moirer; H. Vendler, *The Art of Shakespeare's Sonnets* (1998); *The Oxford Book of Sonnets*, ed. J. Fuller (2000); *Penguin Book of the Sonnet*, ed. P. Levin (2001); *The Making of a Sonnet*, ed. E. Boland and E. Hirsch (2008); *The Reality Street Book of Sonnets*, ed. J. Hilson (2009); S. Burt and D. Mikics, *The Art of the Sonnet* (2010); *The Cambridge Companion to the Sonnet*, ed. P. Howarth (2010).

T.V.F. Brogan; L. J. Zillman; C. Scott; J. Lewin

SONNET SEQUENCE. A subset of the *lyric sequence consisting of a series of *sonnets, of any number, that may be organized according to some fictional or intellectual order. The sequence made entirely of sonnets is rarer than readers often suppose and seldom holds an author's or a culture's attention for long before deliberate variations emerge. The rise of the sonnet sequence in most Eur. langs. coincides with that of Petrarchism: because Petrarch's late 14th-c. *Canzoniere* is made largely but not exclusively of sonnets (317 of 366 poems), many of its imitators and adapters in Fr., Eng., Port., and Sp. saw their roles as involving the domestication of his sonnet form; hence, the first Petrarchans in the vernaculars (e.g., Thomas Wyatt and Henry Howard, the Earl of Surrey, in Eng.) are often the first sonneteers in their langs. as well (e.g., Joachim du Bellay and Pierre de Ronsard in Fr., Francisco Sá de Miranda and Luís de Camões in Port., Juan Boscán and Garcilaso de la Vega in Sp.). The most extreme vogue for sonnet sequences was that of Eng. poets in the later 16th c.: examples include Thomas Watson's *Hekatompathia* of 18-line sonnets (1582); Philip Sidney's *Astrophil and Stella* (written early 1580s, pub. 1591); Edmund Spenser's *Ruins of Rome* (1591—an adaptation of du Bellay's *Antiquités de Rome* [1558] and drawn upon by Shakespeare) and *Amoretti* (with its completing *Epithalamion* [1595]); Henry Constable's *Diana* (1592); Samuel Daniel's *Delia* (1592); Michael Drayton's much revised *Idea* (1593); and Shakespeare's *Sonnets* (written 1590s, pub. 1609). In the 17th c., while poets such as the Spaniard Francisco de Quevedo, Sidney's niece Mary Wroth, and the Mexican nun Sor Juana Inés de la Cruz continue to extend the reach of the amatory and philosophical sonnet sequence, the orientation of the sequence at large (like that of the lyric sequence) turns toward *devotional poetry. Aside from Quevedo and John Donne, notable religious sonneteers incl. the Ger. Andreas Gryphius, the It. Tommaso Campanella, the Dutchman Constantijn Huygens, and the Frenchman Jean de La Ceppède.

In the early mod. period generally, the sonnet sequence is often thought to have a special, almost automatic claim to overall integrity—whether topical (as in du Bellay's *Les Regrets* [1558]), meditative (as in the "corona" used by Donne and others), or vaguely chronological (as in the common usage of the Eng. word *century* for 100 sonnets). As scholars such as Warley and Alduy have demonstrated, the sonnet sequence can be as much a political and economic as a literary construction—an arena or marketplace for the working out of collective interests; earlier scholars have dwelt on its character as a ritual experience, a type of public space, and an art form with analogues in painting, religion, and architecture, among other disciplines. The job

of cultural mediation enacted by the sonnet sequence perhaps indicates why poetic amateurs of note—such as the It. sculptor and painter Michelangelo Buonarroti in the 1530s and 1540s, the Eng. Puritan polemicist Henry Lock in the 1590s, or the Am. philosopher George Santayana in the 1890s—are drawn to this form as a uniquely deprivileged space: it enables them to think through emotional, philosophical, or religious issues in a formally determined, publicly accessible medium. In fact, the first sonnet sequence in Eng.—Anne Lock's *Meditation of a Penitent Sinner* (1560), inspired by the Scottish Puritan John Knox—is the ideologically charged work of a poetic amateur, intervening in contemp. religious debates in the mode of a deeply personal meditation (Roche).

Like the lyric sequence, the sonnet sequence seems to have had few important instances in the 18th c. but became a major romantic and postromantic vehicle. Notable examples incl. William Wordworth's several sonnet sequences; E. B. Browning's *Sonnets from the Portuguese* (1850); George Meredith's narrative *Modern Love* (1862), in which the "sonnets" have 16 lines; D. G. Rossetti's *House of Life* (1881); Rubén Darío's "sonetos" and "medallones" in *Azul . . .* (1888), the book that impelled Sp.-Am. *modernismo*, which had a recurrent fascination with the sonnet in loosely organized collocations; Fernando Pessoa's *35 Sonnets* in Eng. (1918); R. M. Rilke's *Sonette an Orpheus* (1923); and e. e. cummings's several sonnet sequences in his early volumes *Tulips and Chimneys* (1923), *&* (1925), and *XLI Poems* (1925). With the 20th c. and modernism came another hiatus, followed by a renewed sense of the sonnet sequence's potential for organizing experience, esp. love, though, in the later 20th c., it was perhaps impossible for the sonnet sequence to occur without formal irony, cultural critique, or anachronistic pathos. Thus, Nicolás Guillén's political volumes are founded on his early experiments as a sonneteer, a role to which he returns for ironic effect (as in "El abuelo" in *West Indies, Ltd.* [1934]); and John Berryman's adulterous *Sonnets* (written 1940s, pub. 1968) seek out a self-conscious Petrarchism (esp. 15, an adaptation of *Canzoniere* 189). Robert Lowell became all but exclusively a sonneteer in late career: his experiments in recasting the sonnet sequence *Notebook 1967–68* as *Notebook* (1970), *History* (1973), and *For Lizzie and Harriet* (1973) might be considered the climax of his work, culminating in *The Dolphin* (1973) and

Day by Day (1977). Among late-c. adaptations in Eng. are Seamus Heaney's ten "Glanmore Sonnets" (in *Field Work*, 1979) and his eight-sonnet elegy "Clearances" (in *The Haw Lantern*, 1987); Tony Harrison's dissonant rewriting of the formal trad. in *Continuous: 50 Sonnets from the School of Eloquence* (1982); Marilyn Hacker's amatory *Love, Death, and the Changing of the Seasons* (1986), incl. an updated crown of sonnets; and Bill Knott's cultural polemic in *Outremer* (1989).

■ *Elizabethan Sonnet-Cycles*, ed. M. F. Crow (1896); L. C. John, *The English Sonnet Sequences* (1938); W. Mönch, *Das Sonett: Gestalt und Geschichte* (1955); *European Metaphysical Poetry*, ed. F. J. Warnke (1961); D. Stone, *Ronsard's Sonnet Cycles* (1966); B. Stirling, *The Shakespeare Sonnet Order* (1968); S. Booth, *An Essay on Shakespeare's Sonnets* (1969); T. Cave, *Devotional Poetry in France 1570–1613* (1969); essays on Ronsard, Scève, and du Bellay in *YFS* 47 (1972); T. Cave, *The Cornucopian Text* (1979); J. de La Ceppède, *From the Theorems*, trans. K. Bosley (1983); R. A. Katz, *The Ordered Text* (1985)—du Bellay's sonnet sequences; J. Fineman, *Shakespeare's Perjured Eye* (1986); Hollier; T. P. Roche Jr., *Petrarch and the English Sonnet Sequences* (1989); G. Warkentin, "Sonnet Sequence," *The Spenser Encyclopedia*, ed. A.C. Hamilton et al. (1990); W. C. Johnson, *Spenser's "Amoretti"* (1990); A. R. Jones, *The Currency of Eros: Women's Love Lyric in Europe, 1540–1620* (1990); R. Greene, *Post-Petrarchism* (1991); E. Hanson, "Boredom and Whoredom: Reading Renaissance Women's Sonnet Sequences," *Yale Journal of Criticism* 10 (1997); R. Kuin, *Chamber Music: Elizabethan Sonnet Sequences and the Pleasure of Criticism* (1998); J. Holmes, *Dante Gabriel Rossetti and the Late Victorian Sonnet Sequence* (2005); C. Warley, *Sonnet Sequences and Social Distinction in Renaissance England* (2005); C. Alduy, *Politique des "Amours" (1544–1560)* (2007), and "Lyric Economies: Manufacturing Values in French Petrarchan Collections," *RQ* 63 (2010).

R. Greene

SOUND

I. Theoretical Overview. This synthetic account of sound in poetry will recognize important devels. in poetry, poetics, literary theory and crit., ling., acoustics, and cognitive science without attempting to privilege one kind of knowledge over another. The topic of sound in poetry often raises an unresolvable theoretical controversy about the nature of poetry, namely, where the *poem exists: concretely on the page, temporally as a spoken verbal utterance, or liminally between the two. If a poem simply exists on the page, then what do its auditory qualities mean? If, as Paul Valéry argued, the poem should be approached as a musical score to be performed aloud, what happens to the poem when it is closed in a book and ceases to be read? The recent profusion of poetry in electronic and recorded media, which seems to present a new medium, a new type of textuality, or what Ong has called a "secondary orality," nevertheless falls into the same two categories of visual representation on a screen or as hypertext and as oral performance recorded or streamed live. For present purposes, this philosophical antinomy may be resolved pragmatically: the poem exists in tension between the extremes of audible speech and silent reading.

The prosodies of different langs. focus on different qualities of sound (see PROSODY), and *meter typically focuses on one phonological element of lang.—stress, pitch, or length (i.e., *quantity)—reducing the varying levels of such elements to a binary of more or less prominence. Some meters incorporate a second element in subsidiary patterns. This process, at work in every lang. and developed over time, is not subject to the whims of a poet since the element is intrinsic to the lang. Attempts by poets to select a different marker for the lang. (e.g., Eng. Ren. poets writing in *syllabic verse or quantitative meters) are generally academic exercises, because the lang.'s phonological features will, as Fussell has shown, overrun the intended metrical effect. While such attempts have played a constitutive role in the evolution of poetry and while poets consistently experiment with the limits of a given lang., nevertheless, the phonological limitations on the metrical resources of a lang. will dictate a native speaker's *performance of a poem or experience of one. In short, the rhythm of Eng. will trump syllabic length. Thus, the phonology of a lang. not only decides the meter but also typically locks the poet into the inherited trad.

II. Articulation, Acoustics, and Cognition

A. Articulation. The place and manner of articulation of vowels in the mouth are often graphically represented by a trapezoid broken into nine sections, high to low and front to back. Consonants are created by impeding, through the use of the tongue, lips, and palate, the flow of air at different positions of articulation.

B. *Acoustics.* According to the science of acoustics, sounds are waves passing through a medium. In the case of voiced poetry, that medium is air (with the Fr. lettrist group of the 1950s, the It. poet Arrigo Lora-Totino experimented with vocalizing poetry through water; see SOUND POETRY). A wave from one crest to another is a single cycle, while the number of cycles per second is the *frequency* of a sound and is measured in Hertz (Hz). Although the human voice ranges from 100 to 200 Hz, the ear can perceive a range from 20 to 20,000 Hz. Middle C is 261 Hz. The higher the *frequency*, the higher the *pitch*. The intensity of the sound, known as *stress*, is measured in decibels, i.e., amplitude or a sound's overall power (the height and depth of a wave's crests and peaks). *Quantity* refers to the duration of a sound. Meter is at stake when these phenomena are applied to syllabic lang. and patterned in accordance—or in opposition to—its rules.

C. *Cognition.* Contemp. cognitive science holds that the hemispheres of the brain process sound in different ways or to different degrees. While the left hemisphere, which possesses logical and analytical functions, interprets ling. sounds for meaning, the right hemisphere processes ambient sounds and music. Simultaneous words and music, as in song, are analyzed by both hemispheres of the brain at once. For poetry, both hemispheres function in the apprehension and analysis of ling. and aesthetic sounds. The left hemisphere processes speech rhythm and lexical-semantic sounds, while the right analyzes poetic sound patterning and the aesthetics of poetry (Turner attempts to show the relation of cognition to meter). Thus, poetry, using both hemispheres at once, makes use of both ling. sound and poetic sound, mapping both lexical pattern and designed aesthetic patterns. In brain functions themselves exists the dichotomy of the sensuous and the semantic, of sound and sense.

III. Recent Approaches to Sound. The ascendancy of deconstruction during the late 20th c. largely relegated scholarship on sound to linguists and prosodists. Deconstruction's privileging of writing over speech left sound as a large gap in the analysis of poetry. The difference between langs. suggests that words are determined differentially. The difference in a single lang. between words like *bit* and *bat*, *puck* and *puke*, *lock* and *lick* suggested to Saussure that lang. was grounded through differentials, not the presence of word features. As Saussure himself observed, however, the etymological trad. does solidify meaning in practice (see also the discussion of *onomatopoeia below). Meaning depends on both the nature of signifiers and their hist. Change clearly occurs through time, and the various forces of historical ling. are always at work (e.g., Grimm's law, vowel shifts). Transubstantiated as *textualité*, speech generally becomes a nonissue for deconstructionists and those who read poetry as they do, whether knowingly or not. *L'écriture* (writing) trumps *lecture* (speech) every time for Jacques Derrida; sound becomes a secondary matter in lang., if it matters at all.

However, beyond the meanings that may or may not be produced through the opposition of signifier and signified, lang. can also mean obliquely through *metaphor. Typically, when there is not a word for something, we do not feel the need to invent one, since no one else would know what it means. Rather, metaphor, *simile, and analogy generate meaning where there was none before (see Ricoeur). Metaphorical truth moves beyond arbitrary word-truth and encapsulates a role of poetry. It concedes or ignores the truth of the arbitrary signifier and moves in the opposite direction. While meaning can be perceived as just as unstable within metaphor as in lang., metaphor transcends the sign (sound-image and concept), and meaning at the edge of lang. emerges. The meaning of the tenor and the meaning of the vehicle, when combined, produce something that was not in the originals when they were separate, namely, a poetic meaning). Poetic lang. revels in words, while their representational function is diminished. Poets give primary importance to phonological patterning and sound effects. When lang. is transformed into poetry, when pattern is made through sound, and when poetic effects are produced by sound, words construct meaning through their effects on each other and the reader. The following W. B. Yeats line (from

"The Lake Isle of Innisfree") aggregates meanings through sound juxtapositions that did not inhere individually in words like *lap, lake, low, sound, shore, hear*: "I hear lake water lapping with low sounds by the shore." Meaning, constructed and resilient through sound, is produced in poetry outside the signifier-signified dichotomy.

In *La révolution du langage poétique* (1974), Julia Kristeva gives poetic lang. a sexually charged, prerational, and bodily importance. Essentially, she agrees with both Ezra Pound, i.e., that poetry is lang. charged with meaning to the highest degree (see "How to Read," *Literary Essays*, 1968), and Jakobson, i.e., that poetic lang. represents standard lang. charged with its infinite possibilities—its study comprehends the becoming of signification, i.e., meaning. She divides the semiotic (i.e., nonverbal signifying systems) from the symbolic but insists that both are inseparable from the signifying process. Kristeva privileges the semiotic as preverbal, libidinal, and corporeal, in opposition to Alexander Pope's rational sound symbolism, as expressed in his *Essay on Criticism* (1711). The semiotic, however, includes rhythm (its effect on the body) in a variation on Mallarméan poetic mystery and power. According to Kristeva, the communication of libidinal subjectivity is the ultimate object of poetic lang. The sounds of words become their expressive desire and expressive meaning. Thus, they do not echo sense in a rational way but rather echo an individual's unconscious, chthonic drives. Where Pope locates the importance of sound in the mimetic imitation of the meaning of a line, Kristeva finds that poetic sound vibrates deeply in the core of one's being, ultimately agreeing with Roethke and complementing Turner's discussion of poetic rhythm and the brain.

It is also important to recognize the emergence of a poetry that is concerned almost exclusively with the sound of words and not, or at least not primarily, with their meaning. Twentieth-c. devels. in *sound poetry and later Language poetry exploit the disjunction between signifier and signified, transforming signs into mere sounds divorced from semantic content. The Dada poems of Hugo Ball or Kurt Schwitters are among the many important forerunners of this line of poetic inquiry. Similarly, Bernstein (1992) has questioned when it is that noise becomes semantically meaningful. There are all varieties of meanings composed at the subsemantic or sublexical units of lang. production

(i.e., onomatopoeia, grunts, groans, nonlexical voicings of dissent and agreement, etc.). Where Bernstein disappointingly finds meaning self-embodied by the whole poem, he does provide a starting point for the discussion of nonlexical elements, though not always sound based, within a poem. Such questions find a predecessor in early 20th-c. avant-garde music and the futurist noise-art of Luigi Russolo.

Slam poetry, on the other hand, is to a far greater degree concerned with semantic meaning, often a poem's political or moral message. Such poetry, frequently memorized, is located almost exclusively as an oral phenomenon and later disseminated in textual transcription or recorded performance. Emerging from the convergence of a textual avant-garde, popular music, and the poetry reading, slam poetry created its own oral trad. with its clearest analogues in the 1950s Beat poets. Its sonic qualities are most typically *alliteration, *assonance, *anaphora, and paromoiosis; thus, its difference from traditional poetry lies mostly in locale.

IV. Expressivity. One debate about sound and poetry, dating to Plato's *Cratylus*, concerns the inherent meaning in sound; i.e., does sound express meaning? The answer is no, but with numerous qualifications that have fascinated poets. Meaning can clearly be evoked or connoted by sounds as in onomatopoeia (see also the concept of the ideophone in Tedlock), but this kind of meaning in large part corresponds to a historical train of significance. If words are signifying abstractions, onomatopoetic effects seem to express a generalized meaning based on natural phenomena such as animal sounds or water. Ultimately, however, when we examine the written words that langs. have for the sounds animals make, the *trope descends almost to the arbitrariness of most words, e.g., the Eng. *woof* and the Fr. *ouah ouah* for the sounds of a dog; likewise, the Gr. *barbaros* for *barbarians* was derived from the sounds the Greeks ascribed to other langs. While such words stem etymologically from sound imitation, their meanings are virtually as arbitrary as those of any other signifier, given their subsequent devel.

Iconicity, the concept that there is an analogy or resemblance between a word and the object to which it refers, was propagated by C. S. Peirce. Mimetic sound effects accordingly become central to the representational system of lang. Subsequent research in the 20th

c. demonstrated its existence in all langs. and at every level of ling. structure. For Peirce, the icon, one of three types of representation, is a sign that resembles its object, however inexactly (*pop, hiss, murmur*—the names of sounds tend to be onomatopoetic). The phonestheme (a term coined by J. R. Firth) is a phoneme that has a recognizable semantic association because it appears in numerous words with similar meanings and sounds. Such words seem to have a familiar, natural force on a reader and seem mimetically expressive. In "Vowel and Consonant Patterns in Poetry," Masson has observed this phenomenon in the different connotations of the word for *night* across langs. Wellek and Warren use the term *orchestration* for such morphemic echoing in poetry. Perhaps more useful to poetry is kinesthetics, which associates the sound produced or being produced with a semantic meaning (i.e., traditional sound symbolism). Richards (1929) and Ransom (1936) demonstrated, through a dummy version of stanza 15 of John Milton's "On the Morning of Christ's Nativity" and a *parody of Alfred, Lord Tennyson's "Come Down, O Maid," respectively, that the same sounds and the same rhythm, when divorced from original meaning, lose their expressivity. (For an approach to sound expressiveness via pragmatic theory and relevance theory, see Pilkington.)

V. Sound Effects and Sound Patterning in Poetry.
However arbitrary sound expressivity may be, readers may often experience an echo of sense in lines like Homer's "para thina poluphloisboio thalasses" (*Iliad* 1.34) and Matthew Arnold's "roar / Of pebbles which the waves draw back, and fling, . . . / Begin, and cease, and then again begin" ("Dover Beach," 9–10, 12), both purporting to imitate the actual sound of waves. Likewise, Milton's fricatives also accentuate meaning, as in "Out of my sight, thou Serpent, that name best / Befits thee with him leagu'd, thyself as false / And hateful" (*Paradise Lost*, 10.867–69). Any attempt to ascribe meaning to sound, however, should heed the warning proferred by Ransom's parody. Tennyson's "The moan of doves in immemorial elms, / The murmuring of innumerable bees" (30–31) becomes "The murdering of innumerable beeves," which demonstrates that, while sound may well echo sense, the same sounds in different words do not generate the same meanings. Sound as mimetic representation, thus, clearly entails a reader's recognition of

the meaning of a line before the meaning of a sound pattern.

There are certain associations made with particular sounds, though there are invariably exceptions. High vowels tend toward brightness, highness, vivacity, sharpness. P. B. Shelley's "To a Skylark" begins on a shrieking fever pitch of the four highest vowels, "Hail to thee, blithe spirit," setting the tone for the poem. In John Keats's "Ode to a Nightingale," the poet addresses the nightingale in appropriately high vowels in response to the bird's high-pitched song: "light-wingèd Dryad of the trees." By contrast, low vowels tend to convey wholeness, roundness, downness, heaviness, or darkness. Milton's "On the Late Massacre in Piedmont," e.g., is full of low vowels. In the final lines of the *sonnet, Milton's curse on the It. fields is set low, and the last line presents a steady descent "that from these may grow / A hundredfold, who having learnt thy way / Early may fly the Babylonian woe." Keats's ode similarly begins with low vowels of tubercular sleep before it ascends with the prospect of the nightingale— "drowsy numbness," the hemlock "drunk," the "dull opiate," and the speaker Lethe-ward "sunk." The final line of the first stanza alternates high and mid vowels, without low ones, before a striking ascent in the line's last syllable, "Singest of summer in full-throated ease." These associations are not, strictly speaking, meanings of sounds or abstractions but rather connotations that poets have traditionally embraced.

Consonants, too, have their feelings. Liquids, nasals, fricatives, and plosives produce their own peculiar sound effects and are often combined with alliteration. Yeats's famous lapping lake water illustrates sufficiently. The liquid consonants, *l* and *r* and sometimes *w*, are soft and melodic, giving the impression of water and smoothness, as in the famous Yeats line, or, in Keats's *Endymion*, "Wild thyme, and valley-lilies whiter still / Than Leda's love, and cresses from the rill" (1.157–58), which conveys languor and softness.

Nasals *m*, *n*, and *ng* (as in si*ng*) divert the flow of air into the nasal passage. Tennyson's murmuring bees imitate the insects with the string of nasals. Fricatives include *f*, *th* (both in *th*in and *th*en), *s*, *sh*, *h*, *v*, *z*, and the sound in the middle of the word "mea*s*ure." Milton consistently plays on fricatives; in *Paradise Lost*, book 10, Satan addresses the fallen angels as they turn into serpents: "On all sides, from innumerable tongues / A dismal universal hiss, the sound /

Of public scorn[.] . . . punisht in the shape he sinn'd, / According to his doom: he would have spoke, / But hiss for hiss return'd . . . to Serpents all as accessories" (507–9, 516–18, 520).

The affricates *ch*, and *j* (as in "judge") begin as plosives or stops and then, like the fricatives, rasp through a friction upon airflow. *J* is voiced, which means the vocal cords vibrate in its pronunciation. Philomel, her tongue cut out, throatily cries "jug, jug."

Plosives or stops—*b, d, g, p, t, k*—are the harshest consonants and are probably those the most often used to emphasize sense through sound. Yeats's "King Billy bomb balls" ("Lapis Lazuli") explodes in the speaker's mouth, while Pope twice uses plosives to imply constipation: in the *Essay on Criticism*, poets "Ev'n to the Dregs and *Squeezings* of the *Brain*; / Strain out the last, dull droppings of their Sense, / And Rhyme with all the *Rage* of *Impotence*" (607–9); and in the "Epistle to Dr. Arbuthnot" regarding Ambrose Philips, who "Just writes to make his barrenness appear, / And strains from hardbound brains eight lines a year" (181–82).

In *The Expression of the Emotions in Man and Animal* (1872), Charles Darwin used photographs to examine the facial expressions that occur with particular sounds. While Darwin did not concern himself so much with the actual sounds, Nims uses the photographs to analyze consonant clusters. Darwin reproduced a photograph by Oscar Gustave Rejlander of a woman sneering and exposing part of a canine tooth. Nims observes that most words beginning with the consonant cluster *sn* are as unpleasant as the expression of the woman in the photograph—*sneer* itself, *snitch*, *snob*, *snaggle*, *snort*, and *snarl*. The short *u* can be *ugsome* as in *ugh* and *upchuck*, *slut*, *sludge*, and *pus*, and in a photograph of Rejlander himself hamming an expression as he says the word *disgusted*. Such sounds can, as Nims says, physicalize a poem's meaning.

The use by poets of vowels and consonants to underline meaning in the line is often conjoined with alliteration or other nonfixed sound patterns to emphasize and underline the designed effect. These examples illustrate that, despite the popping of plosives, the mellifluousness of liquids, or the sliding of glides (semivowels *w, y,* and sometimes *j*), there is no inherent meaning within the sounds. The issue of sound expressivity or mimetic sound, while not a tenable theoretical position, provides an enactment of meaning or a gesture toward it. Poets

dramatically associate sounds with the meaning of a word or line for emphasis or effect.

The archetypical demonstration of auditory pyrotechnics in Pope's *Essay on Criticism* delivers, as does the poem in its entirety, both the argument and evidence for the claim that "The *Sound* must seem an *Echo* to the *Sense*" (365). A soft wind must be demonstrated by a soft line, as Pope both says and shows through the repetition of the letter *s* (366–67). The loud, hoarse lines (368–69) likewise enact his own dictum as it roars. However, Pope alliterates with the same *s* sound, though the line is tempered by consonant clusters and heavy with monosyllables. Pope also envelops the two harsh, roaring *couplets (368–71) between the two soft couplets (366–67 and 372–73). The final two couplets of the passage (370–73), while spectacular for mostly metrical reasons, deserve analysis as well:

> When *Ajax* strives, some Rock's vast Weight to throw,
> The Line too *labors*, and the Words move *slow*;
> Not so, when swift *Camilla* scours the Plain,
> Flies o'er th'unbending Corn, and skims along the Main.

Ajax's slow, heavy lines are both loaded with monosyllables and consonants (even the typically mellifluous liquids are overpowered as they shudder and heave into the middle of the third foot). The first line of the Camilla couplet again repeats the alliterating *s* sounds, before moving into the fastest line in the Eng. lang. Line 373 sports more words beginning with vowels than the sole two in the previous Ajax couplet. The *elision and light vowels give the impression of speed. Lines 356–57 before this passage had castigated poets for using needless *alexandrines that are "languishingly slow," but Pope the metrical genius makes his speedy line 373 itself an alexandrine.

Sound pattern, like alliteration, assonance, paromoiosis (the *parallelism between the sounds of words in adjacent clauses or lines), *consonance, and onomatopoeia, can function to tag words of special importance. Sound patterning can then be used to underline the semantic import or key words of a line. Sound schemes are sometimes used to produce a demonstrable pattern on a higher level of design than simple repetition. Masson ("Vowel and Consonant Patterning") observed sequence (*abcabc*) and *chiasmus (*abccba*) at work in sound patterning and found them to be in consistent usage. Envelope (*abba*) and simpler alternation (*abab*) of sound can also have broad application, although analysis of such patterns and their complications deserves further study. Consider, e.g., the Yeats line referenced throughout: "lake water lapping with low." The *l*'s and *w*'s alternate *ababa* at the beginning of each word. Such sound patterns can be used alongside rhythm to coincide or counterpoint, just as, in Lat. prosody, it has been suggested that stress was often patterned to coincide with long syllables in the fixed final feet of dactylic *hexameter.

All such sound-patterning shapes order and intensifies meaning and is, thus, essential to the analysis of a poem. *Rhyme is perhaps the most familiar sound patterning in poetry. According to Levý and others (Wimsatt, Hollander), rhyme, which binds two words that would normally not be connected in a prose sentence, produces secondary semantic effects, incl. ironical contrasts with humorous potential. Lord Byron is a master of this technique ("even when he prayed / He turned from grisly saints, and martyrs hairy, / To the sweet portraits of the Virgin Mary" [*Don Juan*, 2. 149. 6–8]), having learned it from Pope ("But thousands die without or this or that, / Die, and endow a College, or a Cat" ["Epistle to Bathurst," 97–98]). Or as Hopkins said, condensing this matter, "There are two elements in the beauty rhyme has to the mind, the likeness or sameness of sound and the unlikeness or difference of meaning."

VI. Conclusion. Sound, the foundation of lang., ultimately comprises the form and craft of poetry, subsuming meter; the schemes of alliteration, assonance, and rhyme; and the segmental phonemes of vowels and consonants. Such elements of sound have been analyzed with varying degrees of comprehensiveness. (See the only extensive bibl. in Brogan 1981.) There is no appropriate term for sound patterning as there is for *rhythm. Thus, *prosody* is frequently used to incorporate both metrical and segmental sound patterning.

Some have argued that there is a norm or experiential core behind the varying realizations of a single poem. Correct *scansion and recognition of rhyme depend on historical context. The study of recorded readings seems generally to assume this position by tracking the variety and range of differences. This approach ultimately proves, however, that there is no

definitive performance of a poem. While there are a certain number of sounds that a speaker must get right to give a correct reading—the core or norm of the reading of a given poem—there are numerous ling. and nonphonemic differences that can vary from reader to reader while still constituting a perfectly acceptable reading of the poem, as one can discern clearly in the strange-to-modern-ears recordings by Yeats and what can be heard of Tennyson's. This wavering style of recitation, now out of favor, was "author-approved." An analysis of recorded readings should not, of course, be in any way seen as a foray into the realm of authorial *voice or the intentional fallacy, in that the rightness of a sound is a matter of (1) historical devel., (2) an understanding of poetics, and (3) a recognition of design in a poem that is demonstrably patterned. Effects on a reader might vary, but the fact remains that designed effects occur.

Jakobson believes that every verbal element in a line of verse is transformed into an element of poetry or poetic speech. Though Jakobson's argument cannot be falsified, it is noteworthy in that it reminds a reader that both levels of lang., sound and meaning, intersect at all times in any poem and necessitate a synthetic analysis, treating neither in isolation from the other. At the same time, a systematic analysis of every element of sound, meaning, and their nexus at work is daunting. The interplay of sounds between themselves and on meaning fully expresses and accomplishes the craft of verse, as in T. S. Eliot's concept of the auditory imagination. Poetic lang. constitutes the poem and is creative action.

According to Wallace Stevens, the sound of words is their importance in poetry; sound is the principal business of poetry. The poet harnesses reality and makes a reader's or listener's first response an aesthetic one. As Stevens says, "A poet's words are of things that do not exist without the words." We attempt through words to express the truth of our existence, our thoughts, and feelings. And we respond to these words not only with analysis but with our physical senses, as in the case of William Blake's mellifluous phrasing in "To the Evening Star," "to wash the dusk with silver."

■ F. de Saussure, *Cours de linguistique générale* (1916); I. A. Richards, *Practical Criticism* (1929); J. C. Ransom, *The World's Body* (1938); D. I. Masson, "Patterns of Vowel and Consonant in a Rilkean Sonnet," *MLR* 46 (1951); W. Stevens, "The Noble Rider and the Sound of Words," *The*

Necessary Angel (1951); D. I. Masson, "Vowel and Consonant Patterns in Poetry," *JAAC* 12 (1953); "Word and Sound in Yeats's 'Byzantium,'" *ELH* 20 (1953); and "Free Phonetic Patterns in Shakespeare's Sonnets," *Neophilologus* 38 (1954); W. K. Wimsatt, "One Relation of Rhyme to Reason," *The Verbal Icon* (1954); J. Hollander, "The Music of Poetry," *JAAC* 15 (1956); Wellek and Warren; P. Valéry, "Poésie et pensée abstraite," *Oeuvres*, ed. J. Hytier, v. 1 (1957); *The Journals and Papers of Gerard Manley Hopkins*, ed. H. House and G. Storey (1959); D. H. Hymes, "Phonological Aspects of Style," Sebeok; D. I. Masson, "Thematic Analysis of Sound in Poetry," *Proceedings of the Leeds Philosophical and Literary Society-Literary and Historical Section* 9 (1960); C. S. Peirce, "The Icon, Index, and Symbol," *Collected Papers of C. S. Peirce*, v. 2, *Elements of Logic*, ed. C. Hartshorne and P. Weiss (1960); J. Hollander, *The Untuning of the Sky* (1961); D. I. Masson, "Sound Repetition Terms," *Poetics—Poetyka—Poetika*, ed. D. Davie et al. (1961); J. R. Firth, *The Tongues of Men and Speech* (1964); T. Roethke, "Some Remarks on Rhythm," *On the Poet and His Craft* (1965); A. A. Hill, "A Phonological Description of Poetic Ornaments," *L&S* 2 (1969); D. I. Masson, "The Keatsian Incantation," *John Keats*, ed. K. Muir (1969); J. Levý, "The Meanings of Form and the Forms of Meaning," *Paralipomena* (1971); J. C. Ransom, "Positive and Near-Positive Aesthetics," *Beating the Bushes* (1972); T. S. Eliot, "Milton I," *Selected Prose*, ed. F. Kermode (1975); A. A. Hill, "Analogies, Icons, and Images," and "Two Views of Poetic Language and Meaning," *Constituent and Pattern in Poetry* (1976); D. I. Masson, "Poetic Sound-Patterning Reconsidered," *Proceedings of the Leeds Philosophical and Literary Society-Literary and Historical Section* 16 (1976)—Masson's sonal summa and survey of eight national lits.; W. K. Wimsatt, "In Search of Verbal Mimesis," *The Day of the Leopards* (1976); J. M. Lotman, *The Structure of the Artistic Text*, trans. G. Lenhoff and R. Vroon (1977); P. Ricoeur, *The Rule of Metaphor*, trans. R. Czerny (1977); P. Fussell, *Poetic Meter and Poetic Form*, rev. ed. (1979); B. Hrushovski, "The Meaning of Sound Patterns in Poetry," *PoT* 2 (1980); Brogan; W. J. Ong, *Orality and Literacy* (1982); R. Chapman, *The Treatment of Sounds in Language and Literature* (1984); Hollander, "The Poem in the Ear"; F. Turner, "The Neural Lyre," *Natural Classicism* (1985); G. Stewart, *Reading Voices* (1990); C. Bernstein, "Artifice of Absorption," *A Poetics* (1992); J. F. Nims, *Western Wind*, rev. ed. (1992); R. Tsur, *What Makes Sound Patterns Expressive?* (1992); H. Gross and R. McDowell, *Sound and Form in Modern Poetry*, rev. ed. (1996); *Close Listening*, ed. C. Bernstein (1998); R. Tsur, *Poetic Rhythm* (1998); A. Pilkington, *Poetic Effects* (2000); D. Tedlock, "Ideophone," *Key Terms in Language and Culture*, ed. A. Duranti (2001); N. Fabb, *Language and Literary Structure* (2002); A. Hecht, "The Music of Forms," *Melodies Unheard* (2003); C. Noland, "Phonic Matters," *PMLA* 120 (2005); L. Wheeler, *Voicing American Poetry* (2008); *The Sound of Poetry / The Poetry of Sound*, ed. M. Perloff and C. Dworkin (2009); "Wallace Stevens and 'The Less Legible Meanings of Sound,'" *The Wallace Stevens Journal* 33.1 (2009)—spec. iss; R. Tsur, "The Poetic Function and Aesthetic Qualities: Cognitive Poetics and the Jakobsonian Model," *Acta Linguistica Hafniensia* 42.1 (2010)—spec. iss.

D. Wood

SOUND POETRY. If poetry is the verbal art in which *sound and sense are arranged in ideal tension, sound poetry (also "sonorist rhythms," "phonetic poetry," or *poesie sonore*) alters this relationship by multiplying, reducing, or denying semantic reference, while amplifying the phonetic and aural properties of lang. Some sound poems attempt to generate natural signifying relationships between sound and meaning through phonetic symbolism; others use sound as antagonistic or indifferent toward meaning. Sound poems challenge the limits of natural langs. and produce the illusion of lang. before, beyond, or after meaning, from the Adamic to the utopian.

Surveys of sound poetry often furnish it with a long genealogy encompassing all ancient and mod. uses of preverbal speech codes such as *onomatopoeia, glossolalia, the incantations of oral poetry, *nonsense verse like Lewis Carroll's "Jabberwocky," and Stéphane Mallarmé's formulation of *inanité sonore*. While these codes are among sound poetry's principal resources and precedents, the practice of sound poetry has fairly distinct origins in an extensive, international network of avant-garde poets from the late 19th c. into the 1930s, and it has been extended and theorized by neo–avant-garde poets from the 1940s to the present.

In Europe, nearly all the historical avant-garde movements practiced a version of sound poetry. In the pamphlet *Declaration of the*

Word as Such (1913), the Rus. futurist Aleksei Kruchenykh coined the neologism *zaum'* (transrational or beyonsense) to describe poems he had written "in their own language," of which the most notorious example is "Dyr bul schyl," though Velimir Khlebnikov's 1910 "Zaklyatie smekhom" ("Incantation by Laughter") also anticipated this tendency. While Kruchenykh's poems deploy nonce words or write through source texts via lipogrammatic removals of all consonants in the attempt to "destroy language" and install referential indeterminacy, more ambitious zaum' poems, such as Khlebnikov's "Zangezi," dramatize a universal lang. of the future that fixes references at varying planes of psychic evolution, purporting to vocalize the speech of gods, birds, and other nonhuman phenomena. The Chilean poet Vicente Huidobro's *Altazor* (1931), the voyage of a poet-parachutist ejecting himself from the lang. system into what Octavio Paz calls a "post-Babelic" fantasy of ling. reunification, bears comparison.

Experiments contemporaneous to zaum' in Italy include Aldo Palazzeschi's examples of a *poetica del divertimento*, playful poems in which infantile stutters and syllabic refrains are a refuge for the crepuscular poet discarded by the culture of modernity. Although he was briefly associated with It. futurism, Palazzeschi's ludic sound has little in common with F. T. Marinetti's *parole in libertà* (words in freedom), a poetry that attempts to enact a synthetic *mimesis of the city or mod. warfare, most often through martial onomatopoeias such as *Zang Tumb Tuum* (1912). Guillaume Apollinaire voiced a familiar objection in his remark that this scientific notation of machine noise could be faulted as "gags" or *trompe-oreilles*.

In the germanophone context, Dada sound poetry built on examples of nonsense poetry like that of Christian Morgenstern. Most often cited among the many varieties of sound poetry produced by the Dadaists, Hugo Ball's "gadji beri bimba," a cycle of five *lautgedichte* (noise poems) or *verse ohne worte* (wordless verses), posited a primitive refounding of the word in reaction to the commodification of lang. Performed at the Zurich Cabaret Voltaire in 1916, these poems offer a prophetic authority for sound poetry based on a magical "innermost alchemy" of antiquated words and a liturgical performance register, while also suggesting the babbling repetitions of a traumatized soldier. Other Dada sound poetry, such as Kurt Schwitters's lengthy *Ursonate*, established

musical protocols and structuring devices for sound poetry, and Raoul Housmann's "optophonetic poetry" pioneered typographical notation systems for performance volume, tempo, and duration. Tristan Tzara and Richard Hülsenbeck employed the ethnographic imitation of Af. sounds, which North has identified as a ling. form of racial masquerade. Dada had a poorly documented but marked impact on the vanguard poets of the Sp. Caribbean, such as Luis Palés Matos, yet the misappropriation of pseudo-African vocables by Dada *chantes negres* must be sharply distinguished from the sound motifs characteristic of *negrismo* poetry of the late 1920s and 1930s such as that of Nicolás Guillén, who is also identified with the use of the jitanjáfora inaugurated by the Cuban poet Mariano Brull's "Leyenda" (1928).

Despite the increasingly self-aware, international proliferation of sound poetry as a genre—esp. from 1910 to 1930—no poetry advertised itself as such in the Anglo-Am. trad. at that time. Sound play in the work of James Joyce and Gertrude Stein was instrumental to the late modernist notion of "the revolution of the word," and even Louis Armstrong's scat has been proposed as a cousin to sound poetry. However, the emergent orthodoxies of New Critical formalism make T. S. Eliot's 1942 remark a mainstay of the anglophone view well into the postwar period: "We can be deeply stirred by hearing the recitation of a poem in a language of which we understand no word; but if we are then told that the poem is gibberish and has no meaning, we shall consider that we have been deluded—this was no poem, it was merely an imitation of instrumental music." As if anticipating and flounting such objections, Dada *bruitisme* and Rus. zaum' persistently employ xenoglossia as a device. Indeed, the deliberate use of incomprehensible foreign langs. is a primary asemantic speech code in which sound poetry traffics, often in open response to the diasporic displacements of global cultures. Performed in the langs. of three warring nations at once, Tzara's 1916 "Simultaneist" poem "L'amiral cherche une maison à louer" (The Admiral Searches for a House to Rent) dilates this technique.

While even its staunchest proponents, such as Jolas, considered sound poetry to be a limited ling. strategy in the wake of World War II, the genre has a rich postwar life in Fr. *lettrisme*, esp. in the work of Isidore Isou (1925–2007) and Henri Chopin (1922–2008), as well as in that of Bob Cobbing (1920–2002) in England, Ernst Jandl (1925–2000) in Austria, Jackson Mac Low (1922–2004) in the U.S., and later bpNichol (1944–88) and Steve McCaffery (b. 1947) in Canada. McCaffery, alongside Chopin and Fluxus artist Dick Higgins (1938–98), have been instrumental to the validation of sound poetry as a historical genre and performance practice. The U.S. Language poets emergent in the 1970s bear out that influence, as in Bernstein's remark in "Artifice of Absorption" that "there is no fixed / threshold at which noise becomes phonically / significant; the further back this threshold is / pushed, the greater the resonance at the cutting / edge." With some exceptions, Chopin's distinction holds that sound poetry before World War II is phonetic poetry, preserving an attachment to words and syllables as compositional units, while, after the war, lettrisme arbitrarily assigns phonic values to letters, moving sound poetry toward performance scores for "sub-phonemic" levels of noise. Postwar practitioners have placed greater emphasis on nontextual performance and recording media, often disseminating poems by tape recorder as in the works of François Dufrêne and stressing ambitious research programs over ludic play. Still, much *concrete poetry includes an active sound component, and the long *visual poetry trad. runs in tandem with that of sound poetry, as typographical innovations often enhance or dictate performance standards.

*Voice has become a major theoretical issue for sound poetry. Antonin Artaud's scream poems and Michael McClure's "beast language" offer an affiliation to sound poetry that reconnects the voice to biological priorities, while McCaffery has rethought the voice as a "paleotechnic" instrument in a wider media ecology. A third critical view, exemplified by the philosopher Giorgio Agamben, holds that written, asemantic speech codes are the textual figuration of embodied voice, opening poetry to an "unheard dimension sustained in the pure breath of the voice, in mere *vox* as insignificant will to signify." A countertendency could be located in a group of sound collagists and aleators working in the trad. of John Cage, for whom the approximation of lang. to noise often eschews the voice as a unifying performance principle in favor of random and found materials.

Sound poetry has a complex but coherent status in the hist. of poetic forms, but it should be stressed that sound poetry also belongs to a hist. of dissonance and noise in 20th-c. cinema, music, phonographic reproduction, and radio, and emerges not by coincidence in a transformative historical period for auditory technologies. The generation of sound poets now reaching maturity, such as the Canadian poet Christian Bök (b. 1966), has suggested that the "theurgical," antitechnological reaction of early sound poets such as Hugo Ball is untenable for contemp. poets who may be the first "who can reasonably expect in our lifetime to write poems for a machinic audience." Bök's work in progress *The Cyborg Opera* refigures the sound poetry inheritance for an "undreamt poetics of electronica" or a "spoken techno" that he allies with the technical virtuosity of beatboxers such as Razhel. Bök reimagines sound poems as participants in a "growing digital culture," as in his lettristic drum kit notation systems ("Bhm--T-Nsh--tpt'Bhm--T--Nsh [thsss]"), and he also systematically plumbs vernacular phonetic patterns: "my tongue muttering / an unsung lettering."

■ A. Reyes, "Las jitanjáforas," in *La experiencia literaria* (1942); I. Isou, *Introduction à une Nouvelle Poésie et une Nouvelle Musique* (1947); E. Jolas, "From the Jabberwocky to Lettrisme," *Transition* 1 (1948); G. Apollinaire, "The New Spirit and the Poets," *Selected Writings*, trans. R. Shattuck (1950); T. S. Eliot, "The Music of Poetry," *Selected Prose,* ed. F. Kermode (1975); H. Chopin, *Poésie Sonore Internationale* (1979); *Sound Poetry,* ed. S. McCaffery and bpNichol (1979); J. Schnapp, "Politics and Poetics in F. T. Marinetti's *Zang Tumb Tuuum,*" *Stanford Italian Review* 5.1 (1985); O. Paz, *Convergences,* trans. H. Lane (1987); C. Bernstein, "Artifice of Absorption," *A Poetics* (1992); G. Janecek, *Zaum* (1996); M. North, *The Dialect of Modernism* (1997); G. Agamben, "Pascoli and the Thought of the Voice," *The End of the Poem,* trans. D. Heller-Roazen (1999); D. Kahn, *Noise, Water, Meat: A History of Sound in the Arts* (1999); S. McCaffery, *Prior to Meaning* (2001); T. J. Demos, "Circulations: In and Around Zurich Dada," *October* 105 (2003); C. Dworkin, "To Destroy Language," *Textual Practice* 18 (2004); *The Sound of Poetry / The Poetry of Sound,* ed. M. Perloff and C. Dworkin (2009).

■ **Discography/Web Resources**: *Text Sound Compositions,* RELP 1049, 1054, 1072–74, 1102–03 (1968–70)—seven records of the Stockholm festivals of sound poetry (partly available on UbuWeb); *Futura: Poesia Sonora,* ed. A. Lora-Totino, Cramps 5206-301–307 (1978)—six-record international anthol., available on Ubu

Web, http://www.ubu.com (best audio resource on sound poetry).

■ **Periodicals:** *Ou*, ed. H. Chopin (1963–68); *Stereo Headphones,* ed. N. Zurbrugg (1969–)—most issues include records.

H. FEINSOD

SPEAKER. *See* PERSONA; VOICE.

SPENSERIAN STANZA. The Spenserian stanza has been taken up by poets from Robert Burns to John Keats to Alfred, Lord Tennyson; but as its name suggests, it has never escaped association with its inventor, Edmund Spenser (1552–99). Its combination of versatility and idiosyncrasy may be unmatched: nine lines long, with a mix of alternating rhyme and *couplets (*ababbcbcc*), it proceeds in strict *pentameter up to its concluding *alexandrine. Spenser's principal sources were doubtless the Chaucerian *rhyme-royal stanza, which shifts, like his, to couplets at the fifth line (*ababbcc*), and the *ottava rima* of It. epic (*abababcc*). The stanza is also shaped by the manifold narrative, imagistic, argumentative, and visionary uses to which *The Faerie Queene* puts it.

The first jolt the stanza gives its reader is that unexpected couplet. At the beginning of book 1, we learn that Red Cross's armor bears "The cruell markes of many a bloudy fielde," and in the next breath, "Yet armes till that time did he neuer wield" (1.1.1). It is the first of many double takes. That fifth line can also usher in a new stage of argument or a new event; it can drive a point home with double force; it can offer a resting place in the middle of the stanza. Any rest, however, is provisional at best, for the alternating rhymes promptly resume.

Some version of the same effect happens at the stanza's end, but this time, the line that completes the couplet has an extra foot. Length gives a sense of finality, and the alexandrine makes a good home for the poem's frequently sententious pronouncements ("That blisse may not abide in state of mortal men" [1.13.44]). There is authority in the nod to epic *hexameter and in the evenhandedness of the usual medial *caesura. That split down the middle, however, can also have a contrary effect, introducing, with the help of an unstated *beat at the joint, the native jounce and narrative carry of *ballad meter ("She turnd her bote about, and from them rowed quite" [2.12.16]).

Spenser uses this peculiar stanza to think with, and it suits his epic's self-critical habits of mind: sometimes careening but more often pausing to doubt, to declare, and then to doubt again. Other poets have variously adapted these potentials. James Thomson's *Castle of Indolence* is full of Spenserian stops and starts; Keats's "Eve of St. Agnes" is more apt to swoon through the middle of the stanza without taking a breath, as Tennyson does in "The Lotus Eaters." Some of the stanza's inheritors conjure Spenser's resuscitated medievalism, some his dreamy storytelling; all of them conjure Spenser, who can never be cast out of the strange room he built.

■ Empson; P. Alpers, *The Poetry of "The Faerie Queene"* (1967); J. Dolven, "The Method of Spenser's Stanza," *Spenser Studies* 21 (2004).

J. DOLVEN

SPLIT LINES. Originating in cl. drama, split lines are metrically complete lines shared by two or more speakers, often producing an effect of rapidity in the exchange between them. Examples include exchanges between Oedipus and Creon in Sophocles' *Oedipus Rex* and between Medea and her nurse in Seneca's *Medea*. In his essay on Senecan tragedy in Elizabethan trans., T. S. Eliot quotes the latter, calling the split lines "minimum antiphonal units." Split lines became a feature of Elizabethan drama, with Thomas Kyd, Christopher Marlowe, John Webster, and Ben Jonson among those using them, in addition to Shakespeare, whose plays show a steady increase in the percentage of split lines over his career—the late plays contain from 15 to almost 20%, peaking in *Antony and Cleopatra* and *Coriolanus*—as the point of breaking in the line steadily moves to the right. Whereas the First Folio of Shakespeare's plays does not distinguish split lines visually, they appear with a distinct visual format—the second part of the line indented beyond the end of the first after an intervening strophic boundary—in William Wordsworth's "Tintern Abbey," in which the visible break signals some transition in the speaker's thought or feeling, rather than an exchange between two speakers. Among the modernists, visible split lines appear in the poems of Robert Frost (his two-speaker dramatic poems), Wallace Stevens, Ezra Pound, W. C. Williams, and Eliot, among others. But often in the case of Williams or Pound, a question arises: in verse without a metrical norm, how can one distinguish between, on the one hand, two or more parts of a single line and, on the other, two or more lines with visual formatting that uses indentation? In the later 20th c., Charles Wright made split lines his signature technique (as in *Half-life*, 1988), speaking of the "dropped line" or "low rider" and signaling the intralinear status of his breaks by capitalizing the first words of left-justified lines.

■ T. S. Eliot, *Elizabethan Dramatists* (1963); M. G. Tarlinskaja, *Shakespeare's Verse* (1987), ch. 4; G. T. Wright, *Shakespeare's Metrical Art* (1988), ch. 8.

T.V.F. BROGAN; G. BRADEN; S. CUSHMAN

SPOKEN WORD. *See* PERFORMANCE.

SPONDEE (Gr., "used at a libation," i.e., poured to the accompaniment of the two long notes). In classical prosody, a metrical unit consisting of two long syllables; in the mod. accentually based prosodies, a *foot of two stressed syllables. Cl. meters entirely composed of spondees—*versus spondaicus* (spondaic verse)—are rare but do occur (West). But normally, as in the dactylic hexameter, the spondee is an optional substitution for a *dactyl in the first five feet and obligatory in the last (metrical marking of closure is a widely attested phenomenon). Allen, therefore, thinks the spondee "can hardly be termed a 'foot' in its own right," since it does not manifest internal opposition or contrast of members, and cites Pohlsander, who holds that the spondee "has no real existence of its own . . . but must always be considered the contracted form of some other metrical unit."

In the prosodies of the mod. Germanic langs., which have been traditionally scanned in feet, the existence of spondaic feet is disputed. Several knowledgable and sensible mod. metrists (J. B. Mayor, George Saintsbury, Fitzroy Pyle, Clive Scott, G. T. Wright) have long held that the foot of two heavy syllables is a legitimate variation in iambic verse: they point to examples such as the last two syllables of the following lines: "The dove pursues the griffon, the mild hind" (Shakespeare, *A Midsummer Night's Dream* 2.1.232), or "The long day wanes, the slow moon climbs" (Alfred, Lord Tennyson, "Ulysses"), or "Silence, ye troubl'd waves, and thou Deep, peace" (John Milton, *Paradise Lost* 7.216), or the third and fourth syllables of "That in one speech two negatives affirm" (Philip Sidney, *Astrophil and Stella* 63.14). Absolutists, these metrists hold that, if two contiguous odd-even stresses in a line are both strong—perhaps not perfectly equal in

strength (though that is certainly possible) but nearly so—then they should both be counted as strong, and the foot is, thus, a spondee. That is, if both stresses are, on a scale of four degrees of stress (1 strongest, 4 weakest), 1s or 2s (i.e., either the sequence 1-2 or 2-1), then *scansion should reflect the fact that these levels are both above 3 and 4. As in the examples from Tennyson and Milton, such alleged instances of spondees are often made possible by two adjacent monosyllables or, more clearly, by a major syntactic juncture within the foot.

Other mod. metrists (e.g., Edwin Guest, W. W. Skeat, Jakob Schipper, Derek Attridge, Susanne Woods), esp. those who base their theories on ling., deny the existence of the spondee and *pyrrhic in mod. verse, either on the basis of their definition of the foot itself as an element of metrical theory or else on the basis of Otto Jespersen's Relative Stress Principle (RSP), which explicitly prohibits absolute weighting of stress (hence, two heavy syllables within one foot). Jespersen's relativity principle assumed the existence of metrical feet and amounted to the claim that stress matters only in relation to immediately contiguous syllables, esp. the one syllable preceding. Hence, for him, the sequence "and thou Deep, peace" amounts to two iambs—unequal ones, perhaps, but iambs. The RSP yielded, for many metrists, elegant and subtle scansions that preserved both extensive metrical conformity (it allowed only iambs and trochees, in effect) and expressive readings. But it did this at the expense of variety in feet and of, some felt, due recognition of weighting in the line. Pyle rightly identifies the underlying issue at stake as being the question of "how far does the metre actually influence our rendering of stress as we read?" Readers and metrists who grant a strong influence will deny the existence of spondees (McAuley), those a weak influence, affirm (Pyle). Relativist scansion more accurately tracks the shape of line movement; absolutist scansion more accurately takes account of which syllables are heavy and which not.

It is evident that, in certain contexts where full syllable realization is granted every syllable, spondaic words can occur (Fussell gives the example of "Amen"), but these may represent an unusual performance mode and so be exceptions. In any event, the normal processes of stress alternation and reduction operate so systematically in Eng. phonology that, in compound words or in phrases of any length, spondees are difficult at best. Still, absolutists in scansion can produce strong examples, as Wright does from Shakespeare. Of course, mod. imitations of cl. meters such as the *hexameter attempt to reproduce spondees either accentually or by some theory of quantities.

■ P. Fussell, *Poetic Meter and Poetic Form* (1965); J. McAuley, *Versification* (1966); F. Pyle, "Pyrrhic and Spondee," *Hermathena* 107 (1968); Allen; West; Scott; Attridge, *Rhythms*; G. T. Wright, *Shakespeare's Metrical Art* (1988); *Meter in English: A Critical Engagement*, ed. D. Baker (1996); C. Addison, "Stress Felt, Stroke Dealt: The Spondee, the Text, and the Reader," *Style* 39 (2005).

T.V.F. Brogan

SPRUNG RHYTHM. G. M. Hopkins coined the term *sprung rhythm* to characterize the poetic rhythm that he used first in his great ode "The Wreck of the Deutschland" and in numerous subsequent poems, incl. most of his best known. Hopkins describes the rhythm most valuably in his Author's Preface, composed for the later poems, "Deutschland" and after, and in a long letter to his poet-friend, Canon Richard Watson Dixon (October 5, 1878). He tells Dixon the "echo" of the rhythm long "haunted" his ear before he "realized [it] on paper" in the ode. To explain how poetic rhythm may be "sprung," he instances the work of John Milton, "the great standard in the use of counterpoint." Counterpoint is prominent in *Paradise Lost* and *Paradise Regained*, and then Milton carries it much further in the choruses of *Samson Agonistes*, which are "counterpointed throughout" so that each line "has two different coexisting scansions. But when you reach that point the secondary or 'mounted rhythm,' which is necessarily a sprung rhythm, overpowers the original or conventional one and then this becomes superfluous." Sprung rhythm, as Hopkins points out, cannot be counterpointed.

Hopkins tells Dixon that sprung rhythm "consists in scanning by accents or stresses alone . . . so that a foot may be one strong syllable or it may be many light and one strong." His imprecision does not mean, however, that the foot patterns are in his mind arbitrary or of no importance, as his explanation in his Author's Preface shows. Except for "particular effect," the sprung-rhythm foot will have one to four syllables. The nuclear stress may come at any point in the foot, but "it is a great convenience to follow the example of music and take the stress always first," producing "four sorts of feet, a

monosyllable and the so-called accentual Trochee, Dactyl, and the First Paeon [four syllables (´xxx)]. And there will be four corresponding natural rhythms." However, labeling a poem's rhythm accordingly, as, for instance, the poet's headnote identifying "The Windhover" as "falling paeonic," seems of minimal practical help for *scansion. It is more useful to consider the effect that the poet aims for with sprung rhythm.

Hopkins wants his poetry to be "logaoedic," to combine the advantages of prose and verse. Writing to Robert Bridges (August 21, 1877), he states he uses sprung rhythm "because it is the nearest to the rhythm of prose, that is the native and natural rhythm of speech, the least forced, the most rhetorical and emphatic of all possible rhythms, combining, as it seems to me, opposite and, one wd. have thought, incompatible excellences, markedness of rhythm—that is rhythm's self—and naturalness of expression." In sprung rhythm, two kinds of verbal music happily intersect: on the one hand, it has marked rhythm, requiring a clearly defined recurrence of stress; on the other hand, it has naturalness, the stress pattern of natural speech. The paeon is of particular interest to Hopkins. In his lecture notes on "Rhythm and Other Structural Parts of Rhetoric," he observes that the foot patterns that Aristotle prescribes for oratory are the first and fourth paeon, neither of which can make "meters" (verse lines) in the common ("running") rhythms. Sprung rhythm, however, makes the metrical paeon possible.

The naturalness of sprung rhythm results importantly from its free mixing of foot types, producing both adjacent and widely separated stress, thereby obscuring the underlying regularity of the rhythm. Hopkins emphasizes that his rhythm does not result from laxity in timing, but rather is carefully planned. He contrasts his rhythm with Walt Whitman's, whose verse he admired: Whitman's verses verge on "decomposition into common prose," while his own are "very highly wrought. . . . Everything is weighed and timed in them" (letter to Bridges, Oct. 18, 1882). "The native and natural rhythm of speech" that Hopkins aims for with sprung rhythm, then, does not arise from imitating ordinary linguistic intonation. Instead, it comes from an artful reconstitution of it. He tells his brother Everard in a late letter (Nov. 5, 1885), "Sprung rhythm makes verse stressy; it purges it to an emphasis as much brighter, livelier, more lustrous than the regular emphasis of common rhythm as poetry in general is brighter than common speech." A reading of sprung rhythm verse will be "poetical" rather than rhetorical; in his Author's Preface, he instructs the reader of sprung rhythm "strongly to mark the beats of the measure . . . not disguising the rhythm and the rhyme, as some readers do, who treat poetry as if it were prose fantastically written to rule . . . , but laying on the beat too much stress rather than too little." He declares to Bridges (May 21, 1878), "Stress is the life of it."

■ *Correspondence of Gerard Manley Hopkins and R. W. Dixon,* ed. C. C. Abbott (1935); *Letters of Gerard Manley Hopkins to Robert Bridges,* ed. C. C. Abbott (1935); M. Holloway, *Prosodic Theory of Gerard Manley Hopkins* (1947); W. Ong, "Hopkins' Sprung Rhythm and the Life of English Poetry," *Immortal Diamond,* ed. N. Weyand (1949); *Journals and Papers of Gerard Manley Hopkins,* ed. H. House and G. Storey (1959); E. Schneider, *Dragon in the Gate* (1968); C. Scott, *A Question of Syllables* (1986), ch. 5; P. Kiparsky, "Sprung Rhythm," *Rhythm and Meter,* ed. P. Kiparsky and G. Youmans (1989); N. MacKenzie, "Metrical Marks," *Poetical Works of Gerard Manley Hopkins,* 5th ed. (1990); J. I. Wimsatt, "Alliteration and Hopkins's Sprung Rhythm," *PoT* 19 (1998), and *Hopkins's Poetics of Speech Sound* (2006).

J. I. Wimsatt

STANZA. A unit of poetic lines organized by a specific principle or set of principles. The possibilities include *alliteration, *syntax, lineation, *meter, arc of thought, although most familiarly in Eng., the end rhyme fashions a stanza. Stanzas are sequential: they are identified as such by the intervals and by the other units of lines (often isomorphic with the first stanza) before and after them. They are periodic, guiding the reader alternately through a sojourn in their organized lines, then through the suspensions of stanzaic intervals. Traditionally, they are partitioned from each other by techniques of closure, e.g., a tag in another lang., *couplet or strong rhyme, *refrain or *envoi, *proverb or aphorism, *dialogue, lengthened or shortened line, or tail rhyme. Longer, nonisomorphic groups of lines are sometimes referred to as *strophes.

Stanzas are found in poetic cultures both written and oral. They may emerge from a *song tradition in which words are composed to accompany a preexisting melody—an origin asserted in poetics from George Puttenham to

Ezra Pound and manifest in the practice of poets like Thomas Campion and George Herbert. Stanzas arise also within the widespread professional cultures of compositional virtuosity like the bardic and skaldic guilds of northwest Europe, the troubadour culture of southern Europe, or late med. clerical and courtly milieux; these are often stanzas of technical intricacy. Stanza forms are also continually developed by major poet-thinkers of form (e.g., in Eng., the *Gawain/Pearl*-poet, Chaucer, Edmund Spenser, Ben Jonson, the John Keats of the odes, Thomas Hardy, Langston Hughes, A. R. Ammons, and Jorie Graham). In Eng., end rhyme has been the chief means of binding the massed lines of a stanza for more than 600 years, though poetries in other langs., as well as earlier alliterative work in OE and modernist and postmod. practice, manifest other ways of conceiving stanzaic form. Stanzas may hew to a simple pattern, three or four lines with one or two rhyme sounds, e.g., the *blues stanza or the *ballad stanza; a stanza may have identical or varying line lengths within a single stanza (isometric or heterometric, respectively); Eng. line lengths themselves may be as brief as one or two syllables, as long as a William Blake or a C.K. Williams can extend them. In spacious stanza forms—e.g., ballade and pseudo-ballade, long-line alliterative stanzas, *ottava rima*, *rhyme royal, the more ambitious tail-rhyme stanzas, *Spenserian stanza—rhyme patterns and groupings of line create dynamic complexities of internal movement. Such complexity is also evident in terse stanzas like the skaldic eight-line form *drottkvaett* or the Eng. common meter in the hands of Emily Dickinson. Syntax threads pathwise through the enclosed space of the stanza; the flexible play of syntax in relation to rhyme and line creates variety and movement through sequences of stanzas, while metrical structure maintained and repeated through sequences creates stability.

The relationship between the stanza and its interval offers flexible resources for shaping the stanza's *closure and the reader's temporal experience of periodicity; stanzas often deploy verb forms, tense, mood, and aspect as means to slow, to quicken, to close off, or to open upon the interval. (The Spenserian stanzas of P. B. Shelley and Lord Byron are swift-moving and climactic; the Spenserian stanzas of Keats are weightier and noun-based; those of Spenser himself are characterized by verbs of temporal extensivity, marking actions habitual, sustained, or repeated.)

Most descriptive and taxonomic work on Eur. stanza forms focuses on the stanza as an object or chunk of matter, a box-like unit, a "room" of poetic discourse in which aural elements governed by rules are lodged and fixed. Apropos of Eng. stanzas, this tendency to take the stanza as object or structure is intensified by defining stanzas chiefly in relation to their rhyme scheme. Stanzas have thus been evaluated by the degree to which they demonstrate internal coherence or integrity, in terms of form, syntax, content, and figuration. Readers who require this sense of stanzaic integrity are often disappointed with stanzaic devels. in the 20th and 21st cs., when aesthetics and philosophy articulate an opposition to the spatialization of time in preference to process and duration; when organicism inherited from romantic poetics, *free verse, and field poetics challenge set forms; and when Western poets' encounters in the first half of the 20th c. with Chinese poetry and poetics give them access to a syntactic freedom and spareness that releases them from their sense of Eur. stanzaic traditions' enervation. But in light of early med., modernist, and postmod. practice as well as research in ethnopoetics, no account of stanzas can be limited to the single story of form versus freedom; a global account would include multiple stories of stanzas' changeful work in mediating temporal experience.

Specific stanza forms arise and thrive in specific moments and cultures. They are always being embroiled in debates about form and freedom. But the political and ideological implications of specific stanza forms are never intrinsic, nor their future life predictable. The rigid form of the *sestina, which had pretty well disappeared from Eur. poetries after two decades of popularity in the 16th c., was revitalized in 20th-c. Am. poetry; the Persian *ghazal* with its single rhyme and its couplets has come into Eng. in the late 20th and 21st cs.; traditional Eng. poetry and free verse have shaken up 20th-c. Chinese poetry just as cl. Chinese poetry did Eng. modernism; Alexander Pushkin's Onegin stanza now does interesting work in verse and novel all over the world; the engagements of Af. Am. and Caribbean writers with Eng. stanza trads. demonstrate the shifting and generative work of stanzaic form.

■ Schipper, *History*; P. Martinon, *Les Strophes: Études historiques et critiques sur les formes de la poésie lyrique on France depuis la Renaissance* (1912); I. Frank, *Répertoire métrique de la poésie des troubadours*, 2 v. (1953–57); Maas; W. Pfrommer, *Grundzüge der Strophenentwicklung in derfranzösischen Lyric von Baudelaire zu Apollinaire*, diss., Tübingen (1963); Koster; T. Navarro, *Repertorio de estrofas españolas* (1968); U. Mölk and F. Wolfzettel, *Répertoire métrique de la poésie lyrique française des origines à 1350* (1972); F. Schlawe, *Die deutsche Strophenformen: Systematisch-chronologische Register zur deutschen Lyrik 1600–1950* (1972); Wimsatt; S. Ranawake, *Höfische Strophenkunst: Vergleichende Untersuchungen zur Formen-typologie von Minnesang und Trouverelied an der Wende zum Spatmittelalter* (1976); Tarlinskaja; E. Häublein, *The Stanza* (1978); H. J. Frank, *Handbuch der deutsche Strophenformen* (1980); A. Solimena, *Repertorio metrico dello Stil novo* (1980); T.V.F. Brogan, *English Versification, 1570–1980: A Reference Guide with Global Appendix* (1981); F. P. Memmo, *Dizionario di metrica italiana* (1983); G. S. Smith, "The Stanza Typology of Russian Poetry 1735–1816: A General Survey," *Russian Literature* 13.2 (1983); T.V.F. Brogan, *Verseform: A Comparative Bibliography* (1989); Gasparov, *History*; P. Seital, *The Power of Genre: Interpreting Haya Oral Literature* (1999); A. Addison, "Little Boxes: The Effects of the Stanza on Poetic Narrative," *Style* 37.2 (2003); D. Hymes, *Now I Know Only So Far: Essays in Ethnopoetics* (2003); J. Boffey and A.S.G. Edwards, *A New Index of Middle English Verse* (2005).

T. Krier

STICHOMYTHIA (Gr., "line-speech"). Refers to a highly formalized kind of *dialogue in Gr. and Lat. drama in which each speech is confined to a single metrical line. Equally formalized are two related phenomena: *distichomythia*, in which the exchanges are each exactly two lines long, and repartee in *split lines (the split line being called *antilabé*) in which one of two speakers gets the beginning of a line and the other gets the end (we might call this *hemistichomythia*). Every one of the 33 extant Gr. tragedies makes use of stichomythia (50, 75, or 100 lines of stichomythia occur), and many use the other two kinds as well. Long passages of stichomythia or distichomythia are not characteristic of Aristophanes or of Menander, who likes to start speeches midline. This naturalism was passed on to the Roman comic poets, who make no use of stichomythia. The fragments of the Roman tragic poets before Seneca show no traces of it. It was revived by Seneca, who uses it in most of his plays, though the long runs of stichomythia characteristic of Gr. tragedy are rare.

Seneca's use of stichomythia and antilabé for repartee influenced William Shakespeare (e.g., *Richard III* 4.4 and *Hamlet* 3.4) and Molière. J. W. Goethe uses stichomythia in *Iphigenia auf Tauris*. An adaptation of stichomythia to another genre is the amoebean verse contest in *pastoral poetry (e.g. Theocritus, *Idyll* 5, and John Milton, *Comus*). There is a hilarious parody of tragic stichomythia and distichomythia in A. E. Housman's "Fragment of a Tragedy" (Burnett).

■ A. Gross, *Die Stichomythie in der griechischen Tragödie und Komödie* (1905); J. L. Hancock, *Studies in Stichomythia* (1917); J. Myres, *The Structure of Stichomythia in Attic Tragedy* (1950); W. Jens, *Die Stichomythie in der frühen griechischen Tragödie* (1955); E.-R. Schwinge, *Die Verwendung der Stichomythie in den Dramen des Euripides* (1968); B. Seidensticker, *Die Gesprächsverdichtung in den Tragödien Senecas* (1968), and "Die Stichomythie," *Die Bauformen der griechischen Tragödie,* ed. W. Jens (1971); S. Ireland, "Stichomythia in Aeschylus," *Hermes* 102 (1974); D. J. Mastronarde, *Contact and Discontinuity* (1979), chs. 3 and 4; *The Poems of A. E. Housman,* ed. A. Burnett (1997).

W. H. RACE; D. KOVACS

STROPHE. From the Gr. for *turn* or *bend,* a defined unit of movement with song performed in ancient Gr. drama by the chorus as it turned now one way (strophe), then another (*antistrophe), then stood (*epode). Strophe and antistrophe were of identical metrical and musical structure, with the epode of a different structure. In cl. antiquity and later poetry modeled on it, the term came to refer to a structural unit of a poem, like a *stanza, with varying line-length, notably in *odes with their expansive strophes (e.g., Pindar, Horace, Ben Jonson, Thomas Gray, John Keats). But a strophe could be brief, as with the two-line dactylic distich or the four-line *sapphic strophe; other cl. forms included the elegiac strophe, the alcaic strophe, and the asclepiadean strophe. In all of these, a crucial feature is the repetition, at least once, of the first strophe's metrical pattern. In analysis of song and poetry derived from song, a strophe is one of a metrically and melodically identical set of stanzas; thus, popular song, troubadour song, Ger. lieder, *blues stanzas, verse-and-refrain forms

like the muwashshaḥ and the *zéjel* proceed by adding new strophes to the melody of the first strophe. In contemp. usage about Eng.-lang. poetries, *strophe* is sometimes used for long, nonisomorphic units, *stanza* for more regular ones. Biblical scholars speak of several strophes gathered together into a single stanza, but the unit definitions are not airtight. Discourses about Gr. and Lat. drama and poetics, about Ar. and Andalusian med. song and performance practice, about Semitic poetries, about music forms, and ethnopoetic studies in sub-Saharan Af. poetries often use *strophe* for its flexibility in discussing poetic performance with music, gesture, dance, and breath. In either case, *stanza* carries a long-standing implication of fixed "rooms" or boxes of verse; "strophe" implies movement of speakers/singers, currents, alternation of speakers, shared or exchanged parts.

See DACTYL, ELEGIAC DISTICH.

■ F. M. Warren, "The Troubadour *canso* and Latin Lyric Poetry," *MP* 9 (1912); D. C. Clarke, "Miscellaneous Strophe Forms in the Fifteenth-Century Court Lyric," *Hispanic Review* 16.2 (1948); G. Rouget, "African Traditional Non-Prose Forms: Reciting, Declaiming, Singing, and Strophic Structure," *Proceedings of a Conference on African Languages and Literatures,* ed. J. Berry, R. P. Armstrong, and J. Povey (1966); R. H. Finnegan, *Oral Literature in Africa* (1970); S. M. Stern, *Hispano-Arabic Strophic Poetry: Studies,* ed. L. P. Harvey (1974); Halporn et al; *A Handbook of the Troubadours,* ed. F.R.P. Akehurst and J. M. Davis (1995); J. P. Fokkelman, *Reading Biblical Poetry: An Introductory Guide,* trans. Ineke Smit (2001); H. Heijkoop and O. Zwartjes, *Muwassah, Zajal, Kharja: Bibliography of Strophic Poetry and Music from al-Andalus and Their Influence in East and West* (2004).

T. KRIER

STYLE. *Style* is the way something is done or made: not the what, but the how; not the method, but the manner. This rudimentary definition has been current for millennia, but the word commands interest not least for its contradictions. It has been used to define the distinctive voice of an individual and also the common features that identify the works of particular places, times, groups, or schools; for the holistic charisma of first impressions and the scrupling analyses of stylistics; for the highest artistic achievement (having a style) and the season's passing fashions. That range is a challenge for theory and suggests (as such contradictions do) how much cultural work *style* does, defining how we recognize likeness and difference, community and individuality, present and past in our works and in one another.

In the Western trad., style was treated first as a department of rhet. *Style* for Aristotle consists of those aspects of lang.—*syntax, *diction, figuration—that can be adapted to suit a persuasive occasion. He bequeathed this emphasis on decorum to Cicero, whose *Orator* codifies the flexibility of style in three *genera dicendi*, or kinds of speech: high, middle, and low. The high style, "forceful, versatile, copious and grave," suits affairs of state; the low, "refined, concise [and] stripped of ornament," is "clear rather than impressive" and serves for explanation and familiar talk. The middle is a compromise (never as clearly defined as its neighbors, in Cicero or in the trad. that followed him). This tripartite scheme offers a set of rhetorical strategies that may be taught to anyone, and though variations were proposed (like Hermogenes' 2d-c. *Seven Types of Style*), it remained central to rhetorical instruction through the Middle Ages and into the Ren. Its flexibility encourages a conceptual distinction between manner and matter, as though a single subject could be dressed (a common metaphor) in a variety of styles. Similarly persistent was the promise of a normative or best style: Cicero himself held that role for many Ren. humanists, and it was the characteristic aim of 18th-c. rhetorical manuals.

Cicero might also be said to be the source of a rival strand of the trad. His *De oratore*, written ten years before the *Orator*, asks, "Do you not expect that we shall find almost as many styles of oratory as orators?" Here is style as the mark of an individual, a signature (to take up the metaphor implicit in the Lat. *stilus*, or pen). The idea of individual style, cultivated or innate, was a persistent undercurrent in Eur. letters through the 18th c. and became a critical preoccupation in the 19th. Style simultaneously developed into a central category for historical understanding. Ren. historicism arguably began in the recognition of stylistic difference, as eds. of cl. texts learned to date them (and to unmask forgeries) by changes in lang. over time. Art historians of the 18th and 19th cs. elaborated taxonomies of style to define periods and schools. Indeed, style, understood as the recognition of origins, might be said to be the most vivid way that historical stratification is present in daily life (Ginzburg): we are surrounded by things that look like the time and place they were made or pretend to have been made.

In the 20th c., ling. and technology transformed the study of style for literary analysis. The revolution of Noam Chomsky's generative grammar gave rise to a subdiscipline of stylistics that considers stylistic variation in relation to deep structure. Computers permitted ambitious statistical portraits of texts, providing evidence for dating and even attribution to individuals. In breaking texts down into features (like relative letter frequency) that no reader could be expected to notice, much less quantify, computer-assisted stylometrics has moved far away from the immediate power of style. That extension from total impression to incidental, telltale element has been a provocation to theorists, and philosophical thinking of the last 50 years has centered around a few recurring questions. Do texts, objects, or people have specifically stylistic features? This question is a version of the matter and manner problem: can we separate the subject of a poem, say, or its form, from what defines its style? Mod. opinion has tended to reject any a priori distinction—saying in advance what features of a text can and cannot count as stylistic—but there have been many attempts to set criteria. Stylistic features may be those, e.g., that express or solicit an affective response (Bally) or that express the psychology of the maker (Wollheim, Gilmore) or that convey the way something was made (Walton). Another common question is whether style requires a choice among possible alternatives. Would style be intelligible if there were only one style; is having a style necessarily a conscious choice? Other theorists have treated stylistic difference as the deviation from a norm, so that style, choice or no, is necessarily supplementary to the usual or the merely useful (Barthes, Todorov). The unity of style has attracted comment, too, much of it engaging the work of Spitzer. If a novel has a style, is that style necessarily present in each of its details? Is unity—which the critic discovers by traveling Spitzer's hermeneutic circle, moving from detail to whole and around again—the criterion of style?

Such theoretical questions coexist with a popular conversation about style that makes its social aspects particularly obvious. Style defines communities of people who dress similarly and read similar books, as well as communities that make similar poems. Having a style affords all of them a certain ease or at least a way of knowing what to do or how to do it. That goes for membership in a group as well as for individual style, insofar as a poet with a recognizable style can be said to imitate himself or herself. (The word's adaptability both to singling out and to collecting allows for delicate calibrations of affiliation and independence, in art and life.) In a social context, it becomes clear that the affiliations we perceive when we recognize a style are more than merely formal. We also register something like charisma: style impresses us when we see not only a way of proceeding but how someone might want to act or dress or make something that way (whether we ourselves would want to or not). Much of our life with works of art involves such negotiations of imitative desire, as we map the stylistic variety of our world, its communities and its hist., and define the boundaries of taste within which we will live.

For all this attention and interest, the concept of style, still vital in art hist. and musicology, has been relatively peripheral to lit. crit. of the last 50 years. The New Criticism often treated stylistic description as a distraction from the interpretive challenges of the particular text. Neither poststructuralism nor historicism found terms for reviving its currency. But the bearing toward the world that style names is perdurably important to literary experience, and reading for the style—for who wrote the text, where it comes from, but also for what the writer's life might be like and what it might offer our own—is arguably far more widespread than formal interpretation. Style has great promise for contemp. crit. as a neglected connection among form, society, and hist.

■ W. Pater, "Style," *Appreciations* (1889); L. Spitzer, *Linguistics and Literary History* (1948); C. Bally, *Traité de stylistique française*, 3d ed. (1951); S. Ullman, *Language and Style* (1964); S. Sontag, "On Style," *Against Interpretation* (1966); E. Gombrich, "Style," *International Encyclopedia of the Social Sciences*, ed. D. L. Sills (1968); G. Hough, *Style and Stylistics* (1969); *Literary Style: A Symposium*, ed. S. Chatman (1971)—see esp. R. Barthes, "Style and Its Image," and T. Todorov, "The Place of Style in the Structure of the Text"; R. Lanham, *Style: An Anti-Textbook* (1974); N. Goodman, "The Status of Style," *CritI* 1 (1975); D. Russell, "Theories of Style," *Criticism in Antiquity* (1981); W. Sauerländer, "From Stilus to Style," *Art History* 6 (1983); *The Concept of Style*, ed. B. Lang, rev. ed. (1987)—see esp. K. Walton, "Style and the Products and Processes of Art," and R. Wollheim, "Pictorial Style: Two Views";

G. Genette, *Fiction and Diction*, trans. C. Porter (1993); C. Ginzburg, "Style as Inclusion, Style as Exclusion," *Picturing Science, Producing Art*, ed. P. Gallison and C. A. Jones (1998); J. Gilmore, *The Life of a Style* (2000).

J. DOLVEN

SUBLIME

I. Classical
II. Enlightenment to Modern

I. Classical. *Sublime* (Lat. *sublimis*, "[on] high, lofty, elevated") owes its currency as a critical and aesthetic term to the anonymous Gr. treatise *Peri hypsous* (*On the Sublime*; *hypsos*, "height, elevation") once ascribed to the rhetorician Longinus of the 3d c. CE but now generally agreed to belong to the 1st c., perhaps around 50 CE. Whatever his name and origin, its author was certainly a rhetorician and a teacher of the art, but one of uncommon mold. His treatise, with its intimacy of tone (it is addressed to a favorite pupil, a young Roman) and breadth of spirit, stands more or less isolated in its own time but has had a recurrent fascination for the mod. mind since the 17th c.

The idea of sublimity had its roots in the rhetorical distinction, well established before Longinus, of three levels of *style—high, middle, and low. His achievement was to draw it out of the technical sphere, where it had to do primarily with style, and to associate it with the general phenomenon of greatness in lit., prose and poetry alike. The author regards sublimity above all as a thing of the spirit, a spark that leaps from the soul of the writer to the soul of his reader and only secondarily as a matter of technique and expression. "Sublimity is the echo of greatness of spirit." Being of the soul, it may pervade a whole work (speech, hist., or poem: the author pays little attention to generic distinctions), or it may flash out at particular moments. "Father Zeus, kill us if thou wilt, but kill us in the light." "God said, 'Let there be light,' and there was light." In such quotations as these, Longinus shows among other things his sharp eye for the particular passage and his capacity for empathy with the actual work, qualities that are, in fact, rare in ancient crit. and that presage the mod. spirit.

The distinguishing mark of sublimity for this ancient author is a certain quality of feeling. But he will not allow it to be identified simply with emotion, for not all emotions are true or noble. Only art can guard against exaggerated or misplaced feeling. Nevertheless, art is subordinated to genius in his thinking. He enumerates five sources of the sublime: great thoughts, noble feeling, lofty figures, *diction, and arrangement. The first two, the crucial ones, are the gift of nature, not art. He even prefers the faults of a great spirit, a Homer, a Plato, or a Demosthenes, to the faultless mediocrity that is achieved by following rules.

In later antiquity and the Middle Ages, the treatise remained unknown, or at least exercised little influence. In the Ren., it was first published by Francesco Robortello in 1554, then translated into Lat. in 1572 and into Eng. in 1652 by John Hall. But it made no great impression until the late 17th c. Paradoxically enough, it was Nicolas Boileau, the high priest of Fr. neoclassicism, who launched the *Peri hypsous* on its great mod. career and thus helped to prepare the ultimate downfall of classicism. His trans. (1674) had immense reverberation, esp. in England. The Eng., always restive under the so-called Fr. rules, instinctively welcomed Longinus as an ally. As neoclassicism advanced and subjectivity became increasingly central to Eng. thinking, not only about lit. but about art in general, the sublime became a key concept in the rise of romanticism in poetry and the concurrent establishment of aesthetics as a new, separate branch of philosophy.

II. Enlightenment to Modern. In the 18th c., the sublime represented merely one type of experience that could be described under the general philosophical rubric of sensationism. For a host of writers producing everything from aesthetic treatises to Gothic novels, it was synonymous with irresistible forces that produced overwhelming sensations. In the 18th and 19th cs., *sublime* came increasingly to be a term of aesthetic approbation, as attested by the interest in both sublime landscapes and paintings of sublime landscapes. In the popular view, the term amounted to a description: it represented primarily a subject matter, the wild and desolate natural scene or the natural force that dwarfed the individual human figure. Its effect was simultaneously to make one conscious of one's own comparative weakness in the face of natural might and to produce a sense of the strength of one's own faculties. As John Baillie put it in his *Essay on the Sublime* (1747), "Vast Objects occasion vast Sensations, and vast Sensations give the Mind a higher Idea of her own Powers."

Along with the increasing currency of the term in the 18th c., two particularly strong arguments about the place of the sublime and sublime nature emerged: Edmund Burke's *Philosophical Enquiry into the Origin of Our Ideas of the Sublime and the Beautiful* (1757) and Immanuel Kant's *Critique of Judgment* (1790; commonly referred to as his Third Critique, after the *Critique of Pure Reason* [1781] and *Critique of Practical Reason* [1788]). In the hist. of what we now call *aesthetics*, these two works were esp. important for according significance to pleasure in objects that were not, strictly speaking, beautiful. Burke developed the sensationist position into an affectivism that continually connected the sublime with the issue of an individual's relationship to society, and Kant made his discussion of the sublime a cornerstone of a formalist account of aesthetics.

Burke's *Enquiry* sets out the affectivist position on the sublime in an argument that emphasizes the power of experience. In the "Introduction on Taste" added to the 2d ed. (1759), Burke made two claims for the importance of taste. First, his emphasis on the regular operation of the senses makes taste as meaningful and as generalizable as reason: "as the conformation of their organs are nearly, or altogether the same in all men, so the manner of perceiving external objects is in all men the same, or with little difference." Second, his emphasis on the origin of the passions treats taste as a field of determinate knowledge in which the "remembrance of the original natural causes of pleasure" can be distinguished from the acquired tastes that fashion and habit promote. People, he observes, are not likely to be mistaken in their reactions to sensation even though they may often be confused in their reasoning about them.

Burke traced the attractions of the beautiful and the sublime to human impulses that are ultimately utilitarian. The beautiful he saw as a manifestation of the human instinct toward sociability, with sociability, in turn, serving the purpose of the continuation of the species. The sublime he treated as a manifestation of the instinct for self-preservation, the response of terror that "anticipates our reasonings, and hurries us on by an irresistible force." The beautiful represents what we love (and love specifically for submitting to us and flattering our sense of our own power); the sublime represents all that we fear for being greater and more powerful than we are.

If the notion of sympathy had for writers like Adam Smith suggested how persons might identify with the interests of others, Burke's discussion of the sublime and the beautiful emphasizes relations between individuals and objects far more than intersubjective relations. Yet Burke argues for the social utility of our feelings of the sublime and beautiful. He increasingly aligns the beautiful not merely with the sociable and pleasing but with a relaxation of the bodily functions that eventually becomes disabling. The sublime, by contrast, presents difficulties that require "exercise or labour" to be overcome. Although the sublime feelings of astonishment or awe may resemble pain, the excitation and exertion that they produce yield a very real pleasure—a consciousness of one's own powers and even a physical exercise that keeps the various organs of sensation in tone. Burke's account may be empiricist in suggesting that objects have regular and predictable operations on the senses, but it ultimately de-emphasizes knowledge of the external world and stresses instead the uses of objects in gratifying and challenging the individual human organism.

Kant, in his *Critical Observations on the Feeling of the Beautiful and Sublime* (1784), does not depart strikingly from the Burkean position. He identifies the beautiful and the sublime as terms under which contrasting kinds of objects of experience might be subsumed; and he sees the enjoyment or displeasure in these objects as having essentially a psychological dimension. In this, his remarks are consistent with the familiar critical view that shifted discussions of pleasure in art and nature from an emphasis on production—what the artist must do to achieve certain effects—to an emphasis on reception—how the response to certain objects raises questions of a viewer's or reader's psychology.

With the Third Critique, however, Kant reoriented aesthetic discussion. Burke and other writers (incl. the Kant of the *Observations*) had described the sublime and the beautiful in terms of both natural and human-made objects; Homeric and Miltonic poetry could serve as examples of sublimity as well as the seemingly infinite expanse of the ocean or a powerful animal in whom "the terrible and sublime blaze out together." Kant reduced the metaphorical reach of the term *sublime* and identified it exclusively with natural objects. The effect of this reduction was to enable him to argue that the sublime is not—or not particularly—important for establishing human inferiority relative to natural might. Rather, the pleasure that one takes in sublime nature reveals a pleasure in judging objects that are not the vehicles of a message and not expressions of anyone's intentions. If a poem or a statue cannot exist without the intentional action of its maker, natural sublimity appeals to human viewers in a fashion that stands outside such communication of intention.

Kant's claim for sublime intentionlessness obviously opposes itself to the "argument from design," which reads the book of nature as revealing divine intention. Its primary significance, however, is not so much to argue against belief in divinity as to identify aesthetic judgment as a faculty that is, in interesting ways, unable to ground itself in claims about the prior value of external objects. The sublime becomes the primary vehicle for the Kantian argument about the importance of "purposiveness without purpose" in aesthetic objects. While natural beauty might appear to have been formed by design (echoing Joseph Addison's sense of the mutually enhancing relationship of art and nature to one another), the sublime, lacking the form of beautiful nature, bespeaks pleasure in an object that is without bounds not merely in appearing infinite but in having no form. The aesthetic judgment, i.e., does not respond to the intrinsic beauty of an object in appreciating natural sublimity, but neither does it merely provide a screen on which individual psychology is projected. Rather, the sublime in its intentionlessness and formlessness makes visible the judgment's role as a form-giving faculty.

In the 1970s and after, the sublime gained prominence in poststructuralism, rhetorical crit., and continental philosophy. In the work of Jacques Derrida, for instance, it figured in his challenge to Kantian formalism. Indeed, for many critics it came to represent something like an inversion of the Kantian claim about it: namely, the view that the sublime represents an "excess" in lang. that keeps it from ever assuming any fixed form or meaning. More recently, the Fr. philosopher Jean-François Lyotard revisited the Kantian sublime as an Enlightenment anticipation of the epistemological complexity associated with postmodernism, while the Slovenian philosopher Slavoj Žižek has argued that political regimes depend on extrapolitical "sublime objects" (such as the state or religion) to frame their subjects' worldview. Meanwhile, many literary scholars have been concerned to develop the material, psychological, and transhistorical dimensions of the sublime.

■ T. R. Henn, *Longinus and English Criticism* (1934); S. H. Monk, *The Sublime: A Study of Critical Theories in XVIII-Century England* (1935); B. Weinberg, "Translations and Commentaries on Longinus to 1600, A Bibliography," *MP* 47 (1949–50); F. Wehrli, "Der erhabene und der schlichte Stil in der poetisch-rhetorischen Theorie der Antike," *Phylobolia fauur P. von der Mauuhll* (1946); E. Olson, "The Argument of Longinus' *On the Sublime*," Crane; Wimsatt and Brooks, esp. chs. 6, 14; W. J. Hipple, *The Beautiful, The Sublime, and the Picturesque* (1957); J. Brody, *Boileau and Longinus* (1958); M. H. Nicolson, *Mountain Gloom and Mountain Glory* (1959); E. Tuveson, *The Imagination as a Means of Grace* (1960); M. Price, "The Sublime Poem," *Yale Review* 58 (1969); Saisselin; A. Litman, *Le Sublime en France, 1666–1714* (1971); D. B. Morris, *The Religious Sublime* (1972); T.E.B. Wood, *The Word "Sublime" and Its Context, 1650–1760* (1972); A. O. Wlecke, *Wordsworth and the Sublime* (1973); W. P. Albrecht, *The Sublime Pleasures of Tragedy* (1975); T. Weiskel, *The Romantic Sublime* (1976); J. Derrida, "Economimesis," trans. R. Klein, *Diacritics* 11 (1981); P. H. Fry, *The Reach of Criticism* (1983); P. de Man, "Hegel on the Sublime," *Displacement*, ed. M. Krupnick (1983); A. Leighton, *Shelley and the Sublime* (1984); N. Hertz, *The End of the Line* (1985); E. Escoubas, "Kant ou la simplicité du sublime," *Poésie* 32 (1985); S. Knapp, *Personification and the Sublime: Milton to Coleridge* (1985); "The Sublime and the Beautiful: Reconsiderations," *NLH* 16.2 (1985)—spec. iss.; *The American Sublime*, ed. M. Arensberg (1986); P. Lacoue-Labarthe, "La Verité sublime," *Poésie* 38 (1986); L. W. Marvick, *Mallarmé and the Sublime* (1986); J. Derrida, *The Truth in Painting*, trans. G. Bennington and I. McLeod (1987); *La Via al Sublime*, ed. M. Brown et al. (1987); T. M. Kelley, *Wordsworth's Revisionary Aesthetics* (1988); P. Boitani, *The Tragic and the Sublime in Medieval Literature* (1989); P. Crowther, *The Kantian Sublime* (1989); *Das Erhabene*, ed. C. Pries (1989); J.-F. Lyotard, *The Differend*, trans. G. Van Den Abbeele (1988); and "The Sublime and the Avant-Garde," *The Lyotard Reader*, ed. A. Benjamin (1989); J. Ramazani, "Yeats: Tragic Joy and the Sublime," *PMLA* 104 (1989); S. Guerlac, *The Impersonal Sublime*

(1990); R. Wilson, *American Sublime* (1991); V. A. De Luca, *Words of Eternity: Blake and the Poetics of the Sublime* (1991); F. Ferguson, *Solitude and the Sublime* (1992); N. A. Halmi, "From Hierarchy to Opposition: Allegory and the Sublime," *CL* 44 (1992); J.-L. Nancy, "The Sublime Offering," *Of the Sublime*, trans. J. S. Librett (1993); *Eighteenth-Century Studies* 28.1 (1994)—several essays on the sublime in France and Germany; M. Lollini, *Le muse, le maschere e il sublime* (1994); J.-F. Lyotard, *Lessons on the Analytic of the Sublime*, trans. E. Rottenberg (1994); *Beauty and the Critic*, ed. J. Soderholm (1997); D. Bromwich, "The Sublime before Aesthetics and Politics," *Raritan* 16 (1997); E. Baker, "Fables of the Sublime: Kant, Schiller, Kleist," *MLN* 113 (1998); S. Budick, *The Western Theory of Tradition* (2000); M. Donougho, "Stages of the Sublime in North America," *MLN* 115 (2000); J. Turner, "Wordsworth and the Psychogenesis of the Sublime," *Romanticism* 6 (2000); R. Gasché, "The Sublime, Ontologically Speaking," *YFS* 99 (2001); I. Balfour, "The Sublime between History and Theory: Hegel, de Man, and Beyond," *After Poststructuralism*, ed. T. Rajan and M. J. O'Driscoll (2002), and "The Sublime Sonnet in European Romanticism," *Romantic Poetry*, ed. A. Esterhammer (2002); M. Blackwell, "The Sublimity of Taste in Edmund Burke's *A Philosophical Enquiry into the Origin of Our Ideas of the Sublime and Beautiful*," *PQ* 82 (2003); H. Ram, *The Imperial Sublime: A Russian Poetics of Empire* (2003); *Georgia Review* 58.2 (2004)—symposium on the poetic sublime; C. Duffy, *Shelley and the Revolutionary Sublime* (2005); *Phrasis* 46.1 (2005)—several essays on the sublime; I. Balfour, "Torso: (The) Sublime Sex, Beautiful Bodies, and the Matter of the Text," *Eighteenth-Century Studies* 39 (2006); A. J. Cascardi, "The Genealogy of the Sublime in the Aesthetics of the Spanish Baroque," *Reason and Its Others*, ed. D. Castillo and M. Lollini (2006); B. Kim, "Generating a National Sublime: Wordsworth's *The River Duddon* and *The Guide to the Lakes*," *SIR* 45 (2006); C. Battersby, *The Sublime, Terror and Human Difference* (2007); R. Rothman, "Modernism, Postmodernism, and the Two Sublimes of Surrealism," *Modernism and Theory*, ed. S. Ross (2009); S. Žižek, *The Sublime Object of Ideology*, 2d ed. (2009); R. A. Barney, "The Splenetic Sublime: Anne Finch, Melancholic Psychology, and Post/Modernity," *Studies in Eighteenth-Century Culture* 39 (2010);

A. Richardson, *The Neural Sublime* (2010);
C. Stokes, *Coleridge, Language, and the Sublime*
(2011).

G. F. Else, T.V.F. Brogan (cl.);
F. Ferguson, R. Greene (mod.)

SYLLABIC VERSE

I. System of Versification
II. English

I. System of Versification. Syllabic verse is one
of the earliest and most widespread modes of
versifying: it is evidenced in Old Iranian, Sanskrit, ancient Gr., and the earliest Chinese and
Japanese poems. Its defining feature is that the
lines match (or, more rarely, contrast) only in
the number of syllables they contain. The syllabic line's rhythm is termed a *simple primary
rhythm* because a single type of *event*, a syllable,
is repeated. A passage of syllabic verse is, thus, a
series of fours, sixes, or eights or whatever line
length the poet chooses.

Versifying by counting syllables alone has serious drawbacks, the first of which is that some
syllables have no consonant at their boundary with the next, and the result may be pronounced as one syllable or two. This has largely
been left to fashion: in cl. verse, such adjacent
vowels counted as one syllable (by *elision or
synaloepha); in med. Lat., they counted as two
(by *hiatus); and in mod. romance verse, they
almost always count as one.

The other drawbacks of syllabic verse are
more fundamental. One reflects the psychological limits to human counting: we can learn
to recognize a series of threes, sixes, or even
eights intuitively, but a series of tens or fifteens
is beyond us. For that reason, syllabic meters
must be either short (up to eight syllables)
or compound (made up of regular subunits
each with no more than eight syllables). The
second drawback is that the syllables of most
langs. have properties that are more obvious
than their number, such as length, stress (see
ACCENT), and pitch. The moment poets begin
to regularize any of these, the verse is no longer
simply syllabic, and for this reason, most syllabic meters have developed into something
rather more complex.

Gr., Sanskrit, and Chinese poets soon de-
parted from strictly syllabic verse and introduced patterns in the duration or the pitch
of their syllables. Japanese poets introduced
the refinement of recognizing long vowels as

two syllables. Lat. poets seem at first to have
counted words, not syllables; but by the 2d c.
BCE, they had adopted the Gr. system with its
contrasts between long and short syllables. By
the 3d c. CE, most Lat. speakers had lost any in-
tuitive sense of the difference between long and
short vowels, and for several centuries, some
Lat. poets composed in the old meters but with
the wrong length given to some of their syllables. Most Lat. poets, however, followed the
example of the composers of popular hymns
and wrote syllabic verse.

There were also new forces influencing versification: *assonance and *rhyme, which were
occasional devices in cl. Lat., became mandatory in the new syllabic meters; and stress,
which had played a minor role in cl. Lat. meters, became a vital element. The essence of
systematic assonance and rhyme is stress: thus,
rhymes are either oxytonic (*cat/mat*) or paroxytonic (*horses/courses*), depending on whether a
posttonic syllable follows the stressed, rhymed
syllable.

Much med. Lat. verse is syllabic, although
some poets clearly favored certain positions
in their lines for stress, esp. between 1100 and
1500. And in the 11th c., Fr. verse became syllabic: from then on, only the final stresses of
lines and *hemistichs had metrical significance.
Syllabic verse fits well the mod. Fr. lang., where
only phrasal stress has survived.

When poets of other langs. tried to adopt Fr.
syllabic metrics, they faced the problem of word
stresses in midline, which interfered with the
reader's perception of the syllabic pattern. Hispanic and It. poets used these midline stresses
to produce a variety of rhythms in their lines,
but Eng. poets used them to create regular patterns—that is, *accentual-syllabic verse.

Rhyme and syllable count entered Eng. verse
after the Norman Conquest, but in England,
something happened to strict syllable count.
It began in Anglo-Norman (the official lang.
from 1066 to 1363), where the ubiquitous *octosyllabe* was often a syllable short or in excess
(see OCTOSYLLABLE). Eng. audiences had always
counted stresses, not syllables, and many poets
and scribes in this period tolerated lines with
approximately eight syllables, providing they
had four stresses. Eng. poets never really accepted syllabic verse in their own lang., having
incorporated stress patterns from the very first.

These two distinctions have remained:
most Eng. verse is *accentual-syllabic, most
Fr. syllabic. Mod. Fr. metrists argue that the

syllable-timed delivery of their lang. means that syllabic lines occupy equal time in performance and that such equal-time units are the essence of Fr. verse rhythm. Eng. with its stress-timing offers no such isochrony, and the prevalence of *syncope in the lang. leaves the syllabification of many words ambiguous (thus, *mystery* may be two syllables or three). But this has not prevented mod. Eng.-lang. poets from attempting syllabic meters, incl. W. B. Yeats, W. H. Auden, and Marianne Moore.

II. English. In many poetries, including Japanese and those of the Romance languages, meter is organized around the counting of syllables, known as syllabism (see METER, 1.B.). The prevalence of this principle, however, is qualified by the fact that purely syllabic meters are uncommon. Traditional Japanese prosody, which depends on the regulation of syllables or morae in the line and favors five- and seven-syllable lines as in the 31-syllable tanka, is perhaps the most thoroughly syllabic of any major lang.

As Martin Duffell observes, "in the verse traditions of most languages syllabism came to be compounded or replaced by the regulation of some other suprasegmental feature, such as duration/weight (as in Sanskrit and Ancient Greek), pitch (as in Chinese), or stress (as in Iranian, Greek, Romance, and the Slavonic languages), and some evidence of such regulation is often present in the earliest surviving texts in these languages." Duffell notes that purely syllabic meters are "fragile," and that syllable counts alone are not "obvious" enough for readers and listeners. Even med. Lat. verse, where syllabism arose after 300 CE in the ruins of quantitative prosody, often depends on stress patterning and rhyme to support the less perceptible syllable count. OF versification took note of the regulation of word stress in med. Lat., and came to include the principle that the final position in each line (and in longer lines, the final position in each hemistich) must contain a stress. While the location of the stress itself is regulated by the syllable count (e.g. in an *octosyllable* it must occur in the last of eight positions), it also in turn defines the end of the line for metrical purposes; where additional syllables occur after the stress, they are not counted, and therefore the syllabic line is negotiated rather than strictly empirical. "This metre," Duffell writes, "although it regulates phrasal stress, is termed syllabic in traditional French metrics"; its phrasal-stress versification became the basis

for syllabism in many languages "from Italian and Spanish in the South to Polish and Russian in the North." The devel. of particular syllabic meters often involved further negotiations with local conditions, especially an accommodation of word stress in those languages where it was phonologically prominent.

In Eng., syllabic verse is not so much a metrical program as an experiment or even a curiosity. Many poets and scholars have doubted that verse lines in Eng. regulated by nothing more than identity of numbers of syllables would be perceived by auditors as verse, for there would be nothing to mark them as such except for end-of-line pauses in performance, if that (though Robert Beum argues otherwise). Paul Fussell and others have questioned whether syllabic versification accords with the accentual nature of Eng. Notwithstanding such skepticism on the part of prosodists troubled by the auditory elusiveness of syllabic verse, the number of syllabic poems in Eng., already considerable, continues to grow.

Aside from some debatable Ren. examples, the practice is a mod. one, pioneered by Robert Bridges in the late 19th and early 20th cs. Bridges wrote nearly 5,000 lines of syllabic *alexandrines, esp. for *New Verse* (1925) and *The Testament of Beauty* (1929), the longest syllabic-verse poem in the lang. In the 1910s, Adelaide Crapsey invented the cinquain. Beginning in the same decade, Marianne Moore, the Am. poet best known for the practice, wrote poems in elaborate syllabic stanzas featuring wide variations in line length, complex patterns of rhyme or half rhyme, and conspicuous use of prose rhythms. This last point, highlighted by Roy Fuller and others, suggests that Moore's version of syllabic verse has affinities with the verset and the *prose poem. From the mid-20th c. on, notable syllabic poems have been written by Elizabeth Daryush, Dylan Thomas, W. H. Auden, Donald Justice, Thom Gunn, Richard Howard, Robert Wells, and others. Some have used haiku as stanzas; Richard Wilbur in doing so rhymes the first and third lines of each. As Steele notes, most poets working in syllabic verse in Eng. attempt to avoid sustained regular (particularly iambic) rhythms, although, for expressive purposes, these may be admitted. Syllabic verse can, in fact, be so accommodating to audible patterns that it can be mistaken for other forms: some of Daryush's syllabic poems can be read as accentual-syllabic with minor variations, and Justice's "For the

Suicides," in seven-syllable lines, can be read as an accentual poem because the three beats in each line, though variably placed, are invariably prominent. That which makes syllabic verse conceptually dubious to some prosodists has made it artistically inviting to a widening array of poets, some of whom view it as a half measure between traditional meter and *free verse, and all of whom exploit its paradoxical combination of constraint (in the strict syllable count) and freedom (in the possibility of shifting rhythms at will within the syllabic matrix). The term *syllabic verse* used in relation to Ir. and Welsh prosody is not a categorically exclusive designation, since in these systems, the syllable count of a line is but one of a number of required prosodic features.

■ **Versification:** G. B. Pighi, *Studi di ritmica e metrica* (1970); M. L. West, "Greek Poetry 2000–700 BC," *CQ* 23 (1973), and "Indo-European Metre," *Glotta* 51 (1973); S. Oliva, *Mètrica catalana* (1980); P. M. Bertinetto, *Strutture prosodiche dell' italiano* (1981); P. G. Beltrami, *La metrica italiana* (1991); B. de Cornulier, *Art poëtique* (1995); M. L. Gasparov, *A History of European Versification*, trans. and ed. G. S. Smith, M. Tarlinskaja, and L. Holford-Strevens (1996); R. Pensom, *Accent and Metre in French, 1100–1900* (1998); J. Domínguez Caparrós, *Métrica española*, 2d ed. (2000); M. J. Duffell, "French Symmetry, Germanic Rhythm, and Spanish Metre," *Chaucer and the Challenges of Medievalism*, ed. D. Minkova and T. Tinkle (2003); *Syllable and Accent: Studies on Medieval Hispanic Metrics* (2007); and Duffell.

■ **English:** R. Bridges, "New Verse: Explanation of the Prosody of My Late Syllabic 'Free Verse'," *Collected Essays*, v. 2 (1933); E. C. Wright, *Metaphor, Sound and Meaning in Bridges' "Testament of Beauty"* (1951); R. Beum, "Syllabic Verse in English," *Prairie Schooner* 31 (1957); R. Beloof, "Prosody and Tone," *KR* 20 (1958); Sr. M. G. Berg, *The Prosodic Structure of Robert Bridges' "Neo-Miltonic Syllabics"* (1962); R. Fuller, "An Artifice of Versification," *Owls and Artificers* (1971); E. Daryush, "Note on Syllabic Metres," *Collected Poems* (1976); P. Fussell Jr., *Poetic Meter and Poetic Form*, rev. ed. (1979); Brogan; T. Steele, *All the Fun's in How You Say a Thing* (1999); M. Holley, "Syllabics: Sweeter Melodies," Finch and Varnes; M. J. Duffell, "The Metric Cleansing of Hispanic Verse," *BHS* 76 (1999); Duffell; Gasparov, *History*; R. H. Brower, "Japanese," A. B. Giamatti,

"Italian," L. Nelson, Jr., "Spanish," and J. Flescher, "French"—all in Wimsatt.

> M. J. DUFFELL (VERSIFICATION);
> T.V.F. BROGAN; R. B. SHAW (ENG.)

SYMBOL

I. In Culture
II. In Poetry

In literary studies, the term *symbol* (Gr. verb *symballein*, "to put together," and the related noun *symbolon*, "mark," "token," or "sign," referring to the half coin carried away as a pledge by each of the two parties to an agreement) has had a broad range of applications and interpretations. In the study of lang., e.g., words are symbols of what they stand for, but the more common ling. terminology after Ferdinand de Saussure is sign, which joins a signifier and a signified. *Sign* generally refers to a relatively specific representation of one thing by another—a red traffic light, e.g., means "stop"—while *symbol* refers to a more polysemous representation of one thing by another—as when the sea, e.g., is used to stand for such different feelings as the danger of being overwhelmed (by analogy with drowning) or the excitement and anxiety of making a transition (as in a journey) or the power and fulfillment of strength (as in mighty), and so on.

For the present purpose, however, the meanings and uses of *symbolism* can be analyzed in terms of two main categories: on the one hand is the study of the symbol in such larger contexts as lang. and the interpretation of lang. (philology, rhet., ling., semantics, semiotics, hermeneutics), of philosophy (metaphysics, epistemology, aesthetics), of social science (sociology, anthropology, psychology), and of hist. and religion; on the other hand is the study of the symbol in its discrete contexts as an aspect of art, of literary theory and crit., and of poetry (Wimsatt 1965, Hayes).

I. In Culture. Historically as well as logically, the larger field comes first. Where people once tended habitually to see the physical world in terms of emotional and spiritual values, they now tend to separate their values from the world. It has become one of the clichés of mod. crit. that, due to the anti-imagistic crusade of the Protestant Reformation, the growth of science and its search for "objective" knowledge, the changes in focus from sacred to secular gradually effected in school curricula, and the mere passage of time, many traditional symbols have been rendered meaningless to poets and readers alike. Thus, received symbolism was called in the 20th c. the "lost" or "forgotten" lang. (Bayley, Fromm).

It may be said, then, that the evolution of symbolism began with the evolution of primitive humanity. It was not until the med. period, however, that symbols and the interpretation of symbols became a branch of learning. The patristic trad. of biblical exegesis, heavily under the influence of the Platonic and Neoplatonic schools of thought, developed standards and procedures for the doctrinal interpretation of scripture according to four levels of meaning—literal, allegorical, moral and tropological, and anagogic. The purpose was twofold: to reconcile the OT with the NT and to reconcile various difficult portions of each with Catholic teaching. Thus, e.g., while the Song of Songs is a mildly erotic wedding poem on the literal level, its true meaning on the allegorical level is the "marriage" of Christ and the Church.

This exegetical trad. evolved during the 16th c. into Ren. nature philosophy and, under the influence of the mysticism of the Ger. Jakob Boehme (1575–1624) and the Swede Emanuel Swedenborg (1688–1772), into the doctrine of correspondences, which viewed the external world as a system of symbols revealing the spiritual world in material form. By the romantic period, the view that nature is the visual lang. of God or spirit became established as one of the mainstays of poetry, but two fundamental shifts had occurred: the material and spiritual worlds were seen as merged rather than related simply as representation to the thing represented; and, as a result, the meaning of symbols became less fixed and more ambiguous (Seward, Sewell, Hirst, Wimsatt, Todorov, and Adams).

Out of this romantic trad. grew a large and influential 20th-c. movement that tried to re-unite what the Reformation and science ostensibly had sundered. Following the lead of such writers as Urban, Cassirer, Langer, and Wheelwright, mod. philosophers and critics developed a set of concepts whereby the lang. of symbols can be regarded as having as much epistemological status as—if not more than—the lang. of fact and reason. The question, therefore, is as follows: if the latter refers to the "real" or "objective" world, and is subject to test and verification, what does the former refer to, and does it too have analogous evaluative procedures?

The answers range along a spectrum: at the one extreme are the positivists, who say that the lang. of fact and science is the only true lang. and, therefore, that all other langs. are nonsense; at the other end are the mystics, who claim that the lang. of fact and science is trivial and that the only true lang. is that of symbols. Northrop Frye, in *Anatomy of Criticism*, however, falls off the spectrum altogether: neither world for him, at least as literary critic, exists. He simply postulates that there is an "order" of lit., that this order has an objective existence in the totality of literary texts, and that it is based on the fundamental seasonal monomyth of death and rebirth.

Closer to the center are two other positions that seek either to balance this subject-object split or to reconcile it. The first is exemplified by I. A. Richards, who accepted the distinction between scientific and poetic lang. but then proceeded to accord to the latter a status and value of its own. Thus, he distinguished between "referential" lang., the lang. of fact and science, and "emotive" lang., the lang. of poetry. The status and value of the latter were found in its ability to arouse and organize our emotions, thus giving poetry some sort of psychological and therapeutic if not metaphysical "truth." The New Criticism, not entirely satisfied with this distinction, claimed further that poetry gives us another and "higher" kind of truth, a truth of human existence that is more complex and profound than that of mere fact and science.

The reconcilers, exemplified chiefly by Cassirer and Langer and their followers, claim that *all* langs., whether of science or poetry, or of any in between, are various ways in which the human mind constructs reality for itself and, therefore, that all our knowledges give *pictures* of reality rather than reality *itself*. For this school, humanity has not "lost" or "forgotten" the lang. of symbols; it has merely come to prefer one kind of symbolic lang. to another.

Such is the process of hist., however, that this ambitious theory itself has been turned inside out, and later movements have claimed that, since all our langs. are equally symbolic, they are all equally meaningless—at least insofar as the quest for "objective" truth is concerned. Thus, we find the theory of "paradigms" in the philosophy of science (Kuhn, Rorty), which says that scientific hypotheses are merely arbitrary constructs that may appear true in one era but are supplanted by other hypotheses in another era—"truth" being more a matter of cultural convenience, mental set, and consensus than of objective verifiability. And we find the theory of deconstruction in ling. and lit. theory and crit. (Culler), which claims that, since the relation between signifier and signified is arbitrary, lang. itself carries multiple meanings.

Another and somewhat more "rational" approach, represented by Wimsatt (1954), Kermode, and Fingesten, and anticipated by Whitehead, is that symbols, since they come between ourselves and reality, can be the agents of distortion and error as well as of knowledge and insight. Thus, they urge that the subjective be balanced by the objective.

II. In Poetry. To the reader considering how to recognize and interpret symbols in poetry, these philosophical disputes may seem not only bewildering but irrelevant. However, one's practical approach to symbols will be governed in large part by one's theory, for a critic's use of any given term is determined by the assumptions he or she makes about lit., lang., and reality, and by the kind of knowledge sought.

Olson (in Crane), e.g., as a neo-Aristotelian, is primarily concerned with literary works in their aspect as artistic wholes of certain kinds; therefore, he regards symbolism as a device that is sometimes used in the service of the work's artistic effect—to aid in the expression of remote ideas, to vivify what otherwise would be faint, to aid in framing the reader's emotional reactions, and the like. Yeats, by contrast, is primarily interested in the suggestive powers of poetry, so he extends his definition of *symbolism* to include not only images, *metaphors, and myths, but all the "musical relations" of a poem—*rhythm, *diction, *rhyme, *sound. Or again, Wheelwright, Langer, Cassirer, and Urban, as antipositivists, are concerned to defend poetry as having epistemological status, so they stress symbolism's powers of bodying forth nondiscursive meaning, truth, or vision. Burke, as a student of lang. in terms of human motives, deduces the form of a literary work from speculations as to how it functions in relation to the poet's inner life, so he emphasizes how various elements of that work symbolize an enactment of the poet's psychological tensions.

But the simplest way to begin interpretation is to regard symbols, although they may derive from literal or figurative images or both, as a kind of figurative lang. in which what is shown (normally referring to something material)

means, by virtue of some sort of resemblance, suggestion, or association, something *more* or something else (normally immaterial).

A. *Identification.* When interpreting symbols in a poem, it is helpful to begin by identifying its figuration—incl. metaphor, *metonymy, and *synecdoche—and analyzing the source of those figures in experience, whether from the natural world, the human body, human-made artifacts, or so on. We then proceed to ask how the figures in question are something other than literal. A figure may present itself as figurative in several ways, notably (1) it may be presented as if it were literal, but as it develops we see that it is, rather, a dream, a vision, a fantasy, or an imaginary action and, hence, must be understood entirely on a symbolic level, as is the case in W. B. Yeats's "Sailing to Byzantium," where the speaker talks about crossing the sea and coming to the holy city, which seems literally improbable; (2) there is a literal action and situation, but certain metaphors and *similes are presented in relation to one another and to the literal action so as to produce an additional level of meaning—by way of expanded, recurring, or clustered figures (Burke, Brower).

Thus, symbolism resembles figures of speech in having a basic doubleness of meaning between what is meant and what is said (tenor and vehicle, but it differs in that what is said is *also* what is meant. The "vehicle" is also a "tenor," so a symbolism may be said to be a metaphor in reverse, where the vehicle has been expanded and put in place of the tenor, while the tenor has been left to implication [cf. Bartel]). And this applies even to recurring figures within a literal action, because such figures are embedded in a context of more complex relationships within the work as a whole rather than occurring simply as figures per se.

Similarly, symbolism resembles allegory. Technically, *allegory* refers to the use of personified abstractions in a literary work. Edmund Spenser's *The Faerie Queene* is a standard example: the Redcrosse Knight represents the Christian soul, Duessa the duplicity of temptation, Una the true Church, and so on. Not only the characters may be allegorical, however; the setting and actions may follow suit. Thus, the work in its entirety may be allegorical. The difference between this form and symbolic works is that allegory begins with the tenor, the vehicle being constructed to fit, while symbol begins with the vehicle and the tenor is discovered, elicited, or evoked from it. Beginning with J. W. Goethe and S. T. Coleridge, this distinction was turned into a value judgment, with allegory being condemned as didactic and artificial and symbol being praised as natural and organic. This judgment became a commonplace of romantic and mod. crit., until a line of defense was established for allegory by more recent critics such as Honig, Fletcher, Hayes, de Man, Brett, Bloomfield, Todorov, and Adams. De Man, in particular, developed a detailed contrast between symbol and allegory as modes of representation distinguished by their avoidance and acknowledgment, respectively, of temporality in human existence; he proceeded from this contrast to build a critique of romantic ideology, esp. the romantics' celebration of symbol over allegory.

B. *Interpretation.* Once we know that something in the figurative inventory of a poem is symbolic, we need to see how it became so and, therefore, what it means. As a final practical suggestion, we will inquire into the various ways in which links may be established between a figure and an idea to form a symbol.

(1) The connection, as in metaphor and simile, may be based on resemblance, as mentioned above. A great many natural and universal symbols arise in this way: accomplishing something is like climbing a mountain, making a transition in life is like a journey to a new land, and so on. Examples are to be found everywhere in poetry (Bevan, Kimpel, Frye, Douglas, Embler), as well as in everyday usage.

(2) The link may evolve into an associative connection by virtue of repetition, as when a metaphor or simile is repeated so often, either in the work of a single author or in literary trad., that the vehicle can be used alone to summon up the tenor to which it was usually attached, somewhat in the manner of a code. An example is found by comparing Stéphane Mallarmé's swan imagery in "Le Vierge, le vivace et le bel aujourd'hui" with Yeats's in "Leda and the Swan" and "Among School Children."

(3) The connection may be based on the internal relationships that obtain among the elements of a given work, whereby one thing becomes associated with another by virtue of structural emphasis, arrangement, position, or devel. (which is, of course, true to some degree in all works containing symbols). Examples are the wall as division between the primitive and civilized in Robert Frost, the guitar and the color blue as the aesthetic imagination in

Wallace Stevens, and the island as complacency and the sea as courage in W. H. Auden.

(4) The connection may be based on primitive and magical associations, as when the loss of a man's hair symbolizes the loss of strength (Samson) or the rejection of worldly desires (monastic and ascetic practice), not because of any resemblance between them but rather because a mythic and ritualistic relationship has been established among secondary sex characteristics, virility, and desire. The underlying sterility/fertility symbolism in T. S. Eliot's *The Waste Land* is a conspicuous example.

(5) The connection may be derived from a particular historical convention, such as the transmutation of lead to gold as redemption, the lily as chastity and the rose as passion, or the fish as Christ (Hirst). A noted poetic instance is Yeats's use of the Rosy Cross, derived from Rosicrucianism, to symbolize the joining of flesh and spirit.

(6) The connection may derive from some private system invented by the poet—e.g., the phases of the moon as the cycles of hist. combined with the psychology of individuals in Yeats, or embalmment as an obstacle that cannot be overcome in the attempt to resurrect the spirit in Dylan Thomas (Olson 1954).

Critics rightly warn that symbolic associations should be neither too explicit nor too fixed, for implications of this sort are better felt than explained and they vary from work to work depending on the individual context (see, e.g., Carlson, Mischel, Cary, Wimsatt 1965, and Todorov).

See CONVENTION.

■ W. B. Yeats, "The Symbolism of Poetry," *Ideas of Good and Evil* (1903); H. Bayley, *The Lost Language of Symbolism*, 2 v. (1912); D. A. Mackenzie, *The Migration of Symbols* (1926); I. A. Richards, *Science and Poetry* (1926); A. N. Whitehead, *Symbolism* (1927); H. F. Dunbar, *Symbolism in Medieval Thought* (1929); E. Bevan, *Symbolism and Belief* (1938); W. M. Urban, *Language and Reality* (1939); K. Burke, *The Philosophy of Literary Form* (1941); S. K. Langer, *Philosophy in a New Key* (1942); C. M. Bowra, *The Heritage of Symbolism* (1943); E. Cassirer, *An Essay on Man* (1944), and *Language and Myth*, trans. S. Langer (1946); E. W. Carlson, "The Range of Symbolism in Poetry," *South Atlantic Quarterly* 48 (1949); M. Foss, *Symbol and Metaphor in Human Experience* (1949); R. Hertz, *Chance and Symbol* (1949); R. A. Brower, *The Fields of Light* (1951); E. Fromm,

The Forgotten Language (1951); T. Mischel, "The Meanings of 'Symbol' in Literature," *Arizona Quarterly* 8 (1952); E. Olson, "A Dialogue on Symbolism," Crane; "Symbol and Symbolism," spec. iss., *YFS* 9 (1952); H. D. Duncan, *Language and Literature in Society* (1953); C. Feidelson Jr., *Symbolism in American Literature* (1953); "Symbolism," spec. iss., *JAAC* 12 (1953); E. Cassirer, *The Philosophy of Symbolic Forms*, trans. R. Manheim, 3 v. (1953–57); B. Kimpel, *The Symbols of Religious Faith* (1954); E. Olson, *The Poetry of Dylan Thomas* (1954); P. Wheelwright, *The Burning Fountain* (1954); W. K. Wimsatt, *The Verbal Icon* (1954); *Symbols and Values* (1954) and *Symbols and Society* (1955), both ed. L. Bryson et al.; F. F. Nesbit, *Language, Meaning and Reality* (1955); W. Y. Tindall, *The Literary Symbol* (1955); Wellek and Warren, ch. 15; Frye; F. Kermode, *Romantic Image* (1957); S. K. Langer, *Problems of Art* (1957); J. Cary, *Art and Reality* (1958); E. Honig, *Dark Conceit* (1959); J. W. Beach, *Obsessive Images* (1960); *Literary Symbolism*, ed. M. Beebe (1960); *Metaphor and Symbolism*, ed. L. C. Knights and B. Cottle (1960); B. Seward, *The Symbolic Rose* (1960); *Symbolism in Religion and Literature*, ed. R. May (1960); H. Musurillo, *Symbol and Myth in Ancient Poetry* (1961); E. Sewell, *The Orphic Voice* (1961); T. J. Kuhn, *The Structure of Scientific Revolutions* (1962); R. Ross, *Symbols and Civilization* (1962); *Truth, Myth, and Symbol*, ed. T.J.J. Altizer et al. (1962); P. Wheelwright, *Metaphor and Reality* (1962); *Myth and Symbol*, ed. B. Slote (1963); A. Fletcher, *Allegory* (1964); D. Hirst, *Hidden Riches* (1964); E. Sewell, *The Human Metaphor* (1964); *Literary Symbolism*, ed. H. Rehder (1965); W. K. Wimsatt, *Hateful Contraries* (1965); K. Burke, *Language as Symbolic Action* (1966); W. Embler, *Metaphor and Meaning* (1966); G. Hough, *An Essay on Criticism* (1966); N. Goodman, *Languages of Art* (1968); *Perspectives on Literary Symbolism*, ed. J. P. Strelka (1968); R. Wellek, "Symbol and Symbolism in Literature," *DHI*; R. L. Brett, *Fancy and Imagination* (1969); H. D. Duncan, *Symbols and Social Theory* (1969); C. Hayes, "Symbol and Allegory," *Germanic Review* 44 (1969); *Interpretation*, ed. C. S. Singleton (1969); M. Douglas, *Natural Symbols* (1970); P. Fingesten, *The Eclipse of Symbolism* (1970); C. Chadwick, *Symbolism* (1971); J. R. Barth, *The Symbolic Imagination* (1977); R. Rorty, *Philosophy and the Mirror of Nature* (1979); *Symbol, Myth, and Culture*, ed. D. P. Verene (1979); *Literature, Criticism and Myth*,

ed. J. P. Strelka (1980); *Allegory, Myth, and Symbol*, ed. M. Bloomfield (1981); J. D. Culler, *On Deconstruction* (1982); T. Todorov, *Theories of the Symbol*, and *Symbolism and Interpretation*, both trans. C. Porter (1982); H. Adams, *Philosophy of the Literary Symbolic* (1983); R. Bartel, *Metaphors and Symbols* (1983); de Man, "The Rhetoric of Temporality"; J. Whitman, "From the Textual to the Temporal: Early Christian 'Allegory' and Early Romantic 'Symbol,'" *NLH* 22 (1991); Morier; D. Fried, "The Politics of the Coleridgean Symbol," *SEL* 46 (2006); N. Halmi, *The Genesis of the Romantic Symbol* (2007); R. E. Innis, "The Making of the Literary Symbol: Taking Note of Langer," *Semiotica* 165 (2007).

N. FRIEDMAN

SYNAERESIS (Gr., "drawing together"). The coalescing of two contiguous vowels within a word, usually for metrical purposes, e.g., *theoi* for *thĕoi* (*Iliad* 1.18) or *Thĕudōsiŭs* for *Thĕōdŏsiŭs*. Strictly speaking, synaeresis in Gr. denotes coalescing, where the second vowel is iota or upsilon, in order to form a diphthong. This is indicated in Gr. by the cornois mark (equivalent to smooth breathing). The term is often confused with or synonymous with synizesis, *syncope, and *synaloepha. An Eng. example would be "seest" for "seĕst." In the opening line of *Paradise Lost*, "Of Man's First Disobedience, and the Fruit," the *ie* in "Disobedience" changes to what is called a "y-glide," reducing the word from five syllables to four. But to some degree, synaeresis is simply a normal linguistic process frequently carried on in ordinary speech, of which the poet takes advantage for writing verse with regulated syllable count: several words have syllabically alternative forms, e.g., "heaven" as both disyllable and monosyllable. Coalescing of vowels across a word boundary (end of one word, beginning of next) is synaloepha.

See ELISION.

■ Allen; Morier; West.

T.V.F. BROGAN; R. A. HORNSBY; J. W. HALPORN

SYNAESTHESIA. The phenomenon in which one sense is felt, perceived, or described in terms of another, e.g., describing a voice as velvety or sweet or a trumpet blast as scarlet ("To the bugle," says Emily Dickinson, "every color is red"). In poetics, it is usually considered a species of *metaphor. Evidence for synaesthesia in lit. is ancient and cross-cultural; its critical conceptualization in the West, however, dates from the 18th c., and a specific term for it appeared only in 1891 (*Century Dictionary*). In the literary sense, it seems to have been first employed by Jules Millet in 1892. Synaesthesia was popularized by two *sonnets, Charles Baudelaire's "Correspondances" (1857) and Arthur Rimbaud's "Voyelles" (1871), as well as by J.-K. Huysmans's novel *À rebours* (1884); from these sources, it became one of the central tenets of symbolism. The device had been widely employed earlier in Ger. and Eng. romantic poetry, and it also can be found in some of the earliest lit. of the West (in the *Iliad* 3.152, the voices of the old Trojans are likened to the "lily-like" voices of cicadas; in the *Iliad* 3.222, Odysseus's words fall like winter snowflakes; and in the *Odyssey* 12.187, in the "honey-voice" of the Sirens). In Aeschylus's *Persians* (395), "the trumpet set all the shores ablaze with its sound." In the Bible, Heb. 6.5 and Rev. 1.12 refer to "tasting" the word of God and "seeing" a voice. Dante refers to a place "where the sun is silent" (*Inferno* 1.60). John Donne mentions a "loud perfume," Richard Crashaw a "sparkling noyse." P. B. Shelley refers to the fragrance of the hyacinth as "music," Heinrich Heine to words "sweet as moonlight and delicate as the scent of the rose."

Synaesthesia as the expression of intersense analogues has been exploited in lit. for a variety of effects, particularly increase of textural richness, complication, and unification. It is evident that other kinds of metaphor, esp. in the tenor and vehicle model, and *simile can also approximate the same kinds of suggestion, albeit in looser and more taxonomic forms. Shelley, one of the first Eng. poets to use synaesthesia extensively, employs it particularly in connection with visionary and mystical states of transcendental union ("Alastor," "Epipsychidion," "The Triumph of Life"); in these, synaesthesia suggests not only a greater "refinement and complexity of sensuous experience" but a "harmony or synthesis of all sensations" and a kind of "supersensuous unity" (O'Malley 1964). Cf. Baudelaire's "métamorphose mystique / De tous mes sens fondus en un" ("Toute Entière").

Because of its susceptibility to modify "inappropriate" objects (Meltzer), color has a long hist. of metaphorical richness, and the critical lit. has paid particular attention to it. One important species of synaesthesia is *audition colorée*, in which sound (or even silence)

is described in terms of colors. Silence is "perfumed" (Rimbaud), "black" (Pindar, Peretz Markish), "dark" (James Macpherson, *Ossian*), "green" (Giosuè Carducci, Georg Trakl), "silver" (Oscar Wilde), "blue" (Gabriele D'Annunzio), "purple" (David Fogel), "chill" (Edith Sitwell), "green water" (Louis Aragon). Perhaps the most famous example of the use of synaesthesia in poetry is Rimbaud's sonnet "Voyelles" (Vowels) beginning "A noir, E blanc, I rouge, U vert, O bleu, voyelles . . ." Such terms as "golden voice," *coloratura soprano*, "chromatic scale," Ger. *Klangfarbe* (sound-color) show the assimilation of audition colorée into both common and scholarly usage. More important still is the "light–dark" opposition in vowels first demonstrated by Köhler in 1910 and subsequently shown to exist in many of the world's langs.: Köhler argued that this opposition is not merely metaphorical but, in fact, a feature of all the senses resulting from some "central physiological perceptual correlate."

The related term *synaesthesis* appears in the late 19th c. in the course of evolving psychological theories of beauty to mean a wholeness in perception or anti-atomism in epistemology. I. A. Richards takes up this term for his psychological theory of crit. as part of his neurologically derived account of literary value (*Principles of Literary Criticism*, 1925): he too uses it in the sense of "wholeness" to refer to the synergistic nature of sense-experience, wherein wholes, "sensation-complexes," are greater than the sum of their parts.

The increasing interest in synaesthesia not only in psychology but in neuroscience, ling., and other fields has enhanced the interest in, and study of, literary synaesthesia. Literary critics have begun looking at various kinds of pseudosynaesthesia or "conceptual synaesthesia" (Sacks)—i.e., the use of concepts or other nonsensory objects as sensory data—to understand better the metaphorical relationships between the senses and how this metaphorical resource is used in the construction of poetic discourses.

■ **Criticism, General**: W. Köhler, "Akustische Untersuchungen," *Zeits. für Psychologie* 54–72 (1910–15); J. E. Downey, "Literary Synesthesia," *Journal of Philosophy, Psychology and Scientific Methods* 9 (1912); A. Wellek, "Das Doppelempfinden im abendländischen Altertum und Mittelalter," and "Zur Geschichte und Kritik des Synästhesie-Forschung," *Archiv für die gesamte Psychologie* 79–80 (1931); W. B. Stanford, *Greek Metaphor* (1936) and "Synaesthetic

Metaphor," *Comparative Literature Studies* 6–7 (1942); A. G. Engstrom, "In Defense of Synaesthesia in Literature," *PQ* 25 (1946); S. Ullmann, *The Principles of Semantics* (1951); G. O'Malley, "Literary Synesthesia," *JAAC* 15 (1957); L. Schrader, *Sinne und Sinnesverknüpfungen* (1969)—synaesthesia in It., Sp., and Fr.; P. Ostwald, *The Semiotics of Human Sound* (1973); P. E. Dombi, "Synaesthesia and Poetry," *Poetics* 3 (1974); L. Vinge, *The Five Senses* (1975); S. Sandbank, *Shtei Breikhot Ba-ya'ar* (Two Pools in the Wood, 1976); L. E. Marks, *The Unity of the Senses* (1978); D. Johnson, "The Role of Synaesthesia in Jakobson's Theory of Language," *International Journal of Slavic Linguistics and Poetics* 25–26 (1982); L. E. Marks, "Synesthetic Perception and Poetic Metaphor," *Journal of Experimental Psychology: Human Perception and Performance* 8 (1982); L. E. Marks, "Synesthetic and the Arts," *Advances in Psychology* 19 (1984); J. H. Ryalls, "Synaesthesia," *Semiotica* 58 (1986); J. P. Russo, *I. A. Richards* (1989); R. Tsur, "Literary Synaesthesia," *Hebrew Linguistics* 28–30 (1990); J. Harrison and S. Baron-Cohen, "Synaesthesia," *Leonardo* 27 (1994); R. Tsur, "Picture Poetry, Mannerism, and Sign Relationships," *PoT* 21 (2000); A. Motoyoshi, "Sensibility and Synaesthesia," *Journal of Arabic Literature* 32 (2001); R. E. Cytowic, *Synesthesia* (2002); O. Sacks, *Musicophilia* (2008).

■ **Criticism, Poets:** W. Silz, "Heine's Synaesthesia," *PMLA* 57 (1942); E. Noulet, *Le premier visage de Rimbaud* (1953); C. F. Roeding, "Baudelaire and Synaesthesia," *Kentucky Foreign Language Quarterly* 5 (1958); G. Guder, "The Meaning of Colour in Else Lasker-Schüler's Poetry," *German Life and Letters* 14 (1961); R. H. Fogle, "Synaesthetic Imagery in Keats," *Keats*, ed. W. J. Bate (1964); G. O'Malley, *Shelley and Synaesthesia* (1964); R. Étiemble, *Le Sonnet des voyelles* (1968); G. Cambon, "Synaesthesia in the *Divine Comedy*," *Dante Studies with the Annual Report of the Dante Society* 88 (1970); N. Ruddick, "Synaesthesia in Emily Dickinson's Poetry," *PoT* 5 (1984); J. Finkin, "Markish, Trakl, and the Temporaesthetic," *Modernism/Modernity* 15 (2008).

■ **Criticism, Senses and Movements:** J. Millet, *Audition colorée* (1892); V. Ségalen, "Les synesthésies et l'école symboliste," *Mercure de France* 42 (1902); I. Babbitt, *The New Laokoön* (1910)—attacks synaesthesia as decadent; E. von Erhardt-Siebold, "Synäksthesien in der englischen Dichtung des 19. Jahrhunderts,"

Englische Studien 53 (1919–20); A. Argelander, *Das Farbenhören und der synästhetische Faktor der Wahrnehmung* (1927); E. von Erhardt-Siebold, "Harmony of the Senses in English, German, and French Romanticism," *PMLA* 47 (1932); S. de Ullmann, "Romanticism and Synaesthesia," *PMLA* 60 (1945); A. H. Whitney, "Synaesthesia in Twentieth-Century Hungarian Poetry," *Slavonic and East European Review* 30 (1952); K. Mautz, "Dir Farbensprache der expressionistischen Lyrik," *Deutsche Vierteljahrschrift für Literaturwissenschaft und Geistesgeschichte* 31 (1957); M. Chastaing, "Audition colorée," *Vie et langage* 105, 112 (1960, 1961); F. Meltzer, "Color Cognition in Symbolist Verse," *CritI* 5 (1978).

T.V.F. Brogan; A. G. Engstrom; J. Finkin

SYNCOPE (Gr., "a cutting up"). The omission of a letter, syllable, or a sound from the middle of a word, related to aphaeresis (initial omission) or apocope (final omission). Punctuation is often used ("e'er" for "ever," "giv'n" for "given") to indicate syncope. Shakespeare's double syncope of "overtaken" removes excess syllables and exposes a rhyme: "She might have been o'erta'en; and yet she writes, / Pursuit would be but vain" (*All's Well That Ends Well*, 3.4). It may be used solely to approximate the sounds of speech. Paul Laurence Dunbar's "A Warm Day in Winter" offers both: "Missis gone a-drivin', / Mastah gone to shoot; / Ev'ry da'ky lazin' / In de sun to boot," where "Ev'ry" is shortened for either metrical rhythm or speed of dialect, but "da'ky" (for "darky") is strictly dialect.

See ELISION.

K. McFadden

SYNECDOCHE (Gr., "act of taking together," "understanding one thing with another"). A *trope (change of meaning) in which part is substituted for whole (hired "hands" for hired men); species for genus (live by the "sword" for weapons) or vice versa; or individual for group (the "Romans" won for the Roman army). Lausberg and Group μ, discussed below, would limit synecdoche to these types. In cl. rhet., synecdoche also includes material for the object made of it ("steel" for sword) and abstract quality for its possessor ("pride" for the person displaying it).

In 20th-c. attempts to organize the terminology inherited from rhet., one group of critics held that there are four basic tropes, and another claimed that there are only two. For discussion of these views, see METAPHOR and METONYMY. Definitions of synecdoche and metonymy have always overlapped. Both entail a material, factual, or conceptual connection to the literal meaning evoked. Genette and Eco show that the name of the trope can depend on how the example is interpreted.

Ruwet and Le Guern argue that most examples of synecdoche are not figurative: they either are part of ordinary usage or can be understood literally. The use of "tree" or "oak" for oak tree or "weapon" for pistol need not be considered synecdoche since the generic name can be applied literally to the species. Linguists find that purported instances of synecdoche often result from *ellipsis—deletion of a phrase that, if included, would be redundant. "A herd of thirty head" does not require "of cattle." "The animal that laughs" (man) and "the gods of blood and salt" (Mars and Neptune) can be classified as *periphrasis rather than as synecdoche with qualification. Thus, synecdoche can often be viewed as a stylistic phenomenon, its effect being dependent on whether it is expected in its context (Klinkenberg).

Todorov and Group μ reawakened interest in synecdoche with their claim that it is the fundamental figure, based on an increase or decrease of a word's semes (lexical features), from which metaphor and metonymy are derived. They found four possible changes of meaning in synecdoche: generalizing or particularizing, and material (part-whole) or conceptual (species-genus). "The enemy," meaning the enemies, is particularizing; the cl. example of part for whole is "sail" for ship; "mortal" for man is species for the genus.

Attempting to draw a clear distinction between metonymy and synecdoche, Sato and Seto suggest that synecdoche be limited to semantic or conceptual relations, with all material connections, such as part–whole, being assigned to metonymy. Meyer (1985) would limit the latter to contextual or accidental connections, synecdoche being a more abstract relation. Others see synecdoche as a figure of integration, metonymy representing fragmentation or reduction. Each of these views has something to recommend it, but evidence and logic do not show that any of them is correct. In popular usage and handbooks, "metonymy" usually includes all tropes that have been called synecdoche. This is especially true in ling. and fields such as conceptual metaphor theory and cognitive ling.

Synecdoche does remain important in one area of literary study. Like Burke, practitioners of New Historicism show how lit. and life produce events representing the social structure as a whole. Burke's examples of the importance of synecdoche range from the traditional idea of microcosm and macrocosm to crucial issues of political representation. A character named Synecdoche in a Restoration play says, "By me a single Monarch makes himself a multitude . . . a whole Kingdome fits in Parliament at once." By the absolute ruler, as Thomas Hobbes said, "a multitude of men are made one person" (Christiansen, Baldo). Further examples of such representations appear in studies of synecdoche in Shakespeare's plays. The trope remains important in both sociology and anthropology (Parsons, Fernandez). Attempts to assign part-whole and species-genus relations to either metonymy or synecdoche eliminate the crucial space of their interaction, which is ideology. This is clear in anthropological studies, where synecdoche mediates between groups in the social structure and the species and genera found in nature. Analogous situations appear today. Synecdoche has become a crucial trope in arguments between environmentalists and commercial interests (Moore). Often appearing as a particular example representing the norm or ideal of the genus, synecdoche remains important in poetics, rhet., and other disciplines.

■ K. Burke, "Four Master Tropes," *A Grammar of Motives* (1945); T. Todorov, "Synecdoques," *Communications* 16 (1970); M. Le Guern, *Sémantique de la métaphore et de la métonymie* (1973); N. Ruwet, "Synecdoques et métonymies," *Poétique* 6 (1975); A. Parsons, "Interpretive Sociology," *Human Studies* 1 (1978); N. Sato, "Synecdoque, un trope suspect," *Revue d'esthétique* 1 (1979); B. Meyer, "Synecdoques du genre?" *Poétique* 57 (1980); Group μ; G. Genette, "Rhetoric Restrained," *Figures of Literary Discourse*, trans. A. Sheridan, 2d ed. (1982); J. Klinkenberg, D. Bouverot, B. Meyer, G. Silingardi, J.-P. Schmitz in *Le Français moderne* 51 (1983); B. Meyer, "La synecdoque d'espèce," *Langues et Littératures* 3 (1983); U. Eco, "Metaphor, Dictionary, and Encyclopedia," *NLH* 15 (1984); B. Meyer, "Sous les pavés, la plage: Autour de la synecdoque du tout," *Poétique* 62 (1985); *Beyond Metaphor*, ed. J. Fernandez (1991); M. Moore, "Constructing Irreconcilable Conflict," *Communication Monographs* 60 (1993); J. Baldo, "Ophelia's Rhetoric, or Partial to Synecdoche," *Criticism* 37 (1995);

Lausberg; K. Seto, "Distinguishing Metonymy from Synecdoche," *Metonymy in Language and Thought*, ed. K.-U. Panther and G. Radden (1999); N. Christiansen, "Synecdoche, Tropic Violence and Shakespeare's *Imitatio* in *Titus Andronicus*," *Style* 34 (2000); K. Acheson, "Hamlet, Synecdoche and History," *College Literature* 31 (2004).

W. MARTIN

SYNTAX, POETIC (Gr., *syntaxis*, "a putting together in order"). All oral and written lang. uses that fall under culturally specific definitions of poetry have *syntax*, if that term is defined as a meaning-making arrangement of words in a sequence. But not all poetries, oral or written, are distinguished from other discourses in ways that would allow us to say that they have poetic syntax, as opposed to syntax in general; nor is there scholarly consensus about what that former (poetic syntax) phrase might mean across different times, places, and langs. Mod. linguists have, for instance, noted parallels among ancient Gr., Ar., and Indian (Sanskrit) concepts of the *proposition* or *sentence*, a unit that Aristotle defined in his *Rhetoric* as expressing a "complete" thought and that has been foundational to many theories of syntax. But cross-cultural generalizations about syntax are difficult: problems of trans. arise not only between what linguists call *natural* langs. but also between competing professional metalanguages for describing syntactic features in relation to sometimes overlapping ones assigned to related areas such as grammar, morphology, phonemics, semantics, and rhetoric, with its many rules aimed at classifying and controlling the use of *tropes. Tropes in some taxonomic systems include a specific category of syntactic figures (figures of speech) recognized as such by virtue of their alleged deviation from what is thought to be ordinary or normal lang. use.

As a term that denotes both an object and a field of study, *syntax* has been decisively marked by the origins of the word itself in ancient Greece. The earliest uses of *syntaxis* have to do not with words or mathematical symbols but with soldiers. But many scholars have seen issues of hierarchy, governance, and obedience as no less critical to the workings of ling. syntax than they are to the workings of armies and of the societies that armies are thought to serve. Deutscher compares sentences to military maneuvers; in both, "chaos would prevail" without a chain of command subordinating some elements to others through rules that can be specified.

Metaphysically and socially charged debates about order are at the center of a Greco-Eur.-Eng. trad. of thinking about syntax in relation to poetry, a trad. that this article constructs provisionally and, of necessity, by relying in part on a terminology for syntax that some mod. theorists have critiqued as fundamentally inadequate to the understanding of ling. phenomena. The critiques come chiefly from those associated with the structuralist movement in ling. led by Ferdinand de Saussure; this movement turns away—in conjunction with similar turns in many areas of modernist thought—from a mimetic or "substantialist" theory of lang. inscribed into the very notion of the noun as a "substantive." Structuralism directs us to a view of lang. as a fluid system constituted by differential relations among various elements. Acknowledging the philosophical problems in the substantialist trad. but acknowledging at the same time the continuing importance of that trad. for those who write, read, recite, hear, and reflect on poetry, this entry attempts a dialectical approach to the topic. The differential relations of "poetic syntax" are here considered as arising not only from a system of discourse that can be analyzed synchronically in terms of key binary oppositions (between "ordinary" and "extraordinary" word order, or poetry and prose, or poetry and science, or poetry and "not poetry"); the relations also arise along vectors of time, space, and trans. among some of the world's more than 6,000 (now extant) langs. We cannot know in how many of these langs. "syntax" and "poetry" exist as loci of historical influence, current practice, and reflection. The present entry assumes that what linguists call a "natural" lang. is not a unified entity; differently positioned and differently educated practitioners within a certain lang. field have construed and indeed encountered poetic syntax differently.

In the Greco-Eur.-Eng. trad. discussed here, "appropriate" syntactic arrangements have typically been seen as imitating an order given by nature or by logic. The latter is sometimes conceived as a subset of the former, but sometimes these two key strands of a "mimetic" trad. diverge, with interesting consequences for views of syntax (see MIMESIS). Those who see syntax primarily as reflecting an external reality have tended to focus on an *iconic* dimension of syntax, i.e., on ways in which the placement of words, phrases, clauses, and other units can be interpreted as imitating—and indeed as being determined by—a real sequence of events in "Nature" or in hist. Deutscher invokes Caesar's famous series of parallel clauses, *veni, vidi, vici* (I came, I saw, I conquered), to illustrate the principle that "the order in which events are expressed in language mirrors the order in which they occur in reality." (For Deutscher, it is only a joke, not a threat to Caesar's principle, that the first clause, in Lat. or in Eng., has a bawdy figurative meaning that allows the premise of a single natural order to expand into nine possibilities for ostensibly mimetic clause arrangement.)

A second major mimetic principle of syntax has been adduced—also debatably—to explain why grammatical subjects precede verbs and objects in a "majority" of the world's langs. (Dirven and Verspoor, Deutscher). A natural hierarchy in which the human actor and particularly the self are of supreme importance is said to be recognized by "most" speakers' preferences for arrangements in which the subject precedes the verb and object; linguists writing in Eng. term these SVO or SOV patterns and find them predominating in all but a handful of langs. Deutcher mentions Welsh, biblical Heb., and Maori as exceptions to this rule of (human) subject-first. But many other exceptions can be and have been adduced in ways that do not accept the premise of exceptionality. Some scholars of written Ar. consider a "verb-subject-object" pattern typical, for instance, while other scholars see case endings as more important than word order for understanding this lang. Peled observes that, among students of written Ar., sentence types and word order have been a focus for debate since med. times. Inflected langs. such as Lat., Ger., and Gr. do not exhibit a clear tendency toward subject-first syntactic arrangements in declarative sentences, at least if one considers the partial evidence about lang. use provided by the written record. A sentence pattern that puts the "object" or predicate first, followed by a subject and verb—which may well be expressed in one rather than two words—is clearly familiar to poets working in many langs.; it was known to poets writing in Eng. for centuries from their grammar-school study of Lat. classics, incl. Virgil's *Aeneid*, which begins, "Arma virumque cano" (arms and the man I sing). We need not accept foundationalist claims for the relation between syntax and the world to recognize that

many poets have experimented with syntactic patterns in ways that might be called "mimetic" but that might also be called "thematic": interpreters have found syntactic patterns mimicking both natural spaces (dells, for instance) and culturally charged objects (Christ's cross can be evoked by a "chiastic" pattern in a line or couplet; see CHIASMUS).

Poetic theories and practices also cluster around a second major strand of thought about mimetic syntax that stretches back to the ancient Greeks: this is the theory that sees syntax "following" logic or reason (the Gr. term *logos*, which becomes central to Christian theological discourses). On this view, syntax illuminates the workings of a rational order assumed to precede lang. and to have universal qualities. Although this line of thought is sometimes expressed as a corollary to the first, the two strands of the mimetic theory at times diverge in consequential ways. Both Land and Cohen have traced one historical instance of divergence in 17th- and 18th-c. Eng. writing about lang., a movement from a "grammar of things" focused on relations among signs and their referents to a "grammar of the mind" focused on "bundles" of words and on those parts of speech that have no obvious analogues in the world. John Locke illustrates this tendency in his *Essay Concerning Human Understanding* (1690), which holds that knowledge "consists in propositions." For Locke, as for the Port-Royal group of lang. philosophers in 17th-c. Paris, the verb takes priority over the noun because it is seen as critical to acts of judgment; moreover, there is a marked interest in the "syntax of connectives" (Cohen). Locke argues that the humble particle has been unjustly neglected; he approaches syntactic relations as windows into the way in which the mind pursues "connexion, restriction, distinction, opposition, emphasis, etc." (*Essay* 3.7.2). A number of scholars have found a significant correlation between such a philosophical view of syntax and features of neoclassical poetry, particularly the use of parallel and antithetical clauses in the rhymed *couplets of John Dryden, Jean Racine, Pierre Corneille, and Alexander Pope.

For the major strands of Occidental speculation that conceive of syntax as imitating a corresponding order of reality, tropes are anomalous; paradoxically, they are also typical of poetry perceived as a form of discourse granted "license" to deviate from ordinary lang. "Aside from figurative speech," as Chomsky states the central idea of the Port-Royal grammarians, "the sequence of words follows an 'ordre naturel,' which conforms "à l'expression naturelle de nos pensées' [to the natural expression of our thoughts]." It can be argued, however, that poetic syntax, which stresses questions of figurative lang., is constitutive of, rather than marginal to, syntax as an object of multicultural knowledge with Gr. roots. This is so partly because theorists from Aristotle on define the basic units of syntax as phenomena that, when correctly performed in speech or writing, reflect reality in ways that reveal both completeness of thought (*dianoia*) and elegance of expression (*lexis,* sometimes trans. as *"diction"). Moreover, as Basset has shown, when Aristotle discusses syntactic units such as the *colon or the period in terms of such qualities as elegance and completeness, it is hard to know whether he is judging such units for their rhythmic, grammatical, or logical properties, or for a combination of these in which "appropriateness" of tropes plays a role.

By the 1st c. BCE, *syntaxis* began to be used by Gr. grammarians and philosophers in ways that encompassed discussions of "parts" of speech and relations of "agreement" among forms of words signaling such concepts as gender, tense, mood, number, and grammatical case. The first extant Gr. treatise on syntax, *Peri Syntaxeôs* (2d c. CE), sees syntactic irregularities as corruptions of a rule that reflects reason and that can be traced back to a pristine natural past. Written by Apollonios Dyskolos (the "surly"), who worked as a teacher of grammar in Alexandria, the treatise analyzes examples of "ungrammaticality" (*akatallēlia*) drawn both from ordinary usage and from poetry, esp. the Homeric epics. As Blank shows, Apollonios oscillates between correcting errors and explaining them (away) when they occur in Homer. Deeply influenced by Stoic logic, which distinguished between "complete" and "deficient" propositions and which saw the former as demonstrating an ethical ideal of self-sufficiency (*autoteleia*), Apollonios repeatedly discusses syntactic issues by contrasting arrangements of words that are morphologically, syntactically, and semantically akin.

The subject of syntax as Apollonios constructs it is dependent on comparative judgments; it becomes even more complexly comparative when Gr. discourses on syntax are appropriated by Roman poets and educators and, subsequently, by later Eur. and Eng. writers

extensively educated in Lat. grammar, poetry, and rhet. In treatises that variously transliterate the Gr. word *syntaxis* into Roman letters or render it in the Lat. words *constructio, dispositio,* or *ordinatio,* the subject of syntax retains its focus on the illustration and discussion of errors in lang., whether these occur in single words or in larger signifying units. Though the names for these errors are legion and the category distinctions among them are often perplexing—esp. as the examples begin to appear in both Gr. and Lat. forms—there is considerable continuity in this discursive trad. focused on right and wrong syntax. The trad. mingles poetical examples with pedagogical and philosophical precepts. Priscian, whose influential 6th-c. CE discussion of syntax in the final two books of his *Institutionem Grammaticorum* appropriates many points from Apollonios, repeatedly asks his readers "whether a phrase is right or wrong" ("recta sit an non," 17:14). Priscian's analysis of "irregularities" (*incongruae* or *inconcinnae*), however, conceives lang. as a phenomenon with a past. This may complicate present judgments of correct usage. Priscian cites many poetic lines illustrating "uncommon" usages that are, he acknowledges, "preferred by old communities" (2:122). His use of ancient Gr. examples along with his awareness of ling. "preferences" among old Lat.-speaking communities highlights how hist. impinges on a theory or practice of syntax considered primarily as a set of rules.

Moreover, Priscian's *Institutio* contributes to a continuing question about the place of syntax in a course of study: is it a subset of grammar, as Joseph Aiken indicated in his *British Grammar* (1693), where the subject is divided into orthography, prosody, etymology, and syntax? Or is syntax a step above grammar in a hierarchy that points further up toward the study of poetry or *bonae literae* (good letters, a humanist ideal) in Lat. and in those vernacular langs. lexically and syntactically indebted to Lat.? In many 16th-c. Eng. grammar schools, syntax was studied by boys in the third form after basic Lat. grammar and before poetry approached as a matter to be translated from Lat. to Eng. and back again. According to the *OED,* as late as the 19th c., the term *syntax* denoted a school subject below poetry and above grammar.

Wherever syntax is placed in school curricula, it has often been viewed as a surly and difficult subject. This perception derives in part from the fact that syntactic analysis requires a historical education in several taxonomic schemes and in multilingual terminologies for rhetorical tropes involving varying perceptions of "transgressive" behavior in the construction of sentences. The figure of *hyperbaton, for instance, denoting "various forms of departure from ordinary word order" (Lanham), is called *transgressio* in Lat. and "the trespasser" by George Puttenham in *The Arte of English Poesie* (1589). Despite or perhaps because of the fact that there is no stable or single concept of ordinary (or common or natural) syntax that crosses from Gr. to Lat. to the Eur. vernaculars, the notion of difficult syntax—as a written and later a printed phenomenon that members of an educated elite can appreciate as something different from "vulgar" speech—has been valued by writers such as Torquato Tasso, Giovanni della Casa, Luis de Góngora, Sor Juana Inés de la Cruz, Maurice Scève, and John Milton, as well as by mod. poets such as Stéphane Mallarmé, Giuseppe Ungaretti, R. M. Rilke, e. e. cummings, and Ezra Pound. Different instances of a poetic syntax designed to deviate conspicuously from vernacular usages may, of course, refract quite different political and philosophical views about ordinary lang. and the people who are thought to speak it.

In his *Institutio oratoria* (1st c. CE), Quintilian suggests that a "difficult" style might appropriately be described as "Virgilian" or even as "rhythmical"—the latter quality presented in a way that admits of no clear division between admirable poetry and artistically crafted prose. The best way we have of making our speech (*sermonem*) rhythmical (*numerosum*), writes Quintilian, is by "opportune change[s] of [word] order" (8.6. 64–65). Such changes clearly raise questions about the appropriate limits of poetic license both for the writer and the reader. Quintilian avers that "language would very often be rough, harsh, limp, or disjointed if the words were constrained as their natural order demands" (*si ad necessitate ordinis sui verba redigantur*; 8.6.62); however, he also insists that the freedom exhibited in hyperbaton and related syntactic figures would not be allowed in *oratio* (rendered as "prose" by one Eng. translator at 8.6.66). *Oratio*, however, can also be translated as "speech," and Quintilian in the same passage praises Plato for trying out many different patterns of word order in his prose sentences (8.6.64). Worrying that errors may arise from *hyperbata* that are too long, Quintilian does not say exactly how long is too long; nor does he distinguish clearly between

aesthetic and moral dimensions of appropriate and inappropriate syntax. Finally, he relies on tropes to explain what counts as "good" syntax: "Words," he writes, are to be "moved from one place to another so as to join where they fit best, just as, in constructions made of unhewn stones, the irregularity itself (*ipsa enormitas*) suggests the right stones which each piece can fit or rest upon" (9.4.27).

Many poems in various langs. create effects of "irregularity" in ways that call attention to poetic form while asking the reader or listener to reflect on what often began as his or her subconscious knowledge of verbal regularity in a given lang. Such calling attention to the medium is central to what Jakobson defines as the poetic function of lang. The writer's or linguist's or literary critic's educated perspective on what constitutes regular and irregular patterns in a given evidentiary field makes poetic syntax into an object of study but seldom warrants generalizations about it across cultures. An exception might be in those cases where we can hypothesize a foreign influence on an Eng. poetic construction that can be observed in numerous examples from a certain era. An example is the "absolute participial" construction that occurs with some frequency in med. and early mod. Eng. lit.—in this line of *Hamlet*, for instance: "The passion ending, doth the purpose lose" (3.2.185). Some linguists have explained the apparent irregularity of this line—what is its grammatical subject and how does that "agree" with the verb form?—as a sign of the significant influence of Lat. or Fr. syntax on Eng. poetry.

In a famous letter, John Keats deplored the "gallicisms" of Chaucer's poetry and found Milton's *Paradise Lost* a "corruption" of the Eng. lang. But Keats himself had been criticized for "bad" writing, and many of his lines imitate Milton's in syntax and diction. For poets and their interpreters, the distinction between proper and improper usages is fluid and usually open to testing, as is the distinction between native and foreign. Inversions of word order, so critical to Quintilian's understanding of what makes an admirable high style like Virgil's, occur as often in Pope's poetry as in Milton's, according to Brogan; and such "inversions" also occur in poems by those who explicitly reject a high style. S. T. Coleridge described one of his conversation poems, for instance—"Reflections on Having Left a Place of Retirement"—as a "poem which affects not to be Poetry"; he elaborates the paradox in that phrase with his first line, which conspicuously departs from what many feel is the usual word order of Eng.: "Low was our pretty Cot!" In versions printed after 1797, moreover, Coleridge's poem begins with a Lat. epigraph: "Sermoni propriora." Charles Lamb jokingly translated this as "properer for a sermon," whereas others—more seriously but not necessarily more correctly—have rendered it "more suitable for conversation/prose." The adjective in its original context, however (Horace's Satire 4) is spelled differently: *propiora*, which is usually translated into Eng. as "nearer." Coleridge plays with the meaning of the Eng. word *proper* as "one's own." Is a low style, nearer to prose, more properly Eng. than a high style? Like many other poets, Coleridge poses the question without providing a definitive answer.

As this story of trans. indicates, matters of poetic syntax invite analysis in relation to other aspects of a poem or the culture where it was produced and where it continues to be interpreted. Chomsky proclaimed the existence of an "autonomous syntax principle" and of a phenomenon he named ling. "competence" and defined as an "innate" knowledge of syntactic and grammatical rules possessed by every speaker of a natural lang. His theory, frequently revised, is important because it calls attention to the issue of constraints on syntax without moralizing them—but also without considering them in relation to educational institutions or to the entire domain of what Chomsky called "performance" and defined as a set of specific utterances produced by *native* speakers. Chomsky's "performance," which some critics have allied with Saussure's "parole," is conceived without reference to the institution of the theater or to some cultures' trads. of oral poetic performances. For poetic syntax considered in a comparative context, there is no "autonomous" principle of syntax, ontological or hermeneutic. There is, however, a useful heuristic notion (also a spatial metaphor) proffered by structuralist theorists in the 20th c.: the notion of the "syntagmatic" and "paradigmatic" axes of lang. Formulated by Saussure for the field of semiotics and elaborated for poetry by Jakobson, Jameson, Silverman, Culler, and others, this interpretive schema relies on Gr. terms but departs from Gr. presuppositions concerning syntax as mimesis and tropes as instances of both culpable and admirable erring. The notion of the two axes—often visually represented as a horizontal (syntagmatic) line crossed by numerous vertical (paradigmatic) ones—allows

Saussure to explain how ling. meaning arises from two kinds of difference: that which we might provisionally see as occurring in a syntactic unit (a clause or a sentence) as extended in the time of speech or the space/time of the text; and that which arises in the reader's or hearer's mind from the relations between a sign and other elements in its "system." The vertical axis, which Saussure called "associative," works with the syntagmatic axis to create sequences of various degrees of complexity. The paradigmatic axis may include case endings or parts of speech other than the ones actualized in the words of a given sentence or clause; the paradigmatic axis is more commonly thought of as "supplying" the missing terms of a *metaphor or alternate sounds or letters of a rhyme or a pun. Any word, *line, couplet, or *stanza of poetry can be analyzed with reference to these axes, with syntactic elements now construed as aspects of lang. working in concert (via forms of *parallelism incl. tropes such as *isocolon) but also in tension with other elements of the poetic line and/or with other signifying units.

Many syntactic units are, of course, smaller or larger than the sentence; and many poets have worked against as well as with the traditional idea, inherited from Aristotle and the Stoics in many elegantly circular forms, that a *proper* sentence or clause "reflects" a *complete* thought. One could indeed say that the enigmatic idea of a proper sentence (as memory or expectation or pedagogical rule) exists on the paradigmatic axis created jointly by many Eng. poems and their readers and hearers; consider, for instance Pound's "In a Station of the Metro," which consists of two syntagms (incl. the title) that traditional Western grammarians would call *sentence fragments*. Inspired in part by Japanese and Chinese poems, Pound uses the fragment to present a new reality; in one of his manifestos for imagism, he contrasts poetic "presenting" with painterly "describing" ("A Retrospect," 1913). But his fragment poem relies on the reader's knowledge of what counts as a complete sentence, as do many poems that delay a main verb in long invocations of a muse who figures inspiration.

An approach to poetic syntax that is at once structuralist (synchronic) and historical (diachronic) is difficult, as Jameson observes in his *Prison-House of Language* (1972); but attempting it allows us to construct a paradigmatic axis that extends over time and space to encompass a recurring contrast between theories and practices of "difficult" syntax and those devoted to a style that aspires to plainness and that presents features of colloquial, even dialectal, speech, the vulgar or "mother" tongue (see PLAIN STYLE). Under a different figure, this is what William Wordsworth, in the Preface to the 2d ed. of *Lyrical Ballads* (1800), called lang. "really spoken by men." But which lang. is that? And does it exist except as it has been historically (re)constructed in relation to a poetic lang. marked by "irregularities" such as *elision and inverted word order?

Elision and inversion are perennially interesting and conceptually difficult for a comparative approach to poetic syntax or to syntax in general. Lacking evidence of normal speech patterns for many past cultures and some present ones, we cannot securely distinguish between approved omissions of words (elisions) and ones that are classified as errors (*vitia*) in the Occidental written record, often under such Gr. terms as *barbarism* and *solecism*. Like children, foreigners, and jokesters, poets often use lang. in ways that have been deemed transgressive; but for past cultures, even in the West, we do not know who would have judged a transgression playful, enigmatic (because the sign of textual corruption), or inept. Some forms of elision have been named, noticed, and generally approved as achieving effects of wit. Elision combines with complex figuration in *zeugma or syllepsis: consider, e.g., Pope's famous couplet comparing, contrasting, and compressing the idiomatic Eng. phrases "take counsel" and "take tea" (*The Rape of the Lock*, 1714). Other forms of elision arise from syntactic arrangements extending over many lines and often creating instances of double syntax: a syntagm that starts by inviting one interpretation but grows to invite a second reading that conceptually revises the first; see, e.g., the first four lines of cummings's "since feeling is first" or the transition between stanzas 3 and 4 of Emily Dickinson's "A bird came down the walk" (Empson, Ferguson). Elisions of main-clause verbs in Eng. and Am. poetry have sometimes accompanied semantic inquiries into domination and subordination, disobedience and obedience to rules, and the relation of parts to putative wholes. An example is W. C. Williams's "The Young Sycamore," which uses ambiguous syntax to explore whether a sapling is an independent entity or is not (yet). The rhetorical figures of anapodoton (omitting a main clause from a conditional sentence) and

aposiopesis (breaking off suddenly in the middle of speaking) are important to poems that explore and dramatize relations between syntax and a fictional speaker's emotional states; Virgil, for instance, illustrates the sea god Neptune's anger—and his ability to control it—in a famous aposiopesis in the *Aeneid*: "quos ego—! sed motos praestat componere fluctus" (whom I—! But better it is to calm the troubled waves [1.135]). Milton combines anapodoton and aposiopesis in Satan's opening address to Beelzebub in *Paradise Lost* ("If thou beest he; But oh how falln, how changed / From him . . .). The initial subordinate conditional clause breaks off, and Satan (as represented by the narrator) seems to forget his conventional obligation to complete his thought with a main clause.

Like Milton's Satan, many poets have conspicuously failed to obey the rules of the "well-formed" sentence, and sometimes they have done so by following the incompletely codified and imperfectly translated rules of tropes. Sometimes, however, poets transgress in ways that strain even the cl. notion of poetic license, which relies on hypotheses about the poet's intention and about the poem's ultimate intelligibility. In "Adonais" (51–53), P. B. Shelley, for instance, often writes sentences that are "almost impenetrable" (Austin 1993):

> Thy extreme hope, the loveliest and the last,
> The bloom, whose petals nipped before they blew
> Died on the promise of the fruit, is waste.

What rules of (Eng.) syntax is Shelley breaking or bending here? How are historically variable conventions of printing and punctuation (here, the absence of the expected "closing" comma after "blew") implicated in our perceptions of what is and is not an intelligible sentence? Shelley's sentence appears to illustrate Chomsky's argument that a "well-formed" sentence, one operating correctly by a recursive rule of sentence formation, may nonetheless be "unacceptable." Indeed, Shelley's sentence appears to illustrate the phenomenon of "center-embedding" that Chomsky uses to explain the distinction between grammaticality and acceptability; an example is "The man who the boys who the students recognized pointed out is a friend of mine." Such a sentence fails to be acceptable to an Eng. speaker, Chomsky suggests, because of a problem in the domain of performance, not competence. In MacCabe's paraphrase of Chomsky, "the body is simply unable to store the necessary bits of information to decode the sentence although it does have the necessary decoding mechanisms." Shelley's lines, however, like the prose passage by James Joyce that MacCabe analyzes to show "center-embedding" at work, challenge us to think recursively, testing the human memory encountering something like a sentence in the medium of print. Shelley's lines counter common assumptions about lang. as communication while suggesting the social value of puzzles and *riddles, traditionally close kin to certain experiments in extreme syntax.

Poetic syntax, like unmodified syntax, has seemed a surly subject to many school children taught to attend to lang. through syntactic categories. But poets shaped by multilingual educational theories and practices have been in constant conversation with philosophers, teachers, and linguists on the question of what is a proper sentence—in the senses both of being correct and of belonging to one's own ling. trad. Chomsky generated a mod. chapter in this conversation when, in his *Syntactic Structures* (1957), he gave an example of a syntactically correct sentence that is "unacceptable" because it makes no sense: "Colorless green ideas sleep furiously." A number of writers, incl. Chinese linguist Yuen Ren Chao and Am. poets John Hollander and Clive James, have contested Chomsky's point by using figuration and recontextualization to make his string of words legible after all, if not necessarily on first glance. In so doing, such writers participate in a long-enduring and multicultural game that exploits the resources of syntax and tropes—the "colors" of rhet.—to test the boundaries between sense and nonsense, figurative and proper meanings, practices and theories of lang., and last but not least, between prose and poetry. Hollander's poem makes Chomsky's sentence into a subordinate clause in a larger syntactic unit titled "Coiled Alizarine." The title serves as an apt concluding emblem for the transformational powers of poetic syntax. "Coiled" like a snake, with the potential for fuller extensions in the future, poetic syntax has metamorphic powers like those of alizarine: an organic dye used in the past, and still used today, to change the colors of various paints and inks.

See ELLIPSIS, HYPOTAXIS AND PARATAXIS.

■ E. Pound, "A Few Don'ts by an Imagiste," *Poetry* 1 (1913); and *ABC of Reading* (1934); F. T. Prince, *The Italian Element in Milton's Verse* (1953); Empson; D. Davie, *Articulate Energy* (1955); J. Miles, *Eras and Modes in English Poetry* (1957); C. Brooke-Rose, *A Grammar of Metaphor* (1958); F. Perry, *Poet's Grammar* (1958); E. Wasserman, *The Subtler Language* (1959); S. Levin, *Linguistic Structures in Poetry* (1962); W. Nowottny, *The Language Poets Use* (1962); C. Ricks, *Milton's Grand Style* (1963); N. Chomsky, *Aspects of a Theory of Syntax* (1965); R. Levin, "Internal and External Deviation in Poetry," *Word* 21 (1965); F. T. Visser, *An Historical Syntax of the English Language* (1966); W. Baker, *Syntax in English Poetry, 1879–1930* (1967); W. N. Francis, "Syntax and Literary Interpretation," *Essays in the Language of Literature*, ed. S. Chatman and S. Levin (1967); J.-C. Chevalier, *Histoire de la syntaxe . . . (1530–1750)* (1968); B. H. Smith, *Poetic Closure* (1968); R. Mitchell, "Toward a System of Grammatical Scansion," *Lang&S* 3 (1970); I. Michael, *English Grammatical Categories and the Tradition to 1800* (1971); F. Jameson, *Prison-House of Language* (1972); J. M. Sinclair, "Lines and 'Lines,'" *Current Trends in Stylistics*, ed. B. Kachru and H.F.W. Stahlke (1972); J. S. Borck, "Blake's 'The Lamb': The Punctuation of Innocence," *TSL* 19 (1974); S. K. Land, *From Signs to Propositions* (1974); Culler; G. Dillon, "Inversions and Deletions in English Poetry," *Lang&S* 8 (1975); and "Literary Transformations and Poetic Word Order," *Poetics* 5 (1976); I. Fairley, *E. E. Cummings and Ungrammar* (1975); D. C. Freeman, "Iconic Syntax in Poetry: A Note on Blake's 'Ah! Sun-Flower,'" *University of Massachusetts Occasional Papers in Linguistics* 2 (1976); J. M. Lipski, "Poetic Deviance and Generative Grammar," *PTL* 2 (1977); J. M. Lotman, *The Structure of the Artistic Text*, trans. G. Lenhoff and R. Vroon (1977); E. Kintgen, "Perceiving Poetic Syntax," *CE* 40 (1978); M. Borroff, *The Language and the Poet* (1979); M. Cohen, *Sensible Words: Linguistic Practice in England, 1640–1785* (1979); R. Cureton, "e. e. cummings: A Study of the Poetic Use of Deviant Morphology," *PoT* 1 (1979); H. Golomb, *Enjambment in Poetry* (1979); D. Simpson, *Irony and Authority in Romantic Poetry* (1979); R. Cureton, "'He danced his did': An Analysis," *JL* 16 (1980); and "Poetic Syntax and Aesthetic Form," *Style* 14 (1980); Brogan; R. Cureton, "e. e. cummings: A Case Study of Iconic Syntax," *Lang&S* 14 (1981); R. Jakobson, "The Poetry of Grammar and Grammar of Poetry," Jakobson, v. 3; J. Moulton and G. M. Robinson, *The Organization of Language* (1981); G. Roscow, *Syntax and Style in Chaucer's*

Poetry (1981); D. Blank, *Ancient Philosophy and Grammar* (1982); A. Easthope, *Poetry as Discourse* (1983); K. Silverman, *The Subject of Semiotics* (1983); M. Sirridge, "Socrates' Hood: Lexical Meaning and Syntax in Jordanus and Kilwardby," *Cahiers de l'Institut du Moyen-Âge Grec et Latin* 44 (1983); T. R. Austin, *Language Crafted* (1984); V. Bers, *Greek Poetic Syntax in the Classical Age* (1984); D. Donoghue, *Style in Old English Poetry* (1984); M. Tarlinskaja, "Rhythm–morphology–syntax–rhythm," *Style* 18 (1984); R. Cureton, "Poetry, Grammar, and Epistemology: The Order of Prenominal Modifiers in the Poetry of e. e. cummings," *Lang&S* 18 (1985); M.A.K. Halliday, *An Introduction to Functional Grammar* (1985); R. Hasan, *Linguistics, Language, and Verbal Art* (1985); Hollander; C. Miller, *Emily Dickinson: A Poet's Grammar* (1987); J. P. Houston, *Shakespearean Sentences* (1988); A. Kaster, *Guardians of Language* (1988); R. M. Baratin, *La naissance de la syntaxe à Rome* (1989); H. Pinkster, *Latin Syntax and Semantics* (1990); D. Lateiner, "Mimetic Syntax: Metaphor from Word Order, Especially in Ovid," *AJP* 3 (1990); Lanham; R. Cureton, *Rhythmic Phrasing in English Verse* (1992); T. R. Austin, "Syntax, Poetic," *The New Princeton Encyclopedia of Poetry and Poetics*, ed. A. Preminger and T.V.F. Brogan (1993); R. Cureton, "Poetry, Language, and Literary Study: The Unfinished Tasks of Stylistics," *Language and Literature* 21 (1996); T. J. Taylor and M. Toolan, "Recent Trends in Stylistics," *The Stylistics Reader*, ed. J. J. Weber (1996); R. Cureton, "Linguistics, Stylistics, and Poetics," *Language and Literature* 22 (1997), and "Toward a Temporal Theory of Language," *Journal of English Linguistics* 25 (1997); F. J. Newmeyer, *Language Form and Language Function* (1998); M. Collins, "On Syntax in Poetry," *Field* (1999); R. Dirven and M. Verspoor, *Cognitive Explorations in Language and Linguistics* (1999); R. Cribiore, *Gymnastics of the Mind* (2001); M. De Grazia, "Shakespeare and the Craft of Language," *The Cambridge Companion to Shakespeare*, ed. M. de Grazia and S. Wells (2001); *Cambridge Grammar of the English Language*, ed. R. Huddleston and G. K. Pullum et al. (2002); C. MacCabe, *James Joyce and the Revolution of the Word*, 2d ed. (2003); Z. Pickard, "Milton's Latinisms" (2003): http://www.chass.utoronto.ca/~cpercy/courses/6362Pickard1.htm; *Syntax in Antiquity*, ed. P. Swiggers and A. Wouters (2003)—see esp. L. Basset, "Aristote et la Syntaxe"; A. Luhtala, "Syntax and Dialectic in Late Antiquity"; P. Swiggers and A. Wouters, "Réflexions à propos de (l'absence de?) la syntaxe dans la grammaire Gréco-Latine"; and T. Viljamaa, "Colon and Comma. Dionysius of Halicarnassus on the Sentence Structure"; G. Deutscher, *The Unfolding of Language* (2005); M. Ferguson, "Poetic Syntax," *The Norton Anthology of Poetry*, ed. M. Ferguson, M. J. Salter, J. Stallworthy, 5th ed. (2005); A. Luhtala, *Grammar and Philosophy in Late Antiquity* (2005); A. M. Devine and L. D. Stephens, *Latin Word Order* (2006); Y. Peled, *Sentence Types and Word-Order Patterns in Written Arabic* (2009).

M. W. FERGUSON

T

TERCET. A verse unit of three lines, usually rhymed, most often employed as a stanzaic form. It was first developed systematically in It. poetry (*terzina*): Dante chose the tercet with interlocking rhymes (*terza rima) for the stanza of the *Divine Comedy*, whence it spread to the other vernacular poetries. In those versions of the *sonnet derived from It., the *sestet is made up of two tercets rhyming (often) *cdecde*. Eng. users of tercets or terza rima include Thomas Wyatt, John Donne, Robert Herrick ("Whenas in Silks my Julia Goes") and P. B. Shelley ("Ode to the West Wind," "The Triumph of Life"). The tercet became the major form of the mature Wallace Stevens: fully half of the poems in his last three books of poetry use it, incl. nearly all of the major poems ("Notes toward a Supreme Fiction," "Auroras of Autumn," "Sea Surface Full of Clouds"). W. C. Williams uses a variant "triadic stanza" as his staple form. Monorhymed tercets in stichic verse are triplets. Though three-line stanzas are less common in the poetries of the world than *quatrain, they are important nonetheless: the Fr. *villanelle comprises five tercets and a quatrain, and two forms of Welsh *englynion* are in tercets, incl. most of the work of Llywarch Hen (6th c.). Western adaptations of the Japanese *haiku normally set it as a tercet of five-, seven-, and five-syllable lines, unrhymed.

■ E. Berry, "W. C. Williams' Triadic-Line Verse," *Twentieth-Century Literature* 35 (1989).

T.V.F. BROGAN

TERZA RIMA. It. verse form consisting of interlinked *tercets, in which the second line of each tercet rhymes with the first and third lines of the one following, *aba bcb cdc*, etc. The sequence of tercets formed in this way may be of any length and is usually brought to a conclusion by a single final line, which rhymes with the second line of the tercet preceding it, *aba a*. Terza rima has a powerful forward momentum, while the concatenated rhymes provide a reassuring structure of woven continuity, which may on occasion, however, imprison the poet in a movement of cyclical repression or driven mindlessness (Alfred de Vigny, "Les Destinées"; Hugo von Hofmannsthal, "Ballade des äusseren

Lebens"). In all its realizations, terza rima suggests processes without beginning or end, an irresistible *perpetuum mobile*.

Terza rima (in *hendecasyllables) was introduced by Dante as an appropriate stanza form for his *Divina commedia*. Its symbolic reference to the Holy Trinity, its other numerological implications, and the overtones of tireless quest and of the interconnectedness of things were particularly apposite. Most probably Dante developed terza rima from the tercets of the *sirventes*, but whatever the origin of the form, it found immediate popularity with Giovanni Boccaccio, who used it in his uncompleted *Amorosa visione*, and with Petrarch (*I Trionfi*). After Dante, terza rima became the preferred verse form for allegorical and didactic poems such as Fazio degli Uberti's *Dittamondo* and Federico Frezzi's *Quadriregio*. But its implicit difficulty discouraged its widespread use after the 14th c., although Vincenzo Monti in the late 18th c. and Ugo Foscolo in the early 19th c. had recourse to it.

In France, terza rima first appeared in the work of Jean Lemaire de Belges ("Le Temple d'honneur et de vertus," 1503; "La Concorde des deux langages," 1511) and was taken up by poets of the Pléiade—Pontus de Tyard, Étienne Jodelle, Jean-Antoine de Baïf. The *decasyllable almost invariably used by these 16th-c. poets yielded to the *alexandrine in the form's 19th-c. revival, which was subscribed to by Parnassians (Théodore de Banville, Charles-Marie Leconte de Lisle) and symbolists alike.

The form makes even greater demands on poets who write in a lang. less rich in rhymes than It. or Fr. Chaucer first experimented with terza rima in Eng. for parts of his early "Complaint to His Lady," but its first significant use is by Thomas Wyatt, followed by Philip Sidney and Samuel Daniel. The romantics experimented with it, Lord Byron for "The Prophecy of Dante" and P. B. Shelley for "Prince Athanase" and "The Triumph of Life." Shelley's "Ode to the West Wind" is composed of five sections, each rhyming *aba bcb cdc ded ee*. Since the romantics, it has been used, sometimes with variation of line length and looser rhymes, by Thomas Hardy, W. B. Yeats, T. S. Eliot, W. H. Auden ("The Sea and the Mirror"), Roy Fuller

("Centaurs"; "To My Brother"), and Archibald MacLeish ("Conquistador"). More recently, in Derek Walcott's *Omeros* (1990), an almost free-rhyming terza rima ("Dantesque design") is combined with a polymorphous *hexameter (Homer); in this "undone" state, terza rima supports a thematics of woundedness and of the difficult curing of the present by the past, but still manages to embody the poem's final line: "When he left the beach the sea was still going on."

■ L. E. Kastner, "A History of the Terza Rima in France," *ZFSL* 26 (1904); J.S.P. Tatlock, "Dante's *Terza Rima*," *PMLA* 51 (1936); L. Binyon, "Terza Rima in English Poetry," *English* 3 (1940); J. Wain, "Terza Rima," *Rivista di Letterature Moderne* 1 (1950); R. Bernheim, *Die Terzine in der deutschen Dichtung* (1954); M. Fubini, "La Terzina della *Commedia*," *DDJ* 43 (1965); P. Boyde, *Dante's Style in His Lyric Poetry* (1971); J. D. Bone, "On 'Influence' and on Byron and Shelley's Use of Terza Rima in 1819," *KSMB* 32 (1982); J. Freccero, "The Significance of Terza Rima," *Dante, Petrarch, Boccaccio*, ed. A. S. Bernardo and A. L. Pellegrini (1983); P. Breslin, "Epic Amnesia: Healing and Memory in *Omeros*," *Nobody's Nation: Reading Derek Walcott* (2001); M. Hurley, "Interpreting Dante's *Terza Rima*," *FMLS* 41 (2005).

L. J. ZILLMAN; C. SCOTT

TETRAMETER (Gr., "of four measures").

I. Classical
II. Modern

I. Classical. In Gr. and Lat., the basic meter for recitation forms is the trochaic tetrameter catalectic, i.e., four trochaic metra (units of measurement): $- \cup - x \mid - \cup - x \mid - \cup - x \mid - \cup - x$ where x = anceps (a syllable that, independently of its real metrical value, can be counted as long or short, according to the requirements of the meter), with truncation (see CATALEXIS) of the final anceps. There is a diaeresis (coincidence of a word ending with the end of a metrical unit) after the second anceps, which in comedy is sometimes replaced by a *caesura before it or, more rarely, the third breve. In Gr. drama, this meter is often associated with scenes of excitement. Several prosodic phenomena, such as (1) the occasional responsion of $- \cup \cup \cup$ with a trochaic metron in Aristophanes; (2) the fact that even in the strict versification of Solon, Havet's bridge in his tetrameters is slightly less stringent than Porson's bridge in his trimeters; and (3) the lower rate of the substitution of $\cup \cup$ for $\cup$ or x as compared to the *trimeter suggest that the trochaic tetrameter was less constrained in its access to the rhythms of Gr. speech than some other meters. Ancient trad. (e.g., Aristotle, *Rhetoric* 1407; Marius Victorinus 4.44) considered the trochaic tetrameter a faster meter than the iambic trimeter. At any rate, the greater speed of the tetrameter is probably more than a matter of conventional performance tempo and may reflect a universal feature of falling rhythm in ordinary speech. The trochaic tetrameter catalectic was employed by the archaic iambographers (writers of *iambs); Aristotle (*Poetics* 1449a2) states that it was used in tragedy before the iambic trimeter, but in extant drama, it is much less frequent than the latter.

Besides its use in trochaic, the tetrameter length was also used in antiquity with anapestic and iambic metra. The anapestic tetrameter catalectic is used in comic dialogue. It is characterized by metron diaeresis as well as regular median diaeresis, frequent contraction of all but the last pair of *brevia*, and resolution of *longa*. The iambic tetrameter catalectic was used by Hipponax and is fairly frequent in comedy for the entrance and exits of choruses and for contest scenes. Diaeresis after the second metron is preferred but caesura after the third anceps is common; resolution and substitution are frequent. The acatalectic iambic tetrameter is used only by Sophocles in the *Ichneutai* and in Ion's satyr-play *Omphale*.

The Lat. adaptation of the Gr. trochaic tetrameter catalectic is the trochaic *septenarius*, used commonly for comic dialogue and favored by Plautus. It stands in the same relation to its Gr. model as does the *senarius*, showing the same regard for linguistic stress. The absence of polysyllabic oxytones (words whose last syllable is stressed) and infrequency of proparoxytones (words stressed on the antepenultimate syllable) in Lat. means that the frequent trochaic closes of paroxytonic words (stressed on the penultimate syllable) will effect a prevailingly trochaic rhythm. As a popular form, it is known as the *versus quadratus*. Beare summarizes the long-held view that it was this meter, widely used for popular verse forms such as the marching songs of Caesar's legions, and common in late antiquity, that became the basis for much of med. Lat. versification. It is the meter of the *Pervigilium veneris* and a number of Christian *hymns, notably Venantius Fortunatus's *Pange lingua*, and was surpassed only by the iambic dimeter hymn quatrain (itself octosyllabic when regular) and the sequence as the most popular meter of the Middle Ages.

II. Modern. In mod. langs., the tetrameter is based on feet rather than metra; hence, it is but half as long as the cl. type. The mod. vernacular tetrameter, strictly speaking, is a verse line of four regular metrical feet; with freer metrical patterning, it is simply an *octosyllable as in Fr. and Sp. versification, or else stress verse, as in *ballad meter and hymn meter. The Fr. *tétramètre*, however, is a 12-syllable line with four divisions. In Eng. poetry, the tetrameter is second only to iambic pentameter in wideness of use; it is employed frequently in popular verse, nursery rhymes, songs, *hymns, and *ballads, as well as literary verse. Eng. tetrameters are chiefly in iambic rhythm, although trochaic tetrameters are also common. Eng. and Scottish traditional ballads usually consist of four-line stanzas that alternate iambic tetrameter and trimeter. Considerably less common than iambic and trochaic tetrameters, anapestic and dactylic tetrameters were popular during the romantic period; the most famous example is Lord Byron's "The Destruction of Sennacherib," in anapestic rhythm. Eng. tetrameter is almost always rhymed: in a famous footnote to his 1933 Leslie Stephen lecture, A. E. Housman singles out as one of the mysteries of versification "why, while blank verse can be written in lines of ten or six syllables, a series of octosyllables ceases to be verse if they are not rhymed." Well-known examples of iambic tetrameter verse in Eng. include one (only) of William Shakespeare's sonnets (145), John Donne's "The Extasie," Andrew Marvell's "To His Coy Mistress," William Wordsworth's "I Wandered Lonely as a Cloud," Alfred, Lord Tennyson's *In Memoriam*, and Robert Frost's "Stopping by Woods on a Snowy Evening." Something of a literary curiosity, Herman Melville's *Clarel: A Poem and Pilgrimage in the Holy Land* (1876), at nearly 18,000 lines the longest poem in Am. lit., is composed (except for its epilogue) in iambic tetrameter.

Rus. poetry features iambic tetrameter most famously and successfully in the work of Alexander Pushkin, who wrote nearly 22,000 tetrameters, over half his entire output, for *The Bronze Horseman* (1833) and *Evgenij Onegin* (1825–32).

Trochaic tetrameters are almost as common in Eng. as iambic, a fact of interest because trochaic pentameters, e.g., are almost nonexistent (see PENTAMETER). One of the more notorious and frequently parodied instances of mod. trochaic tetrameter is H. W. Longfellow's *Song of Hiawatha* (1855). Eng. poems in trochaic tetrameter frequently employ catalexis, truncating the second syllable of the line's last foot. Examples include Thomas Carew's "A Prayer to the Wind" and W. H. Auden's "Lullaby." Other famous poems in tetrameter combine iambic and trochaic feet along with catalexis: John Milton's "L'Allegro" and "Il Penseroso" and P. B. Shelley's "Lines Written among the Euganean Hills."

■ **Classical:** J. Rumpel, "Der trochäische Tetrameter bei den griechischen Lyrikern und Dramatikern," *Philologus* 28 (1869); H. J. Kanz, *De tetrametro trochaico* (1913); Beare; F. Crusius, *Römische Metrik*, 2d ed. (1955); F. Perusino, *Il tetrametro giambico catalettico nella commedia greca* (1968); West; A. M. Devine and L. D. Stephens, *Language and Metre* (1984).

■ **Modern:** Schipper, *History*; W. L. Schramm, "Time and Intensity in English Tetrameter Verse," *PQ* 13 (1934); P. Habermann, "Tetrameter," *Reallexikon I*; V. Nabokov, *Notes on Prosody* (1964); J. Bailey, *Toward a Statistical Analysis of English Verse* (1975); Attridge, *Rhythms*; M. Tarlinskaja, "Meter and Meaning: The Semantic 'Halo' of Verse Form in English Romantic Lyrical Poems (Iambic and Trochaic Tetrameter)," *AJS* 4 (1986); Morier.

A. M. DEVINE, L. D. STEPHENS (CLASSICAL); T.V.F. BROGAN, E. T. JOHNSTON (MODERN)

TONE (Gr. *tonos*, Lat. *tonus*, "stretching"). *Tone* primarily refers to the perceptible quality (pitch, intensity or loudness, and inflection) of *sound, particularly of the spoken or sung human voice. While all langs. use tone to convey meaning, phonetics distinguishes nontonal langs., in which tone is primarily a syntactical determinant, from tonal langs., such as Mandarin Chinese, in which tone is also an essential feature of the meaning of individual words (lexical tone). While the notion of a literary tone is relatively recent, it has important precedents in cl. Gr. and Lat. rhet. and philosophy.

Cl. treatments of tone in rhet. are informed by the view that the tone of the human voice naturally expresses the emotions and attitudes of the speaker. Aristotle in the *Rhetoric* complains that earlier rhetoricians had not paid sufficient attention to the "delivery" of their oration, which is "a matter of voice, as to the mode in which it should be used for each particular emotion; when it should be loud, when low, when intermediate; and how the tones (*tonoi*), i.e., shrill, deep, and intermediate, should be used" (1403b). Aristotle's discussion relies on the notion that the tone of the human voice should be in tune with human emotion, an idea indebted to the Pythagorean-Platonist philosophy that uses a mathematical model of music to interpret the universe and the human being in terms of harmony (Spitzer). The notion that the human voice, and indeed the body, is a musical instrument that expresses the emotions tonally becomes, after Aristotle, a crucial aspect of the third and final part of rhet. (*pronunciatio* or *actio*). The mathematical-musical model is reflected in Cicero's discussion of delivery, which he finds "the dominant factor in oratory" in *De oratore*: "nature has assigned to every emotion a particular look and tone of voice and bearing of its own; and the whole of a person's frame and every look on his face and utterance of his voice are like the strings of a harp, and sound according as they are struck by each successive emotion" (3.212, 216). The sense that the tone of the human voice expresses the emotional state of the speaker is carried by the first vernacular variations of the word (12th c. in Fr., 14th c. in Eng.), and it is reflected by the psychological descriptors often used with the word. Although cl. rhet. discusses the significance of sound in oratory, treatments of tone are largely restrained to the literal sense of *tone* as the material quality of the human voice, and as such they remain part of the third and final part of rhet. (Vega Ramos).

While in the cl. rhetorical trad. discussions of the tone of the voice belong to delivery, mod. literary discourse has applied the term to written texts. From the perspective of cl. rhet., this may be considered a category mistake, and it certainly leads to complications in the mod. use of the concept. In both tonal and nontonal langs., the tone of the voice may be used to enhance and complement the semantic content of the utterance, as well as to add to, modify, or even reverse it (as in the case of *irony). While some uses of vocal tone support meaning that may be grammatically codified and may appear in script (from sentence types to emphases), the mod. literary use of *tone* usually refers precisely to those aspects of written lang. that are neither lexical nor syntactical, but that appear, at least at first, somewhat intangibly, as a quality of the text as a whole, or of a significant part of it.

This mod. usage of *tone* is often considered a metaphorical use of the original concept, but it also goes back to the original meaning of the Gr. *tonos* as "stretching" and "tension." Indeed, the Pythagorean-Platonist concept of the human being as instrument was not restrained to the human voice or even to sound in general, and the notion that nonaural phenomena may have tone is central in Stoic philosophy, where *tone* is used to describe a tensile force that holds together inimical elements at both cosmological and psychological levels. This sense of *tone* as a cohesive force and harmony is evident in cl. and Christian philosophy through the Middle Ages and the Ren. (Spitzer).

In the 17th c., some Eur. vernaculars began to use *tone* to refer to a person's character, style, and manners, as well as to the air and mood of a phenomenon or a person. Parallel with this devel., the concept was also applied to written text, often in the same sense as an expression of the author's personality, manners, or mood; Madame Sévigné wrote, in 1691, that "[mes lettres] ont des tons, et ne sont pas supportables quand elles sont ânnonées" (my letters have tones, and they are intolerable when read monotonously). This application of *tone* to written texts implies a shift in what may be called the rhet. of tone: while in cl. rhet., the tone of the voice belongs to the actual vocal delivery of the oration, the mod. literary sense of *tone* belongs to what cl. rhet. discussed under the category of style (*elocutio*).

Within this trad. that takes tone as a feature of the written text, we may distinguish two distinct views. In the first, tone is associated with the mood or general atmosphere of the written text. This view is esp. prominent within the Ger. trad. after J. W. Goethe, and its most important and controversial proponent is the romantic poet Friedrich Hölderlin, who in a series of difficult theoretical writings produced a theory of poetry as tonal movement (the so-called *Tönewechsel* doctrine). In Hölderlin's theory, the three "basic" tones of poetry correspond to the three basic genres: the heroic tone to the tragic genre, the idealist tone to the lyric genre, and the naïve tone to the epic genre. Hölderlin uses the Ger. word *Ton* (tone, sound) essentially synonymously with the word *Stimmung* (mood, attunement), a word crucial to both the poetics and the philosophy of the postromantic era.

The other trad., by contrast, tends to associate the tone of the written text with a personal attitude, whether that of the author or of an implied speaker within the text. The most influential theorist of this position in Eng. lit. crit. is Richards, who in *Practical Criticism* identified tone as one of the "Four Kinds of Meanings." Besides sense, feeling, and intention, Richards codified the term *tone* to refer to that aspect of the utterance that "reflects [the speaker's] awareness of [his] relation [to his listener], his sense of how he stands toward those he is addressing." Richards's definition is remarkable in its profound debt to cl. rhet.: tone in *Practical Criticism* refers to that aspect of the poem that reflects the author's awareness of how an audience might receive his discourse. While Richards's definition thus conflates the Aristotelian notions of *ethos* (the orator's character constructed in the oratorical performance) and *pathos* (the emotional response that the orator tries to obtain from an audience), it essentially identifies the tone of the text with the style of the text. Indeed, it is as such an index of authorial self-awareness that Richards considers tone to be one of the most important and most difficult aspects of poetry: "many of the secrets of 'style' could, I believe, be shown to be matters of tone, of the perfect recognition of the writer's relation to the reader in view of what is being said and their joint feelings about it." Finally, this also implies that Richards can locate the cl. rhetorical notion of propriety in the tone of the text; tone can be proper or improper, and "faults of tone are much more than mere superficial blemishes. They may indicate a very deep disorder."

While Richards's attempt to codify the literary meaning of *tone* had an enormous influence on New Criticism, in more recent lit. crit. the concept has received considerably less attention, partly because of the psychological assumptions that support it in Richards's definition. Attempts have been made to sever the concept from Richards's psychological framework; thus, Ngai theorizes a notion of tone that allows one "to generalize, totalize, and abstract the 'world' of the literary object, in a way that seems particularly conducive to the analysis of ideology." Yet in an essay on treatments of lyric poetry after the New Critics, Culler has argued that, even for a critic like Smith, to interpret the poem is to "identify the concerns to which the speaker is responding and the tone of the response." If lyric poems are fictional representations of personal utterances, Culler states, "the methodological heritage of the New Critics encourages us to focus above all on the complexities of the speaker's attitude revealed over the course of the overheard utterance, and on the culmination of the poem in what Cleanth Brooks calls the 'total and governing attitude.'" He goes on to suggest that, while continental theorists were instrumental in the shift from the New Critical interest in poetic tone to a structuralist investment in narrative voice and mood (Genette), the post-New Critical era has not produced a general theory of the lyric.

The recent reluctance to use *tone* as an analytical concept is probably due to difficulties implied in the application of the term for written lang.: most conspicuous in Richards's definition of *tone* as an expression of the author's attitude to an audience is the fact that the tone of a written text is identified not in particular textual features but by its alleged effect on the reader. On the other hand, the hist. of the concept shows that tone began to be used for written texts precisely in order to refer to that intangible quality of the text that cannot be immediately accessed through an analysis of individual textual features; it is, rather, a holistic quality, something that belongs to the text as such. Indeed, the New Critics' concept of tone was never an analytical tool for poetry only; rather, *tone* in their sense might be characterized as a rhetorical effect common to all ling. utterances. A more accurately poetic concept of tone is implied in Stewart's discussion of sound. She asserts that, in the case of written texts, to speak about sound is to speak about the recollection of sound that the written text evokes from the reader. Stewart goes on to discuss G. M. Hopkins's theoretical writings, which define the poem as "the figure of spoken sound" and which ultimately suggest that "emotional intonation" is produced in the poem by the tension between the rhythms of speech and the poetic meter. Although this method of rhythmic dissonance has been analyzed in the works of many other poets, it has rarely been considered as the "tone" of the poem, even though it would be a proper recycling of the term's connotation as "stretching" and "tension" for the purposes of poetics.

■ I. A. Richards, *Practical Criticism* (1929); G. M. Hopkins, "Rhythm and the Other Structural Parts of Rhetoric—Verse," *The Journals and Papers of Gerard Manley Hopkins*, ed. H. House (1959); L. Spitzer, *Classical and Christian Ideas of World Harmony: Prolegomena to an Interpretation of the Word "Stimmung"* (1963); G. Genette, *Figures of Literary Discourse*, trans.

A. Sheridan (1981); B. H. Smith, *On the Margins of Discourse* (1981); J. Culler, "Changes in the Study of the Lyric," *Lyric Poetry: Beyond New Criticism*, ed. C. Hošek and P. Parker (1985); S. Stewart, "Letter on Sound," *Close Listening: Poetry and the Performed World*, ed. C. Bernstein (1998); "Tone," *A Dictionary of Linguistics and Phonetics*, ed. D. Crystal (1992); "Tönerhetorik," *Historisches Wörterbuch der Rhetorik*, ed. G. Ueding (1992–); M. J. Vega Ramos, *El secreto artificio* (1992); "Tone Languages" *The Encyclopedia of Language and Linguistics*, ed. R. E. Asher (1994); D. Wellbery, "Stimmung," *Ästhetische Grundbegriffe*, ed. K. Barck (2003); S. Ngai, *Ugly Feelings* (2005); "Ton," *Le dictionnaire culturel en langue française*, ed. A. Rey (2005).

D. MARNO

TRIMETER (Gr., "of three measures"). Aristotle (*Poetics* 1449a24, *Rhetoric* 1408b33) regards the iambic trimeter as the most speech-like of Gr. meters (see IAMBIC). It is first employed mixed with dactylic hexameters in the *Margites* ascribed to Homer, though some scholars regard the first line of the "Nestor's cup" inscription, ca. 750–700 BCE, as a trimeter. Despite ancient trad. (e.g., Pseudo-Plutarch, *De musica* 28), Archilochus (fl. 650 BCE) is not its inventor, although he was the first to use the word *iamb* and developed the trimeter as a medium for personal *invective, a practice in which he was followed by Semonides. The Athenian lawgiver Solon used the trimeter for political poetry. The trimeter is the basic dialogue meter of Gr. tragedy, satyr-play, and comedy. It consists of three iambic metra (units of measurement) (x represents anceps [a syllable which, independently of its real metrical value, can be counted as long or short, according to the requirements of the meter]): $x - \cup - \mid x - \cup - \mid x - \cup -$. The penthemimeral *caesura (after the fifth position [second anceps]) is much more frequent than the hephthemimeral (after the seventh position [second breve]); median diaeresis (coincidence of a word ending with the end of a metrical unit) is permitted occasionally in tragedy, though in Euripides only when accompanied by *elision (omission or blurring of a final unstressed vowel followed by a vowel or mute consonant). Resolution of a *longum* (long syllable) is permitted at differing rates in all feet but the last. The final element may be short (*brevis in longo*). Most of these departures from the basic iambic pattern are subject to a complex of finely graded phonological, lexical, and syntactic constraints that form a hierarchy of strictness that decreases from the archaic iambographers (writers of iambs) through early tragedy and later Euripides to satyr-play and finally comedy. The trimeter is subject to a number of bridges, the strictness of which follows the same generic and stylistic hierarchy.

The Lat. adaptation of the Gr. trimeter is the *senarius*, first used by Livius Andronicus. The senarius is a common dialogue meter of early Lat. drama and was frequently used in funerary inscriptions. This version of the trimeter, however, is organized as six feet rather than three metra. The most striking departure from the Gr. trimeter is the permissibility of *spondees in the second and fourth feet. This variation and many differing constraints on word boundaries are motivated by the differing nature of the Lat. stress accent. Iambic-shaped words, even those of the type not regularly subject to *iambic shortening, are severely restricted in the interior of the line, since otherwise they would produce conflict of accent with metrical ictus. Spondee-shaped (or -ending) words, however, could be permitted in trochaic segments of the verse, since their stress pattern would preserve the iambic rhythm. In contrast to the senarius, the Lat. lyric poets, such as Catullus and Horace, and Seneca in his dramas, follow the pattern of the Gr. trimeter more closely, excluding spondees in even feet, restricting resolution and substitution, and not admitting iambic shortening.

The prosodies of the mod. vernacular followed the Lat. metrical practice of scanning in feet rather than metra, so that the trimeter of the Germanic langs. (incl. Eng.) of the later Middle Ages, Ren., and mod. period is most often a very short line of three binary feet or six syllables—too short to be capable of sustained effects in *narrative or *dramatic verse, but very suitable for song and for humor or *satire. Literary examples include a dozen songs by Thomas Wyatt ("I will and yet I may not," "Me list no more to sing"); Henry Howard, the Earl of Surrey; Ben Jonson's "Dedication of the King's New Cellar" (with feminine rhymes); Elizabeth Barrett Browning's "The Mourning Mother"; a dozen poems by P. B. Shelley (incl. "When the Lamp Is Shattered," and another of them, "To a Skylark," trochaic trimeter with an *alexandrine close), and Theodore Roethke's "My Papa's Waltz" (with occasional extra syllables at the ends of lines). In French prosody, the line now called the *trimètre* is not a trimeter

in this sense: it is an *alexandrine of 12 syllables divided into three rhythmical phrases and
made its appearance only with the advent of
romanticism.

■ Schipper, *History*; F. Lang, *Platen's Trim-
eter* (1924); J. Descroix, *Le Trimètre iambique*
(1931); G. Rosenthal, *Der Trimeter als deutsche
Versmasse* (1934); P. W. Harsh, *Iambic Words
and Regard for Accent in Plautus* (1949); Maas;
D. S. Raven, *Latin Metre* (1965); C. Questa,
Introduzione alla metrica di Plauto (1967);
Allen; S. L. Schein, *The Iambic Trimeter in
Aeschylus and Sophocles* (1979); West; A. M.
Devine and L. D. Stephens, *Language and
Metre* (1984); M. Lotman, "The Ancient
Iambic Trimeters: A Disbalanced Harmony,"
Formal Approaches to Poetry, ed. B. E. Dresher
and N. Friedberg (2006).

A. M. Devine; L. D. Stephens;
T.V.F. Brogan; E. T. Johnston

TROCHAIC (Gr., *trochee, choree*, respectively,
"running," "belonging to the dance"). A term
used for both metrical units and whole *meters
having the rhythm "marked–unmarked" in series. In the mod. accentual meters, a *trochee* is a
*foot comprising a stressed syllable followed by
an unstressed; in the quantitative meters of the
cl. langs., however, the elements were long and
short. In Lat., the trochaic foot comprised one
long syllable followed by one short, whereas in
Gr., the unit was the trochaic metron, $- \cup - x$
(x denotes *anceps*). Trochaic measures were used
in archaic Gr. poetry at least from the time of
Archilochus; and in Gr. tragedy and comedy,
they appear in both choral lyric and spoken
dialogue. In Lat. comedy, the trochaic seems to
have lent itself esp. well to rapid movement and
dancing; the most common meter of Plautus
and Terence is the trochaic tetrameter catalectic
or septenarius. This is the meter also used by
Caesar's legions for marching songs (Beare). In
all these registers, it seems to maintain close ties
with popular speech and popular verse genres.

In mod. verse, trochaic meter used for entire poems is far less common than *iambic and
does not appear until the Ren.: the first clearly
accentual trochaics in Eng. are by Philip Sidney
(*Certain Sonnets* 7, 26, 27), followed by Nicholas Breton. From Sidney's example, they became
more popular in the 1590s, though still mainly
in *tetrameters. King Lear's "Never, never,
never, never, never" is an exception meant to
reaffirm the iambic rule. On the other hand,
trochaic meters are quite common in many

*songs and chants; in idioms, formulaic expres-
sions, *proverbs, *riddles, slogans, jingles, and
cheers; and in much popular and folk verse. In
short, trochaic verse is rare in literary poetry but
common in popular. The most obvious explanation for this difference would be that most
of these forms have some close relation to song.
They are either sung to music, recited in a singsong chant, or originally derived from song.
In music, trochaic rhythm is structural since a
stress begins every bar. It is presumed that the
use of trochaic meters for text simplifies the fitting of the words to music.

Some metrists (e.g., Boris Tomashevsky,
V. E. Xolsevnikov) have denied that there is any
difference between iambic and trochaic meters
except for the first syllable. But, in fact, poets
make it very clear that they perceive a radical
distinction between the two meters. Whole
poems in trochaic meter are relatively rare in
any mod. verse trad. (Saintsbury, 3.529; Gasparov 1974), and trochaic meter is clearly associated with only certain kinds of genres, subjects,
and rhythmic movements. The distribution of
line forms is also quite different; trochaic pentameter is almost unheard of, while trochaic
tetrameters are as common as iambic, if not
more so. Poems where metrical code switching
between iambic and trochaic is systematic are
rare (in Marina Tsvetaeva in Rus.; in the verse
known as "8s and 7s" in Eng.). And internal
line dynamics differ radically: first-foot stress
reversals are four times more common in iambic verse (12%) than in trochaic (3%) in Eng.
and 30 times more common in Rus. There is a
widespread perception among poets and prosodists that trochaic meters are in some way more
rigid, more brittle, "more difficult to maintain"
(Hascall) than iambic ones.

In Eng., there is a mixed iambo-trochaic
form known as "8s and 7s," instanced most
famously in John Milton's "L'Allegro" and "Il
Penseroso," which seems to mix iambic and trochaic lines seamlessly or else to mix normal iambic lines with acephalous ones that only *seem* to
be trochaic. This problem points up the importance of distinguishing between trochaic *meters*
and trochaic *rhythms* in iambic meters. Traditional Eng. metrics would say that an iambic
pentameter line such as "And quickly jumping
backward, raised his shield," although in iambic
meter, has a "falling rhythm" that is the result
of trochaic word shapes. While meter organizes
lang. on the phonological level, it nevertheless
affects, and is affected by, morphology as well.

There is some evidence that trochaic rhythms predominate in certain speech contexts, esp. children's speech, and that trochaic rhythms are easier both to produce and to perceive. But it is disputed whether Eng. as a lang. is essentially iambic or trochaic in character. Comprehensive data on word shapes in the lexicon (i.e., how many are monosyllabic, disyllabic iambic, disyllabic trochaic, trisyllabic, polysyllabic) and the frequencies of these words in ordinary speech versus poetry (many words in the dictionary will never appear in poetry), along with comparable data on the shapes of Eng. phrases and their frequencies, are difficult to come by, even for one lang. Gil makes a global distinction between iambic and trochaic langs.: iambic "are characterized by subject-verb-object (SVO) word order, simple syllable structures, high consonant-vowel ratios, and the absence of phonemic tones," while trochaic have SOV, complex syllable structures, low C-V ratios, and phonemic tone.

Several efforts have been made to analyze the frequency of word types both in iambic versus trochaic verse and in these as set against the norm of the lang. to try to discover significant statistical deviations (e.g., Jones; Tarlinskaja, following Gasparov). Some striking statistics have emerged. But the very idea of a ling. "norm" against which poetic lang. "deviates" is an approach now viewed as suspect. Lexical selection is not the only or even perhaps the central issue; certainly, poets think in terms of significant words, but more generally these must be woven into the fabric in syntactically predetermined ways. Analyzing word-shape rhythms in relation to line rhythms misses the crucial point that lines are not formed by stringing words together but, rather, mainly by putting phrases together: most words come in packaged phrasal containers of relatively fixed rhythmic shape—prepositional phrases, noun phrases, compound verbs. And once a poet selects a word in a line, the range of relevant words for that or even following lines is constrained by the chosen semantic field. It is precisely the power of iambic verse, e.g., that an iambic line may comprise two monosyllables and four trochaic words. Word shapes are the elements, and, certainly, these vary in significant ways; but it is the stitching that counts.

See PYRRHIC, SPONDEE.

■ Schipper 2.375–98; W. Brown, *Time in English Verse Rhythm* (1908); H. Woodrow, *A Quantitative Study of Rhythm* (1909); Schipper, *History*, chs. 13, 14.2; J.E.W. Wallin, "Experimental Studies of Rhythm and Time," *Psychology Review* 18 (1911), 19 (1912); J. W. White, *The Verse of Greek Comedy* (1912); Wilamowitz, pt. 2, ch. 5; K. Taranovski, *Ruski dvodelni ritmovi* (1953); P. Fraisse, *Les Structures rythmiques* (1956); Beare; Norberg, 73 ff.; C. L. Drage, "Trochaic Metres in Early Russian Syllabo-Tonic Poetry," *Slavonic and Eastern European Review* 38 (1960); Saintsbury, *Prosody*; P. Fraisse, *The Psychology of Time*, trans. J. Leith (1963); Koster, ch. 6; C. Questa, *Introduzione alla metrica di Plauto* (1967); Dale; G. Faure, *Les Élements du rythme poétique en anglaise moderne* (1970); D. L. Hascall, "Trochaic Meter," *CE* 33 (1971); P. Fraisse, *Psychologie du rythme* (1974); M. L. Gasparov, *Sovremennyj russkij stix* (1974); R. P. Newton, "Trochaic and Iambic," *Lang&S* 8 (1975); Tarlinskaja; D. Laferrière, "Iambic versus Trochaic: The Case of Russian," *International Review of Slavic Linguistics* 4 (1979); R. G. Jones, "Linguistic and Metrical Constraints in Verse," *Linguistic and Literary Studies in Honor of A. A. Hill*, ed. M. ali Jazayery et al., v. 4 (1979); Halporn et al.; Snell; West; D. Gil, "A Prosodic Typology of Language," *Folia Linguistica* 20 (1986); G. T. Wright, *Shakespeare's Metrical Art* (1988), ch. 13; B. Bjorklund, "Iambic and Trochaic Verse," *Rhythm and Meter*, ed. P. Kiparsky and G. Youmans (1989); *CHCL*, v.1.5; M. L. Gasparov, "The Semantic Halo of the Russian Trochaic Pentameter: Thirty Years of the Problem," *Elementa* 2 (1996); D. Zec, "The Prosodic Word as a Unit in Poetic Meter," *The Nature of the Word*, ed. K. Hanson and S. Inkelas (2009).

T.V.F. BROGAN

TROPE (Gr., "turn"). In its most restricted definition, a *trope* is a figure of speech that uses a word or phrase in a sense other than what is proper to it. Cl. rhetoricians describe this change in meaning as a movement: the artful deviation of a word from its ordinary signification, a deviation that usually involves the substitution of one word or concept for another. As devices of rhetorical *style, tropes give lang. what Aristotle calls a "foreign air" (*xénos*), using strange words to refer to familiar concepts or assigning novel meaning to ordinary words (*Rhetoric*). Quintilian distinguishes tropes from other figures of speech by defining them as stylistic deviations that affect only a word or a small group of words (*Institutio oratoria*). According to this understanding, tropes such as "the Lord is my shepherd" (*metaphor), "from the cradle to the grave" (*metonymy), and "the face that launched a thousand ships" (*synecdoche) operate by changing the signification of the words "shepherd," "cradle," "grave," and "face." Tropes allow lang. to mean *more* or *something other*, leading to Richards's position that a metaphor allows two or more ideas to be carried by a single word or expression (the vehicle), its meaning (the tenor) resulting from their "interaction" on the basis of a relation (the ground).

In order to define *trope* as a figure of speech, cl. rhet. naturalizes ordinary locutions as the basic norms of lang., as when Quintilian identifies *trope* as "language transferred from its natural and principal meaning to another for the sake of embellishment" (*Institutio oratoria*). This depiction of figuration as movement from a fixed location recurs in definitions of *trope* from antiquity forward, as tropes "transport" words from their normal, familiar habitat. As Barthes observes, the distinction between proper and figured lang. frequently becomes expressed as a distinction between the native and the foreign or the normal and the strange. Definitions of *trope* are thus themselves inescapably metaphorical, that is, relying on an idea of "home" (*oikos*) to theorize the ling. transports of figures of speech, as when César Chesneau Dumarsais defines *metaphor* as occupying a "borrowed home" (*Traité des Tropes*, 1730).

The cl. definition of *trope* as deviation from a ling. norm (variously defined as the ordinary, proper, or familiar) has repeatedly been challenged in the mod. era, first by romantic critics (Johann Georg Hamann, Jean-Jacques Rousseau, and Friedrich Nietzsche), and still more aggressively by linguistically oriented literary theorists (Jakobson, Barthes, Genette, Todorov, Derrida, de Man). While cl. rhet. presumes the existence of two langs., one proper and one figured, mod. literary theory identifies *trope* as a fundamental structure of a single ling. system, rather than

an exception or deviation from a prior norm. From the romantic point of view, tropes such as metaphor comprise our most basic mechanisms of thought and expression: we have no way of understanding "the Lord" except through the application of metaphors such as "shepherd." From a deconstructive perspective, "the Lord" does not exist prior to the "shepherd" metaphor; rather, the trope confers an illusory presence on what it signifies (its signified). The argument that trope is *the* principle of thought and verbal organization leads to the claim that lit. is a privileged vehicle for access to the problems that lang. poses for understanding (de Man).

See CATACHRESIS, SCHEME.

■ I. A. Richards, *The Philosophy of Rhetoric* (1936); K. Burke, "Four Master Tropes," *A Grammar of Motives* (1945); Jakobson and Halle, "Two Aspects of Language and Two Types of Aphasic Disturbances"; E. Auerbach, "Figura," trans. R. Manheim, *Scenes from the Drama of European Literature* (1959); J. L. Austin, "The Meaning of a Word," *Philosophical Papers* (1961); O. Ducrot and T. Todorov, *Encyclopedic Dictionary of the Sciences of Language*, trans. C. Porter (1979); G. Genette, *Figures of Literary Discourse*, trans. A. Sheridan, 3 v. (1981); P. Ricoeur, *The Rule of Metaphor*, trans. R. Czerny et al. (1981); P. de Man, "The Rhetoric of Temporality," "The Rhetoric of Blindness," *Blindness and Insight*; and "Anthropomorphism and Trope in the Lyric," *The Rhetoric of Romanticism* (1984); and "Hypogram and Inscription" and "The Resistance to Theory," *The Resistance to Theory* (1986); J. Derrida, "White Mythology," *Margins of Philosophy*, trans. A. Bass (1986); Vickers, *Defence*; R. Barthes, "The Old Rhetoric," *The Semiotic Challenge*, trans. R. Howard (1988); P. Parker, "Metaphor and Catachresis," *The Ends of Rhetoric*, ed. J. Bender and D. Wellbery (1990); Lanham; *Tropical Truth(s): The Epistemology of Metaphor and Other Tropes*, ed. A. Burkhardt and B. Nerlich (2010).

T. BAHTI; J. C. MANN

U

UT PICTURA POESIS. In Horace's *Ars poetica*, the phrase *ut pictura poesis* (as is painting, so is poetry) offers an analogy to painting to describe the effects of poetry. Some texts, Horace argues, reveal their value when scrutinized more closely than others; some please on one encounter, while others bear repeated examination. This comparison of painting and poetry has precedents, as in Simonides' formulation that "painting is mute poetry and poetry a speaking picture." Over time, however, Horace's dictum has moved from designating a comparison, to outlining a contest between the arts, and then to functioning prescriptively rather than descriptively, commanding that poetry and painting resemble each other. It has also faced questions about the validity of the initial analogy and participated in theories of representation that blur the boundaries between different categories of signs.

The relationship between painting and poetry underwent various early forms of examination, such as Dion of Prusa (Chrysostom)'s statement that a poem develops in time, unlike a painting. (The dichotomy of space and time would continue to inform discussions of ut pictura poesis throughout its hist.) During the Middle Ages, orthodox Christian culture asserted the text's superiority over the image, mistrusting the latter's potential falsity. At the same time, poetry continued to interact with visual art, as in Petrarch's reference to Homer as a painter. In the Ren., Leonardo da Vinci's *paragone* made the competition between the two arts explicit. Reasoning that sight is the most direct sense and that the sequentiality of writing divides up the experience of the beautiful, da Vinci argued for painting's superiority. The Ren. also explored emblems as a means of approaching the goal of ut pictura poesis, offering poetry that functioned in visually "hieroglyphic" ways (Hagstrum). Early mod. and baroque painters seemed to use the terms of poetics to legitimize and ennoble their tasks, Nicolas Poussin being esp. renowned for his learning and his interartistic approach to theorizing painting. But, according to Lee, painters' work was often more deeply informed by earlier visual trads. G. E. Lessing's *Laokoön* (1766), an important critique of ut pictura poesis, disapproved of the use of

painting as a metaphor for poetry. For Lessing, the more a poem tries to be visually descriptive, the more it shows how it cannot be—if short, it lacks sufficient detail; if long, it becomes too sequential. But rebuttals to Lessing followed, such as J. G. Herder's contention that poetry, not describing action, lacks sequentiality. During the romantic period, according to Steiner, the importance of the painting-poetry analogy waned, and discussions of these arts focused less than they had earlier on either's connections to empirical reality. In the mod. and postmod. periods, the work of art's self-conscious materiality encouraged reexamination of the interartistic comparison. Multimedia artistic objects have also complicated such comparisons. Even if, in these cases as well, one form ultimately dominates the other (Wimsatt), such art develops Friedrich Schlegel's and others' earlier interest in relations of accompaniment and simultaneity between the arts, rather than analogical comparison.

Throughout this hist., analogy and metaphor surface as important but problematic terms. Lessing's misgivings about critical attempts to literalize artistic metaphor through ut pictura poesis. These are revisited in contemp. critiques of the vagueness of metaphors comparing different arts. Analogical and metaphorical comparisons between the arts, Wellek and Warren note, cannot trace patterns of influence and devel. At the same time, ut pictura poesis has consistently wielded power in discussions of poetics. For Krieger, metaphors of space and visuality "inevitably" inflect the critic's lang. for describing poetic *form. And while arguments of analogy and *metaphor impose certain limits on investigations of the interaction between painting and poetry, they also suggest a provocative challenge to transcend the analogy itself in the examination of the "sister arts."

Interartistic crit. and practice move beyond analogy in part by providing a forum to discuss representation and signs. Plato's writings on poetry and painting regarded representation itself as a tool of analysis; to Plato, painting's and poetry's capacity as representational arts also exposed their deceptiveness. Rather than critiquing *mimesis, Aristotle sought in each art the achievement of a form with its own unity (*energeia*) through, for instance, plot in drama or design in painting. Plutarch privileged the vividness of imitation (*enargeia*) available to painting and poetry, holding up painting as the art form with the closest relationship to reality. For Joshua Reynolds, a painting's representation of reality was a "sign," like the signs used in poetry; but in separate ways, each art should activate an encompassing imagination, rising above the specular faculty. Markiewicz asserts that, while Lessing emphasized the material differences between poetry's and painting's respective signs, he also saw the potential for arbitrary signs to become natural signs, particularly in drama. For Mitchell, the Blakean "art of both language and vision" addresses the contrast wherein the signs of writing signify through difference and absence, whereas the visual image does so through similitude and presence.

These visually oriented issues surrounding ut pictura poesis suggest further questions about the nature of the image and the imagination. E.g., how do we define the images that painting and poetry each produce? One approach to the image appears in Hagstrum's "literary pictorialism," the relationship between a poem's evocation of a visual *image and its overall structure. Richards, however, points out that different readers perceive the images in a literary work differently; thus, a poetic image cannot be evaluated for its pictorial potential. Ut pictura poesis potentially asserts the image-making quality of lit. (explored in Marxist studies), yet it also exposes questions about the possibility of mental images. Assessing the mental image requires a turn to the beholder, another topic preoccupying interartistic discourse. Horace's dictum has been called a species of reception theory by Gadoin, with Trimpi asserting that its terms reveal a mistrust of "excessive scrupulosity" as an analytical method. For some, e.g., Gombrich and Faust, the intersection of the arts demands attention to the role of the viewer's imagination in constructing visual or verbal objects. Ut pictura poesis involves a specifically visual imagination (as distinct from the romantic imagina-

tion) and a need to investigate and transcend its own analogy. In response, we might conceive of an interdisciplinary poetics: art speaking about poetic representation in its own visual terms (Davidson, Chaganti), rather than having its visual features converted through the verbal machinery of metaphor.

■ I. Babbitt, *The New Laokoön* (1910); I. A. Richards, *Principles of Literary Criticism* (1924); R. Wellek and A. Warren, "Literature and the Other Arts," *Theory of Literature* (1949); J. H. Hagstrum, *The Sister Arts* (1958); R. W. Lee, *Ut Pictura Poesis* (1967); H. D. Goldstein, "*Ut Poesis Pictura*: Reynolds on Imitation and Imagination," *Eighteenth-Century Studies* 1 (1968); M. Krieger, "Ekphrasis and the Still Movement of Poetry: or, *Laokoön* Revisited," *Perspectives on Poetry*, ed. J. L. Calderwood and H. E. Toliver (1968); E. Panofsky, *Idea*, trans. J. S. Peake (1968); W. K. Wimsatt, *Day of the Leopards* (1976)—esp. "Laokoön: An Oracle Reconsulted" and "In Search of Verbal Mimesis"; W. Trimpi, "Horace's 'Ut Pictura Poesis': The Argument for Stylistic Decorum," *Traditio* 34 (1978); J.-M. Croisille, *Poésie et art figuré de Néron aux Flaviens* (1982), and rev. in *Journal of Roman Studies* 73 (1983); R. A. Goodrich, "Plato on Poetry and Painting," *BJA* 22 (1982); W. Steiner, *The Colors of Rhetoric* (1982); M. Davidson, "Ekphrasis and the Postmodern Painter Poem," *JAAC* 42 (1983); D. E. Wellbery, *Lessing's "Laocoön"* (1984); N. Bryson, "Intertextuality and Visual Poetics," *Style* 22 (1988); H. Markiewicz, "*Ut pictura poesis*: A History of the Topos and the Problem," *NLH* 18 (1987); G. E. Lessing, *Laocoön*, trans. E. A. McCormick (1989); W.J.T. Mitchell, *Picture Theory* (1994); E. H. Gombrich, *Art and Illusion*, 3d ed. (2000); I. Gadoin, "Re-reading Lessing's *Laocoön*," *Études Britannique Contemporaines* 31 (2006); J. Faust, "Blurring the Boundaries: *Ut pictura poesis* and Marvell's Liminal Mower," *SP* 104 (2007); S. Chaganti, *The Medieval Poetics of the Reliquary* (2008).

S. CHAGANTI

V

VARIABLE FOOT. A term associated with W. C. Williams, who first used it to explain the triadic stanzas of his *Paterson* 2.3 (1948), later reprinted separately as "The Descent." Claiming that the concept of the foot had to be altered to suit a newly relativistic world, Williams insisted that the variable foot allowed both order and variability in so-called *free verse, which he claimed could never be truly free. The variable foot, he asserted, supplanted the fixed foot of traditional Eng. prosody in order to represent more accurately the speech rhythms of the mod. Am. idiom. Attempting to demonstrate his measurement of the variable foot, Williams explained that he counted "a single beat" for each line of his three-line stanzas so as to regulate the "musical pace" of his verse, though, in fact, his lines contain varying numbers of stresses and syllables. But, as his nine-poem sequence "Some Simple Measures in the American Idiom and the Variable Foot" (1959) shows, Williams did not always identify the variable foot with the triadic stanza form. Because his own explanations of the device often lack precision and consistency, subsequent critics have questioned the legitimacy of the concept of the variable foot, one remarking that the variable foot in verse is as impossible as a variable inch on a yardstick; an alternative approach to Williams's prosody lies in treating it as primarily visual (see VISUAL POETRY). E. A. Poe had used the term to describe the *caesura; for Poe, the caesura was "a perfect foot," the length of which would vary in accordance with the time it takes to pronounce other feet in the line. Williams read Poe's essays on prosody, which apparently influenced his conception of verse structure.

■ E. A. Poe, "The Rationale of Verse," *Complete Works*, ed. J. A. Harrison, v. 14 (1902); W. C. Williams, Letter to R. Eberhart (May 23, 1954), *Selected Letters*, (1957); *I Wanted to Write a Poem*, ed. E. Heal (1958); "The American Idiom," *Interviews with W. C. Williams*, ed. L. Wagner (1976); H. M. Sayre, *The Visual Text of W. C. Williams* (1983); S. Cushman, *W. C. Williams and the Meanings of Measure* (1985); R. Gates, "Forging an American Poetry from Speech Rhythms: Williams after Whitman," *PoT* 8 (1987); E. Berry, "W. C. Williams' Triadic-Line Verse," *Twentieth Century*

Literature 35 (1989); R. Bradford, *The Look of It* (1993); N. Gerber, "Getting the 'Squiggly Tunes Down' on the Page: Williams's Triadic-Line Verse and American Intonation," *Rigor of Beauty,* ed. I. Copestake (2004).

S. CUSHMAN

VERISIMILITUDE. *See* MIMESIS.

VERSE DRAMA. *See* DRAMATIC POETRY.

VERSE EPISTLE (Gr. *epistole,* Lat. *epistula*). A poem addressed to a friend, lover, or patron, written in familiar style and in *hexameters (cl.) or their mod. equivalents. Two types of verse epistles exist: the one on moral and philosophical subjects, which stems from Horace's *Epistles*, and the other on romantic and sentimental subjects, which stems from Ovid's *Heroides*. Though the verse epistle may be found as early as 146 BCE (L. Mummius Achaicus's letters from Corinth and some of the satires of Lucullus), Horace perfected the form, employing common *diction, personal details, and a plain style to lend familiarity to his philosophical subjects. His letters to the Lucius Calpurnius Piso and his sons (ca. 10 BCE) on the art of poetry, known since Quintilian as the *Ars poetica*, became a standard genre of the Middle Ages and after. Ovid used the same style for his *Tristia* and *Ex Ponto* but developed the sentimental epistle in his *Heroides*, which are fictional letters from the legendary women of antiquity—e.g., Helen, Medea, Dido—to their lovers. Throughout the Middle Ages, the latter seems to have been the more popular type, for it had an influence on the poets of courtly love and subsequently inspired Samuel Daniel to introduce the form into Eng., e.g., his "Letter from Octavia to Marcus Antonius." Such also was the source for John Donne's large body of memorable verse epistles ("Sir, more than Kisses, letters mingle souls") and Alexander Pope's "Eloisa to Abelard."

But it was the Horatian epistle that had the greater effect on Ren. and mod. poetry. Petrarch, the first humanist to know Horace, wrote his influential *Epistulae metricae* in Lat. Subsequently, Ludovico Ariosto's *Satires* in *terza rima* employed the form in vernacular It. In all these epistles, Christian sentiment made itself felt. In Spain, Garcilaso de la Vega's "Epístola a Boscán" (1543) in *blank verse and the "Epístola moral a Fabio" in terza rima introduced and perfected the form. Fr. writers esp. cultivated it for its "graceful precision and dignified familiarity"; Nicolas Boileau's 12 epistles in couplets (1668–95) are considered the finest examples. Ben Jonson began the Eng. use of the Horatian form (*The Forest*, 1616) and was followed by others, e.g. Henry Vaughan, John Dryden, and William Congreve. But the finest examples in Eng. are Pope's *Moral Essays* and the "Epistle to Dr. Arbuthnot" in *heroic couplets. The romantics did not value the verse epistle, though P. B. Shelley, John Keats, and W. S. Landor on occasion wrote them. Examples in the 20th c. incl. W. H. Auden's *New Year Letter* and Auden and Louis MacNeice's *Letters from Iceland.*

■ H. Peter, *Der Brief in der römische Litteratur* (1901); J. Vianey, *Les Epéítres de Marot* (1935); W. Grenzmann, "Briefgedicht," *Reallexikon II*; J. A. Levine, "The Status of the Verse Epistle before Pope," *SP* 59 (1962); W. Trimpi, *Ben Jonson's Poems* (1962); J. Norton-Smith, "Chaucer's Epistolary Style," *Essays on Style and Language*, ed. R. Fowler (1966); *John Donne: The Satires, Epigrams and Verse Letters,* ed. W. Milgate (1967); N. C. de Nagy, *Michael Drayton's "England's Heroical Epistles"* (1968); R. S. Matteson, "English Verse Epistles, 1660–1758," *DAI* 28 (1968); D. J. Palmer, "The Verse Epistle," *Metaphysical Poetry*, ed. M. Bradbury and D. Palmer (1970); M. Motsch, *Die poetische Epistel* (1974); A. B. Cameron, "Donne's Deliberative Verse Epistles," *English Literary Renaissance* 6 (1976); M. R. Sperberg-McQueen, "Martin Opitz and the Tradition of the Renaissance Poetic Epistle," *Daphnis* 11 (1982); J. E. Brown, "The Verse Epistles of A. S. Pushkin," *DAI* 45 (1984); C. Guillén, "Notes toward the Study of the Renaissance Letter," *Renaissance Genres*, ed. B. K. Lewalski (1986); M. Camargo, *The Middle English Verse Love Epistle* (1991); W. C. Dowling, *The Epistolary Moment* (1991)—on the 18th c.; D. Aers, "'Darke Texts Need Notes': Versions of Self in Donne's Verse Epistles," *Critical Essays on John Donne*, ed. A. Marotti (1994); B. Overton, "Aphra Behn and the Verse Epistle," *Women's Writing* 16 (2009).

R. A. HORNSBY; T.V.F. BROGAN

VERSE NOVEL. *See* NARRATIVE POETRY.

VERSE PARAGRAPH. If a paragraph is defined as one or more sentences unified by a dominant mood or thought, then poetry, like prose, can be seen as moving forward in units that could be called paragraphs. Typically, the term *verse paragraph* is used to designate a group of lines that lacks regular stanzaic form and contains a nonstandardized number of lines and that is separated from the other verse paragraphs of a poem through indentation or blank space. Rhymed verse paragraphs do occur (e.g., the irregular *canzoni* of John Milton's "Lycidas" or the indented sections of varying numbers of couplets within the subdivisions of Alexander Pope's *Essay on Man*), but the term is used most frequently in relation to *blank verse. Lacking the somewhat arbitrary organization provided by an established *rhyme scheme, blank verse must provide units supporting the organization of idea such that the narration, description, or exposition unfolds in a series of stages felt as justly proportioned. In this sense, the verse paragraph is a syntactic period, frequently a single complex or periodic sentence, deployed in enjambed stichic verse so that the beginnings and ends of the syntactic frames conspicuously do not coincide with those of the metrical frames (the lines), with the result that meter and syntax are in counterpoint or tension.

The verse paragraph is a common feature of Old Germanic heroic poetry and is an important element in Eng. poetry as early as *Beowulf*, where sentences often begin at the *caesura. But by general consent, the greatest master of the verse paragraph is Milton, who, in writing *Paradise Lost*, needed "to devise a formal unit not regularly rhymed, not necessarily brief, sufficiently coherent but sufficiently flexible, intermediate between the line and the book" (Weismiller 189). Many of the most characteristic effects of *Paradise Lost*—its majesty, its epic sweep, its rich counterpoint of line and sentence rhythms—are produced or enhanced by Milton's verse paragraphs. Certain shorter poems in Eng., such as William Wordsworth's "Tintern Abbey," also make use of the verse paragraph. In addition, many *free verse poems, such as Walt Whitman's "Out of the Cradle Endlessly Rocking," which operate without a rhyme scheme or other regular structural organization, can be described as being composed of verse paragraphs.

■ G. Hübner, *Die stilistische Spannung in Milton's Paradise Lost* (1913); R. D. Havens, *The*

Influence of Milton on English Poetry (1922); J. Whaler, *Counterpoint and Symbol* (1956); E. Weismiller, "Blank Verse," *A Milton Encyclopedia*, ed. W. B. Hunter Jr., et al. (1978); W. H. Beale, "Rhetoric in the OE Verse Paragraph," *NM* 80 (1979); J. Hollander, "'Sense Variously Drawn Out'" in Hollander; J. K. Hale, *Milton's Languages* (1997).

A. Preminger; E. R. Weismiller;
T.V.F. Brogan; P. Kline

VERSE SYSTEMS. *See* meter.

VERSIFICATION. Versification refers to the making of verse or verse craft. Derived from the Lat. *versificatio,* a form combining *versus* (turning a plow at the ends of successive furrows, which, by analogy, suggest lines of writing) and *facio* (make), *versification* for a long time meant making lines. With the advent of mod. *free verse, esp. of composition by open field, the original sense of versification as making lines according to some measure, or *meter (Gr. *metron,* OE *mete*) has expanded to include all aspects of making poetry, from the smallest aspects of *sound to *stanzas to whole-poem forms and genres.

Versification is still sometimes defined and used as synonymous with *prosody (Gr. *prosodia,* the song accompaniment to words, pitch variation as spoken; Lat., *prosodia,* the marking of accent on a syllable). Prosody has referred to the sound patterns of lang. since the early Ren. and with verse practice since the mid-Ren. (*OED*). With the Ren., experiments with Romance models spurred close attention to rules for making lines and stanzas. By the late Ren., when poetry followed the taste for strict versions of metrical conformity, *prosodie* referred to both the practice of marking accents and to the rules for duration in pronunciation (*OED*). The marking of accents in making meters was a primary and necessary part of making verse, so the two terms served equally in discussing verse and became conflated. To the present, the two terms are sometimes interchangeable. W. K. Wimsatt (in 1972), e.g., was still using versification to mean the craft of making metrical poetry, even while John Hollander (in 1981) was distinguishing verse, as metered lines, from a mod. sense of poetry, as requiring the making of new metaphors.

With energetic Ren. experiments in adapting duration-based cl., It., and Fr. forms to the pitch-based prosody of Eng., versification was often a matter both of counting syllables and, in some cases, of determining their lengths as either "short" or "long"; thus, a versifier was largely occupied with prosodic considerations. Med. and Ren. grammars regarded prosody as pronunciation and often placed verse within the province of prosody. Because verse was an oral as well as a written art, pronunciation was a central concern.

With the expansion of styles and forms over the past century, individual poets and critics may use versification to refer to various aspects of poetry, incl. rhetorical structure, point of view, figuration, *diction, *syntax, fixed forms (such as the *sonnet), and the use of a particular lyric *genre or mode (such as *ode, *elegy, dramatic monologue), as well as sound patterning (e.g., *rhythm, *meter, *assonance, *consonance, *rhyme), visual patterning (see VISUAL POETRY), or the blending of the auditory and the visual, as in the case of *line or stanza integrity. The historical emergence of free verse, along with the expanded construing of *poetry* to signify many kinds of linguistic *poiēsis, has largely rendered *versification* outmoded as a term in its original sense.

Contributing to the declining value and significance of the term *versification* are the ongoing reconsiderations of some of the basic terms associated with the craft of verse. The traditional metered line came under attack during modernism, when a wave of experimentation with verse broke the consistency of meters, loosened them, or attempted to define and use new measures. Unlike Ren. innovations, modernism exploited the prosodic potentials in the lang. medium; the importation of foreign-lang. forms accounted for but a small portion of new line and verse forms (e.g., from OE and ME, Japanese, and Chinese). The line as it had been conceived until 1910 was exploded, freeing it to be redefined as metrical, nonmetrical, visual, or newly defined, as in W. C. Williams's poetry. The breakdown of the traditional meters, with the *prose poem and *concrete poetry being the extreme forms, spurred a reactive need to redefine the line and assert its priority as the most distinguishing marker of poetry. Accordingly, James Longenbach and others have argued for discarding the term *line breaks* for the more accurate *fulfillment,* since a line is not "broken"; it simply ends before another begins. The value placed on line integrity requires that a line be "fulfilled," i.e., that it have reason for being a piece of meaning, affect, and sound, as opposed to a randomly sliced bit of chopped prose. Similarly, a stanza (It. for "room") needs to be organized as a room of its own at the same time that it contributes to the whole. For Hollander and others, a verbal work must achieve the figurative level of metaphor to be a poem. These aspects of poetry point more clearly to the qualitative ends of verse craft: principles, assumptions, rules, guidelines, etc., exist for the writing of *good* poetry. When poetry was largely synonymous with *verse* and *verse* meant *metered lines*, versification pertained mostly to descriptions of craft. Now that boundaries between verse and prose have become less distinct and poetry, for many, serves as a general term for artful lang., discussions of versification have necessarily become more prescriptive, as they advance particular views of what poetry is or should be.

■ Wimsatt; P. Fussell, *Poetic Meter and Poetic Form*, rev. ed. (1979); J. Hollander, *Figure of Echo* (1981), and *Rhyme's Reason: A Guide to English Verse* (1981); Attridge, *Rhythms*; *The Line in Postmodern Poetry*, ed. R. J. Frank and H. M. Sayre (1988); G. T. Wright, *Shakespeare's Metrical Art* (1988); J. McCorkle, ed., *Conversant Essays, Contemporary Poets on Poetry* (1990); T. Steele, *Missing Measures: Modern Poetry and the Revolt against Meter* (1990); S. Cushman, *Fictions of Form in American Poetry* (1993); Gasparov, *History*; H. Gross, *Sound and Form in Modern Poetry*, 2d ed. (1996); Finch and Varnes; R. Abbott, "T. S. Eliot's Ghostly Footfalls: The Versification of 'Four Quartets,'" *Cambridge Quarterly* 4 (2005); 365–85; *Radiant Lyre: Essays on Lyric Poetry*, ed. D. Baker and A. Townsend (2007); J. Longenbach, *The Art of the Poetic Line* (2008).

R. WINSLOW

VERS LIBRE. Because of its prosodic relatedness to *vers libres classiques* and *vers libéré*, this term is best reserved for 19th-c. Fr. *free verse and those modernist free-verse prosodies that acknowledge a debt to it (e.g., It. futurism; the Anglo-Am. *vers libristes* Ezra Pound and T. S. Eliot; and imagism). The directions mapped out by the vers libristes of the late 19th c., mostly advocates of the fashionable aesthetic of symbolism with its emphasis on musicality, were variously explored and adapted by 20th-c. practitioners such as Guillaume Apollinaire, Blaise Cendrars, Pierre-Jean Jouve, Pierre Reverdy, Paul Éluard, Robert Desnos, René Char, Yves Bonnefoy, and Michel Deguy.

The emergence of vers libre is specifically datable to 1886, the year in which the review *La Vogue*, ed. by Gustave Kahn, published, in rapid succession, Arthur Rimbaud's free-verse *Illuminations*, "Marine," and "Mouvement" (possibly written in May 1873); trans. of some of Walt Whitman's *Leaves of Grass* by Jules Laforgue; Kahn's series of poems titled "Intermède" (to become part of his *Les Palais nomades*, 1887); ten of Laforgue's own free-verse poems (later collected in his posthumous *Derniers Vers* (Last verses), 1890); and further examples by Paul Adam and Jean Moréas. To this list of initiators, Jean Ajalbert, Édouard Dujardin, Albert Mockel, Francis Vielé-Griffin, Émile Verhaeren, Adolphe Retté, Maurice Maeterlinck, Camille Mauclair, and Stuart Merrill added their names in the years immediately following. Vers libre caused either considerable enthusiasm or anxiety, since its rejection of a traditional metrical order in favor of unbridled individuality appeared highly subversive in the context of Third Republican efforts to eradicate difference and create a stable, unified national identity; Mauclair, in F. T. Marinetti's *Enquête internationale sur le vers libre* (*International survey on free verse*, 1909), writes, "There are as many kinds of free verse as there are poets," while Laforgue claims, "My keyboard is constantly changing, and there is no other identical to mine. All keyboards are legitimate" (*Mélanges posthumes*, 1903). The conservative Catulle Mendès, however, in his governmentally commissioned *Rapport sur le mouvement poétique français 1867–1900* (Report on the French Poetic Movement, 1902) blames such rampant anarchy on the influence of foreigners and women, such as the Peruvian exile Della Rocca de Vergalo (*Poétique nouvelle*, 1880) and the Polish Jew Marie Krysinska (*Rythmes pittoresques*, 1890).

One might believe that the relative freedoms of vers libres classiques combined with those of vers libéré would produce the absolute freedom of vers libre, but this is not quite so. Certainly, vers libre is *heterometric and rhymes freely, and its lines are rhythmically unstable. But it goes further still; it rejects the indispensability of *rhyme with its line-demarcative function and instead relates lineation not to number of syllables but to the coincidence of units of meaning and units of rhythm or to integral impulses of utterance or else simply to the optimal expressive disposition of its textual raw materials. And indeed, the vers-libristes seek to abandon the principle of syllabism itself, by making the number of syllables in a line either irrelevant or indeterminable or both (see SYL- LABIC VERSE). The undermining of the syllabic system is facilitated by the ambiguous syllabic status of the *eatone* (mute *e*)—should it be counted when unelided?—and by doubts about the syllabic value of contiguous vowels. La- forgue summarizes the *tabula rasa* of vers libre in a letter to Kahn of July 1886: "I forget to rhyme, I forget about the number of syllables, I forget about stanzaic structure."

Paradoxically, however, syllabic amorphous- ness produces rhythmic polymorphousness and polysemy; in other words, a single line of vers libre is potentially several lines, each with its own inherited modalities. In addition, because of its heterometricity, vers libre can maximize rhythmic shifts between lines, creating a verse texture of multiplied tonalities. Within this paradox lies another fruitful contradiction. One of the original justifications for vers libre was its inimitability, its resistance to abstraction and systemization; thus, it could theoretically mold itself to the uniqueness of a personality, a psyche, a mood. Again Kahn: "For a long time I had been seeking to discover in myself a personal rhythm capable of communicating my lyric impulses with the cadence and music which I judged indispensable to them" (Préface to *Premiers Poèmes*, 1897). Yet, vers libre equally proposes a range of rhythmic possibilities that the reader is left to resolve into any one of a number of specific recitations. Given the sig- nificance of typographical arrangement in vers libre, this contradiction might be reformulated as a polarization of the visual and the oral, of the ling. and the paralinguistic, of the text as text, demanding to be read on its own terms, and the text as script, a set of incomplete in- structions to the reader's *voice. One further contradiction might be mentioned: for all vers libre's ambiguation of syllabic number, with its transference of focus from syllable to accent, from number of syllables to number of mea- sures, many free-verse poems are constructed on a "constante rythmique" (rhythmic con- stant), an intermittently recurrent measure that can be defined only syllabically.

Two broad currents of devel. can be distin- guished in vers libre: one derives its rhythmic purchase from its varying approximation to, and distance from, recognizably regular lines and often cultivates ironic modes of utterance;

the other seeks to undermine the primacy of the line by promoting rhythmic units larger than the line—the *verset* or the *stanza—or smaller than the line—the individual measure; this lat- ter strain is often informed by a rhapsodic voice. But in both currents, the line's role as guardian of metrical authority and guarantor of verse as ritual and self-transcendence is removed.

In both currents, too, the stanza finds itself without pedigree, infinitely elastic, ensuring no structural continuity. The stanza of vers libre ends not in conformity with some visible struc- tural imperative—though who may say what invisible imperatives operate—but because a movement of utterance comes to an end and because only by ending can a sequence of lines define its own field of structural and prosodic activity. The stanzas of vers libre are a pursuit of unique kinds of formality constantly renewed, not the repeated confirmation of a certain stan- zaic blueprint.

Vers libre can claim, with some justification, to have "psychologized" verse structure, to have made the act of writing apparently simultane- ous with the changing movements of mind: "a poem is not a feeling communicated just as it was conceived before the act of writing. Let us acknowledge the small felicities of rhyme, and the deviations caused by the chances of inven- tion, the whole unforeseen symphony which comes to accompany the subject" (Laforgue, *Mélanges posthumes*). By allowing the aleatory and the improvised to inhabit verse, by exploit- ing the psychological layering produced by variable rhyme interval and variable margin, by locating verse at the intersection of multiplied coordinates (rhyme, rhymelessness, *repetition, the metrical, the nonmetrical), by using ling. structures to attract and activate paralinguistic features (tempo, pause, *tone, accentual varia- tion, emotional coloring), vers libre establishes its affinities with the stream of consciousness of contemp. fiction and proffers a stream of con- sciousness of poetic reading.

■ Thieme 386; T. M. Dondo, *Vers Libre: A Logical Development of French Verse* (1922); E. Dujardin, *Les Premiers Poètes du vers libre* (1922); J. Hytier, *Les Techniques modernes du vers français* (1923); Patterson; L.-P. Thomas, *Le Vers moderne: ses moyens d'expression, son esthétique* (1943); H. Morier, *Le Rythme du vers libre sym- boliste*, 3 v. (1944); P. M. Jones, *The Background of Modern French Poetry* (1951), pt. 2; Z. Czerny, "Le Vers libre français et son art structural," *Poet- ics, Poetyka, Poetika*, ed. D. Davie et al. (1961);

T. S. Eliot, "Reflections on *Vers Libre*" (1917), *To Criticize the Critic* (1965); *Le Vers français au 20e siècle*, ed. M. Parent (1967); F. Carmody, "La Doctrine du vers libre de Gustave Kahn," *Cahiers de l'Association Internationale des Etudes Françaises* 21 (1969); J. Mazaleyrat, "Problèmes de scansion du vers libre," *Philologische Studien für Joseph M. Piel* (1969); J. Filliolet, "Problématique du vers libre," *Poétique du vers français*, ed. H. Meschonnic (1974); Elwert; Scott; Mazaleyrat; D. Grojnowski, "Poétique du vers libre: *Derniers Vers* de Jules Laforgue (1886)," *Revue d'histoire littéraire de la France* 84 (1984); C. Scott, *A Question of Syllables* (1986), *Vers Libre: The Emergence of Free Verse in France* (1990), and *Reading the Rhythm: The Poetics of French Free Verse 1910–1930* (1993); Morier; M. Murat, *Le Vers libre* (2008).

C. Scott; D. Evans

VILLANELLE (from It. *villanella*, a rustic song, *villano*, a peasant). As known today, a 19-line poem with two rhymes and two *refrain lines, in the form $A_1bA_2\ abA_1\ abA_2\ abA_1\ abA_2\ abA_1\ A_2$, where capital letters indicate refrains. Fr. poet Théodore de Banville compared the interweaving *a*, *b*, and refrain lines to "a braid of silver and gold threads, crossed with a third thread the color of a rose." Also distinctive is the *quatrain occurring at the end of a series of *tercets, the extra line in the last stanza furnishing a sense of closure to the repetitive pattern with a conclusive *couplet. In the 16th c., however, the villanelle had no set form other than the presence of a refrain after each verse. When Fr. poets such as Joachim du Bellay and Philippe Desportes began writing lyric poems in the spirit of the *villanella*—a trendy It. style of song that imitated rustic dance tunes from the oral trad., although its composers were courtly and literate—the rhyme schemes varied widely, the refrain could be one to five lines in length, and there could be any number of verses, although four was the most common in both the musical and poetic versions. Many of the 16th-c. poetic villanelles were set to music by composers of the time, and references to the villanelle through the 17th c. portray it as a musical and not poetic genre.

Throughout the 18th c., the same single example of the villanelle was frequently cited: Jean Passerat's 19-line alternating-refrain "Villanelle" ("J'ay perdu ma Tourterelle"), first pub. in 1606. Most 18th-c. texts defined the villanelle simply as a "peasant song," but an obscure 1722

Fr. grammar by Denis Gaullyer asserted that the villanelle required the first and last lines of the first verse to alternate as refrains. A similar claim in Pierre-Charles Berthelin's 1751 rev. ed. of Pierre Richelet's authoritative rhyming dictionary and prosody manual probably had more influence. Nineteenth-c. Fr. dictionaries, grammars, encyclopedias, and handbooks subsequently defined the villanelle as a traditional schematic poetic form, but Passerat's form was one of a kind until Banville's "Villanelle de Buloz" of 1845. Significantly fortified by Banville's popular handbook *Petit traité de poésie française*, the mistaken belief that the villanelle was an antique form persisted tenaciously throughout the 19th and 20th cs.

Enthusiasm for med. and Ren. forms in the 19th c. also helped establish the villanelle among authentic antique Fr. forms such as the triolet, *rondeau, and ballade. French Parnassian poets believed that a villanelle might be any length (like a poem written in *terza rima*); but in 1878, Joseph Boulmier published an entire volume of 19-line villanelles on the Passerat template, arguing in an intro. that this was the best length. Boulmier also pointed out that the villanelle was not a poetic form in the Ren., but this correction went largely unnoticed. Eng. aestheticism also admired archaic forms, and in the 1870s, Edmund Gosse helped make the villanelle a staple of light verse. Poets such as Oscar Wilde, Andrew Lang, and (in America) E. A. Robinson wrote 19-line villanelles, which established that length as a rule.

Hardly any Fr. poets wrote villanelles after the 19th c., but the form gradually became surprisingly important in Eng.—though Eng. writers continued to refer to the villanelle as a "French form." James Joyce's 1916 *Portrait of the Artist as a Young Man* included a scene about the composition of a villanelle in which Joyce's mod. stream-of-consciousness prose contrasts starkly with the outdated fin de siècle theme and form of his hero's poem. But William Empson's "Villanelle" ("It is the pain, it is the pain endures") of 1928 was highly mod.; and when W. H. Auden adopted the form, his villanelles, like Empson's, were *pentameter: almost all earlier Eng. villanelles are *tetrameter or *trimeter. Dylan Thomas's first villanelle was a 1942 *parody of Empson titled "Request to Leda," but it was Thomas's 1951 "Do not go gentle into that good night" that ensured the villanelle's survival and status in Eng. poetry. Throughout the 1950s, 1960s, and 1970s, major poets occasionally wrote villanelles.

Elizabeth Bishop's 1976 villanelle "One Art," along with the emergence of New Formalism, introduced what might be called the postmod. villanelle. In the last quarter of the 20th c., poet after poet adopted the villanelle, often making use of a new license to use *near rhyme and near refrain and overtly obeying or challenging to the supposedly strict, traditional rules of the form. Poets also began to invent similar forms, most unique but some not: the prose villanelle, the *terzanelle* (a hybrid with terza rima), and, most notably, a ludicrously repetitive form invented by Billy Collins. The *paradelle*, which Collins claimed was a *langue d'oc* form of the 11th c., is a "parody villanelle" whose origin story is only slightly falser than the one commonly told of the "real" villanelle.

■ J. Passerat, *Recueil des oeuvres poétiques* (1606); D. Gaullyer, *Abregé de la grammaire françoise* (1722); P. Richelet, *Dictionnaire des rimes*, ed. P. C. Berthelin (1751); T. de Banville, *Petit traité de poésie française* (1872); E. Gosse, "A Plea for Certain Exotic Forms of Verse," *Cornhill Magazine* 36 (1877); J. Boulmier, *Villanelles* (1878); C. Scott, *French Verse-Art* (1980); D. G. Cardamone, *The Canzone Villanesa alla Napolitana and Related Forms, 1537–1570* (1981); R. F. McFarland, *The Villanelle* (1987); J. Kane, "The Myth of the Fixed-Form Villanelle," *MLQ* 64 (2003); *The Paradelle*, ed. T. W. Welford (2006); A. L. French, "Edmund Gosse and the Stubborn Villanelle Blunder," *VP* 48 (2010).

J. KANE; A. L. FRENCH

VIRELAI (also called *chanson baladée* and *vireli*). Originally a variant of the common dance song with refrain, of which the *rondeau is the most prominent type, this med. Fr. lyric form developed in the 13th c. and at first may have been performed by one or more leading voices and a chorus. It begins with a *refrain, followed by a stanza of four lines of which the first two have a musical line (repeated) different from that of the refrain. The last two lines of the stanza return to the music of the refrain. The opening refrain, words and music, is then sung again. The *virelai* usually continues with two more stanzas presented in this same way. A virelai with only one stanza would be a *bergerette*. In Italy, the 13th-c. *lauda* and, in Spain, the *cantiga*, follow the same form. The syllables *vireli* and *virelai* were probably nonsense refrains that later came to designate the type.

The large number of variations and optional elements both in the *lai* and in the virelai (as practiced by Guillaume de Machaut, Jean Froissart, Christine de Pizan, and Eustache Deschamps) produced much uncertainty among recent prosodists about how both forms should be defined, so that one must approach any mod. definition with great caution. Most recent commentators follow Théodore de Banville (*Petit traité de poésie française*, 1872), who, relying on the authority of the 17th-c. prosodist le Père Mourgues (*Traité de la poésie française*, 1685), tried to settle matters by defining the lai as a poem in which each stanza is a combination of three-line groups, two longer lines followed by a shorter one, with the longer lines sharing one rhyme sound and the shorter lines another (*aabaabaab ccdccdccd*, etc.). Then, calling on a false etymology of *virelai*—from *virer* (to turn) and *lai*—he defined the virelai as a lai in which the rhyme sounds are "turned" from stanza to stanza; i.e., the rhyme of the shorter lines becomes the rhyme of the longer lines in the following stanza (*aabaabaab, bbcbbcbbc*, etc.). Calling the virelai thus defined the *virelai ancien*, Banville goes on to describe the *virelai nouveau*, which bears no relation to the virelai ancien and is, if anything, more like the *villanelle. The virelai nouveau opens with a refrain, whose two lines then recur separately and alternately as the refrains of the stanzas following, reappearing together again only at the end of the final stanza, but with their order reversed. The stanzas of the virelai nouveau may be of any length and employ any rhyme scheme, but the poem is limited to two rhyme sounds only. Here again, Banville merely follows le Père Mourgues, whose "Le Rimeur rebuté" is used as an illustration. John Payne's "Spring Sadness" (virelai ancien) and Austin Dobson's "July" (virelai nouveau) are the only evidence that these two forms have excited any interest.

■ E. Gosse, "A Plea for Certain Exotic Forms of Verse," *Cornhill Magazine* 36 (1877); G. White, *Ballades and Rondeaus* (1887); Kastner; H. L. Cohen, *Lyric Forms from France* (1922); Le Gentil; P. Le Gentil, *Le Virelai et le villancico* (1954); M. Françon, "On the Nature of the Virelai," *Symposium* 9 (1955); G. Reaney, "The Development of the Rondeau, Virelai, and Ballade," *Festschrift Karl Gustav Fellerer* (1962); F. Gennrich, *Das altfranzösische Rondeau und V. im 12. und 13. Jahrhundert* (1963); F. Gennrich and G. Reaney, "Virelai," *MGG* 13.1802–11; N. Wilkins, "Virelai," *New Grove*; Morier;

R. Mullally, "Vireli, Virelai," *Neuphilologische Mitteilungen* 101 (2000); J.-F. Kosta-Théfaine, "Les Virelais de Christine de Pizan," *Moyen Français* 48 (2001).

U. T. Holmes; C. Scott

VISUAL ARTS AND POETRY. *See* concrete poetry; ekphrasis; ut pictura poesis; visual poetry.

VISUAL POETRY

I. Forms
II. Free Verse

Visual poetry is poetry composed for the eye as well as, or more than, for the ear. All written and printed poetry is visual poetry in a broad sense, in that, when we read the poem, the visual form affects how we read it and so contributes to our experience of its sound, movement, and meaning. The overwhelming majority of lyric poems are meant to fit on a codex page, hence, to meet the reader's eye as a simultaneously apprehensible whole. As Mooij points out, "written poetry allows for devices of foregrounding not available to oral poetry." Among these devices are lineation, line length, line grouping, indentation, intra- and interlinear white space, punctuation, capitalization, and size and style of type. In traditional verse, however, the written text serves mainly a notational role, and its visual aspects are subordinate to the oral form they represent. In visual poetry in the strict sense, the visual form of the text becomes an object for apprehension in its own right. In some visual poetry, text is combined with nontextual graphic elements.

I. Forms. In general, the visual form of a poem may be figurative or nonfigurative; if figurative, it may be mimetic or abstract. In cl. and Ren. pattern poetry, we find figurative visual form that is mimetic, the printed text taking the shape of objects; the best-known examples are two poems by George Herbert, "The Altar" and "Easter Wings." There are also some 20th-c. examples of mimetic visual form, among them the calligrammes of Guillaume Apollinaire and some *concrete poetry. Poems in the shape of geometric figures such as circles and lozenges, another kind of pattern poetry, realize the possibility of figurative visual form that is abstract: in the Ren., 15 such forms are enumerated by George Puttenham. Less rigidly geometric forms are not uncommon in conventional poetry (Ranta).

The visual form of most poems is nonfigurative: such poems are isometrical or heterometrical, hence, consist of regular or irregular blocks of long and/or short lines. Open arrangements of lines in the page space are usually also nonfigurative. Such nonfigurative visual form may contribute significantly to the effect of the poem. In the case of short poems, the shape of the whole poem is apprehended immediately as open or dense, balanced or imbalanced, even or uneven, simple or intricate. In stanzaic poems, the regular partitioning of the text may convey a sense of order and control and generate an expectation of regular closure. Further, the individual stanzas themselves are apprehensible visual units. Stanzas in symmetrical shapes may suggest stability or stillness, while asymmetrical shapes may suggest instability or movement in a direction. Stanzas of complex shape may convey a sense of elaborate artifice. Stanzas where lines of different lengths, or with different rhymes, are indented by different amounts, as in John Donne's *Songs and Sonnets*, may appear esp. highly ordered. For the reader steeped in poetry, the visual forms of stanzas may also recall antecedent poems written in stanzas of similar shape. The basic shape of the *sapphic stanza, e.g., is recognizable even in extreme variations.

II. Free Verse. Visual form plays a more important role in the prosody of *free verse than in that of metrical verse. One distinguishing feature of much modernist free verse—the eschewal of line-initial capitals—is a purely visual feature. On the one hand, besides serving to label the verse as nonmetrical, the use of lowercase letters at the beginnings of lines (unless they are also beginnings of sentences) may have the effect of reducing the visual prominence of the line as a unit. On the other hand, where lineation and line grouping are not determined by meter and rhyme, lines and line groups may be constitutively visual units. Even where lines are phonological, syntactical, and/or semantic units as well, their visual aspect may be important to their effect.

In most cases, visual form in free verse assumes a subservient, pattern-marking role. E.g., lineation, in its visual aspect, may serve to juxtapose images, as in Ezra Pound's classic imagist poem "In a Station of the Metro." Lineation, layout, and other visual features may serve to score the text for oral performance. Charles Olson, in his 1950 essay "Projective Verse," claimed that there should be a direct relationship between the amount of white space and the length of pause. Regardless of whether it signals pause, intra- or interlinear white space can work mimetically, expressively, and rhetorically. Many free-verse poets exploit these possibilities through arrangement of text in the page space, as does Denise Levertov in this passage from "The Five-Day Rain":

Sequence broken, tension
of sunlight broken.
        So light a rain
fine shreds
pending above the rigid leaves.

Less commonly, the visual form takes on a privileged, pattern-making role. Where lines do not coincide with units of the text's linguistic structure, they may, esp. in the case of short lines, set up a counterpoint to it. Free-verse poets, notably W. C. Williams, sometimes arrange their lines in "sight-stanzas," perceptible as stanzas only by virtue of having equal numbers of lines and creating iterated visual patterns. Here, the visual order of the stanzas may compensate aesthetically for considerable density or sprawl in syntax or argument. In other free-verse poems, white space serves to defamiliarize split or isolated textual elements, as in these lines from the Canadian poet bpNichol's *The Martyrology*:

hand

the h &
what else

■ G. Puttenham, *The Arte of English Poesie* (1589), rpt. in Smith; J. Sparrow, *Visible Words* (1969); R. Massin, *La Lettre et l'image*, 2d ed. (1973); *Speaking Pictures*, ed. M. Klonsky (1975)—anthol.; J.J.A. Mooij, "On the 'Foregrounding' of Graphic Elements in Poetry," *Comparative Poetics*, ed. D. W. Fokkema et al. (1976); J. Ranta, "Geometry, Vision, and Poetic Form," *CE* 39 (1978); *Visual Literature Criticism*, ed. R. Kostelanetz (1979); R. Kostelanetz, *The Old Poetries and the New* (1981); Morier, under "Blanchissement," "Vide"; R. Shusterman, "Aesthetic Blindness to Textual Visuality," *JAAC* 41 (1982); M. Cummings and R. Simmons, "Graphology," *The Language of Literature* (1983); H. M. Sayre, *The Visual Text of W. C. Williams* (1983); S. Cushman, *W. C. Williams and the Meanings of Measure* (1985), ch. 2; C. Taylor, *A Poetics of Seeing* (1985);

Hollander; W. Bohn, *The Aesthetics of Visual Poetry, 1914–1928* (1986); R. Cureton, "Visual Form in e. e. cummings' *No Thanks*," *Word & Image* 2 (1986); J. Adler and U. Ernst, *Text als Figur* (1987); *The Line in Postmodern Poetry*, ed. R. Frank and H. Sayre (1988); "Material Poetry of the Renaissance / The Renaissance of Material Poetry," ed. R. Greene, *Harvard Library Bulletin* NS 3.2 (1992); *Experimental—Visual—Concrete*, ed. K. D Jackson et al. (1996); *Visuelle Poesie*, ed. H. L. Arnold and H. Korte (1997); J. Drucker, *Figuring the Word* (1998); *New Media Poetics*, ed. A. Morris and T. Swiss (2006).

E. BERRY

VISUAL RHYME. *See* EYE RHYME.

VOICE. To define *voice* in written poetry immediately poses a problem, for there is no literal voice in the poem: voice is an oral *metaphor employed in the description and analysis of the written word. It is not just any metaphor, however, but one that foregrounds fundamental distinctions underpinning Western culture: orality and literacy, speaking and writing. Regardless of how much one insists that writing is not speaking and that voice is not literally present in the poem, literary critics have persistently relied on metaphors of voice to analyze writing; it is difficult to imagine how one would go about discussing poetry in particular if we were forbidden to use the terms *voice*, *speaker*, and other vocal terms like *monologue* or *song*, to give a few examples. Teachers, students, and scholars regularly say that poetry "speaks" and readers "listen." The hist. of lit. crit. is saturated with more or less self-conscious uses of oral and aural terms for poetry. Though there are theories of narrative "voice"—see the work of Bakhtin and Genette, e.g.—poetry is regularly imagined to be the privileged site of vocal presence; those who seek to demystify that presence work to dislodge or trouble oral metaphors that cleave far closer to poetry than to fiction, nonfiction, or perhaps even drama.

Studies of orality offer one approach to explaining why voice is so closely affiliated with poetry. These studies tend to agree that poetry is a crucial vehicle for the transmission of information in oral cultures. The repetitive sound structures that define poetry—*rhythm, *rhyme, *refrain, *alliteration, *assonance, *parallelism, *anaphora—are a central technology of cultural memory and historical transmission. In the absence of written documentation, sound patterns form a lang. system that enables recollection and recitation. Though oral cultures are certainly not extinct and though oral practices coexist alongside written practices in literate cultures, there is an abundance of work on the historical transition from orality to literacy in Western culture. Havelock, e.g., offers a theory of the "literate revolution" in Greece in the 7th to 4th cs. BCE that accounts for the saturation of vocal and aural figures in Gr. lit. During that time, oral strategies—singing, recitation, memorization—were not simply supplanted by a literate culture's documentary practices; instead, the two modes entered into "competition and collision." The jostling of literacy by the traces of orality never ended: "the Muse never became the discarded mistress of Greece. She learned to write and read while she continued to sing." Metaphors of orality continue to inhabit, unsettle, and complicate the textual realm to the present day. The earlier, crucial functions of poetry, however, have been replaced by more peripheral, optional practices. Rather than a warehouse for a culture's knowledge, poetry now serves, e.g., as an entertaining pastime, a form of individualized or collective aesthetic expression, or a tool in commercial marketing.

See DRAMATIC POETRY.

■ T. S. Eliot, *On Poetry and Poets* (1957); F. Berry, *Poetry and the Physical Voice* (1962); W. J. Ong, *The Barbarian Within* (1962); M. M. Bakhtin, *The Dialogic Imagination*, ed. M. Holquist, trans. C. Emerson and M. Holquist (1981); W. R. Johnson, *The Idea of Lyric* (1982); G. Genette, *Narrative Discourse*, trans. J. E. Lewin (1983); P. de Man,

The Rhetoric of Romanticism (1984); H. Tucker, "Dramatic Monologue and the Overhearing of Lyric," *Lyric Poetry: Beyond New Criticism*, ed. C. Hošek and P. Parker (1985); J. Goldberg, *Voice Terminal Echo: Postmodernism and English Renaissance Texts* (1986); E. Havelock, *The Muse Learns to Write: Reflections on Orality and Literacy from Antiquity to the Present* (1986); E. Griffiths, *The Printed Voice of Victorian Poetry* (1989); F. A. Kittler, *Discourse Networks 1800/1900*, trans. M. Metteer (1990); P. Zumthor, *Oral Poetry*, trans. K. Murphy-Judy (1990); B. R. Smith, *The Acoustic World of Early Modern England* (1999); Y. Prins, "Voice Inverse," *VP* 42 (2004); C. Mazzio, *The Inarticulate Renaissance* (2008); J. A. Peraino, *Giving Voice to Love: Song and Self-Expression from the Troubadours to Guillaume de Machaut* (2011).

E. RICHARDS

VOLTA, *volte* (It., "turn"). A musical and prosodic term for a turn, particularly the transition point between the *octave and *sestet of the *sonnet, which, in its It. form, usually rhymes *abbaabba cdecde*: the *volta* is significant because both the particular rhymes unifying the two quatrains of the octave and also the envelope scheme are abandoned simultaneously, regardless of whether this break is further reinforced syntactically by a full stop at the end of the octave (though usually it is), creating a decisive "turn in thought." By extension, the term is applied to the gap or break at line nine of any sonnet type, though in the Shakespearean form, e.g., the type of rhyming (*cross rhyme) is not abandoned at that point.

T.V.F. BROGAN

Z

ZEUGMA (Gr., "means of binding"; cf. Gr. *zeugos*, "yoke"). Form of brachylogy in which multiple clauses are governed by a single word, most often a noun or verb. According to Quintilian (*Institutio oratoria* 9.3.62), who calls the figure *synezeugmenon*, the governing word is always a verb (e.g., "Lust conquered shame, audacity fear, madness reason"). The *Rhetorica ad Herennium* (4, 27:37–38) allows for noun governance as well, a construction it labels *diazeugmenon* (e.g., "The Roman people destroyed Numantia, razed Carthage, and overthrew Fregellae").

Later rhetoricians extended the definition of zeugma to the "yoking" together of any two parts of speech by means of any other. Following Quintilian, George Puttenham (*The Arte of English Poesie* [1589], book 3, ch. 12) and other Ren. rhetoricians (e.g., Johannes Susenbrotus, *Epitome troporum ac schematum* [1541], and Henry Peacham, *The Garden of Eloquence* [1577]) distinguished three zeugmatic constructions according to whether the governing word precedes the words it governs (*prozeugma*); stands between them (*mesozeugma*, e.g., "Much he the place admired, the person more"— Milton, *Paradise Lost* 9.444); or follows them (*hypozeugma*).

There is little consensus regarding the distinction between zeugma and syllepsis.

Puttenham argues that, whereas in zeugma the governing word agrees grammatically with each of the governed clauses, in syllepsis, it agrees with only one, thus producing what he calls the "double supply," a semantic sleight-of-hand. What seems clear is that zeugma, unlike syllepsis, requires an ellipsis. Peacham and others (e.g., A. Quinn, *Figures of Speech* [1982], 98) thus view zeugma as the opposite of *hypozeuxis,* in which the governing words are repeated in each clause (e.g., Winston Churchill's "We shall fight on the beaches, we shall fight on the landing grounds, we shall fight in the fields and in the streets. . . ."). Considered in relation to hypozeuxis, zeugma can be seen as an efficient means of emphasis (i.e., it lacks iteration).

Alexander Pope favors the figure, and he frequently employs mixed zeugmas (e.g., "See Pan with flocks, with fruit Pomona crowned" [*Windsor Forest*, 37], which relies on both hypozeugma and prozeugma to produce a *chiasmus).

■ C. Walz, *Rhetores Graeci*, 9 v. (1832–36), 8.474, 686, 709; M. Joseph, *Shakespeare's Use of the Arts of Language* (1947); L. A. Sonnino, *Handbook to 16th-Century Rhetoric* (1968); Lausberg, sect. 702–7; Vickers.

C. H. MOORE

Index

Page numbers in **boldface** indicate article titles.

NourbeSe Philip, M., 266
Nourritures terrestres (Gide), 277
Nouvelles Impressiones d'Afrique (Roussel), 47
Novak, Helga, 277
Novalis, 187, 277
novel, 10, 132, 134, 186, 216; ekphrasis, 87; epic
    precedent, 106, 107, 110, 111; Menippean satire
    precedent, 313; narrative poetry precedent, 214;
    pastoral, 243
novel in verse. *See* narrative poetry
Nowottny, Winifred, 68, 69
number. *See* meter
Nykrog, Per, 119

Oakden, J. P., 95
"O Captain! My Captain!" (Whitman), 42
occasional poetry, 271
Occitan poetry, 100, 152; alba, 5; courtly love, 175;
    enueg, 50; jongleur, 247; octave, 223; rhyme,
    170, 295; troubadour, 5, 179, 223, 224, 247
O'Connell, Eileen, 169–70
O'Conor, Michael Patrick, 235
octave, **223**
octosyllable, 59, 94, 119, **223–24**, 352, 372
ode, 97, 180, **225–27**, 269; hymn and psalm ante-
    cedent, 225; meter, 223
"Ode: Intimations of Immortality" (Wordsworth),
    227
"Ode on a Grecian Urn" (Keats), 157–58, 227, 283
"Ode on the Death of Sir Lucius Cary and Sir H.
    Morison" (Jonson), 226
"Ode on the Death of the Duke of Wellington"
    (Tennyson), 227
"Ode on the Poetical Character" (Collins), 225
"Ode on Solitude" (Pope), 309
Odes (Horace), 42, 92, 114, 225, 289, 309, 314
Odes en son honneur (Verlaine), 226
"Ode to a Nightingale" (Keats), 2, 205, 227, 335
"Ode to Death" (Smith), 163
"Ode to Joy" (Schiller), 226
"Ode to Psyche" (Keats), 225
"Ode to the Confederate Dead" (Tate), 227
"Ode to the Memory of Mrs. Anne Killigrew"
    (Dryden), 226
"Ode to the West Wind" (Shelley), 227, 283, 370
"Ode upon a Question moved, An" (Herbert), 162
"Ode, Written in the Beginning of the Year, 1746"
    (Collins), 253
Odi barbare (Carducci), 226, 309
Odyssey (Homer), 101–3, 105–8, 214, 215; lament,
    169; modern adaptations, 111; oral origin, 101;
    pastoral, 241; structure, 103; synaesthesia, 359;
    translations, 32, 138, 139, 142
Oedipus Rex (Sophocles), 166, 341
Oehlenschläger, Adam, 33

"Of De Witt Williams on his way to Lincoln Cem-
    etery" (Brooks), 24
O'Hara, Frank, 54, 187
Okigbo, Christopher, 181
Okot p'Bitek, 290
Old English prosody. *See* English prosody
"Old Lem" (Brown), 290–91
Olds, Sharon, 54
Olive, L' (Bellay), 329
Oliver, Mary, 9
Olson, Charles: composition by field, 50, 125,
    248; free verse, 125; line, 39; performance, 248;
    projective verse, 50, 174, 248, 388–89
Olson, Elder, 356
"O Maria, Deu maire" (song), 5
Omeros (Walcott), 111, 217, 371
Omphale (Ion), 371
"One Art" (Bishop), 1, 17, 387
Onegin stanza. *See* Pushkin, Alexander
"One Word More" (Browning), 246
Ong, Walter, 246, 332
"On My First Daughter" (Jonson), 114
"On My First Son" (Jonson), 113, 114
onomatopoeia, **227–29**, 334–35
Ono no Komachi, 180
"On the Death of a Fair Infant Dying of a Cough"
    (Milton), 299, 320
"On the Late Massacre in Piedmont" (Milton), 335
"On the Morning of Christ's Nativity" (Milton),
    226, 299, 335
"On Translations of Homer" (Tennyson), 143
open form, 50–51
Opitz, Martin, 51, 321
oral-formulaic theory, 101
oral poetry, 71, 124, 127, 215, 223, 236, 246, 249;
    epic, 101, 270; folk song, 20, 23, 203, 270, 303,
    326; orality, 389–90; periphrasis, 251; refrain,
    290; repetition, 291, 292. *See also* ballad; epic;
    performance
orchestration, 335
Order and Disorder (Hutchinson), 106
organicism, 50, 122–23, 125, 129, 157–58, 180,
    193, 265, 293, 345, 357
Orlando furioso (Ariosto), 103–6, 109, 215, 229, 264
Ormulum (ME poem), 138
Orpheus (Buchner), 61
Orphic Hymns, 145
Orwell, George, 310
Ossian (Macpherson), 110, 111, 359
Ossi di Seppia (Montale), 187
Othello (Shakespeare), 13, 79, 80, 92, 211, 276
Other, 35
ottava rima, 59, 215, 223, **229–30**; rhyme royal, 298
"Our Eunuch Dreams" (Thomas), 56
"Out, Out—" (Frost), 150

soliloquy, 211
"Solitary Reaper, The" (Wordsworth), 114
Solon, 371, 375
Somervile, William, 134
"Some Simple Measures in the American Idiom and
  the Variable Foot" (Williams), 381
"Son, The" (Herbert), 240
Sonette an Orpheus, Die (Rilke), 329, 331
Sonette aus Venedig (Platen), 329
song, 20, **324–27**, 344
"Song (Go and Catch a falling Star)" (Donne), 296
"Song for St. Cecilia's Day, A" (Dryden), 47, 226
Song of Hiawatha (Longfellow), 372
"Song of Myself" (Whitman), 292, 326
Song of Roland. See *Chanson de Roland*
Song of Songs (Heb. OT), 65, 115, 152, 176, 178,
  258, 355
"Song of the Harper" (anon.), 42
"Song of the Merchant Kalashnikov" (Lermontov), 34
Songs and Sonnets (Donne), 96, 233
Songs of Innocence and Experience (Blake), 31, 326
"Songs of the Western Slavs" (Pushkin), 34
sonnet, 131–32, 179, **327–30**; caudate, 328; corona,
  328, 331; curtal, 328; English (Shakespearean),
  112, 327–28, 329, 390; epigram, 112; French,
  329; German, 329; Italian (Petrarchan), 132,
  162, 179, 189, 327–28, 329, 370, 390; meter,
  327; octave, 223, 320, 327; rhyme scheme,
  327–28; sestet, 320, 327–28; Sicilian school,
  328; Spanish, 75, 328–29; Spenserian, 327–28,
  329; terza rima, 328; variations, 328. *See also*
  sonnet sequence
"Sonnet Reversed" (Brooke), 328
Sonnets (Shakespeare), 8, 13, 45, 131–32, 187, 193,
  206, 215, 249, 329; antithesis, 15; apostrophe,
  16; Bellay source, 329, 331; blason, 52; conceit,
  52; couplet, 59; enjambment, 99; polyptoton,
  275; polysyndeton, 276; repetition, 275, 291;
  rhyme scheme, 299; simile, 323
Sonnets, The (Berrigan), 188
sonnet sequence, 29, 113, 132, 179, 188, 260, 329,
  330–32
Sonnets from the Portuguese (Browning), 118, 329,
  331
Sonnets pour Hélène (Ronsard), 187
Sontag, Susan, 238
Sophocles, 74, 169, 371
Sophonisba (Trissino), 28
Sophron, 66, 241
Sor Juana. See Cruz, Sor Juana Inés de la
Sosa, Roberto, 181
Sotades, 163
sound, 278–79, **332–38**
sound poetry, 174, 248–49, 334, **338–41**
Southey, Robert, 100, 143, 309

Soyinka, Wole, 76
"Spain" (Auden), 14
Spain, poetry of, 31–32, 135, 328–29, 331
Spanish prosody, 137, 224
Spanish Tragedy, The (Kyd), 50
Spargo, R. Clifton, 90
"Spaziergang, Der" (Schiller), 90
speaker. *See* persona; voice
Spedding, James, 172–73
speech act theory, 16, 196
Spender, Stephen, 219
Spenser, Edmund: alliteration, 8; archaism, 70;
  canon, 41; carpe diem, 43; catalog, 45; chain
  rhyme, 46; complaint, 50; couplet, 59; decasyllable, 63, 96; dialogue, 67; diction, 68; difficulty,
  72; eclogue, 85; elegiac distich, 88; epic, 43,
  43, 45, 103–6, 108, 109; epithalamium, 116;
  epithet, 117; hymn, 146; hyperbaton, 148;
  influence of, 31, 96; lament, 169; meter, 217;
  narrative poetry, 214, 215, 217; ottava rima, 229;
  palinode, 231; paronomasia, 240; pastoral, 241;
  personification, 253; polyptoton, 275; refrain,
  291; rhyme, 217; rhyme royal, 299; rich rhyme,
  304; satire, 310; simile, 323; sonnet, 46, 122,
  216, 275, 329, 331
Spenserian stanza, 122, 216, 329, **341**, 344–45
Spitzer, Leo, 10, 347
Spivak, Gayatri Chakravorty, 44
split lines, 30, 33, 136, 173, 218, **341–42**, 345
spondee, 120, 314, 318, **342–43**, 375
Spoon River Anthology (Masters), 66, 115, 216
"Spring and All" (Williams), 100
"Spring Images" (Wright), 127
"Spring Sadness" (Payne), 387
Sprung, Mervyn, 245
sprung rhythm, 97, 100, 152, 202, 217, **343–44**
Stagnelius, Erik Johan, 34
"Stagolee" (ballad), 23, 36
Stampa, Gaspara, 321, 328
Stanford formalists, 31
Stanislavski, Konstantin, 78–79, 81
Stanyhurst, Richard, 142–43
stanza, 289, **344–45**, 384; free verse, 126–27, 345,
  385; "sight stanza," 389; vs. strophe, 346
"Stanzas for Music" (Byron), 138
"Starlight of Night, The" (Hopkins), 57
"Star-Spangled Banner, The" (Key), 226
Statius, 19, 102
Steele, Joshua, 303
Steele, Timothy, 353
Stein, Gertrude: dramatic poetry, 76, 77, 78; epi-
  thalamium, 116; imagery, 158; prose poem, 277;
  repetition, 291; sound play, 339
Steiner, Wendy, 379
Stephanus, Henricus (Henri Estienne), 12